The Twilight Zone

Unlocking the Door to A Television Classic

Martin Grams, Jr.

Published in the USA by:
OTR Publishing, LLC
PO Box 252
Churchville, MD 21028
www.martingrams.com and www.amazon.com

ISBN 13: 978-0-9703310-9-0
ISBN 10: 0-9703310-9-6

Printed in the United States of America.

Book & cover design by Darlene & Dan Swanson of Van-garde Imagery, Inc.

Contents:

A BELATED LETTER TO ROD SERLING

by George Clayton Johnson

September 22, 2008
Mr. Rod Serling
Somewhere in *The Twilight Zone*

Dear Rod:
I believe that your name, Rod Serling, has become as recognizable as the title of your landmark show itself. I also believe that someone who wanted to carry on the *Twilight Zone* tradition might call their new series simply "The Rod Serling Show" without infringing the CBS trademark title and still reach *the Twilight Zone* audience.

By now, having watched most of the episodes several times I can easily picture you in my imagination as a character, very dapper in your neat black suit, living in cyberspace made out of pixels like Max Headroom knowing everything that is happening on the World Wide Web and in the lives of the people who log on ready to intrude into the scene itself with a trenchant commentary to provide a necessary moral dimension to the lives of those young cell-phone viewers who love surfing the net and will track down the show if those new stories are any good.

Congratulations, Rod, on your well-deserved Global celebrity. A lot of people are now giving you a lot of attention, including one fellow in particular. You may be aware that one of your devoted fans, writer Martin Grams Jr., has been working his butt off forever on a massive book about the making of *The Twilight Zone* television series for that self-same audience. He showed me part of his manuscript. I believe you will be pleased. I congratulate the guy for his admirable dedication to getting the details straight. I also praise OTR Publishing for having the wisdom to recognize the singular contribution that you have made to television history. The book will get a lot of attention from the fans of the show of which, as you know, there are many. Next year is the 50th anniversary of your series and the show is as hot as ever with all of the episodes available on DVD from Image Entertainment. Barry Hoffman of Gauntlet Press is publishing *The Complete Twilight Zone Scripts of Rod Serling* in many volumes. Almost all of the other scripts are now in print and selling well. They show up here and there with increasing frequency as stage-plays.

What an astonishing shelf-life for a piece of television entertainment and a great testament to the timeless nature of the program and the quality production you brought to the project.

At first, *The Twilight Zone* had a small audience which helped keep executive hands off, thankfully, and allowed you and Buck Houghton to run things the way you wanted.

Although you were legally obligated to write the bulk of the scripts you were permitted to hire other writers to help out which brings in Charles Beaumont and Richard Matheson to take up the slack but as fast and as good as these two gifted men were there was a need occasionally for other writers to add their sparkle to *The Twilight Zone* which brings in Earl Hamner and Reginald Rose and Montgomery Pittman and a few others including me.

This was long ago when, with my wife Lola's permission, who said, "You can't tie a man's legs together and expect him to run," I had quit my drafting job at U.S. Steel after buying a house on the G.I. Bill with neither of us knowing how we'd make the necessary monthly payments without a regular income.

I'd then spent five solid, anxiety-ridden years becoming a beatnik existentialist trying to write slightly surreal off-beat short stories without any success whatever.

By that time my house was facing foreclosure and I was in debt with doors closing on all sides.

When I got that $500 check from Cayuga Productions as payment for the non-exclusive right for you to adapt my story "All Of Us Are Dying" into an episode of your excellent television series, *The Twilight Zone*, it heartened me as you can well imagine.

"All Of Us Are Dying" was my first sale to television, indeed, my first short-story sale and it was, fortunately, enough money for me to pay several months of delinquent house payments and to buy groceries besides. It gave me hope.

The suspenseful job you did with my story transforming it into "The Four Of Us Are Dying" episode of *The Twilight Zone* taught me a lot about television drama.

The episode aired on New Year's day, 1960.

Change was in the air.

I noticed that many of your finest pieces and many of the stories you bought to adapt were basically filmed stage plays which was something I believed I could learn to write. You and Buck Houghton gave me a chance to prove I could do it with "A Penny For Your Thoughts."

Your acceptance of my script put me on a permanent search for story ideas dealing with the imaginary — some of which found their way to the screen. The hidden hand was at work that day for your decision to buy my material had far-reaching consequences still at work now. That precious house is paid for, I haven't any debts and I find the door open to me wherever I go, all stemming from your generous act.

I find that for me, Rod, some things have to be put in writing for them to be real. And so:

For all of your kindness to a beginning writer and for the powerful influence you have had on my life with Lola's, with heartfelt gratitude, both Lola and I thank you for letting me play in your brilliant game and for allowing me to shine by your reflected light.

Sincerely,

George Clayton Johnson
Pacoima, California

INTRODUCTION

The year was 1959. Bill Veeck, head of a group that purchased a controlling interest in the Chicago White Sox, presented an unexpected specialty one afternoon in Comiskey Park. Little spacemen showed up to capture Luis Aparicio and Nellie Fox, proving that the bizarre and unexpected would be accepted by the crowd who cheered with amusement.

In the November 7, 1959 issue of *TV Guide*, Rod Serling commented, "Here's what *The Twilight Zone* is: It's an anthology series, half-hour in length, that delves into the odd, the bizarre, the unexpected. It probes into the dimension of imagination but with a concern for taste and for an adult audience too long considered to have I.Q.s in negative figures. *The Twilight Zone* is what it implies: that shadowy area of the almost-but-not-quite; the unbelievable told in terms that can be believed. Here's what the program isn't: It's not a monster rally or a spook show. There will be nothing formula'd in it, nothing telegraphed, nothing so nostalgically familiar that an audience can usually join actors in duets."

Writer George Clayton Johnson probably described *Twilight Zone* best when he referred to the series as "wisdom fiction." In 1959, Rod Serling told Clarence E. Flick, supervisor of the *Radio-Television Curriculum* at San Jose State College, that the series was inspired and designed for that "willing suspension of disbelief." For more than fifty years, *The Twilight Zone* has become an established landmark on the map of television history.

As a fan of the series, I read a lot of books and magazine articles about the program. I absorbed the wealth of information that came from those periodicals. Over the years, I purchased and collected a large number of papers related to Serling and *The Twilight Zone*, including production sheets, casting call sheets; internal correspondence, tax forms, contracts and many other sources I consider of value from private collectors and eBay. After reviewing the materials, I started to realize that many of the books and magazine articles were printing misinformation. One example was Marc Scott Zicree's *The Twilight Zone Companion*, which had producer William Froug recall purchasing the French film, "An Occurrence at Owl Creek Bridge," for $10,000. The fact is, according to Cayuga's financial papers, the film was purchased for $20,000 plus an additional expense of almost $5,000 for editing and sound sync fees. Worse, I began noticing how many books were consulting previous publications (rather than consulting studio and archival documents), resulting in the reprint of the same misinformation.

While every book about Rod Serling or *The Twilight Zone* has offered something new and fresh, whether it be unpublished *Zone* scripts or exclusive interviews with cast and crew, I never found any book that did not have some major error within the pages. It is a known fact that no book ever published is flawless, so stating corrections to previously published material is important as preserving the 35mm nitrate films housed at CBS.

The origin of this tome began four years ago when I submitted an article for a film magazine that corrected many of the errors that I had observed in other books, and citing the sources for these corrections. Someone representing the magazine sent me a rejection. I later discovered that one of the members of magazine's staff had written a book about *The Twilight Zone* and without knowing it beforehand, was citing a mistake from their own effort.

My next option? Write a book. Document the series with as many facts as I could glean from the materials and whenever possible, correct the errors that continue to be reprinted in other books. And this is what you hold in your hands. Every bit of information within the pages of his book originated from "reliable" materials in my personal archive. For the reasons stated above, I decided it would be unwise to consult previously published books on Rod Serling or *The Twilight Zone*. As a friend of mine once told me, "just because it's found in four different books does not make it a fact."

It is important to note that this book is about *The Twilight Zone* and not a biography about Rod Serling. Some publications have blended both themes, discussing personal opinions as fact when describing another person's thoughts or feelings. I have avoided this technique. Any statements alluded to Serling, such as "Serling felt comfortable," are not opinions based on my own interpretation of the research material. They are based on facts, such as a letter from Serling to a friend, expressing the very words that he "felt comfortable."

This book is not meant to offer a critical analysis of the episodes, nor approach the psychological aspect of fictional characters and how they were portrayed on screen. There is no exploration of Freudian terms or suggested sexual overtones, unless it involved a documented censorship issue. This book will not question the science and physics within the content of the episodes. Why did I choose to avoid this? Because Serling specifically asked the viewers to suspend disbelief in order to enjoy the stories and the morals they were designed to elucidate.

If there is a moral to be learned from watching an episode of *The Twilight Zone*, it comes across when viewed at home. There will be some information and trivia that fans of the program will find repetitive. This is unavoidable – especially since, at this late date, there have been a number of books and magazine articles about Rod Serling and *The Twilight Zone*. What I can assure you is that to the best of my ability, it is complete, accurate, and extensive. I consulted no books or websites for the sake of maintaining the accuracy of the contents in this book. Every piece of information in this book can be backed up and in most cases, verified using more than one reliable source.

As I was completing the rough draft of the book, I sought out help from a few "authorities" on *The Twilight Zone* that came recommended to me by word-of-mouth, in the hopes that they would lend a guiding hand. Instead, I received opposition in both verbal and written form: If Rod Serling was alive today, I am sure he would have been disappointed to learn that some people have taken a hobby and turned it into a religion. Along the way, however, I met another soul who had the same intentions as I, and he, too, received similar opposition. To finish the project, it soon became apparent that I should consult only close friends who I have known for years. They made suggestions, offered advice and they are without a doubt the best friends I could ever ask for.

With this in mind, I would like to thank many individuals who contributed to this book. In no particular order: Donald Ramlow, for his suggestions and review; Jim Widner, for his knowledge in all things science fiction; Ben Ohmart for his friendship and putting me in touch with many actors; June Foray; Roger Davis; Mariette Hartley; Michael Berger; R.R. King; William Allendoerfer; Brooke Hayward; Roy Bright, for his guidance and friendship; Warren Stevens; Jack French; Jacqueline Scott; Jen and Ken Stockinger; Cliff Robertson; Natalie Trundy; Patricia Breslin; Patricia Crowley; Tom Reese; Ruta Lee; Margarita Cordiva; Gail Kobe; Noah Keen; Marvin H. Petal; John Crawford; John Tomerlin; Walter E. Grauman; Russell Johnson; Orson Bean; Joseph Ruskin; Barbara Stuart; Jimmy Lydon; Josip Elic; Derek Tague, who assisted me at the New York Public Library for the Performing Arts, at Lincoln Center, Billy Rose Theater Collection; Lois Nettleton; Bob Cockrum; Clorinda Thompson; David Macklin; Virginia Trimble; Patrick Lucanio; Peter Mark Richman; James Callahan; Earl Hamner, Jr.; Professor John Furia, Jr., B.A.; Bill Jaker, Theodore Bikel; Ned Comstock; Paul Comi; Bill Sasser; Larry Floyd; Michelle Katherine; Gene Blottner; Richard Devon; H.W. Wynant; Kenneth Field; Karl Schadow; Rodney Bowcock; Mickey Rooney; Carol Summers and Jim Rosen, who put me in touch with many of the actors and directors from the television series; Jim Sheldon; Joanne Linville; Bill Seabrook; Scott Brogan; Bill Abbott; Bob Klein; James Best; Mike Tiefenbacher and Scott Shaw for helping assist me with the comic books; Wright King; Robert Redford; Nico Minardos; John Dunning; Mike Korologos; Marvin Petal; Jonathan Winters; Richard Fry; Rick Keating; Anne Francis; Charlie Summers and the OTR Digest; William Windom; Bill Mumy; Arlene Osborne; Martin Landau; Morgan Brittany; Joseph Ruskin; Laurie Jacobson; Jean Carson; Steve Kostelecky; Jack Klugman; Chuck Hicks; Richard Donner; Shelley Berman; Nancy Malone; Barry Nelson; George Takei; Jack Grinnage; Curt Phillips; Del Reisman; Buck Houghton; Suzanne Lloyd; Kermyt Anderson; Tim Matheson; Paul Adomites; Susan Gordon; George Grizzard; Scott Livingston; Henri Lanoë; the staff at Lazy River Books; W. Gary Wetstein; Dara Hoffman; Jonathan Harris; Ted Post; Richard Erdman; Antoinette Bower; Bill Idelson; Mary Wood for sharing a few of the letters and telegrams she collected over the years; Jeff Pirtle and LeeAnn Platner of NBC Universal; Seth T. Smolinske; George Barris; Joji A. Barris; Barry Hoffman; Richard L. Bare; Earl Holliman; Beverly Garland; Kevin McCarthy; Orson Bean; and Joyce Van Patten.

The following people were responsible for helping me with research for the music scores in this book: Graham Newton, whose knowledge of the CBS Music Stock Library is beyond comprehension; Mike Biel, a good friend who put me in touch with Graham; the library staff at USC; Lauren Buisson and her staff of the UCLA Performing Arts Special Collections; and Carson Cohen, Philip Sternenburg, Paul Giammarco and Matt Vandermast for clarifying a number of music cues.

For generously providing permission for the use of photos, quotations, letters, and literary material: Steve Boisson; Matthew R. Bradley; Stephen Tippie of *The Chicago Tribune*; Hugh Hefner; Susan Ramer at Congdon and Associates; Christopher Beaumont; Heather Penn of NEA, Inc.; Tom Weaver; Richard Matheson and his son Richard Christian Matheson; Lisa DeMille of the J. Willard Marriott Library; Noel Sturgeon, Chris Lotts, and Adam Lefton of the Theodore Sturgeon Trust; Richard Kiel; the staff of *Variety*; Mark Phillips; Lynn Eaton at Duke University for assisting me with the Dan Seymour Papers; Francis M. Nevins, a good friend and expert on copyright law (he teaches it); Frances Pardee of the Jerry Sohl Estate and Trust; Carl Amari of Falcon Picture Group who was also instrumental in getting me in touch with Jeff Nemerovski, Roni Mueler, Risa Kessler and Grace Goldblatt of CBS; Ray Bradbury; William F. Nolan; George Clayton Johnson; and Lisa Chambers and Brooke Fairey of *TV Guide*.

Photos in this book were provided by a number of individuals: of actors, writers and directors who were involved with the actual productions and were kind enough to mail me the photos from their personal collection. I also want to thank Darlene K. Swanson and Dan Swanson of Van-garde Imagery, Inc. for the hard work they put into each page of the book.

The one person I am most indebted to is Terry Salomonson. I met Terry along the well-traveled road and he spent countless hours assisting me in the research for this book. He offered suggestions, double checked facts by reviewing various prints of the television episodes, and drove a ton of Serling memorabilia from a private collector's archive to my house. My wife likes to say that our house is God's house. Terry's Michigan-based generosity not only earned him a key to our front door, but to our hearts as well.

Any hobby, whether it be collecting stamps, collecting old-time radio shows or viewing *The Twilight Zone*, lends itself a form of gratitude to the fan clubs, newsletters, websites and books published on the subject. Without these, any hobby would diminish in size. There have been a bazillion books written on *The Twilight Zone* already, and there will probably be a bazillion more. Each one contributes something of importance to those who appreciate the program, and it is my hope that this book augments these contributions.

Regarding the subject of contributions . . . this book was a labor of love for me. I never wrote it for the purpose of name glory or financial profit. With this in mind, I have arranged with the publishers to donate my royalties (the standard percentage of net profits for any author) to the Johns Hopkins Comprehensive Cancer Center. Some people dismiss cancer as a six-letter word, until they observe a friend or family relative suffering from the disease. Johns Hopkins is a leading contributor to the fight and prevention of cancer. Through this arrangement, the book will contribute much more than a few pages of text.

If I may close on a positive note, this marks my 17th successfully published book. Every book has been a learning experience and with the completion of each project, I realize I made new friends. *The Twilight Zone* is no exception. For everyone who helped me along, I offer my sincere appreciation.

Now let us travel down that road toward the signpost up ahead . . .

Martin Grams Jr.
August 2007

History of *The Twilight Zone*

CHAPTER ONE

Dr. Christian Meets Rod Serling

While many maintain that *The Twilight Zone* influenced a great number of authors, television producers, scriptwriters and fans in general, the television program was influenced by the standards of the broadcast networks. Rod Serling worked first in radio and then moved on to television in Cincinnati (teaching himself, through actual writing, whatever he learned of playwriting). Wanting to make a profession of writing, he was at the radio's speaker, often favoring good dramas and programs of serious horror and science fiction. Shows such as *Suspense* and *The Mysterious Traveler* may well have been influences for the types of stories of which he grew fond.

One of Serling's earliest jobs was as an unsalaried volunteer writer and actor with WNYC, a New York City radio station. Later he worked for stations in Marion and Springfield, Ohio, as well as his native Binghamton, N.Y., and Cincinnati.

"In 1946, I started writing for radio at a New York City station and thereafter did radio writing at other small stations," he recalled. "It was experience, but incidental experience. I learned 'time,' writing for a medium that is measured in seconds. Radio and its offspring, television, are unique in the stringency of the time factor. Radio and TV stations gave me a look-see at the factory that would produce my product. I got to understand the basic workings of cameras, lights and microphones. I got a sense of the space that could be utilized and the number of people who might be accommodated in that space. This was all to the good."

The radio programs Serling wrote for, however, were not broadcast nationally on a coast-to-coast hookup. They were not sponsored. In fact, almost all of them were sustained, that is, the production costs were borne by the network rather than a sponsor. Cheap to produce, these programs required no major film stars to pay, and there was no shortage of radio actors willing to work for union scale. For him, this was experience needed for a writer with no credits to his name, to get his foot in the door for programs that paid much more – courtesy of well-heeled sponsors willing to pick up the tab.

The Chesebrough Manufacturing Company, for example, sponsored a long-running radio program titled *Dr. Christian*. The program featured top-quality dramas of a country doctor who applied the Golden Rule approach to life when facing obstacles that required his inner strength for support.

In the beginning, the *Dr. Christian* radio program came from various scriptwriters, among them Ruth Adams Knight. In 1942, the producers tried a new approach: a contest in which listeners could submit scripts and be eligible for large cash prizes. This may have been the most significant factor in the program's long 17-year history. Suddenly, everyone in the country was a scriptwriter. Weekly awards ranged from $150 to $500, good money in 1942, and the grand prize won the author $2,000. It soon became *The Vaseline Program*, "the only show in radio where the audience writes the script." *Newsweek* reported that 7,697 scripts were received in 1947; sometimes that number went as high as 10,000. Many were called, however, but few were chosen.

The scripts that made it to the air continued the appeal of traditional values, showing Dr. Christian as the symbol of good will, as a philanthropist and an unabashed Cupid. The subject matter would include anything – even fantasy. One show was about a mermaid; on another, a human-like jalopy named Betsy fell in love with a black Packard owned by a woman chief of police. Only when murder was the theme of a script did listeners complain; they liked the show when it was mellow. The 1947 prize play concerned Dr. Christian's effort to convince an unborn child that Earth was not so bad after all.

At Antioch College in Yellow Springs, Ohio, Rod Serling majored in language and literature and began writing scripts for radio. He became manager of the Antioch Broadcasting System's radio workshop where he wrote, directed and acted in weekly full-scale radio productions broadcast over WJEM, Springfield. With confidence on his shoulder, during the 1948-49 school year, the entire output of the workshop was written by Serling. With the exception of one adaptation, all of the radio scripts were entirely original. Later he would look back and call this work some "pretty bad stuff."

For the broadcast of May 18, 1949, the eighth annual scriptwriting contest of *Dr. Christian* ended with a special broadcast revealing the year's winners. Among the guests on that particular program was Rod Serling, who at the time was attending Antioch College. The producers of the radio show even paid him $76.56 to reimburse his expenses in getting to CBS in New York City to appear on the *Dr. Christian* program. His submission, titled "To Live a Dream," had won approval of the judges and been accepted by producer Dorothy McCann. Serling's script helped him place in the radio contest that netted him a $500 award.

Serling brought along his wife, Carol, to attend the radio broadcast. Among the cast on stage were star Jean Hersholt, Helen Claire as nurse Judy Price, and prizewinners Russell F. Johnson, Maree Dow Gagne, Mrs. Aida Cromwell, Miss Terry McCoog, Earl Hamner, Jr. and Mrs. Halle Truitt Yenni. The program, still sponsored by Chesebrough, was the 546th broadcast of the series. Russell F. Johnson of Thomaston, Connecticut won the $2,000 first prize for his script titled, "Stolen Glory." Mrs. Lillian Kerr of Tillamook, Oregon, won $500 for her script titled, "Angel with a Black Eye." Earl Hamner, Jr. of Cincinnati, Ohio (the same Hamner who would later write scripts for *The Twilight Zone*), won $500 for his script titled "All Things Come Home." This was not Hamner's first time winning the contest. He had been on the show previous for his award-winning scripts, "Now That Spring is There" and "Who Would Not Sing for David?"

One by one, the prizewinners were announced and interviewed on stage. Biographical background, professional endeavors and their writing ambitions were discussed. Halfway through the broadcast, Rod Serling came to the microphone.

HERSHOLT: *Hello, Rod . . . and congratulations. I read your winning script, "To Live a Dream," and I thought it was a fine job of writing.*

SERLING: *Thank you, Mr. Hersholt. You've no idea how thrilled I am to know that you and the judges selected my script as one of the winners.*

HERSHOLT: *Now tell us a little about yourself, Rod.*

SERLING: *Well . . . I first saw the light of day in Syracuse, New York, graduated from Binghamton High School, at Binghamton, New York . . . And am now in my third year of college at Antioch College, Yellow Springs, Ohio.*

HERSHOLT: *You covered an awful lot of years in an awfully few words. What happened during all that time?*

SERLING: *Well . . . before the war I did some staff work at a Binghamton radio station . . . tried to write . . . but never had anything published.*

HERSHOLT: *And during the war?*

SERLING: *I was in the same place as Russell Johnson . . . the Pacific . . . with the Army.*

HERSHOLT: *What did you do in the Army?*

SERLING: *I was a paratrooper.*

HERSHOLT: *Where did you get the idea for this fine story you wrote?*

SERLING: *Well . . . I've always been fond of boxing . . . tried my hand in the Golden Gloves. And well . . . since you've read my story, you know where it all ties in.*

HERSHOLT: *Indeed I do. And do you intend to follow writing as a profession?*

SERLING: *I'd like to, Mr. Hersholt. In fact, the ambition of my wife and I . . .*

HERSHOLT: *Oh . . . another married man!*

SERLING: *How did Russell Johnson say it? Yes, sir!*

HERSHOLT: *And is your wife sitting out front, too?*

SERLING: *Yes, sir . . . right there.*

HERSHOLT: *Well, let's have her stand up and take a bow, too . . . Mrs. Rod Serling . . .*

(Applause)

HERSHOLT: *Well, well, you ex-G.I.s certainly specialize in beautiful brides. And now, back to that ambition of yours.*

SERLING: *Well, we want to live in a large house, in the suburb of a large city, raise a family, a lot of dogs . . . and write!*

HERSHOLT: *And I certainly hope you realize such a fine American ambition, Mr. Serling. Maybe this check for five hundred dollars will go toward part of the down payment on that dream! Congratulations . . . and good luck to you!*

SERLING: *Thank you, Mr. Hersholt.*

The Radio Scripts

Serling's success earned him a credit that would gain the attention of other radio producers, when he included a cover letter with a submission. Broadcasting standards during the 1940s were much different from the standards enforced by the late 1950s. The policy of reviewing and accepting unsolicited radio scripts and plot proposals varied from one producer to the next. While many programs had a staff of writers, other programs occasionally purchased submissions from the open market. *Suspense*, a radio anthology specializing in thrilling crime dramas, for example, bought scripts from a deaf mute in Brooklyn, a night watchman from Chicago, a cowhand in Wyoming, and one script from a former inmate of San Quentin.

By the 1950s, however, a few who submitted plot proposals and scripts were seeking vengeance for their rejected submissions. They filed lawsuits against the producers and the networks whenever they heard a program of similar nature, claiming their ideas were "stolen" without due compensation. The networks began enforcing policies, in agreement with radio and television producers, not to review or accept any outside submissions. For scriptwriters offering their work in the hopes of making a sale it became a bit more complicated.

The success of the *Dr. Christian* radio script led to multiple attempts on Serling's part to submit more proposals to other coast-to-coast radio programs.

"I just kept on," he recalled years later to a newspaper columnist. "I had to earn a living and took a staff writing job on a Cincinnati radio station; but during every spare moment I turned out more free-lance scripts. Finally, I sold three others, but for each play accepted there were at least three or more turned down."

With success came the eventual edge of defeat. On September 8, 1949, Serling's radio script "Potter's Paradise" was rejected by the advertising agency, Wallace-Ferry-Hanly Company, for the *First Nighter Program*. Ira L. Avery, producer for Armstrong's *Theatre of Today*, rejected his script "The Memory" in October, because "in the handling of familiar plots and themes, selection needs to be placed on a level determined by the volume and quality of submissions. We regret that, in the light of heavy competition, we do not find this story suited to our current needs."

After peddling a football script titled "Cupid at Left Half" to *Curtain Time* and finding that script rejected, he wrote to Myron Golden, script editor of the radio program, to ask why he had failed to sell a single script to *Curtain Time*. On October 10, 1949, he sent the following candid reply: "This particular script lacks a professional quality. The dialog is spotty, the plot is loose, and the whole thing lacks verisimilitude . . . It appears to be a standard plot that writers somehow or other manage to pluck out of the public domain." *

On August 10, 1949, producer/director Martin Horrell of *Grand Central Station* rejected Serling's prizefight script titled "Winner Take Nothing." The script was "better than average" Horrell admitted, but the ladies who listened to his program on Saturday afternoons "have told us in no uncertain terms that prize fight stories aren't what they like most." In a letter, Horrell offered him what may have been the best advice given to the young Ohio resident. "I have a feeling that the script

---

* Two of Serling's earliest attempts to sell scripts to a national radio program are evident in "Look to the Sky," dated July 13, 1947, and "The Most Dangerous Game," dated June 22, 1947. The latter script was adapted from the Richard Connell short story of the same name.

would be far better for sight than for sound only, because in any radio presentation, the fights are not seen. Perhaps this is a baby you should try on some of the producers of television shows."

"Those were discouraging, frustrating years," he told a columnist in early 1960. "I wanted to quit many times. But there was something within me that made me go on. I continued writing and submitting scripts without pay and, what is even worse, most of the time, without recognition. Then at last I came up with two plays that were bought by the old *Grand Central Station* series on CBS Radio. I thought that now surely I was in. But I wasn't. Day after day, I continued to pound the typewriter, with no result."

Grand Central Station was a radio anthology consisting of light comedies and fluffy romance. Serling's first sale to the program was "The Local is a Very Slow Train." Broadcast on September 10, 1949, under the new title of "Hop Off the Express and Grab a Local," the story concerned two young men, Joey and Steve, who became involved in a murder case while trying to escape the slums of the city where they live. His second sale for the series was "The Welcome Home," broadcast on December 31, 1949, and concerned the story of Bill Grant, a crusading reporter for the fictional New York *Globe*.

While his first sale was the prize-winning *Dr. Christian* script, the first script to be dramatized nationally on radio was the September 10, 1949 broadcast of *Grand Central Station*. In early November, his luck hung on long enough for him to receive a letter from Rita Franklin of the *Dr. Christian* program, alerting him that his prize-winning "To Live a Dream," would finally be broadcast on December 7, 1949. Scheduling conflicts pushed the script ahead a week to November 30, 1949, and Rod Serling's name was once again referenced on the *Dr. Christian* radio program. *

Serling began working at radio stations such as WJEL in Springfield, Ohio, and WMRN in Marion, Ohio. Months later, in the spring of 1950, he graduated from college, and his first job was at WLW in Cincinnati, the Crosley Broadcasting Corporation's flagship station. The college radio work had paid $45 to $50 a week, but WLW was offering $75 weekly and the young playwright accepted the job. Members of the program's casts were students of the radio department at the College of Music in Cincinnati, and he often found himself playing a role or two for some of the broadcasts. It should be noted that among the leaders of the entertainment industry who began their careers at WLW were Rosemary Clooney, Betty Clooney, Red Skelton, Red Barber, Jane Froman, The Mills Brothers, Virginia Payne, Doris Day, Durward Kirby, Eddie Albert, and Janette Davis.**

Sometime in 1950 or 1951, Serling sold Crosley a number of scripts for dramatization on both radio and television. It is not clear whether the dramas made it to the airwaves, but he did revise the scripts slightly and sold them to various television anthologies. Among the scripts were "Grady Everett for the People," "Law Nine Concerning Christmas," "The Sands of Tom," "The Time Element,"

---

* Serling later submitted a second script to the *Dr. Christian* radio program that was originally titled "The Power of Abner Doubleday" (for reasons unknown the title changed to "The Power of Willie Doubleday") but failed to make the sale.

** The Crosley Broadcasting Corporation, founded by radio manufacturing pioneer Powel Crosley, Jr., was an early operator of radio stations in the U.S. During World War II, it operated as many as five shortwave stations, using the call signs WLWK, WLWL, WLWO, WLWR and WLWS. In 1945, the Crosley interests were purchased by the Aviation Corporation. The radio and appliance manufacturing arm changed its name to Avco, but the broadcast operations continued to operate under the Crosley name. From the 1950s through the 1970s, Crosley (or Avco) operated a small television network in which programs were produced at one of its stations and broadcast on the other Crosley stations in the Midwest, and occasionally by non-Crosley stations.

"The Carlson Legend," "The Face of Autumn," "The Hill," "A Time for Heroes," "The Keeper of the Chair," "Aftermath" and "The Steel Casket."

Serling also composed a number of radio scripts for a proposed radio series titled *It Happens to You*. Among the scripts for this series were "Mr. Finchley Versus the Bomb" and "You Be the Bad Guy" (both of which were later dramatized on *The Lux Video Theater*); "And Then Came Jones," about the mishaps of Wendell Jones, who had papers claiming ownership to all the area within six and a half miles of Times Square; "The Gallant Breed of Men," about Captain Peter Bruce, an ex-captain in the Merchant Marine with a conscience; and "Law Nine Concerning Christmas," details of which can be found under the episode entry for "The Obsolete Man."

From October 14, 1950 to February 17, 1951, Serling authored a weekly program titled *Adventure Express*, which dramatized the exciting travels of Billy, Betty and their Uncle Jim, who traveled by train across the country seeking high adventure. Each week they stopped at a different town and got involved with the locals. One episode, for example, took place in the wooded countryside of Kansas, and another took place in the state of Florida. From July 23, 1951 to August 23, 1951, he wrote a number of scripts for a weekly program titled *Leave it to Kathy*. From September to October of 1951, *Our America* presented historical biographies of American historical figures such as Jefferson Davis, General Custer and Lewis and Clark. From November 24, 1951 to December 8, 1951, a similar radio program titled *Builders of Destiny* gave him the opportunity to dramatize biographies of Zane Grey and General Philip Sheridan. *

On November 25, 1949, John Driscoll, story editor for *The Cavalcade of America*, rejected Serling's plot outline titled "Father of the Common School," which he would later rewrite for an episode of the short-run historical dramas broadcast over WLW.

"From a writing point of view, radio ate up ideas that might have put food on the table for weeks at a future freelancing date," he later said. "The minute you tie yourself down to a radio or TV station, you write around the clock. You rip out ideas, many of them irreplaceable. They go on and consequently can never go on again. And you've sold them for $50 a week. You can't afford to give away ideas – they're too damn hard to come by. If I had it to do over, I wouldn't staff-write at all. I'd find some other way to support myself while getting a start as a writer."

Blanche Gaines

On July 31, 1950, through the advice of friends and rejection letters, Rod Serling wrote to Blanche Gaines in New York – an agent who specialized in handling about two dozen clients attempting to sell scripts to both radio and television. Blanche was the widow of Charles Gaines, who had died in 1947. He was vice president of the World Broadcasting System, a pioneer in the production of recorded radio series. Among her clients were Frank Gilroy, Jerome Ross, Nelson Bond and Helen Cotton. He included a few scripts ("Vertical Deep," "The Air is Free," and "Look to the Sky"), as samples of his work and a résumé of successful sales to *Dr. Christian* and *Grand Central Station*. Gaines reviewed the material and gave her opinion regarding the plots and the prose, suggesting a

---

* The dates of broadcast are accurate in this paragraph, but may not necessarily be the exact premiere and concluding airdates. A complete set of scripts was not available during research and it was determined to list the earliest and latest known dates of broadcast for those particular series.

variety of programs for which to submit them, most notably television's *Lights Out!* and the radio anthology, *Suspense*. She agreed to handle his material on a 15 percent commission basis. "It is more difficult to work with a writer who is living so far away from New York," she explained, "but I think your stuff has merit and am willing to try and see what I can do with it."

Serling wrote back saying that he was concerned about the 15 percent fee, but Gaines assured him that it was not permanent. After the tenth sale by the same writer, she reduced her commission to 10 percent, explaining that earliest efforts often brought about more rejections, and the 5 percent difference offset the costs involved. In the meantime, she submitted scripts such as "Temptation," "The Air is Free," "Look to the Sky" and "Vertical Deep" to *Suspense*, which were all promptly rejected for various reasons.

On November 11, 1950, Rod Serling composed a general outline of a television series titled *Monday Morning Quarterback*. The program, he proposed, would involve an emcee, studio guests and film shots consisting of the highlights of a comparatively old football game. While the film was being shown, the emcee narrated the actions on the screen. At one point in the game when the offensive team was about to make a crucial decision, the film would be stopped as the team went out of its huddle and to the line for a play. At this point the emcee would ask the studio guests (professional football players, well-known coaches, sports writers, etc.) what play they would call under the circumstances. He was unable to make the sale.

Serling wrote a teleplay titled "Sweeney," and managed on his own to sell it to television's *Stars Over Hollywood*, broadcast under the title "Merry Christmas From Sweeney" on December 20, 1950. A months before, he had sold the producers another teleplay, "Grady Everett for the People," broadcast on September 13, 1950. Blanche Gaines soon learned about the sale and insisted he sign up because "an agent can make a better business arrangement for you than you can yourself."

Serling agreed and Blanche Gaines not only encouraged the young playwright to continue writing scripts, but also presented his best efforts to producers who were open to submissions from the open market. "Blanche Gaines represents 10 percent of everything from my budget to my libido," he commented a couple years later, "but an agent is nigh on to irreplaceable in television writing. Most buying programs prefer submissions from agents. In this way, they eliminate the crackpot element whose writing is more therapeutic than economic or artistic."

The method of operation for dramatic programs was for the writer to compose a plot synopsis (between one and 20-plus pages), dictating not just the plot, but also the message being sent through the story, special camera techniques, and other important factors related to the broadcast. If a producer or story editor accepted the treatment, he would purchase the story and then commission a member of their staff (or the person who submitted the plot outline, if they have experience) to write the script.

"After learning the physical technique of splitting a page, indicating stage action, and suggesting basic camera shots – all that's left is a story," Serling explained for a magazine in the mid-1950s. "You can be supplied with the techniques – tools, if you will – but the telling is your baby and you do it your way. Secondly, and this follows, you're dealing with ideas and you can't be taught an original idea. Thirdly, your writing will cover a multitude of plots, people, attitudes and motives. All these components you get from observation, not from lectures. A general course in any of the humanities serves you better stead than a dozen applied writing courses. This plus listening, looking, feeling and imagining – all add up to subject matter."

The year 1952 promoted Serling to a level of success that he failed to achieve the previous year. The major reason was Blanche Gaines. For every script he finished, she sent a formal submission to story editors and producers of radio and television programs that were on her lists. Every script that was rejected by one program was resubmitted to a different program. No effort was wasted and sales started growing.

On January 2, 1952, the *Dr. Christian* radio program presented "The Long Black Night," which was a major rewrite of Serling's earlier prize-winning script, "To Live a Dream."

The *Lux Video Theater* purchased a number of scripts, resulting in five telecasts that year with Serling's name acknowledged as the author. "Mr. Finchley Versus the Bomb" (January 7, 1952) was a comedy featuring Henry Hull as Jason W. Finchley, the sole occupant of a ghost town who refused to leave when the Army selected it as an A-bomb site, and Arlene Francis as a reporter who became personally involved in his story. "Welcome Home, Lefty" (June 23, 1952), featured Chester Morris in the title role, as a pitcher who returned home after playing 17 years in the major leagues. "You Be the Bad Guy" (August 18, 1952) starred Macdonald Carey as a policeman demoted for not being tough enough on criminals, and his kid brother, a ne'er-do-well with a chip on his shoulder. "The Face of Autumn" (November 3, 1952) featured Pat O'Brien as a down-on-his luck fight manager who persisted in trying to find a champion, while his wife begged him to give up the boxing racket. In "The Hill" (November 24, 1952), Mercedes McCambridge played a war correspondent covering the attempt of soldiers to secure a strategic battle position during the Korean War. *

The Television Scripts

"You can make good money in television," Serling recalled. "Not swimming pool-capital gains kind of money – but enough so your kid can go to college and your wife can buy a fur coat without your having a trauma. The budgetary problem involves learning how to stretch out the good months to cover the not so good. The high part of the hog is meaty but not endless. Eat well but put some meat in the freezer."

Additional sales that year included a plot proposal titled "Ward 8," sold to the *Armstrong Circle Theater* on March 7, 1952. The story concerned a sergeant, suffering a head wound, who is brought into the same hospital ward as four soldiers from his platoon; those four are the only survivors from a platoon of 40 men. They blame the sergeant for his poor leadership in battle, despite his prior record of heroism. Roger Garis wrote the teleplay as adapted from his story, and it aired on April 29, 1952, under the title "The Sergeant."

The *Hallmark Hall of Fame* purchased two teleplays. In "The Carlson Legend," telecast on August 3, 1952, a young state senator runs into a moral problem while conducting a cleanup campaign. In "I Lift Up My Lamp," telecast August 17, 1952, a young Czech girl in the United States faces the choice of returning to her family behind the Iron Curtain, or remaining free in America.

Despite both positive and bad reviews, whether his name was spelled "Sterling" or "Serling" in those reviews, he was always given to deprecating himself (with a good deal of charm) and reached the point where, as Blanche Gaines defined it to a newspaper columnist, "He can run himself down with some assurance."

---

*If you change the sport from baseball to boxing in "Welcome Home, Lefty," and expand the length of the teleplay, the premise of the *Lux* presentation was in many respects, an early rendition of what would later become "Requiem for a Heavyweight" for *Playhouse 90*.

Rod Serling took a standard B.A. in a liberal arts college, Ohio's Antioch, with a nominal number of applied writing courses. He drew daily from his college education that included psychology and political science, as well as literature. Shakespeare's "psychology" and "unity of time and place," Milton's "good-evil," as well as the entire chronological line of classic to realistic drama provided a background for his television writing. It was in 1953 that Serling stylistically and thematically used all of these for his latest teleplays. The *Lux* presentation "You Be the Bad Guy" was thematically a story of fratricide. In the spring of 1953, he sold a script called "Next of Kin," telecast on the *Kraft Television Theater*, which dealt in part with marital infidelity.

"I read in the newspaper about three men from the Greater Cincinnati area who were missing in action," he recalled. "The account mentioned names, addresses, names of parents. One guy was from the Bottoms, one from a ritzy section of town, the third from some nondescript suburb. I got to thinking. How does each family react? Is it a universal emotion or does each family react according to its economic station? In my play, three different types of families receive 'missing in action' telegrams from the War Department."

"Next of Kin" was a successful production. Taken straight from the headlines, it was not the typical boy-meets-girl premise. "I read in *Variety* not long ago that film producers on the West Coast admit to a much narrower thematic field than their live sisters in the East," he recalled. "Check your film shows. With a few exceptions they seem to be lukewarm stuff, always ending on a happy note. I don't object to happiness. I do object to its being a requirement in drama."

"In television, the hour long program is the better paying and provides the most prestige," Serling wrote for a magazine article in December of 1953. "In addition, you get a creative kick out of having 50-odd minutes to work a plot, delineate characters, provide motivation and resolve." Serling's pay for his earliest efforts was $1,250 on average for a first time sale. *Kraft* paid $1,000. Half-hour shows paid, on average, $700 to $750 per script.

Kraft Television Theatre had earned a reputation for being one of television's most prestigious showcases, winning top ratings and awards. When Ed Rice began buying Serling's teleplays, the critics did not overlook the subject matter. In "The Blues for Joey Menotti" (August 26, 1953) Serling scripted a prostitute as the female lead. "A Long Time Till Dawn" (November 11, 1953) concerned itself with paranoia and homicide.

For all practical purposes, the television business was located in two places, and Rod Serling had become weary of commuting to both coasts from Cincinnati. In 1954, he and his wife, two children and two dogs moved to Westport, Connecticut, on the advice of Blanche Gaines. The Serling family enjoyed a new nine-room house in a section of town that was not particularly exclusive. By this time, he dismissed writing radio dramas and focused primarily on television. Moreover, for every rejection, he wrote another play and continued to revise rejected scripts.

"The writer who's stubborn," an advertising agency executive observed with the finality of a man fronting for a sponsor, "sells relatively few scripts. The writer most frequently employed is (1) a man of talent and (2) ready to be reasonable. Aside from that, if we get one script a year that's 100 percent ready to go, it's time to declare a legal holiday." The judgment of those concerned with Serling's "Patterns," all of them working for the *Kraft Television Theatre* at J. Walter Thompson Advertising Agency at the time, was that when the script was submitted, it was, in the words of Arthur Heineman, one of the script editors, "50 or 60 percent ready to go."

In its original form, it made more of the protagonist's wife than the protagonist. The story's resolution – the confrontation of old tycoon by young tycoon – was handled differently. Consideration for the proper industrial atmosphere was lacking. By the time "Patterns" went on the air in January of 1955, the drive had been shifted from wife to husband (by the agreement of all hands). The atmosphere had been supplied by Fielder Cook, the director, who was then working for *Kraft* and who borrowed much of the Thompson physical layout for "Patterns." The ending had been worked out by, Arthur Singer, another story editor. Serling not merely accepted these decisions but, with a forthrightness that unquestionably must have lacerated his spirit, praised them.

On the evening of January 12, 1955, *Kraft Television Theater* presented "Patterns," the story of the clash between a decent but ambitious young man, and an indecent older man in an industrial empire. The story was a favorite one at the time of "live" broadcasting. It allowed for the possibility of dramatic conflict, of psychological probing (not far removed from the surface), and of rapid characterization. At the same time, it avoided all of the things considered controversial in television: race, politics and sticky social problems. It made no troublesome comment on the American way, carefully confining itself to the paring of slices of life.

"The atmosphere and mood, plus some of the finest camera work and direction I have ever seen, were his," Serling recalled of Cook. "It turned out to be one of the play's biggest features. I fought against them both; I'm glad I lost." Rod Serling and his wife had gone out for the evening, leaving the babysitter to handle their two children, Jodi and Nan. Having recently moved into the house, the Serlings were certain that the phone would remain silent all evening. They returned to discover the phone started ringing and did not stop.

"From '*Patterns*' on," he recalled, "I suffered what every writer's suffered from a single big success – the expectations that go with it, the publicity, the attention given to everything he does. This is as it should be. You've got to pay for success as well as achieve it. So much of what I put on after that was dictated by economic considerations, too. I had to live. Unlike a legitimate theatre man, I don't have 18 months to three years for another success. I've got weeks."

"But the critics and the audience who put me up there in that 80 percent bracket shouldn't be expected to make allowances for that," he went on resolutely. "So what did I do? I took assignments right and left, because they were waiting for me in a way they never had been, and also because I'm the kind of guy who depends on impetus, or I'll swear my brain's going to atrophy. That's why I never take long vacations."

A contract through CBS dated September 1, 1955, granted the network an exclusive on Rod Serling, which he signed because the offer was too good to pass up. The contract required him to submit to the network (and the programs they televised) a maximum of 12 different ideas; a minimum of these nine had to be full outlines. There were to be at least six full scripts and four adaptations completed. He had the right to reject up to two adaptations, and the network had the right to offer two additional. In compensation, he would be paid $1,500 for every adaptation, $2,500 for every script accepted by the network, and a guarantee of $288.46 per week for one year. At the end of the first year, CBS had the option to renew his contract within 30 days prior notice. Serling then had the option to accept or reject within 21 days. The second year, should the contract be renewed, guaranteed the playwright $18,000 ($3,000 per script, $1,750 per adaptation). Year 3, should the contract be renewed again, guaranteed $20,000 ($3,333.33 per script, $2,000 per adaptation).

Under the contract, CBS received first option for any program ideas he would create. If the network rejected any of his proposals, Serling then had the right to submit his proposal to another network.

The successful playwright soon found himself writing scripts to satisfy the volume of demand and meet his contractual obligation. In one week of November 1955, for example, three of his plays were telecast. *The U.S. Steel Hour* presented "Incident in an Alley" on the evening of November 23, "Portrait in Celluloid" the following night on *Climax!*, and "The Man Who Caught the Ball at Coogan's Bluff" for *Studio One* on November 28.

Between trying to live up to expectations, fighting down fears of mental atrophy and trying to make money, his output swelled and its quality, in the opinion of critics, thinned. From February of 1955, when "Patterns" was shown for a second time, until "Requiem for a Heavyweight" won unanimously excellent reviews, 13 of his plays or adaptations were televised. Only one or two were well received. A Philadelphia reviewer wrote that he had "cluttered TV channels with a dismaying collection of junk."

His reaction (particularly in the week when three of his shows failed) was not uncommon. "I felt I was not a good writer," he said. "I felt that I couldn't capture the universality of my material." Although he staked everything on "Requiem for a Heavyweight" as a sort of rehabilitation project, there was no permanent damage to his ego, as his next remark showed. "I felt that what I did in the future would be plays that would be good audience shows or good critical shows, but not both."

Rod Serling was honored with a number of awards for "Patterns" and "Requiem for a Heavyweight," but the top honors came when he was bestowed the Sylvania Award for "Best Television Writing" and the Academy of Television Arts & Sciences handed out the Emmy Award for "Best Teleplay Writing." "Requiem" had proven to critics and television producers that "Patterns" was not the playwright's one-hit wonder.

Robert Redford in "Nothing in the Dark"

The Tale of the Metal Monster

From August 3, 1951 to June 12, 1953, ABC-TV offered an adult science fiction anthology titled *Tales of Tomorrow*. The stories ranged from time-travel to alien invasions, supernatural happenings and adaptations of classic works of literature. In 1952, Serling submitted what became his earliest efforts to write science fiction for television. As an admirer of the series, he contacted Mort Abrahams in New York City with two plot outlines called "The Oath" and "A Gift for a Metal Monster." "The Oath," dealt with a sensitive Czech surgeon, a "reflective little man" who spent a number of years in concentration camps for political beliefs. During that time and in the process of his political "rehabilitation," his captors broke his fingers and he never again was able to perform brain surgery.

Called into the cellar headquarters of the Prague Underground to administer to a young man hurt in a shooting foray, the surgeon discovers the events also resulted in the wounding of the local commissar who was much-hated in that area. In the cellar, the television audience would get a studied view of the underground – the courage of the men and women, the pathos of their existence and the almost religious fervor of even the littlest person among them. They inform the doctor of what has transpired with the commissar. It happens that he is well known to the doctor from previous years when they attended college together.

Later, the doctor is summoned clandestinely to the home of the commissar. He is weak to the point of dying, but he is conscious enough to have his cronies contact the doctor and call him in for consultation and eventual surgery. The doctor balks. With his broken, stiff, out-of-practice fingers, he does not dare attempt anything as complex and demanding as the operation necessary to save the commissar. In addition, his conscience stops at the prospect of saving the life of a butcher.

The people in the underground, informed of the situation, berate the doctor for even considering operating on their enemy – that in a sense he would be undoing what they had spent many painstaking months planning and finally executing. The doctor, however, faces a conflict of ideas and emotions. The commissar has appealed to him on quite another level than politics – as an old friend and a human being. Deep down, for the doctor, is the professional pride of a surgeon who was once great – a medical man who took the Hippocratic Oath to administer to anyone requiring his skill.

Confronted by the forces of conscience on one side and the forces of practical, common sense on the other, it appeared that he alone could save the life of the butcher. He finally agrees to the operation – over the objections of those in the underground who have done everything they can to prevent it. On the table in a dimly lit cellar, the surgeon performs the operation, and is successful. The people of the underground, upon hearing the news, turn their backs on the doctor – unwilling to reconcile what he has accomplished.

The upshot is that the commissar goes from operating table to liquidation by his own party. They assume that because an underground doctor operated that the patient is politically unreliable. They cannot think in terms of this being a human act. Their minds cannot conceive of this kind of humanity. Therefore, the surgeon accomplishes two things. He saves his conscience and he rids the country of a mortal enemy.

In "A Gift for a Metal Monster," Dr. Leslie Craig resides in a secluded laboratory in the Northwest woods. Craig has been experimenting with guided electrical impulses with the aim of creating a mechanical man. Not the circus freak who in a grotesque, metallic voice adds five and five and counts up to 10, this robot possesses the one thing that no other man-made creature ever possessed – the ability to reason, a brain whereby the robot can think for himself. Craig, however, discovers that his experiment is a failure. Before retiring, he meets a similar metal man, who explains to the doctor that he came from "outside Earth" who is representing a race of superior beings who utilize mechanical men. They are a race that long ago conquered evil by curbing what natural evil lies in human nature – itself. They have been sending their robots from planet to planet, taking over in order to save the planet from itself by eliminating its wars, its quarreling factions, its hell-weapons.

This particular robot's assignment was Earth, and it has found enough evidence to justify returning to his masters with the recommendation of immediate "subjugation." The robots will arrive to take over every phase of existence from government to social order. He tells the doctor that he plans to remain for a few days longer to acquaint himself further with Earthly customs before returning home. The good doctor pleads with the robot for the freedom of humankind, using as his argument the basic decency that exists in all men. The robot scoffs at this, pointing out that there is no room for improvement. The metal man's assumptions are founded when government officials come to check out Craig's failed robot and explain their purpose for seeing the experiment.

On Christmas Eve, Craig's wife and young daughter arrive to spend the holiday with him. They go about trimming the tree joyfully, preparing gifts and generally partaking of the traditional Yule joys, unconscious of impending tragedy. In a climactic scene, Craig desperately pleads to the robot, in private, for more time, accusing the metal man of not understanding the minds and feelings of humans. The robot pays no attention to Craig's final cry that Earth's hope does not rest on a race of supermen, but on its young, its future generations.

That night, Craig and his family unwrap their gifts. Craig is almost numb with fear and despair and tries to hide it from his family. His young daughter leaves the room and goes outside where the robot stands. With the amazing discernment of the young, she tells him that she knows "Daddy didn't make him" and that she realizes he is angry or at least unhappy about something and that she thinks she understands why. It is because "he didn't get any presents for Christmas." And with this, she kisses the robot and wishes him a merry Christmas. "I don't know where you're from," she says, "but they must have Christmas everyplace." The robot slowly touches his metal face where the child kissed him and stands there in utter wonderment.

When Craig comes out looking for his daughter, she is gone ... leaving the robot behind to state that he received a gift for Christmas, a kiss. For the first time the metal man has probed the depths of the human make-up – to see love and unselfishness that surely exist. The robot tells Craig that perhaps he was too quick to judge. He will recommend that Earth be given a longer period to find itself – until, he explains, "The children can grow up and see what they can do."

Before the robot leaves, he touches Craig's shoulder and wishes him a merry Christmas. Craig returns to join his family, singing in joyful thanksgiving.

It was Serling's hope that Abrahams would commission him to write the teleplays. Both plot proposals were rejected.

The Keeper of the Chair

While these were some of Serling's earliest attempts at fantasy and science fiction for television, they would not be his last. His love for this kind of stories was evident in a number of early teleplays. In his unsold "The Keeper of the Chair," he told the tale of a condemned man named Paul, who spends his last moments on death row talking to his executioner, George Frank, about how many people Paul had put to death, and how many Paul felt were guilty of murder and deserved to die. However, a murder has occurred, the result of a prank, and when the warden talks to a guard, looking over the dead body, he questions why Paul shouted out "George Frank" before he died. They had no guard named George Frank. There was a convict by that name executed in 1942, and new evidence presented in 1943 proved his innocence. Paul was the state executioner, whose mind snapped over the years, having been unable to cope with sending a man to the chair for a crime he never committed, and he spent his remaining moments hallucinating – a guilt complex in the form of his own execution.

In late 1949, when Serling was still at Antioch College, he submitted his radio play of the same name to John Meston, the story editor for radio's *Suspense*. On December 1, 1949, Meston returned the script, explaining, "After careful consideration, the Script Committee has decided that the story is not suitable for *Suspense*." On April 27, 1950, John Meston sent another rejection letter to Serling regarding the same script, as he had submitted it for radio's *Escape*. By November of 1950, Rod Serling was living (at 5016 Sidney Road) in Cincinnati, Ohio, and had adapted his radio script into a teleplay, for television's *Lights Out!* program. The script editor sent a rejection stating, "This is not well written and does not sufficiently get around its basic fallacy that the executioner, rather than the jury, is responsible for the death of an innocent man."

The Flying Saucers

In the summer of 1947, reports of unidentified flying objects (UFOs) went from obscure Air Force investigations to a pop culture phenomenon when pilot Kenneth Arnold witnessed what he claimed were nine unusual objects resembling flat saucers, hovering in the air. While the U.S. Army Air Force dismissed what he saw as a mirage, newspapers coined the phrase, "flying saucer" and the rest is history. Science fiction writers influenced by the reports in varied periodicals, began incorporating flying saucers in their stories – and Rod Serling was among them.

In July of 1953, Blanche Gaines sold one of his teleplays, "Nightmare at Ground Zero," to television's *Suspense*, for $300. The story told of the strange things that resulted during an atomic bomb test when a mild mannequin maker decided to create lifelike dummies for the target house. By the summer of 1953, more than 10 of Serling's scripts had been sold, and Gaines was only collecting 10 percent of the profits her client was earning, instead of 15 percent. In June of 1954, a script titled "U.F.O." was purchased by *Westinghouse Summer Theatre* for $1,250.00. Telecast on September 6, 1954, it was an amusing story of what happened in Bradleyville, a town that became "stagnant" from inactivity. In order to create a bit of excitement and put Bradleyville "on the map," editor Pinches of The Bugle (circulation 80) kept printing and phoning into the state wire service stories he had dreamed up: a rooster that sang, a two-headed calf, and flying saucers — just a little publicity to prove that Bradleyville wasn't becoming a ghost town. His efforts were wasted until a movie-prop flying saucer fell from its cargo truck overnight in Mr. Pinches' field, in the care of Mike, a writer-hitch-hiker. The result of the ensuing confusion was the stirring up of Bradleyville and its citizens – as well as the outside world.

Science fiction, as a whole, was not widely accepted by the mainstream until the late forties and early fifties, when a breed of young writers such as Bradbury and Vonnegut began to find their short stories published in widely circulated magazines such as *Collier's* and *The Saturday Evening Post*. It was after the Second World War that science fiction sprouted from the early visionaries of centuries past, and into a genre of its own when the pulp magazines and comics were considered an indulgence for juveniles. As the world entered a decade of global technology, jet planes, satellites, color television and the atomic bomb, science fiction drew attention to itself. The chance meetings of visitors from outer space were blame-shifted toward sightings of flying saucers – which made their way into Hollywood theaters that drew hoards of teenagers longing for excitement from such classics as *The Day the Earth Stood Still* (1951), *The Thing From Another World* (1951), *Invasion of the Saucer Men* (1957) and *Earth vs. the Flying Saucers* (1956).

On March 17, 1956, L.H. Stringfield, director of the monthly newsletter C.R.I.F.O. (Civilian Research, Interplanetary Flying Objects) wrote to Rod Serling, congratulating the playwright for his excellent television scripts. "Once, while watching 'Incident in an Alley' and seeing your name mentioned, I thought of the days you worked for WLW in Cincinnati," wrote Stringfield. "For some reason or another, I got the idea that I'd like to see a production on the subject of flying saucers – one where justice was done to the subject, a rarity."

"Today, most media fear saucers and the subject never reaches the dignified stage. This is unfortunate for the material exists in superabundance and is relatively untouched," continued Stringfield.

"I am not referring to the kind that appeals to the lunatics or pipe-dreamers either – I mean the good, bona fide material, the kind which concerns the Air Force. In the massive bulk of [flying] saucer information there should be many top-notch stories. I would like to see you take hold of the situation."

On April 8, Serling wrote back from his home in Westport. Serling shared his enthusiasm, if not his knowledge of interplanetary flying objects. He pointed out that he had a show called 'U.F.O.' on the *Westinghouse Summer Theatre* two summers previous. Shortly thereafter, having read Kehoe's first book on the subject, he broached the idea of a very serious treatment of the subject matter to CBS, and the idea was duly tossed around for a while. "It's their feeling that this subject is of limited interest, and they didn't want to peruse it any further than that," he explained. "Actually, I think the subject is absolutely universal in its scope and interest, and I haven't given up yet. Your issue of *Orbit* was fascinating stuff and I appreciate your sending it along to me. With your permission I'm going to keep your name at the top of my list and will probably contact you before very long if I can push a 'saucer' story across to one of the networks."

If there was ever a space-race on dramatic television, *Robert Montgomery Presents* beat Serling to the punch. The anthology series gave the public a sound and sane story on flying saucers, on the evening of January 26, 1953, in a presentation titled "The Outer Limit." Adapted from the Graham Doar short story of the same name, originally published in the December 24, 1949, issue of *The Saturday Evening Post*, Jackie Cooper played a young U.S. Air Force pilot who tests a new rocket ship. As he zooms through the interplanetary regions, a patrol ship of the Intergalactic Council scoops him up and takes him prisoner. The Councilors convey to him their unhappiness over the way men of Earth are using atomic weapons. Afraid that these new engines of war will upset the balance of surrounding planets, they send him back to Earth with a warning to his people.

Science Fiction Theatre, a syndicated television program produced by Ivan Tors and packaged by ZIV Television, offered that rare glimpse of the scientific "what if" in their fantastic tales. Viewers were treated to a number of flying saucer episodes. In "Beyond," a test pilot flying at twice the speed of sound meets face-to-face with a torpedo-shaped flying object. Afraid of collision, the pilot bails out. Medical experts examine the pilot, putting him through a series of lie detector tests, hypnosis and various mental and physical examinations. Prominent scientists, in the meantime, arrive at the conclusion that the pilot experienced hallucinations caused by atmospheric conditions both inside and outside the cockpit. When pieces of the wrecked airplane are recovered in the desert, the metal is highly magnetized, indicating that the plane brushed against something traveling along magnetic lines of force – possibly a flying saucer. *

In the episode "Hour of Nightmare," Mel and Verda Wingate, two free-lance photographers, are sent into Mexico by an American picture magazine to investigate rumors of mysterious flying objects reported over the mountains. They photograph an object and lights, but feel what they saw was due to optical illusions. In the morning, they stumble across the dead body of a creature so strangely formed that it could not be of their planet. The photographers head back to the village with their amazing discovery. That night the lights again appear in the sky. It is plain that the spaceships are looking for their comrade. Hours later, the evidence – including the dead body – vanishes. Their

_____

* The program was syndicated across the country, so the initial telecast varied from one television station to another and the exact date of telecast for each episode cannot be determined. The series premiered nationally in April of 1955.

film is fogged, eliminating any chance of confirming their adventure. Phoning the magazine editor, they "confirm" the editor's theory that there is "no proof" of the existence of flying saucers.

From October 28, 1951 to January 13, 1952, CBS Television broadcast a short-run science fiction series called *Out There*, which lasted a mere 12 episodes. The live anthology series offered adaptations of short stories penned by such masters as Ray Bradbury and Theodore Sturgeon. Designed to entertain adults as well as young children, almost every show featured spaceships traveling through space (in similar production values as *Tom Corbett, Space Cadet* and *Space Patrol*) and alien visitation. Science fiction classics such as Graham Doar's "The Outer Limit" and Robert A. Heinlein's "The Green Hills of Earth" were among the telecasts.

The December 28, 1957 issue of TV Guide reported, "A kept-quiet test film has been completed for an Air Force series titled *Flight*. It is planned to cover everything from "Jennys to flying saucers," according to producer Al Simon, "and to be Hollywood TV's first serious space-age series." The series premiered on November 4, 1958, running a full season of 39 episodes. While most dealt with Air Force technical subjects (such as test-flying experimental aircraft and how Air Force pilots cope with domestic issues at home), one show dealt with the subject of flying saucers.

With the exception of these minor efforts, the subject of UFOs was limited to such programs as *Space Patrol, Captain Video, Rod Brown of the Rocket Rangers* and *Tom Corbett, Space Cadet*, all geared toward a juvenile audience. Serious science fiction was shunned by the networks, which assumed that potential sponsors would show only a temporary interest – especially when the ratings indicated a lack of popularity for the genre. Viewers crying for adult science fiction were contained within a limited percentage of the total viewing audience – hence, unsatisfactory ratings. *Tales of Tomorrow* was the only program to prove otherwise, and even the contractual arrangements to keep the series on the air limited producers Mort Abrahams, Richard Gordon and George F. Foley, Jr. to the type of stories that could be presented without interference from the sponsors and the ABC Television.

The M-G-M Deal

With many of the dramatic television programs making the shift to California (producers favored filming the dramas on the West Coast instead of "live" telecasts from the East), so went the writers. Hollywood beckoned and the scriptwriters answered the call. According to *Variety*, on January 14, 1956, Rod Serling inked a deal with M-G-M involving approximately $250,000, for a four-year, non-exclusive pact as a screenwriter. He had recently finished a two-year ticket calling for two pictures at the Culver City lot. According to the article, "in addition to those two films, however, he also wrote the screenplay on *Company of Cowards*, and is currently polishing *No Blade of Grass*." The agreement between Serling and Loew's, Inc. was for the playwright to submit one feasible screenplay per year for four years. *

Rod Serling made at least two trips to California so he could work on *Saddle the Wind*, and each visit to the West Coast lasted three months. As a sort of testing ground for the Serling family, to decide whether to commit to moving to the Golden State on a more permanent basis, the Serling household moved west with him for one of the trips.

---

* Rod Serling once commented that *No Blade of Grass*, while never produced, was "a beautiful science fiction yarn, and I'm sorry it never got off the ground."

Saddle the Wind went before the cameras, and during the weeks of production, he toured the movie studio to inspect its facilities. It was during this first visit to M-G-M that he was exposed to the vast departments and sound stages. The backstage tour and experience gave him the knowledge he needed to understand the inner workings of film production.

Serling had also written two treatments and three screenplays (dated between May 20, 1957 and June 19, 1958) from Jack Schaefer's 1957 novel *Company of Cowards*, and Schaefer's own treatment, dated October 16, 1956. He also wrote one script adapted from John Christopher's 1956 novel *No Blade of Grass*, and two revisions (dated between November 14, 1957 and January 23, 1958).

Goodbye to Gaines

It was during his California trip that he met and negotiated with representatives of the Ashley-Steiner Agency, which wanted to represent the playwright for future projects. This would mean having to dismiss Blanche Gaines, the same woman who was responsible for helping him establish a reputation for quality dramatic programs.

On May 2, 1957, Rod Serling again drafted his letter to Blanche Gaines, explaining his motives: "This letter has been started and restarted a dozen times in the past couple of days which should suggest the content to you," Serling wrote. "I was going to tell you this when I got home – tell you reasonably, logically and in a manner which would be far less jarring than a letter. But on the phone the other day, when you told me about leaving for your tour on Thursday, I decided that it would be much better that this particular piece of news didn't come to you on the eve of a well-deserved vacation and, if not spoil it, at least throw a little gray over it. It is simply this, Blanche: I have decided to sign with Ashley-Steiner for one year commencing in August. The basic reason for this is that I feel most of my operation will be West Coast for the next two or three years anyway and it seems impractical to have representation in an area where it's not needed."

The Serling family shifted residence from Westport to the West Coast during the Christmas season of 1957.

Eight years before, TV spawned a hard-working, serious cult of writers, termed by one columnist as "The Dirty-Shirt" school of writing. They dealt in realism served up in great expansive lumps. Two of its more publicized members were Paddy Chayefsky and Rod Serling, who were turning out dramas with machine gun rapidity. From critical points of view, these dramas were elected the cream of that era's TV fare and they catapulted the writers to fame and fortune.

By January of 1958, Rod Serling was 33 years old. He had a happy 10-year marriage with Caroline Kramer, and together they shared two lovely daughters, Judy, 5, and Nan, 2. His scripts for radio and television were dramatized on all the major networks, including the programs of which critics took notice: *Kraft Television Theater, United States Steel Hour, Playhouse 90* and *Studio One*.

While negotiations with CBS regarding *The Twilight Zone* began as early as May of 1957, it was not until January of 1958 that word leaked out that Rod Serling, was going to premiere a new science fiction television anthology that would exceed viewer expectations.

The January 22, 1958 issue of *The Daily Register* featured a brief mention that "Rod Serling is preparing a new science fiction series, *Twilight Zone*, for CBS TV airing next fall."

The day before, on January 21, Serling formed his own production company, Jo-Nan Productions, to shoot the hour-long series. Jo-Nan Productions was named after his two daughters, Jodi and Anne (Nan was her family nickname).

The pilot for *The Twilight Zone* was "I Shot An Arrow Into the Air" (not the same story as the Rod Taylor vehicle filmed a year-and-a-half later) and scheduled to roll before the cameras within the next two months. Serling and CBS negotiated the terms, and series ownership would probably be 50-50. A producer had not yet been selected, but according to an exchange of letters, John Frankenheimer was slated to direct the pilot.

Serling consented to a number of interviews with reporters and magazine and newspaper columnists about wanting to have his own program – besides his love for science fiction stories.

"The sponsor is king in television," he said grudgingly. "And he always will be. It's a fact of life we must live with. I never got along with sponsors when I was a writer. That's why I'm producing my own show. There still are restrictions, but now I'm dealing directly with the sponsor and running into less trouble.

"The situation finally reached the heights of stupidity when normal words couldn't be mentioned because of competing products. I had to take a line out of a script that read, 'Have you got a match?' The show was sponsored by a lighter company. Nobody can be 'lucky' on a program that is sponsored by a cigarette firm, and criminals cannot go to the gas chamber if the guys picking up the check manufactures gas stoves.

"I began producing so I could write for myself, have a hand in the casting, and meet sponsors on their own ground," he concluded.

"There were no trumpets, no kettle drums, not even the usual two-inch headlines," wrote Charles Beaumont. "Just a simple notice, buried in the Trades, to the effect the eminent TV writer Rod Serling was preparing 'a series of imaginative stories.' Nothing more. Is it any wonder that we scoffed? Sure, he could rip off an occasional Emmy-winning *Playhouse 90* script, but did that give him any right to invade our domain? Answer: Yes."

The publicity was favored by critics, but as the hundreds of plot proposals, story ideas, and printed submissions arrived in February and March, he found himself bombarded with a large number of submissions from literary agents including Carolyn Willyoung Stagg of Lester Lewis Associates and Geraldine Cassidy of Los Angeles, among others. Serling sent a personal rejection to every person who wrote to him, because the pilot had not been filmed. "We are shooting the proposed series pilot in March and there will probably be a period of a couple of months at least while the process of sale goes on," Serling explained. He asked many to be patient and resend their proposals in a few months, when definite word about the series being picked up became official.

In an issue of *TV Guide*, Rod Serling recounted, "When the first publicity came out on the series, I was inundated by submissions from agents offering me 6-foot-9 actors with long necks through which electrodes could easily be attached. One agent told me that he had an actor so versed in horror movies that he'd taken to sleeping in a box in the basement. That's an oblique way of getting around to the fact the anthology has been misnomered as a cross between scaly reptiles that walk on two feet and come from the planet Alpha Centauri, and 'I Was a Teenage Vampire for the Federal Communications Commission.'"

Among the submitters were a few kind souls of notoriety who offered not story submissions, but advice for a man who was venturing into the field of "executive producer." In television during the '50s, an executive producer had more power than any other credited crewmember – this was the case with Serling. Credited as the creator of the series and serving as an influential staff writer on the show, his role was to guide the overall creative progress over the course of a season – basically, the de facto creative director of the show – and all creative decisions, (from casting to script approval) went through him.

Robert P. Mills, editor at *Venture Science Fiction* sent Serling a copy of his magazine with Theodore Sturgeon's editorial titled "A Defiance of Time," which appeared in the March 1958 issue of *Venture*. Sturgeon defended science fiction in his essay, and this particular article is of interest to fans because it contains one of the first published references to what is now called "Sturgeon's Law." About the same time the magazine appeared on newsstands, Sturgeon privately pleaded a similar case to him, in a letter from his home in Truro, Massachusetts, dated February 10, 1958:

Dear Mr. Serling:
The fast-talking buck-hungry times in which we live force me to be exceedingly blunt at the outset, to wit:

1. I don't want a job or a "position" or a handout. I'm content where I am with what I'm doing.
2. If you don't know who I am, you haven't done enough reading in the sci-fantasy field to do full justice to *Twilight Zone*.

Now I can get off the bald-and-surly kick and write you the way I want to write you, wherein a compliment is not sweet-talk and a brag makes a point, not a point-of-sale.

First of all, many warm congratulations on *Twilight Zone*. I think you have picked the right time for it; I think you are the right person to tackle it; and I think that the series can be, and probably will be, superb, valuable in several coins, and a great delight. I am especially pleased with your design to produce fantasy as well as science fiction, which latter, in the public mind, is for kids with fishbowls on their heads and consists of monsters from 20,000 cheap and careless movies.

For twenty years I have been involved in sci-fantasy, and it has been my greatest desire to break down this zap-gun syndrome in the public mind. Without fawning, I submit herewith that with your first 39 shows you will do more to that end than I have been able to do in two decades, and I am enormously enthusiastic about it.

I know what you are against. In '50 and '51, I was involved in a science fiction TV series: *Tales of Tomorrow* was originally my show. And with Johnny Haggott, now with the *Theater Guild* and *U.S. Steel Theater*, I started *Out There* for CBS. You will not have to face some of the pitfalls of those early days: $12,000 budgets, fly-by-night packagers, heavy-handed sponsors (one of ours would not permit any script which showed an extra-terrestrial who was smarter or stronger than an Earthman) and the burden of no "name." But certain others are going to climb your back. Among them:

With few exceptions, any actor dressed up to look like an extra-terrestrial looks like an actor dressed up as an extra-terrestrial.

Science fiction sets and costumes are inordinately hard to design. Eighty times out of eighty-one, the viewer who sees someone else's idea of another planet or of the future, just doesn't believe it.

You cannot do science fiction for the technically-minded (and that's a monumental slice of the American public) and expect to get away with flights to the planet Itshy Ahmpitz in two hours and seven minutes; not unless you are willing to invent and describe a convincing faster-than-light drive. This and other savage violations of elementary logic (not to say science) never did help the genre; from here on out they will harm it and, more immediately, the show which commits them. The man on the street now knows what orbital velocity is; tomorrow he will understand escape velocity. This is no time to play footsie with science: too many people are getting devout on the subject. In this area there is hope. Axiom: There is always clear scientific justification for any script situation if you can only think of it.

A simple rule which I know you know and I doubt you could violate: Good science fiction is good fiction. Good fiction is simply the understandable solution, by people, of real people's real problems.

In the area of fantasy, there are vast unmined lodes. But what is it? Fletcher Pratt once said, "All fiction is fantasy." John Campbell came out with an implied definition which pleases me most, however. It was back in the days when he edited both *Astounding* and the late-lamented, much beloved, *Unknown*, a fantasy magazine. "For *Astounding*," he would tell his writers, "I want stories which are logical, possible, and good. For *Unknown* I want stories which are logical and good."

There are breeds of fantasy which have never been touched in TV, or which have remained untouched for altogether too long. Here's the single-assumption fantasy, where one unbelievable fact is plunked down in a realistic world (like that delightful movie *A Guy Named Joe*, with its talking dog, or *Mr. Peabody and the Mermaid*.) There's the hyperbolic, or sheer slapstick fantasy, as in those wonderful old silent films wherein railroad trains would leap over houses or pranksters would hitch a balloon to a building and haul it 3,000 feet up unbeknownst to the occupants, or where a man's car stalls and he pushes it against a parked car ahead, which pushes one ahead of it, and so on until he is single-handedly and innocently trundling fifteen automobiles, all of which ultimately go over a cliff. There were gag fantasy ideas, like the hair-restorer gimmicks and the I-swallowed-a-jumping-bean thing, and "vanishing cream" which . . . Well, you know.

Also, we have exploited far too little that variety of fantasy-horror which asks the audience to use its own imagination. Remember the harrowing just-off-camera leopard in *The Cat People* with Simone Simon, and a superb story by Anthony Boucher, from *Unknown*, which does that: it's called *They Bite*, and that's all you ever really know about "them." One of the best suspense structures I have ever seen lies in the first third of *The Thing*; and it lies right down and dies as soon as the Thing actually appears on the screen. (Incidentally, that was made from John Campbell's fine story, *Who Goes There?* and so drastically altered that the original could still be done as a "new" story – and a beauty.) The same thing applies to Harry Bates' *Farewell to the Master*, source of *The Day the Earth Stood Still*, a highly visual novelette containing the dog-gondest punch line in science – or any other fiction. (Speaking of punch lines: do you know Damon Knight's *To Serve Man*?)

There's one kind of anything-can-happen fantasy which does not violate the single-assumption rule (never ask your audience to believe more than one impossible thing). The all-time unstoppable peak of that idea is Fredric Brown's *What Mad Universe?* (which of course you couldn't use) but here's one. There's a circa-1915 children's book by Evelyn Nesbitt called *Five Children and It*. "It" is an animal these kids discover, which can grant one wish every day – any wish. Now, supposed this were brought up to date, and some adults got hold of it? One of the gimmicks in the book was that the kids had to watch their mouths every day before they decided on what to wish. They'd sit around for an hour arguing about it and one might say absently, "I wish Nana would hurry with our tea," and that would be that for today. Or some family crisis might depend on the fulfillment of a wish, and someone would get careless, and wish for a sugar-plum or something, and there they were, stuck with the crisis. So: in the updated version, here are people walking around saying, "Oh,

I wish I was dead!" and "I wish I was a kid again," and for that situation where the wish is planned-for and crucial, someone calls out, "Hey Joe, I wish you'd pass the salt."

I could go on for eleventeen pages with this, but this is more than ample for now. I'm taking the liberty of asking my good friend and cohort Robert Mills, editor of *Venture Science Fiction*, to send you a copy (or tear sheets) of the current issue and my book column, wherein I advance an idea for doing something about the above-mentioned "zap-gun syndrome." Meanwhile, thanks – really, thanks for *Twilight Zone* (a grand title), and may it turn out to be the biggest thing that has ever happened to you.

And, bearing sharply in mind my rude opening statement (1), I wish you'd call on me for anything you might want or need in this project. I will happily do anything in my power to help. The very, very best of luck to you. (Or is it "break a leg"?)

Sincerely,
Theodore Sturgeon

Laura Templeton (Pippa Scott) reminds us what was so great about the Roaring 20s in "The Trouble with Templeton."

CHAPTER TWO

The First Pilot Script

The initial proposal with CBS was for Serling to co-produce a series of science fiction and fantasy dramas, with negotiations exchanged between CBS, Lee Moselle at the law office of Katz, Moselle and Schier in New York City, and Arthur Joel Katz of Serling's new agent, Ashley-Steiner. Jack K. Katz of the law office was a relation to Arthur Joel Katz and represented the agency, freelance.

Among those at Ashley-Steiner was Frederick Lee Engel, who helped Serling with the formation of the television series.

"I started out as a clerk at MCA," recalled Engel. "When the mail arrived, I sorted the envelopes and made the deliveries. Lew Wasserman, then head of MCA before he bought out Universal, needed a chauffeur for a few months so I took the job. [laughs] I really did! Later I went to work at Ashley. My task was to find literary material for producers and directors and story editors. We had clients like Mel Brooks, Perry Como, and Rod, who was a gentle man. Smoked too much and had a great sense of humor. Sharp wit. Only time we had issues between us was professional, not personal. I had a hand in choosing some of the stories, and he would look over them. Some of the stories I nudged his way, of course, were owned by clients of ours, but that was the way of the business."

Ashley-Steiner became a force on the West Coast, securing names from other agencies that represented the best in showbiz. After signing some of MCA's best clients, Ashley-Steiner merged with Famous Artists in 1962 and strengthened its position in motion pictures. The name of the company then changed to Ashley-Steiner-Famous Artists, Inc.

According to letters exchanged between Rod Serling and Olga Lee (theatrical agent representing actor James Daly), he had polished an hour-long teleplay about an advertising executive whose only escape from the high pressures of work was in his dreams while commuting from New York City to his residence in Connecticut. He sent the teleplay to Olga, in the hopes that James Daly would play the lead.

"Jim read *The Twilight Zone* and is most enthusiastic about it, as am I," Olga Lee wrote to Serling on February 18, 1958. "It is so good to read this type of script that is concerned with character rather than the usual gimmicks. Jim didn't seem quite sure whether this was a pilot or the first of a series. I think the part of Williams would be fine for Jim."

On February 21, Serling explained to Olga Lee the hour-long series prospectus in more detail.

"The script in question that I gave to Jim Daly to look over is the pilot of a proposed film series that I am co-producing with CBS Television. The tentative shooting date for this is on or around March the 1st. As I told Jim, my personal preference is for him to take the role of Williams in the script. This is subject to approval by the powers that be at CBS who, as you can imagine, have a great deal of prerogatives in terms of casting and everything else. We intend to have a casting meeting early next week to make a final decision and I will wire you as to the decision. And also to find out from you Jim's availability."

The negotiations for this pilot fell through. Jo-Nan Productions was closed on a permanent basis. (A second production company was formed, Palisades Productions, named after Serling's two-story house in Pacific Palisades.) Determined that only Daly should play the lead, Serling temporarily shelved the teleplay for a future date. According to a memo to William Self, Serling felt that when the series went to production in the near future, Daly would again be approached. In the meantime, he composed a second script in early March, titled "The Happy Place." On March 25, 1958, he revised some of the pages to perfect the dialogue and scene scenario for the teleplay, causing the script to run a total of 61 ½ pages in length.

I Shot An Arrow Into the Air

Serling's second pilot was titled "I Shot An Arrow Into the Air," a touching story about humanity's first contact with an alien race and a young boy's friendship with a visitor from outer space. Even though the teleplay did not include any opening or closing narration, his proposed series opener is featured on the first page.

"There is a sixth dimension beyond that which is known to man. It lies in a boundless area full of light and shadow. Between what man has experienced and what man can dream. Between his grasp and his reach. Between science and superstition. Between the pit of his fears and the sunlight of his knowledge. This area can be called the Twilight Zone!"

The episode opens with a wire mesh of a gate and a collection of faces of onlookers staring at something behind the camera through the fence.

This is the story of the Arrow One, an American satellite launched into Earth's orbit and destined to travel the planet's orbit for thirty days, a long journey in orbit around the globe. One of the onlookers, who lived five miles away from the launching site, was David Henniker, age 12, a small, misshapen little boy with a withered leg and a hunched back. David's parents, Edna and Paul, care for the lad, but while Edna applies a loving hand, Paul pushes the boy around.

On the satellite's sixth orbit, the Space Agency loses contact with the satellite, and starts to ponder what kind of malfunction could have caused the problem. After 48 hours pass, the scientists are mystified when they discover that the satellite had come back to Earth, having landed just five miles from where it was launched.

When Dr. Gibbons (a name used in "Of Late I Think of Cliffordville," "The Happy Place" and "He's Alive") and his assistant check out the satellite with their own eyes, they discover a horrifying secret. The craft was operated manually. The metal is not steel or aluminum or any known alloy. It did not come back because it was never sent up. It is a satellite all right, but it isn't theirs!

When the military arrives on the scene, one of the soldiers wounds a creature that originated from the fallen satellite, and they take pursuit. Across the woods, young David is beaten up by some of the neighbor kids and is saved by the stranger, who scares off the kids. David is not scared of the visitor, who introduces himself as John Williams. Realizing the man is bleeding (albeit green blood), David takes him home and uses a first aid kit to repair the wound. David's father shows up and orders Mr. Williams to leave, not taking a liking to a stranger in his house and ignoring the boy's request to help shelter Mr. Williams because he's his friend. The stranger leaves without any hesitation. The sheriff arrives, courtesy of a phone call, and takes Mr. Williams in.

Dr. Gibbons introduces himself to the space visitor and begins to ask questions, including the whereabouts of their satellite, which had recently vanished. Before the visitor tells everything he knows, he realizes that he is not alone, and fakes a story about being a farm laborer who was shot and wounded by soldiers. Late at night alone Williams receives a visit from a single ball of light burning in the center of the room. A voice originates from the light. The Controller, deep and resonant, tells Williams that the alien race was premature. Having observed the inhabitants of Earth for some time, it has been decided that the human race is a frightened and deadly breed. They intended to give gifts of knowledge to the Earthlings, but fearing these gifts would be used for hostile purposes, the aliens intend to return home without assisting the human race. They repair the satellite and instruct Williams to return as soon as he can.

Later, when Williams manages to escape, he seeks out young David and explains the purpose of his visit. He came from another place, from another star. His race has always known about the existence of Earthlings, but knew very little else. When they saw Earth put a satellite in orbit, the alien race thought this might be a good time to let Earth know they existed. Unfortunately, they had trouble with their satellite in the atmosphere and crashed back on Earth. There were three of his race, and his two friends went in other directions. They looked around, did a lot of checking, and then made their report to the Controller. The Controller is the individual who took charge of the operation. Their general feeling now is that the human race is not yet ready for the inventions and ideas of their planet. Perhaps they will when the humans no longer has hatred in its heart for their fellow men across the oceans.

Meeting with his fellow beings, John Williams explains why they should wait 20 years to return and find a contact. Choosing young David as the man to whom to make contact, he bestows on the boy a strange light – great knowledge of formulas and ideas – knowing that years later, David will give humankind their ideas and knowledge to reach the stars. Though David does not know what John Williams bestowed on him, the lad is heartbroken to see his friend depart – but with the promise that they shall meet again.

The story concludes 20 years later, when David is now Dr. Henniker, the first man to pilot a satellite in orbit. Mr. and Mrs. Henniker, David's parents, are invited into the control center to watch the launch, which is a success. A small light representing David's vessel blinks on the control panel. Suddenly another dot of light appears close by. The men in the room crowd around the screen. The voices are up in excitement. It is another satellite, and this one joins the one David pilots in orbit. They are making contact.

This pilot teleplay was never filmed, but the story was rewritten three years later and filmed, in modified form, for the *Twilight Zone* episode, "The Gift."

Pacific Palisades and "The Happy Place"

A few weeks before completing the third pilot script, "The Happy Place," William Self was promoted to the development area of CBS, courtesy of Bill Dozier. His first project scheduled to go into development was *The Twilight Zone.* "I knew Bill Dozier as a big name," Self recalled to interviewer and author Tom Weaver. "He'd been head of Universal Pictures, he'd been head of RKO Pictures, and then he went over eventually to become head of the West Coast for CBS. I don't think I had ever met him during that period. When *The Frank Sinatra Show* closed, I wrote Dozier a letter and said that I was looking for a job at a network. I had no network experience other than producing shows. He responded and we had an interview, and he hired me for CBS. I went there as a program executive – kind of a vague title [laughs] – and I was primarily in the development field, looking for new programs and making pilots."

On March 28, Frank Morris of CBS Television sent Serling a list of censorship concerns regarding "The Happy Place" script. One was his repeated use of the term "clubfoot." Believing there were thousands of individuals and families who felt the word had a very personal and probably painful significance, the network wanted to avoid the "unnecessary discomfort to those afflicted persons and their families" through the mention of their deformities by name. The network wanted him to replace the term with something else throughout the script. It was also requested that the words "damned" and "God" be deleted. This latter request would become all too familiar for Rod Serling as he neglected to refrain from using "hell," "damn" and "God." *

On March 21, 1958, lawyer Bayard F. Berman of Kaplan, Livingston, Goodwin & Berkowitz, submitted an outline of the proposed deal between Palisades Productions, Inc. and CBS with respect to *The Twilight Zone* series. The contract stated that Palisades would begin principal filming of the pilot between April 1, 1958 and April 15, 1958. The budget for the pilot film was fixed at approximately $75,000. CBS would agree to advance Palisades a sum equal to the total cost of the pilot, up to the $75,000 figure. CBS would have complete control over the exclusive rights to negotiate and make a national network sale to a sponsor during a period ending on December 15, 1958. Palisades would own the rights to the film under two stipulations:

(a)   In the event that Palisades made a sale of the series during the period of December 16, 1958 through September 15, 1959, Palisades would be obligated to reimburse CBS for the cost of the pilot.

(b)   If Palisades failed to sell the series during the same period, CBS would have the right to use the pilot in one of its regular hour-long television anthologies to recoup the cost of making it.

If CBS made a national network sale on or prior to December 15, 1958, the network had the right to exercise its option for the first year of the series by written notice to Palisades. The first telecast of the series would begin within 120 days after CBS advised Palisades that it was exercising its option. Additionally, CBS would then be obligated either to: (a) order and pay for 26 one-hour films from Palisades during the first year, or (b) pay Palisades what would equal to $2,000 as an "unproduced picture penalty" to compensate for loss of profits.

Palisades would own the copyrights and all other intellectual properties for each film of the

---

* The censorship of blasphemous words was not directed to Serling specifically. All television scripts, even comedies, were looked over by the network in an effort to prevent hate letters and potential lawsuits that could potentially harm the network. Richard Matheson also recalled how words and phrases were censored from his scripts.

proposed television series. Net profits derived from the distribution of the series would be divided as follows: 40 percent to Palisades and 60 percent to CBS. If CBS exercised its option for the first year of the series, the network also had four successive options to extend the contract for an additional period of one year per option. *

Palisades was legally bound to acquire and provide everyone and everything (including literary and musical material, cast, production and other rights, properties and services) necessary to the preparation, production and delivery to CBS of the films ordered by the network, including the pilot. Palisades would be obligated to submit to CBS the name of the individual whom Palisades proposed to employ as producer of each film of the series, and the network had the right of final approval of the selection. The same had to be submitted and approved for the associate producer, director, and the featured members of the cast for each film. If CBS disapproved of the company's choice of any of those people, the decision of the producer would be final.

Serling was contractually obligated to write and deliver at least 12 shooting scripts for the first year, 10 scripts for the second year, and eight scripts for the third, fourth and fifth year, if CBS renewed each season. He was also obligated to supervise the preparation of the scripts by other writers for the remaining films during each season.

Palisades would be obligated to submit to CBS, for the network's approval, an outline of each story that Palisades proposed to use together with the name of the writer (other than Rod Serling) who Palisades proposed to employ. If CBS disapproved of the first two submissions, the network was obligated to accept the third story outline submitted to it by Palisades with respect to the same film. CBS also had the right to approve each script and to require revisions to it or a completely new script, provided that CBS reimburse Palisades for any additional costs. The network also had the right to reject scripts written by Serling, which were subject to certain limitations.

Should CBS choose to release any of the episodes on a theatrical exhibition, CBS would pay Palisades a percentage of the profits. The network retained merchandising rights, which were all subject to the network's approval, and the worldwide rights for the purpose of syndication. The network would distribute the episodes on a syndication basis in accordance with its current distribution fee schedule, which was set forth in a formal agreement approved by both parties. If CBS failed to begin distribution on a syndication basis within 24 months following the final telecast of the national network run of the series, Palisades had the right to cancel the network's distribution rights to distribute, and the power to syndicate would revert to Palisades.

On a somber note, if, during the years *The Twilight Zone* was in production, Palisades was unable to provide the required number of Rod Serling scripts by reason of Serling's death, incapacity or refusal to perform, the parties' obligations under the contract would continue throughout the balance of the year. One exception to this clause was that Palisades would furnish, in substitution for the remaining unwritten Serling scripts, scripts written by another writer (to be approved by CBS) of the same standing and ability comparable to Rod Serling and Palisades would provide the services of that other writer to supervise the writing of the remaining scripts during the balance of the year.

The terms of the contract were standard for most programs produced and broadcast for the Columbia Broadcasting System. Serling's exclusivity was the only unique aspect that varied from

---

* According to network standards, in all legal documents, and clarified in the contract, a "broadcast year" was defined as a 12-month period commencing on the date of the first telecast.

normal agreements between production companies and the network. Before the contract was signed, the deal fell through – apparently because of the script he submitted, titled "The Happy Place." As William Self recalled to interviewer Tom Weaver, "We got off to a very bad start. Serling had written a script called 'The Happy Place' for the pilot, and I had read it."

The script concerned a futuristic society in which the State, in full control of the people, dictated the age limit of individuals and humanely exterminated those who reached that age. The story opens with Mr. and Mrs. Gibbons, age 66 and 64, who are escorted by armed guards to an estate labeled as the "Division of Relaxation and Contentment, Department for Aged Citizens, North American Section." The director of this section is Mr. Harris, who assures the old couple that every conceivable thing has been done to make them comfortable and content during their remaining years. The couple is escorted to an empty elevator, where, as the doors suddenly begin to close rapidly, a deadly gas spews from a metal grill. The old pair sink slowly to the floor, while their suitcase is catalogued and assigned for burning. Across the ante room, Mr. Harris welcomes the next old couple, Mr. and Mrs. Wilson, assuring them that the State will make sure their "remaining years are as happy and fruitful as possible."

SERLING: *"Your first introduction to the day after tomorrow – a forceful society of the future in which the ground rules have changed. Morality, as we know it, has been given a paint job. Things of value . . . have been re-assessed. There is a new God in this society – it's called 'Perfection.'"*

Mr. Harris, however, finds his job less appealing when the State changes the mandatory age limit of 65 to 60. His father, a surgeon who respects human life, is 58 and challenges the State by ordering medication restricted to patients of a certain age limit. After losing a patient, the surgeon speaks out against the State. Fletcher, Harris' supervisor, feels his position threatened when Harris proves to be a dedicated employee of the State. In an attempt to force Harris to resign, Fletcher changes the age of his surgeon-father, executing orders to put the good doctor on report for 'The Happy Place.' Of course, the error could be corrected . . .

Mr. Harris is forced to choose between his position of employment and the life of his father. Before he can make a judgment call, the surgeon makes his escape. Finding his father hiding in a warehouse, Harris brings the escapee clothes, food and a gun. The State, however, tracks the old man's whereabouts, and during a confrontation, gunfire is exchanged. The old man is killed for his beliefs, and Harris, thinking of his wife and son, pretends to aid the guards in the apprehension of his father. Wishing to steal credit where credit is due, Fletcher finds Harris' young son, Paul, in a position to take the claim – it was he who phoned the State regarding the whereabouts of his grandfather. "I've found that to be sort of a rule with older people," young Paul explains. "They like to take credit for things they don't deserve." On the way back home, Harris attempts to explain to his son that the State is wrong – there is a deity above that dictates the age limit of human beings. Paul, however, has been brainwashed by the teachings of the State-operated school. Sixty is much too high, Paul explains. "Fifty-five would be more like it. Or maybe even fifty." Paul leaves Harris alone in the streets to pray to God, asking for deliverance – to save mankind . . . and his son.

SERLING: *"The Time is the day after tomorrow. Man has lived through his wars, his bombs, and*

> *his rockets. And this is a society of the future. It is a forceful society where nothing remains static. The process of living operates from different rules now. And there is a new God . . . Called Perfection! [a pause] But this God is only . . . temporary."* *

Serling worked with Ashley-Steiner for a number of months, to see what potential could come from a working relationship with Ashley-Steiner, and on August 7, 1959, signed contracts to make their partnership official.

Notes about "The Happy Place"

The opening of the script revealed Serling's initial intention for the thematic season premiere, described in the script as "A long stretch of highway, flanked by a barren, nondescript landscape – gnarled trees with bony supplicating branches silhouetted against an off-color gray sky. The camera moves down this road at an indescribably fast speed."

SERLING'S VOICE *(over the camera movement)*

> *This is a highway into a land of strangeness – a place of shadow.*
> *To reach it – you ride the dream. To enter it – you need only your imagination.*
> *The place is called . . .*

At this moment the camera reaches the end of the road, and the words 'The Twilight Zone' come up suddenly as if on hinges. The camera hurtles through them, smashing them into falling pieces.

SERLINGS' VOICE *(concurrent with the appearance of the letters)*

> *. . . The Twilight Zone.*

The camera has begun to pan down until it passes the horizon and is flush on the opening shot (each week the opening shot of the play).

Mr. Denton was a guard in the story, forced to admit that he was a member of a rebellion group – which received punishment through brainwashing and through which Denton would become a "slave" of the State. One of Rod Serling's childhood friends, Herbert Denton, was the inspiration for the name. Serling would use the name "Denton" again as the title character in "Mr. Denton on Doomsday."

Taking place in the future, guards working for the State are able to voice a request through a speaker system from behind a door, such as asking to be allowed to enter. (This concept was later used for the *Twilight Zone* episode "To Serve Man.")

The premise itself would be given a drastic revision for "The Obsolete Man," in which a futuristic society, dictated by the State, determined who was ready for extermination because they were

---

* Serling's former closing narration before the March 25 revision read: *"Time – the future. Place – immaterial. It's anywhere where men construct idols and call them, 'God' . . . forgetting the most basic truth of all . . . that man-made gods are temporal and never last. Tonight's exercise in government and reason . . . from The Twilight Zone."*

considered "obsolete." This, of course, meant old people – with Serling making sure no commentary was implied in the script about age. When *The Twilight Zone* later expanded to an hour-long format for the fourth season, he dusted off this script once again and attempted to have it approved by CBS – and again the network turned it down. *

"The Time Element"

"Dozier set up a meeting for me and Serling," continued Self. "I had never met Serling [previously]. Serling came into my office at CBS, at Beverly and Fairfax in Hollywood, and he asked, 'How'd you like the script?' I said I hated it. He was, obviously, kind of shocked. 'My God,' he said, 'everybody else loves it! Including your boss Bill Dozier and *his* boss Hubbell Robinson [then the New York head of CBS Programming]. You hate it?' I said, 'Well, I hate it because, Rod, you're going into a commercial thing. It's not *Playhouse 90*. You're gonna have to have an advertiser, and I don't think the Buick people, or any other advertiser, will want to sponsor a show where, in

Jack Weston shows off his little black book in "The Bard."

the first episode, you kill nice old people.' He left the room in a huff. He went to Dozier, who later called me and said, 'My God, what happened? Serling wants you off the project.' I said, 'Well, I'm sorry to hear that 'cause I admire him, I think he's a tremendous talent, I'd love to work on the show. But I had to tell him what I thought.' Dozier said, 'Well . . . Stay away from him. Don't try to contact him. I'll see if I can put it back together. But . . . Rod really wants you off the show.'"

Negotiations regarding *The Twilight Zone* between CBS and Pacific Palisades ended on April 27, 1958. The network would have nothing to do with a teleplay about old people being euthanized, regardless of how humane the execution. On April 28, Serling quit his assignment at M-G-M for a movie Serling scripted titled *The Immortal* for Lauder Motion Pictures, Inc., having written a treatment on April 21.

"I was director of program sales for the CBS-TV Network," recalled Bob Hoag. "We had on our hands a singular and unique program titled *The Twilight Zone*. And I couldn't sell it. A gentleman named Bill Dozier asked me if I would introduce the author to New York advertising agencies in an attempt to sell it. After meeting the lad who wrote this, I walked him around Central Park for a few laps to cool him off and then entered him in the race."

---

* "The Happy Place" was reminiscent of an hour-long teleplay scripted by Ray Bradbury, "The Jail." The script was produced through Alfred Hitchcock's Shamley Productions, the same company responsible for producing *Alfred Hitchcock Presents* and *The Alfred Hitchcock Hour*. It was telecast on the evening of February 6, 1962 on *Alcoa Premiere*. The story was set in the future (c. 2002), where a series of computers dictated whether citizens of the State were guilty or not and sentenced the guilty parties to trade bodies (à la *The Twilight Zone*'s "The Trade-Ins"). A few citizens were quietly making plans to rebel, and the protagonist spent a lot of time trying to get his youthful body back before the old man's body gave out from fatigue. The episode was a pilot that never went anywhere.

Amidst all the hectic attempts to get *The Twilight Zone* off the ground, a personal tragedy hit the Serling home. Esther Serling, Rod's mother, died on March 5, 1958, in a Miami hospital after suffering a stroke. Mrs. Serling, 65, had been under a doctor's care for high blood pressure. Her passing may have been a contributing factor to the stress he was feeling.

"A couple of days later and I honestly do think it was only a couple of days, Serling came to me, unannounced," Self continued. "He came into my office and threw a new script on my desk and said, 'You're right, and I've written another story.' And that became the pilot." The new teleplay was titled "The Time Element" and it had been adapted from a previous script of the same name he wrote during his Cincinnati scriptwriting days.

In a letter to Blanche Gaines dated April 8, 1958, Serling thanked his ex-agent for submitting stories for his proposed series, and he explained that he would take them into consideration. "You'd best hold up sending any more stuff for the time being until things get a little bit more finalized here," he wrote. "It was CBS's idea that we do my second script on tape as part of *Studio One*'s regular programming. I didn't go for the idea, but was willing to at least listen to their proposition. As it stands now however, I've written yet a third pilot script which is probably the best of the bunch and which they think they will film very, very soon."

The earliest documented news of his third script for the proposed *Twilight Zone* series was on April 23, 1958, when *Variety* magazine reported, "Pilot for Rod Serling's new hour-long film series for CBS will roll the early part of May, probably at U.I., and negotiations are on for Jack Warden to essay the lead in the initialed, 'The Time Element.' Bob Parrish, theatrical film director-writer, will make his TV debut directing the segment which will be co-produced by Serling and Charles Russell. Format of the series is scientification and fantasy."

On May 12, 1958, Ira Steiner of Ashley-Steiner wrote to Serling, "Over the weekend I re-read *The Twilight Zone.* I think it's a hell of a script. Although it looks like we have lost this year, I think we ought to put it in the bank and sell it next year." By May, the network had already settled on a number of pilots for the fall season, and even with a commitment and advance preparation, the late date would not have guaranteed sufficient quality for a series to premiere in the fall.

On June 3, William Dozier announced that the deal had been inked. "The Columbia Broadcasting System has signed Rod Serling, writer, to a one-year exclusive television contract beginning next fall," *Variety* reported. The new contract for *The Twilight Zone* was not too different from the proposal described previously. Notable changes included making the series a half-hour instead of a full-hour, adjusting the cost factor because of the length of films, and switching to a third production company now called Cayuga Productions. Palisades Productions, like the former Jo-Nan Productions, folded.

"The name of Cayuga was chosen for sentimental reasons," Serling explained. "I grew up in Binghamton, New York, and presently have a summer cottage on Cayuga Lake which my wife and I go to every July."

The contract with CBS also required Serling to deliver a minimum of three *Playhouse 90* scenarios for the 1959-60 season. One was probably going to be "The Mogul," a drama of life in Hollywood. The script had been scheduled for the 1958-59 season, but was postponed until the next year – and ultimately was never dramatized. "In the Presence of Mine Enemies," however, was accepted and dramatized on the *Playhouse 90* program, and marked the final broadcast of the series.

Rod Serling was also preparing a Broadway stage production based on his teleplay, "Requiem for a Heavyweight," which was planned for a fall 1958 premiere. CBS granted him permission to further his efforts for the stage production, with no limits or restrictions. The contract also acknowledged his present arrangement with Loew's, Inc. by which he was obligated to write a screenplay for one M-G-M theatrical motion picture a year, for four years, beginning in 1958. The CBS deal did not interfere with the Loew's contract. No limits or restrictions were applied against him. *

Regarding the change in length for the series, the June 4, 1958 issue of *The New York Times* confirmed, "A pilot film treatment for a half-hour science fiction series, *Twilight Zone*, is also to be delivered by Mr. Serling to the network. Originally, this idea was conceived as an hour program, but CBS felt it would be better in thirty-minute form. An hour scenario titled 'Time Element,' already completed, is being considered by *Studio One* for presentation at the end of the summer."

Serling explained to columnist Leo Guild of *The New York Herald Tribune* that the program was "a half-hour show and normally I don't like half-hour shows. There isn't enough time to tell a story. But I was convinced after a while there were certain stories we could do within that framework and frankly, it's working out alright *[sic]*."

Days before the premiere of *The Twilight Zone*, Serling asserted his commitment to columnist Les Brown of *Variety* that *The Twilight Zone* was going to prove that, even in the 30-minute limit, the plays could still be as thought provoking. "In any case the half-hour form is a fact of life," he explained, "and as long as we have to live with it, we might as well try to do something meaningful in it. Even if they fail, I think my shows will be better than *My Little Margie*, and if it weren't for my shows we might have two *My Little Margies*. I don't like to single out that that's symptomatic of the negative side of TV, the raunchy mediocrity of the medium."

In July of 1958, a typographical error caused the name of the script, "The Time Element," to read "The Time Machine." Rod Serling wrote to Mel Bloom of Ashley-Steiner reminding them that the name change could cause a problem since the H.G. Wells property of the same name was copyrighted. Bloom informed him that it was a typographical error, only in paperwork sent to him and that, "Desilu had the right name for the project anyhow."

In that same month, Bob Parrish gave Serling much more of which to be concerned. "While I was in Bert's [Granet] office, the phone rang. It was somebody from Westinghouse," Parrish recalled. "Bert put his hand over the phone and said, 'Bob, is it true that Westinghouse turned down 'The Time Element' for *Studio One*?' I said not to my knowledge and even if they did, what difference did it make? He said 'You're right . . . we like the show and Goldsmith, we're going to do it.' He said it bravely, like we were representing the first uncensored gang-fuck in living color. I asked him what the problem was. He said, 'No problem. I'll get into it with Ira.'"

McCann-Erickson (the advertising agency representing Westinghouse) rejected the script, with strong protest to Bert Granet, using the studio rep to communicate their concerns to Serling. Westinghouse had many contracts with the Defense Department, and did not want the Army pictured in the light of brushing a time traveler off as a crackpot. For this reason, the script was rejected. One of the earlier drafts of "The Time Element" (dated June 13, 1958) had Jenson trying to convince Army brass that they would be attacked on the morning of Pearl Harbor. "Another area that worries me a trifle," Granet suggested to him, "literally has been brought about by the Mid-East crisis and the pe-

---

* As mentioned previously, Serling wrote a number of screenplays, but only one – *Saddle the Wind* – was filmed and released theatrically. The studio shelved the remainder of his efforts.

culiar temper of the times that hits the public at troubled moments. The cupidity of the Army when Jenson speaks his piece seems to go too far. After Jenson leaves the office, we see the only portion of the dream when he is not present. Call it what you will but a turn of political events can suddenly make this Army scene a trifle unpalatable and damaging to a wonderful story. Essentially, this could be easily cured by subduing or shortening the Army scenes and throwing more to the ensign and his wife, which in turn would serve to enhance Jenson's character."

Serling took Granet's advice and rewrote pages of the script (revision dated July 2, 1958). He deleted the pages in which Jenson speaks boldly to the Army brass, and replaced it with Jenson having concern for the young newlyweds and their inevitable future. The newer version also featured Jenson visiting a local newspaper to tip them about the attack, but they brush him off, explaining they do not want to get involved in Army red tape. Thanks to Granet's insistence, the rejection was recalled.

Incidentally, Westinghouse had rejected a number of Serling's scripts in the past for the *Studio One* program, including "Patterns," which scored a tremendous hit on *Kraft*. Reginald Rose's "Tragedy in a Temporary Town" was also rejected by *Studio One*, but later became a critical success when presented on *The Alcoa Hour*.

Other complications began. Bob Parrish, who directed *Saddle the Wind*, was Serling's initial choice for director. Parrish, however, deserted the series, and "The Time Element," for flying down to Mexico for the summer. D.R.M. Productions hired Parrish to direct *The Wonderful Country* (1959), which was filmed on location in Durango, Mexico.

Suggesting replacements, Serling requested Don Weiss direct "The Time Element," but Weiss was unavailable for the dates of filming. Fiedler Cook's name was also suggested, but Cook was in Ireland and unable to return for the show. Fourth choice Allen Reisner was selected to direct the episode.

Westinghouse, having recently shifted its television broadcasts from the East Coast to the West Coast, discovered the change was not well received by television critics and there were faltering ratings. Opting for filmed presentations instead, the company signed a deal with Desilu Productions, which at the time was considered one of the most successful production companies in Hollywood – thanks to Desi Arnaz's unusual business style. To cinch the deal and convince Westinghouse, Arnaz granted three exclusive conditions. The title would change from *Studio One* to *Westinghouse Desilu Playhouse*, Lucille Ball and Desi Arnaz would appear in comical mis-adventures as hour-long extensions of the former *I Love Lucy* series every few weeks in between the anthology dramas, and Arnaz himself would play host.

Bert Granet fought the executives at CBS to keep "The Time Element," regardless of the series change, and then consulted Serling regarding the upcoming filming schedule. Granet asked him to write an additional 45 seconds of prologue Desi Arnaz needed to speak on film for the introduction of "The Time Element." Granet forwarded to a two-page example from another script for the Westinghouse series, in which Arnaz holds a pair of wooden shoes and explains the connection between the shoes and the story that follows. Serling, using the same formula, scripted Arnaz with a metronome, an instrument used to produce a regulated audible pulse so musicians can keep a steady beat.

"Obviously the story was designed series-wise and the narrator was the method of utilizing the *Twilight Zone* pattern for all the stories," Granet pointed out to Serling in a letter dated August 1. "In order to obtain the release of 'Time Element' from CBS, Desilu had to forego any usage or mention of the title *Twilight Zone*, even amongst our closest relatives, since it rightfully is an infringement on your series idea and we have no intention of disturbing anything concerning your contemplated show. So my relatives will never hear the magic words, *Twilight Zone*." All references to his series were removed from the script, but Serling and CBS made sure the network, the television critics and potential sponsors knew that the pilot was for a program titled *The Twilight Zone*.

During the last weekend of October 1958, a reporter for *Variety* remarked that Serling "will never again write a TV film drama (except for his own upcoming series), following rigid censorship [of "The Time Element]." The inside back cover of the November 15-21, 1958 issue of *TV Guide* reported, "Rod Serling, who wrote "The Time Element" for *Desilu Playhouse*, says it has been so watered down that he'll never write another line for filmed TV."

Actress Carolyn Kearney, who would later appear in the *Twilight Zone* episode "Ninety Years Without Slumbering," was also in the cast of "The Time Element." "I'd met Rod Serling when I did a *Desilu Playhouse*," she recalled to author Tom Weaver. "William Bendix had the lead, and I remember he was very 'ready' – he had all his lines learned! And Jesse White was always joking around and being very funny. Rod Serling was on the set all the time – I don't know why, but he was there."

On November 14, 1958, CBS issued a number of press releases for "The Time Element." Actor Martin Balsam is quoted in the press release: "In the play, I give Bill a real bad time – in fact, I treat him as a looney. But, frankly, I'm not sure that's the way I'd treat someone who really came to me with a story like that. I suppose people today are overly skeptical. Maybe because we live so close to danger that we can't get excited about a little extra. Or perhaps there are too many people telling too many wild tales for us to be able to judge the truth any longer." *

The Welcome Reception

According to Jeanne Marshall's seminar notes from early 1963, Rod Serling told his class that he got the idea of *The Twilight Zone* because "he wanted to do an imaginative series, using all the strength his mind could conceive of . . . real people set against an odd, tilt background." When he tried to sell the series to CBS, they laughed at him and told him it was "too odd." When "The Time Element" aired on the *Desilu Playhouse*, the network received 64,000 letters within 48 hours.

In the summer of 1976, William Self was interviewed for *The New York Daily News*, explaining that networks did not like anthology series because of the cost. Unlike a situation comedy in which the same living room set could be used week-in-week-out, an anthology required a different set every week. Critics took notice, however, and the network saw the letters addressing the bizarre presentation.

Just a few hours after viewing the telecast, at 12:41 a.m., actor and comedian Phil Baker sent the following telegram to Rod Serling:

DEAR ROD
MAN OH MAN TIME ELEMENT HAD ALL THE ELEMENTS OF THE MOST THRILL-
ING HOUR I'VE SEEN ON TV IN YEARS I RING THIS ONE UP AS ANOTHER OR-
CHID IN YOUR GARDEN OF HITS AT THE RISK OF BEING GAUCHE I'D LIKE TO
DROP A MICKEY ON DESI'S TAMALE FOR NOT MENTIONING THE WRITER IN
HIS TRITE PAYOFF
        SINCERELY
        PHIL BAKER

---

* © Desilu Productions, Inc., September 18, 1958, LP13066, renewal RE-291-610.

The November 25, 1958 issue of *The New York Times* reviewed:

> Rod Serling is one of the pioneer television writers who still stays in the medium even though he is as articulate as video's expatriates about television's limitations. Last night he once again came up with an unusual and absorbing drama, 'The Time Element,' in which William Bendix showed anew that he is a fine serious actor as well as a clown.
>
> Mr. Serling's story was about a man visiting a psychiatrist. The patient complains of recurrent dreams in which he imagines he is living in Hawaii just before the attack of Pearl Harbor. In a series of flashbacks, the man is shown living with his knowledge of what has happened in the seventeen years since. He bets on sure winners in sports events, for example. But more particularly he seeks to warn a newly-wed couple, newspaper editors and anyone else who will listen that they will be attacked by the Japanese. But everyone is either too interested in a good time or too determinedly patriotic to give heed; the man only gets punched in the jaw.
>
> In a highly tricky ending, the psychiatrist is left looking at a blank couch and to steady his own nerves, he goes to a bar to get a drink. There, he learns his patient was killed at Pearl Harbor. The humor and sincerity of Mr. Serling's dialogue made "The Time Element" consistently arresting. And Mr. Serling wisely left the individual viewer to work out for himself whether the play's meaning was that even with fresh knowledge of the past no one will heed its lesson, that to be out of step with the crowd is to only invite ridicule.
>
> Mr. Serling had his troubles in Hollywood over script censorship. But where other dramatists either capitulate or retire, he manages to achieve a great deal through the subtlety of his approach. What he might do with no shackles could be most exciting.

On November 25, Blanche Gaines wrote to Rod Serling, "Of course I saw 'The Time Element.' Though scraps of paper may change relationships, old habits persist and watching Serling shows has been one of mine for years. I thought it was a good show. It held my interest continuously despite my familiarity with the story, though the trick ending left me as baffled as it did with the psychiatrist. Heaven help us if the head shrinkers become incapable of distinguishing between their own dreams and reality! ... Perhaps it was just as well that Westinghouse did not allow you to attack 'the stupidity of the brass.' Bet you would have gone to town with some oratory on that."

On November 26, Albert McCleery, an executive producer at the National Broadcasting Company, wrote the following to Serling: "My wife came in twice during the showing of 'The Time Element' to ask me who I was swearing at (I have a habit of talking to characters if I believe in them), and I had to admit that I was so wrought up at the story that I was swearing at how stupid people could be not to have sense enough to know what has happened. I was engrossed from the very beginning to the final touching ending and it left me completely shattered."

"In some 11 years of writing for this medium, I think I've written exactly four film shows," he remarked. "I've always thought TV film was a kind of factory operation in which the product is ground up in a vat, poured out on a belt, pasted together with clichés and spewed out to an audience that has seen it before. This anthology is not an assembly-line operation. Each show is a carefully conceived and wrought piece of drama, cast with competent people; directed by creative, quality-conscious guys, and shot with an eye toward mood and reality. You don't often see a preoccupation with mood and reality in a filmed TV show because mood and reality are usually incompatible with budget, and the canned TV show usually owes its existence to the economy of its production – and rarely to the quality of the production."

According to columnist Leo Guild of *The New York Herald Tribune*, the background of *The Twilight Zone* began with Rod Serling, who "had this idea for three years. Ray Bradbury, famous science fiction writer, tried to sell a similar idea but after a pilot was made the network officials scoffed. They said the public wouldn't sit still for a whole series about such subjects as food that makes a man invisible and Saturn dwarfs attack Pittsburgh. When Bradbury was turned down, Rod felt his project was impossible."

Don Rickles tries to force Burgess Meredith to see things his way.

CHAPTER THREE

"Where is Everybody?"

Having read an article in the May 26, 1958 issue of *Time* magazine about isolation experiments on astronaut trainees, Serling was inspired to write a script he titled "Where is Everybody?" The story concerned a man wandering the empty streets of a town, completely devoid of human life, with suggested impressions that the occupants were in hiding. The mystery is rationalized with various theories, until the solution is revealed. The protagonist is an Air Force trainee suffering a nightmare, the result of side effects from an isolation experiment.

" . . . I read Serling's first script. It was, or seemed to be, an end-of-the-world story," recalled Charles Beaumont. "Resisting the impulse to throw the wretched thing across the room, I read on. A man is alone in a town that shows every sign of having been recently occupied. He finds cigarettes burning in ashtrays. Stoves are still warm. Chimneys are smoking. But no one is there, only this one frightened man who can't even remember his name . . . Old stuff? Of course. I thought so at the time, and I think so now. But there was one element in the story which kept me from my customary bitterness. The element was quality. Quality shone on every page. It shone in the dialogue and in the scene set-ups. And because of this, the story seemed fresh and new and powerful. There was one compromise, but it was made for the purpose of selling the series."

"Where is Everybody?" was filmed at the back lot of Universal-International (formerly Universal Studios). By 1958, MCA's television subsidiary, Revue Productions, had outgrown its production facility, which was the former Republic Studio lot, so MCA head Lew Wasserman purchased the entire Universal-International lot as a wise move for expansion. Universal-International would use and reuse the back lot for a number of motion pictures such as *It Came From Outer Space* (1953), *Tarantula* (1955) and *The Monolith Monsters* (1957), all of which may appear familiar when viewed consecutively with these movies. The pilot also features the famed Courthouse Square, which had been featured in numerous motion pictures including *Gremlins* (1984), *Back to the Future* (1985) and *Batman and Robin* (1997).

Hired to narrate only the pilot film was Westbrook Van Voorhis, perhaps best known as "the Voice of Doom," and for his popular catchphrase, "Time . . . marches on!"

"Before we decided on Rod, there was a lot of effort to find the right narrator," recalled William Self. "We actually went to Orson Welles and we went to Westbrook Van Voorhis, the voice of the *March of Time* films. But they all sounded a little pompous, like they were talking down to this audience that might not understand what the show was about – which a lot of people didn't [understand]! . . . Meanwhile, Rod kept saying, 'Y'know, I'd like to narrate this . . .,' and we – 'we' being CBS – kept saying, 'Well, we're lookin' for somebody.' And then we finally settled on Rod, which was a lucky decision. Rod brought to it a kind of an 'everyman quality.'" *

"I forget the date that my friend Charles Beaumont and I first went to CBS Studios to view the pilot film of *The Twilight Zone* and meet its creator Rod Serling," recalled Richard Matheson in the introduction to *Rod Serling's Other Worlds*, published in March 1978 (with no stories written or adapted by Serling). "It was a momentous day for Chuck and myself, for it led not only to five years of most enjoyable writing assignments for us but to many more pleasurable years knowing and working with Rod, one of the most talented craftsmen the television medium has ever produced and one of the kindest, most feeling men I have ever known."

Cayuga Productions

On December 12, 1958, while the Serlings were in Miami, Florida, Sam Kaplan of Ashley-Steiner contacted Rod. In order to protect the tax position of Serling's corporation, Kaplan bludgeoned CBS into funneling all money, even for the pilot, through the corporation. This meant that CBS would make payment to Cayuga Productions for all costs on the pilot and Cayuga Productions would make all payments for the pilot on its own checks. Cayuga would not be officially formed until March, but clarification and approval from him was needed to set up the paperwork.

The officers of the corporation were Rod Serling as president, Ira Steiner as vice president, Carol Serling as secretary-treasurer, and Sam Kaplan as assistant treasurer. Bill Freedman was also authorized to withdraw funds from the corporation, providing Ira Steiner or Sam Kaplan co-signed.

CBS, having first option under contract, accepted the series and helped arrange for the pilot to be shown to a number of potential sponsors. The March 8, 1959 issue of *The New York Times* reported that, "an order for sponsorship has been placed by the General Foods Corporation, although a time period is still subject to negotiations between the advertiser and the network." The same news brief described the series as offering the type of stories that "lie somewhere between down-to-earth reality and outer space. Mr. Serling hopes to pack his plays with unusually imaginative happenings designed to seem neither completely real nor wholly unreal."

Having a sponsor six months in advance of premiere time was "unprecedented" according to *Variety*, which also reported, "GF is taking the show on an every week basis for a full 52-week commitment."

Cayuga Productions, Inc. was formed in March of 1959 through the law office of Kaplan, Livingston, Goodwin & Berkowitz in Beverly Hills, California. It would be Cayuga Productions that handled all the contracts and made all the payments. Under the agreement between Cayuga and

---

* Regardless of what multiple reference books state, Welles was never considered a host when the series was conceived. The suggestion was not brought up until the end of the first season, when the advertising agency representing General Foods suggested Welles be the narrator for the new, upcoming season. The May 28, 1960 issue of *TV Guide* reported, "Host for *The Twilight Zone* next season may be Orson Welles, who has been invited to take over from creator-writer Rod Serling. His critique of himself as an on-camera personality: 'I look like a scared Sicilian prizefighter.'" He was against the idea of Welles as narrator, and he made two separate trips to New York (the second was from May 15 through May 18) to talk the sponsors out of getting Welles for the series. Had Welles been hired, another $2,000 a week would come out of the show's budget, plus $600 to $800 for the still frame effect that would involve a blue backdrop and transparent film. The network, concerned over the expenses above all else, accepted Serling's appeal.

CBS, 100 percent of the legal title to copyright and film was in Cayuga's hand. Profit sharing was 60-40 split in CBS's favor. Serling's fee was $2,250 per script, and $750 as a production fee for each episode for supervisory duties and script consulting, whether Serling wrote the script or not. Residuals on both the script and production fee were 100 percent of the initial sum spread over six reruns. Excess beyond $1,540 per script writing residuals constituted an advance against profits. He was contracted to write a minimum of 11 shows for the first year, 10 the second year, and eight each year thereafter, but he could write as many additional scripts as he wished. The minimum order each year was for 26 films, with CBS having the option to increase that number up to a total of 40 annually. CBS was responsible for deciding whether the program would be renewed, and it could option renewals for a maximum of five years.

CBS provided all the financing, retaining the rights to approval terms and budget. CBS also had an exclusive distribution for 50 years.

Plot Proposals and Story Selection

When asked by the editor of *Gamma* magazine why he chose to do a series on fantasy and science fiction, when he had little prior experience with the genre, Serling remarked, "Because I loved this area of imaginative storytelling – and because there had never been a TV series like it. The strength of *Twilight Zone* is that through parable, or controversial theme against fantasy background you can make a point, which not if more blatantly stated in a realistic frame, would be acceptable. Because of this, from time to time, we've been able to make some pertinent social comments on conformity, on prejudice, on political ideologies, without sponsor interference. It offered a whole new outlet, a new approach."

"What we discovered, first of all," Buck Houghton explained to a reporter for *The Appleton Wisconsin Post-Crescent*, "was that there are relatively few dramatic contrivances that distinguish fantasy from a realistic telling of the same idea."

"The test of a good story must be whether there is a character to go with it," Serling explained to the same reporter. "If there is no attachment to the character, no way for his development, then there is no way to do the story." He received submissions from agents and authors as early as February 1958 because of the initial (and premature) press release. Author Dick Ashby, who had sold a number of short stories to a variety of science fiction magazines, such as *Astounding* and Anthony Boucher's *Fantasy and Science Fiction*, wrote to Rod Serling on March 17, 1958, asking about submitting plot ideas for his program. Ashby did not have a television agent, but that was not the reason why Serling sent him a rejection letter. A pilot had not until then been filmed, and he chose not to look at any story submissions until a pilot was in the can.

Throughout the month of April in 1958 Serling replied to a number of requests to submit plot ideas for his up-coming series. "We will consider unsolicited manuscripts from any writer," Serling told them. "Our criteria will be simply the value of each piece of writing – and not the credits or lack of credits of the submitting author. Unfortunately, however, the series is still in a very embryonic stage without even a pilot shot as yet. So I will ask your indulgence for the time being, keeping your letter, with a promise to let you know when submissions will be requested."

That same month, Harold L. Zimmer, a scriptwriter in St. Louis, Missouri, whose credits included selling a dozen scripts to Banner Films, of Paramount, for the1950s *Night Court* television program, wrote to Serling asking for a job. Zimmer had read conflicting rumors about *The Twilight Zone* episode and decided to ask the famed playwright himself. Serling replied, politely explaining that the pilot had not yet been filmed, and would not be looking at submissions for story ideas until fall or early winter. In November, Zimmer wrote another letter. "I have a nice, crisp, brand-new hour story treatment for *The Twilight Zone* I'd like to send you. It's a fantasy that I had originally planned to work into a short novel, but I've been holding up, waiting to hear from you." It is not known what reply Serling sent, but Zimmer never sold a story idea or premise for the series. *

On June 26, 1958, comedian Steve Allen (then located at 729 Seventh Ave., 8ᵗʰ Floor, New York 19, N.Y.) wrote the following to Rod Serling, living in Pacific Palisades, California:

Dear Rod:
I was just reading the story about you in this week's *Time* and happened to come across references to a forth-coming science fiction series titled *Twilight Zone*.

This called to my mind a short story I wrote a couple of years back which was originally published in *Bluebook Magazine* and was eventually selected as one of the top science fiction stories of the year and was included in a science fiction anthology.

Oddly enough, I did not think of it as science fiction at all when I wrote it, but in any event I am sending you herewith a copy of my book, *Fourteen for Tonight*, which includes the story. It is titled 'The Public Hating' and it occurs to me that you might want to consider it for inclusion in your *Twilight Zone* series. * *

Congratulations, by the way, on the great things you have been doing. As long as I'm at it, I think I will also enclose another book I did: *The Girls on the 10ᵗʰ Floor*, because it includes a southern lynching-type story with a new twist.

Best regards,
Steve Allen

On July 14, 1958, John J. Boyd, Sr., president of the Boyd Specialty Company in Columbus, Ohio, wrote to Rod Serling, asking the playwright to consider cross-marketing a game they created (still in the planning stages) that could use the name of "Twilight Zone" and be featured on the series as a form of advertising. "It is more interesting than Monopoly will ever be," the letter explained, "and you and those concerned could reap results that would be astounding as when offered for sale with your show, that we can get publicity in every science and fiction publication all over the world for free."

On August 5, 1958, Serling wrote back, stating that while the idea of coordinating a television series with a popular game was "interesting," it was premature at the time to discuss this kind of

---

* Whether Zimmer completed his novel remains unknown, but there is no evidence it was published. Another story that remains a mystery originates from the November 1, 1959 issue of *Pictorial TView* which mentioned that "one upcoming episode concerns a man who discovers a tombstone with his name being carved into it by a stranger whom he has never seen before." No such episode was ever filmed, but it is assumed that the plot was an adaptation a short story by W. F. Harvey titled "August Heat."

** "The Public Hating" (originally published in the January 1955 issue of *Bluebook*) by Steve Allen is a story about people gathering in a stadium for what appears to be a festive celebration, but it is actually the site for a public execution. People are silenced and asked to focus their hatred toward the man on the platform. Suddenly, he begins to shrivel and die, as he writhes in pain from all the hatred.

operation. Since they had not yet shot a pilot for the series, and the basic concept had not really been formulated, Serling suggested Boyd contact CBS Television directly with a general idea of what he had in mind and work with them on it. "My job will be principally in the creation of the series and in the writing of several of the shows and I would have little time to consider any other aspect. The gentleman you might write to is Mr. William Dozier, head of programming on the West Coast. The address is simply CBS-Television City, Hollywood, California. I hope you can work something out with him."

On September 16, 1958, Bob Somerfeld of the Petersen Publishing Company, submitted to Serling a number of books, pointing out one or two stories which Somerfeld felt would fit the mold of the proposed series. One book written by Richard Matheson, contained two short stories, "The Test" and "Steel," the latter of which Somerfeld wrote, "it's offbeat as hell and has a clean dramatic structure, as does "The Test." In case you like either or both of these for the series, but for some reason are unable to do the adaptation, I suggest Matheson himself for the job."

"The Test" by Richard Matheson, was originally published in the November 1954 issue of *Fantasy & Science Fiction*. It is a tale of age and survival. Upon reaching a certain age, the elderly must undergo a final exam of sorts. To pass means continuing to live; to fail leads to euthanasia. *

Somerfeld also suggested John Collier's collection of science fantasy, *Fancies and Goodnights*, which contained Walter Van Tilburg Clark's short story, "The Portable Phonograph," originally published in the Spring 1941 issue of *Yale Review*. This is an end-of-the-world tale in which the last handful of survivors on Earth conflict over possession of a portable phonograph. He also suggested Roald Dahl's "Someone Like You" (Alfred A. Knopf, 1953), about a man who invents a machine that can hear the sounds of plants and other things.

Serling wrote to Somerfeld, complimenting him on his taste. Through Serling's eyes, "Test" had the substance of "an especially good television play." He commented that if he could get a hold of the rights, he would do some substantial changing in the characters, but the basic structure would be left alone. By far the best story in the whole book, in Serling's opinion, was "Steel," but unfortunately Serling considered this "un-shootable for our purposes." It may be possible that "The Test" suited Rod Serling because it mirrored his concept within the rejected teleplay, "The Happy Place."

On November 9, 1958, John Mandola of the Bronx, New York, wrote to Serling proposing "a story about two men who perfect a supersonic moving camera and accidentally discover a race of men living on Earth that can't be seen with the eye."

On November 24, 1958, science fiction author Raymond E. Banks wrote a letter suggesting Serling look over a few of his short stories. "The Happiness Effect" was first published in the November 1953 issue of *Astounding Science Fiction Magazine* and told the story about a futuristic society with the perfect answer to problem humans – brain writing. Their brains arranged to conform to what society universally thinks is correct. It begins to come undone when an artist gets on the bad side of the brain writer and it becomes necessary to alter the artist's brain. This was the first of four short stories Banks submitted with his letter. While the story had never been anthologized at the time, it had been dramatized twice on radio. Once it was done as a 10-minute "quickie" for the Mutual Network, with Peter Lorre doing the narration and acting. It was also dramatized in early 1958 on John Campbell's NBC Radio program, *Exploring Tomorrow*.

---

* Matheson's "The Test" was apparently adapted years later as an episode of *I Racconti di Fantascienza di Blasetti*, the Italian anthology show from famed filmmaker Alessandro Blasetti, in 1978-1979.

The other three short stories were looked over by Serling, but rejected as he felt they did not fit the mold of what he intended to use for the *Twilight Zone*. "The Short Ones" was originally published in the March 1955 issue of *Fantasy & Science Fiction* and appeared in book form in *Best from Fantasy & Science Fiction, Fifth Series*, which had been selected in December 1957 as an offering of the Doubleday Science Fiction Book Club. "The Critic," by Raymond E. Banks, was originally published in the November 1955 issue of *Imaginative Tales*, an amusing story about sociological change and "competitive leisure." "Christmas Trombone" was first printed in the 1955 issue of *Best Science Fiction*, published in France, and had been translated into German, but never actually published there.

Banks' letter went on to suggest other authors and their works for *The Twilight Zone*. "Charles Beaumont has a pocketbook collection of stories that you ought to look at," Banks wrote Serling. "He is an arrived writer under contract to *Playboy* and working for the same agency that handles Herman Wouk and Ray Bradbury. Probably one of the best since Bradbury to rise up from the science fiction ranks. For some strange reason, Hollywood and television have been slow to utilize his talents."

Charles Beaumont admired Bradbury, having read many of Bradbury's stories, and often submitted his own to the literary giant for advice and criticism before they were submitted and sold to magazines such as *Playboy*. "There's a light Bradbury and there's a dark Bradbury. He's got his cruel streak in him, you know," recalled George Clayton Johnson to interviewer Matthew R. Bradley. "You see that in *Ray Bradbury Theater*. That and *Twilight Zone* aren't much different in their sensibility; they're mostly technological differences. When I saw Rod doing Ray's act, but within his style, I said, 'Well, that's very easy to do. I'm going to adopt the script style of Rod Serling, write just like him, and enjoy the sort of things that he does.' He's got a dark edge to him, too. He likes things that are grim and tense, and everybody is sort of whispering because if it gets out, we're all in trouble – this kind of anger and tension all being compressed because it's got to be quiet."

"Serling came over to the house one night and told me what he was doing," recalled Ray Bradbury, in an interview with author Mark Phillips. "He said, 'Can you suggest some writers?' I said, 'Sure!' I went down to my basement and came back with paperback copies by Richard Matheson, Charles Beaumont, George Clayton Johnson and John Collier. I said, 'These are good people. And you can use me, too.' The series went on shortly afterwards, and it's been running ever since."

Banks' letter also reveals Serling's introduction to Forrest J. Ackerman, a literary agent who, represented Beaumont and Bradbury. Ackerman would eventually sell "Time Enough at Last" to Serling, which became one of the most memorable first-season episodes. "Forrest J. Ackerman is known as 'Mr. Science Fiction' and with good reason," Banks explained. "Agent and fan, he has the world's most complete library of science fiction material, and he is an astonishing walking encyclopedia of science fiction stories going back to Year One. He operates as an agent – he is something of a character, which means not very business-like. If you were to spend a day in his house with its fabulous library on Sherbourne Street in Beverly Hills, you would learn more about science fiction than spending a year in talking to writers and editors."

Enter stage left, Charles Beaumont. Chicago-born in 1929, he was struck down by spinal meningitis as a child, and "forced into reading about the land of OZ, which ignited a fire that is till burning in me," recounted Beaumont. He made his fictional debut in Amazing Stories early in 1951. It wasn't long until the floodgates finally opened and the acceptance checks began pouring in — establishing him as a top name in and out of the field of fantasy.

"With great misgivings, and after a suitable period of grousing about outsiders and why didn't the networks buy our shows, we – Richard Matheson, Ray Bradbury, and I – agreed to discuss the possibility of joining the program," wrote Charles Beaumont for *The Magazine of Fantasy and Science Fiction*. "I don't know what we expected Serling to be like, but we were all surprised to find that he was a nice guy who happened to love good science fiction and fantasy and saw no reason why it shouldn't be brought to the screen. My own resentment vanished during that first meeting. But I still had doubts. Serling's talk was good, but what about the scripts? The first nine were written by him, based on his story ideas. Wasn't this a bit cheeky?"

"Yes," said Serling. "However, I had no choice. My promise to write most of the scripts was a very big factor in the network's acceptance of the project."

"I took the nine home with me, determined to hate them," remarked Beaumont. "At midnight, when I'd finished reading the material, I knew that Serling was an 'outsider' only in terms of experience; in terms of instinct, he was a veteran. Bradbury and Matheson read the scripts also, and in very little time we all decided to join the *Twilight Zone* team."

Lawrence S. Cruikshank of the Lawrence Cruikshank Agency, in Los Angeles, wrote to Cayuga Productions, proposing a number of his clients who had experience scripting teleplays. Among the names was Merwin Gerard, whose credits included a number of television anthologies and was billed as the creator and associate producer for *One Step Beyond*. Hiring someone to write scripts for *The Twilight Zone*, from an eerie anthology that was considered competition, ruled Gerard out immediately.

Cruikshank also suggested the services of: Arthur Fitz-Richard, who wrote teleplays for *Hawkeye and the Mohicans*, *Science Fiction Theatre*, *I Led Three Lives* and *Lassie*, was proposed. Fitz-Richard was formerly a story analyst at Warner Bros., Universal, 20th Century Fox and M-G-M. Charles Larson's credits included a number of teleplays for *Climax!* and *General Electric Theater*, and 65 published short stories. Bob Mitchell's credits were an impressive array, which included *Maverick*, *I Led Three Lives*, *Sheriff of Cochise*, *Front Page Detective*, and his "Shark on the Mountain" teleplay on the *DuPont Cavalcade Theater* which was nominated for best anthology teleplay of 1958. On radio, Mitchell wrote for *Gunsmoke*, *The Whistler*, *Murder by Experts*, *Box 13*, *Diary of Fate* and 104 scripts of *Philip Marlowe*. Arthur Orloff wrote pilot scripts and created formats for *Racket Squad* and *Public Defender* and wrote teleplays for *Ellery Queen*, *Mr. and Mrs. North*, *Perry Mason* and *The Texan*. Gene Roddenberry's name was even proposed to Serling; his teleplay credits up to that time included *Mr. District Attorney*, *Dragnet*, *Boots and Saddles*, *Have Gun-Will Travel* and *Highway Patrol*. Cayuga accepted none of the Cruikshank nominees.

When Cruikshank learned that Richard L. Bare was hired to direct a couple episodes, he proposed Frederic Brady, because Brady wrote the teleplay "All Our Yesterdays," which won Bare a Screen Directors' Guild Award. Again, Cayuga turned Brady down.

Rod Serling wanted to secure the rights to feature Philip K. Dick's story, "Imposter," which was about a scientist who worked for a top secret government project. He is sent undercover to discover the identity of an android that has infiltrated the project's facility and taken the place of a worker. However, he is accused of being an android himself and must clear his name and reveal the identity of the traitor.

On February 10, 1959, Alden Schwimmer of Ashley-Steiner wrote to Serling, explaining about the screen rights to "Imposter." *Galaxy* magazine made a deal with a producer named Larry White in which all of *Galaxy*'s stories were to be packaged in a potential series. In short, the story was not available. However, Schwimmer was an old friend of White, and he called the producer to ask him to release the one story. White said he would, but the people at *Galaxy* wanted $1,500 for it. On February 13, Serling wrote to Schwimmer, explaining that Fred Engel had probably already contacted him about how anxious he was to latch onto the rights to "The Imposter" by Philip Dick. Fifteen hundred bucks was a high price tag, Serling remarked, "but it's a wonderful story and I think we might as well go ahead with it." On February 20, Schwimmer wrote back. "On '[The] Imposter,' Larry White tells me that the *Galaxy Magazine* people will not accept any kind of an option deal. They will only sell the story on the basis of a firm $1,500 purchase." On March 9, Fred Engel of Ashley-Steiner told Serling that the story is tied up with *Galaxy Magazine* and Larry White may not be able to get them the rights.

Fred Engel submitted a number of published stories to help Rod Serling with the selection of first-season story material. On February 18, 1959, he submitted "Hangover" by John D. MacDonald and "The Two of Them" by William Brandon, and in the cover letter included with the submissions Engel remarked to Serling, "for your perusal, pursuant to *Twilight Zone.*"

Serling wrote to Schwimmer on March 9, 1959, having looked over the list of possible stories Schwimmer had copied for him. Serling requested to look at the following:

"The Custodian" from *Of All Possible Worlds* by William Tenn, Ballantine Books
"Breaking Strain" from *Expedition to Earth* by Arthur C. Clarke, Ballantine Books
"Exile of the Eons" from *Expedition to Earth* by Arthur C. Clarke, Ballantine Books
"The Wheel" by John Wyndham
"Far Centaurus" by A.E. Van Vogt
"Vintage Season" by Laurence O'Donnell
"–And He Built a Crooked House–" by Robert Heinlein
"The Nine Billion Names of God" by Arthur C. Clarke
"Don't Look Now" by Henry Kuttner, *Better Publications,*
"Here There is Tygers" from *New Tales of Space and Time* by Ray Bradbury and
"The Cold Equations" from *Astounding Stories* by Tom Goodwin

"The Custodian" was first printed in the November 1953 issue of *If.* Written by William Tenn, it tells the story after the Earth has been abandoned because the sun is predicted to go nova. One man chooses to remain, a man who has been dubbed a "custodian" because he is interested in things that are not merely useful, unlike the pragmatic Affirmers, a sort of religious sect that seems to have organized the evacuation of the planet.

"Breaking Strain" was first printed in the December 1949 issue of *Thrilling Wonder Stories.* Written by Arthur C. Clarke, it tells the story about a ship on a run from Earth to Venus, which is struck by a meteor. The oxygen supply is damaged. There is only enough oxygen for one of two of the multiple crewmembers. Eventually, only two remain and it has to be decided who will live and who will die. Because some must die to save others, it is decided to randomly poison cups of coffee.

"Vintage Season" was first printed in the September 1946 issue of *Astounding Science Fiction*. Written by Lawrence O'Donnell (a pseudonym for Henry Kuttner and C.L. Moore), it tells about Oliver, who rents his home to strange out-of-town visitors, who speak very formally and wear strange clothes. He soon learns that his renters are time travelers from the future who visit major catastrophes of the past. When a comet crashes and devastates the town, Oliver's home is one of the few that survive, which was why the time travelers chose it. He comes to despise the renters because of their uncaring nature for the victims of the catastrophe.

"–And He Built a Crooked House–" was first published in the February 1941 issue of *Astounding Science Fiction*. Written by Robert Heinlein, it tells the story of architect Quintus Teal and his desire to build a four dimensional house for his friends Homer Bailey and his wife. The house is constructed in an inverted double cross shape. The day after it is finished, he plans to take them to the house. When they arrive, they see one cube out of the eight original cubes. At first thinking the rest of the house was somehow stolen, they find upon entering, that an earthquake the night before has caused the house to fold into itself becoming a true four-dimensional home.

Arthur C. Clarke's "The Nine Billion Names of God" was also selected by Serling. Originally published in 1953, the story told of a Buddhist monastery whose monks have engineered, with the assistance of "Westerners," a computer that will apply a number of calculations that, given a long time period, eliminate all of the possibilities of the Lord's name, existence will become meaningless, and God himself will "wind up" the universe. The computer operators, fearing the final hours, flee the monastery. They look behind them and "overhead, without any fuss, the stars were going out." According to a progress report dated July 1, 1959, Cayuga had a six-month option to purchase the short story for $1,500. Serling did compose a feasible teleplay, but the film was never produced.

"Far Centaurus" was first published in the January 1944 issue of *Astounding Science Fiction*. Written by A.E. Van Vogt, it tells the story of a spaceship sent from Earth to travel for 500 years to Alpha Centauri. The four men on the ship take pills which will keep them asleep for periods of 50 to 150 years at a time. This way each one can wake up at different times to report back. By the time they arrive, Earth has already developed advanced time travel over 500 years and the system is already populated by Earth beings. Because they smell strange to these future inhabitants, they are kept isolated. Bored, the four men set off to explore the galaxy.

"Don't Look Now" was first published in 1948. Written by Henry Kuttner, it tells the tale of a man named Lyman who is sitting in a bar with another man, a reporter. Lyman tells the man about the Martians that he sees that no one else seems to see. He knows they are Martians because occasionally he sees a third eye in the middle of their forehead, which is normally invisible. After much suspicion, the reporter believes he too has seen them but not directly – more as a little suggestion of movement in the corner of his eye. He has photographs, however, that he has accidentally taken. The two agree to meet again the next night since they do not seem to suspect each other. Lyman, however, is a Martian and his efforts were merely a means of covering up the secret. *

Ray Bradbury's story, "Here There Be Tygers," was a favorite of Serling's. The story concerns an expedition to another planet, where human spacemen are searching for natural resources that

---

* This story was adapted and performed twice for the television horror anthology program, *Lights Out!*, with Burgess Meredith in the role of Lyman. Serling looked into purchasing this story, but discovered a conflict regarding the ownership of the rights and dismissed the story for possible use on *Twilight Zone*.

Kevin McCarthy meets up with his
past in "Long Live Walter Jameson."

could be harvested for people back on Earth. They discover the planet is a literal Garden of Eden and soon realize that the planet, untouched by the destructive forces of man, should stay that way. They return to Earth, intent on falsifying a report that the planet was hostile and contained no natural resources. Bradbury promised to write the script in June, when he would be free from a contractual obligation. By July 1, Bradbury began working on the script. (More about this later.)

"The Cold Equations" was first published in *Astounding Magazine* in 1954. Written by Tom Godwin, the short story tells of a starship making the rounds of Earth colonies, delivering much needed medical supplies to a frontier planet. When the pilot discovers a stowaway on board, an 18-year-old named Marilyn, who wants to see her brother at the colony, he realizes a bigger problem ahead for them. The ship only has enough fuel for the pilot and the cargo. Marilyn's weight and mass will prevent the starship from reaching its destination. Marilyn accepts the consequences of her mistake, writes a farewell letter to her parents, talks to her brother by radio, and then enters the airlock – ready to be jettisoned into space. While this story was never used on the original series, the 1985-89 revival of *The Twilight Zone* featured an adaptation of this short story.

On March 24, 1959, Sylvia Hirsch of the William Morris Agency submitted an hour-long teleplay titled "Tomorrow is Here" by Whitfield Cook. On March 25, Fred Engel proposed "The Black Hound of Bailundu" by Paul I. Wellman. Serling rejected both of these.

On April 7, 1959, the radio play "Return to Dust" was considered for inclusion in the *Twilight Zone* series. Originally broadcast on *Suspense*, the George Bamber story concerned a biologist's efforts to decrease cancer cells, and through an accident in the lab, found himself slowly shrinking in size. The majority of the drama (making the most effective use for the medium of radio) was the biologist's effort to leave a recorded message explaining his situation and where his lab associates could find him, should they play back the recording. In the end, however, the scientist is down to the size of a bug and still shrinking, though he never gets to microscopic size because a bird mistakes him for an insect and makes a feast of him.

Also submitted for Serling's approval on April 7 was "The Boy Who Saved the World" by Roland A. Martone, which was originally published in the December 1956 issue of *Boys' Life*.

On that same day, Melvin Korshak of Shasta Publishers submitted to Fred Engel a number of books for possible use on *The Twilight Zone*. While most of the novels were not even read due to time restraints, the short story anthologies were checked out: Fredric Brown and Mack Reynolds' *Science Fiction Carnival* and editor Melvin Korshak's *Let's Ride a Rocket*.

According to a progress report dated April 9, 1959, Robert Heinlein's "Life-Line" was one of many stories Serling wanted to include in the *Twilight Zone* lineup. Originally published in the August 1939 issue of *Astounding Science Fiction Magazine*, it tells the story of one Hugo Panero, scientist and entrepreneur, who discovers a method of accurately predicting one's death. The insurance industry begins to find this discovery a threat to its very survival and begins to take action. On March 27, 1959, Cayuga attempted to contact Heinlein's New York agent, Lurton Blassingame, to purchase the story. Leonard Freeman rejected the offer, suggesting that Heinlein had a "moral commitment" to write a screenplay.

On April 16, 1959, Serling received a *New Yorker* anthology with the short story "I Am Waiting," which was recommended to him. Serling rejected the story.

On April 17, 1959, Reece Halsey at the Reece Halsey Agency in Los Angeles submitted a story to Serling, titled "The Little Girl at the Window" by Rik Vollaerts. The story was based on the widely publicized disappearance of a little boy during a hiking trip, two years before. "It would make an absorbing show, under your expert supervision," said Halsey. Serling obliged and on April 21, wrote a reply to Halsey thanking him for the enclosed, but found it a little wide off the mark for *The Twilight Zone*. Serling did suggest Halsey submit the story to Alcoa's *One Step Beyond*.

Cayuga attempted to purchase "7 Days to Live," a short story by Jack Finney that was originally published in the January 10, 1959 issue of *The Saturday Evening Post*. A condemned man awaiting execution within a week requests paints and brushes. He then passes the time away by painting a door that, to the amazement of the guards and other prisoners, takes on realism never before captured by oils. Just minutes prior to his execution, he escapes through the painting.

In mid-April 1959, Buck Houghton discovered that Harry Lewis represented Finney, but Finney had no television screenplay credits and no particular wish to adapt the material, but he was willing to try it. By April 30, Finney submitted speculatively a teleplay based on his story, which Cayuga felt was "no good for our purposes." According to a progress report that day, "We are inspecting other Finney material to see if there is another story or two of his that would enhance our purchase prospects." According to a May 11 interoffice memo, Jack Finney did his own adaptation and wanted to try for a while longer to sell it before considering Cayuga's offer to buy the original story material only.

Finney's short story, "The Third Level," originally published in the October 1950 issue of *Collier's* and which appeared in the book of the same name from Reinhart & Co., Inc., interested Serling, so Cayuga attempted to buy the story in the hopes that a dual purchase might move him from holding on to "7 Days to Live." They failed in convincing Finney to release the rights to both stories. "The Third Level" was a time travel story about a man named Charley, who finds himself in a non-existing third level of Grand Central Station in 1894. After he discovers his way back, Charley reveals his fantastic story to his wife, and together they attempt to find the same passage – but fail. Days later, Charley suspects his adventure might have been a dream, until he finds an old letter addressed to him, from the year 1894.

Under consideration was Aldous Huxley's "Voices," a short story that appeared in *Atlantic*. Another being considered was Ray Bradbury's "Hail and Farewell," the story of a young boy who would not age, could not grow up, and was forced to run away from home every few years to prevent the adopted parents from discovering his circumstance. Bradbury, who insisted on writing the teleplays based on his stories, did not make the story available to Serling.

Also under deliberation, according to interoffice correspondence, Bradbury's 1953 collection of short stories, *The Golden Apples of the Sun*, published by Doubleday & Company. Among the short stories, two were favored for adaptation – "The Fruit at the Bottom of the Bowl" (1948) and "Invisible Boy" (1945). In the former tale, Mr. Acton commits a cold-blooded murder and in an effort to wipe away all the fingerprints in the house, forgets his true objective and is ultimately arrested. In the second story, a young boy runs away from home and finds himself held captive by a witch who renders him invisible.

On June 29, 1959, Jack Stewart & Associates, representatives of William N. Robson, wrote to Rod Serling, in care of Metro-Goldwyn-Mayer Studios:

Dear Mr. Serling:
William Robson, who is director-producer and sometime writer for CBS's Suspense, has a backlog of science stories which he owns. You probably know Bill by reputation. He, along with Norman Corwin and Arch Oboler, changed the whole technique of radio with their wonderful shows. Recently Bill won the Mystery Writers of America – Special Award – for "Best Suspense Series." Will you please let me know when it would be convenient for you to talk to him?

Very cordially yours,
Jack Stewart

On July 8, 1959, Rod Serling replied, acknowledging Robson's reputation and confessed that he was a fan of the producer/director. Unfortunately, at the moment, he had over purchased the number of story materials beyond the actual production commitments. He explained that it would be a waste of time for the two to talk on what would be a very problematical level, but offered a sympathetic and interested ear. "Should our situation change and we are once more in the market for material, I'd consider it a privilege to meet Robson because I recognize it as a fact that he was doing wonderful things when I was just still hoping."

William F. Nolan submitted "Small World" to Serling in August of 1959, and that, too, was rejected. He found it "just a little too wild for us and a little too tough to do."

On April 19, 1961, Fred Engel of Ashley-Steiner contacted Buck Houghton with a copy of "Rat Race" by Sid Mandel and Sol Drucker. The script supposedly was written specifically for *The Twilight Zone*, and Engel felt it was "of superior quality."

In mid-late August of 1959, Russell Stoneham at CBS Television forwarded to Bill Self a copy of a radio script penned by Irving Reis, titled "Man of Tomorrow." Self liked the story, and passed it on to Serling for review. The script has been performed twice on CBS Radio – the *Escape* broadcast of August 23, 1953, and on *Suspense* on September 1, 1957. Serling rejected the idea and had the script sent back to CBS. The story concerned an Air Force pilot who returns from Korea and agrees to an immoral experiment that ultimately surpasses his five senses, granting him the opportunity of experiencing a sixth sense.

In April of 1960, Blanche Gaines submitted an original half-hour teleplay titled "The Man with the Diamond," which she felt was a "dilly" and would fit beautifully into the format of the series. Serling was an ardent fan of Frank Gilroy's work and asked her to send it to him. Serling loved the adaptation and forwarded the script to editor and associate producer Del Reisman for review. Reisman reported to Serling with a negative opinion. The teleplay was apparently an adaptation of a brief in the newspaper, and the rights holder was Stan Opotowsky of *The New York Post*. Reisman would not contact Opotowsky, believing the story was not up to standards for the program, so the story was shelved.

"As a story editor on *Playhouse 90*, I met Rod a number of times. He wrote a number of scripts for the program," recalled Del Reisman. "I was the story editor for the program. I wrote a couple teleplays for the series. We became good friends so one day he phoned me and said he was looking for some help with his *Twilight Zone* series. He was the only man in charge of story selection. Buck was producing the show, but had little involvement with the stories. That was left up to Rod. He told me he needed help, and asked if I would come on board for some script help. This was in the middle of the first season of *Twilight Zone*, so I told him I couldn't. I was tied up with the *Playhouse 90* series, but when the season was over, I would come help him. I did for the second season of the *Twilight Zone*."

On October 27, 1960, Charles R. Steers of Chicago suggested to Serling by way of a fan letter that he check out "A Fall of Glass" by Stanley R. Lee, which had recently appeared in the October 1960 issue of *Galaxy* magazine. Due to the previous failed attempt to buy properties from *Galaxy*, Serling may have read the story, but acquiring the basic rights would have been a dead end, and the story was never purchased. Steers even suggested Charles Laughton and Elsa Lanchester in the leads. Serling sent the usual rejection letter, politely claiming that he already purchased all the material needed for the current season and was no longer in the market for stories.

On September 15, 1959, Serling had Buck Houghton begin preliminaries in purchasing a short story called "The Walker Through Walls" by Marcel Ayme. The story originally appeared in a collection of Ayme's short stories called *Across Paris and Other Stories*, published by Harper & Brothers. In the book, the copyright was indicated as jointly Harper & Brothers and Librairie Galliamard. Ayme was a French author and it was uncertain at the time whether Ayme was in the country. Serling was interested in adapting the story into a feasible teleplay. The story also had appeared in a recent issue of *Fantasy and Science Fiction Magazine*.

"Never Ask a Lady Her Age"
On October 12, 1958, Rod Serling wrote to William Dozier, head of programming on the West Coast, who resided at the Hampshire House at 150 Central Park South in New York. He submitted more than six plot proposals, and one of them was a three-paragraph plot titled "Never Ask a Lady Her Age."

On February 8, 1961, Serling would adapt the proposal into a *Twilight Zone* script called "The Black Letter Day." Judging by the partial script and internal documented evidence, he stopped at page 15 and never finished the script.

This was a story about an amateur hypnotist who, as a party favor, mesmerized people. As the custom of modern hypnosis, he asked his "patients" to regress by writing their names at progressively earlier ages. For example, he told a woman she was 30 and asked her to write her name. Then he told her she was 25 and 20 and so on down the line, as his audience marveled at how her handwriting changed to coincide with the age group she imagined herself to be. One evening for kicks, he reversed the process of hypnosis and told one woman to write her name as she progressively grew older. He told her she was 35 and she wrote her name in a slightly different way then she was accustomed. Then he told her she was 40, 45, 46, 47, and each time the handwriting altered to become a little shakier and a little less firm. Finally, when she reached the age of 54, he asked her to write her name and she was unable to do so. She could write nothing.

"Why don't you write?" he asked.

"I can't. I can't write anything," she answered.

"Why not?"

There is a long silence as everyone in the room inched closer. She looked up and spoke, "Because I am dead." There was a sudden intake of breath and then a mass hush fell over the crowd. The hypnotist was shaken. Immediately as a post-hypnotic suggestion, he told the woman that she would remember nothing that had occurred in the past few moments. He did not want to frighten her particularly since he could not explain the phenomena. Everyone in the room was sworn to secrecy before the woman was snapped out of the mesmerism. The party seemed to be going on as before with hardly a hint of the disquiet caused.

A year or two pass and the hypnotist had almost forgotten the occurrence at the party. He had been keeping himself busy with other areas. He was in the process of putting the bite on a wealthy widow when he found himself in almost the identical social situation as he was a number of years before. Again, the process was the same and this time the hypnotist was, in turn, hypnotized. He was asked to regress by writing his name and then at later stages. The age crept up from 38 to 39, and then he himself was unable to write his name, because he told people he was dead. This time, his hypnotist was too shaken by the incident to suggest the subject post-hypnotically would not remember the incident. There was no falsehood with the subject. What happened was unexplainable.

The thing stayed on him destructively, worrying, until he finally decided to hurry up the process of fleecing the widow and leave the country. His situation became even more frantic when he learned of the death of the woman he had hypnotized years ago and that her age coincided with her revelation under hypnosis. Now, desperately frightened, he booked passage on a ship to get out of the country. He told the confidante that he was taking the safest boat afloat and would lock himself in the cabin because the date that he himself had picked as his death under hypnosis was to take place while he was on the high seas. Nothing and no one could possibly cause his death under such security. The ocean provided him with a feeling of contentment. On board the luxury liner, he bid farewell and retreated to his cabin. As the ship pulled out, the television viewers could see written on her bow, "The Titanic."

In the February 1961 script, the hypnotist was named Harvey, and his first victim was named Doreen. While "The Black Letter Day," (formerly "Never Ask a Lady Her Age") never fleshed into a feasible episode for *The Twilight Zone*, a similar premise was applied in an episode of Rod Serling's *Night Gallery*, titled "The Dead Man," adapted from a short story by Fritz Leiber. The story concerned a doctor who, using a posthypnotic trance, induced or cured the symptoms of a disease. Considered a "variation on a theme," the *Twilight Zone* rarely delved into the subject of hypnotism. "The Black Letter Day" was never completed, but Serling did compose his opening narration after the opening scene:

"Picture of a man playing with fire. Mr. Harvey Cranston who thinks hypnosis, like spin-the-bottle, is a rather light-hearted diversion to be pulled off at parties and other social gatherings. He, of course, does not realize it at the moment – as do very few people – but hypnosis, like any excursion into the mind, is not for amateurs. It happens to be a serious and in large measure an unexplored science that requires medical

knowledge. It was Goethe who said it . . . in effect – nothing is worse than ignorance with spurs. And what we're soon to see happen here is precisely that. An excursion into terror as a living proof that a little knowledge can be a most dangerous thing. In just a moment, Miss Doreen Spruance will take an extended walk into the darker regions which we call . . . the Twilight Zone."

Franchot Tone is shocked to learn he lost his bet in "The Silence."

CHAPTER FOUR

Production Begins

A lot of the *Twilight Zone* crew, almost the entire crew for the run of that series, came from Meridian Productions and the *Schlitz Playhouse of Stars*," recalled William Self for author Tom Weaver. "The cameraman George Clemens was from Meridian, the assistant director Eddie Denault was from Meridian, the production manager Ralph W. Nelson was from Meridian. Generally speaking, all the way down to the gaffer who worked with George Clemens, they had all worked on *Schlitz*. I gave Rod all those names, that was my contribution. . . . Incidentally, after the pilot sold, Serling wanted me to join Cayuga Productions and produce the series. But I had only been with CBS a short period of time and I was reluctant to go with a production company headed by one guy – Serling. If anything went wrong, that was the end of my job! I thought I'd better stay with CBS, which I did."

With Rod Serling's role as executive producer, the actual task of producing was assigned to Buck Houghton. "Buck Houghton was a very capable young producer assistant at RKO when I first came out here," Self recalled. "When I started the *Schlitz Playhouse of Stars* and reached a point where I could afford a story editor, I hired Buck Houghton to do that . . . I suggested Buck Houghton as a possible producer, because he was very knowledgeable about making a television show and Rod Serling was very knowledgeable about writing a television show. I thought it was a good combination, and that turned out to be true."

Houghton's primary role as producer was to coordinate and control all aspects of production, ranging from shoot supervision to fact checking. He supervised the quality of the films, working closely with the casting director, the hiring of the director, the set designs, and the financial business matters such as budgets and contracts.

Houghton worked almost hand-in-hand with Serling, fully understanding the scope of the series, leaving his taste in scripts and stories up to the playwright. "The scripts I handled were thoroughly entertaining and thought-provoking," Houghton recalled. "That was my standard of what was going to please the average TV viewer. After all, I was a perfectly average fellow, minding my own business, when I was asked to read the first scripts. Fantasy or not, they were damn good."

Houghton and Serling quickly agreed that, financially, it was better to film the teleplays at a movie studio where costumes and props were at their disposal; it would be less expensive than forming their own studio for television production. Having had a movie contract with M-G-M and familiar with the back lots and sound studios, Serling felt comfortable knowing the company was capable of providing their every need.

By the mid-1950s, the studio was not the dream factory Hollywood made it out to be. Ticket sales were down, and television was the major culprit. In 1955, Metro-Goldwyn-Mayer, Inc. counteracted by launching Metro-Goldwyn-Mayer Television as a survival tactic to venture in television series production. That same year, *Twentieth Century-Fox Hour* played on CBS and *M-G-M Parade* on ABC. In addition to *Parade*, M-G-M Television offered *Northwest Passage*, but by 1960, its own television production showed very little profit. A solution came in the form of in-house projects and joint ventures to make use of the sets, lots, costumes and props, allowing production chiefs to rent them to produce their own programs.

An agreement was struck with the studio chiefs and Houghton and Serling then began focusing their efforts on directors. In late April 1959, Self, Serling and Houghton began to make lists of the directors they favored, and penciled in who would helm which script. Houghton commented in an interoffice memo that "we must choose people who have a good, firm chance of meeting our production schedule and that we must also have imaginative directors who will rise to the theatrically and bizarre elements in our scripts."

Self and Houghton created the following list, though Houghton was dead set against Robert Florey "because I believe he gives actors no help whatsoever."

Justus Addiss	Montgomery Pittman
Walter Doniger	Richard Sale
Robert Florey	Robert Stevens
Christian Nyby	

The following list of men had worked for CBS and had experience in film. Houghton approved Reisner because he was favored by many production companies, "and will probably be wanted on at least two or three of our shows."

Buzz Kulik	Allen Reisner
Allen Miner	Sheldon Leonard
Sidney Lumet	

Houghton made an additional list of whom he had heard very good reports and offered them for consideration:

Robert Altman	Jack Arnold
Douglas Heyes	Jack Smight
Richard Wilson	

"There are several young men, many raised in the *Matinee Theatre* school, whom I think have done very good work," Houghton explained. "They seem to be especially notable for injecting a great deal of life and vivacity into their films." In the list below of Houghton's, Sagal was one of his favorites. "I've had two personal experiences with Sagal and would like very much to use him in this series."

Walter Grauman	David O. McDearmon

Boris Sagal   Jeffrey Hayden
Lamont Johnson

There were several men still active, who, over a long period of years, had established reputations of great style. Girard and Peyser were younger men whom Houghton referred to as "less dependable than the others; under the discipline by which they do their best work, they are perhaps better than the others."

James Neilson   Lazlo Benedek
John Brahm   Bernard Girard
Arthur Ripley   John Peyser
Harry Horner

Should *The Twilight Zone* do a comedy (which they did a number of times), the following were directors considered:

Rod Amateau   Richard Kinon
Hy Averback   Oscar Rudolph

Houghton either had experience with the directors listed below, or direct detailed reports of their work, and were the names Houghton personally recommended to Serling:

Richard L. Bare   Gene Fowler, Jr.
Leslie Martinson   Robert Parrish
Robert Stevens   Boris Sagal
Richard Sale   Paul Stewart
Anton Morris Leader   Hugo Haas
Michael Gordon   Alvin Ganzer
Hugo Fregonese

Two names that Houghton brought up for consideration were rejected for various reasons, though they were, for a brief spell, considered: Livia Granito and Paul Stanley. Granito was a bright young woman who directed about 60 of the *Matinee Theatre* episodes and had a long work record in live television. She never shot film, which turned out to be her downside. Houghton had arranged to get a direct report of her work, in the hopes that she might be excellent in a story where a woman's point of view would add materially to the total effect. Stanley did Rod Serling's "The Last Night in August" on *Pursuit*, and several of the *Third Man* television episodes, with which National Telefilm Associates (NTA) was very pleased. Though he had recently finished a feature for Hecht-Hill-Lancaster called *Cry Tough*, his name was tossed aside for the more experienced directors on the lists.

On the final days of August 1959, Harold Rose of Famous Artists Corporation wrote to Serling, proposing director William Russell, who was under exclusive contract to CBS and was presently shooting one of the *Perry Mason* episodes. According to Rose's proposal, Russell was quite eager to work with Cayuga on *The Twilight Zone*, but after a discussion between Bill Dozier and Buck Houghton, it decided not to hire Russell.

So the agency publicity staff would understand the subject matter of the show, formulate a strong point of view for their campaign, and the probable cost to the sponsor (and CBS) for publicity, Buck Houghton hosted a showing of the "Where is Everybody?" pilot on April 15, 1959 to Milton Samuels of Young & Rubicam and several of his staff.

Millie Gusse was hired by Cayuga Productions as the casting director. Working closely with both Serling and Houghton, her main task was to fill the roles of all spoken and silent bit parts – and to oversee the hiring of all extras. While Serling and Houghton had suggestions for some of the roles, it was Gusse who made the arrangements and drew up the contracts for the stars to sign. Contractually, her employment began on May 4, 1959, for at least 15 shows with a guarantee of 12 shows. Her salary was $275 for each episode.

On May 6, 1959, Bill Robinson of Ashley-Steiner submitted a list of nine actors and actresses who could be available for *The Twilight Zone*: Lloyd Nolan, Walter Slezak, James Donald, Jan Sterling, Anne Francis, Glynis Johns, Linda Darnell, Cyril Ritchard, Martin Balsam and Eric Portman.

By May 14, Serling, Houghton and Hal Graham had worked out a format for *The Twilight Zone*, a blueprint for the opening narration, the teaser for the drama, the three commercials, the length of time for the two acts, Serling on camera setting the stage for next week, end credits and billboard, all making up the time allotted for the series.

It was about this same time that the question of whether Rod Serling would appear on camera in the beginning of each episode was decided by the majority involved. Wick Crider of Young & Rubicam, Ed Ebel of General Foods, and Tom Brennen of Foote, Cone & Belding, were all against Serling appearing before the camera, except for the teaser for next week's episode. Serling, however, felt their decision was wrong. He wanted to appear on the screen as host. Truman Bradley welcomed viewers before each drama on *Science Fiction Theatre*. Alfred Hitchcock was a household name because of his series. John Newland walked on to the set in the beginning of each of his *One Step Beyond* presentations (and this format resembled closest with Serling's intention). During his days at radio station WLW in Cincinnati, Serling wrote himself in as a narrator for a large number of scripts.

The original draft of the script (and revised pages dated November 26, 1958), featured the narrator's voice off screen, introducing the play while Mike Ferris enters the diner.

"We are looking at a Male Caucasian, age approximately thirty-one, height, approximately 5' 11". As to his name, where he is, and what he's doing there – this even he doesn't know . . ."

On Tuesday, May 19, Serling was filmed for a four-minute sales presentation, using a sound stage as the background. A camera, mike boom and lights were in evidence as was a partially constructed set. He used props from upcoming pictures as cues to tell a little about each one. The actual script was not written until that weekend and, therefore, not available for review by William Dozier or Bill Self until Monday. The estimated cost of shooting the scene was $2,500. The promo was originally intended to be four minutes long, but Serling felt he could not explain the episodes – or the series in general – in depth. Instead, the presentation ran 10 minutes. Also filmed on May 19 was a test closing of him telling about the next week's show, shot against some kind of non-descript background, possibly just a

---

* Sometime after (exact year unknown), Serling was filmed before the cameras for another sales pitch, this time to a television network for the Netherlands and another for the United Kingdom. The promo film was shot in New York City, with the host/creator standing behind the desk, surrounded by a bookcase. After complimenting Holland and the Netherlands (England for the U.K. version), he explained in the 4 ½-minute sales promo what the series was about. The promotional film was not scripted by Serling, who was apparently following cue cards to the right side of the camera, facing him, and notes on the desk. In the U.K. version, a shadow of the man holding cue cards is visible.

drape. The reason was that UPA had not yet come up with any concrete suggestions that might clash with their storyboards. Serling also recorded his voice (audio only) to replace Westbrook Van Voorhis. If Serling was to become the host of the program, he would certainly be heard off screen. *

During the same day, the director filmed a medium close-up shot of Serling standing against a black background and invited the audience to stay tuned for *The Twilight Zone*. This promo was shown between the closing credits of the concluding program and the CBS eye logo moments before the show's premiere.

"Good evening. I'm Rod Serling. Like all writers I like a good story and this will be a series devoted to story-telling. We think special stories told in rather a special way. In just a moment . . . please be my guest . . . to watch Earl Holliman and James Gregory appear in what I call . . . Where is Everybody?"

The first of what would become many trailers promoting "next week's show" was recorded the same day as well. The trailer, medium-close again on Serling surrounded in black as he touts "Judgment Night," was never used.

"Next week we offer you passage on a very unique boat ride. The ship will be a tramp steamer. The ocean's the Atlantic. The time is 1942. It's the story of a long nightmarish night. One perhaps difficult to believe . . . but one we think will fasten itself in your mind not to leave for sometime to come. I hope we'll see you next week for a play called 'Judgment Night' . . . on The Twilight Zone. Until next week then, good night."

On May 21, 1959, Houghton sought approval from Leo Lefcourt, at the request of Self and Serling, to employ the services of the De Forest Research Company, managed by Kellam De Forest with offices at Desilu-Gower. The basic charge was $30 per script, for which he read the story and did the necessary research to confirm or deny facts, figures and other matters in the script and then submitted a report. On average, researching a script took 10 hours, during which his staff looked into every detail. If it should develop that he devoted more time than that, the fee would be subject to adjustment, but never retroactively. The research company submitted a bill at the end of each month. Lefcourt gave his approval, so Serling began submitting scripts to the company for review.

Serling was first introduced to De Forest Research while working on "The Time Element." Desilu was the company's first major client, and it looked over scripts for such series as *The Untouchables*, *Mission: Impossible* and *Star Trek*. The firm would become the largest independent research consultant on the West Coast by the 1970s.

In April of 1959, William Dozier put Serling in touch with James E. McGinnis, M.D., in Pasadena, California. Feeling certain that during the shooting of the series that there would be odd times when technical advice of a medical or psychiatric nature might be required, Serling requested McGinnis be a free-lance consultant when the occasion required his expert advice. McGinnis agreed to offer any assistance, but as the months passed, Serling apparently never found reason or cause to consult McGinnis, with De Forest proving to cover that same area of expertise.

On June 12, 1959, the General Foods sales presentation met with unanimous approval in New York, and the alternate sponsor asked William Self and Cayuga Productions to make two corrections at its expense. The first request was to dissolve where Serling disappeared, so that the illusion was much slower. They felt his dissolve should begin earlier in the walk. Second, they wanted Serling to add a verbal line over the same scene that mentioned the brand name: "And this is nothing compared to the way Instant Sanka will be disappearing off shelves come this fall!" Serling reported to M-G-M to have his voice recorded, and the sales presentation was re-edited to the sponsor's request. Because Kimberly-Clark wanted to use the same film, a second version without the Sanka line was constructed.

On the same June day, the UPA story board was made for the first season opener, and was approved by Young & Rubicam, General Foods, Foote, Cone & Belding and Kimberly-Clark with the following changes:

1. The mountain background should be revised so that it does not suggest this is a horror show.
2. It was also suggested that the background illustrating the narration "and it lies between the pit of man's fears and the sunlight of his knowledge" perhaps should be a pit rather than a mountain.
3. *The Twilight Zone* lettering seemed to imply Dracula, Frankenstein, etc. and should be changed.

The narration was recorded by Rod Serling on June 17, 1959:

> *"There is a fifth dimension . . . beyond that which is known to man. It is a dimension as vast as space, and as timeless as infinity. It is the middle ground between light and shadow – between science and superstition. And it lies between the pit of man's fears and the summit of his knowledge. This is the dimension of imagination. It is an area which we call, The Twilight Zone."*

After reviewing a number of openers, this was considered final. Reps Herbert Klynn and Rudy La Riva of UPA took the audio recording and timed it with the illustrative background to the reading. According to one interoffice memo, Serling's narrative ran a total of 24.6 seconds.

He wrote a number of original openers, and for various degrees of reason and opinion, they were rewritten, thrown aside, and disregarded. Two of them were:

> *"You've all been on this road. It's concrete or asphalt or macadam, and it always leads to a place or from a place and it's a well-traveled route to reality. But this highway you don't find on maps or on road signs. It is a road that leads to a strange and wondrous land of imagination and it is paved with wishes . . . with dreams . . . With the endless, boundless infinity that is the human mind. Ladies and gentlemen, your next stop is . . . (we hit the sign and smash into it winding up in the stars) . . . The Twilight Zone.*

And

> *"There is a sixth dimension . . . beyond that which is known to man. It is a dimension as vast as space, and as timeless as infinity. It is the middle ground between light and shadow – and it lies between the pit of man's fears and the sunlight of his knowledge. This is the dimension of imagination. It is an area that might be called, The Twilight Zone." **

---

* This alternate opener was recorded on May 19, 1959. When William Self heard the line, he asked Serling to name the five dimensions, commenting he was only aware of four. Serling was prompted to rewrite the opening and record a new narration, beginning with "There is a fifth dimension . . ."

On June 15, 1959, a policy regarding fan mail was established. William Self informed Serling and Houghton that "we [CBS] are attempting to improve our public relations in the area of mail received regarding each program and would appreciate it if you would set up the following procedure. All mail which the producer does not wish to personally answer should be forwarded to Bob Blake. Bob will see that letters which require a policy reply in terms of violence, minority groups, juvenile delinquency, teenage crime, religious criticism, etc., are forwarded to Bill Tankersley who, in turn, will arrange for the necessary answer, or comment. For all those other letters of thanks, appreciation, boredom and just critics of quality, etc., Bob Blake will arrange for a card reply."

On the afternoon of the same day, Darryl S. Jerlow of the James McHugh, Jr. Agency in Beverly Hills submitted the following list of actors and actresses, and English clients, who Houghton and Serling could employ and consider for acting roles. A meeting with Millie Gusse helped eliminate some names and mark others as "possible."

Actresses

Louise Albritton	Vanessa Brown	Barbara Ruick
Constance Bennett	Brook Byron	Dorothy Stickney
Barbara Banning	Rosemary DeCamp	Peggy Webber
Mari Blanchard	Louise Lorimer	Ce Ce Whitney

Actors

Wolfe Barzell	Byron Foulger	Michael Lipton
Don Beddoe	Douglas Fowley	Ralph Purdum
Harry Bellaver	Forrest Johnson	Ernest Sarracino
Joseph Calleia	Stephen Joyce	Arthur Shields
Sam Capuano	Don Keefer	Regis Toomey
Nick Dennis	Brian Keith	James Westerfield
Paul Donovan	John Lawrence	Peter Wright
Buddy Ebsen		

English Actresses

Jean Anderson	Hermione Baddeley	Suzanne Flon
Angela Baddeley	Rosalie Crutchley	Muriel Pavlow
		Anne Vernon

English Actors

Robin Bailey	David Farrar	Moultrie Kelsall
John Chandos	John Glen	Bernard Miles
Maurice Denham	Colin Gordon	William Squire
Francis De Wolff	Malcolm Keen	Nigel Stock

In July of 1959, Ashley-Steiner, the same agency that represented Serling, submitted a list of actors and actresses to him who were available for guest spots on the television anthology.

Actresses

Gertrude Berg	Betty Furness	Elsa Lanchester
Edna Best	Betty Garde	Kathleen MaGuire
Ilka Chase	Signe Hasso	Edith Meiser
Marianne Demming	Joan Greenwood	Susan Morrow
Joan Evans	Arlene Howell	Cornelia Otis Skinner
Virginia Field	Isabel Jeans	Nancy Walker
Anne Francis	Patricia Jessel	Alida Valli
	Glynis Johns	

Actors

Max Adrian	William Hickey	Willard Parker
Edward Andrews	Frank Holms	Eric Portman
Martin Balsam	Wilfred Hyde-White	William Prince
Clive Brook	Richard Johnson	Cyril Ritchard
Yul Brynner	John Kerr	Alfred Ryder
Frank Campanella	Robert Q. Lewis	William Shatner
Jerome Cowan	Michael Lord	Walter Slezak
Joe Cronin	Harry Millard	Torin Thatcher
Thayer David	James Millhollin	Bill Travers
James Donald	Jules Munshin	Mike Wallace
Walter Fitzgerald	Lloyd Nolan	Donald Wolfit
Leo Genn	Warren Oates	Keenan Wynn

On Thursday, June 18, Mr. Steinberg, vice president in charge of information services for CBS (meaning he was the top publicity man) expressed his regard for *The Twilight Zone* as "the most prestigious half-hour show the network has" and his intentions to give it all he had. On Friday, June 19, Serling was asked to come up with some by-liners so that CBS could ensure a successful publicity campaign. That same month, he also was asked to write a 200-word piece for a national magazine that intended to use the piece as an introduction to its drama section in which *The Twilight Zone* would be highlighted. Serling agreed to the job, knowing full well that the magazine wanted the piece in hand by July 27 in order to appear in print by the time the series premiered. On July 6, he drafted what he referred to as "a slightly over-long article" for the TV magazine, and most of it was used for the column.

The August 12, 1959 issue of *Variety* reported, "Rod Serling and CBS-TV have agreed on terms of a new three-year deal which will guarantee the writer $100,000 annually. Deal, providing for Serling's exclusive television services, is with both Serling as an individual and with his Cayuga Productions, currently producing *Twilight Zone* for the network. Cayuga will develop pilots for the network, in which it will share ownership with CBS, and Serling himself will deliver at least one *Playhouse 90* script a year to CBS, devoting himself otherwise to *Twilight Zone* and the new Cayuga properties. His previous one-year deal with the web expires this month."

On September 4, 1959, Buck Houghton began working with Serling regarding the order in which the episodes were going to be broadcast. The initial preliminary schedule was:

October 2, 1959	"Where is Everybody?"
October 9, 1959	"One for the Angels"
October 16, 1959	"Mr. Denton on Doomsday"
October 23, 1959	"The Sixteen Millimeter Shrine"
October 30, 1959	"Walking Distance"
November 6, 1959	"Escape Clause"
November 13, 1959	"The Purple Testament"
November 20, 1959	"Perchance to Dream"
November 27, 1959	"Time Enough at Last"
December 4, 1959	"The Hitch-Hiker"

The early broadcasts on the list were aired as originally intended, but beginning with November 13, the order was different: "The Lonely" aired on that date, "Time Enough At Last" aired November 20, and so on. The reason for the initial selection was to put episodes with name stars first, and episodes light in star value afterwards. "The Mighty Casey" was withheld for a possible December 25 broadcast, but it did not air then.

On September 8, Rod Serling appeared in person at a studio to film his narration for the first batch of *Twilight Zone* episodes. This also included his closing trailers for "next week's episodes." On October 8 and October 28, he returned to the studio for more, making up a total of 25 segments for the series.

On September 11, Serling was informed that Kimberly-Clark intended to use the corner of the screen during the closing credits to display a product ad. This practice was not uncommon on television programs during the late 1950s and early 1960s, but Serling was against the idea. "I can't impress upon you enough how miserably vitiating an effect this will have on the entire mood of the closing moments of the show," he wrote to Buck Houghton. Houghton agreed, and had a discussion with Tom Brennen of Kimberly-Clark, explaining their joint thoughts in the matter and how much care and thought was devised in the closings. "It's my personal feeling," Serling remarked, "that any product identification at this point in the format can do nothing but hurt . . . sticking a picture of a roll of toilet paper on a screen with closing credits is the absolute essence of tastelessness."

For the next week, Houghton humored both sponsors by arranging for one of each of the sponsor's products to be placed in the lower left-hand corner of the closing credits, so executives could judge for themselves. On September 18, he reported to Serling and William Self of CBS that the sponsor, General Foods, having seen a can of Sanka coffee on the screen, decided not to use the product identification in the end credits. There was a stipulation, however: If Kimberly-Clark decided to keep its products on the screen during the closing credits, then General Foods would feel compelled to do the same.

Serling wrote to Tom Brennen personally to plead his case, and Kimberly-Clark agreed to go with the same decision General Foods made the week before.

The Publicity Tour

Before the program's premiere, Rod Serling went on tour to help publicize the television series. The excursion was conducted jointly by Young & Rubicam, Foote, Cone & Belding and CBS Television. Serling was met at airport by Owen Comora of Y&R and Jerry Collins of CBS. He left Los Angeles on September 12 at 11:15 p.m. and arrived at Idlewild at 7:10 a.m. He stayed at the Hotel Plaza.

New York City, New York
Sunday, September 13

2:00 p.m.	Telephone interview with Bob Williams of *The New York Post*.
3:00 p.m.	Serling interviewed by Lionel Olay, a member of Mike Wallace's staff.
5:00 p.m.	Cocktail interview with Paul Molloy of *The Chicago Sun-Times*.

Monday, September 14

9:15 a.m.	Interview with Stanley Frank for *The Saturday Evening Post* – free lance.
10:00 a.m.	Telephone interview with Bernie Harrison of *The Washington Star*.
11:00 a.m.	Interview with Nan Langman of *McCall's Magazine*, at her apartment.
12:30 p.m.	Interview with Russell Kane of *The Cleveland Plain Dealer*.
1:00 p.m.	Lunch with Jack Shanley of *The New York Times*.
2:30 p.m.	Interview with Bill Ewald of *Newsweek*, at the Hotel Plaza.
3:30 p.m.	Taped audio and video spots at CBS for television promotion.
5:00 p.m.	Cocktail interview with Harriet Van Horne of *The World Telegram*.
6:00 p.m.	Cocktail party by General Foods.
8:30 p.m.	*The Mike Wallace Show*, half-hour taped interview, to be telecast on the evening of Tuesday, Sept. 22. Was taped at Tele-Studios at 1481 Broadway (between 42nd and 43rd streets).

Tuesday, September 15

9:30 a.m.	Interview with Mary Hazard of *Scholastic Magazine*.
11:30 a.m.	Interview with Ben Kubasik of *Newsday*.
12:30 p.m.	Lunch interview with Hal Boyle of the Associated Press.
3:30 p.m.	Interview with John Crosby of *The New York Herald Tribune*, at the Plaza.
5:10 p.m.	Left for La Guardia Airport, and departed 6:25 p.m.

Pittsburgh, Pennsylvania
Tuesday, September 15

8:00 p.m.	Serling and Comora met at Pittsburgh airport at 8:06 p.m. with Peter Thornton of KDKA-TV.
8:45 p.m.	Dinner interview at Colony Restaurant with John Patterson, magazine editor of *The Pittsburgh Press* and Bill Gill TV columnist for *The Pittsburgh Press*.

Wednesday, September 16

10:00 a.m.	Press conference in Serling's suite at Carlton House. Two of *The Twilight Zone* films were screened for Arnold Zeitlin of *The Sun-Telegraph* and Winn Fanning of *The Post-Gazette*. Newsreel coverage run on KDKA-TV late news.
12:20 p.m.	Serling appeared as a guest for ten minutes on *The Faye Parker Show* on KDKA-TV to discuss *The Twilight Zone*.

| 12:30 p.m. | Serling met with station officials and Paul Long to discuss thirty-minute program, *Sound-Off*, taped at 2:30 p.m. Serling had an opportunity to air views via intelligent questioning from college students and moderator Paul Long. Program press- – reviewed to be shown on KDKA-TV on Saturday, October 3 at 5:00 p.m. |
| 6:15 p.m. | Departed Pittsburgh Airport for Cleveland. |

Cleveland, Ohio
Wednesday, September 16

| 7:00 p.m. | Serling and Comora arrived at Cleveland Airport, met by Bud Mertens of WJW-TV and driven to the Carter Hotel. |

Thursday, September 17

9:00 a.m.	Appearance on *Watch & Win* on WJW-TV. Six minute interview with Serling.
10:30 a.m.	Serling cut promotion spots to be used by WJW-TV to promote *Twilight Zone*.
11:00 a.m.	Taping of special seminar program between Serling and prominent Cleveland personalities. Topic was "Where do we go from here in TV?" Program titled *Conversation* was probably telecast during the second week of October.
12:15 p.m.	Press luncheon and screening of pilot film at Carter Hotel.
3:00 p.m.	Taped five-minute interview with Tom Griffiths of WNOB-FM.
7:20 p.m.	Departed Cleveland Airport for Detroit.

Detroit, Michigan
Thursday, September 17

| 7:05 p.m. | Arrived at Detroit (Metropolitan Airport). Met by Al Weisman. |
| | Stayed at Sheraton-Cadillac Hotel. |

Friday, September 18

9:15 a.m.	Serling appeared on local TV show, *Daytime Frolics*, over WJBK-TV. Tape to be used on day of show.
9:30 a.m.	Phone interview with Ray Oviatt, TV editor of *The Toledo Blade*.
10:00 a.m.	Interview with Betty Lou Peterson of *The Detroit Free Press*.
2:30 p.m.	Interview with Floyd Judge of *The Detroit News*.
3:00 p.m.	Serling cut promotional 10 and 20-second spots for *The Twilight Zone*.
5:15 p.m.	Departed Detroit for Chicago.

Chicago, Illinois
Friday, September 18

6:30 p.m.	Arrived at Chicago Midway. Serling stayed at the Ambassador East.
7:15 p.m.	Serling was a guest on *Frankly Speaking* on WBVM-TV with Les Brown and a Northwestern University Professor.
10:00 p.m.	Appearance on Tony Weitzel's radio program for interview. Weitzel is a columnist for *The Chicago Daily News*.
12:30 a.m.	Late night (early morning) interview with Jack Eigan of WMAQ-NBC Radio.

Saturday, September 19

12 noon	Luncheon with writer from Norman Ross' *V.I.P.* show.
2:00 p.m.	Interview with Janet Kern of *The Chicago American*.
3:00 a.m.	Late night (early morning) taping for Serling appearance on Irv Kupcinet's *At Random* TV show for WBBM-TV. This was a round-table discussion program similar to *The David Susskind Show*.

Sunday, September 20

2:00 p.m.	Serling interviewed by Norman Ross on *V.I.P.*, highest-rated prestige TV show in Midwest. Taped for viewing Sunday night at 8:30 p.m., over WBKB. This was a full half-hour coverage (there are usually two, 15-minute interviews).

Monday, September 21

8:30 a.m.	Serling interview for eight minutes by Don McNeill of *The Breakfast Club* on ABC radio network, 300 stations.
11:00 a.m.	Interview with Fran Allison, WGN-TV, five minutes.
12:15 p.m.	Interview of Rod on *Shopping with Miss Lee*, six minutes, broadcast live.
12:35 p.m.	Serling was guest speaker at luncheon meeting of Chicago chapter of the Television Academy of Arts and Sciences at the Sheraton Hotel. Spoke on the general state of affairs of television, dramatic programs, etc. Estimated crowd of 300 attended. Spoke for 20 minutes. Kimberly-Clark attended.
7:10 p.m.	Departed Chicago Midway for Cincinnati, Ohio.

Cincinnati, Ohio
Monday, September 21

8:30 p.m.	Met at airport by Mary Wood of *The Cincinnati Times Post* and E.B. Radcliffe of *The Enquirer*. Photographs were taken and used next day in *The Enquirer*.
11:30 p.m.	Interview with Paul Jones on *Late Movie Theater* for 15 minutes on WKRC-TV.

| 12 midnight | Radio interview with Jack Remington on WKRC. |

Tuesday, September 22

9:30 a.m.	Mayor's office key to the city. "Rod Serling Day" photos were taken and newsreels were used on late news WKRC-TV.
12 noon	Interview with Ruth Lyons program WLW-TV for 25 minutes.
3:30 p.m.	Cut promotion spots for WKRC-TV. Spots were used on three other Taft owned stations in Columbus, Dayton and Akron.
5:30 p.m.	Cocktail party at station for General Foods and Kimberly-Clark reps in Cincinnati.
6:00 p.m.	Dinner party at Mary Wood's home, *The Cincinnati Post*, with old friends.
6:30 p.m.	Jane Lynn Show, *Ladies Home Theater* over WKRC-TV. During show Serling was made lifetime member of Cincinnati Kiwanis Club.

Wednesday, September 23

| 11:30 a.m. | Departed Cincinnati Airport for Los Angeles International. |
| 5:10 p.m. | Serling returned home. |

The dinner party at Mary Wood's home on Tuesday, September 22, in Cincinnati was to be, according to a letter he wrote to Miss Wood on September 10, a highlight of his trip. "I'm told by my various mentors from the agencies who're handling this publicity tour that you'd intended to have a dinner party while I was in Cincinnati. Frankly, Mary, this is the singular thing I can look forward to on this bull shit tour, and I hope you're not doing this under duress."

Mary Wood began as a writer at Crosley Broadcasting where she worked with many local talents. Noted for her long-running radio and TV reporting for *The Cincinnati Post*, she became a major influence in the state of Ohio. "Rod Serling was never relaxed," she called. "He was always on the go. Unless he was stationed in front of a typewriter, he never sat for a lengthy period of time. His wife loved to throw parties. If you thought he smoked a lot when he was working, you should have seen him relaxed at the parties. [laughs] Rod started out as a writer at WLW and he wanted to write television plays. He wrote a number of scripts for *The Storm* . . . featured a lot of local actors and talent. That was Channel 12 . . . I'll tell you a funny story about Rod and *The Storm*. Rod was writing script after script. They probably bought every one he wrote. The series was "live" in those days, so I don't think any films exist. One day he had brass to ask for a raise. Instead, he got fired from WLW. Now I do not know if it was a contract issue, but for a rational reason they would not let him have his scripts back. Several people who worked at the station started stealing the scripts when they could do so without getting caught and gave them back to Rod. I was a faithful viewer of *The Storm* so I can tell you that many of the stories he wrote for *Playhouse 90* and *Lux Video* were the same stories broadcast on *The Storm*. He was reusing the same stories."

The Mike Wallace Show

Of all the publicity generated by Serling's tour, none was more important than the coast-to-coast telecast of *The Mike Wallace Show*, which aired on the evening of Tuesday, September 22. Wallace and Serling discussed censorship in television, through involvement with the sponsors and the networks.

After a few examples, citing *Playhouse 90* telecasts, *The Twilight Zone* was brought to light, where Serling commented, "We have what I think, at least theoretically anyway, because it hasn't really been put into practice yet, a good working relationship, wherein questions of taste and questions of the art form itself and questions of drama [then] – I'm the judge, because this is my medium and I understand it. I'm a dramatist for television. This is the area I know; I've been trained for it. I've worked for it for 12 years, and the sponsor knows his product but he doesn't know mine. So when it comes to the commercials, I leave that up to him. When it comes to the story content, he leaves it up to me."

TV-Time, a company specializing in radio and television recordings, located in White Plains, New York, offered to make a kinescope recording of the broadcast. Serling paid the $225 fee for a 16 mm sound film, made direct from the original videotape, to be processed and shipped to him for posterity. The tape went into syndication (all the better for promoting *The Twilight Zone*), so the kinescope was made two weeks later than scheduled.

Hype of the Premiere

In the September issue of *Writer's Digest*, playwright Stirling Silliphant focused on television's half-hour shows, comparing them to the short story form in fiction. In line with this, he gave a nice plug to Serling's *Twilight Zone*:

"A new sun-ray on the dark horizon is Rod Serling's *Twilight Zone*, a half-hour series to debut this fall on CBS. Mr. Serling is writing the series and it is hoped he will devote his time to writing all of them, because if this series is successful in the ratings stampede, it may well open up the door for better writing in the half-hour field."

Days before the premiere, the September 28, 1959 issue of *Broadcasting* commented, "On the basis of its initial episode, *The Twilight Zone* is perhaps the best new show out of CBS-TV this season and certainly among the best of all the new network entries. It is notable evidence that talent rather than money makes good entertainment." The same issue

William Shatner in "Nightmare at 20,000 Feet"

of *Broadcasting*, however, contradicted itself when the estimated production budget per episode was put at $54,000 – rather expensive when compared with other programs debuting on CBS that fall.

Mr. Lucky $40,000	*The Many Loves of Dobie Gillis* $40,000
Johnny Ringo $45,000	*The Betty Hutton Show* $50,000
Men Into Space $50,000	*The Dennis O'Keefe Show* $45,000
Hotel de Paree $40,000	

Of the prime-time programs that CBS carried in the autumn of 1959, only one had a larger budget than *The Twilight Zone*, and that was *The Lineup* with an estimated $90,000 per show!

CHAPTER FIVE

The Premiere: Reviews

The December 1959 issue of *The Magazine of Fantasy and Science Fiction* (which appeared on newsstands before December, naturally) featured a column titled "The Seeing I," written by Charles Beaumont. In his column, Beaumont wrote:

On October 2, 1959, a new television series will be launched. If it is anywhere as successful as certain powers are betting, the dream of every green-blooded science fiction fan will come true and we'll have, for the first time, decent science fiction and fantasy drama on a regular basis. If the series turns out to be as successful as hoped, then something like a revolution will occur. . . . The series that will spark this revolution is called *The Twilight Zone.* . . . If the show fails, it won't be because we haven't tried. Even now, producers all over Hollywood wait poised, ready to jump aboard. They only want to see if it's a band wagon or a funeral cortege.

Columnist Walter Hawver of *The Knickerbocker News* (Albany, New York), wrote in his October 2, 1959, "TV-Radio in Review" column that he had never done so before, "but I consider tonight's premiere episode of *Twilight Zone* so outstanding that I would be remiss if I did not recommend it to all viewers. The play was written and produced by Rod Serling. . . . In my opinion, it is the greatest half-hour TV drama ever made."

Ben Gross of *The New York Daily News* reviewed in his October 3, 1959, "What's On?" column, "The premiere episode of Rod Serling's *Twilight Zone*, under the obvious title of 'Where is Everybody?' was a suspenseful, tautly-written story of an Air Force officer who finds himself in a completely deserted town. This is still an interesting theme, even though it has been used in other works, including the current movie, *The World, the Flesh and the Devil.*"

Time magazine commented the *Twilight Zone* was "a fresh idea presented by people with a decent respect for the medium and the audience." The same review said, "Whether the hero is an Air Force officer suffering hallucinations after more than 400 hours of isolation, or a tired old pitchman bargaining with 'Mr. Death,' tales from the *Twilight Zone* are proof that a little talent and imagination can atone for a lot of television."

Paul Molloy of *The Chicago Sun-Times* predicted in his October 5, 1959 column, "The weekend premiere of *Twilight Zone*, anthology of the unusual, suggests this series will have little difficulty scoring a hit. It is written and produced by multiple award winner Rod Serling and the debut plainly promises a care for quality in casting and direction. Earl Holliman was painfully convincing as the last man on earth in an episode that brilliantly exploited those story line details the eye and ear remember long after the fadeout."

Variety's review appeared in the October 5, 1959 issue. "It may well turn out to be one of CBS-TV's strongest entries, generic in its appeal and with the arresting quality of skirting the current cycles. It gives TV a new and much-needed dimension, far off the beaten path of western and private eyes. If the word hasn't been abused, it could be honestly labeled adult drama. Serling has stood for qualitative writing and here, in his own venture, he is inspired to heights corresponding with the moon phase of the story."

Harriet Van Horne of *The New York World-Telegraph and Sun* commented that the *Twilight Zone* premiere "got off to a splendid, eerie start with a nightmare – in depth. Earl Holliman was starred in what was virtually a monodrama and he was first rate."

"I've never failed in my TV writing from lack of effort," Serling commented weeks before the premiere. "I promise that in this television series I have no intention of being satisfied with what would be considered second best. I'm concerned first with quality. . . . Professionally, I don't think *Twilight Zone* will hurt me. But I must admit I don't think it will help me, either. After all, it's a series primarily designed to entertain. Writing for it will certainly be much easier on me. I won't require the effort and probing a 90-minute script does."

Writing the Scripts

"Creating, producing and writing a half-hour series doesn't necessarily run counter to the demands of integrity," Serling told columnist Ed Misurell. "We won't be able to do any 'idea' shows and we'll not deal in areas of controversy, but we can still handle thought-provoking, adult, meaningful themes and handle them artistically and well."

In a guest column for Allen Rich, he gave a similar statement, "*The Twilight Zone* is in the process of handling thought provoking, adult, meaningful themes without being too arty, too obtuse, too pretentiously intellectual. I think *The Twilight Zone* is different than most anthology series. Its major difference, I think, is in the handling of story."

How tough of a theme was acceptable to both sponsor and network, and how tough its treatment, could be varied from one script to another. Some shows dug into a conflict with both hands; others flit around edges with veiled hints and guarded implications. The climax came into the script with no more impact than before because every preceding speech had been a climax unto itself. By writing, rewriting and through self-analysis and his own professional criticism, Serling established a style for *The Twilight Zone*, and as the selector of stories for the series, he now found himself on the other side of the television market — a buyer of ideas and scripts. While he still chose the stories, delineated the characters, and provided motivation and resolutions, he found himself rejecting teleplays from those submitted for his approval.

"The first draft is right off the top," he explained for the September 5, 1963 issue of *The New York Morning-Telegraph*. "I do it very fast. I think about it three or four weeks, and then do the first draft practically overnight."

By September 10, 1959, Serling had viewed 15 of the first 18 episodes that were in the can. "The consensus is that these are very top drawer, high quality and very different television programs," Serling explained to James W. Andrews, of the Maxwell House Division of General Foods. As a thankful expression of its appreciation, Maxwell House mailed a case of Sanka coffee to the Serling household. He remained in constant contact with Andrews, who wrote to the series' creator on September 2, one month before the premiere. "As the big night approaches, I grow more and more confident that this show will be an outstanding success. The continuing high level of the scripts, the impressive roster of stars and directors, the great reports we've been getting on the production of the shows – all of these factors add to my enthusiasm."

On September 11, Serling sent a telegram to assistant director Eddie DeNault on Stage 19 of M-G-M Studios in Culver City:

DEAR EDDIE AND CREW,
I'M SPENDING THE DAY GETTING TUBES AND KNIVES STUCK IN MY EARS AND ONLY THE MEDICAL PROFESSION KEEPS ME FROM JOINING YOU GUYS TO HOIST A FEW IN COMMEMORATION OF FINISHING OUR FIRST CYCLE OF FILMS. AS A MOST INEXPERI-ENCED EXECUTIVE PRODUCER I REALIZE MY VISITS TO THE SET HAVE BEEN FEW AND MY COMMENTS EVEN SPARSER BUT I WANTED YOU ALL TO KNOW AND I MEAN EVERYONE INVOLVED, THAT I APPRECIATE MORE THAN ANY LANGUAGE CAN DESCRIBE ALL YOUR TALENTS, YOUR HARD WORK AND YOUR CONTRIBUTIONS TO MAKING OUR SERIES A WINNER. THANK YOU AND GOD BLESS YOU ALL AND TAKE A COUPLE OF SWIGS FOR THE SHORT DARK MAN WHO PROBABLY MAKES ALL YOUR LIVES MISERABLE WITH THE DE-MANDS HE MAKES BUT WHO AT THIS MOMENT IS OFFERING SEVERAL SILENT PRAYERS OF THANKSGIVING THAT YOU PEOPLE ARE THE ONES BRINGING THE TWILIGHT ZONE TO LIFE.
WITH ETERNAL GRATITUDE,
ROD SERLING

Ratings and Response

The pain of ear surgery would be minor compared to what he would feel when the first ratings came. Despite all of the excitement about how well the first episodes had turned out, and all of the ecstatic press, the early episodes did not do well in total viewers. The first week the show scored low in the eyes of the sponsors.

On October 21, Serling saw the ratings for the first few episodes and wrote a personal letter to Owen S. Comora of Young & Rubicam, saying, "I'm still battling against the depression that comes every time ratings are announced and you are a most gentle and compassionate man to keep trying to buoy me up. I think it boils down to my having to develop my own crocodile skin, not to mention patience!"

According to a reliable studio press release, when Serling heard that the series garnered a crawl-ing rating, he lamented, "Fifteen million viewers! More than saw *Oklahoma!* during its entire run on Broadway – and they want to cancel!"

Charles Beaumont commented at the time, "Maybe that's because kids are hungry for the full play of their imagination while their elders are inclined to fear it." And Buck Houghton recalled, "We were always on the edge of getting canceled."

According to one periodical from November 1959, Serling worked about 18 hours a day on the series. A number of these hours were spent dictating his scripts into a recording machine and the rest taken up with his production chores at M-G-M. Questioned about the dangers of spreading himself too thin with the multiple chores, he agreed that such pitfalls existed. "There are three principal occupational hazards that I am aware of," he said with a smile, "ulcers, falling hair and hypertension. I hope I can ward off all three until we shoot at least 39 shows."

The November 7, 1959 issue of *TV Guide* featured a two-page article written by Serling, explaining why he created the series and what he intended to prove.

When *Gunsmoke* corrals an audience, the next season will see a herd of imitators varying in title and star but painfully similar. Peter Gunn goes off on a caper, and the next season 14 other actors take out private-eye licenses, and the television audience is exposed to a diet of sameness that makes dial-switching superfluous.

The exciting thing about our medium is its potential, the fact that it doesn't have to be imitative. The horizons of what it can do and where it can go stretch out beyond vision. What it can produce in terms of novelty and ingenuity had barely been scratched. This is a medium that can spread out experimentally to whole new concepts. And that's what we're trying to do with *The Twilight Zone*. We want to tell stories that are different. We want to prove that television, even in its half-hour form, can be both commercial and worthwhile. At the same time, perhaps only as a side effect, a point can be made that the fresh and the untried can carry more infinite appeal than a palpable imitation of the already proved.

It was this crusading spirit that gave the television series a loyal following that took the time to submit feedback.

In the November 15, 1959 issue of *The Oakland Tribune*, Serling was asked how to define the program. "It's difficult to give a genetic classification, a single definition of the series. I guess you can say it's stories of imagination. They all tilt from the center – unreal, told in terms of reality."

In the November 29, 1959 issue of *The Radio-Television Curriculum* of San Jose State College, columnist Clarence E. Flick commented:

"Already the soothsayers in this screwball business are laying wreaths on Rod's show. 'It's too far out,' says one. 'It's a think show and viewers don't want to think,' says another. At a party recently, Rod was confronted by an executive from ABC who said, 'Rod, that's a humdinger of a show, but you're doomed because you can't compete with *The Detectives*.' In one of the rating polls, Rod's series came within one point of ABC's *The Detectives*, but sponsors have been known to drop a series which trailed by a single point. It is ridiculous, of course, because no rating service takes a big enough sample to be that accurate – but that's the way the game is played." *

"It's true," said Serling, "that *Twilight Zone* is a think show. You can't afford to miss a line of dialogue without maybe losing the plot. But is this a crime? Ninety percent of TV talks down to the audience. I'm just trying to get TV to take off those trench coats and get the shooter half of those horses. *Twilight Zone* isn't attempting to uplift or enlighten the viewers but simply entertain them in a little different manner."

---

* During the month of February, the ratings began leaning in Serling's favor. For the broadcast of February 5, *The Twilight Zone* earned an audience share of 37.1 and *The Detectives* posted a 34 share; February 12 – *The Twilight Zone* 37.2, *The Detectives* 32.2; February 19 – *The Twilight Zone* 37, *The Detectives* 30; March 4, *The Twilight Zone* 43.3, *The Detectives* 27.7.

Hal Humphrey, syndicated columnist of "Viewing TV" wrote in early December 1959 that Serling was pleased with the outcome of *The Twilight Zone*. "My faith in TV viewers has been reaffirmed," he quoted Serling. The cause for the rather oratorical outburst, according to Humphey, was "a huge bundle of mail (more than 2,500 pieces so far) which has accumulated in a corner of his M-G-M studio office during the past three weeks. It was the result of a plea which Serling made through this column after being nettled by some critics who liked his shows, but predicted the series was doomed because it was over the heads of 'the masses.'" *

Serling went through each letter and composed a brief personal reply to every one of them. Though he hadn't gone through 2,500 by the time Humphrey reported the news, he had sifted through a considerable number and found only eight viewers writing to knock *Twilight Zone*. "They had some very aware comments about their dislike for the series," he commented. "Two of the eight made valid points about the characters being too vague in some instances."

Nearly all of the comments included a complete disenchantment with most of the private eye and western television programs; they welcomed *The Twilight Zone* as a challenge to do a little thinking, and they could remember the plots the next day. Mrs. H. Diehl of Toledo, Ohio, summed it all up for many viewers, "As of now I feel capable of being an assistant to any of the private eyes on TV – in fact, Pappy and I can predict the next move and even some of the conversation that follows. The plots of the westerns are pretty well worn and tiresome, and those, too, we can predict. I'm all for a 'think show' and heartedly endorse them before I become a total vegetable in the living room. By all means, give us a program that takes concentration for a change!"

"The sponsors and CBS are impressed by this mail," Serling told columnist Humphrey. "In fact, one of the sponsors has gone on record to tell me the chances are 90 to 1 that he will renew for next season."

Among the fan mail received during the initial rush was a three-page missive from a girl asking him for a date and assuring him that "I am no ugly duckling." Three people asked for jobs and 11 submitted manuscripts. "I heard from two Army buddies that I had lost track of since the war, too," he remarked. Bill Baur of *TV Guide* once commented that Serling received more fan mail than any other TV performer, adding that "a great deal of this fan mail is from neighboring planets."

The largest number of letters came from housewives, but many were from people with professions (doctors, dentists, ministers, etc.) as well as teenagers, farmers, and groups of office workers and television writing classes who wrote in petition-like form.

All of the complaints received were minor. Some disliked the title of the show. Others wished the show could be moved to an earlier hour or another weeknight. Some science fiction addicts wished the story material was more "out." One viewer complained he could no longer sleep through

---

* On November 13, 1961, Serling wrote to Stirling Silliphant, revealing his mistake regarding the public call for opportunity. For the first year and a half of the *Twilight Zone*'s existence, Cayuga opened the gates wide to submissions from anyone. Serling had been screaming about the dearth of writing talent for years, laying claim to a deep-seated belief on his part that there were ample battalions of writers, but no channels through which they could get recognition. "Well, Stirling, my money went precisely where my mouth was and I almost choked to death. We received at least two hundred manuscripts a week and the bulk of them – the sizable bulk were simply bad therapeutic exercises. Unprofessional and untalented people who had no story sense and simply no writing training. It also reached the point where we could no longer handle the flow of material because it became prohibitive trying to analytically read as many manuscripts as there were, overflowing on the desks." Serling admitted that things had reached the stage now where CBS was almost stripped bare of its story department of readers.

the show because he was so engrossed. Surprisingly, according to one report from secretary Connie Olmsted, "All of the viewers were incensed that the show was considered too intelligent for them."

Practically all the responses were intelligent, thought-out answers (not merely "it's a great show"), and the viewers were extremely appreciative that this kind of program was now available. Many said if pay-TV came into existence, *The Twilight Zone* would definitely be one show they would pay to see. Many doubted the accuracy of the ratings, from what they read in trade papers, and most had never been polled. Some said they would never buy the sponsor's products if the show were dropped. One, however, commented on the tasteful presentation of the Sanka commercial. Many claimed the show had received little publicity and said more people would have seen it sooner if there had been more advertising.

Even 12-year-olds who wrote in understood the show and welcomed the opportunity to have something to discuss – thus showing television could be a medium not only of entertainment but education and stimulation as well.

Besides the usual adjectives of "encore, bravo, great, refreshing, delightful, wonderful, unusual, unique," there were other expressions of praise and gratitude:

"It is so refreshing to be entertained at an adult level."

"The acting is the best on television."

"*The Twilight Zone* is the only time in the week I don't get powder burn…"

"*The Twilight Zone* is one small lifeboat in that sea of slag pouring out of picture tubes across the country."

"One large vote for the quality television you champion. Let's hope some of the weak-kneed television sponsors quit conspiring with the unfortunately large, mediocre segment of the American public to lower the intellectual standards of American culture."

"It's about time that we got a series that is deserving of the prime time on the TV timetable."

The Music

"Many of the things I tried would not have been possible in any other atmosphere, but on *The Twilight Zone* I had this freedom – thanks, mainly, to Buck Houghton and Rod," director Douglas Heyes recalled to interviewer Ben Herndon. "I sat in on every cutting session. They worked right with you on the cutting, and it came out the way you wanted it. I was spoiled early on because, both on *Maverick* and *Twilight Zone*, producer Roy Huggins and Rod encouraged me to do everything I could."

After the rough cut was edited, the film was submitted to Eugene Feldman, who supervised the music scores. The music for each film was either specially composed and conducted, or sliced together courtesy of sound clips from the CBS stock music library. During the early 1950s, CBS began collecting a number of music scores for its library, with the intention of reusing the scores for future television productions. Every score composed by a musician on the CBS payroll was recorded and saved, and as the years passed, the library grew. Sections and bridges from these recorded scores were reused for many television productions, and after a while musicians discovered their scores cut down on the demand for original compositions. A strike was called by the musicians, claiming an unfair labor practice, and by July of 1957, a resolution was established. For a television season consisting of 39 episodes, a minimum of 13 had to feature original scores. The remaining 26 could feature music owned by the network.

Lud Gluskin, a staff musician at CBS, has been credited in past publications for choosing and selecting the stock music for various *Twilight Zone* productions, but it was actually Feldman, working closely with Buck Houghton, who chose which episodes deserved original music scores, who would compose the scores, and which episodes would draw their music from the stock library. Gluskin was in charge of the music department, but in a supervisory position, except when conducting the orchestra for various music scores.

Tommy Morgan, who scored a number of original pieces for the series, recalled to Paul Giammarco: "In those years, the composers would go to the studio to view that episode to be scored. A music editor was with you, as well as the head of the music department. During this 'spotting session,' all would join in in deciding where the music was to be used in the show. After viewing the episode, the editor would take the film and break it down for each music cue, giving times along the way when things happened during the scenes you were to score. In virtually all cases, the composer assigned titles to all of the cues."

Among the more notable music cues in the library featured repeatedly on *The Twilight Zone* was Bernard Herrmann's "Brave New World." The composition was commissioned by William Froug, producer and director of *The CBS Radio Workshop* and the same William Froug who would later produce the last half of the fifth season of *Twilight Zone*. The radio program offered a two-part adaptation of Aldous Huxley's novel, *Brave New World*, as the premiere for the series; Herrmann composed and conducted his original music score for the drama, broadcast over CBS Radio on January 27 and February 3, 1956.

Two of Herrmann's earlier music contributions for radio was "The Hitch-Hiker" and "Moat Farm Murder" for *The Mercury Summer Theater on the Air*, produced and occasionally directed by Orson Welles, a short-run summer radio program. Music scores from both presentations were added to the CBS library of stock music, and brief cues from those scores were often repeated on *The Twilight Zone*.

Other music pulled from the stock library and used on episodes of *The Twilight Zone* were sections of music scores specially composed for *Gunsmoke*, *Perry Mason*, and *Have Gun – Will Travel*, among others. The system also worked the other way. Specially composed music scores for episodes of *The Twilight Zone* often found their way into the stock library, and segments from those scores were reused for episodes of *Perry Mason*, *Gunsmoke* and *Have Gun – Will Travel*. Radio programs such as *Suspense* and *Hello Americans* during the late 1940s and early 1950s featured music scores by Lucien Moraweck and René Garriguenc, with Lud Gluskin often conducting the music scores. For a number of *Twilight Zone* productions, this same partnership took place – Gluskin conducted the CBS Orchestra for other people's music scores.

Much of the stock music was also recorded in Europe to avoid paying excessive fees imposed on the networks. On December 2, 1961, Herman Kenin, head of the American Federation of Musicians, called for a government ban against the use of foreign music recordings as background for United States television shows. Kenin made his plea in testimony before a House labor subcommittee studying the effects of foreign trade on American employment. By 1961, half of the television shows being produced in the United States used background music recorded abroad at cut rates. The use of such tapes in 35 series currently being filmed was costing American musicians $742,500 in wages. *The Twilight Zone* was among the list of shows that were using foreign "canned" music.

The producers of many television shows sent their music scores overseas, then had them recorded in Europe and the tapes flown back. This was in order to take advantage of foreign costs of approximately $40 a minute for the finished tape as against the $120 a minute in the United States. This practice was fought and protested during the years *The Twilight Zone* was initially telecast, but a solution never came until years later when the musicians won a decisive battle against television and film producers. But by then, CBS had built a large enough library to use and reuse. From 1974 to 1982, producer/director Himan Brown borrowed heavily from the stock library, for use on every one of his 1,600-plus radio broadcasts of *The CBS Radio Mystery Theatre*, and many of the original scores for *The Twilight Zone* can be heard repeatedly in the recordings.

The Theme Music

The original "Twilight Zone Theme" for the first season episodes was composed by Bernard Herrmann (copyright registration date: February 9, 1959. Official CBS Score No. CPN6035. Copyright Registration Number: EU 561-560 *). Often described as a "misty visual opening," the score featured chords of E minor above a D-sharp minor, which alternates with the D-sharp minor above the E minor in the lower notes. This shifts over a changing bass line of G, E and C-sharp. According to Herrmann's manuscript in the CBS Collection at UCLA, the closing theme uses the same score, but has a second ending which extends the piece a few additional bars, resolving finally on a unison E bass note. Obviously inspired by a few of the pieces from Gustav Holst's "The Planets", the theme remained constant until the opening title was revised towards the end of the first season.

In June of 1960, with CBS agreeing to a second season, Buck Houghton was rehired by Cayuga, and among the changes enforced for the second season was Serling's insistence that the new opening title and theme be replaced again. One of the previously-conceived openers, similar to the revised one, in which a sun comes in with hard, definite edges that then acquire a little nimbus and then goes back to hard edges, was chosen. A new music score was required for the new title. Jerry Goldsmith and Leith Stevens contributed one each, while Bernard Herrmann composed two. Eugene Feldman worked with music director Lud Gluskin to create a new score, preferably from the stock library.

Feldman took two music cues from the library, "Etrange No. 3" and "Milieu No. 2," originally composed by Marius Constant, and combined them to form a single score for the new *Twilight Zone* theme. The pieces were composed and recorded in Paris years before, avoiding the U.S. musician union re-use fees, which were 100 percent of the original session fee for any subsequent use. Supposedly, Gluskin himself went to Paris a number of times to find and record the music tracks that the network could add to its stock library.

The original music scores, lasting mere seconds each, were never intended to be used as a theme for a television series. The decision to use them for this purpose was not until years after the pieces were added to the library. **

The First Season

On October 21, 1959, Ben Irwin observed there was a problem relating "to our finding some means

---

* Renewal date: May 22, 1987, RE 337-981.

** "Twilight Zone (theme)" Copyright date: November 23, 1979. PA 54-066. Copyright was part of a Performing Arts copyright for the motion picture filed as: "King Nine Will Not Return, Episode of The Twilight Zone including Twilight Zone Theme," by Cayuga Productions, Inc.

of calling special attention to our *Zone* photos of newspaper TV editors who receive reams of pictures and copy each week. We obviously need some gimmick to accomplish this." Irwin suggested using off-beat photos of sexy women (most of them in bikinis) – but with a twist. One suggestion was to have the girl bending over to pick up a beach ball with two hands. A third hand reaches from behind her to scratch her back. The caption provided: "Think this girl is unique? Then wait until you see the story on this week's *Twilight Zone*." Another suggestion was of a naked woman putting on lipstick and looking into a mirror, possibly for the upcoming show, "Mirror Image." Serling, however, disregarded the idea, declaring that only photos of actors that actually have something to do with the series be used.

On October 26, 1959, Irwin discussed briefly with Buck Houghton the opportunities in upcoming episodes to cast people in major or minor roles who could gain additional promotional and publicity mileage for the program based on their offbeat or unusual casting. "Perfect examples of the 'off-beat' casting in the star category would be Eddie Cantor as a heavy, William Boyd in a sophisticated role, Tony Randall in a serious role, etc.," explained Irwin. "Sports figures always make for good copy, even though they might be cast in minor roles. Some suggestions might be Floyd Patterson, Rocky Marciano, any of the Dodger heroes, Willie Mays, Althea Gibson, any of a number of champions in some of our more popular sports . . . this also holds true of public figures in the news such as ex-governor Goodwin Knight."

During the first full week of November 1959, Serling participated in a radio interview for Dick Strout's *Young Hollywood*. Promoting *The Twilight Zone*, Serling explained his love of science fiction and fantasy, and what he felt made his program unique among the rest of the television offerings. This radio program was later syndicated to and used by over 600 radio stations from coast-to-coast.

On December 2, 1959, Houghton took an inventory of the first season's story properties. Ray Bradbury's "And Here There Be Tygers" cost Cayuga $2,500 for the rights to the story, and it was decided to temporarily shelve the idea of adapting it into a feasible teleplay for a later date. "A Most Unusual Camera" had been given a production number, but never went to film. George Clayton Johnson's story, *The Hanging of Jason Black*, was a story property Serling asked Houghton in late November to purchase for a future episode. He had expressed interest in *The Walker Through Walls* back in September, but was no longer eager to adapt the story and asked Houghton to freeze until a later time whatever progress he had made toward purchasing the story.

There were numerous short stories that, while they possibly fit the *Twilight Zone* mold, were too difficult to adapt into teleplays. A viewer named Willard Bailey from Ada, Ohio, wrote to Serling on February 13. "I'll bet you ten dollars you can't do Ray Bradbury's 'A Sound of Thunder' on *The Twilight Zone*." On February 25, he wrote back. "You win before we even make the bet. I tried to purchase Ray Bradbury's 'A Sound of Thunder' but Ray tells me he has other plans for the property – probably a movie. But I tried Mr. Bailey, I tried!"

After the first season's episodes, Terry Vernon, television columnist for the Long Beach, California *Press-Telegram* commented, "Count me among the few who don't think *The Twilight Zone* series is consistently good. Too often the scripts merely take one theme and belabor it to the point of boredom."

In January 1960, the Screen Producers' Guild named *The Twilight Zone* as the best-produced television film series of 1959 at its annual Milestone Award dinner. Considering the series premiered in October, the award revealed how high of a caliber the series impressed the judges in three months of broadcasts. Producer Buck Houghton was on hand to receive the award from actress Jane Wyman.

The Twilight Zone was selected from a field of nine television film series.

On January 7, 1960, Harold Hourihan of the CBS sales department contacted Houghton to provide him with prints of what Houghton and Serling considered the three best pictures then available. It was routine for the sales department to have three shows on hand for sales purposes, regardless of whether the show was renewed in the present market. Their request was immediate, so Houghton, unable to await Serling's return from a trip, selected "Time Enough at Last," "Walking Distance" and "The Four of Us Are Dying." The sales department had specifically requested not to have the pilot, feeling it had considerable exposure in the original sales effort.

On February 9, 1960, Jan Hartman of Harvard College, Massachusetts, wrote to Rod Serling, recalling their luncheon conversation they shared back in September. Hartman had read in the February 9 issue of *The New York Times* that *The Twilight Zone* had been renewed by the sponsors.

On February 12, 1960, Nelson Bond wrote to Serling mentioning, "It is refreshing to find that there can be television entertainment without shoot 'em-up or mayhem." Bond, an author of science fiction stories, submitted a number of short stories to Serling for his approval, none of which were purchased because, as he explained in his February 23 reply, "We were only renewed for ten additional shows and as of the first of February I had written or bought the necessary ten to wind up the season. As to future plans, at this moment they're very, very 'ify.' The show seems to have captured a rather large coterie of very loyal and enthusiastic supporters. But to date the numbers in this group do not constitute 'success,' as understood in television jargon." Of the stories submitted, he did decide to hold on to at least two or three that interested him, in the hopes that in the future he could adapt them into feasible *Twilight Zone* scripts. Among the submissions:

"The Bookshop" (*Blue Book*, October 1941) was the story of a death-faced man who wanders into the mystic bookshop on the shelves of which he finds all the great, unwritten volumes: Shakespeare's *Agamemnon*, *Darkling Moors* by Charlotte Bronte . . . and his own not-yet-begun masterpiece. He escapes the bookshop, clutching his "completed" volumes, only to meet the inexorable fate awaiting him outside.

"The Dark Door" (*Blue Book*, May 1932) was the tale of a man haunted all his life by the vision of a dark and sinister doorway, the sight of which always serves as a deterrent to his rash impulses. When finally he does not permit the vision to dissuade him from a wrong deed, he commits a murder . . . and finally encounters the true dark door at the end of the narrow passage – the death chamber.

"Vital Factor" (*Esquire*, August 1957) tells the tale of a wealthy man who wants to build the first spaceship so he may conquer not only Earth but the universe. A quiet little stranger is able to build the ship for him, and together they make a successful test flight. But they do not return, for the little stranger is a Martian, and the vital factor in his desire to conquer space was not the lust of conquest, but homesickness.

"It is a pleasure to report that *The Twilight Zone*, a Rod Serling enterprise filmed in Hollywood and broadcast on Friday nights by CBS, is the most refreshing new anthology series in some time," wrote a reviewer for the February 27, 1960 issue of *TV Guide*. "It has imagination, highly competent production and excellent acting. There isn't much meat in it, but, for a mulligan stew, it is a tasty dish indeed. . . . So far a highly competent group of actors has been employed on *The Twilight Zone* – Burgess Meredith, Everett Sloane, Dan Duryea, Ed Wynn, fellows like that. But the real star of the series is its creator, chief writer, executive producer and narrator, Serling himself. It is the Serling touch that brings *The Twilight Zone* out of the everyday – and into the beyond."

In the March 13, 1960 issue of *The New York Sunday News*, Serling commented that "I read every new script submitted to me. So far I've waded through 200 and here's what I've found: some

90 percent were poorly written by non-pros; most of the others were sent in by pros and sized up merely as smooth hack work. Still, I continue reading." When asked how many scripts he bought from unknowns, he commented, "I hate to confess it – not one."

On March 14, 1960, Serling received the following request from the Office of the Director of Instruction, U.S. Army Transportation School in Fort Eustis, Virginia:

Dear Mr. Serling:

I am in the process of writing an article which I hope to have published in one of the military magazines, probably "Army," because of its wide circulation among the top officials for whom the article is intended.

In an endeavor to emphasize a critical void in our logistical system, namely the mobility aspects so necessary to the new tactical concepts around which our "New Look" Army is patterned, I would like your permission to apply the term 'Twilight Zone' to the era in which our Army Aviation system now finds itself. In other words, we are so completely tied up in "red tape," politics, and selfish interests that it's almost like being in another world. I feel that the term 'Twilight Zone' is most appropriate.

Perhaps I should introduce myself at this point. I am an Army Transportation Corps officer, stationed here at the U.S. Army Transportation School where Army Aviation concepts, doctrine, policies, and procedures often originate, and are taught along with the many other transportation subjects, and I happen to be one who is more than a little concerned over a critical weakness in our otherwise highly efficient fighting forces.

I don't wish to bore you with details, but do want to assure you that the contents of my article will justify your generosity in permitting me to use the term in the body of the article. I say that because I will also propose a solution to the situation. It is the fantastically simple process of tying together items of currently available equipment, ideas, and machines, some of which were either mistakenly discarded or are painfully slow in being recognized, into a single system for rapid mobility.

In using the term "Twilight Zone," I am counting on your program being as popular with high military officials as it is in my household. If so, it will be an excellent means of illustrating a major point I wish to make.

Thank you for your kind attention. I am looking forward to your answer with great anxiety.

Very truly yours,
Lt. Col. Gus S. Zinnecker

On March 28, Serling replied with positive favoritism, granting permission for the application of the term "Twilight Zone" in any way he saw fit.

On May 11, 1960, CBS announced *The Twilight Zone* would be renewed for a second season – but only for 10 additional episodes.

The Profits

"The guaranteed income from this show is considerably less than I get for doing a picture a year,"

Serling told a columnist in late 1959. "Potentially the take will be large if the show is the kind of success I hope it will be. I won't deny the prospect of a bank account, a trust fund for my kids, a fur coat for my wife aren't delightful to contemplate. They most certainly are. But *The Twilight Zone* doesn't walk hand and hand with a budget. I'm doing it because it's an exciting show and different in its approach and technique than what I've done before."

Since Serling staked half interest in Cayuga Productions, *The Twilight Zone* gave him income through a number of responsibilities. He received a $750 fee per episode for supervising the selection of teleplays and stories, and $2,250 for every script written by him (including adaptations) – both netting him a total of $66,750. There was additional income for supplying the narrations for each episode. Not bad for having complete control of a series that bore his own name, and his reputation. Back in 1956, his net income totaled $85,570.83, but since the average salary for an American household in 1959 was about $3,000, he was now living quite comfortably while working on a television series he defined as a labor of love.

Vera Miles verifies her sanity in "Mirror Image."

On June 24, 1960, a breakdown of the past 14 episodes was put together and submitted to Serling, from Pat Hogan of Young & Rubicam, Inc. The breakdown was of *Twilight Zone*-publicized shows as compared with unpublicized shows. "We think this points up graphically, more than any other show that we've ever had in the shop, the advantages of publicity on a series," wrote Hogan.

"THE TWILIGHT ZONE"
PUBLICIZED AND UNPUBLISHED DURING 14-WEEK PERIOD
JANUARY 1 – APRIL 1, 1960

DATE OF SHOW	NEILSEN AVERAGE AUDIENCE RATING	PUBLICITY
January 1	18.0	None
January 8	19.7	Y&R Publicity
January 15	18.0	None
January 22	19.1	Y&R Publicity
January 29	17.7	None
February 5	21.1	Y&R Publicity
February 12	19.0	None
February 19	22.2	Y&R Publicity

February 26	19.9	None
March 4	23.5	Y&R Publicity
March 11	20.8	None
March 18	19.9	Y&R Publicity
March 25	19.9	None
April 1	21.2	Y&R Publicity

In reaching any conclusion that might explain the consistently higher ratings of *The Twilight Zone* on its publicized programs, it was necessary to determine the influence of two factors: (1) station lineup and (2) competing programs.

The publicized programs were carried in five more markets than the unpublicized shows. Amarillo, Texas, was the largest of these markets. The radio-TV research section said the influence of these markets on a national basis would be nil.

The "Friday Night Fights," which fluctuated in their attraction was considered as an influencing factor. However, on the night of its biggest attraction, a publicized show week – *The Twilight Zone* picked up its usual two rating points over the preceding unpublicized week. Also indicative was the rating for the week of March 4. The publicity operation for that was considerably more than for any other publicized week and the program received its highest rating, 23.5.

The average rating for unpublicized weeks was 19.0 compared to 21.0 for publicized weeks. In conclusion, *The Twilight Zone*'s publicized programs achieved the following:

1. Reached 900,000 more homes per program than the unpublicized shows, or 1,800,222 more viewers.
2. In terms of cost, these 900,000 additional homes were bought at a rate of $2 per thousand homes as compared with the actual show cost of $3.67 per thousand.

The Eye Opener

In response to suggestions from one of the sponsors, a new opening was written by Rod Serling on December 17, 1959. Once again Serling, talking with Buck Houghton, proposed the original introduction he conceived before the series premiered, opening with the sketch in which the audience looks across a desert with rocks toward a sunlit horizon (the shadows from the rocks are at full length). Down the center, stretching from the bottom of the screen to the horizon would be added a highway with center marker. Shortly after the scene is clear on the screen, the audience would start down the road quickly as if in a car traveling it.

"As we reach the end of the narration we should be closely approaching the horizon at which point a card would swing toward our eyes as if it were hinged toward the bottom of the screen," explained Houghton to George Amy. This card would have stars with the words "The Twilight Zone" on it. Movement into the screen would continue until the audience crashes into the card at which point the words fragment and leave the audience in clear stars for the pull down at the opening of the show.

Regrettably, Serling's initial concept was once again discarded for a different opener. The new one imagined a dark line advancing across the bottom of the screen, in solid chunks in tempo to music. The lid of an eye closes while itself dissolving, although the sun in the background remains unaffected. The white object that appears was a true sun with halation, and not merely a white cut-out.

The gray twilight sky grows darker, so when the lettering "Twilight Zone" fades out, the audience is left with the stars for the pan down to the first scene in the picture.

An estimate based on a new storyboard was received from Pacific Title on January 2, 1960. At $1,800 it was high and there was some indecision as to whether a new opening was financially worthwhile. Houghton sought approval from CBS, as well as to learn who would foot the bill – the sponsor, the network? On January 12, Norman Glenn brought up the subject again and offered the ideas of Stephen Frankfort of the Young & Rubicam New York office. It took a number of weeks, concluding February 25, before the Photostats of the storyboard were prepared by Frankfort.

An interoffice memo from Buck Houghton and Norman Felton about the decision explained the new opener, which had been storyboarded and approved by Serling. "It is clean; it has style and distinctiveness," Houghton wrote. "Most importantly, it communicates something of the nature of *The Twilight Zone*." Using the new opener entailed many problems. First, the entry would have to be done in the same 40 seconds as the show's present opening used – to avoid formidable expenses in preparing the earlier pictures for rerun in a different order.

Then, it was a cost decision as to whether they put the new opening onto former pictures; the alternative being that in rerun, *The Twilight Zone* would have different openings capriciously from week to week. It would cost Cayuga a large sum to have 26 fine-grain prints made to accomplish this, so that a duplicate negative could replace each of the 35 mm negatives for former pictures; also there was the cost of redubbing the first reel of each of the former pictures.

Frankfort's effects house looked at the storyboard and estimated $5,700 for the finished product, plus $2,000 for music, but this did not include the rerun costs. Houghton felt the cost was too high, so he went to M-G-M and Pacific Title to get an estimate. Should the notion be approved within a few days, the new opener would conceivably appear on the air no sooner than the April 8th broadcast, perhaps that of April 15, according to the interoffice memo. With 14 reruns, the new opening would appear 21 or 22 times. "I would like very much to see this opening on our shows," Houghton wrote. "Prudence makes me wonder whether a change in mid-season (and its resultant costs in fixing earlier pictures) is wise. Putting them on next season, at its [correct] length, would signify something of a 'new' season of *The Twilight Zone*, and no reprise would have to be made to the first season's episodes."

During the final week of February, Guy Della Cioppa of CBS attempted to get permission from the clients to continue with the old opening. On March 1, 1960, Norman Felton wrote to Buck Houghton, explaining that "the $2,000 as suggested figure for music can, for all intents and purposes, be eliminated, for I'm sure we all agree we should continue with our present theme. In this regard, I have discussed the matter with Lud Gluskin, who informed me that it is quite flexible . . . However, you must discuss the footage with him so that the new title can be developed in terms of the existing music." Felton also informed Houghton that if he could get the estimate for the new opener around $3,000 or less, CBS would approve because the possible $8,000 price tag was a bit steep.

On March 2, Houghton received the go-ahead by a phone call. Having received estimates on the new storyboard prepared by Pacific Title and M-G-M, and since the lowest bid was from Metro, Houghton closed the figure of $800 on March 7. Because CBS had a verbal understanding with Pacific Title that it would have all title and optical work done exclusively by Pacific Title at a money advantage, there was a three-or-four day delay while contracts were adjusted to give half of the business to M-G-M and half of the business to Pacific Title. Metro handled the camera work and Pacific Title handled the optical work.

For M-G-M, there were four photographic elements involved in the titles:
(1) a close up of a girl's eye which closes slowly.
(2) a sun which comes in with hard, definite edges that then acquired a little nimbus and then goes back to hard edges.
(3) a transition from the white of the girl's skin to the dark of *The Twilight Zone* night in which the sky is full of stars.
(4) the accumulation of stars by small groups as gray moves to black.

The making of these four elements was a long and boring process of day-to-day viewing, printing and reprinting. The selection of a girl took four interviews alone, and the camera crew could not light her eye strongly enough for a quadruple speed camera without injury to her eye. They opted for double speed and had to print double frames to slow down the closing of the eye. There were three tests of the sun, four tests of the gray scale and three tests of stars. Lud Gluskin assured Houghton that he could do the music work within the same period to exact counts.

The title was of different length than the former one, and since all the episodes filmed and ready for the new opener were of the exact length, a 10-second public service announcement and a five-second stretch had to go somewhere during the commercial break.

According to an April 15, 1960 interoffice memo from Houghton to Felton, the client was applying pressure on all parties involved for a new opener and had expressed an "indignant surprise" that the new opener was not yet ready or on the pictures. Felton understood Houghton's position, and on April 19 explained in a letter that Houghton was doing a good job and hoped the new title would appear on the last six shows.

The day after, Houghton admitted the choice of this specific new opener was a bad one. "Historically every thought and idea for an opening to *The Twilight Zone* has had some complications to it," he explained to Felton on April 20. "It has never been simple lettering against a plain background. Nevertheless I thought the present new opening would be relatively simple in as much as its components are real and observable in nature – eyes, stars, sun. Nevertheless it has proven to me that the real night stars move while you are photographing them and that the real sun fogs the camera; from an inch away an eye is not necessarily an eye. I am merely trying to point out that we thought we had a less complex new opening than others that had been suggested."

One of the proposals rejected for the eye-sun-stars opener was the long highway:

"The artwork will represent a long highway-like thruway. It stretches out toward what appeared to be an abyss. There is something highly unspecific about the highway and whatever flanks it. The sense of artwork, however, is not only the odd quality of the background and the place but the fact that there is constant movement the moment we pick up the scene. An audience is traveling this road getting closer and closer to its end. Over this movement shot we hear the following narration:

"This is a highway to a destination that lies on the shadowy tip of reality. It's a through route to a strange and bizarre land of the different, the odd, the bizarre. You can go as far as you like on this road. Its limits are those limits of the human mind itself. Whatever is the breadth of your imagination – that represents the mileage it takes to get into . . . THE TWILIGHT ZONE."

"At this moment the camera reaches the end of the road and runs smack dab into the lettering that spells out 'The Twilight Zone,' then hurdles through it into the starry night from which we pan down to the opening shot of the show . . . At the end of each episode now we will pan up to this same starry background and the lettering, finally to move away and retrace our steps in reverse down the road as in the beginning."

The new opening sequence premiered with the episode "Mr. Bevis," telecast on June 6, 1960. The new sequence appeared throughout the remainder of the first season episodes, "The After Hours," "The Mighty Casey" and "A World of His Own," and the rerun of "Mr. Denton on Doomsday," the latter of which cost Cayuga $1,675.92 to re-edit the opener with the new sequence. The cost factor in re-editing other first-season episodes for the summer reruns was weighed, and the idea was not favored, making "Mr. Denton on Doomsday" the only episode produced for the first season to have two different opening sequences.

Buck Houghton

On April 27, 1960, Sam Kaplan of Cayuga Productions, Inc. drafted a formal letter to Buck Houghton informing him that, "in accordance with our phone conversation of this morning, this will serve as official notice that Cayuga Productions, Inc. hereby exercises its right to suspend your services effective May 7, 1960, in accordance with Paragraph 5 of the Employment Agreement between you and Cayuga Productions, Inc. dated April 6, 1959, as amended by Letters of Amendment dated January 8, 1960 and January 15, 1960, respectively. Permit me to take this opportunity once again on behalf of the company and specifically on behalf of Rod Serling and myself to thank you for your contribution to the series this year and to express our hope that the series will be re-sold or renewed for next year so that we will once again have the opportunity to work with you."

It was apparent that as of late April 1960, there was an uncertainty as to whether *The Twilight Zone* would be renewed by CBS for an additional year. The original contract dated April 6, 1959, stated that Houghton was employed for a period of five consecutive production years or five consecutive broadcast years, whichever should expire later. However, Cayuga had the right to terminate his employment at the end of any production schedule. While Houghton's compensation for the first production year was $550 per week, effective April 4, 1960, his salary went up to $650 per week.

Buck Houghton, incidentally, had won an award from the Producers' Guild of America earlier in the year. On January 27, 1960, director Richard L. Bare wrote to Serling, congratulating him and Houghton for the Producer's Award. "You and Buck have done a terrific job and the joy that I receive in watching the show is only exceeded by the pleasure of working on it."

Inspired Imitators

Rod Serling may have had difficulties fighting with CBS in his attempt to get *The Twilight Zone* on the air, but months after the program premiered, the opinion of the "powers that be" started leaning toward his direction. While no television program was created purposely to capture the same audience *Zone* was garnering, the attempts did not go unnoticed.

In January of 1960, Four Star Productions urged Aaron Spelling to reactivate his *Tales of the Unknown* as an hour-long pilot. Spelling wrote the first script himself, and lest he be accused of stealing the series idea from *Twilight Zone*, wanted it known that he created *Unknown* two years before, "but there were no takers," he explained to the trade papers.

In late May of 1960, a test film went into production for a new series, *Operation: Moon*, described as science-factual rather than science fiction. *TV Guide* took up one full sentence to report the news of the pilot, and did not fail to include *The Twilight Zone* on the same page.

In the September 1960 issue of *The Nonconformist Fanzine*, published and edited irregularly from *Saginaw Magazine*, a lengthy review of *The Twilight Zone* appeared in a column titled "The One-Eyed Monster." The review was also a commentary on the science fiction and horror that was then gracing the television screens:

> It might be noted here that more and more of our so-called 'leaders' are, and have been, invading the television world. At first it was Charles Beaumont, Richard Matheson, and Ray Bradbury in *The Twilight Zone*, along with Rod Serling, of course. But now it has expanded to include Fritz Leiber, whose "Conjure Wife" I recently saw on *Moment of Fear*, Isaac Asimov, whose "Caves of Steel" is scheduled for the same program and of course, 'Mr. Mystery' himself, Robert Bloch, who more or less writes regularly for *Alfred Hitchcock Presents*.
>
> I think most of this growing acceptance of science fiction on television was caused by Rod Serling's switchover to *Twilight Zone* from occasional *Playhouse 90*s. When a person as well-liked and respected as he moves into science fiction, some kind of reaction is in store. In this case, it has helped somewhat to bring sci-fi to television.

Serling Answers Questions

When columnist Marie Torre went on vacation, Rod Serling filled in for her column, *Marie Torre Reports*, answering questions faithful readers had submitted. The Monday, August 8, 1960 issue of *The New York Herald Tribune* had fans asking questions that required firm, solid answers, and he took the time to answer them publicly.

The Twilight Zone' stories are uniformly offbeat. How do you manage to find enough ideas?
We haven't even scraped the surface of ideas. What we're dealing with here is imagination and the scope of this approach is broad, wide, deep and almost unfathomable. This is possibly the one anthology format that is not self-limiting. We can travel as high or as deep as the human imagination and the material for this kind of dramatic excursion is limitless.

Any changes in 'The Twilight Zone' next season?
A higher rating, I hope. But in terms of its approach, few changes at all. We'll do some lighter and not as many "far out" stories. But by and large the format will remain the same.

Most of TV's successful playwrights have moved on to Broadway and Hollywood. What makes you stay in television?
A weekly series called *The Twilight Zone* is the answer. Most of the other TV playwrights lost interest in the medium and had no interest in half-hour scripts. Quite legitimately and logically they've moved over to different areas of writing. I'll probably follow them after this series is over.

Why do the creative dramatists withdraw from TV?
Lack of market is one reason. A limited thematic area from which to draw and create. Mistakenly, it's been said that the exodus of most of the major TV dramatists had been dictated by bank accounts.

This is simply not the case. I know of no TV writers who go to Broadway or to motion pictures for a buck. Most of the time writing a legitimate play is far more speculative and far less guaranteed in its resultant financial security than TV drama. This exodus can best be explained for artistic reasons. They should prefer to write in a freer atmosphere. They want to say what they want in the way they want to. The legitimate playwright is protected by the Dramatists Guild. The television writer has no such protection. His lines can be altered, his meanings diluted, his concepts diluted and vitiated by other people. This isn't possible on a Broadway stage.

Is there a market for dramatic originals in TV?
Yes, the market's there, but it's gradually shrinking. The receptivity on the part of producers, agents and networks to "new writing" has shrunk with each passing season until the medium has now reached a point where it's almost impossible for new talent to break in.

Are writers' complaints about TV censorship and sponsorship interference valid?
In most cases I believe firmly that they are. On *The Twilight Zone*, I've had considerably more freedom of approach than in any other television writing I've done. But much of this stems from my own pre-censorship – the fact that I'm knowledgeable about those areas which would create a storm and which are considered controversial. I simply don't touch these areas and as a result have far less trouble. But censorship and intrusion are more the rule in television than the exception.

Explanation of First Season Costs
In a letter drafted to Norman Felton dated April 20, 1960, Buck Houghton explained, "With regard to the overall budget on these last ten pictures, I have a strong feeling that the final figures will be very, very close to the money allotted; it must be remembered that $500,000 spent with pin-point accuracy is nearly impossible." This, of course, was an understatement. According to Houghton's figures, unforeseen expenses were added to the lineup. Central Casting was late getting the bills recorded. Due to an actors strike headed by the Screen Actors' Guild, M-G-M had to add $100 per shooting day to the cost to defer their expenses in keeping supervisory personnel on salary which only the television companies needed. For 16 days, this totaled $1,600.

Art directors, set designers, set decorators and the department accounts, including set estimating, blue-printing, etc., were calculated for Houghton by the head of the art department as $30 over the initial estimate. The rental, purchase and manning of props and set decorations was reported by the head of that department as under budget between $300 and $500 per picture. Cayuga used about $300 worth of stock shots where $2,000 was estimated for the 10 pictures. Ninety-seven dollars worth of process shooting was figured per picture and none had been used. Houghton cast the pictures and made allowances for extra actors, for a net savings in the neighborhood of $15,000. The bills for M-G-M stages and production services had always been on budget. The area in which the production went over was a grab bag account called "set operations," in which the moving of dressing rooms and sweeping out stages and providing booms and camera dollies had run over. Lighting was a hard account to control because, in the hurly burly of a big studio, platforms that one had figured to be in place for Cayuga had been moved to another set – and so with them, the lights.

The Hugo Awards

On June 3, 1960, Mrs. Arthur G. Archer, on behalf of the 18th World Science Fiction Convention, to be held in Pittsburgh, Pennsylvania, invited Serling to attend as their guest. In mid-July, he declined the offer. "Unfortunately, the date of the convention and my availability don't jibe. I shall be back on the Coast shooting the series and it would be physically impossible for me to make the trip. As a suggestion, why not Charles Beaumont or Richard Matheson, both of whom have written for our series and other television, and are certainly well-respected S-F writers."

Realizing Serling was not going to attend, on July 18, 1960, Mrs. Archer told him that *The Twilight Zone* had won the Hugo Award for "Best Dramatic Work of 1959" in the science fiction field. "Some English votes may still wander in," she explained, "correctly postmarked, but *Twilight Zone* received such an overwhelming majority nothing can possibly change the result of the voting at this date." The Hugo Awards was relatively new in 1960, the first ceremony held a few years previous, so the Hugo did not have the prestige it would gain over the years. Serling felt appreciative of the advance notice and submitted the following acceptance speech for a designated speaker to read in his place:

"Ladies and gentlemen, in some fourteen years of writing for television, I have managed to acquire by one means or another, a motley collection of metal doo-dads, jim crackery, plaques and some flamboyant certificates which variously grace the inside of seldom used desk drawers, my kid's play room, or on a few rarer occasions, a rather pretentious niche on the mantelpiece. It is disturbing commentary on television that the majority of awards are a result of a popularity contest or whatever politics are extant at the time. On too few occasions can they be equated with quality or do their auspices carry with it the innate dignity that any award should have. It's for this reason that the notification of *The Twilight Zone* winning this Hugo Award was a source of very special satisfaction for myself and for a legion of unheralded people who produce the show. Admittedly, I'm a Johnny-come-lately in the science fiction-fantasy field and in this case I feel I have been judged not by a jury of peers, but rather by a courthouse full of senior-status professionals who were gracious enough to overlook the fact that I just happened to sneak in through the back door long after my predecessors had made this area of fiction the meaningful important and qualitative adjunct to American literature that it is. It makes this recognition that much more exciting and it makes my gratitude that much more heartfelt. Thank you for a singular honor."

This would not be the last time Serling would be bestowed the Hugo Award because of *The Twilight Zone*. He would win the award again in 1961 and 1962. In August of 1962, after learning that he was going to be bestowed the Hugo for the third consecutive year, he apologized again for not attending the September ceremonies. "I think I shall have to establish a new record for recipience in not attending the awards," he joked. "September will find me en route to Ohio for a teaching-residency at Antioch College with simply no chance for a detour to Chicago." Serling did, however, consent to a telephone taped interview, but did so with some reluctance. "With no phony humility, I'm hardly in the league with Bradbury or Arthur C. Clarke," he commented.

For 1963, *The Twilight Zone* was nominated in the same category, but no Hugo Award was awarded to anyone for "Best Dramatic Presentation" that year. The rules for the Hugo Award require that "no award" always appear on the ballot, and if "no award" won the election by majority, no award was presented in that category.

Varied Awards

Hosted by the Academy of Television Arts and Sciences, the annual Emmy Awards recognize the highest achievements in television broadcasting. Emmy Awards were first given in 1949 for the 1948 broadcast year, and the Academy has continued awarding statuettes to this day. *The Twilight Zone* achieved a number of nominations and awards.

On June 10, 1960, at NBC's Burbank Studios and the Ziegfeld Theatre in New York, the 1960 Emmy Awards was telecast on NBC. For programs broadcast between March 1, 1959 and March 31, 1960, a 35-year-old Rod Serling took home his fourth prize and what would become the first Emmy Award for *The Twilight Zone*. His acceptance speech was brief. "I don't know how deserving I am, but I do know how grateful. Thank you so very much."

On May 16, 1961, at the Moulin Rouge in Hollywood and the Ziegfeld Theatre in New York, the 1961 Emmy Awards was telecast on NBC. For programs broadcast between April 1, 1960 and April 15, 1961, *The Twilight Zone* gained more prizes than the year before. Serling won for a second time in a row for "Outstanding Writing Achievement in Drama," besting pal Reginald Rose for "The Sacco and Vanzetti Story." According to author Thomas O'Neil, TV observers "wondered aloud if this meant that live television was dead." The episode submitted to the Academy as best representing *The Twilight Zone* was "Eye of the Beholder." George Clemens won an award for "Outstanding Achievement in Cinematography for Television" because of that same episode. *The Twilight Zone* was nominated, but lost to the *Hallmark Hall of Fame* for "Outstanding Program Achievement in the Field of Drama."

On May 22, 1962, at the Hollywood Palladium, the Astor Hotel in New York, and the Sheraton-Park Hotel in Washington, D.C., the 1962 Emmy Awards was telecast on NBC. For programs broadcast between April 16, 1961 and April 14, 1962, *The Twilight Zone* gained three nominations, but no wins. Philip Barber was nominated for "Outstanding Achievement in Art Direction and Scenic Design." Serling received a nomination for "Outstanding Writing Achievement in Drama" and lost to Reginald Rose, whom he had defeated the year before. George Clemens also received a nomination for "Outstanding Achievement in Cinematography for Television." For the 1963 Emmy Awards, Clemens, along with Robert W. Pittack, were the only *Twilight Zone* persons nominated.

In November of 1960, days after the classic "Eye of the Beholder" episode aired on CBS, Owen Comora told Rod Serling that "I'm keeping my fingers crossed about Sanka giving you some extra coin to publicize the alternate weeks. This would be the best of all possible occurrences." On Saturday evening, November 26, Serling was honored by Hollywood Lodge of B'nai B'rith for the coveted "Max M. Berick Service Award."

In 1961, *The Twilight Zone* received the annual Unity Award for "Outstanding Contributions to Better Race Relations." Buck Houghton would receive the Producers' Guild Award for "Best Produced Series" for his work on *The Twilight Zone*. John Brahm would win a Directors' Guild Award for his work on "Time Enough at Last."

The Kimberly-Clark Corporation

Kimberly-Clark was the alternating sponsor for the first season. The company devoted its airtime on *The Twilight Zone* pitching Kleenex paper products such as facial tissue, bathroom tissues and table napkins. Foote, Cone & Belding in Chicago was the advertising agency representing Kimberly-Clark, and Serling struck up a strong friendship with the advertising agency's Albert Weisman. The primary concern of Tom Brennen of Kimberly-Clark was not the quality of the films, but the ratings, which, in his opinion, was the method to determine sales profits.

On January 14, 1960, Serling wrote to Weisman. Judging from the nature of the phone call he got from Tom Brennen the day before, their relationship may well have been totally social after the end of the month. "He was somewhat depressing as to the fortunes of our show with regards to the gentlemen in Neenah who make toilet paper," Serling commented. "So all our efforts notwithstanding, we just didn't make it sufficiently in the ratings or in Mr. Kimberly's dramatic enjoyment to warrant a continuation." Serling gathered this was their point of view and that the chances of a renewal were somewhat less than 50-50.

Serling's stance had changed by March 14 when he wrote another letter to Weisman. The Neilsen had been good to him. For the first time the series went over 20 since the second month of the show. For the sixth week in a row they topped Taylor on Arbitron, by a minimum four points and while this may not have meant the series was on its way to success, ratings were a lot healthier than they were two months previous. Serling, thinking positively, commented: "You also have the benefit (that is, Kimberly-Clark does) of three of our best, best, best films. 'The Big, Tall Wish,' 'A Stop at Willoughby' and 'A Passage for Trumpet.' I think they're the best we will have done or at least, they shape up that way now."

The rise in ratings was not enough, and Kimberly-Clark dropped sponsorship after the summer reruns for the first season concluded in September of 1960. It should be noted that Kimberly-Clark had previously turned down such programs as *Rawhide* and *Black Saddle*, because the company that sold toilet tissue could not figure how to work their product in with a western. Kimberly-Clark bowed out after the first season of the science fiction program, as one newspaper journalist commented, "because Mr. Kimberly didn't understand it."

The Colgate-Palmolive Company

By May 27, CBS had reached a decision regarding a renewal of a second season – but with only 10 episodes to start and the option for additional films if the ratings proved promising. Serling had requested formally in writing that Buck Houghton's services be arranged for the coming year, and Robert Goldfarb of the Frank Cooper Associates Agency helped make the arrangements. Replacing Kimberly-Clark, beginning with the second season, was Colgate-Palmolive.

During the billboards and commercial breaks, Colgate advertised a variety of products: Toothpaste with the promotion jingle, "Helps Clean Your Breath"; Halo Shampoo, the "new dry hair formula"; Wildroot Cream Oil; Palmolive Soap; Palmolive Rapid-Shave Cream; and Veto Roll-On Deodorant.

On June 9, 1960, George T. Laboda, director of the Radio and Television department of Colgate-Palmolive Company in New York, contacted Rod Serling (who was then residing in Pacific Palisades, California), to make certain that the Serling household was well-stocked with Colgate-Palmolive products. Laboda made certain a number of people put together an assortment of virtually every item the company produced and had them shipped to the family residence.

Months into the second season, upon learning that the ratings were good enough to warrant additional episodes by the network, Serling wrote to Weisman, noting that the program was growing a steadfast and loyal following: "Does Kimberly-Clark realize what they missed? There I could have done an entire toilet paper commercial with unblushing professionalism which would have sent people into their bathrooms helter skelter and willy nilly or to their supermarkets screaming for Delsey.... In all truth, they done me dirt and CBS sold me out before I had a chance to remonstrate. First we were renewed and then it was very subtly suggested to me that the renewal hinged on my assuming the pitchman's mantel. I hate the shit, but I've only got 26 more weeks to go. Hell, I can do that standing on my head. (Which would make for kind of a unique commercial!)"

Colgate-Palmolive dropped sponsorship at the end of the second season, citing it wanted to shift to "the hard sell," but the final episode sponsored by Colgate was "Two," actually the premiere episode of the third season. Contracts between Cayuga, CBS and the sponsor conflicted, granting Colgate sponsorship of the third season's first show, broadcast on September 15, 1961. Trade papers received separate press releases and news items during the summer of 1961, alerting them of the season premiere and Colgate's exit from sponsorship. Nonetheless, trade papers such as *Variety* and *The Hollywood Reporter* that generally specialize in reviewing season premieres ultimately reviewed "The Arrival," which aired the week after, overlooking the true season premiere, "Two."

The General Foods Corporation

General Foods was the first to sign up to sponsor *The Twilight Zone* and remained on board through-out the entire first season and most of the second season. Before CBS could confirm a second season renewal, General Foods exercised a contract clause that allowed them to bow out after the summer reruns. On May 6, 1960, James W. Andrews of Maxwell House Division of General Foods wrote to Serling:

Dear Rod,

It was certainly most thoughtful of you to write, and I'm sorry that the television partnership between the Maxwell House Division and your enterprise is coming to an end. Let's hope this is just a temporary situation, because I'm certain that you will produce many outstanding proper-ties in the years ahead; and with our interest in television being what it is, it's most probable that we can look forward to other partnerships in the future.

I'm delighted to hear that *Twilight Zone* is being continued by CBS as it's always been one of my favorites – biased though I may be – and I do think it's been an excellent vehicle for Instant Sanka during this year.

My best wishes to you and your charming wife.

Sincerely yours,
James W. Andrews

The letter was premature. CBS did renew the program for a second season, so General Foods continued into the second season, promoting the same "newest coffee sensation," Sanka Coffee, dur-ing the commercial breaks. The commercials were similar in both seasons, and a few shown during the second season airings were the same commercials used during the first.)

Before the end of 1960, General Foods exercised its option to drop sponsorship in March – the earliest date it could contractually vacate. In January of 1961, newspapers began reporting that *The Twilight Zone* had been restored to full sponsorship status with the inking of tobacco giant Liggett & Myers to replace the alternate-week sponsorship being vacated by General Foods. Colgate stayed on as the alternate sponsor, and the television series remained in its Friday night berth. The final broadcast sponsored by General Foods was on March 31, 1961, titled "Long Distance Call."

In the premiere issue of *Gamma* magazine, dated 1963, Serling was asked when *The Twilight Zone* was dropped by the sponsors after the first season, didn't a lot of fans write in to complain of this? His answer: "Not exactly. We knew we had a strong show, so we sent out appeals to the viewers, asking them to write us if they wanted *Zone* to continue. We got over 2,500 cards and letters in response, all of them urging us to stay on TV. This sold the sponsors, and we were able to continue."

On Valentine's Day 1961, Owen S. Comora of Young & Rubicam, the advertising agency representing General Foods, wrote to Serling, expressing his sorrow for leaving the program. "The past two years have gone much too quickly, but that's the way it is with anything you enjoy. And I have enjoyed every minute of our association."

According to the June 30, 1962 issue of *TV Guide*, General Foods said the show "wasn't doing a job for us." While this may have been an official stance by the former sponsor, the date of their statement remains unknown because the periodical could have been quoting a statement from the year before. The debate over the effectiveness of television commercials gained the attention of the advertising community in March of 1962 when Young & Rubicam released the results of an extensive survey that indicated program content did not influence commercial recall. "A given commercial will attain the same level of recall and sales point scores in any program category," Young & Rubicam concluded.

The Liggett & Myers Tobacco Company

Beginning in April of 1961, Liggett & Myers began promoting its products, Oasis Cigarettes and Chesterfield Kings. A switch to Wednesday nights had been under consideration during negotiations with CBS when L&M expressed an interest in *The Twilight Zone*. One reason was that it would give the cigarette company a contiguity deal, since it was the alternate sponsor of the new Jackie Gleason show on Friday nights at 9:30, just ahead of *The Twilight Zone*.

But more important in killing the change of nights was that a move to lure *Peter Gunn* away from ABC-TV didn't prove successful. Had *Peter Gunn* moved, *Twilight Zone* would have replaced *My Sister Eileen* on Wednesdays at 9 p.m. for Colgate, and *Peter Gunn* would have followed at 9:30 under its sponsors, Bristol-Myers and R.J. Reynolds. What would have replaced *Twilight Zone's* 10 p.m. time slot? *I've Got a Secret*, sponsored by the same pair, which would have made the shift. (Source: *Variety*, January 11, 1961)

There was more than a gleam in the eye of CBS about the *Peter Gunn* move. Bristol-Myers was all for the schedule change, and Reynolds liked the idea. But L&M optioned a clause in its contract because of the Friday switch for *Secret*. Reynolds felt it already had too much Friday night exposure for the Winston brand, which also was on ABC-TV's *The Flintstones*.

Summer of 1960

Getting ready for the second season, Serling and Houghton began choosing literary properties for adaptation and teleplay assignments for both Richard Matheson and Charles Beaumont. On April 5, 1960, Serling told a fan of the program that "next season we hope to use writers like Sheckley, Bradbury, et al." but no adaptations of Robert Sheckley or Ray Bradbury stories went before the cameras.

According to a progress report dated June 7, 1960, Script #42 was originally meant to be an adaptation of "Dory" by Gabrielle Upton, with the first draft due June 6. The first draft was completed by August, with the intention of being mimeographed by September 1. A production report dated June 30 stated a final polish was due any day. Cayuga Productions paid $2,000.00 for the rights to the story, but the cameras never rolled for it; the screen rights remained the property of Cayuga Productions until 1965, when the television series was sold to CBS.

According to the same June 7 progress report, Serling attempted to purchase the rights to compose an adaptation of "The Open Window," by Hector Hugo Munro, who wrote the story under the pen name of Saki. The story told of Framton Nuttel, a man who visits a small village to call upon a lady his sister used to know. For a few minutes he is left alone with her niece, who has quite an active imagination. She tells Framton the story about the tragedy of the lady's husband and two younger brothers, who had gone hunting three years earlier and never returned. The bodies were never found, and because of this the window from which they left is always kept open. When indeed they do return that very night, Frampton – who has suffered from nerves in the past – runs out of the house, and the niece explains his sudden departure to her relatives with an equally imaginative fiction.

Charles Beaumont was committed to five original teleplays, the last due by August 10, 1960. The first was already written by June 7, a teleplay titled "The Young Folks." His second was already selected by that time, an adaptation of "The Howling Man." By June 30, Beaumont had proposed "Venus in the Garage," slated as Script #47 and due by July 5, 1960.

In late August 1960, Serling took Matheson's "One for the Books" under consideration, requesting a copy of the short story from Matheson.

Serling himself had been committed to complete a teleplay titled "McClintock's Machine," slated as script #51, due by July 15, 1960. Neither of the two scripts ever became episodes of the series.

On July 28, 1960, Henry Colman, former director of program development for General Artists Corporation, offered his services as a "television consultant" to Serling. "My firm is a Producer's Representative, servicing television production companies at the network and advertising agency level," Colman explained. He rejected the offer, explaining that "I doubt very much if this is either practical or required. The show has only one more season to go and to date we've felt no need of any consultant help on any level. But I do thank you for your interest and wish you all good things."

In the July 20 issue of *Variety*, the annual "Review and Preview" feature was released on newsstands. Consisting of what happened in the past year on television and the predictions for the near future, both Houghton and Serling agreed to pay for advertising from Cayuga funds to ensure *The Twilight Zone* was represented in that edition.

On August 31, 1960, Rod Serling recorded "stay-tuned" spots, all under 10 seconds, for the close of other television programs to promote the new season:

"Next" Spots
1. This is Rod Serling, gatekeeper for television's most exclusive district – *The Twilight Zone*. Enter. Next on most of these stations.
2. This is Rod Serling, welcoming committee of one at the portals of *The Twilight Zone*. My duties begin momentarily – on most of these stations.
3. Cast off the ties of the prosaic world. Give your imagination free rein. Ahead lies *The Twilight Zone* – next on most of these stations.

4. This is Rod Serling. In a moment on most of these stations, imagination takes flight. Destination: *The Twilight Zone*. Brace yourselves.

"Later Tonight" Spots

1. This is Rod Serling. Later tonight on most of these stations, I conduct a field trip into the back-country of man's imagination: *The Twilight Zone*.
2. This is Rod Serling, with an invitation to join me for tonight's tale of *The Twilight Zone* – later, on most of these stations.

"Tomorrow" Spots

1. This is Rod Serling, taking reservations for tomorrow's excursion into *The Twilight Zone*. Check the departure time, on most of these stations.
2. This is Rod Serling. Tomorrow night, most of these stations present *The Twilight Zone*. Shall we rendezvous in this most remarkable domain?

Lieutenant Mason (Ross Martin) greets his daughter when
he discovers he is back on Earth.

CHAPTER SIX

The Second Season

For the second season of *The Twilight Zone*, Serling and Houghton needed to convince the network to keep the budget no less than the year's before. The network, having a financial stake in the cost of production, wanted to lower the budget slightly to offset what it felt were unnecessary expenses. "In order to get extra dough from these tight bastards, I had to commit to three pilots and exclusivity for another year in the area of new program development," Serling told Bill Dozier in a letter dated April 14, 1960. "This totally mitigates against any deal between us for the next 12 months (and probably ends our friendship.)" Among the pilots he wrote was an hour-long teleplay for *The Loner*, a television western for which he would attempt to secure Bob Cummings as the star.

By November of 1960, Serling was communicating with Guy Della Cioppa, requesting he not supply the network with series ideas, citing, "The experience of *Twilight Zone* has proven to me that writing a pilot is a quick walk around the block. It's the further requirements of scripts from me that have proven itself such an assault on my physical condition and my sanity. On *Zone*, I'm just starting my forty-fourth script and I find myself feeling like a potato sack that's been out in the sun for the better part of July."

Discussing plans for the second season of *The Twilight Zone*, Serling told a reporter for the July 17, 1960 issue of *The Louisville, Kentucky Courier-Journal*, "Every communications medium in history has discovered the truth of those two maxims. . . . You cannot fool an audience forever. The audience demands not only original stories and ideas. It demands variety and originality in the presentation. It does not want, each week, to recognize the trappings in which an idea – even a new one – is presented."

Columnist Bill Ladd acknowledged that, "Serling promised at the beginning of the season to give us something different, and he has done that."

"Some of the shows were too different," commented Serling in the same *Courier-Journal* article. "Of the first 36, I think I am proud of about 18. There are others I liked, and there were some I wished we had never heard of in the first place." Serling admitted that the first season had taught some lessons which would be observed for the second season. The audience had indicated in letters to him that a desirable thing would be more balance between light stories and the "down-beat" type. "We will do more of our shows with tongue-in-cheek," he said. "We will also have more women as leading characters next season. We will avoid some of the 'real-far-out' endings which leave no alternatives for the viewer. We have found our audience wants to think. I don't mean we will have no ending at all, but we will have final scenes which will give the viewer a chance to decide for himself if there was a logical explanation for what happened."

In a guest column for Allen Rich, Serling wrote: "This is the season of the professional knocker. Television's detractors come out like millions of ground hogs looking for shadows and because so much of what we disseminate to an audience is pap and pabulum, or violent bone-jarring, blood-slicing shoot-'em-ups, there are ample shadows to contend with. But it remains a fact that television with all its faults and foibles, with its rigged quizzes, with its painful imitations, with its propensity for filling up gigantic blocks of time with carbon copies of what went before and what follows, it is nonetheless a medium of promise, of creativity and of exciting entertainment. It has provided enough solid, qualitative hours of memorable moments already to justify this claim. It's for this reason that I stick with it. It may well leave me – but I doubt if I shall ever leave it."

The Stars Requested

Phyllis Standish, a young aspiring actress who played the role of an Indian girl in the episode "Little Heathen" on TV's *Buckskin*, and a teenager in the motion picture, *The Beat Generation* (1959), wrote to Rod Serling on October 20, 1959, asking to play a role in his television series. "I have spoken of you to my mother at great length," she wrote, "and she feels – as do I – that it is high time that you include a well-trained, competent and well-tested woman in one of your scripts." Standish did not make an appearance on *The Twilight Zone*, but she left an impression with him; they exchanged a number of letters as pen pals for a time.

In December of 1959, Chester Morris wrote to Serling, requesting a part on a Twilight Zone production. By mid-December, Serling was suffering exhaustion and ordered to bed by his doctor, so he spent the day composing letters. He told Morris, "As soon as I conjure up a meaty, demanding and substantial role, I shall be contacting you so that the Serling-Morris axis can once again roll." Morris had played the role in the Lux Video Theatre presentation of "Welcome Home, Lefty," which was scripted by Serling. In early January 1960, Serling met up with Richard L. Bare, temporary producer-writer of the television series The Islanders. Serling recommended Morris get a role on The Islanders in order to compensate for not being able to immediately find a role for Morris on The Twilight Zone. Bare was enthusiastic and was surprised that he had not thought of Morris before. By early March, Serling apologized to Morris for not getting him a role on The Twilight Zone, explaining that "because of the [actors] strike, we had to rush into production, cast in a vast hurry, and there was no time to contact you."

On June 20, 1960, an agent at the Paul Wilkins Agency in Hollywood, wrote to Rod Serling, explaining how the Wednesday, June 15th issues of both *Variety* and the *Hollywood Reporter* reviewed *333 Montgomery Street*, which starred his client DeForest Kelley. "His performance in the show was so impressive that he has been receiving fan letters from many of the actors in the industry commending him on his work," the agent said. "Mr. Kelley is also a fan of *Twilight Zone* and would like very much to meet with you and discuss the possibility of doing one of your shows."

On December 10, 1960, actor Jack Lord contacted Rod Serling through a personal, handwritten letter on official stationery:

Dear Rod –
I used to write letters like this when I was a struggling actor in New York, trying to crash Broadway. I resume now because I know of no other way to tell you that *Twilight Zone* is one of my favorite of all television shows and I want very much to do one for you. What else can I say?
Sincerely,
Jack

P.S. This is personal letter to you and would appreciate it if you would treat it as such. You may care to check with Bill Warren on your lot, regarding my work. I just did a second *Rawhide* for him.

On December 27, Serling drafted a reply to Lord, informing him that the bio material was not necessary, since he knew his work well and happened to be a fan. "Just why our paths didn't cross on *The Twilight Zone* is quite beyond me. I normally take very little part in casting, but I know for a fact that your name was broached on a number of occasions and engendered some very pleasant comment as to your capabilities. If *The Twilight Zone* continues (at the moment it appears to be dubious) and we go back into production, rest assured something will be done."

Serling may have been aware of an incident Jack Lord caused on a former *Studio One*. In the closing scene of the episode, Lord was supposed to shy away from the camera, but instead he chose to steal the scene by breaking down and crying, keeping the camera focused on himself and changing the ending to the story.

On February 27, 1961, Rosemary DeCamp, a character actress who played the nurse Judy Price on the radio program *Dr. Christian*, wrote to Serling, recalling with fondness their first meeting when he was a winner in 1949 for the radio script that won him $500 prize money. She was presently residing in Redondo Beach, California, and was conducting an original one-act playwriting contest at Torrance High School. She had written to him to ask if he would have the time, in between his *Twilight Zone* productions, to attend as a guest to critique the students' award-winning productions. Serling apologized, explaining that he would be in New York on the date she requested, but wished her all the luck, offering her a rain check for a future date.

In November and December of 1961, Martin Goodman Productions, Inc. attempted to solicit actress Arlene Francis for a guest star appearance on *The Twilight Zone*. This attempt, however, was made too late. Weeks after, Buck Houghton left and Serling went east, and the offer was never relayed to the new producer, Herbert Hirschman, until many months later when the series was picked up for a fourth season.

On March 18, 1960, Laurence Schwab, who directed Serling's script, "O'Toole From Moscow" for *Matinee Theatre*, wrote to the playwright, explaining how he watched a few episodes and offering his directing skills for a few productions. On April 5, Serling apologized, explaining that he already had signed up all of his directors for the balance of the required filming. He added, "Conscience dictates the following candor. I remember with horror 'O'Toole from Moscow.' I must tell you, Larry, that I thought it was a heavy-handed, depressing directorial job which left me ice cold. God, friend, why bring that up when suggesting your qualifications to work with me further?"

Sue Mengers of Tom Korman Associates, Inc., an agency representing actors and actresses for motion pictures, telefilms and stage productions, was responsible for securing Jack Klugman in May of 1963 for the episode "In Praise of Pip." Days before, she attempted to solicit two other fine actors for *The Twilight Zone*, Rip Torn and Claudia McNeil – neither of whom made an appearance on *Twilight Zone*.

Some movie stars contacted Serling through gentle notes and letters, if not for the intention of winning good graces to appear in an episode of *The Twilight Zone*, but to inform him that fans come from all fashions – and legends. In December of 1963, Clara Bow, the famed "It Girl," residing in Culver City, California, sent Serling a Christmas card.

Rod Serling, the Celebrity

The second season featured a new opening sequence, a variation of the sun setting (sans female eye), one of the rejected proposals from the first season's revised title sequence. With CBS unsure of committing itself to renewing a complete second season, only 10 episodes were commissioned for the initial request. Obviously, additional episodes were ordered by the network, but CBS, in taking too long to get back to Buck Houghton regarding the official notice, forced Cayuga to insert four reruns from the first season into the prime-time lineup. These episodes were re-edited to feature the new opening sequence, so the opening titles did not vary week-by-week. The same opening sequence also was edited into the first season episodes for the summer of 1961. (This explains why some commercial releases and television syndication prints, on occasion, will contain a different opening sequence that does not match the season it was initially telecast.)

Besides the new opener with the now-popular theme, the most notable difference between the first season and the second was Rod Serling's appearance on camera. Having made a humorous cameo in "A World of Difference," it was agreed that he could appear as the host.

"There was no running character we could use as host, so CBS picked me," Serling commented in an interview with Charles E. Fritch, editor of *Gamma* magazine. "I had done some promotional films for them and they looked at these and decided on giving me a try. Actually, I photograph better than I look. Now people see me on the street and they say, 'Gee, we thought you were six foot one,' and I know they're thinking 'God, this kid is only five feet five and he's got a broken nose!' But I think I've improved a lot since the first season, and the ham in me is pleased with this."

On June 8, 1960, Mark Nichols, entertainment editor of *Coronet Magazine*, wanted to do a story on Serling as *The Twilight Zone* host. However, Nichols felt that his participation at the end of the show wasn't long enough and wondered why he did not appear to introduce each show. By coincidence, the final cut of "A World of Difference" had been viewed and it had been decided by network and sponsor to start featuring Serling as the host on screen, seeing how well he handled himself in the final episode of the first season. "In view of last week's events," Owen S. Comora of Young & Rubicam wrote, "I called Mark this morning to tell him that your host role for next season has been expanded considerably. He was quite happy to hear this and readily agreed to do a story on you."

Beginning with the second season, the closing credits reflected Serling as the creator of the television series – something that was not displayed on the screen during any of the first season telecasts. In a letter Serling wrote to Buck Houghton dated August 12, 1960, "One small point and I hope this can be handled, but if it gives you trouble – let me know. Instead of an executive producer credit on the screen, Buck, could I have a credit which reads 'Created by Rod Serling'? This is for no other reason than plain, simple ego. I want to continue to be associated with the show in as close public terms as possible. And this 'Created by' credit would accomplish this handsomely. Let me know if this screws up anything or if you can proceed to get this thing effected."

Back in early November of 1959, a meeting with the new publicity director for CBS Television, Ernie Stern, led to a surprising result. CBS agreed with the need for building Serling's image as the "star" of the show, even though by November 3, only a few episodes had been broadcast. Along these lines, CBS insisted the show should always be referred to in publicity releases as "Rod Serling's *The Twilight Zone*."

On September 16, 1960, Serling signed an agreement with B. Kuppenheimer & Company, Inc. to use his name and likeness in publicity and point-of-sale advertising specifically involving counter and window cards, direct mail, newspaper, magazine and television advertising as well as editorial publicity. Rod Serling and *The Twilight Zone* program received credit printed on all such uses.

"I liked to tie the *Twilight Zone* introductions into the show," director Douglas Heyes recounted to interviewer Ben Herndon. "If I possibly could get hold of Rod – if he wasn't in New York or somewhere – I would try to get him in with the actors and with the people on the set. I thought that Rod's appearance in those things was part – really was *The Twilight Zone*. Where he appeared from and how he appeared was important. For example, in 'Dust' we worked out the thing where they were testing the gallows. The sacks flop down – BAM! – with a tremendous impact, and they hit the end of the rope. And as we pan down with it, we bring in Rod Serling, who's standing there at the base of the gallows, and he starts talking."

In early September 1960, John F. Moore of *The Binghamton Press* wrote a letter to Serling, revealing that *The Twilight Zone* was not being broadcast in Serling's hometown of Binghamton, New York. Serling contacted Robert B. Hoag of CBS, asking if he could look into the matter, to discover why affiliate WNBK did not carry his program. On September 22, Hoag sent the following reply to Serling. "The station in your home town is a primary ABC affiliate, and as such, [they're] pretty much forced to take Robert Taylor. The station offered to carry *Twilight Zone* at a delayed time, but apparently it was such a poor time period that both Colgate and General Foods refused to accept it."

Ralph W. Nelson, the production manager, took ill during the first few weeks of production for the second season, leaving Houghton to handle more paperwork than usual until Nelson returned. In a memo dated August 19, 1960, to Howard Barnes of CBS, Houghton explained the budgetary progress for the first batch of films completed for the second season.

"We plan the production prudently and carefully and then budget the expenses of executing those plans at average levels – neither optimistically nor pessimistically; but there are so far as I know no allowances nor hidden figures for emergency, crisis, nor accident. Yet any picture, anywhere, will have its bad breaks or reverses or accidents. Budgeting tightly this way makes it an almost dead certainty that the final cost will be a little in excess of the show estimate but I believe this is the proper way to budget. You will note that several pictures are over their estimate on account of extra shooting hours or mechanical phases of production that did not work as quickly as anticipated; I could have cushioned these events with extra money here and there, but as long as the ultimate event is still controllably under series estimate I believe it is wise to budget according to optimum performance."

In October of 1960, Serling drafted a letter to Hoag but, on second thought, withheld mailing it. He explained to CBS that while they had to deal with an ill Nelson, whom Serling referred to as "a highly efficient production manager," he lodged a complaint that the network's interference in productions due to costs was harming the quality of the episodes. "I won't short-shrift this show," Serling explained. "Our sincere concern in this area has very specifically been shown in our tentative shelving of a couple of high-budgeted scripts, which have been replaced by me with more economical productions." *

The letter Serling withheld also revealed his feelings for the producer. "Buck Houghton is doing a masterful job keeping this show moving, while concurrently retaining its richness while econo-

---

* On June 23, 1960, an arrangement was made with Ralph W. Nelson as the unit production manager for the second season, starting June 27, at the rate of $500 per week.

mizing whenever it's even remotely possible to do. When he's phoned, Bob, as often as he's being phoned, and is badgered, reminded, told, ordered, warned, threatened, et al, he is taken off his job of putting a show together, and sent off to dark corners searching for a thousand bucks here, an explanation of another thousand bucks there, and what have you. Speaking as a network partner in this deal, I really must voice a strong and urgent request that we be left alone in this matter unless there is an ample indication that we are going over budget because of slovenly and careless operation. . . . If their concern continues on this same level of constant meddling and disapprobation, I believe it would be much more practical and realistic of me to take my wares and what talent I have elsewhere where, perhaps there is a concern over budget, but not this constant preoccupation."

The September 20, 1959 issue of *The New York Times* reported that "television audiences will be able to get a good look at Rod Serling" and commented that he would "be on camera at the beginning and the end of each of the filmed telecasts in the role of narrator."

Physically, Serling was nothing to blur the portrait of the archetype, being only slightly shorter than average, 5 feet 5 inches tall, and correspondingly a light 137 pounds. His nose was sometimes described as "hawk like" (by a television dramatist); his eyebrows were black and beetling, and his mouth was usually compressed purposefully and dramatically into thin lines, thus giving him what *The New York Times* wrote, "a facial expression of unusual intensity, combined with an anxiety to please, and just anxiety."

Serling was nervous behind the camera, tensing up when filming for the episodes commenced. On many occasion he slipped and had to start his narration over again, solely because he was nervous at the time he recited his lines. He was most comfortable delivering his lines when sitting in a chair in a lounge or behind a desk. While he looked tall standing on screen with nothing purposely on camera of a specific height to compare him with, much of the television audience was unaware of his height. "I really don't like to do hosting. I do it by default. I have to," Serling explained to a reporter of United Press International in August of 1963. "If I had my druthers, I wouldn't do it. If I had to go on live, of course, I'd never do it."

Kuppenheimer and Eagle Clothing

On January 22, 1960, Eagle Clothes, Inc., one of the top custom-styled manufacturers in the United States, offered to supply the leading star of each episode of *The Twilight Zone* with a wardrobe of high-fashion suits. Having been responsible for supplying suits for a number of motion pictures, including *The Man in the Gray Flannel Suit* (1956) and *Paris Holiday* (1958), Eagle attempted to branch out into television. "We realize the importance of a star's appearance, both on and off camera, and feel confident he would be pleased with an Eagle wardrobe," explained Laurence Laurie, director of public relations for Rogers & Cowan, Inc. Eagle also offered Rod Serling a selection of suits to wear during the trailers for "next week's episode," ranging in fabrics from Turkish mohair to silk to pure Australian wool. These same suits, off the rack, sold for an average of $100 or more (depending on the retail chains). The offer was extended to Serling through Monte Factor in Beverly Hills, a noted retailer who handled the Eagle line. In return, Eagle asked only for credit on the end titles of *The Twilight Zone*, for supplying each actor's wardrobe.

On January 24, details were forwarded to Serling, offering three suits plus one overcoat, or if he preferred, two suits, one sport coat and one overcoat. On January 28, 1960, Serling personally sent a rejection, explaining that "unfortunately, network policy prohibits the kind of tie-in you suggest with Eagle Clothes . . . I'm sorry I can't oblige you, but I thank you for your consideration."

Part of the reason for Serling's rejection was because two months previous, A.R. Green, vice president of Kuppenheimer Clothes in Chicago, had already beaten Eagle to the punch by offering him a tour of the manufacturing plant, as well as taking measurements for tailor-made suits, for a purpose similar to Eagle's. Serling agreed to Kuppenheimer's terms, but unlike the Eagle offer, the complimentary suits were extended to him only – not the guest actors. Serling enjoyed the educative couple hours at the plant and signed a contract with the publicity and marketing department of Kuppenheimer. The new wardrobe arrived in his hands by December 8, 1960.

Eagle Clothing, in the meantime, sent Serling suits from its factory and arranged for a contract to guarantee onscreen credit, to appear as early as February 1961. This, however, caused a conflict. By February 1961, Kuppenheimer was enjoying the promotional product placement with the company receiving onscreen credit. In fact, the closing credits for the entire second season acknowledged Kuppenheimer. Episodes from the first season, rerun in between new telecasts of second season episodes, were re-edited to reflect the new opening title screen and music theme, but the closing credits were not changed, avoiding wardrobe credit. To satisfy both companies, Serling offered a solution, which would begin with the third season. On a rotating basis, both would receive clothing credit on an almost equal number of episodes.

On May 2, 1961, as the second season was about to conclude, and word about a third season renewal had reached the trade columns, Joseph Castor of Castor and Associates, representing Kuppenheimer, confirmed its desire to continue the arrangement, but with the assurance that the company receive screen credit for the entire third season – not partial as Serling proposed. Unable to meet the request, Serling was forced to drop Kuppenheimer, and beginning with the third season, Eagle Clothing received onscreen credit. Eagle would remain credited on *The Twilight Zone* throughout the remainder of the series. Serling received 10 additional suits, sport coats or topcoats every year in agreement for the onscreen credit. (When "Nothing in the Dark" and "The Grave," filmed during the second season, were scheduled for broadcast during the third season, the closing credits were adjusted to reflect Eagle Clothing instead of Kuppenheimer, even though the suits were Kuppenheimer's.) *

Advertisement for Kuppenheimer.

---

* Rod Serling, in a jovial mood swing, once referred to Eagle Clothing as "Evil" Clothing, suggesting there may have been a bit of conflict between the two.

The Charity of Rod Serling

During the first week of February, 1961, Rod Serling recorded an "over credit" plug for the Easter Seals for Art Linkletter, to be included at the end of one of Linkletter's upcoming television productions. Later that month, on February 26, he attended a banquet in Cincinnati honoring WLW for its 40 years of pioneering development of the medium. Weeks later, on April 7, he appeared at a Central High School assembly in Binghamton, New York. His appearance was brief, informal, and unheralded in local papers. Having attended the school in his youth, he enjoyed the opportunity to revisit the campus.

In February of 1960, Miss Eleanor R. Roche of Chatham, New Jersey, wrote a fan letter to Serling with a most unusual request. "I write to you this letter with high hopes and a fervent hand. I am 22 and a student in my final year at Parsons School of Design, (connected with N.Y.U. for a B.F.A. degree) in N.Y.C. I am in the Interior Design and Architecture Department and have become greatly interested in set design and art direction. I speak with everyone I can on the subject, see all the TV shows, plays, and motion pictures of value, viewing all with an eye for sets, props, background and art direction. I will be in the Los Angeles area on my Easter vacation around the middle of April and I would like to know if it would be at all possible for me to see (or peek at) your set design and/ or Art Department? It would mean the world to me if I could get an idea of how an operation like yours works and how I could best fit myself into one like it in the future."

On February 26, Serling wrote to Miss Roche. "I'll try to spring our set designer long enough to sit down and talk to you and perhaps acquaint you with some of the designing concepts operative in filming. If you'll phone me when you arrive, I'll see what can be worked out. My home number is Granite 8-7759."

The Community Fund Spot

In 1960 (exact date unknown), Rod Serling was filmed for a 60-second community fund spot, which aired over CBS during the closing of various programs. While simply standing on the set, Serling remarked:

I'm Rod Serling, creator of *The Twilight Zone*. Just as space pioneers continue to probe and explore the outer atmosphere, we continue to find new regions of *The Twilight Zone*. These regions are concepts and ideas about man's role in time and space – and they continue to provide the basis for fascinating drama on our program. We hope that you'll join us on our next journey into . . . *The Twilight Zone* – Friday night on most of these stations.

Now about something in our own time, dimension and place. In your community the problems are real enough . . . and for many people, too real. Families, children, young people, the sick, the elderly: they often run head in into problems that are too much for them. And many people . . . of all ages . . . get help from the health and welfare services supported by your United Fund or Community Chest. That means it's up to you. It's your community . . . here and now. Give your fair share too. Give the United Way.

The Popularity Grows

In 1960, the Armed Forces Radio and Television Services (AFRTS) was busy preparing new television programs for broadcast for troops stationed in the Far East. According to the *Pacific Stars and Stripes*, a newspaper published daily in Tokyo, Captain John J. Brown, on a one-month visit of the AFRTS stations, announced that *The Twilight Zone* would be among the newest additions of programs syndicated overseas for the troops, who were otherwise missing the programs broadcast back home. Other television programs presented for troops were *The Untouchables*, *The Man Called X*, *Doctor Christian*, *Harbor Command*, and *Martin Kane*.

On February 11 – 13, 1961, a new restaurant and lounge in Austin, Illinois, at 904 N. Pulaski, conducted its grand opening, featuring Italian-American cuisine. The restaurant, inspired by the popular television series, was named "The Twilight Zone." Hosts John Castrovillari and Sam Eremo held the three-day gala, which

Vintage advertisement taking advantage of the Twilight Zone name.

offered customers spaghetti, devil fish, clams on the half shell, and lasagna. Many of the citizens nicknamed it the "Twilight Lounge."

Fred Croste of Oelwein, Iowa, wrote to a television columnist for his local newspaper, commenting: "Those fantastic fiction stories like *The Twilight Zone* should be dropped, they're too far-fetched. They're not true to life and stretch the imagination almost to the breaking point."

The May 14, 1961 issue of the Syracuse, New York, *The Post-Standard* reported that "In a recent poll of Los Angeles schoolchildren, the favorite show of all age groups turned out to be *The Twilight Zone*. This seems strange because the imaginative series comes on at 10 p.m. Friday on the CBS-TV Network, and it would appear to be too late for most youngsters. Maybe, simply because *Twilight Zone* is a good show, parents let their kids stay up for it."

In the January 29, 1962 issue of *Radio-Television Daily*, a total of 422 radio and television critics, feature writers and editors serving America's leading newspapers, magazines and fan publications, voted Rod Serling "Writer of the Year" for the second year in a row.

The Twilight Zone Shakespearean Sonnet

One of the frequent viewers of the television series, Lucille Robinson of Spokane, Washington, and a member of Poetry Scribes of Spokane, submitted the following Shakespearean sonnet to Serling:

There is a fifth dimension to record,
Imagination plays the leading role
Into the dark recesses unexplored,
Dimension of psychic, questing soul;
A journey through the superstitious mist
That clouds the concept of the human mind
Into the realm of psychic physicist,
With elements Almighty God designed;
A scientific search to understand
The thought transmittance of telepathy,
Untapped frontiers of knowledge to command;
One step into the extra-sensory.
A visit to a time and place unknown,
The fifth dimension called The Twilight Zone!

The Fan Clubs

On June 21, 1960, Carol Rosenthal of Lynbrook, Long Island, New York, received Serling's formal blessing to have a fan club. "Writers are notoriously anonymous people who usually get lost in the shuffle; therefore, the distinction of a fan club is a most gratifying thing to contemplate."

By March of 1961, a *Twilight Zone* fan club had been established in Belleville, Illinois. In October 1961, Richard Steel of Fall River, Massachusetts, wrote to Rod Serling. "Some months ago I wrote telling you I was starting a fan club. You asked me to give you the names of the members. Please send autographed pictures to the below people. In addition I would like, if it isn't too much trouble to have monthly reports of your activities and the *Twilight Zone*." Club members named were Richard Steel, Henry Dumont, Pat Merola, Margaret Oliver, Theresa Flanagan, Joel Cabral, Theresa Dumont, Hilda McGraw and Linda Steel. On October 18, Serling wrote back to Mr. Steel, including autographed photos. "Unfortunately, I just don't have the time to send you a monthly report of our *Twilight Zone* activities," he explained. "Normally, you can read of upcoming shows in *TV Guide* or your local paper."

On July 2, 1962, Bob Curley, Jack Guillon, Alan R. Evans and James W. Harris Jr., students at the Binghamton Central High School, wrote to Rod Serling, asking permission to organize a Rod Serling Fan Club in their vicinity. He wrote back, giving them permission and wished them luck.

The Twilight Zone Album

In November of 1960, CBS Records (also known as Columbia Records) produced a long-playing record album titled *The Twilight Zone*, from which Cayuga Productions would receive a royalty of 2 percent of the retail selling price. Since the record would not contain any of the music from the show, but simply exploit the name of the series, Sam Kaplan of Ashley-Steiner felt it was a fair arrangement. The money to be received by the series was subject to a 25 percent handling fee to which CBS was entitled for the exploitation of subsidiary rights. The balance was split evenly between CBS and Cayuga.

Marty Manning, who got his start during the Big Band era, was an arranger and conducted pop music during the late 1950s and early 1960s. He was assigned to compose a series of space age sounds, with space age pop names, inspired by *The Twilight Zone*. Mundell Lowe performed on the guitar, Lois Hunt sang the ethereal wordless vocals, Jerry Murad supplied the harmonica, Harry Breuer played the vibes, and Phil Kraus offered percussion. Manning provided the keyboard.

The LP contained 12 music scores; the first titled "The Twilight Zone." The remaining pieces featured "Shangri-La," "The Lost Weekend Theme," "Forbidden Planet," "Spellbound Concerto," "The Moon is Low" and others. The variation of the *Twilight Zone* theme was arranged by Marty Manning and Ernie Altschuler. The liner notes read: "To pluck such sounds out of *The Twilight Zone* and give them expression, an astounding group of musical instruments was brought together. The familiar tones of woodwinds, trumpet, piano and guitar were expanded and given shapes through electronic sorcery. And to them were added exotic instruments that seem to have been invented for, and even in, *The Twilight Zone*; the Martinot, the Ondioline, the bongos and the whole spectrum of percussion instruments. A vast library of sound effects added further intriguing notes. All of these were employed by arranger Manning to produce sounds that are musical, witty and beyond question other worldly."

Months later, Serling commented publicly about the album. "This is exceptional music and it carries with it the mood, the feeling, the pulse of the show. It seems to combine that which the show strives for – a marriage between reality and the different; the haunting, bittersweet nostalgia of something warm and rich and beautiful that has gone by and the piquant, titillating question mark of an experience yet to come."

In October of 1963, an album was released through Warner Bros. Records, titled *Out of Limits*, performed by The Marketts. Considered a surf record, the album contained a number of songs including "Collision Course," "Out of Limits" and "Twilight City." The Marketts was not a real group – they were a bunch of Los Angeles session musicians assembled by producer Joe Saraceno. He created the group to capitalize on the surf music craze that was ruling the radio airwaves. Their biggest success was their No. 3 hit, "Out of Limits," which was clearly influenced by the *Twilight Zone* theme by Marius Constant.

On November 15, Gerald H. Saltsman of Ashley-Steiner wrote to attorney Sol Rosenthal after having purchased the LP for comparison to the Columbia Records release that Cayuga and CBS were offering. "As I indicated to you, we feel that there is much too great a similarity in the basic themes of the two compositions. If you agree with us, will you please send out legal letters to the necessary parties? We have been told that the "Out of Limits" record has been played very frequently on radio station KFWB in particular." While Cayuga and CBS attempted to protect their property, no lawsuit arose from this, and the matter was eventually dropped.

The Logistics of the System

Submitted for the approval of Twilight Zone fans: a list of materials regarding Rod Serling's business affairs and the routine activities at the Serling home and office that were part of the success from Twilight Zone.

William Freedman of Beverly Hills was Serling's personal business manager and accountant. Nina Bruce was Freedman's secretary. Rod wrote out his own checks, but once a month sent his bank statement (after he checked it) to Nina. All bank deposit slips were sent to her with check stubs or a note explaining the deposit for their records. Freeman made a quarterly report regarding the finances of Cayuga Productions, including all cost factors incorporated into each television production. The Serlings deposited their money into numerous banks across Pacific Palisades and Beverly Hills, such as the Glendale Federal Savings, the Beverly Hills Federal Savings & Loan Association, and the Gibraltar Savings & Loan Association. Freedman handled the accounting, but the Serlings handled the funds earned from Cayuga Productions and other income from Serling's teleplays.

Serling's personal letterhead and envelopes were ordered through Beverly Stationers. The company delivered to his house or office any and all of the office supplies he requested. After much experimenting with the electronic typewriter, Serling chose two types of Eatons Corrasable Bond. #416-1 to use as his first ribbon copy, and #413-1 to use for all carbons.

IBM delivered ribbons and carbon paper quarterly on a yearly supply order. Carbons (five boxes quarterly) were intermediate weight, intense finish, Code 641. Ribbons (three quarterly) black nylon, "clean clip" style. The typewriter was under IBM service, under the company name, and received three regular inspections a year on a maintenance agreement. Whenever there were urgent problems, which was extremely rare, service representative Don Cockrell was called in.

The Cayuga production office was located at M-G-M Studios. Most correspondence between Cayuga and anyone else of a business nature went out on Cayuga stationery and the return address was either M-G-M or Ashley-Steiner. In order to maintain his privacy, his personal stationery never carried his residential address or his telephone number.

During the five years spanning *The Twilight Zone*, Serling had two secretaries. Patricia Riley Temple was his private secretary for three years. She had permission to drive the company car, a 1960 Mercury station wagon (temporary license #0385727), and handled much of his correspondence. Fan letters that were often generic and, on occasion, included story submissions, were tended to by Temple without Serling reviewing the submissions. The reply was often the same, thanking the viewer for their interest and apologizing for no interest in the story since all of the story material was purchased for the season. Depending on the time of year, Temple would change the excuse to informing the viewer that production and filming of the present season had already come to a close, and there was no certainty that the program would be renewed an additional season.

When Patricia Temple departed to the East in 1961, she was replaced by Connie Olmsted. Olmsted worked from her home and visited the Serling house twice a week to receive new secretarial assignments and pick up and deliver materials. Occasionally an unsolicited story submission was delivered to the house, and they were immediately forwarded to Del Reisman and Dick McDonagh, the story editors at M-G-M, to handle the rejections. Serling would, on occasion, read a submission made through an agent or a writer whose work he liked. Serling personally answered the submission and kept a record of the title for legal purposes.

Serling's publicity photos came from Picwood Camera, located then at Pico & Westwood Blvds. The company did not deliver; negatives were taken in and usually 100 prints at a time were ordered and picked up. One-hundred copies cost $48, plus tax, after a 20 percent discount for the bulk order. Serling had no charge account, so he paid by check.

Script folders, embossed, were ordered from California Bookbinding, located at 6369 Selma Avenue in Hollywood. Mr. Gausman in Hollywood handled the orders. (Red for *Twilight Zone* and black for motion pictures and other television scripts). They, too, were picked up.

Ashley-Steiner, Inc. in Beverly Hills represented Serling. The main contact was Ira Steiner, and his secretary was Kathy. They also paid bills and conducted other business for Cayuga Productions. Sam Kaplan was the agency lawyer and handled all of Cayuga's legal matters. Hene (pronounced Hen-ya) Bercovich was the bookkeeper. Alden Schwimmer was the local contact. The New York office at 579 Fifth Avenue was handled by Ted Ashley.

Carol Serling ran the household. Jessie Wheeler, the live-in maid, had Sundays and Mondays off. Harriet Burns came every Thursday and cleaned the office on that day. The gardener, Louis Gallegos, came on Monday, Wednesday and Friday. The pool man, George, came on the same days.

Serling had a passion for automobiles. Reaping the rewards for his hard labors, he was able to afford these luxuries. His auto club membership card was #D-20948. Ed Silvera at the local Texaco station took care of the cars. He usually came three times a week to wash them. Lynch Motors handled any major repairs. The Serling household also had dogs. Usually the Blue Cross Animal Hospital in the Palisades handled the grooming and care of Beau, an Irish Setter, and George, a beagle.

Playboy Gets Involved

In February of 1961, Charles Beaumont, who had a working relationship with the magazine, encouraged his friend Ray Russell to convince Rod Serling that submitting short fiction to *Playboy* might give the television series a few advantages. The primary reason was for publicity. Serling suggested submitting a few short story versions of forthcoming *Twilight Zone* scripts. A.C. Spectorsky, associate publisher and editorial publisher of *Playboy*, informed Serling that while this proposal could be arranged, the magazine would want to feature the story in their issue before the television version aired. This, naturally, would have put him in the position of submitting fiction on speculation and present a tricky matter of timing. Spectorsky suggested to him that submissions might be stories in mind or on paper that were not quite right for *The Twilight Zone*, but might be right for the monthly magazine.

In a letter to Spectorsky dated February 21, Serling commented, "I'm rather excited by the prospect. And after this hopeful note of beginning, I must temper this enthusiasm with a few mitigating and rather harsh realities. Writing speculatively for the magazine does not frighten me a bit, nor does it offend any deep-rooted sensitivities. Finding the time to do such is yet another story. This damned *Twilight Zone* occupied the bulk of my working day and just when I could sit down and try some other fiction." Serling filed the letter away, believing that if the door opened on his schedule, he would make a good-faith effort to compose a short fiction story for the magazine.

On August 26, in Interlaken, New York, he wrote to Spectorsky, rejecting the offer. "I had intended to create the world's greatest short story while sojourning here in the Finger Lakes, but as the fates would have it, I contracted for a new book with Bantam and since fiction writing is about as easy for me as poking hot butter up a wildcat's —, I'm afraid I must renege on my offer of submitting a short story, at least for the time being."

The Complications

"Once I asked to have two actors work for me and found out they were blacklisted and I couldn't use them," recalled Serling for a trade paper in late 1961. "In this case, we submitted their names to the network. The network told us that these two actors were not hirable and I found out later that one was a mistake in name, which happens all the time. In the other case it was a guy – you know – a little, two-bit walk-on that I wanted to use. I picked him because I liked his face, I didn't know what his politics were. And then all hell broke loose. The network knocked his name off the cast list. The agency said *they* didn't have a blacklist and yet these men remain un-hirable. So there must be somebody's list." In November of 1964, he recounted this same example, remarking "they only knew there was some sort of a cloud over them."

On occasion, Serling tried to fight the network about the content of his scripts, and the cast and crew who put the films together. But he rarely won. As he explained, "I'm not that kind of a crusader. I've got enough trouble trying to get this thing on the air. If I started to stop in my tracks and started fighting big social battles, I couldn't do it. This doesn't speak too well of any intrepid guts of mine, but it happens to be a fact. There isn't any time."

"Chuck Beaumont and I had a similar take on fantasy. I never made any social commentary in my *Twilight Zones*," recalled Richard Matheson to interviewer Matthew R. Bradley. "They were all just stories and character studies, whereas, very often, Serling's had a social commentary. I don't think Chuck Beaumont did that either – his were just plain stories, too, because when we were in print, with the stories we wrote for magazines, that's what they were. Once in a blue moon, I wrote a story ["Full Circle," first published in 1953] about a reporter who covers a puppet show. But it isn't a puppet show, it's little Martians doing 'Rip Van Winkle.' Then he goes back and interviews the leader of the 'living marionettes,' Larg, an older man who is very wise, tired and exhausted. So he writes this harsh story about the terrible plight of this little Martian. But his editor doesn't print any of it, so that was, obviously, social commentary. But I didn't do many of those, and unless I'm wrong, none for *The Twilight Zone*."

For the March 6, 1960 issue of *The New York Sunday News*, Serling explained that television writers "can for the most part, write only about things that are bland, conventional, safe and completely uncontroversial. He does a script, but before it goes before the cameras, the networks, the sponsors, the Madison Avenue and agency men tinker with it, censor it; so that by the time it's seen on the home screen a great deal or all of the real life juices have been squeezed out of it."

"I encountered censorship – sometimes picayune, in other instances important – until I began doing my own series, *The Twilight Zone*," Serling continued. "In this I have a free hand. But before that I learned: If your play, for example, is sponsored by Chevy, you can't have a character 'ford' a river."

The Six Taped Shows

Television shows recorded on tape and played back at the push of a button – once a laboratory dream – became a reality in 1957 when both CBS and NBC planned to put their tape recording machines to work on a regular schedule, taping live New York shows for rebroadcast on the West Coast three hours later. The two previous methods before the advent of videotape were to restage and perform the same drama a second time a few hours later, for a coast-to-coast hook-up, or to film the broadcast via kinescope. Sports events and news were videotaped, because the network found the method economical, but dramatic programs were trickier – involving unions and guilds and producer cooperation.

This all concerned itself with "live" telecasts and not filmed productions. But recording a television episode on videotape instead on 35mm film was a technological advancement predicted by the networks. CBS, like its competitors, had a financial stake in the cost of television production. When the advantages of videotape reduced those costs, the networks took a serious stance on expanding videotape production.

Videotape basically was an extension of the tape used in audio tape recorders. Besides transcribing onto tape TV's sounds, the videotape could also record the video, or sight signals. Thus, any show televised by standard live cameras could be recorded on tape in its entirety and rebroadcast almost immediately or stored for future use.

The beauty of videotape was that the picture quality was virtually as good as a live show. "The difference between videotape and a kinescope is the same as the difference between a scratchy old phonograph record and a new hi-fi recording," said one engineer. A complete swing over from film to tape would have required costly retooling of Hollywood's TV film studios, and no studio head was willing to pay out the huge amount of funds to make that transition.

Generally, tape saved networks and sponsors hundreds of thousands of dollars annually, money the networks claimed could be used elsewhere. Tape also had advantages and disadvantages – while the program could be edited on site and reviewed on screen (rather than wait for the film to be processed), the production could not be made on location. So each episode had to be taped in its entirety at a single studio.

When CBS, which had as much of a financial stake as Cayuga, decided to cut costs by recording entire episodes with a TV camera plugged into a videotape recorder, Houghton and Serling were not in favor of the experiment.

On August 12, 1960, while Rod Serling was in Interlaken, New York, he wrote to Houghton saying, "I do think that in terms of Beaumont's or Matheson's next script, or even mine after the Christmas thing, we should consider locales and themes which might lend themselves to tape. It appears very likely that we'll have to go into six of them whether we like it or not, if only to satisfy CBS's vast and ever present budget concerns. I had rather hoped we could hold down the film averages to such a great degree that taping would become academic. Unfortunately, though – and no one to blame either – this does not seem to be the case. I think we'll be fortunate to come in at a forty-nine figure as an average which, of course, pretty much makes mandatory our taping six shows at the end."

The decision was not a surprise, or random by choice. *The Twilight Zone* had a much higher budget than most of the dramatic prime-time programs. The late-night time slot meant the network did not favor the series too strongly to consider top quality an issue. Programs slated at an earlier time slot of say, 8 p.m., were strong contenders, designed to keep the audience tuned to the same network for the 9 p.m. show. Putting the best shows last at 10 p.m. was not a wise scheduling move, so experimenting with videotape on a program less critical than the early-evening programs was also a factor.

On September 24, 1960, Houghton sent an interoffice memo to Serling, explaining where they stood on the cost of production on the most recently completed episodes and a few of the ones to come. "'Acceleration' is tough to contain," he explained, "so is 'Reluctant Genius'... unless early ratings or reviews overwhelm CBS, I don't see how we can support a plea for film. It does no good to be dubious about tape costs for the peculiarities of *Twilight Zone* – CBS ain't dubious. Six tapes look like $42,000 in the bank to them [compared to the $70,000+ budget per episode]. I can't believe it, if I continue to make the quality-motivated decisions I have made in the past; but they do."

Russell Stoneham of CBS-TV in New York wrote to Serling on September 25, 1959, as the two remained good friends for a number of years. "As you know, I always had grave doubts about the wisdom of using tape to save money without an apparent concern for matching the creative quality of film," he explained to Serling. His judgment would prove to be correct because the productions were limited to the scope of a single studio, causing both critics and fans today to disregard the videotape productions as the program's lesser efforts.

"In those days, the 1960s, videotape was difficult to edit, actually," recalled director Jim Sheldon. "The process is simple today, but in those days the main reason *The Twilight Zone* was done on videotape was because CBS had built Television City [in Los Angeles] and had all that empty space. Since the program was partnered with Serling, rather than pay for the use of the M-G-M Studio facilities, they decided to cut costs by producing the episodes in their studio. Rod objected for various reasons and he was justified doing so. If we were to make a wrong cut back then, and we wanted to edit or tighten the film, we did not have the leeway that normally came when shooting on film. Tape had just come in and was useable, but not editable."

On November 2, in a letter to Guy Della Cioppa, Serling lodged a complaint against the network, claiming the problem was the network's preoccupation with profit and budget, "almost at the exclusion of program quality. Forcing *The Twilight Zone* into tape (the only show in the country to do so) cannot help but hurt the overall appearance of the show. I went along with it on advice from all sides, but I frankly hope that a renewal will not be forthcoming if it carries with it an obligation to do further taping rather than film."

"The six scripts set to videotape were not adventuresome, because they were limited to the square feet inside the studio," explained Jim Sheldon. "Of the ones I directed, 'The Whole Truth' was done completely in one large studio using three or four cameras. The entire story took place on the car lot. For 'Long Distance Call,' that was done on a set built with an upstairs and downstairs of the house. It was all there. Boy, when we filmed on M-G-M, the sets were more elaborate."

The impact of videotape on television and advertising, in addition to its many new applications in the fields of education and industry, had created a need for more advanced and flexible videotape facilities. Previously limited to use within the confines of the television studio, videotape productions were slowly starting to expand beyond the studio. To extend the scope and flexibility of videotape, IVT (International Video Tape Recording & Production, Inc.) sent Rod Serling an invitation to a dinner in Los Angeles, on Tuesday, November 22, 1960. Serling declined the invitation.

On November 21, 1960, Alden Schwimmer, representing director Alex March, submitted his client for Serling's approval. The previous season, March functioned as associate producer of the *NBC Sunday Showcase*, he also directed three of the programs, one of which was, "Murder and the Android," a futuristic piece by Alfred Bester. "I sincerely feel that Alex could do a hell of a job on *Twilight Zone*," Schwimmer explained. "His only lack is film experience and I don't know how much of a lack you feel that is." On November 29, Serling sent a polite reply, admitting he knew March very well, though not as a director. He worked with March years before on *Westinghouse Summer Theatre* and he thought then that March "was a most creative guy." Unfortunately, the letter had arrived too late. "We've only got three more shows to tape," Serling remarked, "and then we wind up until Spring and maybe forever. If the renewal is there, and if it comes in my terms, I'd like to consider Alex for a taping job. I doubt very much if I'd want to try him on film. We found over and over again that experience is of the essence when it comes to keeping a film show on budget and inexperience invariably winds us up on the red side of the book."

When production was completed for the six taped shows, it was decided not to tape any more, thus spoiling Alex March's efforts to direct an episode of *The Twilight Zone*.

On December 19, 1960, Serling told Dick Connelly and Owen Comora at Young & Rubicam that "we are now in the process of winding up our sixth taped show and I must tell you in all candor that the taped stuff is simply inferior to what we did on film. The Christmas show, for example, is an abomination and looks for all the world like a rough dress rehearsal that is a couple days from coming around. This, unfortunately, is not the exception to the rule – but seems to be the innate problem of the live show versus the film. I'm sure some anthology, whose action is principally an interior one, would take to tape naturally and well; *The Twilight Zone* desperately needs the flexibility and the perfection that comes with film."

The situation by December 1960 was this: the series was sold to General Foods and to Colgate on the basis of 16 films and six taped, with the renewal period calling for 10 additional tapes and three reruns. Serling went back to CBS and insisted that if a renewal came, it must be done at a reasonable budget, at least a thousand dollars more than the present operating status, and it must be done totally on film. CBS took his request under advisement and told him they would get back with a formal status shortly.

"I can't help but have noted a general decline in the quality of the series this season, Dick," Serling continued. "Where last year every third show seemed to be something special – this season we're lucky to hit one out of five – or so it seems. As to what are the contributing factors in this decline – I can only surmise. I think one of the problems is that I've written too much and for too protracted a period of time and that as a result my writing has become blunted and my perspective has become shot. I think perhaps this general dulling process is visible in the other areas of the production as well – principally the direction. It appears to me that the whole crew was just plain fagged out and that general fatigue showed up on the screen. I'm kind of an edict-type guy and too often my preoccupation with perfection is more of a hindrance than a help and this too, I think, has been one of the reasons that the series has suffered."

Serling confessed that while he wanted to give up on the series altogether, the financial rewards outweighed his decision of cancellation. Having by this time fulfilled his writing commitments for the current season; he risked losing the program in its entirety by lodging his issue about tape vs. film to CBS. "At the moment my feeling is that the network will not or cannot afford to put us back on film and that therefore, *The Twilight Zone* will fade into obscurity. I must say with further candor that I'm not altogether sure that this isn't what I'd prefer. It's been a back-breaking, torturous schedule, Dick, and both my health and my point of view have suffered irreparably as a result of it."

CBS gave Serling an offer to script a totally different anthology program, operating in an hour-long time slot, for the next season. He rejected the offer, because the demands on his health – and experience with *The Twilight Zone* earned him that lesson – required he take a break for a spell. "Upon serious perusal and after-thinking, it seems quite obvious that an hour show would be even twice as hard as doing *The Twilight Zone*," he explained to Ashley-Steiner on December 27.

Conflict Within The Zone

Censorship and the fight against videotaping future productions were not the only battlegrounds Serling fought during the month of December 1960. As a writer, he was subject to scrutiny by his peers and his friends. They had good reason, too, since he was under constant demands to "create" top-notch stories equivalent to about one script every two weeks. While almost any original story of fiction can be praised by television viewers and reviewers of the trades, a previously published story penned by another author could be brought out for comparison. Case in point, December 3, 1960. Charles Beaumont wrote a letter to Rod Serling, explaining how, after a number of months, he was getting tired of defending Serling from accusations of plagiarism.

"I don't believe you're a plagiarist," Beaumont wrote. "I have said so to you and to a great many other people and I have been saying it for almost a year. But, very frankly, the defense is becoming a bit hysterical; and again frankly, a bit hollow-sounding." What prompted Beaumont to write the letter was his viewing of the episode, "The Lateness of the Hour," which Beaumont found to be a copy of his published short story, "In His Image." Beaumont admitted that paths were bound to be re-traveled in a small cow pasture, and there was nothing new under the sun, but the telecast gave Beaumont a reason to express his feelings in the form of a letter.

Citing examples, Beaumont told Serling that "Walking Distance" was "a clear steal from Bradbury. The theme, the mood, the merry-go-round, the idea of a man going back in time and seeing himself as a child, the business of convincing his parents he is their son . . . all obviously Bradbury." For another first season episode, "The Lonely," Beaumont claimed Bradbury again, citing the short story "Marionettes, Inc." as being a possible influence, as well as his own short story, "Mother's Day," and William Nolan's "Joy of Living," about a robot which hungers for human compassion. "The After Hours" was another example, which Beaumont firmly believed was a take-off on John Collier's *Evening Primrose*. "I argued the plots were different," Beaumont explained, "but it was pointed out to me – again by several people, all outraged – that the theme of an animated mannequin was not at all general, that Collier made his reputation by coming up with fresh, new gimmicks, and that this is one of his best known stories."

For "Escape Clause," Beaumont claimed that his short story, "Hair of Dog," which was about a hypochondriac who made a deal with Satan, was the inspiration. In Serling's version, he is granted immortality and ends up with a life sentence for the crime of murder. In Beaumont's, he wishes for immortality but is instead, granted as many years of life as he had hairs on his head, after which he starts to go bald. "After this show, I was called by at least six people who spotted the nearness of the characters, mood, theme and plot," remarked Beaumont.

For "The Man in the Bottle," the premise of be-careful-what-you-wish-for story had been explored numerous times in W.W. Jacobs' "The Monkey's Paw" and was certainly public property, but when the hero wished for power, he became Adolph Hitler. In the published story, "The Howling Man," Beaumont's villain turned out to be Hitler, and Beaumont himself pointed this out in the letter.

"As I said at the beginning of this letter, I don't believe you are a plagiarist, Rod," Beaumont wrote. "But neither do I believe, any more, that it's coincidence. Instead, I think it's clearly the second half of my 'defense' – that you have assimilated a great deal of material and that some of it lodged deep in the works, whence spring all of our ideas, and that from time to time you are definitely drawing on someone else's literary account.

"When you get an idea, tell it to me, or to Dick, or to George, or to someone who knows the field. Any one of us could spot a 'source,' if such existed, and we'd all be delighted to serve. If a friend is a friend, he goes out on a limb occasionally. In telling you all of this straightforwardly, I'm climbing out to the tip of the tallest. Don't break the limb by taking it as anything but a sincere gesture of friendship."

The next afternoon, Beaumont had dinner with Serling, and while the dinner focused on *The Twilight Zone* and personal matters involving their families, Beaumont asked his friend not to open the letter till he got home. Serling agreed. On December 5, having read Beaumont's words, Serling composed an eight-page letter (after eight abortive attempts to compose a proper reply). Serling opened his letter thanking Beaumont for being "man enough and friend enough" to broach the subject to his face. No matter what Serling's reply stated and no matter what temper it would suggest, he respected Beaumont's act of friendship to take the guts and innate decency to write to him. Then Serling began to reject almost everything to which he was accused of and categorically deny the excuses that Beaumont took on Serling's defense.

"Number one, and first and foremost, I am not a plagiarist," Serling defended. "I have never stolen another writer's line, theme, dialogue, mood or concept. I have never knowingly put down on paper what is either the sum total of a fraction of another man's work. And when you say that I have consistently, through a process of some kind of osmosis and subconscious assimilation, taken other people's central ideas and unwittingly claimed them for my own is charitable but wholly euphemistic."

Serling took each of Beaumont's examples and explained, one-by-one, how they were not related to the teleplays in question. For Beaumont's "Hair of Dog," Serling admitted that he was totally unfamiliar with the story, and cited a number of short fiction in which a man strikes a deal with the Devil. As for "The Man in the Bottle" taking an unpleasant familiarity to "The Howling Man" because the villain turns out to be Hitler . . . "These two stories beyond the fact that they utilize the figure of Hitler as a symbol of evil, are absolutely, totally and down-the-line dissimilar." Serling's story was about a man who received three wishes. Beaumont's is the story about a man who seeks out the Devil, finally finds him and then discovers him to be Hitler.

"I think the allegations began and now are snow-balling to a point where if there is even the vaguest suggestion of similarity, I am now held up as suspect or worse, judged and condemned," Serling continued. Defending himself, Serling explained that he has been accused by two different people of theft. "The eminent Frank Gruber says that I copped the story from one of his and then you told me that Collier was suing me because it was close to his. I am frankly appalled, Chuck, at this particular revelation. How in Christ's name can Collier sue me when our stories are a world apart?"

"Evening Primrose" dealt with a girl who sought out the confines of a department store at night because she wanted to hide from society and found that a department store could make her self-sustaining. She discovered that other human beings had precisely the same idea and have set up a kind of strange night society. In "The After Hours," the television viewers watched a story that dealt specifically with a girl who assumed she was a human and then found out that she was a mannequin. Once a month each mannequin went out into society and lived as a human being until his or her turn is over, to be thereupon replaced by yet another mannequin. "If Mr. Collier feels in his heart that I can be sued for plagiarism on this score, I would welcome such a suit," Serling wrote. "He'd have about as much chance of winning it or even having it heard in a courtroom as I would have suing you because your script, 'Acceleration,' deals with breaking the sound barrier as did two stories of mine ten years ago." Collier, for the record, never sued Serling.

For "Walking Distance," Serling admitted that he was unfamiliar with any Bradbury story involved time travel and a merry-go-round. For "The Lonely," he admitted he never read "Marionettes, Inc.," and explained that the business of the prisoner on the asteroid had been done a hundred times. The concept of a robot who seeks human qualities had been copied in numerous distinct stories.

"I realize now what you must have been going through each Friday night when the calls came in and the people gathered and the chorus of accusations thundered down on you. That you defended me is an expression of faith that I bless you for," Serling concluded. "But obviously even in your own mind, you find that your defense is going stale, sagging around the middle from strain, and appearing with less and less conviction as each accusation is thrown. So it strikes me, Chuck, that you should stop the defense and perhaps, if your heart and mind dictates it to you, join in the accusations. It struck me that in your letter quite involuntarily and almost unconsciously, you had picked up a cudgel and already joined the chorus. But at least, Chuck, you had the grace, the manners and the manliness to bring it face to face. You did not dagger me to death in other people's kitchens and living rooms without my knowledge. That someone I thought was a friend is doing precisely this is a source of shock and hurt which I have not yet gotten over and probably won't for a long time to come."

"I had personal knowledge of this," recalled William F. Nolan in an article he wrote for *Outré*. "I recall that a letter from Rod was delivered late one night at Beaumont's home when I was present. Chuck opened the letter and read it aloud. It contained an abject apology from Serling for his inadvertent 'borrowing' of certain Beaumont stories. Chuck was very forgiving and phoned Rod that same evening, telling him not to worry, and that he understood how something like this could happen. As Chuck said to me later that night, 'I'd be crazy to make an issue out of this after all that Rod's done for me as a writer. I told him to forget it and I'd do the same.'"

With their friendship strengthened, Beaumont continued to defend Serling from the numerous people who claimed the young playwright was stealing ideas from past masters, and little – if nothing else – was brought up about the matter again. In private, Beaumont named a few people who were among the antagonists, one major influence being Ray Bradbury. Serling sat down to type a four-page letter to Bradbury, making sure not to mention Beaumont by name, which was also dated December 5. In the letter, Serling defended himself regarding the two cases of "plagiarism," namely "Walking Distance" and "The Lonely," in the same manner he explained to Beaumont. Serling then brought to light a number of issues in which Bradbury was claiming the television playwright was stealing ideas from other writers. The rumors had spread across town and to his ears, and Beaumont's letter prompted him to confront Bradbury, retaining a professional stance and admiration for the science fiction author.

"Some weeks ago, little things were said to me obliquely by mutual friends of comments made by you which were frankly both damning and accusative," Serling wrote. "I chose to slough these things off believing that if any such accusations festered inside you, you would not relegate them to cocktail conversation, but would rather bring them to me face to face and give me the opportunity to hear you out, listen to your judgments, and as two honorable men sit down and iron things out. . . . It is for this reason that your public assassination of my character in return without giving me the simple basic courtesy of telling me rather than others, is so shocking."

"And this final item which, if things that have been told me are to be believed, should delight you no end. A few days ago I resigned from CBS Television and gave up *The Twilight Zone*. In large measure, it was your accusations and those of a few others that were contributory to this decision. I did not realize that science fiction was so exclusive a fraternity that newcomers would suffer an entrance at their own risk and would take on a stigma of thieving Johnny-come-latelies because they had the temerity and the gall to enter this very private domain. The basic regret of all this, Ray, is not that you thought me a thief because in my heart of hearts I know that I'm no such thing. What is the most agonizing thing of all is that you did not see fit to make this accusation to me directly, but rather spread it around in other people's houses and in your own."

After receiving the letter, Ray Bradbury contacted Serling and the two discussed the accusations. Apologies were exchanged from both sides, and Serling did not give up *The Twilight Zone*. Instead, he told Bradbury to write an original teleplay and he would ensure that unlike Bradbury's previous attempts, the new submission would be produced. But during this time Serling was facing threatening lawsuits for plagiarism regarding "Long Distance Call," "Static" and "The After Hours," which were adding to his stress.

Respect between the storytellers remained strong throughout the series, even into the final season. When Serling won the Emmy award for the second year in a row, for outstanding writing, he acknowledged the primary contributors for the series publicly on the air. "To three writing gremlins named Charles Beaumont, George Clayton Johnson and Dick Matheson, who do much of the writing on the kooky *Twilight Zone*, many thanks fellas, come on over and we'll carve it up like a turkey."

End of Second Season

During negotiations, Serling won the battle against the network's insistence that videotaping future episodes would lower the budget. Instead of an order of 10 additional films, however, it was agreed that nine would be produced – and two of them, "The Rip Van Winkle Caper" and "A Hundred Yards Over the Rim," would be produced back-to-back to help offset the rising costs.

The earliest indication of a third season renewal was on February 27, 1961, when *The Hollywood Reporter* announced that "Sponsors are already talking a third season for *Twilight Zone*." This was news to Houghton and Serling, so on March 1, 1961, Houghton wrote to Guy Della Cioppa inquiring about a firm position on the status of a renewal. Asking Della Cioppa if he would consider the advisability of authorizing 10 advance scripts against the next season of *The Twilight Zone*, Houghton explained that "Rod is available at this moment to write and to play his considerable editorial part in the work of others." Serling had written a Broadway play and his commitment for the stage production would keep him away from *The Twilight Zone* during the latter half of July and all of August and September. No scripts had been stockpiled. "I want to remind you of the advantages to all financially, and the sponsors as well qualitatively, [that] if we have an early sale, [with] scripts ahead, and are able to start shooting for next season in May," Houghton explained. "CBS Sales might well press these advantages upon the attention of a potential sponsor. Production activity in Hollywood, and specifically at M-G-M, will be at an annual low . . . If the encouraging rumors that reach me, Guy, are even likely, much less true, that *The Twilight Zone* will be on next season, I urge you to authorize a small gamble that will pay off handsomely."

The March 8, 1961 issue of *The Hollywood Reporter* then featured a much lengthier blurb about the possibility of a renewal:

Best indication that Rod Serling's *Twilight Zone* will shoo-in for a third season is the fact that producer Buck Houghton isn't thinking about other project offers, even though he has but nine more segs to roll for wrapping the current skein. Through two seasons, Houghton's kept all his opportunity eggs in the 'Zone' basket because he unabashedly feels Serling's is one of the few prestige weekly series around, a pardonable point of pride since critics are unanimous in echoing those sentiments – not to mention the fact that Houghton can't think of one star or director who hasn't wanted to come back for seconds on the series. Burgess Meredith, for instance, who oftener than not has refused to leave his Gotham hideout for guesting pleas here, will eagerly wing in soon for his third 'Zone.' Not one to pass this Buck, Serling's large measure of respect for Houghton's efforts is proved by the fact that he's insisted on no 'executive producer' crawl credit so's no one will underestimate Houghton's major contribution to the series.

In early-to-mid March, Malcolm Stuart, an agent from Preminger-Stuart-Feins Agency representing both Beaumont and Matheson, spent a few hours with Serling at Beaumont's house. He wanted to arrange for both Matheson and Beaumont to write five episodes for the third season. Since CBS had yet to give them notice of a renewal, Serling asked to wait until a renewal came in.

When Bob Williams of *The New York Post* contacted Serling by phone in early March, attempting to get verification of *Twilight Zone*'s renewal, he wrote back on March 13 with the following confirmation: "It does appear *The Twilight Zone* will stay alive for another season. I don't know whether to cheer or cut my wrists. But I did want to assure you of how deeply appreciative I am of your interest and willingness to give us a hand."

By May of 1961, the series was granted a renewal, regardless of Serling's public comments of the past that he was tired and would be happy to quit. Houghton told reporters, "Rod says he wants to quit and enjoy himself, but he can't. He'll have a new idea for a story, and shortly we'll have a completed script. He just has to write."

With CBS concerned over the cost of productions, Houghton's insistence that an early commitment for a renewal of a third season would offset rising costs seemed to please the network. Liggett & Myers also signed on for sponsorship, on alternating weeks, for the third season, helping to reaffirm the network's confidence (and the sponsor pretty much cinched a verbal agreement that Serling would be filmed for additional testimonials for the camera sometime during the third season). But rushing into production caused a number of complications. With nine additional films in the can, and only seven slots for telecast (partly because CBS was late in ordering the additional films and it took time to shoot the episodes), two of the productions were shelved for use on the third season – "Nothing in the Dark" and "The Grave."

Serling felt that each episode should be told in a tight, crisp, 30-minute format, with "one miracle to a customer." Producer Houghton was under the guidelines that, as Rod had said, "If we've got to explain things we're in deep trouble." Houghton admitted once that he did receive a number of letters from viewers complaining that they failed to understand the ending or that the important segment hadn't been sufficiently clear. "I believe in playing fair," Houghton explained to a reporter for *The Salina (Kansas) Journal*. "We generally make our point by telling it twice. I do admit that a viewer has to pay attention and he can miss something by going to the refrigerator for a beer."

"The fact a man is on Mars is enough for a 30-minute show," Houghton continued. "Then comes the point of drama. If we had to explain and explain we couldn't hold the audience. Now I'm not a writer, but I have a feeling the writing is easier on this series because we have fewer restrictions. We say, 'here's a man who can change his face at will,' and then we move into the story. My suspicion is that doing a story in this vein takes the wraps off a writer's imagination."

An oil man by profession once told Houghton, "What I like about the series is that I find myself thinking about what goes on after the story is over."

According to a progress report dated June 12, 1961, Rod Serling was attempting to buy two literary properties for adaptation for *The Twilight Zone*: "A Length of Rope" by Chester S. Geier and "None Before Me" by Sidney Carroll.

Original Intention

On March 8, 1961, Buck Houghton drew up a release schedule for the remainder of the second season, the summer run, and the third season openers.: the following below is that proposal:

Proposed Release Schedule

Sequence	Air Date	Title	Sponsor
1	4-7-61	"A Hundred Yards Over the Rim"	Liggett & Myers
2	4-14-61	"The Mighty Casey" (rerun)	Colgate
3	4-21-61	"The Rip Van Winkle Caper"	Liggett & Myers
4	4-28-61	"The Silence"	Colgate
5	5-5-61	"Shadow Play"	Liggett & Myers
6	5-12-61	"The Mind and the Matter"	Colgate
7	5-19-61	*pre-emption*	Liggett & Myers
8	5-26-61	"Nobody Here But Us Martians"*	Colgate
9	6-2-61	"Nothing in the Dark"	Liggett & Myers
10	6-9-61	"Where is Everybody?" (rerun)	Colgate
11	6-16-61	"Perchance to Dream" (rerun)	Liggett & Myers
12	6-23-61	"I Shot An Arrow Into the Air" (rerun)	Colgate
13	6-30-61	"Escape Clause" (rerun)	Liggett & Myers
14	7-7-61	"A World of Difference" (rerun)	Colgate
15	7-14-61	"The Fever" (rerun)	Liggett & Myers
16	7-21-61	"The Purple Testament" (rerun)	Colgate
17	7-28-61	"Elegy" (rerun)	Liggett & Myers
18	8-4-61	"Mirror Image" (rerun)	Colgate
19	8-11-61	"One for the Angels" (rerun)	Liggett & Myers
20	8-18-61	"The Big, Tall Wish" (rerun)	Colgate
21	8-25-61	"Nightmare as a Child" (rerun)	Liggett & Myers
22	9-1-61	"The Chaser" (rerun)	Colgate
23	9-8-61	"A World of His Own" (rerun)	Liggett & Myers
24	9-15-61	"The Grave"	Colgate
25	9-22-61	"The Obsolete Man"	Liggett & Myers

"Where is Everybody?" was the first episode aired during the summer rerun. Rod Serling was filmed on camera for a trailer promoting the episode on "next week's program," and the trailer featured a clip of the empty town. According to a release schedule dated August 25, 1960, this episode was supposed to be broadcast on November 25, 1960, but CBS instead aired an hour-long special on that date. On August 24, 1961, Allen Parr drew up a release schedule for the opening months of the third season.

Proposed Release Schedule

Sequence	Air Date	Prod. No.	Title	
1	9-29-61	4803	"The Shelter"	*variety*
2	10-6-61	4817	"The Passersby"	Liggett & Myers
3	10-13-61	4815	"A Game of Pool"	*variety*

---

* Production title for "Will the Real Martian Please Stand Up?"

4	10-20-61	4819	"The Mirror"	Liggett & Myers
5	10-27-61	3656	"The Grave"	*variety*
6	11-3-61	4804	"Deaths-Head Revisited"	Liggett & Myers
7	11-10-61	4818	"The Midnight Sun"	*variety*
8	11-17-61	4820	"Once Upon A Time"	Liggett & Myers
9	11-24-61	4801	"It's a Good Life"	*variety*
10	12-1-61	4806	"The Jungle"	Liggett & Myers
	12-8-61	pre-emption	*Westinghouse Special*	*variety*
11	12-15-61	4808	"Still Valley"	Liggett & Myers
12	12-22-61	4805	"Five Characters in Search…"	*variety*
13	12-29-61	3662	"Nothing in the Dark"	Liggett & Myers
14	1-5-62	4809	"A Quality of Mercy"	*variety*
15	1-12-62	4816	"The Fugitive"	Liggett & Myers

Days later, Serling and Houghton, having looked over the list, made revisions, so in late August, a revised schedule was composed, reprinted below.

Proposed Release Schedule

Sequence	Air Date	Prod. No.	Title	Sponsor
1	9-15-61	4802	"Two"	Colgate
2	9-22-61	4803	"The Shelter"	Liggett & Myers
3	9-29-61	4817	"The Passersby"	*variety*
4	10-6-61	4814	"The Arrival"	Liggett & Myers
5	10-13-61	4804	"Deaths-Head Revisited"	*variety*
6	10-20-61	3656	"The Grave"	Liggett & Myers
7	10-27-61	4819	"The Mirror"	*variety*
8	11-3-61	4818	"The Midnight Sun"	Liggett & Myers
9	11-10-61	xxxx *	"Once Upon a Time"	*variety*
10	11-17-61	4806	"The Jungle"	Liggett & Myers
11	11-24-61	4815	"A Game of Pool"	*variety*
12	12-1-61	4801	"It's a Good Life"	Liggett & Myers
	12-8-61	pre-emption	*Westinghouse Special*	*variety*
13	12-15-61	4808	"Still Valley"	Liggett & Myers
14	12-22-61	4805	"Five Characters in Search…"	*variety*
15	12-29-61	3662	"Nothing in the Dark"	Liggett & Myers
16	1-5-62	4809	"A Quality of Mercy"	*variety*
17	1-12-62	4816	"The Fugitive"	Liggett & Myers

---

* "Once Upon a Time" had not been assigned a production number at the time this schedule was drawn up. Of the 17 titles scheduled above, 15 of them never aired on the dates originally proposed. "Five Characters in Search of an Exit" was a Christmas episode, so the December 22 date was set in stone. Serling easily convinced Buck Houghton that the festive episode should air for the pre-Christmas broadcast spot. Buck Houghton, however, mentioned in a letter that "Nothing in the Dark" should be broadcast before the end of the year because the film was made during the second season, and financial paperwork carrying over the costs of the production needed to be eliminated.

The initial intention was to begin the season premiere on September 29, along with the rest of the CBS lineup that premiered that season, *Ichabod & Me* and *Father of the Bride*. According to Buck Houghton in an interoffice memo, the contention was that if two good episodes were already telecast before CBS premiered the new season of prime-time shows, the jump-start might be beneficial and keep the viewers tuned in for the remainder of the season.

John McGiver poses for the camera in between takes of "Sounds and Silences."

CHAPTER SEVEN

The Third Season

The October 1961 issue of *Show* magazine hailed the return of the third season as "one of the great favorites, and for good reasons. The show offers good scripts, impeccable choice of material, and always sound casting. Beyond that, it often soars beyond mere fact and everyday fiction into the supernatural, depositing the viewer in a cloudland where reality gets turned inside out. For the jaded soul, the fresh view can have remarkable restorative effects."

In the November 28, 1961 issue of *Show Business Illustrated*, Serling committed during a candid conversation with the magazine. When asked if he was satisfied with the series as his only outlet on television, Serling replied, "I think it ran out last year, although it will be with us another season. I'm tired of it – as most people are when they do a series for three years. I was tired after the fourth show. It's been a good series. It's not been consistently good, but I don't know of any one series that is consistently good when you shoot it in three days. We've been trying gradually to get away from the necessity of a gimmick, but the show has the stamp of the gimmick and it's looked for now. It's tough to come up with them, week after week. . . . In terms of a track record I would guess that a third of them have been pretty damn good shows. Another third have been passable. Another third are dogs – which I think is a little bit better batting average than the average film show. But to be honest, it's not as good as we thought or expected it might be."

Earlier that same month, Serling talked to a staff correspondent of *The New York Morning Telegraph*, expressing his desire to close the door on *The Twilight Zone* after the third season. "The 36-year-old creator-writer of the CBS program has simple, honest reasons that are refreshing in the midst of the TV rate race: he takes pride in quality. And he is running out of material," the article reported.

"This is our third year, and it seems like 10 or 11 to me," he commented. "The first year is kind of a vacation – exciting. The second is like a vacation without pay. The third is just a tough grind, trying to come up with material." So why did the show continue for a third year? "I have no choice," he explained. "It's half-owned by the network, and as long as somebody wants to buy it, we're in business."

"If only I could take off for about six months and replenish the well. But I guess all of us who complain, including me, get a little idiotic saying we want to quit. We never had it so good. We're well paid for our fatigue." Serling's wish was granted when CBS did not renew the series for a fourth season, giving him a few months to visit Ohio in search of a teaching job.

In December of 1961, columnist John Phillips analyzed *One Step Beyond* and *The Twilight Zone*, which he described as "two shows with similar themes." While each dealt with supernatural occurrences, the difference was that *One Step Beyond* was real, inasmuch as each presentation involved a documented, although almost — if not altogether — unbelievable incident, or series of incidents. Material was created to weave the recounting into a whole and presentable story. The other, *The Twilight Zone*, was wholly made up of figments of imagination. Phillips felt that *One Step Beyond* was "a more fascinating, enthralling series" than *The Twilight Zone* and was annoyed that the series was canceled, leaving *The Twilight Zone* on its continued course on CBS.

Before the third season completed airing the initial telecasts, word already spread that *The Twilight Zone* was not going to be picked up for an additional season. Serling had said publicly he wanted to take *The Twilight Zone* off the air at the end of the season because it had gone astray from what he originally conceived it to be.

Because no sponsor signed on for a fourth season, the series was not included in the fall schedule. Houghton accepted an offer to work for Four Star Productions on the new *The Richard Boone Show*. Serling accepted a teaching job at his alma mater, which would take up most of his time from September 1962 to January 1963.

"My title will be 'writer in residence.' That means I will be free to devote my time to writing when I'm not teaching," explained Serling to Vernon Scott, a columnist for UPI. "Carol and I graduated from Antioch and we're anxious to get back to small town living." He became a member of the faculty for about five months beginning in September at Antioch College, lecturing on play writing and the history of mass media, radio and television.

"I have three reasons," Serling explained. "First is extreme fatigue. Secondly, I'm desperate for a change of scene, and third, is a chance to exhale with the opportunity for picking up a little knowledge instead of trying to spew it out. . . . I might die in limbo from lack of activity. But if I don't take this step now I never will. At the moment, my perspective is shot. I think that is evident at times in the lack of quality in some of the *Twilight Zone* scripts. And, frankly, I'd like to be able to do my best work all the time. Who wouldn't?"

In the June 1963 issue of *Writer's Digest*, Serling was asked what his intention was for his teaching course. "I didn't try to 'teach' writing because it cannot be taught. There has to be innate talent and all we can do with this talent is sharpen, broaden it, let it find its own level. The one thing I pushed constantly was style. If there is so-called truth in any writing it is precisely this – the writer's style."

"The bulk of the episodes were written by Rod," Houghton recalled, "and by the end of the third year, he was getting a bit pooped! We also had some fine scripts from people such as Richard Matheson and E. Jack Neuman. As a producer, I knew how lucky I was to be getting these kinds of scripts. You hardly ever ran into that caliber of writing."

"My show died an unlamented death at CBS," Serling continued. "But odds are pretty good we may go for an hour *Twilight Zone* next January or perhaps in September of 1963. I've already written three shows and have two others ready to go."

While Serling was in New York beating the drums for the motion picture, *Requiem for a Heavyweight*, he chatted with newspaper columnist Harvey Pack of the *Waterloo* (Iowa) *Daily Courier*. He explained that in Hollywood he was not really a celebrity but in Yellow Springs, Ohio, people noticed him. "My little girl even said to me last week that she'd like to go out for a soda with me without people staring at us. But in Hollywood I had a different experience. She came home one day and said that one of her classmates had given out autographed pictures of his dad. It turned out to be Jim Arness. I jokingly suggested that she give out my picture and she said, 'Who'd know you?' So you see fame is simply a matter of geography."

By June 30, 1962, the usual monthly statement of cash receipts and disbursements of the non-production cash account of Cayuga Productions was drawn up, revealing the financial end of the corporation's profits. Rerun fee income alone totaled $46,357.38.

Exit Liggett & Myers Tobacco Company

In January of 1962, Rod Serling had received a solid gold Zippo from Liggett & Myers as a token of their appreciation for the hard work he put into the filmed cigarette testimonials. Towards the end of the third season, when word that the program was officially canceled, Lawrence W. Bruff, vice president of Liggett & Myers, wrote to him on March 16, 1962. Bruff was an upstater himself from Ithaca, New York, and perhaps had more than a normal interest in Cayuga Productions. "One of the strange parts of the television end of this business is that a satisfied client very seldom these days has any say at all as to whether a program in which he is interested will stay put in its time period. Personally, I think *Twilight Zone* is one of television's really rewarding moments and I liked it at 10:00 o'clock on Friday. It is different for us to consider *Twilight Zone* on a 52-week basis in a 7:30 time period, so we must exit. I regret it deeply."

On March 22, Serling replied, "I share your disappointment in the termination of our association. In all sincerity I can say that it has been a most satisfying, and tremendously rewarding, relationship – and one that I'm quite certain I'll be hard pressed to see duplicated in future projects. I do, of course, understand your company's feelings in terms of the earlier time slot for *Twilight Zone*. I, myself, had hoped we would remain in the ten o'clock Friday slot, where we seemed reasonably well entrenched with, if not the largest bulk audience available – at least a healthy and loyal coterie of viewers that would have remained with us."

Liggett & Myers continued sponsoring the series throughout the third season and the summer of reruns.

Summer Reruns Between Third and Fourth Season

On March 30, 1962, a schedule was drawn up, using input from Rod Serling and Buck Houghton, as to which half-hour episodes were to be rerun during the summer hiatus. On April 24, a revised table was drawn up (reprinted below) for Allen Parr of CBS Television in Los Angeles. One noticeable difference with the summer reruns was the broadcast of June 15, titled "A Private World of Darkness," which was formerly "Eye of the Beholder." Due to the conflict with General Electric, Cayuga went through additional expense to change the title during the closing credits, and the repeat broadcast reflected that change.

1. "The Odyssey of Flight 33"
2. "A Private World of Darkness"
3. "King Nine Will Not Return"
4. "The Trouble with Templeton"
5. "Dust"
6. "The Howling Man"
7. "A Most Unusual Camera"
8. "People Are Alike All Over"
9. "Nick of Time"
10. "The Silence"
11. "The Night of the Meek"
12. "The Obsolete Man"
13. "The Whole Truth"
14. "Hundred Yards Over the Rim"
15. "The Invaders"

The March 30 draft originally had "A Thing About Machines" in the 10th slot, but Serling, dissatisfied with the finished product, requested it be removed from the reruns, and instead, what was in the 11th position moved up to 10th, adding "The Invaders" at the bottom of the list. The first two episodes were permanent, agreed to by everyone, because of the publicity department's efforts.

WBNS-TV in Columbus

Trading in the fantasies of *The Twilight Zone* for the harsh realities of Hollywood flicks, beginning the evening of September 27, 1962, Serling premiered as host of WBNS-TV's new *10 O'Clock Theater*. Not only did he introduce recent, first-time-on-local-TV movies on the show, but he also made comments on what made them unusual film fare. A representative of WBNS contacted him in June of 1962 and then proposed the idea in writing on June 25.

Ohio State University Ph.D. candidate Dave Parker did all the research, sent it to Serling, who then wrote the scripts he would use for the taped introductions. Each movie aired Thursday night beginning 10 p.m. and usually ran until 15 minutes after midnight. The movie would stop at 11 p.m., when he announced a 15-minute rest stop for the 11 p.m. news, weather and sports. After the news, the feature continued. Classic movies included *East of Eden* (1955), *Young at Heart* (1954), *I Confess* (1953), *Force of Arms* (1951), *The Bad and the Beautiful* (1952) and *Captain Horatio Hornblower R.N.* (1951).

"The Time Element" Movie

From October to December of 1962, Rod Serling exchanged a number of correspondences with actor Kirk Douglas, proposing to work a joint venture for a motion picture adapted from the teleplay, "The Time Element." His intention was to have John Frankenheimer direct. Having sold the script to Desilu for production and broadcast on the former *Westinghouse* program, Serling asked Sam Kaplan of Ashley-Steiner to secure permission from Desilu. On January 11, 1963, Kaplan sent a formal request and on January 15, Bernard Weitzman of Desilu Productions called Kaplan to discuss the project. On January 16, executives at Desilu exercised its first refusal rights to any motion picture, per the original 1958 contract. "After discussing your request to waive our rights, it was Desilu's feeling that what Rod Serling intends to use in his original concept for the feature film to star Kirk Douglas, is the main theme and most important element of 'The Time Element' script," wrote Weitzman. "Therefore, unless we can see how he intends to use the material in the actual shooting script, it is difficult to determine how extensive the similarity may be. If Rod's people feel there is no similarity, and proceed to do the picture without first offering us the deal, then he assumes the risk of any subsequent consequences."

The Twilight Zone Spin-Off

In preparation for the hour-long season, Rod Serling wanted to adapt "A Child is Crying," a short story by John D. MacDonald, which was originally published in the December 1948 issue of *Thrilling Wonder Stories*. The story is about Billy, a child super-genius who not only is more knowledgeable than any other human, he has extraordinary powers and can see the future. He comes into the hands of the U.S. Military which discovers he is an evolutionary answer to atomics, designed to save the world from militaristic nuclear wars.

On October 2, 1962, Alden Schwimmer of Ashley-Steiner wrote to Serling, explaining that the literary property was currently controlled by Mort Abrahams through a previous deal with Coogamooga, Pat Boone's production company. Abrahams owned the rights to the story, having purchased it for adaptation for the television anthology, *Tales of Tomorrow*. The story had been dramatized previously on August 17, 1951. According to Abrahams, "something like $15,000" had already been invested. While this made it difficult for him to purchase the story as a single-shot television program as he intended, Abrahams proposed a counter-offer – to use the story as a spin-off on *Twilight Zone*. According to Schwimmer, "You might ask a spin-off for what, and the only answer that I could give you is a science fiction anthology."

Schwimmer admitted that while he saw no demand for a science fiction anthology, especially with *Twilight Zone* presently sitting in the wings, "if we could do it without much cost, get a good *Twilight Zone* out of it, and have a chance for another series – why not? What it would take is the additional money for an original opening and closing and perhaps the hiring of somebody to serve as host. Mort's interest is obviously in being proprietor of the new series. I am not sure the script is worth all the effort, but here it is."

December 1962 Drunk Driving Campaign

In the fall of 1962, the state of New York's Department of Motor Vehicles decided to prepare a December campaign for the holiday season, when residents of both state and city celebrate with a few drinks. "The real problem in traffic safety is not the out-and-out drunk, but the fellow who has had just enough to feel like a king," wrote Robert Shelford of New York's public information office. "The fellow who is high must learn to recognize – while in his state of intoxication – that his judgment and reflexes are impaired no matter how good he feels. He must recognize that if he is going to drive, despite his impairment, he must compensate for that impairment by being extra cautious, rather than yielding to feelings of reckless joy."

Confrontation with a ghost in "Ring-A-Ding Girl."

In October of 1962, Shelford approached Serling, inquiring whether the creator of *The Twilight Zone* could help them with the December campaign to try to reduce the traffic accidents attributable to drinking and driving. "We believe that the dangers of driving with just a few drinks can be emphasized through use of the expression 'Two Drink Twilight Zone'," explained Shelford.

Shelford originally wanted him to provide a master film, if he could make a visit to New York, but a hectic schedule would not allow the time. Instead, an audio tape of Rod Serling was made, lasting about 16 seconds. The message was seen in adjoining states and was used on some networks, with filmed footage of automobiles, highways and alcohol. The message was delivered to all television stations in the state of New York without regard for network affiliation.

This is Rod Serling. The Twilight Zone is a world of fantasy – occasionally a pleasant world. But for drivers, the alcohol Twilight Zone is a world of danger. Don't kid yourself. You're not a better driver with a couple of drinks – you're a menace. The Two Drink Twilight Zone is a danger zone – keep out.

CHAPTER EIGHT

The Fourth (Hour-Long) Season

In a letter dated November 9, 1959, Serling told a fan, "Many thanks for your kind card. I hope you stick with *The Twilight Zone* because I think the shows get better and better. I share your wish that it would be an hour show but the Gods and the network were of another mind."

Answering another fan letter on September 12, 1960, Serling explained why the show was not broadcast in an hour-long treatment. "I share your feeling as to the length of *The Twilight Zone*. I, too, would prefer the hour format, but unfortunately the network has only the half-hour available."

The expansion from a half-hour format to an hour was discussed between CBS and producer Buck Houghton toward the end of the second season. In a newspaper column in *The Post-Standard* penned by columnist Charles Witbeck, dated May 14, 1961: "There was a rumor *The Twilight Zone* would stretch out to an hour next season, but this has been dispelled. 'I was very anxious when I first heard it,' said Houghton. 'I think we and the public are better off with our present limit.'"

The May 23, 1961 issue of *The Salina (Kansas) Journal* reported the same news, verifying that the network had insisted on an hour-long format before the initial telecasts of the second season's episodes were completed. The hour-long format did not become a reality, however, until after the third season.

Serling began preproduction for the hour-long series with an episode called "The Thirty Fathom Grave" as early as March of 1962 – when he commissioned the De Forest Research Company to investigate the logistics of a destroyer locating a submarine. "If ocean depth is from 75 to 250 feet and there is sandy bottom, then the destroyer's sonar equipment can pick up the shape of an object and determine if it is metal," explained the report. "When ship's screws are stopped it can also hear voices or noises in a submarine or sunken vessel." The research report sent to him also gave a sample of the dialogue for a sonar operator noting an object on his sonar equipment, pointing out the fact that the captain went to the sonar shack and determined whether to investigate, and the procedure by which the captain and crew would handle a situation if he felt it worthy of investigation. The same report explained how a deep sea diver would approach the sub and the procedure for reporting back to the ship via underwater telephone, which worked liked a walkie-talkie and had no wires.

The May 29, 1962 issue of *The New York Times* reported that "although the present series of half-hour fantasies is not scheduled to continue next fall, the Columbia Broadcasting System television network and Mr. Serling are discussing plans to film a series of hour-long shows. The expanded version of *Twilight Zone* would go on the air possibly midway of the 1962-63 season or in the fall of 1963. Both Mr. Serling and CBS confirmed last week that negotiations were in progress."

"We are very close to an agreement," said Serling to columnist Val Adams. "We're working out a deal and I think we will make one," said Hubbell Robinson, senior vice president of programs for CBS-Television. It was reported, however, that at least one major issue remained to be settled. He wanted CBS to commit itself of nearly $2,000,000. For the time being, the network preferred to finance an hour-long pilot film and a few scripts to be held in readiness."

When asked why the expanded format, Serling explained, "It would give us a chance for much more probing in the story line. We could put much more emphasis on character. Right now we have to emphasize plot." According to a *New York Times* article, he had received "several thousand letters of protest" from viewers since it had become known the show would not be on the air next fall, even with the chance of making an appearance in an hour-long format.

In December of 1960, Serling had submitted to Buck Houghton a number of proposals for other television programs, asking him to look over them for a valued opinion and to verify whether he wanted to go in on a joint venture for filming the pilots. One was a prison series, which Houghton commented, "I think it is less than is expected of you, and less than you expect of yourself." Serling also proposed a weekly hour anthology titled "Serling Presents 60" or "The Serling Sixty," meant to capture the essence of *Playhouse 90*. Houghton did not dismiss the idea, but remarked that "such an effort by Cayuga would call for an increase in the organization size and a full-time job from you, without excursions into book writing, Broadway or anything else, for the production period of fifty weeks." Houghton explained that if he truly wanted to take on such a project, he should consider producing only four out of every nine teleplays, while the remaining five would be produced from loosely allied organizations such as Four Star, Spartan and Sheldon Leonard. *

This notion never came to be, and by spring of 1962, Serling had accepted the position at Antioch, leaving Houghton to find another job elsewhere. Houghton had been offered a position as producer for two television series being planned at ZIV-UA the year before, *Small Town D.A.* and *The Everglades*. Houghton was not impressed with the script of *Small Town D.A.*, and having learned that ZIV Television wanted to speed up the process of finishing the pilot, backed down. As for *The Everglades*, he knew nothing about it except the novelist and short story writer who was dramatizing the series.

In April of 1962, Houghton was making his departure from *The Twilight Zone* after serving three faithful years. CBS took its time settling with the vital details of when the series would return, and Houghton, unclear of his immediate future, decided to accept a job producing a new program in development, *The Richard Boone Show*. Boone was leaving the CBS western, *Have Gun – Will Travel*, for a chance to work on a television repertory company series that, each week, employed the same cast of actors playing different roles. Houghton moved over to NBC for the task, leaving the producing chair empty for the fourth season – if the network were to renew the program.

In accordance with the employment agreement between Houghton and Cayuga Productions, dated April 17, 1961, Houghton was entitled to a percentage of the profits derived from the reruns

---

* It is possible that Serling, at one time, planned to do a series of 90-minute anthology films to be shot in England, according to one interoffice memo.

of the *Twilight Zone* broadcasts. With respect to the programs produced for the initial network broadcast during the 1959-60 and the 1960-61 television seasons, he was entitled to an number equal to 5 percent of the net profits. With respect to the third season (1961-62), Houghton was titled to 10 percent of the net profits. *

On May 8, 1962, Serling told Hubbell Robinson that "I'm struggling to keep a nucleus of my staff, including our unit man, Ralph W. Nelson, and our cameraman, George Clemens, plus at least one of our cutters. The earlier you can come up with a decision, the more secure I'll feel in turning out a qualitative product." Having lost Buck Houghton, Serling assured the network that the best men working for him would also be finding other jobs if a renewal guarantee was not given. Serling himself, having been uncertain of the series' future, had accepted the college teaching job at Antioch. His term would begin in the fall, giving him a few months to finish necessary paperwork related to the closing of the *Zone*'s third season and to complete production on the 13 hour-long shows before leaving for college. **

In April of 1962, negotiations were underway for the new hour-long series. Under the old half-hour deal, ownership of the films remained in Cayuga's holdings, and profits were divided 50-50 with the network. CBS had agreed to charge the "Cavender is Coming" pilot against the third season's financial paperwork, giving Cayuga a clean slate to start with for the fourth season.

Under a new deal, which would override the previous legal agreements (except for the financial arrangements), Cayuga would deliver two sample one-hour scripts to CBS, the first no later than May 18, 1962, and the second no later than June 1. CBS had 30 days following delivery of the second script to order a minimum of 13 one-hour episodes. If CBS failed to give notice within a month, the network forfeited all rights to the program, except for the former half-hour series, and Serling and Cayuga had the right to look for another network.

Naturally, CBS did order 13 episodes and optioned to start the hour-long series as a mid-season replacement, with a commitment date no later than April 5, 1963. If the network chose to premiere the hour-long series in the beginning of the 1962-63 season, a minimum of 26 episodes were to be ordered by the network, and the order for an additional 13 would be delivered no later than November 1. If the hour-long series were to be picked up for additional seasons, a minimum of 26 episodes were guaranteed to be ordered by the network, and the contract stipulated options for a second, third and fourth season.

CBS had the option within each contract year to require additional production beyond 26 programs for up to a maximum of nine additional and a total yearly maximum of 35 programs. Rod Serling's personal obligation to the series consisted of rendering services as host and executive producer on all programs produced, and would primarily be involved in the script area. He would contractually be obligated to write a minimum of four episodes out of the first 13 in any one year, and if yearly production went beyond 13, and not more than 26, he would write a minimum total of

---

* On February 24, 1964, Sam Kaplan handled the royalties as contracted and Houghton's first royalty check was payable in the amount of $4,909.59, representing his share of profits received by Cayuga Productions to date.

** While in Yellow Springs, Ohio, the Serling household took advantage of an invitation from Stephen Kelley, curator at the Columbus Municipal Zoo. The zoo was closed for the season, and not scheduled to re-open until April 13. "It is my wish that you take advantage of this invitation now while we are closed, believing this might better satisfy your desire for privacy.... We can show you a world of animals which the casual visitor seldom sees."

six episodes. If the yearly production exceeded 26, he would be obligated to write a minimum yearly total of eight. Cayuga had the right to employ him to write as many additional scripts beyond the minimum guarantee.

In the premiere issue of *Gamma* magazine, dated 1963, Serling was interviewed by the publisher and editor, Charles E. Fritch, and asked how large a contribution he made toward the script writing for the series. "Under my contract I had to write 80 percent of the first two season's shows. Now the pressure is off, which is a helluva big help. The grind was more than I'd bargained for. As exec producer as well as writer I had to sweat out all kinds of stuff – ratings, set costs, casting, locations, budgets . . . Time was a luxury. If I dropped a pencil and stooped to pick it up I was five minutes behind schedule."

Also, under contract, he would be prohibited from performing as host on any continuing basis for any other series. He could not render continuing services as a writer on any series. "Continuing writing services" was defined as more than three writing assignments for any series within one broadcast year. For any scripts Serling wrote that were adaptations of previously published material, his fee would be reduced by the cost of the basic material purchase so the script fee would not exceed the amount. Initially the fee was $7,500 per script, but during negotiations, the fee was upped to $10,000 per script.

By mid-May, Serling and the Columbia Broadcasting System finally reached an agreement for the 13 hour-long episodes. The third half-hour season had not even finished airing when he began planning the latest adventures down the dark corridor. CBS, however, would not confirm the start date for airing the hour-long series, promising him that if the program did not premiere in the fall, a mid-season premiere would be assured. During the first week of April, Serling requested that Perry Lafferty be the new producer, by virtue of his abilities, experience and availability. CBS gave an official rejection, citing Perry was simply too valuable a man for them to lose. In late May, he arranged to have Bert Granet place the same request, and again CBS rejected for the same reason.

On May 31, 1962, CBS Television's West Coast program chief Robert Lewine closed a two-pronged deal with producer Herbert Hirschman and his Double H Productions, Inc. The deal called for Double H to loan out Hirschman to CBS to serve as producer of the hour-long *Twilight Zone* series, replacing Houghton. In order to entice and secure Hirschman, the deal also involved Double H producing as a joint venture with CBS, a minimum of two hour-long pilots for the fall season.

Serling, however, had moved to Yellow Springs, leaving Hirschman completely in charge of overseeing production on the West Coast. He had to deal with both his college job and production of the *Twilight Zone* at the same time, but unlike the previous three seasons, he would not be on site offering his personal touch and supervision, leaving everything in the capable hands of Hirschman. Numerous letters were mailed to him almost daily from Hirschman, with updates and reports regarding the status of production, and he composed a daily reply.

By July 12, Art Wallace's "A Little Piece of Clay" had been accepted by Serling, but Hirschman reviewed the story and rejected it. Cayuga productions negotiated for John Cecil Holm's "The Other Side of Yesterday" (for which the first draft was written and awaiting a revision by August 1.) The script concerns Jeremy King, a novelist, who purchases a home in the country, far away from the city. After discovering the house has remained untouched for almost 40 years, he finds an antique telephone, and a telephone directory dated 1918. The operator on the other end is friendly enough to help him place calls, but he soon discovers that he is talking to the past – 1918, to be exact. After falling in love with the voice on the other end, he spends considerable time trying to prove it a hoax. Regrettably, he is unable to meet, touch or love the operator because of the difference in time. After studying the history of the town, he learns when she will die. He is forced to withhold the information, believing she will not believe his story.

On July 27, 1962, Herbert Hirschman apologized to Serling, who was then residing at Interlaken, New York, for a mistake regarding the availability of a John Collier story titled "Sleeping Beauty." Serling wanted to adapt it for *Twilight Zone*, but upon checking with Collier's agent, Hirschman discovered that was one of two stories which Collier had reserved for himself, with the intention of writing a feature screenplay.

By July 28, Hirschman was expressing some concerns with the script of "The Other Side of Yesterday," so he postponed that production awaiting further work and revisions. Since it was intended to be the second production of the season, Serling's "No Time Like the Past" was moved up the schedule.

For the script "The Thirty Fathom Grave," Herbert Hirschman was dead set against the line delivered by Captain Beecham, " . . . or maybe it's our imagination." Serling argued that the line should remain in the script. "This is a kind of *Twilight Zone* line," he explained. "Obviously it isn't their imagination but is a throw-away line in which Beecham, devoid of any practical explanation, makes a grim joke. Very Twilight Zoneish, believe me." Hirschman began questioning Serling's script regarding the plausibility of true-to-life characters suspecting that someone might still be alive in the sub. He explained, "again, a *Twilight Zone* point of view. It must remain as is. Herb, boobie, live with me on this. I know I'm right."

As a producer, Hirschman had his own style and method for *Twilight Zone*, and Serling, over 2,000 miles away from California, was unable to supervise the productions. Hirschman shared the same vision as the network regarding the uncertainty of science fiction and fantasy. Hirschman critiqued the scripts, often finding fault in what Serling found satisfaction, and the two did not see eye-to-eye. The hour-long script also took longer for Serling to compose than the half-hour, so his efforts were stretched to the breaking point.

"In the half-hour form we depended heavily on the old O. Henry twist," Serling told *TV Guide*. "So the question is: Can we retain the *Twilight Zone* flavor in an hour? We may come up with something totally different."

The New Opening

On June 27, 1962, Ralph W. Nelson wrote to both Herbert Hirschman and Rod Serling, explaining, "Kaplan said not to do anything about music at this time as they are considering possibly using Leonard Bernstein for the new theme music behind the title." If Bernstein composed a new theme, it was never used for the series. Constant's theme from the second and third season was still used, though a new rendition of his two pieces was recorded to form a single new recording. Two renditions were made; each differed in length by one to two seconds, to fit the length of the opening and closing credits.

Serling asked to have the road trip visual he intended from the very beginning, but Nelson explained in the same letter that "I would consider a suitable road or air strip for shooting the basic material for the title, but I have not gone to Edwards Air Force Base as yet. There is an abandoned Air Force strip near Lone Pine where the desert brush has grown very heavy alongside of the taxi strip, which is about 50 feet wide, and also has come up in all of the tar divider strips along the concrete. I thought perhaps we could clear some of this brush, leaving it heavy on one side and filled in a bit on the opposite side, paint a blank line and use a camera car going at high speed with under-cranked camera. Bare trees could be spotted at appropriate footages on each side of this strip."

"But the fact remains that even if this method would work out to everyone's satisfaction, it would probably cost around $3,500 because of air transportation for survey and photographic crews, nursery and construction personnel, and then still might not be usable due to the up and down jiggle of the camera," Nelson concluded. "Also, it would be impossible for any camera car driver to keep an absolute straight course in following the black line and there is bound to be a certain amount of side away. I have talked to a location representative in Lone Pine and tomorrow will have a couple of probably not too good pictures of the brush-grown strip which might give a better idea of how this method might be used."

A new opening was designed in late July, but it did not involve the airstrip and speeding road-way Serling intended. On August 1, he was informed by letter that the following objects would be floating past the camera:

- A glass eye with eyelashes over it. As the eye approaches the camera, the eyelashes open, disclosing the eye staring at you.
- A mathematical equation in three dimensional wooden letters that tumbles and floats.
- An articulated mannequin or doll with long hair that floats in the breeze.
- A pendulum clock with the pendulum swinging.

On August 20, 1962, Hirschman wrote to Serling. "The question has been raised as to whether the series should be known as 'The Twilight Zone' or 'Twilight Zone.' I must say my own inclination, for no real reason, is to prefer 'Twilight Zone.' However, I will certainly defer to your wishes in this regard." Serling's reply remains unknown, but Hirschman may have been the reason for the first word to be dropped from the title.

Production

On Wednesday, August 15, 1962, Rod Serling reported to Stage 22 at the M-G-M Studio for shooting the teasers, and recording the opening and closing narrations for the following episodes: "Death Ship," "In His Image," "The Bard," "The Thirty Fathom Grave" and "No Time Like the Past."

On September 19, 1962, Herbert Hirschman wrote to Rod Serling, who was then residing in Yellow Springs, explaining how smoothly filming was progressing, and how pleased he was to see the dailies on "He's Alive," and the Navy approval for "The Thirty Fathom Grave." Quite humorously, he explained to him: "We are very busy here today shooting scenes with Hitler on one stage, a spaceship on another, and a leopard on a third."

The productions were faulted on a minor level by the lack of Serling's presence on the West Coast. Thirteen hour-long shows were produced for which Serling was not present during the bulk of the shooting. A number of page revisions for some of the scripts went by without his even knowing about them. Directors and cast were chosen with no prior communication to him and no consultation of any kind.

For the previous three seasons, Serling took major responsibility for script material. Buck

Houghton was consulted and, on many occasions, gave opinions and editorial aid. As he described it, "At the rock bottom decision level – they came out of my hip pocket and no one else's."

In October of 1962, Rod and Carol Serling flew to Japan for sort of a publicity junket for *The Twilight Zone*, and returning from the tour, he told reporters "the series has been good to me. It's made me a public personality and I like that very much." When asked to comment on the new hour-long series, he remarked "the network wants us to go way out next fall. Our stories will be wilder."

The October 20, 1962 issue of *The Hagerstown Herald-Mail* reported that a plot for a weekly comedy series starring Jerry Van Dyke was under development and would be produced by Herbert Hirschman and directed by Perry Lafferty. The program was intended to debut next season and was one of two pilots Hirschman was contracted to furnish the network through his Double H Productions, Inc.

When Serling returned to the United States in late October, Hirschman's involvement with the *Twilight Zone* series was starting to annoy him, and the playwright wondered if Hirschman was the wrong man for the job. While he was not expecting the efficiency of Houghton, the constant nit-picking by Hirschman and problems causing productions costs to rise were intolerable. Serling privately phoned Ralph W. Nelson to address his concerns. During the month of October, Nelson and Serling exchanged a number of private conversations regarding Hirschman. By early November, Hirschman was approached and the concerns were addressed.

Serling admitted that "the whole hour concept is too back-breaking and too difficult to warrant a complicated chain of command beginning with Boris Kaplan, working its way through Bert Granet, and then frittering around on the executive level at CBS. I don't see any alternative at all beyond CBS giving me total carte blanche – or forgetting the thing out of hand."

On November 8, 1962, Serling's letter to Nelson commented, "I'm not sure just what Herb's plans are but I would very much like to consider Perry Lafferty. I think he'd be a real asset to us and it's my personal feeling (very entre nous) that he thinks more like we do than does Herb. To this end I shall certainly work – particularly if Herb leaves the scene."

During the first full week of December, it was decided that Perry Lafferty was not going to hop on board as producer, but Bert Granet was a candidate. "Under duress from CBS, I was placed on the hour *Twilight Zone*, and much the same pressure was exerted on me with *The Great Adventure* later," explained Granet in a letter to Serling, dated October 2, 1963.

On December 11, Granet accepted the position, with Nelson as production manager, under the stipulation that Granet wanted to be connected with the dubbing of any of Hirschman's shows, even though the dubbing process went into January and February.

On December 13, Serling told Robert Lewine of CBS Television, "My feeling about Bert Granet is roughly the same as with Herb Hirschman. They are both qualitative and intelligent gentlemen, well-versed in production. But they are not versed in the concept of the *Twilight Zone*."

On November 29, Nelson wrote to Serling. "I understand from Bob Norvet, they have talked to various producers, including Roy Huggins – of all people. Hirschman is definitely finished and they are paying off his $50,000 deal, of which Cayuga has absorbed $32,500 and CBS is stuck with $17,500 in order to get rid of him. Both of his contemplated projects of *The Gate* pilot and *The Jerry Van Dyke Show* are off."

Hirschman went to London to help produce a spy drama titled *Espionage*, which would be telecast over NBC beginning in October of 1963.

By the end of November 1962, the decision when to premiere the new hour-long series was still up in the air. Primary filming for the contracted 13 episodes was already completed and in the can. Ralph W. Nelson sat down with Bob Norvet of CBS late in the afternoon of November 28 regarding the pickup and starting date. CBS was trying to start the new season as late as possible so they could get a rating on the first two or three episodes broadcast, on which to base their decision on whether to order additional episodes or leave the effort at 13. If CBS canceled, the network would face expenditures of $20,000 or more. But since Hirschman was out of the program, and no additional scripts had been approved, CBS was scrambling for a new producer for Serling. Hirschman, however, remained for a time to finish the episodes he had started, and serve with CBS under the terms of his contract, to arrange for the episodes he worked on to be polished for broadcast.

Serling, meanwhile, was attempting to finish two additional scripts for the hour-long season. Very little is known about these scripts except that one was a "robot idea," which may have resulted in the script "Uncle Simon," later produced for the fifth season, and a 707 airplane story that he went so far as to commission the De Forest Research Company for technicals related to the plot proposal. Serling assured Nelson that the 707 airplane story would not require an aircraft crashing, "simply winging over as a result of a nuclear blast from below, and then recovering and going back on course as before." He could not conceive of any film clips that could be doctored up to create the illusion, so the stunt would require original filming.

By December 1, a tentative release schedule was designed by Hirschman and Kaplan, with the first two episodes completed and in the can set for the initial airings. The remaining episodes did not air as originally intended.

January 3, 1963	"In His Image"
January 10, 1963	"The Thirty Fathom Grave"
January 17, 1963	"Mute"
January 24, 1963	"Jess-Belle"
January 31, 1963	"Death Ship"
February 7, 1963	"He's Alive"
February 14, 1963	"Miniature"
February 21, 1963	"Printer's Devil"
February 28, 1963	"Valley of the Shadow"
March 7, 1963	"No Time Like the Past"
March 14, 1963	"The Incredible World of Horace Ford"
March 21, 1963	"I Dream of Genie"
March 28, 1963	"The Bard"

"I was working at CBS when they asked me to take over for Hirschman," recalled Bert Granet in a phone interview with the author. "*The Twilight Zone* was a costly affair for the network. They did not want to disappoint Rod Serling so I came on and we got along professionally. Of course, I left months later and he felt I was deserting the ship. Personally, he was not happy with me leaving and he took it personal."

CBS did commission five additional hour-long episodes, so Serling attempted to get two more scripts approved. "I told Lewine that I wanted to shoot both 'The Happy Place,' and "The Parallel'," Serling explained to Nelson in a letter. "The latter I don't think we have any problem with. The former, since Hubbell Robinson already knocked it out once; I contemplate some resistance on the part of the net. But I'm contacting my agent in New York to help me push this through."

On December 3, 1962, Nelson wrote to Serling. "Bob Norvet did tell me that he had been told that Perry Lafferty had been considered but then discarded. He said he asked them to seriously reconsider Perry again – for the reasons I mentioned in my last letter – nine weeks is not very practical to keep a continuing air schedule." Hirschman and George Amy completed the dubbing and sound for the 13 films produced, while Nelson remained the only person to communicate with Serling during the fiasco. CBS would not commit to additional films until they scheduled the first 13, assured that there would be a need to air additional episodes.

The same December 3 memo told Serling, "I think John Conwell did an excellent job in selection of cast and in making deals, and that he is not entirely responsible for some of the casting mistakes that were made on the last thirteen."

On December 12, Ralph W. Nelson told Serling that "*Twilight Zone* is no longer *Twilight Zone* with you gone, and the new producers, the knick-knacking and interference of CBS – particularly in the cutting situation." Nelson also suggested that it would be a waste of money to put someone in the associate producer spot for the five remaining episodes.

Correspondence between Serling and Nelson and Robert Lewine, the CBS vice president of programs in Hollywood showed, that he preferred "Death Ship" as the season opener instead of "In His Image," feeling the space travel episode was far more intriguing. The selection was not changed, however, by command of Lewine, who explained to Serling, ". . . the first two pictures to be finished were 'In His Image' and 'The Thirty Fathom Grave.' Because of this, these were the two programs shown to our sales department and to prospective advertisers and, incidentally, both have been highly praised."

In November of 1962, Serling received the latest story to appear in *The Saturday Evening Post*, and though he considered the story a "lulu," his concern was with the author. "It involves Jack Finney who we've gone to before," he informed Nelson, "and he is pretty hard-nosed about signing deals with us – unless he collects an arm [and a leg] plus additional other concessions that make it pretty much totally prohibitive to buy anything from him."

On December 4, 1962, Serling received word from CBS that additional episodes were requested and filming could commence. He told Lewine, "There are two scripts available – one in good condition – the other, possible to be put in good condition on relatively short notice. A script is mine called 'The Happy Place,' is a definite necessity for shooting. It's a good, sound, solid piece of writing – not overly expensive to do, and very much a part of the show idea. This is one I will fight for down the line as a definite entry. The next script is called 'Parallel,' which Herb rejected out of hand. This requires considerable work, but still represents a good entry into the next group. Charlie Beaumont has an exceptionally good idea for a wax museum story which he will start work on the moment you give him the word."

The day after, Lewine informed Serling that "The Happy Place" was rejected. "My vague recollection that there was a sound reason for this rejection has been borne out by the information that this was originally submitted as a *Playhouse 90*, and was turned down. This doesn't mean it won't be reconsidered, but it does mean that we had the opportunity to do it in this cycle of thirteen and passed."

On December 10, Serling admitted "since Hubbell Robinson already knocked it out once, I contemplate some resistance on the part of the net. But I'm contacting my agent in New York to help me push this through."

In January of 1963, Serling wrote to John Guedel of John Guedel Productions, inviting him to submit a few original scripts for the new hour-long series. On January 15, Guedel wrote back, politely explaining that while he did not have any script to offer, he had a free notion which had been haunting him. "I was talking to a blind person the other day – blind since birth," he explained. "She said that she would give anything to be able to see for just one day. Then she would store up the memories of that day and would know what so many things looked like (reminiscent of the one day that the 12-year-old girl was allowed to come back on earth in *Our Town* – which, to me, remains the most poignant scene in the theater. The question: What would you choose to see? Apparently, those who become blind later in life feel they are more fortunate because they at least had a chance to look. The message is there of course – for all sighted persons to more fully appreciate what we see every day."

This idea might possibly have been the genesis for a script Serling would later compose after the cancellation of *The Twilight Zone*, about a blind spinster who receives an operation granting her a limited number of hours of sight. The awful twist is that after the successful operation, the city faces a power outage and she is condemned to spend most of her hours in the dark – until the sun starts to rise and her sight returns to darkness. The segment, titled "Eyes," would be contemplated for a *Twilight Zone* movie he intended to do after the series went off the air, and though the project never became a *Zone* feature, it was used in the pilot movie of *Night Gallery* in 1969.

Republic Studios

After most of the production and dubbing was completed, Nelson informed Serling that he would probably be working with Buzz Kulik and Bob Banner on a pilot they wanted to shoot early in January. (Nelson later managed to get himself away from that pilot.) At Bob Norvet's request, Nelson surveyed Republic Studios "to see whether it is practical to make *Twilight Zone* there in the future." Nelson was to take inventory of the types of sets, wooded exteriors, costumes and the like – but Nelson already made up his mind, even before seeing the place, that the scope was so limited and the lack of available standing sets would have cut down production values.

In a deal made by CBS earlier in the year, the network leased the 70-acre Republic Studios lot for 10-years with an option to buy. For at least two-and-a-half years, however, the network had to share the facilities with Four Star Productions, which already was ensconced on the lot with a contract of its own. The first CBS series to move in was *Rawhide*, and the network felt that if Cayuga could move from M-G-M to Republic, production costs would be minimized – no rental fees for use of studio or props.

Serling disapproved, stating "that Republic would be a lousy place to go back to shoot. Their back lot is so skimpy, as compared to Metro, and their available standing sets also so inferior that my own personal feeling is that we'd be making a desperate mistake."

By December 12, Nelson admitted that while he had the deal with Republic 90 percent closed, the final decision was based on what the requirements were in the way of available sets and back lot. The price tag was also not acceptable, as the savings would have been a mere $2,500 per episode, hardly enough to warrant filming at another studio that had apparent limitations.

The Jack Benny Program

On Tuesday morning, November 13, 1962, Serling attended a reading for a half-hour teleplay of *The Jack Benny Program*. He had agreed to participate in a spoof of *The Twilight Zone*, which was scheduled for telecast in January.

Serling was summoned to play the role of a sophisticated writer who could add a little polish to Jack's program. Concerned that his staff writers weren't delivering the quality he demanded, the famed comedian hires Serling. But unaware of how comedy is devised, he apologizes to Benny, explaining that the television program doesn't make any sense. Jack confesses that *The Twilight Zone* never made any sense to him. When he returns home, Jack discovers that no one, not even his servant, Rochester – recognizes him. Spoofing the *Twilight Zone* episode "A World of Difference," Benny struggles to prove his identity and that Mr. Zone (played by Serling) did not really reside in his house.

Paid $1,000 plus scale residuals for his appearance, Serling attended the rehearsal from 10 a.m. to 12 noon at Revue Studios on Wednesday, with filming from 3 p.m. to 9:30 p.m. on Friday, November 16. On November 18, 1962, he returned from the West Coast to Yellow Springs, Ohio, to continue teaching at Antioch College.

Co-sponsored by State Farm Insurance and Jell-O and broadcast on the CBS Television Network, Serling's appearance doubled as publicity for his anthology program. Initially telecast on the evening of January 15, 1963, the script was titled "Twilight Zone Sketch" and was written by George Balzer, Hal Goldman, Al Gordon and Sam Perrin.

An Homage to *The Twilight Zone*

The Jack Benny Program was not the only television series to feature a spoof, salute or homage to the anthology series. In the episode "It May Look Like a Walnut," on *The Dick Van Dyke Show*, initially telecast on February 6, 1963, Dick Van Dyke watches a late-night horror movie on the boob tube and falls asleep, suffering from an unusual nightmare. Now a resident of "The Twilo Zone," he discovers that an alien race has succeeded in taking over the world and can be distinguished by their lack of thumbs and by an extra eye in the back of their heads. The aliens have a fetish for walnuts. The show's climax occurs when Van Dyke opens the hall closet and thousands of walnuts pour out, with his wife (played by Mary Tyler Moore) smilingly swimming among them. On a later episode, "Young Man with a Shoehorn," telecast February 24, 1965, *The Twilight Zone* is referenced again, but only through a brief, smart remark.

In the episode "Beaver on TV," on *Leave it to Beaver*, first telecast on February 21, 1963, Beaver Cleaver is a contestant on a television quiz show and excused from school for the taping. But circumstances force the show to be broadcast a week later than scheduled. When Beaver returns to school the next day, his friends and schoolteachers suspect he made up the story to have the day off. Gilbert, a friend of Beaver's, suggests: "Boy, Beave, this is kinda like the *Twilight Zone* with that guy Rod Serling." The camera zooms in for an eerie close-up of the Beaver as the *Twilight Zone* theme music is heard in the background.

The Twilight Zone is mentioned twice on *The Andy Griffith Show*. In "The Haunted House," initially shown on October 7, 1963, Opie's baseball flies into a spooky house, and Barney and Gomer attempt to retrieve the ball. Barney comments, "There's plenty going on right now in *The Twilight Zone* that we don't know anything about and I think we oughta stay clear!" In the episode "Citizen's Arrest," broadcast December 16, 1963, Barney is behind cell bars, under arrest for making an illegal U-turn. Attempting to get Otis to unlock the door, Barney informs Otis that he's on the outside and it is Otis who is trapped within. His excuse is "I'm in *The Twilight Zone!*"

In the episode "Lucy Gets Amnesia," on *The Lucy Show*, first seen on October 12, 1964, Lucille Ball suffers from a temporary case of amnesia. When she snaps out, she questions where the brand new fur coat came from, and Vivian explains, "That arrived while you were in *The Twilight Zone.*"

In "Erika Tiffany Smith to the Rescue," on *Gilligan's Island,* telecast on December 30, 1965, Zsa Zsa Gabor arrives on the island with the intention of scouting a new location to build a resort, and remarks, "This place is so far off the map it isn't even listed in *The Twilight Zone.*"

In "Excuse Me, May I Cut In?" on *Laverne & Shirley,* initially telecast October 26, 1976, the television set breaks down, and the girls stare at a blank screen, sarcastically commenting about which shows they do not want to miss – including *The Twilight Zone.*

There were numerous other mentions of *The Twilight Zone,* on *The Jeffersons, The Wonder Years, Night Court,* the pilot movie of *MacGyver, Quantum Leap* and *Frasier,* among many others.

On the November 20, 1976 telecast of *Saturday Night Live,* Dan Aykroyd parodies the role of Rod Serling, who cleverly promises three aspiring actresses to visit a hotel room where he can give each of them a tryout for his television series – with a few drinks of champagne to start the ball rolling.

The 1963 situation comedy series *Harry's Girls* told the story of Harry Burns, a vaudeville entertainer with an act that featured three beautiful girl dancers, Rusty, Lois and Terry. In addition to being the star of the act, Harry had to do the booking, handle finances, and try to keep tabs on the girls. The last was not so easy. In the script titled "Fresh Air and Sunshine," Harry and the girls go on a camping trip. Harry is sleeping on the ground. While sleeping, the girls put him in a sleeping bag. After a moment, Harry begins to mumble in his sleep, and then suddenly his eyes open wide in a stare. He moves his head a little and realizes his arms are pinned to his sides. Believing he is in a strait-jacket, he begins to cry for help – and makes a reference to being in "the Outdoor Twilight Zone!" The series ran a mere 15 episodes because NBC did not renew the contract for additional episodes. This *Twilight Zone* reference is unique in that, while filmed and edited, it was never broadcast, preventing a *Twilight Zone* reference from reaching the airwaves.

Making Room for *The Twilight Zone*

Meanwhile, news of *Twilight Zone*'s return went public on November 18, 1962, as *The New York Times* reported that *Fair Exchange,* a comedy series about American and English families who exchange their teenage daughters for a year, might be discontinued December 28 by CBS. It would be replaced on January 4 by a new one-hour version of *Twilight Zone.* The cancellation of *Fair Exchange* was reported the week before as "highly probable," although CBS sought a way to improve the program's rating. After its debut on September 21, the show received more acclaim from the critics than any other new program on the network, but its rating had been far below what was believed a show at that hour should obtain.

Bringing *Twilight Zone* back to the airwaves involved the shifting of two other programs. *The Alfred Hitchcock Hour,* on Thursday evening, would make a move into the Friday night time slot replacing *Fair Exchange.* The Hitchcock program had been competing against Andy Williams and the Fred Astaire anthology series. *The Nurses* would move into the old Hitchcock time slot. CBS admitted that *The Nurses* was getting walloped by *McHale's Navy* and *Hazel* on competing networks. *The Twilight Zone* would take up the slot formerly occupied by *The Nurses.* The maneuvering was part of the cutthroat battling among the networks to protect their expensive prime-time hours. The reasoning at CBS was that *The Nurses,* a new series that had premiered a few months previous, stood a better chance against the Fred Astaire anthology and the Williams show. *The Alfred Hitchcock Hour* and *The Twilight Zone* were expected to carry their own loyal audiences wherever they were scheduled.

CBS predicted in advance that *Fair Exchange* would most likely tank in the ratings and announced in a press release that if the series did not show promise by mid-season, *The Twilight Zone* would move in for the remainder of the 1962-63 season. Support for CBS was validated by a television critic for *The Winnipeg Free Press*, who explained to a query submitted from a reader in his September 15, 1962 column that *The Twilight Zone* "may show up during the 1962-63 season as a replacement for a new series that doesn't make it through the ratings race."

Sponsorship
After Colgate dropped sponsorship at the end of the second season, Liggett & Myers (the American Tobacco Company), remained as the alternate sponsor for the third season, promoting Oasis and Chesterfield. The alternate weeks were assigned to an assortment of companies who wanted to advertise on the series, but did not want to sign up for the entire season. The viewing audience was treated to a variety of products ranging from Pepsi-Cola, Polaroid, and Mobil Gas and Oil.

For the fourth season, the hour-long time slot allowed for more than one product to be advertised during the program, instead of a sole sponsor on alternating weeks. This allowed the companies to promote weekly instead of bi-weekly. Johnson & Johnson was the largest contributor, promoting baby powder, Band-Aid and Micrin Antiseptic Mouthwash. The Studebaker Corporation also shared advertising minutes, along with U.S. Royal Tires, Pepsi-Cola, and Liggett & Myers. When *The Twilight Zone* returned to a half-hour format with the fifth season, the format of one sponsor per program advertising on alternate weeks also returned. L&M continued hawking Tareyton, Lucky Strike and Pall Mall cigarettes. Procter & Gamble promoted Milk Wave Lilt, Push Button Lilt, Crest Toothpaste and Prell Shampoo.

Summary of the Hour-Long Season
Of the 18 episodes produced for the one-hour *Twilight Zone*, Serling wrote eight scripts. He was paid for two of them, "The Thirty Fathom Grave" at $10,000 and "The Happy Place" at $6,000. These were the so-called pilot scripts delivered to CBS before the option was picked up on the one-hour series. "The Happy Place" was used in the series, a rewrite of an old hour script originally written for CBS before the initial sale of the show. Serling had already been paid $4,000 for it by the network. "The Thirty Fathom Grave" constituted the other pilot script which was a rewrite of a half-hour version he had done at the end of the third series pending a pick-up of the show in half-hour form for a fourth year. Serling wrote three such half-hours for which he was never paid at the half-hour price which would have been $2,925. Two others were expanded and used in the hour scripts.

So, having written eight one-hour scripts (seven had been used and he had been paid for two), five of the remaining six netted Serling $10,000 per script, with one at the rate of $9,500. The difference was attributed to a story purchase of $500, which under the hour deal came out of his fee. Hence in the script area alone, by April of 1963, he was due $59,000 income. In addition, at the rate of $350 per show for 18 shows he accrued for supervising, he also picked up $6,300 for hosting services, netting him a total of $65,800.

The hour-long season did not hurt the prestige of *Twilight Zone*. Seeing that the program received an Emmy nomination for cinematography, the president of the Academy of Television Arts and Sciences Foundation, Harry S. Ackerman, sent Serling a personal congratulations. "It goes without saying that this most excellent program should be included in the permanent archives of the industry," Ackerman wrote. On November 27, 1963, Ackerman informed him that the Academy was responsible for the Television Library of the Hollywood Museum, the repository of films, tapes and artifacts relating to telecasting. "Now, with the Museum an actuality, and with the New York and Washington, D.C. branches of the Foundation's Library organized, it becomes vital that no outstanding examples of television be omitted. May we ask that you please make the necessary arrangements to provide us with three copies of 16mm prints of an episode most representative of the Cinematographers' work and of the series, and thus give you and the Academy the satisfaction of making its techniques available to students and researchers on both coasts in the years to come."

The Twilight Zone of Other Nations

In France, *The Twilight Zone* was broadcast under the title *La Quantrième Dimension* (*The Fourth Dimension*). In Latin America, the series was referred to as *La Dimension Desconocida* (*The Unknown Dimension*).

Rod Serling composed a program announcement for syndication in Australia:

Hello . . . I'm Rod Serling, the executive producer of the program we call The Twilight Zone; *and one we are delighted to send over to Australia for you to share with us.* The Twilight Zone *is that wondrous area of light and shadow . . . the unique, the bizarre, the strange, the unexpected. A hearty greeting to our friends down under . . . from those of us in* The Twilight Zone.

Hannes Lutz of Munchen, Germany, wrote to Serling in September of 1963, proposing a remake of the *Twilight Zone* to be filmed abroad. Since Serling was off on a combination business and pleasure trip to Manila, Hong Kong, Australia and Japan, on September 26, 1963, George D. Faber, the director of client relations for CBS Films, Inc., replied, "We have already given out the rights in various languages, including German, and are unable to grant your request."

During the month of October 1963, Serling and wife took a tour of the Orient, sort of a publicity junket for *The Twilight Zone* which was a big hit there. "In Japan, *Twilight Zone* is called *Mystery Zone*," he explained, "only because the Japanese alphabet doesn't have an 'l' in it."

In early 1963, Cayuga Productions ventured into the field of international syndication for *The Twilight Zone*. George Amy, Boris Kaplan, Buck Houghton and Serling agreed to put together a syndication package for the series to be distributed in the United Kingdom. Rather than offer half-hour shows, Cayuga packaged the series as an hour-long program with two half-hour episodes. Ralph W. Nelson was heavily involved with the project, making all the arrangements from incorporating brief seconds between the two dramas to the BBC's use of a station announcer for the opening and a revised title card reading, "Rod Serling's Twilight Zone." Beth Wheeler of the CBS music department looked into the aspect of music rights, and Lud Gluskin consulted Leo Lefcourt regarding possible payments to the Musicians Trust Fund for the music on the productions.

A total of 14 episodes were planned, with the half-hours combined to form a similar theme for each week's presentation. "Walking Distance" and "A Stop at Willoughby" were put together for one production; "Third From the Sun" and "People Are Alike All Over" for another; "The Odyssey of Flight 33" and "The Arrival" for another, and so on. Serling was scheduled to be filmed for the new introductions, bridging between the two productions, which he composed himself.

On November 11, 1963, the introductions were filmed for the BBC airings. Despite all preparation that went into the proposed series, the BBC telecasts never aired.

Rod Serling Business Trips – 1961 through 1963

As an indication of how busy Serling's schedule was, here are his business trips for the years of 1961 through 1963.

Dec. 29 – Jan. 2, 1961	Chicago, Columbus and Dayton *Twilight Zone* publicity.
January 7, 1961	Santa Barbara, California Dinner with Frank Kelly, Fund for the Republic.
Jan. 4 – Jan. 18, 1961	New York City Meetings with McCann-Erickson and CBS.
Jan. 19 – Jan. 22, 1961	Phoenix and Tucson, Arizona TWA Awards Dinner and Advertising Council Western States speech.
Feb. 26 – Feb. 28, 1961	New York City Meetings with NBC and CBS affiliates.
Feb. 28 and Mar. 1, 1961	Washington, D.C. Meeting with John Chambers, Federal Aviation Agency.
March 29 – April 2, 1961	San Diego and Coronado Tour of aircraft carrier and meeting with Navy Personnel.
April 6 – April 8, 1961	Binghamton, New York Chamber of Commerce recognition meeting.
April 8, 1961	Newark, Atlanta, Tallahassee *Twilight Zone* publicity.
April 9 – April 12, 1961	Tallahassee, Florida Speeches and *Twilight Zone* publicity.
April 13, 1961	Miami, Florida *Twilight Zone* publicity.
May 4 – May 6, 1961	New York City Bantam Books meeting and CBS-TV meeting.
June 27, 1961	New York City Meeting with Ashley-Steiner.
June 30, 1961	Washington, D.C. Discussions with John Chambers, Federal Aviation Agency.

July 16 – July 30, 1961	California Shooting host spots for *Twilight Zone* and scenes for various television series.
August 7, 1961	New York City Publicity Pictures for Eagle Clothes and meeting with Bantam Books.
September 5, 1961	Los Angeles (unknown)
October 19, 1961	Dayton, Ohio Job discussions with Antioch College.
Oct. 21 – Nov. 6, 1961	New York City *Requiem for a Heavyweight* rehearsals and shooting.
Dec. 3 – Dec. 7, 1961	New York City Additional shooting for movie and meeting with Famous Writers School.
Dec. 27 – Jan. 2, 1962	Dayton & Columbus, Ohio Interviews and *Twilight Zone* publicity.
Jan. 1 and 2, 1962	Columbus, Ohio Discussions with WBNS-TV for hosting a late-night television show.
Jan. 13 and 14, 1962	Phoenix, Arizona Publicity appearance – Trans World Airway dinner Discussed use of TWA mock-up aircraft for *Twilight Zone* productions. Entertained Thomas Bell, vice president of TWA.
Feb. 12 – 14, 1962	San Francisco, California Speeches for Television Academy and Writer's Group in Berkley.
February 19, 1962	San Diego, California Speech at the Television Improvement League.
March 26, 1962	Columbus, Ohio Speech at Unitarian Church. Continued discussions with John Haldi, Program Director at WNBS-TV concerning local late-night show.
March 27, 1962	Yellow Springs, Ohio Meeting with W.B. Alexander, vice president of Antioch College. Discussed faculty position for following year.

March 28 – 30, 1962	New York City Meetings with Ashley-Steiner and Hubbell Robinson with Robert Lewine of CBS Television Meetings with David Suskind, and meetings with Eagle Clothing and agency rep.
April 18 and 19, 1962	Palm Springs, California Meetings with Ernest Lehman and John Gay at M-G-M.
May 12 – 23, 1962	Seattle, Washington Creative Writing Symposium with Ray Bradbury at the Seattle World's Fair.
May 14 – 19, 1962	New York City Meetings with David Susskind. Meeting with Dick Roberts of Bantam Books. Shot Schlitz Beer Commercial.
June 8 and 9, 1962	St. Louis, Missouri Speech for Television Academy.
June 23, 1962	New York City Meetings with Ted Ashley on CBS contract.
July 2, 1962	Binghamton, New York Speech in front of Brandeis University alumni.
July 15 – 23, 1962	Los Angeles, California Shot host and recorded narrations for *Twilight Zone*.
July 25, 1962	Syracuse, New York Press interview for upstate New York papers.
August 5 – 16, 1962	Los Angles, California Filmed host and narration for *Twilight Zone*. Also initial conversations with director John Frankenheimer for *Seven Days in May*.
September 9 – 15, 1962	Chicago, Illinois Appearance on Kupcinet show, then plane to L.A. for *Seven Days in May* Discussions – Edward Lewis, producer, and John Frankenheimer; then plane back to Chicago for personal appearance CBS affiliate to publicize the *Twilight Zone*.
September 18, 1962	Columbus, Ohio Taped late movie host intros – WBNS-TV.

September 22, 1962	Marion, Ohio Speech – Women's Radio and Television Group.
October 3, 1962	New York City *Requiem for a Heavyweight* publicity. Radio interviews.
October 17, 1962	Columbus, Ohio Taping host spots, WBNS-TV. Speech at the Television Academy of Columbus.
October 19 and 20, 1962	Chicago, Illinois *Requiem for a Heavyweight* publicity tour.
October 21 and 22, 1962	Cleveland, Ohio *Requiem for a Heavyweight* publicity tour.
October 23 and 24, 1962	Pittsburgh, Pennsylvania *Requiem for a Heavyweight* publicity tour. Speech in front of Carnegie Tech.
November 1, 1962	Springfield, Ohio *Requiem for a Heavyweight* publicity tour. Appearance in front of Service groups.
November 3, 1962	Columbus, Ohio Taped late movie host intros – WBNS-TV.
November 7, 1962	Chicago, Illinois Press interviews. Taped local CBS station tie-ins for *Twilight Zone*.
November 9 – 16, 1962	Los Angeles, California Meetings with CBS. Rehearsals and taping for appearance on Jack Benny.
November 21, 1962	Columbus, Ohio Taped late movie host intros – WBNS-TV.
January 14 – 19, 1963	Los Angeles, California Conferences and rewrite for *Seven Days in May*.
January 22, 1963	Columbus, Ohio Taped late movie host intros – WBNS-TV.
January 31, 1963	Taped late movie host intros – WBNS-TV.
February 1, 1963	Returned to Los Angeles.
Feb. 28 and March 1	New York City Discussed clothing deal with Ted Bernstein Associates for wardrobe credit – *Twilight Zone*.

March 1, 1963	Westport, Connecticut Meeting of Famous Writers School faculty.
March 1 and 2, 1963	Washington, D.C. Discussions with Pentagon office on *Seven Days in May.*
March 16 – 29, 1963	Hawaii (mostly pleasure) Two meetings to discuss possible shooting sites for motion picture.
March 30 – April 5, 1963	Venezuela Publicity opening – Sheraton Hotel.
April 5 and 6, 1963	Miami, Florida Interviews and television appearances.
April 23 and 24, 1963	New York City Meetings with Ely Landau on *Forbidden Area.*
April 28, 1963	San Francisco, California United Airlines tour through maintenance and mock up.
May 8 – 11, 1963	New York City Meetings with CBS. Attended a CBS affiliates conference.
June 3 – 5, 1963	New York City Panel Show – *The Match Game*
June 5, 1963	Binghamton, New York *Twilight Zone* interviews – WNBF-TV.

CHAPTER NINE

The Fifth Season

Richard Matheson recalled, "We were all glad it went back to a half-hour for the last season."

"*Twilight Zone* in the half-hour form is quite simply plot stories with kicker endings," commented Serling to the *Ohio-Pennsylvania Derrick* newspaper. "You just can't do an hour show with a kicker ending."

The March 1964 issue of *Show* recapped the history for their readers. "Rod Serling's *Twilight Zone* began as a half-hour quickie in 1959, went off the air for 13 weeks in '62, returned as a full hour in '63 and last fall snapped back in its original length. Through it all, the handsome host of the macabre and his wizard entourage of offbeat writers have been consistent in scaring the wits out of a goodly portion of their audience."

Paperwork and package agreements were signed and initialed by Serling for Cayuga Productions, and the new half-hour format became official in April of 1963. Negotiations in February were designed for the best interests of CBS and Serling. Merritt Coleman of CBS requested that besides a renewal of a half-hour season of *Twilight Zone*, a separate agreement between Serling and CBS give the network certain first negotiation and first refusal rights for any television series concepts that he might develop or create during the term of Cayuga's agreement with CBS.

To accommodate Merritt Coleman and to retain the excellent relationship that he and Cayuga had with the network, on the advice of Sam Kaplan, Serling sent a letter to CBS, constituting a simple statement of intention to take new projects to the network and stating the letter would have no legally binding effect.

Under the new deal, Cayuga would be contracted to deliver a minimum of 13 programs, with the network's option for additional episodes – a maximum of 40 if they requested. CBS also retained the option for two additional years in each of which Cayuga would be obligated to deliver a minimum of 26 half-hour programs and a maximum of 40. CBS had until completion of the 11th program that year to order a minimum of 13 additional shows. Interoffice memos exchanged between Sam Kaplan and William Freedman suggested CBS had intentions from the get-go of scheduling 32 new shows.

Cayuga and CBS continued to split the profits on the new project, 50-50. However, under the new arrangement, the new season came off the network at break even. On the one hand, Cayuga did not bear any loss that might have been occasioned by the original network use (including intermixed and summer repeats), but on the other hand, Cayuga was guaranteed that after network exhibition, after deducting distributed fees and expenses, the balance from the programs would constitute profits subject to profit sharing.

Serling's writing obligation for the first year was to write five scripts out of the first 13; five out of the second 13 and two additional scripts if CBS ordered over 26. If the series was to be picked up for a sixth and a seventh season, his commitment was four scripts out of the first 26 and one script if the order went beyond 26. The minimum number of scripts he would write was dictated by his assurance to Sam Kaplan that he would not write more than 12 scripts for the initial broadcast year, and no more than five for each subsequent year. For each script written in the first year, Cayuga received $4,000, whether it was an original or an adaptation. CBS financed separately the cost of any basic story purchase in conjunction with a script. The script prices escalated to $4,250 in the second year and $4,500 for the third. Reruns were paid for as percentages of the initial fees: first rerun – 25 percent; second rerun – 25 percent; third rerun – 20 percent; fourth and fifth reruns – 15 percent each.

Cayuga was to receive a production fee for each program produced in the first year of $2,250. For each program produced in the second and third years, the production fee was $2,000. Cayuga was to be paid for reruns, a percentage of $1,400: first rerun – 35 percent; second rerun – 30 percent; third, fourth and fifth reruns – 25 percent each.

No separate fee was specified for legal and accounting services, which was to be borne by Cayuga out of its production fee. No separate fee was specified for the services of the continuing host (Serling), which was to be paid out of the Cayuga production fee.

For the fifth and final season, Serling wrote a total of 16 scripts. His creativity was running dry, and even today, fans of the program criticize how many of his efforts for the final season were previous episodes being re-written. "The Last Night of a Jockey" is considered by many as a redo of "Nervous Man in a Four Dollar Room." "A Short Drink from a Certain Fountain" and "The Jeopardy Room" were composed from material shelved years before. "A Kind of a Stopwatch" and "Mr. Garrity and the Graves" were adaptations from unpublished story submissions from viewers. "Overall, it's just more than you really should do," he commented to a reporter for *The New York Morning Telegraph*. "You can't retain quality. You start borrowing from yourself, making your own clichés. I notice that more and more."

"I have no illusions about our show," Serling continued. "It's not the legitimate theatre – this is sheer entertainment, done as intelligently as possible. You have only 23 minutes, and you can't get too darned artistic and create valid people and situations. So the best you can hope for is a well-told tale done with class."

In late August of 1963, Robert F. Lewine, vice president of television programs for CBS, announced in a press release that William Froug would become the new producer for *The Twilight Zone*, succeeding Bert Granet, who in turn was appointed producer of the new hour-long series, *The Great Adventure*. Froug had produced *The Alcoa-Goodyear Playhouse* in 1957-58 and won a Screen Producers' Guild award for an episode which also won Emmys for the series, its director and its writer. He also produced the Sam Benedict series and most recently had been a producer for the *Mr. Novak* series at M-G-M, where *Twilight Zone* was filmed. His credentials with television production and familiarity with the studio qualified him for Serling's approval.

The Great Adventure, a series of American history dramas, found producer John Houseman's services terminated. CBS suits were nervous over the budgets and the quality. To succeed Houseman, the network hired Granet, who had begun his career as a student in Yale University's drama department. Since William Froug replaced Granet as producer for *Twilight Zone*, newspaper columnist Frank Langley of *The Troy* (New York) *Record* remarked the switch as "sort of a TV producers' game of musical chairs."

The Fifth Season Promotional Campaign

The 1963-64 season of *Twilight Zone* involved publicity and promotion problems that constituted a challenge for Rogers & Cowan, Inc., a public relations organization. Since *Twilight Zone* was changing the time slot to Friday night at 9:30 and returning to the half-hour format, the rating picture was important to Procter & Gamble, the new sponsor. The lead-in strength depended on how well *Route 66* stood up against *The Bob Hope Show* and *The Millionaire Detective.* "We believe that these problems can be solved with a creative, hard-hitting publicity and promotion campaign, designed to stimulate new interest in *Twilight Zone*," a representative for Rogers & Cowan, Inc. commented in an interoffice memo dated May 28, 1963. "There has been a lack of excitement about *Twilight Zone* since its first season when it hit the airwaves as an innovation in television programming. It is possible to revive that excitement through promotion. All the elements are there."

Rogers & Cowan designed a consistent publicity campaign for September 1, 1963 through January 31, 1964. Divided chronologically with a number of different steps, the campaign included a traveling exhibit and a "Princess Twilight" scheme known as "Miss Twilight Zone."

The first step was the opening campaign. Despite editors of publications being inundated with material on new shows, there was always space for good, creative material. A byline article was submitted to TV editors, written by Serling, accompanied with special photography in which he indicated that "science imagination" had become "science reality."

The Traveling *Twilight Zone* Exhibit

Throughout the country there was a yawning expanse of time to be filled on local television shows. To nail down that time for *Twilight Zone*, one only needed to be creative and far-thinking. "We believe we have the concept for a *Twilight Zone* exhibit which can be sent on national tour early in the season and which is fascinating, visual, and also expressive of the *Twilight Zone* theme and appeal as well," wrote an executive at Rogers & Cowan. According to his spiel . . .

Twilight Zone is not science fiction . . . It is "science imagination." Part of the appeal of "science imagination," apart from the intrinsic entertainment value, is the fact that it borders on what is real and what is possible. Science fiction does not tread this delicate line and therefore does not have the distinctive quality of *Twilight Zone*. "Science imagination" has a great and glorious tradition, and in many instances "science imagination" has anticipated, or even aided, the advent of "science reality."

The plan was to compile an exhibit of examples of "science imagination" of the past which had anticipated "science reality." There was much material upon which to draw in devising this "SI to SR" display. The exhibit would be sent on tour and placed at the disposal of promotion managers at each station for placement on leading TV shows, coverage by local papers and even display at local museums, banks or central locations. One of the sources for this exhibit would be Jules Verne. His drawings anticipated rocket-powered space travel, submarines and radar. Back copies of the "Buck Rogers" comic strip would be obtained and placed side-by-side with photos of the Bell Aerosystems' Bell Rocket Belt, which was then operational and so closely approximated Buck Rogers' customary means of transportation.

Other fruitful sources included H.G. Wells and Greek mythology. Especially visual was reference to the remarkable predictions of the early French movie magician, George Melies. Melies produced movies 65 years before, predicting rocket travel and other dreams of the times. Other early films anticipated aerial bombardment, ground-to-air rocket missiles, and numerous other things. Especially appealing to TV interview shows was that much of the exhibit could consist of film clips which could be shown. The early Melies films could be contrasted with those of present applications of the wonders he predicted. Clips could be obtained showing Bell's rocket belt in action.

It was intended that Serling be tied in very closely with the *Twilight Zone* exhibit. In some instances it might have been arranged for telephone interviews to be done with him during the showing of the exhibit on local TV shows. Tie-ins with local boards of education could expose schoolchildren to the exhibit, and as a result, special awards of commendation could be presented to the show. To date, there is nothing to verify such a tour was designed or sent out to any major cities across the country. Cost may have been a factor. Nevertheless, the aspect of a publicity tour was conceived at least one time during the *Twilight Zone*'s initial telecast.

The Woman of Tomorrow Tour – Princess Twilight

"Take one accurately designed woman of tomorrow, conjured up five hundred years before her time; outfit her, decorate her and equip her for her future times as authentically as the best informed minds of today can predict; send her to key markets across the country and the result is infinite possibility for interviews not only with television editors, but women editors, food editors, automotive editors and science editors, as well as visually exciting material for up to thirty minutes of interview on local and national television and radio shows."

That's how a publicity campaign proposal read and not even Rod Serling would have conceived that such a notion be seriously considered – but it was. In early July, the idea was suggested to him. He gave it some thought and had multiple discussions with Dick Isreal at CBS press relations. "We talked at length of this 'Miss Twilight Zone' idea where a six-foot-six broad will traipse around the country pushing the show in as literate a fashion as possible," Serling wrote. "After these few hours of perusal, I think the idea is a bum one. First of all, it creates a carnival atmosphere which at the very best is somewhat demeaning to the show. The audience we seek and the audience we'll ultimately get are not the kind of people who respond to this kind of publicity goose. Also, you're not pushing for a motion picture now. You're trying to create a sustaining audience for a television show week after week. Though I have no statistics to back this up, I seriously doubt if the presence of even the most bizarre and beautiful young woman will create sufficient lasting interest to compensate for her cost and the cost of the tour. In short, I think the whole idea is an expensive one and one of very questionable virtue."

Rogers & Cowan, publicity agents, were responsible for creating the idea of the tour. While Serling had reasonable doubts, Betty O'Hara of Dancer-Fitzgerald-Sample, Inc. worked with Henry C. Rogers to create the necessary details and plans for the "Miss Twilight Zone" tour. "This idea for creating a Princess Twilight, the first woman of tomorrow, to tour nationally to promote the *Twilight Zone*, is a realistic possibility," according to the proposal. "We have researched the idea and found that, with further research and authentication, we actually can provide a young lady with all of the information, apparel and accoutrements which would make her a close approximation of the probable woman of tomorrow."

This tour was proposed for October and November of 1963 to fasten attention on *Twilight Zone* at the crucial point of the year when viewers stop experimenting in their selections and finalize their viewing habits for the winter months. The famed Edith Head was approached, and she provided designs for the probable attire of the woman of 500 years later, complete with details for revolutionary fabrics. Wally Westmore projected the trends in makeup and devised the likely makeup design of the period. George Masters was approached to design the coiffure of the future. An architect was asked to design a futuristic house, projecting the appliances and other miracles that would ease and compliment the life of a future woman.

The contents of a woman's handbag, the promoters agreed, would evoke interest, including the handbag itself. Food pills would be displayed as her daily diet, tiny electronic devices were packed into the handbag, including radios and other tools of thumbnail-sized packages, and the handbag itself utilized a recently developed lock opened only by a special electronic wavelength.

It was intended to furnish the house of the future with furniture designed by a manufacturer, Charles Eames, but the company never had time to design a working model of a transportable futuristic chair in which Princess Twilight would sit during interviews.

"An essential aspect of the promotion would be the establishing of Princess Twilight's raison d'etre and her close association with *Twilight Zone*," according to Henry C. Rogers of Rogers & Cowan. "It would be given a role in one of the shows and it would be presented that her national tour as a visitor from the future derived from a chance conversation she had with Rod Serling." Serling, they proposed, would write all of the material she would speak during interviews. But with his insistence the idea was a "bum one," the proposal was debated. Betty O'Hara wrote a reply to him, saying that, "If I were only a phone call away, I think I could allay any misgivings you might have that we were going only for the bizarre in our *Twilight Zone* girl promotion."

Nineteen-year-old Virginia Trimble, a UCLA astrophysics major, was selected to play the lead. "Rogers & Cowan asked the UCLA dean of students (or some such) to find a possible person," recalled Trimble. "The then head of student counseling thought of me because of the *Life Magazine* article the previous year – so she knew I photographed reasonably well, and because I was part of the gifted students' program I could probably be trusted not to say anything terribly stupid that would embarrass UCLA. The one thing I remember doing badly was an attempt to defend the folks who were fighting to keep their own homes in Vietnam against U.S. invaders."

"By the time I was on board, the 'princess' title concept had completely disappeared, as had any thought of 500 years in future. The focus was science of today and how *Twilight Zone* interfaced with it. I was 5 feet 7 ½ inches, not 6 feet tall (and did not wear more than modestly high heels). All the words I spoke were my own (and I was not scolded for attempting to defend the Viet Cong's fight to keep their homes, perhaps because I didn't do it as well as I would now!)"

Serling's insistence on avoiding the far-out, futuristic approach was taken into consideration. There was no futuristic furniture and no far-out handbags. Virginia Trimble carried her own, a plain black leather one with lots of compartments. She wore no fancy hair style or makeup. She wore her everyday cosmetics – Max Factor Pancake in Tan No. 2, Maybelline eyebrow pencil and mascara; sometimes eye shadow in a color matching her dress. Her hairstyle was of a daily style and the clothing was her own – standard UCLA co-ed – mostly sheath-style dresses, some princess seamed, some with waistlines, in bright colors and black, plus a green Scot's plaid dress with pleated skirt to wear on airplanes.

"What we did was a sweep through all the Nielsen cities, two-to-three days each, in a slightly odd order (Houston, Dallas, Chicago, Cincinnati, Pittsburgh, New York, Boston, Washington, Cleveland, San Francisco, and Los Angeles)," continued Trimble, who participated in newspaper interviews for women, society and entertainment sections. She appeared on morning wake-up shows on radio and local television stations.

"R&C made all the arrangements and sent me with a 'bringer' whose job was to see that I arrived on time for everything, looking the way R&C thought I should. One of the bringers introduced me to Black Russians and Brandy Alexanders (yeah, I was underage), and his battle cry 'stand tall' still echoes in my ears when I go out on a stage to give a public lecture!

"I spent one afternoon with Serling at his home. Something of a ladies' man, but a couple of inches shorter than I. Luckily, it was a problem the photographer had dealt with before, and we posed, for instance, with me looking over his shoulder while he sat at a desk, pointing to some script item or other. I actually read quite a few scripts, made a few suggestions (sorting out the difference between a galaxy and a solar system for instance) and a few were taken.

"I have no idea whether the project did what it was supposed to for ratings (one cannot, after all, do a controlled experiment with such things), but they paid me enough for a few weeks work to cover the next couple of semesters of fees and books at UCLA."

Now a Professor of astronomy, history of science and scientometrics, Virginia Trimble received her B.A. from UCLA in 1964 and her M.S. and Ph.D. degrees from the California Institute of Technology in 1965 and 1968 respectively. She joined the UCI faculty in 1971, after a year's teaching at Smith College and two postdoctoral fellowship years at Cambridge University (M.A. 1969). She received the 1986 National Academy of Sciences Award for scientific reviewing and currently serves as vice president of the International Astronomical Union; vice president of the American Astronomical Society and Chair of its Historical Astronomy Division;

George Grizzard questions his identity in "In His Image."

and member of the Executive Board of the American Physical Society and chair-elect of its Division of Astrophysics.

A Departure from *The Twilight Zone*

In February of 1964, columnist and television critic Edwin Matesky gave a review of the fifth season in his weekly column, "Looking and Listening," stating his high opinion for the series and his disappointment for the hour-long format:

Twilight Zone, Rod Serling's prize-winning creation of seasons past has fallen on hard times this season. For Friday evening after Friday evening I have faithfully watched the current version of the series. And for Friday evening after Friday evening I have come away disappointed. This season's *Twilight Zone* is, literally, in twilight compared to past years. It is but a pale imitation of the stellar *Twilight Zone* offerings of yesteryear.

My reaction to the Serling series this season – after having been "spoiled" by a bumper crop of fine, imaginative *Twilight Zones* last season – is analogous to someone discovering on a skid row a once prosperous, talented friend who is only a shadow of his former self. While the comparison may sound severe, bear in mind that it stems from an erstwhile devoted follower of the series whose affection this season has been rebuffed by some rather mediocre *Twilight Zones*.

Actually, there have been a few good *Twilight Zones* this season but they have been too few and too far between to save the series as a series. In fairness to the series it must be said that most of the fault apparently lies with forces beyond Mr. Serling's control. The chief culprit is abbreviation of the program from its former 60-minute length to 30 minutes. Apparently this was done at the behest of the network moguls who normally make such decisions. Brevity, someone once said, is the soul of wit. In this case, of *Twilight Zone*, brevity is anathema.

The 30-minute time period is best suited for the quickie comedy, the light drama, the quip, the anecdote. It is not made for the epic, the highly-inventive type stuff which requires an intricate weaving and integration of moods, thoughts and ideas. *

The fifth and final season came with noticeable restrictions on both the writers and producers. "We use a number of writers on the show," Serling commented in 1964. "Generally they are men whose literary talents are well known to us; and almost all of them, without exception, are published in other literary fields. At the moment, there have been roughly twenty men involved in more or less regular employment in this regard. We are forced to limit the size of our cast because of budget problems. Ours is a show which suffers one of the smallest budget allotments of any anthology extant. Therefore, it is much to our advantage if we can hold down the speaking roles in any given production to approximately five or six. Our shooting schedule is a straight three-day schedule. Prior to this year, we were able to have one day of rehearsal. This, too, for economic reasons has gone by the board. The snags that are often run into as to ideas or interpretation are usually production problems. We are asked to film patently difficult areas of drama, which for reasons of budget force us into more accommodating areas."

Serling still took the time to assist fans and viewers with their requests when not restricted by the network. Phyllis L. Pipitone, an adult senior majoring in speech at the University of Akron, chose for a project in her speech seminar class the writing of a "Twilight Zone-type" script. On February 11, 1964, she wrote to him asking if he could answer a few questions and supply a complimentary script to work with. On February 27, he answered her questions and forwarded a copy of the script, "There Goes Bunny Blake," the title of which would later be revised as "Ring-A-Ding Girl."

By June of 1964, the series was coming to a close and Serling offered both an apology and explanation to his fans. "Toward the end of the *Twilight Zone* it appeared that we hit fewer and fewer

---

* It should be noted that this critic was probably one of the very few who felt the hour-long format was best suited for *Twilight Zone*. Almost everyone else felt the 30 minute format was advantageous.

truths and our probing became conspicuously shallow. I do believe, however, that this is simply time and attrition operative. Five years is a long time to delve in anything meaningful on a weekly basis. So I believe it is with no sense of lament that we leave the air."

Influences

Shortly before the premiere of the fifth and final season, Rod Serling was quoted by the United Press International as being proud of the series. "We're part of the language now. Archie Moore, when he last got knocked out, said he felt like he was in the 'twilight zone.' Secretary of State Dean Rusk spoke of the 'twilight zone' in a speech of international diplomacy. There is a 'twilight zone' defense in basketball."

In the October 29, 1964 issue of *The Burlington* (North Carolina) *Daily Times-News*, a columnist wrote an article describing why he felt Halloween is so much fun. "There's an incredible appeal about the shadowy world of the occult that has attracted poets, playwrights and authors for centuries. And, throughout the history of mankind, this appeal has spelled success in the entertainment business – from William Shakespeare, with the ghost of Hamlet's father, to Rod Serling and his probes of the *Twilight Zone*."

On the occasion of Mao Tse-Tung's death in 1976, American diplomat John S. Service referred to the "twilight zone" of Chinese-American relations in a *New York Times* article.

In late 1962, the current house magazine of Television Shares Management Corp., *Keeping Up*, led off with a story about an airborne infrared "eye" that saw the past as well as the present. What this particular instrument accomplished was this: Operating from a height of some 40,000 feet, according to the article quoting from *Science News Letter*'s story by Lillian Levy, the "eye" looked down and reflected images of people and objects not then present but were there on the previous day. Developed by the Department of Defense to gather information on missile bases in Cuba, the TV-like "eye" somehow picked up reflections of activity and things from some time before, transferring them to an operating film camera. For instance, the "eye" would pass over an empty parking lot to capture pictures of the spot when it was filled with autos during the day. In a late November 1962 issue of *The Los Angeles Sunday Herald-Examiner*, Bob Hull remarked about the article, concluding: "If Rod Serling doesn't pick up this gimmick as the substance for one of his *Twilight Zone* stories, he's missing a good theme."

Serling may not have picked up on the idea, but producer Joseph Stefano or scriptwriter Meyer Dolinksy may have for the episode "O.B.I.T.," televised in November of 1963 on *The Outer Limits*.

The Cancellation

In the Sunday, November 1, 1959 issue of *Pictorial TView*, Serling told columnist Ed Misurell that "I'm sticking to television because of all the media with the exception of the legitimate stage, it provides the writer with the closest association with his craft. . . . The fact remains television is an exciting medium. I won't leave it – it could only happen that it might leave me."

Two years later, Serling told a columnist, "The things that encourage me the most are the things I've seen already done, which suggest potentially what can be done on television – what it's capable of doing. It's a hell of a medium and there is so much we can do and have done that I can't sell it out completely."

On March 30, 1964, Serling became the latest victim of television's continual struggle with creative juices. His show "just got booted off" CBS, as he phrased it, "for reasons totally unknown to me." Having been "booted off" once before, he was used to it. This time however, he did not expect to get a new lease on life. "The other time we were tossed off with the knowledge that we might come back in hour form," he recalled to a reporter for the United Press International. "This time we have no assurances that we'll ever come back, even as a five-minute commercial."

"In a strange way, I don't really blame them," Serling continued. "To this extent, we've been on five years and I think the show took on kind of an aged look. . . . We had differences of opinion. CBS didn't even give me a chance to change the format. I think they're preoccupying themselves with comedy fare."

Though the reason for the cancellation was not clear or direct from CBS, Serling's attempt to sell another anthology series to another network may have been one of the reasons. During the first week of March 1964, Bob Foster of *The San Mateo Times* reported that "ABC has approached the author and emcee of the series, Rod Serling, to do the show next season on the A.B.C. Network. At the moment, according to Serling, his show is being kept in reserve by CBS. He is currently trying to get them to release it for showing on ABC."

William E. Sarmento's May 11, 1964 column of "And Relax" in *The Lowell* (Massachusetts) *Sun* reported, "Today the Serling fans can smile indeed, for he has escaped the clutches of CBS and will be on the ABC network next season with a brand new show. It would seem that every year at this time Serling and his loyal fans would be waiting the decision from CBS as to whether *Twilight Zone* would be renewed. And usually it was put back in the schedule as a last minute filler or as a substitution for a flop. To be sure, *Twilight Zone* has had its share of obvious plots this year, but when Serling is in top form, the stories made some barbed and thought-provoking observations."

In late February and early March, weeks before CBS gave the cancellation, Serling discussed a proposal for a new TV series, titled *Witches, Warlocks and Werewolves*, which was originally slated to occupy the fall Friday evening time period. Knowing full well that CBS was not renewing *The Twilight Zone* for a sixth season, Serling went hard to work to propose the new anthology series. But ABC scrapped the project because of a difference of opinion between Serling and ABC's programming head, Tom Moore. "We have buried the project," Moore said to the press on March 19, 1964, and the comment pre-dates *Twilight Zone*'s cancellation by a week and a half. Serling, in Hollywood, told reporters that he was notified by ABC that "they had no further interest in continuing negotiations with me."

According to Serling, Moore reacted sensitively to an interview he gave to a West Coast *Variety* reporter. In it he said they did not see eye-to-eye on the series' concept. "I was quoted as saying that by preoccupying ourselves with ghouls, graves and walking death, we'd hook ourselves in a Class C concept. What Mr. Moore is looking for is a series about ghouls. I prefer to do a more adult type show with occasional social comment. I was even opposed to the title. 'Weird, Wild and Wondrous' would have been more in keeping with my idea. I'm sorry if I humiliated Mr. Moore with the interview, but in this business I did not expect such sensitivity. My next step, I guess, is to go fishing or seek out a plot in Forest Lawn." Serling also drafted an apology letter on March 19 to Moore, personally offering an explanation. "While the sense of my remarks was properly laid down, there was a belligerence and a harshness implicit in my tone which did not properly represent the frame of reference. There were some deletions of modifying adjectives which would have softened my remarks considerably, and served to eradicate any impression of either anger or reproval. . . . I did not deliberately set out to damage you in any way." ABC, in the meantime, replaced his proposed series with a new situation comedy starring Mickey Rooney, titled *Mickey*.

On March 26, 1964, Raymond A. Klune, vice president and general manager of M-G-M Studios, wrote a personal letter to Serling. "I can't recall how many times since *Twilight Zone* first started that there seemed to be some question about its continuance. Always and inevitably, however, it seemed as if [the series] not only continued, but additional shows were added each season. Finally we almost became convinced that here was a television series with an eternal life. There are many, indeed, who certainly believe that it should have had just that, but, alas, it has fallen victim to the same fate that we mortals do – unhappily. I do want you to know how much we enjoyed having *Twilight Zone* at our studio through these years. We are also more than a little proud to have had it here. I do hope that sometime we shall be considered in the role of host to one of your other undertakings. With all good wishes to you."

On April 7, Serling acknowledged the letter, explaining, "Our tenure at M-G-M was an altogether satisfying and productive one, and for all your efforts and those of the Metro team, we are deeply indebted. Needless to say, if another idea pulses its way out of my head – we'll be right back at your doorstep knocking to get in."

Serling was working on plans for a *Twilight Zone* motion picture as early as August of 1961. "The picture as I see it can be one of two things; either a quick, slick, capitalization of the name *Twilight Zone* and an attempt to cash in on a unique and successful television series, or an attempt to do a first class imaginative motion picture stemming very loosely from the basic philosophy that gave birth to the *Twilight Zone* television series," Alden Schwimmer of Ashley-Steiner wrote to Serling. "Buck Houghton should, in my opinion, be the producer of a *Twilight Zone* motion picture. He should not necessarily be the producer of a motion picture built out of your imagination and designed to stand on its own as a first class motion picture." In the same month, Serling acknowledged that he was figuring out a treatment for it, pointing out direction and plot.

The relationship with the agency, however, was growing worse with each passing month. When a fan asked Serling for recommendations for an agency that would get them in the field, the reply was course. "I don't know who the hell you can talk to. Agents are agents. They vary not a whit. Mine is Ashley-Steiner-Famous Artists, Inc. My contact there is Alden Schwimmer. But I don't even know whether he'll give you the time of day. Feel free to mention my name but I doubt if it'll even push the door open a crack. I wish this weren't so negative. But this is one of the strange phenomena of our business. They scream for new talent and provide not one single, lousy channel through which that talent can get recognition."

In March or April of 1963, Serling approached Schwimmer to clear with CBS the use of a theatrical motion picture called *The Twilight Zone* done in trilogy form. At first, Schwimmer wanted to do this on the basis of hooking it to a pilot for CBS so that they would be "properly sweetened and in a permissive frame of mind" to relinquish the rights for a nominal figure. The pilot died, and there was no chance of securing any kind of CBS cooperation without what Serling referred to as "paying through the nose" for it.

In July of 1964, he proposed the "three-part feature length *Twilight Zone*," to Schwimmer again, keeping an eye toward getting the rights to use the "Twilight Zone" on a film title as a kind of fulcrum. "It has much more appeal to me than embarking on another series at the moment," he explained. Schwimmer declined. In a letter dated August 17, Serling wrote to Ted Ashley of Ashley-Steiner. "The point of this is, Ted, that I want to do that film and I want to do it badly. I have in mind three exceptionally good story lines that would make a walloping good motion picture."

On Christmas Eve, 1964, Serling wrote to director Robert Parrish, asking if he wanted to be involved with the motion picture. "It goes like this," Serling wrote. "I'm in the process of selling a trilogy to Paramount called *The Twilight Zone* . . . or something like it. Three separate stories, each a kind of Hitchcock-ish (there he goes – coining again) very visual and I think quite exciting. It would be a spring project and a good opening number for the two of us to get back together on. . . . I just think that now that the years have gone by and *Saddle the Wind* has sort of faded off into merciful memory, it's time we did another. I don't know exactly what kind of deal I'm going to make but I rather think you can have participation if you want it." (He had written to Parrish in June of 1964 proposing the same thing, and Parrish agreed to participate, under one stipulation. Parrish could not commit himself until after Christmas, since he was working for Fox on a motion picture that required considerable time to produce.)

The story content for Serling's proposal for a motion picture under the *Twilight Zone* varied. With each rejection, he revised the selection of stories. Looking over the number of proposals, the trilogies included such tales as an ex-Nazi in hiding, and a blind woman facing retribution when an operation gives her the chance to regain her sight for a few hours. These two tales were later used for the pilot movie of *Night Gallery*, in 1969.

Other tales included a revision of "I Shot an Arrow Into the Air," about a young boy who befriends a visitor from outer space, who is being hunted by the U.S. Military, in what becomes Earth's first contact with extraterrestrials.

One untitled story told of a hot dog vendor who dreams he is a legend at Shea Stadium, during the after hours at the ballpark. Another untitled story concerned a woman who witnesses her life flashing before her eyes in a movie theater.

Another untitled plot synopsis involved Selena Brockman, an evil, old woman who, applying empathic powers, sucked the youth out of her young niece, Diane. When the mansion burns to the ground, Selena perishes and Diane regains her youthful beauty. This plot synopsis would later be scripted by J. Michael Straczynski, to form the episode "Our Sylena Is Dying," for an episode of the 1980s revival series of *The Twilight Zone*.

In one fascinating tale, two researchers travel back in time to 1871, in the hopes of discovering the cure to a modern day epidemic that plagued the city of Chicago a hundred years previous. While this story never made it to a *Twilight Zone* motion picture, producer Irwin Allen bought the script and arranged for the production to go before the cameras. In an effort to keep production costs down, many of the props and sets used in Allen's former television series, *The Time Tunnel*, were used for the production. The pilot movie, titled *Time Travelers*, was telecast on the evening of March 19, 1976.

Days after CBS made the cancellation official, Serling jumped out of an airplane. "I'm jumping out of an airplane for the 82nd Airborne Division. They sent me a note and said if I had the guts they had the plane." He left for Fort Bragg on March 31 and jumped the following afternoon on April 1. Though 39 years old, he had experience as a World War II paratrooper.

On April 1, 1964, John T. Reynolds, senior vice president of CBS Television, wrote a letter to Serling, expressing his condolences. "I did not want to pass the opportunity to tell you how much we on the West Coast regret the passing of *Twilight Zone* – into the twilight zone," he wrote. "It has been an honor to have such an illustrious program on the CBS Television Network and I might add it has been a personal pleasure for me to have been associated with such an outstanding professional and good friend as you have been during our relationship at Television City. I'm sure this is only a momentary good-bye as we at CBS certainly look forward to new and even more exciting projects to come from you and to appear during the interim period." The letter accompanied a bottle of champagne.

On April 15, Serling wrote to Bob Hoag. "Though the impersonality of our business has probably kept people from telling you that you were appreciated – the appreciation is nonetheless there in abundance."

In May of 1964, *The Twilight Zone* was still being marketed. The Ideal Toy Corporation produced a board game adapted from the television series. Serling was coming back from Europe (to be more specific, the New York to Los Angeles part of the trip) and sat next to a passenger from Ideal Toy, who was telling him about the game. Never having heard of it, Serling was quietly preparing legal action in advance. When he returned from his trip, he found two complimentary board games at his house in Pacific Palisades, waiting for him, sent over by Murray Benson, director of licensing and development for CBS. He dismissed the idea of a lawsuit with the understanding that the board game was licensed.

Rod Serling's Epitaph

On July 31, 1961, Serling's secretary, Patricia Temple, forwarded to Dick Isreal of the press information department of CBS-Television City an epitaph which was prematurely suited for the demise of the series:

> Here lies the body of a fella named Rod,
> Who lies under posies deep down in the sod.
> He had all his battles with sponsors and nets,
> Over what should come on and come off on the sets.
> The ad men will not miss his baitings,
> But at least under ground he won't worry about ratings.

The Season That Wasn't

On February 5, 1964, Rod Serling wrote to Alden Schwimmer of Ashley-Steiner, with a projection of what he planned to do for the new season. He confessed the intention to do some very exciting two-parters. Serling had made arrangements to shoot in the Thousand Islands using a vast unfinished island mansion called Boldt Castle, which he described as "the most incredible and eminently shootable piece of ruined masonry on the face of the earth." Serling acknowledged an invitation to visit the Vandenberg missile establishment and he had intended, with the cooperation of the employees, do considerably more dabbling in the space exploration theme, "possibly utilizing some never before seen footage that would have been made available to us." In line with the emphasis of space, he planned to do considerably more extra-terrestrial stuff – stories that took place on other planets. Not the "scaly monster business," but some credible suspense items that Serling favored with extreme intensity.

Serling also explained that he received a rundown on several story properties never before available. One was a short story entitled "The Devil and Sam Shay," written by Robert Arthur. Serling felt positive that the new season would offer more excitement and a "new flavor." He sent his proposals to Mike Dan of CBS Television, for review.

The short story called "The Devil and Sam Shay" dealt with a professional gambler who plays against the Devil. After losing three bets in a row, Satan furiously curses Shay so the gambler will never again win another wager. Opposed to honest labor, Shay gives the Devil and his myrmidons a real run for their money – by spending several weeks making all kinds of outlandish and extremely complicated wagers. This creates a hassle for Satan's minions, as it requires hundreds of them to be on hand at a minute's notice in order to make sure that Shay never wins a wager. The amount of sin occurring elsewhere is drastically reduced in the world since so many of them are busy with Shay. Gambling with the chance that Satan would not see his plan, Shay succeeds.

The Sale of *The Twilight Zone*

Newspapers at the time featured CBS reporting a lack of profits with *The Twilight Zone* and that may have been another of ABC's deciding factors to not pick up Serling's *Witches, Warlocks and Werewolves*.

In the November 2, 1964 issue of *The New York Times*, Serling was quoted as explaining "Television has left me frustrated and fatigued . . . Toward the end I was writing so much that I felt I had begun to lose my perspective on what was good or bad."

On November 13, 1964, he drafted a resignation request to Ted Ashley and Alden Schwimmer of the Ashley-Steiner Agency. "In essence, it is a notification to you that I've become disenchanted with my representation at Ashley and I think at this moment I'd like out." Among his complaints was how *The Twilight Zone* had not yet gone into syndication, while other programs with shorter life-spans had already made the jump. One critical complaint from him suggested money was an issue. "I think you guys have been less than frank with me in terms of the Agency's financial arrangements with the network. It has come back to me that though Ted told me how readily Ashley-Steiner cut its package fee to keep *The Twilight Zone* on the air – it was not broached that after the initial deal was made by Ira, Ted upped the ante at CBS to get a more sizable figure. This was cut down later on to keep the show on the air – but a sizable figure was operative. And never once have either of you told me what has been your cut in this deal. I understand now it's close to three-quarters of a million dollars. I don't begrudge you this dough. I know how you worked your asses off to make the deal. And the deal was a brilliant one. But where the hell is my cut? I spent five bleeding years knocking out close to a hundred scripts for this series – a series, mind you, that I created all by my lonesome – and now I'd like to get some gravy from it."

In fact, the *Twilight Zone* was already being syndicated by CBS. On December 27, 1964, *The New York Times* mentioned that Channel 9 in New York had recently purchased a syndication package for showing.

In March of 1965, negotiations were made to sell *The Twilight Zone* outright. According to numerous letters both personal and professional dated late 1964 through early 1965, Serling was upset about the overall quality of the final season and the cancellation. For financial reasons, he had hoped to continue the anthology. For personal reasons, he wanted to walk away from *Twilight Zone* for good. On the advice of agents, his lawyer and his accountant, Rod agreed to sell the series to CBS for a one-time payment.

On April 1, 1965, Serling attended a meeting with Gerald Mehlman and Roger Sherman of CBS and William Freedman of Freedman & Freedman, to work out the details of the purchase agreement to grant him an opportunity to create, exclusively for CBS, a number of television pilots over the coming years. This later agreement was to accommodate Merritt Coleman, who requested a little less than a year earlier that he commit to in a legally binding agreement to give the network first and exclusive opportunity to negotiate the pilots. He would only commit in a non-binding letter, but this time CBS got its wish. Among the pilots Serling would conceive:

The Jeopardy Run – Script dated December 16, 1963. A secret agent-type of series involving CIA men, a casket being carried across the ocean on a junk and an action-packed climax on the bridge of a ship. The company wanted to visit Hong Kong to film the adventure pilot for CBS, and get permission from the Mandarin Hotel to film on location, but the pilot ultimately was never filmed. Designed to be an attempt to cash in on the success of the James Bond motion pictures, the proposal gave the appearance of imitation.

Garrett's Ghost – Serling turned to friend John C. Champion for a television western about a sheriff named Pat Garrett, who shoots and kills a famous outlaw named Web Banister. The year was 1865, and the place was El Paso, Texas. After the death, Garrett discovers he is plagued by the ghost of the dead man, who helps assist him with his comical adventures, in a western version of *Topper* and *Here Comes Mr. Jordan*.

The Chase – "Each individual episode of *The Chase* is a case history of trouble. It's the story of the Soviet defectee or the American turncoat or any one of twenty-five dozen other stories of intrigue, or suspense, and of jeopardy," he wrote in a proposal for this series. It centered on an American named McGough, a former O.S.S. man and "is probably closest to the James Bond concept than anything else." Each week McGough was to go off on an assignment – the last 10 minutes of the shows devoted to a chase scene, hence the title. He proposed most of the series could be filmed in studios, and that "the authors will have complete control over story concepts."

According to columnist David Jampel in *Variety*, "If the show rolls, Serling would be its exec producer, a position he downgrades as 'titular,' and would write the first five scripts for the initial season."

Almost two years after *The Twilight Zone* went off the air, Serling wrote to Alden Schwimmer on August 12, 1966, explaining how he used two specific episodes of *The Twilight Zone* as pilots to fulfill his contractual obligations. "The CBS chaps looked at the two *Twilight Zone* films and tell me that neither one of them do anything in particular to suggest the kind of series that they are thinking about. As I understand it the kind of series they are thinking about lies more in the general area of a strange element in known surroundings rather than moving off into space. I believe they described *The Invaders* program to you as the prototype."

Cleaning Out the Closet

On March 15, 1965, an inventory was made on the literary properties purchased by Cayuga Productions with the intention of adapting them into feasible teleplays. Bought throughout the previous five years, the inventory gives a glimpse of stories Serling intended to produce.

"A Length of Rope" by Chester S. Geier was intended for a third-season episode. Basic rights were purchased for $350. Originally published in the April 1941 issue of *Unknown Worlds*, it tells the story of a man who saves the life of a stranger by pulling him out of the path of a speeding truck. The stranger turns out to be Satan, who insists on offering a gift to the man who saved his life; a length of rope that has magical qualities, as well as a history of having strangled to death several previous owners.

"The Devil and Sam Shay," written by Robert Arthur, was submitted during production of the third season. Cayuga purchased only basic rights. The short story was originally published as "Satan and Sam Shay," in the August 1942 issue of *The Elks Magazine*. Arthur had adapted the short story for *Buckingham Theatre* in 1950, one of the most prestigious coast-to-coast Canadian radio programs.

"The Uninvited Guest" by Pat O'Neil came with a $500 price tag, and production reports suggest an adaptation was scheduled for filming between July 1, 1961 and December 31, 1961.

George Clayton Johnson was paid $1,125 for the first draft of the script titled "Dream Flight." Co-written with William F. Nolan, this script was intended for a third season entry, but was never produced. The story told of Helen Cady, who suffers from a recurring nightmare as a passenger on board Trans Globe Airlines flight 88 en route to Chicago. She dreams that all four engines on the craft die out one-by-one, till the plane takes a nosedive and the passengers scream as they plunge to their deaths. As a passenger on the very same plane, Helen fears her dream was a premonition, and shortly after takeoff, the engines start to die out one at a time. With every sequence matching the exact scene experienced in her recurring nightmares, Helen suggests changing the pattern, so the event does not occur, and her lover, David, breaks the chain by kissing her. Only after he kisses her does the plane soar into safe territory and the passengers can breathe a sigh of relief.

Charles Beaumont was paid $1,125 for his story, "Free Dirt," intended for use on the fifth season. The short story was originally published in the May 1955 issue of *The Magazine of Fantasy and Science Fiction*. It told the story of a man who uses the free soil from recently dug graves to grow his own fruits and vegetables, only to discover horrifying results.

Another story proposal purchased during the third season was "Nevermore" by Ocee Ritch. Edmond H. North's story "The Triggerman" was bought for use on the series, and like the rest, never went before the cameras. Additional scripts purchased by Cayuga included "The Other Side of Yesterday" by John Cecil Holm, "What the Devil?" by Arch Oboler, and "The Doll" by Richard Matheson. (More about "The Doll" and "What the Devil?" in the episode guide.)

CBS Gains Control

According to Spencer Harrison's memorandum of March 31, 1965, in connection with the winding up of Cayuga Productions, Inc., Cayuga would be paid $280,000 by CBS for the purchase of Cayuga's interest in the films and in production rerun fees. A portion of this sum would be subject to corporate income tax and some to corporate capital gains tax. The amount, after corporate taxes, would be added to the existing net worth of approximately $130,000 and would be distributed to Serling, who would pay capital gains tax. He was left with approximately $210,000, after taxes, on this distribution.

In addition, CBS would pay Serling $225,000 as payment in full for all of his rerun fees as writer and host of *The Twilight Zone*, plus $25,000 per year for three years for exclusivity and $50,000 per year for three years for the delivery of three television pilot scripts per year. These payments by CBS totaled $450,000. Assuming he could not deliver three television pilot scripts each year for three years, he would receive a total of $350,000.

The agreements were drawn to provide that Serling would be paid the $350,000 at the rate of $35,000 per year commencing 1967. If the total exceeded $350,000, the additional sums would be payable at the rate of $35,000 per year starting with the 11th year.

The total of all the payments equaled $730,000. Since he had cash of approximately $130,000 in Cayuga Productions, the total position was approximately $860,000.

In early July 1965, Cayuga Productions, Inc. received from CBS a check for $280,000 for its interest in the *Twilight Zone* series. When the check arrived, William Freedman, Serling's accountant, put the money into Treasury bills so that interest could be earned immediately.

What Serling never counted on was the longevity of his beloved television series. "Fame is short-lived," he told a reporter for a syndicated trade column seven months previous to the sale. "One year after this show goes off the air, they'll never remember who I am. And I don't care a bit. Anonymity is fine with me. My place is as a writer."

After *The Twilight Zone*

In October of 1962, David M. Knauf, director of the Wisconsin Center for Theatre Research, sent out a number of letters to television legends: Reginald Rose, Adrian Spies, John Frankenheimer, Ernest Kinoy, and of course, Rod Serling. The Center was attempting to assemble and preserve the papers and manuscripts of distinguished contributors to the American theatre, Knauf explained, "in order to prevent the loss, through circumstance, of irreplaceable materials of great interest to future scholars, biographers, and historians." Serling agreed to donate scripts, letters, and other paperwork, especially since the donation was tax-deductible. On May 13, 1963, Milton Luboviski composed an appraisal of the manuscripts, part of which was contributed to the University of Wisconsin on June 7, 1963, and the remainder on January 27, 1964. When he agreed to sell his 50 percent share of Cayuga to CBS, he was advised to donate additional materials, again for a tax deduction, due to the lump sum he would receive from the network for the sale. On March 15, 1965, Luboviski appraised the additional manuscripts, which were contributed to the university on March 26, 1965. Each of the appraisals contained a number of *Twilight Zone* scripts.

On September 29, 1965, Serling wrote to Russell Stoneham of CBS-TV in New York, giving the impression that he was pleased with being able to walk away from the series. "It is my dubious pleasure to tell you that CBS now owns all of *Twilight Zone*. Films — comic books – spacemen T-shirts – Rod Serling masks . . ."

In the fall of 1965, CBS put *The Twilight Zone* into syndication. George D. Faber, director of client relations at CBS Films, Inc., talked with Jim Victory in New York to learn that the syndication was "sensational." The ratings everywhere were excellent.

The Twilight Zone became an instant success across the globe. Since its inception through June 30, 1964, the total number of sales internationally grossed a total of $494,789.81. Television stations across the country were paying for the episodes to air on the network. While every country purchased first and second-season episodes, only 11 purchased episodes from the third season, two countries (Canada and Sweden) chose to purchase the hour-long episodes from the fourth season, and only three countries (Canada, Finland and Sweden) opted for fifth-season episodes. The most profitable countries were Canada, Australia and Japan. Canada grossed CBS a total of $145,259.92 in sales; Australia grossed $115,709.99; and Japan grossed $72,340. (The country of Gibraltar only grossed $325 and Jamaica only grossed $78, making them the least profitable countries for syndication sales.) *

---

* Sales figures compiled and dated October 28, 1964.

Serling was still making guest appearances on television programs, even after *Twilight Zone* was no longer on the air. *The Tonight Show* on June 8, 1965, and *The Mike Douglas Television Show* on September 22, 1965, are two such examples.

On May 19, 1966, Mr. Sonkin, bookkeeper of Ashley-Steiner, sent Rod Serling a check in the amount of $148,748.92, which represented his one-half share of the sale of Cayuga Productions, Inc. The same day Sonkin also sent to Carol Serling, as the other half shareholder in Cayuga, a check made out for a penny more than her husband's.

Ashley-Steiner did not receive any commission fees, according to a letter from Alden Schwimmer to Serling, dated April 1, 1966, from the $280,000 attributable to buying right, title and interest in the "Twilight Zone" films, or the $130,000 that Cayuga had in the bank at the time of the deal.

They did commission at 5 percent the $225,000 that was attributable to rerun fees as host and as writer on the theory that because Serling sold the reruns at a bargain rate, "we ought to commission them at a bargain rate."

Monday, December 5, 1966, Serling attended a cocktail party at the Beverly Hills Hotel – the occasion was a CBS Films sales conference in the hotel, attended by the men who sold *Twilight Zone* domestically in such cities as Chicago and Detroit.

Rod Serling's Untimely Passing

On June 27, 1975, Rod Serling suffered two severe heart attacks en route to Strong Memorial Hospital in Rochester, New York. During heart bypass surgery, he suffered a third heart attack and died the following day. He was 50 years old.

He had recently remarked to an interviewer, "You just can't do social significance on television. The medium will never have an Ibsen." Yet, having served a two-year term as president of the National Academy of Television Arts and Sciences, and as a winner of six Emmy Awards, his death was not overlooked by newspaper columnists and by Robert E. Lewine, then president of the National Academy of Television Arts and Sciences, who wrote, "As members of the entire television community, we are the beneficiaries of his rare talents. His legacy may serve us well but he will be sorely missed."

Serling's body was interred at the cemetery in Interlaken, New York. He left his estate in trust to his widow, Carol, and his two daughters, according to a petition for probate of his will filed July 23 in the Los Angeles Superior Court. The estimated value of the estate, according to a public news item, revealed real estate property and personal property, each in excess of $50,000 with a probable annual income of more than $10,000. The real estate was purchased using the profits from Cayuga Productions, which he wisely invested.

The Syndicated Reruns

Serling lived to see his brainchild acquire cult status through first-run syndication, but according to a columnist in the July 17, 2005 issue of *The New York Times*, he was disappointed in the edits revealed in the syndicated cuts. "You wouldn't recognize what series it was," he explained. "Full scenes were deleted. It looked like a long, protracted commercial separated by fragmentary moments of indistinct drama." The cuts were made for a number of reasons. First, all of his cigarette testimonials at the end of some teasers were removed, to avoid conflict with the new sponsors. In many cases, his teasers for "next week's episodes" were removed. As the years went on, the films began to get shorter and shorter – from 24 and 25 minutes to 21 and 22 minutes, allowing more room for commercials.

The practice of syndication continues today. Airings on some cable networks broadcast *The Twilight Zone* in shorter lengths. In other instances, a little thought was exercised to remove a scene without the viewer being aware of the edit. Other instances, the cut was careless, removing key scenes from an episode and confusing viewers who are left with questions that might otherwise have been answered. Commercial home video and DVD marketers have released the episodes in their true form, uncut and unedited, so fans of the series can enjoy the films as Rod Serling and his crew intended back in 1959.

Spoofs and Salutes

The trailer for the movie *Neighbors* (1981) featured a salute to *The Twilight Zone*. A disco record by Manhattan Transfer featured the familiar *Twilight Zone* theme. In 1982, a four-panel comic strip of "Bloom County," inked by Berke Breathed, featured its own salute to *The Twilight Zone*. Throughout the mid-80s, the comic strip *Robotman* would, on occasion, feature a homage to the television program, as the main character, a robot, found himself in bizarre situations. At least three "Robotman" funnies from the Sunday paper recognized the cult status of *The Twilight Zone*.

Over the past few years, a number of movies have featured references to *The Twilight Zone*. The character of Steve gets an idea for a *Twilight Zone* episode in *A Night at the Roxbury* (1998). The captain of a doomed ship denies the strange incident as being part of the television series. In *Under*

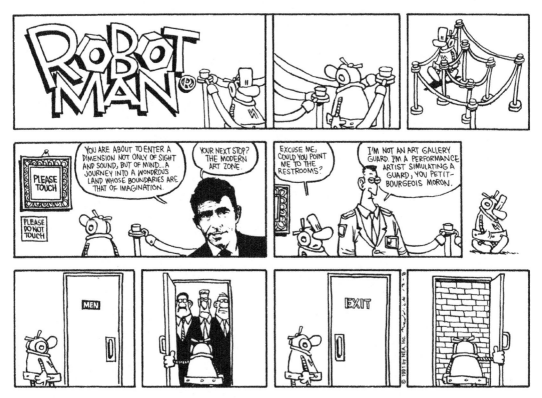

Robotman panel from December 8, 1991, featuring a spoof on *The Twilight Zone*.
Robotman © by Newspaper Enterprise Association, Inc. Reprinted with permission.

Siege II: Dark Territory (1995), the villain does a good Rod Serling impersonation, suggesting he had seen a number of *Twilight Zone* episodes.

Passing references to *The Twilight Zone* appear in *Mystery Science Theater 3000*, *Futurama*, *Ellen*, *The X-Files*, *Family Guy*, *Caroline in the City*, *Cosby*, *Ed*, *Dawson's Creek* and *Birds of Prey*.

The animated cartoon series *Johnny Bravo* featured a three-segment episode spoofing a number of *Twilight Zone* episodes. Initially broadcast on December 8, 1997, the first segment, titled "The Man Who Cried Clown," Johnny attempts to convince other people that a clown is tearing apart one of the engines on the jet airplane. In "Johnny Real Good," Johnny baby-sits a young boy who possesses the same power as Anthony from "It's a Good Life." In the third and final segment, "Little Talky Tabitha," Johnny has to combat a vicious doll that has come to life.

In the episode "Sci-Fi Zoned" on the television series *Weird Science*, initially telecast on June 17, 1995, the lead characters find themselves trapped within a television series that mirrors *The Twilight Zone* and spoof a number of scenes and characters from "Escape Clause," "The Rip Van Winkle Caper," "Living Doll," "Kick the Can," "Eye of the Beholder," "Stopover in a Quiet Town," "Time Enough at Last" and "Will the Real Martian Please Stand Up?"

The theme song of *The Twilight Zone* (the classic Constant theme) was featured in the motion pictures *Lucky Numbers* (2000), *E.T.: The Extra-Terrestrial* (1982), and *Dream A Little Dream* (1989). Verbal references to *The Twilight Zone* are mentioned in: *In and Out* (1997), *Good Morning, Vietnam* (1987), *The Golden Child* (1986) and *The Breakfast Club* (1985).

The Twilight Zone Magazine

On the morning of May 16, 1963, Sam Kaplan had a phone conversation with Murray Benson, authorizing CBS, on behalf of Cayuga Productions, to enter into negotiations for the publication of a magazine intended to bear the title, *Rod Serling's Stories from the Twilight Zone*. From the beginning, the magazine was designed not to contain any stories or storylines actually written by Rod Serling. By July 3, Division Publications proceeded with *The Twilight Zone Magazine* – an advance of $5,000 was made for the start-up of the magazine – Cayuga Productions received $2,500 (half of the income) and CBS kept the other half.

In a letter dated October 29, 1963, Benson wrote to Gerald Saltsman of Ashley-Steiner explaining, "*The Twilight Zone* magazine licensee has been unbelievably delinquent in getting the magazines to the presses and, in fact, we are attempting to legally sever our relationship if at all possible. Of course, the advance of $5,000 is forfeited by the licensee under any circumstance."

In March of 1981, with T.E.D. Klein as editor, a new *The Twilight Zone Magazine* premiered on newsstands. This long-running monthly publication magazine featured a variety of items designed to intrigue any casual fan of science fiction and horror. The issues contained news briefs, previews of up-and-coming motion pictures, short fiction, book reviews, story contests, and exclusive interviews with writers, directors and actors. The magazine was published pursuant to a license from Carol Serling and Viacom Enterprises, a division of Viacom International, Inc. Carol Serling was the associate publisher. *

The magazine was perhaps most prominent for featuring an episode guide compiled by Marc

---

* The FCC had ordered the networks to get out of the syndication business. CBS spun its rerun properties off into a new company, Viacom, in 1971, just in time for the huge syndication boom brought on by the advent of cheap satellite distribution and the birth of the cable TV universe. The CBS library, ranging from *Gunsmoke* to *All In The Family*, was so valuable that Viacom would eventually buy CBS as well as Paramount Pictures, the MTV networks, Nickelodeon and Comedy Central.

Scott Zicree and reprints of many Serling-scripted *Twilight Zone* teleplays. The magazine was responsible for granting fiction writers the opportunity to submit their work on a free-lance basis. It was influential in promoting *The Twilight Zone Companion* by Zicree, which was published months after the magazine's premiere and heavily promoted within the pages. When *The Twilight Zone* received a revival in the mid-80s, the magazine was instrumental in promoting the new series with photos from various episodes, interviews with cast and crew, and news briefs about upcoming episodes.

1984 Was the Year of *The Twilight Zone*

The January 4, 1984 issue of *Variety* reported, "CBS has filed suit in New York Federal Court against Marius Constant, a composer, over the rights to the theme music for *The Twilight Zone*. The suit says CBS commissioned Constant to write the theme in 1960. CBS claims it remains the rights holder to the music, under copyright, throughout the world."

From February 24 through May 3, 1984, the Museum of Broadcasting in New York presented "Rod Serling: Dimensions of Imagination," an exhibition of more than 60 hours of programming, and a special evening panel presentation featuring Carol Serling, Buck Houghton, Bert Granet, Cliff Robertson, Earl Holliman, George Clayton Johnson, Richard Matheson, and others. The exhibition included episodes from *The Twilight Zone* and some of Serling's major 1950s television plays such as "Patterns" and "Requiem for a Heavyweight."

Three episodes of *The Twilight Zone* which, having been held back from syndication, were broadcast on the evening of October 20, 1984, for a two-hour television special titled, *The Twilight Zone Silver Anniversary Special*. Two of the episodes were kept from syndication because they were tied up in litigation over disputes of authorship. Patrick O'Neal, who starred in one of the episodes, "A Short Drink from a Certain Fountain," hosted the two-hour program. "Sounds and Silences" and "Miniature" were the two other episodes. In a first for *Twilight Zone*, one of the original black and white episodes was transformed into color by a computer process. The effect was similar to the hand-colored photographs that were popular before the days of color film. The pastel tints are appropriate to the 19th century romantic spirit of the story. The doll house scenes in "Miniature" were colorized, while the rest of the episode remained in black and white.

Charliex

When Columbia House, a home video company in Terre Haute, Indiana, began sublicensing *The Twilight Zone* on the commercial home video market on a subscription basis, the company turned to Charliex in New York, a company famous for the *Saturday Night Live* opening and a number of Cherry Coke commercials, to create the video preface for the beginning of each and every video. Using an Ultimatte™ Ampex Digital Optics (the ADO), the Paintbox, and good old imagination, an electronic collage of live images and artwork had virtually become a Charliex trademark. For CBS Video, Charliex has created a colored tribute to *I Love Lucy*, featuring great moments from the show. The characters were colored on the Paintbox frame, but the black and white surroundings were preserved for a magical, nostalgic effect. A computer-animated title sequence for a batch of *Star Trek* episodes followed, which was quite successful for CBS. *The Twilight Zone* montage was a natural follow-up. *

---

* The Ultimatte™ ADO was a patented process and device which cleanly keys one element (usually live action) over a background. The name Ultimatte™ is a registered trademark of the Ultimatte Corporation. Reprinted with permission.

The team for the project consisted of Alex Weil, Chris Harvey, John Semerad, and Bill Weber. Based on ideas by Carol Serling and with the assistance of Harry Elias of CBS, a project formed to take various scenes from classic episodes and blend them together into a montage saluting the best of the series. "After many meetings, it was Alex's idea to use great moments from great episodes and to use 'film cutouts,'" explained Chris Harvey. "Beyond that, he left it up to me, working closely with him, to make all the audio and visual selects and pair them together."

Chris Harvey had all the episodes on one-inch masters, and many rough cuts of various audio and video montages were created. The rough cuts were then screened with Alex Weil and CBS. After the consultation, Paintbox artist John Semerad created the background behind the characters. It was made from frames of the holocaust landscape from the episode "Time Enough at Last." The inventive tribute has been featured on commercial home video and is today still being offered on commercial DVDs.

The Twilight Zone Trademark
CBS, Inc. filed a number of trademarks for "The Twilight Zone." The first was Registration # 1,398,021, filed in 1985 and issued in 1986. The paperwork claimed the date of first use was October 2, 1959. The second was Registration # 1,696,570, filed in 1991 and issued in 1992. The second trademark was for "The Twilight Zone" logo, specially stylized words against a starry sky. A third registration was filed, Registration # 1,935,619, issued in 1995 for clothing using the *Twilight Zone* name and logo. The fourth and final registration was # 1,732,656, issued in 1991, but allowed to lapse as of May 24, 1999. It was for the logo design to be used on videocassettes and videotapes.

The Hollywood Walk of Fame
At precisely 6:39 p.m. on Thursday, October 6, 1988, Rod Serling was honored with a star on the fabled Hollywood Walk of Fame. Over 300 friends and admirers gathered at the ceremony on Hollywood Boulevard. Staff of the original *Twilight Zone* series, writers and actors were in attendance. After Carol Serling unveiled the gleaming bronze star and those who had known and respected Serling spoke of his life and legacy, the guests adjourned to the nearby club "Hollywood Live" for a festive reception sponsored by MGM/UA Telecommunications, syndicator of the 1980s revival series.

The Video Game
1988 was the same year that First Row Software, Inc., a software publishing company located in King of Prussia, Pennsylvania, commercially released a popular and successful computer game titled, "The Twilight Zone." Featuring the familiar music and soundtrack from the original series, the title screen included the ticking watch, open door and Einstein equation from the fourth and fifth season opening title sequence.

The Twilight Zone Radio Dramas
Four decades after *The Twilight Zone* premiered on CBS-TV, producer Carl Amari decided to present new dramatizations based on this classic program. A lifelong fan of old-time radio, Amari decided to revive the series not as a nostalgic recreation of radio as it once was. Instead, Amari commissioned fresh radio adaptations based on the original 156 teleplays along with new story ideas never seen or heard on *The Twilight Zone*. Among the prolific writers responsible for adapting the teleplays into

feasible radio scripts are World Fantasy Award-winning writer Dennis Etchison. Recorded in digital stereo, narrated by Stacy Keach and starring a remarkable cast of actors, these exciting productions take the art of audio drama to an audience that may not have seen the *Twilight Zone* productions when they were first telecast from 1959 – 1964.

Among the radio dramas are adaptations of teleplays written by Charles Beaumont and Jerry Sohl that were commissioned but never produced, such as "Free Dirt" and "Who Am I?" The program has been syndicated across the country on XM and Sirius Satellite Radio, as well as a number of local radio stations.

Looking Back

"He had a story to tell, but there were so many taboos," recalled Carol Serling. "When he wanted to do something socially relevant, the networks, sponsors and ad agencies said: 'You can't do that. You'll step on too many toes.'"

"It was timeless. Today there isn't anything like it on the air because those damn folks at the networks are too stupid to duplicate it," recalled Steven King, author of numerous best-selling horror novels, in the June 20, 1983 issue of *The New York Post*. "Sometimes the show was fantastic, but mostly it was shlock."

A press release for *Twilight Zone: The Movie*, the Warner Bros. big-screen motion picture, stated, "It would seem as if the original *Twilight Zone* was born with a silver spoon in its mouth, but the head-spinning popularity and widespread influence the series ultimately enjoyed is worthy of a second look."

With the continued success of *Twilight Zone* marathons on television stations across the country and Serling seminars held at various colleges, universities and film/nostalgia conventions, the universal appeal of Rod Serling's brain child continues to live on.

The Episode Guide

Bernard Herrmann Orchestrations

- "Where is Everybody?" — 6 violins, 4 horns, 2 violas, 2 celli, 2 clarinets, 2 harps, 2 basses, 1 flute, 1 oboe, 1 English horn, 1 bass clarinet and 1 vibe.

- "The Lonely" — 2 vibraphones, 2 harps, 3 trumpets, 3 trombones and 1 hammond organ.

- "Eye of the Beholder" — 4 horns, 3 "C" trumpets, 3 trombones, 2 tubas, 2 harps, 1 timp and 1 cymbal.

- "Little Girl Lost" — 4 harps, 4 flutes, 2 tam tams, 1 viola, 1 tambourine and 1 vibraphone.

- "Living Doll" — 2 harps, 1 celeste and 1 bass clarinet.

- "90 Years Without Slumbering" — 2 clarinets, 1 bass clarinet, 1 harp and 1 vibe.

FIRST SEASON PRODUCTION COSTS

Producer (Buck Houghton): $17,400.00
Unit Manager: $850.00
Messenger Service: $1,775.15
Insurance: $4,956.80
Property Taxes, etc.: $2,509.80
Less: Erroneous non-Cayuga credits from California Studios, Inc. – $130.72
Total Preproduction and Unallocated Costs: $54,949.56

Secretaries: $2,485.00
Office Supplies and Telephone: $3,080.88
Payroll Taxes, etc.: $17,342.65
Titles: $4,680.00
Total Charges: $55,080.28

Adding the preproduction and unallocated costs, and the unassigned literary properties (totaling $6,220.00), and the costs of production for each episode, the total cost to produce the 36 episodes from the first season totaled $1,955,399.41. A total under two million.*

Production #3601 "WHERE IS EVERYBODY?"
(Initial telecast: October 2, 1959)
© Cayuga Productions, Inc., October 1, 1959, LP15007 (in notice: 1958)
Supposedly one day of rehearsal and eight days of filming, during the first two weeks of December.
Script #1 dated: November 20, 1958, with revised pages dated November 25, 26 and December 1, 1958.
Shooting script dated: December 1, 1958

Story and Secretary: $2,250.00
Cast: $8,895.29
Agents Commission: $5,185.55
Payroll Taxes, etc. $569.97
Below the line charges (other): $66,618.41

Director: $2,500.00
Production Fee: $750.00
Legal and Accounting: $250.00
Below the line charges (M-G-M): $2,506.51
Total Production Costs: $89,525.73

---

* All summary of production costs listed for first season episodes according to production files dated June 30, 1960.

Cast: John Conwell (the Colonel); James Gregory (Air Force General); Earl Holliman (Mike Ferris); Jim Johnson (Staff Sergeant); Paul Langton (the doctor); James McCallion (Reporter #3); Carter Mullaly (the Captain); Jay Overholt (Reporter #2); and Gary Walberg (Reporter #1).

Original Music Score Composed and Conducted by Bernard Herrmann: Main Title (:34); The Man (:16); Turkish Delight (by Eric Cook, 1:52); Comin' Thru the Rye (by Robert Burns, :11); The Station (:07); The Door (:32); The Truck (:1:26); The Telephone (:32); The Phone Booth (:36); The Station House (:49); The Cell (:29); The Sun (:16); The Mirror (:35); The Book Rack (1:05); The Lights (:53); The Film (:40); The Bicycle (:29); The Breakdown (:32); The Button (:41); and Finale (:59).

Director of Photography: Joseph LaShelle, a.s.c.
Art Direction: Alex Golitzen and
    Robert Clatworthy
Set Decorations: Russell A. Gausman
    and Ruby Levitt
Sound: Leslie I. Carey and Vernon W. Kramer

Film Editor: Roland Gross, a.c.e.
Assistant Director: Joseph E. Kenny
Makeup: Bud Westmore
Directed by Robert Stevens.
Teleplay by Rod Serling.

"The place is here, the time is now – and the journey into the shadows that we're about to watch could be our journey."

Plot: Mike Ferris wanders into a deserted town, unable to remember who he is or where he came from. All appearances suggest he is not the only person in town. The church bell rings, but no one is present in the church. A half-burned cigar is found burning in an ashtray. A jukebox was left playing in a café. A pot of coffee was left boiling on the stove. A phone rings in a phone booth, but no one is on the line. Ferris briefly mistakes a mannequin as a passenger in a truck. After hours of solitary loneliness, Ferris cracks under the strain. The U.S. Air Force comes to Ferris' rescue – unplugging him from an isolation booth and waking him from a nightmare. As the General explains to members of the press, the Air Force can send a man into orbit, pump oxygen in and waste out, and provide microfilm for recreation . . . but the one barrier they cannot crack is loneliness. The General assures the men present that if they themselves were confined in a box five-feet square for two weeks, their imagination would start to run away with them, too. Next time, Ferris will be alone in the real deal.

"Up there . . . up there in the vastness of space, in the void that is sky . . . up there is an enemy known as isolation. It sits there in the stars waiting . . . waiting with the patience of eons . . . forever waiting . . . in the Twilight Zone."

Trailer: *"I'm about to show you a picture of something that isn't what it looks like. Pleasant little town? It isn't this at all. It's a nightmare. It's a chilling, frightening journey of one man into a mystifying unknown. You're invited to join that man in a most unique experience. Next week, Earl Holliman asks, and you'll ask with him, 'Where is Everybody?' Here's an item we forgot. A moment for the people who pay the tab. It's often said that 'a picture is worth a thousand words.' Case in point. Before we meet again, try Oasis. You'll know what I mean."*

Trivia, etc. The time period in which this episode aired was amidst the space race, in which the United States and the Soviet Union competed to explore outer space with artificial satellites, sending humans into space, and landing a man on the moon. On September 13, 1959, the Luna 2, a Russian spacecraft, crashed onto the moon, man's first physical contact with our orbiting neighbor. On October 7, the Luna 3 sent back the first-ever photos of the far side of the moon. On October 2, Mike Ferris snapped out of an isolation experiment on network television, and *The Twilight Zone* left a large impact on society pop culture.

The premiere episode of the series was described by New York television critic John Crosby, "... I was thoroughly disappointed in the ending, but it was a beautifully directed and produced and written and photographed story – and it still lives with me."

"I got the idea walking through an empty village set at the back lot of a movie studio," Rod Serling recalled. "There was all the evidence of a community ... But no people. I felt at the time a kind of encroaching loneliness and desolation and a feeling of how nightmarish it would be for a man to wind up in a city without inhabitants." Serling admitted a number of times over the years that scenes for this episode also stemmed from a moment when he trapped himself in a phone booth at an airport and reading an article in *Time* about isolation experiments conducted on astronaut trainees.

Earl Holliman had previously co-starred in the *Playhouse 90* production of "The Dark Side of the Earth," and months later, Serling met up with him on a parking lot at the M-G-M Studios. After a brief conversation, Serling promised to send the actor a script for the pilot of a television series he was working on. He fulfilled his promise and Holliman was secured. "Bob Stevens, who directed that episode, was a good friend of mine," Holliman recalled. "But he never gave me any direction. He was busy doing something with someone. I was left to myself to decide how to play the character."

Filmed at Universal-International Studios, the entire production took longer than intended for a variety of reasons. Toward the end of the first day of filming, it was discovered that a mistake was made, so all the film was never developed, and the scenes had to be re-shot. Being the pilot, extra care was taken for the set decorations, lighting, and camera work. The smashed clock that Holliman taps in the isolation booth was foreshadowed a number of times, including the opening scene in the diner – revealing the intricate detail put into the production.

When filming was completed, Westbrook Van Voorhis was hired as narrator for the series. The unaired pilot shown to potential sponsors (and the network) features Van Voorhis in the opening sequence, panning across the stars and galaxies in the universe, and commenting that "There is a sixth dimension ..."

Replacing Van Voorhis' narration, Serling's off-screen voice for the pilot was recorded on May 19, 1959. For the newly recorded voice-overs, and title screen sequence, Serling had changed the opener to "There is a fifth dimension ...." Serling also recorded off-screen narration for the opening of the second act, which would have been seen by the television audience immediately after mid-commercial. The narration was never put into the finished film.

"The barrier of loneliness. The palpable, desperate need of the human animal to be with his fellow man."

Serling's original draft contained two major sequences that were written out during script revisions. One was of Mike Ferris entering an empty bank and setting off the alarm; realizing not even the police are coming to answer the call, he rips out the wires to the alarm to stop the loud ringing. Ferris then steals a large amount of cash and uses one of the bills to light a cigar. Another scene was the phone booth. Rather than figure out he was supposed to pull instead of push, Ferris broke out of the booth by breaking the glass, cutting his hand. (A similar scene managed to find its way into a later first-season episode, "Execution," in which Caswell smashes through the phone booth by breaking the glass.)

The earliest draft of this script instructs the editor to superimpose the title "Where is Everybody?" on the screen after the first commercial break, along with the major credits, during the scene of Mike walking down a street which is devoid of any kind of movement whatsoever.

Shortly before Serling recorded the narrations, the original closer was planned as the following:

"Up there in the vastness of space is an enemy known as isolation. It sits there in the stars waiting with the patience of eons . . . forever waiting . . . in The Twilight Zone."

An early draft featured the following closing narration, which Serling recorded, but was not a part of the final cut that aired on CBS in October of 1959:

"The barrier of loneliness. The palpable, desperate need of the human animal to be with his fellow man. Up there . . . up there in the vastness of space, in the void that is sky . . . up there is an enemy known as isolation. It sits there in the stars waiting . . . waiting with the patience of eons . . . forever waiting . . . in the Twilight Zone."

CBS staff announcer Roy Rowan is heard at the end of a variation of the unaired pilot, reminding viewers that Rod Serling, creator of *The Twilight Zone*, would return after the commercial break to tell the audience about next week's story. This was Rowan's only contribution to the series, as another announcer (Marvin Miller) took his place when the program went into production.

Other brief differences between the unaired pilot and the version that aired on network television include Mike Ferris walking through the diner singing "Comin' Thru the Rye." In the network telecast, the film fades to black for a commercial break, deleting the scene.

Serling's trailer for next week's episode was recorded for "Where is Everybody?" only because of the rerun and not the initial telecast. The trailer was recorded on the morning of March 20, 1961, and featured at the end of the initial telecast for "The Obsolete Man."

The movie theater named "The Savoy" is referenced throughout *The Twilight Zone* series, including "The Trouble With Templeton" and "The Dummy." Serling's constant reuse of names (both places and people) was not so much a lack of creativity, but for legal purposes. If the name of a movie theater matched a real one in existence, legal issues could arise. After researching to discover there was no "Savoy" in the United States (there was one in England), Serling later used the name again to continue avoiding legal issues. Most television viewers would not be observant enough to catch the repeated theater name simply because it was prominently used only once each season.

Jay Overholts, formerly a cast member for many of Serling's radio scripts in Ohio during the early 1950s, makes his first of many appearances on *The Twilight Zone*, and the only episode to accidentally misspell his name "Jay Overholt."

The October 5, 1959 issue of *The Hollywood Reporter* reviewed this episode. "The lonely literati of TV's Word Watchers and Significance Seekers Marching Society may be constrained to discover that, contrary to coffee house gossip, Rod Serling, first class Frankenstein to the electronic monster, can commit himself to a weekly series without necessarily compromising his craft on the altar of commercialism. This debut scored with dramatic impact infrequently found when the TV camera attempts to focus on the fringes of fantasy, and while short on insight, it was strong on style and solidly suspenseful."

The Syracuse Post-Standard commented that, "the ending is not quite up to the beginning, but it's still a tremendous effective production."

Variety magazine, which carried more weight than any of the other trade papers at the time, reviewed this episode. "Obviously these flights of imagination can only be as good and as ingenious as the writer. . . . Since the zinger lies in the denouement, it is here where Serling lets down his audience by providing a completely plausible and logical explanation. Somehow the viewer can't help but feel cheated, even though Serling gives it a topicality attuned to the current human experimentations in preparation for space travel. A science fiction ending would be more in the realm of the imagination. . . . Everything about *Twilight Zone* suggests solid production values, with director Robert Stevens extracting maximum performance in this one-man (almost right up to the end) journey into shadow."

"Serling has stood for qualitative writing and here, in his own venture, he is inspired to heights corresponding with the moon phase of the story," continued *Variety*. "Compelling drama that never released its taut grip, the writing and narration of Serling and Holliman's realistic pretense of terror gave it an epic dimension of greatness in an early season of mediocrity. . . . General Foods and Kimberly-Clark have a winner going for them."

In an issue of *TV Guide*, Rod Serling remarked about Holliman's virtual one-man performance. "On the surface Earl appears to be colorless, bland, because when he's on a set he indulges in no horseplay, no card-playing, no asides. Whether it's self-doubt or self-improvement or maybe old-fashioned gutsy dedication, Earl is just about the hardest-working actor I know."

On October 21, 1959, Serling wrote a thank-you letter to Earl Holliman, saying, "your performance was outstanding, full of dimension, shading and a fantastic believability. In short, Holliman, you're one hell of an actor! Some rich and gracious producers send wristwatches and things like that as expressions of appreciation. Gracious I am – rich I ain't, so accept these few clippings as evidence of my thinking about you."

The March 4, 1960 issue of *The Hollywood Reporter* announced that "CBS will rerun 'Zone' season opener 'Where is Everybody?' in a frank push to parlay Emmy consideration for Rod Serling, the series and Earl Holliman, who starred the initialer." The rerun never came to be, due to scheduling conflicts, but Serling nevertheless won an Emmy for "Outstanding Writing Achievement in Drama" that year – without the nudge of the pilot.

In 1989, an organization called "Cable in the Classroom" was founded, assisting the cable television industry in providing educational content to public and private schools. It allows educators to record the filmed presentations, and later play them back as learning tools for students. This episode of *The Twilight Zone*, among a few others, was chosen for use with the program. Like most courses offered to school systems, a suggested lesson plan was submitted to classroom teachers. Social deprivation and isolation are key factors in the lesson plan, and it was hoped it would help students who might have been affected, psychologically, at home.

Production #3608 "ONE FOR THE ANGELS" (Initial telecast: October 9, 1959)

Copyright Registration: © Cayuga Productions, Inc., October 8, 1959, LP15008
Dates of Rehearsal: July 6 and 7, 1959
Dates of Filming: July 8, 9 and 10, 1959
Script #8 dated: May 18, 1959, with revised pages dated June 29, July 3, 6 and 7, 1959.
Shooting script dated: July 7, 1959

Producer and Secretary: $660.00
Director: $1,250.00
Unit Manager and Secretary: $520.00
Agents Commission: $5,185.55
Below the line charges (M-G-M): $28,622.84
Total Production Costs: $51,327.17

Story and Secretary: $2,598.05
Cast: $7,296.83
Production Fee: $750.00
Legal and Accounting: $250.00
Below the line charges (other): $4,193.90

Cast: Merritt Bohn (the truck driver); Dana Dillaway (Maggie Polansky); Murray Hamilton (Mr. Death); Mickey Maga (the little boy); Jay Overholts (the doctor); and Ed Wynn (Lewis J. Bookman).

Stock Music Cues: Main Title (by Bernard Hermann, :39); Middletown – Average Size City Music (by Willis Schaefer, 1:06); House on K Street – Fade In (by Herrmann, :12); Middletown – Average Size City Music (by Schaefer, :22); House on K Street – Fade In (by Herrmann, :12); Rain Clouds – Western Suite (by Herrmann, 1:03); Piano Sweetener (anonymous, :08); Night Suspense – Western Suite (by Herrmann, 1:29); House on K Street – Fade In (reprise); Prelude I – Outer Space Suite (by Herrmann, :25 and 1:10); Sputnick #2 (by Guy Luypaertz, :48); House on K Street – Fade In (reprise); Rain Clouds – Western Suite (by Herrmann, :29); Bad Man – Western Suite (by Herrmann, :10); Rain Clouds – Western Suite (by Herrmann, :30); Prelude I – Outer Space Suite (by Herrmann, :20); House on K Street – Fade In (by Herrmann, :12); Rain Clouds – Western Suite (by Herrmann, :22); Time Suspense – Outer Space Suite (by Herrmann, 3:32); Starlight – Outer Space Suite (by Herrmann, 1:08); Police Force Opening (by Herrmann, :05); The Ambush – Western Suite (by Herrmann, :05); and End Title (by Herrmann, 1:00).

Director of Photography: George T. Clemens, a.s.c.
Production Manager: Ralph W. Nelson
Art Directors: George W. Davis and
    William Ferrari
Set Decorations: Henry Grace and Rudy Butler
Sound: Franklin Milton and Jean Valentino

Film Editor: Lyle Boyer
Assistant Director: Edward Denault
Casting Director: Mildred Gusse
Directed by Robert Parrish
Teleplay by Rod Serling

"Street scene . . . summer . . .the present. Man on a sidewalk named Lew Bookman – age sixtyish; occupation – pitchman. Lew Bookman. A fixture of the summer. A rather minor component to a hot July. A nondescript, commonplace little man whose life is a treadmill built out of sidewalks. In just a moment Lew Bookman will have to concern himself with survival. Because as of three o'clock this hot July afternoon he'll be stalked by . . . Mr. Death."

Plot: When Lew Bookman's time has come to face the ultimate betrayal of life, he manages to out-con Mr. Death, convincing the suited stranger that he has unfinished business here on Earth. Speaking from the heart, Lew explains that one thing he has always wanted to do before he passes on is to make a sales pitch that would be "one for the angels." It would mean for that one moment his life would have meaning. Mr. Death accepts the terms and promises to return when Lew has fulfilled his errant wish. Moments later, a young girl is hit by a car. With her injuries severe, the doctor admits it isn't looking good, and Lew watches as Mr. Death lingers about, ready to take his next victim. Late that evening, 20 minutes before his scheduled appointment with the girl, Mr. Death finds the sidewalk peddler standing outside the front steps, setting up shop. Explaining that he often makes sales this late at night, Lew begins to demonstrate the quality of his wares, and one-by-one, the demon starts buying ties and trinkets. Lew's sales pitch is so strong that just seconds after midnight, Mr. Death realizes he missed his scheduled appointment. Lew takes a deep sigh of relief. He has made a pitch in which the heavens took notice. Mr. Death, realizing what Lew has done, escorts a contented pitchman down the street.

"Lewis J. Bookman. Age, sixtyish. Occupation: pitchman. Formerly a fixture of the summer. Formerly a rather minor component to a hot July. But throughout his life a man beloved by the children, and therefore . . . a most important man. Couldn't happen, you say? Probably not in most places. But it did happen . . . in the Twilight Zone."

Trailer: *"Next week I'll have a reunion with a unique talent and a valued friend. Our first since 'Requiem for a Heavyweight'. Next week on The Twilight Zone, Mr. Ed Wynn stars in "One for the Angels," playing an old pitchman who sells mechanical toys like this, but who's competition is Mr. Death. We hope you'll join us then. Thank you and good night."*

Trivia, etc. "Humor is something that is true," explained Ed Wynn. "Wit is an exaggeration of the truth. The jokes I used to tell I'd call wit; the kind of acting I do now is more closely akin to humor – or at least a sense of humor. Actually, most people don't understand what a sense of humor is. It has little to do with the ability to tell a joke or even laugh at a joke. It's something which comes to your defense in times of adversity. Back in 1953, when the big theatrical curtain rang down on me, it was my sense of humor – my ability to laugh at myself – that saved me."

The first time Ed Wynn and Rod Serling worked together on a television show, it resulted in a new career for comedian-turned-actor and an Emmy Award for Serling. The year was 1956 and Serling's teleplay "Requiem for a Heavyweight" was presented on *Playhouse 90* over CBS. That was Wynn's first dramatic role. The two men, two generations apart in age, had a high regard for each other. "Rod's a wonderful writer," Wynn explained to a representative of CBS' publicity department, "which is no news to anyone. He's also a wonderful person." Serling felt Wynn's timing was "flawless." The origin of "One for the Angels," however, dates back two years previous.

The script "One for the Angels" was dramatized previously on *Danger*, a CBS television anthology, on September 14, 1954. Before that, it was dramatized on the television program, *The Storm*, on WKRC-TV in Cincinnati. The original tale told of a pitchman named Lou, a 37-year-old pitchman who specialized in selling trinkets – including wind-up walking men – on the street. Lou couldn't hold a crowd if it were cemented to the sidewalk and took to the bottle every night. He wasn't a very good salesman – he sold two the other day, at less than cost, out of desperation to ensure he could make a sale. His father, Andy, was a cripple who lived in the apartment under Lou's care. Vinnie, his younger brother, in his early 20s, knocked Lou for not getting into his line of work as an errand boy for big-time bookies. *

Lou feels concern for his younger brother, admitting to his old man that he would prefer to light a brighter path for Vinnie before it's too late.

LOU: *I can't sell quarter toys. How can I tell Vinnie right from wrong? It figures. Someplace down deep inside me I know I've got the words. They're in there someplace.*

ANDY: *The words?*

LOU: *The words for the pitch. The big pitch. The one that counts. A pitch so big that . . . that the sky has to listen. A pitch for the . . . for the angels!*

One afternoon, Vinnie visits the apartment and is scared to come out. His boss, Archie, found out Vinnie was holding back bet money, so he and his men want to murder him. After observing the gunmen in the street, Lou assures Vinnie that he won't be shot in broad daylight in front of witnesses. However, if he waits until dark, when the streets clear, the gunmen will march up the steps and pay him a private visit. With no other option, Vinnie goes along with his brother, into the street. Lou sets up shop with his satchel of toys and portable stand, and begins his pitch to keep a crowd gathered around.

Lou's success as a pitchman works. People gather, listen to him pitch the trinkets, and one-by-one the wind-up walking men are purchased. When it comes down to the last walking man, Lou starts sweating. After this, he will not be able to attract a crowd. In desperation, Lou removes his wrist watch, in place of the last toy sold. Vinnie, meanwhile, who's been watching Archie and his boys move closer, suddenly succumbs to fright and bolts away from the group and down the sidewalk. The sound of a gunshots stop Lou from his spiel. Vinnie stops, sways, and falls forward. A woman screams. Archie grins, drops his cigarette, grinds it with his heel, and walks off in the opposite direction. A crowd gathers over Vinnie's body. Lou rushes through them and kneels beside the body. The sound of a siren and an ambulance pulling to a stop meets up with a policeman arriving at the scene. Back in the apartment, Lou has a talk with his father.

ANDY: *Way down deep, Lou – he was jealous of you. You know?*

LOU: *Of me? Sure, Pop. He was jealous of me. Why, Pop? What could he be jealous of?*

ANDY: *Don't you know, Lou? He seen it tonight. He seen you make the pitch for him. He musta been proud of you. This I know. He musta been proud of you.*

LOU: *Tonight I made a pitch to the angels. Too late. One night too late. All my life I wanted to make that kid proud of me. For one hour before he died he was proud of me.*

"I had this idea for a long, long time and did a variation of it on *Danger* many years ago," Serling later recalled to a reporter in 1959. "It was one of the few scripts in the series that I wrote with someone specifically in mind as an actor. I tailored it for Ed Wynn." When Serling said "tailored," what he meant was adding an element of fantasy by giving Lew a similar reason to make a pitch, but for someone different – to cheat Death not once, but twice.

---

* The broadcast date for this particular episode of *Danger* has repeatedly been listed inaccurately as September 19, 1954. Another reference source inaccurately cites the title of the drama as "The Pitch." This alternative title was what Serling submitted to the story editor for *Danger*, but changed to "One for the Angels" between the purchase of the plot proposal and the shooting script. Also note, in the *Danger* version of the story, the main character's name was spelled "Lou" but was changed to "Lew" in *The Twilight Zone* script.

The television columnist for *The Syracuse Post-Standard*, who went by the name of "The TV Scout," reviewed this episode, commenting that it "isn't quite up to last week's opener, but it's still a good show. It has its good moments, particularly those involving Ed Wynn as the old man, but there is no surprise ending and it really never hits home." An independent critic for *The Troy Record* commented, "a nice part for the Wynn charm to take over. Watch for his hand gestures as he winds up toys."

According to production papers dated April 24 and May 8, 1959, Robert Stevens was originally slated to direct this episode, with tentative dates of filming for July 3, 6 and 7. The dates were later rescheduled for filming on July 17, 20 and 21, with rehearsal dates July 15 and 16. Finally, Robert Parrish took the helm and the dates were changed again.

Ed Wynn's salary was $5,000 for his role of Lew Bookman for this episode, making Wynn one of the highest-paid actors on the five-year history of *The Twilight Zone* . (The policy of paying lead actors as much as $5,000 per episode would quickly be lowered after the first few productions.) Residuals were to be set up in the following manner: 1st rerun, $1,000; 2nd rerun, $750; 3rd rerun, $750; 4th rerun, $750; and 5th rerun, $250. (No residuals after the 5th rerun for this and following productions.)

Ed Wynn's talent agreement included a "Favored Nations" clause covering the TV season of 1959-60 in connection with his salary. The term "Favored Nations" refers to an individually negotiated agreement between a producer and an actor, which generally indicates that if other actors in the show receive better terms, then this individual will be titled to those same terms. Hence, Ed Wynn was guaranteed that no one else would be paid more money than he for his work on this production. Many of the lead actors required the "Favored Nations" clause in their contract, including Ida Lupino, Burgess Meredith, Howard Duff and Robert Cummings. Minimum theatrical reruns applied with a "Favored Nations" clause.

The arrangement by which actors were signed to play the roles is a case history in itself. To sum it up in one brief paragraph, the casting director was responsible for the hiring and contract negotiations for actors. Oftentimes the producer, scriptwriter or director made suggestions for casting, and the casting director was responsible for making the arrangements. (For this episode, Serling strongly requested that Wynn play the lead). Negotiations often included salary, the minimum and maximum number of days the actor would be required for filming, and how his name would appear on screen in the closing credits. Under contract, Ed Wynn was to be sole star and to be billed on a separate card (you'll notice his name is not shared with any other actor on the screen), and no succeeding player was to be billed in the same size type.

Murray Hamilton was paid $850 for his role of "The Stranger." Minimum film residuals and minimum TV reruns applied. Dana Dillaway was paid $400 for her role of "Little Girl." Minimum film residuals and minimum TV reruns applied. She was a minor (8 years old) at the time the episode was made, so her scenes were limited because of laws prohibiting young children from working more than a specific number of hours per day.

The original script called for Lew to be selling radio tubes. While radio tubes were not uncommon back in the early 1950s, by 1959 the practice had changed. A radio tube was usually tested when purchased as it was an unlikely item for a peddler to stock, so Serling revised the script to match what Lou sold in the *Danger* presentation — wind-up toys. The original script also called for men to carry Maggie after being badly injured. On July 2, the De Forest Research Group informed

Serling that it was unlikely that men would move a badly injured accident victim before medical aid arrived to ascertain the extent of the injury, so the pages describing the men carrying the little girl were revised and her relocation was replaced by a fade-to-black for the commercial break between the first and second act. The original script also called for the clock to read 11:45, but with the July 7 revision, the time was changed on the script to 11:40.

The same De Forest Research report suggested a number of other changes. One was to change the birth place of Lew's father to Warsaw, Poland, explaining that it was "doubtful that both parents were born in this country. For example, if his father had been born in Detroit, it is improbable that he would back track to New York unless he had a profession. As a whole, this profession (peddling) stems from the foreign-born." In response to this suggestion, Serling's solution to this explanation was to have Mr. Death claim Lew's mother was from Syracuse.

Another suggestion was to eliminate the street children addressing the old man as "Hi, Lew," and make reference to "Mr. Bookman." "Despite slum conditions it is unlikely that the children described would address one of their elders by his first name, especially when they show so much respect for him." Serling kept the references unchanged. The doctor, when leaving the apartment house, referred briefly to the hit-and-run and Maggie's condition as a "crisis." De Forest Research suggested the word be removed because "no doctor would make a statement like this under the given circumstances. Medically she is not 'sick,' but injured. The extant of her internal injuries could not be known until after she recovered from shock and was examined and tested." Serling made the required changes.

The original opening narration in the June 29, 1959, revision was different from what actually was featured in the finished product:

"Street scene . . . summer . . .the present. Man on a sidewalk – age, sixtyish; occupation – pitchman. Name – Lew Bookman. A fixture of the summer. A rather minor component to a hot July. A nondescript, commonplace little man whose life is a treadmill built out of sidewalks. Lew Bookman – a walking rebuttal to the American dream that states that success can be carved, gouged and grubbed out of log cabins and tenements. Because Lew Bookman had not even a nodding acquaintance with success and his dreams only extend from the curb to the sidewalk. But in just a moment Lew Bookman will have something to occupy his time which transcends both success and failure. He'll have to concern himself with survival. Because as of three o'clock this hot July, Mr. Bookman will be stalked by . . . Mr. Death!"

Filmed at M-G-M, all of the interiors of the buildings were shot on Stage 23. All of the exterior scenes were shot on Lot 2, including the tenement street where Lew makes his sales pitches, which would be seen in numerous *Twilight Zone* productions, such as "The Big, Tall Wish," "The Fugitive," "The Jungle," and "Five Characters in Search of an Exit."

Normally, exterior scenes that required night shots were filmed in the evening, after the sun set. Ed Wynn was unable to stay up late for filming, so scaffolding and tarps were rented (at a total cost of $1,300 for the tarps and $160 for the scaffolding) to simulate the evening scenes, blocking out the sun, giving the illusion of night. Designing the interior of Lew's room cost $800 in set decorations, while the interior of the foyer and the stairs cost $1,300.

A clock and a sign in a window across the street read "It's Later Than You Think." While a few have written in publications that this was an original artistic attempt to foreshadow Bookman's death, written specifically for this episode, the sign was among Serling's directions in the original *Danger* script which foreshadowed the death of Lew's brother, not Lew. The direction calling for the sign was reproduced for *The Twilight Zone* teleplay, but was not originally conceived for this series. *

Among the wind-up robot toys Bookman is selling in this episode is the 1958 wind-up action toy of Robby the Robot, which was being sold in stores for kids who favored the popular character from the motion picture, *Forbidden Planet*. For reasons unknown, the prop man placed a sticker of an eyeball on the top plastic dome, which was not part of the original toy.

A number of skins were purchased, at the cost of $5.00, to "cover M-G-M name on doors," as it read on a production work order. It remains unknown just why M-G-M's name would have been on any doors on the sets in the first place.

Shortly after this telecast, television columnist Bill Fiest asked his readers how many have watched the first two broadcasts and what they thought of them. "It isn't science fiction and it isn't the supernatural," he commented. "It's one of the scant few TV series which isn't a copy of something else. Rarely can a television columnist come out flatly and urge viewers to watch a weekly program, but this one is getting rave reviews."

Variety magazine commented, "Wynn plays it with whimsical abandon and the tone never gets heavy. Murray Hamilton as Mr. Death is as mortal as Wynn without any of the bizarre effects. The duel for survival gives the play its impact without the shattering emotions. Dana Dillaway as the tyke is a youngster of high promise. Direction of Robert Parrish avoided the macabre to effect the calm that comes at twilight."

Months after the initial telecast, on Friday, April 15, 1960, the *Westinghouse Desilu Playhouse* presented an hour-long drama titled "The Man in the Funny Suit," which marked Rod Serling's dramatic television debut (weeks before he made his first on-screen appearance in the *Twilight Zone* episode, "A World of Difference"). Serling appeared as himself in the teleplay, which dealt with the true father-son conflict between Ed and Keenan Wynn and the dramatic behind-the-scenes events leading up to the memorable presentation of Serling's "Requiem for a Heavyweight" dramatized on *Playhouse 90*. "It was a strange way to start, not only to be playing oneself but also to be acting out scenes that actually happened and are remembered so clearly," Serling recalled. "I learned that the actor must have complete confidence in his role and in his director if he is to do his best work. If there are doubts, even subconscious ones, they are almost certain to affect his portrayal."

Rod at first hesitated to repeat some of his lines, even though he had spoken them when the events in the drama actually took place. They were harsh words about Ed Wynn, uttered in moments of extreme anxiety, when Ed's ineptness seemed almost certain to turn "Requiem for a Heavyweight" into an appalling debacle. Since then, he had developed a profound affection and respect for the famed old comedian, who came through with such a magnificent dramatic debut in "Requiem." "We owed it to him to admit that we also badly underestimated such a great performer as Ed Wynn," Serling concluded.

---

* Since Rod Serling admired the great playwrights of radio broadcasting (Norman Corwin, Arch Oboler, etc.), it is possible that the inclusion was in homage to the signature line "It is later than you think" from the popular *Lights Out!* radio program written, produced and directed by Arch Oboler.

Production #3609 "MR. DENTON ON DOOMSDAY"
(Initial telecast: October 16, 1959)
Copyright Registration: © Cayuga Productions, Inc., October 15, 1959, LP15009
Dates of Rehearsal: June 29 and 30, 1959
Dates of Filming: July 1, 2, 3 and 6, 1959
Script #9 dated: June 1, 1959, with revised pages dated June 25, 26, 29 and July 3, 1959.
Revised script dated: July 1, 1959
Shooting script dated: July 3, 1959

Producer and Secretary: $660.00
Director: $1,000.00
Unit Manager and Secretary: $520.00
Agents Commission: $5,185.55
Below the line charges (M-G-M): $36,005.48
Total Production Costs: $63,197.84

Story and Secretary: $2,476.95
Cast: $11,806.48
Production Fee: $750.00
Legal and Accounting: $250.00
Below the line charges (other): $4,543.38

Cast: Malcolm Atterbury (Henry J. Fate); Arthur Batanides (the leader); Robert Burton (the doctor); Jeanne Cooper (Liz Smith); Dan Duryea (Al Denton); Bill Erwin (the man); Martin Landau (Dan Hotaling); Ken Lynch (Charlie, the bartender); and Doug McClure (Pete Grant).

Stock Music Cues: Main Title (by Bernard Herrmann, :45); Stenka Razin (anonymous Russian folk song, :36); How Dry I Am (anonymous, :02 and :20); Stenka Razin (anonymous, :57); Chime Note (anonymous, :09); Zither Chord Diminished (anonymous, :05); Stenka Razin (anonymous, :17); Zither Chord Diminished (anonymous, :18); How Dry I Am (anonymous, :18); Reflection #4 (by Lucien Moraweck, :39); Stenka Razin (anonymous, 1:45); Zither Diminished Chords (anonymous, :07); Night in the Desert (Dimitri Tiomkin and Rene Garriguenc, :21); Albany – Ethan Allen Suite (by Herrmann, 1:27); Night in the Desert (by Tiomkin & Garriguenc, :18); The Button (by Herrmann, :35); The Mirror (by Herrmann, :26); Reflection #4 (by Moraweck, :45); Zither Diminished Chords (anonymous, :08); Albany – Ethan Allen Suite (by Herrmann, :44); by Tympany Beat (anonymous, :45); Composite Track #4 With Piano – Fear #2 (by Moraweck, :48); Night in the Desert (by Garriguenc, :22); Stenka Razin (anonymous, :52); and End Title (by Herrmann, :39).

Director of Photography: George T.
    Clemens, a.s.c.
Art Directors: George W. Davis and
    William Ferrari
Set Decorations: Henry Grace and
    Rudy Butler
Teleplay by Rod Serling

Production Manager: Ralph W. Nelson
Film Editor: Bill Mosher
Assistant Director: Edward Denault
Casting Director: Mildred Gusse
Sound: Franklin Milton and Jean Valentino
Directed by Allen Reisner

"Portrait of a town drunk named Al Denton. This is a man who's begun his dying early. A long agonizing route through a maze of bottles. Al Denton, who would probably give an arm or a leg or a part of his soul to have another chance, to be able to rise up and shake the dirt from his body and the bad dreams that

infest his consciousness. In the parlance of the time – this is a peddler, a rather fanciful-looking little man in a black frock coat. And this is the third principal character of our story. Its function? Perhaps to give Mr. Al Denton his second chance."

Plot: Al Denton was pretty good with a gun in his day, but has turned to the bottle since he learned that one of his victims was a 16-year-old boy. Eventually, Denton lost his good name and earned a reputation for being the town drunk. One afternoon, fate rides into town – Henry J. Fate – who gives Denton a small nudge and an opportunity to gain redemption. After wounding the town bully, with gun in hand, Denton finds himself facing an ultimatum: leave town or face the next fast-gun who wants to earn a reputation for out-drawing Denton. In a private discussion with Mr. Fate, Denton is given a bottle that, when drunk, supposedly makes him the fastest draw in the land . . . but only for a few seconds. Late that evening, Denton faces off with his challenger, only to discover the young kid drank the same potion from a similar bottle. The men draw and fire. They wound each other's gun hand. Denton tells the kid that they are "blessed," for no longer will they have to deal with any gun play. The kid doesn't fully understand, riding out of town, but Mr. Fate smiles, knowing Denton has redeemed himself.

"Mr. Henry Fate, dealer in utensils, and pots and pans. Liniments and potions. A fanciful little man in a black frock coat who can help a man climbing out of a pit . . . or another man from falling into one. Because, you see, fate can work that way . . . in the Twilight Zone."

Trailer: *"Next week we invite you to take a walk down a western frontier street at the Elbora doomed gunman, whose salvation relies in nothing less a magic potion and a colt .45. Mr. Dan Duryea stars in 'Mr. Denton on Doomsday' next week on The Twilight Zone. We hope you'll be able to be with us. Thank you, and good night."*

Trivia, etc. "I got this idea watching a collection of westerns over a period of a couple weeks," Serling recalled. "In many ways it was almost a spoof of the classic high-noon, walk-down-the-middle-of-the-street gun battle." Another origin for this episode dates back to October 12, 1958, when Serling wrote to William Dozier, head of CBS programming on the West Coast, with plot proposals that would "represent the kind of variety I'd want to get on the series." Among the proposals was "You Too Can Be a Fast Gun," a four-paragraph plot synopsis Serling sent for Dozier's approval. This was the same plot which Serling mentioned in passing during the 10-minute promotional sales film that was attached to the "Where is Everybody?" pilot, which Serling referred to as "Death, Destry and Mr. Dingle."

The proposed plot idea varied slightly from the actual film, and the central character remained unnamed. He was a schoolteacher in a western frontier town during the late 1880s, a peace loving little guy who as Serling described, "perhaps has delusions of grandeur that are part and parcel of the times." The schoolteacher liked to think of himself as a top gun and a rugged cowboy, but was really scared to death of violence and guns. One day, he inadvertently picks up a gun and kills a snake at 200 yards. This feat is witnessed by a small boy who tells the rest of the town and the story grows like wildfire until the little schoolteacher is rumored to be a reformed gunman. News of the top gun gets around and a champ gunner heads toward the little town for a showdown with the schoolteacher. Upon learning the news, the little man is petrified because he realizes he couldn't out-draw a one-armed man with the palsy.

Enter stage left an itinerant medicine man who learns of the situation and sells the school-teacher what he purports to be a vial full of magic liquid that can turn a man into whatever he wants to be, if drunk at a specific time prior to whatever action is to take place. He scoffs at this at first but then is given a successful demonstration by the medicine man. The schoolteacher buys the vial.

The night of the showdown, the schoolteacher is at the local saloon, the townspeople rallied around him. He excuses the small vial as a shot of his own special whiskey. He has planned in his mind how long it will take to move the gunman out of a conversation and into a draw, and exactly what moment he should drink the vial. The gunman arrives, stands a few feet away from him at the bar and it is then that we see that the gunman himself is perturbed and frightened. Both men see each other's identical vial at the same moment and both turn to run in opposite directions. The schoolteacher bangs up against a table, trips, his gun falls out of the holster and is fired, knocking the gun out of the top gun's hand so that the legend remains intact. He then states publicly that he'll never wear a gun again and he sticks to his promise. He walks out into the street that evening only to meet the medicine man who has yet other vials to sell. Love potions and the like. The last moment of the play occurs when the schoolteacher buys one of the potions because throughout the piece he's been trying to woo the sheriff's daughter to no avail.

Judging by the date of the promotional film and the plot proposal, Serling initially intended to name the protagonist of this story, Dingle. That never came to be, but Burgess Meredith did play the role of Dingle in "Mr. Dingle, the Strong."

The title character, Al Denton, was named after one of Rod Serling's childhood friends, Herbert Denton. An episode of *Playhouse 90* titled "A Town Has Turned to Dust," also scripted by Serling, telecast years before, featured the character of a makeshift sheriff named Harvey Denton.

With the revisions of June 26, the names of certain characters were changed. The main character of Walter Denton was changed to Al Denton. The reason for the change remains unknown, but another character of the same name on a CBS television comedy may have been the cause. Richard Crenna played the role of Walter Denton on the radio and television program, *Our Miss Brooks*. Pete Grant was previously listed as Pete Grenville. All references to the peddler (Henry Fate) originally called him a drummer (nameless). The doctor was originally a sheriff in the first draft of the script, and the bartender was originally a piano player.

The original (first) draft of this script featured different opening and closing narrations, as well as a new name for the character:

"Portrait of a town drunk named Walter Denton. [a pause] This is a man who's begun his dying early. A long agonizing route through a maze of bottles. [a pause] Walter Denton who would probably give an arm or a leg or a part of his soul to have another chance. In the parlance of the time – this is a drummer. And this is the third principal character of our story. Its name – Colt. Its caliber – .45. Its function – perhaps to give Mr. Walter Denton his second chance!"

"Mr. Henry Fate, dealer in utensils, and pots and pans. Liniments and potions. A fanciful man in a black frock coat who also deals in second chances. And while there are some who say he doesn't exist – except in the imagination ... the dreams of men – he does exist if only in ... the Twilight Zone."

The exterior of the street (referred to in production sheets as "ghost town" was filmed on Lot 3 at M-G-M. This same street was featured in a number of television episodes for the westerns *Northwest Passage, The Man from Shenandoah* and *Hondo.* The interior of the saloon was filmed on Stage 5. The total cost of set decorations for this episode was $2,075. All of the evening scenes (Denton on the street confronting Mr. Fate) were filmed on the evening of the second day. The role of the bartender, Ken Lynch, was not hired until the morning the role was needed for filming.

On the morning of the third day, an evening campfire scene was filmed on Stage 22, for a scene which ultimately ended up on the cutting room floor with the rough cut of July 15. In this scene, the messenger arrives at the camp to inform Grenville that he delivered the message. Grenville asks how Denton looked, since people say he's as good as he ever was. "Fast as he is," the messenger explains, "with a case of nerves. Nerves like a sickness. I'm glad I ain't him!" A morning scene has the heavies waking at sunrise and they saddle up. Three horses were used for this scene.

The still shot which was to serve as the background for the end titles was originally to be a close-up of Duryea's hand holding the potion bottle. In late August 1959, George Amy, Serling and Houghton agreed on a close-up of the empty bottle on the bar counter instead. It was decided that since the closing credits would be white, the background should have as much of a darker image so the words could stand out. Duryea's hand would have covered up a bit of the words, making it difficult for viewers to read the closing credits.

Publicity for this episode made best bets with Chuck Denton of *The Examiner* who gave it a special plug (lead in his Friday column) as did Bob Hull of *The Herald Express* and Allen Rich of *The Valley Times*. To help publicize the episode, a wire was sent to TV editors in all Trendex cities, signed by Rod Serling, sent by Cleary-Strauss & Irwin:

THIS TYPE OF MESSAGE MARKS A FIRST FOR ME. IT'S BEING SENT ONLY BECAUSE I BELIEVE DAN DURYEA DELIVERS WHAT MAY WELL BE THE MOST BRILLIANT PERFORMANCE IN HIS DISTINGUISHED CAREER FRIDAY NIGHT (OCT. 16) IN TWILIGHT ZONE'S MR. DENTON ON DOOMSDAY OVER CBS-TV. HOPE YOU'LL WATCH IT AND JUDGE FOR YOURSELF.

Dan Duryea was paid $5,000 for his role of Al Denton. There was to be a "Favored Nations" clause. However, in the event the "Favored Nations" clause was invoked, the residual payments to Duryea would not exceed 50 percent of his original fee to be set up as follows: 1st rerun, $1,000; 2nd rerun, $750; 3rd rerun, $750; 4th rerun, $750; and 5th rerun, $250. (The fifth rerun buys into perpetuity.) Minimum theatrical reruns applied.

Jeanne Cooper was paid $600 for her role of Liz. Martin Landau was paid $850 for his role of Hotaling. "The M-G-M back lot was in Culver," Landau recalled. "Everyone was making the move to California while I was still acting back in New York, so I made the move myself for a few productions. I remember doing a bunch of television westerns at that time. The Denton episode was the first of two *Twilight Zones* I did for Rod. We all sat down to do a reading, and then we rehearsed. Rod was on the set, and at the reading, and some of us were making suggestions and he was taking notes. I remember the next day he came back to the set and had some pages of the script revised. Rod was a really nice guy and it's a shame he died so early."

Like any television production, bloopers can be found courtesy of repeat viewings. The time period for this episode was the Old West, but in the background of one shot, radio and television antennas can be seen. These can be found quite easily for anyone looking out for them.

During the number of times he pitched this story to executives, Serling avoided selling the fictional character of Henry J. Fate. "Since the whole concept delves into fantasy, it automatically makes it untellable and of little interest to the powers that be," Serling explained once. The network originally assumed this was going to be a straight western drama, and had no expectations of a fantasy element until the actual script was submitted for censorship review. Beforehand, the network was oblivious to Serling's intention, and sent a memo to Houghton and Serling on June 15 requesting all scripts with elements of fantasy be given the minimal treatment in fear of "viewership disapproval."

In 1994, Martin Landau commented in an interview that he had recently been honored in France at the Grand Prix Theatre, where he spent an evening there for his television work. Among the films presented was *The Twilight Zone*. In 1998, Van Morrison's album, *The Philosopher's Stone*, featured a song titled "Twilight Zone," with lyrics about a cowboy who got his wish, making reference to "Mr. Denton on Doomsday," and a party call referencing the fifth season episode, "Night Call."

Production #3610 "THE SIXTEEN MILLIMETER SHRINE"
(Initial telecast: October 23, 1959)
Copyright Registration: © Cayuga Productions, Inc., October 22, 1959, LP15010
Dates of Rehearsal: August 20 and 21, 1959
Dates of Filming: August 24, 25 and 26, 1959
Script #10 dated: June 10, 1959
Revised draft dated: June 22, 1959, with revised pages dated August 21 and 24, 1959.
Shooting draft dated: August 24, 1959

Producer and Secretary: $660.00
Director: $1,250.00
Unit Manager and Secretary: $520.00
Agents Commission: $5,185.55
Below the line charges (M-G-M): $27,781.94
Total Production Costs: $53,344.82

Story and Secretary: $2,503.65
Cast: $8,301.50
Production Fee: $750.00
Legal and Accounting: $250.00
Below the line charges (other): $6,142.18

Cast: Martin Balsam (Danny Weiss); John Clarke (Jerry on celluloid); Jerome Cowan (Jerry Hearndan); Ted de Corsia (Marty Sall); Alice Frost (Sally, the servant); and Ida Lupino (Barbara Jean Trenton).

Original Music Score Composed and Conducted by Franz Waxman (Score No. CPN5825): Main Title (by Bernard Herrmann, :34); Prologue (arr. by Leonid Raab, 1:01); Alone (:47); Twilight Shimmer (arr. by Leonid Raab, :31); The End (arr. by Leonid Raab, :12); This is 1959 (arr. by Leonid Raab, :28); The Producer (arr. by Leonid Raab, :05); The Past (arr. by Leonid Raab, :12); The Penthouse (arr. by Leonid Raab, :21); The Penthouse – Continued (arr. by Leonid Raab, 1:24); A Visitor (:45); Back to the Past (:41); Champagne (arr. by Leonid Raab, :19); Shrine – Part 1 (arr. by Leonid Raab, :57); Twilight Shimmer (arr. by Leonid Raab, :13); Shrine – Part 2 (arr. by Leonid Raab, 1:21); and End Title (by Herrmann, :39).

Director of Photography: George T. Clemens, a.s.c.

Production Manager: Ralph W. Nelson
Film Editor: Bill Mosher

Art Directors: George W. Davis and
   William Ferrari
Set Decorations: Henry Grace and Rudy Butler
Sound: Franklin Milton and Jean Valentino

Assistant Director: Edward Denault
Casting Director: Mildred Gusse
Directed by Mitchell Leisen
Teleplay by Rod Serling

"Picture of a woman looking at a picture. Movie great of another time – once brilliant star in a firmament no longer a part of the sky. Eclipsed by the movement of earth and time. (a pause) Barbara Jean Trenton whose world is a projection room; whose dreams are made out of celluloid. Barbara Jean Trenton – struck down by hit and run years and lying on the unhappy pavement, trying desperately to get the license number of fleeting fame."

Plot: Barbara Jean Trenton is an aging queen of the silver screen who withdraws into a make-believe world of 25 years ago. Embittered by the passing of time, she endeavors to preserve those days by keeping herself bottled up with booze and a movie projector in a dark room. In the mirrored form of Norma Desmond, she sits in her theater watching the same old movies repeatedly, much to the disapproval of both her servant and her agent – who tries his best to get her bit parts in B-class pictures. To lift her spirits, her agent, Danny Weiss, arranges for a meeting with Jerry Hearndon, her old co-star from the golden years. But when she discovers her leading man runs a chain of supermarkets and has no interest in revisiting the past, Barbara Jean orders him out of her house. She retreats to her dark room. Hours later, when her servant enters to serve some coffee, the room is empty except for the projector operating. She observes the Barbara Jean of today up on the movie screen with the by-gone actors of yesterday. Danny arrives and witnessing the same miracle on the screen, pleads for her to return but the film ends as Barbara Jean walks off the screen – immortalized on celluloid for all time.

"To the wishes that come true. To the strange mystic strength of the human animal who can take a wishful dream and give it a dimension of its own. To Barbara Jean Trenton, movie queen of another era, who has changed the blank tomb of an empty projection screen into a private world. It can happen . . . in the Twilight Zone."

Trailer: *"This motion picture projector and this film provide a background to next week's story when a most distinguished actress takes a journey into The Twilight Zone. Miss Ida Lupino stars in "The Sixteen Millimeter Shrine." A haunting story of a haunted woman that I think you'll find interesting and perhaps shocking. We hope you'll join us then. Thank you, and good night."*

Trivia, etc. "I don't mean to sound temperamental," Serling explained in an interview, "but I don't want to be put on the block every time I write a play. What people don't seem to realize is I can't write a 'Requiem for a Heavyweight' or a 'Patterns' every time 'round." This episode best suited Serling's opinion when, after viewing the rough cut, he discovered that the finished film did not meet his expectations. What a writer puts to paper doesn't come out exactly as he envisioned.

    In the November 5, 1959 issue of *The Washington Post*, Lawrence Laurent told his readers that Rod Serling wanted to hear their opinions on *The Twilight Zone*. Raymond Frye of Washington, D.C., took him up on the offer, writing: "It's generally superior entertainment, but sometimes a bit too far 'out.' Prime example: the show starring Ida Lupino. The dialogue was good, the acting excellent; but I found the ending just a bit disappointing." Serling, after reading Frye's opinion, wrote a reply to the televiewer, agreeing with his analysis of the show, "which I disliked intensely. But stick with us, the best is yet to come."

A little more than a year after writing this script, Rod Serling was asked to account for the story origin, for a reporter at *TV Guide*, in June 1960. Serling remarked (which was never published in the magazine): "I don't know where the hell I got this idea, but I wish I'd never gotten it."

The inspiration may have come from *Sunset Boulevard* (1950), as both episodes featured a faded film star, who refused to face the realities of life and, instead, lived in her own little world of greatness. She sat day and night running off old pictures of her glories when she was both young and desirable. Musician Franz Waxman is credited for supplying the music for this episode (the same Waxman responsible for the music score for *Sunset Boulevard*), but Leonid Raab remains an unaccredited partner in the composition of the music score. Credited as Leon and Leonard in a number of motion pictures, Raab got his start at M-G-M Studios in 1934 as an uncredited orchestrator. His task for this *Twilight Zone* episode (his only contribution for the series) was to arrange the music score so the footage of the vintage Hollywood picture on the screen would feature something reminiscent of 1930s cinema.

The star that shined in this episode was Ida Lupino. Her role was flawless and behind the scenes, she was extremely professional. "A dame can stop to powder her nose at the wrong time and $3,000 goes down the drain," remarked actor Dick Powell. "Lupino knows when to powder and when not to powder."

"Miss Lupino is a professional," added television director Roy Kellino. "She is never late. She always knows her lines. She knows how to improvise." Ida Lupino was paid $5,000 for her role of Barbara Jean Trenton. She was given a "Favored Nations" clause covering this episode, and residuals were to be set up in the following manner: 1st rerun, $1,000; 2nd rerun, $750; 3rd rerun, $750; 4th rerun, $750; and 5th rerun, $250. (The fifth rerun buys into perpetuity.)

According to production papers dated April 24 and May 8, 1959, Robert Stevens was originally slated to direct this episode, with tentative dates of filming for July 15, 16 and 17, with rehearsal dates July 13 and 14. The dates were later rescheduled for filming on July 29, 30 and 31, with rehearsal dates July 27 and 28. The production was eventually pushed to late August.

The entire episode was filmed on Stage 19, except for Marty Sall's office, which was filmed on Stage 24. The soldier love scenes were filmed on the afternoon of the first day's filming. Originally the love scenes were intended for Stage 5, but was filmed on Stage 19 like the rest of the episode. The first day's filming was immediately developed by the morning of the third day, with some scratches added to the film, so it could be projected on the wall for insert shots and the scene with Barbara stepping out from behind the screen. For clarification, the vintage love scenes were described in Serling's script as a garden outside of a hospital or a recuperating center, during World War I, in Italy.

The closing narration in the original draft was different from what is heard in the final film:

"To the wishes that come true. To the strange mystic strength of the human animal who walks that thin line between reality and the shadows and can somehow make one merge with another. To Barbara Jean Trenton, movie queen of another era . . . and no longer of this one."

Days after this episode was telecast, Ben Irwin discussed briefly with Buck Houghton the possibility of using stars of yesteryear for lead roles. "From a publicity standpoint, regardless of role," he explained, "[this] would be old-time stars making a return to show business, like Mary Pickford, Ramon Novarro, etc."

Variety reviewed, "What the agency feared is happening. Rod Serling's writing is 'too far out' for the masses that spell out ratings. No question about them being well done under Serling's astute stewardship from mill to market. The simplicity that is the mark of westerns has no place here. This is what Serling calls 'the dimension of imagination' and makes each issue a think piece. What sets Serling apart from contemporary writers in TV is his crisp dialog and well-turned phrases such as 'she was struck down by hit-and-run years,' or 'an aging broad with only a scrap book' or 'keeps wishing for things that are dead'."

On November 25, 1969, Tom Brown of Towson, Maryland, wrote to Rod Serling (care of Grosset and Dunlap, Inc. in New York). "I am in the ninth grade, and an active member of the Dramatics Club. Last Tuesday, I was confronted with an interesting problem. Come up with a suitable, impressive play for our Club. My mind wandered, as it usually does, to the subject of horror and the supernatural. That brought up you. I hastily flipped through your book looking for an appropriate, but not too long tale of the supernatural that I could adapt for use as an intriguing play. 'The 16-Millimeter Shrine' is just such a tale. I commenced to work out a script and blocking directions for a magnificent two-act play. I have gotten actors and made arrangements with our Club. All I need now is your permission. If royalties are involved, I [probably will not] be able to pay them. Seeing that our school funds aren't the greatest, I am not sure."

On December 5, Rod Serling composed a reply to Mr. Brown. Very brief, the letter simply stated that he granted permission for the use of his story for the Dramatics Club. He also wished Tom Brown good luck with the project.

In early June 1961, Blanche Gaines, Serling's former agent, submitted "The Editor," a story by Mary Harris that Gaines felt Serling could use on *The Twilight Zone*. On June 13, he wrote the following rejection letter: "I'm returning 'The Editor' simply because it is a very special theme that we've already attempted once (and got badly licked). We did a piece with Ida Lupino whose general theme had to do with the reality of life as contrasted to the reality on film. While the stories are reasonably dissimilar, the approaches and general thematic concepts are too close to try again."

Production #3605 "WALKING DISTANCE" (Initial telecast: October 30, 1959)
© Cayuga Productions, Inc., October 29, 1959, LP15011
Dates of Rehearsal: June 23 and 24, 1959
Dates of Filming: June 25, 26, 29 and 30, 1959
Script #5 dated: April 13, 1959, with revised pages dated June 19, 23, 24 and 25, 1959.

Producer and Secretary: $660.00	Story and Secretary: $2,452.27
Director: $1,250.00	Cast: $11,211.16
Unit Manager and Secretary: $520.00	Production Fee: $750.00
Agents Commission: $5,185.55	Legal and Accounting: $250.00
Below the line charges (M-G-M): $45,810.40	Below the line charges (other): $6,396.30
Total Production Costs: $74,485.68	

Cast: Sheridan Comerate (gas station attendant); Joseph Corey (the soda jerk); Bill Erwin (Mr. Wilcox); Byron Foulger (Charlie); Ronnie Howard (Wilcox boy); Buzz Martin (the teenager); Michael Montgomery (Martin, age 11); Pat O'Malley (Mr. Wilson); Frank Overton (Martin's Father); Nan Peterson (the woman in park); Irene Tedrow (Martin's Mother); and Gig Young (Martin Sloan).

Original Music Score Composed and Conducted by Bernard Herrmann (Music Score No. CPN5809): Main Title (:40); Introduction (:28); The Drugstore (:37); Memories (2:22); The Park (1:40); The House (1:32); Curtain (:20); The Parents (1:40); The Merry-Go-Round (:37); Artists' Life (by Johann Strauss, 1:45); Martin's Summer (1:32); Elegy (3:33); Natural Rock (by Bruce Campbell, :14); Finale (1:00); and End Title (by Herrmann, :45).

Director of Photography: George T. Clemens, a.s.c.	Production Manager: Ralph W. Nelson
Art Directors: George W. Davis and William Ferrari	Film Editor: Joseph Gluck, a.c.e.
Set Decorations: Henry Grace and Rudy Butler	Assistant Director: Edward Denault
Sound: Franklin Milton and Jean Valentino	Casting Director: Mildred Gusse
	Directed by Robert Stevens
	Teleplay by Rod Serling

"Martin Sloan, age thirty-six. Occupation: vice-president, ad agency, in charge of media. This is not just a Sunday drive for Martin Sloan. He perhaps doesn't know it at the time, but it's an exodus. Somewhere up the road he's looking for sanity. And somewhere up the road, he'll find something else."

Plot: New York executive Martin Sloan is unable to cope with the pressures of today, and in a desperate attempt to revisit his childhood, makes a return trip to his hometown. There, he finds the town and the people not as it is today, but as it once was. The smell of cotton candy, the merry-go-rounds, and the band concerts – all part of a moment in time that Martin has longed to embrace again. His mother and father are still alive, and young Martin is spending his summer carving his name into a wood post. In an attempt to share the moment with his younger self, Martin exposes the boy to a severe leg injury. While the boy is back home healing from his wound, Martin's father pays him a visit. He knows who Martin is and where he came from – and there is no room for him in the past. The wisdom comes from his father's lips: Martin has been looking behind him for an escape – perhaps he should be looking ahead. Walking out of town, Martin returns to the present day – content on living his life a bit more relaxed should he choose to do so.

(middle) *"A man can think a lot of thoughts and walk a lot of pavements between afternoon and night. And to a man like Martin Sloan, to whom memory has suddenly become reality, a resolve can become just as clearly and inexorably as stars of a summer night. Martin Sloan is now back in time. And his resolve is to put in a claim to the past."*

"Martin Sloan, age thirty-six. Vice president in charge of media. Successful in most things – but not in the one effort that all men try at some time in their lives – trying to go home again. (a pause) And also like all men perhaps there'll be an occasion . . . maybe a summer night sometime . . . when he'll look up from what he's doing and listen to the distant music of a calliope – and hear the voices and the laughter of the people and places of his past. And perhaps across his mind there will flit a little errant wish . . . that a man might not have to become old – never outgrow the parks and the merry-go-rounds of his youth. (a pause) And he'll smile then too because he'll know it is just an errant wish. Some wisp of memory not too important really. Some laughing ghosts that cross a man's mind . . . that are a part . . . of the Twilight Zone."

Trailer: *"Next week we invite you to take a strange journey back in time with Mr. Gig Young, who tries to make the exodus of all men, in their desperate attempt to relive the past. We offer a most bizarre story called 'Walking Distance.' And we hope you'll be around to share it with us. Thank you, and good night."*

Trivia, etc. Rod Serling recalled a number of times how he came up with the idea for this episode. "This is partly from looking at a park on a movie back lot and partly from a sense of my own nostalgia. Often in the summer I'll go back to my hometown, Binghamton, and go through a place called 'Recreation Park' which I can link to vivid and wondrous memories of growing up. I think there's a little of this bitter-sweet nostalgia in all of us for a time well remembered."

For the September 6, 1959 issue of *The Sunday News*, Serling recalled in the "What's On?" column: "I was walking on a set at M-G-M when I was suddenly hit by the similarity of it to my hometown. Feeling an overwhelming sense of nostalgia, it struck me that all of us have a deep longing to go back – not to our home as it is today, but as we remember it. It was from this simple incident I wove the story of 'Walking Distance.'"

A year and a half later, Serling remarked how he paid a visit to Recreation Park, where he spent his childhood. "I looked at the merry-go-round, now condemned, overgrown by weeds, and I had that bittersweet recollection of that wondrous time of growing up."

In Binghamton, New York, Serling was raised in the loving care of an average middle-class family. In the same house with the same friends throughout his youth, Serling did not hesitate to tell people that he led a happy life. He never felt the need for analysis, skirting the possibility of being classed with the current trend of "couch" writers who purged themselves in print. Serling's purpose with this episode was to probe his dramatic characterizations. As he explained, "thoughtfulness doesn't necessarily suggest oddness."

An early draft of this script featured a variation of the opening narration:

"The mirror image of Martin Sloan. Age thirty-six. Occupation – vice president, ad agency, in charge of media. This is not just a Sunday drive for Martin Sloan. He perhaps doesn't know it at the time, but it's an exodus. Somewhere up the road he's looking for sanity. (a pause) And somewhere up the road – he'll find something else."

The first draft of the script, dated April 13, 1959, was reviewed by the CBS Television Network. It's main concern was to have the production crew observe customary caution to avoid visual identification of commercial brand names in the gas station set and in the malt shop. This included, of course, the cigarette machine outside the gas station. CBS also insisted to "please direct camera angles to obscure any view of Martin Sloan's mangled leg." Two brief passages spoken in Martin Sloan's dialogue were also censored: "… going back to the womb" and "Oh, my God!"

Originally, this episode was script #6, dated April 13, 1959, and script #5 was to be Bradbury's "And There Be Tygers," for which, according to a progress report dated April 9, 1959, Bradbury was going to script the teleplay. Since this fell apart, "Walking Distance" was quickly renumbered.

Gig Young was paid $5,000 for his role as Martin Sloan. There was to be a "Favored Nations" clause. However, in the event the "Favored Nations" clause was invoked, the residual payments to Young would not exceed 50 percent of his original fee to be set up as follows: 1st rerun, $1,000; 2nd rerun, $750; 3rd rerun, $750; 4th rerun, $750; and 5th rerun, $250. (The fifth rerun buys into perpetuity.) Minimum theatrical reruns applied.

Frank Overton was paid $1,000 for playing the role of Martin's father for this episode. He also received first-class New York round-trip transportation since he was performing on the East Coast.

Filming was originally scheduled to begin on or about July 6, 1959, but was pushed back a week to accommodate the director and actors' schedules as production fell into place.

Production Schedule at M-G-M

Day #1	Drug Store scenes (Stage 5)
	Exterior of the Park and Pavillion (day and night on Lot #2)
Day #2	Nighttime scenes near the calliope (Stage 26)
	Exterior of the gas station and road (Lot #3)
Day #3	Exterior street shots for the Wilcox and Sloan House (day and night on Lot #3)

The opening scene at the gas station was filmed on Lot 3, for a cost of $600 in materials, signs and props. This was the same gas station used for the evening scene in the second act of "The Hitch-Hiker." The sign hanging above the gas station in the opening scene read "Service Station: Ralph N. Nelson, Prop." This was a tip of the hat to Ralph W. Nelson, the unit production manager for *The Twilight Zone*. To film outside, a generator was rented to power the cameras and equipment. There were intentions of filming scenes inside the gas station, shortly after Martin arrived, but that was changed before production began.

The car the mechanic was working on at the gas station was the same featured on the side of the street in the opening scenes of "The Monsters Are Due on Maple Street." While Gig Young can be seen sitting inside the car during Serling's narration, the opening shot of the car speeding toward the station did not feature Young. A stunt driver was hired (at the cost of $50) to drive the rental, with precision, down the dirt road. Someone evidently caused damage to the seat cushion inside the car – Cayuga fronted a repair bill for 10 dollars.

Originally the interiors of the drug store (both old and new) were scheduled to be filmed on Stage 26 at M-G-M. Hours before production began, however, the set decorator and his crew moved all the props and settings to Stage 5 to accommodate the studio's error in paperwork, granting another television production use of the same Stage 26 on the same day. Rental fees for food, signs, chairs, tables, mirrors and other props for both drug stores cost Cayuga a total of $1,800.

The music coming from the jukebox in the drug store is Bruce Campbell's "Natural Rock," which originated from the CBS stock music library. In the episode "From Agnes – With Love," in the scene where Elwood returns to Walter's apartment, the same music can be heard coming from behind the door while Millie is dancing. This is also the same music Flora dances around the apartment in "A Short Drink from a Certain Fountain."

The exterior of the park (a.k.a. the Pavillion) was filmed on Lot 2 at M-G-M. The cost for props, including an ice cream cart, a baby carriage, balloons and other props cost $1,050. An extra company prop man was hired (at the cost of $75) for June 25 and 26, to handle the scenes that required many extras (including children). An organ grinder and a monkey were hired for some of the scenes, costing $75 for the day, but whether they were filmed remains unknown – he does not appear in the finished film. (They do, however, make an appearance in "Mr. Bevis.")

The residential street prominently displaying the Wilcox and Sloan House was located on Lot 3, which had been built specifically for the 1944 motion picture, *Meet Me in St. Louis*. The movie was produced from 1943 to 1944 with a total budget of $1,707,561.14. The cost of building the street was $208,275. Located at Jefferson and Overland Boulevards in Culver City, the street became known at the studio as "The St. Louis Street." The scene in which Martin Sloan walks the street where he grew up and recalls the names of the neighbors and their corresponding houses contains two in-jokes. Rooney was a tip of the hat to Serling's good friend Mickey Rooney. Dr. Bradbury was referencing science fiction author Ray Bradbury.

To capture the cinematography that director Robert Stevens was looking for in one key scene, he needed the entire bandstand and carousel to be disassembled and reassembled from Lot 2 to Stage 26. The director's request was forwarded to Buck Houghton, who approved it, at the expense of $450, charged against Cayuga. On the morning of June 26, the carousel shots were filmed, providing cinematography that emphasized Martin's insecurity after the accident.

Between takes, one of the young children, Michael Patterson, while running around the stage on the morning of June 26, ran into a bench and hurt his leg. A studio physician was called over to the set to look at the injury. After putting on a bandage, the doctor said the child was fine, and the incident did not cost the company any loss of time during production.

When Martin Sloan encounters his younger self, carving his name on the wooden post, a blooper can be seen – and was overlooked by the film editor, Bill Mosher, and his supervisor, Joseph Gluck. In one shot, young Martin is carving the letter S to indicate his last name, and has yet to spell the rest of the letters, L-O-A-N. In another shot, the last name is already carved, and young Martin is still working on the letter S. In the third shot, he is still working on the same letter, but the other letters have yet to be completed.

There were three shots of the carousel horses taken from the transition sequence between the youthful Martin's injuries and the arrival of his father. The darkest shot of the three was chosen for use as the background end titles, solely because the closing credits, which were white, would show up best on the screen.

Assorted Production Costs
(According to M-G-M Interoffice Communication dated July 1, 1959)
Sound Recording Channel $400
Sound Dubbing Channel $200
Projection $20

Bernard Herrmann not only composed and conducted the dream-like *Twilight Zone* themes featured in the beginning of every first season episode, but he composed the music for this episode on August 15, 1959. It is considered by many viewers as one of the most memorable scores on the series. Pieces of Herrmann's original compositions for "Where is Everybody?" and "Walking Distance" were frequently reused a number of times throughout the series. According to notes at the University of California, the music score for this episode featured a total of 10 violins, 3 violas, 3 celli, 2 basses and 1 harp.

Serling had watched the rough cut of July 17, and throughout the month of September, expressed to Buck Houghton his concerns relative to the scoring. Per Serling's suggestions – but not without a fight from Herrmann – the following changes were made to the music score, to emphasize key scenes in the episode.

(1) The curtain music to the teaser in the beginning needed an uplift. Herrmann objected to doing this, even when Serling stated "at present it just seems to dwindle off suggesting nothing in the way of tension to follow."

(2) There was originally no music in the scene when the drugstore clerk goes up to Mr. Wilson to request reordering supplies. At Serling's insistence, music was added to help the audience associate with the oddness of the situation.

(3) Serling insisted that the sound of the calliope be heard in act two, right after Martin's mother slaps him, and he looks off hearing something for the first time. "It was my feeling that the calliope is a signatory kind of sound," Serling explained.

(4) When Martin left the drugstore a second time near the closing of the episode, there was no music. Serling insisted that music "perhaps partly nostalgic and partly haunting" would suggest not only the pathos of the moment, but the oddness of the whole story.

"I know all these suggestions go against your grain, Bucko," Serling wrote to Houghton, "and in most of our disagreements I've always felt that we could reach compromises and have done so most successfully. But in this particular instance I feel so strongly about this music situation that I hope you'll grant me a little extra prerogative here and see what you can do even under protest. Which is a helluva oblique way of reiterating how tremendous I think this film is and how beautiful I think the music is or at least ninety five percent of it."

Houghton went to Lud Gluskin, head of the music department at CBS, to explain Serling's concern. Gluskin offered two options. First was to select stock music cues to deal with each issue and then re-dub the picture. These, of course, would not be consistent with Herrmann's musical structure, be very costly, and Herrmann would probably be offended to the point of being unwilling to ever do another *Twilight Zone*. The second option was more expensive – have Bernard Herrmann rescore at the four points, call for another orchestral session as well as redubbing. This second option, through Serling's insistence, was implemented and Herrmann composed the new music consistent with the old.

To keep peace with Herrmann, Serling wrote a thank-you letter on October 6. "This is belated congratulatory tome to acknowledge what is one of the most beautiful music scores I've been privileged to hear. I'm referring to the background music to 'Walking Distance.' If you can tell me how I can get this on a recording to keep, I'd much appreciate it. It is a lovely, sensitive and most inspiring theme. Thank you for lending a great talent to our project."

"Writing music for 'Walking Distance' afforded me a most stimulating and rewarding experience, for the nostalgia of the play lent itself most readily to music, and music is always able to communicate most expressively when it assumes an emotional role rather than, as is usual, a descriptive one," replied Herrmann. "It is very rarely that one has an opportunity to write music of a lyrical temperament."

Combined with music and script, *The Twilight Zone* was being praised by a number of viewers. "I have a tough, literary hide to penetrate," wrote Edmund Brophy, a successful scriptwriter for CBS Radio, "but in your third act of 'Walking Distance,' in the scene between father and son, you achieved some rare and piercing dialog, as close to poetry and truth as the stratospheric flier, who 'reached out my hand to touch the face of God.' Stay with it. We will stay with you."

"The Ida Lupino piece on the aging star who refused to yield to time and projected her wishes and the advertising executive who yearned to recapture his boyhood were just great," wrote Henry von Morpurgo of the Pacific Coast Club in Los Angeles. "You seem to stir and stimulate something that is strange and deep and beautiful and profound and inchoate in all of us. Something that is marvelous and mysterious and yet which we ordinary people cannot express. The magic of your great talents, Rod, articulate these feelings, make them seem understandable and enable us better to understand ourselves and our friends."

In a letter dated October 16, 1959, Owen S. Comora of Young & Rubicam, Inc., the advertising agency representing the General Foods Corp., wrote to Rod Serling to explain his concern regarding the listings in *TV Guide*. The advertising agency felt the listings were not large enough coverage for the magazine's readers, so Comora spoke with the editor of *TV Guide* to inquire about the possibility of getting a better listing. Previously the magazine was listing a one-or two-sentence plot description and mention of the actors appearing in large roles. "Those listings have been sent in by the *TV Guide* West Coast office," Comora explained. "In the future they will be done in New York. We hope to be getting a little more space starting with the Gig Young show of October 30." The listings, however, did not get any more coverage than the weeks before, and Comora's efforts faced a dead end.

On October 21, 1959, Serling asked Comora to incorporate the following lines to any promotional materials sent out: "From the standpoint of story development, performance, and film technique, it's my honest feeling that 'Walking Distance' stacks up as one of the most meaningful and poignant half-hour dramas ever produced. It dramatizes flavor, color and dimension to a kind of wondrous, bittersweet attachment the human being has for the past. Bob Stevens' direction and Gig Young's performance prove that the half-hour television form can also be a legitimate story-telling form. When my name was attached to this one – it was put on with pride!"

Variety magazine reviewed, "Well written and equally well performed, the level may be too high for those who make up the ratings. It hasn't reached the payoff point yet. Serling's plays need more than his explanations, fore and aft. It's a serious takeoff on Alfred Hitchcock's caricature, but doesn't help the watcher to un-track himself." The same review added: "Direction of Robert Stevens had good movement."

Production #3603 "ESCAPE CLAUSE" (Initial telecast: November 6, 1959)
Copyright Registration: © Cayuga Productions, Inc., November 5, 1959, LP15233
Dates of Rehearsal: June 17 and 18, 1959
Dates of Filming: June 19, 22 and 23, 1959
Script #3 dated: February 10, 1959, with revised pages dated June 12 and 17, 1959.
Revised pages typed and dated June 12, 1959
Shooting script dated: June 17, 1959

Producer and Secretary: $660.00
Director: $1,250.00
Unit Manager and Secretary: $520.00
Agents Commission: $5,185.55
Below the line charges (M-G-M): $22,638.23
Total Production Costs: $48,018.31

Story and Secretary: $2,469.85
Cast: $9,449.04
Production Fee: $750.00
Legal and Accounting: $250.00
Below the line charges (other): $4,845.64

Cast: Raymond Bailey (the doctor); George Baxter (the judge); Nesden Booth (prison guard); Virginia Christine (Ethel Bedeker); Joe Flynn (adjuster #2); Thomas Gomez (Cadwallader); Wendell Holmes (Mr. Cooper); Allan Lurie (the subway guard); Bob McCord (man in subway); David Wayne (Walter Bedeker); and Dick Wilson (adjuster #1).

Stock Music Cues: Main Title (by Bernard Herrmann, :45); Blues Pantomime #2 (by Arthur Wilkinson, :34); The Search #3 (by Lucien Moraweck, :13); Dream Effects #1 (anonymous, :28); Vibraphone (anonymous, :20); Anticipation (by Jerry Goldsmith, :11); Animation Comedy (by Spence Moore, :05); Market Town (by Wilkinson, :14); Punctuation D2 and D3 (by Moraweck, :10); Slide #5 (by M. Gordon, :06); Wow #3 (by Gordon, :12); Dream Effects #1 (anonymous, :18); Market Town (by Wilkinson, :05); Comedy Tag #4 (by Guy Luypaertz, :04); Blues Pantomime #2 (by Wilkinson, :04); Blues Pantomime #1 (by Wilkinson, :04); Too Many Ideas (by Goldsmith, :22); Kitten and the Bird (by John Gart, :19); Too Many Ideas (by Goldsmith, :14); String Flareout (anonymous, :06); Too Many Ideas (by Goldsmith, :28); December Bride (by Wilbur Hatch, :07); The Big Time (by Goldsmith, :10); The Meeting (by Goldsmith, :10); Too Many Ideas (by Goldsmith, :07); The Giant Killer (by Goldsmith, :07); Too Many Ideas (by Goldsmith, :08); Dream Effects #1 (anonymous, 1:07); Vibraphone (anonymous, :20); Soldiers on Strings (by Bruce Campbell, :05); Wow #3 (chord only, by Gordon, :06); Main Title (by Herrmann, :03); and End Title (by Herrmann, :39).

Director of Photography: George T.
    Clemens, a.s.c.
Art Directors: George W. Davis and
    William Ferrari
Set Decorations: Henry Grace and Rudy Butler
Sound: Franklin Milton and Jean Valentino

Production Manager: Ralph W. Nelson
Film Editor: Bill Mosher
Assistant Director: Edward Denault
Casting Director: Mildred Gusse
Directed by Mitchell Leisen
Teleplay by Rod Serling

"You're about to meet a hypochondriac. Witness Mr. Walter Bedeker, age forty-four. Afraid of the following. Death, disease, other people, germs, draft, and everything else. He has one interest in life – and that's Walter Bedeker. One preoccupation – the life and well-being of Walter Bedeker; one abiding concern about society – that if Walter Bedeker should die, how will it survive without him?"

Plot: A hypochondriac named Walter Bedeker suffers from imagined ailments. Remaining in his bed day after day, he is frightened by the prospect that a man has to die after living such a short lifespan. Late one evening, the devil, under the guise of Cadwallader, pays Bedeker a visit. In exchange for his soul, Bedeker will be granted complete immortality and indestructibility. The hypochondriac agrees, but as the weeks pass, he soon discovers no reason for continued living. After 14 separate accidents, including bus accidents, fires, and jumping in front of a subway train, Bedeker is bored with life. There is no more excitement. After his wife, Ethel, dies in an accident, Bedeker phones the police to confess to her murder, in an effort to give the electric chair a whirl. His attorney, however, manages to get his client off with a sentence of life imprisonment. Bedeker, realizing his plans went afoul, now sits behind prison bars ready to be transported to the penitentiary. Cadwallader materializes and offers Bedeker the chance to exercise an "escape clause" they had in the contract. Bedeker agrees and promptly dies of a heart attack.

"There is a saying . . . 'Every man is put on Earth condemned to die. Time and method of execution unknown.' (a pause) Perhaps this is as it should be. Case in point – Walter Bedeker, lately deceased. A little man with such a yen to live. Beaten by the Devil . . . by his own boredom . . . and by the scheme of things in this . . . the Twilight Zone."

Trivia, etc. Virginia Christine was paid $750 for her role of Ethel, with minimum film residuals and minimum theatrical reruns applied. Her participation for this episode ran over a few additional hours than contracted, so to compensate, her salary was raised to $1,000. David Wayne, who played Walter Bedeker, was paid $1,000 for his work. Thomas Gomez, however, with the least amount of screen time between them, drew the largest pay – $1,200.

In the original script, the episode opens with the janitor fixing the radiator, ensuring Bedeker that he will have enough heat to keep him warm. Bedeker, however, has a bad disposition, that causes the grumpy old janitor to exit, informing him that "If you die Bedeker – and you go where you're goin' – as far as the temperature goes, you ain't gonna be able to tell the difference!" Before leaving, the janitor warned Bedeker's wife to avoid touching the radiator, claiming it would burn her hands off. This adds more meaning when Bedeker later places his hands on the radiator to test his newly-developed gift. Actor Paul E. Burns played the role of the janitor. The scene was filmed but ended up on the cutting room floor.

A scene in which a neighbor who heard the screams, testifying on the stand, was filmed but also ended up on the cutting room floor. The same court room scene featured a blonde and a bailiff. The original draft of this episode featured two policemen arriving at Bedeker's house, but the roles were later replaced with insurance men. Stock footage of an airplane was ordered and paid for, but it was decided that keeping Bedeker within the confines of the city, getting his thrills and collecting insurance, was better for the story.

On June 16, a number of script revisions were made, most of which were deletions since the script ran more than 28 pages in length and the amount of dialogue in the script would have amounted to as much as 37 minutes of screen time. Thomas Gomez got off a bit of whimsy of his own, which director Mitchell Leisen kept in. It occurred when Gomez, as the Devil, stopped to mop his brow with a handkerchief and said to Wayne, "You sure keep it hot in here."

"That," said Gomez, "was true, too. It was hot on that stage. I'm not kidding when I say I felt like the Devil." The impromptu remained in the final film, even though it was not in the script.

The original script called for the Devil to wear a bow tie, sharp suit, and a Stetson hat. The wardrobe department, however, made their own changes when actor Thomas Gomez was suited for the role. The Bedeker character was also more ruthless in the original script – with his wife confessing that she only married him out of pity, believing he was suffering from a severe case of tuberculosis, and Walter thought he only had one week to live.

Frank Morris of CBS reviewed the script for censorship purposes, and on February 17, 1959, asked that the words "idiot" and "crazy" be removed from Walter's lines, early in the script. "CBS Television takes the position that the use of terms are permissible provided they are not found in a context dealing with actual mental illness," Morris explained. "However, too-frequent incidence of these derogatory terms, even in a non-relevant context, can cause us trouble." Serling kept the lines intact.

BEDEKER:	". . . with a handful of years and then eternity in a casket down under the ground. The cold, dark ground."
CADWALLADER:	"With worms, yet."
BEDEKER:	"Of course with worms."

"The little colloquy between Bedeker and Cadwallader on page 11, while good-natured, could be profoundly disturbing to many persons whose families have been touched by death, and especially to those recently bereaved," Morris explained. "Would you rephrase the above?" Serling made no change in the script, and the lines were delivered as written in the script.

The premise of a man becoming immortal and then being sentenced to life imprisonment was done previous on *Inner Sanctum Mystery*, a radio crime thriller broadcast from 1941 to 1952. On February 12, 1946, a script by Emile C. Tepperman titled "Elixir Number Four," was dramatized featuring Richard Widmark as a young man who murders a brilliant chemist, so he can steal and drink an experimental elixir that grants immortality. His plan goes afoul, however, when the murder is uncovered, and the young man is sentenced to life imprisonment. Many of Serling's *Twilight Zone* episodes resembled plots from radio thrillers, of which he was an ardent listener, suggesting yet another link to radio dramas as being an influence for this television series.

In October of 1958, Serling composed a one-and-one-quarter-page plot synopsis titled "The Condemned Man Ate a Million Breakfasts." The story concerned Frank Connacher, a petty, egocentric and pompous bore who had one abiding interest in life – himself. In his middle thirties, he suddenly develops a phobia about disease and dying, and the thought of death is a constant preoccupation. Satan pays him a visit, a suave gentleman who dresses and acts like a top-notch automobile salesman full of glitter and gas, and he sells Connacher on the idea of immortality – in exchange for his soul. After the deal is struck, always an innate coward, Connacher now shows a courage and daredevilry without precedent. He becomes a world-renowned figure with a fulfilled life, having flown all the test planes, deliberately exposed himself to fire, flood, famine, anything. But as the years go by, he is bored. Never a very moral man, his lasting power forces him into several criminal acts for which, of course, he's rarely caught. After a charge of homicide, however, Connacher laughs in court. Who can electrocute him? Who can hang him? Finally, being found guilty, his sentence is passed. Mr. Connacher gets life imprisonment. Banging his head on the stone walls of the cell, it is then that Connacher turns to see a smiling gentleman in a black robe at the far end of this cell who smiles and beckons, asking, "Are you ready?" It was this plot synopsis that later, with a number of revisions, became the episode known as "Escape Clause."

Nesdon Booth, who played the role of the prison guard in the closing scenes, was the father of art director and property master Nesdon Foye Booth and Deena Lynn Booth. Nesdon's name appeared in the credits of both motion pictures and television programs as Ned Booth and Nesdon Booth, but this episode marks what is probably the only time his first name was misspelled as Nesden.

The rooftop was not really the top of a building, but a set created on stage. The glass skylight on the rooftop shown in this episode was a prop reused and seen again in "The Big, Tall Wish" and "A Passage for Trumpet." The entire episode was filmed in three 10-hour days. The same rooftop set had been previously used for the climax of "Plague of Pigeons," an episode of *The Thin Man*, initial telecast December 5, 1958.

It was during the week this episode aired on CBS that Serling did an interview for Dick Strout's *Young Hollywood*. The recording was syndicated to over 600 radio stations.

Variety reviewed, "Here was a little gem. Good work, Rod Serling. This little piece about a hypochondriac who gets tangled up with an obese, clerical devil ranked with the best that has ever been accomplished in half-hour filmed television. One almost wished Serling hadn't wasted it on a 30-minute job. It had that elusive virtue of an artistically sound drama embodied in a commercial, unquestionably marketable offering."

The *Twilight Zone Tower of Terror*™ at the Walt Disney World Resorts makes a reference to this episode in the basement. The elevator contains a plaque revealing the date of October 2, 1959 (the date of *Zone*'s premiere), and was last inspected by Mr. Cadwallader. The amusement park ride features a large number of references to *Twilight Zone* episodes. To accurately capture the mood of the classic television series, Walt Disney Imagineers screened each of the 156 episodes of *The Twilight Zone* at least twice. *

Production #3602 "THE LONELY" (Initial telecast: November 13, 1959)

© Cayuga Productions, Inc., November 12, 1959, LP15234
Dates of Rehearsal: June 11 and 12, 1959
Dates of Filming: June 15, 16 and 17, 1959
Script #2 dated: March 27, 1959
Second draft completed by April 9 (exact date of script unknown).
Shooting script dated: June 10, 1959

Producer and Secretary: $660.00	Story and Secretary: $2,534.48
Director: $1,250.00	Cast: $6,359.54
Unit Manager and Secretary: $482.00	Production Fee: $750.00
Agents Commission: $5,185.55	Legal and Accounting: $250.00
Payroll Taxes, etc. $569.97	Below the line charges (M-G-M): $33,758.45
Below the line charges (other): $9,281.74	Total Production Costs: $60,511.76

Cast: John Dehner (Captain Allenby); Ted Knight (Adams); Jean Marsh (Alicia); James Turley (Carstairs); and Jack Warden (James A. Corry).

---

* *The Twilight Zone Tower of Terror*™ is a registered trademark. Reprinted with permission.
© 2008, Disney. All rights reserved.

Original Music Score Composed and Conducted by Bernard Herrmann (Score No. CPN5808): Twilight Zone Theme – Lonely (:40); Introduction (1:14); The Waiting (1:19); The Box (1:11); Alicia (1:12); George's Bar (by Eric Cook, 1:41); Mockery (1:49); Eleven Months (:54); The Stars (1:27); Fear (:47); Farewell (2:08); Finale (:39); and End Title (by Herrmann, :45).

Director of Photography: George T. Clemens, a.s.c.	Production Manager: Ralph W. Nelson
Art Directors: George W. Davis and William Ferrari	Film Editor: Joseph Gluck, a.c.e.
	Assistant Director: Edward Denault
	Casting Director: Mildred Gusse
Set Decorations: Henry Grace and Rudy Butler	Sound: Franklin Milton and Jean Valentino
Directed by Jack Smight	Teleplay by Rod Serling

"Witness if you will a dungeon, made out of mountains, salt flats and sand that stretch to infinity. The dungeon has an inmate: James A. Corry. And this is his residence: a metal shack. An old touring car that squats in the sun and goes nowhere, for there is nowhere to go. For the record, let it be known that James A. Corry is a convicted criminal placed in solitary confinement. Confinement in this case stretches as far as the eye can see, because this particular dungeon is on an asteroid nine million miles from the Earth. Now witness if you will a man's mind and body shriveling in the sun . . . a man dying of loneliness."

Plot: Set in the far future, James Corry is presently serving the fourth year of a 50-year prison sentence on an deserted asteroid, having been convicted of homicide. Bored out of his mind, suffering from loneliness, Corry confesses that he will go insane before he finishes his sentence. When Captain Allenby arrives to drop off three months of supplies, he explains that public pressure back home regarding the imprisonment of convicts on deserted asteroids has not forced the powers-that-be to consider a change. Allenby breaks the rules by leaving the prisoner with a stack of paperback books and a large wooden crate that might help him pass the time. The crate contains a female robot, complete with all the required features to make Corry forget that she is anything but human. Corry initially resents the android, named Alicia, but out of desperation he begins to fall in love with her. Many months later, Corry receives a visit from Allenby and his crew, explaining that he has been granted a full pardon. Allenby explains to Corry that even with the ship stripped to the bare minimum, there is only enough room and weight for 15 pounds of personal effects. Corry, however, will not leave without Alicia and pleads for Allenby to make an exception. Allenby shoots Alicia in the face, pulling Corry back into reality – and guides him back to the ship destined for home.

"On a microscopic piece of sand that floats through space is a fragment of a man's life. Left to rust is the place he lived in and the machines he used. Without use they will disintegrate from the wind and the sand and the years that act upon them. All of Mr. Corry's machines . . . including the one made in his image, kept alive by love, but now . . . obsolete . . . in The Twilight Zone."

Trailer: *"One of next week's stars is alongside me now. She'll appear in an unusual tale called 'The Lonely.' It is a story that takes place on* [Woman's Voice: *an asteroid and it's a most intriguing premise.*] *It sounds it. Next week on The Twilight Zone . . . Jack Warden, John Dehner and Jean Marsh appear in a bizarre tale of a man and . . . a woman? I don't understand it either. Thank you and good night."*

Trivia, etc. "The difference between New York and Death Valley was the unbearable heat," recalled Jean Marsh. "I don't recall any tempers flaring up because of the heat. The entire crew and Rod Serling, who was on the set, wore shorts and T-shirts! Everyone was very accommodating because, well, I guess because I was a woman and naturally, everyone was concerned for me. Jack Warden had a wonderful sense of humor and stuck close to me. He was constantly offering me advice on the set, especially after dark, that one evening, to keep the insects away from the sleeping quarters. The makeup man was constantly rushing between takes to keep me from sweating on the camera. Imagine a robot sweating in the desert!"

Jean Marsh had not been in the country long when she began doing television dramas. According to one trade column, Marsh left England because she didn't look English enough. "I had trouble finding dramatic roles," she explained. "In America, it doesn't matter. There is no 'American' look. Everyone is different." Marsh was 21 years old when she arrived in the United States, and after spending two years in New York, she took on the role of a Tahitian girl in "The Moon and Sixpence," a color special broadcast on NBC. "That was my first dramatic role," Marsh recalled. Shortly after, she was hired to appear on a television western, and the role of Alicia on *The Twilight Zone*. Columnist Harold Stern of *The Syracuse Herald-American* interviewed her shortly after her arrival, and she told the columnist that in making this episode of *The Twilight Zone*, she encountered a big disappointment. "They didn't have postcards!" she laughed.

Perhaps her biggest compliment was printed in the December 9, 1959 issue of *The Oakland Tribune*. A reader with the initials J.J.M. of Oakland, California, wrote to the television columnist, asking, "I'd like to know about the woman robot on *Twilight Zone* a couple of weeks ago. Is there any chance of my getting one?" The columnist replied, "Probably this will come as a terrible shock, what with half the men around saving their money to buy one, but the robot wasn't really a robot. It was Jean Marsh, a real, live human girl."

Serling recalled how he came up with the idea for this episode: "This one was created from whole cloth. Again triggered by the sense of poignancy that comes with loneliness."

On May 29, 1959, De Forest Research sent Serling a list of corrections that needed to be made to the March 27 draft, known as script #2 in the series. Most notable was the original name of the protagonist in this episode. Originally Serling made him James W. Corry, but the researchers commented that "There is a James W. Corry who is Chairman of the Board of the Reliance Electric and Engineering Company, Cleveland, Ohio." It was suggested he change the name to something such as John W. Corry or James W. Morry. On June 10, Serling changed the name to James A. Corry. Also in the original draft of this script, Allenby commented that he brought Corry "some microfilm" and "some old vintage movies...." This was deleted when the script was revised because of temperature and age would not cooperate with vintage movies. Regarding the words Corry reads, "To all intent and purpose this creature is a woman," the De Forest report commented, "Since 'creature' refers to a living being, this line states that the robot has become a woman and thus is subject to moral laws." The report suggested deleting the word "creature," but Serling kept the line intact.

Another revision to the original script, proposed by De Forest Research, was the change in materials for Corry's shack from driftwood and steel to aluminum, explaining that carrying steel on board a spaceship would have been a weight issue, but aluminum was considerably lighter in weight. The asteroid would have been treeless, so driftwood would not have been available for use in constructing the shack. The wind-up Victrola was replaced with a record player, because, as the report explained, "in the future this item would be a collector's item. Since power is available why not an electric phonograph?" The ice box was replaced with a refrigerator and the gas-powered generator was replaced with a solar-powered generator.

On February 17, 1959, Frank Morris of CBS requested that the word "hell" be removed from one of Corry's lines. He also addressed a concern that would become a repeated request, in writing, for many of Serling's scripts. "The use of the Name of the Diety, if irreverent or casual, always draws a blast of public indignation. The Name of God is frequently employed throughout the script, and we can defend it in all but two instances . . . where it is used in a not-strictly-reverent sense. Would you please delete these?" Serling never made the changes, and both Corry and Allenby make reference to God, including Allenby's "Oh my dear God, I forgot her."

Another concern Morris had was the closing scene. "Practically speaking, Alicia the 'robot' is a human being, and for the purpose of enjoying the play, the viewer will go along with the fiction that she is not. However, it verges upon horror to have the camera show us fragments of her shattered face. Would you confine these odd bits of physiognomy to strictly mechanical props: wires, levers, gears, springs, etc., unrecognizable as eyes, ears or portions of human anatomy?"

This episode was filmed on location at M-G-M Studios and at Desolation Canyon in the Death Valley National Monument, courtesy of the Department of the Interior. The inside of the shack and the exterior of the spaceship were filmed on Stage 6 during the third and final day of shooting, while the rest of the episode was filmed on the first two days on location at Death Valley. There were a number of expenses because of filming on location. To erect the shack cost $240 in materials and labor. Fake rocks were placed in position for various scenes at an expense of $50. A sanitary unit was rented for $240. Flight insurance cost $45 (the cast and some of the crew flew out to Death Valley). A faulty camera, blamed on the heat, was charged to CBS at $150. Rental of a mannequin for the closing shot with Alicia's face blown off cost $25 in rental fees.

"Death Valley was 116 degrees with a ground temperature of 139," commented Serling to a reporter. "We lost seven people off of the crew including the cameraman, the sound man, and the script girl by six o'clock the first night from heat prostration. I thought New Guinea was hot but it was like Fairbanks compared to what we had to put up with there. But we got some beautiful pictures there, albeit somewhat over budgeted pictures."

On June 29, 1959, director Jack Smight wrote to Serling. "I haven't yet had the opportunity to tell you what a distinct pleasure it was working with you. I'll be back on the coast in about a week, and at that time would very much like to have dinner with you we can really talk and get acquainted. I spent some time with Joe Gluck after the rough cut of 'The Lonely,' and I'm sure with tightening and your new approach to the opening narration that the film will be fine. I never thought we'd even finish in that 132 degree heat!"

The opening narration Smight was referring to was the one featured in the early draft, and would be substituted for a different narration:

"The residence of Mr. James W. Corry; a shack, a shed and an old sedan. With a front yard made up of sand and scrub that stretches to infinity. There is a ritual even to loneliness. For twice a day Corry will leave his shack, go over to look at the car . . . touch it . . . sit in its front seat, stare out of its windshield and perhaps succumb to a wishful daydream that he was at the wheel and the car was on a highway and there was someplace to go. (a pause) This would have to be just a wish because where this man is, there are no highways, and there are no places to go, no people to see, no spots to visit. Mr. Corry is all alone . . . For the record, let it *be known that James W. Corry is a convicted criminal placed in solitary confinement. And it matters little that this confinement in this case stretches as far as the eye can see. This is a prison without people; without talk and their laughter; without sound save the wind. It is an exile far worse than a dungeon at the far end of the earth. Because Mr. Corry has been banished to a place beyond the earth!"*

Serling had originally composed a different trailer for this episode:

"One of next week's stars is alongside me now. She'll appear in an unusual tale called 'The Lonely.' It is a story that takes place on [Woman's Voice: *an asteroid. I'm brought there to comfort a man condemned to a life-time of solitary confinement.*] *A most intriguing premise. Next week on The Twilight Zone . . . Jack Warden, John Dehner and Jean Marsh appear in a bizarre tale of a man and a woman or more accurately – flesh and machine. Thank you and good night."*

In the September 6, 1959 issue of *The Sunday News*, Serling commented for the "What's On?" column that while he hoped to build a protective wall around himself with the filmed show, he was entering an area that had not been attempted successfully on television – that of science fiction and fantasy. He believed that such programs thus far had focused upon the fantasy rather than on the people. He planned to remedy this, concentrating his efforts on telling first a story about people; the situation would be secondary. "The Lonely" was such an example.

Bill Fiest, a television critic with a syndicated column titled "The TV People," previewed the episode, and absolutely taken by the drama, devoted his entire column describing the plot and Corry's thesis about man and woman. He never gave away the closing of the story, but did comment that "many of the stories for *Twilight Zone* are being written by Rod Serling. They're offbeat but meaningful and if nothing else they'll titillate the imagination."

Many years after the telecast, Serling would compliment Warden's performance in an interview with Linda Brevelle in March of 1975: "I've been blessed frequently by having good actors. You get certain guys like Klugman – Jack Klugman – Jack Warden, Marty Balsam – solid, dependable, consummately skilled men, who invariably take lines and breathe great life into them, and great vibrance, and great truth." Jack Warden was paid $3,500 for his role of James A. Corry for this episode. Film residuals are as follows: 1st rerun, $700; 2nd rerun, $500; 3rd rerun, $500; 4th rerun, $500; and 5th rerun, $200. (The fifth rerun buys into perpetuity.)

Jean Marsh received $600 for her role of Alicia. Her billing was as second featured player. Minimum film residuals and minimum theatrical reruns applied.

Bernard Herrmann's original music score, dated August 5, 1959, features Eric Cook's "Turkish Delight," pulled from the CBS stock music library. Excerpts from the same music piece can be heard coming from the jukeboxes in "Where is Everybody?" and "Execution."

"The Lonely" was the first episode of the series (not counting "Where is Everybody?") to reach the scoring sessions. After Bernard Herrmann composed and conducted the music, he was apparently not satisfied with the way the theme came out. For the next episode, he rescored the theme music, using different instrumentation that would become the standard opening music for most of the first season. This is why "The Lonely" has a variation of the first season theme music for both the beginning and end credits.

Variety reviewed, "In your wildest flight of imagination you'll never quite catch up with what worms out of Rod Serling's typewriter. Your nightmares even pale by comparison. Yet, they are so well done from script through enactment that *Twilight Zone* is becoming a Friday night habit in millions of homes. . . . Strange and eerie in its concept, it gets added impact from the disarming comments of Serling and has the power to grip. Warden kept his emotions in check to avoid the temptation of going berserk, which also redounds to the credit of director Jack Smight. John Dehner and Miss Marsh were competent abettors and distinguishing marks were left by Bernard Herrmann's scoring and the sets designed by George W. Davis and William Ferrari."

When Serling adapted his teleplay for *More Stories from The Twilight Zone*, a paperback collection of short stories for Bantam Books in April of 1961, Serling added details regarding Corry's crime that got him sentenced to the asteroid. Corry witnessed the death of his wife from a speeding car, which wrecked shortly after. Corry dragged the driver out of the vehicle and choked him to death. In the teleplay, the only reference to Corry's crime is when the convict remarked that it was "self-defense."

A few years after the initial telecast of *The Twilight Zone*, Serling wrote a film script based on Lord Dunsay's novel, *The Last Revolution*, (originally published in the United Kingdom, Jarolds, 1951). The working title of the script was "Gresham's People" and told the story of a female robot with feelings, very much resembled this episode of *The Twilight Zone*. The novel told of a well-off clubman who makes his living by designing gadgets. He decides to build a crablike robot which proves to be intelligent enough to beat him at chess and is sufficiently endowed with emotion to be jealous of the attention its maker gives to his fiancée. The inventor is blinded to the ability of the machine as it learns to create others in its own image. Also, it can somehow play on the sympathy of lesser machinery like trains and motorbikes, subverting them with the spirit of 'The Last Revolution' in which mechanical slaves will throw off their oppressive human masters.

Production #3614 "TIME ENOUGH AT LAST"
(Initial telecast: November 20, 1959)
© Cayuga Productions, Inc., November 19, 1959, LP15235
Dates of Rehearsal: July 30 and 31, 1959
Dates of Filming: August 3, 4 and 5, 1959
Script #14 dated: July 14, 1959, with revised pages dated July 29 and 31, 1959.
Shooting script dated: July 31, 1959

Producer and Secretary: $660.00	Story and Secretary: $2,955.60
Director: $1,250.00	Cast: $7,317.75
Unit Manager and Secretary: $520.00	Production Fee: $750.00
Agents Commission: $5,185.55	Legal and Accounting: $250.00
Below the line charges (M-G-M): $30,574.65	Below the line charges (other): $7,580.61
Total Production Costs: $57,044.16	

Cast: Lela Bliss (woman in the bank); Jaqueline deWit (Helen Bemis); Burgess Meredith (Henry Bemis); and Vaughn Taylor (Mr. Carsville).

Original Music Score Composed and Conducted by Leith Stevens (Score No. CPN5835): Main Title (by Bernard Herrmann, :40); TZ Opening (:12); The President Commands (:30); Introduction (:08); Good Day Bemis (:24); Caught (:43); Lunch Time (1:10); Atom Bomb (:06); Atom Bomb II (:10); A Dead World (2:10); The Market (2:31); Solitude (2:38); There Was Time (1:12); and End Title (by Herrmann, :39).

Director of Photography: George T. Clemens, a.s.c.
Art Directors: George W. Davis and William Ferrari
Set Decorations: Henry Grace and Rudy Butler
Sound: Franklin Milton and Jean Valentino

Production Manager: Ralph W. Nelson
Film Editor: Bill Mosher
Assistant Director: Edward Denault
Casting Director: Mildred Gusse
Directed by John Brahm

Teleplay by Rod Serling, based on the short story of the same name by Lynn Venable, originally published in the January 1953 issue of *If: Worlds of Science Fiction*.

"Witness Mr. Henry Bemis, a charter member in the fraternity of dreamers. A bookish little man whose passion is the printed page, but who is conspired against by a bank president and a wife and a world full of tongue-cluckers and the unrelenting hands of a clock. But in just a moment Mr. Bemis will enter a world without bank presidents or wives or clocks or anything else. He'll have a world all to himself . . . without anyone."

Plot: A mousy little bank teller named Henry Bemis is constantly scolded at work by the bank president and at home by his wife for his habit of losing himself in a good book. With a newspaper in hand, he takes his lunch break one afternoon, locking himself in the bank vault. An H-bomb capable of total destruction devastates the entire area, and when Mr. Bemis surfaces, he discovers he is the only living soul left. Wandering amid the rubble for any sign of life, foraging for food, he begins to despair of his loneliness – even contemplating suicide, until he catches a glimpse of a library in the ruins. His eyes light up at the sight of thousands of books, enough to last him years and years. Beside himself with happiness, Bemis has time enough at last to read to his heart's content and with nobody to order him otherwise. But it's all short-lived, for on top of a major tragedy comes a minor one – while reaching for a book, he stumbles over the ruins, causing his glasses to fall to the ground and shatter. Unable to see clearly enough to read, he cries toward the heavens. "It's not fair," he protests, "It's not fair!"

(middle) *"Seconds, minutes, hours. They crawl by on hands and knees for Mr. Henry Bemis, who looks for a spark in the ashes of a dead world. A telephone connected to nothingness. A neighborhood bar, a movie, a baseball diamond, a hardware store, the mailbox at what was once his house and is now rubble. They lie at his feet as battered monuments to what was but is no more. Mr. Henry Bemis, on an eight-hour tour of a graveyard."*

"The best laid plans of mice and men . . . and Henry Bemis, the small man in the glasses who wanted nothing but time. Henry Bemis . . . now just a part of a smashed landscape. Just a piece of the rubble. Just a fragment of what man has deeded to himself. Mr. Henry Bemis . . . in the Twilight Zone."

Trailer: *"Next week a distinguished actor lends us his talents as Mr. Burgess Meredith stars in 'Time Enough at Last.' The story of a man who seeks salvation in the rubble of a ruined world. We hope you'll share this very strange experience with us. Thank you and good night."*

Trivia, etc. This was the only episode of the series to earn a Directors' Guild Award nomination. Regardless of what appears in numerous reference guides, John Brahm did not win the award. He lost to Phil Karlson for *The Untouchables*. This episode, however, helped cinch *The Twilight Zone* as the recipient of the 1960 Hugo Award for "Best Dramatic Presentation." The television program would win the same award in 1961 and 1962. This same episode helped Buck Houghton win a Producers' Guild Award.

On October 12, 1958, Rod Serling wrote to William Dozier, head of CBS West Coat programming. One of the plot proposals was "The Bomb Fell on Thursday," which was adapted into teleplay and was never produced, most likely because the first season episode "Time Enough at Last" already covered the threat of mass extermination through the use of a bomb. Two stories of the same subject matter would not have given Serling what he intended to offer on *The Twilight Zone* – variety.

In the teleplay dated May 4, 1958, a handful of people are touring an underground cavern much like Howe's outside of Albany. When they return to the surface, the world as they knew it has changed. A bomb has been detonated, leveling most of the scenery and killing off most of mankind. The nearest village is partially destroyed and they soon discover that they represent the last human beings on planet Earth. They struggle to make ends meet, sending out small search parties who come back always with the same story – no sign of life, utter destruction. Gradually the things that they believed in crumble in front of their eyes. At the very end of the piece a man they sent out comes back with a newborn baby he'd discovered on a broken highway somewhere near Atlanta. The mother was found dead. The tiny infant seems to instill new life and new hope in the survivors. After building a crib for the newborn, they try once again to grow things out of the ground and find that plants are sprouting. They hear on the truck radio the sound of others calling them from the north. All is not destroyed. There are yet others living, seeking out companions to try to rebuild what has been lost.

Serling also composed a four-page synopsis titled "The Survivors," which was pretty much the same story as above, except told in more detail and how the survivors, upon reaching the surface, spend a number of weeks trying to adapt to the new world. After discovering there is nothing to live for, they contemplate suicide, until the arrival of a newborn reminds them that some things are worth living for. The date of the plot synopsis remains unknown, and it is not clear whether Serling intended to adapt the synopsis into a feasible *Twilight Zone* teleplay, but "The Bomb Fell on Thursday" was definitely proposed for the anthology series.

After reading Lynn Venable's short story, on which this episode was based, Serling commissioned Alden Schwimmer of Ashley-Steiner to seek the rights to the short story. On February 5, 1959, Schwimmer informed Serling that "Time Enough at Last" was sold to the Quinn Publishing Company of Kingston, New York, by an agent named Forrest Ackerman, who lived at 915 South Sherbourne Drive, Los Angeles 35, California. Through Serling's insistence, a contract was drawn up in mid-March and sent to Venable, care of Forest Ackerman, same address.

After the purchase went through, Ackerman submitted additional short stories in the hopes one of them would interest Serling. "Pompeii in an Elevator" by Terence Kilpatrick; "8:01 from Rosedell" by Arnold Peyser; "Moon Madness" by Wallace Munroe (originally published in the September 1915 of *Snappy Stories*); "Old Spacemen Never Die!" by John Jakes (originally published in the October 1951 issue of *Astounding Science Fiction*); "One Shall Be Taken" by Belle Beatty (originally published in the July 1929 issue of *Breezy Stories*); and "Progress Report" by John H. Pomeroy. After reading the stories, Serling rejected all of them, feeling they did not fit the mold of what he intended to create for *The Twilight Zone*.

According to a progress report dated April 9, 1959, Serling originally intended to have this as the third episode broadcast on the series, but before the end of that same month, the selection of the order in which the episodes would be broadcast changed and this episode was pushed ahead a few weeks.

In an early draft of the script, the opening narration was longer:

"The time is the day after tomorrow; the place is anywhere so long as it can accommodate a bank, a main street and a library – along with a myopic little man named Henry Bemis who has only one passion in life and that is to read. (a pause) Mr. Henry Bemis – conspired against by brow-beaters and hen-peckers and by clocks whose hands waggle disapprovingly at him and always disallow the moments he'd love to use to read what he would. (a pause) In a moment from now, however, Mr. Bemis will have his chance to read in a world much different than the one he knows – a world without clocks or bank presidents; a world for that matter, without anyone!"

Another version of the opening narration read:

"Witness Mr. Henry Bemis, a charter member in the fraternity of dreamers. A bookish little man whose passion is the printed page, but who is conspired against by a bank president and a wife and a world full of tongue-cluckers who cannot sympathize with Mr. Bemis' preoccupation with literature and in just a moment Mr. Bemis will enter a world without bank presidents or wives or clocks or anything else. He'll have a world all to himself . . . without anyone."

Set Decoration Production Costs	
Interior of the Bank $750	Interior of Carsville Office $450
Interior of Bemis Living Room $75	Interior of the Vault $900
Interior of Break-a-way $200	Interior of the Bank (wrecked) $200
Exterior of the Bank (wrecked) $200	Exterior of the Phone Booth $50
Interior of Carsville's Office (wrecked) $300	Exterior of the Bemis House $75
	Exterior of the Walking Shots $750
Interior and Exterior of the Grocery Store $250	Exterior of the Hole $50
	Exterior of the Convertible $50
Interior and Exterior of the Library $650	Exterior of the Sporting Goods $250
	Total $5,450

The Bemis living room was shot on Stage 8, and the library scene toward the end of the episode was shot on Lot 3. The steps of the library on Lot 3 was the same featured in the episode "A Nice Place to Visit," and the 1960 motion picture, *The Time Machine*. The rest of the entire episode was filmed on Stage 10 at M-G-M. Originally, production called for a scene where Bemis finds a large hole or crater in the ground and this was scheduled to be filmed on Lot 3. Whether the scene was filmed or not remains unknown. If it was, the footage never made it to the final cut during the editing process.

Two wrecked cars were rented for this episode, costing Cayuga a total $35 in rental fees. Special effects for this episode (smoke, mist and ashes) cost Cayuga a total of $500.

Official paperwork labels the composition date for the music score as November 2, 1959. This seems a bit too close to the scheduled broadcast date and may have been a clerical error.

On August 9, 1959, Burgess Meredith sent the following telegram to Rod Serling:

ROD SERLING PRODUCTIONS
METRO GOLDWYN MAYER CULVER CITY CALIF
I ENJOYED THE FEW DAYS THERE BECAUSE THE SCRIPT WAS SO GOOD AND
JOHN BRAHM WAS SO HELPFUL AND EVERYBODY SO FRIENDLY I THOUGHT
I OUGHT TO TELL YOU HOW I FELT HOPE IT TURNS OUT AS GOOD AS IT DE-
SERVES REGARDS
MEREDITH

On September 10, 1959, Serling wrote to Meredith, who was in Pomona, New York, to praise the actor's performance. "You did a superb job for us and from the rough cut, I'd say that this is one of our most effective shows. Thanks and bless you and should you ever need a writer as a kind of a personal side man, may I volunteer?"

Variety commented, "Meredith was capitol as the pitiful little bookworm." Burgess Meredith was previously married to Helen Derby from 1933 to 1935. The Bemis character in this episode was married to a woman named Helen. It is not known if Serling did this on purpose in the teleplay, but Meredith was obviously aware of the name connection and the fact that it was not changed meant Meredith approved. Serling's closing commentary makes reference to John Steinbeck's 1937 novel, *Of Mice and Men*. Burgess Meredith played the role of George in the 1939 motion picture based on the same novel. Coincidence? Maybe. Years later, Meredith would become the narrator for *Twilight Zone: The Movie* (1983) and in the beginning of that same movie, Albert Brooks and Dan Aykroyd made a reference to this particular episode.

It should also be noted that Meredith, as Bemis, speaks perfect English throughout the entire episode because he was a reader of so many books.

"I am very grateful to Rod Serling," recalled Meredith for a Serling tribute at the Museum of Broadcasting in 1984. "He provided me with several of the best scripts I ever had the luck to perform. In one case, the role of Mr. Bemis. There isn't a fortnight goes by I don't hear a compliment about it. Year after year, Rod used to have a part for me every season and every one of them [was] extraordinary."

On July 26, 1960, Serling replied to a fan letter to J.E. Wolfe of Knoxville, Tennessee, who felt

Burgess Meredith as the
perplexed Henry Bemis.

offended by the production of "Time Enough at Last," though she commented how beautiful the story was conceived. Serling replied on October 26 with "we were attempting irony and in the view of many of the audience, we created only sadism."

The episode was the central figure of an editorial that appeared in the Saturday, May 21, 1960 issue of *The Stamford Advocate*. Vilius Brazenas commented about the youth of America and how they were being exposed to distorted facts in schools and on television. Brazenas claimed part of the problem was that juveniles, fostered by shows like this, lacked an understanding of "the enemy," faltered by shows like this. "By atom horror shows and movies we are being gradually scared into surrender without being told or shown what that surrender would mean.

Why couldn't those brilliant scriptwriters and producers make a movie about American victims in Korea?"

> **Production Schedule at M-G-M**
> Day 1 –   Interior of the Bank and Interior of Carsville's Office (both good on Stage 10)
> The Bemis Living Room (good on Stage 8)
>
> Day 2 –   Exterior of the Library (rubble on Lot 3)
> Interior of the Vault and Stairway (good) and Interior of the Bank (rubble on Stage 10)
> Carsville's Office (wrecked) and the Phone Booth (rubble on Stage 10)
>
> Day 3 –   Interior of the Vault and Stairway (wrecked), Streets (rubble), Bemis House and Hole (night), Exterior Walking Shot, Grocery Store (night and day shot), Sporting Goods (rubble), and Shots of Bemis Superimposed over the Ruins (all on Lot 10)

This episode was spoofed numerous times on various television programs. On an episode of *The Drew Carey Show* titled "Y2K, You're OK," initially telecast on September 22, 1999, Carey is the last living man on Earth, after the bomb is dropped, but remains content in his bomb shelter because he has all the *Playboy* magazines he could ever want to read. About to browse the July 1999 issue, Carey sneezes, causing his glasses to fall to the ground and shatter, giving Carey reason to cry.

On an episode of *The Simpsons*, titled "Strong Arms of the Ma," initially telecast on February 2, 2003, a postal carrier breaks his glasses amidst delivering the latest issue of *The Twilight Zone Magazine*, and Constant's music theme can be heard in the background. On an episode of *Futurama*, Bemis breaks his glasses, cries "It's not fair!" and then discovers that his eyesight isn't as bad as he thought – until his eyeballs fall out. After deciding to read books in Braille, his hands fall off.

On an episode of *Family Guy*, titled "Wasted Talent," brain cells are fried by a man's drinking binge, except for the lone survivor, wearing glasses, excited to be able to read books. On *The Adventures of Jimmy Neutron: Boy Genius*, in the episode "Return of the Nanobots," a parody on this episode features the character of Hugh being the last man on Earth and breaking his glasses. The PC video game *Fallout Tactics*, released in March of 2001, features an epic post-apocalyptic storyline. At one point during the game, a man comes on the screen asking the role player to help him find his missing glasses, so he can read the books he longs to enjoy.

Production #3616 "PERCHANCE TO DREAM"
(Initial telecast: November 27, 1959)
© Cayuga Productions, Inc., November 26, 1959, LP15236
Dates of Rehearsal: August 14 and 17, 1959
Dates of Filming: August 18, 19 and 20, 1959
Script #16 dated: July 29, 1959, with revised pages dated August 14 and 17, 1959
Shooting script dated: August 17, 1959

Producer and Secretary: $660.00

Director: $1,250.00

Story and Secretary: $2,209.45

Cast: $7,525.00

Unit Manager and Secretary: $520.00

Agents Commission: $5,185.55

Below the line charges (M-G-M): $27,658.40

Total Production Costs: $53,955.00

Production Fee: $750.00

Legal and Accounting: $250.00

Below the line charges (other): $7,946.60

Cast: Richard Conte (Edward Hall); John Larch (Eliot Rathman, M.D.); Suzanne Lloyd (Miss Thomas / Maya, the Cat Girl); Eddie Marr (the sideshow barker); Ted Stanhope (the stranger on the street); and Russell Trent (rifle range barker).

Original Music Score Composed and Conducted by Nathan Van Cleave (Score No. CPN5837): Main Title (by Bernard Herrmann, :40); Prelude (1:22); Sleep (:58); What's Funny? (:33); The Picture (1:46); The Crash (1:55); Stage Opening (:09); Coney Island – Part 1 (:47); Coney Island – Part 2 (:24); Drum Solo (:58); Maya – Part 1 (:10); Maya – Part 2 (:24); Maya – Part 3 (1:05); The Fun House (1:48); The Roller Coaster (2:36); Untitled (:57); Finale (:46); and End Title (by Herrmann, :39).

Director of Photography: George T.
    Clemens, a.s.c.

Art Directors: George W. Davis and
    William Ferrari

Set Decorations: Henry Grace and Rudy Butler

Sound: Franklin Milton and Philip Mitchell

Production Manager: Ralph W. Nelson

Film Editor: Joseph Gluck, a.c.e.

Assistant Director: Edward Denault

Casting Director: Mildred Gusse

Directed by Robert Florey

Teleplay by Charles Beaumont, based on his short story of the same name, originally published in the October 1958 issue of *Playboy*.

"Twelve O'Clock noon. An ordinary scene, an ordinary city. Lunchtime for thousands of ordinary people. To most of them, this hour will be a rest, a pleasant break in the day's routine. To most, but not all. To Edward Hall, time is an enemy, and the hour to come is a matter of life and death."

Plot: Edward Hall, a draftsman by profession, visits a prominent psychiatrist in the hopes of finding a cure for an unusual problem. Claiming he hasn't slept for days, Edward explains that he has a rheumatic heart and doctors have advised him to avoid any strenuous exercise and any kind of shock. Every evening, however, Edward experiences a recurring nightmare, episodic in form, where he spends his time at an amusement park he describes as the kind where everything is twisted out of shape. He spends time with an exotic vixen known as "Maya, the Cat Girl," who informs him that she is aware he is dreaming and then tempts him onto rides that he could not take in real life. His last dream ended with a joy ride on a roller coaster and Maya laughs and screams for him to "jump." Edward explains to the psychiatrist that if he falls asleep again, he'll pick up where he last left off, but if he stays awake any longer, the strain will be too much for his heart. The psychiatrist cannot offer any suggestions. Edward, disappointed, leaves the office and is shocked to see the receptionist (he didn't even glance at her when he had entered) is the same vixen from his dreams! Scared, he runs across the office and jumps out the window to his death. In the office, the psychiatrist calls his receptionist in to examine the dead body of Edward Hall. The psychiatrist explains that the patient came in, lay down and before dying in his sleep, screamed – possibly from a nightmare.

"They say a dream takes only a second or so, and yet in that second a man can live a lifetime. He can suffer and die, and who's to say which is the greater reality; the one we know or the one in dreams, between heaven, the sky, the earth in . . . the Twilight Zone."

Trailer: *"Next week we enlisted the considerable literary talents of Mr. Charles Beaumont, and invite you to join us in a strange and shocking dream. Our story is called 'Perchance to Dream' and stars Richard Conte. I hope you'll be able to join next week's excursion into The Twilight Zone. Thank you and good night."*

Trivia, etc. In the December 1959 issue of *The Magazine of Fantasy and Science Fiction*, Charles Beaumont wrote, "My *Playboy* story, 'Perchance to Dream,' was selected for production a few months ago. Serling told me to dramatize it but to make no changes. He advised me to forget everything I had learned about television taboos. They didn't exist on *Twilight Zone*. I should do the script the way I saw it. Believing the instructions to be well-meant, but hardly to be taken seriously, I nonetheless did write the script precisely as I saw it. To my amazement, it was happily accepted. Nothing was changed. Not one line. Not one word. Not even the wild technical directions, which called for an impressionistic amusement park, a roller coaster ride and a car crash."

"It was filmed exactly as written," Beaumont concluded. "I know because I was on the set, watching, unable to believe that any of this was truly happening. An author was seeing his work treated with respect."

Beaumont's short story, "Perchance to Dream," appeared in *Playboy* some months previous, which Cayuga insisted Beaumont adapt as a feasible teleplay, since he had prior credits for writing for the screen. Beaumont was represented as to writing employment by Malcolm Stuart of the Preminger-Stuart Agency and was represented as to his stories by Don Condon of the Harold Matson office, New York City. For reasons of his own, Beaumont asked the agents to stay out of the negotiations. Stuart understood the difficulty Cayuga would have in buying a short story from one agent and seeking the services of the same author from another agent, when Cayuga merely wanted to arrive at an equitable total price. Stuart promised that he would try to get Condon's permission to conclude the negotiations on his own. Stuart was also Richard Matheson's agent, so the price was close to the same for both authors.

Among Charles Beaumont's entry in *The Twilight Zone* were small bits of macabre humor such as the climax, when the protagonist jumps out the window from the 13th floor. While the room number is 1410, most buildings do not have a 13th floor, so on a technical level, Edward jumped from the 13th floor. The line "We've been expecting you, Mr. Hall," was spoken both by the receptionist and Maya, revealing to the audience early on that both are the same women.

Historically, director Robert Florey was originally slated to take the helm of *Frankenstein*, released theatrically in 1931, giving Universal Studios one of their more profitable and influential horror movies. For the sake of nostalgia, a dummy of the Frankenstein monster was brought to the set and displayed in the house of horrors. According to an interoffice memo, Houghton was concerned about using the monster, in fear of a legal issue with Universal Studios – which may have been the reason why the monster never made the final cut during editing.

"Throughout the TV filming, Florey strove for quality," Beaumont wrote. "It might have been the most expensive M-G-M feature. He rooted out the meanings of certain lines, frequently surprising me with symbols and shadings I'd neither planned nor suspected. The set was truly impressionistic, recalling the days of *Caligari* and *Liliom*. The costumes were generally perfect. And in the starring role, Richard Conte gave a performance which displays both intensity and subtlety."

Set Decoration Production Costs

Exterior of the Goodman Building $200	Interior of the Lobby $800
Interior of Dr. Rathman's Office $350	Exterior of the Rifle Range $300
Exterior of the Girlie Tent $240	Exterior of the Fun House $100
Exterior of the Fortune Teller $150	Interior of the Fun House $400
Exterior of the Roller Coast (booth and car) $150	Interior of the Secretary's Office $250
Total $2,940	

All of the scenes in the Goodman Building and Dr. Rathman's office were filmed on Stage 10 at M-G-M Studios. The exterior of the girlie show, the exterior of the fortune teller's window and the rifle range concession were also filmed on Stage 10. All of the rest of the scenes, the roller coaster booth, the fun house, the canyon road and the roller coaster itself, were filmed on Stage 9 on the third and last day of shooting.

The cars for the roller coaster were rented for the scenes with Edward and Maya to ride in, at cost of $150. While much of the music specially composed for this episode was reused in a number of later *Twilight Zone* episodes, the music featured in the "Coney Island" sequence was reused superbly in "The Incredible World of Horace Ford."

"The role of Maya was a delight to me. It was different from anything I had ever hoped to be able to do. I studied ballet for a year, once a week, and had to drop out because I wanted to pass my exams," recalled Suzanne Lloyd, whose experience helped with the exotic dancing scene on stage. She won the part of Maya, the Cat Girl, and she augmented her previous training by observing the motions of a leopard. "Except for the office scenes, they had the camera tilted throughout. I recall spending long hours trying to get that laugh just right and their efforts to capture close-ups of Richard Conte's face. *The Twilight Zone* is one of my all-time favorites. I was very lucky to be cast in it."

According to an interoffice memo from Buck Houghton to Bill Self, George Amy and Rod Serling, the editing department's Jesse Alexander viewed the final undubbed cut of the episode and approved the film for late evening viewing only, "because of terror portrayed in dream sequences." Since the *Twilight Zone* series was already being broadcast in the 10 p.m. (EST) time slot, this meant it was being "censored" to be aired at an even later time. "This is a picture of terror and must be cut, dubbed, and have music that underwrites mounting terror," Houghton explained. "Nevertheless I have asked Mr. Alexander to be sure and see the answer print in order to be positive that this restriction is just. I feel that in as much as the terror is created by a beautiful woman that this does not fall into the class of monsters, ghouls, and dripping blood; in short, I feel that the restriction should be removed for subsequent showings in earlier time slots."

Suzanne Lloyd concluded, "The fondest memory of the show was that I had the opportunity to work with consummate actors who were dedicated to their craft and to be directed by a man who understood exactly what Buck Houghton was striving for. We were all on the same page. The joy of that is hard to explain unless you have worked on shows where people have their own understanding of how a scene should be and no one agrees. This was not the case on *The Twilight Zone*. This was heaven. It allowed all of us to focus on our characters and to honor the written word."

Music Trivia

Nathan Van Cleave apparently composed two music scores for 'Perchance to Dream.' For reasons unknown, the first one was not satisfactory for the finished film, so it was revised on November 5, 1959. The Score Number for the first composition was CPN5831 and the second was Score Number CPN5837.

Production #3604 "JUDGMENT NIGHT" (Initial telecast: December 4, 1959)
© Cayuga Productions, Inc., December 3, 1959, LP15237
Dates of Rehearsal: July 9 and 10, 1959
Dates of Filming: July 13, 14 and 15, 1959
Script #4 dated: February 16, 1959
Second draft was completed by March 27, 1959, with revised pages dated June 29, 1959.
Shooting script dated: July 10, 1959

Producer and Secretary: $660.00
Director: $1,250.00
Unit Manager and Secretary: $520.00
Agents Commission: $5,185.55
Below the line charges (M-G-M): $27,720.11
Total Production Costs: $53,257.07

Story and Secretary: $2,468.05
Cast: $6,844.10
Production Fee: $750.00
Legal and Accounting: $250.00
Below the line charges (other): $7,609.26

Cast: Barry Bernard (the engineer); Leslie Bradley (Major Devereaux); James Franciscus (Lt. Mueller); Kendrick Huxham (the bartender); Donald Journeaux (the second steward); Debbie Joyce (the little girl); Patrick Macnee (the first officer); Bob McCord (crewman); Deirdre Owen (Barbara); Richard Peel (the first steward); Nehemiah Persoff (Carl Lanser); Hugh Sanders (Mr. Potter of the War Production Board); and Ben Wright (Captain Wilbur).

Stock Music Cues: Main Title (by Bernard Herrmann, :45); Rain Clouds – Western Suite (by Herrmann, 1:08 and :32); Moonscape 9 (by Herrmann, :30); Moonscape – Outer Space Suite (by Herrmann, 1:55); Rain Clouds – Western Suite (by Herrmann, 3:03); Snare Soli (anonymous, :05); Shock Therapy #3 (by Rene Garriguenc, :12); Snare Soli (anonymous, :13); The Book Rack (by Herrmann, :04); Rain Clouds – Western Suite (by Herrmann, :12); Moonscape – Outer Space Suite (by Herrmann, 1:25); Shock Therapy #4 (by Garriguenc, :48); Shock Therapy #3 (by Garriguenc, :35 and :28); Snare Soli (anonymous, 2:11); The Rocks – Have Gun-Will Travel (by Herrmann, :32); Rain Clouds – Western Suite (by Herrmann, 1:06); and End Title (by Herrmann, :39).

Director of Photography: George T.
    Clemens, a.s.c.
Art Directors: George W. Davis and

Production Manager: Ralph W. Nelson
Film Editor: Bill Mosher
Assistant Director: Edward Denault

William Ferrari   Casting Director: Mildred Gusse
Set Decorations: Henry Grace and Rudy Butler   Sound: Franklin Milton and Jean Valentino
Directed by John Brahm   Teleplay by Rod Serling

"Her name is the S.S. Queen of Glasgow. Her registry: British. Gross tonnage: five thousand. Age: indeterminate. At this moment she's one day out of Liverpool, her destination New York. Duly recorded on this ship's log is the sailing time, course to destination, weather conditions, temperature, longitude and latitude. But what is never recorded in a log is the fear that washes over a deck like fog and ocean spray. Fear like the throbbing strokes of engine pistons, each like a heartbeat, parceling out every hour into breathless minutes of watching, waiting and dreading. For the year is 1942, and this particular ship has lost its convoy. It travels alone like an aged blind thing groping through the unfriendly dark, stalked by unseen periscopes of steel killers. Yes, the Queen of Glasgow is a frightened ship, and she carries with her a premonition of . . . death."

Plot: Carl Lanser, a passenger on the S.S. Queen of Glasgow, is suffering from a severe case of déjà vu. He doesn't seem to recall how he got on board, but he knows who he is and where he was born. He feels as if he is in a nightmare and a preying fear of wolfpacks converging on the vessel. His knowledge of German submarines causes the ship's captain to wonder if Lanser isn't acting too much "like a U-Boat Commander." The captain realizes he has engine problems and knows full well that German submarines are out there, stalking the ship's every move. Lanser also suffers from a premonition that at 1:15 in the morning something bad will happen. Unable to shake away the feeling of uneasiness, he tries to warn the crew on board, but none will heed his warnings until it is too late – a German U-boat surfaces and sinks the English ship, killing all of the passengers. On board the submarine, Carl Lanser, the Kapitan Leutnant, of the Kriegsmarine, has a discussion with his lieutenant. The lieutenant finds it difficult to reconcile the killing of women and children without warning. In the eyes of God, he believes they are damned – a special kind of hell now awaits him and his fellow submariners. "Perhaps to be damned is to have a fate like the people on that ship, to suffer as they suffer, and to die as they die," he theorizes. Lanser scoffs at the idea, unaware that he will be riding the ghost of that same ship every night – for eternity.

"The S.S. Queen of Glasgow, heading for New York, and the time is 1942. For one man, it is always 1942 . . . and this man will ride the ghost of that ship every night for eternity. This is what is meant by paying the fiddler. This is the comeuppance awaiting every man when the ledger of his life is opened and examined, the tally made, and then the reward or the penalty paid. And in the case of Carl Lanser, former Kapitan Leutnant, Navy of the Third Reich, this is the penalty. This is the justice meted out. This is judgment night in The Twilight Zone."

Trailer: *"Once upon a time there was a ship sailing from Liverpool, England to New York. It never got there and one man on board knows why. Next week we tell this man's story. The distinguished actor Nehemiah Persoff plays the role of Carl Lanser, a haunted man in a haunted story called 'Judgment Night.' This ship sails next week and we hope you'll see it off. Thank you, and good night."*

Trivia, etc. Rod Serling once recalled how he got the idea for this story: "I got it while listening to a sermon about the hereafter. I've never been able to stomach a concept of 'hell,' at least the Dante version. It struck me that purgatory can be given modern dress, which is what happened in this show."

Serling's fight over control of censorship usually dealt with the sponsors, not the networks. In an issue of *TV Guide*, Serling remarked, "If you sell to *The Saturday Evening Post*, your name goes on the story and it stays on it. It's your story, not the *Post*'s or the sponsor's. The *Post* is also an example of the comparative freedom from this censorship of other mediums. It's a popular, mass medium, too, but I guess people don't associate product with content the way they associate product with a TV show. If a *Post* story deals with infidelity and it's continued to where Seiberling has a tire ad, people who disapprove of infidelity don't stop buying Seiberling tires. If Seiberling sponsored the same story on TV, I guess they might."

While the standard procedure was to send both the network and the advertising agency representing the sponsor a first draft of all the scripts for feedback before the final revision and polish, Serling only had one direct conflict with the sponsor, Sanka, during the first season. In an interview with Mike Wallace on September 22, 1959, Serling explained, "In 18 scripts, Mike, we have had one line changed, which, again, was a little ludicrous but of insufficient basic concern within the context of the story to put up a fight. On a bridge of a British ship, a sailor calls down to the galley and asks in my script for a pot of tea, because I believe that it's constitutionally acceptable in the British Navy to drink tea. One of my sponsors happens to sell instant coffee, and he took great umbrage, or at least minor umbrage anyway, with the idea of saying tea. Well, we had a couple of swings back and forth, nothing serious, and we decided we'd ask for a tray to be sent up to the bridge. But in 18 scripts, that's the only conflict we've had."

The initial draft called for a "coffee urn," but was later changed to "tea pot" on June 29. It was after the June 29 revision that the sponsor reviewed the script and asked for all references to "tea" be removed because the sponsor feared the viewers might associate with their competition, who sold tea. On July 10, Serling made a more drastic change – not just to please the sponsor, but to avoid any association of liquids – "tea" was replaced with "tray of food." The captain, when entering the lounge, originally spoke, "Thought I'd just have a cup of tea," but the line was changed to "I did want to say hello to some of you." A later reference in the script, "pot of tea" was replaced with "the tray for the bridge, please."

The De Forest Research Group gave Serling their comments on July 2, 1959. Among the concerns and suggestions: the antique clock that Lanser views when counting down the minutes was supposed to have a pendulum, as instructed in the script – but it was replaced with a clock with no pendulum. The proper German spelling of lieutenant was "leutnant," and Serling made the appropriate changes. It was also pointed out that the man serving at the bar would most likely be a regular seaman doing extra duty for pay, not a bartender as such. Serling also made a number of other changes, such as changing lines "Yes, Sir" to "Aye, aye, sir." The word "fixed" was replaced with "repaired."

Like "The Sixteen Millimeter Shrine," Serling felt negative about this episode. "'Judgment Night' in its original script form was a better than average flight of fantasy," he recalled after reviewing the final cut. "It's filming left it so considerably less than that." The production values, however, can be listed as above-average to most viewers – most notably how the camera tilts slowly during Carl Lanser's escapade on board the ship as 1:15 approaches.

The closing narration was different in the early draft of this script:

"They talk about paying the fiddler, the comeuppance awaiting every man when the ledger of his life

is opened and examined. The credits and debits added up, a tally made, and then the reward or the penalty paid. And in the case of Carl Lanser, former Kapitan Lieutenant, U-boat commander, Navy of the Third Reich, this is the penalty. This is the justice meted out. This is judgment night in The Twilight Zone."

The closing narration was later revised and recorded by Serling, but a shorter version was used after the final cut was completed, so the narration would fit within the proper time frame:

"The S. S. Queen of Glasgow, registry British, destined for New York and the time is 1942. For one man . . . it is always 1942. And this man will ride the ghost of that ship every night for eternity. This is what is meant by "paying the fiddler." This is the comeuppance awaiting every man when the ledger of his life is opened and examined. The credits and debits added up. The tally made and then the reward of the penalty paid. And in the case of Carl Lanser, former Kapitan Leutant, U-boat commander, Navy of the Third Reich, this is the penalty. This is the justice meted out. This is Judgment Night in The Twilight Zone."

In April of 1959, Rod Serling requested that Ralph Nelson or Franklin Shaffner direct this episode. Shaffner had directed three of his teleplays for *Studio One*: "Buffalo Bill is Dead" (telecast Nov. 23, 1953); "Herman Came By Bomber" (Feb. 1, 1954); and "The Strike" (June 7, 1954). Houghton suggested to Serling that a complete script and a concrete proposal detailing the production be submitted to both men, because he did not want to "saddle either one of these gentlemen with production problems." Neither man directed – Shaffner never got to direct a single *Twilight Zone*, but Nelson helmed one later in the year, "A World of His Own." Serling also suggested "Escape Clause," "A Most Unusual Camera" and "The Last Flight" be offered to Nelson and Schaffner – nothing ever came of those suggestions.

The reason Houghton had turned down the two directors for these scripts, he explained in a letter, was because he felt that "Escape Clause" and "A Most Unusual Camera" gave the impression of a light touch and would not be the directors' greatest strengths. Houghton did suggest offering "The Lonely" to Nelson and "Walking Distance" to Shaffner – this never came to be.

Nehemiah Persoff was paid $2,000 for his role as Carl Lanser. After the episode was filmed, Persoff went to New York to star in *Only in America* on stage, and through the office of Young & Rubicam, was set up to do a number of interviews in New York to plug his appearance on this episode.

"I was very busy working on that episode as there was much to do," recalled Persoff. "My stand-in was from Germany. I had one phrase to say in German –'Fuer Frei' (fire at will). I asked my stand-in Freddie how to pronounce it and he told me. From the moment he instructed me on the proper pronunciation he kept drilling me and testing me and correcting me, and naturally I grew tired of it and told him that it wasn't that important to get it perfectly right. If it was close to right, it's ok. Freddie's feelings were hurt and he backed off. Yet he was much concerned, as if the whole show depended on my saying the phrase as if I was a high-class German commanding the ship."

"As you may know, after the director calls action, no one and I do mean no one calls cut except the director," Persoff continued. "We prepared to shoot the scene in which I call 'Fuer Frei.' The director, John Brahm (who is also a German refugee), called 'action,' and we played the scene and I called 'fuer frei,' at which point Freddie stepped on stage and called 'Cut! Cut! This is not the way a cultured man would call fuer frei!' Now this is unheard of. First of all, nobody but the director calls 'cut' and certainly not a stand-in. Everybody was shocked. I winced and I thought poor Freddie just lost his job. At which point John Brahm, who knew Freddie was in the concentration camps, walked over to Freddie, and in a gentle voice said, 'Freddie, I agree with you that ordinarily a captain of a ship would be from among the upper class Germans, but the captain Mr. Persoff is playing, came up from the ranks, he comes from a working class background.' We went back to shooting the scene, as if nothing happened. Back in the dressing room Freddie apologized profusely. I assured him that I valued his loyalty, that I knew he wanted me to be good in the role and could not contain himself. Freddie was in poor health and passed on several months later."

When *The San Antonio Light* reviewed the episode, the television critic commented that "the production is excellent and Nehemiah Persoff is properly puzzling as the haunted German."

Clarence E. Flick of San Jose State College, however, had a different opinion. Flick commented after viewing this episode, "The excellent mood which was established was suddenly interrupted by the Little-Lulu-Indian comic commercial – would have been improved somewhat if they had reversed the commercials in the program. Then we came back to reality until the shock and surprise of the identity of the submarine commander established the theme. The total impression of the program was of too much visual reality. The few effects used were standard."

On December 5, Murray F. Sleeper, a minister of the North Congregational Church in New Hartford, Connecticut, wrote to Rod Serling after this episode aired, asking if it would be possible to obtain a copy of the portion of the script that contained the closing discussion between the seaman and the Captain. "The basic idea that each of us might have our judgment in the form of eternally facing what we have 'dished out' to others was intriguing, and I would like to use your development of it as the spring-board for a sermon, sometime in the future." On December 24, Serling obliged and sent a copy to Mr. Sleeper. From an inspired sermon came this script, which in turn inspired another sermon.

Regardless of Serling's opinion of the finished product, and the sponsor's request to eliminate any references that could have been related to its competition, five days after this episode was broadcast, on December 9, James W. Andrews, product manager of Maxwell House, wrote to Rod Serling at his Pacific Palisades home. "Just a short line to let you know that I caught last Friday's show starring Nehemiah Persoff. I thought it was excellent, and I thought that Persoff particularly did a fine job."

Assorted Production Costs
Footage of the ship in the fog-enshrouded waters was lifted from *The Wreck of the Mary Deare* starring Gary Cooper and Charlton Heston, a film shot in color but the footage remained black and white in this *Twilight Zone* episode. The motion picture had been released theatrically four weeks before this television episode aired. The cost to use the stock shot was $500. The fog effect for the scenes that took place on the deck of the ship cost $150.

Production #3611 "AND WHEN THE SKY WAS OPENED"
(Initial telecast: December 11, 1959)
© Cayuga Productions, Inc., December 10, 1959, LP15579 (under the title "When the Sky Was Opened")
Dates of Rehearsal: July 20 and 21, 1959
Dates of Filming: July 22, 23 and 24, 1959

Script #11 dated: July 1, 1959
Producer and Secretary: $660.00
Story and Secretary: $3,455.73 (story purchased for $1,000)

Director: $1,250.00
Unit Manager and Secretary: $520.00
Agents Commission: $5,185.55
Below the line charges (M-G-M): $19,437.45
Total Production Costs: $43,301.93

Cast: $4,996.98
Production Fee: $750.00
Legal and Accounting: $250.00
Below the line charges (other): $6,796.22

Cast: Charles Aidman (Colonel Ed Harrington); Joe Bassett (the medical officer); Paul Bryar (the bartender); Maxine Cooper (Amy Riker); Logan Field (the investigator); Elizabeth Fielding (the second nurse); James Hutton (Major William Gart); S. John Launer (Mr. Harrington); Oliver McGowan (the officer); Gloria Pall (the girl in the bar); Sue Randall (the first nurse); and Rod Taylor (Lt. Colonel Clegg Forbes).

Original Music Score Composed and Conducted by Leonard Rosenman (Music Score No. CPN5846): Main Title (by Bernard Herrmann, :40); First Narration (:37); Second Narration (:12); First Hospital Scene (:14); Confusion (1:16); The Missing Colonel (1:05); Desperation (:15); Flashback (:20); No Tricks (by Bruce Campbell, :54); Celestial Call (1:52); It's Never June (by Campbell, :38); Ed Disappears (1:17); No Trace (:33); Waiting for a Phone Call (:14); The Telegram (:54); Back to the Scene of the Crime (:58); Ed Come Back (:23); Celestial Call #3 (1:15); Celestial Call #4 (:47); The Empty Room (:13); Final Celestial Call (:38); and End Title (by Herrmann, :39).

Director of Photography: George T.
    Clemens, a.s.c.
Art Directors: George W. Davis and
    William Ferrari
Set Decorations: Henry Grace and
    Rudy Butler

Production Manager: Ralph W. Nelson
Film Editor: Fred Maguire
Assistant Director: Edward Denault
Casting Director: Mildred Gusse
Sound: Franklin Milton and Jean Valentino
Directed by Douglas Heyes

Teleplay by Rod Serling, based on the short story "Disappearing Act" by Richard Matheson, originally published in the March 1953 issue of *The Magazine of Fantasy and Science Fiction*.

"Her name: X-20. Her type – an experimental interceptor. Recent history – a crash landing in the Mojave Desert after a thirty-one hour flight, nine hundred miles into space. Incidental data: the ship with the men who flew her, disappeared from the radar screen for twenty-four hours. But the shrouds that cover mysteries are not always made out of a tarpaulin, as this man will soon find out on the other side of the hospital door."

Plot: Colonel Forbes visits his good friend Major Gart, who lies recouping from a crash-landing in the desert. Forbes, on the verge of a nervous breakdown, tries to convince Gart that the experimental aircraft originally carried three U.S. Air Force space pilots, not two. Gart doesn't recall any third man, and swears it was the two of them. Forbes recounts that 24 hours previous, he and Colonel Harrington were out drinking at a bar when Harrington started having a strange feeling that he did not belong. Harrington held no reflection in the mirror, his parents claimed they never had a son, and the newspaper reported the craft held only two pilots. Harrington theorized that someone (or some thing) made a mistake — that no one was supposed to come back, and the mistake is being corrected by eliminating all existence of the spacemen's return. Shortly thereafter, Harrington disappears and Gart discovers all evidence of his existence slowly disappearing. Unable to convince Gart, Colonel Forbes runs out of the hospital screaming. Gart soon discovers truth in his friend's story, when the nurse insists he was the only Air Force pilot on the mission, and the newspaper headlines Gart as the survivor of a one-man flight. Gart, too, begins to panic, but it is too late – the doctor and nurse plan to use the hospital room and verify the number of empty beds – three. As for the experimental craft in the hanger, it too has vanished and no trace of either the craft or the crew remains on Earth.

"Once upon a time, there was a man named Harrington . . . a man named Forbes . . . a man named Gart. They used to exist, but don't any longer. Someone . . . or some thing . . . took them somewhere. At least, they are no longer a part of the memory of man. And as to the X-20 supposed to be housed here in this hangar . . . this too does not exist. And if any of you have any questions concerning an aircraft and three men who flew her – speak softly of them . . . and only in . . . the Twilight Zone."

Trailer: *"Next week three men return from a flight into space only to discover that their nightmare has just begun. Rod Taylor, James Hutton and Charles Aidman appear in 'And When the Sky Was Opened.' What happens to these men once they're picked up in the desert . . . [Serling vanishes] . . . Well, that gives you a rough idea. You'll see next week on the Twilight Zone. Thank you and good night."*

Trivia, etc. The most expensive set for the entire episode was the bar, costing $450 in rentals, props, actual liquids to substitute for liquor, and other necessities. The interior of the bar was filmed on Stage 21 at M-G-M, while the rest of the episode was filmed on Stage 23. The first day's filming was completely devoted to all the scenes in Gart's hospital room (the cheapest set for the episode, costing a mere $75). The second day of filming was devoted to scenes in the hospital corridor and the interior of the bar. The third and final day of filming was devoted to the interior of the hotel room, Harrington's room and the interior of the empty hangar.

The February 27, 1960 issue of *TV Guide* raved about this episode. "Serling's gifts as a narrator are easily recognizable. Serling's point of view here is a little obscure, but as pure horror the episode can stand right up there with the best of Poe, Bierce and Sheridan LeFanu."

Apparently this episode was also called "The Aftermath" according to some production paperwork, before the name was later changed to "Disappearing Act," which is the title featured on all paperwork during production. The original short story was about a common citizen who suspected that he was either losing his mind or his friends and family were slowly ceasing to exist. His memories remained intact, but all evidence of their existence had vanished. The story concluded with the first person narrative ending in the middle of a sentence – suggesting he himself ceased to exist. No rational explanation was given for the anomaly, and Serling loved the concept.

An early draft of this script opened with the shrouded aircraft having just been covered with a tarpaulin, part of a cracked wing and bent tail protruding, the wing bearing the remnants of an Air Force star. An Air Force officer questions an investigator. The investigator says the aircraft came in on

Rod

		START PRODUCTION						
		CASTING CALL SHEET						MGM FORM 522

METRO-GOLDWYN-MAYER PICTURES
CULVER CITY CALIFORNIA

Todays date __7/21/59__

Page one of __1__ pages

PROD. __3611TV__   DIRECTOR __HEYES__   TITLE __"DISAPPEARING ACT"__

CALL IS FOR – DAY __WEDNESDAY__   DATE __7/22/59__

WEATHER CONDITIONS: __R or S__

1ST SET	INT. HOSPITAL ROOM (D)	SCS	4 thru 18 – 19 – 51 thru 54 56 – 59 thru 64 – 67	LOC. #23
2ND SET	INSERTS FOR PROD. #3609	SCS.		LOC. "
3RD SET		SCS.		LOC.
4TH SET		SCS.		LOC.

CALLED	NAME	CHARACTER – WARDROBE	GATE	MKUP	WARD	SET
X	ROD TAYLOR	FORBES – Wdb. on Stg.		8am	7:45	8:30
X	JAMES HUTTON	GART – Same as above		7:45	8:15	8:30
X	CHUCK AIDMAN	HARRINGTON – Same as above		10:45	10:30	11am
C	SUE RANDALL	NURSE LT. – Same as above		2pm	3pm	3:30
	ATMOSPHERE					
	NONE					
	STANDINS					
X	BOB McCORD	UTILITY	7:45			
C	PAUL DENTON	UTILITY	"			

Production sheet for this episode verifies that the title was "Disappearing Act" during production. Production sheets were composed for every day of filming for every episode produced by Cayuga.

her belly at something close to 300 miles an hour, which is why the wing looked the way it did. The officer explains the plane was tracked on radar for the first couple of hours and then disappeared for 24 hours. Next, there was an explosion on the desert, and it was the aircraft. None of the crew remembers anything about the landing, possibly having blacked out during reentry to the atmosphere.

The above scene was written but never filmed. Instead, the camera panned down to the craft already covered by the tarpaulin, under armed guard. The name of the craft in an early draft was the X-6 but this was later changed to the X-20.

It was about the time that the X-20 Dyna-Soar (short for "Dynamic Soarer") was designed by the U.S. Air Force for a variety of military missions, including reconnaissance, space rescue, satellite maintenance and the sabotage of enemy satellites. The program ran from October 24, 1957 to December 10, 1963, costing $660 million. Now considered one of the great "what if" projects of early spaceflight, it was what *The Twilight Zone* needed to establish credibility and reality with the viewers. Serling, having read an article about the new experimental spacecraft, combined real science with Matheson's fiction, changing the protagonist to an astronaut. Serling himself explained the difference between the short story and his script. "I felt there was no rationale there. At least if I'm dealing in outer space, I can say something [or] someone." And leaving what was responsible to the imagination of the audience helped make this one of the better episodes of the first season.

A few years after this episode aired, Serling looked back on this film and admitted that the use of sound, such as the sound of footsteps on broken glass, made this one of his favorites.

The interior of the hangar featured in the opening scene, with the experimental spacecraft, and the closing scene without it, was filmed on an empty stage at M-G-M. Which stage remains unknown, because the studio granted Houghton and his crew permission to use whatever stage was available in the afternoon of July 24.

When Richard Matheson first submitted this short story to a reading agent for review, the story was returned to him, torn into pieces. Undiscouraged, Matheson continued to submit the story to other agents, unchanged, and it eventually found its way into *The Magazine of Science Fiction and Fantasy*, and was ultimately purchased by Serling for *The Twilight Zone*.

"Actually, ["Disappearing Act" and "Third from the Sun"] are the only two stories I sold them for many years, because I wanted to just do original [teleplays] and hold onto my stories," Matheson recalled to author Matthew R. Bradley. "Then later on I sold some of the stories, because all my early [scripts], if you notice, are originals . . . I think if it was filmed as written, it would be great . . . [but] there was no point [in trying to adapt it personally], because I didn't own it. I sold the story to *The Twilight Zone*. I would have liked to [adapt it myself]."

According to a progress report dated April 9, 1959, Serling originally intended to have this as the second episode broadcast on the series, but before the end of that same month, the selection of what order the episodes would be broadcast changed. Serling was exposed to this episode and "Third From the Sun," not from the magazines they originally appeared in, but from the "Third From the Sun" anthology published by Bantam in 1955, Matheson's first paperback collection.

It wasn't until production was completed that it would be retitled "And When the Sky Was Open." When conceiving the trailer, he even referred to this episode by the present tense instead of past tense, but that changed before the film was completed and made ready for broadcast. Serling's original dialogue for the trailer was "That's exactly right. One by one . . . they disappear. Next week on *The Twilight Zone* we'll show you why. Thank you and good night."

> **Blooper!** When Col. Forbes looks in the mirror and discovers to his horror that he no longer casts any reflection, he panics and flees out of fright. While the director and camera crew decided to film the shot at an angle to eliminate the reflection, his elbow and hand can actually be seen in the mirror.

"Doug Heyes sent me the script with a letter asking me to play the lead," recalled Rod Taylor. "I did a *Playhouse 90* that probably brought me to Serling's attention, but I don't think he wrote the script. With his name on the *Twilight Zone*, I did not want to miss the opportunity, but I suspect he had me in mind from the start. I do know that Doug Heyes was the man who contacted me. Doug was a true professional, all the way. As an actor you have to give the cameraman specific cues for the action scenes, so he can follow. If, while filming, I got off camera, then we would have had to do a retake. Doug told me where to go and what to do, but only for the camera. The rest was up to me."

"My part was originally different than what you saw. I was supposed to be sitting at a table with two other girls," recalled Gloria Pall. "Rod Serling was on the set for the two days I was there and when he saw me, he had the director change it so I was moved up to the bar. Rod Taylor was a rising star at the time I worked with him and I was more in awe of Taylor than of Serling. Odd thing, I got my real estate license in the late 1950s and opened my own office on the Sunset Strip, Jim Hutton, one of the actors on *The Twilight Zone*, whom I never got to share any scenes with, was one of my clients. When I took him around to show him some houses, we got pulled over for speeding and I got a ticket. Jim told me not to worry about it, that he would take care of it, and he never did."

The closing comments by Serling were not exactly the same as in the finished film, but much of the narration remained intact. Among his closing comment is a reference to the X-6, not the X-20. "As to the aircraft . . . the X-6 . . . It's supposed to be housed here in this hangar. It hasn't been built yet. It's on a drawing board some place."

Production #3622 "WHAT YOU NEED"
(Initial telecast: December 25, 1959)
© Cayuga Productions, Inc., December 24, 1959, LP15580
Dates of Rehearsal: October 7 and 8, 1959
Dates of Filming: October 9, 12 and 13, 1959
Script #22 dated: September 14, 1959
Shooting script dated: October 1, 1959

Producer and Secretary: $660.00
Director: $1,250.00
Unit Manager and Secretary: $520.00
Agents Commission: $5,185.55
Below the line charges (M-G-M): $19,971.70
Total Production Costs: $45,706.94

Story and Secretary: $3,145.00
Cast: $9,153.13
Production Fee: $750.00
Legal and Accounting: $250.00
Below the line charges (other): $4,821.56

> *The Twilight Zone* was not telecast on the evening of December 18, 1959, so that an hour-long documentary, part of the *CBS Reports* series, could be shown in the same time slot. This was the third in a short-run series of television specials which had already presented "Biography of a Missile" and "The Population Explosion." This episode was titled "Iran: Brittle Ally" and CBS news correspondents Edward R. Murrow and Winston Burdett examined the effectiveness of American military and economic aid, and explored the Shah's own efforts to end feudalism and resist Communist pressure in this oil-rich outpost of the free world on the Soviet border.

Cast: Frank Allocca (the waiter); Don Anderson (man in bar); Dick Barber (man in street); Robert Barry (man in street); Steve Cochran (Fred Renard); Evelyn Coner (woman in street); Paul Cristo (man in bar); Paul Denton (man exiting the bar); William Edmonson (the bartender); Judy Ellis (woman on street); Lois James (woman in bar); Doris Karnes (the woman customer); Kenner G. Kemp (man in bar); Fred Kruger (man on street); Dale Logue (man in bar); Bob McCord (silent paramedic); Beryl McCutcheon (woman in bar); Read Morgan (Lefty); Ron Nyman (man in street); John Pedrini (man in street); Arline Sax (girl in bar); Norman Sturgis (the night clerk); Mark Sunday (the photographer); and Ernest Truex (Pedott).

Original Music Score Composed and Conducted by Nathan Van Cleave (Score No. CPN5856): Main Title (by Bernard Herrmann, :40); Blues (by John Hawksworth and Stan Stracey, 1:34); Second Act Opening (:15); The First Vision (:41); The Second Vision (:38); The Vision Comes True (1:51); Trouble Starts (:42); Help (:43); Third Act Opening (:24); The Proposition (1:06); The Fountain Pen (:50); How Heavy (2:11); New Shoes (2:06); The Comb (:50); Finale (:37); and End Title (by Herrmann, :39).

Director of Photography: George T. Clemens, a.s.c.	Production Manager: Ralph W. Nelson
	Film Editor: Joseph Gluck, a.c.e.
Art Directors: George W. Davis and William Ferrari	Assistant Director: Edward Denault
	Casting Director: Mildred Gusse
Set Decorations: Henry Grace and Rudy Butler	Sound: Franklin Milton and Jean Valentino

Directed by Alvin Ganzer.

Teleplay by Rod Serling, based on the short story "We Have What You Need" by Lewis Padgett (a pseudonym of authors Henry Kuttner and C.L. Moore), originally published in the October 1945 issue of *Astounding Science Fiction*.

"You're looking at Mr. Fred Renard, who carries on his shoulder a chip the size of the national debt. This is a sour man; a friendless man; a lonely man; a grasping, compulsive, nervous man. This is a man who has lived thirty-six undistinguished, meaningless, pointless, failure-laden years and who at this moment looks for an escape . . . any escape. Any way, anything, anybody . . . to get out of the rut. And this little old man is just what Mr. Renard is waiting for."

Plot: An old man named Pedott makes a comfortable living peddling small essentials to customers on the street and in bars and taverns. When Fred Renard discovers the old man possesses the rare gift of seeing the near future and giving people what they need to make their lives a bit more comfortable, he attempts to take advantage of the old man. Forcing Pedott into giving him things *he* needs, Renard is handed a pair of scissors. The sharp instrument saves his neck when his scarf gets caught in an elevator. Next, he receives a leaky old pen that predicts the winner of races. Renard, however, is not satisfied with his meager earnings from the pen, so he visits Pedott a third time for another item, forcing the old man into a delicate situation. The third item of value is a new pair of shoes, which Renard accepts with glee, but discovers to his horror they are too slippery when worn on the wet road. An oncoming car hits and runs, killing Renard. The shoes, apparently were not for Renard, but for Pedott – they were what he needed.

"Street scene . . . night . . . traffic accident . . . victim named Fred Renard . . . gentleman with a sour face to whom contentment came with difficulty. Fred Renard, who took all that was needed . . . in the Twilight Zone."

Trailer: *"This is the season of gift-giving. Big gifts and little gifts, and expensive ones and not-so-expensive ones. Well next time, the Twilight Zone gives you its own peculiar, oddball brand of gift-giving. Mr. Steve Cochran and Mr. Ernest Truex combine talents to tell a story about a little man, who has what you need. Our next offering on The Twilight Zone."*

Trivia, etc. Buck Houghton chose the short story from which this episode originated and told the plot to Serling over the phone, who agreed to purchase the tale. The story came to Houghton's attention in the course of standard coverage by the story department. It appeared in a collection of Padgett's works called *Line of Tomorrow*, a Bantam collection of 1954. The short story had originally been published in the October 1945 issue of *Astounding Science Fiction*, published by Street & Smith, authored by Henry Kuttner and C.L. Moore. The same short story had been adapted for the television series *Tales of Tomorrow* (1951 – 1953) – for which Serling not only submitted plot ideas, but was a frequent viewer as well. It is more than likely that Serling was already familiar with the story before Houghton's suggestion. The original short story concerned a machine that could foretell the future, much in the same way a later *Twilight Zone* episode, "Nick of Time," would later be conceived. In adapting the story, Serling replaced the machine with a street peddler who could do the same.

Originally Serling intended to use the following for the trailer, but it was considered too lengthy, and needed to be trimmed down:

"This is the season of gifts. Big gifts and little gifts, expensive ones and not-so-expensive ones. Next week the Twilight Zone gives you its own peculiar brand of gift-giving. Mr. Steve Cochran and Mr. Ernest Truex combine talents to tell a story about a little man who has what you need. Rather simple on the face of it, except the gifts we're talking about now and that you'll see next week have to do with life or death. Next week we'll open up a package that will explode in the air. As for our next offering in The Twilight Zone, we give you, 'What You Need' with this parenthetic guarantee . . . 'What You Need' will not easily be forgotten. See you next week. Thank you and good night."

An early draft of the script featured a lengthier opening narration, describing Fred Renard:

"You're looking at Mr. Fred Renard – age thirty-six, who carries on his shoulder a chip the size of the national debt. This is an antagonism directed against the world, those who people it, the taste of his food,

the temperature of his coffee, the fact that he has lost eleven jobs in the past year and three girl friends in the past month. Beyond that is just a general displeasure that is as much a part of the man as his eyes, nose and ears. This is a sour man, a friendless man, a lonely man, a grasping, compulsive, nervous man. This is a man who has lived thirty-six undistinguished, meaningless, pointless, failure-laden years and who at this moment looks for an escape. Any escape. Any route out of the norm. Any channel out of the sameness slop of his living. Any way. Anything. Anybody . . . to get out of the rut. And this little old man . . . is just what Mr. Renard is waiting for!"

The opening remark about having a chip on the shoulder the size of the national debt was re-used for the opening narration for the first of four sequences in *Twilight Zone: The Movie* (1983).

All of the street scenes were shot on Lot 2 at M-G-M on the evening of the first day's filming. The interior and exterior of the bar was filmed on Stage 29 during the second day of filming. Renard's hotel room and the hotel lobby and elevator were filmed on Stage 6 at M-G-M on the third and final day. The interior of Pedott's bedroom was filmed on Stage 29 on the morning of the final day.

The automobile that ran over Renard was not a Ford. Almost all of the vehicles featured on screen during the first season were Ford motor vehicles, courtesy of "product placement." (Even antiques got into the act. In "The Lonely," a Model A Ford was parked outside the metal shack.) Since automobile manufacturers promote the safety features on their products, and Ford gave Cayuga free use of their vehicles, it seemed appropriate to have an automobile other than a Ford be used for that scene. If you look carefully, the stuntman filling in for the actor is wearing protective padding on his back, underneath the jacket.

Actor Norman Sturgis, who resided in Hollywood, wrote to Rod Serling on October 28, 1959, expressing "my appreciation for the opportunity of working in *Twilight Zone*. I enjoyed being the night clerk in the 'What You Need' script. Laura, who read the script over my shoulder as soon as I brought it in, enjoyed the treatment of the story – as I did."

"My role as the girl in the bar was very important to the story. The dialogue was easy to remember. I only had a few lines to say," recalled Arline Martel, billed as Arline Sax in the credits. "I did a lot of television at the time. I was Tiger in a number of *Hogan's Heroes*. But do you think I get more fan mail because of my recurring role on *Hogan's Heroes*? No. Those few days of filming for *Twilight Zone* has brought me more fan mail than any other."

> **Set Decoration Production Costs**
> Interior and Exterior of the Bar (Stage 29) $450
> Exterior of the Street (Lot 2) $150
> Interior of the Elevator (Stage 6) $100
> Interior of the Hotel Lobby (Stage 6) $305
> Interior of Pedott's Bed Room (Stage 29) $113
> Interior of Renard's Hotel Room (Stage 6) $246
> Total $1,364

The television columnist for *The Hammond Times* reviewed this episode as "a Christmas show that's just a little different. As usual, there's a switch ending, but it's justified."

The racing sheet depicted in the newspaper that the leaky pen spills ink on features a list of horses and their jockeys, pre-arranged for the next day's race which Mr. Renard uses to gamble with. The names of the jockeys is an inside joke for the cast and crew. Thirteen different last names are listed (a few are repeated if you look closely on the screen) and they all represent crewmembers for Cayuga Productions. Boyle, Serling, Hagar, Clemens, Denault, Houghton, Gallegly, Swain, Williams, Van den Ecker, Butler, and Ryan. The top of the racing sheet states "Nelson's Selections," which represents Ralph W. Nelson, the Unit Production Manager.

The newspaper brought to Fred Renard's room features the same front-page headline ("H Bomb Capable of Total Destruction") from the previously telecast episode, "Time Enough at Last." When Fred Renard kicks the door closed in his room, the painting and the wall move a little, revealing how frail the set construction was.

In the 1985 album, *This Nation's Saving Grace*, performed by the rock group known as "The Fall," a song of the same name was apparently inspired by this particular *Twilight Zone* episode.

In the stage musical, *Rent*, musician Jonathan Larson composed the song, "What You Own," which was inspired by this episode of *The Twilight Zone*, even featuring the name of the program within the lyrics.

Production #3618 "THE FOUR OF US ARE DYING"
(Initial telecast: January 1, 1960)
Copyright Registration: © Cayuga Productions, Inc., December 31, 1959, LP15581
Dates of Rehearsal: August 31 and September 1, 1959
Dates of Filming: September 2, 3 and 4, 1959
Script #18 dated: August 6, 1959
Second draft dated: August 14, 1959

Shooting script dated: August 27, 1959
Story and Secretary: $2,937.40 (story
    purchased for $500)
Unit Manager and Secretary: $520.00
Agents Commission: $5,185.55
Below the line charges (M-G-M): $29,017.09
Total Production Costs: $54,821.13

Producer and Secretary: $660.00
Director: $1,250.00
Cast: $6,936.39
Production Fee: $750.00
Legal and Accounting: $250.00
Below the line charges (other): $7,314.70

Cast: Jeonne Baker (silent part); Peter Brocco (Pop Marshak); Pat Comiskey (man number two); Paul Denton (clerk in hotel lobby); Bernard Fein (Penell); Milton Frome (the detective); Beverly Garland (Maggie); Don Gordon (Hammer as Marshak); Jimmy Gray (bellboy in hotel lobby); Bob Hopkins (man in bar); Harry Jackson (the trumpet player); Marco Lopez (silent bit in hotel); Ross Martin (Hammer as Foster); Phillip Pine (Hammer as Virgil Sterig); Sam Rawlins (the busboy); Tony Rosa (silent part); James Selwyn (man in street); and Harry Townes (Arch Hammer).

Original Music Score Composed and Conducted by Jerry Goldsmith (Score No. CPN5850):
Main Title (by Bernard Herrmann, :40); Meet Archie (1:44); Nite Life #1 (1:06); Nite Life #2 (:36); One For My Baby (by Johnny Mercer and Harold Arlen, :49); Ad Lib Piano (by Sam Furman, :31);

Sam's Riff (by Furman, 5:17); Pretty Girl #1 (:06); Too Marvelous for Words (by Richard Whiting and Johnny Mercer, :54); Pretty Girl #2 (:59); The Visit (:17); Getaway #1 (:53); Getaway #2 (1:16); The Pinch (1:36); The Pinch (reprise, :09); Dead Man (2:16) and End Title (by Herrmann, :39).

Director of Photography: George T. Clemens, a.s.c.

Art Directors: George W. Davis and William Ferrari

Set Decorations: Henry Grace and Rudy Butler

Production Manager: Ralph W. Nelson

Film Editor: Joseph Gluck, a.c.e.

Assistant Director: Edward Denault

Casting Director: Mildred Gusse

Sound: Franklin Milton and Jean Valentino

Directed by John Brahm

Teleplay by Rod Serling, based on an original short story submission titled "All of Us Are Dying" / "Rubberface" by George Clayton Johnson.

"His name is Arch Hammer, he's 36 years old. He's been a salesman, a dispatcher, a truck driver, a con man, a bookie, and a part-time bartender. This is a cheap man. A nickel-and-dime man with a cheapness that goes past the suit and the shirt; a cheapness of mind. A cheapness of taste. A tawdry little shine on the seat of his conscience and a dark-room squint at a world whose sunlight has never gotten through to him. But Mr. Hammer has a talent discovered at a very early age. This much he does have. He can make his face change. He can twitch a muscle, move a jaw, concentrate on the cast of his eyes. And he can change his face. He can change it into anything he wants. Mr. Archie Hammer, jack-of-all-trades, has just checked in at three-eighty a night, with two bags, some newspaper clippings, a most odd talent, and a master plan to destroy some lives."

Plot: With a talent for replicating the face of any man he sees, Archie Hammer uses his gift to profit from the dead, using photos in the local obituaries. As Johnny Foster, a former trumpet player, Archie makes love to Johnny's lover and makes plans with her to run away to Chicago. Knowing full well that he needs money to finance their "fling," he imitates Virgil Sterig, a local hoodlum. Using the newspaper obit, Archie fools a mob boss into thinking he is the ghost of Virgil and conducts a brief "business meeting," stealing the money Virgil was killed for – with interest for the attempted murder. When gunmen give chase, Archie imitates Andy Marshak, a local boxer, to fool the gunmen into thinking they were chasing the wrong person. Later that evening, a detective from Michigan catches up to the con man, but Archie makes a slick getaway, reprising the face of Andy Marshak. In the streets, Andy's father meets who he thinks is his son, and wanting to exact vengeance on his kin, shoots the young man dead, killing Archie's chances of a new life.

"He was Arch Hammer, a cheap little man who just checked in. He was Johnny Foster, who played a trumpet and was loved beyond words. He was Virgil Sterig, with money in his pocket. He was Andy Marshak, who got some of his agony back on a sidewalk in front of a cheap hotel...Hammer...Foster...Sterig ...Marshak...and all four of them are dying."

Trailer: *"Next week on The Twilight Zone one of the most bizarre and unusual tales we've told yet. One man with four faces. Four separate and adventuresome lives that must be seen to be believed. Harry Townes, Philip Pine, Ross Martin and Don Gordon star in 'The Four of Us Are Dying.' This is a story designed for goose bumps. I hope we'll see you next week. Good night."*

Set Decoration Production Costs
Exterior of the Stylized Street $1,200
Interior of the Hotel Lobby $150
Interior of the Hotel Room and Bath $400
Interior and Exterior of the Bar $750
Exterior of "Armstrong Towers" (Sign) $75
Interior of the Elevators $50
Interior of the Penell Apartment $75
Interior of the Alley $150
Exterior of the News Stand (Sign) $75
Exterior of the Hotel $250
Total $3,175

Trivia, etc. "At first I thought we could use one actor and have him change his appearance," Millie Gusse, the casting director, explained. "But this was ruled out when we timed it. One actor would be in the make-up room longer than he would be before the cameras." So the search for four actors started.

The first step was to determine the physical characteristics of the actors. Serling, director John Brahm and Millie Gusse decided the characters should all be 5-feet-10-inches tall, weigh 150 pounds and have dark hair. All four men would have to be equally good actors, able to pick up characteristics from the actor who preceded him and to leave the next actor certain traits to duplicate.

"Each actor had to give and take from the other," Gusse explained. "All four had to possess the same drive, and none could be a 'grandstander.'" From her extensive files she selected 12 actors she felt would do justice to the roles. "I called them all to be interviewed. They were told to dress alike: dark suits and ties, white shirts. I'm sure they all thought they were going to a party or a wedding. When they arrived, we immediately eliminated two of them because of their light eyes. And then we changed the interviewing procedure we usually follow. It is our custom to interview each individually. This time, we lined them up in chairs against one wall and allowed them to ask us questions like: 'What's the story all about?' or 'Why will four of us be needed for one role?' After the questioning period ended, we knew the four who were similar enough in drive and ability to play the roles. We signed Harry Townes, Phillip Pine, Ross Martin and Don Gordon for the part that begins with Arch Hammer and progresses through three other characters."

While many scenes in this episode take place outside in the city streets, not a second of footage was filmed outside. Every scene was shot on stage in the M-G-M Studios. The set decorator had his hands full, having to redecorate city streets, including original signs and a newsstand. Newspapers for the newsstand were purchased at the cost of $100. The sign for the stand was custom, setting production back $75. The "Armstrong Towers" sign cost the same.

Marty Sall's office in "The Sixteen Millimeter Shrine" was filmed on Stage 24. The same set was redecorated to serve as Penell's Apartment for this episode. Months before both episodes of *The Twilight Zone* went before the cameras, the same set served as a gangster's suite in "Cherchez la Sexpot," an episode of *The Thin Man* telecast on June 19, 1959.

Production Schedule at M-G-M

Day 1 – Exterior of the Street and Mouth of Alley (Stage 11)
Exterior of the Alley (Stage 11)
Exterior of the Street and the Newsstand (Stage 11)
Exterior of the Street and the Hotel (Stage 10)

Day 2 – Interior of the Bar (Stage 24)
Exterior of the Street and the Bar (Stage 24)
Interior of the Pennell's Apartment (Stage 24)
Exterior of the Street and the Newsstand (Stage 11)

Day 3 – Interior of the Hotel Lobby (Stage 10)
Interior of the Elevator (Stage 10)
Interior of the Hotel Room (Stage 10)
Exterior of the Street and Hotel (Stage 10)
Exterior of the Street and Armstrong Towers (Stage 10)

The photographic background during the closing credits is of the numerous newspaper clippings Hammer used to compose his facial figures. Originally it was planned to use the shot outside Beverly Garland's bar in which Hammer stands silhouetted full figure; this is at the end of the Garland sequence. However, that was scrapped for the photo of the newspaper clippings.

Beverly Garland sang Harold Arlen and Johnny Mercer's 1943 classic, "One for My Baby (and One More for the Road)," first performed by Fred Astaire and later popularized by Frank Sinatra. This episode marked Beverly Garland's TV singing debut, playing the role of a torch singer. She recorded her voice tracks specifically for this episode. The cost for the music discs to be made was $50 and were dubbed into the episode's sound track separately from Jerry Goldsmith's original music score.

"They were concerned about whether or not my voice would be acceptable," recalled Beverly Garland. "I think they were considering another actress or singer for the sound track, and then record the song into the soundtrack. But that's me singing in that episode."

When Rod Serling was being filmed for the trailers, they were done in batches. For this episode, Serling displayed four masks of men's faces, and introduced the teaser for next week's episode. On the same morning, Serling was filmed for trailers for other episodes including "The Lonely," "The Purple Testament," "The Last Flight," "Third From the Sun," "Judgment Night" and the initial production of "The Mighty Casey."

"Suppose you're an unknown and send a copy of a magazine or a novel to a book publisher. It'll be read and considered," Serling commented to Ben Gross of *The New York Sunday News.* "However, most TV program producers won't even look at a script, unless it's submitted by an accredited agent. But most good agents won't read a TV play unless the writer has credits, that is unless he is already a professional. Of course, there still are a few outlets. For example, CBS has a workshop project which, I understand, does read the scripts of unknowns, but how many others?"

One of the lucky few was George Clayton Johnson, who recalled to author Matthew R. Bradley, "Ray Bradbury inspired me by reading my stories, and my notes, and he encouraged me to do more. He was concerned with my career so he motivated me. Ray Bradbury was my mentor. Charles Beaumont was too. I kept my mouth shut and watched how Charles Beaumont did the scripts and I learned how the business worked and eventually I was on my own and Rod and Buck was buying some of my stories. I met Rod at Charles Beaumont's house one day. Rod had bought the rights to adapt my story. Rod was contracted to write most of the scripts for the first season. But he could only come up with so many stories. It takes time to develop a story. So he bought my story, and then a second one called 'Execution.'"

In the August 1981 issue of *The Twilight Zone Magazine*, Johnson recalled how his original three-page story, "All of Us Are Dying," was purchased for the television series. "After the first half-dozen stories had been written, part of the hustle was getting an agent. Through those years I found several who would let me use their names, though few cared to sign a contract with me. One of these men, Jay Richards – at the time head of the television department of the Famous Artists Agency, long since absorbed by I.F.A. (International Famous Agency), and since embedded in I.C.M. (International Creative Management), which represents me now in television and movies – agreed to read something. I showed Jay 'All of Us Are Dying.' After reading it, he crossed out the title with a ballpoint pen and wrote in 'Rubber Face!' Then he sent it to Rod Serling, who had a new series that season called *The Twilight Zone*."

The production went under the title of "Rubber Face" and a July 1, 1959 progress report also stated this as the title of the script. On June 23, Buck Houghton began making preparations to buy the story, which was submitted to him by Jay Richards.

"There was my name up on the screen," continued Johnson. "I had entered into Hollywood, now had a credit, and had one on the goddamn *Twilight Zone*, in a collaboration with Rod Serling. I was utterly thrilled and looked forward to how it would work. This thing was cracking open a door for me, making me acceptable, even though *Twilight Zone* was very much a borderline success. It was shown at odd hours, and had a very small, but very loyal following. It had done only a few shows, and this was like the tail end of the first season. So, I look at it, see that he's taken my short story and used it like a kind of an armature on which to build his tale, and I realize, of course, that's what he must do. This whole damn game is really kicked off by what I'm doing, and keeps the theme or the idea or the point, and maybe some sense of the structure and the characters' names, but not necessarily."

The unpublished story, "All of Us Are Dying," was printed in the May 1982 issue of *The Twilight Zone*, for fans to read the initial plot proposal. It was accompanied by a reprint of Rod Serling's teleplay for this episode.

"Serling really ripened the story. He was a great man," concluded Johnson. "Bradbury was a great man too, but now I was immortalized on the television screen. I was surrounded by creative people who motivated me. My story contributed to *The Twilight Zone*, and *The Twilight Zone* – and you are obviously too young to have lived through the decade – played just as much a part of the renaissance transformation of the 1960s that included rock music and marijuana."

Production #3615 "THIRD FROM THE SUN" (Initial telecast: January 8, 1960)

© Cayuga Productions, Inc., January 7, 1960, LP15582 (in notice: 1959)
Dates of Rehearsal: August 4 and 5, 1959
Dates of Filming: August 6, 7 and 10, 1959
Script dated: July 16, 1959, with revised pages dated August 4 and 6, 1959.

Shooting script dated: August 6, 1959

Producer and Secretary: $660.00

Story and Secretary: $3,457.70 (story
    purchased for $1,000)

Production Fee: $750.00

Legal and Accounting: $250.00

Below the line charges (other): $4,507.53

Director: $1,250.00

Cast: $6,007.75

Unit Manager and Secretary: $520.00

Agents Commission: $5,185.55

Below the line charges (M-G-M): $24,420.83

Total Production Costs: $47,009.36

Cast: Denise Alexander (Jody Sturka); Edward Andrews (Carling); Jeanne Evans (Ann Riden); S. John Launer (voice over the loudspeaker); Lori March (Eve Sturka); Joe Maross (Jerry Riden); Fritz Weaver (William Sturka); and Will J. White (one of the guards).

Stock Music Cues: Main Title (by Bernard Herrmann, :40); Sonce (by Rene Challan, :18); Time Passage – Outer Space Suite (by Herrmann, :09 and :18); Light Rain (by Marius Constant, 1:58); Teddy Blues (by Jacques Lasry, :43); Spoutnik #1 (by Guy Luypaertz, :36); Time Passage – Outer Space Suite (by Herrmann, :45); Light Rain (by Constant, :15); Time Suspense – Outer Space Suite (by Herrmann, :43); Time Passage – Outer Space Suite (by Herrmann, 3:40); Starlight – Outer Space Suite (by Herrmann, :12); Danger – Outer Space Suite (by Herrmann, :26); Light Rain (by Constant, :56); The Ambush – Western Suite (by Herrmann, :56); The Ambush (by Herrmann, :56); Utility Cues (by Bruce Campbell, :10); Light Rain (by Constant, :48); and End Title (by Herrmann, :39).

Director of Photography: Harry Wild, a.s.c.

Art Directors: George W. Davis and
    William Ferrari

Set Decorations: Henry Grace and Rudy Butler

Sound: Franklin Milton and Philip Mitchell

Production Manager: Ralph W. Nelson

Film Editor: Bill Mosher

Assistant Director: Edward Denault

Casting Director: Mildred Gusse

Directed by Richard L. Bare

Teleplay by Rod Serling, based on the short story of the same name by Richard Matheson, originally published in the October 1950 issue of *Galaxy Science Fiction*.

"Quitting time at the plant. Time for supper now. Time for families. Time for a cool drink on a porch. Time for the quiet rustle of leaf-laden trees that screen out the moon. And underneath it all, behind the eyes of the men . . . hanging invisible over the summer night, is a horror without words. For this is the stillness before storm; this is the eve of the end."

Plot: William Sturka works for the nation's defense department. Working from the inside, Sturka learns that the "enemy" will be launching an assault within 48 hours. Sturka's employers plan to beat them to the punch with missiles and bombs properly aimed and skillfully carried out. As a scientist, Sturka knows the result will be a holocaust. With his friend Jerry, the two use their positions at the plant to plan an escape from the planet using an experimental aircraft designed to visit other worlds. They also make plans to bring along their wives and Sturka's young daughter, Jody. Having made contact with the inhabitants of an alien planet, they learn their new hosts speak a language not too dissimilar to their own, and welcome them as guests with open arms. Security Officer Carling, however, suspects Sturka and Jerry's intentions and shadows their every move. With a little help and a little luck, the men and their wives race to the test site and make contact with the guard they quietly paid. The five of them are surprised, however, when the guard turns out to be Carling, armed with a gun. He forces the families back to the car, where Jody gives them the upper hand and the men knock out their intrepid assailant. Dodging bullets and fighting armed guards, the five board the craft and blast off before Armageddon begins. A few hours later, Jerry is making his calculations while Sturka pilots the craft. Their destination is the brightest star on the right – a planet the inhabitants call "Earth."

"Behind a tiny ship heading into space is a doomed planet on the verge of suicide. Ahead lies a place called Earth. The third planet from the sun and for William Sturka and the men and women with him . . . it's the eve of the beginning . . . in the Twilight Zone."

Trailer: *"Next week we'll give you a lesson in astronomy, but the kind of lesson not taught in schools. Fritz Weaver, Edward Andrews and Joe Maross appear in 'Third from the Sun.' This is the story that takes place on the eve of doomsday. We hope you'll join us on the Twilight Zone. Thank you and good night."*

Trivia, etc. "Third From the Sun" was Richard Matheson's second published story and appeared in the very first issue of *Galaxy Science Fiction*. Matheson was paid $50 for the story, and was quite pleased at the time. When the short story was purchased by Cayuga for *The Twilight Zone*, the price tag was $1,000. While the costs involved with the story may appear to be fantastic, the production was far more complex.

The exterior of the field in which the families made a race for survival required the removal and replacing of nursery plants on Stage 22, at a cost of $400. All of the exterior scenes (except for the location shot) were filmed on Stage 22. The interior of the spaceship and Sturka's garage and bedroom were filmed on Stage 7, while the rest of Sturka's house was filmed on Stage 8.

The interior of the spaceship is indeed the same set used for the United Planets Cruiser C-57D in the 1956 motion picture, *Forbidden Planet*. The same glass dome centered at the controls was also from the same movie, and used in the *Twilight Zone* episode "Hocus-Pocus and Frisby." The registering gauges along the wall of the spaceship's interiors, replicating the shape of the Paramount Studio logo, were props from the Krell laboratory from the same motion picture. (The same props appear in the opening scenes in the background of the control room in the next *Twilight Zone* episode, "I Shot An Arrow Into the Air," inside the wrecked spaceship in "People Are Alike All Over" and the laboratory in "In His Image.") The initial glimpse of the flying saucer in this episode was a matte painting left over from the *Forbidden Planet* props at M-G-M, a huge painting formerly in storage and removed for the one scene; it was deliberately lighted to hide the desert landscape that surrounded the spaceship. The flying saucer effect flying through space was stock footage lifted from *Forbidden Planet* and cost Cayuga a total of $500.

Richard L. Bare, who had recently won a Directors' Guild Award for the best-directed television film of 1958 (for "All Our Yesterdays" which was produced by Warner Bros.), took command of this *Twilight Zone* episode. To help make the ending more believable for the viewers, the camera crew, under the direction of Bare, allowed the viewers to assume the setting was on planet Earth, but applied a number of techniques to create an "unearthly" feel similar to our own. Various camera lenses

Set Decoration Production Costs

Exterior of the Ministry of Science $125   Interior of the Bedroom $350
Interior of the Sturka's House $85   Interior of the Garage $300
Exterior of the Field $275   Interior of the Spaceship $775
Exterior of the Saucer (stock footage) $500
Exterior of the Flying Saucer $1,940
Total $4,350

were switched, replacing those most directors would normally use for a number of scenes. Props such as the decorations hanging on the wall, the bizarre "flight" pattern the car took when racing across the field (and the sound of jet engines when the car sped), and the tilted camera angles helped establish the believability of the twist ending when revealed to the audience.

The automobile which Sturka and Jerry use to flee with their family was the "Blue Danube," designed and built by George Barris, who customized the Buick (and a number of others) for use in a key scene in *The Time Machine*. Again, it was another prop reused from a motion picture produced on the M-G-M lot and reused on *The Twilight Zone*.

"Teddy Blues" is the bizarre atmospheric music heard in this episode until Sturka shuts the music machine off. The music was composed by Jacques Lasry. The "Time Passage" theme used frequently throughout the episode was part of Bernard Herrmann's *Outer Space Suite*. This same music was featured in the *Have Gun – Will Travel* episode, "The Monster of Moon Ridge," also telecast on CBS.

The telephone Sturka uses to answer the call was a new model recently made available to the public designed to appear futuristic, but the model never caught on. The prop was used because it could pass for a telephone on both Earth and an alien planet. This same phone would be featured in the episode "One More Pallbearer."

The sign posted on the gate in the beginning of the episode, stating "Security Gate 22," might *possibly* have been an inside joke. Later in the episode, while Sturka and Jerry attempt to get their family to the spaceship and are forced to confront and struggle with Carling, the confrontation was filmed on Stage 22. The confrontation at the gate in the beginning of the episode cost $125 in production expense. Since the next episode to go before the cameras was "People Are Alike All Over," the gate (and the signs on the gate) were reused for the opening scene in that episode.

The opening shot for this episode, with William Sturka exiting the security plant (Ministry of Science), was filmed on location at the Southern California Edison Substation, located at Culver and Overland Boulevards in Culver City, adjoining the M-G-M Transportation Pool. Permission was granted by Mr. John Davies, district superintendent, and Mr. Aughy (pronounced "Oye"), in charge of the substation. There was no charge for use of filming on the location. One M-G-M police officer was positioned inside the substation fence to keep studio personnel from "wandering," since the area had to remain secure. This scene was filmed on the morning of the third day of filming. *

Actress Jeanne Evans, who played the role of Ann, was the real-life wife of Richard L. Bare, the director. Two years later, when Bare directed the episode "To Serve Man," he would arrange for his

---

* Information regarding filming at the substation originates from a Location Department report dated August 7, 1959.

wife to again play a supporting role on the series. Evans played the role of Ann, and Denise Alexander played the role of Jodi – both characters named after Rod Serling's daughters, Jodi and Anne.

This episode prompted a letter from Robert N. Lambeck, editor-publisher of the fanzine *Exconn*, who wrote to Rod Serling on January 20, 1960. "The show of the 8th, I believe, didn't quite gel with me. The switch ending of having the people heading for Earth and away from some other planet rather than the opposite, as the audience had naturally assumed, was an anticlimax and seemed to me to make the entire show quite pointless. I expect that *The Twilight Zone* will either win a Hugo award at the next world science fiction convention or come very near to doing so."

Lambeck, however, was one of the very few who felt cheated by the twist ending. "Third from the Sun" was responsible for the most favorable reaction of any episode from the first season. Serling wrote a reply to Lambeck, explaining that the episode to date was the most favorable feature of the season, judging by the fan mail. "I guess this is what makes ballgames and church attendance." (Serling would later use a variation-on-a-theme of his closing comment in the letter for a line delivered by Julius Moomer in the fourth season episode, "The Bard.")

"I have vivid memories of Rod Serling during the making of *The Twilight Zone*s I was in," Fritz Weaver commented during the 1984 Rod Serling retrospective at the Museum of Broadcasting. "[He was] hanging around like a kid on the set, radiating excitement, having fun. He was generous to performers: he listened, he took suggestions, he gave everybody a free hand. His wide-ranging imagination allowed him to experiment, to take chances, and this was unique."

This episode's concept was lifted a number of times, most notably on the original *Battlestar Galactica* television series. A newspaper article from June 20, 1983, reported this episode was Stephen King's favorite. In his book, *Danse Macabre* (1981), he recalled how " . . . most viewers can remember the snap of that ending to this day. It was the episode which marks the point at which many occasional tuners-in became addicts. Here, for once, was something completely new and different."

Production #3626 "I SHOT AN ARROW INTO THE AIR"
(Initial telecast: January 15, 1960)
Copyright Registration: © Cayuga Productions, Inc., January 14, 1960, LP15583 (in notice: 1959)
Copyright title: "I Shot an Arrow Into the Air (The Conquerors)"
Date of Rehearsal: November 2, 1959
Dates of Filming: November 3, 4, 5 and 6, 1959
Script dated: October 20, 1959, with revised paged October 29 and November 2, 1959.

Producer and Secretary: $660.00	Story and Secretary: $3,035.00
Director: $1,000.00	Cast: $6,762.00
Unit Manager and Secretary: $425.00	Production Fee: $750.00
Agents Commission: $5,185.55	Legal and Accounting: $250.00
Below the line charges (M-G-M): $36,944.43	Below the line charges (other): $4,580.21
Total Production Costs: $59,592.19	

Cast: Leslie Barrett (Brandt); Harry Bartell (Langford); Edward Binns (Colonel Donlin); Boyed Cabeen (man charting or writing on board at mission control center); John Clark (man at mission control center); Paul Denton (wounded and dead man); Kenneth DuMain (played the dead man);

Dewey Martin (Flight Officer Corey); Bob McCord (stunt man); Tom Murray (man at mission control center); and Ted Otis (Flight Officer Pearson).

Stock Music Cues: Main Title (by Bernard Herrmann, :40); Climactic Close (by Herrmann, :08); Short Tags (by Rene Garriguenc, :02); The Fortress (by Lucien Moraweck, :35); Ostinato Suspense (by Garriguenc, 1:09); Soliloquy #4 (by Moraweck, :09); Soliloquy #3 (by Moraweck, :12); Neuro (by Garriguenc, :36); Finale (by Herrmann, :16); Soliloquy #3 (by Moraweck, :52); Neuro (by Garriguenc, 1:04); The Desert #1 (by Garriguenc, :26); Eerie Theme (by Moraweck, :42); The Desert #1 (by Garriguenc, :52); The Gold Hand (by Herrmann, :02); Soliloquy #4 (by Moraweck, :32); Neuro (by Garriguenc, :43); Man of Decision #2 (by Moraweck, :03); Shock Chord (by Moraweck, :08); The Desert #1 (by Garriguenc, :30); Eerie Theme (by Moraweck, 1:45); Brave New World Chord (by Herrmann, 1:45); The Return (by Herrmann, :12); Accent – Walt Whitman Suite (by Herrmann, :14); Mad Harpsichord (anonymous, :05); Thomas Wolfe (by Herrmann, :28); and End Title (by Herrmann, :39).

Director of Photography: George T. Clemens, a.s.c.	Production Manager: Ralph W. Nelson
Art Directors: George W. Davis and William Ferrari	Film Editor: Bill Mosher
	Assistant Director: Edward Denault
	Casting Director: Mildred Gusse
Set Decorations: Henry Grace and Jerry Wunderlich	Sound: Franklin Milton and Jean Valentino
	Directed by Stuart Rosenberg

Teleplay by Rod Serling, based on an original story concept by Madeline Champion.

"Her name is the Arrow One. She represents four and a half years of planning, preparation and training, and a thousand years of science and mathematics and the projected dreams and hopes of not only a nation but a world. She is the first manned aircraft into space. And this is the countdown, the last five seconds before man shot an arrow into the air."

Plot: On what appears to be a rocky, desert landscape of a barren asteroid, four survivors of an eight-man crew debate about the equal balance of water in the canteens. During the initial launch into space, something went wrong and now they must battle the elements – and themselves – in order to survive. One of the desperate is Flight Officer Corey, who shows no heart for the wounded and vents against the orders delivered by Colonel Donlin. After one of the men dies of serious wounds, the three men decide to split up to explore the vast landscape in an effort to find something that might help them survive. Corey returns, but he is not tired. Colonel Donlin thinks Corey should be begging for water, and he suspects foul play because Pearson has not returned with him. Forcing Corey to the place where Pearson was last seen, the colonel learns too late what kind of desperate measures Corey is willing to take in order to survive. Corey shoots his superior in cold blood, justifying his actions by claiming that his superior was looking for morality in the wrong place. As the lone survivor, he takes the remaining water and heads for the hills in the direction Pearson attempted to point with his dying breath. Corey treks through the rocky landscape saving all the water he can, till he finally reaches what Pearson was attempting to describe. Poetic irony laughs as Corey sees telephone poles and a sign pointing to Reno, Nevada, 97 miles away.

(middle) *"Now you make tracks Mr. Corey. You move out and up like some kind of ghostly billy club was tapping at your ankles and telling you that it was later than you think. You scramble up rock hills and feel hot sand underneath your feet and every now and then, take a look over your shoulder at a giant sun suspended in a dead and motionless sky . . . like an unblinking eye that probes at the back of your head in a prolonged accusation. Mr. Corey, last remaining member of a doomed crew – keep moving. Make tracks Mr. Corey. Push up and push out. Because if you stop . . . if you stop, maybe sanity will get you by the throat. Maybe realization will pry open your mind and the horror you left down in the sand will seep in. Yeah, Mr. Corey, yeah, you better keep moving. That's the order of the moment. Keep moving."*

"Practical joke perpetrated by Mother Nature and a combination of improbable events. Practical joke wearing the trappings of nightmare, of terror, of desperation. Small human drama played out in a desert ninety-seven miles from Reno, Nevada, U.S.A., continent of North America, the Earth, and of course . . . the Twilight Zone."

Trailer: *"There's a Longfellow poem. 'I shot an arrow into the air. It fell to Earth I know not where.' In our story next week, we shoot a spaceship into the air and where it fell, only you and I will know. Starring will be Mr. Dewey Martin and Mr. Edward Binns. Next week we promise you a most exciting journey into space. Don't miss the takeoff. Thank you, and good night."*

Trivia, etc. "This was one of the few stories I bought from a story suggestion of a non-professional," Rod Serling later recalled. "The wife of a friend of mine got a basic idea of how incredibly bizarre it would be to have some spacemen land on what they assumed was an asteroid, only to find that they were just a few miles from civilization." According to Rod's brother, Robert Serling, Madeline Champion proposed the story idea during dinner at Rod's house. He paid her back with a new refrigerator.

To secure the premise legally in June of 1959, Cayuga negotiated the purchase of an original story and partial teleplay titled "The Conquerors." There were no agents involved with the deal, since it had been handled personally by Rod and John Champion, and the literary assignment was officially signed over to Cayuga on July 10, 1959, for $750. Madeline and John Champion resided at 160 N. Thurston Ave. in Bel Air, California. After the story purchase, Serling was contracted to complete the first draft of a script by August 12, 1959, according to a progress report dated July 1. *

After Serling submitted the first draft of the script, on October 23, 1959, the De Forest Research Group reported to Serling on the science that needed to be clarified in the script. It was pointed out that a rocket is not considered an aircraft since it was designed to travel in space where there is no air. There was, at the time the script was written, a Captain William E. Donlon in the U.S. Air Force, so it was suggested to change the name of the character. While the last name was not changed, the rank was – from captain to colonel, because astronauts then in training programs all had the ranks of captain or above. Longfellow's poem was not considered a "nursery rhyme," so it was suggested to change the reference in the dialogue to simply "a rhyme." The first entry of a log book detailed information prior to departure, so it was suggested to delete "first entry" in the voice over. It was also

---

* A few reference guides have mistakenly stated the purchase price was $500, paid immediately after she came up with the idea. Cancelled checks, a check book ledger and progress reports verify the accuracy of the information.

suggested to change the road sign displayed at the end of the episode because highway signs did not name the state and would include other towns. It was suggested to change the sign to read "Needles 98, Las Vegas 134." There were other suggestions, but very few were optioned by Serling after the report was turned in, so very little change was made to the script after he received the report.

Originally Serling intended to use the following for the trailer, but it was considered too lengthy, and needed to be trimmed:

"There's a Longfellow poem. 'I shot an arrow into the air. It fell to Earth I know not where.' In our story next week, we shoot a spaceship into the air and where it fell – only you and I will know where. And where it fell . . . provides the most exciting background that must be seen to be believed. See anyway. I'm not at all sure you will believe. Our story will star Mr. Dewey Martin and Mr. Edward Binns. Next week we promise you a most exciting journey into space. Don't miss the takeoff. Thank you and good night."

The first three days of filming was shot on location at Death Valley National Park, where scenes for "The Lonely" were also filmed. Permission to shoot in Death Valley was granted by Mr. Danielson, assistant superintendent, and a fee totaling $1,740 was paid to the government. All of the camera equipment, generators used to power the equipment, costumes and props were loaded on the trucks on Friday afternoon, October 30. On Sunday, November 1, Buck Houghton, Ralph W. Nelson and Stuart Rosenberg left for Death Valley by car. The construction truck containing the wreckage of the spaceship (which cost a total of $75 in materials) left for Death Valley the same day. On Monday, November 2, the executive producer, the cast, second assistant director and construction crew flew to Death Valley on two DC-3 planes. Later that afternoon, the wreckage and the graves were constructed, while the cast rehearsed their roles. Arrangements were made with Furnace Creek Ranch for three single rooms and one double for the lead actors.

Sheriff's deputies and Monument rangers were on location for both security purposes and to enforce the strict policies preventing the production crew from causing any destruction to the property. The first day of filming, Tuesday, November 3, all of the footage involving the desert campfire, desert walking shots (close-ups of the feet marching through the rock and sand), and the control/monitor room was shot on Stage 29. On Wednesday, all of the footage near the base of the mountain, the exterior of the mountain landscape and daytime walking shots through the desert were filmed. On November 5, the equipment was packed up and the crew returned to the studio so that the next day, the remaining close-up shots were filmed without having to deal with the extreme heat of the desert.

Stand-in Bob McCord, who appeared in more *Twilight Zone* episodes than anyone else, was originally slated to play a stand-in for the control room, but he was promoted to a non-script stunt on location. The scene with Colonel Donlin rolling down the hill and a scene with Pearson falling down the hill (which never made it to the final cut), were played by McCord.

The scene in the beginning of the episode, featuring actor Harry Bartell, was produced on the fourth and final day of filming on Stage 29. Among the Props featured in the background of the Space Agency is the same used for the interior of the spaceship in the previous episode, "Third From the Sun."

After the final cut was previewed, it was decided that additional narration needed to be added to the scene where Corey treks across the desert before finding the state highway. The middle narration for this episode, in which Serling plays the voice of conscience plaguing and urging Corey through the rocky desert was composed separately to fill the time of the flight officer's wanderings through the rocky landscape.

This was the first episode of the series produced that did not feature Rod Serling on the set during filming. Instead, on November 6, 1959, Serling sent a telegram addressed to Dewey Martin at M-G-M Studios, expressing his appreciation for the hard work they put into the production:

"May I impose upon your considerable talents to read just these few additional lines of dialogue to the various guys who are standing around you at this given moment. Because I'm rather a sentimental little bastard, I dislike goodbyes, farewells, au revoirs of any kind. But I couldn't let this last day of shooting go by without expressing to all of you how much I appreciate your talent, your concern, your contribution to *The Twilight Zone*. I have never before seen a group of people work so hard and so loyally to assure the success of a venture as you people have on this series. I hope this first twenty-six is only the beginning of many more to come and that when next I walk on the set, I'll see the very same faces I've been accustomed to over the past twenty-six weeks. Thank you all, God bless you all and every good luck and good fortune to all of you."

The photographic background for the end credits was originally intended to be a POV shot from the Death Valley location, chosen by film editor Bill Mosher, but a photo of the water canteen was used instead.

At the end of the episode, one of the three highway signs reads "Nelson's Motel: Eats, Gas & Oil." This was a tip of the hat to the unit production manager, Ralph W. Nelson.

A television critic for *The Palladium Times* referred to this episode as a "weird space tale," and remarked "this episode was shot on the desert and appears bleak enough to suit the story."

When this episode was rerun on June 23, 1961, it prompted Guy Koenigsberger, in charge of advertising and promotion of KRNT-TV in Des Moines, Iowa, to request Serling send him a print of this episode, for use by the Central Presbyterian Church. Serling was forced to forward the request to Guy Della Cioppa of CBS to handle the request, because the network by that time established a policy of not providing prints for people, due to the many number of requests received and few copies of the film available.

The rerun also prompted Mattin Stolzoff, an attorney representing a man named Col. Gordon, to contact CBS regarding a settlement on the grounds of a charge against Rod Serling for plagiarism. Col. Gordon had kept a record of all submissions, including that which his literary agent attempted to handle for him. While there were no records from either party verifying the story was ever submitted to Cayuga, but Col. Gordon accused Serling of somehow acquiring his story and of stealing the idea for the television series without due compensation. Stolzoff indicated that Col. Gordon's story was practically identical to the plot of the *Twilight Zone* script. The attorneys representing Cayuga productions, the office of Lillick, Geary, McHose, Roethke & Myers, defended Cayuga against the claims, turning to the liability insurance policy issued by The Firemen's Fund. After comparing the script, the reps for Cayuga found very little similarity between both stories, and after verifying that Cayuga never received any submission, the matter was promptly dropped.

Production #3612 "THE HITCH-HIKER"
(Initial telecast: January 22, 1960)
Copyright Registration: © Cayuga Productions, Inc., January 21, 1960, LP16035 (in notice: 1959)
Dates of Rehearsal: July 24 and 27, 1959
Dates of Filming: July 28, 29 and 30, 1959
Script #12 dated: July 7, 1959
Shooting script dated: July 27, 1959

Producer and Secretary: $660.00

Director: $1,250.00

Unit Manager and Secretary: $520.00

Agents Commission: $5,185.55

Below the line charges (M-G-M): $24,872.77

Total Production Costs: $47,721.63

Story and Secretary: $4,454.00

Cast: $5,962.50

Production Fee: $750.00

Legal and Accounting: $250.00

Below the line charges (other): $3,816.81

Cast: Eleanor Audley (voice over telephone, Mrs. Whitney); Russ Bender (the counterman); Lew Gallo (the mechanic); Mitzi McCall (the waitress); George Mitchell (gas station attendant); Inger Stevens (Nan Adams); Leonard Strong (the hitch-hiker); Dwight Townsend (highway flag man); and Adam Williams (the sailor).

Stock Music Cues: Main Title (by Bernard Herrmann, :40); Summer Scene (by Bruce Campbell, :59 and :06); Mysterioso (by Gino Marinuzzi, :31); Star Chords (by Jerry Goldsmith, :04); Summer Scene (by Campbell, :14); The Knife (by Herrmann, :08); Hitch-Hiker – Part 3 (by Herrmann, :23); Tympani Punctuations (by Rene Garriguenc, :02); Thrust in the Dark (by Goldsmith, :14); Utility Cues (by Campbell, :17); Hitch-Hiker – Part 6 (by Herrmann, :08); Investigation #2 (by Garriguenc, 1:03); Passage of Time (by Garriguenc, :15); Hitch-Hiker – Part 3 (by Herrmann, :25); Passage of Time #2 (by Garriquenc, :14); Hitch-Hiker – Part 1 (by Herrmann, :13); Somber Apprehension (by Lucien Moraweck, :22); The Gold Hand (by Herrmann, :06); Knife Chord (by Goldsmith, :08); Somber Apprehension (by Moraweck, :48); High-to-Low Punctuations (by Moraweck, :08); The Search #3 (by Moraweck, :15); Hitch-Hiker – Part 6 (by Herrmann, :08); Hitch-Hiker – Part 4 (by Herrmann, :40); Shock Therapy #2 (by Garriguenc, :23); The Station (by Herrmann, :05); Menace Ahead #2 (by Moraweck, :28); Discouragement #2 (by Moraweck, :17); Rapid Flight (by Goldsmith, :35); Somber Apprehension (by Moraweck, :10); Shock Therapy #4 (by Garriguenc, :35); Shock Therapy #2 (by Garriguenc, :15); Ran Afoul (by Goldsmith, :12); The Knife (by Herrmann, :08); Hitch-Hiker – Part 6 (by Herrmann, :09); Mad Harpsichord (anonymous, :05); Doom (by Goldsmith, :05); Run for Cover (by Goldsmith, :38); Strange Visit (by Goldsmith, :10); Into Danger (by Goldsmith, :17); Puncuation (by Moraweck, :05); The Secret Room (by Goldsmith, :59); The Secret Circle (by Goldsmith, :45); Hitch-Hiker – Part 7 (by Herrmann, :39); Hitch-Hiker – Part 8 (by Herrmann, 1:05); Hitch-Hiker – Part 7 (by Herrmann, :05); and End Title (by Herrmann, :39).

Director of Photography: George T.
  Clemens, a.s.c.

Art Directors: George W. Davis and
  William Ferrari

Set Decorations: Henry Grace and Rudy Butler

Production Manager: Ralph W. Nelson

Film Editor: Bill Mosher

Assistant Director: Edward Denault

Casting Director: Mildred Gusse

Sound: Franklin Milton and Jean Valentino

Directed by Alvin Ganzer

Teleplay by Rod Serling, based on the radio play of the same name by Lucille Fletcher.

"Her name is Nan Adams. She's twenty-seven years old. Her occupation – buyer at a New York department store. At present on vacation, driving cross-country to Los Angeles, California, from Manhattan. Minor incident on Highway 11 in Pennsylvania. Perhaps to be filed away under 'accidents you walk away

from.' But from this moment on, Nan Adams' companion on a trip to California will be terror; her route – fear . . . her destination . . . quite unknown."

Plot: Shortly after having a blowout serviced along the highway, Nan Adams finds herself being haunted by an omnipresent, bedraggled hitch-hiker. While he poses no threat of physical harm, the thin grey man in a cheap shabby suit keeps appearing along the side of the road. The more she ponders how the hitch-hiker manages to accomplish being ahead of her, the more scared she gets. In fear, she spends three days and three nights driving non-stop. Towns without names, landscapes without form, all closing in on her. She picks up a different hitch-hiker, a young boy recently released from the military, to keep her company. But when he finds her acting peculiar, he exits the vehicle quickly. Finally, to keep her sanity, Nan stops off at a diner in Tucson, Arizona, to phone her mother, only to discover she is in a hospital after suffering a nervous breakdown following the death of her daughter. Apparently Nan never survived the accident in Pennsylvania when a tire blew out and the car overturned. In a daze with a feeling of emptiness, Nan returns to her car. Seeing the hitch-hiker in the back seat, she agrees to take him where he wants to go.

"Nan Adams, age twenty-seven. She was driving to California. To Los Angeles. She didn't make it. There was a detour . . . through the Twilight Zone."

Trailer: *"Next week you'll drive with Miss Inger Stevens, who starts out on what begins as a vacation and ends as a desperate flight. She begins her trip next week on The Twilight Zone. And you'll be with her when she meets . . . The Hitch-Hiker. We hope you'll be alongside. Good night."*

Trivia, etc. "This is not science fiction; it's sheer fantasy we're doing," Serling told columnist John Crosby. "One of the real strengths of the show is that we've written the scripts with specific people in mind and most of the actors we've approached have accepted the roles."

Inger Stevens was formerly under contract with Paramount Studios, but was put under suspension shortly before this episode went into production. She had refused to accept roles of "artistic mediocrity," insisting that theatrical performers had the right and obligation to stand up for their personal and artistic convictions. Unable to appear in motion pictures, she accepted a number of roles in television programs that suited her fancy. "I want to be happy in my work," she explained.

Inger Stevens is plagued by the visions of an omnipresent hitch-hiker.

"By making yourself happy through dramatic achievement, I believe you can make other people happy."

Inger Stevens apparently took pleasure in her performance for this episode. The television critic for *The Modesto Bee* remarked, "Miss Stevens doesn't overdo her role and keeps fans wondering just what is wrong."

According to a progress report dated April 30, 1959, this radio script was "under consideration" for purchase. On May 4, 1959, at the request of Rod Serling, Buck Houghton made arrangements to secure the purchase of Lucille Fletcher's radio script, "The Hitch-Hiker," for use on the *Twilight Zone*.

The original radio script, as chilling as the *Twilight Zone* screen adaptation, was dramatized on three separate occasions with Orson Welles playing the lead for each performance. The first time was on a summer filler called *Suspense* (which would later become a long-running anthology program for 20 years), broadcast on September 2, 1942. The popularity of that particular *Suspense* broadcast demanded a repeat performance, so Welles obliged a month later on *The Philip Morris Playhouse*, on October 15, 1942. Four years later, Orson Welles restaged the same radio play for *The Mercury Summer Theater on the Air* on June 21, 1946. *

"People listened in those days, and the voices of Agnes Moorehead and Orson Welles set the complete mood for a half hour. And along with the marvelous sound effects and music. I mourn the passing of good radio drama," Lucille Fletcher recalled to columnist Robert Wahls in 1972.

Bernard Herrmann composed and conducted the music for all three radio productions of "The Hitch-Hiker" because he was married to Fletcher at the time they were dramatized. Their marriage ended in divorce in 1948, but excerpts for his rendition for the 1946 radio broadcast (not the 1942 broadcasts) was used for this episode of *The Twilight Zone*.

It is not clear which of the broadcasts exposed Rod Serling to the chilling story, but he certainly remembered it and wanted to adapt it for *The Twilight Zone*. Lucille Fletcher was represented by the William Morris office, so Buck Houghton made arrangements to negotiate the price. "In view of the prominence of this particular play, I think it unlikely that we will get it for under $1,000," Houghton wrote. "May I suggest that we start at $750 and move to $1,000, if we must."

One week later, the offer was rejected and Houghton wrote to Rod Serling, asking how desperate he wanted the story. "Lucille Fletcher has turned down $2,000 for 'The Hitch-Hiker,' when Alfred Hitchcock offered it," Houghton explained. "I don't know how much further we would have to go to get the property, but I think it is too high for us to explore." Leo Lefcourt, the attorney for Cayuga Productions, however, was able to secure a firm price for the story through the William Morris Agency, and completed the purchase for *The Twilight Zone*. The price was $2,000 and a standard W.G.A. percentage rerun pattern based on $1,100. The story had not been done on television, either live or on film, giving *The Twilight Zone* an exclusive.

By July 1, the purchase was settled and Serling had intentions of finishing the first draft by July 17. He completed it 10 days ahead of schedule. According to production papers dated April 24,

---

* Too many books continue to reprint the same misinformation that the radio play was dramatized on *The Mercury Theater on the Air* in 1941. (One reference guide incorrectly states 1942.) For the record, there were two separate programs: *The Mercury Theater on the Air* (1938-1939) and *The Mercury Summer Theater on the Air* (1946). Not only have previous publications been reprinting the wrong year, but also the wrong title of the program.

1959, Robert Stevens was originally slated to direct the episode, with tentative dates of filming for July 27, 28 and 29, with rehearsal dates July 23 and 24. Alvin Ganzer took the helm and the dates changed slightly.

The main protagonist of the radio play was a man, but Serling changed the sex to a woman, "because it's pertinent and it's dramatic to make it a woman," he explained. "Nan" was a nickname of one of his daughters, Anne. If a press release from early January 1960 is accurate, Serling wrote the teleplay under six hours.

In an early draft of the script, Serling revealed Nan Adams as being 31 years old (not 27) and the opening narration explained, "minor incident just beyond the Pulaski Skyway that stretches over the Jersey Flats."

Inger Stevens arrived in New York on Monday, November 30, to appear as a guest in a number of interviews, helping to plug her appearance on the program. The interviews were all recorded and shelved for a January broadcast. Special art was designed for a January issue of *The Chicago Tribune*, with a picture of both Rod Serling and Inger Stevens, to help publicize this episode. According to a progress report, this episode was originally slated for an initial telecast of December 4, 1959. Even issues of *TV Guide* erroneously reported this broadcast date. For reasons unknown, this episode was rescheduled to a later broadcast date.

Leonard Strong, who played the role of the hitch-hiker, made a career out of playing Asians in both motion pictures and television programs. During the Second World War, Strong got his acting break playing Japanese officers in a number of films, which led to his casting for roles of Chinese, Monks and foreign enemy spies.

A scene with Nan and a waitress was filmed (actress Mitzi McCall played the role of the waitress) in an early scene, but this never made the final cut.

A large number of permissions and payments were made to acquire the rights to film on both public and private property. On the first day of filming, the scene involving the railroad crossing required two motorcycle officers of the Los Angeles Police Department, courtesy of arrangements made through Floyd Alexander at $3.78 per hour (plus $10 cash for rental of motorcycles for each of the officers). This was not just for the safety of the cast and crew – the officers kept traffic detoured momentarily while filming commenced. One Los Angeles County fireman was on hand, paid $24 for his time. Filming began at 7:45 a.m. before heavy traffic flooded the road at the crossing. Mr. Raymond Fansett of the S&P Railroad granted the filming crew permission to film on the tracks, provided the crew was insured in the event of an accident.

The second scene to be filmed on the first day was the service station where Nan noticed the funny-looking hitch-hiker in the mirror of her case and thanked the attendant for fixing her flat and checking the car's fluids. This scene was filmed at the Enchanto Turnoff Chevron Service Station in Agoura, California (Cornell Corners). The service station was closed to the public during filming, which began at 11:30 a.m. Two Ventura County sheriff's officers met Bill Venegas (the man in charge of the arrangements made for location filming), who earned a $3.00 per hour fee for ensuring traffic would not drive into the scene and interfere with filming. The manager of the service station received a $100 payment to accommodate for the temporary inconvenience and loss of revenue from the lack of customers.

The rest of the first day of filming was devoted to a highway montage and shots of an underpass. Various country roads were filmed. Two California State Highway Patrol officers from the West Los Angeles office were responsible for directing traffic during filming.

The second day of filming was devoted to the remainder of the highway scenes and the road-block detour scene. Once again, two state highway patrolmen were on hand during the filming. Two men from the Ventura County Sheriff's Department were available as well, paid by the location department of M-G-M $25.00 each for the second day of filming, made payable to the State Highway Recreation Fund. Cayuga and M-G-M both secured two single-day insurance policies at $2.50 each for both days of location filming. These permits, purchased consecutively from the Los Angeles Police Department, West Valley Division, and the Los Angeles Road Department (permits No. 311018 and 311019) cost Cayuga Productions $50.00 each.

After all the location shots were completed, the entire cast and crew returned to the M-G-M lot where the scene with Nan and the sailor was filmed in a mock-up of the car on Stage 22.

The third and final day of filming included the interior of the diner and Mrs. Whitney talking to Nan on the phone (both filmed on Stage 4 at M-G-M); the exterior of the diner and the phone booth on Stage 22; and the exterior of the highway and gas station (night scenes) on Lot 3.

If the gas station where Nan first meets the sailor appears familiar, it should. It was the same gas station seen in "Walking Distance," also filmed on Lot 3. The sign hanging above read "Service Station: John Thompson, Prop." This was a tip of the hat to John Thompson, one of the art directors for *The Twilight Zone*. The "Lubrication" sign is the same featured in "Walking Distance." (Even the front windows of the fake station remained unchanged.)

Before Inger Stevens was dismissed on the third and final day, her narration track was recorded on Stage 22, shortly after the phone booth scene was completed. She recorded her narration twice – each on separate tracks to ensure if one got lost or damaged, there was still a backup copy.

On June 15, 1959, William Freedman, public accountant for Cayuga Productions, contacted Sam Kaplan of Ashley-Steiner to report that Ford Motors delivered to Cayuga at M-G-M for its use, a 1959 Ford Country Sedan (serial number G-9LG-109267). The car was kept at M-G-M for company business and for filming on shows or at times on location trips. This was one of those episodes that put the car to use. While Inger Stevens drove a 1959 Mercury in this episode (with a fake New York license plate, see below), the Sedan was used to transport some of the actors and crew to locations. Ford retained in its name the registration and legal ownership of the car, and James Lang of M-G-M's insurance department and Lynn Welvert of Ebenstein & Company verified that Cayuga was covered for non-owned vehicles under its comprehensive general liability policy.

The generosity of Ford was an act of product placement. Houghton and the crew under employment of Cayuga ensured that most – if not all – of the vehicles in the episodes were Ford automobiles. This included Ford cars in "Walking Distance" and "The Monsters Are Due on Maple Street." By the third season of *The Twilight Zone*, Ford was being acknowledged in the closing credits (including "Five Characters in Search of a Exit" where the audience only catches a glimpse of a Ford car in the closing scenes).

The license plate on this car, New York State 2D 7876 was a prop and can be seen on the 1955 Lincoln concept car in the 1959 motion picture, *It Started with a Kiss*, produced by Arcola Pictures. The only license plate on the M-G-M lot that was off limits to any motion picture or television production was NICK-1, featured on the television program *The Thin Man*. The license plate was made of cardboard (also described as cardstock), and marked accordingly on the back so that other producers would know when the plate was last used, to ensure its reuse would not be too often or recent.

Rod Serling's teleplay made a return visit to television in April of 1997, when a remake of this

Set Decoration Production Costs
Interior of Diner (Stage 4) $400
Exterior of Gas Station (Lot 3) $250
Interior of Nan's Car with Sailor (Stage 22) $50
Exterior of Road with Hitch-hiker (Stage 22) $100
Exterior of Phone Booth (Stage 22) $125
Total $925

classic *Twilight Zone* episode, titled "End of the Road," featured an updated take on the chilling story. Actress Nora Rickert played the role of Nan Adams, a college student on a road trip, who finds herself being terrorized by a mysterious hitch-hiker, played by Matthew Sutton. Scott Henkel directed the film.

In the episode "Why Are We Here?" of *Everybody Loves Raymond*, initially telecast on April 7, 1997, Robert has Debra call the local station to learn what episode of *The Twilight Zone* is scheduled for broadcast that evening. Debra learns that it's "The Hitch-Hiker," and Robert remarks how genius it was for death to be a little guy instead of a large, looming figure.

Production #3627 "THE FEVER" (Initial telecast: January 29, 1960)
Copyright Registration: © Cayuga Productions, Inc., January 28, 1960, LP16036 (in notice: 1959)
Dates of Rehearsal: October 16 and 19, 1959
Dates of Filming: October 20, 21 and 22, 1959
Script dated: October 12, 1959
Shooting script dated: October 15, 1959

Producer and Secretary: $660.00
Director: $1,250.00
Unit Manager and Secretary: $425.00
Agents Commission: $5,185.55
Below the line charges (M-G-M): $30,959.26
Total Production Costs: $55,480.73

Story and Secretary: $2,395.00
Cast: $6,822.38
Production Fee: $750.00
Legal and Accounting: $250.00
Below the line charges (other): $6,783.54

Cast: Vivi Janiss (Flora Gibbs); William Kendis (public relations man); Carole Kent (the girl); Art Lewis (the drunk); Lee Millar (the photograher); Arthur Peterson (the sheriff); Lee Sands (the floor manager); Jeffrey Sayre (the croupier); Everett Sloane (Franklin Gibbs); and Marc Towers (the cashier).

Stock Music Cues: Main Title (by Bernard Herrmann, :40); Hollywood Hustle – Version 2 (by Lyn Murray, :32), Spoutnik #2 (by Guy Luypaertz, :11); The Meeting (by Jerry Goldsmith, :48); The Giant Killer (by Goldsmith, :12); Street Moods in Jazz (by Rene Garriguenc, 1:12); Deserted Street (by Russ Garcia, :13); Street Moods in Jazz (by Garriguenc, :48); A New Office (by Goldsmith, 1:02); The Meeting (by Goldsmith, :05); Street Moods in Jazz (by Garriguenc, 2:11); The Meeting (by Goldsmith, :58); and End Title (by Herrmann, :39).

Director of Photography: George T.
    Clemens, a.s.c.
Art Directors: George W. Davis and
    William Ferrari
Set Decorations: Henry Grace and Rudy Butler
Directed by Robert Florey

Production Manager: Ralph W. Nelson
Film Editor: Joseph Gluck, a.c.e.
Assistant Director: Edward Denault
Casting Director: Mildred Gusse
Sound: Franklin Milton and Jean Valentino
Teleplay by Rod Serling

"Mr. and Mrs. Franklin Gibbs, three days and two nights, all expenses paid, at a Las Vegas hotel, won by virtue of Mrs. Gibbs' knack with a phrase. But unbeknownst to either Mr. or Mrs. Gibbs is the fact that there's a prize in their package neither expected nor bargained for. In just a moment, one of them will succumb to an illness worse than any virus can produce, a most inoperative, deadly, life-shattering affliction known . . . as The Fever."

Plot: Franklin Gibbs and his wife is given a free trip to Vegas. Though he scorns the slot machines as immoral, he is given a free tug at the dollar machine and by a lucky chance, wins. Late that evening, lying in bed with a troubled conscience, Franklin fools himself into believing he must put the dishonest money back into the machine. Then he begins to lose. After cashing many personal checks throughout the night into the early morning hours, Franklin starts hearing the one-armed bandit calling out his name. Coin after coin, Franklin continues to go deeper into debt. He claims the machine is mocking him, and when he breaks down from the strain, he is forced to return to his hotel room. Still mumbling about this traumatic experience, Franklin is chased by a ghostly slot machine right out of his room and out the window, falling to his death. Lying dead in the courtyard, the corpse cannot hear the machine, which – after the medics leave – returns the same coin Franklin initially forfeited.

"Mr. Franklin Gibbs, visitor to Las Vegas – who lost his money . . . his reason . . . and finally his life to an inanimate metal machine variously described as . . . a one-armed bandit . . . a slot machine . . . or in Mr. Franklin Gibbs' words –a monster with a will all its own. For our purposes, we'll stick with the latter definition, because . . . we're in the Twilight Zone."

Trailer: *"Specie of machine known variously as slot machine or one-armed bandit. And if you've ever played with one of these things for a while you've probably gotten a peculiar feeling that this is a machine with a mind and a will of its own. This is precisely what happens when Everett Sloane contacts a fatal ailment we call 'The Fever.' You'll be an eye-witness to it next week on The Twilight Zone."*

Trivia, etc. To celebrate the signing and sale of *The Twilight Zone*, Rod Serling and his wife Carol spent a weekend in Las Vegas. "I got this idea about three o'clock in the morning in a Las Vegas gambling casino," he recalled. "I'd been about sixty minutes battling a one-armed-bandit and I got a feeling of what an extension of this kind of weakness might be to somebody a little different than I am . . . making an assumption, of course, that there is someone weaker than I in this nefarious area."

When this episode was rerun in July of 1961, a television columnist remarked that CBS was "repeating a telefilm that probably got banned in Las Vegas." While the CBS affiliate in Vegas did not censor this episode, no casinos helped in making the production. The exterior scenes of the Las Vegas street was stock footage.

The first two days of filming were devoted to the casino scenes, shot on Stage 20 at M-G-M. The total cost to design the interior of the casino was $1,300, plus $250 for rental of gambling equipment (all but the slot machines) that was brought to M-G-M from an outside gambling establishment. The third and final day of filming was for miscellaneous shots of the slot machine, filmed on Stage 21; the interior of the hotel room also filmed on Stage 21 and all the exterior shots of the window and courtyard on Lot 1.

M-G-M Studios had a number of slot machines available for use in this episode. Only one was needed and used for the scenes in which Franklin is visited by the beckoning one-armed bandit. In the episode "The Prime Mover," one of these same slot machines was used again – but most likely it was not the same one used to terrorize Franklin in the hotel room scene.

The photographic background for the end credit, the close-up shot of the slot machine, was chosen by film editor Joe Gluck when the rest of production team remained undecided what shot to use.

The Oasis sign hanging in the background of the interior of the casino is the same used for the street scenes of "Execution" and "The Four of Us Are Dying."

Small sections of "Deserted Street," composed by prominent jazz arranger Russ Garcia, are featured in this episode. A childhood musical prodigy, Garcia got his start on network radio when the lead musician of a patriotic radio broadcast titled *This is America*, took ill, and Garcia was asked to fill in. Garcia's career grew from that evening. In 1957, he served as arranger and musical director on Louis Armstrong and Ella Fitzgerald's classic *Porgy and Bess* sessions. He scored the music for the 1960 motion picture, *The Time Machine*, and the 1961 classic *Atlantis, the Lost Continent*. His love for jazz granted him the chance to compose a number of music scores for the CBS stock library, where the sound clip for this episode originated. Garcia's jazzy works appears in another episode of *The Twilight Zone*, "A Nice Place to Visit."

When Serling wrote a short story adaptation based on this teleplay for the 1960 publication, *Stories From the Twilight Zone*, he added the following text at the end of the story: "Flora Gibbs flew back to Elgin, Kansas, to pick up the broken crockery of her life. She lived a silent, patient life from then on and gave no one any trouble. Only once did anything unusual happen and that was a year later. The church had a bazaar and someone brought in an old used one-armed bandit. It had taken three of her friends from the Women's Alliance to stop her screaming and get her back home to bed. It had cast rather a pall over the evening."

The change of hometown in the short story, compared with the filmed episode, originates from the earliest draft of the script, which pointed out that Gibbs was from Elgin, Kansas.

Originally Serling intended to use the following for the trailer, but it was considered too lengthy, and needed to be trimmed:

"Specie of machine known variously as slot machine or one-armed bandit or, if you've played it for any protracted period of time and lost on it – which is usually the case – you may have gotten a peculiar feeling that this is a machine with a mind and will of its own. This is precisely what happens when Everett Sloane visits Las Vegas and engages one of these in a life or death struggle. He gets what is an ailment common to people out for a buck via the gambling route. An ailment as deadly as any virus. An ailment we call . . . 'The Fever.' You'll be an eye-witness to the disease next week on The Twilight Zone. Please join us for a most unusual experience. Thank you and good night."

An episode of the animated television series, *Spongebob SquarePants* titled "Skill Crane," features a spoof of this *Twilight Zone* episode. A crane game machine with a swinging claw for a handle chases one of the cartoon characters about, calling out his name, with the sound of coins in the soundtrack.

Production #3607 "THE LAST FLIGHT" (Initial telecast: February 5, 1960)

© Cayuga Productions, Inc., February 4, 1960, LP16037 (in notice: 1959)
Dates of Rehearsal: July 14 and 15, 1959
Dates of Filming: July 16, 17 and 20, 1959
Script #18 dated: May 18, 1959, titled "Flight"
Shooting script dated: July 16, 1959

Producer and Secretary: $660.00
Director: $1,000.00
Unit Manager and Secretary: $520.00
Agents Commission: $5,185.55
Below the line charges (M-G-M): $24,463.75
Total Production Costs: $44,868.76

Story and Secretary: $1,935.80
Cast: $6,207.11
Production Fee: $750.00
Legal and Accounting: $250.00
Below the line charges (other): $3,896.55

Cast: Paul Baxley (the jeep driver); Jerry Catron (the guard); Kenneth Haigh (Flight Lt. Decker); Paul Mantz (the stunt pilot); Jack Perkins (the truck driver); Harry Raybould (the Corporal); Simon Scott (Major Wilson); Alexander Scourby (General Harper); and Robert Warwick (Air Marshall Mackaye);

Original Music Score Composed and Conducted by Bernard Herrmann: Main Title (:40); Funeral March (:19 and :18); Main Title – Collector's Item (:09); The Truck (:19); Religious Bridge – Walt Whitman (:09); The Mirror (1:15); Funeral March (:41); The Mirror (:08); Funeral March (:08); The Mirror (:18 and :34); Funeral March (:24); The Lights (:03); The Mirror (1:17); Funeral March (:08 and :08); The Bicycle (:22); The Cell (:13); The Bicycle (:42); Funeral March (:17); The Cell (:23); Funeral March (:21); The Book Rack (1:13); Police Force Openings (:05); The Ambush – Ambush Suite (:05); and End Title (by Herrmann, :39).

Director of Photography: George T.
   Clemens, a.s.c.
Art Directors: George W. Davis and
   William Ferrari
Set Decorations: Henry Grace and Rudy Butler
Directed by William Claxton

Production Manager: Ralph W. Nelson
Film Editor: Joseph Gluck, a.c.e.
Assistant Director: Edward Denault
Casting Director: Mildred Gusse
Sound: Franklin Milton and Jean Valentino
Teleplay by Richard Matheson

"*Witness Flight Lieutenant William Terrance Decker, Royal Flying Corps, returning from a patrol somewhere over France. The year is 1917. The problem is that the Lieutenant is hopelessly lost. Lieutenant Decker will soon discover that a man can be lost not only in terms of maps and miles... but also in time... and time in this case can be measured in eternities.*"

Plot: Second Lieutenant William Decker lands his Nieuport at a U.S. Air Force base in Reims, France, on March 5, 1959. Naturally, the Air Force takes action and escorts Decker to Major General George Harper, who begins questioning the visitor. Decker claims to be a member of the Royal Flying Corps from March 5, 1917. As soon as Decker learns that Air Marshal Alexander Mackaye is soon to arrive on base, Decker confesses that he was good friends with Mackaye, even referring to him as "old lead bottom" – a joke between friends. Decker confesses that he is a born coward who always hoped for enough time to pass so he could avoid fighting against the enemy. It was he who deserted Mackaye and flew into the mysterious cloud that brought him to 1959. In fear of facing his past, Decker makes a daring escape back to his plane, assisted by Major Wilson, and flies back into the clouds from whence he came. Back on the base, Wilson is reprimanded for assisting in the escape – until Air Marshal Mackaye arrives and looking over Decker's personal belongings, confirms the truth – Decker died in 1917 in an effort to save Mackaye's life, for which the Air Marshall will be eternally grateful.

Lieutenant William Decker finds himself displaced in time.

"Dialogue from a play, Hamlet to Horatio: 'There are more things in heaven and earth than are dreamt of in your philosophy.' Dialogue from a play written long before men took to the sky. There are more things in heaven and earth, and in the sky, that perhaps can be dreamt of. And somewhere in between heaven, the sky, the earth . . . lies the Twilight Zone."

Trailer: *"This is the model of a Nieuport – fighter aircraft vintage World War One. Next week it's flown on a patrol over France in 1917 and its pilot discovers that time has passed him by. Kenneth Haigh stars next week in Richard Matheson's exciting story of 'The Last Flight,' on the Twilight Zone. We hope you'll join us. Thank you and good night."*

Trivia, etc. "After the show is on the air and other professional writers get an idea of what we're after," Serling explained back in September, "I'm sure that we will be using some scripts from the outside." The first of those scripts was by Charles Beaumont and Richard Matheson, both of whom made an impression with producer Buck Houghton and Rod Serling, earning them the opportunity to script additional episodes.

On April 9, 1959, Matheson verbally proposed the idea for this episode, about a lost World War I flyer, who lands at a modern U.S. Air Force base and finds himself displaced in time. It was the story of a man and his flight from cowardice, his flight from the past to the future, and a second chance. "I don't know how many times I actually went in," recalled Matheson to interviewer Matthew R. Bradley. "I know I had to go in and pitch the first one, which was extremely simple: 'World War I pilot gets lost, lands, and he's in a 1959 SAC base.' That was enough. I didn't have a story, I didn't know where it was going to go. I had to figure that out, but because the image was so vivid, they said, 'Yeah, go ahead.' I had been published, and they knew, more or less, what I could do. It wasn't as if they were taking that big [of a] chance."

Buck Houghton loved the story idea, as well as Serling, so Leo Lefcourt contacted Gordon Levey of the Preminger-Stuart Agency to negotiate a deal for Matheson to write the full outline, with the possibility of composing the teleplay. On April 14, Matheson signed a contract and on Monday, April 20, he delivered the story outline entitled "Flight." Houghton then asked Lefcourt to take advantage of the option on the contract that Matheson write the teleplay, due within 14 days.

The first draft of the script was initially contracted to be turned in by April 27, but an extension was granted for completion by May 6. Matheson was paid $1,750.00 for his teleplay. This would be the lowest fee paid for his services on *The Twilight Zone*. For his episode "A World of Difference," Matheson would be paid $2,000, the same fee Charles Beaumont was paid for his scripts. (Both men had the same agent, hence the reason why the pay hike to make it equal to both parties.)

When Serling learned of Matheson's proposal, he brought to light a radio anthology titled *Quiet, Please*, scripted by Wyllis Cooper. On November 21, 1948, the program offered a similar story titled "One for the Book," about an Air Force major who hit Mach 12 in an experimental rocket plane in 1957 and found himself as an Air Force sergeant in 1937. Serling remarked that Matheson's story "was down-the-line almost a twin," and the two considered tracking down Wyllis Cooper to purchase the rights and cover their bases, but unable to do so, the teleplay went into production without further consideration.

On May 21, 1959, Buck Houghton forwarded two copies of the revised script to Captain Damon Eckles of the Air Force, in the hopes that Eckles, acting as a consultant, would help arrange for both the planes and an airfield to accomplish the required filming. The first script submitted was for his approval, but the second was in case he needed permission and clearance from Washington. *

Eckles looked over the pages, especially the matters that Houghton felt needed straightened out – such as what kind of planes one would expect to find at an airbase in France, both resident planes and those in transit status, and what kind of planes Cayuga Productions could expect to find on hand at Riverside or March, nearby airports in California. "Probably the World War I Nieuport referred to would come from Paul Mantz, and there is the matter of clearing permission for it to land at whatever field we select," Houghton wrote. "I presume France is not much like Southern California, and we should select the most verdant of the airbases available to us locally."

There were a number of Nieuport planes in World War I (Nieuport 11, Nieuport 17, Nieuport 24 and the Nieuport 27), but with the limited availability of any Nieuport this meant using whatever was available. The exact replica of the fabric-covered biplane in which U.S. ace Captain Eddie Rickenbacker knocked down his first German aircraft was no newcomer to television and motion picture cameras. According to a CBS press release, it emerged unscathed from countless dogfights

---

* Assistance of the Department of Defense and the Department of the Air Force in the making of this film was acknowledged during the closing credits.

with the "Boche" in such WWI aviation epics as *The Dawn Patrol* (1938), *The Lost Squadron* (1932), and *Lafayette Escadrille* (1958).

Owner Frank Gifford Tallman, whose collection of 16 aged aircraft ran from a 1910 Bleriot to a World War II P-51 fighter, proudly claimed his nifty Nieuport was capable of executing any stunting maneuver in the books. Tallman had put it through every acrobatic test from an Immelmann turn to a snap-roll while flying in 10 major motion pictures. He made the arrangements to have the plane brought in at the Norton Air Force Base near San Bernadino, California, where the scenes were to be shot.

Rigged and braced for stunting, with its wings clipped from a normal 26 feet, 9 inches to 23 feet, the Nieuport scout had a "strength load factor" nearly equal of a 707 jet airliner, according to Tallman. In layman's language, that meant it could stand physical stresses and strains approaching those of jet-age aircraft.

The Nieuport came through with flying colors on a long distance flight in 1957 when Tallman flew it coast-to-coast in six days to celebrate the Air Force's 50th Anniversary. The vintage aircraft was powered by a modern 220-horsepower engine and could hit a top speed of 150 miles an hour. The original Nieuport 28 achieved only 140 m.p.h. with its 160-horsepower Gnome rotary power plant.

To do a story about a WWI pilot landing a Nieuport at a Strategic Air Command base in France, Serling recalled, "We got a hold of a stunt flier *and* the last existing Nieuport, I gather, in the whole world. It was a most effective job."

While Frank Gifford Tallman took credit for supplying the Nieuport, the stunt flier was Paul Mantz, a former member of the U.S. Army Air Corps, who made a career as a stunt flier for Hollywood producers. Among his more notable achievements was piloting a Boeing B-17 for the belly-landing scenes in *Twelve O'Clock High* (1949), and the official stunt pilot for the juvenile television program, *Sky King*. While Mantz did the actual piloting for this *Twilight Zone* production, it would be more than a year later before he began officially collaborating with Tallman for supplying airplanes along with their personal stunt flying scenes to movie and television productions.

Originally this episode was titled "Flight," and remained so through production. The title was not changed until after filming was completed. Production was originally scheduled to start on July 17, but later changed when a director was assigned to the script. All of the scenes in the general's office were filmed on the first day on Stage 23 at M-G-M. The second day of filming was on location at the Norton AFB. The heads of the base granted the crew one day of filming there for a flat fee of $150. On the third day, filming resumed back at Stage 23. A Nieuport mock-up was created at a cost of $125 for scenes filmed there.

Kenneth Haigh, who played the lead in this episode, was paid $2,000 for his role of William Smith Decker. Minimum film residuals and minimum TV reruns applied. This was a far cry from the $5,000 fee actors Ida Lupino and Ed Wynn were paid for their roles in earlier *Twilight Zone* productions. "The money factor was always taken into consideration," recalled Buck Houghton. "Most producers altered the scripts to limit the cost of production. On *Twilight Zone* we worked with the script first, and then juggled the figures. We went over on a few but we made allowances on others to justify the difference. Once in a while Rod or the scriptwriter had an actor in mind, and if we could secure their services . . . I worked closely with the casting director who had lists and we picked the best actor suitable for the role. Price was negotiable but I do recall lowering the salary for the leads after the first few went into production because we realized we were paying more than we should have. Building a reputation for high salaries wasn't what we wanted to pass off to the actors."

By this time, Houghton had a discussion with Serling regarding production costs. Realizing that actors would do the same for half, it was agreed to put the $5,000 figure out of mind. "I think we must recognize that Rod has given a good deal of effective thought to writing on-budget scripts," Houghton wrote to Ira Steiner of Ashley-Steiner. "Three of his are sure-fire economies; four should come very close to budget; none are of extravagant demands. The three we've agreed to buy outside are each below-budget thinking."

"I liked 'Flight'," recalled Matheson to author Matthew R. Bradley. "It was his flight from his cowardice, and a flight from the past to the future, and so on. 'The Last Flight' sort of narrows it down. That's always fun to do that, you know, 'Nick of Time,' that's good. 'Steel' refers to the strength of his personality plus the fact that these [robot prizefighters] are made out of steel, and 'Spur of the Moment.' I love titles like that. Usually, if you can think of a title you can do it right away, and you're very happy with it. If you have to spend a lot of time thinking about it, you never get it right."

Serling's original opening narration for this episode was different from the final revision:

"There is a loneliness to sky, a sense of isolation, a rootless bewilderment translated into fear when a pilot is lost as this man is. His name is William Smith Decker, Royal Flying Corps. He's returning from patrol somewhere over France. He's hopelessly, desperately lost. This is 1919. (after he lands) *As of this moment Lieutenant Decker will begin a process of learning. He will find out that there are degrees to being lost. Degrees not just to be measured in miles . . . but in years. A lot of years. To be exact . . . forty-two of them!*

On March 10, 1960, Blanche Gaines submitted a short story to Serling titled "The Wild Cat" by Neil Tardio, for possible use on *The Twilight Zone*. The story, as Gaines explained to Serling, "is interesting and baffling enough to be just your cup of tea for *Twilight Zone*. Of course the Defense Department might crack down on you, but then again they might like it very much and ask for the rights to screen it for security purposes." Tardio was a television commercial producer at McCann-Erickson for three years and was a former Army officer with the United Nations Forces in Korea. He served in the capacities of regimental intelligence officer and G2 Air, and finished his tour as an infantry company commander.

Set Decoration Production Costs
Exterior of the Plane (Nieuport mock-up, Stage 23) $200
Exterior of the Airfield (on location) $150
Interior of Harper's Office (Stage 23) $250
Interior of the Hallway (Stage 23) $250
Interior of the Detention Room (Stage 23) $150
Total $1,000

On March 21, Serling wrote back to Gaines, pointing out that she was apparently not watching the series. "Last month we did a script by Richard Matheson called 'The Last Flight' which was down the line and in almost every aspect a twin to the enclosed. It does prove, however, that your instincts are right even if the timing was a little off. Mr. Tardio's story was a beaut!"

On March 30, Neil Tardio expressed his opinion, having seen the episode. "Two weeks after I finished 'The Wild Cat,' I saw 'The Last Flight' on *The Twilight Zone* and was a little disturbed over it. Although both stories share a similar opening, they are in no way parallel. *The Twilight Zone* story dealt with a WWI pilot who is reincarnated for a day, and then flies back into the *Zone*. 'The Wild Cat' represents a situation that actually happens today to protect our national security. Since I greatly admire Mr. Serling for the way he presents himself as a person, and for the quality of excellence of his work, I would appreciate the opportunity to work for and learn from such a man, hoping to make an increasing contribution to his organization." Gaines encouraged Tardio to write a resume so she could submit his references to Serling, but by the time it was submitted, Cayuga Productions finished filming for the first season and it was then unclear whether the series would be picked up for a second season, so Tardio's quest for employment was thwarted by bad timing.

Production #3619 "THE PURPLE TESTAMENT"
(Initial telecast: February 12, 1960)
© Cayuga Productions, Inc., February 12, 1960, LP16038 (in notice: 1959)
Date of Rehearsal: September 8, 1959
Dates of Filming: September 9, 10 and 11, 1959
Shooting script #19 dated: August 18, 1959

Producer and Secretary: $660.00	Story and Secretary: $2,492.55
Director: $1,250.00	Cast: $5,646.08
Unit Manager and Secretary: $520.00	Production Fee: $750.00
Agents Commission: $5,185.55	Legal and Accounting: $250.00
Below the line charges (M-G-M): $22,354.22	Below the line charges (other): $7,036.14
Total Production Costs: $46,144.54	

Cast: Marc Cavell (Freeman); S. John Launer (the Colonel); Ron Masak (soldier with harmonica); Paul Mazurky (the orderly); Bob McCord (man in hospital); Warren Oates (the jeep driver); Barney Phillips (Captain E.L. Gunther, Medical Officer); William Phipps (the sergeant); William Reynolds (Lt. William Fitzgerald); Michael Vandever (Smitty); and Dick York (Captain Riker).

Original Music Score Composed by Lucien Moraweck (Score No. CPN5868) and Conducted by Lud Gluskin: Main Title (by Bernard Herrmann, :40); Prologue (by Edmund L. Gruber, arr. by Lucien Moraweck, :54); Battle Fatique (by Gruber, arr. by Moraweck, 1:35); Premonition (2:08); The Hospital (:07); Prophet of Doom (1:09); Uneasiness (1:04); Night Camp (by Gruber, arr. by Moraweck, :14); Vision of Death – Version 2 (by Antonín Dvořák, arr. by Moraweck, 1:46); The Trucks (by Gruber, arr. by Moraweck, :10); After Death C (:19); Reflection of Doom (2:27); Symphony No. 9 in E Minor "Z Noveho Sveta" ["From the New World"] Opus 92, 2nd Movement (excerpt by Dvořák, :28); The Mine (from New World Symphony, by Dvořák, arr. by Moraweck, :47); and End Title (by Herrmann, :39).

Director of Photography: George T. Clemens, a.s.c.
Art Directors: George W. Davis and William Ferrari
Set Decorations: Henry Grace and Rudy Butler
Directed by Richard L. Bare

Production Manager: Ralph W. Nelson
Film Editor: Bill Mosher
Assistant Director: Edward Denault
Casting Director: Mildred Gusse
Sound: Franklin Milton and Jean Valentino
Teleplay by Rod Serling

"Infantry platoon, U.S. Army, Philippine Islands, 1945. These are the faces of the young men who fight, as if some omniscient painter had mixed a tube of oils that were at one time earth brown, dust gray, blood red, beard black and fear yellow-white. And these men were the models. For this is the province of combat, and these are the faces of war."

Plot: Lieutenant Fitzgerald, stationed in the Philippines during the war, is having trouble coping with the recent deaths of four men in his platoon. As he explains to his commanding officer, Captain Riker, he has recently developed a sixth sense and can tell by reading the faces of the men who will soon die. The medics believe Fitz is a man cracking under the strain. Fitz, however, says he's been given a gift they don't teach during training. Before the platoon makes another advance, Fitz warns Riker that he will not return. When the platoon returns from their advances against the guerillas, Riker does not return because of sniper fire. Captain Gunther arrives to pass on the new orders – Fitz is to report back to division for a medical examination. Before leaving, Fitz sees his reflection in the mirror and the same look of death on the driver of the jeep. Moments later, down the road, the jeep hits a land mine, killing both men.

"From William Shakespeare, 'Richard the Third,' a small excerpt. The line reads, 'He has come to open the purple testament of bleeding war.' And for Lieutenant William Fitzgerald, 'A' Company, First Platoon . . . the testament is closed. (a pause) Lieutenant Fitzgerald has found . . . the Twilight Zone."

Trailer: *"Next week we show you the face of war, but the kind of portrait we venture to say you've never seen before. Dick York and William Reynolds star in 'The Purple Testament,' the story of a man who can forecast death. That's next week on The Twilight Zone – 'The Purple Testament.' We hope you'll join us. Thank you and good night."*

Trivia, etc. Serling had no idea he wanted to be a writer until after serving as a paratrooper in the 11th Airborne Division. Afterward, he went to Antioch College in Ohio and felt a compulsion to write about the war. "It was a catharsis. Then, thank God, I became interested in other things and expanded." He applied his knowledge of the Second World War and his experiences in the service as material for numerous radio scripts and teleplays.

An early draft of the script said the setting was Luzon, Philippine Islands, 1944, but this was changed by the time the episode went before the cameras and Serling recorded his opening narration. The entire episode, including exterior scenes, was filmed on Stage 22 at M-G-M during the first two days of filming. All of the interior scenes in the station hospital were filmed on the third day on Stage 19.

In the script, scene 13, the exterior of the hospital was described as follows: "This is an old beat-up schoolhouse commandeered by the U.S. Army and utilized as a hospital. An ambulance is just pulling away as we start to dolly in toward its entrance." A scene of the exterior of the station hospital was filmed, but this was discarded. Instead, stock footage was used. Serling would make a similar description of a schoolhouse being converted into a hospital for the opening scene in, "In Praise of Pip."

The cost for set decoration in the hallway of the station hospital was $100. The interior of Riker's tent (which also doubled for Fitz' tent) was a mere $50. The cost of the 15 pup tents, one pyramid tent, one kitchen fly, camouflage netting and plant life to create the illusion of the exterior of the camp ran a total of $1,975.

If the set where Captain Gunther and Fitzsimmons confront each other at the Station Hospital seems familiar, it should. This scene was filmed on Stage 19 featuring a flight of stairs leading up to the second story. This was the same stairway featured in the hallway outside Barbara's movie room in "The Sixteen Millimeter Shrine" and would be featured in a brief scene in "Elegy," where the spacemen find town citizens cheering a newly elected official at the top of the stairs. The stairway and doors leading to the backyard remained a permanent fixture on the set, but the décor, including the bulletin board, was part of the redecoration to prevent viewers from realizing the same sets were being reused.

William Reynolds recalled for interviewer/author Tom Weaver, "I remember that I got the part in 'The Purple Testament' as a consequence of another actor, Dean Stockwell, turning it down, and that the director Dick Bare then suggested me. I'd worked with Dick at Warner Brothers and done the pilot for the M-G-M TV series, *The Islanders*, with him. I was elated when I got 'The Purple Testament.' It was a go, like, the next day. I believe it was the next day. And as you know, I had a lot of words [dialogue]. Rod Serling was great. He was hands-on on the set and kinda gagged around with [co-star] Dick York and me, keeping people loose. But he was a pretty intense guy. His narrations were indicative of the kind of intensity he projected. A chain-smoker, a very creative and dynamic kind of guy, obviously, and remarkably prolific.

"After 'The Purple Testament,' Dick and I were in Jamaica doing background shots for *The Islanders* – shots of running through a jungle and swimming in a lagoon and landing the Grumman Goose [seaplane] in various places – to inter-cut with the stuff that we would do on the M-G-M back lot. We were flying back to the United States on the 12th of February 1960, the day that 'The Purple Testament' was scheduled to run. We were in level flight, I don't know how high, maybe 1,000 feet, and everything was cool, and I guess the pilot switched from one gas tank to the other – and the engines stopped. All of a sudden there was silence, except the sound of diving toward the water, which we could see through the open cockpit door. The Grumman Goose is not terribly airworthy absent power."

Director Richard L. Bare recalled, "I explained to the studio that if a small crew and I went to Jamaica to film scenic shots, rather than use stage sets for much of the picture, the pilot would impress the networks. They approved and a few of us went south. Filming was completed for *The Islanders*, so I was relatively surprised that they gave me the go-ahead because a trip to Jamaica for . . . oh, I guess it was about five of us . . . was costly for the studio. An unnecessary expense, they felt, but they went for it."

"We had time to buckle up, and I presume the pilot was trying to get some kind of a glide angle so he could land belly-up," continued Reynolds. "Apparently he succeeded, and the Goose split right in the middle. One moment I was buckled in my seat and the next, I was still in my seat, but I was spinning around underwater – I had been thrown clear of the fuselage. I could see light above me, sunlight, so I unbuckled and swam up to the surface, a few miles off the coast of Jamaica. The point of my telling this story, as related to *The Twilight Zone*, is the fact that back in Hollywood, [the TZ people] heard a news flash that our plane had crashed and they didn't know whether I had survived. I guess they were sensitive to the fact that I had a daughter who was a year and a half, and a two-week-old baby, and a wife, and they knew that it would have been a little macabre to show 'The Purple Testament,' an episode in which I see my own death, on the day that I had perhaps died in a plane crash. So out of respect for the feelings of my family, instead of taking advantage of what had happened, they took the show off the air that night."

The February 12, 1960 issue of *The Greeley Daily Fortune* reported four of the five men were rescued. Bare and Reynolds were unconscious hours after the crash. The assistant cameraman, Glen Kirkpatrick, was cut across the eyebrows. William Reynolds suffered severe cuts on the legs, and his right ankle was broken, along with several ribs. The pilot, Howard Smith, was the most seriously injured, suffering internal injuries in the chest and abdomen. George Schmidt bled to death in the hospital.

"At the little hospital in Annotto Bay, this woman in a flower dress stitched my hand," concluded Reynolds. "My left hand was pretty much like raw meat, and [laughs] she was stitching it up like a seamstress, like she was stitching up a dress! And their medication was cognac and morphine [laughs]. Also, they taped up my ribs, but apparently they had flipped my x-rays, because when I got back to the States and went to a doctor, he said, 'They taped up the wrong side!' [laughs] So much for medicine down there, but they were marvelous, friendly, great people!"

This same story was recounted to author Marc Scott Zicree, and while the tragic events of the accident truly happened, and on the very same evening of the telecast, this particular *Twilight Zone* episode was broadcast on CBS that evening, and there is no evidence CBS ever considered removing it from the schedule. The incident, however, did handicap Cayuga momentarily, as director Richard L. Bare was unavailable for a few months. At least one teleplay, "The Chase," had to be rescheduled and handed over to another director.

"The Purple Testament" aired on schedule on both East and West Coast affiliates, and three days after the telecast, on February 15, 1960, *The Hollywood Reporter* reviewed, "Writer-narrator Rod Serling celebrating the announcement that the series he created had been picked up for another 52 weeks by his non-censoring sponsors, General Foods and Kimberly-Clark, scripted a quickie about a battle-fatigued lieutenant who gets premonitions of death. As polished as ever, this segment, directed by Richard L. Bare, contained fewer surprises than expected, and the cast was successful neither in creating the illusion of reality nor the delusions of unreality."

On September 4, 1959, Buck Houghton began working with Serling regarding the order of which the episodes in production and already in the can would be broadcast. According to a release schedule drawn up by Hal Graham dated September 15, 1959, this episode was initially intended to be telecast on the evening of November 13, 1959. A revised schedule dated October 2, replaced "The Lonely" for that date. 'The Purple Testament' was pushed ahead a few months when Serling and Houghton felt other episodes were best suited for earlier broadcast dates, so this episode was rescheduled for February.

The photographic background for the end credits was initially planned to be the shot of the shaving mirror on its tripod from the leading man's point of view; where his face has not yet appeared in the mirror in the frame to be selected. That photo was not used. Instead, the producers chose the C.P. Company "A" Headquarters sign as the background photo.

> **Blooper!** While Serling credits Shakespeare's *Richard the Third* for an excerpt that explains the title of this episode, the passage originates from *Richard the Second*.

After viewing this episode, Loring Fiske in Los Angeles mailed a letter to Serling dated February 12, telling the playwright, "this is the poorest excuse for a story I have seen in months." The letter also suggested Serling was making good on a promise for an old war buddy, perhaps suffering from a hangover, and suggested Serling change the name of the episode to "Much Ado About Nothing." On February 25, Serling drafted a reply. "I regret we were unable to please. Of the several hundred letters received commentative on 'The Purple Testament,' yours was in the distinct minority though I must say none of the other letters, pro or con, came even remotely close to the hysteria of yours. Why not Robert Taylor's *The Detectives*? They're on at the same time, and I rather imagine they would please you more."

Production #3625 "ELEGY" (Initial telecast: February 19, 1960)
Copyright Registration: © Cayuga Productions, Inc., February 18, 1960, LP16039 (in notice: 1959)
Dates of Rehearsal: October 22, 1959
Dates of Filming: October 23, 26, 27 and 28, 1959
Shooting script dated: October 23, 1959

Producer and Secretary: $660.00
Director: $1,250.00
Unit Manager and Secretary: $425.00
Agents Commission: $5,185.55
Below the line charges (M-G-M): $34,637.88
Total Production Costs: $58,075.64

Story and Secretary: $2,245.00
Cast: $6,406.57
Production Fee: $750.00
Legal and Accounting: $250.00
Below the line charges (other): $6,265.64

Cast: Don Dubbins (Peter Kirby); Kevin Hagen (Captain James Webber); Cecil Kellaway (Jeremy Wickwire); and Jeff Morrow (Kurt Meyers).

Original Music Score Composed and Conducted by Nathan Van Cleave (Score No. CPN5869):
Main Title (by Bernard Herrmann, :40); Prelude (:25); Second Act Opening (:16); The Happy Farmer (:29); The Happy Fisherman (:35); There'll Be A Hot Time in the Old Town Tonight (by Theodore Metz and Joe Hayden, :42); Trouble (1:00); Dramatic Tension (:55); Dramatic Tension Tag (:46); Fascination (a.k.a. Valse Tzigane, by F.D. Marchetti, :52); The Beauty Contest (1:16); Second Act Tag (:09); Third Act Opening (:35); Lonesome Town (:39); Nice Old Man (:50); The Martini (:53); We've Had It (2:03); Billy Piano (1:02); The Caretaker (:27); Finale (:32); and End Title (by Herrmann, :39).

Director of Photography: George T.   Production Manager: Ralph W. Nelson

Clemens, a.s.c.

Art Directors: George W. Davis and
   William Ferrari

Set Decorations: Henry Grace and
   Budd S. Friend

Film Editor: Joseph Gluck, a.c.e.

Assistant Director: Edward Denault

Casting Director: Mildred Gusse

Sound: Franklin Milton and Jean Valentino

Directed by Douglas Heyes

Teleplay by Charles Beaumont, based on his short story of the same name, originally published in the February 1953 issue of *Imagination*.

"The time is the day after tomorrow. The place: a far corner of the universe. The cast of characters: three men lost amongst the stars, three men sharing the common urgency of all men lost . . . they're looking for home. And in a moment they'll find home, not a home that is a place to be seen but a strange, unexplainable experience to be felt."

Plot: The year is 2185. Three spacemen on a routine geological mission travel through an asteroid storm and are forced to land on a planet 655 million miles from Earth, only to discover their surroundings not too different from the real thing. With the exception of two suns, the planet resembles 20th century Earth – right down to the music, the costumes, and the frozen figures of flesh and blood that are spread out across the town, fishing holes and farm fields. After spending a couple hours wandering the streets and buildings, they find hundreds of frozen figures, but no sign of life. The solution to the mystery is revealed in the form of Mr. Jeremy Wickwire, the only apparent form of life that walks and talks. Wickwire invites the spacemen into his house, learns who they are and offers them a drink while he offers an explanation. They have landed in a cemetery. This is the place where your dreams come true, after you stop dreaming, he explains. Rather than have the cemetery on Earth, it was established here on another planet to ensure everlasting peace. Wickwire is the caretaker, and wakes only when the residents are disturbed, or routine maintenance is required. Realizing they have been poisoned, the spacemen start to lose strength and fall to the ground. The eternalizing fluid courses through their veins. Wickwire explains his motive: while there are men, there can be no peace. Weeks later, Mr. Wickwire arrives on the spaceship to dust off the frozen figures of the spacemen, positioned in the same manner they dreamed before their demise.

"Kirby, Webber, and Meyers, three men lost. They shared a common wish, a simple one, really – they wanted to be aboard their ship headed for home. And fate – a laughing fate – a practical jokester with a smile that stretched across the stars, saw to it that they got their wish, with just one reservation: the wish came true, but only in . . . the Twilight Zone."

Trailer: *"Next week on the Twilight Zone we offer you the unbelievable along with an explanation. Three men visit a strange new world of people, cars, houses – the works. But something is wrong on the scene. Something very abnormal and it's the normal. You'll see what I mean when next week we bring you 'Elegy' by Charles Beaumont. It stars Cecil Kellaway. Thank you and good night."*

Trivia, etc. Days before "Elegy" was telecast, Nelson Bond submitted a number of plot proposals for possible use on the program. Production on a batch of episodes had been recently completed and whether the series would be renewed was still in question, so Serling politely rejected the offer to purchase the rights to any of Bond's short stories. One of the tales, however, coincidently resembled one of Kurt's comments suggesting the possibility that time is moving slowly, like the hands of a clock.

The short story was "The Silent Planet" (originally published in *Blue Book*, May 1951) and told the tale of space explorers who find a strange planet where apparently death in a mysterious way struck suddenly, turning all creatures into frozen statues in a world where even the seas are carved into motionless waves. When they attempt to pick up and carry home one of these humanoid statues, it crumbles into ashes in their hands. Turns out the explorers are not Earthmen, but aliens who live at a rate of speed we cannot conceive, and the next day the New York papers carry the headline, "Yankee Shortstop Disappears from Infield!"

Originally this episode was scheduled for a three-day shoot, but production ran over into a fourth day. There are production notes from director Douglas Heyes specifically asking the cameraman to keep the camera moving slowly, panning across a set or stage, and the lead actors to continuously move about on the sets, to help counteract any slight movements from the still figures.

"The big trick was to use these crowds of thirty or forty people – motion picture extras – and not have them move," recalled director Douglas Heyes to interviewer Ben Herndon. "I decided that this was impossible, that they would have to move a little if they were human. You just don't take people off the street and expect them to totally freeze. But they could stand reasonably still, so I decided that the camera had to move while these people were standing still. That way, if you saw any slight movement, you'd think it was the camera's fault, not theirs. You never had a chance to analyze whether these people were standing absolutely still. That was why I took that episode – to see if it would work."*

The numerous actors playing the roles of the still figures were courtesy of a casting call. Most of the actors were paid $22.05 for their appearance, and only one actor, Luke Saucier, was used for more than one day's work (and probably appears in two separate scenes as a frozen figure). While there is no paperwork to suggest a connection, more than half of the names on the casting call sheet were extras in *Around the World in Eighty Days* (1956).

The first day of filming was devoted to the entire second half of the show, the interior of the living room and the hotel corridor, on Stage 9, so Cecil Kellaway was only required for the first day of filming. The second and third day were devoted to the spacemen and their exploration of the graveyard surroundings. Day two consisted of the 1940 farmhouse and the exterior of the St. Louis Street, both on Lot 3. (The street was named after the movie *Meet Me in St. Louis*, filmed in 1944.) The exterior of the lake and the exterior of the hotel were filmed on Lot 2. The second day of filming was supposed to conclude with the interior and exterior of the spaceship, but relocating the crew and equipment from the various settings took more time than anticipated. Day three began with the spaceship scenes. The remaining scenes (including the spaceship) were filmed on Stage 29 and filming was completed on the afternoon of the fourth day.

----

* While Heyes arranged to keep the camera moving, there were a few obvious mistakes. One is the scene with the young lady and older man, holding glasses of champagne in their hands. While the figures may appear to be frozen in place, the liquid is clearly moving about in the glasses.

The following people played the silent bit parts in "Elegy" but remained un-accredited: Sally Arnell, Walter Bacon, Frank Baker, Bonnie Barlow, Shelby Benson, Jack Bonigul, George Boyce, Barbara Chrysler, Walter Clinton, Robert Dayo, Alfonso Dubois, Doris Edwards, Joseph Glick, David Greene, Paul Gustine, Carol Holleck, Chester Hayes, James W. Horan, Paul Kruger, Jack Lee, Paul Louis, Charles Lunard, Jack Mattis, June McCall, William Meada, Walter O'Donnell, Patilu Palmer, Luke Saucier, Jerry Schumacher, Stephen Soldi, Jack Stoney, Martin Strader, Dennis Sullivan, George Tatar, and Walton Walker. Among the silent bit parts was Chester Hayes, a former professional wrestler who turned actor/stunt man in the late 1940s. He was not related to director Douglas Heyes (different spelling of last name). Luke Saucier was an alligator wrestler and movie studio reptile handler, and made an appearance as a passenger in the bus in "Mirror Image."

While the spacemen explore the surroundings, they come upon a scene where a group of people are cheering for Mayor Finch. This is the same set and stairs used for the outside of Barbara's dark room in "The Sixteen Millimeter Shrine" and the hospital scene in "The Purple Testament." The same set could be glimpsed through the door of Walter Jameson's classroom in "Long Live Walter Jameson."

The opening and closing narratives in the first draft were revised after Beaumont's initial submission. During revisions, Serling deliberately replaced the opening narration with a variation of the closing narrative from his unused *Twilight Zone* teleplay, "The Happy Place," reprinted below:

"The Time is the day after tomorrow. Man has lived through his wars, his bombs, and his rockets. And this is a society of the future. It is a forceful society where nothing remains static. The process of living operates from different rules now. And there is a new God ... Called Perfection! [a pause] But this God is only ... temporary."

Originally Serling intended to use the following for the trailer, but it was considered too lengthy and needed to be cut:

"There are some experiences which people go through that defy any kind of explanation. What occurs is so unusual, so unique, so unbelievable that at best we push them into the back of our minds in lieu of an explanation. But next week on the Twilight Zone we offer you the unbelievable ... along with an explanation. Three men visit a strange new world of people, buildings, farms, cars, houses – the works. But something's wrong on the scene. Something very abnormal amidst the normal. You'll see what I mean when next week we bring you 'Elegy' by Charles Beaumont. It will star Cecil Kellaway, Jeff Morrow, Don Dubbins and Kevin Hagen. See you next week."

Production #3623 "MIRROR IMAGE" (Initial telecast: February 26, 1960)
© Cayuga Productions, Inc., February 25, 1960, LP16336 (in notice: 1959)
Date of Rehearsal: October 28, 1959
Dates of Filming: October 29 and 30, and November 2, 1959

Script #23 dated: September 30, 1959

Producer and Secretary: $660.00
Director: $1,250.00
Unit Manager and Secretary: $425.00
Agents Commission: $5,185.55
Below the line charges (M-G-M): $17,950.19
Total Production Costs: $40,850.00

Story and Secretary: $2,385.00
Cast: $8,410.01
Production Fee: $750.00
Legal and Accounting: $250.00
Below the line charges (other): $3,584.25

Cast: Max Cutler (bus passenger); Joe Hamilton (the ticket agent); Terese Lyon (the old woman/ wife); Bob McCord (bus passenger); Vera Miles (Millicent Barnes); Martin Milner (Paul Grinstead); Edwin Rand (the bus driver); Tony Renando (bus passenger); Grace Rickey (bus passenger); Luke Saucier (bus passenger); Naomi Stevens (the woman station attendant); and Ferris Taylor (the husband).

Stock Music Cues: Main Title (by Bernard Herrmann, :40); Silent Flight C (by Jerry Goldsmith, :41); Silent Flight BC (by Goldsmith, :47); Brave New World – Chord (by Herrmann, :04); Brave New World (by Herrmann, :22); Brave New World – Chord (:14); Brave New World (by Herrmann, :06); Silent Flight ABD (by Goldsmith, 1:00 and :57); Brave New World – Chord (by Herrmann, :04); Brave New World (by Herrmann, :09); Shock Therapy #3 (by Garriguenc, :05); Brave New World (by Herrmann, :30); Buildup #2 – Man of Decision (by Lucien Moraweck, :07); Brave New World (by Herrmann, :14); Brave New World – Chord (by Herrmann, :14); Brave New World (by Herrmann, :06); Shock Therapy #3 – Man of Decision (by Garriguenc, :14); Brave New World (by Herrmann, :22); Silent Flight BC (by Goldsmith, 1:15); Shock Therapy #3 (by Garriguenc, :05); Silent Flight AD (by Goldsmith, :12); Silent Flight (by Goldsmith, 1:12); Silent Flight AD (by Goldsmith, :34); Brave New World – Chord (by Herrmann, :040; Brave New World (by Herrmann, :06, :36 and :26); Brave New World Chord (by Herrmann, :06), and End Title (by Herrmann, :39).

Director of Photography: George T.
    Clemens, a.s.c.
Art Directors: George W. Davis and
    William Ferrari
Set Decorations: Henry Grace and
    Budd S. Friend
Teleplay by Rod Serling

Production Manager: Ralph W. Nelson
Film Editor: Bill Mosher
Assistant Director: Edward Denault
Casting Director: Mildred Gusse
Sound: Franklin Milton and Jean Valentino
Directed by John Brahm

"Millicent Barnes, age twenty-five, young woman waiting for a bus on a rainy November night. Not a very imaginative type is Miss Barnes; not given to undue anxiety or fears or for that matter even the most temporal flights of fancy. Like most young career women, she has a generic classification as a quote, girl with a head on her shoulders, end of quote. All of which is mentioned now because in just a moment the head on Miss Barnes's shoulders will be put to a test. Circumstances will assault her sense of reality; and a chain of nightmares will put her sanity on a block. Millicent Barnes, who in one minute will wonder if she's going mad!"

Plot: Late one night, while waiting for the bus to Cortland, Millicent Barnes starts doubting her sanity. The ticket man at the bus depot claims she checked her bag, but Millicent has no recollection of doing so. The cleaning lady claims Millicent was in the bathroom only moments before, but again, Millicent has no recollection. When a young man named Paul listens to her story and how she caught a glimpse of herself in the bathroom mirror – a duplicate of her in the lobby – he suspects she is suffering from delusions. When the bus arrives, Millicent prepares to board until she sees a duplicate of herself already a passenger. Panicking, she runs back into the station. After the bus leaves, Millicent wakes to find herself alone in the depot with Paul. She begins recalling something she read or heard about a long time ago about twin planes of existence. Two parallel worlds that exist side-by-side and how everyone has a counterpart in the other world. Sometimes, through unexplained causes, the identical twin crosses over into our world. In order to survive, the duplicate finds it necessary to take over – push the original out in order to live. Paul finds this too metaphysical for him and secretly phones the police. Taking Millicent outside for some fresh air, he hands her over to the police for safekeeping. Returning to the empty depot, Paul shakes his head and gets a drink of water. After witnessing someone running off with his bag, John begins to take chase after someone who looks exactly like him . . .

"Obscure metaphysical explanation to cover a phenomena. Reasons dredged out of the shadows to explain away that which cannot be explained. Call it parallel planes . . . or just insanity . . . whatever it is . . . you find it in the Twilight Zone."

Trailer: *"Next week I try to sell an argument to the effect that I'm not at my best when writing scripts for women. Miss Vera Miles takes my side, in a most unusual and unique story we call 'Mirror Image.' I hope to see you next week – you in your living room, and Miss Vera Miles and the rest of us, in the Twilight Zone."*

Trivia, etc. "I got this idea during a publicity tour last fall," Rod Serling later recalled for *TV Guide*. "I was sitting in a Cleveland, Ohio, airport when I noticed a person walking past me carrying a bag very similar to my own. I looked up and saw the person from the back. The build, the back of the head, etc., were identical to my own, and while I never did see who the unlucky guy was, it provided a springboard to an idea whereby a woman keeps seeing evidence of a twin to herself and ultimately seeing herself."

"Last summer I was in the Cleveland airport when I saw a bag at the claim station which looked much like my own," Serling recalled in less detail in the July 17, 1960 issue of

Vera Miles and Martin Milner faces
their fears in "Mirror Image."

The Louisville Courier-Journal. "A man claimed it, and I saw him only from behind. He was rather short, dark-haired, and looked much like me. I said, 'Gosh, what would it be like to see myself walk up and claim my own baggage while I sat in an airport.' From that came one of our stories in which a woman met herself face-to-face."

While the actual location of the bus station is not directly revealed in this episode, fans have been trying to figure out the exact location. Answering a letter from one viewer concerning this episode, Serling explained, "My wife and I have a summer cottage on Cayuga Lake and I'm a native of Binghamton so that the whole area is familiar stamping ground for me." The setting was described in the first draft of the script as "a typical waiting room of a small city bus station." The location could also be pinned down courtesy of a report dated October 8, 1959, from the De Forest Research Group. The report explained to Serling that the only two places between Binghamton and Cortland (which are mentioned in the episode) is Marathon, with a population of 545, and Ithaca, population 29,164. It was suggested that the bus going to Cortland and Syracuse does not go on to Buffalo. A change in Syracuse would be necessary. Suggestion: delete "Buffalo." Regardless of what town the events take place, the story did take place somewhere in the state of New York.

Serling's first draft also described the ladies room with vanities, but the same report pointed out that ladies rooms in bus stations did not have vanities. They did, however, often have a chair or couch.

The entire episode was filmed on Stage 25, both interior and exterior of the bus station, and the bathroom (which was a permanent fixture on stage). This was the same stage used for Beechcroft's office in the episode "The Mind and the Matter."

Vera Miles' appearance on this episode dates back to August of 1953. While casting a story called "The Soil" for CBS' *Schlitz Playhouse of Stars*, producer William Self came up against a familiar problem: an open part calling for the services of an experienced actress and only a few hundred dollars to offer her. An agent suggested Vera Miles, who had been featured in four movies since she arrived in Hollywood as Miss Kansas of 1948. Miles was under contract to a major film studio and they were not at that time, lending their stars for television production. But Self decided to make the offer anyway. To his surprise, he learned that her studio had recently dropped her.

Thus it was that Vera Miles, ditched by the movies as a poor and unlikely investment in stardom, made appearances on television programs. Her work on *Ford Theater*, *Four Star Playhouse* and *Crown Theater* led to her co-starring role in *The Searchers* (1956) with John Wayne. After seeing her as a cancer victim on *Medic*, Alfred Hitchcock offered her the lead, the role of a psychotic woman, in the first of his television suspense series. This was Hitchcock's way of offering a screen test. Satisfied, he gave her a five-year-contract and cast her in *The Wrong Man* with Henry Fonda.

Months before "Mirror Image" went into production, William Self suggested to Serling that Vera Miles be used for an up-coming episode. His suggestion may have been the reason for her casting.

Days after filming was completed, Buck Houghton explained to Sam Kaplan of Ashley-Steiner that on numerous occasions, he, Serling and Self discussed the numerous camera tricks and "theatrics" applied on the films, and confessed they were as creative as they could possibly be expressed under the circumstances. Realizing that they needed an art director and production designer who could lend a greater air of creativity, Houghton hired Serge Krizman to study this episode and "The Fever." Krizman later gave the men a list of suggestions that could be applied in future productions.

The scene with the suitcase disappearing while Paul gets a drink of water was called for in the script as two shots, but director John Brahm created a simple method of accomplishing the trick in one continuous shot. The suitcase was removed courtesy of a thin string that could not be visible on the camera. Millicent's view of seeing her duplicate from the bathroom mirror was a standard camera trick applied with the assistance of the film editor.

Blake Chatfield of Young & Rubicam provided all TV editors with a photo spread of Vera Miles in connection with this episode. Glamour photos were taken on the set, as well as a few supplied by her agent, to be accompanied with the press release. *TV Guide* rejected a proposal regarding a layout on Vera Miles and the different wigs she wore (playing different roles on television episodes), so Ben Irwin of Cleary-Strauss & Irwin, public relations, made the same pitch to *Life* and *This Week* magazine.

Originally Serling intended to use the following for the trailer, but it was considered too lengthy and needed to be shortened:

(Suitcase on a bench) *"Sometimes you look at things like this suitcase on a waiting room bench. All very normal, hardly worth a second glance. But some things require a second glance.* [Point back to where the bench now sits up on end. The suitcase resting atop it.] *Something of this nature happens next week*

Mirrors played an important part of story telling throughout the first season episodes – a practice that was soon dropped after the premiere of the second season. Mike Ferris runs into a mirror in "Where is Everybody?" Martin Sloan went back in time through the earliest glimpses of the mirror in the drugstore. The mirror provided the poignant demise of the protagonist in "The Purple Testament." The prizefighter observes the scars in his face in "The Big, Tall Wish." Anne Francis, in the role of Marsha White, is frightened by a reflection in a mirror in "The After Hours." Nan Adams catches a glimpse of the hitch-hiker more than once in a mirror in "The Hitch-Hiker." The shaving scene in "The Four of Us Are Dying" reveals the protagonist's special talent. Franklin is plagued by the one-armed bandit when a glimpse is caught in the mirror in "The Fever." James Daly smashes a mirror in "A Stop at Willoughby." Lt. Colonel Clegg Forbes witnesses the loss of his reflection in "And When the Sky Was Opened." Death cannot be seen in the mirror in "One For the Angels." The mirrors in bedrooms in "Escape Clause" and "Third From the Sun" play an important part of the drama, as well.

---

on The Twilight Zone. Something like this . . . But much more so. A distinguished actress, Miss Vera Miles, plays the part of a young woman on whose head toppled the fragments of reality and sanity. Watch this one. It's a corker. Vera Miles in 'Mirror Image' next week on The Twilight Zone."

Production #3620 "THE MONSTERS ARE DUE ON MAPLE STREET" (Initial telecast: March 4, 1960)

© Cayuga Productions, Inc., March 3, 1960, LP16337 (in notice: 1959)
Date of Rehearsal: September 28, 1959
Dates of Filming: September 29, 30, October 1 and 2, 1959
Script #20 dated: September 8, 1959, with revised pages dated September 24 and November 12, 1959.

Producer and Secretary: $660.00
Director: $840.00
Unit Manager and Secretary: $520.00
Agents Commission: $5,185.55
Below the line charges (M-G-M): $32,135.73
Total Production Costs: $56,888.77

Story and Secretary: $2,395.00
Cast: $8,459.50
Production Fee: $750.00
Legal and Accounting: $250.00
Below the line charges (other): $5,692.99

Cast: Claude Akins (Steve Brand); Sheldon Allman (Space Alien #1); Barry Atwater (Mr. Goodman); Anne Barton (Mrs. Brand); Joan Boston (silent bit part); Paul Denton (silent bit part); Ben Erway (Pete Van Horn); Mary Gregory (Tommy's Mother); Lyn Guild (Charlie's Wife); Jan Handzlik (young Tommy); Jim Jacobs (silent bit part); Jason Johnson (man one); Diane Livesey (silent bit part); Bob McCord (the ice cream vendor); Beryl McCutcheon (silent bit part); Burt Metcalfe (Don); William Moran (silent bit part); Vinita Murdock (silent bit part); Amzie Strickland (first woman); Joan Sudlow (woman next door); Lea Waggner (Mrs. Goodman); William Walsh (Space Alien #2); George Washburn (silent bit part); and Jack Weston (Charlie).

Original Music Score Composed by Rene Garriguenc and Conducted by Lud Gluskin (Score No. CPN5882): Main Title (by Bernard Herrmann, :40); Maple Street (:30); What Was It? (:21); The Power's Off (1:01); Tommy's Outer Space Story (2:02); Uneasyness on Maple Street (1:15); Reaction (:08); A Kind of Madness (:07); Ruminating Suspicion (1:44); The Needling (1:01); Footsteps (:07); Lights and Suspicion (:57); Lights and Hysteria (1:30); One to the Other (:47); and End Title (by Herrmann, :39).

Director of Photography: George T.
    Clemens, a.s.c.
Art Directors: George W. Davis and
    William Ferrari
Set Decorations: Henry Grace and Rudy Butler
Directed by Ronald Winston

Production Manager: Ralph W. Nelson
Film Editor: Bill Mosher
Assistant Director: Edward Denault
Casting Director: Mildred Gusse
Sound: Franklin Milton and Jean Valentino
Teleplay by Rod Serling

"Maple Street, U.S.A., late summer. A tree-lined little world of front porch gliders, barbeques, the laughter of children, and the bell of an ice-cream vendor. At the sound of the roar and the flash of light, it will be precisely six-forty-three PM on Maple Street ... This is Maple Street on a late Saturday afternoon. Maple Street – in the last calm and reflective moment ... before the monsters came!"

Plot: Shortly after a mysterious flash of light hovers over Maple Street, late one afternoon, the power goes out – appliances, power tools, radios, even automobiles. Before Charlie and Steve can walk into the next town to learn the source of the power failure, young Tommy warns the citizens of Maple Street that aliens from outer space are responsible. The young boy suggests that a few of them might already be living among their community. As the hours pass, suspicion grows as Les Goodman's automobile starts up automatically, the lights in Charlie's house come on, and everyone starts pointing accusatory fingers at each other. Charlie is quick to point a finger and ends up shooting Pete Van Horn in the streets, mistaking him for an alien. Charlie blames young Tommy for the comic book scare and the inhabitants become a mob. Stones are thrown and gun shots ring through the streets while the entire neighborhood turns into a murderous frenzy. High above on top of a grassy hillside, two aliens observe the massacre. One being explains to the other that if they turn off the power and throw the humans into darkness for a short while, they will find their own worst enemy – themselves. Having seen the results first-hand, the alien race plans to go from one Maple Street to the other until all of mankind has killed itself off.

"The tools of conquest do not necessarily come with bombs and explosions and fall-out. There are weapons that are simply thoughts, attitudes, prejudices – to be found only in the minds of men. For the record, prejudices can kill, and suspicion can destroy and a thoughtless, frightened search for a scapegoat has a fall-out all of its own for the children . . . and the children yet unborn. And the pity of it is . . . that these things cannot be confined to . . . The Twilight Zone."

Trailer: *"Next week on The Twilight Zone we put you on a front porch – summer evening, tree-lined street, typical small town. And then we pull the rug out from under your feet and we throw a nightmare at you. Claude Akins, Jack Weston and Barry Atwater are your neighbors just at that moment when 'The Monsters are Due on Maple Street.' Don't chicken out. See you next week."*

Trivia, etc. The year was 1951. Rod Serling wrote a radio script titled "The Button Pushers," a futuristic science fiction drama set in a future Earth, 1970. Huge television screens substituted for advertising billboards in Times Square, air-way rocket trains carried commuters overhead, and the fear of rival nations separated by a large ocean covered the front page headlines. A bloodthirsty general urges a brilliant scientist to complete the development of a new weapon, best described as a "doomsday bomb." The enemy overseas, reportedly, has already developed a similar weapon. The general asks the scientist to complete the weapon so that it could be fired with the push of a single button – no secondary protocols required. The scientist, fearing his weapon could start a war that would erase the existence of mankind on the entire planet, contemplated the centuries of progress – ancient civilizations that built the pyramids, the deserted Mayan temples and the skyscrapers of today. After 15 minutes contemplating the beauty and wonder Earth had to offer, he completes the weapon and the Army takes over. Against his warnings, the button is pushed. The enemy does the same, and the countdown for contact begins.

The ending featured a series of explosions on the surface of planet Earth, and two aliens on another planet across the universe start the following discussion:

VOICE 1:	*Ah, Verus . . . Have you see the little planet – Earth?*
VOICE 2:	*Why no . . . come to think of it, Felovius I haven't seen it . . . In a few hundred light years. Seems to have just disappeared all of a sudden.*
VOICE 1:	*Ah . . . Then I win my bet.*
VOICE 2:	*Bet?*
VOICE 1:	*Yes, I bet the keeper of the North Star that the little Earth would destroy itself before the next billion years had gone by . . . and she has. She seems to have just blown herself up . . .*

> disintegrated. . . she no longer exists. Tch, tch . . . Pity . . . she was a lovely little planet. Wonder what caused it?

VOICE 2:   *That is a question . . .*

VOICE 1:   *Oh, what am I thinking of . . . I know what destroyed it. It had human beings on it. I'd forgotten.*

VOICE 2:   *Well then, that explains it . . . Those pesky little things can't live side by side very long. Shall we go back and tell the others?*

VOICE 1:   *Why take the trouble? As if anyone cared about tiny Earth . . . So unimportant a speck . . . so insignificant a dot in the universe. Who cares?*

VOICE 2:   *I guess you're right. (sighs) Nice night . . . So quiet . . . So uneventful.*

"*The Twilight Zone* I have, with varying degrees of success or failure, attempted to touch upon moral themes utilizing the device of the parable," Serling concluded. "In other words, I have tried to insert subtly what I hope to be a message, but couched it in such a manner that it becomes almost an unconscious effect. Hence, I will tell a story about an invasion from outer space, but tell it with an implicit suggestion that human beings are prone to inordinate suspicions and prejudices about things that are 'different.'"

Shortly before the premiere of *The Twilight Zone*, Serling assured columnist John P. Shanley of *The New York Times* that, "I'm not writing any material that lies in the danger zone. There won't be anything controversial in the new series." This episode, however, left a commentary that could have been considered "controversial" by a percentage of the viewers. Serling indicated that he was no longer inclined to battle the forces that had drawn his fire in the past. "Now we're petulant aging men. It no longer behooves us to bite the hand that feeds us. Not a meek conformist but a tired nonconformist. The facts of life are these: the creative person is not in control in a creative medium nor shall he ever be, except possibly in the legitimate theatre."

"You can spend half your life fighting points instead of writing points," he continued. "I think you can get adult drama without controversy. In the past when I was doing something even remotely controversial, I've been knocked for it. They said I vitiated it, diluted it. My attitude now is – rather something than nothing."

About the time this episode aired, when asked early in the series what kind of program *The Twilight Zone* was, Serling replied, "they're not vehicles of social criticism. One story, 'The Monsters Are Due on Maple Street,' is a strange oblique commentary on prejudice. The minorities always need

Talent Fees For This Episode:
Minimum film residuals and minimum theatrical reruns applied.
Claude Akins ($500) as Steve   Jack Weston ($850) as Charlie
Anne Barton ($500) as Mrs. Brand   Amzie Strickland ($500) as Woman One
Jason Johnson ($500) as Man One   Burt Metcalfe ($500) as Don
Jan Handzlik ($500) as Tommy   Others varied from $75 to $100 per day.

a scapegoat to explain their own weaknesses."

The entire episode was filmed on the New England Street on Lot 2 at M-G-M. Two outside prop rentals were required for this episode – a vending bike and a power mower, which cost Cayuga $50. Set designs including the "Maple Street" sign for the sign post, landscapes, automobiles and other props cost a total of $750. The exterior of the spaceship was filmed on the evening of the third day. Electronic instruments, garden tools and the illusion of the scenic view of Maple Street and the inhabitants in a panic, cost $1,000.

This episode, like all of the *Twilight Zone* productions, featured in contracts and separate title sheets the size of the names and the screen cards which would feature the cast during the closing credits. According to Jan Handzlik's contract (also known as a "Talent Agreement"), she was 14 years old at the time and was to receive no less than fourth co-star billing in the same size of type and on the same card used to display the names of other co-stars. Claude Akins was to receive first co-star billing. Weston was to receive no less than third co-star billing in same size of type and on the same card used to display the names of other co-stars.

Serling intended to use the following for the trailer, but it was considered too lengthy, and needed to be trimmed down:

"Next week on 'The Twilight Zone' we put you in a glider on a warm summer evening, front porch, tree lined street, typical small town. We let you look at ice cream salesman, listen to kids laugh and play, listen to housewives gossip over porch railings. And then . . . then we pull the rug out from under your feet and we throw a nightmare at you that we venture to say will not be easily set aside. Next week Claude Akens, Jack Weston and Barry Atwater are your neighbors just at the moment when 'The Monsters Are Due on Maple Street.' Don't chicken out. See you next week."

According to a letter dated November 28, 1959, "Along with schedule changes, 'The Monsters Are Due on Maple Street' has been delayed until a February or March date because of production problems." This may explain why revised pages are dated November 12, weeks after filming was completed. It is possible that insert shots and revised scenes were refilmed before the final film was put together.

Herb Luft of the Jewish Telegraphic Agency (syndicated to over 100 Anglo Jewish newspapers) interviewed Serling for a plug for this episode, and the interview went out to help promote the program and this specific episode.

On March 5, 1960, Earl Kemp of the Chicago Science Fiction League wrote to Serling as an "unashamed fan letter." In the letter, Kemp regarded *The Twilight Zone* as "a piece of rare magnificence, combining integrity and taste in the right proportions for relaxing enjoyment. . . . You have always dealt completely honestly with the field of science fiction and fantasy, adding to the prestige of the genre rather than detracting from it. Of course, I do have complaints, too. I'm pretty damn tired of seeing M-G-M's overworked *Forbidden Planet* saucer, and the same astronomicals. I am extremely tired of the odd-angle and screw-ball shots that add not one single thing to the photography but a desire that it should cease."

Serling defended, "While I don't think the camera on it was exceptionally good, I cannot defend the M-G-M saucer. Unfortunately, with budget problems, you have to fall back on standard overworked devices too often."

The Waterloo Daily Courier described the episode being an "excellent production." Other television critics raved about the telecast, but viewers of education took note, and began writing in their praises.

Joseph Janovsky, principal of a school in Brooklyn, New York, felt that the program contained the essence of a "Human Relations" course and requested in writing to Serling and Oscar Katz (vice president in charge of programming in New York) that he acquire a 16mm print of the episode for future courses and classes. Janovsky was not the only person to request a copy of the episode. John Bauer, Ph.D., a professor at City College of New York, felt that his classes would benefit greatly with an opportunity to review the production. "One of the outstanding frustrations in my attempt to further the education of my students is the solidly encased 'It can't happen here' attitude which prevails among today's college youth," Bauer wrote. "Your play might help to break through the unrealistic complacency which marks their thoughts regarding most psycho-social disruptive forces." Serling referred Bauer to Guy Della Cioppa of CBS at Television City in Hollywood, suggesting this might help Bauer avoid any red tape and acquire a print.

By April 14, 1960, Serling was getting tired of the numerous requests from viewers asking for a copy of the script or a 16mm print of the film. In a letter addressed to Miss Pat Thomas of the WAC Department at Fort Monmouth, New Jersey, in response to a request from the chaplain at the U.S. Army, dated that same day, Serling explained to his sorrow: "CBS is no longer allowing films from the series to be shown to public or private groups for whatever reason. We've had so many requests for 'The Monsters Are Due on Maple Street' and found out along the way that there were more requests than there were films. So they've just taken a blanket position of no films to anyone. If he wants to pursue this further, have him write to Guy Della Cioppa, CBS Television City, Hollywood, and explain the situation."

In September of 1960, Gregory Guroff of *Decision Magazine* at Princeton University wrote to Serling, asking for a complimentary copy of the script, for use as the basis of either a story or parable. Serling obliged, explaining that, "since this is a file copy and one of only two in my possession, I would greatly appreciate its return to me after your perusal."

When this script was adapted into a short story for *Stories from the Twilight Zone* by Bantam Books, Serling made one noticeable change at the conclusion. He described how the sunrise revealed the remains of dead bodies draped about the streets and porches, and how, hours later, new residents had arrived to move in – with two heads for each new resident. The script itself has become a textbook standard, having been reprinted in a number of scholastic books over the years, so children of various ages could be exposed to the moral Serling emphasized.

The pattern of conflict in a street when contact with the rest of the world is cut off closely resembled that of a teenage science fiction book titled *The Year When Stardust Fell* (1958), written by Raymond F. Jones and published by the John C. Winston Company. When a viewer brought this to Serling's attention, he confessed that he was unaware of the book and sought out a copy to check its contents and settle his curiosity. The book concerned a mysterious comet that appears in the sky and is apparently the cause of all car engines, worldwide, to mysteriously overheat. By the next day, airplanes, trains, generators and other machinery does not function. Nearly in a state of panic, hys-

---

Recurring Product Placement
Three automobiles are featured in this episode: a 1959 Ford Sedan and a 1959 Ford Station Wagon. The station wagon was the same one the mechanic was working on in "Walking Distance" (verified by registration numbers).

teria and superstition, the people of the Earth resort to mob rule in a fight for survival. In 1962, a book reviewer for *Show* magazine reviewed the book, and claimed it mirrored too much like Serling's teleplay, unaware that the initial publication year pre-dated the *Twilight Zone* production.

The premise of power shutting off all machinery to make a point was also explored in *The Day the Earth Stood Still* (1951), which may have been a brief inspiration for this episode.

In the episode "Boom Boom Out Goes the Ed" of the animated television series *Ed, Edd n' Eddy*, initially telecast November 11, 2005, the lead characters start to panic when the power goes out, and Ed claims the blackout is a result of evil mole people. As the neighbors start to panic, á la spoof of this *Twilight Zone*, the children soon discover that the only way to stop the escalating panic is to take matters into their own hands.

Cold War hysteria at its best was paid a second visit on the evening of February 19, 2003, when a remake of this same teleplay was telecast on a newer rendition of *The Twilight Zone*. One notable difference between the remake and the original was the driving force behind the hysteria. Instead of visitors from outer space, employees from a special branch of the U.S. government were responsible for the power blackouts. The government was conducting tests to see how small town America would react in the face of foreign terrorism.

Production #3624 "A WORLD OF DIFFERENCE" (Initial telecast: March 11, 1960)
© Cayuga Productions, Inc., March 10, 1960, LP16338 (in notice: 1959)
Date of Rehearsal: October 13, 1959
Dates of Filming: October 14, 15 and 16, 1959
Script #24 dated: October 2, 1959, with revised pages dated October 9, 1959
Shooting script dated: October 9, 1959

Producer and Secretary: $660.00
Director: $1,370.00
Unit Manager and Secretary: $520.00
Agents Commission: $5,185.55
Below the line charges (M-G-M): $21,712.52
Total Production Costs: $46,237.76

Story and Secretary: $2,145.00
Cast: $9,502.20
Production Fee: $750.00
Legal and Accounting: $250.00
Below the line charges (other): $4,142.49

Cast: Chester Brandenburg (silent bit part); Susan Dorn (Marian); Howard Duff (Arthur Curtis / Gerald Raigan); William Idelson (Kelly); Gail Kobe (Sally); Frank Maxwell (Marty); Beryl McCutcheon (silent bit part); Joe Norden (film technician); Eileen Ryan (Nora); Jerry Schumacher (silent bit part); Peter Walker (Endicott); and David White (Mr. Brinkley).

Original Music Score Composed and Conducted by Nathan Van Cleave (Score No. CPN5879):
Main Title (by Bernard Herrmann, :40); Prologue (:34); Comin' Thru the Rye (:16); Life's But a Stage (:51); Meet Marty Fisher (:22); I Don't Know You (:36); The Home Telephone (1:47); The Car (:18); Jerry's Wife (:37); The Agent (:28); Where is Home (:41); The Little Girl (:54); You Are Home (:53); The Office Telephone (1:09); Don't Strike the Set (:19); The Ride (1:08); The Office (1:28); Finale (:45); and End Title (by Herrmann, :39).

Director of Photography: Harkness Smith
Art Directors: George W. Davis and
    William Ferrari
Set Decorations: Henry Grace and Rudy Butler
Sound: Franklin Milton and Jean Valentino
Teleplay by Richard Matheson

Production Manager: Ralph W. Nelson
Film Editor: Joseph Gluck, a.c.e.
Assistant Director: Edward Denault
Casting Director: Mildred Gusse
Directed by Ted Post

"You're looking at a tableau of reality . . . things of substance, of physical material: a desk, a window, a light. These things exist and have dimension. Now this is Arthur Curtis, age thirty-six, who also is real. He has flesh and blood, muscle and mind. But in just a moment we will see how thin a line separates that which we assume to be real with that manufactured inside of a mind."

Plot: Arthur Curtis, a successful businessman living in Woodland Hills, with a beautiful wife and young daughter, discovers one afternoon that his private life has become a work of fiction. Mistaken for a movie actor named Gerald Raigan, Curtis finds himself not in his office, but a replica on a sound stage at a movie studio. Spending the afternoon attempting to prove to everyone (including himself) that he is not an actor playing the role of Arthur Curtis, he visits the house that isn't his and phones his employers to discover no such man worked for them. His agent informs him he's on the verge of a nervous breakdown and suffering delusions because his life is a total letdown. Upon learning that the set that contains his office is being torn down, Curtis races to the studio in the hopes that somehow he can go back to his life before the confusion started. He succeeds in his attempt. Realizing his wife is standing in his office, he grabs her by the arm and makes a steadfast escape for a vacation, requesting they leave right now. Back at the studio, Gerald Raigan, the actor, is nowhere to be found, but the script, "The Private World of Arthur Curtis" remains behind, suggesting the actor escaped into another world that is much better than the one he left.

"The modus operandi for the departure from life is usually a pine box of such and such dimensions, and this is the ultimate in reality. But there are other ways for a man to exit from life. Take the case of Arthur Curtis, age thirty-six. His departure was along a highway with an exit sign that reads, 'This Way To Escape.' Arthur Curtis, en route . . . to the Twilight Zone."

Trailer: *"Next week, Mr. Richard Matheson lends us his fine writing talents when we bring you a unique and most arresting story of a movie actor who finds himself on that thin line between what is real and what is a dream. Mr. Howard Duff stars in 'World of Difference,' which I think you'll discover is a television play of difference, too. That's next week, a journey into The Twilight Zone. Thank you and good night."*

Trivia, etc. This episode offers the viewers a wonderful tour through the back lot of M-G-M Studios. The first day of filming consisted of the exterior street scenes, on Lot 2, also known as the New England Street. The exterior of the Raigan House, where Duff pays a visit after leaving the studio, was also on Lot 2, and known at the studio as the Philadelphia Story House, because it was the same house featured in the 1940 motion picture, *The Philadelphia Story*. (Duff walks up to the very door where Cary Grant pushed Katharine Hepburn to the ground, but turns and walks away so he can face the little girl.) The house had undergone a slight change since 1940 – the exterior brick work had been replaced with white siding.

The second half of the first day of filming consisted of the exterior shots of the M-G-M sound studios. The vehicles parked along the lots are actually owned by the production crew, who were instructed earlier in the week to specially park there to ensure that no automobile owned by someone else would be accidentally caught on camera. The exterior of the studio sound stages was filmed outside stages 21, 22, 23 and 24. (The door to Studio 23 can be seen very clearly in the film.) Rounding out the filming on the first day were the interior scenes of Curtis' office and anteroom, shot on Stage 24. *

The second day of filming consisted of additional scenes in Curtis' office and the fictional sound stage, also shot on Stage 24. The third and final day of filming finished the remaining scenes that were not completed on day two, and all of the interiors of Raigan's hallway, bedroom and study which were shot on Stage 9. The painting hanging in the Raigan House where Sally is trying to force Arthur Curtis to sign the papers is the same painting hanging on the wall in the Sturka House in "Third From the Sun." The same painting makes an appearance in Mr. Penell's suite in "The Four of Us Are Dying."

Originally Serling intended to use the following for the trailer, but it was considered too lengthy:

"Mr. Richard Matheson lends us his fine writing talents when we bring you a unique and most arresting story of a movie actor who finds himself on that thin line between what is real and what is a dream. Mr. Howard Duff stars in 'World of Difference,' which I think you'll discover is a television play of difference, too. Very odd, very exciting, with an ending almost impossible to foresee. That's next week, a journey into The Twilight Zone. Bring your imagination. That's all that's required. Thank you and good night."

Ida Lupino, who starred in "The Sixteen Millimeter Shrine," was in real life married to Howard Duff. After having watched this film telecast, she confessed to Serling her love for Duff's performance – admittedly prejudiced because she felt she had never seen her husband in better form on camera. She requested in writing to buy a copy of a 16 mm print so that, as she explained, some day be able to show it to their daughter, Bridget. Lupino had good reason for concern about Duff's performance. He had lost eight pounds while doing his first live television show on *Climax!* a few years before.

Curtis comments to his secretary about going on a vacation with his wife Saturday night to San Francisco. This is an in-joke as Howard Duff played the role of private detective Sam Spade on *The Adventures of Sam Spade* on the long-running radio program, which took place in San Francisco.

This episode also mirrored an article that had appeared in *Time* magazine years before, about a man who got up one morning, looked into the mirror and didn't recognize himself because he had some strange disease that affected him mentally.

There were a few viewers who did not catch the ending and wrote to Serling and CBS asking for an explanation. Serling forwarded their letters to Richard Matheson, explaining, "these are a couple of many who want egg in their beer. Not satisfied with being entertained, they insist on understanding. You're lucky, old friend. At least eight of mine on the series have resulted in similar reaction. If you can drop these people a note, it would be appreciated."

> The stairway that Jerry runs down was located on Stage 9. The same stairway makes an appearance in Wickwire's house in "Elegy." The same stairway can be seen in the San Francisco hotel lobby in the *One Step Beyond* episode, "Earthquake," initial telecast on January 12, 1960.

---

* The Thunderbird was a studio car rented for $5.00 for the one hour of shooting.

Set Decoration Production Costs
Interior of Curtis' Office $600
Exterior of the Sound Stage $25
Exterior of the Studio Streets $25
Exterior of the Suburban Street $55
Exterior of the Raigan House $75
Interior of the Raigan House $150
Interior of the Raigan Bedroom $125
Exterior of the Studio Gate $25
Total $1,080

This *Twilight Zone* episode was parodied on *Saturday Night Live*, with the cast of the original *Star Trek* television series in denial, when forced to confront their show's cancellation. In the episode titled "Reality Takes a Holiday" (initially telecast in April of 1992) on *Eerie, Indiana*, Marshall Teller discovers the world he knows was purely fiction, and everyone he grew up with was a fictional character on a television series, who refer to him by a different name. He spends much of his time trying to find a way back to the life he knew, before submitting to the alternate reality. Steven King's short story, "Umney's Last Case," features a variation-on-a-theme compared to this *Twilight Zone* episode. Author King confessed once that Matheson and *The Twilight Zone* were two of many influences.

On May 18, 1995, an episode of the television sitcom *Mad About You* presented a salute to this episode of *The Twilight Zone* in a script titled "Up in Smoke." In this episode, Helen Hunt and Paul Reiser, playing the roles of Jamie and Paul Buchman, celebrate their third anniversary at the ritzy Twilight Room and soon discover that all evidence of their true existence has disappeared, and no one recognizes them.

Production #3621 "LONG LIVE WALTER JAMESON" (Initial telecast: March 18, 1960)

© Cayuga Productions, Inc., March 17, 1960, LP16339 (in notice: 1959)
Dates of Rehearsal: October 1 and 2, 1959
Dates of Filming: October 5, 6, 7 and 8, 1959
Shooting script dated: October 1, 1959

Producer and Secretary: $660.00
Lloyd Rogers Director: $1,000.00
Unit Manager and Secretary: $520.00
Agents Commission: $5,185.55
Below the line charges (M-G-M): $22,001.10
Total Production Costs: $42,726.66

Story and Secretary: $2,145.00
Cast: $6,496.34
Production Fee: $750.00
Legal and Accounting: $250.00
Below the line charges (other): $3,718.67

Cast: Charles Arrigo (student #3); Brad Broun (student #4); Geri Chatis (student #1); Paul Denton (student #6); Beverly Englander (student #2); David Harrell (student #5); Dody Heath (Susanna Kittridge); Phil Kaufman (student #7); Kevin McCarthy (Professor Walter Jameson); Bob McCord (bit part); Edgar Stehli (Professor Samuel Kittridge); and Estelle Winwood (Laurette Bowen).

Stock Music Cues: Main Title (by Bernard Herrmann, :40); Gaudiamus Igitur (traditional, :18); Composite Track #2 – Eerie Nightmare (by Lucien Moraweck, :22); Shock Harmonica (by Fred Steiner, :12); Dramatic Scene in New England (by Rene Garriguenc, :08); Composite Track #2 – Eerie Nightmare (by Moraweck, :10); Eerie Dream #2 (by Moraweck, :39, :13, and :47); Harp Shockers (by Steiner, :07); Shock Harmonica (by Steiner, :07); Composite Track #2 – Eerie Nightmare (by Moraweck, :15); Silent Flight – Dark Room (by Jerry Goldsmith, 1:13); Anxiety – Suspense (by Garriguenc, :56 and :57); Eerie Dream #2 (by Moraweck, :22); Shock Harmonics (by Steiner, :11 and :11); Hope – Walt Whitman Suite (by Herrmann, :56); Dream Sequence Loop E, C &E #3 (anonymous, :35 and :22); Shock Chords (by Moraweck, :08); Eerie Dream #2 (by Moraweck, 1:03); and End Title (by Herrmann, :39).

Director of Photography: George T. Clemens, a.s.c.
Art Directors: George W. Davis and William Ferrari
Set Decorations: Henry Grace and Rudy Butler
Makeup: William Tuttle
Teleplay by Charles Beaumont

Production Manager: Ralph W. Nelson
Film Editor: Bill Mosher
Assistant Director: Edward Denault
Casting Director: Mildred Gusse
Sound: Franklin Milton and Jean Valentino
Directed by Anton M. Leader

"You're looking at act one, scene one, of a nightmare. One not restricted to witching hours and dark, rain-swept nights. Professor Walter Jameson, popular beyond words, who talks of the past as if it were the present, who conjures up the dead as if they were alive. In the view of this man, Professor Samuel Kittridge, Walter Jameson has access to knowledge that couldn't come out of a volume of history, but rather from a book on black magic, which is to say that this nightmare begins at noon."

Plot: Professor Walter Jameson has become popular with the students of American history at the university because of the graphic details he displays in his lectures, almost as if he lived through the time periods he discusses. Professor Samuel Kittridge's daughter, Susanna, is engaged to Jameson, so the professor keeps a keen eye on Jameson. Kittridge presents Jameson with damning evidence proving the history professor is older than he claims. Jameson, backed in a corner, is forced to confess he's over 2,000 years old, thanks to an alchemist who granted his wish. He explains to Kittridge that immortality is a curse, not a blessing. All of his loved ones age as he remains young, and so will Susanna. Late that evening, Jameson returns home to find his past catching up to him – an old woman who was once his wife saw his engagement announcement in the paper. Out of anger, she shoots him with a gun and then flees from the scene of the crime. Kittridge arrives, having heard the gunshot, only to find Jameson aging swiftly into 2,000 years of dust and decay, leaving only the clothes behind to tell the tale.

"Last stop on a long journey, as yet another human being returns to the vast nothingness that is the beginning and into the dust that is always the end."

Trailer: *"Next week the culprit is Charles Beaumont, the gentleman responsible for a story unlike any you've ever seen. You talk of immortality – the business of being able to live for as long as one wants. Well next week you'll see Kevin McCarthy at the tail end of a life that's gone on for 2,000 years. The play is called 'Long Live Walter Jameson,' on The Twilight Zone."*

Set Decoration Production Costs
Interior of the Classroom and Hallway $300
Exterior of Jamesons House and Street $100
Interior of the Kittridge House $125
Interior of Jameson's Study $200
Total $725

Trivia, etc. The original title of this script and throughout production was "Forever and a Day." The title was not changed until months after filming was completed. Originally this episode was to be filmed in three days, but it took an extra day to complete production – mainly because of the time involved to construct the proper aging process in Jameson's study.

Originally, William Tuttle conceived the effect of Jameson aging by using a second person in makeup, actor Lloyd Rogers, for a progressive lap-dissolve sequence applied in previous movies such as *The Wolf Man* (1941). The cost for makeup for this scene was $184. After trial and error, this idea was quickly dismissed when another option was applied and exercised – changing colored filters on the lens, enabling the make-up to be gradually exposed and visible during the transformation scene. This same process was applied years before in the 1932 version of *Dr. Jekyll and Mr. Hyde*. The cost of makeup for this transformation scene was a total of $15.50.

"The ten or fifteen seconds on the screen when I age was done with red and green lines on my face," recalled McCarthy. "We shot the film in black and white with red and green filters. When we switched the color filters, the lines that were obscured [then] appeared on the screen and it looks like I age without any special effects. The man who did the makeup on me that day told me when he did the same trick for *Dr. Jekyll and Mr. Hyde*, it cost the studio $5,000. Now he was doing it for *The Twilight Zone* and it was costing them $25,000!"

The opening scene, an exterior of Collins University, was stock footage purchased at a bargain, according to a letter penned by Buck Houghton. The exterior of Jameson's house was filmed on the old Andy Hardy street, featured in numerous episodes of *The Twilight Zone*. The exterior of Jame-

Blooper! Jameson implies to his students that General Sherman ordered the Union Army to set fire to buildings in Atlanta, September 1864, and even started the fires himself. The correct statement should have been that the Confederates, in blowing up the ammunition depots, accidentally set fire to the remainder of the city. If Charles Beaumont had only remembered the facts from Hollywood – the actual situation was correctly depicted in *Gone With the Wind* (1939).

The blooper did not go unnoticed. Numerous viewers wrote to both Serling and CBS, pointing out the mistake, and as Serling himself explained in one reply, "The script in question was written by Charles Beaumont and very likely should have been checked for accuracy before a judgment like the one made was allowed to slip through. Since I don't happen to be a Civil War buff, I'm not at all knowledgeable in this area; but I'm disturbed that any misstatement of fact would occur on my show."

son's house is the same Howard Duff approaches (but never enters) in the first season episode "A World of Difference." It was known as the Philadelphia Story House, because it was the same house that Cary Grant pushed Katharine Hepburn to the ground in the motion picture of the same name.

Reprinted below is the opening narration that was originally intended to be used, but discarded because of the length:

"There are some stories . . . that by their nature . . . because their ingredients add up to nothing but a question mark . . . must begin this way: once upon a time . . . (Into the beginning of Jameson's lecture) So this story must begin once upon a time . . . (a pause) there was a professor named Jameson who talked of the past as if it happened yesterday: who talked of dead things and times and places and men . . . as if he'd known them personally. And while most of the student body found Professor Jameson's lectures an excursion into a new kind of excitement . .

Kevin McCarthy poses for a publicity shot. Photo provided by Kevin McCarthy.

. There were those like Professor Samuel Kittridge who felt a gnawing, disturbing, disquieting sense of wonder as to the youngish looking man in the front of the class room who could lecture about the events of a hundred years past . . . as if he had lived through them. It conjured up a theory that by rights should be left within the pages of a book on black magic . . . but for some, and particularly for Professor Kittredge . . . it loomed up in the room like a kind of specter, a theory that was more like a nightmare. A simple question . . . that for the sake of sanity best remain unanswered. How old was the youngish looking professor who spoke so knowledgeably about the past?

Serling originally intended to use the following trailer, but it was considered too lengthy:

"Charles Beaumont is the culprit next week – the gentleman responsible for a story unlike any you've ever seen. We talk of immortality – the business of being able to live for as long as one wants. Survive wars, famines, accidents – and give battle to the worst enemy longevity has – old age. Next week you'll see Kevin McCarthy at the tail end of a life that's gone on for two thousand years. A play called 'Forever And a Day," and what's more . . . strange as it may sound . . . I think you'll believe it. That's The Twilight Zone, next week at the same stand and in the same shadow land of the different, the bizarre and the unexpected. Thank you and good night."

In the episode "Curiosity Killed," on *Tales from the Crypt*, initially telecast September 16, 1992, actor Kevin McCarthy played the role of Jack, a man whose disagreeable wife wanted the secret of eternal youth. After she kills him with a poison, causing him to turn to dust, she finds herself the victim of an unexpected side effect. The plot obviously mirrored this *Twilight Zone* episode, including McCarthy's horrific demise of aging away to dust. The director was Elliot Silverstein, who took helm of a few *Twilight Zone* productions.

Production #3613 "PEOPLE ARE ALIKE ALL OVER"
(Initial telecast: March 25, 1960)

© Cayuga Productions, Inc., March 24, 1960, LP16340 (in notice: 1959)
Dates of Rehearsal: August 10 and 11, 1959
Dates of Filming: August 12, 13 and 14, 1959
Script #13 dated: July 10, 1959, with revised pages August 4, 5 and 6, 1959.
Revised script dated: August 5 and 6, 1959

Producer and Secretary: $660.00
Director: $1,250.00
Unit Manager and Secretary: $520.00
Agents Commission: $5,185.55
Below the line charges (M-G-M): $28,594.36
Total Production Costs: $55,454,64

Story and Secretary: $5,110.10
Cast: $6,947.48
Production Fee: $750.00
Legal and Accounting: $250.00
Below the line charges (other): $6,187.15

Cast: Paul Comi (Warren Marcusson); Vernon Gray (Martian #3); Roddy McDowall (Samuel Conrad); Byron Morrow (Martian #1); Susan Oliver (Teenya); and Vic Perrin (Martian #2).

Stock Music Cues: Main Title (by Bernard Herrmann, :40); Time Suspense – Outer Space Suite (by Herrmann, :20); Zaphyr 1 (by Marius Constant, :24); Moonscape – Outer Space Suite (by Herrmann, :04); House on K Street – Fade In (by Herrmann, :07); Space Drift – Outer Space Suite (by Herrmann, 2:09); Brouillards (by Constant, :45); Rain Clouds – Western Suite (by Herrmann, 1:22); Utility Cues (by Bruce Campbell, :06); Zephyr 1 (by Constant, :26); House on K Street – Fade In (by Herrmann, :09); Light Rain (by Constant, 1:02); Passage of Time #6 (by Rene Garriguenc, :04); Tycho – Outer Space Suite (by Herrmann, 1:02); Pasage of Time #16 (by Garriguenc, :04); Spinoza 1 (by Constant, 1:15 and :14); Light Rain (by Constant, :01); Au Crepuscle (by Rene Challan, :55); Brouillards (by Constant, :38); Mistral (by Constant, :04); Light Rain (by Constant, 1:10); Build-Up #2 – Man of Decision (by Moraweck, :10); Brouillards (by Constant, :39); and End Title (by Herrmann, :39).

Director of Photography: George T.
    Clemens, a.s.c.
Art Directors: George W. Davis and
    William Ferrari
Set Decorations: Henry Grace and Rudy Butler

Production Manager: Ralph W. Nelson
Film Editor: Fred Maguire
Assistant Director: Edward Denault
Casting Director: Mildred Gusse
Sound: Franklin Milton and Philip Mitchell

Directed by Mitchell Leisen
Teleplay by Rod Serling, based on the short story "Brothers Beyond the Void" by Paul W. Fair-

man, originally published in the March 1952 of *Fantastic Adventures*.

"You're looking at a species of flimsy little two-legged animals with extremely small heads whose name is 'man.' Warren Marcusson, age thirty-five. Samuel A. Conrad, age thirty-one. They're taking a highway into space, man unshackling himself and sending his tiny, groping fingers up into the unknown. Their destination is Mars, and in just a moment we'll land there with them."

Plot: Two intrepid space explorers venture into outer space to plant a flag on planet Mars. Though Marcusson has been trained for the trip, Conrad, a biologist with an inquiring scientific mind, would have preferred to remain behind on Mother Earth. When the spacecraft crash lands on Mars, Marcusson is

Roddy McDowall and Susan Oliver pose for a publicity shot against the landscape of Mars.

severely injured leaving Conrad to sit alone like a frightened rabbit. Someone or something is tapping on the ship from the outside. Marcusson pleads with Conrad to open the door. He has a sixth sense that outside, on the landscape of Mars, there are people and firmly believes that when God made human beings, they were made from a fixed formula. Marcusson, however, dies before learning the identity of the hosts – a race of culturally advanced human beings. After the Martians manage to open the ship, they reassure Conrad that they mean him no harm. To show good will, they bury Marcusson's body and then prepare a place for him not too different from an Earth dwelling. At first, Conrad feels at home with his new surroundings – till he discovers to his horror that he has become a caged animal for an alien zoo. The sign outside his cage reads "Earth Creature in its Native Habitat."

"Specie of animal brought back alive. Interesting similarity in physical characteristics to human beings – in head, trunk, arms, legs, hands, feet. Very tiny undeveloped brain. Comes from primitive planet named Earth. Calls himself Samuel Conrad. And he will remain here in his cage with the running water and the electricity and the central heat as long as he lives. Samuel Conrad . . . has found the Twilight Zone."

Trailer: *"Next week an excursion to Mars with Roddy McDowall and Paul Comi, two men trying to prove a point – a simple proposition that men are alike all over. And on Mars they discover that this is just whistling in the dark. People are not alike and next week on the Twilight Zone you'll see why. I hope you'll be with us. Thank you and good night."*

Trivia, etc. In early March 1959, Serling expressed an interest in the short story, and Fred Engel of Ashley-Steiner dug into the ownership to report that the story was owned by Dudley Pictures. Carl

Dudley was out of the country, so when he returned in mid-April, an offer for purchase was made. Dudley, however, explained that he had used the story as part of a trilogy screenplay he owned, and would not sell the short story for a cheap price. In April of 1959, Dudley, who represented author Paul W. Fairman, was asking too high a price for Cayuga to pay. Houghton asked Serling to forget the story and look over other possible literary properties, but Serling strongly insisted on adapting this episode for *The Twilight Zone* for any price and by any means.

Negotiations were exchanged and eventually the screen rights was purchased – the most costly of the season at $2,500. Additional costs included the $2,250 fee Serling received for drafting the teleplay, the $360.10 for secretarial fees, and Serling's $750-per-script supervision fee as agreed upon under his contract. Total = $5,860.10. (The second most expensive story was "The Hitch-Hiker" which totaled $5,204.)

Before filming commenced on *The Twilight Zone*, and shortly before General Foods signed on as an alternate sponsor, Serling composed a one-page plot summary titled "Human Beings Are Alike All Over," based on Fairman's short story. In Serling's earliest of adaptations, the humanities professor is the only passenger, though he did have a conversation with another man at the launching site shortly before lift-off. He lands safely on Mars and finds himself greeted by two very human-looking figures who are somewhat smaller than he is and have no language. Gradually, through drawings and mathematics, a level of understanding is achieved. He is escorted to a Martian lab, where overnight the Martians construct a perfect replica of an Earth home, complete with fireplace, dishwasher, freezer and refrigerator. When he turns around to thank his hosts, he realizes that he has been left alone. That is when he discovers he is locked inside After pulling aside the heavy drapes that cover the big picture window in front of the living room, he discovers he is the newest addition to the Martian zoo. The Martians are certainly no different than Earthlings.

Revised pages of the script dated August 5 featured a different opening narration, revealing a difference in the age of the two lead characters:

"You're looking at a highway into space soon to be traveled by the flimsy little two-legged animal with the extremely small head whose name is man and who sends his tiny, groping fingers up into the unknown. (a pause) *Man unshackling himself and heading for Mars!* (a pause) *Samuel A. Conrad, age thirty-five; Warren Marcusson, age thirty-one. They are the first to try. And in a moment . . . we'll travel with them."*

The July 1, 1959 progress report calls this script "Brothers Beyond the Void," but the title was changed before the teleplay went to film. The interior and exterior of the rocket ship cost Cayuga $3,500 to produce, reusing props from the M-G-M lot. The interior of the wrecked ship included registering gauges in the background (described as a duplicate of the Paramount Studio logo), which were originally props from the Krell laboratory from the 1956 motion picture, *Forbidden Planet*.

The fence with the barbed-wire top at which Marcusson and Conrad discuss their inevitable future in the opening scene is the same featured in the opening scene of "Third From the Sun." In the former episode, as Sturka left the plant, an "Exit Only" sign behind one of the security guards was reused for the opening shot of this *Twilight Zone* adventure, repositioned, while the "No Smoking" sign remained where it was.

The exterior of the Martian landscape was actually the huge painted cyclorama of the desert landscape of Altair 4, which was originally created for *Forbidden Planet* and took up an entire sound stage at M-G-M.

"I worked with Roddy a number of times. We became good friends," recalled Paul Comi. "I first met Roddy on *The Twilight Zone*. Very intelligent. I was able to pick that up within minutes of our first meeting. He told me stories of the movies he had done before. The director, Mitch Leisen, was a scenic designer for the great Cecil B. DeMille and he also spent some time sharing stories with us. The backdrop used for the Mars landscape was not a flat painting. It was a cyclorama. That helped capture the depth of the landscape on film."

Set Decoration Production Costs
Exterior of the Launching Pad $450
Interior and Exterior of the Rocket $3,500
Interior of the Typical Home $650
Exterior of the Picture Window $350
Total $4,950

Susan Oliver recalled in an issue of *Starlog*, "That was lots of fun. Roddy used to take me to lunch at M-G-M. He had practically grown up there. He used to do all of these hilarious impressions of big movie moguls. Rod Serling was very special. He was a nice, gentle man, very modest and self-effacing. Mitchell Leisen had been a costumer as well as a film director. He picked my costume, a Greek gown, for me to wear as a Martian. He said, 'You can only be so futuristic, and then it comes back to what the classic is.'"

After watching the initial telecast, Walter Chizinsky, Ph. D., Department of Biology at Bennett College in Millbrook, New York, corrected Serling for his repeated grammatical error in this episode, when referring to the singular and plural of species, which would become engraved on Serling's consciousness.

A considerable amount of music featured in this episode originated from the "Outer Space Suite," a musical composition deliberately created in 1957 for CBS' music library. Bernard Herrmann did not compose every segment of the suite, but he has been given credit for authorship in numerous publications.

When this episode was rerun on July 27, 1962, *The Los Angeles Times* featured a color picture advertising this episode.

Production #3628 "EXECUTION" (Initial telecast: April 1, 1960)
Copyright Registration: © Cayuga Productions, Inc., March 31, 1960, LP16772
Date of Rehearsal: February 15 and 16, 1960
Dates of Filming: February 17, 18 and 19, 1960
Script #30 dated: December 28, 1959
Shooting script dated: February 10, 1960

Producer and Secretary: $675.00
Director: $1,250.00
Unit Manager and Secretary: $395.00
Agents Commission: $5,185.55
Below the line charges (M-G-M): $32,359.05
Total Production Costs: $53,149.32

Story and Secretary: $2,865.00
Cast: $5,314.01
Production Fee: $750.00
Legal and Accounting: $250.00
Below the line charges (other): $4,105.71

Cast: Joe Haworth (the cowboy); Russell Johnson (Professor George Manion); Richard Karlan (the bartender); Jon Lormer (the reverend); George Mitchell (the old man); Fay Roope (the judge); Albert Salmi (Joe Caswell); and Than Wyenn (Johnson).

Stock Music Cues: Main Title (by Bernard Herrmann, :40); Prelude–Desert Suite (by Herrmann, :50 and :13); Pursuit Theme (by Herrmann, :25); Shock Harmonics (by Fred Steiner, :28); The Cell (by Herrmann, :05); Harp Stings (by Steiner, :10); The Mesa-Western Saga (by Herrmann, :06); Ran Afoul (by Jerry Goldsmith, :10); Prelude–Desert Suite (by Herrmann, :04 and :28); The Ambush (by Herrmann, 1:08 and 2:11); Climactic Close (by Herrmann, :16); Collector's Item Main Title (by Herrmann, :04); Peeping Creeps (by Goldsmith, :29); Shock Therapy #3 (by Rene Garriguenc, :07); End Title (by Ernest Gold, 1:16); Gunsmoke-Western Saga (by Herrmann, :25); Turkish Delight (by Eric Cook, :21); Opening (by Gold, :21); Wild Knife Chord (by Herrmann, :10); Climactic Close (by Herrmann, :17); Harp Stings (by Steiner, :11); Shock Harmonics (by Steiner, :17); The Ambush (by Herrmann, :46); Shock Harmonics (by Steiner, :08); and End Title (by Herrmann, :39).

Director of Photography: George T. Clemens, a.s.c.
Art Directors: George W. Davis and Merrill Pye
Set Decorations: Henry Grace and Keogh Gleason
Directed by David Orrick McDearmon

Production Manager: Ralph W. Nelson
Film Editor: Joseph Gluck, a.c.e.
Assistant Director: Kurt Neumann
Casting Director: Mildred Gusse
Sound: Franklin Milton and Philip Mitchell

Teleplay written by Rod Serling, based on an original short story proposal by George Clayton Johnson.

"Commonplace, if somewhat grim, unsocial event known as a necktie party. The guest of dishonor – a cowboy named Joe Caswell, just a moment away from a rope, a short dance several feet off the ground, and then . . . the dark eternity of all evil men. Mr. Joe Caswell who, when the good Lord passed out a conscience, a heart, a feeling for fellow men, must have been out for a beer and missed out. Mr. Joe Caswell, in the last quiet moment of a violent life!"

Plot: Eighty years in the past, Joseph Caswell is hanged for murder, but wakes to find himself in the present, New York City. A professor of science explains that he is experimenting with time travel, and Caswell has become the unwilling subject of his experiment. Though Caswell cannot fathom the principles involved, the professor wonders if he made a mistake, having seen the rope marks etched into his neck. The professor doesn't like Caswell's looks and theorizes that he may have put a 19th century primitive into a 20th century jungle. In a confrontation between the men about right and wrong, law and justice, Caswell murders the professor and runs out into the city streets to make an escape. Dodging traffic and panicking from the noise and flashing lights, Caswell smashes a jukebox, shoots up a television set and commits another murder before returning to the professor's laboratory. Pleading to the dead body for help, Caswell is interrupted by an armed robber, who has intentions of his own. The two men struggle, and the robber ultimately strangles Caswell with the rope connected to the window curtains. Alone, the robber sets out to find a wall safe. Accidentally activating the time machine, the robber is sent back to the exact moment where Caswell was picked up . . . at the end of a noose.

"This is November . . . 1880. The aftermath of a necktie party. The victim's name, Paul Johnson, a minor-league criminal and the taker of another human life. No comment on his death save this . . . justice can span years; retribution is not subject to a calendar. Tonight's case in point . . . in the Twilight Zone."

Trailer: *"This may look like some kind of kooky greenhouse. Actually, it happens to be a conveyance, a mode of travel – time travel. And next week you'll see Albert Salmi take an extended journey from 1880 to 1960. I hope then next week you'll be able to take another walk with us into the Twilight Zone. [Serling vanishes] Hey! Where did everybody go?"*

Trivia, etc. Ten days after the CBS editing department received the script, William H. Tankersley, director of editing, sent a report dated January 29, 1960, noting a few concerns and suggestions. Among them: the opening scene in which Caswell referred to the Bible as "that book." CBS requested Serling change the speech to substitute their concern with "your preachin'," but Serling made no change. To compromise, Serling made sure to take out the line that described Caswell spitting, because the network wanted to "avoid distastefulness," or at least, avoid spitting on a tight close-up or while facing the camera.

The rest of the network's concerns were taken into consideration, and Serling made the necessary changes. Among these was the line, "I've been to hell and back" in Caswell's speech, and changed at CBS's suggestion to "I've been to hell and now I'm back." The scenes involving Caswell shooting the driver of a car, and the robber strangling Caswell to death were exercised with caution. "We were informed these scenes will not display excessive violence or morbidity," CBS requested. Lastly, CBS asked Serling and Houghton to show no commercial identification in the bar, on the jukebox or on the television set.

Two incidents that neither could have been foreseen nor avoided (a power failure on the back lot at night and a sudden actor unavailability), put production over a few hours. Actor Neville Brand was originally scheduled to play the role of Caswell. He even attended the rehearsals. The morning this episode was slated to go before the cameras, Brand phoned in sick. Buck Houghton made a few phone calls and secured Albert Salmi for the role.

"I met Albert Salmi on the set," recalled George Clayton Johnson. "He was very quiet, but I think that was because he was bottling up all his emotions for the role. He was a method actor. After seeing what he could do on the set when they filmed, I knew he was a wonderful actor."

During the hanging sequence in the beginning, Salmi grabbed the rope and held tight to it, so when the camera picked up his feet dangling in the air, it would appear as if he was hanged by the neck. The sequence was only done twice – Salmi told the director after the second time that he wasn't sure if his arms could hold him up long enough to do it a third time. The shadow against the Earth was not really Salmi's shadow, but specifically created to help create the illusion of the vanishing effect.

When Caswell runs through the streets, deafened by all the noise, the theater marquee advertises Doris Day in *Please Don't Eat the Daisies*, which was released theatrically six weeks after this episode was filmed. A movie poster for *The Last Time I Saw Paris*, which was released in theaters in 1955, was displayed outside the movie theater. Both films were released through M-G-M Studios, where this episode was filmed.

"I did two terrific episodes of *Twilight Zone*," recalled Russell Johnson for *Filmfax* magazine. "As far as my TV favorites are concerned, it's my *Twilight Zone*. It was considered a 'prestige' show to work on, so I did one and it went well. A year later I got a lead role in another episode . . . [Rod Serling] would come down on the set each day just to see how things were going and to chat. He was a very nice man. He, as a matter of fact, came from Binghamton, New York, not far from where I was born. So we had a little bit in common in terms of talking about the old neighborhood. He was a busy guy. Rod would come down for maybe 15 or 20 minutes in the morning and then go back to his office and pound at the typewriter. Then, he'd show up again at some point in the afternoon after they'd seen the daily rushes. I had no long contact with him, but he was certainly an agreeable, dedicated, and driven man."

Serling's original trailer was never used:

"This item may somewhat resemble an ultra-modern greenhouse. Actually it happens to be a conveyance – that's right – a mode of travel – time travel. And next week you'll see Albert Salmi take an extended journey over land, sea and calendar – from 1880 to 1960. This one we recommend most highly, it's quite unusual. I hope then, next week, you'll be able to take another walk with us into The Twilight Zone."

After the first 26 episodes were filmed, a second batch of episodes was produced to round out the first season. This episode marked the first of the 10 new pictures to be shot. After production was completed, the total budget would come in at about $2,000 over what was originally projected, combining above and below-the-line elements.

The music playing over the jukebox, which Caswell interrupts with the bullets from his gun, is Eric Cook's "Turkish Delight," which originated from the CBS stock music library. This same music can be heard in two other episodes: the juke box in "Where is Everybody?" and the record player Corey uses in his shack in "The Lonely."

Production #3630 "THE BIG, TALL WISH" (Initial telecast: April 8, 1960)
Copyright Registration: © Cayuga Productions, Inc., April 7, 1960, LP16773
Dates of Rehearsal: February 19 and 22, 1960
Dates of Filming: February 23, 24 and 25, 1960
Script #28 dated: December 21, 1959, with revised pages dated January 12, February 12 and 22, 1960
Shooting script dated: February 22, 1960

Producer and Secretary: $675.00	Story and Secretary: $2,365.00
Director: $950.00	Cast: $5,377.05
Unit Manager and Secretary: $525.00	Production Fee: $750.00
Agents Commission: $5,185.55	Legal and Accounting: $250.00
Below the line charges (M-G-M): $21,508.31	Below the line charges (other): $5,867.49
Total Production Costs: $43,453.40	

Cast: Walter Burke (prizefighter assistant); Ivan Dixon (Bolie Jackson); Kim Hamilton (Frances Temple); Charles Hovarth (Bolie's opponent); Carl McIntire (the announcer); Steven Perry (Henry Temple); Henry Scott (Harvey Thomas); Dan Terranova (Rodie); and Frankie Van (the referee).

Original Music Score Composed and Conducted by Jerry Goldsmith (Score No. CPN5896):
Main Title (by Bernard Herrmann, :40); Bolie Jackson (1:13); Good Friends (:10); The Cruel Past (2:04); Concrete World (1:04); Broken Fist (1:34); Knock Out (:16); The Magic (:33); Meeting on

the Roof (1:11); The Champ (1:21); The Realization (2:49); and End Title (by Herrmann, :39).

Director of Photography: George T. Clemens, a.s.c.	Production Manager: Ralph W. Nelson
	Film Editor: Bill Mosher
Art Directors: George W. Davis and Merrill Pye	Assistant Director: Kurt Neumann
Set Decorations: Henry Grace and Keough Gleason	Casting Director: Mildred Gusse
Sound: Franklin Milton and Philip Mitchell	Directed by Ronald Winston.
Teleplay by Rod Serling	

"In this corner of the universe, a prizefighter named Bolie Jackson, one hundred eighty-three pounds and an hour and a half away from a comeback at St. Nick's Arena. Mr. Bolie Jackson, who by the standards of his profession, is an aging, over-the-hill relic of what was, and who now sees a reflection of a man who has left too many pieces of his youth in too many stadiums for too many years before too many screaming people. Mr. Bolie Jackson, who might do well to look for some gentle magic in the hard-surfaced glass that stares back at him."

Plot: A tired old prizefighter named Bolie Jackson wears a scrapbook on his face, with each scar telling a story of past fights that Bolie cares to forget. In an effort to redeem his good name, Bolie sets out to fight the great Consiglio at the St. Nicholas Arena. Bolie's biggest fan is a little boy named Henry, who, with a head full of dreams, intends to make a big, tall wish so his idol will win the bout. Before entering the ring, Bolie smashes four of his knuckles, a sure guarantee that he will go down before the third round. Back at the apartment, young Henry watches the fight on television. When Bolie gets knocked out, Henry grasps at the television screen and makes a big, tall wish. Call it fate or call it magic . . . Bolie and Consiglio switch places. Everyone congratulates Bolie for his winning, but when he confronts young Henry, the boxer learns the truth – Henry made a wish and it was granted. Bolie, however, doesn't believe in magic and swears to the kid that the world is made of cement, heartache and scars. The boy cries, explaining that magic only happens if you believe in it. Since Bolie swears that he cannot believe in magic, the prizefighters switch places in the ring and Bolie is carried out. Returning to the apartment house, the boxer confronts Henry, to discover the boy is still proud of him, but the lad has decided to stop making wishes. He no longer believes in magic. Bolie wonders if maybe the problem in this world is there aren't enough people who believe . . .

"Mr. Bolie Jackson, a hundred and eighty-three pounds, who left a second chance lying in a heap on a rosin-splattered canvas at St. Nick's Arena. Mr. Bolie Jackson, who shares the most common ailment of all men . . . the strange and perverse disinclination to believe in a miracle. The kind of miracle to come from the mind of a little boy perhaps only to be found . . . in the Twilight Zone."

Trailer: *The man who lives in this tenement is an aging fighter named Bolie Jackson. Over the hill at age 36 from leaving too much of himself in too many arenas, for too many years before too many screaming people. And next week he looks for a miracle and he finds it in a little boy. On the Twilight Zone next week, 'The Big Tall Wish.' Something very, very special. I hope we'll see you then."*

Trivia, etc. For the first time since "Requiem for a Heavyweight," Serling again turned his attention to boxing in "The Big, Tall Wish," a poignant story of the relationship between a washed-out prizefighter and a 10-year-old boy. Serling admitted the violent sport lent itself ideally to dramatic situations. "It's the contradiction inherent in the sport that I find fascinating," he explained. "When you talk to ex-fighters, you discover they're a breed of soft-spoken, gentle men. They expend so much violence beating each other's brains out that they have no antagonisms left outside the ring – they're serene people."

Serling's interest in boxing dates back to his childhood in upstate New York and memories of a fading Jack Dempsey training for a comeback at Saratoga Lake. The same day Rod Serling graduated from high school, he enlisted in the U.S. Army 11th Airborne Division as a paratrooper. During basic training, he took up boxing. Fighting in the then catch weight division, he enjoyed a 17-bout winning streak. In the 18th fight, a professional boxer was brought in who broke his nose in two places, sent him to defeat in the third round, and thoroughly convinced him to give up boxing. His personal misadventure didn't dull his taste for the sport.

One fighter dwarfed all others in Serling's memory. That was Joe Louis, whom the playwright regarded as "the greatest fighter, pound-for-pound, who ever lived." While recognizing the sport's evils, Serling refused to subject his audiences to pedantic moralizing on it shortcomings. Instead, he saw its finer side. "A good fighter is a piece of art," Serling once commented.

"My idea of a hero was Joe Louis because he beat up white folks and because he did it with dignity, a kind of crude grace, the way he'd always step back a little before bombing into them," remarked Ivan Dixon, who played the role of Bolie in this boxing-themed episode. Serling was on the set a few hours during the filming. When Dixon smashed his hand into the concrete wall, symbolizing Bolie's remark that the world is made of concrete, Serling insisted that Dixon shake his arm and fist slightly like an old-timer, to add to the realism of the pain.

Supposedly boxer Archie Moore was slated to play the lead but the casting attempt failed. Ironically, months later, when Moore was knocked out by Yvon Durelle in 1961, he publicly described his knockout: "Man, I was in the Twilight Zone!"

In the earliest draft of this script, Serling mentioned Bolie Jackson being 163 pounds, not 183, in the opening narration.

It was about this time that the NAACP (The National Association for the Advancement of Colored People) attacked the movie industry and the broadcasting networks, charging widespread discrimination in employment and grossly unfair portrayals of the Negro's role on the contemporary scene. Edward D. Warren, president of the Los Angeles chapter of the NAACP, warned that movie theatres and television studios might be picketed and that the charges might be turned over to the California Attorney General's office. The charges involved the television industry because a large portion of television series and anthologies were made by or at the movie studios.

"They will show a scene with a baseball crowd and you don't even see a single Negro," Mr. Warren commented. "This is ridiculous. You will see city street scenes and not a single Negro. We are not arguing for Negroes on this matter. We want treatment for Mexicans, Jews or any other group."

"Television, like its big sister, the motion picture, has been guilty of the sin of omission," remarked Serling in an interview about the time this episode was initially telecast. "Hungry for talent, desperate for the so-called 'new face,' constantly searching for a transfusion of new blood, it has overlooked a source of wondrous talent that resides under its nose. This is the Negro actor." Under Serling's guidance, the entire episode was filmed with a cast almost entirely composed of Negro actors.

Director Ronald Winston let the audience's hands tell the story of the fight in the ring – hands tensing around a microphone, hands shielding the eyes, hands grasping the coat sleeve of another, and so on. While few blows are exchanged in the ring, the attendance depicts the fight for the television audience.

To accomplish the shot from below the floor of the boxing ring looking up at the referee, part of the floor was replaced with a sheet of glass, and removed for camera shots looking down from above.

This episode went into production at an estimated savings of $4,957, combining above and below-the-line estimates. It finished shooting on Thursday night, right on budget hours as predicted.

To help publicize this episode, the April 2 issue of *The New York Amsterdam News*, the most influential Negro newspaper in the Greater New York area, featured an article about "The Big, Tall Wish." George Pitts, columnist of *The Pittsburgh Courier*, devoted his entire column of March 26 to an article Serling provided about this episode. *The Courier* had 14 editions around the country and it was carried in all of them.

A couple weeks after this telecast, the National Scholarship Service and Fund for Negro Students in New York sent Serling a letter, praising the episode, and asked if a donation to the non-profit organization could be made. Serling donated $25 to the cause on April 29. A week later, the Committee to Salvage Talent for Negro Actors also asked for the same request, and Serling also sent it a donation. (In December of 1961, he also made a donation to the NAACP.)

In 1961, *The Twilight Zone* received the annual Unity Award for "Outstanding Contributions to Better Race Relations." Two years later, CBS enacted a policy requesting television producers to incorporate a Negro actor in filmed television plays, even if the roles were as minor as background stand-ins. *The Twilight Zone* would join the ranks when, during the program's final two seasons, it began incorporating Negro actors in roles.

In "The Last Round," an episode of television's *One Step Beyond*, guest starring Charles Bronson, a poster is hanging on the wall in the arena manager's office promoting the Bolie Jackson and Consiglio bout. The reason for this was because both programs were filmed at M-G-M and "The Last Round" was filmed shortly after production for this *Twilight Zone* episode was completed.

Production #3632 "A NICE PLACE TO VISIT" (Initial telecast: April 15, 1960)
© Cayuga Productions, Inc., April 14, 1960, LP16774
Dates of Rehearsal: February 25 and 26, 1960
Dates of Filming: February 29, and March 1 and 2, 1960
Script #32 dated: February 2, 1960, with revised pages dated February 15 and 24, 1960.
Shooting script dated: February 24, 1960

Producer and Secretary: $675.00
Director: $1,250.00
Unit Manager and Secretary: $525.00
Agents Commission: $5,185.55
Below the line charges (M-G-M): $28,722.85
Total Production Costs: $48,737.26

Story and Secretary: $2,120.00
Cast: $6,364.00
Production Fee: $750.00
Legal and Accounting: $250.00
Below the line charges (other): $2,894.86

Cast: Larry Blyden (Rocky Valentine); Sebastian Cabot (Mr. Pip); John Close (the policeman); Barbara English (the dancing girl); Peter Hornsby (the crap dealer); Bob McCord (man who serves drinks); Bill Mullikin (the parking lot attendant); Nels Nelson (the midget policeman); Wayne Turner (the croupier); and Sandra Warner (the beautiful girl).

Stock Music Cues: Main Title (by Bernard Herrmann, :40); Lead-In F (by Herrmann, :44); Clue Hunt #2 (by Lucien Moraweck, :26); Raw Tragedy (by Rene Garriguenc, :16); Clue Hunt #2 (by Moraweck, :15); Raw Tragedy (by Garriguenc, :16); The Meadows – Western Suite (by Herrmann, :16); Naughty Doll (by Moraweck, :18); Signals – Outer Space Suite (by Herrmann, :05); Celeste Effects (anonymous, :07 and :05); Naughty Doll (by Moraweck, :19); Celeste Effects (anonymous, :05); Signals – Outer Space Suite (by Herrmann, :23); Celeste Effects (anonymous, :05); Naughty Doll (by Moraweck, :13); Cha Cha Cha Linda (by Garriguenc, :37); Naughty Doll (by Moraweck, :22 and :36); Space Drift – Outer Space Suite (by Herrmann, 1:41); Celeste Effects (anonymous, :06); Naughty Doll (by Moraweck, :14); Celeste Effects (anonymous, :05); Naughty Doll (by Moraweck, :19); The Fight (by Russ Garcia, :11); Signals – Outer Space Suite (by Herrmann, :16); Celeste Effects (anonymous, :06); and End Title (by Herrmann, :39).

Director of Photography: George T. Clemens, a.s.c.
Art Directors: George W. Davis and Merrill Pye
Set Decorations: Henry Grace and Keogh Gleason
Sound: Franklin Milton and Philip Mitchell
Teleplay by Charles Beaumont

Production Manager: Ralph W. Nelson
Film Editor: Joseph Gluck, a.c.e.
Assistant Director: Don Klune
Casting Director: Mildred Gusse
Directed by John Brahm

"Portrait of a man at work, the only work he's ever done, the only work he knows. His name is Henry Francis Valentine, but he calls himself 'Rocky,' because that's the way his life has been – rocky and perilous and uphill at a dead run all the way. He's tired now, tired of running or wanting, of waiting for the breaks that come to others but never to him, never to Rocky Valentine. A scared, angry little man. He thinks it's all over now but he's wrong. For Rocky Valentine, it's just the beginning."

Plot: A street punk and burglar named Rocky Valentine attempts to evade the police and finds himself shot for his troubles. He quickly wakes to find a bearded "guide" in an expensive suit standing over him, named Mr. Pip. Pip modestly explains to the criminal that he was shot and killed and is being summoned for the afterlife. This, however, offers privileges and luxuries branded with Rocky's approval. His own private domain and a pleasure palace stacked with beautiful women at his disposal. During his first few days, Rocky enjoys winning at the roulette wheel, the slot machine and the dice table. He soon feels compelled to lose a few games, because winning every hand isn't all it's cracked up to be. At the hall of records, Rocky reviews his past to find a reason for his rewards, but nothing good can be found, further puzzling him. After a month, Rocky finds himself bored – no excitement, no kicks. Knocking off a bank without any risk of getting caught is tiresome. Being a big guy with a chick isn't bragging rights when it's prearranged. Confronting Pip, Rocky explains that Heaven wasn't what he thought it was going to be, only to learn that he is in "the other place."

"A scared, angry little man who never got a break. Now he has everything he's ever wanted and he's going to have to live with it for eternity . . . in the Twilight Zone."

Trailer: *"Greetings from the low-rent district. Next week we follow the fortunes and misfortunes of Mr. Larry Blyden, who plays the role of one Rocky Valentine, an itinerant second-story man who was shot dead in an alley one night, then goes to his just rewards. This is why I'm here, being one of them. This one you can watch with a tongue in your cheek. It's called 'A Nice Place to Visit.' Next week, on The Twilight Zone."*

Trivia, etc. Rocky Valentine was depicted in this episode quite smoothly by actor Larry Blyden as a man with low class and an unsavory personality. William H. Tankersley, director of editing for CBS, received Beaumont's script titled "The Other Place," on February 3, 1960. On February 15, a report back to Serling requested many of Valentine's lines be changed or removed. The word "broad" was to be replaced with "doll" or "chick." When Rocky asks ". . . you wanna come in an' ball it up a little? . . . ," it was suggested to replace the word "ball" for "party," in order to give the audience "more clarity."

The word "stacked" when Rocky describes women to Pip, was requested by CBS to be replaced with "'built like' or a similar expression." In the casino, Rocky was to slap one of the girls on the thigh, and CBS asked this movement be removed. Yet in the finished film, Rocky makes the movements to do so, but never makes contact. Other concerns raised by Tankersley were to use caution in the placement of Rocky's body "so as not to be shown in a grotesque manner." The network also asked Serling to use caution in the selection of wardrobe for the girls, i.e. "not too low-cut or suggestive."

The closing scenes in the episode were also of concern for CBS. The girl's line asking if there was anything else she could do for him was definitely suggesting a sexual favor, and the network asked Serling to "please be certain that the girl's third speech be delivered in a sweet manner, as described." One of the final lines delivered by Rocky, "scoring with a chick," at the network's suggestion was changed to "being a big guy with a chick."

One of Serling's disappointments was the use of "The Casino" featured on Rocky's bag. Serling, having been to Vegas, felt sure he could secure the name of a real casino to help dismiss any ideas the viewers might have had regarding Rocky being in hell instead of the real world. In a letter to Buck Houghton, Serling felt "certain that a few inquiries emphasizing benefits the casinos would have, would get us permission from the front." But the name "The Casino" remained, as generic as it may be.

On January 29, 1960, Charles Beaumont wrote to Rod Serling, explaining:

Dear Rod:
Tried to get you by phone, couldn't, so:
I've had an absolutely screwball idea. Your first reaction will be one of dumb astonishment, followed by rapid blinking and fantods. If for any reason we can't get Mickey Rooney for 'The Other Place,' why don't you essay the role of Rocky yourself? (Dumb astonishment? Rapid blinking? Fantods?) When I mentioned it to Helen, she said, 'Swell, now he'll think you consider him the cheap crook

The Twilight Zone was not telecast on the evening of April 22, 1960. Instead, CBS presented a special broadcast of *Playhouse 90* titled "Journey to the Day" with Mike Nichols, Mary Astor, James Dunn, James Gregory and Steven Hill.

type.' I cuffed her lightly about the ears, explaining that if I know writers, it's a good bet old Rod has the same secret ambition I do . . . to wit, to act. We're all hams, in our own ways, each of us planning to write himself into a part some day; is it not so? My opinion is that it would be a lot of fun all around, that if you can indeed act you'd be keen in the role, and that the concomitant publicity would be not bad. Anyway, give me your reaction, huh?
Chuck

This episode of *The Twilight Zone* was the inspiration for the song "Hell Hotel," an unreleased track recorded for a 1985 demo tape, by a then-unsigned music group called "They Might Be Giants."

On March 4, 1965, a variation of this *Twilight Zone* episode aired on the radio program, *Theater Five*. "The Land of Milk and Honey" was an almost mirrored copy of the same story, right down to the final surprise ending. In the episode "Chasing It" (initially telecast April 29, 2007) on HBO's *The Sopranos*, this episode was referenced in a remark when Carlo Gervasi finds Tony Soprano's gambling situation similar to that of Rocky. This episode was also spoofed on the animated series, *Futurama*. The web comic *8-Bit Theater* also featured a spoof of this story.

Production #3635 "NIGHTMARE AS A CHILD" (Initial telecast: April 29, 1960)
© Cayuga Productions, Inc., April 28, 1960, LP16775
Dates of Rehearsal: March 2 and 3, 1960
Dates of Filming: March 4, 7 and 8, 1960
Script #35 dated: February 4, 1960

Producer and Secretary: $675.00	Story and Secretary: $2,370.00
Director: $1,250.00	Cast: $4,556.87
Unit Manager and Secretary: $525.00	Production Fee: $750.00
Agents Commission: $5,185.55	Legal and Accounting: $250.00
Below the line charges (M-G-M): $19,009.88	Below the line charges (other): $3,624.81
Total Production Costs: $38,197.11	

Cast: Terry Burnham (Markie); Suzanne Cupito (the little girl); Michael Fox (the doctor); Joe Perry (the police lieutenant); Janice Rule (Helen Foley); and Shepperd Strudwick (Peter Selden).

Original Music Score Composed and Conducted by Jerry Goldsmith: Main Title (by Bernard Herrmann, :40); Miss Marky (:50); Hot Chocolate (1:10); Friendly Talk (:18); The Scar (:46); The Man (:54); Mr. Seldon (:32); The Past (1:32); The Song (:20); Twinkle, Twinkle Little Star (vocals, traditional, :20); The Voice (2:05); Twinkle, Twinkle Little Star (vocals, traditional, 1:30); Nightmare (:53): The Song (:30); Twinkle, Twinkle Little Star (vocals, traditional, :30); The Scar (:30); Peter's Death (1:56); Twinkle, Twinkle Little Star (vocals, traditional, :20); Morning (:31); and End Title (by Herrmann, :06).

Director of Photography: George T.   Production Manager: Ralph W. Nelson

Clemens, a.s.c.

Art Directors: George W. Davis and Merrill Pye

Set Decorations: Henry Grace and Keogh Gleason

Directed by Alvin Ganzer

Assistant Director: Don Klune

Film Editor: Bill Mosher

Sound: Franklin Milton and Philip Mitchell

Teleplay by Rod Serling

"Month of November . . . hot chocolate . . . and a small cameo of a child's face – imperfect only in its solemnity. And these are the improbable ingredients to a human emotion . . . an emotion, say, like . . . fear. But in a moment, this woman, Helen Foley, will realize fear. She will understand what are the properties of terror. A little girl will lead her by the hand and walk with her into a nightmare."

Plot: Schoolteacher Helen Foley finds herself revisiting the past when, as a little girl, she witnessed the murder of her mother from the hands of an unknown stranger. Helen forgot the details of that night and has spent the past 18 or 19 years shrouded in the dark. Doctors told her that in time, her memory will return. After inviting a little girl into her apartment for some hot chocolate, Helen discovers the child has the same nickname she had when she was a child – Markie. Late that evening, Helen recalls the events of the past in a dream and wakes to hear Markie singing on the steps outside her apartment. She soon realizes that the little girl is nothing but a hallucination of her younger self, an effort to recall the details of her mother's murder. Peter Selden shows up at her apartment, having kept tabs on her all these years, because he knew that one day she would put the pieces together and identify him. After a struggle, Selden falls down a flight of stairs, breaking his neck. Helen, free from the history that burdened her subconscious, finds another little girl on the stairs – this one being the real deal and not a figment of her imagination.

"Miss Helen Foley, who has lived in night . . . and who will wake up to morning; Miss Helen Foley, who took a dark spot from the tapestry of her life and rubbed it clean . . . then stepped back a few paces and got a good look . . . at the Twilight Zone."

Trailer: *"Next week, you'll spend a few rather unforgettable hours in this living room watching Miss Janice Rule and Mr. Shepperd Strudwick partake of a dramatic delicacy that is one part nursery rhyme, one part terror. This is designed for those of you who are getting too much sleep. Next week, on The Twilight Zone, 'Nightmare as a Child.' I hope we'll see you then. Thank you and good night."*

Trivia, etc. Having previewed this episode, the television columnist for *The San Antonio Light* remarked it was, "another strange one but if you accept the basic premise and don't ask for explanations, you'll enjoy it."

Actress Janice Rule preferred to play a different role for each television series she guest starred on. Playing a lead character in a series of her own was not to her liking. "I think I'd go mad," she explained. "I could never do the same character week after week with the same people. Your acting has to suffer. All you do is get one script a few days before you finish the preceding one. You'd never see your family. I know I would be making lots of money with a series but it's not worth it. Not to me, anyway."

Janice Rule squeezed in the role of Helen Foley, for this episode – literally. As soon as her shots were completed on Tuesday, March 8, she rushed out of the M-G-M Studio to begin rehearsal for her starring role in the CBS presentation of *The Snows of Kilimanjaro*.

The character of Helen Foley was named after Serling's English, literature and drama teacher from his childhood. The name "Helen Foley" also would be used in the movie adaptation of "It's a Good Life," directed by Joe Dante.

Director Richard L. Bare was originally slated to direct this episode, but due to an airplane crash, Alvin Ganzer was assigned the job. (For details about the airplane incident, see the episode entry for "The Purple Testament.")

Production #3629 "A STOP AT WILLOUGHBY" (Initial telecast: May 6, 1960)

© Cayuga Productions, Inc., May 5, 1960, LP16776
Dates of Rehearsal: March 8 and 9, 1960
Dates of Filming: March 10, 11 and 14, 1960
Sound dubbing completed: April 21, 1960
Script #29 dated: January 4, 1960, with minor revisions on January 12, 1960

Producer and Secretary: $675.00	Story and Secretary: $2,370.00
Director: $1,250.00	Cast: $5,422.86
Unit Manager and Secretary: $525.00	Production Fee: $750.00
Agents Commission: $5,185.55	Legal and Accounting: $250.00
Below the line charges (M-G-M): $31,955.17	Below the line charges (other): $3,117.88
Total Production Costs: $51,501.46	

Cast: Billy Booth (boy #1); James Daly (Gart Williams); Patricia Donahue (Jane Williams); Ryan Hayes (the trainman); Butch Hengen (boy #2); James Maloney (conductor #2); Mavis Neal (Helen, the secretary); Max Slaten (man on wagon); Howard Smith (Mr. Misrell); and Jason Wingreen (conductor #1).

Original Music Score Composed and Conducted by Nathan Scott (Score No. CPN5901): Main Title (by Bernard Herrmann, :40); Board Meeting (:39); Shut Your Mouth (1:41); Gart's Dream (1:15); Alone in 1888 (:22); The Ice Bucket (:33); Very Old Dream (:49); Full Measure (:35); This Stop is Willoughby (:21); Band Concert Medley – "Camptown Races" and "Listen to the Rocking Bird" (anonymous, arr. by Scott, :41); Next Time (:16); More Push-Push (:50); Fed Up (:20); The Plea Fails (:11); Arrival at Willoughby (:13); Oh, Susanna (by S.C. Foster, arr. by Scott, :50); Beautiful Dreamer (by S.C. Foster, arr. by Scott, :32); The Ambulance (1:00); Willoughby? (:32); and End Title (by Herrmann, :39).

Director of Photography: George T. Clemens, a.s.c.	Production Manager: Ralph W. Nelson
	Assistant Director: Don Klune
Art Directors: George W. Davis and Merrill Pye	Film Editor: Joseph Gluck, a.c.e.
Set Decorations: Henry Grace and Keogh Gleason	Sound: Franklin Milton and Philip Mitchell
Directed by Robert Parrish	Teleplay by Rod Serling

"This is Gart Williams, age thirty-eight, a man protected by a suit of armor all held together by one bolt. Just a moment ago, someone removed the bolt, and Mr. Williams' protection fell away from him and left him a naked target. He's been cannonaded this afternoon by all the enemies of his life. His insecurity has shelled him, his sensitivity has straddled him with humiliation, his deep-rooted disquiet about his own worth has zeroed in on him, landed on target, and blown him apart. Mr. Gart Williams, ad agency exec, who in just a moment will move into the Twilight Zone . . . in a desperate search for survival."

Plot: Gart Williams, an advertising agency executive, is suffering from exhaustion, stress and stomach ulcers from the pressures and demands of his raging boss. Traveling to and from work by train every day, during the cold and snowy month of November, Mr. Williams falls asleep and dreams of arriving at a town called Willoughby. The time is 1888 and the setting is a warm July afternoon. Best described as a Courier and Ives painting, complete with bandstand and bicycles, the conductor on the vintage train describes the town as a place that is "peaceful, restful, and where a man can slow down to a walk and live his life to full measure." Back in the real world, Gart suffers the ordeals of more stomach ulcers and pressure from his employer. After quitting his job and learning that his wife is walking out on him, Gart takes a trip back home by train and falls asleep. He wakes to find himself stationed at Willoughby and without hesitation, walks off to meet the residents who welcome him to a life of serenity. Back in reality, the train conductor looks over the dead body of Mr. Williams, explaining to a man next to him that Mr. Williams jumped off the platform on the train, shouting "Willoughby." Unaware of what the name means, they watch as the body of Mr. Williams is hauled off in an ambulance marked "Willoughby & Son, Funeral Home."

"Willoughby? Maybe it's wishful thinking nestled in a hidden part of a man's mind. Or maybe it's the last stop in the vast design of things. Or perhaps, for a man like Mr. Gart Williams, who climbed on a world that went by too fast, it's a place around the bend where he could jump off. Willoughby? Whatever it is, it comes with sunlight and serenity, and is a part . . . of the Twilight Zone."

Trailer: *"This old-fashioned railroad car is about as extinct as the dinosaur, but next week it takes us to a little village that is not only a place, but a state of mind. It's the transportation to what we think is one of the most unique stories we've ever presented. Next week, Mr. James Daly stars in 'A Stop at Willoughby.' We hope you stop with him. Thank you and good night."*

Trivia, etc. Originally conceived as the pilot film for *The Twilight Zone*, scheduling conflicts caused Serling to shelve this script for a time. Shortly after the holiday season of 1959, he revised the script, shortening the length from 60 minutes to 30. Since James Daly was Serling's first choice in 1958, he made arrangements for Daly to again be consulted. This time he succeeded.

Toward the end of the first season, Buck Houghton wrote a memo regarding this episode as Rod Serling's best *Twilight Zone* script. It was, in his opinion, "a good, tight, step-beyond-reality script, with a downbeat ending that might be against it. I like it, however. I think the moral is worthwhile and vividly shown – the background of the script (advertising, Westport, expense account world) is sophisticated – but again I wonder if its very lack of familiarity with the teen-ager makes it stronger, really."

The closing narration in the early draft was different from what appears in the finished film:

"Mr. Gart Williams, who sought respite from torment under a gravestone; who climbed on a world that went by too fast and then . . . jumped off. Mr. Gart Williams who might now tell us what awaits us in the beyond . . . because this too is a part of . . . The Twilight Zone."

Serling's original intention for the trailer was longer, and therefore, never used:

"This is Willoughby, serene, calm, summery. The kind of place where a man could live his life full measure. It forms the basis of one of the most unique stories we have ever told on the Twilight Zone. Mr. James Daly stars next week in, 'A Stop at Willoughby.' And friends, if this one doesn't haunt you, you simply have no hearts. See you next week on The Twilight Zone."

When the Serling household moved from Ohio to further Rod Serling's career for teleplay scripting and to be closer to Blanche Gaines in New York, they resided in Westport, Connecticut. The character of Gart Williams was making the same trek Rod himself made personally between New York City and Westport. Willoughby was the name of a real town in Ohio, which Serling traveled through when commuting from Ohio and New York in his earliest years of writing teleplays. A tip of the hat to Ray Bradbury is referenced in this episode when Gart Williams is discussing "the Bradbury account" over the speakerphone on his desk.

Miss Barbara J. Crompton of the New York Telephone Company wrote to Serling, care of the CBS network, making special notice of a mistake she observed in this episode, regarding the speakerphone used on the show. "It was used incorrectly," she explained. "It was shown with the telephone receiver off the hook. The speakerphone could not possibly work this way, because as soon as the receiver is taken off the hook, the loudspeaker and the microphone automatically disconnect. I just thought I'd call your attention to this fact so that should you intend to use the speakerphone on any subsequent shows, it would be used correctly." This is a legitimate on-camera blooper which still remains on the finished film.

One viewer in Pittsburgh, Pennsylvania, wrote to Serling, complimenting the ending and asked if the closing scene with the funeral parlor ambulance was inspired by another source of concern. Serling wrote back, assuring the viewer that he felt the ending of "A Stop at Willoughby" was not part or parcel of any fear of death. "I thought it was a piece of delightful irony which I had planned in the beginning. What constitutes 'delightful irony' for me is often not received in similar fashion by others."

In the episode "A Stop at Willoughby," in the television series *Thirtysomething*, initially telecast on May 14, 1991, the character of Michael visits a doctor because of chest pains caused by stress from work.

In October of 2000, the made-for-TV movie, *For All Time*, reintroduced the viewers to Serling's touching story of escape, and the longing to go back to a simpler time. Actor Mark Harmon played the role of Charles Lattimer, a man confronting a mid-life crisis, and a failing marriage. Finding an escape route, he prefers to travel back to a time when the world is not moving so fast, and the pressures of present society can be put behind him. Because this film was an adaptation of this *Twilight Zone* episode, Rod Serling was credited on screen.

Production #3636 "THE CHASER" (Initial telecast: May 13, 1960)

Copyright Registration: © Cayuga Productions, Inc., May 12, 1960, LP16777
Dates of Rehearsal: March 14 and 15, 1960
Dates of Filming: March 16, 17 and 18, 1960

Sound dubbing completed: April 27, 1960
Script #36 dated: February 17, 1960

Producer and Secretary: $675.00
Director: $1,250.00
Unit Manager and Secretary: $525.00
Agents Commission: $5,185.55
Below the line charges (M-G-M): $22,193.12
Total Production Costs: $40,228.24

Story and Secretary: $2,130.00
Cast: $5,504.49
Production Fee: $750.00
Legal and Accounting: $250.00
Below the line charges (other): $1,765.08

Cast: Patricia Barry (Leila); Marjorie Bennett (the fat lady); Duane Grey (the bartender); George Grizzard (Roger Shackleforth); John McIntire (Professor A. Daemon); J. Pat O'Malley (Homburg); Barbara Perry (the blonde); and Rusty Westcott (the tall man).

Stock Music Cues: Main Title (by Bernard Herrmann, :40); Jazz (by Eddie Blair, Ron Price, Keith Christie, Johnny Hawksworth, Stan Tracey and Ronnie Verrell, 1:19 and :29); Street Moods in Jazz (by Rene Garriguenc, :58); It's Never June (by Bruce Campbell, 1:53); Happy Girl (by Jerry Goldsmith, :20); Sneak to Tag (by Garriguenc, :23); Romeo and Juliet (by Peter Tschaikowsky, arr. by Garriguenc, 3:19); Street Moods in Jazz (by Garriguenc, :26); City Mood (by Goldsmith, :41); Andante Cantabile – 5th Symphony (by Peter Tschaikowsky, arr. by Garriguenc, 1:45); Trouble Ahead (by Goldsmith, :07); The Big Time (by Goldsmith, :38 and :20); Sneak to Tag (by Garriguenc, :27); and End Title (by Herrmann, :39).

Director of Photography: George T.
    Clemens, a.s.c.
Art Directors: George W. Davis and
    Merrill Pye
Set Decorations: Henry Grace and Keogh
    Gleason

Production Manager: Ralph W. Nelson
Assistant Director: Don Klune
Film Editor: Bill Mosher
Sound: Franklin Milton and Philip Mitchell
Directed by Douglas Heyes

Teleplay by Robert Presnell, Jr., based on the original short story "Duet for Two Actors" by John Collier, originally published in the December 28, 1940 issue of *The New Yorker*.

"Mr. Roger Shackleforth. Age: youthful twenties. Occupation: being in love. Not just in love, but madly, passionately, illogically, miserably, all-consumingly in love, with a young woman named Leila who has a vague recollection of his face and even less than a passing interest. In a moment you'll see a switch, because Mr. Roger Shackleforth, the young gentleman so much in love, will take a short but very meaningful journey . . . into the Twilight Zone."

Plot: Roger is desperately in love with the beautiful Leila, but the woman does not share his enthusiasm. Working on the recommendation of a satisfied customer, Roger visits Professor A. Daemon, a dealer who makes his living selling potions. Roger explains his problem and the professor sells him a love potion guaranteed to ensure Leila will never leave his side. This he ensures is an elementary parlor trick of science that will prove its worth when Leila drinks the champagne spiked with the elixir. The potion only costs a dollar, but the magic is worth every cent. Months later, newly married, Roger finds that Leila's love is a bit too much; a constant love, she hangs on his every word. Returning to the professor, Roger asks for a means of escape and discovers that the only way out is a "glove cleaner" – a murderous poison that is untraceable, containing no odor or flavor. The cost is much more than a single dollar, hence the professor's method for making his living. Returning home, Roger attempts to poison his wife – but drops the poison when he learns that she is expecting, and she assures him this is just the beginning . . .

"Mr. Roger Shackleforth, who has discovered at this late date that love can be as sticky as a vat of molasses, as unpalatable as a hunk of spoiled yeast, and as all-consuming as a six-alarm fire in a bamboo and canvas tent. Case history of a lover boy who should never have entered the Twilight Zone."

Trailer: *"In this library, a certain professor sells things. Ointments, salves, powders, sovereign remedies, nectars, concoctions, decoctions and potions – all guaranteed. Next week, he'll sell one to a loverboy so that he can slip an affectionate mickey into the champagne of his lady love. It sets up a most bizarre and very unexpected chain of events. On the Twilight Zone next week, 'The Chaser.'"*

Trivia, etc. The short story from which this episode was adapted was originally scripted by Robert Presnell Jr. for *Billy Rose's Playbill Theater* and dramatized "live" on February 20, 1951, under the title "Duet for Two Actors." When Rod Serling expressed an interest in adapting the short story for *The Twilight Zone*, Buck Houghton and Leo Lefcourt dug into the case history. John Collier, in selling the rights to the *Playbill Theater*, not only was returned all rights to the story, but was also given complete ownership of the Presnell script. (This was the result of a good agent's attempt to make a second sale of a short story uncomplicated by the contrary ownership of the adaptation.) Jed Harris, the producer of the former series, did not retain the rights to the story, making it possible for Serling and Houghton to secure the rights through Collier direct.

Al Manuel represented Collier, and together the men agreed on a uniform policy of $2,000 per short story for filmed television. At the same time, Lefcourt contacted Manuel to verify whether Collier retained all rights, including Presnell's adaptation, and Lefcourt contacted Robert Goldfarb of the Frank Cooper office, which represented Robert Presnell Jr. "I know that he hopes that we will give Presnell the assignment of adapting the Collier short story based on his former adaptation," wrote Houghton, "making any changes that are wanted." Houghton, however, wanted to merely buy Presnell's existing work, so Rod Serling could compose the adaptation. If Presnell retained the rights to his own teleplay, Houghton wanted to buy them for as little as possible, between $500 and $750.

"Rod Serling feels, that for the sake of the series, he would be willing to forgo his full writing charge and take only his supervision charge, plus any difference between the deal we make and $2,250, in this instance," Houghton explained. The deal was cinched, and the teleplay was re-written by Presnell to fit the mold of a filmed episode instead of a "live" telecast.

The short story, which appeared in *The New Yorker*, was collected in *Presenting Moonshine* (1941), *Fancies and Goodnights* (1951) and *The John Collier Reader* (1972).

Director Douglas Heyes, who had proven himself sufficient in the eyes of Houghton and Serling with "Elegy," was hired in early March for a commitment of two additional episodes (this one and "The After Hours") for the second batch of programs rounding out production of the first season. Heyes was provided to Cayuga, courtesy of the Frank Cooper Associates Agency, as a result of Richard L. Bare's plane accident, which made Bare unavailable for a brief time. The agency represented both Bare and Heyes, and worked with Serling and Houghton in securing Heyes for the two commitments.

In the original script, Roger visits the professor, who removes the love potion from a drawer in his desk and sells it to him. Heyes decided that Roger departs from reality when he visits the professor, so the scene should be out of the ordinary. "We built a very long, narrow set which was very high, with lots of bookcases," Heyes explained to Ben Herndon. "We didn't put a back on these bookcases; instead we covered the backs with gauze and lit it from behind, so that the books stood out in relief against light – which is something they never do in a bookcase. But you don't think about that because it's in the *Twilight Zone* and you accept these weird things. But that subliminally made the whole scene crazy. And the interesting thing was that in *The Twilight Zone*, Buck Houghton, production manager Ralph W. Nelson, and Rod all said, 'Yeah, let's do it that way!' Anyplace else, people would have said, 'Why? Why? Why?'"

A verbal agreement between Serling and Robert Presnell was in exchange for the services and the story, Serling would help Presnell get a teleplay in the hands of other producers. Serling obliged, submitting Presnell's "Fare Thee Well" to television producer Fred Coe, with Serling's stamp of approval and recommendation.

John McIntire, who played the role of Professor A. Daemon (a play on the word "Demon"), received top billing above George Grizzard's name in the closing credits.

The number of on-air advertising spots for this particular *Twilight Zone* episode was increased, because the network and the sponsor felt this episode had the makings of an outstanding half-hour. The arrangement was made on April 7, and additional photos were supplied for a network-wide mailing.

In the episode "Loved to Death," on the television series *Tales from the Crypt*, initially telecast on June 15, 1991, a variation of this *Twilight Zone* was presented. A writer who receives the brush-off from an attractive neighbor purchases a magic potion designed to make her fall in love with him. Only after he starts receiving her affections does he learn that there is such a thing as "too much love."

Production #3633 "A PASSAGE FOR TRUMPET" (Initial telecast: May 20, 1960)
© Cayuga Productions, Inc., May 19, 1960, LP16778
Dates of Rehearsal: March 18 and 21, 1960
Dates of Filming: March 22, 23 and 24, 1960
Sound dubbing completed: May 5, 1960
Script #33 dated: January 29, 1960

Producer and Secretary: $675.00
Director: $1,250.00
Unit Manager and Secretary: $525.00
Agents Commission: $5,185.55
Below the line charges (M-G-M): $31,022.52
Total Production Costs: $49,973.90

Story and Secretary: $2,250.00
Cast: $5,147.76
Production Fee: $750.00
Legal and Accounting: $250.00
Below the line charges (other): $2,918.07

Cast: John Anderson (Gabriel); James Flavin (the truck driver); Ned Glass (Nate, the pawnshop owner); Diane Honodel (the screaming woman); Jack Klugman (Joey Crown); Mary Webster (Nan); and Frank Wolff (Baron, a trumpet player).

Original Music Score Composed and Conducted by Lyn Murray: Main Title (by Bernard Herrmann, :40); Brought (by Jeff Alexander, :39); Take Your Time (2:57); The Lowest (:32); T-Zone Blues (:16); Hock Shop Blues (:26); Reflection – Versions One and Two (:41); Mirrorsville (1:44); Ballad a la Butterfield (by Alexander, :44); Baron's Blues (by Alexander, :22); Song for Gabriel (:35); The Lowest (:25); Limbo'sville (1:05); Call Me Gabe (:19); Girl Called Ann (:27); New York's Ville (:48); and End Title (by Herrmann, :39).

Director of Photography: George T. Clemens, a.s.c.
Art Directors: George W. Davis and Merrill Pye
Set Decorations: Henry Grace and Keogh Gleason

Production Manager: Ralph W. Nelson
Assistant Director: Don Klune
Film Editor: Joseph Gluck, a.c.e.
Sound: Franklin Milton and Philip Mitchell
Directed by Don Medford
Teleplay by Rod Serling

"Joey Crown, musician with an odd, intense face, whose life is a quest for impossible things . . . like flowers in concrete . . . or like trying to pluck a note of music out of the air and put it under a glass to treasure. Joey Crown . . . musician with an odd intense face . . . who in a moment will try to leave the Earth and discover the middle ground . . . the place we call . . . the Twilight Zone."

Plot: Joey Crown, once known for playing the lead with a magic horn, now drowns his sorrows in a bottle. Unable to brush the filth from whence he came and tired of being rejected by the nightclub operators, Joey trades in his trumpet so he can afford to buy his last drink. Longing for a way out, he walks out into the street to become a victim of a hit and run. When he wakes, Joey finds himself ignored by people on the streets – and justifiably so. His reflection cannot be seen in mirrors or windows, and he suspects his attempt at suicide worked – he is now a ghost. Returning to the back alley of the nightclub where Joey once worked, he overhears trumpet music that could make butterflies dance and deaf men cry. The stranger strikes a brief friendship with Joey, explaining that he is not dead – he is in limbo. Joey can only understand meaning through the notes of a trumpet and having heard the music played by the stranger, he confesses he forgot how valuable life is. Offered the choice to go back, Joey accepts. As the stranger walks away, Joey asks the stranger for his name. Gabe – short for Gabriel. Purchasing his trumpet back, Joey returns to the roof top of the tenement, and spends the long evening hours trying to reproduce the music he heard Gabe play. Nan, a new tenant, overhears the music and visits Joey on the rooftop. She is new to the City and wants him to show her the sights. Maybe, just maybe, the two can make some beautiful music together.

"Joey Crown . . . who makes music. And who discovered something about life. That it can be rich and rewarding and full of beauty . . . Just like the music he played. If a person would only pause to look and to listen. Joey Crown . . . who got his clue . . . in the Twilight Zone."

Trailer: *"Next week you'll stand in this alley at the shoulder of Jack Klugman, who plays the role of a trumpet player who has run out of music and run out of dreams. Poignant is the best word for Mr. Klugman's performance. Next week, on the Twilight Zone, 'A Passage for Trumpet.' I think they're unusual notes indeed and we hope you'll be listening to them. Thank you and good night."*

Trivia, etc. The character of Joey, a young man desperate to rise out of the tenements where he grew up, was a character of Serling's since the summer of 1949 when he composed a radio script titled "The Local is a Very Slow Train." He submitted the idea to the producers of the radio anthology, *Grand Central Station*, who purchased the script and re-titled it "Hop Off the Express and Grab a Local." The story concerned two young men of the slums, Joey and Steve, who get involved in a murder. Joey comments not once, but twice, about how depressed he became when he was reminded of the social group in which he grew up, having been raised in the slums of the big city. The episode was broadcast over the CBS Radio Network on September 10, 1949.

On July 14, 1953, Serling sold a script to the *Kraft Television Theater* titled "The Blues for Joey Menotti," for $1,000. Dramatized on the evening of August 26, 1953, Dan Morgan and Constance Ford played the leads in a character study of a sad but talented honky-tonk piano player who reflected his mood with music. The Joey in this production did not play a horn, but the character study into the complexities of man's relationship to his social group remained.

As early as 1954, Serling drafted a script titled "A Passage for Trumpet" for *Studio One*. In this version, a trumpet player named Eddie Bogen tries out for the role in a traveling road show and makes good on his efforts. His father, an ex-fighter named Champ, takes to the bottle and on occasion, takes out his aggressions on young Eddie. But Eddie, with the same complexities as the Joey character on *Kraft*, has misguided virtues when, after being hired, he packs his bags, deserts a girl he once loved and cared for, and shouts to the world that he has finally earned his ticket out of the slums. Later, after the gig has ended, he is informed that his services were only required for a large performance and returns to discover why his father took to the bottle. Realizing finer friends could not be found elsewhere than where he grew up, Eddie makes a return without the aid of divine intervention. The story editor for *Studio One* rejected the script.

Serling then ignored the usual protocol and submitted "A Passage for Trumpet" to Arthur Heinemann, story editor for another television anthology. In rejecting the script, Heinemann returned it not to Serling but, by proper channels, to Serling's agent, Blanche Gaines, noting, "I'm sorry, but I think he has missed in this one. It's a mood piece that doesn't come off, a vignette that is stretched too long, about a character who arouses no sympathy in me. I can see doing a study of a neurotic musician, but I must have some direction to it. Incidentally, I thought Rod's 'Strike' on *Studio One* was a fine job, and I wish we had done it."

On June 15, 1954, Blanche Gaines forwarded Heinemann's comment to Serling, with her own personal comments. "I am not going to harp on the 'I told you so' theme, but I do wish, Rod, that you would not leave bad examples of your work with editors. If you could only learn to evaluate your work more and throw a few things in the wastebasket, I am sure it would help your career in the long

---

* It was this same month that Serling received a check for $1,110.00, for his hour-long script, "U.F.O.," which would be presented on *Westinghouse Summer Theatre*. Actual payment was $1,250, but Gaines kept her 10 percent commission and her previous loan of $15 to Serling.

run. You are not in such a dire financial position that you have to sell everything you write. Practically every writer turns out some bad material at one time or another and accepts that fact in a mature way. Since you know that you are not analytical when it comes to your own writing, I think that you should respect your agent's judgment a little bit more. I am as anxious to sell as you are, but not at the expense of my writer's reputation or my own." *

Actor John Anderson recalled more than once that this film won an award at the Cannes Film Festival, but there are no records to indicate this is accurate. More than likely, someone told Anderson, who felt proud of the fact and repeated this to interviewers over the years.

When Joey was in "a kind of a limbo," he was unable to see his reflection in any mirrors. Technical devices aside, this was accomplished using clever camera angles and a mirrored reproduction of the ticket booth set, complete with twins playing the role of the ticket lady. While one man's reflection is captured on a mirror, Joey stands where there is no mirror, and the twin is mimicking the same actions as her sister, thus fooling the audience into thinking Joey's reflection is not picked up on a non-existing mirror. The production crew succeeds -- except when Joey is at the ticket booth and his reflection is accidentally picked up on camera.

Serling flew to New York covering a period from April 17 through April 22. During this time, he had two major interviews with *The New York Telegram* and United Press International, both set up by CBS for *Playhouse 90* publicity. In addition, he held meetings with Young & Rubicam, sat in on some acting classes with the idea of picking potential talent for the show and also had dinner and cocktails with Jack Klugman for the successful purpose of getting him to agree to do a *Twilight Zone*. Klugman's fee for playing the role of Joey in this episode was $2,500.

"I have a tremendous respect for Rod and his endeavors," commented Klugman. "When you had a starring role on a *Twilight Zone*, you had a role with meat. For 'A Passage for Trumpet,' I spent a number of hours learning how to play the trumpet. There was an expert who taught me how to use my fingers and it wasn't long before I could mimic a real trumpet player."

"That was my favorite episode," Anderson recalled to author Mark Phillips. "They wrote a special music piece for the show. Neither Jack nor I played trumpet, so CBS went to the trouble of sending their musical director to my house with a cassette of the song and the sheet music. On the sheet, it told me what trumpet valves to press as I played. I worked my butt off, learning to play it by pantomime. Later, Jack and I, who are old friends, started rehearsing the scene and said, 'Jack, how did you do the trumpet practice?' He said, 'What practice?' I said, 'Klugman! Are you telling me that you didn't even practice? You're gonna fake it?' he said, 'For Christ's sake, Anderson, who's gonna notice if we're hitting the right valves or not? If the audience is so busy looking at our fingers, then we're really in trouble.' I said, 'Jack you S.O.B.! I worked my butt off to learn the fingers!' and he laughed. But Jack was right. Fact was, you couldn't tell if I'm faking it oor if he's faking it."

The television critic for *The Bennington Evening Banner* commented this episode was "attention holding, although not as compelling as most." *The Hammond Times* described it as "a tight tale with some good moments." Looking back over the years, this episode has been hailed as a classic among fans of the program, proving that regardless of the former rejections and varied attempts to sell a story without a fantasy element, Serling's decision to incorporate a rejected script for his own program was the better choice.

There are a couple in-jokes in this episode. The name of the woman on the rooftop is Nan, a nickname for one of Serling's daughters, Anne. The sign hanging above the scaffolding during a good part of the episode read "Houghton," a tip of the hat to producer Buck Houghton.

The name of "Officer Flaherty" is mentioned by Joey in the beginning of the second act. Though the character never appeared on screen, Serling, who often reused the names of fictional characters, would feature such a character named Officer Flaherty in the holiday offering, "The Night of the Meek."

The framed photo of Cassius Clay hanging on the wall in the bar is the same photo that appears in almost every bar scene on *The Twilight Zone* series, including "A Kind of a Stopwatch" and "What You Need."

Displayed outside the movie theater are a number of movie posters including *Edge of the City* (1957), *Big Leaguer* (1953), *Moonfleet* (1955) and *The Marauders* (1955). These posters belonged to M-G-M releases and were pulled from stock at *Twilight Zone's* home studio.

Production #3631 "MR. BEVIS" (Initial telecast: June 3, 1960)
© Cayuga Productions, Inc., June 2, 1960, LP16779
Dates of Filming: March 28, 29 and 30, 1960
Sound dubbing completed: May 10, 1960
Script #31 dated: January 11, 1960, with revised pages dated March 24 and 25, 1960
Shooting script dated: March 25, 1960

Producer and Secretary: $675.00
Director: $1,250.00
Unit Manager and Secretary: $525.00
Production Fee: $750.00
Agents Commission: $5,185.55
Legal and Accounting: $250.00
Below the line charges (M-G-M): $30,488.76
Below the line charges (other): $1,503.19
Total Production Costs: $50,274.35

Story and Secretary: $2,250.00
Cast: $7,396.85

> *The Twilight Zone* was not telecast on the evening of May 27, 1960. Instead, another entry in the *CBS Reports* series was presented, with Edward R. Murrow as both host and reporter. The title of this presentation about public school integration was "Who Speaks for the South?"

Cast: Orson Bean (James B.W. Bevis); Timmy Cletro (the little boy); Henry Jones (J. Hardy Hempstead); Charles Lane (Mr. Peckinpaugh); Florence MacMichael (Margaret); Horace McMahon (the bartender); Dorothy Neumann (the landlady); Colleen O'Sullivan (the young lady); House Peters, Jr. (the second police officer); William Schallert (the first police officer); and Vito Scotti (the fruit peddler).

Stock Music Cues: Main Title (by Bernard Herrmann, :25); Sidewalks of New York (by Charles B. Lawlor and J.W. Blake, :57); Unidentifiable Whistle (by Orson Bean, improvised, :04); That's My Weakness (by Bud Green and Sam H. Stept, 1:23); Oh, Those Bells – Osgood (by Maurice Carlton, :07); Soliloquy #1 (by Arthur Wilkinson, :25); Angry Steps #2 (by Wilbur Hatch, :18); Soliloquy #1 (by Wilkinson, :18); Easy Going (by Fred Steiner, :01); Soliloquy #1 (by Wilkinson, :31); Brave New World (by Herrmann, :05); Harp Shockers #1 (by Steiner, :05); Brave New World – Chord (by Herrmann, :03); Harp Shockers #2 (by Steiner, :03); Mysterious Liza (by Hatch, arr. by Wilkinson, :14); Robot Rock (by Bruce Campbell, :06); Hiccup (by Carlton, :12); Glockenspiel Note "A" (anonymous, :05); Brave New World – Chord (by Herrmann, :05); Harp Shockers #3 (by Steiner, :05); Vibe Notes "B" (anonymous, :03); Brave New World – Chord (by Herrmann, :03); Soliloquy #1 (by Wilkinson, :12); Blues Pantomime #2 (by Wilkinson, :13); Shakes (by Carlton, :12); Sidewalks of New York (by Lawlor and Blake, :05); Brave New World – Chord (by Herrmann, :05); Harp Shockers #4 (by Steiner, :05); Brave New World – Chord (by Herrmann, :05); Harp Shockers #5 (by Steiner, :05); Night Flight – 4A (by Campbell, :16); Night Flight – 2A (by Campbell, :08); Brave New World – Chord (by Herrmann, :05); Harp Shockers #6 (by Steiner, :08); Soliloquy #1 (by Wilkinson, :37); Soldiers on Strings (by Campbell, :20); Hiccup (by Carlton, :12); Brave New World – Chord (by Herrmann, :05); Harp Shockers #7 (by Steiner, :05); Brave New World – Chord (by Herrmann, :05); Harp Shockers #8 (by Steiner, :05); Brave New World – Chord (by Herrmann, :05); Harp Shockers #10 (by Steiner, :05); Brave New World – Chord (by Herrmann, :05); Harp Shockers #11 (by Steiner, :05); Brave New World – Chord (by Herrmann, :04); Mysterious Liza (by Hatch, arr. by Wilkinson, :04); and End Title (by Herrmann, :52).

Director of Photography: George T.
    Clemens, a.s.c.
Art Directors: George W. Davis and
    Merrill Pye
Set Decorations: Henry Grace and
    Keogh Gleason

Production Manager: Ralph W. Nelson
Assistant Director: Don Klune
Film Editor: Bill Mosher
Sound: Franklin Milton and Philip Mitchell
Directed by William Asher
Teleplay by Rod Serling

"In the parlance of the twentieth century, this is an oddball. His name is James B.W. Bevis and his tastes lean towards stuffed animals, zither music, professional football, Charles Dickens, moose heads, carnivals, dogs, children, and young ladies. Mr. Bevis is accident prone, a little vague, a little discombobulated, with a life that possesses all the security of a floating crap game. But this can be said about Mr. Bevis: without him – without his warmth, without his kindness – the world would be a considerably poorer place . . . albeit perhaps, a little saner. Should it not be obvious by now, James B.W. Bevis is a fixture in his own private, optimistic, hopeful little world. A world that has long ceased being surprised by him. James B.W. Bevis, on whom dame fortune will shortly turn her back, but not before she gives him a paste on the mouth. Mr. James B.W. Bevis, just one block away . . . from the Twilight Zone."

Plot: Mr. Bevis is having a bad day. He lost his sixth job in the past year, his landlord is evicting him for failure to pay the rent, and his automobile is the cause of a traffic accident. Towards the end of the day, Bevis meets J. Hardy Hempstead, his guardian angel, who offers him a second chance to relive the same day over – with noticeable changes. Bevis dresses for success, pays for his rent three weeks in advance, Bevis has been promoted with a raise, and his sports car is the latest fashion. Though the future looks bright, Mr. Bevis isn't satisfied with big dreams – he prefers his old self that collects antiques, enjoys zither music, plays with kids in the street and feels jumping from job to job is worth more than all the pay his boss could possibly raise. Hempstead returns things the way they were and Bevis is more content than he was before. But now he has a guardian angel to look after his needs . . . or nudges, so to speak.

"Mr. James B.W. Bevis, who believes in a magic all his own. The magic of a child's smile . . . the magic of liking and being liked . . . the strange and wondrous mysticism that is the simple act of living. Mr. James B.W. Bevis, species of twentieth-century male who has his own private and special Twilight Zone."

Trailer: *"Next week you'll meet the occupant of this desk, whose name is James B.W. Bevis, a warm and winning 20th century oddball about a mile and a half from the norm. He likes things like zither music, little kids, and stuff like this. Orson Bean stars next week on the Twilight Zone as "Mr. Bevis," and Henry Jones plays his guardian angel. He's this kind of oddball."*

Trivia, etc. Henry Jones, who played the role of the guardian angel, recalled his origins as an actor. "When I was in college, I wanted to be a lawyer. My father, a surgeon,

Orson Bean prepares to lose his job in "Mr. Bevis."

said he didn't care what I became as long as I wasn't a doctor – this was in 1935 and doctors were at the bottom of the financial barrel. I went to several prep schools and colleges and got kicked out of most of them. I had infantile paralysis when I was four and the only thing paralyzed was my throat – I think that is why I have such a funny voice. I also grew up with flat feet and I didn't develop muscles until I was in my late twenties. Any kid could beat me up. But I found out one day that I could be funny and sarcastic and make the kids in class laugh. That was the beginning of my acting career."

Ironically, Henry Jones could have reprised his youthful years for the lead, but that was handed over to Orson Bean, who signed on for the role for $2,500. "It was a wonderful time to work at the studios," recalled Bean. "I was told in advance that it was a pilot and that I would play the lead. Television offered the opportunity of a steady paycheck and I was ready and willing. When I was told that Rod Serling wrote the script, I was impressed. 'My God, Rod Serling?' Henry Jones was a dear man to work with and kept thinking to myself how poorly executed the pilot [was filmed]. Looking back at it today I can see why. The script was not up to Serling standards."

Werner Michel, vice president of the radio-television department of Reach, McClinton & Co., Inc. in New York, representing the Prudential Insurance Company, was one of many sponsors who watched the *Twilight Zone* pilot and Serling sales promo film back in early 1959. Prudential placed

---

* In April of 1959, with General Foods already signed up as one of the alternating sponsors, the Prudential Insurance Company was momentarily interested in becoming the other alternating sponsor. This, of course, did not come to be, so it was in Prudential's interest to view any additional programs Serling might conceive.

an order, but CBS somehow was unable to deliver. Presently sponsoring *The Twentieth Century*, and very happy with the series, Michel wrote to Serling on October 30, 1959, explaining that, "we will want to branch out into nighttime entertainment programming next year – no Westerns, no mysteries." Michel flew out to the West Coast for a week on November 15 and arranged a meeting with Serling, asking for a pilot of a different type of series. This was the origin of "Mr. Bevis." *

During the meeting, Serling admitted that he heard "belatedly of the abortive connection" between Prudential and *The Twilight Zone*, but hoped to design a program that would suit their mutual interests. Serling proposed a series titled "The American," which Werner Michel gave serious consideration for the next television season. "The more I think about this idea – though admittedly embryonic at the time we talked about it – the more I'm getting intrigued," wrote Michel on December 9. Ten days before Christmas, Serling admitted in a letter to Michel that while "The American" remained in embryonic stages, he had a new idea called "Mr. Bemis," which in a lighter way incorporated the concept they discussed previous.

"Mr. Bemis is a 40-year-old kind of bumbling fey, infinitely warm but incredibly accident prone gnome-like little man," Serling explained to Michel. "The accent, of course, is comedic but the idea incorporates a comment on the times. When the presentation is finished and the script written in about two weeks, I'll send you out a copy. If it doesn't do anything for you, I'd be more than happy to pursue the other a step further."

On February 12, 1960, Walter N. Hiller, Jr., of MCA Artists, Ltd., an agency representing television and stage actors, had read a copy of the script, forwarded to him by Buck Houghton, with the understanding that while this was a guest appearance on *The Twilight Zone*, their appearance would also constitute a possible role on a regular weekly television series. Stars who were not willing to commit to a weekly program were not considered. At Hiller's suggestion, the following names were proposed for the role of Mr. Bevis and Mr. Hempstead:

Mr. Bevis	Mr. Hempstead
Shelley Berman	Edward Atienza
Jack Carson	William Demarest
Wendell Corey	Robert Emhardt
Henry Jones	Gale Gordon
Burgess Meredith	Sterling Holloway
Zachary Scott	Henry Jones
Alan Young	Murray Matheson
	Harry Von Zell
	John McGiver
	Paul Hartman

Shortly before Christmas, Serling composed a five-page outline for the series, changing the name from "Bemis" to "Bevis" and soon after, wrote what would become an episode of *The Twilight Zone*. "I like the outline better than the script, but I realize that you have to fit your 'pilot' into an existing format," wrote Michel to Serling in a letter dated February 24. "What intrigues me about Mr. Bevis are his Chaplinesque qualities, a quality often attempted but rarely realized in any form of literature. I even could see this 'little man' operate against the whole big world without the assistance of J. Hardy

Hempstead (which incidentally would probably make it an easier commercial sale). At any rate, I find the project very interesting and have asked CBS to let me know when script 31 goes on the air."

In the outline, Serling described Mr. Bevis as 5' 8", unmarried, in his early 30s, has the face of a 20th century gnome, tends toward the fey and was somewhat vague and absent-minded about things. Mr. Bevis never held a job for longer than two or three weeks and the positions he held have been varied, from selling foreign cars to designing women's dresses. Each job ended abruptly because of his propensity for (1) accidents; (2) the wrong word at the wrong time and (3) his preoccupation with truth. Hence, if a customer asked Mr. Bevis directly how he looked in a given garment, Bevis gave an honest answer.

Mr. Bevis characteristically was gentle, warm, compassionate, bumbling, awkward, unconsciously funny, rigidly honest, and infinitely likeable. He loved children, fairy tales, exotic European dishes, pro football, and beautiful women. He disliked deferential maitre D's, nouveau riche pseudo-sophisticates, prejudice, the Daughters of the American Revolution and crooked politicians.

Mr. Bevis also has a guardian angel! This "gentleman" is J. Hardy Hempstead. Serling proposed that Hempstead received the appointment to look after Mr. Bevis many eons ago because one of Mr. Bevis' ancestors performed a feat of great courage and, as a result, was rewarded by a heavenly statute providing for the nominal protection of a guardian angel to one member of the Bevis progeny in each generation. This protection takes the form of mystic interferences at odd times like plucking Mr. Bevis from out in front of speeding buses. Hempstead also supplies editorial and philosophical comments on Mr. Bevis' weaknesses. Hempstead appears usually in full dimensioned flesh wearing a rather tight, double-breasted kind of Kiwanis officer installation blue suit but only appears to Mr. Bevis and no one else.

Serling composed a number of plot proposals for future episodes. Since the series never came to be, none of the proposals ever made it to script stage.

Plot Proposal #1 – A computer has been designed to pick out an average man, based on material fed into it by the scientists. On the basis of this, the computer projects what mankind will need in the coming years. After all the data has been fed into the computer, the system commences and a tiny card appears. On it is one name – Henry Bevis. The little man is immediately pounced upon by scientists and manufacturers and treated to a most subtle period of intense observation. No matter what he buys, says or does, he is immediately given vast credence as definitive of the coming taste of American society. But because Mr. Bevis is an oddball who likes mayonnaise on ice cream, automobiles with three wheels and zither music, he sets the economy on its ear. It's only at the end of the piece that we realize that someone had turned the wrong dial on the machine.

Plot Proposal #2 – Through a set of circumstances, Mr. Bevis finds himself running for councilman. He is extremely reluctant to get into politics but Mr. Hempstead, long associated with more illustrious Bevises, prods him into accepting the nomination. Bevis accepts on one condition: that his guardian angel will supply no heavenly interferences in garnering a vote. He wants it a clean, unsullied victory. Mr. Hempstead protests, but agrees to let the election run its course with no mystical aids, but goes Bevis one better by making it incumbent upon him to speak only the truth. Hence, for a 24 hour period Mr. Bevis is not allowed even a discoloration of fact, not even a simple exaggeration. Throughout the next day, Mr. Bevis discusses the campaign and every time he tries to say something subtly, it comes out as the whole truth. This also applies to his campaign speeches on the street corners. Mr. Bevis' honesty, albeit somewhat forced, loses him the election. But in the end, the opposition candidate is forced to take a leaf from his book and operate with equal candor, suggesting a cleaner administration will now operate within the city.

Plot Proposal #3 – A little refugee boy moves in on Mr. Bevis' block. This is a kid whose brief 11 years have been spent behind barbed-wires in refugee camps all over Europe. Bevis, always sensitive and compassionate to children, is desperate to make the little boy smile. Because magic is the only thing the little boy believes in, Bevis promises magic. Mr. Hempstead is duly approached to supply the unearthly accomplishments and he refuses because of certain heavenly statutes in force that prohibit any display of miracles. Mr. Bevis tries to implement some make-shift miracles of his own that fall flat and as a result, disillusions the little boy. In the end, through the little boy's eyes, he realizes that the kid responds to what have been the efforts of one little man desperate to give him comfort and solace for the first time in his life. This relief is short-lived when in the last moment of this episode, three more refugee children arrive and Bevis begins the same routine all over again.

Plot Proposal #4 – Bevis has just lost his 13th job of the month and has begun to be assailed by self-doubts. Hempstead enters the picture by giving our hero extraordinary salesmanship powers so that for at least a brief period of time, Bevis can find his faith replenished. This has to do with the ability to sell the new compact cars and thanks to Hempstead, Mr. Bevis becomes the number one salesman. But as things happen, Mr. Bevis goes to ply his new talents in the wrong place. He winds up in an auto salon which sells the European Rolled Roost, a 40-foot limousine with a 500 horsepower engine, bar, back seat television set, hand-woven upholstery, and every absolute luxury that a $27,000 car can offer. A customer in this salon is ushered in by a uniformed doorman and placed in a reclining chair. He is given a highball and then a very soft three-hour sell. He thereupon offers this kind of pitch to the first potential customer, a retired Duke who lives in the Waldorf Towers. He succeeds in alienating the Duke, the owner of the car agency and everyone else, much to Hempstead's chagrin. Once again Bevis finds himself out of a job but sans his self-doubts because the Duke has definitely been swayed by Mr. Bevis' salesmanship and is now riding a motorcycle.

CBS Press Release read:
Orson Bean stars as a lovable eccentric who remains popular even after losing his job, until a visit from his guardian angel changes his personality, in Rod Serling's "Mr. Bevis" on *The Twilight Zone* Friday, June 3 (CBS-TV).

Bean, as the daydreaming Mr. Bevis, drives a 1924 Rickenbacker, loves zither music and keeps stuffed squirrels on his desk. Then he meets J. Hardy Hempstead, his guardian angel (played by Henry Jones), who profoundly affects his way of life. Also featured are Charles Lane as Mr. Peckinpaugh, Bevis' hard-hearted boss; William Schallert as a policeman and Horace McMahon as a bartender.

It was originally planned for Serling to do the trailer in Bevis' apartment house, but scheduling complications prevented Serling from appearing on the set as required, so instead he invited the audience to visit the program next week from Bevis' desk at work. For the trailer promoting next week's episode, the clock in the back of the room read 10:30, the same time *The Twilight Zone* went

> **Blooper!** When Mr. Bevis correctly asked the angel, "Who might you be?" the other character countered with, "Whom, I'm your guardian angel." This objective case was caught and pointed out by more than 80 viewers, according to a letter penned by Serling, who stood corrected and apologized for the error. But the entire episode was a big blooper in Serling's eyes. "It has not the dimension of a pilot nor the production polish that should be attendant," Serling apologized to a potential sponsor. "The budget got destroyed toward the end of the show during the period of the cycle when this was being shot and I think it's reflected in the show itself. But at least it will give you a kind of general idea of direction that I wanted to take, if not necessarily a true picture of the casting."
>
> "I tried to sell the idea of a guardian angel based on something we did in a very rough fashion on the series," Serling later recalled, "and received nothing but cold, blank stares for my efforts. . . . I hated the Bevis show from its rough-cut on to its airing. I thought it a slaughtered version of what potentially could have been very cute and also very definitive of the proposed series."

off the air. In the actual episode, the clock was a different time reflecting when Bevis was arriving late to work – meaning the time set on the clock behind Serling's "teaser" was deliberate.

The street outside Mr. Bevis' apartment is the same featured in "A Penny For Your Thoughts," where Dick York paid for his newspaper. The stairway inside Mr. Bevis' apartment is the same as featured in "Nightmare as a Child" and "Cavender is Coming." The same organ grinder and monkey that were paid to appear in "Walking Distance" make a return visit – this time appearing on the finished film. (Author verified by consulting Cayuga production reports.)

Production #3637 "THE AFTER HOURS" (Initial telecast: June 10, 1960)
Copyright Registration: © Cayuga Productions, Inc., June 9, 1960, LP16780
Dates of Rehearsal: April 5 and 6, 1960
Dates of Filming: April 7, 8 and 11, 1960
Sound dubbing completed: May 10, 1960
Script #37 dated: February 15, 1960

Producer and Secretary: $775.00
Director: $1,450.00
Unit Manager and Secretary: $425.00
Agents Commission: $5,185.55
Below the line charges (M-G-M): $29,461.48
Total Production Costs: $45,685.21

Story and Secretary: $2,250.00
Cast: $4,634.38
Production Fee: $750.00
Legal and Accounting: $250.00
Below the line charges (other): $503.80

Cast: Elizabeth Allen (the saleswoman); John Conwell (the elevator operator); Anne Francis (Marsha White); James Millhollin (Armbruster, the floor walker); Nancy Rennick (Miss Keevers); and Patrick White (Sloan).

Stock Music Cues: Main Title (by Bernard Herrmann, :25); Hustle Bustle – Big City Music (by William Schaeffer (:09); I Can't Get You Off My Mind (by Lucien Moraweck and Frank Perkins, 1:32); The Telephone (by Herrmann, :30 and :09); The Sun (by Herrmann, :13); Tales from the Vienna Woods (by Johann Strauss Jr., arr. by Moraweck, :14); Shock Therapy #3 (by Rene Garriguenc, :06); The Truck (by Herrmann, :08); Bon Bon (by Garriguenc, :54); Shock Therapy #3 (by Garriguenc, :14); The Button (by Herrmann, 1:15); The Mirror (by Herrmann, :33); The Sun (by Herrmann, :32); Emperor Waltz #4 (by Strauss Jr., arr. by Moraweck, :38); The Telephone (by Herrmann, :39); and End Title (by Herrmann, :52).

Director of Photography: George T. Clemens, a.s.c.
Production Manager: Ralph W. Nelson
Art Directors: George W. Davis and Merrill Pye
Assistant Director: Don Klune
Film Editor: Bill Mosher
Set Decorations: Henry Grace and Keogh Gleason
Sound: Franklin Milton and Philip Mitchell
Makeup: William Tuttle
Directed by Douglas Heyes
Teleplay by Rod Serling

> "Looking back on those years, I would say that I get more fan mail related to The Twilight Zone than anything else I have done — including Honey West and Forbidden Planet," recalled Anne Francis.

"Express elevator to the ninth floor of a department store, carrying Miss Marsha White on a most prosaic, ordinary, run-of-the-mill errand. Miss Marsha White on the ninth floor, Specialties department, looking for a gold thimble. The odds are that she'll find it, but there are even better odds that she'll find something else because this isn't just a department store. This happens to be . . . the Twilight Zone."

Plot: Marsha White has a bit of a mystery in her hands. After the elevator operator lets her off on the 9th floor where he says she may purchase the gold thimble she desires, she finds but one saleswoman and, in that vast area, only one item is for sale . . . a gold thimble. She completes her purchase but soon discovers that the thimble is damaged. She complains to the store manager, asking to have the thimble replaced. He is extremely perplexed by her story because the store does not have a 9th floor and they do not carry gold thimbles. Marsha faints when she catches a glimpse of the saleslady and discovers she was talking to a mannequin. Later that evening, Marsha wakes to find herself overlooked and left behind after store hours. Alone by herself, she is terrified inside the darkened store, until she starts to hear voices. The mannequins come to life and the truth is revealed: Marsha is also a mannequin and it was her turn to venture outside in the real world for a month. Only she returned a day late. After being reprimanded in front of the others, Marsha recollects everything and apologizes. She explains that the world was so beautiful outside she forgot her place. The next morning, the store manager is perplexed when he notices a mannequin in a display that resembles Marsha White . . .

"Marsha White, in her normal and natural state. A wooden lady with a painted face, who, one month out of the year, takes on the characteristics of someone as normal and as flesh and blood as you and I. But it makes

you wonder, doesn't it? Just how normal are we? Just who are the people we nod our hellos to as we pass on the street? A rather good question to ask, particularly ... in The Twilight Zone."

Trailer: *"Next week, you'll see our friends here along with Anne Francis and Elizabeth Allen in one of the strangest stories we've yet presented on The Twilight Zone. It's called 'The After Hours' and concerns the shadowy time when normal people go back to their homes and concurrently what happens to those who perhaps are not quite so normal ... or perhaps not quite so human. Intriguing? I think you'll find it so, next week on the Twilight Zone."*

Anne Francis and her plastic double creates confusion.

Trivia, etc. Anne Francis recalled to interviewer Tom Weaver: "Rod Serling was a wonderful man – a brilliant man, with a sense of humor. That was back in the days when we rehearsed the show for a full week before we shot it, so we knew every shot that was going to be done. It was wonderful to be able to do that."

TV Guide featured a photo spread for this episode, about a week before the broadcast, with Anne Francis posing in front of her plastic duplicate. While the caption read "Anne Francis helps manipulate the imagination this Friday," the editors of the magazine carelessly gave away the solution to the mystery, remarking "Miss Francis plays a mannequin who comes to life in CBS' *Twilight Zone*." This obviously upset Houghton and Serling. For future episodes that required the ending to be concealed, Houghton would make sure a memo accompanied press releases and photos, reminding editors of periodicals not to reveal the surprise ending.

"Liz Allen was professional on the set," recalled Anne Francis. "She did a great job on that episode and the actor who was the store manager was also wonderful. He did this double-take that was so good the cameraman specifically wanted to get a number of close-ups of that take. The makeup man did such a great likeness with me for the mannequin that I was in awe. I really was! I still have the head to this day."

Serling's virgin story of mannequins coming to life in a department store after hours was critically taken apart by a couple critics of trade columns for mirroring a short story titled "Evening Primrose," by John Collier. The story told of a woman who went to a department store and became one of the "night people" – a society of humans who had decided to live in the "twilight zone" of locked up stores. Serling may have been exposed to the story from a dramatization on the radio program *Escape*, which featured an adaptation of the Collier story on November 5, 1947. Serling was a frequent listener of the program. While no one representing Collier filed a claim against Serling, Frank Gruber, one of the great pulp writers living in Los Angeles, began filing a claim of his own.

Gruber had written a teleplay titled "The Thirteenth Floor" years before and managed to sell the picture and TV rights to Sam Goldwyn – for a five-year lease. The rights ultimately reverted to Gruber, who by then, having learned that CBS agreed to contract the *Twilight Zone* for the upcoming season, submitted the script to Cayuga through MCA. "Most of the material was handled through

Buck Houghton and I read very little of it," Serling explained. "But I have to repeat and reemphasize, that I was not familiar with this story, I made no subconscious reference beyond the physical similarities [and] find that the plot is totally dissimilar."

Gruber, however, went about social gatherings spreading word that Rod Serling was a plagiarist and this, naturally, reached Serling, who was forced to defend himself at a brief meeting at the Writers' Guild. Gruber's script was different from Serling's "The After Hours," except for the first few pages in which someone enters a department store and ends up on an non-existing 13th floor. The rest of the script was completely different. *

On December 6, 1960, Serling submitted a copy of "The After Hours" script to Gruber, confident that the famed writer would note that beyond the passing similarity of the use of a non-existent floor in a department store, the two stories were miles apart in terms of mood, character and plot development. "If upon reading the enclosed you are not satisfied, I do think we should either sit down and discuss this as two honorable men, or, as in the words of the prophet, 'put your money where your mouth is,' secure a lawyer and make your accusations in a courtroom where I shall have a legitimate forum in which to answer the charges. . . . I'm sure you must know that thievery is no sideline of mine and never has been."

On December 11, Gruber sent a reply to Serling, filling two full pages voicing political differences, before getting down to the reason at hand, explaining that, "the week before 'The After Hours' appeared on TV I received three phone calls, from science fiction fans, asking if this was to be 'The Thirteenth Floor.' They had formed this impression solely from the brief blurb in *TV Guide*. After the *Twilight Zone* story appeared I had no less than eight or nine calls. Having been alerted by the three previous calls, I watched the show myself and after the first four scenes [I] thought you had copied the story, almost verbatim. From that point on there were no similarities. However, basically, I still find it hard to be convinced that you had not read 'The Thirteenth Floor.' The missing floor is not only the theme, but the background is also a department store."

On December 13, Serling wrote another reply. "Frank, it strikes me that my detractors had better stand in line because more than one claims that 'The After Hours' is theirs. I checked with the CBS story department after your last note and was told by someone in Glickman's office that there were six to eight stories that he knew of involving odd floors in buildings that were not actually there and/or mannequins who came alive. I inject this only to insert what I hope is the last nail in the coffin of this argument." It was apparently the last Serling heard from Gruber.

Actress Nancy Rennick played the role of Miss Keevers in this episode, who absentmindedly forgets Martha is in the back room. The floor walker calls out to another sales lady, Miss Pettigrew, and this has caused a number of reference works to erroneously credit Nancy Rennick for the role of Miss Pettigrew.

This same story was remade for the 1985 revival series of *The Twilight Zone*, placing a greater emphasis that all of us – including viewers – will ultimately become mannequins one day.

Production #3617 "THE MIGHTY CASEY" (Initial telecast: June 17, 1960)
© Cayuga Productions, Inc., June 16, 1960, LP16781
Dates of Rehearsal: August 25 and 26, 1959

---

* Also, it should be noted that in Serling's initial draft, the mysterious non-existing floor was the 18th, not the 9th.

Dates of Filming: August 27, 28 and 31, 1959
Script #17 dated: August 12, 1959, with revised pages dated August 24, 1959.
Shooting script dated: August 24, 1959

Producer and Secretary: $660.00
Director: $1,400.00
Unit Manager and Secretary: $520.00
Agents Commission: $5,185.55
Below the line charges (M-G-M): $23,764.51
Total Production Costs: $46,823.40

Story and Secretary: $2,461.55
Cast: $8,431.43
Production Fee: $750.00
Legal and Accounting: $250.00
Below the line charges – other $3,400.36

Cast: Alan Dexter (Beasley); Jonathan Hole (the doctor); Rusty Lane (the baseball commisisoner); Don O'Kelly (Monk); Abraham Sofaer (Dr. Stillman); Robert Sorrells (Casey); and Jack Warden (Mouth McGarry).

Stock Music Cues: Main Title (by Bernard Herrmann, :25); Brave New World (by Herrmann, :29); Takeoff to Space – Departure (by Bruce Campbell, :13); The World Today – Newsreel March (by William Schaffer, :20); Newsreel March (by John Leipold, :23); Punctuation (by Moraweck, :04); Knife Chord to Tail (by Moraweck, :03 and :06); Spoutnik #2 (by Guy Luypaertz, :26); Signals – Outer Space Suite (by Herrmann, :05); Curiosity (by Wilbur Hatch, :06); Oh, Those Bells – Osgood (by Maurice Carlton, :08, :07 and :06); Scherzando (by Rene Garriguenc, :25); The World Today – Newsreel March (by Schaffer, :41); and End Title (by Herrmann, :52).

Director of Photography: George T.
    Clemens, a.s.c.
Art Directors: George W. Davis and
    Merrill Pye
Set Decorations: Henry Grace and
    Keogh Gleason

Production Manager: Ralph W. Nelson
Assistant Director: Don Klune
Film Editor: Joseph Gluck, a.c.e.
Sound: Franklin Milton and Philip Mitchell
Directed by Robert Parrish and Alvin Ganzer
Teleplay by Rod Serling

Production #3687 retakes of "THE MIGHTY CASEY"

Dates of Filming: April 12 and 13, 1960
Sound dubbing completed: May 13, 1960
Narration revised on May 3, 1960
Rough draft dated: April 8, 1960, with revised pages dated April 10 and 11, 1960.
Shooting script dated: April 10, 1960

Producer and Secretary: $50.00
Cast: $5,910.20
Deposit on use of Wrigley Field: $750.00
Below the line charges (other): $32.21

Director: $1,250.00
Unit Manager and Secretary: $210.00
Below the line charges (M-G-M): $12,999.23
Total Production Costs: $21,201.64

"What you're looking at is a ghost. Something once alive . . . but now deceased. Once upon a time it was a baseball stadium that housed a major league ball club known as the Hoboken Zephyrs. Now it houses nothing but memories and a wind that stirs in the high grass of what was once an outfield; a wind that sometimes bears a faint, ghostly resemblance to the roar of a crowd that once sat here. We're back in time now when the Hoboken Zephyrs were still a part of the National League. And this mausoleum of memories was an honest-to-pete stadium. But since this is strictly a story of make believe, it has to start this way: Once upon a time in Hoboken, New Jersey, it was try-out day and though he's not yet on the field . . . you're about to meet a most unusual fella. A left-handed pitcher named Casey."

Plot: On a serious losing streak, a desperate baseball manager for the Hoboken Zephyrs finds a solution in the form of a robot whose pitching is phenomenal. Casey was designed by a clever scientist who wants nothing more than to prove to the scientific community that he can build a race of super humans. Employing Casey as part of the team, the Zephyrs start a winning streak that makes nationwide headlines. The deception is discovered when, upon being injured, the robot is discovered to lack a heart. Since he is not human, he is disqualified from the league. The scientist offers to install a heart, but this ruins his effectiveness as an aggressive pitcher. Casey is no longer able to thwart the ambitions of the batters he faces, so he pitches easy ones. Casey leaves to start a career in social work, and the manager of the Zephyrs starts looking for another job . . . until the blueprints left behind by the scientist gives the baseball manager an idea . . .

"Once upon a time there was a major league baseball team called the Hoboken Zephyrs who during the last year of their existence, wound up in last place and shortly thereafter wound up in oblivion. There is a rumor – unsubstantiated, of course – that a manager named McGarry took them to the West Coast and wound up with several pennants and a couple World's Championships. This team had a pitching staff that made history. Of course, none of them smiled very much, but it happens to be a fact that they pitched like nothing human. And if you are interested as to where these gentlemen came from, you might check under 'B' for baseball in the Twilight Zone."

Trailer: *"This locker and liniment emporium houses a major league baseball team known as the Hoboken Zephyrs, all of which by way of introduction to next week's show, a wild and wooly yarn about the great American pastime. It's called 'The Mighty Casey' and it's all about a left-hander who pitches like nothing human, simply because he isn't. Mr. Jack Warden takes us into the stadium next week for nine fast innings, on The Twilight Zone."*

Trivia, etc. "I root with a vast enthusiasm for the Brooklyn (now Los Angeles) Dodgers and for the Washington Red Skins in pro Football," Serling once wrote to a fan. "This idea stemmed from a general love for the great American sport and a feeling that the series could do with some tongue-in-cheek humor. I thought to myself, how incredible it would be if a baseball team mired in the cellar could derive the services of a robot – somebody whose arm never went lame, legs never went rubbery, and to whom age would have no deleterious effects. Hence – Casey the robot, left hander!"

This was not Rod Serling's first exploration into baseball dramas. Sometime around 1949 to 1951, he wrote a plot synopsis titled "Dependable," about Chris Forrest, a steady center-fielder who performed consistently without being glamorous. The plot was later fleshed into a radio script, but the exact title of the script and the program remain unknown.

"There's no such thing as actors on TV," growled actor Paul Douglas. "Only performers. Get through a scene without blowing a line, and they print it." Douglas had appeared in the motion picture *Angels in the Outfield* (1951), which he regarded as "a really crummy picture."

> **Blooper!** While the story supposedly takes place in New Jersey, palm trees can be seen outside the stadium in a number of shots.

Apparently President Eisenhower did not agree – there were reports that he had seen it several times. Having made a number of appearances on top-notch dramatic programs such as *Playhouse 90*, *Studio One*, and *Climax!*, Douglas' roles in comedy were very limited. "I'm a conscientious ham. I hate unfunny comedy. I guess I'm old-fashioned because I don't mind working for my money."

So what convinced Douglas to star in this episode of *The Twilight Zone*? A personal letter of invitation from Serling to Douglas cinched the deal. Serling was an established name by the time production began with *The Twilight Zone*, and to Douglas, a graduate of *Playhouse 90* and *Studio One*, that meant a guarantee of a role that he could employ his talents.

All of the scenes in the ballpark were filmed on location at Wrigley Field (yes, Los Angeles had its own Wrigley Field, located at 435 E. 42nd Place). Permission to film at the ballpark was granted through Lefty Phillips and Dick Walsh of the L.A. Dodgers. The cost for permission included $750 per shooting day. Approximately $35 was paid per day for the groundskeeper, Jim Williams, to tend to the ground both before and after filming. The actual cost for crews used for cleanup up was to be paid by the location department of M-G-M Studios.

Arnold Tashin was paid $15 per day to operate the scoreboard for filming. One police officer from LAPD to watch over the camera equipment and keep outsiders from sneaking inside the park was $3.15 per hour for an eight-hour day, paid through an M-G-M voucher. It was originally intended for a fireman to be on the set, through arrangement with Chief Degenkolb, but one was not necessary and the notion was scrapped.

Director Alvin Ganzer handled the complete operation, with the assistance of Eddie Denault as the assistant director. The first two days of filming were shot in the ballpark. All of the interior scenes, the hospital, the hospital corridor and the dressing room were shot on the third day, on Stage 10. A sign had to be printed for the ballpark and another sign for the scoreboard, to reflect the New Jersey team, not Los Angeles. The signs cost a total of $75.

Working on an emphasis of humor, this episode features a number of visual gags: the baseball hitting Casey in the head and not being affected, the smoke coming from the pitcher's glove, and the oil can on the hospital bed. Less than two weeks after principal filming was completed for this episode, Paul Douglas passed away. It was intended to possibly air the story for Christmas 1959, since it was of lighter fare, but due to the actor's death, the date was postponed.

Television again proved that it had the same "heart" often attributed to the other, older media of show business. To protect the good name and genuine talent of Douglas, it was decided to film new scenes and literally remake the entire episode. It was estimated that redoing the episode would cost some $40,000, according to one press release sent to newspapers.

Rod Serling was singularly quiet when he talked of Paul Douglas' performance in the original version of this episode. "Paul was a sick man when he filmed the story," he recalled. "He should never have consented to play the role. In the weeks prior to our filming, Paul had lost too much weight; he was a shadow of his former brawny self. He appeared as he was, a tired, haggard, sick man. When I saw the films of the shooting in the projection room, I could only think back to the accomplished acting jobs Paul had turned in for *Born Yesterday* on the stage, for *Letter to Three Wives*, *Clash by Night*, *Executive Suite*, *The Solid Gold Cadillac* and a dozen more films. Paul possessed a propensity to make people laugh or cry, and he always put his full self into his roles. The man I saw on our film was not that Paul Douglas."

Buck Houghton, Serling and other members of the production discussed the situation at great length. "All of us at Cayuga Productions felt that this performance by such a competent actor as Paul Douglas was not one which we could show to the public," Serling stated in the same press release. "We who were associated with him on the set know how hard he tried not to let his loss of health show up in the picture, but the prying, probing eye of the motion picture camera was too cruel. Heaven knows he turned in a performance that was outstanding for a man in his physical condition. Only a fine actor could have done so well in such a state of health."

"The tremendous exploitation and publicity possibilities of having Douglas' final performance on *The Twilight Zone* were pointed out to us by members of our staff," Serling concluded, "but in the final analysis, it was decided to do the thing that was right for Paul and remake the film."

According to a release schedule dated February 3, 1960, this episode was originally scheduled for broadcast on March 25. On February 17, the episode was moved to the June 17 time slot.

Robert Parrish came in to direct the new scenes, using the same schedule – first two days on location, third day at Stage 10 for the hospital and dressing room scenes. There was only one noticeable difference between the first filming and the second. The original production included day and night shots of the exterior of the ballpark, and night scenes of the dugout and the scoreboard. For the new scenes, no night shots were filmed, and very little from the first production was edited into the finished film we see today. No footage from the first film (featuring Paul Douglas) is known to exist.

Jack Warden, who played the lead in a previous *Zone* episode, "The Lonely," was brought in to replace Paul Douglas in the role of Mouth McGarry, manager of the Hoboken Zephyrs, a major league team whose records are only available in *The Twilight Zone*.

The closing narration for the first cut was not the same as featured in the version we see today:

"Once upon a time there was a major league baseball team called the Hoboken Zephyrs who during the last year of their existence, wound up in last place and shortly thereafter wound up in oblivion. There is a rumor . . . unsubstantiated, of course . . . that a manager named McGarry took them to the West Coast and wound up with a pennant and a World's Championship not long after their arrival. This team had a pretty fair pitching staff, several fellahs named Drysdale, Koufax and Sherry . . . [a pause] And if you are interested as to where these gentlemen came from, you might check under 'B' for baseball . . . in the Twilight Zone."

Because of the death of Paul Douglas, the trailer Serling did for this episode was scrapped and replaced with a new one. The unseen trailer is reprinted below:

"Next week we take you into a state of wonderful confusion. The late Mr. Paul Douglas stars in a play we call 'The Mighty Casey.' Bring your imagination as we recount for you the trials and tribulations of a major league ball club called the Hoboken Zephyrs, a put upon manager, and the most fabulous baseball pitcher you'll ever watch in action. Next week on The Twilight Zone – 'The Mighty Casey.'"

With the CBS Television Network owning 50 percent control over the series, their concerns for budget was justified. The network disapproved refilming "The Mighty Casey," so Serling insisted on using Cayuga's funds to produce the revised version. The network took a stance against the decision.

Future productions (especially for the second season) would generate a strain on both Serling and Houghton, as the network would continue to look over the books, attempting to voice prior approval of expenses when the opportunity knocked. Cayuga had a large control over the production costs, but the network took a negative view of refilming an episode it felt was satisfactory and expressed its concern a number of times. Serling voiced his opinion to Guy Della Cioppa months after this episode was telecast. "I'll grant you an inordinate amount of pique on my part with the Network's handling of *The Twilight Zone*. I can't help but feel that it's been short-shifted. Their refusal to re-shoot the Paul Douglas film which was patently unshakable and the ultimate necessity of my having to put out my own money for this purpose makes me think that a future relationship between CBS and Serling might find itself strained at the edges."

Months after this episode was telecast, Serling was offered $5,000 for permission to do "Old McDonald Had a Curve," for *The Shirley Temple Theatre*. The script was one formerly submitted to *The Lux Video Theater* and rejected. The script was then purchased by the producers of *Kraft Television Theater* and broadcast under the same name on August 5, 1953. The story told of a 67-year-old ex-major league baseball pitcher who proves his worth to the team when he develops a curve ball that passes the rule of Major League Baseball and strikes out his competition. Serling admitted in a letter that, "I took the basic idea of this story and put it into a *Twilight Zone* episode called 'The Mighty Casey.'" Serling disclosed this fact to the producers *Shirley Temple*, having offered to buy the rights back from *Kraft*, feeling that the two teleplays were similar.

On May 2, 1961, John M. Hardy of the Central Christian Church in Orlando, Florida, submitted a plot device for *The Twilight Zone*, on the inspiration of the rerun telecast weeks before.

Dear Mr. Serling,
I would like to submit a story idea for your consideration on your program, Twilight Zone. For some months I have been toying with the idea and it came to somewhat of a head in seeing your recent program on "Casey, the Robot Pitcher."

Briefly here it is: The "hero" of this opus is accidentally hit on the head and thereby receives damage to his optic nerve. The only sustained damage is that his vision of moving objects is considerably slowed. All that he sees crawls by at a snail's pace – automobiles traveling at sixty mph seem to be doing about thirty mph. In attending a baseball game he realizes the tremendous potential of his newly found condition. A fast pitch from a big-league pitcher seems to literally float up to the plate. A ball hit by a bat, a line drive that is, lazily makes its way to the outfield.

Robert Sorrells clowns around on the set of "The Mighty Casey."

Seeing everything in slow motion, he decides to offer his services to the team as a shortstop. Imagine the results! No pitcher can strike him out. He has such good timing that he bats 1.000. If they walk him he steals second, third and home. He scores a run every time he comes to bat. At field no ball passes him. In fact, he is so fast a-foot that he can manage to play his own position and cover second, third and most of the shallow out-field.

The twist to this could very well be that one day he gets "beaned" during a turn at bat – perhaps a dust particle gets in his eye. Any way this is the end of the man who batted 1.000.

Please try this on for size and see if you can use it. While I do some writing, I feel that you could take this idea and make somewhat of a classic of it.

I would appreciate hearing from you concerning this idea and knowing whether or not it would be suitable for your fine program.

Thank you for considering this suggestion, I am,

Most cordially yours,

John M. Hardy

Terry Vernon, television columnist for *The Long Beach Press-Telegram* commented that this episode "scores a home run."

In a baseball-themed episode of *The Simpsons*, titled "Homer at the Bat," initially telecast on February 20, 1992, one of the animated characters gets sucked into another dimension and Einstein's equation flies across the television screen.

Production #3634 "A WORLD OF HIS OWN" (Initial telecast: July 1, 1960)

© Cayuga Productions, Inc., June 30, 1960, LP16782

Dates of Rehearsal: March 30 and 31, 1960

Dates of Filming: April 1, 4 and 5, 1960

Sound dubbing completed: May 13, 1960

Script #34 dated: February 25, 1960, with revised pages dated March 26, 1960.

Shooting script dated: March 26, 1960

Producer and Secretary: $725.00	Story and Secretary: $2,000.00
Director: $1,250.00	Cast: $5,900.00
Unit Manager and Secretary: $315.00	Production Fee: $750.00
Legal and Accounting: $250.00	Below the line charges (M-G-M): $22,015.55
Below the line charges (other): $232.52	Total Production Costs: $33,438.07

Cast: Phyllis Kirk (Victoria West); Mary La Roche (Mary); and Keenan Wynn (Gregory West).

Stock Music Cues: Main Title (by Bernard Herrmann, :25); Monday Morning Part 1 – Never Come Monday (by Herrmann, :30); Light Dramatic Series #6 (by Rene Garriguenc, :12); The Search #3 (by Lucien Moraweck, :12); Light Dramatic Series #12 (by Garriguenc, :16); Harpsichord Notes and Chords (anonymous, :05); Bell Notes (anonymous, :04); Robot Rock (by Bruce Campbell, :13); Monday Morning (by Herrmann, :17); Light Dramatic Series #14 (by Garriguenc, :12); Light Dramatic Series #16 (by Garriguenc, :14); Songe (by Rene Challan, :52); Accent (by Herrmann, :12); Wacky (by Wilbur Hatch, :04); Ho-Hum (by Hatch, :02); Robot Rock (by Campbell, :01); Waiting for Babies (by Hatch, :18); Songe (by Challan, :55); Shock Chord (by Moraweck, :02); Shock Harmonics #1 (by Fred Steiner, :13); Accent (by Herrmann, :14); Vibraphone Effects (anonymous, :14); Utility Cues (by Campbell, :08); Shock Harmonics #2 (by Steiner, :04); City Melancholy #2 (by Garriguenc, :11); Hope – Walt Whitman Suite (by Herrmann, :20); Shock Chord (by Moraweck, :03); Shock Harmonics #3 (by Steiner, :15); Brave New World (by Herrmann, :10); Ruthless Ruth (by Hatch, :10 and :06); Songe (by Challan, :54); Vibraphone Effects (anonymous, :05); Shock Harmonics #1 (by Steiner, :02); Monday Morning (by Herrmann, :22); Elegant Liza (by Hatch and Wilkinson, :05); and End Title (by Herrmann, :52).

Director of Photography: George T. Clemens, a.s.c.
Art Directors: George W. Davis and Merrill Pye
Set Decorations: Henry Grace and Keogh Gleason

Production Manager: Ralph W. Nelson
Assistant Director: Don Klune
Film Editor: Joseph Gluck, a.c.e.
Sound: Franklin Milton and Philip Mitchell
Directed by Ralph Nelson
Teleplay by Richard Matheson

"The home of Mr. Gregory West, one of America's most noted playwrights. The office of Mr. Gregory West. Mr. Gregory West: shy, quiet, and at the moment, very happy. Mary: warm, affectionate . . . and the final ingredient: Mrs. Gregory West."

Plot: The wife of Gregory West, a great and famous playwright, swears she saw him in the company with another woman. When she enters his office, the woman is nowhere to be seen. Puzzled, she forces Gregory to reveal how he brings the fictional "Mary" to life. He explains that anytime he describes a character in extreme detail in his Dictaphone, the character comes true to form. To prove this to Victoria, he brings Mary to life and only after he cuts the tape out of the Dictaphone and throws it into the fire does Mary vanish before Victoria's eyes. His wife, however, after seeing the proof, decides to file for a divorce and have him committed. Forced to reveal his hand, Gregory removes an envelope from his wall safe with her name on it, containing a magnetic strip. Victoria doesn't believe a word he says, and stubbornly grabs the envelope and throws it into the fire – which causes her to vanish. Realizing he has the opportunity to change things, Gregory brings back his new love, a woman named "Mary," who will remain with him now on a permanent basis.

"We hope you enjoyed tonight's romantic story on The Twilight Zone. At the same time, we want you to realize that it was, of course, purely fictional. In real life, such ridiculous nonsense could never . . . [Keenan Wynn longs for privacy by throwing a tape designed for Serling into the fireplace] . . . Well, that's the way it goes . . . [Serling vanishes] . . . Leaving Mr. Gregory West, still shy, quiet, very happy and apparently in complete control . . . of The Twilight Zone."

Trailer: *"Next week we take you back into the dark and hidden, unexplored recesses of a writer's mind, and do some probing as to just how this type of bird operates. It's a fascinating excursion into the oddball. On the Twilight Zone next week Keenan Wynn and Phyllis Kirk star in Richard Matheson's 'A World of His Own.'*

And in this particular one – even this kooky writer gets into the act. Good night."

Trivia, etc. When Rod Serling was writing teleplays for live dramatic anthologies like *Kraft Television Theater*, *Playhouse 90* and *Studio One*, he used two typewriters alternately. He was a one-handed, punching typist and hard on machines – the typewriters had a habit of breaking down, and he found them unable to keep up with his creative torrents. So in late 1955, he substituted the typewriters for a dictating machine. (He would use a typewriter to type letters and briefs at times, but for the most part he used the Dictaphone.) He dictated his *Twilight Zone* scripts into the same type of machine seen and used by Keenan Wynn in this episode. Serling, however, did not have a hand in scripting this episode.

Richard Matheson originally wrote the teleplay as a serious story, but after reviewing it, Serling had Buck Houghton request a rewrite so the script could be enacted in lighter fare. Shortly after the rewrite, Matheson realized that the opinion of the story content was not agreed on by both parties. In a very brief note, Matheson wrote to Serling. "A brief note to thank you for your tact and understanding regarding the last rewrite on my script. I certainly didn't want to make trouble. As I said, I was just upset. Your kind words have made me feel very happy about the whole thing. I think you know that I have the greatest of respect for your craft and want only to do the best work I can for your series – which, unless justice is only a word, must succeed tremendously."

On the same day Serling appeared on camera for this episode, he sat on the desk and delivered two trailers, each of different length. When the film was edited down to size, the one of shorter length was used for the finished product. The longer one was never used:

"Next week we take you back into the dark and hidden, unexplored recesses of a writer's mind and shine a twenty five watt bulb on just how these weird, wild kooks operate. It's a fascinating excursion into the oddball. On the Twilight Zone next week Keenan Wynn and Phyllis Kirk star in Richard Matheson's 'A World of His Own.' And in this particular one – even this kooky writer gets into the act."

The lounge with the fireplace where most of the story takes place is the same set featured in "A Stop at Willoughby" where Gart Williams takes a drink and exchanges words with his wife. No statues are seen on the bookshelves in "A Stop at Willoughby" as seen in this episode, but the fireplace and bookshelf were a permanent fixture on the set, redecorated to give the appearance of a totally separate living room. (The fake stairway next to the fireplace in "Willoughby" was removed for this scene.) Ironically, the same fireplace makes an appearance in two separate episodes of *The Thin Man*, which co-starred Phyllis Kirk.

On October 28, 1961, columnist Gilbert Seldes reviewed *The Twilight Zone*, commenting, "I liked best the one in which Keenan Wynn is a great novelist whose wife sees him through the window making a pass at another woman."

The characters Virginia West and Gregory West were an inside-joke. The secretary for producer Buck Houghton was named Virginia Gregory.

Richard Matheson later wrote a short story adapted from this teleplay, titled "And Now I'm Waiting," which was published in an issue of *The Twilight Zone Magazine*.

This episode also marks Serling's first on-screen appearance on the television series, not counting the teasers that appeared at the end of each episode. It may have been this very episode that convinced Buck Houghton and the sponsors that Serling was right for the on-screen host beginning with the second episode.

SUMMER RERUNS

On April 25, a proposed schedule of summer reruns was created. That list is reprinted below:

June 24, 1960	"One for the Angels"	General Foods
July 1, 1960	"A World of His Own" (original)	Kimberly-Clark
July 8, 1960	"The Four of us Are Dying"	General Foods
July 15, 1960	"Mr. Denton on Doomsday"	Kimberly-Clark
July 22, 1960	"The Purple Testament"	General Foods
July 29, 1960	"Walking Distance"	Kimberly-Clark
August 5, 1960	"A World of Difference"	General Foods
August 12, 1960	"The Hitch-Hiker"	Kimberly-Clark
August 19, 1960	"Time Enough at Last"	General Foods
August 26, 1960	"The Monsters Are Due on …"	Kimberly-Clark
September 2, 1960	"Escape Clause"	General Foods
September 9, 1960	"And When the Sky Was Opened"	Kimberly-Clark
September 16, 1960	"The 16 Millimeter Shrine"	General Foods
September 23, 1960	"The Lonely"	Kimberly-Clark

It was "suggested" that "The After Hours" could air on September 16, "A Passage for Trumpet" could air on September 2, and "Where is Everybody?" could air on August 12. According to an interoffice memo from Buck Houghton to Rod Serling, the schedule of reruns was a bit tricky, and the changes were made so the sponsors would be promoted in episodes they did not promote during the first run. "It is highly desirable that the two sponsors change shows. Don't give General Foods first run to them again in a rerun. This pleases the little rascals, I'm told."

It was also decided that the audience had grown considerably since the early weeks of the program. "Therefore, the earlier a show was in first run, the more likely it will be brand new to a directly proportionate segment of our present audience," Houghton explained. "Two of the shows we like for rerun because of their outstanding qualities nevertheless have a snapper at the end; knowing the snapper I think a good many viewers might dial them out because they know what is to come, and because the snapper is their finest quality. These are 'Third From the Sun' and 'Where is Everybody?'"

Amazingly, the eventual schedule of reruns almost contradicts Houghton's suggestions, but nevertheless did not harm the ratings. Serling wrote back the day after seeing the proposed rerun schedule, suggesting the following be run instead:

"Where is Everybody?"	"The Hitch-Hiker"
"Mr. Denton on Doomsday"	"The Last Flight"
"Walking Distance"	"The Lonely"
"Time Enough at Last"	"And When the Sky Was Opened"
"Third from the Sun"	"The Purple Testament"
"A Nice Place to Visit"	"The Big, Tall Wish"
"The Monsters Are Due on Maple Street"	

Looking over some of the first season episodes, Serling critiqued what he felt were inferior. "The following shows cannot be repeated for the following reasons," he explained. "'One for the Angels' was cute, but ineffective and Wynn's performance let us down terribly. 'A World of His Own' turned out to be one of the most obtuse shows we had by way of audience understanding. I don't want to compound what has been a criticism of the show by repeating [these] kinds of questions. I love this baby, but I'm thinking of audience reaction now. 'Escape Clause' was the least original of any of the shows we had on and 'The Sixteen Millimeter Shrine' was simply a bad film, poorly conceived and badly executed."

Following Serling's suggestions, a revised list was made:

July 8, 1960	"Time Enough at Last"	General Foods
July 15, 1960	"Where is Everybody?"	Kimberly-Clark
July 22, 1960	"Third From the Sun"	General Foods
July 29, 1960	"Walking Distance"	Kimberly-Clark
August 5, 1960	"The Purple Testament"	General Foods
August 12, 1960	"And When the Sky Was Opened"	Kimberly-Clark
August 19, 1960	"The Hitch-Hiker"	General Foods
August 26, 1960	"The Last Flight"	Kimberly-Clark
September 2, 1960	"The Monsters Are Due on ..."	General Foods
September 9, 1960	"A Nice Place to Visit"	Kimberly-Clark
September 16, 1960	"The Big, Tall Wish"	General Foods
September 23, 1960	"The Lonely"	Kimberly-Clark

In view of the possibility of a pre-emption of *Twilight Zone* on September 2, Serling and Houghton decided to remove a well received show, "The Monsters Are Due on Maple Street" from September 2, and moved it to August 26, figuring if there was a pre-emption, the acclaimed episode would still air. The following was the next revision:

July 8, 1960	"Time Enough at Last"	General Foods
July 15, 1960	"Where Is Everybody?"	Kimberly-Clark
July 22, 1960	"Third From the Sun"	General Foods
July 29, 1960	"Walking Distance"	Kimberly-Clark
August 5, 1960	"And When the Sky Was Opened"	General Foods
August 12, 1960	"The Hitch-Hiker"	Kimberly-Clark
August 19, 1960	"The Last Flight"	General Foods
August 26, 1960	"The Monsters Are Due on ..."	Kimberly-Clark
September 2, 1960	"The Purple Testament"	General Foods
September 9, 1960	"A Nice Place to Visit"	Kimberly-Clark
September 16, 1960	"The Big, Tall Wish"	General Foods
September 23, 1960	"The Lonely"	Kimberly-Clark

The final list of reruns as actually aired:

Date	**Title**	**Sponsor**
July 8, 1960	**Repeat** "Time Enough at Last"	General Foods
July 15, 1960	*pre-empted due to the Democratic National Convention*	

July 22, 1960	**Repeat** "Third From the Sun"	General Foods
July 29, 1960	**Repeat** "Walking Distance"	Kimberly-Clark
August 5, 1960	**Repeat** "And When the Sky Was Opened"	General Foods
August 12, 1960	**Repeat** "The Hitch-Hiker"	Kimberly-Clark
August 19, 1960	**Repeat** "The Last Flight"	General Foods
August 26, 1960	**Repeat** "The Monsters Are Due on …"	Kimberly-Clark
September 2, 1960	**Repeat** "The Four of Us Are Dying"	General Foods
September 9, 1960	**Repeat** "A Nice Place to Visit"	Kimberly-Clark
September 16, 1960	**Repeat** "The Lonely"	General Foods
September 23, 1960	**Repeat** "Execution"	Kimberly-Clark

First Season Instrumentation for Original Music Scores

- "And When the Sky Was Opened" — 1 Flute, 1 Clarinet, 1 Bass Clarinet, 1 Horn and 1 Trumpet. For Percussion: Vibraphone, Triangle, Tam-Tams, Snare Drum, Bass Drum, Cymbal, Harp, Celeste, Piano, Violin, Cello and 5 string Double Bass.

- "What You Need" — 1 Clarinet, 1 Bass Clarinet, 3 Horns, 3 Cellos, 1 Organ, 1 Piano and 1 Celeste.

- "The Four of Us Are Dying" — 2 Flutes, 3 Clarinets, 2 Alto Saxes, 2 Tenor Saxes, 1 Baritone Sax, 3 Trumpets, 4 Trombones, 1 Piano, and 1 Bass. For Drums/Percussion: Vibraphone, Xylophone, Marimba, Bongo, "Boo-Bams" and Gourd.

- "The Purple Testament" — 1 Harmonica, 1 Flute, 1 Oboe, 1 English Horn, 2 Clarinets, 1 Bass Clarinet, 1 Bassoon, 3 French Horns, 2 Trumpets, 1 Trombone and 1 Bass. For Percussion: Snare Drum, Marimba, Tympani, Vibraphone and Cymbal.

- "Elegy" — 1 Piccolo, 1 Flute, 1 Oboe, 1 English Horn, 1 Clarinet, 1 Tenor Sax, 1 Bassoon, 2 Horns, 2 Trumpets, 1 Trombone, 1 Euphonium, 1 Tuba and 1 Bass (trombone?). For Percussion: Vibraphone, Bass Drum, Cymbal, Snare Drum, 2 Pianos, 3 Violins and Bass.

- "The Monsters Are Due on Maple Street" — 1 Piccolo, 1 Flute, 1 Alto Flute, 1 Oboe, 1 English Horn, 2 Clarinets, 2 Bass Clarinets, 1 Bassoon, 1 Euphonium, 3 Horns, 1 Harp, 1 Tympani, 1 Vibraphone and Bass.

- "A World of Difference" — 2 Oboes, 2 English Horns, 1 Bass Oboe, 1 Clarinet, 1 Bass Clarinet, 1 Bassoon, 2 Trumpets, 1 Horn, 2 Trombones, 1 Violin, 3 Cellos, 1 Organ, 1 Tympani and Vibraphone.

- "The Big Tall Wish" — 1 Flute, 1 Oboe, 1 Clarinet/Bass Clarinet, 1 Bassoon, , 1 Harp, 1 Vibraphone, 1 Harmonica, 3 Violas, 2 Cellos and Contrabass.

- "Nightmare as a Child" — 1 Flute/Alto Flute, 1 Harp, 1 Celeste/Piano and 1 Cello. For Percussion: Vibraphone, Marimba, Xylophone and Glockenspiel.

SECOND SEASON PRODUCTION COSTS

Secretary Salary: $1,166.84
Office Supplies: $1,659.80
Payroll Taxes, etc.: $11,854.78
Layoff Week Salary: $75.00

Unit Manager Salary: $2,255.00
Messenger Service: $344.60
Insurance: $5,041.34
Guild Pension Plans: $13,194.27

Adding the preproduction and unallocated costs, and the unassigned literary properties (totaling $4,500.00), and the costs of production for each episode, the total cost to produce the 31 episodes (which included "Nothing in the Dark" and "The Grave") from the second season's filming totaled $1,567,106.83 – half a million less than the year before.*

Production #3639 "KING NINE WILL NOT RETURN"
(Initial telecast: September 30, 1960)
© Cayuga Productions, Inc., September 30, 1960, LP17899
Dates of Rehearsal: August 5 and 8, 1960
Dates of Filming: August 9, 10 and 11, 1960
Script #39 dated: May 26, 1960, with revised pages dated July 14 and 29, and August 3, 1960.
Revised draft: June 6, 1960
Shooting script dated: August 3, 1960

Producer and Secretary: $1,823.00
Director: $1,250.00
Unit Manager and Secretary: $600.00
Agents Commission: $2,500.00
Below the line charges (M-G-M): $45,405.79
Total Production Costs: $61,812.53

Story and Secretary: $2,630.00
Cast: $4,600.00
Production Fee: $825.00
Legal and Accounting: $250.00
Below the line charges (other): $1,928.74

---

* All summary of production costs listed for second season episodes according to production files dated June 30, 1961.

Cast: Bob Cummings (Captain Robert Embry); Seymour Green (the British officer); Paul Lambert (the doctor); Richard Lupino (the British soldier); Gene Lyons (the psychiatrist); and Jenna McMahon (the nurse).

Original Music Score Composed and Conducted by Fred Steiner (Score No. CPN5928): Etrange #3 (by Marius Constant, :09); Milieu #1 (by Constant, :16); Passacaglia (1:20); Captain Embry (1:17); Capt. Embry A (:42); Puzzles (:51); I'm Alone (:59); First Vision (:22); No Joking (:18); Dead Phones (:10); Hallucinations (:52); Barren Hill (:51); Struggle (1:21); Second Vision (1:03); Prayer (:23); Sand (:36); Etrange #3 (by Constant, :10); and Milieu #2 (by Constant, :30).

Associate Producer: Del Reisman
Art Director: George W. Davis and
    Phil Barber
Director of Photography: George T.
    Clemens, a.s.c.
Production Managers: Ralph W. Nelson
    and E. Darrell Hallenbeck
Set Decorations: Henry Grace and H. Web
    Arrowsmith
Teleplay by Rod Serling

Captain James Embry (Bob Cummings) tries to find reason amidst chaos.

Assistant Director: Kurt Neumann, Jr.
Casting: Ethel Winant
Film Editor: Bill Mosher
Sound: Franklin Milton and Charles Scheid
Directed by Buzz Kulik

"This is Africa, 1943. War spits out its violence overhead . . . and the sandy graveyard swallows it up. Her name is King Nine . . . B-25, medium bomber, 12th Air Force. On a hot still morning she took off from Tunisia to bomb the southern tip of Italy. An errant piece of flak tore a hole in a wing tank and, like a wounded bird, this is where she landed, not to return on this day, or any other day."

Plot: Captain James Embry wakes to find himself alone in the desert, surrounded by the bellied wreckage of the King Nine. Sifting through torn wires, smashed metal and shattered glass, he is unable to find any evidence that his crew is within sight or sound. He seeks rescue with the help of a radio that provides no answer. Suffering from both heat and hallucinations, Embry visions the ghosts of his crew and wonders if his mind has snapped. He finds a grave marker for one of the crewmembers. He witnesses jet aircraft flying overhead, apparently out of place and out of time. Finally he screams from exhaustion and wakes in a hospital bed with a doctor and psychiatrist looking over him. Apparently, a recent article in the local newspaper about a WWII bomber found intact in the desert caused Embry's mind to snap. He has accepted the blame for a crash during the war that caused the death of his crew, which still plagues him. Embry laughs, wondering if maybe he should have been on board the plane that day when it went down and disappeared, but the psychiatrist claims a guilty conscience is to blame. Yet, as the doctor and psychiatrist exit the room, they observe sand falling out of Embry's shoe . . .

"Enigma buried in the sand, a question mark with broken wings that lies in silent grace as a marker in a desert shrine. Odd how the real consorts with the shadows, how the present fuses with the past. How does it happen? The question is on file in the silent desert. And the answer? The answer is waiting for us in the Twilight Zone."

Trailer: *"Next week you'll ride up front in this B-25, you'll crash land in a desert, and you'll go through an incredible experience with a most distinguished actor, Mr. Robert Cummings, who lends us his talents as we once again move into the Twilight Zone and bring you a tale that I doubt will be easily forgotten. Mr. Robert Cummings stars in 'King Nine Will Not Return' . . . next week on The Twilight Zone!"*

Trivia, etc. Serling was inspired to write the teleplay because of recent news events reporting the discovery of the B-24 Liberator bomber known as the "Lady Be Good." Following a bombing raid in April of 1943, the "Lady Be Good" of the 514th Bomb Squadron failed to return to base. After attempts to locate the plane, the nine crewmembers were classified as "Missing In Action" and presumed dead, believed to have perished after crashing in the Mediterranean. Flash forward to February 27, 1959, when a British oil surveyor named Paul Johnson located the wreckage of the "Lady Be Good" in the Sahara Desert, following a first sighting from the air on May 16 and June 15, 1958. The plane was broken into two pieces, was immaculately preserved, with functioning machine guns, working radio, and supplies of food and water. No human remains were found near the aircraft, nor were parachutes found. *

This episode of *The Twilight Zone* was not the only film inspired by the "Lady Be Good" incident. A 1970 made-for-TV movie titled *Sole Survivor* concerned the ghosts of a B-25 bomber crew that crashed in the Libyan desert. The 1964 novel, *Flight of the Phoenix*, features a similar premise but the plot does not involve ghosts, strange visions or a lone survivor. Instead, the story concerns a group of survivors who crash land in the desert and must resort to an arrogant aeronautical engineer to help repair the craft and seek an escape route.

For Rod Serling to make the dialogue in his script as true to form, and preventing viewers who served in the U.S. military from laughing at what could be obvious mistakes, Serling consulted De Forest Research at Desilu Studios. Verbiage of an American reporting a missing aircraft, the operations room, and dialogue from a pilot of a downed craft were given careful attention. The research cost $15.00 (Invoice #333, dated June 2, 1960) and Cayuga Productions paid for the service.

On June 8, 1960, Serling submitted the rough draft of the script to Owen Comora of Young & Rubicam, explaining that, in his opinion, it would serve as a strong opening show for the second season. From the day the script was drafted to the day it was sent to Comora, it was decided that Serling would

* The inspiration for this *Twilight Zone* episode was confirmed by Connie Olmsted, Serling's secretary, answering a fan letter dated November 14, 1960.

begin appearing on camera (Serling described it as "the host-on-camera concept" and "frozen frame idea"). The script did not reflect this change, but Serling made mention that he would be appearing on screen instead of off. "If you get a moment, I'd love to get your reaction to this though it strikes me that, as in the pilot, this will be a more exciting film to watch than to read," he told Comora.

Donald Gotschall of the CBS editing department looked over the first draft of this script, which he received on June 7, 1960. On June 14, he addressed a number of concerns to Buck Houghton, most of which were the descriptive parts. Among the concerns:

- Please exercise extreme caution of the "long animal scream" to avoid excessive shock value.
- Embry's words, "Oh God ... Oh, dear God ... I'm responsible" must be delivered with reverence.
- Please delete the reference to the deity in Embry's speech. We suggest "What in heaven's name" be substituted.
- Please delete the business of Embry clawing at his face.
- Please exercise make-up caution on the ugly looking gash across the young sergeant's forehead.

Gotschall also expressed a concern for certain viewers because of the current news events. "In as much as there is a possibility of identification with this plane and the 'Lady Be Good' bomber that disappeared in the desert during the war, it is assumed the names of the crewmembers in the story are fictitious."

Another concern was to "please exercise caution in the direction of the 'half wild, half meaningless, half nonsensical' laugh." This scene, however, where Embry suspects he doesn't exist any more than the aircraft, is not exercised with caution, giving the viewer the suggestion that Embry has indeed cracked.

Bob Cummings appeared in the season opener, courtesy of negotiations during the first two weeks of June, 1960, between Houghton and Cummings' agent, Jerry Zeitman, who was concerned that the normal half-hour anthology supplied little showcase for an actor of name value. Serling graciously assured Zeitman that there would be a large publicity campaign attending the fall opener. Houghton recalled, "On occasion, an actor's agent would tell our casting director, 'Oh, he doesn't do TV.' We'd give him a copy of the script anyway, and the agent would call back, 'He'll do this one!' We got a lot of positive effect out of the first-rate scripts by Rod Serling."

On August 12, Serling wrote to Houghton asking, "I hope to God the desert thing went fine and that Cummings turned in as good a performance as I know he's capable of. His reading was exciting and Buzz's concept seemed particularly valid and creative." The day before, Serling complimented Cummings: "You're a most uniquely talented man and it's a real honor to work with you. I think we should continue this association."

On the evening of the last day of filming, Cummings made arrangements for Rod Serling to receive a book titled *The Damned*, for which Cummings was heavily involved in securing the screen rights. The proposal was to have Serling write a screenplay adapted from the book and film the entire production in Argentina. Like a lot of screenplays and story purchases that happen in Hollywood, this one was never produced.

Serling wrote a 90-minute script titled "The Vespers," which would later be adapted into an episode of the television series, *The Loner*. Serling intended for Cummings to play the role of Booker, but this also never came to be. (About this time Serling had received another book from another Robert, his brother, who penned *The Probable Cause*. Serling remarked to his brother, "for my money the drama of the book far outshines the somewhat sedentary quality of the cover.")

Two months before this episode went before the cameras, Robert Parrish, who directed four episodes during the first season of *The Twilight Zone*, was originally scheduled to direct. For reasons unknown, he was replaced with Buzz Kulik. Parrish never directed any other episodes for the series. Kulik, who proved his measure, considered Rod Serling a "master stylist" plying his trade "with gusto and skill."

"I was an office boy in an advertising agency in 1947 when I directed my first [live] show," recalled director Buzz Kulik. "That was because no one else was considered menial enough. I was making $35 a week at the time. Many young talented people were given the opportunity to develop as the medium developed. Sure it was exciting. Every show was a cliffhanger. You never knew when an actor would blow a line containing a basic plot point, or your key camera would cease to function during the big scene, or the ingénue would get the jitters, or the set would begin to totter – as it actually did once in *Climax!*'s modern dress version of 'Crime and Punishment.' This, they say, lent an urgency, a fiery air of spontaneity that just can't be duplicated on film. I say nuts. The talent may have been urgent and fiery, but this had little to do with the fact that it was live."

"Filmed TV has the advantage of control," Kulik continued. "I admit I was reluctant to do my first filmed show – a *Gunsmoke* shot in 1957. What little may be lost in 'spontaneity' can be gained in perfection in a medium where you can shoot and re-shoot a scene until you get what you really want. But for this you need people skilled in their trade: actors, writers, technicians; in short, the same ingredients that go into the making of any good show."

Production included one day to travel to the location, two days of location shooting, and one day of shooting on the stage back at M-G-M. A generator was required to operate the camera equipment on location. A nurse was on hand to care for anyone who might suffer from the heat while on location. The episode came in at about $14,000 over budget. $5,000 of the overage was because of King Nine's location and transportation expenses – billed to Houghton in mid-September. The total costs surprised Houghton, according an interoffice memo, and he cited this "would not have happened with Ralph Nelson around."

"Both Houghton and Kulik were ecstatic after seeing the rushes," recalled Cummings. "I don't think it was so much my performance as the way 'the bomber' looked sitting out there all alone in one hundred and thirty degrees, but whatever it was, suffice it to say they were as happy as any two executives I have ever seen coming fresh from the world of dailies."

On September 21, 1960, Serling told Cummings, "Your performance in 'King Nine' is something quite unique and I think you'll share my pleasure in it. I think further we ought to have some kind of social get-together the night of the premiere, September 30th, so I wish you'd put a little mark on the calendar. . . . CBS publicity has been calling me with tremored voices telling me of the fantastic cooperation you've been giving them in publicizing the premiere show. For a man of your stature, this goes well above and beyond the call of duty and it's much, much appreciated."

A 31 second music cue was composed by Steiner, entitled "Jets." The music was supposed to be heard in the soundtrack when Embry looks up and observes modern day jets flying through the sky. The music cue was never used. A possible explanation is that the film editor wanted to ensure the sound of the jets flying through the sky could be picked up in sound track, and the music cue may have deafened the sound of the engines. While composed and never used for this episode, the music cue can be heard in two episodes; "Five Characters in Search of an Exit" right after Serling's intro, as the major is searching the wall, and "Death Ship" as the captain swings around to see that Mason is missing.

The September 20, 1959 issue of *The New York Times* reported that "television audiences will be able to get a good look at Rod Serling" and commented that he would "be on camera at the beginning and the end of each of the filmed telecasts in the role of narrator."

Serling was nervous when standing in front of the camera, tensing up when filming for the episodes commenced. While he looked tall on the screen, his height was five-foot-five and with nothing on camera of a specific height to purposely compare him with, much of the television audience was unaware of this fact. "I really don't like to do hosting. I do it by default. I have to," Serling explained to a reporter from the United Press International in August of 1963. "If I had my druthers, I wouldn't do it. If I had to go on live, of course, I'd never do it."

To promote the new season, on August 31, 1960, Rod Serling recorded the following "stay-tuned" spots, all under 10 seconds, featured during the closing credit sequences of other television programs :

1. This is Rod Serling. Bomber "King Nine" piloted by Robert Cummings, comes down hard in *The Twilight Zone* . . . premiering next on most of these stations.
2. This is Rod Serling. Bomber "King Nine" piloted by Robert Cummings, comes down hard in *The Twilight Zone* . . . premiering later tonight on most of these stations.
3. This is Rod Serling. Bomber "King Nine" piloted by Robert Cummings, comes down hard in *The Twilight Zone* . . . premiering tomorrow on most of these stations.

A newspaper in West Virginia commented in its television column that Bob Cummings gave "one of his best performances."

When *Variety* reviewed this episode, it said, "Apparently inspired by the discovery of a missing World War II bomber last summer in the North African desert, 'King Nine' was a psychological study of an Air Force captain who suffered from a guilt complex for 17 years. Following Serling's brief introductory narrative, the viewer was confronted with the captain who paced about a disabled bomber giant, a stagey desert setting.

"It was an acting tour-de-force for Bob Cummings, but neither his superlative one-man performance nor the script was equal to holding audience attention for some 20 minutes when it at last was revealed the captain was a patient in a mental ward. . . . Sole dramatic impact was provided by Cummings' fine portrayal. The quick windup, after the moody, suspenseful beginning, was a letdown. It gave the impression that Serling had suddenly run out of ideas."

The October 3, 1960 issue of *The Hollywood Reporter* reviewed the season premiere: "Rod Serling's stamp on a script has consistently spelled 'quality' and this seasonal debut of his created series was no exception." One week later, the same paper reported, "Rob Cummings' deal to teeoff *Twilight Zone* this year was strictly payoff. In order to bag Bob, Rod Serling agreed to script a Cummings show cuffo."

When this episode was rerun in June of 1962, the television columnist for *The San Antonio Light* recommended "fans should tune in for this one."

On January 3, 1961, wife Mary Cummings wrote to Rod Serling, explaining that the Cummings household received from the Directors' Guild of America a list of titles which would be considered for nominations for best directorial achievement during 1960 for the Television Academy's Emmy Awards. "King Nine Will Not Return" was not included, and Mary requested Serling talk to Houghton and make whatever arrangements were necessary in getting the episode on the list so members would have a chance to vote on it. Only the producer, not the actor, can make that request.

On January 9, Serling sent the following apology to Mary and Robert Cummings, "Unfortunately and regretfully, I was unable to include 'King Nine' in the Emmy nominations for that time period. Another of our shows called 'Eye of the Beholder' seemed to have been better written. It could not boast the kind of brilliant tour-de-force performance that Bob gave in 'King Nine,' but as an over-all production found more audience favor."

Previously, in March of 1960, Serling proposed *The Loner* to Bert Granet of Desilu Productions, Inc. and found his proposal rejected on the grounds that the premise was too similar to *The Texan* starring Rory Calhoun, already two years into production. In December of 1960, Serling pitched the idea with the star appeal of Robert Cummings, to MCA (Universal Studios Television), who gave Serling a belated rejection after the playwright submitted a number of follow-ups. Cummings was willing to climb on board, having favored the pilot script. This marked the final attempted collaboration between Serling and Cumming.

After *The Twilight Zone*, Serling would later find success in getting *The Loner* on the air with Lloyd Bridges in the lead, not Cummings, who by that time walked away from the television sitcom, *My Living Doll*, after having a dispute with the producer.

Production #3638 "THE MAN IN THE BOTTLE" (Initial telecast: October 7, 1960)
© Cayuga Productions, Inc., October 6, 1960, LP17900
Dates of Rehearsal: July 20 and 21, 1960
Dates of Filming: July 22, 23 and 26, 1960
Script #38 dated: May 23, 1960, with revised pages dated June 13 and 21, 1960.
Revised draft: June 7, 1960
Shooting script dated: July 21, 1960

Producer and Secretary: $1,775.00	Story and Secretary: $2,630.00
Director: $1,250.00	Cast: $6,250.98
Unit Manager and Secretary: $600.00	Production Fee: $825.00
Agents Commission: $2,500.00	Legal and Accounting: $250.00
Below the line charges (M-G-M): $28,227.05	Below the line charges (other); $1,153.97
Total Production Costs: $45,462.00	

Cast: Luther Adler (Arthur Castle); Peter Coe (the German officer); Lisa Golm (Mrs. Gumley); Vivi Janiss (Edna Castle); Joseph Ruskin (the genie); Olan Soulé (the I.R.S. agent); and Albert Szabo (the German officer).

Stock Music Cues: Etrange #3 (by Marius Constant, :09); Milieu #1 (by Constant, :16); The Park (by Bernard Herrmann, :44); Brave New World (by Herrmann, :05); Trouble Starts (by Nathan Van Cleave, :42); The Old Man (by Van Cleave, :06); Finale (by Van Cleave, :11); Brave New World (by Herrmann, :05); Glockenspiel Note "D" (anonymous, :07); Back to the Scene of the Crime (by Leonard Rosenman, :49); Low Chords (by anonymous, :06); Brave New World (by Herrmann, :06); Back to the Scene of the Crime (by Rosenman, :43); Harp Shockers (by Fred Steiner, :07); Brave New World (by Herrmann, :06); Back to the Scene of the Crime (by Rosenman, :38); Brave New World (by Herrmann, :06); Harp Shockers (by Steiner, :07); Hope – Walt Whitman Suite (by Herrmann, :24); Desperation (by Rosenman, :12); El Choclo (by A.G. Villoldo, :15); Finale (by Van Cleave, :22); The Proposition (by Van Cleave, :31); Brave New World (by Herrmann, :02); Harp Shockers (by Steiner, :02); The First Vision (by Van Cleave, :31); Back to the Scene of the Crime (by Rosenman, :30); Drum March (anonymous, :15); Drink of Water #8 (by Herrmann, :15); Mad Harpsichord (anonymous, :05); Brave New World (by Herrmann, :13); Military Drums (anonymous, :52); Low Ominous Background (by Lucien Moraweck, :52); Finale (by Van Cleave, :05); Brave New World (by Herrmann, :05); Harp Shockers (by Steiner, :05 and :06); Brave New World (by Herrmann, :06); Glockenspiel "D" (anonymous, :06); The Park (by Herrmann, :32); New Shoes (by Van Cleave, :05); The Old Man (by Van Cleave, :14); Etrange #3 (by Constant, :10); and Milieu #2 (by Constant, :30).

Associate Producer: Del Reisman
Director of Photography: George T. Clemens, a.s.c.
Art Director: George W. Davis and Phil Barber
Set Decorations: Henry Grace and H. Web Arrowsmith

Production Manager: Ralph W. Nelson
Assistant Director: E. Darrell Hallenbeck
Casting: Ethel Winant
Film Editor: Leon Barsha, a.c.e.
Sound: Franklin Milton and Charles Scheid
Directed by Don Medford
Teleplay by Rod Serling

"Mr. and Mrs. Arthur Castle, gentle and infinitely patient people, whose lives have been a hope chest with a rusty lock and a lost set of keys. But in just a moment that hope chest will be opened, and an improbable phantom will try to bedeck the drabness of these two people's failure-laden lives ... with the gold and precious stones of fulfillment. Mr. and Mrs. Arthur Castle, standing on the outskirts and about to enter ... the Twilight Zone."

Plot: Arthur Castle, owner and operator of an antique shop with a heart as big as his store, is around the corner from bankruptcy because he longs for a more profitable business with cheery surroundings. One afternoon, however, Mr. Castle discovers a genie in a bottle, who offers the Castles four

> **Blooper!** In the scene where Arthur becomes Adolph Hitler, the swastika on the flag hanging on the wall is hanging backwards. The left-facing swastika can be found in Hindu and Buddist tradition, but when it represents the Third Reich, it should be right-facing. This mistake was apparently overlooked by everyone involved with the production, right down to the film editors and Buck Houghton. (The swastika is worn correctly on Arthur's arm in full Hitler garb.)

wishes of "a guaranteed performance." Arthur, at first, disbelieves what he sees, but wishes for a broken glass to be fixed for verification – which is accomplished promptly. Failing to accept the consequences of his wishing, Mr. Castle asks for a million dollars so he can clean up his debt – only to suffer from an accountant at the I.R.S. who confiscates most of the cash. Arthur's third wish is for power – so he can rule a foreign country that cannot vote him out of office – and finds himself transformed into Adolph Hilter during his last moment in charge. Using his fourth and final wish, he returns to his antique shop. Disposing of the bottle – and the genie inside – Arthur is now content with his present debt and the drabness of his store.

"A word to the wise now to the garbage collectors of the world, to the curio seekers, to the antique buffs – to everyone who would try to coax out a miracle from unlikely places. Check that bottle you're taking back for a two-cent deposit. The genie you save might be your own. Case in point: Mr. and Mrs. Arthur Castle, fresh from the briefest of trips . . . into the Twilight Zone."

Trailer: *"Inside this curio shop, next week, from amidst this old-school rococo and some fusty, moth-eaten antiquary, will emerge a bottle – this one. And from it will step a genie to give Mr. Luther Adler four wishes. But he'll discover, as will all of you, that there's an economics to magic . . . a high cost of wishing. Next week, a most intriguing tale, 'The Man in the Bottle.' Thank you and good night."*

Trivia, etc. "My work on *The Twilight Zone* came early in my career here in the West," recalled Ruskin. "I have dined out on pointing out that our first rehearsal of 'Man In the Bottle' was a half day in the producers office at a table read. The next day was a full eight-hour rehearsal on the set, that had already been built, with the three actors and the director. The next day was the same with the addition of the cinematographer and one or two department heads. The next day we shot our scenes in the store, all of which went swimmingly. That was my first and last experience rehearsing fully before shooting a TV show in Hollywood in over forty years. We did rehearse live TV in New York so I did not realize, then, that I was dealing with something extraordinary."

In a letter dated August 19, 1960, Buck Houghton explained that the projected estimated budget for this episode was supposed to be a savings of $3,900. "Due to shooting hours running longer than anticipated, both cast and crew went into overtime to the extent of about $2,400."

On July 19, Serling composed an alternate ending to this episode, in which a nondescript street bum happens upon the garbage can containing the remains of the once-broken glass bottle, which has magically repaired itself. He takes out the bottle, stares at it, then sticks it under his shirt. As the street bum starts to walk away, Serling's voice closes the episode:

"And perhaps this man too will realize that there's an economics to magic too . . . rather a high cost of wishing. He may learn this fact just as he'll soon realize that in a very strange way, all roads lead to . . . The Twilight Zone."

This alternate ending may explain the closing comments we hear on the episode today, in which Serling mentioned "garbage collectors of the world" and "check that bottle you're taking back for a two-cent deposit."

Production #3641 "NERVOUS MAN IN A FOUR DOLLAR ROOM"
(Initial telecast: October 14, 1960)

© Cayuga Productions, Inc., October 13, 1960, LP18458
Dates of Rehearsal: July 14 and 15, 1960
Dates of Filming: July 18, 19 and 20, 1960
Shooting script dated: July 15, 1960

Producer and Secretary: $1,775.00
Director: $1,325.00
Unit Manager and Secretary: $600.00
Agents Commission: $2,500.00
Below the line charges (M-G-M): $23,845.37
Total Production Costs: $38,469.08

Story and Secretary: $2,630.00
Cast: $3,307.70
Production Fee: $825.00
Legal and Accounting: $250.00
Below the line charges (other): $1,411.01

Cast: William D. Gordon (George) and Joe Mantell (Jackie Rhoades).

Original Music Score Composed and Conducted by Jerry Goldsmith (Music No. CPN5924): Etrange #3 (by Marius Constant, :09); Milieu #1 (by Constant, :16); The Jitters (:16); Dead Phone (1:01); The Knock (:20); The Gun (1:05); The Image / Image A (:48); Shadows (:38); The Appointment (:15); Jackie's Escape (1:32); New Man (1:18); Etrange #3 (by Constant, :10); and Milieu #2 (by Constant, :30).

Associate Producer: Del Reisman
Director of Photography: George T.
    Clemens, a.s.c.
Art Director: George W. Davis and
    Phil Barber
Set Decorations: Henry Grace and
    H. Web Arrowsmith

Production Manager: Ralph W. Nelson
Assistant Director: E. Darrell Hallenbeck
Casting: Ethel Winant
Film Editor: Bill Mosher
Sound: Franklin Milton and Charles Scheid
Directed by Douglas Heyes
Teleplay by Rod Serling

"This is Mr. Jackie Rhoades, age thirty-four. And where some men leave a mark of their lives as a record of their fragmentary existence on Earth – this man leaves a blot. A dirty, discolored blemish to document a cheap and undistinguished sojourn amongst his betters. What you are about to watch in this room is a strange, mortal combat between a man . . . and himself. For in just a moment Mr. Jackie Rhoades, whose life has been given over to fighting adversaries, will find his most formidable opponent in a cheap hotel room that is in reality the outskirts . . . of the Twilight Zone."

Plot: Jackie Rhoades, a habitual nail biter, is nothing but a nickel-and-dime man. His record with the police lists minor offenses. George, a shady racketeer, visits Jackie late one evening with a proposition – to knock off an old man who has consistently defied the protection racket. George's torpedoes will be picked up by the police after the killing, so he wants Jackie to do the job this time. George hands the little man a gun and warns him what will happen if the job isn't done. Alone in his hotel room, Jackie ponders whether or not he should commit the murderous act. He starts an argument with his alter ego in the mirror, who pleads for Jackie to let him take over. His alter ego is tired of living an existence in which Jackie makes poor decisions – especially the one he's about to make tonight. After an exchange of words and flared tempers, Jackie finds the guts and goodness to grant his alter ego the opportunity. At 2:30 in the morning, George visits the hotel room to learn why the old man is still breathing. Jackie, now a new man with the name of John, pushes George around and orders him to go away . . . or else. With one problem taken care of, John looks himself in the mirror to see his own reflection – that of Jackie, still biting his nails. Jackie asks what comes next and John, before exiting the room, informs his former ego that now they look for a job and a girl.

"Exit Mr. John Rhoades, formerly a reflection in a mirror – a fragment of someone else's conscience, a wishful thinker made out of glass, but now made of flesh and on his way to join the company of men. Mr. John Rhoades, with one foot through the door and one foot out . . . of the Twilight Zone."

Trailer: *"Next week we take you into this eight-by-eight hotel room and we watch a penny-ante crook make a decision. You better ask the room clerk the number of this room, and then come on up. Mr. Joe Mantell is the 'Nervous Man in a Four Dollar Room.' That's the Twilight Zone . . . next week and we'll be waiting for you. Thank you and good night."*

Trivia, etc. In determining whether an idea for *The Twilight Zone* was suitable for the series, fantasy had to be acceptable to the viewing audience. As producer Buck Houghton explained in an interview for Wisconsin's *Appleton Post-Crescent*, "What we do is to limit ourselves to one fantasy [per] show – one fantasy to a customer. Second, we utilize fantasy only when it helps to tell a story, only when it makes the drama stronger, only when it is pertinent to the action." Houghton's description fits this episode, a tour-de-force performance by Joe Mantell as the "little man," in the episode that Houghton referred to as a "closet show."

"Joe Mantell has been cast as the Nervous Man," Houghton drafted to Robert Hoag in a letter. "I can't think of a finer performer for this part but his price is modest; therefore cast will probably come in $4,733 under budget. Since all other elements above-the-line are per budget, this picture is going in $9,835 below the series allowance."

Houghton was extremely pleased by the finances regarding this episode. The total came in almost $9,000 under budget. Originally in an interoffice memo dated July 12, 1960, the episode had been budgeted by M-G-M at $24,783 below-the-line. By the time they added CBS elements chargeable below-the-line, the figure came to $26,377. This was $5,102 under budget. That of course, was an estimate and the final dollar figure saved was more. By August 19, 1960, Houghton explained that "the necessity of making optical corrections for the process work on the stage that fuzzed due to our need to meet schedule will result in this picture going about $500 over show estimate below-the-line . . . reducing the net to $9,300 under."

Production notes on Serling's script (number 41) remarked: "This set is subject to exhaustive design discussions in order to suit it to the script action; however, it will probably evolve into a set requiring a mirror duplicate set alongside. There is the possibility, growing out of discussions with director and cameraman, of the need for designing two or three split screen shots."

"'Nervous Man' was a challenge because I had always wanted to do a *Prisoner of Zenda*-type dual role with the same actor playing both parts," recalled Douglas Heyes with interviewer Ben Herndon.

"But instead of doing it with a split screen or over another actor's shoulder the easy way, I wanted to do it the hard way – with rear projection. First we photographed every part of Joe Mantell's performance that was in the mirror, and then later he played against himself in rear projection. So when we were photographing the mirror stuff, we also had another actor playing out front who was making Joe's moves, so that Joe in the mirror was actually looking in the direction where Joe the actor would be later, when I photographed it for the second time."

"We had another actor, Brian Hutton, who wanted to learn about directing, play the other end of all the scenes," continued Heyes. "He actually had both parts, but his role was completely cut out. We used him so that Joe could actually play the scene to another actor. Hutton was always off camera. When it became rear projection, Joe was speaking to himself, because we'd cut out the Hutton part. His lines were erased from the soundtrack. It was a totally thankless task. Hutton eventually went on to become a director; he did *Where Eagles Dare* (1968)."

Donald Gotschall of the CBS editing department received the script on June 20, 1960, and on June 23, discussed a few concerns with Del Reisman, the associate producer for *The Twilight Zone*. On June 24, Gotschall made out a report to Houghton, asking for a few changes or revisions – none of which were made to the script as both Houghton and Serling apparently felt the issues addressed were not of serious concern. It was requested that the line "look under the bed or go buy some from a vendor or grow them in a pot" be deleted. The word "guts" appeared a number of times throughout the script, and the network insisted that the word "guts" was objectionable and should be replaced or deleted.

The script called for an instant freeze frame with Jackie standing motionless, so Serling could walk out and give his narration. The director, however, decided to film the hotel room scene from the ceiling, and have that footage developed (along with the mirror reflection scenes), so Serling could make his entrance in a more colorful view – walking on the walls. The film was projected against a backdrop where Serling walked out in front and gave the opening narration.

> *The Twilight Zone* was not telecast on the evening of October 21, 1960. All three major networks carried a debate between Vice President Nixon and Senator Kennedy. In their race for the presidency, the men compared views on the vital issues of the day and replied to questions on foreign affairs.

The opening narration, incidentally, was longer in the script than what appears in the finished product:

"This is Mr. Jackie Rhoades, age thirty-four. If there was a Who's Who for nickel and dime crooks, his chronology would state most simply that he was born in New York City, went to a boy's reformatory at age eleven, a state penal institute at age nineteen. He has been picked up on every count from petty larceny to extortion to assault with a deadly weapon. And where some men leave a mark of their lives as a record of their fragmentary existence on Earth – this man leaves a blot. A dirty, discolored blemish to document a cheap and undistinguished sojourn amongst his betters. What you are about to watch in this room is a strange, mortal combat between a man . . . and himself. For in just a moment Mr. Jackie Rhoades, whose life has been given over to fighting adversaries, will find his most formidable opponent in a cheap hotel room that is in reality the outskirts . . . of the Twilight Zone."

The original closing remarks were also lengthier than what appeared in the finished film:

"Exit Mr. John nee Jackie Rhoades, age thirty-four, about to carve himself a nicer and more acceptable piece of life. And while we do not offer this story as the norm or the rule . . . there is a school of thought that says that there are two people in each of us, so, gentlemen . . . mind who you're shaving tomorrow morning. If you nick yourself . . . and the mirror yells ouch . . . you've arrived . . . in The Twilight Zone!"

The 48 second music cue listed as "Image / Image A" was really two separate scores. As per instructions in the score, it was "played back twice as fast and combined" together for the segment where the mirror spun and Jackie's alter ego grew in size.

In June of 1960, Blanche Gaines, Serling's former agent, submitted a couple teleplays to Serling from promising clients: one of them being "The Two-Sided Triangle" by Tobias and Perkins. The script was embarrassingly close to a script Serling was already working on called "There's Another Gentleman in the Room." It involved a man looking at himself in a mirror and the mirror image gradually taking him over. Beyond this, there seemed to be little similarity in the two scripts, but the likeness was sufficiently close enough for Serling to contemplate throwing away his script to ensure he wouldn't be thought a literary pirate.

On July 13, 1960, Bob Shuford of Raleigh, North Carolina, wrote to Rod Serling, care of Bantam Books. Shuford had submitted an original short story titled "Behind the Glass," which told the tale of Claude Randal, a small-time crook who, after facing defeat in various forms (including holding out for bet money), is introduced to a reflection of himself, who guides him into committing a number of profitable crimes. Every time the reflection gives Claude a tip, he concludes with "touch my hand, I'm so very cold." Claude follows each tip, committing acts of robbery and murder, and the rewards grow with each passing week – expensive cars, champagne and a fine home. One day, Claude faces his fears and after receiving another tip, reaches out and touches the reflection's hand. Instantly the reflection and Claude switch places. Claude discovers he is a prisoner of the mirror, and his only means of escape is to do as his reflection did. The mirror, however, is sold to an antique store, where it is later purchased and hung in a mansion. Late one night, with a burglar about, Claude attempts to give the man a tip that would make him wealthy, but the burglar accidentally smashes the mirror, leaving Claude to remain in his cold, world of darkness.

Serling had written his teleplay, "Nervous Man in a Four Dollar Room," weeks before Shuford mailed his submission. The episode went before the cameras before the letter was forwarded to Serling by Bantam. The coincidence of a guided voice in a mirror remained a minor risk for Serling, who was unable to send a rejection letter because Shuford failed to include a mailing address with his submission. Fearing Shuford might threaten a lawsuit for plagiarism because of the submission, after seeing the episode telecast months later, Serling filed the short story away. No lawsuit or further communication resulted from the broadcast, but this was another example of how viewers were submitting plot ideas for episodes that had already finished production, but not yet aired on the network.

The Bennington, Vermont, *Evening Banner* labeled this episode as an "absorbing drama."

The plot device of a man alone in a room, facing his alter ego, forced to choose what would become his destiny while groping with reality, was reused in "The Last Night of a Jockey." When *The Twilight Zone* was revived in the mid-'80s, Bruce Willis starred in a similar-themed story titled "Shatterday." This was a tale about a man, Peter Jay Novins, who attempts to prevent his life from being taken over by his alter ego . . . and by the time he checks into a hotel room, discovers he has failed in every attempt. In a number of episodes of *Married . . . with Children*, the character of Bud Bundy faces his alter ego in the mirror and becomes a suave, sexual, personality that momentarily takes over. The 1993 album, *The Infotainment Scan*, performed by the music group, The Fall, features a song titled "Paranoia Man in Cheap Shit Room," with lyrics in homage to this particular episode.

Production #3645 "A THING ABOUT MACHINES"
(Initial telecast: October 28, 1960)
© Cayuga Productions, Inc., October 27, 1960, LP18591
Dates of Rehearsal: August 23 and 24, 1960
Dates of Filming: August 25, 26 and 29, 1960
Script #45 dated: July 25, 1960

Producer and Secretary: $2,775.00
Director: $1,250.00
Unit Manager and Secretary: $350.00
Agents Commission: $2,500.00
Below the line charges (M-G-M): $36,787.06
Total Production Costs: $53,591.64

Story and Secretary: $2,830.00
Cast: $5,005.00
Production Fee: $825.00
Legal and Accounting: $250.00
Below the line charges (other): $1,619.58

Cast: Henry Beckman (the policeman); Margarita Cordova (the girl on television); Richard Haydn (Bartlett Finchley); Jay Overholts (the intern); Barney Phillips (the repairman); and Barbara Stuart (Edith, the secretary).

Stock Music Cues: Etrange #3 (by Marius Constant, :09); Milieu #1 (by Constant, :16); City Melancholy (by Rene Garriguenc, :28); Bel Air Outdoors (by Garriguenc, :17); Shooting Lesson #1 (by Garriguenc, :03); Perry Mason Background (by Garriguenc, :03); Bel Air Outdoors (by Garriguenc, :44); Shooting Lesson #3 (by Garriguenc, :03); Glissando and Tremolo (anonymous, :01); Shooting Lesson #1 (by Garriguenc, :03); Twilight Zone Theme Main Title Part 2 (by Constant, :18); Menton 17 (by Bernard Herrmann, :18); Brave New World (by Herrmann, :15); Improvisation Eight (by William Gomez, :43 and :25); Belfort 8 (by Constant, :08); Twilight Zone Finale (by Constant, :40 and :46); Perry Mason Background (by Fred Steiner, :02); Menton 8 (by Constant, :28); High Chords (anonymous, :02); Nemours (by Constant, :10); Soft Cascading Glissando (anonymous, :10); High String Tremolo (by Lucien Moraweck, :15); Bel Air Outdoors (by Garriguenc, :15); Belfort #8 (by Constant, :21); Etrange #3 (by Constant, :10); and Milieu #2 (by Constant, :30).

Associate Producer: Del Reisman
Director of Photography: George T.
    Clemens, a.s.c.
Art Director: George W. Davis and Phil Barber
Set Decorations: Henry Grace and
    H. Web Arrowsmith
Teleplay by Rod Serling

Production Manager: Sidney Van Keuran
Assistant Director: E. Darrell Hallenbeck
Casting: Ethel Winant
Film Editor: Leon Barsha, a.c.e.
Sound: Franklin Milton and Charles Scheid
Directed by David Orrick McDearmon

"This is Mr. Bartlett Finchley, age forty-eight, a practicing sophisticate who writes very special and very precious things for gourmet magazines and the like. He's a bachelor and a recluse. With few friends

– only devotees and adherents to the cause of tart sophistry. He has no interests – save whatever current annoyances he can put his mind to. He has no purpose to his life – except the formulation of day-to-day op- portunities to vent his wrath on mechanical contrivances of an age he abhors. In short, Mr. Bartlett Finchley is a malcontent, born either too late or too early in the century – and who in just a moment will enter a realm where muscles and the will to fight back are not limited to human beings. Next stop for Mr. Bartlett Finchley – the Twilight Zone."

Plot: Bartlett Finchley, with the sensitivity of an alligator, has built a reputation for verbally abusing his fellow man. When things do not work the way he wants, Finchley vents his anger on the appli- ances in his house, giving the local repairmen steady revenue. As he explains to his private secretary, before she walks out on him, he prefers to blame-shift his failures on the machines that fail to work. He fears one day the machines will seek vengeance. His suspicions are confirmed when, late one eve- ning after downing a few drinks, he defends himself in a mortal combat with the household appli- ances. The typewriter types "Get Out Of Here Finchley" on carbon paper; the television set displays a gypsy dancer who delivers the same message; the telephone repeats the same verbal warning, and the electric razor takes on a life of its own. He ventures outside to find himself in a deadly game of cat and mouse with his automobile, which is trying to run him over. In the morning, the coroner and police drag the body of Bartlett Finchley out of his swimming pool. The coroner claims a dead body usually floats on water – but this one stayed on the bottom as if something held him down. The police rule it an "accident," possibly a heart attack or too much alcohol in the system.

"Yes, it could just be. It could just be that Mr. Bartlett Finchley succumbed from a heart attack and a set of delusions. It could just be that he was tormented by an imagination as sharp as his wit and as pointed as his dislikes. But as perceived by those attending . . . this is one explanation that has left the premises with the deceased. Look for it filed under 'M' for machines . . . in the Twilight Zone."

Trailer: *"These are familiar items, I'm sure. Television set, electric razor, clock, typewriter . . . the normal, everyday accouterments that are part and parcel of Twentieth Century progress. But next week you'll see them under different circumstances and in a totally dissimilar guise. They'll be machines . . . but they'll also be mon- sters. Our story is called 'A Thing About Machines' and it'll be here waiting for you in the Twilight Zone."*

Trivia, etc. For this episode, Serling came up with the name of Bartlett Finchley from a combination of two former teleplays. Bartlett was the name of a character from an unsold script, "The Beloved Outcast." The character was similar to the one in this *Twilight Zone* episode, both of whom possessed heartless cruelty and uttered quick-witted insults. The name of Finchley originated from a science fiction drama titled "Mr. Finchley Versus the Bomb."

For the projected radio series *It Happens to You*, Serling's first script in the series (labeled number one on the front page) was titled "Mr. Finchley Versus the Bomb." The tale would have been fitting for *The Twilight Zone*: Jason W. Finchley is an old man who resides in a ramshackle old house with a battered porch, in a section of the desert recently designated as a testing ground for U.S. Army bombs. General Millet, in charge of the program, finds the test inconveniently postponed for a time when his orders to remove all residents are defied. Mr. Finchley finds comfort in his rocking chair, whistling and whittling away. Eddie Sloane, a female reporter, becomes involved with the story and helps support the old man as Millet, on orders from higher up, attempts to evict the old man to a safer area. Millet, however, finds himself against the old man and his league of ever-growing supporters. The U.S. Army found themselves facing opposition.

It Happens to You never came to be so, months later, Serling sold a revised script of the same name, now written specifically for television, to *The Lux Video Theater* (telecast January 7, 1952) with Henry Hull in the lead.

Serling recounted to *TV Guide* how he came up with the idea for this *Twilight Zone* entry. "This one I got trying to shave with a razor during a given morning when three appliances in my house gave out. A washer, a dryer, and a television set. It occurred to me how absolutely vulnerable we are to gadgets, gimmicks and electronic jim-crackery. Then the progression took the form of a story involving a man whose appliances became entities and instead of just stopping on him, they went the full route and actually remonstrated against him. Unfortunately, the show did not live up to its potential." On December 12, 1960, in a letter to Owen Comora of Young & Rubicam, the advertising agency representing the sponsor, Serling backed his statement adding, "Mr. Finchley drowned in his swimming pool. Upon reflecting, I wish I had before I wrote the bloody thing."

Barbara Stuart, who played the secretary in this episode, appeared as the recurring character of Lily, the waitress, in the coffee shop on *The George Burns Show*. She was a casting director for a film-commercial company and used her experience to contact other casting directors for television programs, such as *The Twilight Zone*, to get roles. "I want to be a good supporting actress all my life," she said. "I prefer comedy, but I like to make a living. Naturally, I cast myself every chance I got. You have to be practical about these things."

A few references cite actor Lew Brown as the telephone repairman for this episode. This remains a bit of a mystery as the script did not call for the role of a telephone repairman. The information no doubt originates from a CBS publicity release sent out for possible use in television listings. These press releases were, on occasion, inaccurate with a cast name (or two) for a number of episodes. It is possible that the actor was on set to play the role, but this author could find no scripts verifying such a character. Actor Lew Brown did appear in the episodes "Back There" and "Long Distance Call."

In Serling's original draft, Finchley gets back on his feet during the scene in which the car chases him through the streets. He throws himself into the shadows, his back against the house, as the lights of the car play on him briefly and then pass. He feels a sense of relief, pulls out his keys and begins to unlock the door when he hears the blaring, shrieking sound of a car horn and finds himself bathed in the light of the car headlights. He screams, drops the keys, runs off the porch and into the driveway. The car backs up and turns into the driveway. Finchley races aimlessly toward the garage. Its doors are open. Without thinking, he goes inside. As he races back and forth, upsetting paint buckets, ladders and tools, the lights of the car come closer and closer. With its engine roaring, the car moves in as Finchley, with arms outstretched and backed against the far wall of the garage, screams.

The next morning, a police officer and a white-coated intern stare down at the body of Finchley, lying in the driveway in front of the closed doors of the garage. They suspect it was a heart attack, but the neighbors gathering swear they heard screaming the night before. The police officer explains to the intern that the body was found inside the garage in front of his car, just slumped up against the far wall, eyes wide open, "as if he'd seen a ghost . . . or as if that ghost were chasing him!"

According to a letter from Del Reisman of Cayuga Productions to Serling, dated August 24, 1960, "Here is David McDearmon's version of the final scene of 'A Thing About Machines,' designed to incorporate the swimming pool idea. This will not be shot until Monday night, the 29ᵗʰ. If you have any objections, please yell." Serling's initial climax was never filmed, and the episode was shot with McDearmon's revised closing pages, leaving Serling's closing narration intact.

After the initial telecast, a few viewers failed to understand why Finchley's body did not float in the swimming pool. Failing to notice the water dripping from the Lagonda, viewers did not realize the car landed on top of Finchley. Letters asking for an explanation were many. Michael L. Nash, of Far Rockaway, New York, was among the many who wrote to the network, asking for an explanation. Amidst the hundreds of letters Serling received on a regular basis every month, he took the time to offer a brief explanation to each of the viewers who remained puzzled regarding the conclusion of the story.

The scenes outside the mansion, including the swimming pool, were shot on Lot 2 at M-G-M. This is the same swimming pool featured in "Queen of the Nile," "The Trouble with Templeton" and "The Bewitchin' Pool." The exterior shot of the mansion where Finchley drives up to discover the TV repairman's van in his driveway is the same mansion (slightly redecorated) for the opening shot of "Queen of the Nile."

There were two versions filmed of the trailer promoting the next week's episode. The only difference between the two is the added comment, "Thank you and good night." Apparently the version without the "thank you" was used on the program to keep the running time of the film on key.

All music cues titled "Shooting Lesson" were originally composed and conducted for the CBS-TV Western, *Hotel de Paree*. This episode makes use of those scores more than any other in the series.

Production #3642 "THE HOWLING MAN" (Initial telecast: November 4, 1960)

Copyright Registration: © Cayuga Productions, Inc., November 3, 1960, LP18459
Dates of Rehearsal: August 17 and 18, 1960
Dates of Filming: August 19, 22 and 23, 1960
First draft undated with rewrite requested by June 8, 1960.
Script #42 dated: August 4, 1960, with revised pages dated August 11, 16 and 18, 1960.
Shooting script dated: August 18, 1960

Producer and Secretary: $2,775.00	Story and Secretary: $2,155.00
Director: $1,250.00	Cast: $3,870.21
Unit Manager and Secretary: $432.00	Production Fee: $825.00
Agents Commission: $2,500.00	Legal and Accounting: $250.00
Below the line charges (M-G-M): $31,007.00	Below the line charges (other): $1,149.84
Total Production Costs: $45,614.05	

Cast: John Carradine (Brother Jerome); Robin Hughes (the howling man); Frederic Ledebur (Brother Christopher); Ezelle Poule (elderly housekeeper); and H.M. Wynant (David Ellington).

Stock Music Cues: Etrange #3 (by Marius Constant, :09); Milieu #1 (by Constant, :16); Mysterious Storm (by Jerry Goldsmith, :28); The Book Rack (by Bernard Herrmann, :25); The Sun (by

Herrmann, :05); The Telephone (by Herrmann, :24); The Book Rack (by Herrmann, :41); Shock Therapy #3 (by Rene Garriguenc, :07); Mysterious Storm (by Goldsmith, :07); The Book Rack (by Herrmann, :40); Secret Circle (by Goldsmith, :37); Back to the Scene of the Crime (by Leonard Rosenman, :54); Twilight Zone Theme Opening (by Herrmann, :33); Shock Therapy #2 (by Garriguenc, :17); The Book Rack (by Herrmann, :42); The Sun (by Herrmann, :06); Etrange #3 (by Constant, :10); and Milieu #2 (by Constant, :30).

Associate Producer: Del Reisman

Director of Photography: George T.
    Clemens, a.s.c.

Production Manager: Sidney Van Keuran
    and Ralph W. Nelson

Art Director: George W. Davis and Phil Barber

Sound: Franklin Milton and Charles Scheid

Assistant Director: E. Darrell Hallenbeck

Casting: Ethel Winant

Film Editor: Bill Mosher

Set Decorations: Henry Grace
    and H. Web Arrowsmith

Directed by Douglas Heyes

Teleplay by Charles Beaumont, originally published in the November 1959 issue of *Rogue*, under the pen name of C.B. Lovehill (later reprinted in *Night Ride and Other Journeys* (Bantam, 1960).

"The prostrate form of Mr. David Ellington, scholar, seeker of truth and, regrettably, finder of truth. A man who will shortly arise from his exhaustion to confront a problem that has tormented mankind since the beginning of time. A man who knocked on a door seeking sanctuary and found instead the outer edges of the Twilight Zone."

Plot: One dark and stormy night, a few years after the First World War, while traveling through Central Europe, David Ellington finds himself seeking shelter at a European monastery. There, Ellington is introduced to the "Brothers of Truth," keepers of the hermitage, who are holding a man against his will. Brother Jerome claims their captive is the Devil himself, and the constant howling and shrieks are coming from the dark corridors originating from the prisoner – his own form of torture against his captors. Jerome also explains that since the capture, there have been no world wars, pestilence, plague or unnatural disasters. The prisoner, however, looks nothing like the Devil. Alone with Ellington, he tells a mournful tale of his capture and pleads with the visitor to help him get free. Having heard both sides of the story, Ellington chooses to act. Waking in the middle of the night, he steals the keys and grants the captive freedom by removing the staff of truth from the door . . . and is shocked to witness a transformation before his eyes. Before he could be caught again, Satan, now in his true form, vanishes in a puff of smoke – leaving Ellington a burden to bear knowing he released the Devil back into the world. Many years later, after World War II and the Korean War, a much older Ellington has finally caught up with the howling man and warns his servant to ignore the howling and leave the door locked until he returns with the Brothers from the monastery. The old woman, also skeptical, waits till her master leaves before opening the door . . .

"Ancient folk saying: 'You can catch the Devil, but you can't hold him for long.' Ask Brother Jerome. Ask David Ellington. They know, and they'll go on knowing to the end of their days and beyond . . . in the Twilight Zone."

Trailer: *"Down this hall is a very strange individual locked in a room. He's known by various names and by various forms, and next week on the Twilight Zone you'll be close to the elbow of the people who let him out. Our story is called 'The Howling Man' by Mr. Charles Beaumont. It's designed for the young in heart . . . but the strong of nerve. I hope we'll see you next week along with 'The Howling Man.' Thank you and good night."*

Trivia, etc. "The director filmed a different scene than the one that was in the script," recalled H.M. Wynant. "Robin Hughes, as the prisoner, was supposed to make a wild escape from the castle and the camera was supposed to catch a glimpse of a cloven hoof jumping over the wall. That was to suggest the prisoner was the Devil himself. There was some argument about it, and they spent considerable time making the Devil more traditional than myth. But the film turned out nicely and few people suspect the difference."

"When I was a young kid I was very influenced by films like *Dr. Jekyll and Mr. Hyde* (1932). I loved *Frankenstein* (1931) and *Dracula* (1931)," recalled director Douglas Heyes to interviewer Ben Herndon. "One that influenced me on 'Howling Man' was the *Werewolf of London* (1935), with Henry Hull. In that, he did a slow, moving transition into the werewolf, which I had never seen before. He was walking up a staircase, and as he would move behind pieces of the set, he would come out from behind the next piece of set looking slightly more advanced in his transformation. I'd seen that as a kid, and I always said, 'That's the way to do it.'"

"I had [the Devil] walking very fast down a corridor in the old monastery," continued Heyes. "The cameras were on the outside of the columns and arches along the corridor, and I had him make the entire walk at the same dolly speed every time there was a makeup change. In editing, we could cut from one makeup change to the next in the middle part of each column, where it would be dark. At the end of the corridor he went out the window with a big puff of smoke."

The transformation scene even includes a similar technique applied in a previous episode, "Long Live Walter Jameson." As Robin Hughes leaves his solitary confinement, he strokes his beard seconds before making his grand exit. In the frame while he strokes his beard, the transformation begins on the skin revealing facial features characteristic of the Devil. By way of extra makeup on the face, the features were not revealed on camera until cinematographer George Clemens and his crew turned on a special light that exposed the extra makeup.

This episode was originally planned to be script #40. Charles Beaumont was paid $2,000.00 for his story and the teleplay adaptation.

A photograph of Buck Houghton, standing next to actor Robin Hughes, in the guise of the horned-and-caped Satan, graced the cover of "Progress Report No. 3," printed by the 20th World Science Fiction Convention, which was to be held at the Pick-Congress Hotel from August 31 – September 3, 1962. Serling himself provided the photo for the cover, and the progress report was issued in late May of 1962. The same progress report revealed recent auction material contributions for the upcoming convention: "Richard Matheson has sent the manuscript of his story, 'Little Girl Lost' and it is autographed. Mr. Matheson said, 'the story appeared in *Amazing*, then in my collection *The Shores of Space* and, this year, I adapted it into a *Twilight Zone* script. And speaking of the *Twilight Zone*, as reported in the last progress report, Rod Serling was sending a package to the auction. It has arrived, containing four autographed scripts. You *Twilight Zone* fans will have to fight it out among yourselves. And CBS has supplied several delightful still photos from the show, showing the actors in some of the far-out costumes."

The August 4, 1960 revision of the script featured a number of scene changes and production notes to explain the changes between the first and final draft. "The Abbey has been changed, for policy reasons, to the war-torn ruin of a once great castle. Left little more than a shell by World War One explosives, ransacked, burned, it is a nightmare place barely hinting of past grandeurs. The cells of the monks are therefore reconverted bedrooms, libraries, studies, etc. They can be as stark in the original, but not quite so small, perhaps. Brother Christopher's room was once the library of the Wulfran castle; Jerome's the master bedroom; the Prisoner occupies what was the pantry."

Production #3640 "EYE OF THE BEHOLDER"
(Initial telecast: November 11, 1960)
© Cayuga Productions, Inc., November 10, 1960, LP19931 (under the title "The Private World of Darkness")
Dates of Rehearsal: August 1 and 2, 1960
Dates of Filming: August 3, 4 and 5, 1960
Script #40 dated: June 8, 1960, with revised pages dated August 1, 1960
Shooting script dated: August 1, 1960

Producer and Secretary: $1,775.00
Director: $1,250.00
Unit Manager and Secretary: $600.00
Agents Commission: $2,500.00
Below the line charges (M-G-M): $31,663.49
Total Production Costs: $48,599.00

Story and Secretary: $2,650.00
Cast: $5,294.39
Production Fee: $825.00
Legal and Accounting: $250.00
Below the line charges (other): $1,791.12

Cast: Donna Douglas (Janet Tyler, revealed); William D. Gordon (the doctor); Jennifer Howard (Janet's nurse); Joanna Heyes (the reception nurse); George Keymas (the Leader); Edson Stroll (Walter Smith); and Maxine Stuart (Janet Tyler, bandaged).

Original Music Score Composed and Conducted by Bernard Herrmann (Music No. CPN5926):
Etrange #3 (by Marius Constant, :09); Milieu #1 (by Constant, :16); Patience (:12); The Nurse (:44); The Hospital (:54); The Doctor (:16); The Plea (:46); Lead-In (:06); Declaration (:03); The Bandage (1:50); The Last Bandage (1:31); Hysteria (1:13); The Revelation (1:47); Etrange #3 (by Constant, :10); and Milieu #2 (by Constant, :30).

Associate Producer: Del Reisman
Director of Photography: George T. Clemens, a.s.c.
Production Managers: E. Darrell Hallenbeck and Ralph W. Nelson
Art Director: George W. Davis and Phil Barber
Set Decorations: Henry Grace and H. Web Arrowsmith

Assistant Director: Henry Weinberger
Casting: Ethel Winant
Film Editor: Leon Barsha, a.c.e.
Sound: Franklin Milton and Charles Scheid
Makeup: William Tuttle
Directed by Douglas Heyes
Teleplay by Rod Serling

"Suspended in time and space for a moment. Your introduction to Miss Janet Tyler who lives in a very private world of darkness; a universe whose dimensions are the size, thickness, length of a swath of bandages that cover her face. In a moment we'll go back into this room and also in a moment we'll look under those bandages. Keeping in mind, of course, that we're not to be surprised by what we see, because this isn't just a hospital. And this patient in 307 is not just a woman. This happens to be the Twilight Zone . . . and Miss Janet Tyler, with you, is about to enter it!"

Plot: Janet Tyler has gotten used to having bandages wrapped around her face. She has finished her 11th surgery and while the doctors and surgeons remain hopeful, her condition remains a concern. The State does not allow horribly disfigured people with her bone structure and flesh type to exist in society – banishing them to a village where undesirables are segregated. Eleven is the mandatory number of "experiments" and if this latest surgery fails, the doctors will be forced to give her an ultimatum – banishment or extinction. While the leader of the State speaks "live" on television about "conformity" and a "single morality," the surgeons spend their time cutting away the bandages from Janet Tyler's head. Slowly they work until the last of the bandages is removed and to their horror, there has been no improvement. The lights go on to reveal the truth – she is beautiful – it is the doctors who are the monsters. Janet Tyler, frightened, attempts to flee. Almost as if a hand were guiding her, she runs into Mr. Smith, a representative from the village, who offers her a hand of friendship. He assures her that she will feel comfortable at her new home and will be loved. As Smith assures her, "Beauty is in the eye of the beholder." Hoping for a future life with people of her own kind, she chooses to go with him.

"Now the questions that come to mind . . . where is this place and when is it. What kind of world where ugliness is the norm and beauty the deviation from that norm? You want an answer? The answer is . . . it doesn't make any difference. Because the old saying happens to be true. Beauty is in the eye of the beholder. In this year or a hundred years hence. On this planet or wherever there is human life perhaps out amongst the stars. Beauty is in the eye of the beholder. Lesson to be learned . . . in The Twilight Zone."

Trailer: *"Next week, you'll see these bandages unwrapped and you'll get a good, close look at the face beneath them. It's an excursion into the odd and into the very, very different. Our play is called 'The Eye of the Beholder' and it comes recommended. I hope we'll see you next week on the Twilight Zone. Thank you and good night."*

Trivia, etc. "This is one of those wild ones that I came up with while lying in bed and staring into the darkness," Serling told a reporter for *TV Guide*. "Nothing precipitated it beyond the writer's instinct as to what constitutes an interesting story. Also, as is often the case on *The Twilight Zone*, I would like to make a thematic point. 'The Monsters are Due on Maple Street' was a parable having to do with prejudice. 'Eye of the Beholder' on the other hand made a comment on conformity. No audience likes a writer's opinion thrust down their gullet as simply a tract. It has to be dramatized and made acceptably palatable within a dramatic form. This is how we designed 'Eye of the Beholder' and I think we were successful."

The CBS censors received the script on June 20, 1960. On the morning of June 23, Donald Gotschall of the editing department, having looked over the script page by page, contacted Del Reisman regarding two minor matters that piqued the network's interest. The first was to make sure the cigarette package contained no commercial identification and the title of the magazine was fictitious. For a number of reasons, he suggested the nurse's comment in the beginning of the episode, "If it were mine, I'd bury myself in a grave someplace" be removed. Serling and Houghton were responsible for the decision to remove the line or keep it intact. They did not remove the line from the script.

CBS had two major concerns, however, and on June 24, wrote a report and sent it to Del Reisman, Robert Hoag, George Amy, Buck Houghton, and Rod Serling, explaining that caution should be issued in the delivery of the nurse's speech in the opening scenes, "so as to not offend the Nursing Association. We were informed the nurses would not be portrayed as being in our society, but in a fictitious one." The other major concern was mentioned twice in the same report: to exercise directorial caution in the climatic scenes to avoid any element of shock – and that "the abrupt close ups of the nurses' faces will not be played for shock."

The problem of how to avoid the faces of the doctors and nurses without making it too obvious with the viewers that a secret was being kept from them proved a challenge. "You could have done it all with inserts, but that would have made the audience suspicious," explained director Heyes in an interview with Ben Herndon. "What I wanted to do was try and hold their attention and yet not let them see any faces – without having the audience say, 'Hey, something's wrong. They're not showing the faces.' In other words, there is constantly a very subtle camera movement, so that you're not aware of the fact that when somebody turns around, for example, and starts to turn towards you, someone else walks in front of the camera just at the moment he's turning so that you don't actually see the front of his face."

The tricks applied involved zooming in on a pack of cigarettes on the counter, making sure the only source of light was a lamp by the hospital bed, and the actors turning their faces toward the dark, allowing only the back of their heads exposed to the light. "I had the idea that the voices of these monster people would be very sympathetic," continued Heyes. "Rod was surprised at that. He had not intended them to be that way, but he liked it. So I interviewed the actors for that show without ever seeing them. I sat in a room with my back to the door. They'd come in, and I'd read the part with them and listen only to their voices. I picked the people with the most sympathetic voices I could get. If we are going to believe that these people are the norm, then they have to sound like nice people."

"The opposite is also true," Heyes continued. "Under the bandages, I wanted a voice that suggested it could belong to an ugly person. I wanted a voice with character, harshness, and timbre. So we used a radio actress named Maxine Stuart, a marvelous actress, and she played the part of Janet Tyler under the bandages. Later, when we unwrapped the bandages, Donna Douglas emerged, so the part was actually played by two actresses. I thought we were going to use Maxine's voice afterward as well, dubbing Donna after the bandages came off. But Donna was there throughout all the shooting, watching everything and listening, and she surprised me. When it came time to do the unwrapping scene, she had learned the vocal intonations and did her own dialogue sounding just like Maxine Stuart."

"I was a newcomer from New York," recalled Douglas. "They were looking for a woman of exceptional beauty and they picked me. Looking back I can express how proud I was to be a part of the show. It was fascinating how they put that together. The flesh-colored makeup on the nurses and doctors. They put makeup on me too, but I don't know why since I was supposed to be under the bandages. I don't know why they had someone different underneath the bandages. I would have done that. I guess it was the woman's voice they were going after but I had the same voice."

"Ethel Winant was a friend of mine at the time and she hired me for any show she was involved with. She was a dear," recalled Maxine Stuart. "I was the victim under the bandages who was the most beautiful woman. I always had trouble crying tears on television such as *Philco* [*Television Playhouse*], but I cried tears under the bandages . . . I was into the role so much. They had me come back later and loop my voice to the film and that sound studio was at M-G-M. I could not see anything with the bandages around my face, so the cast or someone – I can't remember – helped me move about. I had to go to the bathroom once and it was embarrassing!"

"Well I was kind of in the dark," Edson Stroll recalled. "I didn't know what they were doing, and it was a bit odd. I suspect Donna Douglas was in on it, because she knew how the story was working, but I was there just for the one scene and then walked away with her, so I wasn't all too sure why there were people with monstrous makeup on their faces. Looking back now I am aware of what they were doing and it certainly was magnificent."

To throw the audience off, in case they were to recognize the brand of cigarettes passed between nurses, a pack of Templeton Cigarettes were used. Templetons are produced by Austria Tabak, a German manufacturing company that manufactured a large variety of cigarettes for European distribution.

All of the actors and actresses were required to wear the makeup at all times, even before the unraveling of the bandages, but there was apparently an exception – the opening scenes in Janet Tyler's room with the nurse before Serling's intro and the scene with the doctor and nurse behind the screen. The actors, in those particular opening scenes, did *not* have any makeup on their faces (confirmed through production notes). Among the cast was Joanna Heyes, as the receptionist who takes the pack of cigarettes off the counter seconds before Rod Serling walked on to the set. Joanna was the wife of Douglas Heyes, and she also played supporting roles in two episodes of television's *Thriller* series that her husband directed. "When she came on the set with the full outfit on, all the makeup and everything, I glanced over and said, 'Hi, honey, shouldn't you be in makeup?' The day did not go well from that point afterward."

Originally, this episode was to grant Cayuga a savings of $10,000 budgetarily, but excessive shooting hours caused this episode to go into overtime, finishing at $3,000 less than anticipated.

Owen S. Comora was the representative of advertising agency Young & Rubicam, on behalf of General Foods. He remained in constant communication with Serling to coordinate arrangements for all printed materials, news briefs, press releases, slide mailings, and all other forms of marketing that would promote the anthology series. For this episode, Comora wrote to Bob Stahl of *TV Guide* to remind him of an "extremely important point regarding all publicity" on this episode. "We must be extremely careful never to tip the most important element of the show," he explained. "Neither the face beneath all those bandages nor the grotesque faces of everyone in the drama can ever be revealed in advance of the show. If they are divulged in either picture, storyline, feature or script form, Rod emphasized, it could ruin the impact of the entire show."

By the end of the first week of October 1960, publicity mailings were sent out regarding "Eye of the Beholder." In addition to photo-storyline and telop-slide mailings, Young & Rubicam arranged to supply nationally an artist's conception of the "Eye" theme (all details regarding the actors faces were, of course, kept secret). Morr Kusnet was the artist, commissioned by Y&R, and his work was mailed to some 450 TV stations.

On October 4, Owen S. Comora wrote to Serling, suggesting they send out a special letter or wire to at least 155 of the nation's top TV editors. "To make it as effective as possible, I'd appreciate a quote from you on this film." Two days latter, Serling told Comora, "There are times when film seems to fulfill its function – that of an eye, a story teller, and a probing machine into the innards of people. 'Eye of the Beholder' seems to us to eminently handle all these assignments and it does so with taste, excitement and meaning. I think it's one of the most unique shows we've ever done on *The Twilight Zone* and conceivably is one of the most unusual ever to appear on television."

TV Guide ran a four-page story titled "Anatomy of a Script." This piece contained the first few pages from the actual script. The idea was to show how a teleplay was written in both style and format. The article was certainly effective because it appeared on the same week "Eye of the Beholder" aired. This fact was pointed out in the introductory text of the article. This was through special arrangement with Merrill Panitt of *TV Guide* on August 12, 1960, with the assistance of Patricia Temple, Serling's secretary.

The CBS network agreed to increase their on-the-air network spot announcements for the show, during this particular week, leading up to the broadcast. On November 14, Comora of Y&R wrote Serling, "I think the publicity on 'Eye of the Beholder' was phenomenal. The seven-city Arbitron seemed to reflect this and the word of mouth on the show had been exceptional – the best of any show this year."

When this episode aired on November 11, 1960, the title on the screen (and on advance publicity) was "Eye of the Beholder." When it was rerun on June 15, 1962, the title card had been altered to read "A Private World of Darkness." Why the titular change? As Serling admitted in a letter dated August 31, 1962, "Eye of the Beholder" had its title changed because of a legal hassle. "There had been a program on the old *General Electric Theatre* a number of years ago utilizing the same title; and in face of threatened litigation, we altered it to 'The Private World of Darkness.'"

On November 7, 1960, upon learning of the title through advance publicity, Stuart Reynolds of Stuart Reynolds Productions, a motion picture company responsible for producing *General Electric Theatre*, *The Cavalcade of America*, *Hong Kong Adventure* and *Wild Bill Hickok*, wrote a letter to Serling, explaining his stance. "This morning, I tried to reach you or Buck Houghton to notify you that your next *Twilight Zone* program to be aired this coming Friday and titled 'Eye of the Beholder' is exactly the same as one which we produced for the *General Electric Theatre* in October of 1953. Our 'Eye of the Beholder' was telecast over the CBS network for G.E. shortly after it was produced and again in the summer of 1954. Also, prints of this film are now being shown all over the world as part of a filmed syndicated anthology series titled *Your Star Showcase*. And, in addition, and equally important, is the fact that we are distributing this film as an educational aid to universities and industry dramatizing the theory of perception – why 'no two people see the same thing in the same way.' Following the initial appearance of our film on CBS, we have spent thousands of dollars in promotion and advertising of this particular film. To have a film bearing the same title appear on such a popular program as *Twilight Zone* on CBS at this time would tend to create confusion and possible injury and loss of revenue to us. As the lawyers would say – 'Please cease and desist from using such title on *Twilight Zone* – but, as friends, we sincerely do urge you to do something about this now, before Friday."

Reynolds phoned Houghton and demanded he speak with Serling personally, but since the playwright was unavailable, Houghton referred Reynolds to attorney Sam Kaplan. On Wednesday,

Reynolds talked to Kaplan, explaining the problem, and upset there was no assurance a correction would be made before airtime, consulted his attorney.

Serling received the letter, forwarded to him from CBS, on Saturday morning. "My first knowledge of the title mix-up came on Thursday evening, via a telephone call from my attorney, Sam Kaplan, at Ashley-Steiner," Serling replied to Reynolds. "Needless to say, I had no prior knowledge whatsoever of the previous usage of 'Eye of the Beholder' on your *General Electric Theatre* or anywhere else. Since its genesis was that of a classic and well-known quote, it seemed a particularly safe choice at the time that I put it in the script." Serling's experience had encompassed the multi-usage of titles on other properties, so it never occurred to him that any kind of legal hassle would result. In an effort to avoid legal issues, he assured Reynolds that Cayuga intended to re-shoot both the title and trailer footage in which the title had previously been used. No further advertising would go out in which the title "Eye of the Beholder" was mentioned.

The episode aired as intended and unaltered. On November 16, Reynolds sent a reply to Serling, blaming CBS, who he felt, "does not keep better records in their title department." The attorney for Reynolds continued to protest the use, even with Serling's confirmation that changes were going to be made. On November 29, Serling explained to the still-persisting Reynolds, "I can well understand your feeling of propriety in the title of 'Eye of the Beholder' and the tone of your letter seemed to indicate that you were aware of my position on the other side of the spectrum. The quote is as eminently public domain as it is eminently well-known and it never occurred to me that anyone had capitalized on it and that my use of it would be detrimental. I'm delighted that the thing seems to be in the process of being ironed out to the satisfaction of all parties."*

Both versions of the episode (each featuring the different closing credits with different title) have been released commercially on home video and DVD over the years, and in subsequent television reruns, offering viewers the opportunity to see the two versions.

The *General Electric Theatre* story of the same name was telecast in December of 1953. The teleplay by Hannah Grad Goodman, presented the story of a talented artist in search of his Madonna. Everyone in town, however, judged him by the way he dressed, walked and talked. The cab driver thought he was a hood. To his mother, he was thoughtless and unappreciative. His landlord thought he was a lunatic, and the perfect model for his inspiration thought he was a square. When the model for his canvas showed up tipsy after a hard night, he remonstrated with her bodily and she fell in a heap, more from her alcoholic content than the roughing. A cleaning woman saw this and sounded the alarm that there had been a murder. Obviously, there was no material that mirrored the *Twilight Zone* production, but the title was enough to cause temporary havoc.

Ironically, months before, on August 8, 1960, *The New York Herald Tribune* published a favored and respected comment by Serling regarding the *G.E. Theatre*. "The half-hour film has always been an imitative, doggy, telegraphed, insipid, assembly-line product since its inception eleven years ago,"

* Ironically, almost two years later, Stuart Reynolds contacted James Aubrey of CBS in an attempt to acquire a negative of "The Monsters Are Due on Maple Street" because of its psychological value, in hopes of distributing the film commercially. Having consulted a group of UCLA professors and having screened many potential films, they found one – and only one – that had any value as an educational film that could merit distribution to schools, colleges and universities. While Serling told Reynolds he would be more than happy to cooperate, Aubrey had the final say because the film was a joint venture between Cayuga and CBS. The network sent Reynolds a rejection letter.

Serling commented. "In the past few years, good anthology shows like *G.E. Theatre* have proven that the half-hour film can make a point tellingly and dramatically. *The Twilight Zone* is attempting this, too. It will often fall on its duff and on occasion will mistake pretension for maturity (a common fault of many of the ninety-minute specs), but the attempt at quality is always there."

On August 1, 1960, while the sets were being designed and built, Serling drafted "The Leader's Voice," which would be featured throughout the second half of the episode. Two speeches were composed and recorded separately from the Janet Tyler scenes, so the Leader's voice could be later added to the soundtrack, and the film placed on large television screens during the editing. The first was used through the bandage removal scene. The second speech was revealed more visually during Janet's attempt to escape through the corridor. These speeches, while heard in sections on this episode, appear in print in their complete form, reprinted below, courtesy of CBS, Inc.:

"Good evening, ladies and gentlemen. Tonight I shall talk to you about glorious conformity . . . About the delight and the ultimate pleasure of our unified society . . . You recall, of course, that directionless, unproductive, over-sentimentalized era of man's history when it was assumed that dissent was some kind of natural and healthy adjunct of society. We also recall that during this period of time there was a strange over-sentimentalized concept that it mattered not that people were different, that ideas were at variance with one another, that a world could exist in some kind of crazy, patch-work kind of make up, with foreign elements glued together in a crazy quilt. We realize, of course, now, that . . ."

"I say to you now . . . I say to you now that there is no such thing as a permissive society, because such a society cannot exist! They will scream at you and rant and rave and conjure up some dead and decadent picture of an ancient time when they said that all men are created equal! But to them equality means an equality of opportunity, an equality of status, an equality of aspiration! And then in what must surely be the pinnacle of insanity; the absolute in inconsistency, they would have had us believe that this equality did not apply to form, to color, to creed. They permitted a polygot, accident-bred, mongol-like mass of diversification to blanket the earth, to infiltrate and weaken! Well we know now that there must be a single purpose! A single norm! A single approach! A single entity of peoples! A single virtue! A single morality! A single frame of reference! A single philosophy of government! We cannot permit . . . we must not permit the encroaching sentimentality of a past age to weaken our resolve. We must cut out all that is different like a cancerous growth!"

The November 14, 1960 issue of *The Hollywood Reporter* reviewed, "The biggest reward for that evening was a *Twilight Zone* that should rank as one of Rod Serling's best scripting efforts. Titled 'Eye of the Beholder,' it combined suspense (through excellent low-key camera work) with some of the most penetrating dialogue we've ever heard – a preachment against 'conformity' in a *Zone* where (at the surprise finish) 'ugliness is the norm and beauty the deviation.' Borrowing the thought of Serling's theme, shall the public at large 'conform' to the tastes of a minority group of intellectuals and pseudo-intellectuals? We think not!"

On January 11, 1961, Serling replied to a request from Peter S. Mallett, director of dramatics at the Bellows Free Academy in St. Albans, Vermont. "We have been forced to make a standard rule rejecting offers of copies of the script since these requests come in on the average of fifty to a hundred each week. To date there have been one hundred and sixteen requests for copies of 'Eye of the Beholder,' and it is for this reason we've been forced to hew to a hard and fast rule rather than grant some requests and then quietly unfairly failing to accommodate others. And after this somewhat negative approach, and in my usual disconnected fashion, I'm enclosing a copy of the script to perform as you see fit. There is no royalty payment required and the only requirement is that no admission be charged for its performance."

On October 25, 1961, Lynn Anderson in San Francisco wrote to Serling, explaining a commercial promoting the television program, which featured numerous close-up shots of the monsters from this *Twilight Zone* episode, and the Devil from "The Howling Man" and "Nick of Time." The commercial was being shown at the end of children's TV programs in the morning and during a circus show early in the evening. "As a result of viewing this macabre presentation, [my son] has had various nightmares involving these horrible faces and is frightened in his room at night with the lights off. He says he's afraid of those people – and describes the commercial."

The letter was forwarded to Serling from CBS, and on November 13, 1961, he sent a reply explaining that *The Twilight Zone* is scheduled for ten o'clock Friday evenings – a time frame designed for adult viewing. "Without my knowledge and certainly without my support, film clips of this program have been shown as promotional material during the daylight hours. I deeply regret that this has been the case but unfortunately have no control whatsoever over the networks promotional planning and programming. Please accept my apologies for this. I'm sending a copy of your letter to the network here on the Coast in the hopes that this particular film clip will be taken out of use during the daytime hours."

In January of 1962, this episode of *The Twilight Zone* was shown at the TV Festival of Monte Carlo. *Paris Match*, a French news magazine, featured photos of the monstrous faces of the doctor and the nurses in one of its issues, to help promote the festival and the television series.

Makeup artist Rick Baker, whose work was responsible for such movies as *An American Werewolf in London* (1981) and *Greystoke* (1984), was influenced early on by this television episode. After viewing the telecast at the age of 15, he managed to reproduce the same makeup job from this episode.

Being one of the most popular episodes of the series, this episode has been referenced and spoofed on numerous television programs from *The Simpsons* to *The Family Guy*. On the evening of April 19, 1997, *Saturday Night Live* featured a parody of this episode, which featured the doctors and nurses unraveling the bandages from Janet Tyler's face. When her face is revealed, Pamela Anderson was the beautiful woman and the doctors all agreed that she really was beautiful. *Sports Illustrated* swimsuit model, Molly Sims was cast in the role of Janet Tyler in a remake of the same episode for the revival *Twilight Zone* series, initially telecast on April 30, 2003.

This episode was selected for use in the "Cable in the Classroom" program. (For details about the program, see the episode entry for "Where is Everybody?") This episode was ranked in the January/February 1998 issue of *Cinescape* as the sixth-best science fiction television episode of all time.

Production #3643 "NICK OF TIME" (Initial telecast: November 18, 1960)
© Cayuga Productions, Inc., November 17, 1960, LP18831
Dates of Rehearsal: August 11 and 12, 1960
Dates of Filming: August 15, 16 and 17, 1960
First draft undated with rewrite requested June 6, 1960.
Script #43 dated: June 22, 1960, with revised pages dated June 27, August 4, 10 and 12, 1960.
Shooting script dated: August 12, 1960

Producer and Secretary: $1,935.00   Story and Secretary: $2,155.00
Director: $1,250.00   Cast: $4,950.03
Unit Manager and Secretary: $600.00   Production Fee: $825.00

Agents Commission: $2,500.00

Legal and Accounting: $250.00

Below the line charges (M-G-M): $28,043.86

Below the line charges (other): $754.16

Total Production Costs: $43,263.05

Cast: Patricia Breslin (Pat Carter); Dee Carroll (the desperate woman); Bob McCord (a customer); Walter Reed (the desperate man); Stafford Repp (the mechanic); William Shatner (Don Carter); and Guy Wilkerson (the counter man).

Stock Music Cues: Etrange #3 (by Marius Constant, :09); Milieu #1 (by Constant, :16); A Summer Eve (by Eric Cook, :44); Goodbye Keith (by William Lava, :03); Strange Return (by Jerry Goldsmith, :33); A Summer Eve (by Cook, 1:39); American Patrol (by F.W. Meacham, arr. by Jerry Gray, 1:16); Eerie Nightmare #2 (by Lucien Moraweck, 1:22); Strange Return (by Goldsmith, 1:14); Hitch-Hiker, Parts 1 and 2 (by Herrmann, :48); Shock Therapy #3 (by Rene Garriguenc, :08); Nervous Tension (by Moraweck, :07); Silent Flight (by Goldsmith, 1:07), Mounting Tension (by Goldsmith, :57); Hitch-Hiker Part 1 (by Herrmann, :58); Etrange #3 (by Constant, :10); and Milieu #2 (by Constant, :30).

Associate Producer: Del Reisman

Assistant Director: E. Darrell Hallenbeck

Director of Photography: George T.

Casting: Ethel Winant

   Clemens, a.s.c.

Film Editor: Leon Barsha, a.c.e.

Production Managers: Sidney Van Keuran

Sound: Franklin Milton and Charles Scheid

   and Ralph W. Nelson

Directed by Richard L. Bare

Art Director: George W. Davis and Phil Barber

Teleplay by Richard Matheson

Set Decorations: Henry Grace and

   H. Web Arrowsmith

"The hand belongs to Mr. Don S. Carter, male member of a honeymoon team on route across the Ohio countryside to New York City. In one moment, they will be subjected to a gift most humans never receive in a lifetime. For one penny, they will be able to look into the future. The time is now. The place is a little diner in Ridgeview, Ohio, and what this young couple doesn't realize is that this town happens to lie on the outskirts . . . of the Twilight Zone."

Plot: Due to automotive troubles, a honeymooning couple, Don and Pat Carter, find themselves temporarily laid over for a few hours in a small country town. While grabbing a bite to eat at a small diner, young Don, with a superstitious instinct, plays with a "mystic seer" on the edge of a table. After six straight answers, and two predictions coming true – including Don pulling his wife from the path of a speeding truck – he starts to suspect the "mystic seer" is more than just a small penny arcade. Pat attempts to explain to her husband that the machine only speaks in riddles – it was he who created the details. A strong believer in coincidence, Pat attempts to prove the machine wrong so that her husband will break the obsession, but she fails to pull him away from the machine. She pleads with Don to believe in luck and fortune – rather than allow a machine dictate his life. Realizing a life with Pat is more important, he agrees to leave . . . while another couple enters the café, making their return trip to the same "mystic seer."

"Counterbalance in the little town of Ridgeview, Ohio. Two people permanently enslaved by the tyranny of fear and superstition, facing the future with a kind of helpless dread. Two others facing the future with confidence, having escaped one of the darker places . . . of the Twilight Zone."

Trailer: *"You've probably run across these penny machines that tell your fortune. You put a penny in . . . and out comes a card. Only this particular machine, which you'll see next week, is a little bit unique in that the fortunes that it tells . . . happen to come true. A most intriguing tale called 'The Nick of Time' by Mr. Richard Matheson and you're invited to partake of it. Thank you and good night."*

Trivia, etc. Richard Matheson recalled the genesis for the idea of this script, to author Matthew R. Bradley. "On 'Nick of Time,' my wife and I were in a coffee shop in the San Fernando Valley, and there was this little [fortune-telling] machine that answered yes or no. . . . And so I just thought, 'Oh, that's an interesting idea.' You know, most of them come – the derivation is something you read. With me, it's mostly something I see in the movies. If it's a lousy movie, I don't leave, which I should, but my mind drifts, and something that I see may just trigger an alternative idea."

Matheson put a few pennies into the machine and the predictions gave the impression of coming true. The art department added the Devil's head for effect, which was not described in the original script.

Matheson was paid $2,000 for the rights to "In the Nick of Time." The title would later be shortened. Originally this was planned to be script #41. Two months before this episode went to film, in early June, Boris Sagal was originally slated to direct. Sagal was unable to commit due to a scheduling conflict, so on July 27, 1960, Richard L. Bare took over the helm. Sagal did manage to do two episodes of the series, "The Silence" and "The Arrival." Filming was completed a few hours less than originally planned.

On November 19, 1960, the day after this episode was telecast, Mrs. Robert Kasanda of Hillside, Illinois, wrote a letter to Rod Serling, concerned about the content of this episode. "Yesterday as my husband and I watched your show, 'Nick of Time,' with William Shatner and Patricia Breslin,

> *The Twilight Zone* was not telecast on the evening of November 25, 1960 because of an hour-long television special, *CBS Reports*. This documentary, titled "Harvest of Shame," was a study on migratory farm workers in the country. Edward R. Murrow served as both host and reporter. The presentation was described by CBS in a press release as: "These are different views of the migrant workers who follow the sun in an endless circle of poverty from Florida to New England, from California to the Pacific Northwest. Tonight, the CBS Television Network will bring you the vivid story of these underpaid, underfed, under-educated Americans who harvest the crops. At the very moment when most of the land is filled with the spirit of Thanksgiving, you will meet the millions of men, women and children whose lives and whose labor are America's 'Harvest of Shame.'" Today, this television special is still considered one of the most heralded TV documentaries of all time.

the actor in answer to the actress – William Shatner said, quote, 'Stop treating me like a retarded child.' My husband and I were stunned at this malicious sounding statement. If you only knew how that statement hurt. Couldn't you have used a different term? I have a feeling we are not alone in feeling this way. We have a retarded darling that God sent us."

Serling sent a prompt reply. "I did not write the script of 'Nick of Time,' but I know the writer personally and professionally and I also know that he is a man of stature and good will who would never knowingly have caused as much personal hurt to you as he obviously did with a thoughtless, throw-away line which to him, meant nothing, but which to you must have been heart rending. Please accept my apologies in this and my assurance that it will never happen again on my show or any program in which I have a part. Too often we go along blithely unaware of the myriad meanings of language amongst people. Where to most, a certain line is general, unspecific and quite innocuous – to others it has a very special meaning and can be both damaging and offensive. I'll be most careful of this in the future and I thank you so very much for calling it to my attention."

On the evening of May 13, 1996, *The Fresh Prince of Bel Air*, a television sit-com starring Will Smith, featured William Shatner as a guest. A reference to Shatner's performance on this *Twilight Zone* episode was not overlooked.

Production #1652-1 "THE LATENESS OF THE HOUR"
(Initial telecast: December 2, 1960)
© Cayuga Productions, Inc., December 1, 1960, LP18552
Dates of Filming: November 12 and 13, 1960
Shooting script dated: November 4, 1960

Producer and Secretary: $2,402.43	Story and Secretary: $2,510.00
Cast: $603.82	Production Fee: $825.00
Agents Commission: $2,500.00	Legal and Accounting: $250.00
Below the line charges (CBS): $33,269.89	Below the line charges (other): $210.95
Total Production Costs: $42,572.09	

Cast: Mary Gregory (Nelda, the maid); John Hoyt (Dr. Loren); Jason Johnson (Jensen, the handyman); Doris Karnes (Gretchen, the cook); Valley Keene (Suzanne, the maid); Tom Palmer (Robert, the butler); Inger Stevens (Jana Loren); and Irene Tedrow (Mrs. Loren).

Stock Music Cues: Etrange #3 (by Marius Constant, :09); Milieu #1 (by Constant, :16); Tarn #1 (by Constant, :54); Menton 17 (by Constant, :24); Day #3 (by Constant, :03); Menton 12 (by Constant, :09); Tarn #1 (by Constant, :31 and :06); Menton 17 (by Constant, :12); Farewell (by Herrmann, :04); Oise #1 (by Constant, :35); Colmar #6 (by Constant, :12); Walking Distance Introduction (by Herrmann, :28); The Drug Store (by Herrmann, :56); Menton 17 (by Constant, :20); Tarn #1 (by Constant, :16); Farewell (by Herrmann, :03); Tarn #1 (by Constant, :21); Marne #1 (by Constant, :17); The Park (by Herrmann, :29); Martin's Summer (by Herrmann, :31); The House (by Herrmann, :24); The Parents (by Herrmann, :19); Mad Harpsichord (anonymous, :05); Tarn #1 (by Constant, :12); Curtain (by Herrmann, :19); Etrange #3 (by Constant, :10); and Milieu #2 (by Constant, :25).

Associate Producer: Del Reisman	Art Director: Craig Smith
Technical Director: Jim Brady	Lighting Director: Tom D. Schamp
Set Decorator: Arthur Jeph Parker	Associate Director: James Clark
Casting: Ethel Winant	Directed by Jack Smight
Teleplay by Rod Serling	

"The residence of Dr. William Loren . . . which is in reality a menagerie for machines. We are about to discover that sometimes the product of man's talent and genius can walk amongst us untouched by the normal ravages of time. These are Dr. Loren's robots. Built to be functional as well as artistic perfection. But in a moment, Dr. William Loren, wife . . . and daughter . . . will discover that perfection is relative. That even robots have to be paid for. And very shortly, will be shown exactly what is the bill."

Plot: Dr. William Loren, a brilliant scientist, has designed a house with every perfect necessity – including robots that spend their time devoted to the comfort and relaxation of their masters. Jana, their daughter, finds herself discontent with the lifestyles her parents have adopted. Isolated from the real world, Jana has never experienced war or pestilence. Her father insists he is only protecting her from harm and disease. Threatening to leave so she can have her freedom, Jana forces her father to make a decision – dismantle all of the servants or lose a daughter. Choosing to keep the daughter he loves, Dr. Loren orders the servants downstairs for termination. Hours later, Jana is extremely happy, suggesting the family go on vacation and, if Jana is lucky, find the right man and get married and have children. This proposal forces Dr. and Mrs. Loren into a situation they hoped would never come – a truth she would not accept . . . Jana is also one of Dr. Loren's creations. Days later, with no servants left to serve their needs, Jana's memory banks are wiped clean, and the daughter they once had has replaced the servants as the new maid.

"Let this be the postscript. Should you be worn out by the rigors of competing in a very competitive world; if you're distraught from having to share your existence with the noises and neuroses of the twentieth century; if you crave serenity, but want it full time and with no strings attached – get yourself a workroom in the base-ment and then drop a note to Dr. and Mrs. William Loren. They're a childless couple who made comfort a life's work. And maybe there are a few Do-It-Yourself pamphlets still available . . . in the Twilight Zone."

Trivia, etc. Of the six episodes that were videotaped, this was the first one to be telecast. The cost-cutting measure was insisted by the network, which owned its own studio. Without the necessity to rent equipment, stages, lots, costumes and props from M-G-M, Cayuga found the figures were indeed much lower than filmed presentations. Film had to be developed and then edited and scored. Videotape had its advantages, such as allowing Jim Brady to edit the taped scenes on the spot and avoid the costs of film development.

Production #3649 "THE TROUBLE WITH TEMPLETON"
(Initial telecast: December 9, 1960)
© Cayuga Productions, Inc., December 8, 1960, LP18553
Dates of Rehearsal: October 4 and 5, 1960
Dates of Filming: October 6, 7 and 10, 1960

Producer and Secretary: $1,775.00
Story and Secretary: $2,393.00
Director: $1,250.00
Cast: $6,450.93
Unit Manager and Secretary: $350.00
Production Fee: $825.00
Agents Commission: $2,500.00
Legal and Accounting: $250.00
Below the line charges (M-G-M): $31,961.89
Below the line charges (other): $2,427.56
Total Production Costs: $50,183.38

Cast: Brian Aherne (Booth Templeton); Larry Blake (Freddie); King Calder (Sid Sperry); Charles Carlson (Barney Flueger); John Kroger (Ed Page); Sydney Pollack (Willis, the director); Pippa Scott (Laura Templeton); David Thorsby (Eddie); and Dave Willock (Marcel).

Laura Templeton (Pippa Scott) and her friends watch as Booth Templeton leaves the speakeasy.

Original Music Score Composed and Conducted by Jeff Alexander (Score No. CPN5943): Etrange #3 (by Marius Constant, :09); Milieu #1 (by Constant, :16); New York Locale (:50); Blue Danube Waltz (by Johann Strauss Jr., :30); The Ashes of Love (:29); Rod's Opinion (:35); Schubert Alley (:25); Autonomy (1:10); Cerebral (1:00); Cerebrum I (:15); Cerebellum II (:51); I Like My Wife, But ... (1:03); Cloche Call (:44); "It" Girl (1:17); Jeff's Jam (1:44); Chicken Inspector (1:12); Medulla Oblongata (:42); Templeton's Hauteur (:38); Templeton's Hauteur Cont'd (1:02); Etrange #3 (by Constant, :10); and Milieu #2 (by Constant, :30).

Associate Producer: Del Reisman
Director of Photography: George T.
    Clemens, a.s.c.
Production Manager: E. Darrell Hallenbeck
Art Director: George W. Davis and Phil Barber
Set Decorations: Henry Grace and
    H. Web Arrowsmith

Assistant Director: Lindsey Parsons, Jr.
Casting: Ethel Winant
Film Editor: Bill Mosher
Sound: Franklin Milton and Charles Scheid
Directed by Buzz Kulik
Teleplay by E. Jack Neuman

"Pleased to present for your consideration Mr. Booth Templeton, serious and successful star of over thirty Broadway plays, who is not quite all right today. Yesterday and its memories is what he wants, and yesterday is what he'll get. Soon his years and his troubles will descend on him in an avalanche. In order not to be crushed, Mr. Booth Templeton will escape from his theater and his world ... and make his debut on another stage in another world that we call ... the Twilight Zone."

Plot: Booth Templeton, an aged, non-content actor of the past, longs for the days when he never had to worry about his flirtatious wife and a stage production run by dictators who directed stars like cattle. Dead set against living a life of modern times, he is escorted to and from his residence and the theater, waiting for the world to pass him by. Recollecting those indescribable moments of life when he was a significant personality, he finds himself magically transported back to 1927 – a contented moment long ago when his wife of faithful dedication was still alive and the Roaring Twenties were full of bustle. While Templeton relives the memories, he discovers that life changes and so has his perceptions. He's now a tired old man who is advised by his late wife to go back home – he is not wanted in the past. Returning to his own time, Templeton realizes that the ghosts of his past were playing their parts in a fictional drama so the aged actor would make a change for the better – live his life to the fullest, which is exactly what Templeton plans to do from this day forward.

"Mr. Booth Templeton, who shared with most human beings the hunger to recapture the past moments . . . the ones that soften with the years. But in his case, the characters of his past blocked him out and sent him back to his own time, which is where we find him now. Mr. Booth Templeton, who had a round-trip ticket . . . into the Twilight Zone."

Trailer: *"An attractive and rather unimposing room, lived in by a man named Templeton and like most rooms suggestive really of only a part of the man – the outside part. Our story next week takes off from here. Mr. Brian Aherne lends us his considerable talents in a script by E. Jack Neuman called, 'The Trouble With Templeton.' It can best be described as poignant, provocative and a highly diverting trip into the Twilight Zone."*

Trivia, etc. The scene at the swimming pool is the same pool at Cohn Park on the M-G-M lot, part of Lot 2 at the studio. This was the same swimming pool featured in *Twilight Zone* episodes "Queen of the Nile" and "The Bewitchin' Pool."

Booth Templeton performs at the "Savoy Theatre," the same theater name featured in "Where is Everybody?" and verbally mentioned by the wooden dummy in "The Dummy," both scripted by Rod Serling. This is another suggestive instance where Serling may have had a hand in revising bits and pieces of teleplays by other writers.

Serling's original trailer was longer, but because of the limited amount of time, was edited down to fit the time frame:

"An attractive and rather unimposing room, lived in by a man named Templeton and like most rooms suggestive really of only a part of the man – the outside part. His taste in furnishings . . . perhaps a hint of at which rung he stands on the ladder of social strata. But our story next week only begins in this room. It goes much further, both in distance and in time. And it also delves deep into the heart of this man. Mr. Brian Aherne lends us his considerable talents in a script by E. Jack Neuman called, 'The Trouble With Templeton.' It can best be described as poignant, provocative and a highly diverting trip into the Twilight Zone."

"I read every new script submitted to me," Serling told Ben Gross of *The New York Sunday News*, in March of 1960. "So far I've waded through 200 and here's what I found: some 90 percent were poorly written by non-pros; most of the others were sent in by pros and sized up merely as smooth hack work. Still, I continue my reading."

While Serling confessed to not buying a single script from any outside submissions, this script must have intrigued Serling for E. Jack Neuman became the first outsider (other than Beaumont and Matheson) to submit a plot synopsis and receive a contract. The plot outline was titled "What Do You Hear?" dated May of 1960, and a first draft of the script contractually due by June 6, 1960. Weeks later, according to a production report dated June 30, 1960, this script was assigned a different script number, #46, and retitled "The Strange Debut," due for submission by July 5. It was still called "The Strange Debut" in August of 1960, and by October 3, 1960, a revised draft titled "The Strange Debut" was completed. By October 7, 1960, it had been retitled to "The Trouble with Templeton."

As of August 18, the episode was scheduled for filming on September 26, 27 and 28, with rehearsal dates September 22 and 23. Don Medford was originally slated to direct. According to a release schedule dated August 25, 1960, "The Strange Debut" was slated for telecast on January 27, 1961.

When this episode was rerun on June 29, 1962, *The Los Angeles Times* featured a color picture advertising the drama.

In the scene when Templeton confronts Laura in the speakeasy and interrupts her dancing, he tears her string of pearls. While she attempts to dance with the broken string of pearls dangling over the back of her neck, he interrupts her dancing again, and before walking away, Laura begins dancing again but this time the string of pearls are whole again. This was an accident overlooked by the film editor, putting together film takes from various shots.

With Ford donating automobiles for most of the *Twilight Zone* productions, it comes as no surprise that the Model T featured in the 1927 scenes is a Ford.

Sydney Pollack, who played the role of a stage director for this episode, was originally slated to direct a 1965 M-G-M motion picture, *A Time of Glory*, a screenplay written by Rod Serling (dated December 8, 1964). Arthur P. Jacobs was supposed to be the producer, but the project never got off the ground. (Jacobs would co-produce *Planet of the Apes* (1968) with a screenplay by Serling, but without Pollack as director.)

Production #3606 "A MOST UNUSUAL CAMERA"
(Initial telecast: December 16, 1960)
© Cayuga Productions, Inc., December 15, 1960, LP18554
Dates of Rehearsal: October 13 and 14, 1960
Dates of Filming: October 17, 18 and 19, 1960
First script dated: April 23, 1959
Revised script dated: October 3, 1960, with revised pages dated October 7, 11 and 14, 1960.
Shooting script: October 14, 1960

Producer and Secretary: $1,775.00
Director: $1,250.00
Unit Manager and Secretary: $100.00
Agents Commission: $2,500.00
Below the line charges (M-G-M): $24,496.31
Total Production Costs: $39,607.47

Story and Secretary: $2,630.00
Cast: $4,784.45
Production Fee: $825.00
Legal and Accounting: $250.00
Below the line charges (other): $996.71

Cast: Jean Carson (Paula Diedrich); Fred Clark (Chester Diedrich); Marcel Hillaire (the French waiter); Artie Lewis (the racetrack tout); and Adam Williams (Woodward).

Stock Music Cues: Etrange #3 (by Marius Constant, :09); Milieu #1 (by Constant, :16); Space Stations – Outer Space Suite (by Bernard Herrmann, :07); Stalagmites #1 (by Bruce Campbell, :45); Space Stations – Outer Space Suite (by Herrmann, :07); Brouillards (by Constant, :15); Stalagmites #1 (by Bruce Campbell, :05); Spoutnik #1 (by Guy Luypaertz, :55); Space Stations – Outer Space Suite (by Herrmann, :07); Spoutnik #1 (by Luypaertz, :45); Space Stations – Outer Space Suite (by Herrmann, :07); Travelling Lightly (by Bernard Green, :09); Stalagmites #1 (by Campbell, :16); Travelling Lightly (by Green, :40); Spoutnik #1 (by Luypaertz, :26); Stalagmites #1 (by Campbell, :31); The Airlock – Outer Space Suite (by Herrmann, :07); Kant #4 (by Constant, :21); Improvised Humming (anonymous, :11); Neuro Background (by Garriguenc, :29); Stalagmites #1 (by Campbell); Etrange #3 (by Constant, :10); and Milieu #2 (by Constant, :30). *

Associate Producer: Del Reisman
Director of Photography: George T.
   Clemens, a.s.c.
Art Director: George W. Davis and Phil Barber
Set Decorations: Henry Grace and
   H. Web Arrowsmith

Assistant Director: E. Darrell Hallenbeck
Casting: Ethel Winant
Film Editor: Bill Mosher
Sound: Franklin Milton and Charles Scheid
Directed by John Rich
Teleplay by Rod Serling

"A hotel suite that in this instance serves as a den of crime. The aftermath of a rather minor event to be noted on a police blotter, an insurance claim, perhaps a three inch box on page twelve of the evening paper. Small addenda to be added to the list of the loot. A camera. A most unimposing addition to the flotsam and jetsam that it came with. Hardly worth mentioning, really, because cameras are cameras. Some expensive, some purchasable at five-and-dime stores. But this camera . . . this one's unusual, because in just a moment we'll watch it inject itself into the destinies of three people. It happens to be a fact that the pictures that it takes can only be developed . . . in The Twilight Zone."

Plot: After taking inventory of the recent loot from a victimized curio shop, three small-time heisters find themselves in possession of a funky-looking camera. A short time later, Chester realizes why the original owners never reported the camera among the list of stolen possessions – the camera is unique because it takes pictures of the near future. Hours later, Chester, Paula and Woodward use the camera to take pictures of the winning board at the race track, and place bets of the soon-to-be winning horse. By the end of the day, the crooks find themselves with more money than they would have earned heisting mom and pop shops. When the French inscription on the camera is deciphered as "10 to a customer," the small-time crooks start to panic because they already used up eight photos. During a struggle over deciding what to do with the remaining pictures, Woodward and Chester waste another photo. Fighting over their mistake, they fall out the window to their deaths. A blackmailing French waiter at the hotel begins stealing the money from Paula, only to plunge to his death out the same window – as does Paula, as predicted on the final photograph.

---

* The music cue "Travelling Lightly" is supposed to be spelled that way, according to original music sheets.

"Object known as a camera. Vintage – uncertain; origin – unknown. But for the greedy . . . the avaricious . . . the fleet of foot who can run a four-minute mile so long as they're chasing a fast buck. It makes believe that it's an ally, but it isn't at all. It's a beckoning come-on for a quick walk-around-the-block . . . in the Twilight Zone."

Trailer: *"In this 28-dollar a day hotel suite live three human beings who have larceny in them from their toes to where they part their hair. Amongst the loot of one evening's caper is this camera which they soon discover has most unique properties. It takes pictures of the future. Stick around for the development next week . . . on the Twilight Zone."*

The December 21, 1960 issue of *The Hollywood Reporter* reported Serling's sale of a radio program to CBS, suggesting the network wanted to broadcast a radio series adapted from television scripts of *The Twilight Zone*. This is not a farfetched notion as some might ponder, because the television series *Have Gun – Will Travel* had been adapted to radio two years previous on the CBS Radio Network.

Trivia, etc. Rod Serling completed the first draft of this script by April 23, 1959, labeled script #6, with the intention of filming it for the first season. On April 29, 1959, CBS sent Bill Self, Buck Houghton and Serling a report asking for a number of changes. One of them was to remove the word "frog" from Chester's comments referring to the French waiter. Serling obliged. Serling's original script called for Chester to pull a switchblade knife from his pocket, but the network objected. "Switchblade knives being illegal weapons in most states," the report explained, "their use in television drama is contrary to CBS Policy. Please substitute a standard jackknife or fixed-blade knife in this scene." Serling also made the appropriate change. The third and final request was to "please refrain the coronary histrionics so as to avoid horrifying or frightening the audience, in particular those among it who might have a heart condition themselves." The coronary scene was replaced with the now oblivious window scene.

A progress report dated July 1, 1959, stated "first draft in abeyance." According to first-season production notes, Robert Stevens was originally slated to direct this episode, with dates of filming scheduled for July 7, 8 and 9, 1959, with rehearsal dates of July 3 and 6. The script, however, was shelved and was revised more than a year later for use on the second season.

In May of 1960, Blanche Gaines, Serling's former agent, submitted a short story titled "The Latest Thing in Cameras" by James Blumgarten. Serling rejected the story proposal, on the grounds that it duplicated in essence this script, which he had written almost a year before, even though the episode had not gone before the cameras yet, and a revised script from the year before had been completed days before receiving Gaines' submission.

In the early draft, Serling had a brief scene in the script with the antique store owner and his wife complaining to a detective about the robbery. The revision, however, did not feature this scene. Serling had deleted it because the costs involved in creating another set and hiring at least three more actors for additional roles would not have been practical. CBS, during production of the second season, was pressuring both Serling and Houghton about keeping the costs down, so Serling obliged for the sake of the network.

"A series can be sustained with top quality writing and acting, but suffers when filmed from economics," Serling commented. "It's rare that a show can shoot in more than three days and it is this too-brief shooting schedule that is reflected in the lack of consistency in film shows. This is particularly true in anthologies. When *The Twilight Zone* came up with a rock on occasion, this was occasionally the net result of sloppy writing, but more often it reflected a lack of time to polish the show properly."

Fred Clark and Serling met at a restaurant one afternoon, and it was this chance meeting that led to Clark being cast for this episode. Jean Carson never played the lead on a television series. She had no problems with playing a supporting role on shows like *The Twilight Zone*. "That doesn't bother me," Carson recalled to a trade column at the time. "With my crazy voice I could never be a leading lady, so why should I kill myself trying? Besides, as a 'second tomato' I have the reward of always being busy. I don't have to sit around for months waiting for the few big jobs that exist. I know stars who absolutely go out of their minds from inactivity."

"I was cast for *The Twilight Zone* because Rod Serling wanted me to play the lead in one of his scripts," Carson recalled. "There was a party near Malibu. I was surprised to learn that he had seen me perform on the stage in *Mrs. Gibbon's Boys*. I told him I was definitely interested, being new to the West Coast. The producer phoned me almost two years later, telling me Rod was fulfilling his promise."

On November 21, 1960, the insert scene with the newspaper was filmed by Bill Mosher for use in the final cut. The newspaper cost $32.50. Originally the trailer for "next week's episode" had Serling say it was a $40-a-day hotel, not $28.

Production #1648-3 "THE NIGHT OF THE MEEK"
(Initial telecast: December 23, 1960)
© Cayuga Productions, Inc., December 22, 1960, LP18764
Date of Rehearsal: November 22, 1960
Dates of Filming: November 26 and 27, 1960
Script dated: September 12, 1960
Revised script dated: November 24, 1960

Producer and Secretary: $2,143.84
Director: 399.20
Production Fee: $825.00
Legal and Accounting: $250.00
Below the line charges (other): $113.93

Story and Secretary: $2,510.00
Cast: $988.09
Agents Commission: $2,500.00
Below the line charges (CBS): $619.55
Total Production Costs: $10,349.61

Cast: Val Avery (the bartender); Art Carney (Henry Corwin); Kay Cousins (the irate mother); Andrea Darvi (kid talking to Santa); John Fiedler (Mr. Dundee); Jimmy Garrett (the street child); Larrian Gillespie (the girl elf); Robert P. Lieb (Officer Flaherty); Matthew McCue (man in skidrow mission); Burt Mustin (Burt, the old man); and Meg Wyllie (Sister Florence).

Stock Music Cues: Etrange #3 (by Marius Constant, :09); Milieu #1 (by Constant, :16); Jingle Bells (by James Lord Pierpont, arr. by Rene Garriguenc, :34); Restless Moment (by Jerry Goldsmith, :13); Jingle Bells Paraphrase (arr. by Garriguenc: 14); Perry Mason Bridge (by Fred Steiner, :04); First Noel Paraphrase (arr. by Garriguenc, :35); Lullaby (by Wilbur Hatch, :40); First Noel Paraphrase (arr. by Garriguenc, :15); Chime Notes (anonymous, :03); Adeste Fidelis Paraphrase (by John Francis Wade, arr. by Garriguenc, :25 and :55); Jingle Bells (reprise, :57); First Noel Paraphrase (arr. by Garriguenc, :19); Soliloquy (by Lucien Moraweck, 1:15); High String Tremolo (by Moraweck, :41); First Noel Paraphrase (arr. by Garriguenc, :12

and :12); Soliloquy (by Moraweck, :22); Ascending Glissandi (anonymous, :01); High String Tremolo (by Moraweck, :38); Adeste Fidelis Paraphrase (arr. by Garriguenc, :33); First Noel Paraphrase (arr. by Garriguenc, :24 and :05); Joy to the World (anonymous, traditional, :30 and :30); Perry Mason Background (by Steiner, :02); Adeste Fidelis Paraphrase (arr. by Garriguenc, :39); Pantomime Drunk (by Jack Cathcart, :22); Another TV (by Maurice Carlton, :26); Adeste Fidelis Paraphrase (arr. by Garriguenc, :28); First Noel Paraphrase (arr. by Garriguenc, :22, :37 and :27); Adeste Fidelis Paraphrase (arr. by Garriguenc, :43 and :32); First Noel Paraphrase (arr. by Garriguenc, :26); Pantomime Drunk (by Carthcart, :15); Adeste Fidelis Paraphrase (arr. by Garriguenc, :16); First Noel Paraphrase (arr. by Garriguenc, :12 and :43); First Noel, Second Version (arr. by Garriguenc, :27); Etrange #3 (by Constant, :09); and Milieu #2 (by Constant, :20).

Associate Producer: Del Reisman

Art Director: Craig Smith

Casting: Ethel Winant

Associate Director: James Clark

Technical Director: Jim Brady

Lighting Director: Tom D. Schamp

Set Decorator: Arthur Jeph Parker

Directed by Jack Smight

Teleplay by Rod Serling

"This is Mr. Henry Corwin, normally unemployed, who once a year takes the lead role in the uniquely popular American institution, that of the department-store Santa Claus in a road company version of 'The Night Before Christmas.' But in just a moment Mr. Henry Corwin, ersatz Santa Claus, will enter a strange kind of North Pole which is one part the wondrous spirit of Christmas and one part the magic that can only be found . . . in the Twilight Zone."

Plot: Henry Corwin, a bum of the streets who finds salvation from the bottom of a bottle, is hired by a department store to play the role of Santa Claus. He loses his job on Christmas Eve when he shows up to work intoxicated and departs with head hanging low. Finding a magic sack in the alley, Corwin becomes the real deal when he begins passing out presents to those in need. Whatever people ask for, the sack provides. The police arrest him on a charge of distributing stolen goods, but when they open the sack, they find nothing but garbage. After Corwin is released from custody, he begins passing out gifts again – until the sack is empty. Having seen the smiles on the faces of the homeless and poor, Corwin wishes he could put the same smiles on the meek every holiday season. Wandering the alleyway late that evening, he is approached by a young elf and a sleigh with reindeer – his wish has been granted and next year Corwin, alias Santa Claus, will spread cheer for those in need.

"A word to the wise to all the children of the twentieth century, whether their concern be pediatrics or geriatrics, whether they crawl on hands and knees and wear diapers or walk with a cane and comb their beards. There's a wondrous magic to Christmas and there's a special power reserved for little people. In short, there's nothing mightier than the meek."

Trailer: *"This may look to you like any dismal, dark and dingy alley that lies skulking off the million mirrored shadowy places off the main drags. Actually, it's the private domain of leprechauns and elves and supplies the locale of next week's Twilight Zone. With us for a very special occasion is Mr. Art Carney, who plays the role a department store Santa Claus. And he plays with the heart, the warmth and the vast talent that is uniquely Carney. On The Twilight Zone next week, 'The Night of the Meek.'"*

Trivia, etc. "I generally deal with people who are underdogs," Serling explained to columnist Stephen Strohman. "Social underdogs, professional underdogs, political underdogs. I've been fortunate in TV utilizing this theme, but the stage or the novel is by far the most legitimate area for this kind of telling."

"I got the idea for this one watching a Santa Claus parade with my two kids a year ago and noticed that on the Santa Claus float the worthy gentleman chosen for the role must have been a last-minute and at least third-string replacement," Serling explained to a columnist for *TV Guide*. "He weighed just a few pounds more than Slim Summerville and his Santa Claus suit must have been dredged out of a canal someplace. It suddenly came to me that perhaps there's a story lurking somewhere in the whole concept of these guys who play Santa Claus for a living. And then I started to conceive of a tale of what would happen to an ersatz Kris Kringle if he suddenly found that he *was* Santa Claus."

This was not Carney's first exposure to a Rod Serling teleplay. Two years previous, Carney starred in "The Velvet Alley," for *Playhouse 90*, which told the inside story of a television writer who fought his way from starvation through the Hollywood jungles inhabited by insidious agents, gutless producers and passionate party-givers to reach the oasis of a Bel-Air mansion, complete with swimming pool. Along the way, Serling's writer lost his integrity, his friends, his wife – and his soul.

This episode also reunited Serling and Carney with director Jack Smight from the same *Playhouse 90* telecast, who most recently directed Carney during his summer stock tour in *The Seven Year Itch* and was also the director of "Full Moon Over Brooklyn," the final show in the series of *Art Carney Specials* the previous season.

Serling admitted to a reporter for *The Hammond Indiana Times* that much of the material in "The Velvet Alley" was autobiographical. "How else can a writer write than from learned knowledge? Of course I drew on my experiences as a television writer in molding the characterization and plot of the teleplay."

Shortly after reading "The Night of the Meek," Owen S. Comora of Young & Rubicam wrote to Alex Kennedy, director of audience promotion at CBS. "I think we have an unbeatable combination here with an original Christmas story by Rod Serling … and with Art Carney playing Santa Claus … I have so much faith in this particular show that I would like you to read the script before deciding how much extra network on-the-air promotion you will devote to it."

Serling referred to this as "A Christmas Story" without a title in August of 1960. The character Henry Corwin was named after the radio playwright, Norman Corwin. When he wrote a short story adapted from his teleplay, he gave Mr. Dundee a first name: Walter.

On December 12, 1960, Serling wrote to Owen Comora of Y&R explaining that "the Christmas show instead of being the sheer delight I had hoped it would be, turned out to be an inconsequential nothing and I rather think it'll be a terrible disappointment to you." Serling's major source of disappointment was that the production had been done on videotape, instead of filmed. Soon after viewing the final cut, Serling remarked the Christmas offering was "an abomination and looks for all the world like a rough dress rehearsal that is a couple days from coming around." Today, however, the episode is favored by many fans of the television series and for some, a tradition to view in their living rooms every holiday season.

The December 27 issue of *The Hollywood Reporter* remarked, "No matter how they debunk Santa Claus, the jolly old gent still rides high, but Rod Serling's hassle with this proposition with jaundiced quaint as dep't store Santa (Art Carney), in shabby regalia, and there he was, cockeyed drunk in a saloon. . . . Carney's soft-pedal drollery gave Yule fable its half-sardonic, half-caricature flavor. Obvious concept, of course, was benevolent."

"I've had the privilege of working with a lot of old timers in different shows, men who have been very big stars at one time but who made the transition gracefully to smaller roles," recalled Carney. "It's a pleasure to watch them, the ones who've mellowed and accepted the transition. They have a solidity and grace which comes from doing what they like to do and not resenting that someone else is, at the moment, number one."

Art Carney complete in Santa Claus costume.

This was not Serling's first exploration into a Christmas drama. While he wrote a number of them during his radio career, one radio play never got produced. "No Christmas This Year" (circa 1949-1951), told the tale of a civilization that dispenses with Christmas. No one knew exactly why this was so, they just knew it was happening, and the mayor of the town claims someone high up was responsible for the decision. Santa, up at the North Pole, has his own problems. The elves are on strike. The factory no longer manufactures toys – they produce crying gas, heavy bombs, fire bombs, and atomic bombs. Worse, he's been shot at when he flies over Palestine and China, and one of his elves got hit by shrapnel over Greece. When Serling wrote "The Night of the Meek," he fashioned the characters for Mr. Dundee and Sister Florence from characters in the radio script.

On December 30, Mrs. Marilyn Lister of Milwaukee, Wisconsin, wrote to Serling, expressing her disappointment in the Christmas show. "I enjoyed the plot, but there were several details of it that I disliked. The one thing I disliked most was the portrayal of the woman at the Mission. I think your characterization of this woman was in bad taste and completely unfair to the people who dedicate their lives to helping men (and women) who are down and out. You could have very easily changed this part of your show without harming the story. Why was it so necessary to put this woman at the mission in a bad light?"

The financial paperwork related to the six taped shows dated June 30, 1961 was incomplete, as evidenced by partial or no figures for the director and cast. The author has chosen to include the following production costs dated October 15, 1962:

	Total Cost per report June 30, 1961	Total Cost as adjusted after CBS Billing
"The Night of the Meek"	$10,349.61	$49,153.39
"Static"	$36,286.66	$43,773.70
"Twenty Two"	$53,824.64	$46,897.57
"Long Distance Call"	$50,747.16	$41,495.61
"The Whole Truth"	$45,581.86	$41,911.80
"Lateness of the Hour"	$42,572.09	$39,937.70

On February 7, Serling offered a belated apology. He assured her that it was not his intention to portray the character of the missionary in any unfavorable light. "Ours is never the job to knowingly offend and I think you read something into the characterization that was not there. I would have no reason whatsoever to slight the men and women who do spend their lives helping others."

CBS did not have all the required props to create the illusion of a department store, so many of the toys and decorations were brought in from the outside. All of the reindeer were furnished by Santa's Village, located in Skyforest, California, a 25-acre theme park that was in its third year of business. The reindeer cost Cayuga and CBS no funds. The arrangement granted Santa's Village ons-creen credit during the closing of the episode. The trains that Corwin wrecks were supplied by the Lionel Corporation, under the same arrangements.

John Fielder recalled to interviewer Tom Weaver, "I loved that. It was a wonderful part and great fun. That was the first time I worked with Art Carney; then, of course, I was on Broadway with him in *The Odd Couple*. It was just a really nice part, and working with him and the director and everything was fun. I had met Rod Serling several times before; he was a very, very nice man."

In December of 1964, Stephen Bobbins of the Eugene A. Tighe School in Margate City, New Jersey, wrote to Serling, thanking him for the wonderful story which the kids decided to put on stage. Traditionally, the school put on "A Christmas Carol" but that changed in December of 1964, when "The Night of the Meek" was loosely adapted at a junior high level for stage production. Upon learning of the school's achievement, Serling, on Christmas Eve 1964, wrote to Mr. Bobbins. "I'm delighted that 'The Night of the Meek' was done by your class and I hope it gave pleasure. All writers have pets amongst their output, and this story is my special one."

When this episode was originally telecast in December of 1960, Serling's closing narration featured a final line, not featured on commercial VHS and DVD releases: "And a Merry Christmas to each and all!" This final line was removed from certain prints for reruns, and is rarely seen. On occasion, the initial telecast version is broadcast, featuring that rarely-heard closing line delivered by Serling's off-screen narration.

Production #3653 "DUST" (Initial telecast: January 6, 1961)

Copyright Registration: © Cayuga Productions, Inc., January 5, 1961, LP18765 (in notice: 1960)
Dates of Rehearsal: 22 and 23, 1960
Dates of Filming: September 26, 27 and 28, 1960
Script #53 dated: August 2, 1960, with revised pages dated September 21, 1960.
Shooting script dated: September 21, 1960

Producer and Secretary: $1,775.00	Story and Secretary: $2,630.00
Director: $1,250.00	Cast: $6,620.63
Unit Manager and Secretary: $350.00	Production Fee: $825.00
Agents Commission: $2,500.00	Legal and Accounting: $250.00
Below the line charges (M-G-M): $35,346.20	Below the line charges (other): $1,542.63
Total Production Costs: $53,089.46	

Cast: Dorothy Adams (Mrs. Canfield); John Alonso (Luis Gallegos); Paul Genge (Mr. Canfield); Thomas Gomez (Sykes); Duane Grey (Rogers, the farmer); Douglas Heyes Jr. (the farmer boy); John

Larch (Sheriff Koch); Jon Lormer (man #1); Andrea Margolis (Estrelita); Bob McCord (Eddie, the villager); Vladimir Sokoloff (Gallegos, the farmer); and Daniel White (man #2).

Original Music Score Composed and Conducted by Jerry Goldsmith (Score No. CPN5938): Etrange #3 (by Marius Constant, :09); Milieu #1 (by Constant, :16); Fate (:15); The Funeral (2:07); The Rock (:37); The Magic Dust (1:45); Forecast (:10); March to the Gallows (:48); Last Hope (1:40); Broken Rope (1:15); The Hanging (3:02); Etrange #3 (by Constant, :10); and Milieu #2 (by Constant, :30).

Associate Producer: Del Reisman	Production Manager: Sidney Van Keuran
Director of Photography: George T.	Casting: Ethel Winant
Clemens, a.s.c.	Film Editor: Bill Mosher
Art Director: George W. Davis and Phil Barber	Sound: Franklin Milton and Charles Scheid
Assistant Director: E. Darrell Hallenbeck	Directed by Douglas Heyes
Set Decorations: Henry Grace and	Teleplay by Rod Serling
H. Web Arrowsmith	

"There was a village . . . built of crumbling clay and rotting wood. And it squatted ugly under a broiling sun like a sick and mangy animal waiting to die. This village had a virus . . . shared by its people. It was the germ of squalor . . . of hopelessness . . . of a loss of faith. For the faithless . . . the hopeless . . . the misery-laden, there is time . . . ample time to engage in one of the other pursuits of men . . . they begin to destroy themselves."

Plot: In a dry, dusty southwestern village, Luis Gallegos, a Mexican villager, got drunk one night and accidentally killed a little girl with his wagon. Having been tried and found guilty, he is sentenced to hang this afternoon. In a town where everyone is sick to the stomach, a public execution is the last thing the sheriff wants to perform – but makes the necessary preparations. Sykes, a traveling peddler and boisterous scheming notion of evil, sells the rope that will be used to hang the young man. Sykes then offers false hope to the condemned man by selling the boy's father some magic dust that will supposedly make hate turn into love. The naïve father believes the peddler and buys the bag for 100 pesos. Moments before Gallegos is to be hanged, his father shouts about, throwing dust on everyone, pleading for love. Sykes, in the background, enjoys the laughs. The ceremony goes on, however, and the trap is sprung. Through the hand of providence, the rope breaks and the boy's life is saved. Some people in the crowd shout for a rehanging. But the parents of the dead girl, seeing the desperation of the father, agree that the boy has been punished enough. The lad is released and everyone goes back home. Sykes, realizing that the rope could not have possibly broken because of Gallegos' weight, suspects divine intervention may have had a hand.

"It was a very small, misery-laden village on the day of a hanging . . . and of little historical consequence. And if there's any moral to it at all . . . let's say that in any quest for magic . . . in any search for sorcery, witchery, legerdemain . . . first check the human heart. For inside this deep place there's a wizardry that costs far more than a few pieces of gold. Tonight's case in point . . . in the Twilight Zone."

Trivia, etc. In 1950, Serling wrote a radio script titled "The Dust By Any Other Name," concerning a character named Abner Bodner, who attempts to build a chemical plant that would produce a magic dust. When breathed, the dust would make mortal enemies forget their hatred. As a result of his efforts, Bodner has an accident that costs him his life, proving to everyone in town that a man who dies in his belief of peace leaves a larger mark on society. He believed in his dream – not the dust. The radio script was rejected weeks after being submitted to the *Dr. Christian* radio program.

On June 19, 1958, CBS presented an episode of *Playhouse 90*, titled "A Town Has Turned to Dust," scripted by Serling. This version told the story of the lynching of a 19-year-old Mexican boy by a mob spurred on by a young merchant, whose hatred of the victim stemmed both from his wife accepting the affection of the doomed boy and from a deep-rooted prejudice against Mexicans. It was also the story of the town sheriff, who gives in feebly to the lynching mob, but stands firm when it comes to hanging the victim's brother after he defies the Jim Crow standards of the town. The brother is saved by the sheriff who, after killing the merchant and also is dying from the merchant's bullet, tells of the time, years ago, when he had led a mob in the ugly lawless murder of another man.

The *Playhouse 90* teleplay was a rewrite of a year-old script titled "Aftermath," which was initially rejected by the sponsors who were afraid it was too controversial. The original story dealt with the southern segregation problem, but Serling revised it to center around a Mexican – and the time was pushed back to the late 19th century.

In July of 1960, Serling took the *Playhouse 90* script and shortened the length (and the title), making a number of revisions. In combining both the *Dr. Christian* and *Playhouse 90* scripts, he explored the motivation of the mob and eliminated any reference to a prior hanging (thus, the sheriff is sick to the stomach in this episode). The character of Sheriff Harvey Denton was renamed Sheriff Koch (purposely named after the scriptwriter famous for penning the *War of the Worlds* panic broadcast, an episode of *The Lux Video Theatre* and the 1942 screenplay, *Casablanca*). Perhaps the largest character in this fantasy involves the peddler Sykes (who replaced Jerry Paul, the victim who rouses the mob in the *Playhouse 90* version), a boisterous, scheming personification of evil, who sells rope for the lynching and then pushes the townsfolk to demand action. Not one to miss another opportunity, he then decides to offer the boy's father, played by Vladimir Sokoloff, a bag of magic dust – profiting not just cash, but for laughs. *

Thomas Gomez, who played the role of Sykes in this episode, was on *A Game of Chess* in 1940, one of the first shows ever telecast from New York. Since then he appeared in numerous television dramas, often playing the heavy. When asked by a columnist at the time what it was like to play the role of the bad guy repeatedly from one television program to another, he commented, "I don't understand those categories. I just call myself a leading man and let it go at that. If you ask me what I like best, I would say a comedy part with some rascality, warmth and dimension – and parts where Latin people are presented with sympathy, or at least with humanity." Gomez was granted his wish with this *Twilight Zone* episode.

A second version of "A Town Has Turned to Dust" was telecast on the BBC less than a month before *The Twilight Zone* version aired in the United States. That version was almost word-for-word perfect from the *Playhouse 90* drama and not the *Twilight Zone* revision. In September of the same year, the Macquarie Broadcasting Service in London inquired about a radio broadcast adapted from the script for broadcast in Australia, but the minimal fee and the question about television rights versus radio broadcast rights gave Serling the opportunity to decline the offer. The matter was looked

* Serling reused the name of Sheriff Koch again in "I Am the Night – Color Me Black."

into, and by December, two weeks before Christmas, Serling's terms were met and the rights for a radio broadcast were secured.

This episode came in about $5,500 over budget. The dates of filming were originally scheduled for October 24, 25 and 26, with rehearsal dates October 20 and 21. When it was decided that Douglas Heyes would not be filming Charles Beaumont's unproduced "Acceleration" in mid-October, the dates were pushed ahead and rescheduled. According to a release schedule dated August 25, 1960, this episode was originally scheduled for broadcast on March 3, 1961.

One of the farmer boys in this episode was actually Doug Heyes, Jr., the younger son of the director, Douglas Heyes. The older brother took ill shortly before filming, so Doug Jr. took the role.

Production #3648 "BACK THERE" (Initial telecast: January 13, 1961)
Copyright Registration: © Cayuga Productions, Inc., January 12, 1961, LP18766 (in notice: 1960)
Dates of Rehearsal: September 16 and 19, 1960
Dates of Filming: September 20, 21 and 22, 1960
Script #48 dated: July 28, 1960, with revised pages dated September 14, 1960.

Producer and Secretary: $1,775.00
Director: $1,250.00
Unit Manager and Secretary: $350.00
Agents Commission: $2,500.00
Below the line charges (M-G-M): $30,050.18
Total Production Costs: $47,090.82

Story and Secretary: $2,630.00
Cast: $4,518.46
Production Fee: $825.00
Legal and Accounting: $250.00
Below the line charges (other): $2,942.18

Cast: Raymond Bailey (Millard); Lew Brown (the lieutenant); John Eldredge (Whitaker); James Gavin (the patrolman); Raymond Greenleaf (Jackson); Paul Hartman (Police Sergeant); Jean Inness (Mrs. Landers); Russell Johnson (Peter Corrigan); Fred Kruger (attendant in 1865); John Lasell (John Wilkes Booth); James Lydon (the patrolman); Nora Marlowe (the chambermaid); Pat O'Malley (attendant in 1961); Bartlett Robinson (William, the butler); and Carol Eve Rossen (the lieutenant's girl).

Original Music Score Composed and Conducted by Jerry Goldsmith (Score No. CPN5935):
Etrange #3 (by Marius Constant, :09); Milieu #1 (by Constant, :16); The Club (:44); The Discussion (:36); Table Talk (:10); Return to the Past (:40); Return to the Past A (2:13); Fords Theatre (:43); Fords Theatre A (:20); Police Station (:23); Mr. Wellington (:31); The Wine (1:16); The Prediction (1:25); The Assassination (1:35); The Homecoming (:37); Old William (1:55); Etrange #3 (by Constant, :10); and Milieu #2 (by Constant, :30).

Associate Producer: Del Reisman
Director of Photography: George T.
    Clemens, a.s.c.
Art Director: George W. Davis and Phil Barber
Set Decorations: Henry Grace and
    H. Web Arrowsmith
Teleplay by Rod Serling

Production Manager: Sidney Van Keuran
Assistant Director: E. Darrell Hallenbeck
Casting: Ethel Winant
Film Editor: Leon Barsha, a.c.e.
Sound: Franklin Milton and Charles Scheid
Directed by David Orrick McDearmon

"Witness a theoretical argument, Washington D.C., the present. Four intelligent men talking about an improbable thing like going back in time. A friendly debate revolving around a simple issue – could a human being change what has happened before? Interesting and theoretical because . . . who ever heard of a man going back in time . . . before tonight, that is. Because this is . . . the Twilight Zone."

Plot: Late one evening, Peter Corrigan discusses the subject of time travel with other members of a private club. One member claims he could alter the course of past events and then profit from his knowledge of the past. Corrigan, however, disagrees with them – believing that if he went back in time, he could only participate in what has already happened – the present day will never be altered. As he exits the building, however, he finds himself transported back to 1865, the very evening President Lincoln will be assassinated. When Corrigan tries to warn people of the on-coming assassination, the police arrest him for being drunk and disorderly. A doctor named Wellington arranges for Corrigan's release, in the hopes of curing the young man of a case of dementia. In Wellington's hotel room, Corrigan's efforts to convince the doctor that the president will be assassinated fails when he discovers he's been drugged. Waking from the effects of the drug, Corrigan learns he is too late. News shouts through the streets of the President's death, and Corrigan discovers Wellington's real name is John Wilkes Booth. Returning to the present, Corrigan discovers a few minor changes. The answer to the question of whether time travel would alter the events of the past is answered – while a man can alter the events on a small scale in his return to the past, the changes will only be noticeable to the time traveler.

"Mr. Peter Corrigan, lately returned from a place 'Back There'; a journey into time with highly questionable results. Proving, on one hand, that the threads of history are woven tightly and the skein of events cannot be undone . . . but, on the other hand, there are small fragments of tapestry that can be altered. Tonight's thesis . . . to be taken as you will . . . in the Twilight Zone."

Trailer: *"In this rather posh club, you'll see a group of men argue a somewhat metaphysical subject like time travel. One of them maintains it's possible to go back in time, make a few changes in history, and as a result, do quite a job on the present, in this case the assassination of one Abraham Lincoln. Next week a story called 'Back There.' I'd like you all to come with us, I think you'll find it a most exciting journey. Thank you and good night."*

Trivia, etc. To conform to the time period of 1865, small changes were made to the first draft Serling wrote. All references to "police captain" were changed to "police sergeant," including Wellington's introduction in the police station. "Police officer" was changed to "patrolman." All references to "landlady" at the hotel where Wellington was staying were changed to "chambermaid." The sign outside the "Washington Club" was changed to the "Potomac Club."

According to a production report, Serling originally conceived this as an hour-long teleplay titled "Afterwards." Guy Della Cioppa, CBS-TV vice president, offered it to the *Armstrong Circle Theatre*, which happened to be the only hour-long anthology series airing that season, but Armstrong was not intrigued with the script. The sponsors for *The Twilight Zone* were not willing to expand their half-hour time slot. As Della Cioppa explained, "Advertisers who have a regular series and who have extra money for Specials always want to escape from their regular series to offer contrasting attractions." For *The Twilight Zone*, Serling resorted to shortening the script to a brief 23 minutes and changed the title to "Back There."

According to a release schedule dated August 25, 1960, this episode was originally planned for broadcast on December 16, 1960.

On September 2, 1960, Robert Longenecker, operating his own agency for actors and actresses, contacted Ethel Winant, the casting director for *The Twilight Zone*, suggesting actor Ray Montgomery for the role of the policeman or Wellington, John Howard for the role of William, Stuart Wade as a possible for Wellington, Will Thornbury and Patricia Kegley for the handsome young couple, and Connie Davis or Mae Ediss for Mrs. Landers.

On April 10, 1959, Mignon McLaughlin (17 East 89th Street, New York) wrote the following proposal to Serling:

Dear Rod:
I've thought up a play idea which Reggie Rose seems to think might be suitable for the new series you're doing.

We open with Lincoln attending Ford's Theatre. John Wilkes Booth takes a shot at him and either misses altogether or only wounds him superficially. Lincoln then goes on to face his bitter foes in the North and South, the hostile press, all the problems of reconstruction. As defeat piles upon defeat and mess upon mess, his mighty spirit is all but crushed. Then, one night he is called on by an Unearthly Visitor, who offers him a chance: to go not ahead but backward in time, to be shot and killed that night by Booth. Lincoln, seeing this as cowardly, rejects the proposition, but the visitor argues eloquently that not only would this preserve Lincoln's enshrined and inspiring place in history – a consideration that does not sway him – but that also just possibly another man might grapple more successfully with the nation's postwar agonies. In the end, this persuades him; he consents; the years are wiped out and we are back at Ford's on the fateful night, and this time Booth's shot succeeds.

I have a thing about period stuff, so I don't want to write it myself. But I hope that perhaps you'll do it, or farm it out to someone. In any case, best wishes –
Mignon McLaughlin

The plot of a man going back in time to 1865 and given the opportunity to prevent the course of events leading to the assassination of Abraham Lincoln has been explored not once – but twice – on radio. The first attempt was on Mutual's *The Mysterious Traveler*. On the evening of February 7, 1950, "The Man Who Tried to Save Lincoln" dramatized the story of a scientist who figures how to transfer a man's thoughts back into time and occupy another man's body. In this version, the time traveler finds himself in the body of John Wilkes Booth. Booth, managing to get the better of the voice in his head, makes a successful effort to assassinate Lincoln. This same script was dramatized again years later for *Suspense*.

On the evening of September 26, 1975, *The CBS Radio Mystery Theater*, a syndicated radio program offering dramatic thrillers five days a week, featured "Assassination in Time." Written by Ian Martin, the story told of a professor who transported his daughter and her fiancé to 1865, the morning of the assassination. The two time travelers attempt to prevent the murder and change the course of history. Martin played supporting roles in thousands of radio broadcasts during the 1950s, and was also among the cast of *The Mysterious Traveler* and *Suspense*, which exposed him to the same premise which was apparently borrowed for his own rendition.

In an episode of *Early Edition*, titled "Hot Time in the Old Town," initially telecast on May 16,

1998, a computer-generated reproduction of Rod Serling appears on the screen, with the same narration used for this broadcast. The plot was similar to *The Twilight Zone*, which is why the producers chose to feature Serling on the screen. While trying to stop a modern-day disaster which would kill hundreds of Chicago residents, the lead protagonist travels back to 1871, days before the great Chicago fire, and ponders whether he could change the course of events.

Production #4283-4 "THE WHOLE TRUTH" (Initial telecast: January 20, 1961)

© Cayuga Productions, Inc., January 19, 1961, LP18767 (in notice: 1960)
Dates of Filming: December 3 and 4, 1960
Script undated with revisions dated November 8, 1960
Shooting script dated: December 1, 1960

Producer and Secretary: $2,120.08	Story and Secretary: $2,510.00
Director: $270.40	Cast: $4,034.82
Production Fee: $825.00	Agents Commission: $2,500.00
Legal and Accounting: $250.00	Below the line charges (CBS): $32,906.11
Below the line charges (other): $165.45	Total Production Costs: $45,581.86

Cast: Jack Carson (Harvey Hunnicut); George Chandler (the old man); Jack Ging (the young man); Arte Johnson (Irv); Nan Peterson (the young woman); Lee Sabinson (The Premier); Loring Smith (Honest Luther Grimbley); and Patrick Westwood (the Premier's Aide).

Stock Music Cues: Etrange #3 (by Marius Constant, :09); Milieu #1 (by Constant, :16); Hustle Bustle (by Willis Schaefer, :39); Traffic (a.k.a. Big Town, by Rene Garriguenc, :26); Crook (by Maurice Carlton, :05); Exit Lam (by Wilbur Hatch and Garriguenc, :10); Future (by Carlton, :10); Mysterious Liza (by Hatch and Arthur Wilkinson, :14); Date (by Carlton, :05); Comedy Punctuations (by Carlton, :03); Hustle (by Carlton, :10); Crook (by Carlton, :08); Pantomime (by Hatch, :23); Pantomime #3 – Wistful Thinking (by Hatch, :09); Hustle (by Carlton, :09); Brouillard (by Constant, :53 and :26); Mysterious Liza (by Hatch and Wilkinson, :20); Pantomime #3 – Wistful Thinking (by Hatch, :11); Brouillard (by Constant, :25, :13 and :05); Mysterious Liza (by Hatch and Wilkinson, :29 and :09); Brouillard (by Constant, :32); Shakes (by Carlton, :14); Hustle (by Carlton, :12); Brouillard (by Constant, :29, :29, and :19); Bridge #4 – Pseudo Hero (by Hatch, :17); Human Robot (by Carlton, :14); Pantomime #2 – Tongue in Cheek (by Hatch, :28); Human Robot (by Carlton, :20); Neutral Pleasant (by Guy Luypaertz, :05); Brouillard (by Constant, :11); Pixie Pantomime (by Hatch, :18); Mysterious Liza (by Hatch and Wilkinson, :04); Etrange #3 (by Constant, :17); and Milieu #2 (by Constant, :23).

Associate Producer: Del Reisman	Art Director: Robert Tyler Lee
Casting: Ethel Winant	Associate Director: James Clark
Technical Director: Jim Brady	Lighting Director: Tom D. Schamp
Set Decorator: Buck Henshaw	Directed by James Sheldon
Teleplay by Rod Serling	

"This, as the banner already has proclaimed, is Mr. Harvey Hunnicut, an expert on commerce and con jobs; a brash, bright, and larceny-loaded wheeler and dealer who, when the good Lord passed out a conscience, must have gone for a beer and missed out. And these are a couple of other characters in our story. A little old man and a Model 'A' car, but not just any old man and not just any Model 'A.' There's something very special about the both of them. As a matter of fact, in just a few moments they'll give Harvey Hunnicut something that he's never experienced before. Through the good offices of a little magic . . . they will unload on Mr. Hunnicut the absolute necessity to tell the truth. Exactly where they come from is conjecture, but as to where they're heading for, this we know, because all of them and you . . . are on the threshold of the Twilight Zone."

Plot: Harvey Hunnicut, a car salesman with a reputation for conning his customers into purchasing junkers off his used car lot, finds himself in a dilemma. After purchasing a Model A Ford from an old man, he discovers the antique is haunted. Since the vehicle rolled off the assembly line, every owner has experienced a peculiar feeling of telling the truth, whenever asked. No matter how hard Hunnicut attempts to push a vehicle on a customer, he manages to reveal every fallacy in his four-wheel products. When he phones his wife to lie about coming home late because he has to take inventory, he tells her he's playing cards with the boys. When his employee asks for a raise, Hunnicut tells him the truth, and loses his employee. Hunnicut finally finds himself cured of the disease when he manages to sell the vehicle to Nikita Khrushchev, the Soviet premiere, who happens to be on tour in the United States.

"Couldn't happen, you say? Far fetched? Way out? Tilt of center? Possible, but the next time you buy an automobile . . . if it happens to look as if it had just gone through the Battle of the Marne and the seller is ready to throw into the bargain one of his arms . . . be particularly careful in explaining to the boss about your grandmother's funeral . . . when you were actually at Chávez Ravine watching the Dodgers. It'll be a fact that you're the proud possessor of an instrument of truth, manufactured and distributed by an exclusive dealer . . . in the Twilight Zone."

Trailer: *"This, in the parlance of the Twentieth Century, is a used car lot. A graveyard of active ghosts who by dint and virtue of some exceptional salesmanship and an Indian rubber stretching of the truth remain as commodities in a world that by rights they should have left generations ago. Mr. Jack Carson plays the role of a larceny-loaded con man suddenly prevented from telling a falsehood. Next week, on the Twilight Zone a most bizarre tale that we call, 'The Whole Truth.'"*

Trivia, etc. According to the December 31, 1960 – January 6, 1961 issue of *TV Guide*, this episode was originally scheduled for broadcast on January 13.

Sometime circa 1951-1954, Blanche Gaines attempted to pitch a teleplay scripted by Serling, titled "The Gab." The story dealt with Davey Fletcher, a young guy in his late 20s, a high pressure boy with a gift of gab. Pappy Paulson, a used car lot operator, discovers the boy's talent and hires the lad to work for him. When the boy discovers that he is being used, he attempts to take matters into his own hands.

The idea for this script originated from two unused plot synopses composed by Serling for the previously proposed Mr. Bevis television series. One proposed plot involved Mr. Bevis being "blessed"

KEEPING AN EYE ON YOU

FROM THE

TWILIGHT ZONE

HOPE YOU HAVE A WONDERFUL CONVENTION

ROD SERLING

◉ **CBS**

Proposed Advertisement for the 20th World
Science Fiction Convention in Chicago, Ill.,
August 31 – September 3, 1962.

by a guardian angel with the ability to tell the truth for 24 hours. The other plot dealt with Mr. Bevis as a car salesman. Naturally, Serling blended the two together to form "The Whole Truth."

In a former draft of this *Twilight Zone* script, Hunnicut's phone call brought on a press conference with Khrushchev answering reporters' questions. A representative of the Los Angeles Gazette asked, "I wonder if you would tell us, sir, what observations you've made in your travels through the United States? How would you compare the United States with the Soviet Union?" The back view of the chubby, baldheaded man facing the press squirms in his seat and after a slow pan over to the translator, whose eyes bug as he begins to perspire, gulps and swallows. "The premiere . . . the premiere feels that," the translator reveals, "well, he seems to feel that even without a trip to Disneyland, it is obvious that the United States has a standard of living far superior to that of the people of the Soviet Union. And Mr. Khruschev wants it understood that the car . . . such as it is . . . and it isn't much . . . is considerably better than that owned by most Russians. The fact that it possesses four wheels puts it ahead of those owned by most Russians . . ."

Months before Serling wrote this script, on June 10 and 11, 1960, the Serling household went to Disneyland with their friends, John and Madeline Champion and family.

On March 9, 1962, Serling sent four autographed copies of *Twilight Zone* scripts to Earl Kemp, chairman of the 20th World Science Fiction Convention in Chicago, for their next event, August 31 – September 3, 1962. The four scripts were "The Shelter," "The Mirror," "Showdown with Rance McGrew," and this episode, "The Whole Truth."

Along with the scripts, Serling included a check in the amount of $12.00 for an advertisement in the Convention Program Book.

Production #3646 "THE INVADERS" (Initial telecast: January 27, 1961)
Copyright Registration: © Cayuga Productions, Inc., January 26, 1961, LP18768 (in notice: 1960)
Date of Rehearsal: October 10, 1960
Dates of Filming: October 11, 12, 13 and 14, 1960
Script #46 dated: August 6, 1960, with revised pages dated August 17, 1960.

Producer and Secretary: $1,775.00   Story and Secretary: $1,935.00
Director: $1,250.00   Cast: $3,240.00

Unit Manager and Secretary: $350.00
Agents Commission: $2,500.00
Below the line charges (M-G-M): $29,750.44
Total Production Costs: $44,912.46

Production Fee: $825.00
Legal and Accounting: $250.00
Below the line charges (other): $3,037.02

Cast: Agnes Moorehead (the woman)

Original Music Score Composed and Conducted by Jerry Goldsmith (Score No. CPN5947):
Etrange #3 (by Marius Constant, :09); Milieu #1 (by Constant, :16); The Old Woman (1:49); Space Ship (1:31); The Gadget (:58); The Wound (1:09); The Hunter (1:33); The Knife (:28); Counterattack Part 1 (1:11); Counterattack Part 2 (2:25); The Victor (1:24); Etrange #3 (by Constant, :10); and Milieu #2 (by Constant, :30).

Associate Producer: Del Reisman
Director of Photography: George T.
    Clemens, a.s.c.
Art Director: George W. Davis and Phil Barber
Set Decorations: Henry Grace and
    H. Web Arrowsmith
Teleplay by Richard Matheson

Production Manager: E. Darrell Hallenbeck
Assistant Director: Lindsey Parsons, Jr.
Casting: Ethel Winant
Film Editor: Leon Barsha, a.c.e.
Sound: Franklin Milton and Charles Scheid
Directed by Douglas Heyes

"This is one of the out-of-the-way places, the unvisited places – bleak, wasted, dying. This is a farmhouse, handmade, crude, a house without electricity or gas, a house untouched by progress. This is the woman who lives in the house, a woman who's been alone for many years. A strong, simple woman whose only problem up until this moment has been that of acquiring enough food to eat. A woman about to face terror which is even now coming at her from . . . the Twilight Zone."

Plot: An old woman living alone in a farmhouse, through somewhat primitive means, finds her peace disturbed by the landing of a small flying saucer on the rooftop. Apprehensive at first, she discovers two small invaders exiting the craft, displaying hostile intentions. Regardless of their size, these invaders from another planet prove to be a challenge for the old woman, who finds herself under attack. The little spacemen have plenty of strength and equipment to leave more than a few scars on the woman. During the battle, the spacemen manage to blow a hole through her wall while the giant of a woman manages to get the better of one of the visitors by beating him to death. When the remaining alien retreats to his vessel, the old woman takes an ax to the ship and destroys any remote possibility the invader has of returning home. As she finishes her task, a voice calls out over the radio alerting the invading army to retreat – this advance scout has discovered a race of giants which has proved too much for the invaders. The only part of the spacecraft the old woman did not destroy was the label attached to the flying saucer that reads: "U.S. Air Force, Space Probe."

"These are the invaders: the tiny beings from the tiny place called Earth, who would take the giant step across the sky to the question marks that sparkle and beckon from the vastness of the universe only to be imagined. The invaders, who found out that a one-way ticket to the stars beyond . . . has the ultimate

price tag. And we have just seen it entered in a ledger that covers all the transactions of the universe, a bill stamped 'paid in full,' and to be found on file . . . in the Twilight Zone."

Trailer: *"Next week, we bring you a show called 'The Invaders,' written by Mr. Richard Matheson. And in this room you'll watch Miss Agnes Moorehead in a tension-riddled attempt at escape . . . from a pair of very improbable housebreakers. This one we recommend to science fiction buffs, fantasy lovers, or to anyone who wants to grip the edge of his seat and take a twenty-four minute trip into the realm of terror."*

Trivia, etc. The earliest documented origin of this episode began with a progress report dated June 30, 1960, revealing that Richard Matheson had been committed to a teleplay titled "Devil Doll," script #49, first draft due for submission by July 5. As Matheson told Stanley Wiater in the commentary for "Prey" in his *Collected Stories*, "I had originally submitted the story – or at least a similar premise – to *The Twilight Zone*. And they rejected it because they thought it was too grim. So I turned it around into a science fiction story – and it became 'The Invaders,' the episode that Agnes Moorehead was in. Because it's the same damn story – except here there's only one doll. Later on I wrote the premise as the short story called 'Prey' and *Playboy* bought it." Published in *Playboy* in April 1969, and memorably adapted by Richard himself as a segment [titled "Amelia"] of the TV-movie *Trilogy of Terror* (1975) with Karen Black, the story tells of a woman terrorized in her apartment by a fetish doll possessed by the spirit of a Zuni warrior.

When a fan wrote to Rod Serling in April of 1960, asking for more out-of-this-world plots, Serling wrote back, "Next season I'll see what I can do about dimensional stories and space travel. My sponsors, being rather uniquely square gentlemen, have taken a somewhat dim view of science fiction. Next season, however, we hope to slip a few by them."

"The reason we cast Aggie for that part in 'The Invaders' was because she had done a very famous radio show called 'Sorry, Wrong Number' in which she talks constantly. A tour-de-force of one woman talking – one voice, nobody else," recalled director Douglas Heyes to interviewer Ben Herndon. When this part on 'The Invaders' came up and the woman was not going to talk at all – there was no dialogue for her – I said, 'This will be the opposite side of the coin. Let's get Aggie Moorehead.' It turned out she had been a student of the mime Marcel Marceau. She chose to play the part like an animal under attack. Her performance built beautifully and got more and more animalistic as she was being attacked. She made sounds when angry and whimpered when hurt, but she never uttered a word."

"I generally chose the scripts that I directed on *The Twilight Zone* for the problems that were involved," continued Heyes explained to Herndon. "The scripts never told you how to do the trick, and sometimes you would have to invent how this would come to pass. You know – how the little people would run around in 'The Invaders.'"

Originally Buck Houghton and Ralph W. Nelson proposed doing trick photography for the little people, using rear projection or building big sets and having real people do them – the kind of photography applied in such movies as *Dr. Cyclops* (1940). Heyes disagreed. "In having the little characters play in the scene with her, she could actually grab hold of them, throw 'em into the fireplace, see one up on the window ledge and give it a hit, and so forth. It was better than cutting away or doing it with trick photography. So we didn't use special effects after the fact."

Director Heyes drew sketches of the visitors from outer space, unique enough to disguise their humanity, but could be later accepted by the viewers as human beings. A shapeless look was what Heyes intended, which led to the idea of an inflated spacesuit. "I got the idea from the little Michelin Tire man," Heyes confessed. William Tuttle then built the space visitors out of a latex-type rubbery plastic material. The whole thing was a hollow shell. Tuttle and his crew made a model of the character, and then cast a number of them from the mold. The backs were cut so technicians could get their hands and fingers inside. The men operating the aliens (one of them included Douglas Heyes), wore a black sleeve to blend in with the background, giving the illusion that the spacemen walked on their own. A small battery attached to wires allowed the ray guns to light up, simply by pushing a small button. The voice at the end of the episode, originating from the surviving space visitor coming from within the ship, was director Doug Heyes.

"I thought [Richard] Donner did an excellent job on 'Nightmare at 20,000 Feet,' and Douglas Heyes, who did the Agnes Moorehead one, 'The Invaders,'" recalled Matheson to author Mathew Bradley. "What's there is good, because I have said many times that I would have liked it if ['The Invaders'] had gone faster. In that and the Buster Keaton thing ['Once Upon a Time'], I had a lot more material – more going on between her and these little critters because the opening I find, to this day, unbearably leisurely. It just takes forever. It takes forever before she hears the noise on the roof, and then it takes forever for her to get up there. I think [the opening] probably could have been cut in half, or by a third. . . . They should have, but I don't think they cut the opening. And I didn't like the little [spacemen], those little roly-poly things. I had them appearing so – just flying past your eye or your attention. They had little space things that made them fly, and you would just see them and then they'd be gone. They weren't just wobbling around."

This episode was not the first scripted by Richard Matheson to take place in real time (hence the story began and ended within a 23-minute time frame). His first season episode "A World of His Own" and the third season episode "Young Man's Fancy" also took place in real time.

According to a production schedule, this episode was supposed to have four days of filming and zero days of rehearsal from October 17 through October 20. It was believed that since there were no lines for Agnes Moorehead to memorize, there would be no need for rehearsal. Douglas Heyes was also scheduled to direct Charles Beaumont's "Acceleration" script from October 12 to 14, allowing the weekend to catch up before filming commenced on "The Invaders" on October 17. Since "Acceleration" was scrapped, the filming for this episode commenced a week earlier, and a day for rehearsal (and to iron out the schematics of the little aliens, camera shots and props and sets) was added.

According to a release schedule dated August 25, 1960, this episode was originally scheduled for broadcast on February 10, 1961.

Serling's closing comments in the script Matheson initially submitted was different from what is featured now in the filmed episode:

This is one of the out-of-the-way places; until now, one of the unvisited places in our solar system – the planet Mars. Bleak. Wasted. Dying. But not quite dead yet.

On January 28, 1961, Arthur Allwood of Whitehall, Michigan, wrote to the network, explaining his interest in the USAF Space Probe featured in the conclusion. "In my spare time I like to do trick photography, just for kicks. For this purpose, and for the reason that I'm still a kid at heart, would you sell me a copy of the blueprints your engineers used to build the model, so I can build one too? If you do sell it to me, would you please include instructions as to how I would go about installing the working parts you had on yours? (The ramp that goes up and down, the blinking lights, etc.)"

On February 22, Connie Olmsted, Serling's secretary, sent the following reply: "Thank you for your interest in our presentation, 'The Invaders.' Unfortunately, we can't honor your request for a copy of the blueprints of the spaceship. This is not available for commercial use but was designed especially for our show."

The flying saucer was one of a handful of props left over from the filming of *Forbidden Planet* (1956). The flying saucer was featured so predominately in the motion picture, that various miniatures were used to acquire the special effects needed. The one featured in this episode, obviously, was trashed by the end of filming.

On February 2, William Dozier, then vice president in charge of West Coast activities of Screen Gems, the television subsidiary of Columbia Pictures Corp., wrote to Serling, offering his rave of this episode, complimenting Matheson. "Loved the Aggie Moorehead show; tough scripting job, I'll bet!"

Production #3650 "A PENNY FOR YOUR THOUGHTS"
(Initial telecast: February 3, 1961)
© Cayuga Productions, Inc., February 2, 1961, LP18769 (in notice: 1960)
Dates of Rehearsal: September 28 and 29, 1960
Dates of Filming: September 30 and October 3 and 4, 1960
Script undated with revised pages dated September 26, 28 and 29, 1960
Shooting script dated: September 29, 1960

Producer and Secretary: $1,775.00
Director: $1,250.00
Unit Manager and Secretary: $350.00
Agents Commission: $2,500.00
Below the line charges (M-G-M): $27,788.15
Total Production Costs: $43,094.57

Story and Secretary: $1,365.00
Cast: $5,575.46
Production Fee: $825.00
Legal and Accounting: $250.00
Below the line charges (other): $1,415.96

Cast: June Dayton (Miss Turner); Cyril Delevanti (Mr. Smithers); Frank London (the driver); James Nolan (Mr. Brand); Anthony Ray (the news boy); Hayden Rorke (Mr. Sykes); Dan Tobin (Mr. Bagby); Patrick Waltz (the smiling woman); and Dick York (Hector B. Poole).

Stock Music Cues: Etrange #3 (by Marius Constant, :09); Milieu #1 (by Constant, :16); Shock Harmonics (by Fred Steiner, :04); Starlight – Outer Space Suite (by Herrmann, :25); Space Stations – Outer Space Suite (by Herrmann, :07); Street Scene #1 (:19); Brave New World (by Herrmann, :07); Alain #3 (by Constant, :25); Brave New World (by Herrmann, 1:05); Light Rain (by Constant, :24); Street Scene #1 (by Garriguenc, :17); Investigation #1 (by Garriguenc, 1:06); Shock Harmonics (by Steiner, :15); Brave New World (by Herrmann, :31); Kant #7 (by Constant, :27); Kant #8 (by Constant, :06); Etrange #3 (by Constant, :10); and Milieu #2 (by Constant, :30).

Associate Producer: Del Reisman
Director of Photography: George T.
    Clemens, a.s.c.
Art Director: George W. Davis and Phil Barber
Set Decorations: Henry Grace and
    H. Web Arrowsmith

Production Manager: E. Darrell Hallenbeck
Assistant Director: Lindsley Parsons, Jr.
Casting: Ethel Winant
Film Editor: Leon Barsha, a.c.e.
Sound: Franklin Milton and Charles Scheid
Directed by James Sheldon

Teleplay by George Clayton Johnson

"Mr. Hector B. Poole, resident of the Twilight Zone. Flip a coin and keep flipping it. What are the odds? Half the time it will come up heads, half the time tails. But in one freakish chance in a million, it'll land on its edge. Mr. Hector B. Poole, a bright human coin, on his way to the bank."

Plot: On his way to work one morning, Hector Poole purchases a newspaper. In doing so, he makes payment by tossing the coin into a box, and instead of landing face down, it lands on its edge. From that moment on, Poole discovers that he can read people's thoughts. At the bank where he works, he spends the afternoon overhearing customers thinking to themselves, both good and evil, realizing that people are different underneath the exterior of a smile. Most important, Poole has reason to believe Mr. Smithers, an employee of 20 years, is planning to rob the bank at 4:30. Mr. Bagby, the bank president, hears Poole out and gives him the benefit of the doubt. Before the old man can walk out of the bank, his case is searched and nothing is found but paperwork and pencils. Poole is fired for his error. In private, Poole learns from Smithers that robbing the bank has always been a dream of his ... just a dream. Cleaning out his desk, Poole learns that he has earned the respect of Miss Helen Turner, an employee at the bank. With her advice (and a little blackmail against his boss), he not only gets his job reinstated, but promoted as well. On the way home, Poole buys the evening paper and in making payment, accidentally knocks the same coin off its edge. The voices stop and Poole has returned to normal.

"One time in a million, a coin will land on its edge, but all it takes to knock it over is a vagrant breeze, a vibration or a slight blow. Hector B. Poole, a human coin, on edge for a brief time in the Twilight Zone."

Trailer: *"Next week on this very spot there commences a very kooky chain of occurrences. The story has to do with a young bank clerk who for some unexplained and most uncanny reason, finds himself able to read other people's minds. And then finds that the power can get him into a peck of trouble and a bushel of travail. Our show is called 'A Penny for Your Thoughts,' and it'll be here waiting for you next week on The Twilight Zone."*

Trivia, etc. By the time this episode aired, *The Palladium-Times* remarked this broadcast was "another good show on a series that deserves higher ratings."

"I was credited, officially, as associate producer for the second season of *Twilight Zone*, but my tasks consisted mainly of being the story editor," recalled Del Reisman. "I reviewed material submitted to Cayuga, Rod and Buck. I worked with the writers, helped Rod find the stories needed, and I also assisted Buck in many of the production details. There were story submissions from viewers, individual writers would contact us, and agents were always pitching ideas. One of the young writers was George Clayton Johnson, who, I am sure, you are familiar with. He had a whole crateful of ideas and Rod finally told him, 'Look, you are friends of Charlie and Richard, but you have never written a teleplay before. How about you write the stories, we'll buy them, and then someone else like Charlie will write the teleplays.' Well, George comes up with this story about a man who can read people's thoughts. Rod tells Buck and me that 'I want Del to work with this guy and get a teleplay out of him.' So I did. And that became 'A Penny For Your Thoughts.'"

George Clayton Johnson received $220 for his narrative synopsis of the same name and much more for writing the teleplay. Charles Beaumont was instrumental in convincing Johnson to contribute for the series. "He was a good friend and he inspired people to try harder," recalled Johnson to interviewer Steve Boisson. "He said, 'Put up or shut up.' He said that I really ought to write something if I'm going to have so many ideas about what's good or bad."

Johnson commented a great deal about this episode to Matthew R. Bradley. "I turned it in, they accepted it, and that is when I decided to use some leverage to get a script. I said to Buck, when he called me up to praise me for the story and say they were gonna do it, 'I can't let you have it until I get a chance to do the first draft.' There were some very stiff silences back and forth as we really were aware of what was going on, because it was clear I was holding him up. He had made a deal, Rod liked it, thought it would make a charming show, and was ready to write it himself, and here I am saying I want to write it. Here's Rod, feeling guilty about this 'Sea Change' story [that they had bought and then been forced to sell back to Johnson, due to reservations from the sponsor], saying, 'Sure, let him write it,' and Buck sort of caught in the middle, not wanting to cede me this power but realizing that I could really throw a monkey wrench into their plans, although I would hurt myself as well. But I was the stubborn and idealistic type, and really felt that I could do it."

"Down goes the phone and then two weeks of solid listening and not hearing a word, with every passing moment reassuring myself with a great truth which was taught to me by Beaumont: 'No news is no news.' When I came to realize that, I tried to calm myself and say, 'It doesn't matter that it's taking longer.' He should have called me. My God, don't they care? Are they gonna say no? Have I blown it, for God's sakes? Is [my wife] Lola going to look at me with those accusing eyes and say, 'George, what did you do here? You had Rod Serling lined up and now it's all fallen apart? What is happening?' I waited, and then I got a call from an attorney named Gerry Saltsman, who subsequently went on to become a big-name person, and in fact may at this very moment be sitting at the top of some tower somewhere in Los Angeles or Hollywood. Gerald called me to say he wanted to have a meeting at Ashley-Steiner, which was the agency of the *Twilight Zone* show. So I went to his office and sat down, and he said that they had decided to buy this story with an option for me to write a teleplay for this additional amount of money, and he was forthwith executing that option. Then it's like, 'You sign here, I'll sign here,' and it was done. There was the check in front of me. He'd already prepared the check, the numbers were all cleared, and I walked out of the room with this assignment and the check and an understanding that I'd better get to it and a couple of weeks would be fine, with me always sort of dragging my feet. But I went home and I stuck patiently to the outline, doing my very best to try and embody it as perfectly as I could, and fortunately for me, they came up with Dick York."

The original script did not feature the toss of a coin in the box. "Dick York, the character of Hector Poole, is hit with a car and later comes to realize that he can hear voices," Johnson recalled. "Well, the budget wouldn't allow them to spend the time or the money to build up a great car accident. Someone on the set comes up with the idea of putting a string on a coin, and he shows it to Serling and Serling says he likes the idea. Well they film this coin trick and it flies through the air and snaps outright, standing up on its edge. A miraculous situation that grants Hector Poole a chance to hear other people's thoughts."

Serling later remarked that this episode was "not unlike another short story I read where a man learns the ability to read thoughts from an aged, musty manuscript which he buys in a used book stall. He proceeds to utilize this knowledge, only to be shot in the end by a crook who didn't think the gun was loaded. . . . And never once did it cross my mind that because one writer deals with X doing Y to Z makes this situation sacrosanct and untouchable by anyone else."

According to a production report dated June 30, 1960, this was script #50. (was script #50. (keeping in mind that the production report varied month by month, so the number may have changed). On September 2, 1960, Robert Longenecker, operating his own agency for actors and actresses, contacted Ethel Winant, the casting director for *The Twilight Zone*, suggesting actor Kip King for the role of the aggressive Mr. Brand; Ed Wilson for the role of Mr. Sykes; and Beverly Brown for the role of Miss Turner. Serling had, by coincidence, met Beverly Brown at a luncheon and wanted to feature her in an episode of *The Twilight Zone*. While she did not get the role of Miss Turner for this episode, Brown did get the role of Stewardess Jane in the episode "The Odyssey of Flight 33."

According to a release schedule dated August 25, 1960, this episode was originally scheduled for broadcast on January 20, 1961.

The original trailer for next week's episode was a bit different:

"Next week on this very spot there commences a most unusual chain of occurrences. Simply stated so as not to tip it and ruin it for you, the story has to do with a young bank clerk who for some unexplained and most uncanny reason finds himself able to read other people's minds. And then finds that the power can get him into a peck of trouble and a bushel of travail. Our show is called 'A Penny for Your Thoughts,' and it'll be here waiting for you next week on The Twilight Zone."

"Now I will tell my favorite *Twilight Zone* and Rod Serling story," remarked Johnson. "I was on the set that day because I was invited. I took Lola with me, and we watched the filming. I introduced myself to James Sheldon, he was the director, and we talked a while and then Rod Serling comes on the set. He's leading a choir of on-lookers like a tour guide for visiting dignitaries and everyone on the set was electrified. No one dared to make a move while he was there. Then he sees me and Lola standing there, and he introduces me to the people, 'And this is George Clayton Johnson, the writer of this absolutely dandy film we are making right now.' And I am hearing my name and the praise. Then Serling introduces the director . . . but he introduced me first. I felt like a king."

In the episode "Samantha Goes South for a Spell," on television's *Bewitched*, initially telecast on October 3, 1968, Darrin (played by Dick York) returns home to find himself in another comical situation involving witchcraft. He remarks, "Oh, this is just great. I come home from work and find out my wife is in *The Twilight Zone*." This was, obviously, an inside joke because both York and Elizabeth Montgomery made guest appearances on the series.

This particular episode of *The Twilight Zone* was referenced by the fictional criminals in the motion picture *Truth or Consequences, N.M.* (1997).

Production #4003-5 "TWENTY TWO" (Initial telecast: February 10, 1961)

© Cayuga Productions, Inc., February 9, 1961, LP19932 (in notice: 1960)
Dates of Filming: December 10 and 11, 1960
Script dated: October 31, 1960
Shooting script dated: December 8, 1960

Producer and Secretary: $2,135.52
Director: $279.70
Production Fee: $825.00

Story and Secretary: $2,510.00
Cast: $6,330.39
Agents Commission: $2,500.00

Legal and Accounting: $250.00
Below the line charges (other): $79.95

Below the line charges (CBS): $38,914.08
Total Production Costs: $53,824.64

Cast: Mary Adams (the day nurse); Carole Conn (double for actress Arline Sax); Norma Connolly (the night burse); Angus Duncan (ticket clerk #1); Jonathan Harris (the doctor); Wesley Lau (the airline agent); Barbara Nichols (Elizabeth Powell); Jay Overholts (the voice on the P.A. system); Joe Sargent (ticket clerk #2); Arline Sax (the nurse in the morgue); and Fredd Wayne (Barney Kaminer).

Stock Music Cues by Nathan Van Cleave unless noted: Etrange #3 (by Marius Constant, :09); Milieu #1 (by Constant, :16); Trouble Elegy (1:39); Dark Room – Silent Flight C (by Jerry Goldsmith, 1:00); Dramatic Tension (:59); Piano Stings (:20); Prelude Elegy (:34); The Happy Farmer (:22); Second Act Opening – Elegy (:06); We've Had It (:38); Nice Old Man (:44); Piano Stings (:10); Expectation (by Rene Garriguenc, :05); Lonesome Town (:35); Second Act Opening – Elegy (:17); Trouble – Elegy (:44); The Martini (:11); Dramatic Tension (:51); Dark Room – Silent Flight C (by Goldsmith, :45); Piano Stings (:11 and :11); Howe's Place (by Fred Steiner, :04); We've Had It (:12); Lonesome Town (:16); Second Act Opening – Elegy (:10); Lonesome Town (:10); The Happy Fisherman (:13); Trouble – Elegy (:08); Dramatic Tension (:49); The Martini (:58); Composite Track #1 – Dark Cell #1 (by Lucien Moraweck, 1:18); We've Had it (:20); Dark Room – Silent Flight C (:20); Buildup Chords (by Moraweck, :32); The Martini (:11); Piano Stings (:11 and :11); Ostinato on C and G Metronome (anonymous, :11); Piano Stings (:08 and :08); Mad Harpsichord (anonymous, :25); We've Had It (:25); Etrange #3 (by Constant, :10); and Milieu #2 (by Constant, :31).

Associate Producer: Del Reisman
Casting: Ethel Winant
Technical Director: Jim Brady
Set Decorator: Arthur Jeph Parker

Art Director: Craig Smith
Associate Director: James Clark
Lighting Director: Tom D. Schamp
Directed by Jack Smight

Teleplay by Rod Serling, based on an anecdote from Bennett Cerf's *Famous Ghost Stories*.

"This is Miss Liz Powell. She's a professional dancer and she's in the hospital as a result of overwork and nervous fatigue. And at this moment we have just finished walking with her in a nightmare. In a moment she'll wake up and we'll remain at her side. The problem here is that both Miss Powell and you will reach a point where it might be difficult to decide which is reality – and which is nightmare. A problem uncommon perhaps . . . but rather peculiar . . . to the Twilight Zone."

Plot: Elizabeth Powell, a stage dancer by profession, has spent the past weeks at a sanitarium for rest and relaxation. Maybe it is her nerves, but she claims that every evening she has the same recurring nightmare, without any variation. In her dream, she wakes to break a glass of water on the floor, hears footsteps outside her room and follows someone to the elevator. Downstairs by the door of the morgue, labeled room 22, she is greeted by a strange woman with a crazy smile who tells Miss Powell, "Room for one more, Honey." Her doctor suggests she attempt to vary the routine in her dream to prevent the same events from happening, believing she would be cured after one good night's rest. She makes a faithful attempt, but finds herself repeating the same scenes as the night before. After checking out of the sanitarium the next day, Miss Powell is escorted to the airport by her agent, where she books a one-way, non-stop flight to Miami . . . on Flight 22. Staring out a window, she starts having a sense of déjà vu, reproducing most of the scenes from her dream, including dropping a glass and taking a long walk down to the airplane. Before getting in, the stewardess steps out – the same woman from Powell's dream – and remarks, "Room for one more, Honey." Miss Powell screams and runs back into the airport. While her agent and the airport staff comfort her, they watch with horror as the plane takes off and bursts into flames . . .

"Miss Elizabeth Powell: profession, dancer; hospital diagnosis – acute anxiety brought on by overwork and fatigue. Prognosis; with rest and care, she'll probably recover. But the cure to some nightmares is not to be found in known medical journals. You look for it under Potions For Bad Dreams, to be found . . . in the Twilight Zone."

Fredd Wayne looks over Barbara Nichols in "Twenty Two."

Trailer: *"This is room 22 and on the other side of its doors lies an adventure that is as fascinating as it is inexplicable. It's a story that comes to us from Mr. Bennett Cerf, who describes it as an age-old horror tale whose origin is unknown. We have dressed it up in some hospital wrappings and enlisted the performance of Miss Barbara Nichols. Next on The Twilight Zone, 'Twenty-Two.' Be prepared to be spooked. It's that kind of story."*

Trivia, etc. This episode originated from a gracious gesture to Serling from friend Bennett Cerf, president of Random House, Inc. Cerf spent the afternoon and evening as a guest at the Serlings' Pacific Palisades home. As a way of saying thanks, Cerf arranged for new Beginner Books and the latest Dr. Seuss release to be shipped to the Serlings in mid-December of 1959. Among the books was an anthology of ghost stories for Rod – and it was one of the short stories contained within that was half the inspiration for this episode.

The other half originated from Mrs. Peter D. Matthews of Needham, Massachusetts. She wrote to Serling on July 26, forwarding two clippings from the July 25 issue of *The Boston Sunday Herald*. The news briefs told of a construction worker who, days before a deadly accident, shook hands with his fellow workers and told them he would be dead before Wednesday. Sure enough, a 120-foot crane smashed down on Decatur Street in East Boston, killing three men, including the man who predicted his own death. The premise was too intriguing in details, so Serling blended the ghost story and the news items into a fictional tale of a woman who suffers a recurring nightmare, foretelling a future accident that just may be the cause of her own death.

After viewing the finished film, actress Barbara Nichols admitted that she was a bit scared for a spell. "I told Mr. Serling I'm always a comedienne," she said. "I told him I'd always wanted to do dramatic roles. So he wrote the show for me. I'm happy as a clam." Because this episode was taped, Barbara Nichols was able to view the scene minutes later on the tape playback. "That was when I scared myself," she said. "There I was in the bed in a hospital nightgown screaming my head off. I had to scream. Real loud. So I just screamed. I'm not a method actor. I didn't practice. I guess a method actor would have gone off in a corner to cogitate or maybe run around the building a few times. Me, I just screamed."

Known for her lusty portrayal of a stripper in the original two-part pilot of *The Untouchables*, Nichols played the same roles before she became an actress. A Long Island girl, she began her trip to stardom by winning beauty contests at Woodrow Wilson High School in Jamaica, New York. Before long she was in the chorus line at the Latin Quarter in New York. "I was a model, a calendar girl and a dancer," she recalled. "I also was Miss Loew's Paradise, Miss Long Island Duckling and Miss Loew's Valencia." She played the role of a stripper in the 1952 revival of *Pal Joey* for Richard Rogers, and it was her stage work in *Pal Joey* that brought her to Hollywood and her career as a succession of dumb blondes. Whether it was the Jack Benny program or Red Skelton, she could not escape the typecast. She posed for a calendar, was the cover girl on at least 50 magazines, a nightclub dancer and in 1956, played the role of a stripper in *Miracle in the Rain*. On the television series, *The Mask*, she played a murdered stripper. On *Studio One* she was a dumb blonde. On *Danger* she was a nightclub singer. On *Circle Theater*, *Pond's Theater* and *The U.S. Steel Hour* she was cast to portray a succession of sweater girls, hat-check girls, chorus girls and movie starlets, and this episode of *The Twilight Zone* kept up her track record.

The nightgown Nichols wore in this episode caused one of the few retakes. It was not an ordinary nightgown by any means. It was a lacy job with a peekaboo front. "Well, anyhow, there was too much peekaboo or too little," she recalled. "Well, we had to redo it. That was just about the only laugh the camera crew had out of the whole show."

In one scene she landed so hard that her knees were bruised and scratched. "I sure was glad no retakes were necessary on that one."

Production #3651 "THE ODYSSEY OF FLIGHT 33"
(Initial telecast: February 24, 1961)
© Cayuga Productions, Inc., February 23, 1961, LP19933 (in notice: 1960)
Dates of Rehearsal: October 18 and 19, 1960
Dates of Filming: October 20, 21 and 24, 1960
Script #51 dated: October 4, 1960, with revised pages dated October 11 and 18, 1960.
Shooting script dated: October 18, 1960

Producer and Secretary: $1,775.00	Story and Secretary: $2,745.00
Director: $1,250.00	Cast: $4,528.62
Production Fee: $825.00	Agents Commission: $2,500.00
Legal and Accounting: $250.00	Below the line charges (M-G-M): $26,872.99
Below the line charges – other $4,790.33	Total Production Costs: $45,536.94

Cast: John Anderson (Captain Farver); Beverly Brown (Stewardess Jane); Paul Comi (First Officer Craig); Lester Fletcher (R.A.F. man); Betty Garde (lady on the plane); Wayne Hefley (Second Officer Wyatt); Sandy Kenyon (Navigator Hatch); Bob McCord (passenger); Harp McGuire (Fight Engineer Parcell); Jay Overholts (a passenger); and Nancy Rennick (Stewardess Paula).

Stock Music Cues: Etrange #3 (by Marius Constant, :09); Milieu #1 (by Constant, :16); Silent Flight (by Jerry Goldsmith, :47 and 1:07); Eerie Nightmare #2 (by Lucien Moraweck, 1:11); Science Fiction #2 (by Rene Garriguenc, :13); Silent Flight (by Goldsmith, :47 and 1:04); Science Fiction #2 (by Garriguenc, 1:24 and :28); Shock Therapy #3 (by Garriguenc, :13); Science Fiction #2 (by Garriguenc, :14, :45, :26, and 1:22); Departure in the Fog (by Goldsmith, :44); Etrange #3 (by Constant, :10); and Milieu #2 (by Constant, :30).

Associate Producer: Del Reisman
Director of Photography: George T.
   Clemens, a.s.c.
Art Director: George W. Davis and Phil Barber
Set Decorations: Henry Grace and
   H. Web Arrowsmith

Assistant Director: E. Darrell Hallenbeck
Casting: Ethel Winant
Film Editor: Bill Mosher
Sound: Franklin Milton and Charles Scheid
Directed by Justus Addiss
Teleplay by Rod Serling

"You're riding on a jet airliner en route from London to New York. You're at thirty-five thousand feet atop an overcast and roughly fifty-five minutes from Idlewild Airport. But what you've seen occur inside the cockpit of this plane is no reflection on the aircraft or the crew. It's a safe, well-engineered, perfectly designed machine. And the men you've just met are a trained, cool, highly efficient team. The problem is simply that the plane is going too fast and there is nothing within the realm of knowledge . . . or at least logic . . . to explain it. Unbeknownst to passengers and crew, this airplane is heading into an un-charted region well off the beaten track of commercial travelers. It's moving into the Twilight Zone. What you're about to see . . . we call 'The Odyssey of Flight 33.'"

Plot: Global Airlines Flight 33, a passenger jet airliner four minutes behind flight plan, picks up a freak tail wind and finds itself traveling at a supersonic speed. After a flash of light and a deafening roar, the passengers and crew find themselves in a situation that could only be written off as an atmospheric phenomenon. No radio contact can be established and in an effort to make visual contact, the plane drops to a lower elevation to discover they have traveled smack dab in the middle of the prehistoric period. Captain Farver, in command of the jet airliner, knows that they cannot possibly land in this era. He orders the crew to attempt a recreation of the same situation that occurred, hoping to travel back to the present. Picking up the same freak tail wind, the airliner manages to travel forward in time, only not far enough – since the 1939 New York World's Fair can be seen from the windows. Realizing they cannot land in 1939, the captain decides to reveal the situation to the panicked passengers and asks them to pray. In desperation, the captain decides to try again, hoping the third time's a charm . . .

"A Global jet airliner en route from London to New York on an uneventful afternoon in the year 1961, but now reported overdue and missing and by now searched for on land, sea and air by anguished human beings fearful of what they'll find. But you and I know where she is. You and I know what's happened. So if some moment . . . any moment . . . you hear the sound of jet engines flying atop the overcast, engines that sound searching and lost, engines that sound desperate . . . shoot up a flare or do something . . .that would be Global 33, trying to get home . . . from the Twilight Zone."

Trailer: *"Next week you'll find each of your names on the passenger manifest of this jet aircraft that travels* *from London to New York City. You'll sit in these seats and you'll go through an experience unique beyond words and tense beyond anything I believe you've ever seen. You'll be departing next week at about this time in a vehicle we call 'The Odyssey of Flight 33,' but be prepared for a stop midway . . . in the Twilight Zone."*

Trivia, etc. Actress Beverly Brown appeared in this episode through a chance meeting at a luncheon she and Rod Serling attended. Taken by her insistence to play a role on *The Twilight Zone*, Serling asked Ethel Winant, the casting director, to remind him of Brown's availability, so she could be on the program. When Robert Longenecker, the agent representing the actress, suggested she play the role of Miss Turner in "A Penny For Your Thoughts," the casting suggestion was turned down. Through Winant and Longenecker, Brown was cast in what has become one of the more popular episodes of the series.

In late February 1962, Brown, who played the role of Jane, personally wrote Serling, in the hopes of appearing in another episode. On March 2 he sent her the following reply: "I'm afraid a meeting with our casting director, Bob Walker, would be somewhat academic. We are finishing up our last three films and will then move on into a very special and personal *Twilight Zone* of our own. We're winding up our thing for good and all. Should any other series come into the horizon and there is a casting man, and I am involved, and God is good, and peace reigns, I'll certainly contact you and see that an introduction is arranged."

"We looked damn serious doing that show," laughed John Anderson, "but we had a blast filming that. The guys playing my co-pilots were great. The director had trouble getting us settled because we were having so much fun. When you see me looking out at the dinosaur, I'm really looking at the poor director. As soon as he'd yell, 'Cut,' we were cracking jokes again. We were confined to this little cockpit. Whenever the director said, 'There's a dinosaur,' we had to pretend that it was out there. I saw the episode recently, and I was amazed I was able to spew out that technical gobbledygook."

The earliest draft of the script labeled it a Trans-Ocean jet airliner, Trans-Ocean 33, but when Serling learned from his brother that there was actually an airline called Trans-Ocean, he changed the name to Trans-Globe. While making the correction in the script was not a problem, Serling had already jumped the gun and submitted a short story adaptation of the same name and quickly contacted Richard E. Roberts, the managing editor of Bantam Books, Inc., in New York City, to make the necessary changes before going to print.

The stop-motion Brontosaurus featured in this episode was credited on screen to Jack H. Harris, but credit should also go to a staff of individuals at Project Unlimited, who were involved with all the stop-motion animation for the Universal release of *Dinosaurus!* in 1960. Wah Chang, Gene Warren, Tim Baar, Tom Holland and Don Sahlin were involved. The two men most likely responsible for the sculpting were Marcel Delgado and his brother Victor. The footage used for this *Twilight Zone* episode was not lifted from the 1960 Universal film. It was made at the same time Project Unlimited was creating footage for the dinosaur movie, and the staff was commissioned to create less than 60 seconds of an animated sequence for use on the television series. The same Brontosaurus, however, was not wasted after all the work was put into the model, so it was used for the motion picture (including the sequence where it gets caught in the mud). The cost of the special effects was a bit pricey at $3,940, almost five times more than the highest-paid actor in this episode.

"When we made that episode, we never saw the dinosaur," recalled Paul Comi. "We played make-believe and imagined it was there and reacted on cue. They made the stop-motion effect separately so I have always assumed the dinosaur scenes were inserted later. I remember watching it on television and remarking how cheap the effect was, and impractical. But I guess it worked and I probably get more letters and phone calls from fans because of *The Twilight Zone* than any other show I have ever done."

This episode aired in the wake of the strike which grounded whole fleets of commercial planes. One week before telecast, on Friday, February 17, all operations of Eastern, American, Trans World, Pan American, National and Western airlines were shut down due to a ruling of the Federal Mediation Board covering union jurisdictions. The board ruled that the flight engineers of United Air Lines must join the same union as the pilots. The flight engineers feared a single union because the pilots could easily outnumber them when it came to decision-making. Secretary of Labor Arthur J. Goldberg maintained consistently that the board's ruling applied to United Air Lines alone, but the flight engineers of the other major airlines walked off their jobs. On the evening of February 23, the day before this episode was broadcast, President Kennedy announced the strike was over, temporarily. A settlement was made in which the union accepted a 90-day truce while a Kennedy probe investigated the situation and agreed to find a solution before the end of the truce.

This episode of *The Twilight Zone* was scheduled for February 24 many weeks before news of the strike even lingered in the newspapers. Despite the recent news events, it was doubtful the story was affected, as viewers wrote in to the network and to Serling, praising the broadcast, and expressing their fondness for similar stories broadcast on the network.

James Abbe, author of the syndicated column, "Abbe Airs It," remarked this episode was "not recommended to televiewers who have booked flights on a jet."

A television columnist for *The Register and Post-Herald, Weekender* in West Virginia commented, "Maybe Rod Serling would know what those 'flakes' were that Glenn and Carpenter saw in orbit."

"With the dramatic development of space aviation these days, I don't know which of us is writing the most unbelievable stuff, my brother Bob or I," commented Serling for a *Long Beach Press-Telegram* column.

His brother, Robert Serling, was the aviation editor for the United Press International in Washington. Winner of many journalism awards for his endeavors, he looked over the script and then wrote back his list of suggestions (dated October 3) and additional flight cockpit dialogue to help make the situation more realistic. "Frankly, it's not 100 percent accurate and it can't be, because the situation you present is so fantastic that you've presented the crew with an almost impossible impasse," Robert Serling wrote. "Air-ground communications have changed so since 1940 that it's

Talent Fees
Paul Comi received $600 for his role of "First Officer Craig"
Harp McGuire received $500 for his role of "Flight Engineer Parcell"
John Anderson received $800 for his role of "Captain Farver"
Wayne Heffley received $500 for his role of "Second Officer Wyatt"
Beverly Brown received $350 for his role of "Stewardess Jane"
Sandy Kenyon received $600 for his role of "Navigator Hatch"

likely that a Boeing 707 with 1960 communications equipment would have one helluva time even raising a control tower with 1940 equipment. Frequencies, for example, are completely different. I've included some stuff on the crew trying to tell LaGuardia they're a 707 ... and asking for a radar vector into Idlewild. This telegraphs the surprise ending and you may want to change it around a bit."

Serling made the adjustments as his brother suggested, and the result was cockpit flight dialogue that was convincing enough for the viewers to accept the gravity of the situation. This was not Robert Serling's final contribution to *The Twilight Zone*, and years later in 1966, Rod turned to his brother again for a television feature, *The Doomsday Flight*.

On October 7, arrangements were made to have this episode directed by Douglas Heyes. He had originally agreed to direct, but days after, for reasons unknown, the job was handed over to Justus Addiss as a last-minute replacement. So while Addiss was behind the camera during rehearsals, on the afternoon of the second day of filming, he signed the necessary commitment papers. This episode was cost-effective because of the set cost and shooting hours.

A week and a half after Serling wrote the first draft of this script, Louis E. Holz, a retired major and present chief of security at the Air Force Ballistic Missile Division in Los Angeles, submitted a few stories to Cayuga through an agent. About two months later, Holz was given a rejection for the stories, because "these are too time machinist." Among the stories was "Snipped Thread," a tale about time travel. On March 1, days after viewing this episode, Holz wrote to Serling, crying plagiarism. "The details were different but the nugget, the hinge, was identical," Holz told Serling. "Rod, this coincidence is not unusual in the teleplay business – creative minds run on the same uncharted lanes but, great guns, fellow, this is too, too coincidental, or so it seems to me." Holz admitted that he had no intention of contacting the Guild or any other entity until Serling spoke to him first.

On March 8, Serling forwarded a copy of the teleplay for "The Odyssey of Flight 33," and a copy of Holz's "Snipped Thread," and explained to Holz that "neither the situations, the characters, the story projection or the conclusion have even the remotest similarity. I find it difficult to understand or, indeed, am I able to figure out just what 'coincidences' you're referring to. In my view, these two stories share not one thing in common ... At least fifteen letter writers each month accuse us of stealing story material from them. Frankly, it has become impractical to even open up manuscripts because the process carries with it the built-in possibility of having to respond to often violent accusations and with it, the added inconvenience of having to devote time trying to explain to the letter writers that we are a legitimate production unit who have enough trouble getting a show on the air without having to spend the time answering correspondence."

Holz offered to submit to Serling over 20 plot ideas, but Serling rejected the option of looking at them. One of Holz's previous story submissions, "Ah, Youth!" was purchased by Serling, solely to keep Holz at bay and avoid legal issues that – regardless of Serling's innocence – would have been costly in a legal issue. During the fifth season of *The Twilight Zone*, Serling would adapt "Ah, Youth!" into the episode "A Short Drink from a Certain Fountain."

In the 1990 novella, *The Langoliers*, by Stephen King, a passenger airliner is suffering from what turns out to be a flight through a time rift, and one of the characters recalls the plot of this very same *Twilight Zone* episode.

Production #3644 "MR. DINGLE, THE STRONG" (Initial telecast: March 3, 1961)
© Cayuga Productions, Inc., March 2, 1961, LP19934 (in notice: 1960)
Dates of Rehearsal: July 26 and 27, 1960
Dates of Filming: July 28, 29 and August 1, 1960
Script #44 dated: June 20, 1960

Producer and Secretary: $1,782.40
Director: $1,250.00
Unit Manager and Secretary: $600.00
Agents Commission: $2,500.00
Below the line charges (M-G-M): $31,268.85
Total Production Costs: $51,777.43

Story and Secretary: $2,648.00
Cast: $9,645.59
Production Fee: $825.00
Legal and Accounting: $250.00
Below the line charges (other): $1,007.59

Cast: Phil Arnold (the first man); Jo Ann Dixon (the nurse); Bob Duggan (the photographer); Douglas Evans (the second man); Michael Fox (Martian's right head); Jay Hector (the boy); Greg Irvin (the second Venusian); Donald Losby (the first Venusian); Bob McCord (home owner who receives football); Burgess Meredith (Luther Dingle); James Millhollin (Jason Abernathy, the TV host); Frank Richards (the third man); Don Rickles (the bettor); Edward Ryder (James Callahan); Douglas Spencer (Martian's left head); and James Westerfield (Anthony O'Toole).

Stock Music Cues: Etrange #3 (by Marius Constant, :09); Milieu #1 (by Constant, :16); Bridge-Neutral (by C. Savina, :27); Essay (by Jerry Goldsmith, :16 and :16); Moonscape – Outer Space Suite (by Herrmann, :22); Celeste Notes (anonymous, :04); Fourmillement Detoiles (by Pierre Henry, :04); Shock Harmonics #1 (by Fred Steiner, :08); Pixie Pantomime (by Wilbur Hatch, :07); Curiosity (by Hatch, :18); Alley Fight (by Hatch, :02); Easy Going (by Steiner, :17); Pixie Pantomime (by Hatch, :04); Horn Stings on A (anonymous, :01); Pixie Pantomime (by Hatch, :04); Getting Gladys' Goat (by Hatch, :04); Ho Hum (by Hatch, :02); Pixie Pantomime (by Hatch, :07); Pantomime #3 – Wistful Thinking (by Hatch, :15); Pixie Pantomime (by Hatch, :08 and :08); Horn Stings on A (anonymous, :03); Glissando Pantomime (by Hatch, :08); Takeoff to Space – Departure (by Bruce Campbell, :13); Soldiers on Strings (by Campbell, :14 and :05); Bridge #4 – Pseudo Hero (by Hatch, :12); Comedy Curtain (by Bernard Herrmann, :04); Bridge #4 – Pseudo Hero (by Hatch, :07); Bridge #7 – Jaunty Character (by Hatch, :08); Soldiers on Strings (by Campbell, :56); Improvised Humming (anonymous, :06); Improvised Humming and Whistling (anonymous, :06); Fourmillement Detoiles (by Pierre Henry, :06); Shock Harmonics #1 (by Steiner, :08); Soldiers on Strings (by Campbell, :20); Sad But Funny, Part 2 (by Bernard Green, :14); Sad But Funny, Part 4 (by Green, :11); Sad But Funny #6 (by Green, :06); Fourmillement Detoiles (by Pierre Henry, :08); Etrange #3 (by Constant, :10); and Milieu #2 (by Constant, :40).

Associate Producer: Del Reisman
Director of Photography: George T. Clemens, a.s.c. and William Skall, a.s.c.
Production Manager: Ralph W. Nelson and E. Darrell Hallenbeck

Assistant Director: Henry Weinberger
Casting: Ethel Winant
Film Editor: Bill Mosher
Sound: Franklin Milton and Charles Scheid
Directed by John Brahm

Art Director: George W. Davis and Phil Barber   Teleplay by Rod Serling
Set Decorations: Henry Grace and
   H. Web Arrowsmith

"Uniquely American institution known as the neighborhood bar. Reading left to right are Mr. Anthony O'Toole, proprietor who waters his drinks like geraniums but who stands foursquare for peace and quiet and for booths for ladies. This is Mr. Joseph J. Callahan, an unregistered bookie, whose entire life is any sporting event with two sides and a set of odds. His idea of a meeting at the summit is any dialogue between a catcher and a pitcher with more than one man on base. And this animated citizen is every anonymous bettor who ever dropped rent money on a horse race, a prize fight, or a floating crap game, and who took out his frustrations and his insolvency on any vulnerable fellow barstool companion within arm's and fist's reach. And this is Mr. Luther Dingle, a vacuum-cleaner salesman whose volume of business is roughly that of a valet at a hobo convention. He's a consummate failure in almost everything but is a good listener and has a prominent jaw. [Narration interrupted by character action and dialogue.] And these two unseen gentlemen are visitors from outer space. They are about to alter the destiny of Luther Dingle by leaving him a legacy – the kind you can't hardly find no more. In just a moment, a sad-faced perennial punching bag who missed even the caboose of life's gravy train, will take a short constitutional into that most unpredictable region that we refer to as . . . the Twilight Zone."

Plot: Luther Dingle, a meek vacuum cleaner salesman, is constantly having to settle disputes between the bettors in a neighborhood bar, receiving a few bruises on the jaw for his participation. Classified by a two-headed alien from the planet Mars as a perfect specimen for a test in human strength and durability, the visitors grant Dingle super-human strength. Now 300 times stronger than the average human being, Dingle finds himself on the other end of the physical abuse and a celebrity, thanks to a local newspaper reporter. Carnival operators and television producers start waving contracts. When Dingle uses his strength for petty exhibition, for a "live" television broadcast, the aliens return to remove the super-human strength so they visit other planets to conduct similar experiments. As the Martian makes his exit, two small aliens from the planet Venus arrive and select Mr. Dingle as a test subject, grant him intelligence 500 times more than the average human.

"Exit Mr. Luther Dingle, formerly vacuum cleaner salesman, strongest man on Earth, and now mental giant. These latter powers will very likely be eliminated before too long, but Mr. Dingle has an appeal to extraterrestrial note-takers as well as to frustrated and insolvent bet-losers. Offhand, I'd say that he was in for a great deal of extremely odd periods. Simply because . . . there are so many inhabited planets who send down observers . . . and also, because of course, Mr. Dingle lives his life with one foot in his mouth and the other . . . in the Twilight Zone."

Trailer: *"I've only got about 18 seconds to tell you that next week, Mr. Burgess Meredith returns to The Twilight Zone as 'Mr. Dingle, The Strong.' He plays the role of an incredible little man who's given the strength of about five hundred men and comes out of it as a kind of a twentieth-century Hercules and Samson all rolled into one. It's designed to send you right from your set into a fast bowl of spinach.* [Serling crushes a telephone that rings on the table.] *It's catching."*

Trivia, etc. As verified by prop numbers on production sheets: The horse painting hanging in the bar is the same one hanging on the wall above Mickey Rooney's bed in "The Last Night of a Jockey." The two spinning lights on the chest of the two-headed alien was the same that flashed above Mr. Chambers' door in "To Serve Man," while he was an occupant of the spacecraft. Some of the framed boxing and sports photographs are the same hanging in the bar in "What You Need." The television camera features the same lens that was used to mount on the wall in Burgess Meredith's bedroom in "The Obsolete Man." (Source: props were verified by prop numbers on production sheets.)

Don Rickles does a double-take for the camera.

The church seen in the background when Mr. Dingle is playing football with the boys is the same church prominently featured in "Stopover in a Quiet Town." The church was located outside the park/town square on Lot 2 at M-G-M. The same statue Dingle lifts in the air for everyone's amusement can be found in the same park in "No Time Like the Past," "Mute," "A Stop at Willoughby" and "I Sing the Body Electric."

The character of Abernathy, the television host, was lifted from an unsold script Rod Serling wrote years before titled "You Be the Bad Guy," for the proposed *It Happens to You* radio series. The story involved a private eye named Dan Shevlin, who had to resort to devious means to solve a case. Along the way, he meets a man named Abernathy. The name of Dingle was Serling's initial choice for the main protagonist in "Mr. Denton on Doomsday."

Michael Fox recalled to interviewer Tom Weaver, "I did a few of those [television shows]. The one that I'm remembered for was the one where I played half of a two-headed monster and that was delightful. I got to know Serling fairly well – he was a charming and most talented man, and one of the few writers who really understood an actor's problems, I thought."

To help publicize this episode, the September 5, 1960 issue of *Life Magazine* featured a photo spread with Greg Irvin and Donny Losby, both 9-year-olds, as the super-smart visitors from the planet Venus. The photo revealed the adult supervisor on the set and a technician, at the makeup set, complete with two mirrors, where the makeup were applied to the juveniles.

Before Don Rickles left the set on the final day of filming, someone of the CBS publicity department asked him to come up with a few one-liners they could use for publicity.

"Serling must do well. I've seen him in a convertible space ship."

"The producer of *Twilight Zone* liked my work so well he gave me a summer home on Venus."

"Serling is a brilliant writer – I know this because he gave me a card that said 'brilliant writer' in color."

"Screw the director. I don't even recall who directed that," recalled Don Rickles. "The main man I remember was Burgess Meredith. He was one of the greats. I'm telling you he played his part so well that Rod Serling is probably shaking his hand to this day. That alien thing was stupid but what the heck, that was *The Twilight Zone*. You know what I remember about Meredith? In between takes he was a warm fellow who had a great sense of humor. We shot jabs at each other and he took 'em as fast as he pitched them. They don't make men like him anymore."

> **Coincidence?** The airline flight in the previous *Twilight Zone* episode was Global Airlines Flight 33 and the taxi cab in this episode is from the Globe Taxi Cab Company, car number 33.

The following are verbal advertisements, composed February 14, 1961, that Rod Serling recorded in a studio for voice-overs during the closing credits on various CBS television programs.

10 Second Spot

Burgess Meredith stars as a weakling who suddenly acquires superhuman strength. But he doesn't come by his power naturally . . . It's a gift from a couple of oddball creatures from another planet . . Watch Burgess Meredith tonight (Tomorrow Night) at _____ P.M., over channel _____ in *The Twilight Zone*.

A couple of creatures from another planet drop in on Earth . . . Object . . . To conduct some scientific experiments on the primitive earthlings . . . Burgess Meredith is singled out as the most likely candidate in this amusing farce . . . Tonight (Tomorrow Night) at _____ P.M., over channel ____ in *The Twilight Zone*.

20 Second Spot

Burgess Meredith returns for his second journey into *The Twilight Zone*. This time he portrays Mr. Dingle, a weak, spindle-framed doormat of a man who suddenly acquires superhuman strength. Mr. Dingle, our modern-day Hercules, has been singled out for scientific experiments by a couple of oddball creatures from another planet. What he does with his new-found power . . . How he evens up a couple of old scores, make for a most amusing tale. But there is much more waiting for him and you in *The Twilight Zone*. See for yourself Tonight (Tomorrow Night) at _____ P.M., over channel _____ in *The Twilight Zone*.

Three different trailers for "next week's episode" were composed, each using a separate stage prop, and all three were filmed. Each of varied length, the film editor timed the finished film and whichever trailer fit the allotted time slot was used. The following are the two trailers filmed but never used:

"Next week the distinguished Mr. Burgess Meredith pays us a return visit and enacts the role of a little man suddenly given the gift of strength. I don't mean like spinach and vitamin pills . . . I'm talking about the strength of five hundred men. Next week on The Twilight Zone, 'Mr. Dingle, The Strong.'" [Serling, fiddling with the barstool, suddenly lifts it up by the bolts] *Aah . . . check please, bartender!* [into camera] *Thank you and see you next week."*

"We're a little short so I only have about eighteen seconds to make an invitation to you to attend the return performance of Mr. Burgess Meredith to The Twilight Zone. He plays the role of an incredible little man who's given the strength of about five hundred men and comes out of it as a kind of a Twentieth Century Hercules and Samson all rolled into one. It's designed to send you right from your set into a fast bowl of spinach. Next week Mr. Burgess Meredith as 'Mr. Dingle, The Strong.'" [Serling reaches over to shut off an alarm clock and crushes it and holds it up for the camera.] *It's catching!"*

Buck Houghton described the filming of this episode as "the mis-adventures of Dingle." Perhaps because this episode ran $1,800 over budget due to the number of special effects and wire gags running into longer hours than foreseen. According to a release schedule dated August 25, 1960, this episode was originally scheduled for broadcast on December 2, 1960. The television critic for *The Palladium-Times* mentioned "comic Don Rickles, in a nice bit of casting, is the braggart of the piece."

The 2007 documentary, *Mr. Warmth: The Don Rickles Project*, directed by John Landis, features a mention of this *Twilight Zone* classic.

Production #1656-2 "STATIC" (Initial telecast: March 10, 1961)

© Cayuga Productions, Inc., March 9, 1961, LP19935 (in notice: 1960)
Dates of Filming: November 19 and 20, 1960
First draft titled "Tune in Yesterday" dated August of 1960.
Script dated: November 18, 1960, with printing on it saying airdate will be January 13, 1961

Producer and Secretary: $3,051.50	Story and Secretary: $2,285.00
Cast: $311.07	Production Fee: $825.00
Agents Commission: $2,500.00	Legal and Accounting: $250.00
Below the line charges (CBS): $26,895.04	Below the line charges (other): $169.05
Total Production Costs: $36,286.66	

Cast: Bob Crane (voice of the disc jockey); Bob Duggan (man #1); Robert Emhardt (Professor Ackerman); Jerry Fuller (the rock n' roll singer); Clegg Hoyt (the shopkeeper); Dean Jagger (Ed Lindsay); Arch W. Johnson (Roscoe Bragg); Eddie Marr (the real estate pitchman); Carmen Mathews (Vinnie Broun); J. Pat O'Malley (Mr. Llewellyn); Lillian O'Malley (Miss Meredith); Jay Overholts (man #2); Alice Pearce (Mrs. Nielson); Roy Rowan (the television/radio announcer); Diane Strom (blonde girl in cigarette commercial); and Stephen Talbot (the boy).

Stock Music Cues: Etrange #3 (by Marius Constant, :09); Milieu #1 (by Constant, :16); Silverstone Mansion (by Fred Steiner, :05); Western Bridge (by Lucien Moraweck, :16); The Horsemen #2 (by Moraweck, :13); The Proposition (by Nathan Van Cleave, :10); Second Act Opening – Need (by Van Cleave, :23); The Vision Comes True (by Van Cleave, :23); Help (by Van Cleave, :22); Algebra Rock (by Wilbur Hatch, :17); I'm Getting Sentimental Over You (by George Bassman and Ned Washington, arr. by Gene Elliott, :41, :08 and :05); Natural Rock (by Bruce Campbell, :05); Big Dipper (by Campbell, :05); Voi Che Sapete (by W.A. Mozart, :05); Second Act Opening – Need (by Van Cleave, :16); The Proposition (by Van Cleave, :40); The Vision Comes True (by Van Cleave, :44); Romantic Opening (by Rene Garriguenc, :24); I'm Getting Sentimental Over You (by Bassman and Washington, arr. by Gene Elliott, :59 and :05); Pantomime #2 – Tongue in Cheek (by Hatch, :09); Help (by Van Cleave, :21); Utility Cues (by Campbell, :03); The Fountain Pen (by Van Cleave, :25); Utility Cues (by Campbell, :02); Help (by Van Cleave, :06); I'm Getting Sentimental Over You (by Bassman and Washington, arr. by Gene Elliott, 1:17); Etrange #3 (by Constant, :09); and Milieu #2 (by Constant, :27).

Associate Producer: Del Reisman	Art Director: Robert Tyler Lee
Associate Director: James Clark	Casting: Ethel Winant
Technical Director: Jim Brady	Lighting Director: Tom D. Schamp
Set Decorator: Buck Henshaw	Directed by Buzz Kulik.

Teleplay by Charles Beaumont, based on an unpublished, original story by OCee Ritch.

"No one ever saw one quite like that, because that's a very special sort of radio. In its day, circa 1935, its

Robert Emhart and Dean Jagger pose for
the photographer in between takes of "Static."

type was one of the most elegant consoles on the market. Now, with its fabric-covered speakers, its peculiar yellow dial, its serrated knobs . . . it looks quaint and a little strange. Mr. Ed Lindsay is going to find out how strange very soon, when he tunes into the Twilight Zone."

Plot: Ed Lindsay, one of the tenants at Vinnie's boarding house, longs for the days when radio was a medium of entertainment. He tires of watching everyone else stay fixated to the television programs that insult his intelligence. Digging out the old radio from the basement, Vinnie carries the unit up to his room and plugs it in. He soon discovers that broadcasts of the past are coming through the speakers. Every time he tries to get someone else to listen with him, however, all that comes through the speakers is static. Vinnie, his old flame, believes Ed is getting sentimental for the past, during their romantic days. But 20 years later, they apparently missed their chance. Avoiding the rest of the tenants, Ed retires every day to the radio to listen to *Let's Pretend* and Kay Kyser, but is heartbroken when he returns from the grocery store one afternoon to find the radio had been sold to a junk dealer. Ed sets out to find the radio and buy it back. He succeeds and, returning the radio to his bedroom and turning it on, finds himself transported back to 1940 where he is 20 years younger – and so is Vinnie.

"Around and around she goes, and where she stops nobody knows. All Ed Lindsay knows is that he desperately wanted a second chance and he finally got it, through a strange and wonderful time machine called a radio . . . in the Twilight Zone."

Trailer: *"Item of consequence – a radio. A carryover from that other era when quiz shows went up to only sixty-four dollars and entertainment was aimed only at the ears. Mr. Charles Beaumont has given us a most unusual story called 'Static.' We invite you to watch Mr. Dean Jagger fiddle with a few of these knobs, change a few stations, and find a couple of programs that are broadcast . . . only in the Twilight Zone."*

Trivia, etc. This was Charles Beaumont's third assignment under his five-teleplay commitment. Based on the Ocee Ritch story, "Tune in Yesterday," the purchase of the short story was made in early August, 1960. (Ocee Ritch was also credited on screen as Oceo Ritch and O.C. Ritch on other television programs and motion pictures.)

Having written for radio, the story appealed to Serling, who felt the nostalgic chance to go back to the by-gone days was perfect hunting ground for *The Twilight Zone*. Days before the episode went before the cameras, he wrote to Ed Wynn, explaining they were doing a show called "Static," which involved the use of famous radio programs of the past. "Since 'The Fire Chief' is an integral as well as beloved part of the memorabilia of the time, it is essential that it be included. So in addition to your permission, I wonder if you could give us or tell us where we might obtain records or transcriptions of any of your old radio shows." Wynn replied by phone, explaining to Serling that while he had no problem of *The Twilight Zone* featuring sound clips from existing recordings, he himself had none in his possession. He recommended Serling contact Texaco, the sponsor of the series. Buck Houghton, upon learning the sad news, explained to Serling that time was of the essence, and instead, used a recording of *The Fred Allen Show* in its place.

The F.D.R. address to the nation, heard in the soundtrack of this episode, was a recording from his fireside chat of April 28, 1935. *The Fred Allen Show* segment with Fred and Portland arriving at "Allen's Alley," was a broadcast from January 6, 1946. Radio Station WPDA, heard over the radio from one of the recordings was referencing radio station WPDA in Cedarburg, New Jersey.

For custom recordings for this production, the role of the real estate salesman on the television set is played by Eddie Marr, a veteran of numerous radio broadcasts from the '40s and '50s. According to a production report dated November 18, the voice of the radio disc jockey is that of Bob Crane, who would later play the starring role of television's *Hogan's Heroes*. Though Crane is heard and not seen, this episode technically marks his television debut. Crane was a local morning disc jockey on a Los Angeles radio station at the time, and he was offered the proposal of supplying the voice needed in the soundtrack.

The scene where Ed Lindsay tells the young boy to go out and buy himself a switchblade, handing him pocket change, was not approved by CBS, who asked Houghton that the line be replaced with "an alternative," suggesting candy or a remote control toy.

Days after this episode was telecast, viewer Fred DeGroter claimed that his former story submission titled "Radio," was the basis of this episode and threatened a suit of plagiarism, citing that CBS Television failed to financially reimburse him for his story and failed to give him on screen credit. This claim was later dismissed.

One comment delivered in this episode that "Tommy Dorsey's dead," prompted a letter from a viewer claiming to be a friend of Dorsey's widow and that the comment was in "bad taste."

Production #3647 "THE PRIME MOVER" (Initial telecast: March 24, 1961)
© Cayuga Productions, Inc., March 23, 1961, LP19936 (in notice: 1960)
Dates of Rehearsal: September 12 and 13, 1960
Dates of Filming: September 14, 15 and 16, 1960
Script #47 dated: August 8, 1960, with revised pages dated September 1, 9 and 14, 1960.
Shooting script dated: September 14, 1960

Producer and Secretary: $1,775.00
Director: $1,250.00
Unit Manager and Secretary: $350.00
Agents Commission: $2,500.00
Below the line charges (M-G-M): $33,609.52
Total Production Costs: $51,327.47

Story and Secretary: $2,155.00
Cast: $7,308.53
Production Fee: $825.00
Legal and Accounting: $250.00
Below the line charges (other): $1,304.42

Cast: Nesdon Booth (Big Phil Nolan); Jane Burgess (Sheila, the gold digger); Dane Clark (Ace Larsen); Clancy Cooper (the trucker); Buddy Ebsen (Jimbo Cobb); William Keene (the desk clerk); Robert Riordan (the hotel manager); Joe Scott (the croupier); and Christine White (Kitty Cavanaugh).

Stock Music Cues: Etrange #3 (by Marius Constant, :09); Milieu #1 (by Constant, :16); Street Moods in Jazz (by Rene Garriguenc, :16); Neuro Background (by Garriguenc, :42); Street Moods in Jazz (by Garriguenc, :12); Brouillard (by Constant, 1:02); The Girl (by Jerry Goldsmith, :10 and :15); Brouillard (by Constant, :45); The Girl (by Goldsmith, :09); Street Moods in Jazz (by Garriguenc, :06); No Time at All #1 (by Jack Douglas, 1:38); Street Moods in Jazz (by Garriguenc, :18, :18 and :26); Brouillard (by Constant, :28); Etrange #3 (by Constant, :10); and Milieu #2 (by Constant, :30).

Associate Producer: Del Reisman
Director of Photography: George T. Clemens, a.s.c.
Production Manager: Sidney Van Keuran and E. Darrell Hallenbeck
Art Director: George W. Davis and Phil Barber
Set Decorations: Henry Grace and H. Web Arrowsmith
Teleplay by Charles Beaumont, based on an idea proposal by George Clayton Johnson.

Assistant Director: Jack Boyer
Casting: Ethel Winant
Film Editor: Bill Mosher
Sound: Franklin Milton and Charles Scheid
Directed by Richard L. Bare

"Portrait of a man who thinks and thereby gets things done. Mr. Jimbo Cobb might be called a prime mover, a talent which has to be seen to be believed. In just a moment, he'll show his friends and you how he keeps both feet on the ground . . . and his head in the Twilight Zone."

Plot: Ace Larsen, co-owner and operator of a roadside diner, pushes a losing streak that no rabbit's foot can cure. When a serious auto accident outside the diner forces Jimbo Cobb to use his brain power and push the wrecked car off live electric wires, Ace discovers his partner possesses a rare gift of moving objects no matter how large or small. Jimbo has kept his power a secret – and prefers not to use it unless necessary. Ace gets a brainstorm and convinces his girlfriend, Kitty, and Jimbo to travel to Las Vegas. Using his talent to ensure the roulette wheel and dice games land to their liking, Jimbo gives Ace the edge he needs to win $200,000 within a few hours. When his expectations run too high, Kitty leaves to return home. The next afternoon, Ace arranges to wager all his winnings with a high-shot Chicago gangster. Before the afternoon is over, Jimbo runs out of steam, causing Ace to lose every dollar. Back at the roadside diner, Ace confesses that his love for Kitty is worth more than all the money in Vegas and proposes marriage. She accepts, knowing full well that Ace has learned his lesson. As for Jimbo, he still has his talent; he just wanted Ace to go back home with Kitty.

"Some people possess talent, others are possessed by it. When that happens, the talent becomes a curse. Jimbo Cobb knew, right from the beginning. But before Ace Larsen learned that simple truth, he had to take a short trip through the Twilight Zone."

Trivia, etc. In late July of 1960, Charles Beaumont wrote to Rod Serling:
"Here is a spec script I wrote some time ago for my own show (now gone the way of all good

and decent projects). Del says he likes it. Buck, as usual, has more reservations than the combined Indian population of America, though, if one listens with the third and fourth ears, one seems to hear a not altogether unenthusiastic note in his tone. I, of course, love it dearly and believe it could make a wonderfully entertaining and possibly moving show. If your reaction is favorable, we'll do it on *Twilight Zone*.

"You'll note two similarities to 'A Nice Place to Visit' – some parts of Ace's character and the gambling sequence. I don't think it's a troublesome thing, but should it bother you, we can fix it easily enough. As this was purely a labor of love (originally planned as the pilot script for my stillborn brain-child), I have no wish to part with it if the enthusiasm and joy that went into it are not echoed by all my Cayuga friends. Already Buck is mumbling to the effect, he likes the basic idea and the characters and the business of moving things with the mind, but, in sorting the peas from the succotash and putting different sauce on the steak (or whatever it was) we should maybe tone down Ace's personality."

"Beaumont was submitting a script to *Wanted – Dead or Alive*, the Steve McQueen series, 'Angels of Vengeance,' which they bought and made," recalled George Clayton Johnson to interviewer Matthew R. Bradley. "It was an original script by me, which Beaumont rewrites based upon a discussion between the two of us, takes the credit, collects the money, and gives me, I think, $600 – which was an enormous sum to me at the time – for being the first-draft guy on that, and not taking the credit [as he did with this *Twilight Zone* episode]. Anything to try to get some writing done, get some experience, get things sold, not to fight for these credits but to understand the business, be willing to make a deal and stick with the deal – all those sorts of things became very important to me. As I watched Beaumont, I could understand what sort of things go on in an office where a writer is, that are different where a stock broker's, or something else."

On August 15, Serling admitted that he just finished reading "The Prime Mover" and told Buck Houghton, "I think Beaumont's job was excellent and I think the script is in neigh on to perfect shape. I hope it's been mimeoed and all set to go. I can't think of a single criticism." In a letter to Charles Beaumont with the same date, Serling commented, "Just finished 'The Prime Mover' and I have simply flipped! It's a honey of a job and I thought, considering all the travail that exists between you and that miserable *Twilight Zone*, it might be a morale booster for you to know that your latest effort is a real corker!"

Upon Serling's insistence, Houghton sent Beaumont a generous contract for this episode. Beaumont was paid $2,000 for the script and his services. Whether it was Beaumont's involvement in securing the legal rights, or a secretarial error, a production oversight was made and George Clayton Johnson's name was omitted from the credits.

"I had to pitch the story first," recalled George Clayton Johnson in a phone interview with Terry Salomonson. "Before I could do that, Charles Beaumont was a good friend and he would take my stories and make the script, and sell it. Later he would tell Buck that it was my story, and Buck took notice. I would tell Rod and Buck different stories and most of the time they would shake their heads. 'No, no George. Why not this one instead?' So I would suggest another story. 'How about this?' And Buck would say, 'No, no, no.' Buck would only hold those meetings once a month so I gathered all my notions and notes and would pay him a return visit. If he liked the idea, but wanted me to do something with it, I went back home and worked on it. That was how I got to write for the series."

"[Charles Beaumont] was the best," Jerry Sohl recalled in an interview with Steve Boisson. "He was able to intimidate producers – something we all wished we could do. For example, he went to see a certain pilot. They were really anxious to get him to write for the show. The first thing he said to the producer was 'You're what's wrong with television. That pilot was a pilot of —' and the guy said, 'Why? What's wrong with it?' 'Well, I'll tell you what's wrong with it . . .' Chuck then went on to some general things. When he got to the point where he said, 'Now I've got a story for you . . .,' they were anxious and waiting to hear. He was able to do that with almost anybody, though not in the same manner."

On September 2, 1960, Robert Longenecker, with his own talent agency, contacted Ethel Winant, the casting director for *The Twilight Zone*, suggesting actor Ed Wilson play the role of Jimbo Cobb or the truck driver, Jeanne Evans for the role of Kitty Cavanaugh, Mary McClure or Sue Casey for Sheila, and Mike Steele for the croupier. None of these casting suggestions came to fruition.

Dane Clark and Buddy Ebsen were the only actors on the set during the two days of rehearsal. Christine White was not on the set during rehearsals. The first day of filming consisted of all the Happy Daze Café scenes, the exterior of the highway (filmed in the studio, not outside) and the interior of the back room where Jimbo demonstrated his "mind over matter" to Ace. Serling's trailer was also filmed on the morning of the first day of filming. The second day of filming consisted of the casino and various tables, the hotel lobby, and the interior of the fifth floor suite. On the third day of filming, only a few scenes were filmed in the interior of the fifth floor hotel suite where Ace loses everything to Nolan.

Years before this telecast, Rod Serling wrote a series of scripts for a radio program titled *Our America* (broadcast in September to October of 1951). The program featured historic biographical dramas of American historical figures such as Jefferson Davis and Lewis and Clark. One of the episodes dramatized a biography of Irvin Shrewsbury Cobb, the famed humorist and newspaperman. It is possible that Serling, remembering the old radio script, took the occasion to change the last name of Buddy Ebsen's character. Serling, on occasion, changed names of fictional characters in scripts written by others, for various reasons (censorship suggestions, De Forest Research, etc.).

According to a release schedule dated August 25, 1960, this episode was originally scheduled for broadcast on January 6, 1961.

According to Prop numbers on a production report, the slot machine is one of the many one-armed bandits featured as a prop in that episode, but not the same one used as the mechanical monster from "The Fever."

The automobile accident with the speeding car hitting the transformer was stock footage, but the scenes with Jimbo and Ace in front of the wreckage were shot for this episode. That stock footage originated from *Thunder Road* (1958) as the climax towards the end of the film when Robert Mitchum is electrocuted. This same stock footage was reused in *Invisible Invaders* (1959) and *They Saved Hitler's Brain* (1963).

On April 11, 1961, Serling received not one, but two letters from Mr. Stanley F. Skeris, claiming that "The Prime Mover" was possibly stolen from his idea. "I wish to bring to your attention the striking similarity between my short story, and your presentation of 'The Prime Mover,' shown March 24, 1961. The story, I have sent you, 'The Powers That Be or Not Be,' was contained in my manuscript sent to Little, Brown & Co. on January 28, 1960. If you have purchased an identical story, in Milwaukee or elsewhere, from a person or persons, other than Stanley F. Skeris, then the seller of this particular story is liable for fraud. If this be the case, I absolve you of all blame in this matter and would not hamper you with any court action whatsoever in connection with this matter. I wrote the short story prior to October 1, 1959."

On May 2, 1961, Serling drafted the following reply. "I'm in receipt of your letter of April 11th with your synopsis of your story 'The Powers That Be or Not Be.' You are obviously quite unaware of the copyright laws as they apply to material allegedly plagiarized. In so far as the similarity between our presentation, 'The Prime Mover,' and your short story – I first of all see only the vaguest of similarity of theme. As a matter of fact the whole area of telekinetic powers is a common one in literature and appears in literally hundreds of stories. Neither ours nor yours is unique in its approach and it once again emphasizes the very non-sacrosanct aspect of the material. In addition, you must realize, of course, Mr. Skeris, that we have no record of receiving your material or indeed having any access to it. Since there is no signed release in your name it seems unquestionably the case that your material was never sent to us. If, of course, you want to pursue this matter further through a lawyer, my own legal representatives would be happy to respond with the necessary action."

No legal action was officially filed against Rod Serling or Cayuga as a result of this broadcast, but Serling was soon discovering that for every story presented on the program, someone wanted to claim suit for infringement. Houghton, Serling and the rest of the staff were innocent of all the plagiarism claims, but this would become an increasing problem.

Production #4439-6 "LONG DISTANCE CALL" (Initial telecast: March 31, 1961)
© Cayuga Productions, Inc., March 28, 1960, LP20453
Dates of Rehearsal: December 12 through 16, 1960
Dates of Filming: December 17 and 18, 1960

Shooting script dated: December 15, 1960
Story and Secretary: $2,437.27
Cast: $5,600.27
Agents Commission: $2,500.00
Below the line charges (CBS): $36,615.76
Total Production Costs: $50,747.16

Producer and Secretary: $2,136.28
Director: $298.23
Production Fee: $825.00
Legal and Accounting: $250.00
Below the line charges (other): $84.35

Cast: Philip Abbott (Chris Bayles); Lew Brown (the fireman); Lili Darvas (Grandma Bayles); Reid Hammond (Mr. Peterson); Henry Hunter (Dr. Unger); Jenny Maxwell (Shirley, the baby sitter); Bob McCord (the first fireman); Billy Mumy (Billy Bayles); Jutta Parr (the nurse); Patricia Smith (Sylvia Bayles); and Jim Turley (the second fireman).

Stock Music Cues: Etrange #3 (by Marius Constant, :09); Milieu #1 (by Constant, :16); Very Odd Dream (by Nathan Scott, :10); This Stop is Willoughby (by Scott, :15); Perry Mason Background (by Fred Steiner, :21); Hitch-Hiker, Part 7 (by Bernard Herrmann, :12); Full Measure (by Scott, :30); Ed Comes Back (by Leonard Rosenman, :20); The Ice Bucket (by Scott, :37); The Hitch-Hiker, Part 7 (by Herrmann, :07); Perry Mason Background (by Steiner, :07); Full Measure (by Scott, :24); Introduction (by Herrmann, :19); Alicia (by Herrmann, :04); Second Narration (by Rosenman, :06); Alicia (by Herrmann, :04); Second Narration (by Rosenman, :02); The Ice Bucket (by Scott, :27); Back to the Scene of the Crime (by Rosenman, :40); Introduction (by Herrmann, :08); Alicia (by Herrmann, :04); Light Dramatic Series #12 (by Rene Garriguenc, :14); Introduction (by Herrmann,

:05); Punctuation and P.O.T. #2 (by Garriguenc, :15); Time Bomb (by Lucien Moraweck, :20); Ed Comes Back (by Rosenman, :20); Back to the Scene of the Crime (by Rosenman, :18); Introduction (by Herrmann, :09); Back to the Scene of the Crime (by Rosenman, :05); Utility Cues (by Bruce Campbell, :03); Shock Therapy #4 (by Garriguenc, :19); Impending Doom #2 (by Moraweck, :13 and :22); Farewell (by Herrmann, :47); Twilight Zone Theme – Lonely (by Herrmann, :19); Desperation (by Rosenman, :17); The Stars (by Herrmann, :24); Suspense Processional – Walt Whitman Suite (by Herrmann, :06); Vibe Notes "E" (anonymous, :06); Vibe Notes "G Sharp" (anonymous, :06); Vibe Notes "B" (anonymous, :06); and Etrange #3 (by Constant, :14); and Milieu #2 (by Constant, :33).

Associate Producer: Del Reisman	Art Director: Robert Tyler Lee
Casting: Ethel Winant	Associate Director: James Clark
Technical Director: Jim Brady	Lighting Director: Tom D. Schamp
Set Decorator: Buck Henshaw	Directed by James Sheldon
Teleplay by Charles Beaumont and William Idelson	

"As must be obvious, this is a house hovered over by Mr. Death – that omnipresent player to the third and final act of every life. And it's been said, and probably rightfully so, that what follows this life is one of the unfathomable mysteries. An area of darkness which we the living reserve for the dead ... or so it is said. For in a moment, a child will try to cross that bridge which separates light and shadow ... and of course, he must take the only known route, that indistinct highway through the region we call ... the Twilight Zone."

Plot: Grandma forms a strong bond with her grandson, Billy, who is celebrating his fifth birthday. After giving him a toy telephone as his gift, Grandma suffers a stroke and dies a few hours later. Before and after the funeral, young Billy pretends to talk to Grandma through the toy telephone. At first, Sylvia and Chris, Billy's parents, humor the child. But when the boy starts to show suicidal tendencies, because Grandma asked him to come join her in the netherworld, the parents take serious note. After failing to die from a hit and run accident, Billy succeeds a second time by drowning in the backyard pool, and Sylvia verifies the old woman's bond by overhearing Grandma on the other end of the toy phone. While the medics try their best to revive the child, Chris goes upstairs and pretends that his mother can hear him through the toy phone, pleading for his son's return. As a lad, Billy never experienced love, playing baseball or driving his first car. "Please give him the chance," Chris pleads. Grandma agrees and the medics are shocked when Billy pulls through.

"A toy telephone ... an act of faith ... a set of improbable circumstances all combine to probe a mystery, to fathom a depth, to send a facet of light into a dark after-region. To be believed or disbelieved depending on your frame of reference. A fact or a fantasy. A substance or a shadow. But all of it very much a part ... of the Twilight Zone."

Trailer: *"Next week, Mr. Charles Beaumont and Mr. William Idelson deliver a story on your doorstep with the title 'Long Distance Call.' It's uniquely a flesh and fantasy tale involving a small boy, a toy telephone, and the incredible faith of a child. I hope you're around next week at the usual time, which, depending on where you are, varies, and in the usual place, the one that never varies, the uncharted regions of the Twilight Zone."*

Trivia, etc. Bill Idelson wrote an original story titled "Party Line," which Idelson and Beaumont jointly adapted into a teleplay. The decision whether this would be a joint teleplay based on the story by Idelson or a solo teleplay adapted by Beaumont was determined by another script Beaumont submitted in early November of 1960, titled "Dead Man's Shoes." Beaumont quickly turned "Dead Man's Shoes" over to Buck Houghton to fulfill his last commitment of a current five-picture contract. Houghton wrote to Sam Kaplan of Ashley-Steiner, explaining his position on the script, "which we feel is extremely difficult to do on tape without extensive revisions – perhaps even then not tailoring it to the demands of tape; at the same time, there is a story deficiency which would also take a good deal of rewriting to correct." Rather than fall behind schedule, since Houghton was attempting to make good on six episodes put to videotape, he agreed with Beaumont that Cayuga take an option on this script for a period of one year at a figure of $500 against an eventual $2,000. In lieu of this project, the men agreed and Beaumont was hired to jointly adapt the story that would become the episode, "Long Distance Call."

"What had happened was I wrote a script and Richard Matheson, who wrote a number of episodes for *The Twilight Zone*, read it and told me that he thought it was good," recalled Bill Idelson. "He told me he was going to show it to Rod Serling. Well, I got a phone call later and it was from Charles Beaumont. He said he got my story and wanted to write the script, and I would get half the money and we both would get credit on the screen. I told him I wrote a script [entitled "Direct Line"], not a story, so he looked into it. I don't think they liked my script, but they liked the story. I got a runaround regarding the whereabouts of my story. I agreed to go along with it because a friend of mine told me a long time ago that to get your foot in the door, sometimes you have to let someone take advantage of you. [laughs] So that is how my story got on *The Twilight Zone*."

On December 6, days before the episode went before the cameras, Houghton sent Idelson a list of suggestions for the final shooting script, requesting that Serling's teaser comment be more "ominous" because it was "too friendly and casual." It was suggested to delete the grandmother's death, explaining the scene "should keep the audience away from actually seeing death." (Houghton suggested focusing the scene on the parents, only to be interrupted by the boy's shout of Grandma, which tells the audience that she was dead.) The scene in which Chris told his son that Grandma was dead needed to be explained more fully, since it was confined to one speech. The name of Paulie was changed to Billy in the revised draft.

Many of the music cues featured in this episode include Bernard Herrmann's scores specifically composed for first season episodes of *The Twilight Zone*, including "The Lonely." In the scene where Chris breaks down and pleads over the toy phone with his mother to let Billy live a full life, a 19 second music cue titled "Twilight Zone Theme – Lonely" can be heard in the soundtrack. This was a variation of the first season theme, with different instrumentation.

Because the initial script did not have narrations that satisfied Serling, two different openers were drafted. Neither of the two was used for the program.

"We are eavesdroppers now standing at the elbow of an unseen personage called Mr. Death. The omnipresent player to the third and final act of every life on every stage. And it has been said, and I suppose proven over and over again, that there is finality and completeness to death ... that whatever new adventure awaits in the darker sphere that is the life after this one ... we have to await the experience ourselves; there is no bridge to the beyond. Or so it is said. But in a moment a child's plaything ... something as simple and as obvious as a play telephone will figure in a probing of the mystery that lies beyond us. A child's telephone connected at one end by a child's faith ... and at the other ... by an operator ... in The Twilight Zone."

"Everyone knows what a telephone is, and what it does . . . but how many of us know why? When we pick up that familiar object and talk to people we've never seen . . . and listen to their voices come flying back to us across thousands of miles . . . how many of us give it a second thought? Not many. But we might, if . . . like Paulie Bayles . . . we found ourselves connected with The Twilight Zone."

"The script was re-written even when it was being filmed," recalled Idelson. "The scene with the father talking to the grandmother on the toy telephone was filmed twice. They took a break long enough for Rod to rewrite the speech. Charles Beaumont was not involved with the rewrite. I didn't know it at the time, but he had Alzheimer's and he couldn't type a word of the script. I still think Richard Matheson was involved with the first script before it was re-written."

"I cannot recall if it was the first day or second day, but we were trying to get a shot just right for the videotape and it just wasn't working," recalled Jim Sheldon. "Mumy of course was a minor and there were strict laws in effect regarding the number of hours we could use a minor, and after a set time, I believe it was six o'clock, we had to get an extension granted by the Board. His mother was the only representative guardian on the set at the time, so I asked her if she wouldn't mind a few additional minutes. She had no problem with that. I can tell that story now, but if the Child Labor people knew what we had done, the network and Buck would have been furious."

After the initial telecast, Rod Serling and Cayuga Productions went under fire by two different people who claimed that Serling stole their story. While there was no truth to the claims, the complaints were a temporary nuisance. On April 1, 1961, the day after the initial telecast, Mr. Allan Amenta of Quaker Hill, Connecticut, sent a letter to Serling, threatening to sue on the grounds of plagiarism. Amenta's synopsis titled, "Dial H for Happiness," was submitted to Serling under cover letter dated December 2, 1960. Serling returned Amenta's synopsis, along with a courtesy letter, on December 13. Sam Kaplan immediately dug into the facts, and wrote two separate replies to Allan Amenta, explaining in detail, the procedure and general manner by which Serling and the producer handled submissions not made by a reputable author's agent.

"Long Distance Call" was written by Charles Beaumont and William Idelson and represented only minor adaptations of an original teleplay by Idleson, who submitted his original teleplay to the producer on September 10, 1960. Since Amenta's letter insisted it was Serling who stole his idea (since it was Serling who received the synopsis in the mail), Kaplan assured Amenta that it takes a number of weeks to complete a draft for a single script, and therefore, any similarity between the *Twilight Zone* production and his synopsis was the result of complete coincidence. Amenta promptly dropped his complaint and (as it turned out), he never saved a copy of his synopsis and wrote a reply to Sam Kaplan asking to have his synopsis returned – which Kaplan obliged.

The second complaint was apparently more serious. In late July of 1961, Maxwell S. Miller turned to Robert Fendler, an attorney representing him, asserting a claim that the *Twilight Zone* episode "Long Distance Call" was also an infringement on the grounds that his synopsis, which was submitted to Serling, was used without permission or financial compensation.

"Rod Serling and *The Twilight Zone* were not the only people to get sued. I was sued and so was Charles Beaumont," recalled Bill Idelson. "I remember we sat down in the office of the guy's attorney, and I had to explain how I came up with the idea for the story. I told him about my son's birthday party and how that was the inspiration for my story. When the attorney heard the whole thing, he said he wouldn't represent someone who could not verify that we stole his story, so the charges was dropped."

A couple weeks after Amenta and Miller filed their claims, Douglas MacCrae submitted a short story titled "Escape Artist," similar to a story that Serling attempted to purchase previously from *The Saturday Evening Post*, about an inmate of a prison who paints a door so realistic that, when completed, grants him the opportunity to escape death row. "We are, at the moment, suffering two legal suits on properties even more remotely similar than these two would be," Serling told MacCrae. "Hence, fortune and bad fate have worked against you in this instance, and I am forced to return this to you."

Coincidentally, Miss Joy Wyse of San Francisco, California, submitted to Serling a short story of the same name, "Long Distance Call," with a different premise, in early December of 1960. On December 9, Serling's secretary, Connie Olmsted, sent Miss Wyse the standard rejection letter sent to almost everyone who submitted a story or script proposal. "Mr. Serling asked me to write and thank you for sending along your script. Unfortunately, we've purchased all the material needed for our current season of *The Twilight Zone* and are no longer reading outside submissions. But Mr. Serling wishes to thank you for your interest." A few people over the years resubmitted their plot proposal a second time and would often find themselves receiving the same rejection letter.

Production #3654 "A HUNDRED YARDS OVER THE RIM"
(Initial telecast: April 7, 1961)
Copyright Registration: © Cayuga Productions, Inc., April 6, 1961, LP19937
Dates of Rehearsal: March 1 and 2, 1961
Dates of Filming: March 3, 6 and 7, 1961
Script #56 dated: January 30, 1961
Revised script dated: February 22, 1961

Producer and Secretary: $1,375.00
Director: $1,250.00
Unit Manager and Secretary: $600.00
Agents Commission: $2,500.00
Below the line charges (M-G-M): $38,888.24
Total Production Costs: $58,879.17

Story and Secretary: $2,630.00
Cast: $7,637.13
Production Fee: $825.00
Legal and Accounting: $250.00
Below the line charges (other): $2,923.80

Cast: John Astin (Charlie); Jennifer Bunker (the woman); John Crawford (Joe); Ken Drake (the man); Evans Evans (Mary Lou); Miranda Jones (Martha Horn); Bob McCord (the sheriff); Ed Platt (the doctor); and Cliff Robertson (Chris Horn).

Original Music Score Composed and Conducted by Fred Steiner (Score No. CPN5978): Etrange #3 (by Marius Constant, :09); Milieu #1 (by Constant, :16); 1847 Scene (1:06); Over the Rim (:54); The Hill (:08); The Road (1:17); Chris Walks (1:46); Joe's Café (1:27); Curiosity (1:51); The Calendar (:22); Mrs. Joe (:25); Chris Jr. (1:24); Chris Runs (1:19); The Wagons (1:59); Chris Returns (:44); Etrange #3 (by Constant, :10); and Milieu #2 (by Constant, :30).

Director of Photography: George T.
   Clemens, a.s.c.

Production Manager: Ralph W. Nelson
Assistant Director: E. Darrell Hallenbeck

Art Director: George W. Davis and Phil Barber   Casting: Stalmaster-Lister
Set Decorations: Henry Grace and   Film Editor: Leon Barsha, a.c.e.
    H. Web Arrowsmith   Directed by Buzz Kulik
Sound: Franklin Milton and Bill Edmondson   Teleplay by Rod Serling

"The year is 1847 – the place is the territory of New Mexico – the people are a tiny handful of men and women with a dream. Eleven months ago they started out from Ohio and headed west. Someone told them about a place called California. About a warm sun and a blue sky. About rich land and fresh air. And at this moment . . . almost a year later . . . they have seen nothing but cold, heat, exhaustion, hunger, and sickness. This man's name is Christian Horn. He has a dying eight year-old son and a heartsick wife. And he's the only one remaining who has even a fragment of the dream left. Mr. Chris Horn . . . who's going over the top of a rim to look for water and sustenance . . . and in a moment will move into . . . the Twilight Zone."

Plot: In the year 1847, Chris Horn leads a covered wagon train across the desert towards a promised land. Instead, the men and women have suffered from exposure to heat and Indians – and Chris's eight-year-old boy is dying of pneumonia. In desperation, Chris takes a walk over a rim about a hundred yards away from the wagons in search of water, and finds himself transported to 1961. Wandering into Joe and Mary Lou's Airflite Café and Gas Station, Chris meets the proprietors. Courtesy of a doctor, Chris is introduced to penicillin and learns there is a natural spring just a short ways ahead. While the general practitioner believes Chris is suffering a delusion, the time traveler discovers in a book that his son will become a famous doctor. Realizing he has no time to hang about and meet the authorities, Chris races back out to the desert. Hurrying back over the rim, he manages to keep ahead of the pursuing police just in time to find himself transported to 1847. Handing his wife the penicillin, he instructs her on how to administer the drugs and then assures them that the future looks bright. Back in 1961, Joe brings the rifle to Mary, which Chris dropped shortly before vanishing from sight – the gun has aged over a hundred years.

"Mr. Christian Horn, one of the hardy breed of men who headed west during a time when there were no concrete highways or the solace of civilization. Mr. Christian Horn and family and party, heading west after a brief detour . . . through the Twilight Zone."

Trailer: *"Next week you'll ride up front in this wagon on a trek west. Your itinerary is across the Great Plains, over the Rockies, to a point in New Mexico. And you'll ride alongside Mr. Cliff Robertson in a strange tale of a handful of American pioneers who made a detour in time and found themselves one afternoon on the fringe of the future. Our story is called 'A Hundred Yards Over the Rim' and believe me . . . it's quite a view. I hope we'll see you then."*

Trivia, etc. Rod Serling's opening narration in the earliest draft of this script mentioned the story taking place in Arizona territory. By the time he composed the trailer for this episode, the story took place in Northern California.

"The Rip Van Winkle Caper" and this episode were filmed back-to-back on location in Lone Pine. Assigned their respective production numbers on February 13, Buck Houghton, Ralph W.

Nelson, Justus Addiss, Phil Barber and Mike Glick went up to Lone Pine on February 16, to survey the area and figure out what materials would need to be shipped to the location.

The February 28, 1961 issue of *The Hollywood Reporter* disclosed Cliff Robertson taking the top spot for *The Twilight Zone*, signing a contract in late February. During the same month, Robertson played a role on the *U.S. Steel Hour* titled "The Two Worlds of Charlie Gordon." Not only did he steal the limelight, but his performance did not go unnoticed. Robertson made headline news for television the following week, and his signing for *The Twilight Zone* only invited further interest.

Owen S. Comora of Young & Rubicam, the sponsor's advertising agency, read about Cliff Robertson being signed to *The Twilight Zone* and on that same afternoon, he came across an eight-year-old biography issued by CBS. Robertson was being criticized by the dean of Antioch College because the biography claimed the actor had won letters in football, basketball, tennis and track. Of course, the college had no inter-collegiate sports programs. Comora dug into the facts and it turned out the biography was distributed by CBS. There were corrections in Robertson's own handwriting, trying to set the record straight way back then. This error was publicly noted and corrected, to ensure no bad publicity would result during Robertson's appearance on the program. "Incidentally, if you run into Cliff again, give him my best," Comora asked Serling. "He may remember me as the fellow who was official Y&R on-the-road escort for *Rod Brown of the Rocket Rangers* during 1953 when the show was sponsored by General Foods for Post Cereals."

On the morning of March 3, John Astin and Cliff Robertson reported to wardrobe for fittings. Afterward, rehearsals and filming were conducted on Stage 10 at M-G-M for the interior diner scenes. Cost to design the interior of the diner set Cayuga back $1,300. (Exterior of the diner only cost $70 in materials.) For the second and third day of filming, the cast was in Lone Pine for scenes on the highway, the exterior of the hotel and the desert hill.

Serling was not on location during filming. His on-screen narration and trailers were filmed on March 13, after the cast and crew returned to the studio, having shot all the preliminary footage.

"After I read the script, I did some research on my character," recalled Cliff Robertson. "What kind of clothes I would wear, what state I would have come from, and the people who went with me on the trek across the desert. And especially what motivated them to make the move. I showed up with a black hat because I read that those who moved to California wore only the clothes they could wear on their back. They wore used clothing if they could. Someone on the set wasn't happy with me wearing the hat, so they placed a call to Rod Serling. He came and saw me wearing it and he loved it. So I got to wear it on the show."

When Chris arrives at the Airflite Café, there is a sign for "Nelson Creamery Products" on the side of the building, a tip of the hat to Ralph W. Nelson, the production manager for the series.

Production #3655 "THE RIP VAN WINKLE CAPER"
(Initial telecast: April 21, 1961)
© Cayuga Productions, Inc., April 18, 1961, LP20227
Dates of Rehearsal: March 6 and 7, 1961
Dates of Filming: March 8, 9 and 10, 1961
Script #54 dated: January 11, 1961

Producer and Secretary: $1,375.00   Story and Secretary: $2,630.00
Director: $1,250.00   Cast: $4,374.20

Unit Manager and Secretary: $600.00
Agents Commission: $2,500.00
Below the line charges (M-G-M): $39,461.32
Total Production Costs: $55,016.62

Production Fee: $825.00
Legal and Accounting: $250.00
Below the line charges (other): $1,751.10

Cast: Oscar Beregi (Farwell); Lew Gallo (Brooks); John Mitchum (Erbie); Simon Oakland (De-Cruz); Shirley O'Hara (woman on the road); and Wallace Rooney (man on the road).

Stock Music Cues: Etrange #3 (by Marius Constant, :09); Milieu #1 (by Constant, :16); Montage (a.k.a. Suspense, by Rene Garriguenc, :46); New Shock (by Nathan Van Cleave, 1:35); Moat Farm Murder (by Bernard Herrmann, :34, :34, and :48); Third Act Opening (by Van Cleave, :21); Moat Farm Murder (by Herrmann, :56); Jailbreak (by Goldsmith, :36); Moat Farm Murder (by :33, 1:12, :30, :45 and :20); Mousson #5 (by Herrmann, :04); The Light (by Herrmann, :50); Finale (by Van Cleave, :38); Etrange #3 (by Constant, :10); and Milieu #2 (by Constant, :30).

Director of Photography: George T.
    Clemens, a.s.c.
Art Director: George W. Davis and Phil Barber
Film Editor: Jason H. Bernie, a.c.e.
Set Decorations: Henry Grace and
    H. Web Arrowsmith

Production Manager: Ralph W. Nelson
Assistant Director: E. Darrell Hallenbeck
Casting: Stalmaster-Lister
Sound: Franklin Milton and Bill Edmondson
Directed by Justus Addiss
Teleplay by Rod Serling

"Introducing four experts in the questionable art of crime. Mr. Farwell, expert on noxious gases. Former professor with a doctorate in both chemistry and physics. Mr. Erbe, expert on mechanical engineering. Mr. Brooks, expert in the use of firearms and other weaponry. And Mr. DeCruz, expert in demolition and various forms of destruction. The time is now. And the place is a mountain cave in Death Valley, U. S. A. In just a moment, these four men will utilize the service of a truck placed in cosmoline, loaded with a hot heist cooled off by a century of sleep, and then take a drive into . . . the Twilight Zone."

Plot: Four criminals commit a daring train robbery, netting them a large fortune in gold. The ingenious plot was masterminded by Farwell, the ringleader. To escape the law with their booty, the criminals agree to follow Farwell's scheme of being placed in suspended animation, so when they wake from their glass chambers a hundred years in the future, they can walk away with wealth and freedom. The plan goes according to Farwell's schedule and the men quickly find themselves in 2061. A crack in the glass of the air-tight case allowed the experimental gas to escape, taking the life of one of the troupe during the past century. While Farwell ponders what kind of world awaits him, DeCruz starts getting greedy. In a deliberate attempt to eliminate his business partners, DeCruz murders Brooks. As Farwell and DeCruz walk along the highway, carrying heavy knapsacks filled with gold, the heat from the sun takes its toll. Farwell, desperate for survival, starts trading his bars of gold for the purchase of water in DeCruz's canteen. After a number of exchanges, the price begins to go up. Out of desperation, Farwell murders DeCruz. Alone along the highway, Farwell continues his trek as the lone survivor, eventually collapsing from exhaustion. An elderly couple in their hovercraft arrive and find Farwell, offering gold in exchange for water. Before any rescue can be made, he dies from exhaustion. The couple are puzzled by the stranger who died clutching his bar of gold as if it were valuable. Since it was discovered how to manufacture gold, the mineral has been considered valueless.

> *"The last of four Rip Van Winkles who all died precisely the way they lived: chasing an idol across the sand to wind up bleached dry in the hot sun as so much desert flotsam, worthless as the gold bullion they built a shrine to. Tonight's lesson . . . in the Twilight Zone."*

Trailer: *"We've told some oddball stories on the Twilight Zone, but none of them any more weird than next week's tale. Four men plan a heist the likes of which have never before been entered into the annals of crime. At which point, according to plan, they take a brief vacation from reality and they spend it in the Twilight Zone. Next week on the Twilight Zone, 'The Rip Van Winkle Caper.' I hope you will be among the bystanders."*

Trivia, etc. One television critic described this episode as "a combination perfect crime and 'One Step Beyond' bit."

Dave Armstrong, who was a stunt double for a number of *Twilight Zone* episodes, made his debut on the series as a double for DeCruz. (Apparently Armstrong's casting for this episode of *The Twilight Zone* was big enough news to warrant a mention in the March 7, 1961 issue of *The Hollywood Reporter*.) Robert L. McCord III, also known as Bob McCord, who played the role of the sheriff pursuing Chris Horn in the previous episode, was the stunt double for the character of Brooks in this episode. James Turley was paid the usual scale of $27.53 to act as a stand-in for this episode (along with stand-in regular Bob McCord), and found his fee upped to a flat $50 for what Buck Houghton referred to on paperwork as a "hazardous assignment." Turley was the man who grabbed the wheel during the abandoned truck sequence.

Because this and the previous episode were filmed back-to-back on location in a desert near Lone Pine, California, it's very obvious that the truck which speeds past Chris in "A Hundred Yards Over the Rim" was the same used by the crooks in this story. (Even the sign on the side of the truck remained unchanged.)

On July 26, 1946, CBS Radio featured an episode of *The Mercury Summer Theatre* on the Air titled "The Moat Farm Murder," starring Orson Welles in a one-man performance, scripted by Norman Corwin. A murder plot described as "a radio documentary," Bernard Herrmann composed and conducted an original music score for the production, which was later recorded separately and stored in the CBS stock music library for use on other radio and television programs. "The Rip Van Winkle Caper" uses a number of segments from that music score, and this marked the first of many *Twilight Zone* episodes to feature music from that 1946 radio broadcast.

The interior of the cave, including the glass cases, raked up Cayuga's production cost $1,500. The exterior of the cave (including the fake door) was filmed on location in Lone Pine. This was constructed at a cost of $335 in materials and labor, and dismantled after the required scenes were shot. Filming on location for this episode required the use of two local policemen and one ranger to be near the set during filming, for security reasons.

The futuristic car that the older couple drives at the conclusion of this episode is the same prop housed at the M-G-M Studio, constructed and featured in the science fiction motion picture, *Forbidden Planet* (1956).

Another alternate closing narration never used for the program (dated March 23, 1961):

The cast of "The Rip Van Winkle Caper"
clown around in the heat.

"Mr. Farwell . . . the last of four Rip Van Winkles who all died precisely the same way they lived . . . chasing an idol across the sand to wind up bleached dry in the hot sun as so much desert flotsam . . . worthless as the gold bullion they built a shrine to. Tonight's lesson . . . in the Twilight Zone."

Originally Serling had composed a much lengthier opening narration for this script. It is hard to conceive Serling on the screen speaking this much dialogue, and perhaps this was the moment when he realized he was writing himself in too much and started to shorten his narrations considerably:

"Introducing four experts in the questionable art of crime. Mr. Farwell, expert on noxious gasses. Former professor with a doctorate in both chemistry and physics. Mr. Erbe, expert in mechanical engineering. Mr. Brooks, expert in the use of firearms and other weaponry. Mr. DeCruz, expert in demolition and various forms of destruction. (a pause) The time is now. And the place is a mountain cave in Death Valley, U.S.A., one hundred and thirteen miles from a railroad track where at this moment a train has been derailed and a baggage car containing one million dollars in gold bullion en route to Fort Knox, Kentucky has been removed and is in the process of being deposited here. (a pause) So far – so normal, but here comes the bizarre part. Because a million dollars in stolen gold bullion will be a rather warm item to dispense with at this stage of the game – Mr. Farwell and his associates now enter the second phase of their master plan. They destroy their vehicles, all but one, a large truck covered with cosmoline . . . that can remain on blocks indefinitely and made to run when convenient. And like the truck . . . Mr. Farwell and companions plan to do the same thing to themselves. They will place themselves in a state of suspended animation until such time as, in the vernacular of their trade – the heat's off. In this case, apropos of the size of the haul – said period being one hundred years from today's date, at which point they will wake up and as Mr. Farwell says, walk the earth as extremely rich men. Bizarre indeed, but what happens to them one hundred years hence or as of the moment they awake . . . is even more bizarre. They think that outside of this cave is Death Valley. It is, of course, but it's also . . . The Twilight Zone."

In *Planet of the Apes* (1968), featuring a screenplay by Rod Serling, four astronauts are put into a deep sleep in glass cases, much like this episode of *The Twilight Zone*. Three of the four astronauts exit to discover one of their own (the only female) is dead – an aged corpse because the glass case was cracked, allowing the gas to escape from the chamber.

Proposed Flight Schedule for Lone Pine Location

Flight #1 –   Monday, March 6, 1961 – two D.C.-3's to leave Clover Field, Santa Monica, with cast and crew as per work order. Take off 5:45 a.m. to land at Manzanar Field near Lone Pine, and one ship to dead-head back to Los Angeles. One ship to lay-over in Lone Pine for following Flight #2.

Flight #2 –   Monday, March 6, 1961 – late p.m. – One D.C.-3 from above Flight #1 to leave Lone Pine to bring back cast parts of "Joe" and "Sheriff," and exposed film.

Flight #3 –   Tuesday, March 7, 1961 – Seven-passenger plan to leave Clover Field with cast parts of "Charlie," "Martha," "Man #1," "Woman #1," Atmosphere Woman and wardrobe woman, at 5:45 a.m. to land at Lone Pine. This plane to dead-head back to Los Angeles.

Flight #4 –   Tuesday, March 7, 1961 – Seven-passenger plane as above with Justus Addiss, director, and cast parts of "Farwell," "DeCruz," "Brooks," and "Erbe," and special effects man to leave Clover Field at 10:30 a.m. This plane to stay at Lone Pine during the day for return late Tuesday p.m. with the following personnel:

Flight #4A – Tuesday, March 7, 1961 – Above plan from Flight #4 to leave Lone Pine in late p.m. with Buzz Kulik, director, and cast parts of "Charlie," "Martha," "Woman #1," "Man #1," Atmosphere Woman and "Horn," and exposed film, to land at Clover Field.

Flight #5 –   Wednesday, March 8, 1961 – Bob White's Cessna plane to leave Lone Pine in late p.m. with part of "Erbe," and two wranglers and exposed film. To land at Clover Field and lay-over until Thursday a.m. for:

Flight #5A – Thursday, March 9, 1961 – Bob white's Cessna plane from Flight #5 above – to leave Clover Field at 5:45 a.m. with cast parts for "Man on Road" and "Woman on Road." To land at Lone Pine.

Flight #6 –   Thursday, March 9, 1961 – One D.C.-3 to arrive at Manzanar Field near Lone Pine at 4:00 p.m. to return with director, cast and certain key people, and exposed film, to land at Clover Field.

Flight #7 –   Friday, March 10 – One D.C.-3 to arrive at Manzanar Field at 7:00 a.m. to return to Clover Field with balance of crew.

Production #3658 "THE SILENCE" (Initial telecast: April 28, 1961)
Dates of Rehearsal: March 22 and 23, 1961
© Cayuga Productions, Inc., April 25, 1961, LP20228
Dates of Filming: March 23, 24 and 27, 1961
Script #57 dated: February 6, 1961, with revised pages dated March 14, 20 and 22, 1961.
Shooting script dated: March 22, 1961

Producer and Secretary: $1,375.00   Story and Secretary: $2,630.00
Director: $1,250.00   Cast: $7,815.90

Unit Manager and Secretary: $600.00
Agents Commission: $2,500.00
Below the line charges (M-G-M): $30,059.36
Total Production Costs: $49,173.82

Production Fee: $825.00
Legal and Accounting: $250.00
Below the line charges (other): $1,868.56

Cast: Cyril Delevanti (Franklin, the butler); Everett Glass (the first man); Jonathan Harris (George Alfred); John Holland (the third man); Michael Lally (workman #1); Felix Locher (the second man); Liam Sullivan (Jamie Tennyson); Franchot Tone (Col. Archie Taylor); and James Turley (workman #2).

Club Members: David Ahdar, John Alban, William Auray, George Bruggeman, John Clark, Paul Gustine, Robert Haines, Edward Haskett, Jean Heremans, Kenner Kemp, Robert Leonard, Bob McCord, Ted O'Shea, Scott Seaton, Arthur Touex, James Turley, and Allen Zeidman. *

Stock Music Cues by Leonard Rosenman unless stated otherwise: Etrange #3 (by Marius Constant, :09); Milieu #1 (by Constant, :16); Twilight Zone Theme, Milieu #2 (by Constant, :22); Twilight Zone Theme, Milieu #1 (by Constant, :14); Desperation (:03); The Missing Colonel (:29); The Telegram (:33); Back to the Scene of the Crime (:26); Desperation (:14); The Telegram (:25); Confusion (:37); Ed Disappears (:35); Back to the Scene of the Crime (:36); Desperation (:11); Confusion (:48); Knife Chord (by Herrmann, :10); Twilight Zone Theme, Milieu #2 (by Constant, :22); Twilight Zone Theme, Milieu #1 (:14); Etrange #3 (by Constant, :10); and Milieu #2 (by Constant, :30).

Director of Photography: George T.
    Clemens, a.s.c.
Art Director: George W. Davis and Phil Barber
Set Decorations: Henry Grace and
    H. Web Arrowsmith
Directed by Boris Sagal

Production Manager: Ralph W. Nelson
Assistant Director: E. Darrell Hallenbeck
Casting: Stalmaster-Lister
Film Editor: Leon Barsha, a.c.e.
Sound: Franklin Milton and Bill Edmondson
Teleplay by Rod Serling

"The note that this man is carrying across a club room is in the form of a proposed wager . . . but it's the kind of wager that comes without precedent. It stands alone in the annals of bet-making as the strangest game of chance ever offered by one man to another. In just a moment, we'll see the terms of the wager and what young Mr. Tennyson does about it. And in the process, we'll witness all parties spin a wheel of chance in a very bizarre casino called . . . the Twilight Zone."

Plot: Jamie Tennyson, a young man with a reputation for squandering his vocal box amongst the members of a club, has become the object of Colonel Taylor's annoyance. In an effort to get some peace and quiet, Taylor wagers half a million dollars that Tennyson cannot go a full year – 365 days – without saying a single word. The wager carries a stipulation: Mr. Tennyson will be placed in a glass

* Only four of the actors playing members of the club were featured more than once (both the beginning and closing of the episode): George Bruggeman, Paul Gustine, Jean Heremans, and Robert Leonard.

room so he can be observed at all times. Tennyson accepts the bet, much to Taylor's pleasure. As the months pass, Tennyson manages to retain his stature. In desperation, Taylor suggests innuendos about the young man's wife, but Tennyson remains silent. One year later, gossip of Taylor's cruel attempts have spread about the club, proving Taylor is the weaker of the two. The damage forces Taylor into an embarrassing confession: He lost most of his money years ago. He is nothing but a fake in disguise. Naturally, he'll resign from the club, but Tennyson, angry for committing to such a bet, explains in writing that to ensure his winning, he had the nerves of his vocal chords severed.

"Mr. Jamie Tennyson, who almost won a bet, but who discovered somewhat belatedly that gambling can be a most unproductive pursuit, even with loaded dice, marked cards, or as in his case some severed vocal cords. For somewhere beyond him a wheel was turned and his number came up black thirteen. If you don't believe it, ask the croupier, the very special one who handles roulette . . . in the Twilight Zone."

Trailer: *"There are all kinds of wagers and all kinds of odds, from the spin of a roulette wheel to a two-dollar across the board at a race track. But next week, on the Twilight Zone, with the aid of Mr. Franchot Tone, we tell the story of possibly the strangest bet ever to occur in the annals of chance. Our program is called 'The Silence.' I hope we'll see you then. Here's something that doesn't require any imagination. It's Oasis. If you just took this puff, you'd agree. It's the softest taste of all. Before we meet again, try Oasis for the softest taste of all."*

Trivia, etc. Once the final script was polished, it was assigned a production number on March 15, 1961, and within a few days it went before the cameras. This was very quick, considering it normally took a while to assign a director, work out the details and sets required for production, and hire the cast. Boris Sagal, who was originally slated to direct "Nick of Time" and never had the opportunity, made his directorial debut on *The Twilight Zone* with this episode. Sagal was formerly one of the story editors for the television anthology, *Fireside Theatre*, broadcast from 1949 to 1963.

In 1952, Serling submitted a plot idea to *Studio One* titled "The Director," a human interest tale about a stage director who becomes obsessed with his job and, desperate to make good with both the network and sponsor, hires an aging ex-stage actor from the past who can't remember his lines. Risking his career on the television production, the director finally acts with human compassion to convince the old man to pull it through on "live" television . . . and in the process, wins the heart of a waitress who is willing to deal with the director's obsession.

The story editor for *Studio One* rejected the idea, so Serling submitted the story to *Fireside Theatre*. Sagal read the four-page plot synopsis and agreed to buy a script based on the synopsis. In a letter from Blanche Gaines to Serling, dated June 26, 1953, Sagal "decidedly feels that you are the kind of writer they could use if your scripts had a little more scope and range for motion pictures." It was the only script penned by Serling for the television anthology, broadcast on September 13, 1955, with Jack Carson, James Barton and Nancy Gates in the leads.

For this *Twilight Zone* production, the tables were turned when it was Serling who had final approval of director for this episode. Sagal even directed Serling for his on-camera role as narrator.

The entire episode was filmed on Stage 3 at Hal Roach Studios. To create the interior of the men's club with prop rentals, newspapers, plants and other materials, Cayuga was billed a total cost of $330. The Solarium where Tennyson was incarcerated for 12 months cost $1,309 to construct.

"This town – the movie producers seem to be about 20 years behind television," commented

Franchot Tone in an interview with *TV Guide*. "Every film script I'm sent to read has me in the same kind of part I was playing 20 years ago. The character's a little older, but they still want me in white tie and tails as a slick, well-groomed, well-educated, well-heeled stuffed shirt. I have to laugh and I tell them no thanks." Tone was selective in the offers to appear on television anthologies. "I've turned down a bunch of other half-hour film series," he continued. "None of them had any distinction. I don't want to play a cowboy or a private detective."

"Oh, I knew Rod Serling for years. I did two of those *Twilight Zone*s and one of them was filmed, the other was taped," recalled Jonathan Harris. "They were not very large roles, though; I wish I had the opportunity to play a lead. Rod was on the set when I worked with Franchot Tone and we chatted a little here and there. He was a very imaginative man, and very gentle. Many years after, I went to work on *The Liars' Club* and Rod was the host. I would make these funny faces and cross my eyes and he would laugh and laugh. He would beg me, repeatedly, not to do it on camera and every time I was evil and he would just laugh."

"Rod was a very quiet fellow on the set," actor Liam Sullivan recalled for author Mark Phillips. "He let the director take over in most things. He was a terrific writer, and after that experience I was a *Twilight Zone* fan. . . . The long speech I had in the opening sequence was three pages. The day of shooting, Rod came up to me and asked if I could memorize an additional page of dialogue on the spot. I was doing so well, he wanted to lengthen the scene. I said if he could write that fast, I could memorize it. He went off into a corner and started scribbling. He handed me the sheets off his notepad. I picked a corner and started memorizing. He was very pleased with the results."

The short-run magazine, *Show*, premiered shortly before *The Twilight Zone* was on the air, and expired shortly after the series was canceled after the fifth season. The magazine, notable for presenting reviews and previews of top-class television, film and stage performances, rarely discussed *The Twilight Zone*. This marked the first of four episodes to be mentioned in the publication. The August 1962 issue recommended its readers catch the rerun on August 10, remarking it is "an atypical trip through *The Twilight Zone*. . . . The denouement may leave the viewer, if not Mr. Tennyson, speechless."

Production #3657 "SHADOW PLAY" (Initial telecast: May 5, 1961)
© Cayuga Productions, Inc., May 1, 1961, LP20229
Dates of Rehearsal: March 16 and 17, 1961
Dates of Filming: March 17, 20 and 21, 1961
Script #62, date unknown

Producer and Secretary: $1,375.00
Director: $1,250.00
Unit Manager and Secretary: $600.0
Agents Commission: $2,500.00
Below the line charges (M-G-M): $31,022.71
Total Production Costs: $50,115.45

Story and Secretary: $2,155.00
Cast: $8,397.26
Production Fee: $825.00
Legal and Accounting: $250.00
Below the line charges (other): $1,740.48

Cast: Anne Barton (Carol Richie); George Bruggeman (police escort – principal guard); John Close (the guard); Delmar Costello (prisoner named Munoz); Howard Culver (jury foreman); Paul Denton (silent bit, adj. bailiff in courtroom); William Edmonson (Jiggs, the Negro prisoner); Bernie

Hamilton (Coley); Jack Hyde (the attorney); Wright King (Paul Carson, the city editor); Bernard Krakow (guard in prison sequence); Bob McCord (attendee in courtroom); Tommy Nello (Phillips); Bob Olen (attendee in courtroom); Bill Pinckard (silent bit, adj. bailiff in courtroom); Gene Roth (the judge); Harry Townes (District Attorney Henry "Hank" Richie); Dennis Weaver (Adam Grant); and Mack Williams (the priest).

Stock Music Cues: Etrange #3 (by Marius Constant, :09); Milieu #1 (by Constant, :16); Second Act Opening – Elegy (by Nathan Van Cleave, :07); Dramatic Tags #2 (by Van Cleave, :07); Shock Therapy #3 (by Rene Garriguenc, :03); Dramatic Tags #2 (by Van Cleave, :06); Pursuit (by Fred Steiner, :40); Red River Valley Reel (traditional, :49); Dramatic Tension – Elegy (by Van Cleave, :57); The Martini (by Van Cleave, :26); Miniature Overture – Nutcracker Suite (by Tschaikovsky, :14); The Martini (by Van Cleave, :26); Second Act Opening – Elegy (by Van Cleave, :17); Trouble – Elegy (by Van Cleave, :53); Second Act Opening – Elegy (by Van Cleave, :06); Dramatic Tension – Elegy (by Van Cleave, :57); Trouble – Elegy (by Van Cleave, :18); Second Act Opening – Elegy (by Van Cleave, :17); Dramatic Tags #2 (by Van Cleave, :07); Shock Therapy #3 (by Garriguenc, :08); Pursuit (by Fred Steiner, :07); Second Act Opening (by Van Cleave, :06); Etrange #3 (by Constant, :10); and Milieu #2 (by Constant, :30).

Director of Photography: George T. Clemens, a.s.c.
Art Director: George W. Davis and Phil Barber
Film Editor: Jason H. Bernie, a.c.e.
Set Decorations: Henry Grace and H. Web Arrowsmith

Production Manager: Ralph W. Nelson
Assistant Director: E. Darrell Hallenbeck
Casting: Stalmaster-Lister
Sound: Franklin Milton and Bill Edmondson
Directed by John Brahm
Teleplay by Charles Beaumont

"Adam Grant: a nondescript kind of man found guilty of murder and sentenced to the electric chair. Like every other criminal caught in the wheels of justice he's scared . . . right down to the marrow of his bones. But it isn't prison that scares him, the long silent nights of waiting, the slow walk to the little room . . . or even death itself. It's something else that holds Adam Grant in the hot, sweaty grip of fear . . . something worse than any punishment this world has to offer . . . something found only in the Twilight Zone."

Plot: Found guilty of murder in the first degree, Adam Grant is sentenced to death by electrocution. Unable to accept the consequences of his actions, Grant believes in a lie that he has conjured up – and warns the district attorney that this is all a nightmare. If he dies, they will no longer exist. The city editor hears Grant out and believes the condemned has a few points of logic to take under consideration. The district attorney visits Grant to learn that they are characters in his recurring dream, which he suffers through night after night. The death house, the time and the scenario is detailed in the form of old clichés – because that's what Grant saw in the movies. The district attorney is finally convinced that Grant is mentally ill and asks the governor to order a stay of execution – but it's too late. Grant has been executed. The lights go out, and when they come back on in the courtroom, the characters are off centered because Grant is reliving the same dream again . . .

"We know that a dream can be real . . . but who ever thought that reality could be a dream? We ex-

Set Decoration Production Costs
Interior of the Courtroom $785
Interior of the Prisoner Death House $1,650
Interior of the Ritchie House $495
Interior of the Prisoner Execution Room $100
Interior of the Ritchie Kitchen $100
Total $3,130

ist, of course. But how? In what way? As we believe . . . as flesh-and-blood human beings . . . or are we simply parts of someone's feverish, complicated nightmare? Think about it. And then ask yourself . . . do you live here, in this country, in this world . . . or do you live, instead . . . in the Twilight Zone."

Trailer: *"Next week on the Twilight Zone, you'll sit in this courtroom and you'll watch what is apparently the standard, everyday turning of the wheels of justice. But because this is the Twilight Zone, don't be fooled by the readily apparent. When the judge enters, the jury rises, the bailiff calls out the case, all of this is the opening salvo to one of our wildest journeys yet. Our program is called 'Shadow Play' and it's written by Mr. Charles Beaumont. It comes well recommended."*

Trivia, etc. "*The Twilight Zone* has few pretenses," Serling once commented. "It is simply an attempt at a quality half-hour vignette once-a-week. On occasion it can fulfill a function as a commentary on a social evil or disparity. But in half-hour form this is a subtle process and is usually a secondary effect to the entertainment involved."

On April 21, 1951, the radio program *Stars Over Hollywood* featured "Curtain Call for Carol" with Phyllis Thaxter in the title role. When Carol Adams appears in a Broadway show backed by her father, she was unmercifully panned by Bill Grant, temporary drama critic for a large metropolitan newspaper. Her anger was further increased when the same Grant offered to teach her how to act, despite the fact that his real specialty was as a sports writer.

This *Twilight Zone* episode was assigned a production number on March 8, 1961. In Beaumont's original script, the lead character was Adam Trask. The name might have been changed as a result of Serling's supervision of the scripts, changed from Adam Trask to Adam Grant, "possibly" a combination taken from the two main characters in the radio drama.

The Richie living room and kitchen were filmed on Stage 5 at the Hal Roach studio. The prison cells, death house and court room were filmed on Stage 19 on the M-G-M lot. One of the recurring props on the series is a small white horse that shows up on living room tables and desks. Used for the purpose of background decoration, this same horse makes an appearance in "A Most Unusual Camera" and "The Jungle." You'll see the same horse on a table in the Richie living room.

"You know what I think is the best show, the one that has, for me, the greatest power? It's the one with Dennis Weaver that Beaumont wrote," recalled George Clayton Johnson to interviewer Matthew R. Bradley.

Actor Wright King recalled, "I am ashamed to admit that I found 'Shadow Play' obscure. I managed to sort out the character's lines of thought in my two or three scenes – well enough to satisfy director John Brahm. I've seen the show two times and have yet to make it out. Truly a first for me. I always enjoyed working with my good friends Dennis Weaver, Harry Townes and Anne Barton, who I worked with many times."

"I had done *Gunsmoke* with Dennis," King continued. "We shot a mini-Western with his kids and mine on the M-G-M back lot once. I worked with Townes on live television from New York at one time and when I moved the family to California, I moved into a house about two blocks away from his. We used to carpool to studio lots so we may have carpooled together for that episode."

One particular scene that was filmed and ended up on the cutting room floor was Trask being prepared for the electric chair. Guards slit Trask's trousers and shave his head. The priest and warden enter the execution room. Among the cast was Jack Lee who played the role of the principal guard for the death scene; Larry Evans and George Ford were the police guards during the death march; and Frank Eldridge was the warden.

In the movie *Vanilla Sky* (2001), the character of David Aames dreams he is in Times Square and playing on the Budweiser Jumbotron is a clip from this episode of *The Twilight Zone*.

Adam Grant fights for his life (and everyone in the courtroom) in "Shadow Play."

Production #3659 "THE MIND AND THE MATTER"
(Initial telecast: May 12, 1961)
© Cayuga Productions, Inc., May 9, 1961, LP20230
Dates of Rehearsal: March 27 and 28, 1961
Dates of Filming: March 29, 30 and 31, 1961
Script #55 dated: January 31, 1961

Producer and Secretary: $1,375.00
Director: $1,250.00
Unit Manager and Secretary: $600.00
Agents Commission: $2,500.00
Below the line charges (M-G-M): $41,265.83
Total Production Costs: $56,970.64

Story and Secretary: $2,630.00
Cast: $5,199.19
Production Fee: $825.00
Legal and Accounting: $250.00
Below the line charges (other): $1,075.62

Cast: Dave Armstrong (man in subway); Roy Aversa (mask principal); Margaret Barstow (woman in office); Shelley Berman (Archibald Beechcroft); Jeannie Dawson (mask principal); Len Erickson (mask principal); William Graffe, Jr. (newsboy); Jack Grinnage (Henry, the office boy); Ralph Grosh (mask principal); Ken Kane (mask principal); Fred Kinney (mask principal); Bob McCord (mask principal / elevator boy); Marilyn Malloy (woman who pushes soft drink machine button); James Niekerk (mask principal); Chester Stratton (Rogers); Ray Strickland (mask principal); James Turley (subway – jostle principal); Dave White (mask principal); Roy Wilson (photo double); and Jeane Wood (the landlady). *

Stock Music Cues: Etrange #3 (by Marius Constant, :09); Milieu #1 (by Constant, :16); Hustle Bustle, Part 1 (by Willis Schaefer, :21); Hustle Bustle, Part 2 (by Schaefer, :13); Hustle Bustle, Part 1 (by Schaefer, :06); Hustle Bustle, Part 2 (by Schaefer, :04); Shakes (by Maurice Carlton, :17); Garden Variety (by Wilbur Hatch, :01); Utility Cues (by Bruce Campbell, :03); Bonbon (by Rene Garriguenc, :30); Oh Those Bells – Osgood #2 (by Tutti Camarata, :07); Misterietto (by Bernard Green, :10); Old Coat (by Fred Steiner, :45 and :29); Shock Harmonics (by Steiner, :10); High String Tremolo (by Lucien Moraweck, :10); Signals – Outer Space Suite (by Bernard Herrmann, :10); Night Vigil #1 (by Moraweck, :07); Old Coat (by Steiner, :08); Miscellaneous Snare Rolls (anonymous, :03); Whistle Gag (by Lyn Murray, :04); Hustle Bustle, Part 1 (by Schaefer, :19); Alone (by Arthur Freed and Nacio Herb Brown, :41); Hitch-Hiker (by Bernard Herrmann, :07); The Telephone (by Bernard Herrmann, :38); The Man (by Herrmann, :19); The Door (by Herrmann, :38); Pantomime #1 "Harvey" (by Lyn Murray, :02); The Bicycle (by Herrmann, :16); Little Fugue (by Steiner, :04); The Bicycle (by Herrmann, :10); Little Fugue (by Steiner, :04); The Bicycle (by Herrmann, :05); Little Fugue (by Steiner, :05); Oh Those Bells – Osgood #2 (by Camarta, :02); Indolent (by Steiner, :10); Night Vigil #1 (by Moraweck, :07); Hustle Bustle, Part 1 (by Schaefer, :05); Getting Gladys' Goat (by Wilbur Hatch, Lee Wainer and Parke Levy, :08); Sad But Funny (by Bernard Green, :40); Hustle Bustle, Part 2 (by Schaefer, :20); Etrange #3 (by Constant, :10); and Milieu #2 (by Constant, :30).

Director of Photography: George T. Clemens, a.s.c.	Production Manager: Ralph W. Nelson
Art Director: George W. Davis and Phil Barber	Assistant Director: E. Darrell Hallenbeck
Film Editor: Jason H. Bernie, a.c.e.	Casting: Stalmaster-Lister
Set Decorations: Henry Grace and H. Web Arrowsmith	Sound: Franklin Milton and Bill Edmondson
	Directed by Buzz Kulik
	Teleplay by Rod Serling

"A brief, if frenetic, introduction to Mr. Archibald Beechcroft – a child of the Twentieth Century – a product of the population explosion and one of the inheritors of the legacy of progress. Mr. Beechcroft again . . . this time act two of his battle for survival. And in just a moment our hero will begin his personal, one-man rebellion against the mechanics of his age. And to do so he will enlist certain aids available only . . . in The Twilight Zone."

Plot: Mr. Beechcroft, an employee of the Park Central Insurance Company, is tired of being pushed around by society. Every day he rides crowded subways, is herded into the elevator like cattle, and having people spill fluids on his clothes. When a friend hands Beechcroft a book titled "The Mind and the Matter: How You can Achieve the Ultimate Power of Concentration," it takes Beechcroft

---

* All of the actors who wore a mask also doubled for elevator, subway and office scenes without the masks, hence, dual roles.

only a few hours to read the contents. Applying wisdom from within the pages, he uses concentration, an underrated power of the universe, to get rid of the people who annoy him. Late one evening, he uses his power to cause his landlady to vanish. When he succeeds, he concentrates on eliminating all the people in the world. Now the ride on the subway train is not crowded, and the office where he works is peaceful and quiet – so quiet that Beechcroft finds himself resorting to folding paper airplanes by the end of the day. While he enjoys the luxury of peace, he is bored to death. With the still emptiness preying on him, he decides to focus his concentration on people he can stand – people like himself. He succeeds in populating a world full of Archibald Beechcrofts. But since he hated people, he now has to live in a world that hates everyone else. Putting everything back the way it was, Beechcroft realizes that if he had the chance to change anything, he wouldn't be more content.

"Mr. Archibald Beechcroft: a child of the Twentieth Century, who has found out through trial and error . . . and mostly error . . . that with all its faults . . . it may well be that this is the best of all possible worlds. People not withstanding – it has much to offer. Tonight's case in point . . . in the Twilight Zone."

Trailer: *"Next week, the very considerable talents of Mr. Shelley Berman are utilized to bring you another in our weekly excursions into the never-never land of the wild, the wooly, and the wondrous. He plays the part of a little man who yearns for the serenity of a world without people, and as it happens, he gets his wish to walk an uninhabited earth and face the consequences. Our story is called 'The Mind and the Matter.' I hope we'll see you then. And this isn't just a word from the sponsor, it's simply a very good suggestion. It stands for real refreshment. Before we meet again, try Oasis, for the softest taste of all."*

Trivia, etc. Telecast on the evening of November 28, 1955, *Studio One* offered "The Man Who Caught the Ball at Coogan's Bluff." Serling's script dramatized the story of George Abernathy, a 50-year-old man who works a standard government job. He is a creature of habit. He's totally passive, selfless and dull. Even his wife controls his finances. One day in mid-August, the pattern of habit George established is altered. The office is closed for renovations so he decides to take in a ballgame at the Polo Grounds. A pitched ball makes its way into the crowd and by some fantastic miracle, George stretches out his arm to protect himself and catches the ball. The crowd goes wild with back-slaps and congratulations, and the TV announcer interviews him. This was an act of destiny – a new purpose in his living. George returns home and suggests to his wife they dine out and go dancing. His clothes go from undertaker gray to flamboyant checks. His speech is peppery and colloquial. He may have kicked the hell out of the habit, but his wife Alice cannot philosophically take the change. They have a scene, and George leaves the house – only to realize the truth. He's been kidding himself. He's been making believe. When he returns home, he chooses to remain quiet and uncomplaining. The next morning the little man goes to work as if nothing ever happened, content with the realization that while the world speeds past him, he will remain content if he goes about the world in his own fashion.

Once again Serling took a previous story premise from an earlier drama and fashioned an air of fantasy in the mix. Instead of a baseball game and a fantastic catch in the stand, the main protagonist changes the world using mind over matter. But, like George Abernathy, it doesn't take long for him to realize that the old way was much better, and he sets out to correct the change.

On June 7, 1960, Martin Dubow of the William Morris Agency approached Serling about the possibility of using Joey Bishop for an episode of *The Twilight Zone*. "Joey is most anxious to do a dramatic appearance," Dubow explained. "I would like you very much to keep Joey Bishop in mind for some of your forthcoming shows." Serling wrote a kind reply, suggesting he would get back to them shortly. After the script "The Mind and the Matter" was completed, Bishop turned out to be unavailable. So Serling tracked down comedian Shelley Berman.

"Well, I received a phone call from Serling one day – and it was a surprise – asking me if I would like to star in an episode of *The Twilight Zone*," recalled Berman. "He told me he had a script tailored for me and with me in mind when he wrote it. I was just surprised and of course I said yes. I think I was dizzy in the head when he phoned me."

The March 20, 1961 issue of *The Hollywood Reporter* alerted show business that "Shelley Berman will star in *The Twilight Zone* especially written for the comedian by Serling." Berman arrived from the East Coast on March 26, flown in the day before rehearsals.

"I never saw the script till I arrived in Hollywood," added Berman. "The scene where I play a woman in the elevator was my idea, you know. Rod was on the set when we were rehearsing – with Buzz Kulik, a fine director by the way – and he asked me what I thought about playing all these roles. I told him, 'Well, it's fine, Rod, but I think you are missing something the audience needs for a laugh.' He asked me what that was and I told him I thought I should be a woman somewhere. He told me, 'I'll fix that for you.' The next day, when we were filming, I learned that I was going to be playing a woman in the elevator."

According to M-G-M production sheets and casting vouchers, an actress named Betty Rosa was hired to play the role of "woman Shelley Berman" but she never appears in this episode. She was filmed for the elevator scene, followed by Berman's role as the woman. After looking over the dailies, Houghton or Serling chose Berman's portrayal the better of the two, and her footage was discarded.

Jack Grinnage played the role of Henry, for $600, contract of employment signed March 28, 1961. "This was an interesting shot for me," recalled Grinnage. "As I not only played the role of Henry, but I was also booked to play the scenes with Shelley when he was talking to himself. I made it possible for Mr. Berman to react with someone. I would be off camera, playing his alter ego. Then they would do the reverse on him, and I would play the other ego. I also remember him talking about his prior experience of having the masks made . . . putting some gooey substance on his face to make the mold. Buzz Kulik was great to work with. As I was doing a revue called *The Billy Barnes People* at that time, and had to make the 8 p.m. curtain, I made each curtain just in time after each day's shoot. It was a fun job."

The script was assigned a production number on March 20, 1961, filmed entirely on three separate sets at M-G-M Studios. The interior of Beechcroft's living room was filmed on Stage 3 and set decorations cost $620. The New York subway station and train was filmed on Stage 20, and was the most costly of the sets, $2,160. This was because subway admission gates had to be rented and the stairway where Beechcroft walked down had to be constructed from scratch. The interior of the office building and the bathroom was filmed on Stage 25. The office, including desks, office supplies, file cabinets and other materials cost $1,215 while the bathroom only required $60. *Twilight Zone* fans might recognize the office and bathroom – it is the same set used as the bus station for the episode "Mirror Image." The paint on the walls was the same as in the station, and the bathroom where Beechcroft washes up is the same as where Millicent saw her duplicate in the mirror.

The Twilight Zone was not telecast on the evening of May 19, 1961, due to an Arthur Godfrey television special titled "On the Go."

On May 17, Henry Strauss of Henry Strauss & Co., Inc., New York, wrote to Serling after viewing this episode, requesting to discuss the possibilities of obtaining 16mm rights for distribution to industry and schools. On May 22, Serling wrote the following (and interesting) reply: "Thank you for your interesting letter. Unfortunately, we intend to do a small, low-budget picture of 'The Mind and the Matter' which I think mitigates against the possibility of using it elsewhere."

Production #3660 "WILL THE REAL MARTIAN PLEASE STAND UP?" (Initial telecast: May 26, 1961)

© Cayuga Productions, Inc., May 23, 1961, LP20231
Date of Rehearsal: April 3, 1961
Dates of Filming: April 4, 5 and 6, 1961
Script dated: February 9, 1961, with revised pages dated March 17, 25 and April 3, 1961.
Script dated: March 17, 1961, with revised pages dated March 25 and April 3, 1961.
Shooting script dated: April 3, 1961

Producer and Secretary: $1,375.00
Director: $1,250.00
Unit Manager and Secretary: $600.00
Agents Commission: $2,500.00
Below the line charges (M-G-M): $27,092.00
Total Production Costs: $44,750.80

Story and Secretary: $2,630.00
Cast: $7,360.32
Production Fee: $825.00
Legal and Accounting: $250.00
Below the line charges (other): $868.48

Cast: John Archer (Trooper Bill Padgett); Jack Elam (Avery); Jill Ellis (Connie Prince); Bill Erwin (Peter Kramer); Gertrude Flynn (Rose Kramer); John Hoyt (Ross); Morgan Jones (Trooper Dan Perry); Bill Kendis (Olmsted); Ron Kipling (George Prince); Barney Phillips (Haley, the café owner); and Jean Willes (Ethel McConnell).

Music Stock Cues: Etrange #3 (by Marius Constant, :09); Milieu #1 (by Constant, :16); Impatience (by Jerry Goldsmith, :31); The Gun – Judge (by Goldsmith, :21); Doc (by Goldsmith, :17); Alicia (by Bernard Herrmann, :04); Lonely Lady (by Bruce Campbell, :40); The Meeting (by Goldsmith, :24 and :20); The Gun (by Goldsmith, :18); The Meeting (by Goldsmith, :35); George's Bar (by Eric Cook, :12); The Meeting (by Goldsmith, :12); Paladin – The Fool (by Herrmann and Nathan Scott, :04); Impatience (by Goldsmith, :08); The Box (by Herrmann, :08); The Meeting (by Goldsmith, :07); George's Bar (by Cook, :16); The Box (by Herrmann, :20); It's Never June (by Campbell, 1:43); Tratonium #19 (by Oska Sala, 1:40); Tratonium #22 (by Sala, :03); Tratonium #20 (by Sala, :10); Punctuated Fond Sinores (by Pierre Henry, :15); Guitare Sourde (by Henry, :20); Etrange #3 (by Constant, :13); and Milieu #2 (by Constant, :35).

Director of Photography: George T.
    Clemens, a.s.c.
Art Director: George W. Davis and Phil Barber
Set Decorations: Henry Grace and
    H. Web Arrowsmith

Production Manager: Ralph W. Nelson
Assistant Director: E. Darrell Hallenbeck
Casting: Stalmaster-Lister
Film Editor: Leon Barsha, a.c.e.
Makeup by William Tuttle

Sound: Franklin Milton and Bill Edmondson   Directed by Montgomery Pittman
Teleplay by Rod Serling

"Wintry February night . . . the present. Order of events – a phone call from a frightened woman no-tating the arrival of an unidentified flying object. And the check-out you've just witnessed with two State Troopers verifying the event, but with nothing more enlightening to add beyond evidence of some tracks leading across the highway to a diner. You've heard of trying to find a needle in a haystack? Well, stay with us now – and you'll be a part of an investigating team whose mission is not to find that proverbial needle. No, their task is even harder. They've got to find a Martian in a diner. And in just a moment you'll search with them because you've just landed . . . in the Twilight Zone."

Plot: Two patrolmen investigate reports of a flying saucer that, with apparent evidence, knocked off the top of trees and submerged into a pond. Tracks from the pond lead to a nearby diner, so the patrolmen visit the café to see if they can find the visitor from outer space. The people in the diner are all passengers of a bus line that has taken a rest while the rickety bridge ahead is checked out. Spooky happenings such as the lights going on and off, sugar containers exploding and the jukebox starting by itself, confirm the suspicion of the patrolmen. After routine questioning, and with no law granting the men authority to retain someone under suspicion of being a visitor from outer space, the patrolmen are forced to let the passengers board the bus. An hour later, one of the passengers returns to the diner and explains to the owner that he is the lone survivor. The bridge was not safe and everything and everyone died in the accident. Using three arms to light his cigarette, the old man confesses that he's an advance scout from the planet Mars, sent ahead for colonization. The diner owner, however, has a surprise for his lone customer – he removes his hat to reveal a third eye. He's from the planet Venus and his friends have intercepted the Martians – so they themselves can begin colonizing.

"Incident on a small island, to be believed or disbelieved. However, if a sour-faced dandy named Ross or a big, good-natured counterman who handles a spatula as if he'd been born with one in his mouth – if either of these two entities walks onto your premises – you'd better hold their hands, all three of them – or check the color of their eyes – all three of them. The gentleman in question might try to pull you into . . . the Twilight Zone."

Trailer: *"It's been said that singularly the most difficult feat of all mankind is to find a needle in a haystack. On the Twilight Zone next time, we do it one better. We pose a problem of finding a Martian in a snow bank. It all adds up to a kind of extraterrestrial who's who with a couple of laughs and more than a couple of tangents. We recommend this to the space buffs and the jigsaw puzzle addicts. Next time on the Twilight Zone, our story is called 'Will the Real Martian Please Stand Up?'"*

Trivia, etc. The origin of this episode dates back to October 12, 1958, when Rod Serling wrote to William Dozier, head of CBS West Coast programming with plot proposals that would "represent the kind of variety I'd want to get on the [*Twilight Zone*] series." He composed a two-paragraph story summary titled "The Night of the Big Rain," which Serling told Dozier, "would make a corker of a show, solid, suspenseful, and yet strangely believable stuff."

In this plot proposal, set in a small New England community, a torrential rain has closed down the two bridges isolating the small area and trapping a handful of people who go to the local diner to wait out the storm. A young patrolman finds what appears to be a meteor that sunk in a swampy bog, and follows the tracks to the local diner. Inside, there are five customers, and the owner/operator of the diner. Each of the customers has a probable story regarding how they came to be at the establishment. In a desperate attempt to discover who is the "thing," he breaks down each of their stories.

After careful corroboration, the people are cleared of any suspicion and the patrolman reluctantly sends them on their way. Unable to prove his theory of a creature from outer space, he rationalizes his theory away by suggesting that maybe they were tracks of a wild animal. The story closes with the audience observing a small, stray dog that was previously established as a new pet of the diner operator. The dog walks outside, freezes in his tracks, and takes on a strange light, signaling a group of other "dogs" as the first beachhead of the alien race rises out of the swamp.

Serling intended to write a script adapted from his plot idea, with the working title of "The Missing Martian," during the summer of 1959. His tasks as executive producer kept him busy, and it wasn't until early 1961 that he returned to his 1958 plot proposal, this time with a more colorful title.

The initial draft for this script (dated February 9, 1961) was "Nobody Here But Us Martians." Assigned a production number on April 3, 1961, the episode kept that title up until the completion of the film, when the title changed to "Will the Real Martian Please Stand Up?" The new title was a spin on the popular television game show *To Tell the Truth*, in which game show host Bud Collyer coined the phrase, "Will the real [secret celebrity] please stand up?"

This episode only required two sets – the interior of the diner (Stage 19 on the M-G-M lot) and the highway countryside (Stage 11) which also included the exterior of the diner. The exteriors cost $350 to design, but the snow effects cost more – $600! The interior of the diner cost $990.

Morgan Jones, who played the role of Trooper Dan Perry, had to record his lines separately later in the month, because after the film was processed and cut, it was discovered that his voice had not been picked up well by the microphone. On the afternoon of April 27, he reported to Sync Room "A" at M-G-M to record his lines so they could be synched into the soundtrack.

Jack Elam did not require much makeup for his role of the eccentric loon in this episode. He already had uneven and discolored teeth, a bumpy nose, a head of hair that was both jet black and receding, and of course the protruding eyes. His left eye was sightless (the result of a boyhood fight) and was gifted to give the appearance that he was always looking over your shoulder while the right eye appeared down like a jabbing finger. The purpose of his role, obviously, was to add an element of mystery to his character – and give the audience someone to suspect as the alien.

John Archer recalled to interviewer Tom Weaver, "Rod Serling was on the set a few times, and he was a very interesting, fast-witted guy. Well, he had to be, because he wrote all those things overnight, practically. He was a nice man."

The name of the bus line, as displayed on the side of the bus in two separate shots outside the diner reads "Cayuga," an in-joke representing Cayuga Productions. The character named Olmsted and the character named Connie Prince were named after Connie Olmsted, Serling's personal secretary. The characters Peter and Rose Kramer was another in-joke. Carol Serling's maiden name was Kramer. The oddball character of Avery was named after Ira L. Avery, a friend of Serling's who had written teleplays for *Armstrong Circle Theatre* and *The Philco Television Playhouse*. The character of Ethel McConnell was named after Ethel Winant, the casting director for the series.

In the script, the third arm and hand of the space visitor was supposed to pick up the menu while the other two hands lit a cigarette. This however, would have been a bit difficult even for three arms and an actor to speak his lines while looking at a menu, so the effect was limited to the lighting of the cigarette.

No doubt due to the sponsor's insistence, this episode features a heavy product placement of Oasis cigarettes. In the diner, five different people are seen smoking cigarettes. In the finale, when Ross reveals he has three arms, the pack of cigarettes is Oasis – which can be clearly made out on the screen. His comment about Earthlings' cigarettes are pleasing to him – "they taste wonderful," is actually the sponsor's slogan. The sponsor's slogan was not even in the script, but the decision of product placement was.

The alien from the planet Venus, played by actor Barney Phillips, was supposed to have four eyes – an extra two on his forehead as indicated in the script. Makeup man William Tuttle was only able to add one eye to the forehead. By rigging a hidden wire designed to allow a man off camera to move the eye left and right, Tuttle was able to add to the realistic appearance of the additional optic.

Tracy's Pond (also referenced as Tracys Pond) was a real pond located in Connecticut, less than an hour from Serling's former home in Westport. Often mistaken for the pond of the same name located in Duchess County, New York, the Connecticut location was verified by a letter from Serling to Houghton dated February 3, 1961.

A number of props from the diner in "A Hundred Yards Over the Rim" can be found in this episode – including signs hanging on the wall, as well as the jukebox.

The music cue "George's Bar" by Eric Cook was the same music coming from James Corry's music box in "The Lonely." The music cues "Impatience," "The Gun," "Doc Judge" and "The Meeting" were originally composed by Jerry Goldsmith for the *Gunsmoke* episode "Doc Judge," originally telecast on February 6, 1960.

Revised pages dated March 25 in the script featured different closing remarks by Serling:

"Incident on a small island, to be believed or disbelieved . . . Depending on your frame of reference, your imagination and whether or not you're from Missouri. But no matter the degree of your skepticism – if a sour faced dandy named Ross who looks like a stocks and bonds salesman; or a big, good natured counter man who handles a spatula as if he'd been born with one in his mouth – if either of these two entities walk onto your premises – you better hold their hands, all three of them – or check the color of their eyes – all four of them. The gentlemen in question might try to pull you into . . . The Twilight Zone."

This episode was referenced in the song "The Twilight Zone," featured in the 1976 album titled *2112* ("Twenty-One Twelve") performed by the Canadian progressive rock group band Rush. The same single, written by Geddy Lee, Alex Lifeson and Neil Peart, also makes reference to the *Twilight Zone* episode, "Stopover in a Quiet Town." The 1979 album, *Extensions*, performed by The Manhattan Transfer, featured two tracks, back to back, titled "Twilight Zone," which reached No. 12 on the Billboard's disco chart. That musical number also made reference to this episode and "The Obsolete Man," "The Last Flight" and "Nightmare at 20,000 Feet."

Production #3678 THE OASIS COMMERCIALS (Filmed: March 20, 1961)

In the December 2, 1956 issue of *The New York Times*, television producer Herbert Brodkin remarked, "Rod has either got to stay commercial or become a discerning artist."

"Will the Real Martian Please Stand Up?" was one of Serling's ways of accepting the commercial end of television production. During the first week of January 1961, Serling agreed to do a series of testimonial commercials for Liggett & Myers on *The Twilight Zone*, the placement of which would be immediately after the teaser for "next week's show." Ted Ashley of Ashley-Steiner wrote to Hal Graham of McCann-Erickson, explaining that there needed to be enough cutting room between the teaser and the testimonial to permit the teaser to be used sans commercial for syndication. An initial testimonial from L&M was submitted to Serling giving the playwright an idea of what they wanted, since Serling was to write the testimonials himself. The initial sample was to have Serling standing in the shadows and deliver his speech while walking to a brightly lit area.

"Step out with me . . . out of the Twilight Zone of smoking to new Oasis. The only filter cigarette that's Oasis cool – Oasis mild – Oasis fresh. The tobacco is soothed for the softest taste of all and menthol misting makes it so. Try Oasis."

It is apparent that Serling did not want to personally appear in filmed commercials for L&M. In a letter dated February 24, 1961, to Graham, Serling explained, "The smell of cordite and battle that must have permeated the ethereal regions of McCann-Erickson came from a few muzzle blasts from the CBS programers on the coast, who reacted somewhat violently to my stepping out of 'character' to peddle Oasis cigarettes on the new crop of *Twilight Zone* shows. It was their contention, and I have to agree with them, that unlike Bob Stack or the other personalities who portray actual dramatic roles, my situation is somewhat unique in that I am Rod Serling to begin with and there is no natural point of transition where I can step over and do a commercial. I understand, however, that the fight was lost and that I will do my fifteen-second bit with what is hopefully a smiling professionalism. I'm sorry we got into the hassle at all, but at least it has been settled and we will break our backs out here trying to figure out a smooth and unobtrusive way of handling it."

Serling, in good humor, concluded the letter with the comment that "some gracious soul at L&M has been sending me two cartons of cigarettes a week. Do you suppose you could find out who's responsible for this so that I can drop them a note of thanks? Also I intend to give them the address of my doctor who every three months counts the spots on my lungs and advises me to start taking it with a needle. I keep telling him that at public gatherings this is a little obvious and somewhat socially frowned upon."

A total of seven 25-second commercials and seven trailers for the next week's episodes included additional dialogue from Serling commenting how good Oasis and Chesterfields felt to the throat. While not all seven were used on the series, Buck Houghton explained in an interoffice communication (dated March 3, 1961) that "the reason for doing an L&M trailer on all nine of the currently shooting pictures is that no one can be confident that the release schedule is firm; in view of that, we must be prepared for a show to become an L&M majority show on short notice." (Originally planned were nine commercials, but by March 10, that was narrowed to seven.)

This means that while Serling was seen twice on the screen hawking Oasis cigarettes in "The Silence," he also filmed commercials for "Shadow Play" in case the rotation of the episodes changed between March and June, and that episode aired on the alternate week that L&M sponsored. Cayuga produced the commercials, at a direct cost to the sponsor for $500 each, plus $95 for Serling's services in the commercial aspect of it.

The sponsor also requested that they shoot five 15-second spots with Serling for use on L&M majority reruns for summer airing. These "testimonials" were all shot at the same time for a cost of $2,725 for facilities, plus $95 paid to Serling for each of these brief commercials (plus $127.60 in tax and $7.60 for M.P.R.F.). Therefore, the five "testimonials" cost the sponsor a total of $3,349.80.

The contract between Serling and L&M guaranteed him a fee for every rerun – $70 for the second use, $60 for the third use and $57 for the forth through the 13th use. Should L&M choose to rerun the commercials beyond 13 (although it did not), Serling would have been entitled to $95 each.

A production number (#3678) was assigned to the commercials on March 15, 1961, shortly after the brief scripts for the Oasis commercials, written by Serling, were approved by the sponsor. All of the commercials for were filmed on the morning of March 20, 1961 on Stage 19 at M-G-M. Justus Addiss directed. Serling did eight 25-second commercials and five 15-second spots on that morning, reporting to the studio at 8:30 to get ready for wardrobe and makeup.

As for the Oasis pitch at the end of his trailers, those were made on the set as each episode was being filmed on their appropriate days and schedules. Serling would take a brief pause between the teaser and the commercial, so if the programs were scheduled for the week of the alternate sponsor, the editors could do a smooth, quick fade-to-black to cut out the commercial part. Trailers without the testimonials were also filmed for rerun purposes.

An analysis of the television schedule sponsored by cigarette firms in 1963 indicated that almost all cigarette firms bought air time during a large number of shows that had audiences consisting of 30 percent or more youth (i.e. persons under the age of 21). The American Tobacco Company had found 30 percent of *Twilight Zone* viewers were under age, and therefore, receptive (and maybe slightly influenced) by the testimonials delivered by Serling.

Production #3661 "THE OBSOLETE MAN" (Initial telecast: June 2, 1961)
Copyright Registration: © Cayuga Productions, Inc., May 30, 1961, LP20232
Dates of Rehearsal: April 6 and 7, 1961
Dates of Filming: April 10, 11 and 12, 1961
Script #59 dated: February 15, 1961, with revised pages dated March 25, 1961.

Producer and Secretary: $1,375.00	Story and Secretary: $2,630.00
Director: $1,380.00	Cast: $7,865.95
Unit Manager and Secretary: $540.00	Production Fee: $825.00
Agents Commission: $2,500.00	Legal and Accounting: $250.00
Below the line charges (M-G-M): $37,918.76	Below the line charges (other): $1,286.04
Total Production Costs: $56,570.75	

Cast: Barry Brooks (the first man); Josip Elic (the subaltern); Harry Fleer (the guard); Harold Innocent (the second man); Bob McCord (the third man); Burgess Meredith (Romney Wordsworth); Jane Romeyn (the woman); and Fritz Weaver (the chancellor). *

Stock Music Cues: Etrange #3 (by Marius Constant, :09); Milieu #1 (by Constant, :16); Funeral March Mondiale (anonymous, 1:29); Brave New World (by Bernard Herrmann, :03); Funeral March Mondiale (anonymous, :05 and :24); Brave New World (by Herrmann, :23, :48, :37, 2:09 and :17); Funeral March Mondiale (anonymous, :25); Brave New World (by Herrmann, :03); Etrange #3 (by Constant, :11); and Milieu #2 (by Constant, :32).

---

* Actor Josip Elic was listed Josep Elic during the closing credits of this episode. He has also been credited as Joseph Elic in some reference guides.

Director of Photography: George T.
  Clemens, a.s.c.
Art Director: George W. Davis and Phil Barber
Set Decorations: Henry Grace and
  H. Web Arrowsmith
Directed by Elliot Silverstein

Production Manager: Ralph W. Nelson
Assistant Director: E. Darrell Hallenbeck
Casting: Stalmaster-Lister
Film Editor: Jason H. Bernie, a.c.e.
Sound: Franklin Milton and Bill Edmondson
Teleplay by Rod Serling

"You walk into this room at your own risk, because it leads to the future, not a future that will be but one that might be. This is not a new world, it is simply an extension of what began in the old one. It has patterned itself after every dictator who has ever planted the ripping imprint of a boot on the pages of history . . . since the beginning of time. It has refinements, technological advancements, and a more sophisticated approach to the destruction of human freedom. But like every one of the super states that preceded it, it has one iron rule: logic is an enemy and truth is a menace. This is Mr. Romney Wordsworth, in his last forty-eight hours on Earth. He's a citizen of the State but will soon have to be eliminated, because he's built out of flesh and because he has a mind. Mr. Romney Wordsworth, who will draw his last breaths . . . in the Twilight Zone."

Plot: A field investigation has found Romney Wordsworth, a librarian, to be obsolete. In the future, the State holds hearings to find out who in society has no value, no purpose, and executes them so the world is purged from the likes of Mr. Wordsworth. A jury reviews the evidence, finds him "obsolete" and sentences him to liquidation within 48 hours. Seeing no form of escape, Wordsworth asks that there be a public viewing of his execution from his room and a private executioner, who remains the only other person who knows the method of his demise. His request is granted. Shortly before midnight the next evening, the chancellor pays a visit to Wordsworth, answering the librarian's request, only to find the tables turned. After an exchange of words, the chancellor learns that a bomb will go off at midnight and the door is locked – trapping the chancellor inside. While the librarian spends his remaining moments reading the Bible in front of the camera, he asks his persecutor how he will spend his remaining hours. No one will come to save him because it would demean the State; out of curiosity, televiewers watch to see how a member of the State handles the pressure, knowing his door to nirvana is about to open. The minutes tick by and Wordsworth reads from the Bible . . . Just seconds before the bomb goes off, the chancellor cracks under the strain and begs for the key to unlock door, pleading in the name of God. Wordsworth hands him the key and is liquidated just as the chancellor makes his escape – or so he thinks. Back at the courtroom, the chancellor finds himself under scrutiny and a judge reviews the evidence on the grounds that he is obsolete . . . and is torn apart by a jury of his peers.

"The chancellor – the late chancellor – was only partly correct. He was obsolete, but so is the State. The entity he worshipped. Any state, any entity, any ideology that fails to recognize the worth . . . the dignity . . . the rights of man . . . that state is obsolete. A case to be filed under 'M' for mankind . . . in the Twilight Zone."

Trailer: *"Mr. Burgess Meredith is no stranger to the Twilight Zone, but his role in next week's story is a unique one, even for him. The time will be the future, the place just about anywhere where men have been taken over by a machine state. Our story is called 'The Obsolete Man.' It may chill, it may provoke, but we're rather certain it will leave a mark. Next week on the Twilight Zone, 'The Obsolete Man.'"*

Trivia, etc. In the November 28, 1961 issue of *Show Business Illustrated*, Serling commented, "There's a propensity in our country to polarize things in black and white concepts. A man is either this or he is that. He's either a Communist or he's on our side, and I think the reverse is true amongst liberals. If a man happens to be militantly and vehemently anti-Communist, this guy is suspect amongst the liberals. I've either got to climb into bed with the John Birch group, or I've got to move far over to the wild left where I don't want to sit either. It's kind of a dilemma of the – you might coin a phrase – conservative liberal. I'd like to dramatize this problem."

This episode of *The Twilight Zone* may just have been Serling's attempt to dramatize the foolishness of a state under dictatorship. The script was a combination of two previously written scripts. The earliest dates back to the early 1950s, when Serling was writing scripts for radio station WLW in Ohio, where he proposed an anthology series titled *It Happens to You*, featuring stories the radio listeners would become engrossed in, whimsical tales not too dissimilar to *The Twilight Zone*. Episode 7 titled "Law Nine Concerning Christmas," explored the notion of a future society in which an unnamed town had a law passed which abolished Christmas, a law against Christ. The church was declared off-limits to the entire village. The mayor, acting much like the chancellor in this *Twilight Zone* episode, tries to explain why such a law has been put into effect. The state did not recognize any such deity, and therefore, neither should the people. Yet, he faced resistance when a crowd gathered at the front door of the church for midnight mass on Christmas Eve. After judging them each for their crimes against the State, he attempts to pass sentence – until a little girl named Pat reminds the mayor that Christ died for a principle, too.

The second source for this episode was "The Happy Place," an hour-long pilot script for *The Twilight Zone* that was formerly rejected by the network. The story, concerning a future society where people who reached a certain age were considered obsolete – unnecessary for continued living – and promptly executed by the government. Serling combined elements from both these plays to form "The Obsolete Man," a nightmarish vision in which the State made decisions as to which citizens were allowed to live because they served a purpose in society, and which ones should be eliminated because they offered no benefit to society. References to Hitler and Stalin were brought to light by the chancellor, as well as a statement regarding the non-existence of God.

The script originally called for a minister to visit Wordsworth in his room before the televised execution, but Serling deleted it from his earliest draft, realizing that a minister defeats the purpose of what he was trying to emphasize with a Godless future.

The closing narration was lengthier in the March 25, 1961 revision:

"The chancellor is only partly correct. He is obsolete. But so is the State. So is the entity he worships. Any system becomes obsolete when it stockpiles the wrong weapons. When it captures countries, but not minds. When it enslaves people, but convinces no one. When it puts on armor and calls it faith . . . when in the eyes of God it is naked of faith. It has no faith at all. Any state, any entity, any ideology that fails to recognize the worth of man . . . his dignity . . . his rights . . . they are obsolete. A case to be filed under 'M' for mankind . . . in the Twilight Zone."

Burgess Meredith received $3,500 for his role of "Wordsworth" for this episode, plus first class air transportation from New York to Los Angeles and a complimentary return trip. The entire episode was filmed on Stage 5 at the Hal Roach Studios. The interior of Wordsworth's apartment cost a mere $420 to construct. The apartment hallway and stairs cost $880. The interior of the cavernous room where the judicial courts were held cost $2,700 to construct. The television lens installed in the librarian's room is the same prop seen in "Mr. Dingle, the Strong" and "To Serve Man." Custom sound effects were created and synched at M-G-M's Sync Room "A" on May 10, 1961, from 9 a.m. to 2 p.m.

On March 8, 1961, Serling apologized to Joseph Schildkraut for not coming through on his promise of appearing in a *Twilight Zone* episode. Months before, Serling promised Schildkraut the starring role in "The Obsolete Man," but it was the opinion of the director and Buck Houghton that the role required an "Anglo-Saxon" man totally divorced from any suggestion of a specific nationality or race. Since the show had to do with prejudice in a futuristic society, it was the feeling because of the nature of the theme involved, "it would be too much on the button to cast even an actor of your stature in a role that was such a fist in the eye, so to speak." Serling explained to Schildkraut, "they were much more interested in casting away from the mold rather than toward it."

This episode was assigned a production number on April 3, 1961, the same time "Nothing in the Dark" was assigned a production number.

According to an interoffice memo dated March 8, 1961 (weeks before it went to film), this episode was originally scheduled for broadcast on September 22, 1961, as the second episode of the third season, provided the series would be renewed and broadcast for a third season. The initial intention, however, was revised. Instead of "Nothing in the Dark" being broadcast as the final episode of the second season, this episode replaced it – pushing "Nothing in the Dark" into the third season's rotation.

The responses from viewers were strong after the initial telecast. On June 6, Serling explained that the feedback ran four to one in favor of the program. The bulk of the negatives were unsigned postcards accusing Serling of Communist leanings. One such postcard read: "We watched your pro-Commy program. Do you believe books can save us? And America the super-state is to be mocked by the cheap likes of you and your Rusky pals? You preach the Commie line now, but when such patriotic societies as our John Birch Society are in power you will find out what obsolescence really is!! Yours, a Patriot."

An angry letter from Edward S. Ulman, of Los Angeles prompted Serling to reply: "Oddly enough your negative reaction was the only bright and analytical response representative of your side . . . But I do think you demean yourself with the categorical self-placement in the so-called lunatic fringe."

W.M. Price of Fallbrook, California, a high school principal, wrote to Serling stating: "What you have done has exceeding great merit. It has purpose, it has power, it has impact, it possesses that rare quality that causes men to think." Rita Krich of North Hollywood, California, found the episode to be "garbage," causing Serling to defend himself. "'The Obsolete Man' had a very simple premise. It was simply that you cannot destroy truth by destroying the printed word. You cannot undignify man by destroying him. You cannot wipe away a belief in God by an edict. And sooner or later every dictatorship must of necessity fall because sooner or later thinking people with courage will overthrow it. This, Mrs. Krich, was the statement explicit in 'The Obsolete Man.'"

On July 9, 1961, Rev. Abbott W. Whitmarsh of the First Baptist Church in West Haven, Connecticut, wrote to Serling, informing him that the offering "has been the talk of my youth groups here at First Baptist and I am sure in other areas too." Rev. Whitmarsh requested a copy of the script for a course on "Drama in Christian Education." On July 13, a copy of the teleplay was mailed to Rev. Whimarsh.

On the same day, V. Neil Wyrick, Jr., the minister of Palmetto Presbyterian Church in Miami,

Florida, wrote to Serling, explaining that he missed the airing, but it "has come to my attention by several members of my church with such favorable comments, that I would like very much to have a copy of same." On July 25, a copy of the teleplay was mailed to him. After reading the script, he wrote back to Serling, asking for permission to put on the play "in churches by our group of players, called The Palmetto Players, on a non-profit basis." Permission was denied, in light of network policy, and the outcries from some viewers who misinterpreted the script for Communist leanings.

SUMMER RERUNS
All of the summer reruns were from the first season. The opening title sequence from the first season was replaced with the second season opener, re-edited to match the rest of the second season openers.

Date	Title	Sponsor
June 9, 1961	**Repeat** "Where is Everybody?"	Colgate
June 16, 1961	**Repeat** "Perchance to Dream"	Liggett & Myers
June 23, 1961	**Repeat** "I Shot an Arrow Into the Air"	Colgate
June 30, 1961	**Repeat** "Escape Clause"	Liggett & Myers
July 7, 1961	**Repeat** "A World of Difference"	Colgate
July 14, 1961	**Repeat** "The Fever"	Liggett & Myers
July 21, 1961	**Repeat** "The Purple Testament"	Colgate
July 28, 1961	**Repeat** "Elegy"	Liggett & Myers
August 4, 1961	**Repeat** "Mirror Image"	Colgate
August 11, 1961	**Repeat** "One for the Angels"	Liggett & Myers
August 18, 1961	**Repeat** "The Big, Tall Wish"	Colgate
August 25, 1961	**Repeat** "The Chaser" *	Liggett & Myers
September 1, 1961	**Repeat** "Nightmare as a Child" *	Colgate
September 8, 1961	**Repeat** "A World of His Own"	Liggett & Myers

---

* According to an interoffice memo dated March 8, "The Chaser" was originally slated for a rerun date of September 1, and "Nightmare as a Child" was originally slated for a rerun date of August 25, but apparently they were switched. As of August 24, 1961, "Two" was slated for the premiere of the third season, followed by "The Arrival," and denotes the change from the former schedule issued April 7, 1961.

THIRD SEASON PRODUCTION COSTS

Season production info below originates from a July 31, 1961 report.

Secretary's Salary: $1,373.90

Guild Pension Plan: $12,087.31

Messenger Service: $1,092.55

Other Taxes: $1,805.77

Unit Manager's Salary: $9,000.00

Office Supplies and Expense: $1,945.96

Payroll Taxes, etc.: $14,157.14

Insurance: $5,250.00

Adding the preproduction and unallocated costs, and the unassigned literary properties (totaling $1,475.00), and the costs of production for each episode, the total cost to produce the 36 episodes from the third season (including "The Grave" and "Nothing in the Dark" produced during the second season) totaled $1,691,483.55.

Summary of production costs listed for third season episodes in the book vary through different reports. The most complete available for individual episodes were used for reference and are noted for every individual episode.

Production #4802 "TWO" (Initial telecast: September 15, 1961)

Copyright Registration: © Cayuga Productions, Inc., September 1, 1961, LP33182

Date of Rehearsal: May 11 and 12, 1961

Dates of Filming: May 15, 16 and 17, 1961

Script #64 dated: April 6, 1961

Producer and Secretary: $1,375.00

Director: $1,250.00

Unit Manager and Secretary: $600.00

Agents Commission: $2,500.00

Below the line charges (M-G-M): $29,365.47

Total Production Costs: $44,943.28 *

Story and Secretary: $2,505.00

Cast: $5,965.00

Production Fee: $900.00

Legal and Accounting: $250.00

Below the line charges (other): $232.81

---

* Total production costs and breakdown from production summary dated July 31, 1961.

Cast: Charles Bronson (the man) and Elizabeth Montgomery (the woman).

Original Music Score Composed and Conducted by Nathan Van Cleave (Score No. CPN5987):
Etrange #3 (by Marius Constant, :09); Milieu #1 (by Constant, :16); The Jungle (:40); Eve (:47); Entre Act (:13); Eve Meets Adam (1:19); What a Gal (2:00); Eve's Awakening (2:19); Adam the Barber (1:42); Male – Female (1:34); Armed Truce (:47); The Dress (:53); The War Posters (1:27); Alone (:27); Go Away (:59); Can't Forget That Man (:59); Two Are One (:24); Etrange #3 (by Constant, :08); and Milieu #2 (by Constant, :18).

Director of Photography: George T.
    Clemens, a.s.c.
Production Manager: Ralph W. Nelson
Art Directors: George W. Davis and Phil Barber
Casting: Stalmaster-Lister
Sound: Franklin Milton and Bill Edmondson
Teleplay by Montgomery Pittman

Set Decorations: H. Web Arrowsmith
Assistant Director: E. Darrell Hallenbeck
Film Editor: Bill Mosher
Directed by Montgomery Pittman

"This is a jungle, a monument built by nature honoring disuse, commemorating a few years of nature being left to its own devices. But it's another kind of jungle . . . the kind that comes in the aftermath of man's battles against himself. Hardly an important battle, not a Gettysburg or a Marne or an Iwo Jima. More like one insignificant corner patch in the crazy quilt of combat. But it was enough to end the existence of this little city. It's been five years since a human being walked these streets. This is the first day of the sixth year . . . as man used to measure time. The time: perhaps a hundred years from now. Or sooner. Or perhaps it's already happened two million years ago. The Place? The signposts are in English so that we may read them more easily, but the place . . . is the Twilight Zone."

Charles Bronson as the man

Plot: A war-torn city of weeds and rubble lies dormant from the effects of a great war. Chemical warfare and a bomb leveled much of the countryside. Two uniformed strangers – a man and a woman – wander the streets scavenging for food. There are no more boundaries, governments or causes, the man rationalizes. The only reason for fighting now is the different colors of their uniforms. The woman cannot speak English, but displays a strong instinct of hatred bred into her from years of war and is cautious regarding his every move. After she uses a weapon against him and misses, the man gives up trying to tame the wild animal and leaves. In the morning, she returns with forgiveness in her eyes and wearing a dress from a store window display. Realizing there is hope, the two walk out of the town together.

"This has been a love story, about two lonely people who found each other . . . in the Twilight Zone."

Trivia, etc. This episode was assigned a production number on April 19, 1961, and preliminary production began on May 10 when the streets and interiors were designed and photographed without the need of actors. The scenes of the deserted streets and still rooms, with no human being in the scene, were filmed on May 10. On that same day, a casting call for eight women and 10 men gave the producer, director and casting agency their choice of people for photography. All of the calendars and posters hanging inside the rooms were created specifically for this episode. Five women were selected for the calendar, and out of three attractive blondes, one was selected to pose in a bikini style costume. Three of the six clean-cut men were selected to wear plain dark suits and two of the remaining four men, blonds, were also selected for the posters.

The first two days of filming were devoted to the street scenes and interior of the barber shop and kitchen, filmed on Stage 5 at the Hal Roach Studio. On the third day, filming in the recruiting office and the exterior of the theater were filmed, as well as the remaining street scenes, on Lot 3. Making this episode was "creepy," according to Elizabeth Montgomery, who played the role of the woman soldier. "I couldn't help thinking what it would be like if I went around the corner and there actually wasn't anyone there – nothing but rubble, grass growing in the streets, the debris of a dead human race."

While this episode made no reference to the enemy being Russian, Elizabeth Montgomery speaks only one word in the episode, "prekrasny," which is Russian for "pretty."

Marilyn Malloy and Bob McCord were stand-ins for the actors. Sharon Lucas was Elizabeth Montgomery's stunt double for this episode.

A CBS press release for this episode featured:

Elizabeth Montgomery, speaking only one word of dialogue, co-stars with Charles Bronson in an episode entitled "Two" on The Twilight Zone Friday, September 15 (CBS-TV). "Two" is the tale of raggedy-uniformed combatants, sole survivors of a world holocaust. The story pits a wild, unkempt – but basically very pretty – girl against a roughneck whose nicer instincts have vanished in the five years that have elapsed since the world conflagration. When their first meeting occurs in the ruins of an old restaurant, deep-seated animosity and hatred spill over into a vicious fight.

Now these two meet the challenge of making their personal peace, neither speaking the language of the other, provides the climax for this unusual story, which was written and directed by Montgomery Pittman and produced by Buck Houghton.

According to an interoffice memo dated March 8, 1961, "The Grave" was originally going to be the season opener, followed by "The Obsolete Man" for the second week, but the schedule was revised (see episode entry for "The Obsolete Man").

Elizabeth Montgomery as the woman

The September 18, 1961 issue of *The Hollywood Reporter* reviewed this episode. "Some confusion at CBS as to whether Friday's *Twilight Zone* was the season's debut, the confusion caused by a sponsor change next week, methinks. . . . But this was the first new one of the season, starring only Charles Bronson and Liz Montgomery in 'Two,' a tale of the only two survivors in an atomic war – Bronson, essaying one of us, and Liz, mute but effective as an enemy soldier . . . Seg was interesting but not as powerful as other short-cast 'Zones,' particularly the one where Robert Cummings carried the whole show solo."

Variety had a policy of reviewing all season premieres of television programs and was also confused. The magazine ended up reviewing next week's episode instead of this one.

This was one of three episodes that were copyrighted in Canada and registered as "Twilight Zone" and not "The Twilight Zone."

Production #4814 "THE ARRIVAL"
(Initial telecast: September 22, 1961)
Copyright Registration: © Cayuga Productions, Inc., September 8, 1961, LP33183
Date of Rehearsal: July 11, 1961
Dates of Filming: July 12, 13 and 14, 1961
Script #76 dated: June 12, 1961

Producer and Secretary: $1,375.00	Story and Secretary: $2,238.00
Director: $1,250.00	Cast: $6,101.64
Unit Manager and Secretary: $600.00	Production Fee: $900.00
Agents Commission: $2,500.00	Legal and Accounting: $250.00
Below the line charges (M-G-M): $19,614.87	Total Production Costs: $34,829.51 *

Cast: Beau Anderson (guard #1); Dave Armstrong (guard #2); Jim Boles (the dispatcher); Jack Bonigul (civilian #3); Robert Brubaker (the tower operator); Bill Brunside (control operator / airline pilot #2); Robert Edmiston (airport workman #2); Hank Faber (guard #2); Sig Frohlich (civilian #2); Robert Karnes (Robbins, the airline official); Noah Keene (Mr. Bengston); Marilyn Malloy (stewardess #1); Jeanne Malone (stewardess #2); Ted O'Shea (civilian #1); Ash Russell (airport workman #1); Bing Russell (Cousins, the ramp attendant); Esther Silvery (the secretary); Harold J. Stone (Grant Sheckly); Kevin Tracy (mechanic #1); James Turley (airline pilot #1); and Fredd Wayne (Paul Malloy).

Stock Music Cues: Etrange #3 (by Marius Constant, :09); Milieu #1 (by Constant, :16); Tension Dramatic Cresendo Thru Chords – Repetitive (by Nathan Van Cleave, 1:19); Blind Alley's End (by Rene Garriguenc, :04); Tension Dramatic Cresendo Thru Chords – Repetitive (by Van Cleave, 1:23); Serling 11 (by Robert Drasnin, :18); Suspense for Perry Mason (by William A. Barnett, 1:15); Serling 11 (by Drasnin, :33); Tension Dramatic Cresendo Thru Chords – Repetitive (by Van Cleave, 1:11); Suspense

---

* Total production costs and breakdown from production summary dated July 31, 1961.

for Perry Mason (by Barnett, :17); Blind Alley's End (by Rene Garriguenc, :48); Chords Montage Minor (by Lucien Moraweck, :20); Shock Harmonics (by Fred Steiner, :20); Serling 11 (by Drasnin, 1:12); Tension Dramatic Crescendo Thru Chords – Repetitive (by Van Cleave, :30); Blind Alley's End (by Garriguenc, :04); Etrange #3 (by Constant, :08); and Milieu #2 (by Constant, :18).

Director of Photography: George T.
   Clemens, a.s.c.
Art Directors: George W. Davis and Phil Barber
Casting: Stalmaster-Lister
Sound: Franklin Milton and Bill Edmondson
Teleplay by Rod Serling

Production Manager: Ralph W. Nelson
Set Decorations: H. Web Arrowsmith
Assistant Director: E. Darrell Hallenbeck
Film Editor: Jason H. Bernie, a.c.e.
Directed by Boris Sagal

"This object, should any of you have lived underground for the better parts of your lives and never had occasion to look toward the sky, is an airplane. Its official designation a DC-3. We offer this rather obvious comment because this particular airplane, the one you're looking at, is a freak. Now, most airplanes take off and land as per scheduled. On rare occasions they crash. But all airplanes can be counted on doing one or the other. Now, yesterday morning this particular airplane ceased to be just a commercial carrier. As of its arrival it became an enigma – a seven-ton puzzle made out of aluminum, steel, wire and a few thousand other component parts, none of which add up to the right thing. In just a moment, we're going to show you the tail end of its history. We're going to give you ninety percent of the jigsaw pieces and you and Mr. Sheckly here of the Federal Aviation Agency will assume the problem of putting them together along with finding the missing pieces. This we offer as an evening's hobby, a little extracurricular diversion which is really the national pastime . . . in the Twilight Zone."

Plot: A small passenger airplane lands with perfect descent at a commercial airport . . . and brings with it an unsolved mystery. No pilots, crew or luggage are found on board. Mr. Scheckly of the Federal Aviation Agency arrives to unearth as many facts as he can. In the 20-odd years he's been investigating aviation puzzles, his record is spotless. Scheckly verifies where the plane took off, the flight plan, and the passenger manifest. Shortly after inspecting the airplane personally, he realizes that what they have is a ghost plane. Each person envisions a different plane – because they were told it landed at the airport – but the plane isn't really there. In order to prove his theory, Scheckly orders a mechanic to start the engines, and he places his arm through the spinning propellers. Unharmed, he witnesses the plane vanish before his eyes . . . and the men surrounding him. The solution to the mystery is revealed – Scheckly was unable to solve the mystery of a vanished DC-3 from 17 years before. His failure to solve the case plagued him until today when he encountered what might best be described as a "ghost plane" that made a successful landing.

"Picture of a man with an Achilles' heel, a mystery that landed in his life and then turned into a heavy weight, dragged across the years to ultimately take the form of an illusion. Now, that's the clinical answer that they put on the tag as they take him away. But if you choose to think that the explanation has to do with an airborne Flying Dutchman, a ghost ship on a fog-enshrouded night on a flight that never ends, then you're doing your business in an old stand . . . in the Twilight Zone."

Trailer: *"Literature is studded with stories of ghost ships and skeleton galleons, and next week on the Twilight Zone, we take the old tale of the Flying Dutchman and give it a coat of fresh paint. This time, the haunted ship is an aircraft. It lands in a typical busy airport and rolls up to the ramp, and it's at this point that you find yourselves on a passenger manifest of a flight that leads only to the Twilight Zone. It's called 'The Arrival.'"*

Trivia, etc. In the October 28, 1961 issue of *TV Guide*, Gilbert Seldes remarked in a review that this episode was one of his favorites. After discussing briefly a couple plots to past *Twilight Zone* offerings, and *Alfred Hitchcock Presents*, Seldes concluded "at their best, both of these programs are first-class entertainment and they are always well-made and thank heaven no one has inflated them beyond their proper length, which is half an hour. I have in recent weeks seen three hour-long dramatic shows which among them hardly contained more entertainment than a single show of either of these."

This episode was assigned a production number on June 30, 1961, before a title was even given to the script. Originally this story was titled "The DC-3" (more likely referred to as "the DC-3 story" than an actual title) and according to a production report dated June 15, 1961, Buzz Kulik was scheduled to direct this episode on August 3, 4 and 7, with rehearsal dates August 1 and 2. Arrangements had to be made at the Santa Monica Airport, especially in the hangar of Clover Field in Santa Monica. When the arrangements were made, the dates selected were in July to accommodate the airport, so the date of production was pushed ahead a couple weeks.

The entire first day and morning of the second day were devoted to filming all the scenes required in the hangar, the operation tower and on the airstrip. On the afternoon of the second day, the cast and crew returned to Stage 5 at M-G-M to film the interior of the Operations Room. On the third day, the remaining scenes in the Operations Room were completed and filming wrapped. (On the morning of July 13, while Sagal and the crew were at the airport, Lamont Johnson and his crew were filming additional scenes of the interior of the barrel for "Five Characters in Search of an Exit," which had been completed the month before, but during the rough cut it was decided to add some insert shots for certain scenes.

The September 27, 1961 issue of *Variety* reviewed: "The show now seems to be feeding itself. In three seasons, it has created its own set of plot clichés, and writer Rod Serling now appears to be weaving them together in multiples with no profounder purpose in mind than to manufacture a provocative show . . . The outing was slick, pat and extravagantly contrived, wholly unworthy of the proven talents of a dramatist like Serling." *Variety* also referred to Harold Stone's character (named after the science-fiction writer) as "a first-rate job."

This was one of three episodes that were copyrighted from Canada and registered as "Twilight Zone" and not "The Twilight Zone."

Production #4803 "THE SHELTER" (Initial telecast: September 29, 1961)

© Cayuga Productions, Inc., September 27, 1961, LP21886
Dates of Rehearsal: May 17 and 18, 1961
Dates of Filming: May 19, 22 and 23, 1961
Script #63 dated: March 9, 1961, with revised pages dated May 3 and 17, 1961.

Producer and Secretary: $1,375.00
Director: $1,250.00
Unit Manager and Secretary: $600.00
Agents Commission: $2,500.00
Below the line charges (M-G-M): $29,981.30
Total Production Costs: $47,708.90 *

Story and Secretary: $2,980.00
Cast: $7,869.15
Production Fee: $900.00
Legal and Accounting: $250.00
Below the line charges (other): $3.45

Cast: Jack Albertson (Jerry Harlowe); Joseph Bernard (Marty Weiss); Michael Burns (Paul Stockton); Larry Gates (Dr. Stockton); Mary Gregory (Mrs. Henderson); Jo Helton (Mrs. Harlowe); Sandy Kenyon (Henderson); John McLiam (the man); Peggy Stewart (Grace Stockton); and Moria Turner (Mrs. Weiss).

Stock Music Cues: Etrange #3 (by Marius Constant, :09); Milieu #1 (by Constant, :16); Good Morning to All (arr. by Bernard Green, :08 and :09); Serling I (by Robert Drasnin, :10, :18 and :05); Serling II (by Drasnin, :14 and :07); Serling I (by Drasnin, :13, :27, :06 and :09); Chester's Plan (by Jerry Goldsmith, :30); Home (by Goldsmith, :52); Free Man (by Goldsmith, :15); Serling III (by Drasnin, :45, :02 and :05); Etrange #3 (by Constant, :08); and Milieu #2 (by Constant, :18).

Director of Photography: George T.
    Clemens, a.s.c.
Art Directors: George W. Davis and Phil Barber
Casting: Stalmaster-Lister
Sound: Franklin Milton and Bill Edmondson
Teleplay by Rod Serling

Production Manager: Ralph W. Nelson
Set Decorations: H. Web Arrowsmith
Assistant Director: E. Darrell Hallenbeck
Film Editor: Jason H. Bernie, a.c.e.
Directed by Lamont Johnson

"What you're about to watch is a nightmare. It is not meant to be prophetic. It need not happen. It's the fervent and urgent prayer of all men of goodwill that it never shall happen. But in this place . . . in this moment . . . it does happen. This is the Twilight Zone."

Plot: Dr. Stockton resides in a suburb where the neighbors are close enough to be considered a part of his family. They celebrate birthday parties together, cookouts and celebrate the achievements of their children. Early one summer evening, when a Conelrad alert from a radio station instructs listeners to take-cover, Stockton ushers his family into a bomb shelter he had specifically constructed. Since the good doctor is the only person on the block with a bomb shelter, the neighbors start migrating to his house. When the doctor tries to explain through the door that there is only enough food, water and room for his wife and his son, the neighbors form a mob. Like a pack of ravaging wolves, the men attempt to break down the door to the shelter. By the time they succeed in barging through, the radio announcer cancels the alert – the missiles were identified as harmless satellites. Even with the standard apologies from the neighbors, Dr. Stockton wonders just what kind of damage has been done.

---

* Total production costs and breakdown from production summary dated July 31, 1961.

"No moral . . . no message . . . no prophetic tract. Just a simple statement of fact. For civilization to survive . . . the human race has to remain civilized. Tonight's very small exercise in logic . . . from the Twilight Zone."

Trailer: *"Next week on the Twilight Zone, we use a camera like an X-ray and look under the skin of a neighborhood of men and women. It's a little experiment in human nature and behavior on the night that a Conelrad broadcast shatters their composure with an announcement of terse terror: a bomb is coming. Most of our stories are a little far out. This one is very close in. You'll see what I mean next week when we present "The Shelter.""*

Trivia, etc. Rod Serling participated in an NBC shelter broadcast in early 1961. It was his meeting with Frank R. Dunbar, survey director of the Los Angeles Shelter Survey, Office of Civil Defense, that Serling asked for background material regarding the construction of a bomb shelter and the details involved to survive an attack from foreign soil. Dunbar was not quick to reply, and by the time he did, Serling confessed that "this show has already been filmed and will be shown sometime next fall. What mistakes are in it, I'm afraid, will remain."

No children were on hand during the two days of rehearsal; only the adult principal characters were involved in a dress rehearsal. This was done for three reasons. One, would have required a welfare worker on the set with limited hours. Two, the expense to have young children on the set during the rehearsals would have been an unnecessary cost. Third, they had no speaking parts so they were not needed until filming commenced.

The exterior of the street was filmed on Lot 2 at M-G-M, the same street seen repeatedly in multiple *Twilight Zone* episodes such as "Elegy" and "Walking Distance." The interior of the dining room, kitchen, basement and bomb shelter were constructed and filmed on Stage 16 at M-G-M.

The production number was assigned on April 19, 1961, and on the morning of May 17, shortly before rehearsals began, Lou Littlefield's voice was taped at M-G-M's Sync Room "A" for the Conelrad voice for the radio spots. On July 19, the same message was recorded again to fit the scenes required, as well as screams and shouts from men and women for the action-packed scene.

As in previous episodes, Serling avoided giving the exact locale of the story. Since one of the characters cites New York City being only 40 miles away, it is assumed that the locale is Westport, Connecticut.

Walter Hiller, Jr. of Ashley-Steiner, described in a letter to Rod Serling, having read the script, "WOW!" In his post-script, Hiller proposed Serling cast Lloyd Nolan in the role of Dr. Stockton, explaining that the character would "come to life" if played by Nolan. That role, however, would be turned over to Larry Gates.

"It was a first-rate script by Rod Serling," recalled Larry Gates to author Mark Phillips. "My character of Dr. Stockton believed he was doing the most reasonable thing with his shelter, but it turned out he had hopelessly misjudged the results of his actions. We had a wonderful cast and an excellent director, a happy company and crew and a fascinating script. When I saw the episode years later, I didn't like my performance. I thought I had overacted. But the script, direction and cast made it work."

When this script was first written, Serling forwarded the play to the De Forest Research Group who looked over the contents and on April 27 and 28, 1961, returned the play to Serling with a number of corrections and suggestions. The name of the main character was Dr. William Stockton. De Forest informed Serling that there was already a Doctor William Stockton with the United States Army Medical Corps. To avoid conflict, they suggested changing the name to Dr. William Stockard or Dr. William Stockwell. Serling never made the correction. Another name that concerned De Forest was Marty Weiss. The research group explained that there was already a Martin Weiss who was chairman and president of the Northwestern Weiss Woodwork Corp. in Milwaukee, but De Forest questioned whether this would even be a problem and admitted that "do not feel this is a conflict."

The major concern the De Forest Research Group had regarding the script was the announcement being broadcast over Conelrad. Comments such as "A state of martial law is hereby declared . . ." was considered inaccurate because no reference to a state of martial law was found in either the yellow or red alert announcements. It was suggested that one comment, ". . . no commercial traffic of any kind will be permitted on streets and highways . . ." be eliminated because a yellow alert did not ban vehicles but rather gave detailed instructions for a local dispersal movement via automobile. Serling suggested in his script that "off in the distance we can see search lights" but De Forest suggested that line be removed because with the high speed and high altitude of modern aircraft and missiles, the searchlight had become obsolete and was no longer used as an anti-aircraft defense. Serling also had in his script, " . . . the angry screaming cries of the people ring in their ears . . ." and De Forest pointed out that the heavy door required by shelters would muffle the outside sound.

Serling's script was never made ready by any governmental agency involved, i.e. the United States Air Force and Civil Defense. No arrangements were made for such a reading either on an official or unofficial basis.

Originally this episode was slated for a November telecast, but was pushed ahead a few weeks since current news regarding Civil Defense was stepping up quickly in September and October. Back in July, President John F. Kennedy spoke about civil defense issues, and many states across the country were establishing their own policy. Exactly one week after this episode of *The Twilight Zone* was telecast, President Kennedy advised American families to build bomb shelters to protect them from atomic fallout in the event of a nuclear exchange with the Soviet Union. Kennedy also assured the public that the U.S. civil defense program would soon begin providing protection for every American.

Carl Jones, a frequent viewer of *The Twilight Zone*, who resided in Brooklyn, New York, wrote to Rod Serling on September 29, 1961, in what was probably the shortest fan letter ever received. It simply read, "I dug your 'The Shelter.'"

In a newspaper editorial in *The Kansas City Star*, one viewer wrote: "I have no intention of buying a shotgun to keep neighbors out of my basement and the thought of 'one out of ten' who have already done so is sickening! It makes a great deal more sense to get together with our neighbors and build together a refuge for each neighborhood. Let's remember the old slogan: United we stand; divided we fall!"

Kenneth H. Campbell, chairman of Civil Defense in Frazier Park, California, wrote: "We thought the film very good, most provocative and thought producing. Due to our distance from Los Angeles, we have met with some apathy here, people believe there would be little danger. However Civil Defense has stressed the need for shelters and the high danger from fallout. We think your film would make people think." Jack B. Schmetterer, assistant director of the Civil Defense Corps in Northbrook, Illinois, expressed how much he enjoyed the telecast, requesting the availability of a print of 'The Shelter.'"

On the morning of this telecast, *The Albuquerque Journal* recommended the program, remarking this as "a show that should not be missed."

In the summer of 1965, Paul L. Millane of Charles Scribner's Sons, a publishing house in New York City, expressed an interest in publishing "The Shelter" in connection with their forthcoming textbook collection of 20 one-act plays. Murray Benson, director of licensing at CBS Films, Inc., was the mediator between Serling and the publishing house, which paid CBS a total of $250 for permission to include the play in its book. The publishing house made minor changes to the play so it would fit the format of the book and made sure to acknowledge within the pages that "The Shelter" was © 1961, Cayuga Productions, Inc. A cast list for the television play and the initial telecast date were also supplied for inclusion of the book.

On *The Simpsons*, the episode "Bart's Comet" parodied this episode of *The Twilight Zone* where the entire neighborhood attempts to escape a meteor destined for Springfield by squeezing into the bomb shelter. There's enough room for everyone – except one person who is forced to stay outside and face Armageddon.

Executive Producer Jon Turtletaub once commented that the television series *Jericho* was drawn from a few post-apocalyptic films, most notably this episode of *The Twilight Zone*.

The Ford Motor Company is credited for supplying the automobiles in this episode. Ford worked out an arrangement with Cayuga Productions to supply vehicles on condition that the company receive acknowledgement during the closing credits whenever an episode could incorporate an automobile in the production.

Production #4817 "THE PASSERSBY" (Initial telecast: October 6, 1961)
© Cayuga Productions, Inc., October 3, 1961, LP20717
Dates of Rehearsal: August 1 and 2, 1961
Dates of Filming: August 3, 4 and 7, 1961
Script #74 dated: June 8, 1961, with revised pages dated July 26, 1961.

Producer and Secretary: $1,625.00	Story and Secretary: $2,820.00
Director: $1,315.00	Cast: $5,479.84
Unit Manager and Secretary: $600.00	Production Fee: $900.00
Agents Commission: $2,500.00	Legal and Accounting: $250.00
Below the line charges (M-G-M): $40,937.56	Below the line charges (other): $3,357.95
Total Production Costs: $59,785.35 *	

Cast: David Garcia (the lieutenant); Austin Green (Abraham Lincoln); James Gregory (the Sergeant); Rex Holman (Charlie); Warren Kimberling (Jud Godwin); Joanne Linville (Lavinia); and Bob McCord (the wounded soldier).

Original Music Score Composed and Conducted by Fred Steiner: Etrange #3 (by Marius Constant, :09); Milieu #1 (by Constant, :16); Passing By (1:55); Improvised Humming (anonymous, :05); Black is the Color of My True Love's Hair (traditional, :28); Improvised Guitar Chords (anon-

---

* Total production costs and breakdown from production summary dated December 31, 1961.

ymous, :10); Lavinia (1:06); Black is the Color of My True Love's Hair (traditional, :33); Broken Dream (:12); Charlie Passes (2:06); Improvised Guitar Chords (anonymous, :02); Black is the Color of My True Love's Hair (traditional, 1:40); Strange Rider (1:25); Blinded Eyes (2:13); Morning (:22); Black is the Color of My True Love's Hair (traditional, :20); Jud's Song (1:40); Reunion (1:46); Etrange #3 (by Constant, :08); and Milieu #2 (by Constant, :18).

Director of Photography: George T. Clemens, a.s.c.
Art Directors: George W. Davis and Phil Barber
Casting: Stalmaster-Lister
Film Editor: Bill Mosher
Directed by Elliot Silverstein

Production Manager: Ralph W. Nelson
Set Decorations: H. Web Arrowsmith
Assistant Director: E. Darrell Hallenbeck
Story Consultant: Richard McDonagh
Sound: Franklin Milton and Bill Edmondson
Teleplay by Rod Serling

"This road is the afterwards of the Civil War. It began at Fort Sumter, South Carolina, and ended at a place called Appomattox. It's littered with the residue of broken battles and shattered dreams. In just a moment, you will enter a strange province that knows neither North nor South, a place we call . . . the Twilight Zone."

Plot: Lavinia relaxes on the front porch of the remnants of what once was her house – partially scorched as a casualty of the American Civil War. A passerby known as the Sergeant stops to rest a spell, striking up a friendly conversation. Day after day she has been watching as the tired and wounded march past her residence, reminding her of the grim repercussions of the bloody war. Among the wounded is a young boy rumored to have been shot in the head and killed at Gettysburg. The man responsible for the death of her husband gives Lavinia ample opportunity to seek vengeance, but the killer passes by when she apparently misses him with a direct gunshot to the face. Eventually the Sergeant figures out why the "wounded" have been slowly marching down the road – they, too, are the war's dead. Thanking her for the hospitality, the Sergeant departs. Lavinia, having succumbed from a fever weeks before, will not accept the inevitable. Even her husband makes an appearance, and like the rest of the walking dead, he is driven by instinct to see what is down at the end of the road, leaving her behind. It takes the wisdom of Abraham Lincoln – the last casualty of the war – to convince her that she, too, should join those walking down the scorched road . . .

"Incident on a dirt road during the month of April, the year 1865. As we've already pointed out . . . it's a road that won't be found on a map. But it's one of many that lead in and out . . . of the Twilight Zone."

Trailer: *"Next week we move back in time to April 1865, the aftermath of the Civil War, at a strange, dusty road that leads to a most unbelievable adventure. On our show next week . . . 'The Passersby.' This one is for the Civil War buffs, the mystics amongst you . . . or any and all who would want a brief vacation . . . in The Twilight Zone."*

Trivia, etc. Years before Serling wrote the first draft of this episode, he composed a six-page plot synopsis titled "The Cause." Human conflict in the same tradition of the *Studio One* and *Playhouse 90* broadcasts was proposed, but with the time period set months after the end the Civil War. A man named Jud, with a passion for tilling the earth, was returning home from the war when he met a beautiful woman wanting to reclaim what still stands, scarred from battle. He agreed to stay and help raise the crops, and the two soon fell in love. Jud was a gifted guitar player, which broke the still of the evening night when the two relaxed on the porch in the hot summer evenings. His cause during the war was different from hers, but the two decided to put the past behind them and move to a brighter future. When a family relative returns home, she finds herself forced to choose between the man she loves or the family that does not sympathize with Jud's leanings. The story was accepted by the producers of *Matinee Theatre*, and the teleplay was dramatized on May 12, 1958, co-starring Lois Smith, Sidney Blackmer and Kent Smith.

For this *Twilight Zone* presentation, Serling created a new premise adding an element of the supernatural, set in the same time period, borrowing one of the names of the fictional characters, and his gift of playing the guitar. (There were no walking dead in "The Cause," but there was a brief mention of soldiers, wounded, marching back home along the same road.)

According to a production schedule dated June 15, 1961, this episode was originally slated for filming on September 14, 15 and 18 (with rehearsal dates September 12 and 13). Shortly after the June 15 schedule was drawn up, the dates for filming this episode were revised and pushed ahead a month when the production schedule was revised. Lamont Johnson was originally slated to direct, but the assignment was handed to Elliot Silverstein. The production number was assigned on July 19.

During filming and production, this episode was titled "The Passerby," singular, not plural. Serling's teaser, trailer and narration for this episode was done on the evening of August 7, after filming was completed.

James Gregory and Joanne Linville reported to wardrobe on the morning of August 1, before they began rehearsals. Rex Holman reported to wardrobe on August 2 before joining rehearsals. The entire episode, which included the exterior of the burned mansion and the road, was filmed on Stage 5 at Hal Roach Studios. A casting call for 30 men to play the wounded Confederate Soldiers gave the casting director the choice of 15 men, mixed ages of 18 to 50 years, lean, haggard, long hair, no crew cuts, and able to wear old clothes for the march scene. A few were selected because they had beards.

The character of Jud Godwin, played by Warren Kimberling, was a tip of the hat to V.J. Godwin of the Buick Motor Division of General Motors. Godwin and Serling had been in the service together for three years during the war, and Godwin often joked that the South really won the Civil War. Godwin's last name was applied to the character for Serling's amusement, and he wrote to the playwright after viewing the telecast, confessing his surprise and considered the in-joke "quite funny."

The second act (following the middle commercial) opens with the Sergeant calling for Lavinia at the front doorway. She flows down the stairs and, seeing that he is carrying his blanket roll and hat, asks if he is leaving. He tells her he is going back on the road . . . to wherever that road leads. In the original script, the second act opened with Lavinia lying on the floor of the kitchen, covered by blankets. She wakes to find the road quiet and empty. She reacts, shouting for the Sergeant. He is standing near the tree in the yard. He answers her call and asks if she needs help with anything. She asks if her sight is correct – that there is no one on the road. He says that it is so, and she is suddenly aware that he is wearing his blanket roll and hat. She then asks the question.

According to M-G-M paperwork, the interior of the mansion kitchen was designed and the scene was filmed on August 4. Paperwork dated before the episode was filmed suggests the production crew "planned" to film the kitchen scene, but for budgetary reasons instead had Lavinia come down the stairs, answering the call of the Sergeant.

"When I played the role of Lavinia, I was thinking to myself, 'This is what it was like to be an actress on the set of *Gone with the Wind*,'" recalled Joanne Linville. "I was doing so much television at the time but usually I stood about and helped someone break jail or played a patient in bed. On *The Twilight Zone*, I was the lead. Well, James Gregory played the lead. We both played the lead. But my role was so much larger than most of the hundred television shows I did. I recall my role was much larger on *Alfred Hitchcock* [*Presents*] and *Star Trek*, but those were the days where you took what you could get and be thankful for the opportunity to act."

There were two previous opening narrations for this episode, one centered on Lavinia Godwin as the central character, but the second was Serling's reference to the time in American History when the story takes place:

"This is the afterwards of the Civil War. And this road began at Fort Sumter, South Carolina, and ended at a place called Appomattox. It is littered with the residue of broken battles and shattered dreams . . . In just a moment you will enter a strange province that knows neither North nor South . . . A place we call . . . The Twilight Zone."

The script called for the Sergeant to sing "Black is the Color (of My True Love's Hair)," which was considered a traditional folk song and in the public domain. The CBS Music Department double-checked the song's copyright status and after determining that the song was in the public domain, agreed to insert the music into the soundtrack. The song was first collected in a book of verses in 1916, but supposedly originated from Scotland and was sung years before in the United States. It does remain possible that the song was too new for the time period the story took place, but the production crew kept the piece in as it was listed in the script.

Production #4815 "A GAME OF POOL" (Initial telecast: October 13, 1961)
Copyright Registration: © Cayuga Productions, Inc., October 10, 1961, LP21340
Dates of Rehearsal: July 26 and 27, 1961
Dates of Filming: July 28, 31 and August 1, 1961
Script dated: June 15, 1961

Producer and Secretary: $1,375.00
Director: $1,250.00
Unit Manager and Secretary: $600.00
Legal and Accounting: $250.00
Total Production Costs: $6,872.28 *

Story and Secretary: $2,000.00
Cast: $375.00
Production Fee: $900.00
Below the line charges (M-G-M): $122.28

Cast: Jack Klugman (Jesse Cardiff) and Jonathan Winters (James Howard Brown, a.k.a. Fats Brown).

Stock Music Cues: Etrange #3 (by Marius Constant, :09); Milieu #1 (by Constant, :16); Lead-In (by Jerry Goldsmith, :16); Alain #3 (by Constant, :25); Menton 17 (by Constant, :24); Day #2 (by Constant, :16); Lead-In (by Goldsmith, :25); Missing Pills (by Goldsmith, :38); Trouble Ahead Tag

* The total production costs and breakdown listed above is incomplete. Info originates from a production summary dated July 31, 1961.

(by Goldsmith, :12); Missing Pills (by Goldsmith, :08); On the Prowl (by Goldsmith, :18); Missing Pills (by Goldsmith, :10); Villers #4 (by Constant, :20); Night Flight – 2A (by Constant, :21); Light Dramatic Series #4 (by Rene Garriguenc, :19); Night Flight – 2A (by Bruce Campbell, :21); Utility Cues (by Campbell, :07); Ad Lib Whistling (anonymous, :04); Belfort #3 (by Constant, :40); Oise #1 (by Constant, :35); Utility Cues (by Campbell, :08); Marne #1 (by Constant, :06); The Robbery (by Goldsmith, :05); Alain #3 (by Constant, :25); Trouble Ahead Tag (by Goldsmith, :25); Etrange #3 (by Constant, :08); and Milieu #2 (by Constant, :18).

Director of Photography: Jack Swain
Art Directors: George W. Davis and Phil Barber
Assistant Director: E. Darrell Hallenbeck
Story Consultant: Richard McDonagh
Sound: Franklin Milton and Bill Edmondson
Teleplay by George Clayton Johnson

Production Manager: Ralph W. Nelson
Set Decorations: H. Web Arrowsmith
Casting: Stalmaster-Lister
Film Editor: Jason H. Bernie, a.c.e.
Directed by Buzz Kulik

"Jesse Cardiff, pool shark. The best on Randolph Street, who will soon learn that trying to be the best at anything carries its own special risks in or out . . . of the Twilight Zone."

Plot: In the after hours of a Chicago pool hall, Jesse Cardiff swears to the heavens that he would give anything to play a game against the late James Howard Brown, a.k.a. "Fats Brown," a legendary pool shark. His wish is granted when the ghost of Brown appears to take up the challenge. To make his long journey worthwhile, Fats wagers Jesse's life on a game of pool. Knowing he cannot make a legend of himself without a little risk, Jesse agrees to the terms. One game, 300 points. The game starts in Jesse's favor, but after the first few racks, Fats proves his worth. During the game, Fats gives Jesse some advice – live a little. There are things more important in life than a game of pool – women, fishing, movies. But to Jesse, a game of pool isn't nice. It's a "win at any price affair." When the game comes to a climax with a simple pocket hanger, Jesse succeeds in sinking the ball, ignoring Fats' warning that if he wins the game, he'll earn more than he bargained for. Years later, after Jesse's untimely demise, he discovers he is another legend in the clouds. He has taken the place of Fats and is now being summoned to another game of pool from another pool shark offering a challenge.

"Mr. Jesse Cardiff, who became a legend by beating one, but who has found out, after his funeral, that being the best of anything carries with it a special obligation to keep on proving it. Mr. Fats Brown, on the other hand, having relinquished the champion's medal . . . has gone fishing. These are the ground rules . . . in the Twilight Zone."

Trailer: *"Next week we engage in 'A Game of Pool.' That's both an activity and a title. A play written by George Clayton Johnson and starring Mr. Jack Klugman and Mr. Jonathan Winters. Its the story about the best pool player living . . . and the best pool player dead. And this one, we submit, will stay with you for quite awhile. Next week on the Twilight Zone, 'A Game of Pool.'"*

Trivia, etc. Jonathan Winters, who was residing at Taylor's Lane in Mamaroneck, New York, wrote to Rod Serling, asking for the opportunity to appear in a future *Twilight Zone* production. Serling

Klugman and Winters pose
for this publicity shot.

worked at it for a few months, and on April 24, Serling answered Winters' follow-up letter. "The silence does not mean that I have forgotten, or that out of sight is out of mind, or any other cliché that happens to cross that incredible mind of yours. I'm still thinking, planning and conjuring up an idea. I don't know how long it will take, but it will come because it always does somehow and in some way. You'll be hearing from me."

This episode was conceived without a typed story outline. By May of 1961, George Clayton Johnson had proven himself to Buck Houghton to be able to pitch a story verbally, in order to receive the go-ahead to write a script. Little did Serling know that soon after, Johnson would provide the solution to Winters' request.

Johnson signed on to write a number of scripts and "The Pool Player" was contractually due by May 1. This was originally intended to be production #4810, according to progress reports dated June 12 and June 15, 1961 (the production number was assigned to "The Pool Player" on July 13). Director Elliot Silverstein was Houghton's first choice, and filming was scheduled for July 6, 7 and 10, with rehearsals on July 3 and 5. Silverstein, however, was assigned to "The Passersby" instead.

The entire episode was filmed on Stage 5 at M-G-M. Only two sets were required for the entire episode: the interior of the pool hall and the "pool hall limbo." The entire company was delayed on August 1, the final day of shooting, due to water dripping from the roof to the stage for "pool hall limbo," forcing the cast and crew to return to film the scene on the morning of August 2.

The original script featured a different ending, in which Jesse loses and Fats chooses not to take his life. Fats only wanted to see how Jesse would stand up against the pressure. The original ending, however, was not filmed. It was rewritten and shot so Jesse would win and replace the veteran as the always-challenged champion.

"I had been in Missouri with my friends Nolan and Beaumont and Ocee Ritch, and a number of other people, to make *The Intruder*," recalled George Clayton Johnson to Matthew R. Bradley. "I was on location when I should have been working on delivering 'Kick the Can,' after having talked about it with a very indecisive kind of an outline, and Buck was waiting for it while filming 'A Game of Pool.' He and Rod had gone over this and wanted to change something that had to do with the ending. I had laid it out to where the young man, Jesse Cardiff, lost, but at least could say threateningly, at the end, to the dead legend, Fats Brown, 'yes, but the thing is, I'm still alive. I still have the chance to get better, and I will get better. I'll practice every day. You'll hear from me again.' That's the tag for my version of it, and now Rod tells me he's changing it. He's going to make the other one – the young guy – win, and all for a gag, a kind of a thing that he had mentally made up, and he thought it was worth this transformation. All of this is being transmitted to me through Buck, without me directly confronting Rod over it, but with me basically hearing Rod's thinking, and then Buck's apologies for Rod's thinking or support of Rod's thinking, and me trying to bear Rod's thinking up, so he would go back to doing it the way I thought I could see it perfectly. Well, Rod thought the idea of a limbo, where there sits the legend waiting to be summoned forth, and to which the newcomer will be doomed to replace him while he goes off to go fishing – you know, that whole visual of a smoky room with a man sitting at a pool table, and a telephonic voice saying, 'Fats Brown, you have been challenged, you have to head to Randolph Street,' and he has to get up and go out – he thought that was cute, and I thought that was dismal. I said, 'No, the whole idea here is that you're trying to suspend disbelief, not jam it down their throats. Let's be sane about this. Just a slight tilt is all you need here.'"

"Those were my arguments to Buck, with me getting more and more stern about it, and him saying, 'Look, we've gotta do it, we're filming right now. If you were here, it would be a different story. If you could find a better way, we'd accept that, but you're not here, you're off there. Where the hell are you? Get back here and do what you're told,' and generally this attitude, with me dragging my heels because what I was doing there, I thought, was important. I wanted to finish it up, I had committed myself to it, and I felt that I could whip out this script on the way back, which, in fact, I did. I started to write 'Kick the Can' in a motel room on the way back from Missouri, while Nolan was finishing up some article that he had agreed to do about the filming and the background behind *The Intruder*."

Apparently Buck Houghton and Buzz Kulik proposed revising a scene in which Fats has a girl with him, during his scenes in the pool hall limbo. Five women were interviewed for the role – all blonde, show-girl types, an age range of 19 to 24, described as "tall and beautiful." A casting call was held on July 31, and Sharon Dee was selected and filmed as Fats' girl. The scene with the girl ended up on the cutting room floor.

Many of the photos hanging on the wall, including the one of the horse standing alone, was reused in many other episodes of *The Twilight Zone*. When Fats is in the pool hall limbo, summoned to the surface, all of the balls on his pool table are black.

The voice of the woman beckoning the legend was Marjorie Lizst, who recorded her voice at M-G-M's Sync Room "B" on September 12, 1961, from 11 to 11:30 am. On this same day, Serling was filmed for the teasers and intros for this episode, as well as "The Passersby," "The Mirror" and "The Midnight Sun."

"I jumped at doing anything that Rod wrote," Jack Klugman explained in a letter. "When my agent told me they wanted me for a *Twilight Zone*, I didn't have to look at the script. I said yes. 'A Game of Pool' is probably my favorite because I was already a pool shooter. John and I got along so beautiful and in between takes he would tell jokes and I would be cracking up on the set."

"It was a very good script," recalled Jonathan Winters. "I was so fortunate to play Fats. They play that episode on holidays on television marathons. I have been told that it is considered one of the best of the series. I was never offered many serious roles; always comedy because I was labeled a comedian. So when the part opened, I was very happy."

"Like *The Devil and Daniel Webster*, in the puffs of pool hall smoke . . . It's a whiz of a pool story," remarked Leonard Hoffman of *The Tucson Daily Citizen*. Jonathan Winters stayed up the evening of the initial telecast to view the finished product. On October 16, he sent the following to Rod Serling: "Enjoyed watching 'The Pool Player' on the air almost as much as working with you and Buzz and your crew in studio. Continued good luck."

Johnson discussed in his interview with Mathew Bradley the remake of this episode, done in 1988 during a writer's strike with Esai Morales in the role of Jesse Cardiff. Johnson's original ending was restored. "It was sort of done with me kicking and screaming and unaware that they had a remake privilege, because I owned all rights to these stories. Rod had only bought the right to make them into one film and then market that film 'til hell and gone, which he had been doing successfully, all was well. But now here they were remaking it, and they had not come to me. Before that, I'd only had to deal with Warner Brothers, who wanted to make *Twilight Zone-The Movie* (1983), and of course they had to come to me because they weren't CBS. But this was CBS International, one arm of a great octopus that was the primary owner of the films. They point to this small print that says, 'Yes, for peanuts and the old 1960s wage scale, we can remake one version of it.' I look at the fine print and, yes indeed, they can do that."

"In a book I put out called *Writing for the Twilight Zone*, which was published by Outré Press in Sacramento, the producers discovered my original script and a little piece of writing that I did about it," Johnson continued. "So they then took that idea and transformed it somehow at their will in this other show, but the way it was directed and written and the general bravura way it was played didn't work for the suspension of disbelief that's so necessary with these kinds of tales, for me. I felt really dismal about it and said, 'My God, now this damn script is cursed, it's never going to get made properly.' So I found a couple of actors, Owen Orr and Michael Green, rehearsed them to play these two characters, borrowed a pool table, walked around it, and planned out all these shots. When it came to shoot the game, I was determined to shoot from below the level of the rail so that you could not see the top of the table. They could just walk around the table and shoot the shots as though they were shot, and later worry about putting in sound effects or what have you, and getting some kind of power from this strange low view of these actors. I did a whole complex business of using videotape that I borrowed, and at CalArts [California Institute of the Arts] what they call their modular theater, some lighting students, and a set designer who helped me make up a big empty box which I lined with white paper. When the lights were hung up above it, snooded down to beam into the box, they went down very hard and cold, hit that white paper, and came up very warm and alive, so that when these actors would lean over the table the light would come blasting up out of it to illuminate them from below. They could control the amount of lights and shadows that were on them after they began to get the feeling for it. It was quite a strange little film that I made, so there actually is a third version of 'A Game of Pool' that I have here as an example of my directing one of my own dramas, because I thought that perhaps it might come in useful at some future time to be prepared to direct something of mine.

"I was astonished at how straight he [Jonathan Winters] played it. I expected him to do some little take somewhere in the midst of it that would let you know that he knew that you knew about his whole schtick, and he sort of modulated down from that," Johnson concluded. "I think it's a very effective play the way they've done it, although the ending rings wrong to me. I would have loved to have seen it done the other way, because I think it would have given Klugman some really great exit lines. He's very good for that, sort of screaming defiantly at the retreating enemy: 'I'll come back, don't worry! You'll hear from me again!' I also had second thoughts and later changed it from Fats to Duke Brown, who was known as John Howard Brown, the Duke of Downtown. That gave it a less offensive quality to me, because Fats was sort of patterned after Minnesota Fats, and I must tell you I was heavily influenced by *The Hustler* [the Walter Tevis novel filmed by Robert Rossen in 1961], although I had the story idea and was working on it before I read it. I grabbed *The Hustler* eagerly when I saw it, because I knew that there was a tremendous amount of drama over that pool table, and the kind of intentions that people have toward each other over it."

Jerry Goldsmith's music cues "Lead-In," "Trouble Ahead Tag" and "On the Prowl" was part of an original music score for *The Sergeant and the Lady*, an unsold 1958 television pilot starring Jack Lord and Peggie Castle as two detectives on the San Diego police force on the trail of the Blue Jeans Bandit.

In the episode "Carbon Creek," on the television series *Enterprise*, initially telecast on September 25, 2002, "A Game of Pool" was referenced.

Production #4819 "THE MIRROR" (Initial telecast: October 20, 1961)

© Cayuga Productions, Inc., October 17, 1961, LP21341
Dates of Rehearsal: August 14, 1961
Dates of Filming: August 15, 16 and 17, 1961
Script #80 dated: July 11, 1961

Producer and Secretary: $1,625.00	Story and Secretary: $2,735.00
Director: $1,315.00	Cast: $7,772.23
Unit Manager and Secretary: $600.00	Production Fee: $900.00
Agents Commission: $2,500.00	Legal and Accounting: $250.00
Below the line charges (M-G-M): $31,899.47	Below the line charges (other): $1,719.76
Total Production Costs: $51,316.46 *	

Cast: Arthur Batanides (Tabal); Antony Carbone (Cristo); Peter Falk (Ramos Clemente); Rodolfo Hoyos (Garcia); Richard Karlan (D'Allesandro); Will Kuluva (General DeCruz); Bob McCord (assistant to priest); Val Ruffino (the guard); and Vladimir Sokoloff (the priest).

Stock Music Cues: Etrange #3 (by Marius Constant, :09); Milieu #1 (by Constant, :16); Twilight Zone Punctuation Showcase #5 (by Nathan Van Cleave, :08); D Story #1 (by Constant, :40); Twilight Zone Punctuation Showcase #5 (by Van Cleave, :08); D Story #1 (by Constant, :02); F Story #5 – Version A (by Constant); Serling II (by Robert Drasnin, :16, :18, :25 and :29); D Story #1 (by Constant, :04); Serling II (by Drasnin, :20); D Story #1 (by Constant, :02 and :15); Serling II (by Drasnin, :16, :10, and :08); D Story #1 (by Constant, :16); Serling II (by Drasnin, :08, :10 and :24); D Story #1 (by Constant, :08); Serling II (by Drasnin, :08 and :29); D Story #1 (by Constant, :02); Serling II (by Drasnin, :26, :08, :12, :08 and :39); D Story #1 (by Constant, :04); Serling II (by Drasnin, :03); Etrange #3 (by Constant, :08); and Milieu #2 (by Constant, :18).

Director of Photography: George T. Clemens, a.s.c.	Production Manager: Ralph W. Nelson
	Set Decorations: H. Web Arrowsmith
Art Directors: George W. Davis and Phil Barber	Assistant Director: E. Darrell Hallenbeck
Casting: Stalmaster-Lister	Story Consultant: Richard McDonagh
Film Editor: Bill Mosher	Sound: Franklin Milton and Bill Edmondson
Directed by Don Medford	Teleplay by Rod Serling

---

* Total production costs and breakdown from production summary dated December 31, 1961.

"This is the face of Ramos Clemente – a year ago a beardless, nameless worker of the dirt who plodded behind a mule, furrowing someone else's land. And he looked up at a hot Central American sun and he pledged the impossible. He made a vow that he would lead an avenging army against the tyranny that put the ache in his back and the anguish in his eyes. And now one year later the dream of the impossible has become a fact. In just a moment we will look deep into this mirror and see the aftermath of a rebellion . . . in the Twilight Zone."

Plot: Cheered by thousands when he took office, a Latin American liberator named Ramos Clemente soon becomes guilty of the same tyranny from which he liberated his people. With the assistance of his four lieutenants, he confronts General DeCruz, the former dictator, who informs Clemente they are of the same breed – they are the keepers of the grab, who will soon suffer from fear of rebellion, disloyalty or assassination. Before being led out for judgment, the general warns Clemente that the mirror hanging on the wall possesses magic – it will reflect the images of his assassins. Clemente laughs at the notion, until he discovers that each decision he makes causes one of his comrades to turn against him. One-by-one his four comrades are murdered at the command of Clemente, each foretold by the reflections in the mirror seen only through Clemente's eyes. A full week goes by as he continues to issue public executions, hoping to purge the streets of his enemies. After receiving a visit from a priest, Clemente learns that his is the story of all tyrants – his greatest enemy is himself. After smashing the mirror, Clemente pulls the trigger of his gun and commits suicide.

"Ramos Clemente. A would-be God in dungarees strangled by an illusion. That will of the wisp mirage that dangles from the sky in front of the eyes of all ambitious men. All tyrants. And any resemblance to tyrants living or dead is hardly coincidental. Whether it be here . . . or in the Twilight Zone."

Trailer: *"We've had some performances of great depth on the Twilight Zone, and next week is no exception. A distinguished and incredibly talented young man lends us his services when Peter Falk stars in 'The Mirror.' This is the story of a tyrant and his assassins, a shattered dream, and the death of a cause. Next week – on the Twilight Zone – 'The Mirror.'"*

Trivia, etc. This script was assigned a production number on July 26, 1961. Don Medford was assigned to direct, shortly after Serling and Houghton reviewed the rough cut of "Deaths-Head Revisited" in early June. The dates of filming were slated for August 3, 4 and 7, with rehearsal dates of August 1 and 2. On July 26, 1961, the script was assigned a production number and it had been decided that Anton M. Leader would direct this segment, and the dates were pushed ahead a couple weeks.

The five leads in this episode went for costume fitting on August 11. Rehearsals were held on August 14. The entire episode was filmed on Stage 19 at M-G-M Studios.

Peter Falk was paid $3,000 for his appearance as Ramos Clemente for this episode. According to the October 17, 1961 issue of *The Hollywood Reporter*, Serling was so impressed with Falk's acting, having seen him on other television programs, that he contractually signed Peter Falk for two additional appearances on *The Twilight Zone*, and this marked his first. It turned out to be his only.

"Peter Falk's character was based loosely on Fidel Castro," recalled Arthur Batanides for *Starlog Magazine*. "It was at the height of the Cuban missile crisis. At one point, we all had to leave the studio dressed in our Latin American outfits. Since there was a lot of anti-Castro bias at the time, we felt insecure walking around the streets in these uniforms. It was definitely not the time to be running around looking like one of Castro's men. I thought somebody might run us down!"

Dave Armstrong is a stunt double for this episode, having appeared unaccredited in numerous episodes. He was the stunt man for the character of DeCruz in the episode "The Rip Van Winkle Caper." Notice that Serling reused the name DeCruz (a character from "The Rip Van Winkle Caper") for a second time. Bob McCord and Jim Turley helped supply some of the off-stage voices.

Originally the trailer was written to read: *"On our next program, a distinguished and incredibly talented young man lends us his services when Peter Falk stars in 'The Mirror.' This is the story of a tyrant and his assassins, a shattered dream, and the death of a cause. Next week – on the Twilight Zone –'The Mirror.'"*

In Serling's earlier draft of the script, his opening narration was longer:

"This is Ramos Clemente who once had a dream. He walked behind a mule furrowing up someone else's land and then looked up at a hot Central American sun and pledged the impossible. He made a vow that he would lead an avenging army against the tyranny that put the ache in his back, the lines in his face, the anguish in his eyes. And one year later the dream of the impossible had become a fact. He rode at the head of an army into a capitol city, cheered along the way by thousands of other dreamers who had an illusion that General Clemente would give them back their freedom. An honest mistake . . . but even honest mistakes must be paid for. In just a moment Clemente, his lieutenants . . . And all of you will look deep into this mirror and see the ugly reflection of a very common specie of men who begin by consecrating their lives to freedom . . . and then forget what they were looking for. We are about to see the aftermath of a rebellion . . . in The Twilight Zone."

The October 20 issue of *The Indiana Evening Gazette* warned viewers in advance that "there is nothing eerie in this drama, aside from the dictator's delusions concerning an ancient mirror said to possess supernatural powers."

Production #3656 "THE GRAVE" (Initial telecast: October 27, 1961)

Copyright Registration: © Cayuga Productions, Inc., October 24, 1961, LP20718
Dates of Rehearsal: March 9 and 10, 1961
Dates of Filming: March 13, 14 and 15, 1961
Script #60 dated: February 27, 1961

Producer and Secretary: $1,375.00	Story and Secretary: $2,155.00
Director: $1,250.00	Cast: $10,389.48
Unit Manager and Secretary: $600.00	Production Fee: $825.00
Agents Commission: $2,500.00	Legal and Accounting: $250.00
Below the line charges (M-G-M): $30,588.71	Below the line charges (other): $1,708.08
Total Production Costs: $51,641.27 *	

Cast: Angelo August (man carrying the body inside); James Best (Johnny Rob Kimmer); William W. Burnside Jr. (western cowboy); William Challee (Jasen); Jack Downs (man carrying the body

---

* Total production costs and breakdown compiled from two production summaries dated June 30, 1961 and February 28, 1962.

inside); Richard Geary (Pinto Sykes); Larry Johns (Corcoran); Strother Martin (Bert Mothershed); Lee Marvin (Conny Miller); Bob McCord (silent bit on rooftop); Stafford Repp (Ira Broadly); James Turley (western cowboy); Lee Van Cleef (Steinhart, the gambler); and Elen Willard (Ione).

Stock Music Cues: Etrange #3 (by Marius Constant, :09); Milieu #1 (by Constant, :16); Pursuit (by Fred Steiner, :34); Chester's Victory (by Goldsmith, :08); The Parson (by Steiner, :35); Pursuit (by Steiner, :16); Mystery Man (by Steiner, :22); Improvised Chords (anonymous, :13, :03, :05, :03, :03 and :03); The Gun (by Goldsmith, :26); Improvised Chords (anonymous, :12, :03, :05 and :03); Suspicion and Mounting Tension (by Rene Garriguenc, :28); Chester's Victory (by Goldsmith, :36); Improvisation on "Sweet Betsie From Pike" (traditional, :10); Bad Man (by Fred Steiner, 1:02); Etrange #3 (by Constant, :10); and Milieu #2 (by Constant, :30).

Director of Photography: George T. Clemens, a.s.c.	Production Manager: Ralph W. Nelson
Art Directors: George W. Davis and Phil Barber	Set Decorations: H. Web Arrowsmith
Casting: Stalmaster-Lister	Assistant Director: E. Darrell Hallenbeck
Sound: Franklin Milton and Bill Edmondson	Film Editor: Leon Barsha, a.c.e.
Teleplay by Rod Serling	Directed by Montgomery Pittman

"Normally, the old man would be correct. This would be the end of the story. We've had the traditional shoot-out on the street, and the bad man will soon be dead. But some men of legend and folk tale have been known to continue having their way even after death. The outlaw and killer, Pinto Sykes, was just such a person. And shortly, we'll see how he introduces the town, and a man named Conny Miller in particular . . . to the Twilight Zone."

Plot: Pinto Sykes, wanted by the law in three states, is shot dead in the streets by a law-abiding committee of eight. Two evenings later, a hired gun named Conny Miller arrives in town, having spent the past few months seeking out Sykes. His friends explain to Miller that on his death bed, Sykes claimed Miller was a coward – having given him the opportunity to face off and Miller was a no-show. In his last dying breath, Sykes swore that if Miller comes near his grave, he'll reach out and grab him. The men in the bar, afraid to visit the grave themselves, bet money against the hired gun that he is afraid of Sykes, dead or alive. To prove his worth, Miller accepts the wager, taking a bowie knife with him to plant in the fresh earth. Alone at midnight, he walks up to the cemetery, finds the grave, removes the knife from his coat and plants the blade firmly into the soil. In the morning, his friends arrive to find Miller dead,

Lee Marvin tries to convince Elen Willard that he isn't afraid of dead men.

lying by the grave. Apparently he had stabbed his coat onto the grave by accident, and when he felt the sudden tug on the coat, his heart gave out, dying of fright. But the wind was blowing the other way ... so how or who grabbed the coat?

"Final comment: you can take this with a grain of salt or a shovel of earth, as shadow or substance. We leave it up to you. And for any further research, check under 'G' for ghosts ... in the Twilight Zone."

Trailer: *"It's traditional in the great American western that the climax of any given story is the gun-down on the main street. Next week Montgomery Pittman has written a story in which we have our gun-down and then go on from there. It's a haunting little item about a top gun as he was alive ... and his operation after death. This is one for rainy nights and power failures, but wherever you watch it, I think it will leave its imprint."*

Trivia, etc. Montgomery Pittman got the inspiration for this story sitting on his father's knee. "I was just a lad growing up on my pappy's ranch in Oklahoma, when I first heard the story of a desperado who swore he would reach out from the grave and get the man who had been tracking him down," Pittman explained in a CBS press release. "It seemed that whenever the wind began to howl, my pappy and his friends would sit around the pot-bellied stove and he would tell the tale. This didn't happen just once, but about anytime the wind was blowing up a storm."

The morning after the telecast, Les M. Kratter of Riverdale, New York, wrote to Serling commenting: "It is an almost exact replica of a short story written by a Russian author. There is nothing wrong with this if it is adapted in an intelligent way. Your program was definitely put into a new format that was very good. The major objection I have to your show is that you gave no credit whatsoever to the original author. I believe that it was Checkov. Your credits in the end gave one the impression that Mr. Pittman wrote the show without help from anyone; this is plagiarism. I am sure that a person of your obvious education must have at some time or another come across this story."

"I was the one responsible for that episode," recalled James Best. "I told Monty Pittman that I was born in Kentucky but raised in Indiana. One of the things I remember most about my childhood was the ghost stories I used to hear. I collected ghost stories. I told Monty a couple stories and suggested he use one for a television series. He told me, 'If I write the script and direct it, I'll have you in the cast.' I told him, 'You do that.' I can't recall how much time passed but one day I get word that I am going to be on a *Twilight Zone*. And I got to work with Lee Van Cleef, Strother Martin and Lee Marvin. And it turns out to be one of those ghost tales. Monty was such a pal and he remembered our agreement and kept his word."

"You know, it got to be that I knew the story by heart," Pittman recalled in a magazine article, "how Pinto Sykes was shot down but left his pledge before he died, how Conny Miller came to town to learn the man he'd been trailing was dead but had left his warning, and how Conny's acquaintances taunted him into visiting the cemetery."

Pittman insisted on the wind blowing during this episode, from the opening shots to the final conclusion. The fan blowing across the graveyard in the closing scenes, however, gener-

Set Decoration Production Costs	
Exterior of Road, Tool Shed, and Graveyard	$2,850
Interior of Saloon	$970
Exterior of Western Street	$150
Total	$3,970

ated too much noise. None of the actors' voices could be heard clear enough on film, especially during the closing scene, so all of the dialogue had to be recorded and synched into the soundtrack. On March 15, Lee Van Cleef, Strother Martin and James Best recorded their voices on Stage 2A. Elen Willard recorded her lines on the same stage on April 19, 1961.

The shots in the western street shown in the opening episode were filmed on Stage 10, and most of the other scenes were filmed on Lot 3 of M-G-M. According to an interoffice memo, this episode was originally intended for the premiere broadcast of the third season. As the schedule was revised, the episode was pushed into the month of October, as a Halloween offering. The production number was assigned on March 6, 1961, and originally the dates of filming were scheduled to be March 17, 20 and 21, 1961, but shortly after, it was rescheduled – filmed a week earlier. The dates and production numbers are accurate – this episode and "Nothing in the Dark" was filmed during the production of the second season episodes, but shelved for use on the third season. The closing credits for both "Nothing in the Dark" and "The Grave" are a combination of the second and third season format.

"Lee Marvin was a drinker. There is no way to hide that," recalled James Best. "He would take a few down in the morning when we reported to the set. You could smell it on his breath. But you know, some people have a problem with alcohol and others can hold their liquor. He showed up on the set and knew his lines forwards and backwards."

Fred Steiner's music cues "Bad Man," "Pursuit" and "The Parson" featured in this episode were originally composed for the December 5, 1959 broadcast of *Gunsmoke*, titled "Box o'Rocks."

This was the third of three episodes to use the name Sykes for a character. The name Sykes was featured in "A Penny For Your Thoughts" and "Dust."

Serling had composed an alternate closing narration for this episode, which was never used. Designed to start over Ione's walk, Serling commented:

"Legend, folk tale, or just an apocryphal old wives tale passed down from one naïve young generation to the next – that's all possible. But death . . . just as life itself . . . has little pockets of mystery. Little caves of unexplored depths and uninhabited basements too dark to distinguish what is shadow and what is substance. This one we leave up to you. Does a marker on a mound of earth mean the end? Maybe the answer is in one of the caves, holes or basements of the world. Or maybe it's one that can only be found . . . in The Twilight Zone."

Another alternate closing never used for the program (dated March 23, 1961):

"Legend, folktale, shadow or substance, we leave it up to you. Take it with tongue in cheek or question mark in mind, but if you plan to put it to a test . . . find a friendly grave and make your overtures in daylight. That's tonight suggestion . . . from the Twilight Zone."

Production #4801 "IT'S A GOOD LIFE" (Initial telecast: November 3, 1961)

Copyright Registration: © Cayuga Productions, Inc., October 31, 1961, LP21342
Dates of Rehearsal: May 5 and 8, 1961
Dates of Filming: May 9, 10 and 11, 1961
Script #65 dated: March 17, 1961

Producer and Secretary: $1,375.00   Story and Secretary: $3,260.00
Director: $1,484.11   Cast: $6,671.92

Unit Manager and Secretary: $600.00

Production Fee: $900.00

Agents Commission: $2,500.00

Legal and Accounting: $250.00

Below the line charges (M-G-M): $30,061.10

Below the line charges (other): $28.00

Total Production Costs: $47,130.13 *

Cast: Casey Adams (Pat Riley); Jeanne Bates (Ethel Hollis); Alice Frost (Aunt Amy); Tom Hatcher (Bill Soames); Don Keefer (Dan Hollis); Lenore Kingston (Thelma Dunn); John Larch (Mr. Fremont); Cloris Leachman (Mrs. Fremont); and Billy Mumy (Anthony Fremont).

Stock Music Cues: Etrange #3 (by Marius Constant, :09); Milieu #1 (by Constant, :16); Bergson #1 (by Constant, :33); Brave New World (by Herrmann, :28 and :41); Mistral #1 (by Constant, :21); Bergson #5 (by Constant, :29); Brave New World (by Herrmann, :30, :28 and :43); Mistral #1 (by Constant, :25 and :20); Brave New World (by Herrmann, :54); Stardust (by Hoagy Carmichael, :18); Brave New World (by Herrmann, :31); Moonglow (by Will Hudson, Eddie De Lange and Irving Mills, :15, :53, 1:06 and :18); Happy Birthday to You (by Mildred J. Hill and Patty S. Hill :16); Brave New World (by Herrmann, :19); Stardust (by Carmichael, :10); You Are My Sunshine (by Jimpie Davis and Charles Mitchell, :11); Mistral #1 (by Constant, 1:19); Brave New World (by Herrmann, :27 and :09); Moonglow (by Hudson, De Lange and Mills, :45); Brave New World (by Herrmann, :39); Kant #3 (by Constant, :08); Etrange #3 (by Constant, :08); and Milieu #2 (by Constant, :18).

Director of Photography: George T.
    Clemens, a.s.c.

Production Manager: Ralph W. Nelson

Set Decorations: H. Web Arrowsmith

Art Directors: George W. Davis and Phil Barber

Assistant Director: E. Darrell Hallenbeck

Casting: Stalmaster-Lister

Story Consultant: Richard McDonagh

Film Editor: Jason H. Bernie, a.c.e.

Sound: Franklin Milton and Bill Edmondson

Directed by James Sheldon

Teleplay by Rod Serling, based the short story of the same name by Jerome Bixby, originally published in *Star Science Fiction Stories* (edited by Frederik Pohl, No. 2 – 1953).

"Tonight's story on The Twilight Zone is somewhat unique and calls for a different kind of introduction. This, as you may recognize, is a map of the United States, and there's a little town there called Peaksville. On a given morning not too long ago, the rest of the world disappeared and Peaksville was left all alone. Its inhabitants were never sure whether the world was destroyed and only Peaksville left untouched . . . or whether the village had somehow been taken away. They were, on the other hand, sure of one thing – the cause. A monster had arrived in the village. Just by using his mind, he took away the automobiles, the electricity, the machines – because they displeased him . . . and he moved an entire community back into the dark ages – just by using his mind. Now I'd like to introduce you to some of the people in Peaksville, Ohio. This is Mr. Fremont. It's in his farmhouse that the monster resides. This is Mrs. Fremont. And this is Aunt Amy, who probably had more control over the monster in the beginning than almost anyone. But one day she forgot . . . she began to sing aloud. Now the monster doesn't like singing, so his mind snapped at her . . . turned her into the smiling, vacant thing you're looking at now. She sings no more. And you'll note that the

---

* Total production costs and breakdown from production summary dated July 31, 1961.

people in Peaksville, Ohio, have to smile; they have to think happy thoughts and say happy things because, once displeased . . . the monster can wish them into a cornfield or change them into a grotesque, walking horror. This particular monster can read minds, you see. He knows every thought, he can feel every emotion. Oh yes . . . I did forget something, didn't I? I forgot to introduce you to the monster. This is the monster. His name is Anthony Fremont. He's a six-year-old, with a cute little-boy face and blue, guileless eyes. But when these eyes look at you – you better start thinking happy thoughts, because the mind behind them is absolutely in charge. This is the Twilight Zone."

Plot: A 6-year-old boy named Anthony Fremont has kept the citizens of Peaksville, Ohio, in constant fear for their lives. Able to make anything happen just by thinking about it, Anthony has become a little demon that is capable of changing pigs into monsters and makings things disappear into the cornfield. Because he is capable of reading other people's minds, the citizens are forced to smile and think happy thoughts when they are in his presence. During a surprise birthday party for Dan Hollis, a resident of Peaksville, Dan downs one glass too many and starts thinking unhappy thoughts about Anthony. While Anthony focuses his mind on Dan, Aunt Amy reaches for a poker by the fireplace in the hopes of ending the nightmare once and for all. Her courage is not strong enough, however, as Anthony gets the best of Dan, transforming the drunk into a jack-in-the-box, and then wishing it away into the cornfield. Everyone in the living room agrees with Anthony's actions, stating it's a good thing Anthony did.

"No comment here. No comment at all. We only wanted to introduce you to one of our very special citizens – little Anthony Fremont, age six, who lives in a place called Peaksville in a place that used to be Ohio. And if by some strange chance you should run across him . . . you had best think only good thoughts. Anything less than that is handled at your own risk. Because if you do meet Anthony you can be sure of one thing. You have entered . . . the Twilight Zone."

Trailer: *"Next week we borrow from the exceptional talent of author Jerome Bixby. It's an adaptation of what has been called one of the most terrifying modern fantasies ever written. What you'll see is in a sense a portrait of a monster as a young boy. Next week's very special excursion into the Twilight Zone is called 'It's a Good Life.' I hope we see you then."*

Trivia, etc. This episode had two days of rehearsals. The first day featured John Larch and Cloris Leachman, while the second day of rehearsal consisted of the entire cast except for Billy Mumy.

The production number was assigned on April 11, 1961, according to an M-G-M work order, without a title. After a week of deliberation as to what title to use, on April 19, it was decided to use the same title as the short story. Principal photography was shot in three days from May 9 to 11. Exterior of the farmhouse was filmed on Lot 3 at M-G-M, while the remainder of the episode was filmed on Stage 8. Inserts for the television screen (the dinosaurs) and the jack-in-the-box were completed on May 18 and inserted into the finished film. Jack Glass and his crew (Virgil Beck as the special effects man, Dick Haager as grip, Cam Rogers as the electrician and Dick Neblett with props) inserted the special effects into the rough cut. The stop-motion dinosaur footage was custom for *The Twilight Zone* by Jack Harris, the same man responsible for supplying the dinosaur footage in the previous *Zone* episode, "The Odyssey of Flight 33."

As Serling explained in the beginning of the episode, the story was somewhat unique and required a different kind of introduction. So different that Serling wrote a number of revisions before settling down with one that worked for the episode. An early draft opened with a panoramic shot of the Ohio countryside and Bill Soames riding his bike to the Fremont house, as Serling began his narration.

This is Peaksville, Ohio, on a hot July afternoon . . .

At this moment an old woman, Aunt Amy, comes out onto the front porch and sits down, rocking slowly back and forth, fanning herself with an old, dilapidated fan.

At a first perfunctory glance and on the surface you may think that this is a town like all towns. And that little boy over there, Anthony by name, appears to be like any little boy.

The camera pans over to Serling who stands near the porch.

But actually none of you have ever seen Peaksville, Ohio. It's a place not to be found on a map. And those fields of grain and wheat and barley that you've seen growing – that isn't the only crop. Something else grows in Peaksville and for want of a better term . . . we're forced to call it simply . . . horror. But let Anthony's father tell you about it. Everybody calls him just 'Dad' Fremont. We'll let him tell the story. And we'll let him describe the horror.

Dad Fremont then breaks the fourth wall and explains to the television viewers how Doc Baker helped deliver Anthony and almost by impulse, attempted to kill the newborn. Anthony, by age 6, had destroyed the world and left only the village. "Anthony's mind will snap at you and he'll do most anything. Most anything at all," he explains to the audience. Dad Fremont explains to the audience how Aunt Amy once yelled at Anthony, and he turned her into the smiling, vacant thing. Anthony introduced to everyone his latest creation, a living, digging creature described by Aunt Amy as "grotesque."

After Bill Soames arrives to make the delivery, Serling's voice closes the scene.

In just a moment we'll get even a closer look at Anthony Fremont and the people of the village and the village itself. Peaksville, Ohio, in a world in which nothing exists except Peaksville. A world that Anthony Fremont manufactured. A nightmare that lies in the center of . . . the Twilight Zone.

The original draft also called for a different kind of television – not an insert shot of dinosaurs. "Hunched over on the floor is Anthony sitting directly in front of it and obviously manipulating it, for on the screen are grotesque color patterns, weird formless lines and shadows. On occasion, a passing face that is only partially humanoid and at intervals there is a sound of some kind of strange, discordant music which Anthony also projects."

The song "Moonglow" was not the original choice of piano music. According to the initial draft, Cole Porter's "Night and Day" was suggested, the same song as featured in the original short story. When Anthony sets his anger toward Dan Hollis, the script did not call for a jack-in-the-box. "As their eyes widen, the women scream. The men turn their heads away. The last close up is that of Ethel who suddenly breaks away from the two men holding her and lets out one long, vast shriek. . . . The shadow of what Dan Hollis is now playing on the wall. It is a wiggly, cobra-like thing which coils and uncoils."

The original short story described the transformation of Dan Hollis "into something like nothing anyone would have believed possible, and then he thought the thing into a grave deep, deep in the cornfield." While the question of "faithful adaptation" is always an arguable point, amongst the additional filming of scenes and revised opening teasers, this episode turned out quite faithful to the short story.

Serling later revised the opening narration, which was recorded but never used:

"I don't know whether you've noticed the looks on the faces of the people you've seen, but what we're

about to show you is one day in their lives and you'll very likely note that the people in Peaksville, Ohio, have to smile. They have to think happy thoughts and say happy things. They have to, by force of will alone, never let the monster know either their hatred, their fear or even the most fleeting fragment of a truth that flits across their minds. Because in Peaksville, Ohio, as you're about to see, men, women and children live in a deep, fathomless pit of burgeoning horror."

After viewing a rough cut, it was decided that additional scenes needed to be filmed and edited for a revised narration written by Rod Serling. Two revisions were composed before it was decided to eliminate Serling's on-screen narration on the farm, and replace it with a separate scene with Serling standing beside a map of the United States. Serling filmed his teaser and opener (with plain background and map of the United States) on May 31.

Having decided to use the opening narrative featured in the episode we see today, the footage of Aunt Amy on the porch was incorporated with additional scenes filmed on June 15, around 1 p.m. on the Farmhouse Street, with two actors in costume (as farmers) walking down the dirt road passing the Fremont farm. On June 16, stills of the empty farmhouse were made. On June 20, 1961, the scene with Billy Mumy on the farmhouse gate was filmed on Stage 5 at Hal Roach Studios, the same gate featured at the end of the episode, "The Last Rites of Jeff Myrtlebank." The scene with Anthony and the gopher tail was also filmed on June 20. "The gopher had hair and it was just truly disgusting," recalled Mumy. "They only used the tail but maybe that was because it was too disgusting and they feared repercussion from the viewers."

Additional scenes with Mumy were going to be filmed on June 21 for inserts, but according to a production sheet, Mumy was ill and unable to visit the studio that morning, so filming of the additional scene was canceled. It was decided later in the afternoon that what had been shot in the can would suffice for the final cut, and Mumy was not asked to return to the set for any additional scenes.

On the same day this episode was initially telecast, *The Hollywood Reporter* featured a half-page advertisement promoting Don Keefer as the star of the evening's *Twilight Zone*.

A few years before his death, Rod Serling wrote a number of drafts for a theatrical motion picture, adapted from the same short story. Alan Landsburg Productions had wanted Serling to narrate a television documentary titled *Chariots of the Gods* and agreed to help with the project. There were a number of scenes described as "graphic" by the few who have read a copy of the screenplay: A rat eats itself into non-existence from the tail up (which was described in Bixby's original story), and the neighbors are grotesquely deformed into monsters. The motion picture never went before the cameras. Joe Dante directed a remake of the same *Twilight Zone* episode, featuring cast members from previous *Twilight Zone* episodes, including Billy Mumy.

When the subject of the filmed remake for *Twilight Zone – The Movie* (1983) came about, Richard Matheson recalled to interviewer Tom Weaver, "I was called to task by a lot of the fans on that one; they cannot stand happy endings, they love to have stories end on a bleak, dark, fatalistic note so that they can all shudder and go, 'Ooo-oo-ooh, wasn't that *wonderful?*' I decided 'Oh, screw it' [laughs] – I wanted to see if I could put a positive ending on it. It didn't work too well, the way it was done, but I still stand by it; up 'til that point I thought that Joe did a marvelous job."

"I had a cameo in the remake," recalled Buck Houghton. "The set of the home had curved tops to door, and the fireplaces were figure eights. It was unlike any house you've ever seen."

In an episode of *The King of Queens*, titled "Tube Stakes," initially telecast on October 18, 1999, the character of Doug gets upset when his television is stolen. He remarks how eerie the possibility

> Many of the props, costumes, paintings and sets in *The Twilight Zone* can commonly be seen in episodes of *The Thin Man*, which was also produced on the M-G-M lot. The marble obelisk that rests on the top of a flight of stairs where Jerry flees past in "A World of Difference" can be seen as a standing prop in *The Thin Man* episode, "A Funny Thing Happened on the Way to the Morgue," initial telecast February 20, 1959.
>
> When Mr. Bevis enters the office of his employer in the episode "Mr. Bevis," the same doors can be seen in the movie studio commissary in *The Thin Man* episode, "The Scene Stealer," initial telecast January 10, 1958.
>
> A television episode of *One Step Beyond* titled "The Stone Cutter" (initial telecast December 8, 1959) featured the same exterior of the Freemont House. The same episode featured a redecorated set of the Sturka living room on Stage 8, from "Third From the Sun." In the episode "Tonight at 12:17" (initial telecast December 5, 1960), the lamp and the painting in the bedroom can also be seen on *The Twilight Zone*.

would be if the television screen had vanished into a cornfield. His wife, uncertain what he is talking about, receives a sarcastic explanation about *The Twilight Zone* and an offer to show her, but he cannot because the television is gone.

In an episode of *The Drew Carey Show*, titled "They're Back," initially telecast on January 8, 1997, Drew wanders into his house looking for his parents, whom he cannot find. He makes a mention in passing that he hopes he did not wish them into the cornfield.

On the evening of February 19, 2003, the UPN Television Network presented a sequel to the original classic, titled "It's Still a Good Life," with Billy Mumy and Cloris Leachman reprising their roles. In the sequel, Bill Mumy plays Anthony Fremont, now a grown man, who has a little girl named Audrey (played by Liliana Mumy), who also possesses the same power. Realizing his daughter may become the problem child he once was, Anthony is forced to succeed with his daughter where others had failed with him and repair the world as it should be.

On the November 3, 1991 telecast of *The Simpsons*, a parody of this episode of *The Twilight Zone* was featured when Bart Simpson took control of the entire town, simply by using his will, and turned his father, Homer, into a jack-in-the-box.

In the episode "Older and Far Away," on the television series *Buffy, the Vampire Slayer*, initially telecast on February 13, 2002, the character of Xander makes a reference to this episode by referring to the cornfield.

Production #4804 "DEATHS-HEAD REVISITED"
(Initial telecast: November 10, 1961)
Copyright Registration: © Cayuga Productions, Inc., November 7, 1961, LP21343
Date of Rehearsal: May 24, 1961
Dates of Filming: May 25, 26 and 29, 1961
Script #67 dated: April 28, 1961, with revised pages dated May 15 and 22, 1961.

Producer and Secretary: $1,375.00

Director: $1,250.00

Unit Manager and Secretary: $600.00

Agents Commission: $2,500.00

Below the line charges (M-G-M): $35,064.26

Story and Secretary: $2,980.00

Cast: $6,386.43

Production Fee: $900.00

Legal and Accounting: $250.00

Total Production Costs: $51,305.69 *

Cast: Oscar Beregi (Captain Gunther Lutze); Robert Boon (the taxi driver); Chuck Fox (the Dauchau victim); Joseph Schildkraut (Alfred Becker); Karen Verne (the hotel clerk); and Ben Wright (the doctor).

Stock Music Cues: Etrange #3 (by Marius Constant, :09); Milieu #1 (by Constant, :16); Silverstone Mansion (by Fred Steiner, :16); Serling II (by Robert Drasnin, :30, :15 and :10); Mysterious Storm (by Jerry Goldsmith, 1:30 and :08); Serling I (by Drasnin, :03); The Meeting (by Goldsmith, :31 and :08); Mysterious Storm (by Goldsmith, :31, 1:01, :04 and :26); Serling I (by Drasnin, :08 and :03); Shock Therapy #1 (by Rene Garriguenc, :02); Shock Therapy #3 (by Garriguenc, :02 and :13); Shock Therapy #4 (by Garriguenc, :31); Shock Therapy #3 (by Garriguenc, :02); Scene of the Crime (by Goldsmith, :39, :08, :12 and :15); Mysterious Storm (by Drasnin, :55); Serling II (by Drasnin, :09); Etrange #3 (by Constant, :08); and Milieu #2 (by Constant, :19).

Director of Photography: Jack Swain

Art Directors: George W. Davis and Phil Barber

Assistant Director: E. Darrell Hallenbeck

Story Consultant: Richard McDonagh

Sound: Franklin Milton and Bill Edmondson

Teleplay by Rod Serling

Production Manager: Ralph W. Nelson

Set Decorations: H. Web Arrowsmith

Casting: Stalmaster-Lister

Film Editor: Bill Mosher

Directed by Don Medford

"Mr. Schmidt, recently arrived in a small Bavarian village which lies eight miles northwest of Munich. A picturesque, delightful little spot onetime known for its scenery . . . but more recently related to other events having to do with some of the less positive pursuits of man. Human slaughter, torture, misery and anguish. Mr. Schmidt, as we will soon perceive, has a vested interest in the ruins of a concentration camp. For once . . . some seventeen years ago, his name was Gunther Lutze. He held the rank of a captain in the S.S. He was a black-uniformed, strutting animal whose function in life was to give pain. And like his colleagues of the time, he shared the one affliction most common amongst that breed known as Nazis . . . he walked the Earth without a heart. And now former S.S. Captain Lutze will revisit his old haunts, satisfied perhaps that all that is awaiting him in the ruins on the hill is an element of nostalgia. What he does not know, of course, is that a place like Dachau cannot exist only in Bavaria. By its nature . . . by its very nature . . . it must be one of the populated areas . . . of the Twilight Zone."

Plot: The small town of Dachau still holds the remains of what was once a concentration camp, left over from the war. While most of the town citizens prefer to burn it to the ground, Captain Gunther Lutze, under the name of Mr. Schmidt, returns to reminisce the days of unforgotten pleasure. While

---

* Total production costs and breakdown from production summary dated July 31, 1961.

wandering the empty buildings, he meets up with Becker, one of his former victims, who tells Captain Lutze that they are beyond the point of forgiveness. Lutze is to be tried for crimes against humanity by a jury of ghosts who linger within the camp. The indictments are brought to light against Lutze, and the wailing of the dead and the crimes charged against him are too much for his ears. The ghosts of his past walk the buildings because their vengeance was not buried deep enough. Within a matter of minutes, Lutze experiences the same tortures he ordered against the anguished – including machine gun bullets, a hangman's noose and inhumane surgery. Some time later, the local doctor commits Lutze to a hospital because the former captain's mind has snapped. Shaking his head, the doctor questions why the camp still stands.

Joseph Schildkraut points an accusatory finger.

"There is an answer to the doctor's question. All the Dachaus must remain standing. The Dachaus, the Belsens, the Buchenwalds, the Auschwitzes. All of them . . . they must remain standing because they are a monument to a moment in time when some men decided to turn the Earth into a graveyard. Into it they shoveled all of their reason, their logic, their knowledge . . . but worst of all, their conscience. And the moment we forget this . . . the moment we cease to be haunted by its remembrance . . . then we become the grave diggers. Something to dwell on and remember . . . not only in the Twilight Zone, but wherever men walk God's Earth."

Trailer: *"This is the lobby of an inn in a small Bavarian town, and next week we'll enter it with a former S.S. officer. It's the first stop on his road back to relive a horror that was Nazi Germany. Mr. Joseph Schildkraut and Mr. Oscar Beregi demonstrate what happens to the monster when it is judged by the victim. Our feeling here is that this is as stark and moving a piece of drama as we have ever presented. I very much hope that you're around to make your own judgment."*

Trivia, etc. Rod Serling was inspired to write this teleplay based on the trial of Otto Adolf Eichmann, referred to by newspaper columnists as "the architect of the Holocaust," who was captured by Israeli Mossad agents in Argentina and put on trial in an Israeli court on 15 criminal charges, including crimes against humanity. Eichmann's trial started on April 11, 1961, and caused a huge international controversy as well as an international sensation. The Israeli government allowed news programs all over the world to broadcast the trial "live" with few restrictions. Within two weeks of the trial's initial telecast in the United States, Serling wrote "Deaths-Head Revisted" – the title was a play on the Evelyn Waugh novel, *Brideshead Revisited*. Various witnesses at the trial included Holocaust survivors, who testified against Eichmann and his role in transporting victims to the extermination camps. Serling borrowed some of that testimony for the dialogue Becker would use against Lutze.

Serling had failed to get Joseph Schildkraut for the lead in "The Obsolete Man," so he offered him the role of Rabbi Heller in the *Playhouse 90* presentation of "In the Presence of Mine Enemies." Schildkraut, through instinct, turned down the role. As Serling later commented, "Laughton, of course, did nothing to help us. How can you show a thin, shabby and yet terribly human sensitivity of a Rabbi in a gross fat-head who eats six meals a day?" In a letter to Schildkraut dated March 8, 1961, Serling apologized for not getting him a role on *The Twilight Zone*, explaining, "I think you're one of the finest talents to come down the pike in the last fifty years. For you to do a show for me would be a unique honor and it's to this end that I'll work."

In the original teleplay, the character of Lutze was named S.S. Lieutenant Oberg, who made his return visit after 18 years after the atrocities. After doing some research about the subject matter, Serling changed the name and made the time frame 17 years.

Assigned a production number on May 11, 1961, this episode featured a Dachau concentration camp, specially created for this production on Lot 3 on M-G-M, where the set of the Gunslinger Fort (used for western movies filmed on the same lot) stood. The cast and crew filmed the interior of the detention camp, the interior of the barracks and the interior of the compound on stage 10 at M-G-M. The the lobby for the hotel in the opening scenes of the episode was filmed on the morning of May 31, on Stage 3 at Hal Roach Studios, with Serling present for his on-screen appearance as host.

The same day that rehearsals began, Serling was on Stage 18 at M-G-M being filmed for promos for season three in the upcoming fall. Sebastian Cabot was also on the same stage being filmed for promos for the *Checkmate* series.

While Schildkraut played the victim and Beregi his tormentor, in truth, the two had been friends for years. Their fathers, also actors, shared billing as well as friendship as far back as 1905, when they worked with the great German director Max Reinhardt. The Beregis moved into the Schildkraut home in Vienna in 1920 when the Schildkrauts moved to America.

"There was a photograph of Pepe (a nickname for Schildkraut) on the wall of the bedroom I occupied," Beregi recalled. "I grew up under that picture for 12 years." The two actually did not meet, however, until 1954, when Beregi arrived in the United States from South America, where he had taken refuge in 1939 from the Nazi regime. Their first professional association was at the La Jolla Playhouse on the Southern California coast, where Schildkraut played the role of Otto Frank in *The Diary of Anne Frank*. Beregi was also in the cast. Later, when the motion picture of the same name was filmed in 1959 for theatrical release, Schildkraut reprised the role he played on stage.

For Beregi, the irony of his *Twilight Zone* appearance was the play's setting – the infamous Nazi camp at Dachau. Beregi narrowly escaped what he assumed would have been a one-way trip there by his timely flight across the Atlantic. Safe in Buenos Aires, Beregi organized the Free German Theatre and a Hungarian exile theatre group. Later, he made Argentina's first anti-Nazi film, *What Happened That Night*.

After filming was completed, on May 31 Schildkraut and Beregi taped loops of their voices on the afternoon because some of the scenes filmed in the yard were not picked up loud enough through the microphone. A final cut was made on June 16, 1961, and on July 7, Schildkraut returned to Sync Room "A" at M-G-M to re-record additional lines that could not be heard clear enough on the finished film.

The November 13, 1961 issue of *The Hollywood Reporter* reviewed this episode of *The Twilight Zone*: "Idea was bold new evidence of author's prowess although action, building to spirit-world version of Eichmann trial with Beregi facing jury of gas chamber specters, seemed less unreal than intended. Impression was that this material called for and got special treatment outside the series format."

This episode prompted a letter from one irate viewer, Mrs. Elmo Holloman of Alexandria, Louisiana, suggesting that Serling had a preoccupation with Nazism on television, might have been an overt act, somehow communist in nature. Serling rejected her notion offhand, and stated "this is simply not true."

Production #4818 "THE MIDNIGHT SUN" (Initial telecast: November 17, 1961)

Copyright Registration: © Cayuga Productions, Inc., November 14, 1961, LP21344
Dates of Rehearsal: August 7 and 8, 1961
Dates of Filming: August 9, 10 and 11, 1961
Script #81 dated: July 21, 1961, with revised pages dated July 31 and August 3, 1961.

Shooting script dated: August 3, 1961
Story and Secretary: $2,855.00
Cast: $4,281.02
Production Fee: $900.00
Legal and Accounting: $250.00
Below the line charges (other): $3,892.03

Producer and Secretary: $1,625.00
Director: $1,315.00
Unit Manager and Secretary: $600.00
Agents Commission: $2,500.00
Below the line charges (M-G-M): $29,314.15
Total Production Costs: $47,532.20 *

Cast: Betty Garde (Mrs. Bronson); June Ellis (the vacating neighbor's wife); William Keene (the doctor); Lois Nettleton (Norma Smith); Tom Reese (the intruder); Robert J. Stevenson (the radio announcer); and Jason Wingreen (the vacating neighbor).

Music Composed and Conducted by Nathan Van Cleave (Score No.CPN6001): Etrange #3 (by Marius Constant, :09); Milieu #1 (by Constant, :16); A Hot Gal (1:48); Here I Stay (1:58); Food (:23); The Frail Human (:45); Beachfront (by Kenyon Hopkins, :48); Paint Cool (:58); Pain (1:06); Thirsty Man (1:04); I'm No Criminal (:57); Exit Mrs. B (1:56); Heat (1:03); Finale (1:14); Etrange #3 (by Constant, :08); and Milieu #2 (by Constant, :18).

Director of Photography: George T.
    Clemens, a.s.c.
Art Directors: George W. Davis and Phil Barber
Casting: Stalmaster-Lister
Film Editor: Jason H. Bernie, a.c.e.
Directed by Anton M. Leader

Production Manager: Ralph W. Nelson
Set Decorations: H. Web Arrowsmith
Assistant Director: E. Darrell Hallenbeck
Story Consultant: Richard McDonagh
Sound: Franklin Milton and Bill Edmondson
Teleplay by Rod Serling

---

* Total production costs and breakdown from production summary dated February 28, 1962.

"The word that Mrs. Bronson is unable to put into the hot, still, sodden air is 'doomed'. . . because the people you've just seen have been handed a death sentence. One month ago, the Earth suddenly changed its elliptical orbit and in doing so began to follow a path which gradually, moment by moment, day by day, took it closer to the sun. And all of man's little devices to stir up the air are now no longer luxuries – they happen to be pitiful and panicky keys to survival. The time is five minutes to twelve, midnight. There is no more darkness. The place is New York City and this is the eve of the end, because even at midnight it's high noon . . . the hottest day in history, and you're about to spend it . . . in the Twilight Zone."

Plot: Case study of a frightened breed known as mankind: doomed to death because, as the scientists theorize, the earth left its orbit and is moving slowly toward the sun. All of the residents of Mrs. Bronson's apartment house have made an attempt to migrate north, except for Norma, a young woman with a passion for painting. As the hours and days pass, the radio announcer starts to lose his marbles, the landlady acts like a wild animal over a cool drink, the electric power stays off for lengthier periods of time, and in one instance, a looter barges into Norma's apartment, driven out of his mind from the present situation. The window sill burns to the touch while Norma cannot paint anything other than the hot sun against the backdrop of a doomed civilization. Eventually the heat is too much when the thermometer explodes, the oils on the canvas start to melt, and Norma screams before collapsing to her death. Waking to discover the whole affair was nothing but a feverish, bad dream, Norma is relieved. In reality, the Earth has left its orbit and is heading away from the sun, and each day will continue to get colder as mankind is doomed to extinction.

"The poles of fear. The extremes of how the Earth might conceivably be doomed. Minor exercise in the care and feeding of a nightmare. Respectfully submitted by all the thermometer watchers . . . in the Twilight Zone."

Trailer: *"Next week we see what will happen to a world that with each passing hour, draws closer and closer to the sun. This is a nightmare in depth in which we watch two doomed women spend their last hours struggling for survival against the fiery orb that moves over the top of a hot, still, deserted city. We call it 'The Midnight Sun,' and we also recommend it most heartily."*

Trivia, etc. Actress Lois Nettleton was reaching stardom by the time this episode of *The Twilight Zone* aired over the network. "I had reached a plateau," she recalled. "I had achieved a certain reputation in show business, but I was not a big name. That meant that I couldn't take parts that weren't good, yet I was not important enough for the major parts. I would audition and be told that I was just right for a part, but I wasn't the name they needed. And I turned down parts offered to me because they weren't big enough for me to take without damaging my reputation."

David B. Graham, of Ashley-Steiner, wrote to Rod Serling on May 20, 1960, pointing out that his client, Lois Nettleton, would be appearing in the title role of "Woman in White" on *Dow Hour of Great Mysteries*, with co-stars Walter Slezak and Arthur Hill. "We strongly urge that you watch Miss Nettleton – she is an extremely talented young woman." This was apparently Serling's initial exposure to the actress. One reference guide incorrectly states that Serling first saw Nettleton in the movie *Period of Adjustment*, but the film was released theatrically in October of 1962. She had found television an ideal medium and appeared on *Naked City*, *Route 66* and this classic episode of *The*

Twilight Zone. "They helped me make a living," she explained, "and when my agent suggested me to M-G-M for *Period of Adjustment*, they knew who I was. They had seen me on *Naked City* and knew me because I made the *Twilight Zone* show at the M-G-M studio."

Lois Nettleton was paid $1,250 for her appearance as Norma Smith. According to paperwork dated August 3, 1961, the name of Norma Smith was supposed to be changed to Norma Forest, but this never happened. Nettleton received first-class round-trip air transportation from New York to Los Angeles. She also received first star billing on the same card as the player receiving the second star billing. "I came out from New York for *The Twilight Zone* and loved every minute of it. The lamps that created the heat on the set helped create the illusion. That's all it was, an illusion. The heat in the studio wasn't enough. Someone was spraying water on our faces between shots. Anton Leader, the director, made all of us feel comfortable on the set. He was the kind of director all method actors longed for on television."

This episode was assigned a production number on July 26, 1961, even though a director had not yet been assigned. Filming commenced on the afternoon of the second day of rehearsals, with scenes of Garde and Nettleton. The entire episode was filmed on Stage 7.

Two scenes filmed for this episode ended up on the cutting room floor due to time restraints. Immediately after the neighbor leaves with his wife and son, and Mrs. Bronson then tells Norma that they are the only two left in the building, a repairman enters the hallway to inform Mrs. Bronson that he has finished fixing the refrigerator in her apartment. He asks if she plans to pay in cash, but she offers a charge card. The repairman explains that his boss ordered him to start collecting cash, under the circumstances. The fee is one hundred dollars. Most outfits, he assures her, are charging double and triple. It's been that way for a month. Mrs. Bronson takes off her wedding ring and offers it as payment, but the repairman cannot accept the ring, and changes his mind, telling her to charge it. Before leaving, he tells her that repairing refrigerators and air conditioning units is only prolonging the inevitable. After the repairman leaves, Norma asks "What happens now?" Mrs. Bronson talks about the scientist on the radio . . . which leads to Serling's opening narration.

The other deleted scene involved a policeman, who arrives wearing his shirt unbuttoned all the way down and with sleeves that have been cut off, ragged and uneven at the elbows. He asks the ladies if they are the only ones in the building. He then explains that the police have been trying to get a public announcement through to everyone left in the city. There will no longer be a police force tomorrow. They are disbanding. He orders them to keep their doors locked. Every wild man, crank and maniac around will be roaming the streets. Asking if they have any weapons, he discovers they don't. The policeman unbuckles his holster and takes a .45 out, handing it to Norma. It's all loaded and the safety is off. All she has to do is pull the trigger. He wishes them luck. Mrs. Bronson stops the officer momentarily to ask what is going to happen to them. He confesses that it's going to get hotter and hotter with each passing day . . . until it is too hot to stand it. Looking meaningfully toward the gun in Norma's hand, he says "then use your own judgment ladies!"

Actor Ned Glass played the role of the refrigerator repairman, and John McLiam played the role of the policeman. McLiam also played the role of the plainclothes detective in the episode "Uncle Simon," and again, for that episode, McLiam's scene ended up on the cutting room floor. Many scenes that ended up on the cutting room floor during production of the third season did survive – including these two scenes. Spliced together to form a brief eight minutes, the unused footage has been screened at film festivals.

On September 12, 1961, additional insert shots were filmed for this episode, which included the thermometer against the window and snow, the heat scenes when the thermometer reached 110, 112 and 118 degrees, and the bursting of the thermometer. An oil painting was furnished, and a woman's hands with a paint brush, were filmed. Close-ups were made of a clock on the table reading 11:45, the radio on the shelf, an electric fan running and then shutting off, and the air conditioner with ribbons extended and the power being cut off. "I can tell you how they accomplished the painting that melted from the heat," revealed Nettleton. "They used wax instead of paint. They put a heater behind the painting and when the wax started to melt, they used that to make the audience believe the heat was causing the oils on canvas to melt."

At one scene towards the end of the episode, Mrs. Bronson crawls over to the painting of a waterfall and remarks how she knew of a waterfall just like that one in Ithaca, New York. This was one of Serling's numerous references to the towns where he grew up.

Serling "may" have gotten the idea for the title (not the plot) from a letter he received on New Year's Eve, 1959, from Jack Kuney of CBS, who described his 12-year-old son's first attempt at stage direction in New Haven, Connecticut – a play called "Midnight Sun." Whether the title was a coincidence or shades of faded memory, it fits well with the subject matter for this episode.

Mr. and Mrs. Schuster's little girl in this episode was selected from a casting call that gave the casting director 6 different girls to choose from, all about 4-years-old in age, and one was selected because she had a somewhat "pleading face."

In March of 1960, Jack Matthews of the E.F. MacDonald Company, specializing in merchandise prize and travel award incentive plans, submitted a brief plot synopsis to Rod Serling, titled "The Sky's the Limit." His tale of Armageddon was considerably different from "The Midnight Sun" and told of a young New York couple, John and Betty Townsend, who faced a desperate race for survival when the gravitational pull of the Earth suddenly gave way. At first, furniture and objects about the house smashed into the ceiling. Manhole covers, sewage, liquids, automobiles and people were whisked into the sky. Buildings such as the one John and Betty resided in, still fastened to the ground, were all that remained. After seeking means of survival and witnessing buildings across the street roaring into the air one-by-one, they realize their hours are dwindling to minutes. In the ensuing deathly stillness, they are suddenly conscious of the faint strains of music. It is coming from another apartment in the building. Following the sound, they make their way through the hallways to the door where laughter can be heard from behind. After knocking and entering, they discover a man with a young girl by his side, standing on the floor (not the ceiling), laughing. The camera closes in for a tight shot of the metal name plate on the door, which reads upside down of course, "Dr. Thomas Barton."

Serling agreed to read the story because Matthews reminded the playwright that many years before, the same company failed to hire a young Antioch student due to his lack of creative ability – or so they thought at the time. Also, Serling agreed to read the story as a gesture to show no ill towards the company, but afterwards he rejected the submission because it did not fit the mold of *The Twilight Zone*.

A film clip of Rod Serling, from this episode, is featured in the episode "Still Life," on *Medium*, initially telecast on November 21, 2005. In the episode, the lead character of Allison witnesses a series of paintings coming to life, one of which features Rod Serling.

Production #4808 "STILL VALLEY" (Initial telecast: November 24, 1961)
Copyright Registration: © Cayuga Productions, Inc., November 21, 1961, LP21345
Dates of Rehearsal: June 21 and 22, 1961
Dates of Filming: June 25, 26 and 27, 1961
Script #70 dated: May 11, 1961
Revised script dated: May 22, 1961

Producer and Secretary: $1,375.00	Story and Secretary: $3,680.00
Director: $1,250.00	Cast: $6,777.31
Unit Manager and Secretary: $600.00	Production Fee: $900.00
Agents Commission: $2,500.00	Legal and Accounting: $250.00
Below the line charges (M-G-M): $30,058.13	Below the line charges (other): $12.75
Total Production Costs: $44,903.19 *	

Cast: Ben Cooper (Dauger); Jack Mann (Mallory); Gary Merrill (Joseph Paradine); Addison Myers (the sentry); Mark Tapscott (the lieutenant); and Vaughn Taylor (the old man).

Original Music Score Composed and Conducted by Wilbur Hatch (Score No. CPN5997): Etrange #3 (by Marius Constant, :09); Milieu #1 (by Constant, :16); Still Valley (:40); Paradine Scouts Enemy (1:17); Deserted Village (1:12); Shock Harmonics (by Fred Steiner, :16); Mysterious Hand (:37); Old Man (:35); Paradine Bewitched (1:55); Witchcraft (1:32); Paradine's Magic (:53); Devil's Bargain (:44); Gettysburg (:33); Etrange #3 (by Constant, :08); and Milieu #2 (by Constant, :18).

Director of Photography: Jack Swain	Production Manager: Ralph W. Nelson
Art Directors: George W. Davis and Phil Barber	Set Decorations: H. Web Arrowsmith
Assistant Director: E. Darrell Hallenbeck	Casting: Stalmaster-Lister
Story Consultant: Richard McDonagh	Film Editor: Bill Mosher
Sound: Franklin Milton and Bill Edmondson	Directed by James Sheldon

Teleplay by Rod Serling, based on the short story "The Valley Was Still" by Manley Wade Wellman, originally published in the August 1939 issue of *Weird Tales*.

"The time is 1863. The place the State of Virginia. The event is a mass blood-letting known as the Civil War. A tragic moment in time when a nation was split into two fragments – each fragment deeming itself a nation. This is Joseph Paradine, Confederate Cavalry, as he heads down toward a small town in the middle of a valley. But very shortly, Joseph Paradine will make contact with the enemy. He will also make contact with an outpost not found on a military map. An outpost called . . . the Twilight Zone."

Plot: A scout for the Confederates, Joseph Paradine, wanders into a small town at the bottom of Channow Valley, only to find every Union soldier frozen in his tracks in the middle of the streets. He rules out all the possibilities . . . a virus, a plague, and time certainly isn't standing still. Seeking

---

* Total production costs and breakdown from production summary dated July 31, 1961.

a rational explanation, he finds an old man, a former resident of the town, who claims he was solely responsible for the deed. As the seventh son of a seventh son, he made a practice of witchcraft like his father before him and uses words from his special book to freeze the Yanks in their tracks. He proposes freezing the entire Union Army in its tracks and end the war, but he won't – he can smell death around the corner and knows he won't be alive come sunrise. Passing the book of witchcraft to Paradine, he gives the scout an opportunity to serve his cause. Paradine takes the book back to camp and makes his reports to the lieutenant. Paradine convinces his commander that while there is something not clean about the whole affair – being in league with the Devil – he can conjure up a spell and guarantee the success of the Confederate Army. After an exchange of words, Paradine throws the book into the fire, sending their chances up in flames – believing that if the book is used, they will be damned, a risk he dares not accept.

"On the following morning, Sergeant Paradine and the rest of these men were moved up north to a little town in Pennsylvania, an obscure little place where a battle was brewing, a town called Gettysburg . . . and this one was fought without the help of the Devil. Small historical note not to be found in any known books, but part of the records . . . in the Twilight Zone."

Trailer: *"Next week we move back into time – back to 1863. A distinguished actor, Mr. Gary Merrill, plays the role of a Confederate scout who goes off on a patrol and winds up smack dab in the center of The Twilight Zone. Our story is an adaptation of a strange tale by Manley Wade Wellman called 'The Still Valley.' This one is for Civil War buffs and the students of the occult. I hope you're around to take a look at it."*

Trivia, etc. After Serling revised his script on May 22, he forwarded the draft to the De Forest Research Group, which studied the contents and reported back to Serling on May 31, 1961, with a number of suggestions. In the beginning of the script, when Paradine and Dauger exchange words, Dauger proposed they "wave an undershirt," but De Forest suggested the line be changed to "wave a shirt," since an undershirt was not a common article of clothing during the time period. Serling made the change.

Before Paradine rides into town, he informs Dauger that "if you hear a rifle shot that means" to return and report to the commander in charge. The line was changed to: "if you hear a shot" because cavalrymen were armed with carbines.

When the old man tells Paradine that he could clear a path straight to Washington, D.C., the report explained that the nation's capital was not admitted to the union till 1889. Serling changed it to read simply "Washington," with the initials deleted.

Serling's opening narrative placed the setting in May of 1863, but the month was removed when the De Forest pointed out that the battle was not intended, and therefore no one could know of it until July 1. Serling left the year in place, but removed the month.

Paradine's line suggesting "hypnotism" was not accepted by De Forest, who said that "in 1863, the term most popularly applied to the phenomena we now call hypnotism was mesmerism. The word hypnotism did not come into popular usage until circa 1880." Serling, however, kept the word "hypnotism" in the script.

The short story from which this episode was adapted was described by George Clayton Johnson as "surrealism" and regarded by the writer as an elegant piece of writing.

The production number was assigned to this episode on June 13, 1961. The first day of filming took place on Lot #3 at M-G-M, in the boomtown area, for the exterior of the village street. All of the street scenes were filmed on this lot. The second and third day of filming took place on Stage 5 at the Hal Roach Studios, for the exterior of the porch, the campfire site and the Confederate camp.

Addison Myers and Mark Tapscott went in for wardrobe on May 26, the day before their scenes were required for filming. For the Union soldiers standing still in the street, 50 men were interviewed for the freeze effect and 35 were selected. Call sheets required no heavyset or pot bellies. Extras had to be lean, healthy types, with long hair and no crew cuts. Three of them were selected for Union generals. Among the men posing as still figures were Dave Armstrong, Ron Brown, Craig Harding, James Kessler, Bob McCord and James Turley.

In the original draft of the script, after the book is tossed into the fire, Paradine learns from Dauger that they will be moving on to a little town called Gettysburg. "Gettysburg," Paradine remarks, "Well, this one we'll have to fight without the Devil." After that, Serling commented:

"In a time to come during what will be Joseph Paradine's old and garrulous years . . . he'll tell anyone willing to listen that the Civil War wasn't lost at Antietam or Gettysburg or Shiloh. Rather, he'll insist, the Confederacy was buried in a little valley hamlet called Channow. People will probably laugh or pity him when he insists that the South lost a war because they refused a certain alliance. But we need neither laugh nor pity because we know the nature of that alliance. Such alliances are the norm rather than the exception . . . in the Twilight Zone."

"I was in awe of Gary Merrill at the time," recalled Ben Cooper, when he was a guest at the 2000 Knoxville Film Festival. "Merrill was a veteran. He was on the set on time, he knew his lines, and he knew how to overplay his role. I assumed that Merrill researched the subject, and Civil War scouts were like that, because of the tasks they had to perform. Jim, the director, is a good friend of mine. We had been friends for years. Jim told me aside that I was to play my role down a bit, so Gary Merrill would shine on stage.

The 34-star flag in this episode was accurate for the year 1863. One reference guide claims the flag showed 50 stars but this is inaccurate. Civil War historians have viewed the footage from this episode and verified the number of stars was accurate.

Production #4806 "THE JUNGLE" (Initial telecast: December 1, 1961)

Copyright Registration: © Cayuga Productions, Inc., November 28, 1961, LP21346
Date of Rehearsal: June 16, 1961
Dates of Filming: June 19, 20, 21 and 22 1961
Script dated: May 22, 1961, with revised pages dated June 13, 1961.

Producer and Secretary: $1,625.00   Story and Secretary: $2,755.00
Director: $1,250.00   Cast: $5,672.50
Unit Manager and Secretary: $600.00   Production Fee: $900.00
Agents Commission: $2,500.00   Legal and Accounting: $250.00
Below the line charges (M-G-M): $43,642.98   Below the line charges (other): $1,570.63
Total Production Costs: $60,766.11 *

---

* Total production costs and breakdown from production summary dated February 28, 1962.

Cast: Jay Adler (the street vagrant); Walter Brooke (Chad Cooper); John Dehner (Alan Richards); Donald Foster (Mr. Sinclair); Bob McCord (bartender); Emily McLaughlin (Doris Richards); Jay Overholts (the taxi driver); Hugh Sanders (Mr. Templeton); and Howard Wright (Mr. Hardy).

Stock Music Cues: Etrange #3 (by Marius Constant, :09); Milieu #1 (by Constant, :16); Big City Moods, Version A (by Fred Steiner, :14); Shock Chord (by Lucien Moraweck, :05); Passacaglia (by Steiner, :40); Captain Embry (by Steiner, :37); Mad Harpsichord (anonymous, :02); Indochinese Gong (anonymous, :02); Batterie Exotique (a.k.a. "Exotic Drums" by Pierre Henry, :25); Serling III (by Robert Drasnin, :22); Threatening Anger (by Rene Garriguenc, :03); Big City Moods, Version A (by Steiner, :18); Six Shot Dissolves, Version A6 (by Nathan Van Cleave, :08); Beverly Hills (by Alan Bristow, 1:45); Emotional Suspense – Walt Whitman Suite (by Bernard Herrmann, :05); No Joking (by Steiner, :05); Shock Chord (by Moraweck, :02); Agony (by Garriguenc, :05); Sand (by Steiner, :16); Etrange #3 (by Constant, :08); and Milieu #2 (by Constant, :18).

Director of Photography: George T. Clemens, a.s.c.
Art Directors: George W. Davis and Phil Barber
Casting: Stalmaster-Lister
Film Editor: Jason H. Bernie, a.c.e.
Automobiles Supplied by Ford Motor Company

Production Manager: Ralph W. Nelson
Set Decorations: H. Web Arrowsmith
Assistant Director: E. Darrell Hallenbeck
Story Consultant: Richard McDonagh
Sound: Franklin Milton and Bill Edmondson
Directed by William Claxton

Teleplay by Charles Beaumont, based on his short story of the same name, originally published in the December 1954 issue of *If* magazine.

"The carcass of a goat, a dead finger, a few bits of broken glass and stone . . . and Mr. Alan Richards, a modern man of a modern age, hating with all his heart something in which he cannot believe . . . and preparing . . . although he doesn't know it . . . to take the longest walk of his life, right down to the center of the Twilight Zone."

Plot: Alan and Doris Richards have recently returned from a trip to Africa, because Alan is an engineer for a hydroelectric plant being constructed in the heart of the continent. Though he's not a superstitious man, Alan soon finds himself suffering from the ill effects of a curse placed on him (and the company he works for) by a witch doctor who is against the project. Forced to walk home alone through the silence of the sleeping city, Alan hears the sounds of drums and animal cries roaring through the streets. The city itself becomes a jungle as Alan makes a desperate attempt to reach home safely. The impending danger grows when he attempts to walk through the park to get to his apartment and races as fast as his legs can take him. Back home, Alan feels secure in the knowledge that a witch doctor's curse couldn't possibly reach him inside his own house . . . until he opens the door of his bedroom. A lion jumps off the bed and shreds him to death.

"Some superstitions kept alive by the long night of ignorance have their own special power. You'll hear of it through a jungle grapevine in a remote corner . . . of the Twilight Zone."

Trailer: *"Next week on the Twilight Zone, we once again borrow the talents of Mr. Charles Beaumont, who's written a script especially for us called 'The Jungle.' Now this is designed for the reasonably impressionable* *amongst you who find nothing to laugh about when somebody mentions the words 'black magic.' Mr. John Dehner stars in another small excursion into the darker regions of the imagination. Next week, 'The Jungle.'"*

Trivia, etc. When Beaumont submitted the story to Buck Houghton during production of the second season, they argued over the devices needed to pull it off on film. The score was zero to zero – in Houghton's favor. "Basically his point seems to be that the original story is right the way it is, only we can't afford to do the original story, and my ideas for revision are workable but not too exciting," Beaumont told Serling. "He thinks there are too many concessions, too many watering-downs, too little that is new and fresh."

Beaumont's proposed treating was to open the story in New York, where the protagonist has returned from Africa. A scientific society dinner is being held for him in honor of his splendid achievements on the Dark Continent. These achievements, when completed, will have desecrated holy territories and bring shame, possibly death, upon large groups of people. As a scientist, he cares little about the cost of human life in his effort to further science. His wife, having seen tiny gods pop up in their penthouse apartment, begs her husband to call off his work. He does not heed the warnings, and returning from a trip out of the city, he discovers the silence of a sleeping New York giving way to the sounds of the jungle. He refuses to take a taxi. Madly, he rushes to his apartment, shutting the door at the last moment before something invisible pounds in the hallway. Silence in the penthouse is interrupted by noise from the bedroom. He finds an African lion standing over the fallen figure of his wife, and the lion springs. Man and beast fill the camera with blackness, and they fall out of the scene. The audience is left seeing only the lion's tail, thrashing madly, and hearing the sounds of feeding . . .

Serling talked to Houghton and Del Reisman (who was story editor at the time) and encouraged them that the story should be adapted for *The Twilight Zone*, against their better judgment. Months later, during production of the third season, the story was reconsidered and the first draft of the script was due contractually by Charles Beaumont by April 27, 1961. After turning it over to Houghton, Serling looked over the script and made a few suggestions. The initial script referred to the company Alan worked for as the "International Development Projects" but at the advice of CBS, to ensure no similarity to a real company of the same name, it was simply referred to as "the company." When Alan tells the cab driver that he wants to be taken to the Schuyler House, the name was changed on the June 13 revision to Schuller House to avoid possible legal issues, as there was a Schuyler House in New York City.

"I recall Bill [the director] telling me that I had the sort of character that had to believe that voodoo stuff," recalled John Dehner. "I was instructed not to smile during the entire film. . . . Take everything serious. I guess it was my saturnine face that cinched it for me. The real challenge was to stay within the marks. They had me run through a park and it was late at night. The sun had set so they placed these markers in the earth so I would run within view of the camera. My job was to keep looking behind me, because something was chasing me through the park. I had difficulty

The Twilight Zone was not telecast on the evening of December 8, 1961. In this time slot, CBS offered the second in a series of original, full-hour dramas for *Westinghouse Presents*. Titled "Come Again to Carthage," Piper Laurie, Ann Harding, Arthur Hill and Joan Hackett joined special guest star Maurice Evans.

looking behind me and down in front of me to see the markers without Bill shouting for me to stop and do another take. The camera was moving alongside of me as I ran, but I kept getting out of range. I couldn't look at the markers and look behind me at the same time. As I recall we spent quite a while getting the run through and I got home way after midnight."

This episode was assigned a production number on June 5, 1961. The interior of the council room was filmed on Stage 4. The interior of Reilly's bar was intended to be shot on Stage 27, instead it was located on Stage 16. Production was intended for a three-day shoot, but ran an additional day. Dehner was the only actor required for the extra day, for shots of Cohn Park on Lot 2 and the interior of the Richards apartment on Stage 20. The jungle sounds of monkeys, bird calls and the lion were synched into the soundtrack on the afternoon of August 7, 1961, at M-G-M's Sync Room "A."

Production sheet prop numbers show the small white horse used as a decoration on the table in the living room was the same featured in "The Silence" and "A Most Unusual Camera." One of the framed photos hanging on the wall in the bar is the same featured on the wall in the bar scene of "Person or Persons Unknown." The jukebox in the bar is the same one from "Mr. Dingle, the Strong." The street scene in which Richards walks at night is the same street on Lot 2 used for the entrance of the apartment house in "The Fugitive" and where Lou Bookman pitched to Mr. Death in "One for the Angels."

The music group "The Queers" recorded an album in 1994 titled *Beat Off*, which contains the song "Voodoo Doll," in homage to this specific episode of *The Twilight Zone*.

Production #4820 "ONCE UPON A TIME" (Initial telecast: December 15, 1961)

Copyright Registration: © Cayuga Productions, Inc., December 12, 1961, LP21470
Dates of Rehearsal: September 6 and 7, 1961
Dates of Filming: September 8, 11 and 12, 1961
First draft dated: June 23, 1961
Script #81 dated: August 4, 1961

Producer and Secretary: $1,625.00
Director: $1,750.00
Unit Manager and Secretary: $600.00
Agents Commission: $2,500.00
Below the line charges (M-G-M): $48,217.62
Total Production Costs: $67,250.76 *

Story and Secretary: $2,405.00
Cast: $7,056.67
Production Fee: $900.00
Legal and Accounting: $250.00
Below the line charges (other): $1,946.47

Cast: Stanley Adams (Rollo); Beau Anderson (man in car); Dave Armstrong (man in car); Jim Crevoy (boy on skates); Jack Clinton (man in car); Hank Faver (man in car); James Flavin (policeman from 1962); Harry Fleer (the second policeman from 1962); Buster Keaton (Woodrow Mulligan); Gil Lamb (policeman from 1890); Bob McCord (utility man in car); Warren Parker (the clothing store manager); Milton Parsons (Professor Gilbert); George E. Stone (Fenwick); Jim Turley (man in car); and Jesse White (Jack, the fix-it-shop owner).

---

* Total production costs and breakdown from production summary dated February 28, 1962.

Original Music Score Composed by William Lava (Score No. CPN6017), performed on piano by Ray Turner: Etrange #3 (by Marius Constant, :09); Milieu #1 (by Constant, :16); Setting the Scene (by Lava, 1:35); Old MacDonald (traditional, arr. by Lava, :06); Assembly (traditional, abb. by Lava, :04); Anvil Chorus (by Giuseppe Verdi, arr. Lava, :08); Old Grey Mare (traditional, arr. by Lava, :06); Kersplash (by Lava, :19); Wring Them Clothes (by Lava, :31); Into the Basement, Ka Poof (by Lava, 3:20); Poet and Peasant (by F. Von Suppe, arr. by Lava, :24); John's Jump (by Johnny Dankworth, :05); Back to 1890 (by Lava, :45); One Week Later (by Lava, 2:13); Ruben and Rachel (traditional, arr. by Lava, :04); Ka Poof Again (by Lava, :30); Etrange #3 (by Constant, :08); and Milieu #2 (by Constant, :18).

Director of Photography: George T. Clemens, a.s.c.	Production Manager: Ralph W. Nelson
Art Directors: George W. Davis and Phil Barber	Assistant Director: E. Darrell Hallenbeck
Set Decorations: Phil Barber and H. Web Arrowsmith	Casting: Stalmaster-Lister
Sound: Franklin Milton and Bill Edmondson	Story Consultant: Richard McDonagh
Automobiles Supplied by the Ford Motor Company	Film Editor: Jason H. Bernie, a.c.e.
	Directed by Norman Z. McLeod
	Teleplay by Richard Matheson

"Mr. Mulligan, a rather dour critic of his times, is shortly to discover the import of that old phrase, 'Out of the frying pan, into the fire' . . . said fire burning brightly at all times . . . in the Twilight Zone."

Plot: Woodrow Mulligan, a resident of New York 1890, is not content with the progress of time. The speed limit has been raised to 8 miles per hour, the cost of living is going up, and oh – the noise from the blacksmith and street peddlers! Working under the employment of Professor Gilbert, Mulligan tries on a new invention — a time helmet designed to transport the wearer to another time, but only for 30 minutes. He finds himself whisked to 1962 where the high cost of living is substantially more and the noise is intolerable. When Mulligan realizes the time helmet is damaged, he goes through a series of comedic efforts with an electronics expert to have the helmet repaired before the 30 minutes expires. He succeeds in his task, returning to 1890, now content with the time period he lives in. As for the scientist from 1961, who traveled back to 1890 with Mulligan, he finds the decade barbaric with few of the conveniences to which he was accustomed. Mulligan uses the helmet to send him back.

"'To each his own' So goes another old phrase to which Mr. Woodrow Mulligan would heartily subscribe, for he has learned, definitely the hard way, that there is much wisdom in a third old phrase which goes as follows: 'Stay in your own backyard.' To which it might be added – And, if possible, assist others to stay in theirs – via, of course, the Twilight Zone."

Trailer: *"Next week on the Twilight Zone, we bring to the television cameras a most unique gentleman . . . whose own very special brand of clown-ship has long ago become a milestone in American humor. Mr. Buster Keaton appears in 'Once Upon A Time,' a script written especially for him by Richard Matheson. This one is wild, woolly, and most unpredictable. On the Twilight Zone next week, Mr. Buster Keaton in 'Once Upon A Time.'"*

Trivia, etc. Comedies did not crop up too often on *The Twilight Zone*. "It's really just a matter of how absurd we want to make the stories," Buck Houghton explained to a reporter. "Obviously, if we establish Buster Keaton as a janitor living in 1890 who accidentally puts a helmet on his head and suddenly discovers himself in 1962, in the middle of a busy intersection without his pants on, then comedy will have a field day."

Norman McLeod had directed W.C. Fields, Groucho Marx, Danny Kaye, Bob Hope and Red Skelton during his 40 years in Hollywood, but it wasn't until this *Twilight Zone* episode that he worked with a comedian that pre-dated them all – Buster Keaton. Although McLeod and Keaton both arrived in Hollywood four decades previous, they had only been social friends, never once sharing screen billing.

"Buster always seemed to have a staff of directors swarming about him," McLeod told Dick Isreal, publicity man of CBS, on the set during a break in filming. McLeod directed such famous comedy films as *Topper* (1937) and *Topper Takes a Trip* (1938), plus *If I Had a Million* (1932) and *It's a Gift* (1934), the last two starring W.C. Fields. "Bill Fields was without doubt the greatest comedian of all time," McLeod remarked. "His talent really took on an indescribable quality. He knew his limitations and that was the key to his success plus his delivery. Bill disliked gag situations and gag writers."

McLeod was in semi-retirement at the time he was asked to direct this episode of *The Twilight Zone*. He took on occasional television directing assignments for pocket money when the jobs interested him. This production marked his final contribution behind the camera as his health took a steady decline after filming.

After costume fittings, Keaton and Adams rehearsed their scenes for two days before filming commenced (though McLeod did film a few shots on the evening of the second day).

Richard Matheson wrote the script (original title on the June 23, 1961 draft was "The Buster Keaton Story") with Keaton in mind. Matheson knew the actor through his friend and fellow writer, William R. Cox. Matheson was paid $1,125.00 for his story and for the first and final draft of the script. The initial script varied considerably from what we view today. The 1890 scenes were not filmed with the intention of playing like a silent movie. The episode opened with Serling's narration lengthier than the finished film.

Witness now the approach of one Mr. Woodrow Mulligan – resident of the good town of Harmony, New Jersey in this, the year of our Lord, 1890. The saturnine Mr. Mulligan is en route to his duties as a janitor for Harmony's one and only inventor. Mr. Mulligan is a rather dour critic of his times – a critic, be it added, who is, shortly, to discover the import of that old phrase: 'Out of the frying man into the fire.' Said fire burning brightly at all times – in The Twilight Zone.

All of the 1890 scenes featured spoken dialogue, with Mulligan's discontent of the government's spending, citizens owning horseless carriages, and the cost of sirloin steak. When used in the finished film, the necessary dialogue was replaced with on-screen intertitles. His confrontation with the policeman and the man on the bicycle was preserved, as was his visit to Professor Gilbert's laboratory where the professor, with trembling hand, announces "The Helmet of Tomorrow."

In the initial draft, Rollo and Mulligan spend most of the 1962 scenes running about in a food market, with Rollo making the adjustments and corrections during the comedic scenes. The purpose of the food market was because Rollo needed to purchase a replacement for a television tube, which was installed on the helmet. The police officer who was spending time looking for Mulligan, catches up to the time traveler in the store, and when Mulligan explains to Rollo that he brought a chicken with him, just by holding it, Rollo disbelieves him and runs out of the food market.

After viewing the rough cut, Buck Houghton and Rod Serling admitted the film needed something unique. Someone on the production crew came up with the idea of taking all of the 1890 scenes and altering them to replicate a silent film. There would be no synchronized sound for dialogue and on-screen intertitles would be inserted. Until the standardization of the projection speed in 1926, most silent films appeared unnaturally fast and jerky. To recreate this effect, the film editor cut out a frame here and there from the film. Piano music substituted the spoken dialogue, specially composed to comment on the action. The effect was magic and television audiences were treated to what appeared to be a silent film pulled from the vaults.

Serling's introductory narration, however, was already filmed before the decision was made to create the 1890 scenes in silent film form. To adjust for this, his introduction was shortened, and his onscreen role was placed at the end of the first few scenes, in sound, briefly breaking the silent movie illusion. The signpost next to him during this scene is out of the era (a blooper that the editors either overlooked, or hoped the audience would not catch).

On October 27, 1961, Keaton returned to M-G-M Studios to film additional scenes. It had been decided that the food market scenes were to be replaced with scenes in a fix-it shop. Some exterior scenes on Boomtown Street on Lot #3, exterior scenes of the small town street on Lot 2 and interior shots of the fix-it shop on Stage 19 were filmed. This was for additional scenes of the 1890s period blacksmith, a thin-faced boy of 18 or 19 to fake playing the clarinet, and scenes with Adams and White in the shop toying with the tools. Les Goodwins directed those scenes.

Any observant folks who have watched this episode more than once may have noticed that the 1890 scenes filmed on Boomtown Street featured the same landmarks where Rance McGrew and Jesse James faced off in the episode "Showdown with Rance McGrew."

Variety reviewed, "To excellent effect, the 1890 sequences were done in the silent vogue with perfect piano accomp by some unsung 88er. Most striking was the contrast between the silence and sound as Keaton projected himself ahead 80 years. A much older clown attacked the sight gags and pratfalls with real courage, allowing for some fine nostalgia."

This episode was assigned a production number on August 14, 1961. Except for the additional retakes in October, 80 lunches were provided for the cast and crew, which included tables and benches, coffee and donuts for all three days.

The final shot in this episode, as the camera pans up to the stars, reveals the top of the wall that was specially constructed on Stage 18. The film editor was supposed to fade the scene out, and the stars were to fade in, but apparently not quick enough before the audience is allowed a glimpse of the top of the set, revealing no ceiling in the basement laboratory. The final chords of William Lava's composition, performed on piano in that same closing scene, features a rendition of Constant's "Etrange #3" for a few seconds.

The sign posted on the brick wall in the beginning of the episode, advertising "Nelson's Buggy Whips, Est. 1836," was a tip of the hat to Ralph W. Nelson, the production manager.

Production #4805 "FIVE CHARACTERS IN SEARCH OF AN EXIT"
(Initial telecast: December 22, 1961)
Copyright Registration: © Cayuga Productions, Inc., December 19, 1961, LP21471
Dates of Rehearsal: June 5 and 6, 1961
Dates of Filming: June 7, 8 and 9, 1961

Script #68 dated: May 16, 1961

Producer and Secretary: $1,625.00
Director: $1,250.00
Unit Manager and Secretary: $600.00
Agents Commission: $2,500.00
Below the line charges (M-G-M): $36,003.42
Total Production Costs: $54,736.51 *

Story and Secretary: $3,455.00
Cast: $6,760.80
Production Fee: $900.00
Legal and Accounting: $250.00
Below the line charges (other): $1,392.29

Cast: Clark Allen (the bagpipe player); Kelton Garwood (the hobo); Susan Harrison (the ballerina); Carol Hill (the woman); Mona Houghton (the little girl); Murray Matheson (the clown); and William Windom (the Army major).

Stock Music Cues: Etrange #3 (by Marius Constant, :09); Milieu #1 (by Constant, :16); Chris Walks (by Fred Steiner, 1:07 and :03); Bagpipe Improvisation (anonymous, :34); Curiosity (by Steiner, 1:06); Jets (by Steiner, :36); Auld Lang Syne (traditional, :05); Bagpipe Improvisation (anonymous, :14); Serling III (by Robert Drasnin, :45): Serling I (by Drasnin, :03); Tension Dramatic Crescendo Through Chords (by Nathan Van Cleave, 1:12); Chris Jr. (by Steiner, :33); Tension Dramatic Crescendo Through Chords (by Van Cleave, :36); Chris Walks (by Steiner, :03); Prayer (by Steiner, :29); Curiosity (by Steiner, :48); Serling III (by Drasnin, :03 and :02); Etrange #3 (by Constant, :08); and Milieu #2 (by Constant, :18).

Director of Photography: George T.
    Clemens, a.s.c.
Art Directors: George W. Davis and Phil Barber
Casting: Stalmaster-Lister
Makeup: William Tuttle
Sound: Franklin Milton and Bill Edmondson

Production Manager: Ralph W. Nelson
Set Decorations: H. Web Arrowsmith
Assistant Director: E. Darrell Hallenbeck
Story Consultant: Richard McDonagh
Film Editor: Bill Mosher
Directed by Lamont Johnson

Teleplay by Rod Serling, based on an original short story titled "The Depository" by Marvin H. Petal.

"Clown, hobo, ballet dancer, bagpiper and an Army Major. A collection of question marks. Five improbable entities stuck together into a pit of darkness. No logic. No reason. No explanation. Just a prolonged nightmare in which fear, loneliness, and the unexplainable walk hand-in-hand through the shadows. In a moment we'll start collecting clues as to the why's, the what's, and the where's. We will not end the nightmare . . . we'll only explain it. Because this . . . is the Twilight Zone."

Plot: Five people wake to find themselves in a deep, circular pit, unaware of who they are, where they are, how they got there and how long they will remain. Judging by the costumes they wear, their professions are truly varied – a bagpipe player, a clown, a ballerina, an Army major and a hobo. Not only do they question their identities, but their prison as well. Could they be in an alien spacecraft? Could this be a mirage? Perhaps they are dead and this is limbo. The only thing certain is the loud

---

* Total production costs and breakdown from production summary dated February 28, 1962.

ringing that echoes in their ears every so often, and the only exit is up above. In desperation, the five of them stand on each other's shoulders to reach the top of the pit. After two attempts they succeed. The Army major reaches the top, losing his balance and falls over the edge. Outside in the snow, a little girl picks up a small doll of an Army major and puts it back in the barrel. Their identities revealed: they are merely unwanted dolls donated to the Viewpark Girls Home for the 17th Annual Christmas Doll Drive. Down inside the barrel, the dolls remain motionless, and the ballerina sheds a tear for she is aware of her identity and the fact that they were all unwanted.

"Just a barrel . . . a dark depository where are kept the counterfeit, make-believe pieces of plaster and cloth wrought in the distorted image of human life. But this added hopeful note . . . perhaps they are unloved only for the moment. In the arms of children . . . there can be nothing but love. A clown, a tramp, a bagpipe player, a ballet dancer and a major. Tonight's cast of players on the odd stage known as . . . the Twilight Zone."

Trailer: *"Next week on the Twilight Zone, you'll find yourself inexplicably entangled in this dark dungeon. You'll meet an incredible group of people who, like you, will be quite unable to explain how they got there, why they got there, or how they're going to get out. And at the end, we're going to belt you with one of the most surprising endings we've ever had. Next week, 'Five Characters in Search of an Exit,' on the Twilight Zone."*

Trivia, etc. "I was trying out a career as a young writer," recalled Marvin Petal. "I wrote several sports shows and a syndicated documentary series called *Confidential File*. I also wrote for a series of court cases called *Youth Court*, about the juvenile court system and another called *Municipal Court*. It was broadcast on my local station, KTLA, Channel 5, the key station of the Paramount network. I was going with a young lady at the time, whose brother-in-law was an attorney for Universal Studios. Through him I attended a Democratic Rally held at the home of Robert Ryan. That was about 1960, I guess, and it was for the Democratic Party in general. I knew Rod Serling was going to be there so I typed a synopsis about 4 or 5 pages called 'The Depository' and wrote the whole scenario on speculation, mostly with dialogue. I approached Serling at the party and said, 'Listen, I have a story that I think would make a great script for Twilight Zone.' Serling said, 'Well, submit it to my producer, Buck Houghton.' So I did and they said 'Okay, we'll buy it but Rod wants to do the script' which I believe paid about $2,000. I was paid only $250 and no residuals. As many times as that episode has been re-run on television, I regret not getting any residuals."

On May 29, 1961, "The Depository" was assigned a production number and on May 31, the title was officially changed to "Five Characters in Search of an Exit," a play on the title of Luigi Pirandello's 1921 stage drama, *Six Characters in Search of an Author*.

On May 29, actor Kelton Garwood reported to the

Production Schedule at M-G-M

Day 1 – Exterior of Main Street, Exterior of the Business District, and the Busy Intersection (Lot #2) Keaton in the Interior of the Science Lab and Cellar (Stage 20)

Day 2 – Exterior of Main Street (Lot #2) Exterior of the Small Town (Lot #3)

Day 3 – Exterior of the Warehouse Alley (Lot #2) Interior of the Fix-it Shop and Interior of the Cellar and Lab (Stage 18) makeup department at M-G-M so an imprint of his face could be made. From this, a mask in his image would be furnished, so in the closing scene, the body of the hobo on the life-size doll would appear as realistic as possible. The other actors would soon follow. On June 5 and 6, rehearsals were done with the five principal players, on Stage 5 in a set specially constructed to resemble the interior of a barrel.

"They changed the title of the original story because, as they explained to me, they felt it sounded too much like 'suppository,'" Petal recounted. "So they changed the title," recalled Petal. "Rod kept the story pretty damn close to how I had it. I believe he took out one character, but it was pretty much the same as I had written it. I recall they were worried about how they were going to produce it. The vertical climb was a challenge for them, but I suggested they build half of the huge container and make it horizontal and that is how they shot it. I wasn't on the set when they filmed it, but they took my suggestion and went with it. I never saw Serling before that party and I never saw him since."

"When we made that episode at M-G-M, Susan Harrison and I got into a bit of a disagreement," recalled William Windom. "I thought my part was larger than hers, so I wanted top billing, but her agent was pushing back. I forget who got top billing. I also remember how the entire set was constructed so it could be tilted. In the scene when we stand on each other's shoulders, the tube was tilted so we wouldn't hurt each other."

Most of the scene with the dolls standing on top of each other's shoulders were not the real actors. This stunt was supplied by Ray Saunders, Russ Saunders, Patti Saunders, Bill Couch and Chuck Couch in costume. The wardrobe for the cast of characters was also supplied by Patti Saunders, who took on the task while employed at the M-G-M costume department. She only worked for the studio a very brief time, and her career in Hollywood left very little on film except for a brief appearance in an episode of the television series *Peter Gunn*.

Considerable expense went into the construction of the barrel, but only half of one was required since the camera was positioned from the side facing the interior. After filming was completed, the barrel was stored at M-G-M for future productions. The outside of the half-barrel was reused for "No Time Like The Past," placed upside down so Harvey could stand on top and operate the time travel controls. According to a production report for Daystar Productions, in *The Outer Limits* episode "The Inheritors – Part Two," the barrel was altered so it could be used as part of the spaceship being constructed. The same barrel was later cut down to size and again altered so it could be used in another episode of *The Outer Limits*, "The Probe."

The street scenes toward the end of the episode that take place outside the barrel were filmed on Lot 2 at M-G-M. The little girl who picks up the doll and returns it to the barrel is Mona Houghton, daughter of the producer.

The last scene in this episode did not require the actors to lie still at the bottom of the barrel. Mannequins were used for the end sequence, designed to look exactly like the actors who played their counterparts – using masks furnished from the week before.

On December 12, 1963, Ruth Smilan, head of foreign relations of the Israel Broadcasting Service, wrote to CBS, asking for "an English or French text of the play *Cinq personnages qui cherchent une sortie*, by Rod Serling, which was presented by your station to the *Prix Italia 1963*." CBS Television sent an English version text of this episode, after Serling granted approval.

There have been several nods to this classic *Twilight Zone* episode. Actor Murray Matheson would later play the role of Mr. Agee in the "Kick the Can" segment in *Twilight Zone: The Movie*

(1983). The same concept would be explored in "Child's Play," an episode of *Hammer House of Mystery and Suspense*, initially telecast May 2, 1986, involving a family of robot dolls who discover they are trapped inside a doll house. This *Twilight Zone* episode was supposedly an inspiration for the 1997 motion picture, *Cube*.

In "Help for the Lovelorn," an episode of the television series *Felicity*, initially telecast on January 23, 2000, a direct take-off on this *Twilight Zone* episode and "The Chaser" was featured in a loving tribute. Director Lamont Johnson took the helm. The entire episode was presented in black and white, featuring *Twilight Zone*-style screen credits, and music commonly heard on *The Twilight Zone*.

Production #4809 "A QUALITY OF MERCY" (Initial telecast: December 29, 1961)
Copyright Registration: © Cayuga Productions, Inc., December 26, 1961, LP21472
Date of Rehearsal: June 28, 1961
Dates of Filming: June 29, 30 and July 3, 1961
Script #72 dated: May 23, 1961, with revised pages dated May 31, 1961.

Producer and Secretary: $1,625.00
Director: $1,250.00
Unit Manager and Secretary: $600.00
Agents Commission: $2,500.00
Below the line charges (M-G-M): $29,032.00
Total Production Costs: $48,514.18 *

Story and Secretary: $3,206.00
Cast: $7,681.25
Production Fee: $900.00
Legal and Accounting: $250.00
Below the line charges (other): $1,469.93

Cast: Rayford Barnes (Watkins); Peter Beathard (U.S. Infantry #4); Wayne Dehmer (U.S. Infantry #3); Richard Fong (Japanese #1); Gaylord Hsieh (Japanese #2); Konji Inouye (Japanese #3); Dale Ishimoto (Non-Commanding Officer); Thomas Kato (Japanese #4); J.H. Fujiyama (Captain Nakagawa); James Kessler (U.S. Infantry #2); Bob McCord (U.S. Infantry #1); Marlin McKeever (U.S. Infantry #5); Leonard Nimoy (Hansen); Michael Pataki (the jeep driver); Bill Pinckard (U.S. Infantry #6); Dan Saito (Japanese #5); Albert Salmi (Sgt. Causarano); Hank Slade (U.S. Infantry #7); Dean Stockwell (Lt. Katell/Lt. Yamuri); James Turley (U.S. Infantry #8); Ralph Votrian (Hanachek); and Warren Yee (Japanese #6).

Stock Music Cues: Etrange #3 (by Marius Constant, :09); Milieu #1 (by Constant, :16); Lowering Sky (by Laurence Rosenthal, :50 and :28); Convening Jury (by Leonard Rosenman, :28); Enter Paladin (by Rosenman, :25); Day Camp (by Lucien Moraweck, :24); Hanging Offense (by Fred Steiner, :16 and :16); Mystery Man (by Steiner, :18); Shooting Lesson #1 (by Rene Garriguenc, :06); Horn String on E (anonymous, :01); Harp Stings (by Steiner, :01); Celestial Call #4 (by Rosenman, :25); Harp Stings (by Steiner, :03); Desperation (by Rosenman, :15); Fake Pearls (by Jerry Goldsmith, :08); Confusion (by Rosenman, :44); Bad Man (by Steiner, :25); Shooting Lesson #1 (by Garriguenc, :06); Final Celestial Call (by Rosenman, :38); Etrange #3 (by Constant, :08); and Milieu #2 (by Constant, :18).

---

* Total production costs and breakdown from production summary dated February 28, 1962.

Director of Photography: George T.
  Clemens, a.s.c.
Art Directors: George W. Davis and Phil Barber
Casting: Stalmaster-Lister
Film Editor: Jason H. Bernie, a.c.e.
Directed by Buzz Kulik
Teleplay by Rod Serling, based on an original story idea by Sam Rolfe.

Production Manager: Ralph W. Nelson
Set Decorations: H. Web Arrowsmith
Assistant Director: E. Darrell Hallenbeck
Story Consultant: Richard McDonagh
Sound: Franklin Milton and Bill Edmondson

"It's August, 1945. The last grimy pages of a dirty, torn book of war. The place is the Philippine Islands. The men are what's left of a platoon of American infantry whose dulled and tired eyes set deep in dulled and tired faces can now look toward a miracle . . . that moment when the nightmare appears to be coming to an end. But they've got one more battle to fight. And in a moment we'll observe that battle. August, 1945, Philippine Islands . . . but in reality . . . it's high noon . . . in the Twilight Zone."

Plot: Since the war isn't going to end before dinner time, Sergeant Causarano and his men wait to see what can happen to a group of worn-out Japanese who are trapped within a cave, unreachable by heavy weaponry. A bloodthirsty lieutenant named Katell arrives to take command, ordering the battle-fatigued platoon to prepare to advance on the cave. With no concern or dignity for human life, Lieutenant Katell believes that the enemy is destined for a killing, regardless of the plea for compassion from Sergeant Causarano. Before the advance can be made, Lieutenant Katell finds himself misplaced in time – Corregidor, May 1942. He is now a Japanese lieutenant named Yamuri and finds himself being ordered about by Captain Nakagawa, a bloodthirsty commander who wants to eliminate the 20 or 30 wounded Americans trapped inside a cave. Yamuri pleads with the captain to have compassion for the wounded Americans, but his pleas are ignored. Returning to the year 1945, Lieutenant Katell receives news of an atomic bomb dropped on Japan. The new orders are to fall back to see if the war ends in the next couple days. Katell, having worn the shoe on the other foot, agrees to fall back without hesitation.

"'The quality of mercy is not strained. It droppeth as the gentle rain, from heaven upon the place beneath. It blesseth him that gives and him that takes.' Shakespeare, 'The Merchant of Venice,' but applicable to any moment in time, to any group of soldiery, to any nation on the face of the Earth. Or . . . as in this case . . . to the Twilight Zone."

Trailer: *"Next week Mr. Dean Stockwell makes his journey into the Twilight Zone, playing the role of a platoon lieutenant on Corregidor during the last few hours of World War II. What happens to him provides the basis of a weird and yet, we think, haunting excursion into the shadow land of imagination. On the Twilight Zone next week, Mr. Dean Stockwell stars in 'The Quality of Mercy.'"*

Trivia, etc. Sam Rolfe, the co-creator of *Have Gun – Will Travel* and future producer and co-creator of *The Man From U.N.C.L.E.*, submitted this plot idea to Serling, who made arrangements for the purchase. Rolfe was committed to submitting a script based on his plot proposal, but was unable to do so, leaving Serling the task of drafting the teleplay. This was not Rolfe's only intended contribution to the series. One script Rolfe was contracted to deliver was "The Calculator," first draft due contractually by May 8. This was never produced.

This episode was set in a locale where Serling himself was after enlisting in the U.S. Army. Following basic training, he went to the Pacific as part of an assault and demolitions team. In 1945, while he was fighting in the Philippines, his father died of a heart attack at the age of 52. "We notified Rod through the American Red Cross," recalled his brother Bob, for the premiere issue of *Rod Serling's The Twilight Zone Magazine* (April, 1981). "He asked for an emergency leave and was refused."

This sort of rejection would have displeased any man serving abroad – possibly suggesting that the character of Causarano in this episode was the basis for Serling's disgruntlement against military superiors who felt the death of the enemy was more important than moral compassion.

A production number was not assigned to this episode until June 26, which is odd because post production began before the episode was assigned a production number. Wild narrations with Japanese actors for the background soundtrack were recorded on June 21 in Sync Room "A" at 4:30 p.m. The narrations were originally scheduled for June 20, but pushed ahead a day so Serling could use the studio on that day to record his voice-overs. On June 27, Stockwell, Ishimoto, Fujikawa and Barnes went in for wardrobe fittings. On June 28, Salmi and Stockwell conducted rehearsals. Filming commenced on June 29. The scenes of the hilltop were filmed on Stage 5 at Hal Roach Studios. The rock set was filmed on Lot 3 at M-G-M.

In the original script, the opening scene of this episode begins with a jeep pulling up toward the infantry's position, entering the clearing and stopping. Lieutenant Katell arrives almost immediately, described as "a 20-year-old shave-tail whose fatigues shine with creased newness." He climbs out of the jeep, looks around at the bearded, dirty, tired-looking men who survey him, yanks at his duffel bag and sends it falling to the ground. He looks briefly over at Hanachek and makes his entrance. When a number of pages went through a revision, the opening was extended so Katell did not arrive in the opening scene.

Serling's love of writing stories about the war would extend beyond this episode. In the summer of 1964, he approached CBS News president Fred W. Friendly about a "documentary in depth" in which the network proposed Serling write and narrate about Corregidor. He had passed through the Philippine bastion during WWII and, having done a recent personal appearance tour, found it a place of "rack and ruin" and was "tremendously enamored" with the idea. "It was," Serling explained, "historically the low ebb of United States military fortunes and yet has great dignity."

Production #3662 "NOTHING IN THE DARK" (Initial telecast: January 5, 1962)
Copyright Registration: © Cayuga Productions, Inc., January 2, 1962, LP21469
Date of Rehearsal: April 14, 1961
Dates of Filming: April 14, 17 and 18, 1961

Producer and Secretary: $1,375.00	Story and Secretary: $1,685.00
Director: $1,250.00	Cast: $5,599.19
Unit Manager and Secretary: $560.00	Production Fee: $825.00
Agents Commission: $2,500.00	Legal and Accounting: $250.00
Below the line charges (M-G-M): $23,957.07	Below the line charges (other): $1,556.30
Total Production Costs: $39,557.56 *	

---

* Total production costs and breakdown compiled from two production summaries dated June 30, 1961 and February 28, 1962.

Cast: R.G. Armstrong (the man); Gladys Cooper (Wanda Dunn); and Robert Redford (Harold Beldon / Mr. Death).

Stock Music Cues: Etrange #3 (by Marius Constant, :09); Milieu #1 (by Constant, :16); Repeated Major Seconds (anonymous, :17); Eerie Theme (by Lucien Moraweck, 1:52); Howe's Place (by Fred Steiner, :06); Defeat (by Jerry Goldsmith, :24); Shake Down (by Goldsmith, :05); Caught in the Act (by Goldsmith, :26); Confession (by Rene Garriguenc, 2:23); Improvised Humming (anonymous, :12); Secret Circle (by Goldsmith, 1:22); Confession (by Garriguenc, :46 and :14); Magdalena 5 – Legend (by Lyn Murray, :10); Confession (by Goldsmith, :14); Secret Circle (by Goldsmith, :52); Shock Chord (by Lucien Moraweck, :03); Caught in the Act (by Goldsmith, :09); The Plot (by Goldsmith, :34); Confession (by Garriguenc, :12); Perry Mason Background (by Steiner, :08); Deep Thoughts (by Goldsmith, :09); The Plot (by Goldsmith, :06); Secret Circle (by Goldsmith, :36 and :57); The House (by Bernard Herrmann, 1:18); Hitch-Hiker, Part 7 (by Herrmann, :26); Curtain (by Herrmann, :18); Hitch-Hiker, Part 8 (by Herrmann, :03); Etrange #3 (by Constant, :14); and Milieu #2 (by Constant, :25).

Director of Photography: George T. Clemens, a.s.c.
Art Directors: George W. Davis and Phil Barber
Casting: Stalmaster-Lister
Film Editor: Jason H. Bernie, a.c.e.
Directed by Lamont Johnson

Production Manager: Ralph W. Nelson
Set Decorations: H. Web Arrowsmith
Assistant Director: E. Darrell Hallenbeck
Story Consultant: Richard McDonagh
Sound: Franklin Milton and Bill Edmondson
Teleplay by George Clayton Johnson

"An old woman living in a nightmare. An old woman who has fought a thousand battles with death and always won. Now she's faced with a grim decision . . . whether or not to open a door. And in some strange and frightening way she knows that this seemingly ordinary door . . . leads to the Twilight Zone."

Plot: A police officer is shot and wounded outside the front door of an abandoned tenement where a frightened old woman resides. Against her better judgment, she pulls the young man in and nurses his wounds – even fixing him warm tea. She has no telephone to call a doctor. She explains to the young man that Mr. Death is out there, waiting for the opportunity to take her away. In fear of her life, she has spent the past few years fending off people whom she feared was Mr. Death in disguise. Late that afternoon, a city contractor barges into her place to inform her that she has to leave – the building has been condemned and his job is to tear down the old to make room for the new. The contractor leaves, warning her she has just one hour to pack her belongings. Before she can decide what to do, she discovers that her guest went unseen by the contractor – because the young officer is Death himself. In an attempt to reassure her that the running is over, he gains her confidence and takes her by the hand. Looking down at her frail, cold body, her fears are put aside. What she thought would come like an explosion, comes in a whisper . . . and in the afterlife, she has an incredible journey ahead . . .

"There was an old woman who lived in a room and, like all of us, was frightened of the dark. But who had discovered in the minute last fragment of her life that there was nothing in the dark that wasn't there when

the lights were on. Object lesson for the more frightened among us, in or out . . . of the Twilight Zone."

Trailer: *"Next week an excursion into the shadow-land of the hereafter. Miss Gladys Cooper and Mr. Robert Redford combine sizable talents to bring you a script by George Clayton Johnson entitled 'Nothing in the Dark,' the dark in this case being the little nooks, crannies, and closets of those regions presided over by Mr. Death. I hope you'll be with us next week for 'Nothing in the Dark.'"*

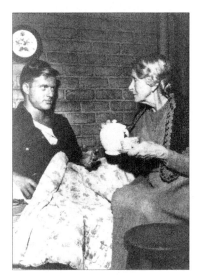

Robert Redford and Gladys Cooper
in "Nothing in the Dark."

Trivia, etc. According to an interoffice memo, this film was originally slated to close the second season on June 2, 1961, but was instead shelved and replaced with "The Obsolete Man." According to a letter from Buck Houghton to CBS, the idea behind removing two new shows from the end of the summer 1961 schedule for use on the new season was to give the series a running jump for season three. The producers were content that there were already two good episodes ready for broadcast before filming of the third season was commissioned.

This episode was assigned a production number on April 3, 1961. Rehearsals began on April 14, and by late afternoon that same day, a few scenes were filmed. The entire episode was produced on Stage 3 at M-G-M. One camera had to be moved to M-G-M from the Hal Roach Studios for this episode (reason for the move remains unknown). The entire set for the tenement apartment cost a total of $890.

"We were invited to watch the screening after the first day of filming and sitting in the back was Robert Redford," recalled George Clayton Johnson. "He was covering his face during most of the showing and when the film was done, he walked out and left without speaking to anyone. Later I was told that Redford did not like himself in the film. But I thought – and still think – that he was absolutely perfect. He was down to earth, attractive, and what you would expect from a man who represented death. When Lamont Johnson played the film for Gladys Cooper later, because she had to rush out and do something else after the filming completed, he told me she kept commenting about her performance, saying 'Oh, that poor old woman . . .'"

"I recall how everyone from the director . . . to the actors . . . to the designers had everything ready from the moment we began filming," recalled Robert Redford. "It was so laid out that by the time we finished the last scene, it felt like a few hours passed by. Gladys Cooper was a wonderful woman to work with, and a pro all the way. That was a good script, too. Of course, no one ever thought then that [the episode] would become a classic and shown around the world like it is today. I don't prefer to look back at my earliest efforts but I have to admit, to this day, I am proud of that one."

Beau Vanden Ecker (last name spelled a variety of ways in numerous television productions) was responsible for the wardrobe for this episode. He handled the wardrobe for other television programs produced at M-G-M, such as *Combat!* and *The Man From U.N.C.L.E.* For this production, he sought out costumes for Gladys Cooper and Robert Redford that were of French design.

"I tend to want to be a perfectionist, because these guys, like Bradbury, have shown me that perfection is possible, and so, therefore, desirable," recalled Johnson to interviewer Matthew R. Bradley. "I must say in all modesty, I have achieved it myself with 'Nothing in the Dark.' I think that Gladys Cooper thing, with Robert Redford, is perfect. I look at it and think, 'What would you change, George? Is there anything in there that would make you flinch, or isn't so good as you can possibly get it, as good as somebody that you would admire would get it? Is this the sort of thing you admire in Bradbury?' I look at this story, as it goes along, and say, 'Yes, this is it.'"

In an episode of *Strange Frequency*, titled "Don't Fear the Reaper," initially telecast on November 11, 2001, one of the characters is watching this *Twilight Zone* episode on the television screen.

Production #4823 "ONE MORE PALLBEARER" (Initial telecast: January 12, 1962)

Copyright Registration: © Cayuga Productions, Inc., January 9, 1962, LP21467 (in notice: 1961)
Date of Rehearsal: September 25, 1961
Dates of Filming: September 26, 27 and 28, 1961
Script #85 dated: September 18, 1961, with revised pages dated September 21, 1961.

Producer and Secretary: $1,625.00
Director: $1,250.00
Unit Manager and Secretary: $600.00
Agents Commission: $2,500.00
Below the line charges (M-G-M): $32,609.33
Total Production Costs: $51,138.58 *

Story and Secretary: $2,855.00
Cast: $6,964.19
Production Fee: $900.00
Legal and Accounting: $250.00
Below the line charges (other): $1,585.06

Cast: Trevor Bardette (Colonel Hawthorne); Gage Clarke (Mr. Hughes, the reverend); Josep Elic (the speaking electrician); Ray Galvin (the policeman); Robert Snyder (the silent electrician); Katherine Squire (Mrs. Langford, the schoolmarm); and Joseph Wiseman (Paul Radin).

Stock Music Cues: Etrange #3 (by Marius Constant, :09); Milieu #1 (by Constant, :16); Dreams, Part 2 (by Wilfred Josephs, :24); Serling I (by Robert Drasnin, :33); Fantasies Parts 1 and 2 (by Josephs, 1:13); Serling II (by Drasnin, :24 and :26); Serling I (by Drasnin, :29); Serling II (by Drasnin, :35); The Hunter (by Jerry Goldsmith, 1:06); The Victor (by Goldsmith, 1:32); Serling III (by Drasnin, :05); Etrange #3 (by Constant, :08); and Milieu #2 (by Constant, :18).

Director of Photography: George T.
    Clemens, a.s.c.
Art Directors: George W. Davis and Phil Barber
Casting: Stalmaster-Lister
Film Editor: Bill Mosher
Produced by Buck Houghton
Directed by Lamont Johnson

Production Manager: Ralph W. Nelson
Set Decorations: George R. Nelson
Assistant Director: E. Darrell Hallenbeck
Story Consultant: Richard McDonagh
Sound: Franklin Milton and Bill Edmondson
Teleplay by Rod Serling

---

* Total production costs and breakdown from production summary dated February 28, 1962.

"What you have just looked at takes place three hundred feet underground, beneath the basement of a New York City skyscraper. It's owned and lived in by one Paul Radin. Mr. Radin is rich, eccentric and single-minded. How rich we can already perceive – how eccentric and single minded, we shall see in a moment, because all of you have just entered . . . the Twilight Zone."

Plot: Wealthy industrialist Paul Radin funds the construction of a fake underground bomb shelter that, for all intents and purposes, is designed to fool anyone who hears the fake sound effects and sees the footage on the view screen. Radin invites three people from whom he feels he unjustly suffered indignities in the past. Hawthorne, his former colonel in the war, was responsible for Radin's court-martial, stripping him of his rank and dishonorably discharging him. Mrs. Langford, a former high school teacher, flunked Radin for cheating and humiliated him in front of an entire class. Mr. Hughes, a reverend, once condemned Radin because the multi-millionaire drove a young girl to suicide to achieve his goals. After Radin's history lesson and an exchange of opinions, the multi-millionaire offers them sanctuary in his shelter in exchange for their unconditional apology. But none of the guests will oblige. Instead, they prefer to head for the surface and be with their loved ones. Upset because he did not receive the apology he expected, Radin's mind snaps, believing that the hydrogen bomb was dropped. He now lives in a fantasy world where he is the sole occupant.

"Mr. Paul Radin . . . a dealer in fantasy . . . who sits in the rubble of his own making and imagines that he's the last man on Earth, doomed to a perdition of unutterable loneliness because a practical joke has turned into a nightmare. Mr. Paul Radin, pallbearer at a funeral that he manufactured himself . . . in the Twilight Zone."

Trailer: *"Next week on the Twilight Zone, we let you in on an extravagant practical joke – a man who wants to convey an illusion that the world is coming to an end. Now there are jokes, and there are jokes, but this one stands all by itself as an exercise in the very different, and the very bizarre. Our play is called 'One More Pallbearer,' and we commend it to you as something quite special."*

Trivia, etc. This episode was assigned a production number on September 19, 1961. The four principal players conducted a rehearsal on September 25. The bare corridor, elevator and bare room were filmed on Stage 10 at M-G-M. All of the scenes involving Radin and his three guests were completed by the afternoon of the second day, whereupon the camera crew and actor Wiseman relocated to Lot 2 at M-G-M to film the exterior of the New York Street. On the morning of the third day, the scenes with Radin and the installers in the shelter were completed on Stage 10, and then the camera crew and Wiseman moved to Stage 27, where the exterior of the wrecked street and bomb wreckage were filmed. Stage 27 was the largest at M-G-M studios, which formerly served as "Munchkin Land" for the 1939 motion picture, *The Wizard of Oz*.

In the first draft of this script, titled "Only One Pallbearer," Serling conceived the story taking place beneath the basement of "a fashionable brownstone on the east side of New York." This was changed to "a New York City skyscraper" by the time the final draft was completed.

The scene in which Mrs. Langford tells Paul Radin what she thought of him and recommended he set up a shrine of mirrors so he would not be lonely was inspired by a scene in *Talk of the Town* (1942), in which actress Jean Arthur, as Miss Nora Shelley, finally stands up to a lawyer played by

Ronald Colman, speaking her mind and recommending he not shave off his beard so his world of perfection would remain unchanged.

Originally Serling conceived of doing a commercial at the end of the trailer, adding: *"Twenty one fine tobaccos, combined to make twenty exceptionally fine smokes. The name is Chesterfield. Once smoked – they're liked, and you come back for more. Put it to a test and see for yourself – Chesterfield."*

The Hollywood Reporter made a very brief mention of this episode, remarking: *"Twilight Zone* sparkled with a fine performance by Joseph Wiseman."

The phone Paul Radin handles in this episode is the same featured in Sturka's house in "Third from the Sun."

To ensure the accuracy of the "Red Alert" that was to be delivered through the speaker system during this episode, Serling commissioned the De Forest Research Group to uncover just what would be said in the event of a real emergency. De Forest put together a two-page radio announcement, and submitted it to Serling on April 28, 1961. None of the actors heard the audio message during rehearsals or filming, since the recording was made separately and sections of the recording were placed into the sound track of the finished film. Director Lamont Johnson gave the cue by reading the lines for the actors to believe they were hearing the "red alert," and they performed accordingly. The red alert was recorded on October 11, 1961 in Sync Room "B" from 6:00 to 6:30 p.m. The following is a reprint of the two-page announcement that was recorded for the series. While only a section of this recording was heard on the episode, the complete text is offered to you now.

RED ALERT

This is your Civil Defense Announcer, (name). Our military authorities have just ordered a take-cover alert. Attack by enemy forces is imminent. Take cover immediately. If you are in your car driving away from your city, continue. Keep on driving. Do not stop. When movement is no longer possible, seek the best available refuge. If you're outdoors on foot, hurry to the nearest shelter but drop to the ground the instant you see a brilliant flash. Face away from the blast and shield your face and hands. As soon as you feel a shock wave pass over you, get up and continue to the nearest shelter. This is your Civil Defense announcer, (name), repeating.

The Air Defense Command has just declared a take-cover signal. This is not a practice warning, not a drill. An attack by enemy forces is expected at any moment. You must seek the nearest shelter immediately. If you are in your home, go to the prepared shelter, or to the basement. If you have no shelter or basement go toward the center of the house, to the first room or hall that will put as many walls as possible between you and the outside of the house. Take your radio with you. If you are in any other type of building, go to the basement or lowest floor and get as close to the center of the building as possible. When you have reached the center of whatever type of building you're in, lie flat, face down under a table, desk or anything else large enough to crawl under. Stay in the building until you are instructed to come out. If you're in your car, keep driving as long as you can, but roll down the windows till you see a brilliant flash of light. Then roll the windows up tight. If you're outdoors on foot, hurry to the best available refuge, but drop to the ground the instant you see a brilliant flash. If possible, drop into a ditch, hole or depression in the ground. Keep your back to the flash. Shield you face and hands as best you can, stay in that position till you feel a shock wave pass over you, then get up and go quickly to the nearest shelter. Do not waste time. Your safety depends on your ability to act calmly, but quickly. This is not a test nor a practice. This is a real, take-cover alert. It has been ordered by the air defense command because attack by enemy forces is expected momentarily. Seek the best available shelter immediately. If you are in your car, do not leave it. Keep driving as long as you can. Roll down the windows until you see a bright flash. Do not look towards the flash. As soon as you see it, roll the windows tight shut. If you're at home go to your prepared shelter or to the basement. If you have no shelter or basement, go towards the center of the house to the first floor hall that will put as many walls as possible between you and the outside of the house. Take your radio with you. If you're in any other type of building, go to the basement or lowest floor and get as close to the center of the building as possible. When you reach the center of whatever building you are in, lie flat, face down under a table, desk or anything else large enough to cover you even partially. If you're outdoors on foot, head for the best available refuge, but the instantly you see a bright flash drop to the ground with your back to the flash. Do not look toward the flash. If possible, drop into a ditch, trench, hole or any depression in the ground. Lie there in a curled up position and shield your face and hands as best as you can. As soon as the shock wave passes over you, get up and hurry to the best available refuge. Whatever type of building you're in, stay there until advised to come out. You will be given advice either by your Conelrad announcer on the radio or by a civil defense worker. We repeat. Do not leave your shelter until told it is safe to do so. This is not a test. This is a real take-cover alert.

Production #4824 "DEAD MAN'S SHOES" (Initial telecast: January 19, 1962)
Copyright Registration: © Cayuga Productions, Inc., January 16, 1962, LP21468 (in notice: 1961)
Date of Rehearsal: October 1, 1961
Dates of Filming: October 2, 3 and 4, 1961
Script #87 dated: September 28, 1961

Producer and Secretary: $1,625.00
Director: $1,250.00
Unit Manager and Secretary: $600.00
Agents Commission: $2,500.00
Below the line charges (M-G-M): $26,424.97
Total Production Costs: $40,956.37 *

Story and Secretary: $1,655.00
Cast: $4,125.00
Production Fee: $900.00
Legal and Accounting: $250.00
Below the line charges (other): $1,626.40

Cast: Dave Armstrong (hood); Jack Bonigal (the bartender); Eugene Borden (the maitre d'); Richard Devon (Bernie Dagget); Billy Gart (bum); Ron Hagerthy (Ben); Marilyn Malloy (pedestrian #1); Florence Marley (Dagget's woman); Joan Marshall (Wilma); Bob McCord (Bernie's assistant); Joe Mell (Jimmy); Murray Pollack (pedestrian #2); Frieda Rentie (piano player); Warren Stevens (Nathan Bledsoe); Harry Swoger (Sam); and Ben Wright (Chips, the bum).

Stock Music Cues: Etrange #3 (by Marius Constant, :09); Milieu #1 (by Constant, :16); Scene of the Crime (by Jerry Goldsmith, :27); The Gun [The Terror] (by Goldsmith, :21); The Caper (by

* Total production costs and breakdown from production summary dated February 28, 1962.

Goldsmith, 3:03 and :20); The Warning (by Goldsmith, :17); The Caper (by Goldsmith, :08); Hopes (by Goldsmith, :03); The Meeting (by Goldsmith, 1:18); The Big Time (by Goldsmith, :34); Hopes (by Goldsmith, :06); The Big Time (by Goldsmith, 1:12); The Caper (by Goldsmith, :30); Hopes (by Goldsmith, :05); The Big Time (by Goldsmith, :52); Too Many Ideas (by Goldsmith, :12); Brother and Sister (by Goldsmith, :30); The Meeting (by Goldsmith, :43 and :18); Serling III (by Robert Drasnin, :02); Piano Improvisation #3 (by Martian Solal, 2:05); Piano Improvisation #2 (by Solal, 2:16); The Meeting (by Goldsmith, 1:09); The Warning (by Goldsmith, :14); Scene of the Crime (by Goldsmith, :24); The Gun (by Goldsmith, :45); The Meeting (by Goldsmith, :23); Serling III (by Goldsmith, :05); Etrange #3 (by Constant, :08); and Milieu #2 (by Constant, :18).

Director of Photography: George T. Clemens, a.s.c.	Production Manager: Ralph W. Nelson
	Set Decorations: H. Web Arrowsmith
Art Directors: George W. Davis and Phil Barber	Assistant Director: E. Darrell Hallenbeck
Casting: Stalmaster-Lister	Story Consultant: Richard McDonagh
Film Editor: Jason H. Bernie, a.c.e.	Sound: Franklin Milton and Bill Edmondson
Automobiles Supplied by the Ford Motor Company	Directed by Montgomery Pittman
	Teleplay by Charles Beaumont

"Nathan Edward Bledsoe, of the Bowery Bledsoes: a man, once – a spectre now, one of those myriad modern-day ghosts that haunt the reeking nights of the city, in search of a flop, a handout, a glass of forget-fulness . . . Nate doesn't know it but his search is about to end. Because those shiny new shoes are going to carry him into the capital . . . of the Twilight Zone."

Plot: The dead body of a hoodlum named Dane is disposed of in an alley. When a panhandler named Nathan steals the shoes and puts them on, the personality of Dane begins to take over. Visiting his apartment for a shower and a shave, Dane (now in the body of Nathan) orders his girl to be there when he gets back, and he sets off to conduct some unfinished business. Visiting a nightclub, he insists on meeting his former business partner, Bernie, to deliver a message. In Bernie's private office, Dane recounts how Bernie attempted to buy his partner out, and when the option failed – he killed Dane. Bernie starts to suspect that the spirit of his ex-partner has come back in the form of another man and tries to eliminate Nathan. Gun shots are exchanged from a hidden panel behind the bookshelf and the body of Nathan drops to the floor. Bernie looks over the body as the man swears to his dying breath that, "I'll be back, Bernie, and I'll keep coming back, again and again." After Bernie and his goons dispose of Nathan's body in the alleyway, another hobo comes along and seeing the shiny pair of shoes, puts them on . . . .

"There's an old saying that goes, 'If the shoe fits, wear it.' But be careful. If you happen to find a pair of size 9 black-and-gray loafers, made to order in the old country, be very careful . . . you might walk right into . . . the Twilight Zone."

Trailer: *"Next week, through the good offices of Mr. Charles Beaumont, we take a walk in some 'Dead Man's Shoes.' It's the story of a hobo who takes some shoes off of a recently deceased hoodlum and then discov-ers that if the shoe fits . . . you have to wear it – and, in this case, you have to do as the shoes do – go where* *they tell you to, and then perform some services above and beyond the norm. I hope we see you next week for ... 'Dead Man's Shoes.'"*

Trivia, etc. Assigned a production number on September 26, the first and second day of filming were shot on Stage 21 at M-G-M, for all the interior shots of the corridor, living room, bath, and the office. On the afternoon of the second day, the cast and crew moved over to Stage 4 for shooting in the nightclub. On the third and last day, filming commenced at 6:30 p.m. and ran through midnight so that the exterior shots of the alley, skid row street and high-class neighborhood could be filmed at night on Lot 2. This was the same lot and alley where Horace Ford would be beaten in "The Incredible World of Horace Ford."

The initial plot synopsis for this story was titled "Venus in the Garage" and later renamed "Down to Earth," before Beaumont settled on "The Reluctant Genius." Basic rights were sold to Cayuga for $500 for this story (which initially concerned a cowboy hat instead of a pair of shoes). An August 16, 1960 progress report said the first draft of script #53, "The Reluctant Genius," was completed. On September 24, 1960, Buck Houghton sent an interoffice memo to Rod Serling, explaining where they stood on the cost of production on the most recently completed episodes, and a few of the ones to come. "'Acceleration' is tough to contain," he explained, "so is 'Reluctant Genius' . . . unless early ratings or reviews overwhelm CBS, I don't see how we can support a plea for film. It does no good to be dubious about tape costs for the peculiarities of *Twilight Zone* – CBS ain't dubious. Six tapes look like $42,000 in the bank to them. I can't believe it, if I continue to make the quality-motivated decisions I have made in the past, but they do."

The script titled "The Reluctant Genius" was originally scheduled for production on October 6, 7 and 10, with rehearsal dates of October 4 and 5. Buzz Kulik was slated as director. But since the script required a rewrite, (according to an October 7, 1960 progress report), the dates of filming pushed ahead a whole year, and once again retitled to "Dead Man's Shoes."*

In July of 1960, Ocee Ritch finished the first draft of the teleplay, since Beaumont was facing the demands of writing other teleplays, short stories and articles for magazines. While Beaumont received credit on screen for the script, Ocee Ritch was responsible for writing the teleplay, based on the story synopsis Beaumont pitched to Houghton. Beaumont envisioned the idea as "a comedy of incongruities," suggesting Wally Cox or Tony Randall play the lead.

(As for "Acceleration," Beaumont was paid $2,000 for the script and story. He wrote to Serling after Houghton rejected it, explaining, "I dig the script and feel strongly that, properly cut and tightened, it could be a hell of a thing. The ending could be melodramatic, but every part of me says, no, this is right, this is what'll kill 'em.")

The script was written for this episode back in late October and early November 1960, when Beaumont quickly turned it over to Houghton to fulfill the last commitment of his current five-picture contract. Houghton wrote to Sam Kaplan of Ashley-Steiner, explaining his position on the script, "which we feel is extremely difficult to do on tape without extensive revisions – perhaps even then not tailoring it

---

* "The Reluctant Genius" was assigned a production number, #3651, and John Rich was assigned as director for filming dates of October 18, 19 and 20, 1960, with rehearsal dates of October 14 and 17. "The Reluctant Genius" was originally slated for telecast on February 24, 1961. "Acceleration" was assigned a production number, #3652, and Douglas Heyes was assigned as director for filming dates of October 24, 25 and 26, 1960, with rehearsal dates of October 20 and 21. "Acceleration" was originally slated for telecast on March 7, 1961.

to the demands of tape; at the same time, there is a story deficiency which would also take a good deal of rewriting to correct." Rather than fall off schedule, since Houghton was attempting to make good on six episodes put to videotape, he agreed that Cayuga take an option on this script for a period of one year at a figure of $500 against an eventual $2,000. In lieu of this

Off-The-Side Trivia
Beaumont wrote to Serling often in a hurried format with careless regard to proper spelling and punctuation in his letters. In one letter, he asked Serling to "give me a growl on the tube" which meant "call on the telephone."

project, the men agreed and Beaumont was, instead, hired to jointly adapt a story that would become the episode, "Long Distance Call."

Warren Stevens shared his recollections of being directed by Montgomery Pittman to interviewer and author Tom Weaver: "Pittman said, 'Listen, I don't know how you should play this. You're on your own!' [laughs] So that was it, I was on my own! I played a bum who put on the shoes of a dead gangster and then 'became' the gangster. I think it should be a joint effort, with suggestions from both parties kind of melding into something that comes out right. So I never forgot Pittman saying to me, 'I don't know what to tell ya!' I met Rod Serling – not on that show, but I met him before. He smoked far too much, but otherwise he was a very personable guy."

Jerry Goldsmith's music scores in this episode, "The Caper," "The Gun," "The Warning," "Scene of the Crime" and "Brother and Sister" were originally written for ""Wake Up to Terror," the premiere episode of the sixth season of *The Lineup*. Many of the other music scores featured in this episode by Goldsmith were originally composed for "The Fair-Haired Boy," initially telecast on *Studio One* on March 3, 1958.

Actor Florence Marly has her name spelled "Florence Marley" in the closing credits, and the same misspelling cropped up for two motion pictures credits as well.

The same story premise was filmed for the revival series of *The Twilight Zone* in the 1980s, with the sex of the protagonist switched from a man to a woman. The title of the remake was "Dead Woman's Shoes."

The trailer for this episode was originally going to feature Serling doing a commercial: *"This is a Chesterfield. Twenty one fine tobaccos make twenty wonderful smokes in every pack. This isn't just a claim – it happens to be a fact. Try it out for size, and I think you will agree it's a good smoke – and you'll enjoy it. The name is Chesterfield."*

The character of Bernie Dagget was originally Bernie Taggart in the initial draft. For anyone wanting to know the details of the shoes, the original script called for "size 9 black and white brogans with perforated uppers and silver buckles." Before Nathan steps on the scale to check his weight, the camera picks up a shot of "Ralph Nelson's Barber Shop," which was a tip of the hat to Ralph W. Nelson, the production manager.

Production #4810 "THE HUNT" (Initial telecast: January 26, 1962)
Copyright Registration: © Cayuga Productions, Inc., January 23, 1962, LP21465 (in notice: 1962)
Dates of Rehearsal: July 3 and 5, 1961
Dates of Filming: July 6, 7 and 10, 1961
Script #75 is undated with revised pages dated May 22, 1961.
First script dated: June 16, 1961

Producer and Secretary: $1,625.00
Director: $1,250.00
Unit Manager and Secretary: $600.00
Agents Commission: $2,500.00
Below the line charges (M-G-M): $39,085.91
Total Production Costs: $56,524.43 *

Story and Secretary: $2,255.00
Cast: $5,197.50
Production Fee: $900.00
Legal and Accounting: $250.00
Below the line charges (other): $2,861.02

Cast: Dexter DuPont (the messenger); Robert Faulk (the gate keeper); Arthur Hunnicutt (Hyder Simpson, the old man); Bob McCord (the pallbearer); Titus Moede (Wesley Miller); Jeanette Nolan (Rachel Simpson, the old woman); Charles Seel (Reverend Wood); and Orville Sherman (Tillman Miller). **

Original Music Score Composed and Conducted by Robert Drasnin: Etrange #3 (by Marius Constant, :09); Milieu #1 (by Constant, :16); Hill Tune (:39); Prelude to Hunt (:42); The Woods (:19); Tragic Waters (:20); Puzzlement (1:49); Tearful, Two (2:07); Hill Tune Cortege (1:21); Walk to Gate (:34); Eternity Road (1:36); Heaven's Door (1:26); and Etrange #3 (by Constant, :08); and Milieu #2 (by Constant, :18).

Director of Photography: George T.
    Clemens, a.s.c.
Art Directors: George W. Davis and Phil Barber
Casting: Stalmaster-Lister
Film Editor: Bill Mosher
Directed by Harold Schuster

Production Manager: Ralph W. Nelson
Set Decorations: H. Web Arrowsmith
Assistant Director: E. Darrell Hallenbeck
Story Consultant: Richard McDonagh
Sound: Franklin Milton and Bill Edmondson
Teleplay by Earl Hamner, Jr.

"An old man and a hound named Rip, off for an evening's pleasure in quest of raccoon. Usually, these evenings end with one tired old man, one battle-scarred hound dog and one or more extremely dead raccoons. But as you may suspect that will not be the case tonight. These hunters won't be coming home from the hill. They're headed for the backwoods . . . of the Twilight Zone."

Plot: An old man and his hound dog spend the evening hunting for raccoons in the mountains, only to walk home empty-handed. It doesn't take long for him to discover that he and his dog died the night before. Following the well-traveled trail alongside a newly erected fence, he comes to a gate where the gatekeeper welcomes him with open arms, but explains that dogs are not permitted. The hound dog doesn't take a liking to the gatekeeper, so the old man stubbornly decides to continue down the road for a possible solution. A passerby meets up with the old man and explains that the entrance he rejected was the gate to hell. The entrance to heaven isn't paved with gold bricks, but they do allow dogs and raccoon hunting. As the passerby explains, people can enter hell with both eyes open, but once the smell of brimstone is in the air, even the Devil cannot fool a dog.

"Travelers to unknown regions would be well advised to take along the family dog. He could just save

---

* Total production costs and breakdown from production summary dated February 28, 1962.

** Actor Robert Foulk is credited as Robert Faulk in the closing credits. This was not necessarily a misspelling. His last name was spelled in a variety of ways on a number of television productions.

you from entering the wrong gate. At least, it happened that way, once, in a mountainous area . . . of the Twilight Zone."

Trailer: *"Perhaps no character, in or out of fiction, has had as much notoriety or publicity as the so-called Grim Reaper. Next week on the Twilight Zone, through the good offices of Mr. Earl Hamner, we present a unique story called 'The Hunt.' It concerns the demise of an old hunter and his dog . . . and this one we rather urgently recommend to people who have lost their senses of humor and who'd like to recover same. As one of my kids says, there's a trillion, trillion ways of telling a story. But there's only one way to tell the Chesterfield story and that's simply to say that great tobaccos make a wonderful smoke. Try Chesterfields. They satisfy."*

Trivia, etc, "I grew up during the depression," recalled Earl Hamner, Jr. "My family was what you considered backwoods folk of Virginia. My father would go hunting for pheasant and quail, and he had a hunting dog he loved. One night the dog ran away and my father spent all night searching for him. It was part of the family, you know, so when he found the dog the next morning, the animal was dead and my father grieved. 'The Hunt' was my first script for *The Twilight Zone* and it is probably my favorite. Not because it was my first, but a part of my family influenced the material I used to write that script."

Three weeks before this episode went before the camera, when it was assigned a production number on June 27, Boris Sagal was originally slated to direct, and the intended filming dates were July 12, 13 and 14, with rehearsal dates July 10 and 11. During rescheduling, the dates were pushed up a few days and newcomer Harold Schuster was offered the job of directing.

Hunnicutt, Nolan and Foulk went in for wardrobe fitting on the morning of July 3, 1961, before rehearsing. The rest of the cast went in for wardrobe fitting on July 5 – including Dexter Depont, Titus Moede, Charles Seel, and Orville Sherman. The entire episode was filmed on Lot 3 at M-G-M, except for the third and last day's filming at Stage 3 at Hal Roach Studios, where the scenes involving the gateway to heaven were filmed. On July 14, on Stage 5, Serling's narration and teaser for this episode were filmed, along with the intro and teasers for "The Last Rites of Jeff Myrtlebank" and "The Arrival."

On January 27, 1962, Charles E. Burgess, a minister for the Nicholls Baptist Church located in Nicholls, Georgia, drafted a written complaint to Serling (care of Metro-Goldwyn-Mayer Studios). Though he admitted that he enjoyed watching the *Twilight Zone*, he condemned this story "with a great deal of disgust," feeling it was misleading to the millions who were "lost" in the path of righteousness. "It had a good moral to the story," Burgess wrote, "but I feel it greatly misconstrued the teaching of The Holy Bible. Mr. Simpson's wife, the old woman, distinctly said, 'Old man was not a member of the church.' Insofar as the story went, the idea presented was that as long as a man leads a good moral life, goes coon hunting with his favorite hound, and does what he can to preserve his dog's life when the need arises, he is assured of the Promised Land. This is completely erroneous! Might I suggest you read Luke 18:18-24. This is a parable taught by Jesus concerning a man who kept all the commandments. I fully realize that your program was purely fictional, but still that does not change the damage that was done. Thousands of ministers stand Sunday after Sunday condemning exactly what the program last night condoned!"

"I realize that perhaps I am in the minority concerning issues like this," Burgess concluded, "and perhaps this is the only letter you will receive concerning 'The Hunt,' but I feel that I owe it to the five hundred people who constitute the Nicholls Baptist Church to express my disapproval of such programs as the one in mention." A copy of this same letter was mailed to WJXT-TV in Jacksonville, Florida, CBS Television in New York, and the sponsors.

Serling replied to Mr. Burgess on March 9, apologizing that he found such questionable elements on the program. Responding with a candor equal to the letter received, Serling explained that a narrow, viewpoint of the Fundamentalist religionists was not the universally accepted approach to the theological view. Since Mr. Burgess quoted the scripture, Serling claimed he reserved the same right, as did the author, to dramatize yet another point of view. "It was [Earl Hamner, Jr.'s] feeling and mine that good work, honesty, and a moral life are not of the essence in considering the whole man – his destiny and his after-life," Serling explained. "While there are certainly thousands of ministers and parishioners who are in disagreement with this point of view, there are equal thousands who support it . . . It is my own sincere feeling that we presented a point of view which probably, though it did not correspond to that of some viewers, was nonetheless a fair and reasoned one."

This letter may have left an impression with Rod Serling, judging by the closing narratives delivered by Serling in "Night Call" and "Probe 7, Over and Out."

Not all followers of all religions took a dislike towards the creepy dramas. Barbara Sharon Emily, wife of Ivan Blaine Emily, minister of the Methodist church in West College Corner, Indiana, wrote to Serling, praising him for his stories. "I do enjoy your work, for it has that unforgettable touch of human compassion which is needed to make such stories come alive," she wrote. "However, there is one character who I have been hoping to meet in your program, in vain. You have done stories about Santa Claus and Satan; you have discussed witchcraft and were-creatures; you have studied parallel worlds and paradoxes; but, to my knowledge, you have never done a story about that familiar creature of the night, the vampire. One story which leaps into my mind as an excellent example is Manly Wade Wellman's 'The Devil is Not Mocked,' an excellent revival of the Dracula legend. And what about Carl Jacobi's 'Revelations in Black?' Of course, there are other famous vampire stories too numerous to mention, but I am sure that you understand what I am trying to say."

The old woman's cabin in this episode was the same cabin featured in a number of television westerns and the opening scenes of "The Hunt."

Production #4812 "SHOWDOWN WITH RANCE McGREW"
(Initial telecast: February 2, 1962)
Copyright Registration: © Cayuga Productions, Inc., January 30, 1962, LP21466 (in notice: 1961)
Dates of Rehearsal: October 16 and 17, 1961
Dates of Filming: October 18, 19 and 20, 1961
Script #86 dated: September 20, 1961, with revised pages dated December 15, 1961

Producer and Secretary: $1,625.00	Story and Secretary: $3,085.00
Director: $1,250.00	Cast: $8,132.04
Unit Manager and Secretary: $600.00	Production Fee: $900.00
Agents Commission: $2,500.00	Legal and Accounting: $250.00
Below the line charges (M-G-M): $30,590.51	Below the line charges (other): $1,553.78
Total Production Costs: $50,486.33 *	

* Total production costs and breakdown from production summary dated February 28, 1962.

Cast: Larry Blyden (Rance McGrew); Jack Boniga (wardrobe man); Robert Cronthwaite (Blattsburg, the director); Hal K. Dawson (the old man); Sandra Downs (wardrobe girl); Billy Gratt Jr. (real cowboy #2); Arch Johnson (Jesse James); James Kessler (for utility); Robert Kline (actor portraying Jesse James); Jack Lorenz (bartender in real world); Bob McCord (real cowboy #1); Beryl McCutcheon (dance hall girl #2); William McLean (the prop man); Troy Melton (movie cowboy #1); Ted O'Chea (workman); Jay Overholts (movie cowboy #2); Lew Smith (makeup man); Robert J. Stevenson (the bartender in fake world); Shirley Swendsen (dance hall girl #1); Jim Turley (McGrew's stunt man); and Sally Yarnell (script supervisor).

Stock Music Cues: Etrange #3 (by Marius Constant, :09); Milieu #1 (by Constant, :16); Explosions (by Fred Steiner, :16); Alone (by Leith Stevens, :33); John's Jump (by John Dankworth, :31); Minnie's Manner (by Steiner, :41); Dax #3 (by Constant, :06); Minnie and Jake (by Steiner, :13); Minnie's Manner (by Steiner, :21); Shooting Lesson #1 (by Rene Garriguenc, :06); Shooting Lesson #2 (by Garriguenc, :07); Shooting Lesson #3 (by Garriguenc, :07); Red River Valley (traditional, :33); Third Corpse (by Steiner, :12); Trapped Twins (by Steiner, :25); Camping Twin (by Steiner, :14); Third Corpse (by Steiner, :06); The Riddle (by Steiner, :07); Minnie's Tune (by Steiner, :22); Minnie's Manner (by Steiner, :49); Rocks (by Steiner, :47); Violence (by Steiner, :28); Anxious Twins (by Steiner, :34); Third Corpse (by Steiner, :11); Drinking Twins (by Steiner, :10); Dax #3 (by Constant, :13); Indian Killers (by Steiner, :17); Anxious Twins (by Steiner, :06); Thoughtful Twins (by Steiner, :13); Camping Twins (by Steiner, :21); Minnie's Manners (by Steiner, :13); Thataway (by Jerome Moross, :10); Etrange #3 (by Constant, :08); and Milieu #2 (by Constant, :18).

Director of Photography: George T. Clemens, a.s.c.	Production Manager: Ralph W. Nelson
Art Directors: George W. Davis and Phil Barber	Set Decorations: H. Web Arrowsmith
Casting: Stalmaster-Lister	Assistant Director: E. Darrell Hallenbeck
Film Editor: Bill Mosher	Story Consultant: Richard McDonagh
Automobiles Supplied by the Ford Motor Company	Sound: Franklin Milton and Bill Edmondson
	Directed by Christian Nyby

Teleplay by Rod Serling, based on an original story idea by Frederic L. Fox.

"Some one hundred odd years ago, a motley collection of tough mustaches galloped across the West, and left behind a raft of legends and legerdemains. And it seems a reasonable conjecture that if there are any television sets up in Cowboy Heaven, any one of these rough-and-wooly nail-eaters could see with what careless abandon their names and exploits are being bandied about – they're very likely turning over in their graves – or worse, getting out of them. Which gives you a clue as to the proceedings that'll begin in just a moment, when one Mr. Rance McGrew, a three-thousand-buck-a-week phony-baloney, discovers that this week's current edition of make-believe is being shot on location – and that location . . . is the Twilight Zone."

Plot: Actor Rance McGrew, the star of his own television western, is late for work, forgets his lines and has a problem quick-drawing his six-shooter. He believes stuntmen are the perfect solution to his faults. One afternoon, while filming a scene for the television program, actor McGrew finds himself misplaced in time, transported to the real Wild West. Here, men roll their own cigarettes, pour alcohol into shot glasses (not from smashed bottles), and disputes are settled quickly with a six-gun in the streets. In a meeting of the minds, the real Jesse James explains to McGrew that the cowboys in heaven upset with the false image his show gives to television viewers. In a showdown in the streets, Jesse challenges McGrew to draw, and injecting a sense of fear, tells the actor to make the television program more realistic – or else. Back on the set, McGrew meets Jesse James, who now serves as his agent, and changes are being made to the scripts – even if McGrew is going to be thrown through the windows without the use of stuntmen.

"The evolution of the so-called 'adult western,' and the metamorphosis of one Rance McGrew, formerly phony-baloney ... now upright citizen with a preoccupation with all things involving tradition, truth and cowpoke predecessors. It's the way the cookie crumbles and the six-gun shoots ... in the Twilight Zone."

Trailer: *"Next week we offer you a Hollywood television cowboy who takes in several bills a week for killing off bad men. Mr. Larry Blyden portrays one of these phony-baloneys who always win in the end. But in this little item, he draws from the hip and realizes his opponent is smack dab out of this world. We invite your attention to 'Showdown With Rance McGrew' – next week's stage coach sojourn ... in the Twilight Zone."*

Trivia, etc. Shortly after an exchange of letters between Rod Serling and Ray Bradbury regarding the plagiarism, Serling promised to Bradbury that he would get a script or two of Bradbury's produced. The first attempt was "A Miracle of Rare Device," a script submitted during the first season, now assigned a production number of #4812 on July 19, 1961, for the third season. Within two months, however, it was decided that the script would not be feasible for filming, so the same production number was reassigned to this episode on September 29, 1961.

The first day of filming was devoted to the scenes in the Western Street on Lot 3 at M-G-M. The second and third day of filming were devoted to the interior of the saloon for the real world and the movie set, on Stage 9. The saloon doors in this episode are the same featured in "Mr. Garrity and the Graves."

Frederic Louis Fox had written a number of stories and teleplays for television westerns including *Johnny Ringo*, *The Rebel*, *Zane Grey Theater*, *Black Saddle* and *Lawman*. Information regarding the origin of the story for this *Twilight Zone* script can be found in a letter dated October 12, 1961, days before the episode went before the camera, in which Rod Serling wrote to Frederic Louis Fox in La Canada, California. Serling thanked Fox for his understanding and patience, having had a recent discussion over the phone. "A few days after its completion, a little persistent gnawing bug crawled into my consciousness, and I finally remembered someone telling me a story at a Strike Meeting last Spring. I don't know if it was your story that pushed this one out of me, or the germ of it made its writing possible, but I do know that in some fifteen years of writing I have never, knowingly, copped someone else's material. I've asked Buck Houghton, our producer, to contact Jay Richards to arrange a price for your outline, and a credit of some sort which will satisfy you."

Actor Robert Cornthwaite was currently appearing in *The Egg* at the Magnolia Theater at the time this episode was being telecast. Cornthwaite played the role of the television director in this episode, and in an early scene, the director placed his hand on a girl. "While we were making this sequence, I stumbled onto something about the relations between actors and extras that I had never known before. And I had been in pictures more than 11 years," commented Cornthwaite. "Chris Nyby, who was directing, casually mentioned that it would be perfectly normal for me, playing the director, to put a

Your introduction to Mr. Jay Overholts . . .

An actor of uncommon talent, with whom Serling had the pleasure of working with at a CBS affiliate in Cincinnati for a number of years, arrived to California in February of 1959. Serling wrote to a number of talent agencies, including the Mitchell Gertz Agency, imposing on them to make a call and set up an appointment so they could meet Overholts and possibly get him a few jobs in television. Serling's efforts were successful, and Overholts began appearing in a number of episodes on *The Twilight Zone*. As one of the passengers in "The Odyssey of Flight 33," a cowboy in "Showdown with Rance McGrew," an intern at the conclusion of "A Thing About Machines," the public address system announcer in "Twenty-Two," the doctor in "One for the Angels," and as a taxi driver in "The Jungle."

hand on the shoulder of the extra girl who played the script clerk when I went over to check a line of dialogue. After three years in Hollywood, I still didn't get his drift. 'Perfectly normal, sure,' I thought, 'but why make such a point of it?' And then I learned that whenever a principal in a scene makes physical contact with an extra in a shot, that extra gets extra. Chris, who is one of the really nice guys in the business, was ensuring this extra girl an 'adjustment' on her daily paycheck."

Nyby also included an inside-joke featured in this episode. As Rance is walking backwards toward the funeral wagon during his showdown in the streets, the sign on one building reads "C. Nyby, Funeral Parlor."

Leonard P. Geer, a fancy saddler and stunt man who specialized in trick horses, made a career doubling for actors on numerous television westerns, including *Laramie*, *Gunsmoke*, *Have Gun-Will Travel* and *Tales of Wells Fargo*. Geer was hired for this episode and brought a trick horse to the set in case it was needed for the production. (Geer also appeared as an extra in the *Twilight Zone* episode "The Old Man in the Cave.")

Almost all of the music scores featured in this episode were originally composed for television westerns *Gunsmoke* and *Hotel de Paree*.

While *The Twilight Zone* offered a parody of the gun-slinging television westerns, comic genius Ernie Kovacs, best known for satire and spoofs on his comedy sketches, produced an offbeat brand of humor in one of his episodes with a *Twilight Zone* western sketch of his own in which bullets turned into bananas.

Production #4821 "KICK THE CAN" (Initial telecast: February 9, 1962)
Copyright Registration: © Cayuga Productions, Inc., February 6, 1962, LP21464 (in notice: 1961)
Dates of Rehearsal: September 12 and 13, 1961
Dates of Filming: September 14, 15 and 18, 1961
Script dated: September 12, 1961

Producer and Secretary: $1,625.00
Director: $1,250.00
Unit Manager and Secretary: $600.00

Story and Secretary: $2,155.00
Cast: $7,731.56
Production Fee: $900.00

Agents Commission: $2,500.00
Below the line charges (M-G-M): $29,268.06
Total Production Costs: $47,964.82 *

Legal and Accounting: $250.00
Below the line charges (other): $1,685.20

Cast: Marjorie Bennett (Mrs. Summers); Russell Collins (Ben Conroy); Earl Hodgins (Agee); John Marley (Mr. Cox); Gregory McCabe (boy #1); Eve McVeagh (the nurse); Burt Mustin (Mr. Carlson); Anne O'Neal (Mrs. Wister); Hank Patterson (Frietag); Lenore Shanewise (Mrs. Densley); Marc Stevens (boy #2); Barry Truex (David Whitley); and Ernest Truex (Charles Whitley).

Stock Music Cues: Etrange #3 (by Marius Constant, :09); Milieu #1 (by Constant, :16); A Country Lane (by Bruce Campbell, :11); A Country Lane, Version A (by Campbell, :05); Neutral Non Active (by Campbell, :35); Pensive to Query (by Campbell, :05); Night Flight – 3A (by Campbell, :10); Night Flight – 2B (by Campbell, :39); Lingering Mists (by Campbell, :24); Utility Cues (by Campbell, :10); A Country Lane (by Campbell, :16); The Drug Store (by Bernard Herrmann, :56); The Old Man (by Nathan Van Cleave, :05); Light Active Agitato (by Campbell, :40); Memories (by Herrmann, :43); Goldfish Bowl (by Campbell, :23); Takeoff to Space – Departure (by Campbell, :30); The Old Man (by Van Cleave, :10); Robot Rock (by Campbell, :07); Summer Scene (by Campbell, :07); Light Active Agitato (by Campbell, :21); Robot Rock, Version 2 (by Campbell, :19); Night Flight – 3A (by Campbell, :16); Night Flight – 4A (by Campbell, :34); Night Flight – 3A (by Campbell, :10); Walking Distance Introduction (by Herrmann, :12); The Drug Store (by Herrmann, :56); Utility Cue, Version 2 (by Campbell, :14); Light Dramatic Series #4 (by Rene Garriguenc, :27); Light Dramatic Series #5 (by Garriguenc, :03); Utility Cue (by Campbell, :18); Goldfish Bowl (by Campbell, :12); Light Active Agitato (by Campbell, :14); The Merry-Go-Round (by Herrmann, :18); The Park (by Herrmann, :34); Finale (by Herrmann, 1:00); The Hill (by Fred Steiner :06); Etrange #3 (by Constant, :08); and Milieu #2 (by Constant, :18).

Director of Photography: George T.
    Clemens, a.s.c.
Art Directors: George W. Davis and Phil Barber
Casting: Stalmaster-Lister
Film Editor: Bill Mosher
Automobiles Supplied by the Ford
    Motor Company

Production Manager: Ralph W. Nelson
Set Decorations: George R. Nelson
Assistant Director: E. Darrell Hallenbeck
Story Consultant: Richard McDonagh
Sound: Franklin Milton and Bill Edmondson
Directed by Lamont Johnson
Teleplay by George Clayton Johnson

"Sunnyvale Rest: a home for the aged. A dying place, and a common children's game called 'kick the can' that will shortly become a refuge for a man who knows he will die in this world if he doesn't escape . . . into the Twilight Zone."

Plot: An old duffer named Charles Whitley longs to escape from the four walls of the Sunnyvale Rest Home, to a place where he isn't confined to vitamin pills and rocking chairs. Attempting to

---

* Total production costs and breakdown from production summary dated February 28, 1962.

relive his youth, Whitley jumps through lawn sprinklers and makes faces at the residents – only to be mistaken as senile. Mr. Conroy, one of the residents, insists that growing old is a fact of life. Whitley believes that the fountain of youth isn't a fountain – it is a way of thinking. Late one summer evening, Whitley encourages most of the residents of Sunnyvale to sneak out and play a game of "Kick the Can." The old people are having a ball outside on the grounds, while Conroy alerts the manager of the retirement home. Outside, however, Conroy watches as young children – one of them the image of a young Whitley – run off into the forest to continue their game . . .

"Sunnyvale Rest, a dying place for ancient people who have forgotten the fragile magic of youth. A dying place for those who have forgotten that childhood, maturity and old age are curiously intertwined . . . and not separate. A dying place for those who have grown too stiff in their thinking to visit . . . the Twilight Zone."

Trailer: *"For all of us, even the most young at heart, I suppose there's a little kernel of want having to do with reliving childhood . . . that grand and glorious moment in time when the biggest guy around is the patrol boy. Next week on The Twilight Zone, this moment is recaptured in George Clayton Johnson's exceptionally sensitive story called 'Kick the Can.' It co-stars Mr. Ernest Truex and Mr. Russell Collins. If the tobaccos in a cigarette is good enough, they alone will give mellow richness and satisfactory mildness. Try Chesterfield and you'll discover 21 great tobaccos make twenty wonderful smokes."*

Trivia, etc. This episode came as a result of George Clayton Johnson's efforts to charm producer Buck Houghton with the evocative idea of a rest home and the types of old people found at such a place. "I wrote a five-page story about an old man who picks up a tin can and tries to remember the rules of the game. He encourages the other people in the old folks home to become young in spirit by playing the game. It was an offbeat story that one might find down the road from where they live. Buck read the story and we would talk about the story and I went home to rework the material. After a while he [told] me that the story was much better and ordered me to write the script. So I went home and wrote the script."

Assigned a production number on September 6, this episode featured Ernest Truex in a return performance for *Twilight Zone*, with his real-life son, actor Barry Truex, in an un-credited role – that of playing his son in the episode as well!

The first day of filming consisted of all the exterior shots of the retirement home, on Lot #3 at M-G-M, filmed in the afternoon and evening. The remainder of filming took place on Stage 18 during the second and third day of filming, with the old folks in the dormitory, corridor and office. The sounds of the kids cheering and playing in the woods were recorded in Sync Room "A" from 9:00 a.m. to noon on October 27.

Hank Patterson, who plays one of the old folks in the home, started out to be a serious musician in his native Texas, but signed on as a piano player with a road show in 1910. Soon he began filling in as an actor "when somebody was drunk or sick or something," and by 1912 he was acting full time. "I started out as [a young guy] playing an old guy," Patterson remarked, and his numerous television appearances always kept him typecast as an old man. "I did so many television shows I cannot remember all of them anymore. *The Twilight Zone* I remember well enough. Ernest Truex wasn't too much older than me, and we got along well on the set."

"Each little piece [of my career], no matter how tiny it is, in some way sort of tends toward the major, because of its association, or the place that it appears, or the notoriety it gets," recalled Johnson to author Matthew R. Bradley. "For example, the remake of 'Kick the Can' for *Twilight Zone-The Movie* (1983) has got Steven Spielberg directing it. Now, that's significant right there. It's one thing to get a remake, but it's another to have *the* Steven Spielberg as the guy who's chosen to direct your work, with me sort of hanging back and saying, 'I'm not so sure, I'd love to have a meeting with Steven,' and Steven through his representative saying, 'No, I do not audition any more,' a take it or leave it sort of attitude. Ultimately I ended up taking their deal, watching the way they put it all together, and feeling somewhat dismayed when I actually saw it. Although I was touched quite a bit by that lady whose husband was Jack Dempsey, not the boxer but Jack Dempsey, and she lost her ring. Right at the end, this ring has become too big and has fallen off of her – that was all very moving to me, but basically I sat there sort of depressed by what they had done with it. I was blessed, though, I ended up making large amounts of money from it. . . . I was fortunate enough to think of an ending for 'Kick the Can' that would make sense, so I typed it up on three pages and took it with me to my little meeting with the producers. Before I signed the deal, I gave them these three pages, so later on when I saw that they had used some of the information from the three pages, I called it to the attention of the business affairs department and they ended up giving me yet more money. So all in all I came away from the experience really satisfied, except for my real disappointment that Spielberg didn't have a clearer idea of stories."

This episode, along with "It's a Good Life" and "Nightmare at 20,000 Feet" was rebroadcast on the evening of Wednesday, July 27, 1983, in an effort to promote *Twilight Zone: The Movie*, which was released theatrically that summer. Carol Serling supplied commentary for the two-hour television special, with brief glimpses and sneak peaks at the motion picture. Kay Gardella of *The New York Daily News* reviewed the production, commenting: "I'm forced to wonder what it was that attracted me to the series after viewing . . . . Even from my memory I could pick better episodes than those three, which could account for the so-so reception critics gave the film."

Production #4825 "A PIANO IN THE HOUSE" (Initial telecast: February 16, 1962)

Copyright Registration: © Cayuga Productions, Inc., February 13, 1962, LP21887 (in notice: 1961)
Date of Rehearsal: October 4 and 5, 1961
Dates of Filming: October 6, 9 and 10, 1961

Producer and Secretary: $1,625.00
Director: $1,250.00
Unit Manager and Secretary: $602.45
Agents Commission: $2,500.00
Below the line charges (M-G-M): $24,871.46
Total Production Costs: $40,833.57 *

Story and Secretary: $2,155.00
Cast: $5,185.04
Production Fee: $900.00
Legal and Accounting: $250.00
Below the line charges (other): $1,494.62

Cast: Philip Coolidge (Mr. Throckmorton, the store owner); Cyril Delevati (Marvin Bridges, the

* Total production costs and breakdown from production summary dated February 28, 1962.

servant); Don Durant (Gregory Walker); Joan Hackett (Esther Fortune); Muriel Landers (Marge Moore); and Barry Morse (Fitzgerald Fortune).

Stock Music Cues: Etrange #3 (by Marius Constant, :09); Milieu #1 (by Constant, :16); Summer Scene (by Campbell, 1:07); I'm in the Mood for Love (by Jimmy McHugh and Dorothy Fields, 1:22); F Story 5, Version A (by Constant, :07); Tragic Loss (by Rene Garriguenc, :41); Prelude – Elegy (by Nathan Van Cleave, :03); F Story 6 (by Constant, :33); Smiles (by J. Will Callahan and Lee Roberts, 1:05); Sabre Dance (by Aram Khatchaturian, 1:14); F Story 5, Version A (by Constant, :09); Tragic Loss (by Garriguenc, :31); Toast to a New Husband (by Nathan Scott, :05); These Foolish Things Remind Me of You (by Holt Marvell, Harry Link and Jack Strachey, 1:25); F Story 5, Version A (by Constant, :06); Tragic Loss (by Garriguenc, :45); Clair De Lune (by Claude Debussy, 2:17); F Story 5, Version A (by Constant, :13); Tragic Loss (by Garriguenc, :29); F Story 6 (by Constant, :16); Lullaby (by Johannes Brahms, 2:25); F Story 6 (by Constant, :21); Reaction to Tag, Version A (by William A. Barnett, :04); Etrange #3 (by Constant, :08); and Milieu #2 (by Constant, :18).

Director of Photography: George T. Clemens, a.s.c.
Art Directors: George W. Davis and Phil Barber
Casting: Stalmaster-Lister
Film Editor: Bill Mosher
Directed by David Greene

Production Manager: Ralph W. Nelson
Set Decorations: H. Web Arrowsmith
Assistant Director: E. Darrell Hallenbeck
Story Consultant: Richard McDonagh
Sound: Franklin Milton and Bill Edmondson
Teleplay by Earl Hamner, Jr.

"Mr. Fitzgerald Fortune, theater critic and cynic at large, on his way to a birthday party. If he knew what is in store for him he probably wouldn't go, because before this evening is over that cranky old piano is going to play those piano roll blues – with some effects that could happen only in . . . the Twilight Zone."

Plot: Fitzgerald Fortune, a theater critic who takes pleasure in cruelty to his fellow man, visits a junk shop with the intention of purchasing a self-playing piano for his wife's birthday – a wife much younger than he. It only takes a moment for Fortune to discover the magical effect the piano has on other people when selected music rolls are played. Believing that everyone has two faces, one we wear and the other we keep hidden, Fortune takes advantage of the guests attending his wife's birthday party. A young man reveals his affections for Fortune's wife, Esther. A fat woman imagines herself as the little girl she never was. The never-smiling servant laughs and cheers. Out of contempt, Esther switches the music sheets to throw the same ploy against her husband – who reveals that he's afraid of the dark. Fortune is nothing more than a frightened boy who hurts others because he envies those who embrace the world in ways he doesn't. He covets the talent of other playwrights, hurting them in his reviews. After having a brief taste of his own medicine, Mr. Fitzgerald Fortune loses the respect of his friends – and his wife.

"Mr. Fitzgerald Fortune, a man who went searching for concealed persons, and found himself . . . in the Twilight Zone."

Trailer: *"Next week on the Twilight Zone, we roll in a musical instrument purchased in this store. Now there are pianos and pianos, but this one was manufactured in our very strange unpredictable factory. It* *comes to you via the typewriter of Mr. Earl Hamner, and it boasts a collection of oddities and oddball doings. Next week you can roll up the rug as we bring you 'A Piano in the House.'"*

Trivia, etc. Rehearsals for this episode were conducted on October 5, involving the five major characters (but not Delevanti, who played the butler). The entire episode was filmed on Stage 19 at M-G-M, including the junk shop and Fortune's New York Apartment. The white walls surrounding the room where most of the story takes place were the same featured in "The Mirror."

This script was originally submitted to Rod Serling under the title "Won't You Play a Simple Melody?" listed as script number 89 with a date of September 26, 1961. The production number was assigned on September 28 and the title changed to "A Piano in the House" officially on October 6, 1961.

The musician responsible for scoring this episode chose the right pieces to represent each of the characters who are subjected to reveal the emotion they hide from the outside world – and themselves. When the song "I'm in the Mood for Love" is played on the piano in the junk shop, the junk dealer, a gruff man, reveals his sentimentality beneath his crude façade. When "Smiles" is played on the piano, the butler, who was gifted in repressing all of his emotions, starts to laugh. "Sabre Dance" was the song that reveals Esther's repressed hysteria. "These Foolish Things" leads Greg to confesses his love for Esther, a foolish act that proves later to be a blessing in disguise. "Clair de Lune" reveals Marge as a dainty, fragile person, and not the jolly vulgar person she was made out to be. The climax revealed Fitzgerald Fortune's fear of other people and the motivation for his cruelty when "Lullaby" is played on the piano, and he cries like a baby.

"It's not hard to be an actress," Joan Hackett commented in an interview for *TV Guide.* "It's not even hard to be a good one, if you care about it and you try. The hard part is persuading yourself that the things you do are of any value." Hackett was born in New York's Harlem district, second child of an Italian mother and an Irish father. The house they lived in was owned by her mother's family, and the top floor of it was rented out to a family of gypsies. "I remember the old grandmother of them," she said. "She would sit all day on the curb across the street, smoking her pipe and watching the house. It used to terrify my grandmother – she was sure the old woman was putting the evil eye on all of us." To play the part for this episode, Hackett managed to keep a straight face by pretending actor Barry Morse was one of the old gypsy women of the past, who was giving her the evil eye.

"Well, Rod and I were residents of Ohio. We both wrote for the *Dr. Christian* program and when I left a job in Cincinnati, he took the position," recalled Earl Hamner. "Years later, I went to Hollywood and Rod introduced me at a party once as the man who gave him his first job. [laughs] That really wasn't how it was, but I let it go at that. He had success with *The Twilight Zone* and I had a problem getting into television," recalled Hamner. "I had written for radio, I had written for live television, and I wrote a few novels. But I could not sell anything for television."

In a 1977 issue of *Writer's Yearbook* with columnist and interviewer Ted Allrich, Hamner remembered, "I had known Rod Serling slightly in New York. One day I called Rod and said I would like to submit some stories for his *Twilight Zone* series. He said that it was an awfully hard

> **Blooper!** When "I'm In The Mood For Love" finishes playing in the junk shop, the observant television audience can catch the lyrics to "These Foolish Things" on the piano.

market to crack, but to give it a try. He promised that all the right people would read my ideas. His producer called back a few days after I submitted some, a nice guy named Buck Houghton. Buck had read the stories and liked them. But he also said, 'I understand you don't write film. Would you like to write these up as little plays?'

"I said, 'No. I'd like to write them up as little television shows.' And I did, and I have not been out of work since."

Production #4811 "THE LAST RITES OF JEFF MYRTLEBANK" (Initial telecast: February 23, 1962)

Copyright Registration: © Cayuga Productions, Inc., February 20, 1962, LP21888 (in notice: 1961)
Dates of Rehearsal: July 14 and 17, 1961
Dates of Filming: July 18, 19 and 20, 1961
Script #73 dated: June 8, 1961

Producer and Secretary: $1,625.00
Director: $1,250.00
Unit Manager and Secretary: $600.00
Agents Commission: $2,500.00
Below the line charges (M-G-M): $32,842.54
Total Production Costs: $50,128.23 *

Story and Secretary: $2,505.00
Cast: $6,752.21
Production Fee: $900.00
Legal and Accounting: $250.00
Below the line charges (other): $903.48

Cast: Beau Anderson (member of mob at gate); Vickie Barnes (Liz Myrtlebank); Jack Bellens (member of mob at gate); James Best (Jefferson Myrtlebank); Edgar Buchanan (Doctor Bolton); John Burnside (member of mob at gate); B. Cates (citizen outside church); Jack Clinton (member of mob at gate); Hank Faber (citizen outside church / member of mob at gate); William Fawcett (Reverend Siddons); Mabel Forrest (Mrs. Ferguson); Lance Fuller (Orgram Gatewood); Pat Hector (Tom); Jim Houghton (Jerry); Sherry Jackson (Comfort Gatewood); Jon Lormer (Mr. Strauss); Gloria Mae (citizen outside church); Lee Montgomery (citizen outside church); Ralph Moody (Pa Myrtlebank); Ezelle Poule (Ma Myrtlebank); Fred Rappaport (citizen outside church); Dub Taylor (Mr. Peters); Barbara Underwood (citizen outside church); Helen Wallace (Ma Gatewood); and Jack Williams (citizen outside church).

Original Music Score Composed and Conducted by Tommy Morgan (Score No. CPN6019):
Etrange #3 (by Marius Constant, :09); Milieu #1 (by Constant, :16); Abide With Me (by W.H. Monk, :43); Jeff in a Casket (:12); I Love You Dear #1 (:19); Afraid of Me? #1 (:21); Afraid of Me? #2 (1:04); I Love You Dear #2 (:36); Mom's Concern (1:28); Country Doctor (:48 and :14); Dead Roses (:19); Comfort's Blue Yodel (1:40); Hit Him, Jeff (1:02); A Warning to Jeff (1:12); Stand Behind Me, Comfort (:28); I Love You Dear #3 (:51); Etrange #3 (by Constant, :08); and Milieu #2 (by Constant, :18).

---

* Total production costs and breakdown from production summary dated February 28, 1962.

Director of Photography: Jack Swain
Art Directors: George W. Davis and Phil Barber
Assistant Director: E. Darrell Hallenbeck
Story Consultant: Richard McDonagh
Sound: Frank Milton and Bill Edmondson
Automobile Supplied by the Ford
    Motor Company.

Production Manager: Ralph W. Nelson
Set Decorations: H. Web Arrowsmith
Casting: Stalmaster-Lister
Film Editor: Bill Mosher
Directed by Montgomery Pittman
Teleplay by Montgomery Pittman

"Time . . . the mid-twenties. Place . . . the Midwest. The southernmost section of the Midwest. We were just witnessing a funeral. A funeral that didn't come off exactly as planned . . . due to a slight fallout . . . from the Twilight Zone."

Plot: During the funeral of Jefferson Myrtlebank, the deceased rises from his coffin to discover he was pronounced dead and just hours away from a Christian burial. Two weeks later, Jeff has expressed a strong desire to work hard, and his eating habits have changed. The town starts spreading stories and rumors, which grow out of proportion. The townsfolk start to wonder if an evil spirit possessed the dead body of Jeff, thus causing the reanimation. A few strange occurrences such as the wilting away of freshly plucked roses and Jeff beating Ardrom in a fist-fight (something Jeff was never able to do) lend credence to the rumors. When the townsfolk decide to take action, Comfort races out to warn Jeff, because she loves him. The mob gathers and asks Jeff to leave for other parts of the country. Comfort turns a deaf ear to the mob and stands behind her man. Jeff insists they are mistaken, but uses their fear as a motive for argument. He tells them he's going to stay and since they insist he's an evil spirit of sorts, he threatens to dry all their wells, kill their crops and burn down their barns. Scared, the members of the mob agree to leave things as they are and drive back to town, promising not to bother the two lovebirds again. After the mob is gone, Jeff lights a match without striking it and smokes his pipe . . .

"Jeff and Comfort are still alive today. And their only son is a United States Senator. He's noted as an uncommonly shrewd politician, and some believe he must have gotten his education . . . in the Twilight Zone."

Trailer: *"A symbol of a sad but rather commonplace event. An impressive funeral, the deceased laid out in a most acceptable manner . . . but in this case, at the last moment deciding that in matters concerning the trip to the great beyond, perhaps this trip wasn't necessary. You'll see it next week on the Twilight Zone when we present Montgomery Pittman's 'The Last Rites of Jeff Myrtlebank.' Very often when you write for a living, you run across blocks. Moments when you can't think of the right thing to say. Now happily there are no blocks to get in the way of the full pleasure of Chesterfield. Great tobaccos make a wonderful smoke. Try 'em. They satisfy."*

Trivia, etc. "Oh yeah, there was a difference between the westerns I did and *Twilight Zone*," recalled James Best. "I cannot recall every television western I did but they were all the same. They filmed so quick an actor could have done two or three shows a week if his schedule permitted. On *The Twilight Zone* they gave me a chance to rehearse before they went to film. That was extremely rare.

Production Schedule at M-G-M and Hal Roach Studios

Day 1 –   Exterior of Gatewood Farm, Exterior of Road and
          Exterior of Church (Lot #3 at M-G-M)
Day 2 –   Interior of Ferguson Parlor and Gatewood Parlor
          (Stage 4 at Hal Roach Studios)
          Myrtlebank's Kitchen and Gatewood Kitchen
          (Stage 4 at Hal Roach Studios)
          Interior of Church (Stage 5 at Hal Roach Studios)
Day 3 –   Exterior of Road and Gate (Stage 5 at Hal Roach Studios)
          Interior of Store (Stage 4 at Hal Roach Studios)

The director had class. The whole show had class. That is probably why, today, thirty . . . forty years later, *The Twilight Zone* is still talked about. I cannot recall the last time anyone asked me about [*The Adventures of*] *Kit Carson* or *West Point Story*. But not a month goes by that someone reminds me about *The Twilight Zone*."

According to James Best, the casket was never fully closed when he was lying inside waiting for the resurrection scene. "I'm not known to being claustrophobic, but when they closed that lid, I stuck a pencil or something small under the lid and told them to leave it there. I didn't get scared laying in there but that pencil did keep the box from getting a bit stuffy."

The cabin where the resurrection occurs in this episode was the same in which the old woman and old man resided in "The Hunt." The gate along the road where the townsfolk meet up with Jeff and Comfort is the same gate little Anthony is playing on in "It's a Good Life."

This episode was assigned a production number on July 13, 1961. The wild lines for the crowd sequences were recorded in Sync Room "A" on December 21, 1961.

An inside joke can be found in this episode. If the viewer looks carefully at the row of mailboxes, the one on the end has "M. Pittman" painted on the side, referring to writer and director Montgomery Pittman.

Production #4807 "TO SERVE MAN" (Initial telecast: March 2, 1962)

Copyright Registration: © Cayuga Productions, Inc., February 27, 1962, LP21889 (in notice: 1961)
Dates of Rehearsal: June 9 and 12, 1961
Dates of Filming: June 13, 14, 15 and 17, 1961
Script #66 dated: April 26, 1961, with revised pages dated June 12, 1961

Producer and Secretary: $1,625.00	Story and Secretary: $3,805.00
Director: $1,588.33	Cast: $7,774.27
Unit Manager and Secretary: $600.00	Production Fee: $900.00
Agents Commission: $2,500.00	Legal and Accounting: $250.00

---

* Total production costs and breakdown from production summary dated February 28, 1962.

Below the line charges (M-G-M): $41,105.47   Below the line charges (other): $971.52
Total Production Costs: $61,119.59 *

Cast: Hardie Albright (the Secretary General); David Armstrong (guest at U.N. #1); Gene Benton (reporter #2); Lloyd Bochner (Mike Chambers); Bill Burnside (TV Cameraman #1); John Burnside (TV Cameraman #2); Susan Cummings (Pat "Penny" Brody); Jeanne Evans (woman #2); J.H. Fujiyama (Japanese delegate); Jean Heremans (Dignitary #3); Richard Kiel (the Kanamits); Theodore Marcuse (Citizen Gregori); Adrienne Marden (woman #1); Bob McCord (Interpreter #1); Nelson Olmsted (the scientist); Ted O'Shea (Dignitary #1); Fred Rappaport (Dignitary #5); Bartlett Robinson (the baldish Colonel); Joseph Ruskin (the voice of the Kanamit); Lomax Study (M. Leveque, French delegate); Robert Tafur (Señor Valdes, Argentine delegate); Charles Tannen (man #1); Jim Turley (TV Cameraman #3); James L. Wellman (man #2); Will J. Wilke (reporter #1); Jack Williams (Dignitary #2); and Carlton Young (Colonel #2).

Cast as Earthlings Boarding the Spaceship: Joan Austin, Joyce Baker, Mary Ellen Batten, Keith Britton, Ellen Brown, B. Cates, Joe Hicks, Lee Montgomery, Bob Peterson, Beau Ramstead, Jack Ramstead, Ester Silvery, Joan Weinstein, Jack Williams, and Sally Yarnell.

Stock Music Cues: Etrange #3 (by Marius Constant, :09); Milieu #1 (by Constant, :16); Counter Attack Part 1 (by Jerry Goldsmith, :42); Return to the Past (by Goldsmith, :47); The Assassination (by Goldsmith, :02); Return to the Past (by Goldsmith, :15); Counter Attack Part 2 (by Goldsmith, :26 and :36); Table Talk (by Goldsmith, :09); The Assasination (by Goldsmith, :02); Counter Attack Part 2 (by Goldsmith, :14); The Prediction (by Goldsmith, :21); Counter Attack Part 2 (by Goldsmith, 1:56); Serling III (by Robert Drasnin, :04); Etrange #3 (by Constant, :08); and Milieu #2 (by Constant, :19).

Director of Photography: George T. Clemens, a.s.c.	Production Manager: Ralph W. Nelson
	Set Decorations: H. Web Arrowsmith
Art Directors: George W. Davis and Phil Barber	Assistant Director: E. Darrell Hallenbeck
Casting: Stalmaster-Lister	Story Consultant: Richard McDonagh
Film Editor: Jason H. Bernie, a.c.e.	Sound: Franklin Milton and Bill Edmondson
Automobiles Supplied by the Ford Motor Company	Directed by Richard L. Bare

Teleplay by Rod Serling, based on the short story of the same name by Damon Knight, originally published in the November 1950 issue of *Galaxy Science Fiction*.

"Respectfully submitted for your perusal – a Kanamit. Height, a little over nine feet. Weight, in the neighborhood of three hundred and fifty pounds. Origin, unknown. Motives? Therein hangs the tale, for in just a moment, we're going to ask you to shake hands... Figuratively... with a Christopher Columbus from another galaxy and another time. This is the Twilight Zone."

Plot: This is the way nightmares begin. On a warm April afternoon, an alien race makes contact with the citizens of planet Earth, offering a hand of friendship. Their intention is to offer peace and prosperity. Within months, deserts become fields of crops, because the Kanamits show how to add a very cheap nitrate to the soil. The threat of war becomes obsolete when all nations implement an invisible force field introduced by the visitors from outer space. While the world slowly transforms into a Garden of Eden, two decoding specialists for the U.S. government, Michael Chambers and Pat Brody, spend long hours trying to decode a book accidentally left behind at the United Nations. The only thing they have been able to crack is the title on the cover – "To Serve Man." One year later, the book still isn't cracked, and Chambers is one of the hundreds of thousands of passengers with a round-trip ticket to the Kanamit's home planet – and fails to make his escape when he is warned at the last minute by Pat that she has finally deciphered the book's meaning – it is a cookbook.

"The recollections of one Michael Chambers, with appropriate flashbacks and soliloquy. Or, more simply stated, the evolution of man. The cycle of going from dust to dessert; the metamorphosis from being the ruler of a planet . . . to an ingredient in someone's soup. It's tonight's bill of fare . . . on the Twilight Zone."

Trailer: *"Next week we burrow deep into the most inner confines of kook-land and hopefully wind up dead center of the oddest portion thereof. We'll bring you a story called 'To Serve Man,' written originally by Damon Knight. If you've ever wondered how we'd react to the arrival of some honest-to-Pete saucers – next week's diet should be your meat. On The Twilight Zone . . . 'To Serve Man.'"*

Trivia, etc. Serling was contractually obligated to turn in the first draft of this script by May 1. The episode was assigned a production number on June 5, 1961. The short story on which this episode is based was retroactively awarded the 1951 "Retro" Hugo Award for "Best Short Story" in 2001. Damon Knight (who then resided in Milford, Pennsylvania), exchanged correspondence with Serling a number of times from 1960 to 1961. Knight submitted short stories and plot proposals for *Twilight Zone*, but this marked his only story to be adapted. A three-page plot outline titled "A Meeting of the Board" was submitted to Serling in June of 1961, but Serling contemplated if it was feasible for use on the series, since the story went nowhere until the very end.

The flying saucer footage featured in the beginning of the episode was borrowed from the 1951 motion picture, *The Day the Earth Stood Still*. The stop-motion footage of the flying saucer taking off into the atmosphere towards the end of the episode was borrowed from the 1956 motion picture, *Earth vs. the Flying Saucers*. The stop-motion effect is credited to Ray Harryhausen, but the closing credits of this episode never acknowledged the famed effects artist.

Richard Kiel, a few hairs over 7-feet tall, was cast by Lynn Stalmaster in the multiple roles of the Kanamits you see throughout the entire episode. "I was still in the middle of shooting *Eegah* (1962) when I got a call from Herman about doing *The Twilight Zone*," recalled Kiel. "Arch Hall was very nice about it, having been an actor himself, and shot around me during the week it took me to do what turned out to be one of the classic episodes, titled 'To Serve Man.'" The role of Lloyd Bochner, however, was director Richard L. Bare's choice, as was actress Jeanne Evans, who played one of the women getting ready to board the ship; she was the real-life wife of director Richard L. Bare.

On June 12, Kiel reported to the men's third floor wardrobe department at M-G-M Studios for makeup tests and costumes. He reported at the studio at 9 a.m., and as soon as the makeup and costumes were completed, Kiel's voice was recorded in Sync Room "A" at M-G-M from 10 a.m. to 10:30 a.m. William Tuttle created the look of the Kanamits, attempting to follow Serling's description from the script: "we are reminded of his size in his relationships to other objects like chairs, tables, ashtrays, etc." Serling's facial description of the alien was a bit different from what turned out on film. "While humanoid in general appearance, it is almost as if someone had been sculpturing it and had left the job prematurely. It has two eyes, very wide apart, a small opening that passes for a nose and a tiny, almost imperceptible circular hole that passes for a mouth."

> **Production Schedule at M-G-M**
> Day 1 –   Interior of Secretary General's Office (Stage 4)
>   Interior of Secretary General's Conference Room (Stage 4)
> Day 2 –   Interior of Code Room (Stage 4)
> Day 3 –   The Lie Detector Room (Stage 4)
>   Spaceship Hangar (Stage 9)
> Day 4 –   Interior of Conference Room (Stage 10)

After makeup, costumes and recorded voice tracks, Kiel then reported to Stage 4 so director Bare and the crew could shoot preliminaries with Kiel in makeup and costume. All of the scenes where a Kanamit first makes his appearance at the U.N. were shot on that afternoon – but only the scenes where only Kiel is seen, not the dignitaries, delegates, interpreters and cameraman.

After viewing the rough cut, Serling was displeased with the effort. "'To Serve Man' turned out piss-poor, a combination of horrible direction and a faithless script bit your back," Serling told Damon Knight on October 12, 1961. "We're re-shooting some scenes and it's my hope that we can at least come within a few hundred yards of your great story."

Richard L. Bare is credited as director on the screen, but he wasn't the only one who had a hand in directing. As Serling described in a letter to Buck Houghton, "I have done this in very rough fashion, offering the suggestions perhaps without proper integration. I'm assuming that we can re-tool this so that on occasion we can go out to film clips of mobs, loudspeakers, et al." Richard L. Bare directed the scenes as the script called for them, as revealed in the M-G-M filming schedule. After a rough cut was made and Richard Kiel's voice was synced with the soundtrack, Serling and Houghton viewed the film and both agreed a major rehaul was needed. So plans were made to add footage, rewrite the Kanamit's dialogue, rerecord the alien's voice, incorporate stock footage and film additional scenes.

The original cut ended abruptly as Pat shouts: "To Serve Man . . . it's a cookbook!" And for a moment, Chambers looked stunned. A zoom into a close-up of his face as the horror takes hold. Slowly a huge hand comes into the frame to touch Chamber's cheek, pinches it lightly as if feeling for tenderness, then the hand gently – but very firmly – turns Chambers around and propels him up the stairs as they slowly close. During the process of this closing, we hear Serling's voice in closing narration:

"The very explicit and very specific differences in points of view. To the wee ones . . . the little folk called man . . . it's a marvelous adventure, a voyage to another planet. An exciting sojourn in another section of the galaxy. But to the very large, granite faced inhabitants known as Kanamits . . . it's nothing more than a cattle car, a very comfortable provisions ship bringing food from the other end of the universe. Like I say . . . it's all in the point of view."

The ending with Chambers being escorted into the spaceship was deleted. Footage of a montage sequence of the Kanamit giving gifts superimposed over the shots of the various newspaper headlines was also deleted, replaced with the delegates offering a token of thanks for the gifts that were bestowed on them. Stock footage of power plants for force fields and crops and deserts was inserted. Serling also composed two additional scenes for the opening and closing of the episode, so the film already shot in the can would become the flashback scenes.

James Sheldon came in to direct the conference room scene on June 17. On October 23, the interior of the spaceship with Kiel and Bochner (composing the opening and closing scenes of the episode) was filmed, as well as a revised scene where Chambers is pushed back onto the stairs as the door to the spaceship closes (which is why Brody and Chambers are not on the screen together in the closing moments). These additional scenes were filmed on Stage 9. Serling also rewrote his narrations and had them rerecorded for this episode.

Serling left for five weeks of vacation, leaving the filming of additional scenes and new cut in the capable hands of Houghton. "Just so long as you know, Buck," Serling wrote before leaving, "how deeply appreciative I am of all your back-breaking labor, your tremendous loyalty and your contributions which consistently and constantly made me look good."

Lloyd Bochner's narrations for the retakes were recorded on January 11, 1962, in Sync Room "B" from 8 a.m. to 9 a.m. By this time, the recordings of Kiel's voice had been tossed aside because of the revision, which required the dialogue to be recorded again. Since Kiel wasn't available, Joseph Ruskin, who played the role of the genie in "The Man in the Bottle," supplied the new voice of the Kanamits. Ruskin's name remained uncredited in the episode.

"I had been told that M-G-M and the producers had the right to use someone else to dub in my lines and that they probably would do that," Kiel recalled in his book, *Making it Big in the Movies* (2002). "I remember driving in directly from Palm Springs and reporting to M-G-M for hours of make-up before beginning the long day of shooting. I was so tired from driving right from one job to another and going through hours of brutal make-up that when they gave me a chance to do the lines myself, I was not prepared and did not do a very good job when I read the lines of the 'Kanamit.' Ultimately, they did use someone else to dub the voice of the Kanamit, and I wasn't surprised, just disappointed in myself."

When he came back from his trip, Serling viewed the revised film and admitted it was much better than before. A number of former insert scenes were deleted. The scene where a group of people boarded the spacecraft (with actor Theodore Marcuse as Citizen Gregori talking about a peaceful coalition) was in editor Jason Bernie's original rough cut, *after* Chambers was put into the spaceship, so the audience would realize that the Earthlings were unaware of what went on across the airfield. Serling favored switching the order of the scenes. *

The flashing light above the door in Chambers' room in the spaceship is the same featured on the chest of the two-headed Martian in "Mr. Dingle, the Strong." The television camera at the U.N. was the same lens installed on Wordsworth's wall in "The Obsolete Man." The private quarters featured in the opening and closing scene inside the spaceship was the same as in "Hocus-Pocus and Frisby," with a different door frame and the addition of lights and drawers.

With the drastic re-edit of this film, an original music score was not recommended by Scott Perry, Jr., the music editor, who decided in favor of using cues from the CBS stock music library.

---

* Among the deleted scenes were inserts of a push panel button, a salesman's hand, gum in a woman's hand, insert of a piano, and young children who received gifts from the Kanamit. Extras who were filmed for the scenes that ultimately got deleted: Bob McCord, Jim Turley, and Shirley Swedsen.

Some of the music is easily recognizable – lifted from the compositions used in "Back There" and "The Invaders."

The footage of New York Times Square was stock footage from 1949. The movie *My Dream is Yours* with Doris Day, Jack Carson and Lee Bowman is advertised at The Strand, and *Champion* with Kirk Douglas is advertised at another movie theater.

Television critic Leonard Hoffman of *The Tucson Daily Citizen* reviewed this episode referring to the story as "mediocre," adding that "the program is saved by television's sometimes unusual ability to reincarnate and even rejuvenate has-been tales and make them enjoyable fare."

On March 9, Damon Knight wrote to Serling, "You have made me a big man around here, and I would hate to try to estimate what your Trendex was in Milford the night you did 'To Serve Man.' My kids thought there ought to have been more to the story, but I thought it was a dandy show; I loved your monster and I treasure your line, 'dust to dessert.' I hear the series has not been renewed, which is a great pity if true, but I trust you are busy and happy. May your tribe increase."

Serling replied on March 13, thanking Knight for the gracious note. "I'm not at all sure we did justice to your exceptional story but the effort was there and the try was a manly one. Actually, the reactions to the show have been quite incredible. The mail pull, for our show anyway, has been quite phenomenal – and the word of mouth unusually positive and extensive. Actually, I think I piddled around with the U.N. too much and was unable to sustain this properly with legitimate production values. If we'd done this as a motion picture, and had a few more dollar bills accessible, it could have been dressed up far more handsomely. But as it is, we've done far worse with fewer results. Apologize to your kids for me, and explain to them what are the pitfalls of novice science fiction writers who run their ham fists all over the works of the legitimate ones. I hope we have a chance to do it again."

Among the television spoofs is *The Simpsons'* annual "Treehouse of Horror" from October of 1990 when elements of "To Serve Man" were implemented with Lisa discovering a book titled "How to Cook Humans." The aliens, however, calm her fears when it is revealed that the book was really titled "How to Cook for Forty Humans." On an episode of *Futurama*, the character of Bender wears an apron that says "To Serve Man."

Lloyd Bochner made his only appearance on *The Twilight Zone* in this episode (though he was offered a lead in "Number 12 Looks Just Like You"), but the actor assisted in what has become probably one of the best spoofs of this classic episode. In the 1991 motion picture, *The Naked Gun 2 ½: The Smell of Fear*, Bochner runs across the screen holding a book, screaming "it's a cookbook!"

In the episode "Sofa So Good," on *Married . . . With Children*, initially telecast January 16, 1994, Al screams off screen "Peg! To Serve Man! It's a cookbook!" In the episode "Space," on *Newsradio*, initially telecast on May 21, 1997, a comical look of the future involves Jimmy distributing copies of a book titled "To Serve Man." The printing is a result of a publishing company he bought out. When someone asks about the title, Jimmy sarcastically comments, "Yeah, it's a cookbook." In the episode "Lessons," on *Buffy, the Vampire Slayer*, initially telecast September 24, 2002, a verbal reference is made about this episode. In the episode "Peace," on *Angel*, initially telecast April 30, 2003, the cast discovers a creature that eats people to sustain life. One of the members, upon learning the news, comments, "It's 'To Serve Man' all over again."

Production #4816 and 4894 "THE FUGITIVE" (Initial telecast: March 9, 1962)
Copyright Registration: © Cayuga Productions, Inc., March 6, 1962, LP21890 (in notice: 1961)
Date of Rehearsal: July 21, 1961
Dates of Filming: July 24, 25 and 26, 1961
First draft dated: June 15, 1961

Producer and Secretary: $1,625.00
Director: $1,458.67
Unit Manager and Secretary: $600.00
Agents Commission: $2,500.00
Below the line charges (M-G-M): $30,032.44
Total Production Costs: $48,012.02 *

Story and Secretary: $2,405.00
Cast: $7,262.50
Production Fee: $900.00
Legal and Accounting: $250.00
Below the line charges (other): $978.41

Cast: Russ Bender (the doctor); Johnny Eiman (the pitcher); Susan Gordon (Jenny); Nancy Kulp (Mrs. Gann); Wesley Lau (the first man); J. Pat O'Malley (Old Ben); Stephen Talbot (Howie); and Paul Tripp (the second man).

The Children: Roger Bramy, Stephen Goodwins, Thomas Greco, John W. Hatley, Gregory McCabe, Eddye Prellwitz, William Rule, Johnny Schultz, Marc Stevens, and Chris Sullivan.

Stock Music Cues: Etrange #3 (by Marius Constant, :09); Milieu #1 (by Constant, :16); Brave New World (by Bernard Hermann, :08); Nemours #3 (by Constant, :03); Dax #1 (by Constant, :08); Colmar #1 (by Constant, :05); Menton 11 (by Constant, :06); Menton 17 (by Constant, :08); Menton 10 (by Constant, :29); Fatherly Advice from Boss (by William Lava, :16); Harp Shockers (by Fred Steiner, :05 and :05); Brothers Lime #4 (by Lyn Murray, :07); Country Wayside (by Lava, :10); Country Wayside – To Coda A (by Lava, :17); Brothers Lime #4 (by Murray :34); Blood Fever (by Murray, :06); Unloaded Gun (by Murray, :25); Menton 4 (by Constant, :05); Brave New World (by Herrmann, :09); Country Wayside (by Lava, :16); Brave New World (by Herrmann, :06); Menton 9 (by Constant, :11); Perry Mason Suspense Background (by Steiner, arr. by William Barnett, :17); Unloaded Gun (by Murray, :34); Tramontane #1 (by Constant, :07); Menton 18 (by Constant, :29); Menton 15 (by Constant, :11); Menton 17 (by Constant, :17); Menton 18 (by Constant, :36); Brave New World (by Herrmann, :18); Country Wayside (by Lava, :28); Menton 12 (by Constant, :05); Bergson #5 (by Constant, :24); Nietzsche #5 (by Constant, :11); Bergson #5 (by Constant, :05); Scherzando (by Rene Garriguenc, :07); Bergson #5 (by Constant, :14); Delfort #5 (by Constant, :15); Etrange #3 (by Constant, :08); and Milieu #2 (by Constant, :18).

Director of Photography: Jack Swain
Art Directors: George W. Davis and Phil Barber
Assistant Director: E. Darrell Hallenbeck
Story Consultant: Richard McDonagh
Sound: Franklin Milton and Bill Edmondson

Production Manager: Ralph W. Nelson
Set Decorations: H. Web Arrowsmith
Casting: Stalmaster-Lister
Film Editor: Jason H. Bernie, a.c.e.
Directed by Richard L. Bare

---

* Total production costs and breakdown from production summary dated February 28, 1962.

Automobiles Supplied by the Ford   Teleplay by Charles Beaumont
   Motor Company

"It's been said that science fiction and fantasy are two different things. Science fiction, the improbable made possible; fantasy, the impossible made probable. What would you have if you put these two different things together? Well, you'd have an old man named Ben who knows a lot of tricks most people don't know and a little girl named Jenny who loves him . . . and a journey into the heart of the Twilight Zone."

Plot: Young Jenny lives with Mrs. Gann, a torturous aunt, but finds happiness in the same building with a tenant known to neighborhood children as "Old Ben." The old man has a unique gift of shape-shifting and performing small feats of magic for their amusement. When two men arrive in search of Old Ben, he reveals his secret to Jenny: he's from another world and needs to flee this world for another. In his final act before leaving, Ben cures Jenny so she'll no longer have a need for the leg brace. When the men looking for Ben notice Jenny is walking without the brace, they cause Jenny to take seriously ill – knowing Ben will return to cure her. Ben does, at the cost of revealing himself to the strangers. It turns out that Ben is a king and the men seeking him are his subjects. Jenny pleads for Ben to either stay or take her with him, but the subjects disapprove – until Jenny comes up with an idea. Alone together, Ben transforms into Jenny – forcing the subjects to take both of them, fearing they might take the wrong one. A charming fantasy that made a monster into a prince, and a cripple a queen.

"Mrs. Gann will be in for a big surprise when she finds this [photo of a young man] *under Jenny's pillow, because Mrs. Gann has more temper than imagination. She'll never dream that this is a picture of Old Ben as he really looks, and it will never occur to her that eventually her niece will grow up to be an honest-to-goodness queen . . . somewhere in the Twilight Zone."*

Trailer: *"Next week on the Twilight Zone, contributor Charles Beaumont provides us with a most charming tale of an old man and some children. An old man who's an exceptional playmate. Exceptional because . . . well, how many old men do you know who can change into monsters? Mr. Beaumont's excellent tasting stew is further seasoned by an element of mystery. It's called 'The Fugitive.' We hope to see you next week."*

Trivia, etc. A production schedule dated June 15, 1961, listed this episode going into production with primary filming on October 2, 3 and 4 (with rehearsal dates of September 28 and 29), but sometime between June 15 and mid-July, it was decided this episode would be produced a few months earlier. Susan Gordon had reported for wardrobe fittings on July 20. "That was one of my favorite roles, if not my favorite," Gordon related years later. "I got to run off with a prince, and I got to be a twin at the end . . . I'd always wanted to be a twin!"

Paul Tripp, who played the role of the "second man" in this episode, appeared courtesy of a fan letter he wrote to Rod Serling, from New York City, on January 17, 1961. "Was so pleased to read that your show had been granted a new lease on life. This is just a rather roundabout way of asking if there would be any chance of appearing in one of your shows while I am out there, next month or so. If it is possible, I shall be very grateful for the opportunity of not only working with you again, but also for the chance to show off my wares."

On January 26, Serling wrote back, asking Tripp to have his agent contact him with the details

> **Production Schedule at M-G-M**
> Day 1 –   Interior of the Gann Apartment
>   and Hallway (Stage 7)
> Day 2 –   Interior of Ben's Room and Interior
>   of the Gann Apartment (Stage 7)
> Day 3 –   Exterior of the City Street (Lot #2)

of his arrival. "Good actors aren't that easy to find and just between you and me and Mr. Nielsen – you're precisely that," Serling commented. Martin Dubow of the William Morris Agency contacted Serling and informed him of when Tripp would be arriving on the West Coast, so the casting director through Serling's influence made the arrangements. On July 20, Dubow sent Serling a thank-you letter for casting Paul Tripp.

When this episode (script #79) was assigned a production number on July 17, 1961, James Sheldon was originally slated to direct. For reasons unknown, the episode was reassigned to Richard L. Bare. The first three days of filming went by smoothly, but on the afternoon of July 26, Susan Gordon was taken to the studio hospital. The doctor in attendance examined the young actress and sent her home. The rest of the cast and crew continued shooting without her for the remainder of the day, using Marilyn Malloy as Gordon's stand-in. Filming did not resume for four days because of her illness. On August 2, 1961, she was well enough to report to Cohn Park on Lot #2 at M-G-M for the remainder of the filming, for the opening scenes of the episode. The final day of filming was assigned a new production number, #4894.

Susan Gordon's strength was not the best, but she managed to pull through long enough for her scenes to be completed. "The last days of shooting were done on the baseball field," recalled Susan Gordon. "It was during those outdoors scenes that I was taken ill – perhaps it was a touch of sunstroke? – and, in the middle of the last scene of the day, I could barely make it through my lines without fainting. When the director yelled, 'Cut!', I walked off the set and collapsed. They carried me off the set on a stretcher as Rod Serling walked in to do his bit. I came '*that close*' to meeting Mr. Serling!"

"One amusing anecdote – well, amusing to me, anyway – happened during the scene with the mouse," added Gordon. "When I held a mouse (supposedly a transformed Old Ben) inside my shirt to hide it from my aunt, the mouse got loose inside my shirt and ran around in there, tickling me silly, before I could catch it. Obviously, the scene had to be re-shot."

After viewing the rough cut, Houghton and Serling felt the opening scene required something more than just the kids in the baseball field. On January 30, 1962, Ralph Nelson directed a helicopter shot of the ballfield for the opening scene. The helicopter was rented from Fred Bowen's Helicopter Company at World Wide Hangar (near Skyways). Jack Glass was on board, pointing the camera straight down and photographing a baseball game in action. The aerial shot did not use actors in a field – it was a real game going on in the city. Joe Roue was the assistant cameraman on board, assisting Glass.

Because Serling appeared on camera for all of the episodes (including the trailers), the Screen Actors' Guild required him to be paid for his appearances. The minimum at the time this episode was filmed (his scene was shot on July 25), according to the S.A.G., was $90, but the figure of $125 was paid to Serling in mid-August.

Serling's original trailer for "next week's episode" was shortened for the actual broadcast. The original was:

"Next week on the Twilight Zone, contributor Charles Beaumont provides us with a most charming

tale of an old man and some children. An old man who's an exceptional playmate. Exceptional because . . . well, how many old men do you know who can change into monsters, exercise magic, or disappear? But Mr. Beaumont's excellent tasting stew is further seasoned by an element of mystery and it's for this reason that this piece is called, 'The Fugitive.' We hope you're gathered around next week to watch it."

Production #4828 "LITTLE GIRL LOST" (Initial telecast: March 16, 1962)

Copyright Registration: © Cayuga Productions, Inc., March 13, 1962, LP21891
Dates of Rehearsal: January 29 and 30, 1962
Dates of Filming: January 31 and February 1 and 2, 1962
Revised Script #92 dated: January 7, 1962

Producer and Secretary: $1,625.00	Story and Secretary: $2,405.00
Director: $1,250.00	Cast: $4,278.41
Unit Manager and Secretary: $600.00	Production Fee: $900.00
Agents Commission: $2,500.00	Legal and Accounting: $250.00
Below the line charges (M-G-M): $32,142.68	Below the line charges (other): $4,084.55
Total Production Costs: $50,035.64 *	

Cast: Charles Aidman (Bill); Sarah Marshall (Ruth Miller); Robert Sampson (Chris Miller); Tracy Stratford (Tina Miller); and Rhoda Williams (Tina's voice).

Original Music Score Composed and Conducted by Bernard Herrmann (Score No. CPN6036):
Etrange #3 (by Marius Constant, :09); Milieu #1 (by Constant, :16); Where Are You? (2:15); Gone (:02); Emptiness (2:02); Dog Gone (:35); Hole in The Wall (:58); Third Dimension (2:05); Coin Disappears (:24); Move Around (:17); Look For Her (1:35); Fourth Dimension (2:54); Half in Zone (:41); Etrange #3 (by Constant, :08); and Milieu #2 (by Constant, :19).

Director of Photography: George T. Clemens, a.s.c.	Production Manager: Ralph W. Nelson
	Set Decorations: Keogh Gleason
Art Directors: George W. Davis and Merill Pye	Assistant Director: E. Darrell Hallenbeck
Casting: Robert Walker	Film Editor: Jason H. Bernie, a.c.e.
Sound: Franklin Milton and Bill Edmondson	Directed by Paul Stewart

Teleplay by Richard Matheson, based on his short story of the same name, originally published in the November 1953 issue of *Amazing Stories*.

"Missing: one frightened, little girl. Name: Bettina Miller. Description: six years of age, average height and build; light brown hair, quite pretty. Last seen: being tucked in bed by her mother a few hours ago. Last heard? Aye, 'there's the rub,' as Hamlet put it. For Bettina Miller can be heard quite clearly – despite the rather curious fact that she can't be seen at all. Present location? Let's say for the moment . . . in the Twilight Zone."

---

* Total production costs and breakdown from production summary dated June 30, 1962.

Plot: The parents of Bettina Miller, a 6-year-old girl, face a problem with a solution that cannot be found in any textbook. In her bedroom, they can hear her cry for help, but they cannot see her. In desperation, Chris Miller phones his friend, Bill, a physicist, to come over to the house and help solve the mystery. When the family dog runs under the bed, he vanishes too. Bill arrives and after exploring a number of options, finds an opening on the wall behind the bed, leading to another dimension – a freak of nature that rarely happens. Since the other side is not laid out like their world, finding Bettina is not as easy as reaching out and grabbing her. In desperation to regain his lost daughter, Chris falls through the portal and taking advantage of the opportunity, calls out to their dog Max, who leads Bettina back to his arms. Bill pulls them back into their world, holding on to half of Chris' body during the rescue. With the entire family safe at home, Chris learns that while he was inside, the door to the other dimension was slowly closing in on him. Half of his body almost left our world for another.

"The other half where? The fourth dimension? The fifth? Perhaps. They never found the answer. Despite a battery of research physicists equipped with every device known to man, electronic and otherwise, no result was ever achieved . . . except perhaps a little more respect for and uncertainty about the mechanisms . . . of the Twilight Zone."

Trailer: *"Next week an excursion into a strange and totally different dimension. We'll bring you a story by Richard Matheson called 'Little Girl Lost' and this one we guarantee is not the kind found on a police docket or in a missing persons bureau. When this little girl is lost, we're talking about out of this world. I hope you can join us next week and find out precisely where she's gone."*

Trivia, etc. Musician Bernard Herrmann is credited before director Paul Stewart. This marks the only episode of the series in which the musician received top billing over the director. Herrmann was in Paris, France, at the time he was approached to do the score. First composed in February 1962, the entire score (including the closing theme) was recorded in Paris on March 6. This also explains why the closing theme is a slightly different rendition from the recording heard normally during the closing of the remaining third-season episodes.

Paul Stewart was an actor-turned-director and helmed the command for this episode. His box-office appeal as an actor had diminished by 1962. "I simply became bored with acting," Stewart recalled. "I'd done all I could with those no dimensional heavies. So I turned to a far more creative kind of work." Stewart started directing television in 1956 "out of disgust with the kind of parts available to an actor." Joan Harrison, producer for *Alfred Hitchcock Presents*, gave him his first chance in TV, and one show led to another.

"Our daughter, our older girl, Tina – the same name as in the story – was crying, and I went into the room," recalled Matheson to interviewer Matthew R. Bradley. "Actually, the apartment was so small, it was just a wooden Army cot she slept on at that time. I felt around the bed and she wasn't on the bed, and I thought, 'Oh, my Lord, the poor kid fell on the floor,' then I felt on the floor, she wasn't there. When I felt under the bed, I couldn't find her. Finally, I found her – she had gone under the bed and rolled all the way to the wall, and that's where I found her, and then, of course, the diabolical writer's mind, you know, after the kid stops crying, you think of a story."

Assigned a production number on January 17, 1962, the episode was filmed on Stage 9 at M-

G-M except for the Fourth Dimension scenes, filmed on the second half of the final day, February 2, on Stage 10. Merrill Pye, one of the art directors for the series, noticed on one of the pages that Matheson described the other world simply as: "Merrill Pye was last seen at a full run down Washington Blvd."

Buck Houghton recalled the day the art director entered his office, having read the script, and asked how they were to create another dimension. He showed Houghton another page in the script where it said, "INTERIOR: LIMBO."

He asked, "What's that supposed to be, Buck?" Houghton's reply was "It's up to you."

The art director went off and created a fourth dimension for the episode. "He broke his neck to make a limbo set," recalled Houghton proudly. "That's challenge and response. That's what the scripts were full of. From the assistant prop man to the cameraman, they worked their ass off. They wanted to do the scripts justice, and that made a lot of difference in how the episodes looked. The crew was absolutely thrilled to see how the shows were going to come off." *

The dog featured in this episode was named "Rags" and was used by the trainer only on the first day of filming. In the story, the dog's name was "Mags," to ensure the dog would react when called, with a name similar to its own. Matheson's script originally called for a young girl with blond hair, but Cayuga arranged for a brunette. When Ruth is asked to produce the box of crayons so Bill can use a black crayon to mark the wall, the production company used a white crayon (or chalk as it appears) against a dark-colored wall. To feature a wall of white would have altered the lighting in the room, so it was decided early on to use a wall with a darkish color.

The role of Tina, played by Tracy Stratford, was unbilled during the closing credits, as was Rhoda Williams, who supplied the voice of Tina. Young Tracy was only needed for the final day of filming, but Williams stayed off camera to supply the voice for the actors to keep on cue. Shortly after filming was completed, Rhoda Williams reported to the recording room at M-G-M to have her voice recorded, to be looped into the soundtrack when the film was edited together. The voice of Tina in this episode was Rhoda Williams until the moment Tina was pulled back into the real world. Williams began her career on radio and was specially trained in voice acting. She played the role of Betty, Robert Young's oldest daughter, on radio's *Father Knows Best* and voiced a number of animatronic creations at Disneyland.

The television critic for *The Bridgeport Post* remarked this episode as "a particularly eerie one for parents," and concluded the review with "a show that will stick in your mind for a while."

Like most filmed television programs, the scenes for this episode were not produced in the sequence they appeared on the finished film. Later scenes involving Bill's attempts to pull Tina out of the fourth dimension were shot before the scenes in which Ruth and Chris discover Tina isn't there. Because of this, at the end of the first day of filming, the chalk marks were removed from the wall and the bed was replaced so Serling's entrance scene could be filmed. In order to ensure the chalk marks matched the next day's filming, light pencil lines were made on the wall tracing the chalk. When the camera picks up Serling's feet and pans up for a portrait shot, Serling can be seen glancing to his left, waiting for the cue to begin talking. In the background, behind Serling, the pencil marks can be seen on the wall.

---

* Source: *Science Fiction Television Series: Episode Guides, Histories, and Casts and Credits for 62 Prime-Time Shows, 1959 through 1989*, by Mark Phillips and Frank Garcia. North Carolina, McFarland & Incorporated, Inc. © 1996. Reprinted with permission.

After viewing the initial telecast of "Nothing in the Dark," Richard Matheson was prompted the next day (January 6) to write the following letter to Houghton:

Dear Buck:

I believe that, generally speaking, I have caused a minimum of problems in the part with regard to my association with *Twilight Zone*. I think I have written some good scripts and have been more than satisfied with our relationship. However, I feel that I must, at this point, raise a brief, polite ruckus as to the treatment my stories have gotten in the past year or so. What brings this on is my admiration for the direction George got on his 'Nothing in the Dark'; which we all saw last night. I feel that I have gotten considerably less on my last three scripts. I thought that Douglas Heyes did a bad job on the Agnes Moorehead story, setting a draggy pace and allowing her to gorge herself on the scenery. I am not too pleased either with 'Young Man's Fancy,' as I feel that Brahm missed a lot of values, that Alex Nicol was badly miscast and that Bare spoiled the ending. Finally, I feel that the Buster Keaton show descended into absolute monotony in the second act and was, generally, badly directed.

For these reasons I would like to – urgently – request that Lamont Johnson direct 'Little Girl Lost.' (I recall you, Buck, mentioning some director you had in mind but do not recall whether it was Johnson or not.) I think that he is the one to do this story since its basic elements are extremely similar to those in George's story – circumscribed area, minimum cast and high emotion. Please let him direct this show – and, in addition, please cast John Alvin for the role of Bill. John is an acquaintance of ours and a fine, professional actor; we have seen much of his work (at the Player's Ring, on *One Step Beyond*, *The Jack Benny Show*, etc.) and have yet to see him do less than a first-rate job. The rest of the casting I leave to your discretion although I have indicated my preference for Shatner and that girl – or someone of their caliber.

I think you know that I am not in the habit of writing letters like this – or of raising issues like this – but, after reviewing the [show last night], to me, rather dismaying deterioration in the presentation of the last three scripts I've done, I feel that I must make myself heard. I have done some good work for *The Twilight Zone*, I hope I have the right to do this.

On January 12, Serling wrote a personal reply, explaining that Houghton took the letter to heart. While Houghton commented to Matheson separately, Serling gave his own personal reply: "I agree with you, of course, that in many cases you did not receive the benefit of professional direction. On the other hand, a couple of your shows I thought got exceptional treatment. The script, 'The Last Flight,' – I thought Bill Claxton did a fine job with. As I recall it, there were a couple rather ecstatic expository scenes that were beautifully directed. I thought Ralph Nelson also treated you handsomely in the Phyllis Kirk and Keenan Wynn show. There's no question but that both the Keaton thing and the Agnes Moorehead thing were damaged rather than helped by the director. But I do think, Dick, that these are the ground rules of the goddamned medium. Doug Heyes was the most singularly successful director we used on the series. He only turned in one bad job and unfortunately that was on your script. I don't want to belabor this or be defensive about it. I'm only broaching all these things to tell you that we're cognizant of your concern, and intent on correcting the problem." Serling also assured Matheson that the next script ("Little Girl Lost") would receive above-average treatment. This may explain why Bernard Herrmann, who was in Paris, was hired to do the music for an episode that any musician in the U.S. could have composed.

Supposedly this episode was the inspiration for the motion picture, *Poltergeist* (1982). Numerous assertions lay claim that the movie owed an unacknowledged debt to "Little Girl Lost." When interviewer Matthew R. Bradley questioned Richard Matheson, the writer explained, "Yeah, I know. But if I'd sued, I would've been clobbered – too much money on the other side. Spielberg asked me if he could see a cassette of 'Little Girl Lost,' and I sent him one, he looked at it, then sent it back, and I never heard until someone said, 'Hey, I see they made your *Twilight Zone* into a movie.' Of course, there was a lot more to the movie but, certainly, that was part of it. I've said it before, I think maybe Spielberg knows this, and always came to me with some kind of offer that would compensate, to repay me, like writing the script for *Twilight Zone – The Movie*, or having me as a consultant on *Amazing Stories*."

In the motion picture, *The Last Action Hero* (1993), the villain puts his hand through the wall in the same fashion as this *Twilight Zone* episode. During this scene, Constant's theme music is played in the background, and Rod Serling's voice can be heard in the soundtrack.

This episode of *The Twilight Zone* was spoofed on *The Simpsons* on one of their annual "Treehouse of Horror" episodes, in which Homer fell into another dimension and described the portal as something from that "twilighty show about that zone." Lawrence Krauss, a physicist who wrote *Hiding in the Mirror*, a 2005 history of speculation about extra dimensions, recalled how this episode had an impact on him when he first saw it as a little boy.

Production #4829 "PERSON OR PERSONS UNKNOWN"
(Initial telecast: March 23, 1962)

Copyright Registration: © Cayuga Productions, Inc., March 20, 1962, LP21892
Dates of Rehearsal: February 2 and 5, 1962
Dates of Filming: February 6, 7 and 8, 1962

Producer and Secretary: $1,625.00
Director: $1,250.00
Unit Manager and Secretary: $600.00
Agents Commission: $2,500.00
Below the line charges (M-G-M): $31,781.51
Total Production Costs: $48,431.82 *

Story and Secretary: $2,405.00
Cast: $5,578.81
Production Fee: $900.00
Legal and Accounting: $250.00
Below the line charges (other): $1,541.50

Cast: Shirley Ballard (Wilma Berenson #1); Ed Glover (Sam Baker); Betty Harford (the woman clerk); Joe Higgins (the bank guard); Clegg Hoyt (Sam, the bartender); Michael Keep (the policeman); Richard Long (David Andrew Gurney); Bob McCord (the truck owner); John Newton (Mr. Cooper); Frank Silvera (Dr. Koslenka); and Julie Van Zandt (Wilma Gurney #2).

Stock Music Cues: Etrange #3 (by Marius Constant, :09); Milieu #1 (by Constant, :16); Soliloquy #1 (by Arthur Wilkinson, :39); Black Mood (by Jerry Goldsmith, :29); Punctuation and Passing of Time #10 (by Rene Garriguenc, :17); Light Dramatic Series #8 (by Garriguenc, :47); Bel Air Outdoors, Part 3 (by Garriguenc, :34); Serling II (by Robert Drasnin, :04 and :04); Light Dramatic Series #4 (by Garriguenc, :32); Light Dramatic Series #1 (by Garriguenc, :24); F Story #7

---

* Total production costs and breakdown from production summary dated June 30, 1962.

(by Constant, :27); Serling I (by Drasnin, :05); Serling II (by Drasnin, :26); Defeat (by Goldsmith, :55); Terror Struck (by Goldsmith, :33 and :39); Light Dramatic Series #4 (by Gariguenc, :25); Light Dramatic Series #10 (by Garriguenc, :11); Black Mood (by Goldsmith, :35); The Robbery (by Goldsmith, :06); Black Mood (by Goldsmith, :42); Serling III (by Drasnin, :05); Etrange #3 (by Constant, :08); and Milieu #2 (by Constant, :19).

Director of Photography: Robert W. Pittack, a.s.c.	Production Manager: Ralph W. Nelson
Art Directors: George W. Davis and Merrill Pye	Set Decorations: Keogh Gleason
Assistant Director: E. Darrell Hallenbeck	Casting: Robert Walker
Film Editor: Bill Mosher	Sound: Franklin Milton and Bill Edmondson
Automobiles Supplied by the Ford Motor Company	Directed by John Brahm
	Teleplay by Charles Beaumont

"Cameo of a man who has just lost his most valuable possession. He doesn't know about the loss yet. In fact, he doesn't even know about the possession. Because, like most people, David Gurney has never really thought about the matter of his identity. But he's going to be thinking a great deal about it from now on, because that is what he's lost. And his search for it is going to take him into the darkest corners . . . of the Twilight Zone."

Plot: David Gurney wakes up one morning to find himself without an identity. His wife of 11 years doesn't recognize him, the employees at the bank where he works don't know him, and all forms of identity, including his driver's license, have vanished. After being picked up by the police for unruly conduct and theft of a vehicle, Gurney finds himself in an asylum where the doctor offers an explanation: sometime last night he suffered a disorientation and a severe case of mistaken identity. Determined to prove he is who he claims, Gurney sets out to find one of the small details that no one could possibly have known or covered up – thus proving the entire stunt was an elaborate practical joke. This attempt fails, and Gurney breaks down crying, only to wake from what appeared to be a nightmare. Now he has to cope with the loss of identity he swore to regain because he cannot recall who he is – and the woman who claims is his wife is unfamiliar to him . . .

"A case of mistaken identity or a nightmare turned inside out? A simple loss of memory or the end of the world? David Gurney may never find the answer, but you can be sure he's looking for it . . . in the Twilight Zone."

Trailer: *"Next week we again borrow from the considerable talents of Charles Beaumont and we take a fast trot on the wild side. Picture if you will, a man who wakes up in a strange world . . . knows everyone, knows everyplace, feels very much at home. The strangeness comes from the fact that no one knows him. Try this one for size on the next Twilight Zone. It's called 'Person or Persons Unknown.' Habit is something you do when pleasure is gone, and certainly this is not the way to smoke. I prefer to smoke Chesterfields and get the rich taste of 21 great tobaccos. Blended mild, not filtered mild. Smoke for pleasure. Smoke Chesterfields."*

Trivia, etc. This episode (script #93) was assigned a production number on January 17, 1962. There were two days of rehearsals for this episode, most of the time devoted to Long and Silvera's scenes together. Actress Shirley Ballard joined the men in rehearsals on February 5.

Days after this episode was filmed, a press release was issued to trade columns attempting to capitalize on the star appeal of Richard Long, reminding readers that Long had co-starred on television's *Bourbon Street Beat* and *77 Sunset Strip* in bygone seasons.

"It's an insane business," Long described for *TV Guide*, regarding his television appearances. "But I have a great deal of respect for it. I see it as a job, a craft. This part turns me on."

The scenes of David Gurney's office were filmed on location outside the Culver City Library where a bank and parking lot were located. The photo of the boxer behind the bar is the same featured in other episodes – "What You Need" and "A Kind of a Stopwatch."

In the episode "The Van Buren Boys," on *Seinfeld*, initially telecast on February 6, 1997, Jerry Seinfeld makes a reference to feeling like a *Twilight Zone* character who woke up and couldn't figure out his identity. When Kramer asked which episode that was, Seinfeld remarked that they were all like that.

Production #4822 "THE LITTLE PEOPLE" (Initial telecast: March 30, 1962)
Copyright Registration: © Cayuga Productions, Inc., March 27, 1962, LP22264
Date of Rehearsal: September 19, 1961
Dates of Filming: September 20, 21 and 22, 1961
Script #84 dated: August 23, 1961, with revised pages dated September 15, 1961

Producer and Secretary: $1,625.00
Director: $1,250.00
Unit Manager and Secretary: $600.00
Agents Commission: $2,500.00
Below the line charges (M-G-M): $28,611.08
Total Production Costs: $43,563.88 *

Story and Secretary: $2,855.00
Cast: $4,112.50
Production Fee: $900.00
Legal and Accounting: $250.00
Below the line charges (other): $860.30

Cast: Claude Akins (William Fletcher); Robert Eaton (spaceman #2, the giant who picks up Craig); Michael Ford (spaceman #1); and Joe Maross (Peter Craig).

Stock Music Cues: Etrange #3 (by Marius Constant, :09); Milieu #1 (by Constant, :16); Fantasies (by Wilfred Josephs, :34 and :10); Mausoleum (by Josephs, 1:11); Mistral #1 (by Constant, :06); Fantasies (by Josephs, :33 and :43); Safe Cracker (by Josephs, :55); Ostinato (by Josephs, :33 and :17); Fantasies (by Josephs, :11); Dreams (by Josephs, :09); Love Vigil (by Josephs, :02); Fantasies (by Josephs, :34); Ostinato (by Josephs, :20); Safe Cracker (by Josephs, :46); Suspense (Neuro) (by Rene Garriguenc, :48); Fantasies (by Josephs, :24); Martenot Improvisation #3 (CBS, :14 and :28); Ostinato (by Josephs, :56); Martenot Improvisation #3 (CBS, :28); Fantasies (by Josephs, :24); Ostinato (by Josephs, :28); Fantasies (by Josephs, :16 and :26); Lone Vigil (by Josephs, :02); Etrange #3 (by Constant, :08); and Milieu #2 (by Constant, :18).

Director of Photography: George T.
   Clemens, a.s.c.
Art Directors: George W. Davis and Phil Barber

Production Manager: Ralph W. Nelson
Set Decorations: H. Web Arrowsmith
Assistant Director: E. Darrell Hallenbeck

---

* Total production costs and breakdown from production summary dated February 28, 1962.

Casting: Stalmaster-Lister
Film Editor: Jason H. Bernie, a.c.e.
Directed by William Claxton

Story Consultant: Richard McDonagh
Sound: Franklin Milton and Bill Edmondson
Teleplay by Rod Serling

"The time is the space age. The place is a barren landscape of a rock-walled canyon that lies millions of miles from the planet Earth. The cast of characters? You've met them: William Fletcher, commander of the spaceship. His co-pilot, Peter Craig. The other characters who inhabit this place, you may never see. But they're there, as these two gentlemen will soon find out. Because they're about to partake in a little exploration into that gray, shaded area in space and time that's known as . . . the Twilight Zone."

Plot: Two astronauts, Fletcher and Craig, land on the floor of a canyon on a deserted asteroid so major repairs can be made to their spacecraft. Craig, tired of being on the receiving end of orders, doesn't assist the commander with the repairs. Instead, he spends his time wandering the rocky landscape and studying a miniature civilization, complete with forests, lakes, rivers, buildings and little people. Having hunger for people at his elbow, on his terms, Craig takes hold of the reins and demands to be a god – believing the little people were created in his image. Fletcher knocks Craig unconscious and finishes repairing the ship, hoping Craig hasn't caused harm to the civilization. Fletcher's efforts for preservation are thwarted when he soon finds himself staring at a life-size statue of Craig and discovers that the little people built it in return for Craig not destroying their buildings. Craig pulls a gun and orders Fletcher to leave, so he can remain behind with "his people." Against his better wishes, Fletcher departs, leaving Craig alone on the asteroid to do what he pleases. Craig bestows a "new order" on the little people, creating a little chaos to remind them of his superior authority. A short time later, Craig hears deafening sounds of another spaceship and when he looks up, he screams for two giant spacemen to go away, unintentionally getting their attention. When one of the giants picks up Craig, he accidentally crushes him to death – and leaves the scene to make repairs on their ship. While Craig's body lies on the ground in a twisted heap, the little people pull the statue down over the dead body of their "god."

"The case of navigator Peter Craig . . . a victim of a delusion. In this case, the dream dies a little harder than the man. A small exercise in space psychology that you can try on for size . . . in the Twilight Zone."

Trailer: *"Next week we take a trip through a galaxy to a few million light years away from your collective television screens. We'll land on an uncharted asteroid and then undergo an experience designed for goose-bumps and palpitations, because, on the Twilight Zone, next time out – you'll see that monsters come in all assorted sizes and shapes. I hope we've whetted your appetite and, if so – we'll see you next week. Our show is called 'The Little People.'"*

Trivia, etc. In a proposed trailer that was never used, Serling was originally going to say, "You'll see monsters come in all assorted sizes and shapes and that good things don't always come in small packages."

Leonard Hoffman of *The Salina Kansas Journal* remarked about this episode, "Host Rod Serling proves again tonight his unique ability as an imaginative and consistently entertaining television writer with an engrossing science fiction tale." The television columnist for *The Register and Post-Herald Weekender* commented that Serling was "having some more fun" with this script.

According to various sources, from *The New York Times* to *The Hollywood Reporter*, the following actors have a *Twilight Zone* connection but never appeared on the series:

February 19, 1963 – Bob Barran had signed on to play the role of a Martian peasant. Barran never appeared on the series and no episode ever contained a Martian peasant!

March 17, 1961 – Anthony George got a hefty salary boost for his role on the second season of *Checkmate*. Sometime during January and February of the same year, George rejected offers to appear on both *Alfred Hitchcock Presents* and *The Twilight Zone*. With a pay hike from the previous season and a guarantee of a limited number of episodes filmed, George was not sobbing.

June 7, 1960 – Martin Dubow of the William Morris Agency approached Rod Serling about the possibility of using Joey Bishop for an episode of *The Twilight Zone*. "Joey is most anxious to do a dramatic appearance," Dubow explained. "I would like you very much to keep Joey Bishop in mind for some of your forthcoming shows."

This episode was assigned a production number on September 12, 1961. The original draft named the main character Peter Knauff, but that was later changed to Peter Craig. The entire episode was filmed on Stage 5 at M-G-M Studios. The first and second day were devoted to Akins and Maross' scenes together, and the evening of the second day was devoted to the exterior cleft of the canyon with actors Michael Ford and Don Rhodes as the giant spacemen. The entire production was slated for three days, but most of the preliminary filming was apparently completed by the end of the second day. Close-up shots of Maross and Akins were scheduled for the third day, but the two men stayed on the set at the end of the second day to complete the job.

The uniforms worn by Fletcher and Craig not only originated from M-G-M's costume department, but were used previously in the episode, "The Lonely." The helmet Fletcher wears is the same featured in "The Lonely," only with noticeable changes – during the two years between filming of these episodes, the helmets were altered both in color and side attachments.

On December 21, 1961, the miniature trick involving the body of Craig in the hand of one of the giants was accomplished by Jack Glass and his camera crew, against black backing. The inserts were shot at 9:30 in the morning. The same trick was applied to the miniature truck in hand.

When originally shot, the scene features Peter Craig running, as Serling described: "tripping as he does so against the ruined head of the statue, toppling over, rolling, then landing in a sitting position, his back against the wall of the canyon. The clump, clump, clump of the mammoth footsteps come closer. He slowly stares up just at the moment a giant shadow covers the sun. His eyes are wide, almost insane with fear. He shakes his head involuntarily, holds up a hand. Now the thumps stop abruptly. The shadow is on him. He continues to stare wide eyed, then very slowly, inching his way to his feet, looking up, then screaming toward the apparition above him . . . He starts to scream."

After a rough cut was viewed, it was decided that the ending would have to be filmed with some revisions. On February 13, 1962, on Stage 24 at M-G-M, actors Don Rhodes and Michael Ford were asked to return to the set to reprise the role of the giant spacemen, but only Ford was available for filming. Actor Robert Eaton took the place of Don Rhodes. The retakes were used for the episode, filmed with an exterior of sky backing. Footage of Craig running was removed, but the scene where he screams remained. The hand insert remained, and the footage with the two new spacemen was incorporated into the finished film.

Eaton and Ford (the men are properly credited on screen) are wearing are the same uniforms featured in *Forbidden Planet* (1956). This episode has been spoofed on *The Simpsons* in the episode "The Genesis Tub," and *Futurama* in the episode "Godfellas." Many fans of *The Outer Limits* believe the premise was lifted for the pilot movie of Showtime Network's remake series, titled "The Sandkings," in which Beau Bridges accepts the position of God to a number of miniature sand creatures that build sculptures in various images at his command.

The musical cue known as "Suspense" by Rene Garriguenc, is not the theme to the radio program of the same name. While it has been mentioned in episode guides that Garriguenc was one of a few responsible for composing music for the radio program, the theme for *Suspense* was never featured in the *Twilight Zone* productions. Often when writing a music cue, it would be titled generically according to the mood it created.

Production #4832 "FOUR O'CLOCK" (Initial telecast: April 6, 1962)

Copyright Registration: © Cayuga Productions, Inc., April 3, 1962, LP22265
Dates of Rehearsal: February 20 and 21, 1962
Dates of Filming: February 22, 23 and 26, 1962
Script #94 dated: "*Received* January 8, 1962"

Producer and Secretary: $1,625.00
Director: $1,250.00
Unit Manager and Secretary: $600.00
Agents Commission: $2,500.00
Below the line charges (M-G-M): $26,532.39
Total Production Costs: $44,279.20 *

Story and Secretary: $3,605.00
Cast: $5,451.81
Production Fee: $900.00
Legal and Accounting: $250.00
Below the line charges (other): $1,565.00

Cast: Theodore Bikel (Oliver Crangle); Linden Chiles (Hall, the FBI Agent); Phyllis Love (Mrs. Lucas); and Moyna MacGill (Mrs. Williams).

Stock Music Cues: Etrange #3 (by Marius Constant, :09); Milieu #1 (by Constant, :16); Confession #2 (by Rene Garriguenc, :26); Eerie Dream (by Lucien Moraweck, 1:10); Villers #4 (by Constant, :21); Fantasies (by Wilfred Josephs, :16); Dreams (by Josephs, :24); Menton (by Constant, :24); Villers #5 (by Constant, :29); Menton (by Constant, :28); Ostinato (by Josephs, :55); Dreams (by Josephs, :50); Moat Farm Murder (by Bernard Herrmann, :06 and :13); Goodbye Keith (by William Lava, :07); Confession #2 (by Garriguenc, :20); Etrange #3 (by Constant, :08); and Milieu #2 (by Constant, :18).

Director of Photography: George T.
    Clemens, a.s.c.

Production Manager: Ralph W. Nelson
Set Decorations: Keogh Gleason

---

* Total production costs and breakdown from production summary dated June 30, 1962.

Art Directors: George W. Davis and Merrill Pye   Assistant Director: E. Darrell Hallenbeck
Casting: Robert Walker   Film Editor: Jason H. Bernie, a.c.e.
Sound: Franklin Milton and Bill Edmondson   Directed by Lamont Johnson
Teleplay by Rod Serling, based on the short story of the same name by Price Day, originally published in the April 1958 issue of *Alfred Hitchcock's Mystery Magazine*.

"That's Oliver Crangle, a dealer in petulance and poison. He's rather arbitrarily chosen four o'clock as his personal Göetterdämerung – and we are about to watch the metamorphosis of a twisted fanatic, poisoned by the gangrene of prejudice – to the status of an avenging angel – upright and omniscient; dedicated and fearsome. Whatever your clocks say – it's four o'clock . . . and wherever you are . . . it happens to be . . . The Twilight Zone."

Plot: Oliver Crangle has taken it upon himself to root out evil and purge immorality from society. Dead set at destroying evil, he spends his time investigating people, cataloging their affiliations and habits, and makes judgments against them. Should he feel they are a menace to society, he places phone calls and mails letters with the intent of exposing evil and stripping it naked in the streets. He even makes late-night phone calls to people, revealing their guilt and then hanging up. Led on by self-delusions, he notifies the FBI that he plans to "will" all the evil people in the world 2-feet tall, so they can easily identify and detain guilty parties off the streets. Rather than gain cooperation, Crangle discovers to his horror that law enforcement suggests he seek psychiatric help. Unaware that he himself is a public nuisance, he shrinks to 2-feet tall when four o'clock comes around, branding him for his crimes against humanity.

"At four o'clock an evil man made his bed and laid in it. A pot called a kettle black. A stone thrower broke the windows of his glass house. You look for this one under 'F' for fanatic and 'J' for justice . . . in The Twilight Zone."

Trailer: *"Next week an exceptionally fine actor named Theodore Bikel portrays a misguided kook who fancies himself some kind of guardian of law and order. He decides that it's his mission in life to eradicate evil the world over. Now this one is to a 'very far-out,' but considering the nature of the times it happens to be 'very close-in.' Next week, an exercise in insanity. It's called 'Four O'Clock.' Set your watches and come on in. This cigarette, Chesterfield King, gives all the advantages of extra length and much more. The great taste of 21 vintage tobaccos, grown mild, aged mild and blended mild. No matter they satisfy so completely."*

Trivia, etc. When Robert Bernstein at Random House first approached Rod Serling in 1959 about the possibility of publishing an anthology of stories from *The Twilight Zone,* he sent a sample of what the books would look like. Bernstein mailed a couple of Hitchcock anthologies that his firm had published. Of the two books, one was *Alfred Hitchcock Presents: My Favorites in Suspense* (Random House, 1959). While Hitchcock never had a hand in the anthologies except for lending his name to the book, the editor, Robert Arthur, chose a short story titled "Four O'Clock" by Price Day. It was this anthology that exposed Serling to the short story.

This episode was assigned a production title on February 8, 1962, exactly one month after Serling submitted his script to Houghton. The entire episode was filmed on Stage 20. A parrot and its trainer were used on all three days of filming. The bird's voice (supplied by a human) was recorded in M-G-M's Sync Room "A" from 4:30 to 4:45 on February 26, 1962.

The original opening narration was never used and was much longer:

"This is Oliver Crangle – a dealer in petulance and poison. A self-appointed, self-designated, self-or-dained, vigilante whose jaundiced eyes peer out at an unholy world, undeserving of anything but judgment and punishment. And Mr. Oliver Crangle, by his lights, is both the judge and the executioner. He's rather arbitrarily chosen four o'clock as his personal Göetterdämerung – and we are about to watch the metamor-phosis of a twisted little gnome of a man, poisoned by the gangrene of prejudice – to the status of an avenging angel – upright and omniscient; dedicated and fearsome. Whatever your clocks say – it's four o'clock. And wherever you are . . . it happens to be . . . The Twilight Zone."

Serling's teaser for next week's episode was originally *"Now this one is very far-out, but consider-ing the nature of the times it happens to be very close-in."* Nervous before the camera, Serling recited his lines three times before succeeding close enough to pass satisfactorily. However, the third take was the one used on the program and Serling delivered his line a little awkward, *"Now this one is to a very far-out, but considering the nature of the times it happens to be very close-in."* The word "very" was never in the trailer sheets, but it was spoken on camera.

"Hollywood is not a town to wait around in," commented Theodore Bikel. A New York actor who played numerous roles on variety and dramatic programs, he went to Hollywood on occasion to make a guest appearance on a television show. "When you're out of work, you become a fourth-rate citizen. In New York, you only become a second-rate citizen. In New York, people smile at you less. Here, they cease to smile. But we are actors. We go where the demands of the profession call us."

The television critic for *The San Antonio Light* reviewed this episode as "a chilling story enhanced by Theodore Bikel's convincing performance as the vindictive man." The TV critic for *The Valley In-dependent* considered this episode "unfortunately, a bit too talky. You should be able to figure out the ending of this show before the first commercial."

"As you may rightly assume, my portrayal of Oliver Crangle stayed in my memory much longer than the many parts I have played on TV and elsewhere," recalled Bikel. "It was a superbly written episode and a wonderful character to get my teeth into. Crangle was, of course, politically the very opposite of where my own convictions lie, then and now. To portray a right wing nut gave me great pleasure."

"You may be interested in an incident that occurred later, not just because of my involvement but because of Rod Serling's reaction," Bikel continued. "He made reference to his own origins while taking a public stand as a citizen and a human being of conscience. Some time (after the episode aired), Rod Ser-ling had an opportunity to defend me against an actual right-wing verbal assault made on a television talk show in which two veteran actors with very reactionary views, Adolphe Menjou and Corinne Griffiths, attacked me. They did so not for the views I espoused – that would have been alright by any civil libertar-ian standards – but they challenged my right to voice them at all on the grounds that I was 'a foreigner'. Not just foreign-born, mind you, but a foreigner who had no right to open his mouth at all. I do not recall whether at that point I was already a citizen or not but that should have made no difference; even resident aliens legally admitted to the United States are titled to all rights and privileges except for the vote.

"A few days later, on the same program, Rod Serling said the following, in part: 'On this program an actor of considerable stature appeared by invitation. Apart from his talents which are consider-able, his reputation as a gentleman and a human being is probably the most unsullied and exemplary of any man in this profession. . . . He was subjected to a vicious and predatory attack by Miss Corinne

Griffiths . . . (because of) the fact that he was of foreign birth. To Miss Griffiths and anyone else who thinks that honor and patriotism can only be equated with those whose roots go deep into the third deck planking of the Mayflower . . . go over the roll call of the Congressional Medal of Honor winners. They read like a check list from Ellis Island.' He concluded by making a reference to his own background: 'A democracy works because its basic tenet is simply the recognition of the dignity of its citizens. The kind of dignity that permits the son of Lithuanian immigrants to say . . . judge a man, Miss Griffiths, as a man. Judge a human being by his works. Judge a human being by his compassion and his sincerity. Judge all of us not by our geography but by our humanity.' I could quote this accurately because Rod sent me a transcript of the show where he made those remarks."

Production #4833 "HOCUS-POCUS AND FRISBY" (Initial telecast: April 13, 1962)

Copyright Registration: © Cayuga Productions, Inc., April 10, 1962, LP22266
Dates of Filming: February 28 and March 1 and 2, 1962
Script #95 undated with revised pages dated January 29, 1962.

Producer and Secretary: $1,625.00
Director: $1,250.00
Unit Manager and Secretary: $600.00
Agents Commission: $2,500.00
Below the line charges (M-G-M): $34,927.13
Total Production Costs: $55,302.46 *

Story and Secretary: $3,205.00
Cast: $7,614.83
Production Fee: $900.00
Legal and Accounting: $250.00
Below the line charges (other): $2,430.50

Cast: Johnnie Albright (spaceman without mask #4); Clem Bevans (the old man); Larry Breitman (Alien #2); Peter Brocco (Alien #3); Max Cutler (spaceman without mask #3); Andy Devine (Somerset Frisby); Morris Drabin (spaceman without mask #2); Dabbs Greer (Scanlan); Howard McNear (Mitchell); Bob O'Sullivan (spaceman without mask #1); and Milton Selzer (Alien #1).

Original Music Score Composed and Conducted by Tom Morgan (Score No. CPN6039):
Etrange #3 (by Marius Constant, :09); Milieu #1 (by Constant, :16); Pitchville Flats #1 (:10); Red River Valley (traditional, :05 and :04); Pitchville Flats #2 (:33); Pitchville Flats #3 (:14); Frisby's Fear #1 (1:26); Frisby's Fear #2 (:56); Frisby's Flying Saucer (:35); Hands (:16); Frisby's Fear #3 (1:33); Death Harmonica #1 (:05); Death Harmonica #2 (:05); Death Harmonica #3 (;05); Death Harmonica #4 (:01); Pitchville Flats #4 (:15); Death Harmonica #5 (:01); Picthville Flats #5 (:15); Etrange #3 (by Constant, :08); and Milieu #2 (by Constant, :18).

Director of Photography: George T.
    Clemens, a.s.c. and Jack Swain
Art Directors: George W. Davis and Merrill Pye
Casting: Robert Walker

Production Manager: Ralph W. Nelson
Set Decorations: Keogh Gleason
Assistant Director: E. Darrell Hallenbeck
Makeup: William Tuttle

---

* Total production costs and breakdown from production summary dated June 30, 1962.

Film Editor: Bill Mosher   Sound: Franklin Milton and Bill Edmondson
Directed by Lamont Johnson
Teleplay by Rod Serling, based on an original unpublished story by Frederic Louis Fox.

"The reluctant gentleman with the sizeable mouth is Mr. Frisby. He has all the drive of a broken cam shaft and the aggressive vinegar of a corpse. As you've no doubt gathered, his big stock in trade is the tall tale. Now, what he doesn't know is that the visitors out front are a very special breed – destined to change his life beyond anything even his fertile imagination could manufacture. The place is Pitchville Flats. The time is the present. But Mr. Frisby is on the first leg of a rather fanciful journey into the place we call . . . the Twilight Zone."

Plot: Mr. Frisby, the proprietor of a general store where the retired members of town hang out, has built a reputation for telling tall tales. While the townsfolk humor him, two visitors arrive in town to check out the man whose reputation precedes the stories. A short time later, they offer Frisby an invitation for adventure, whisking him away to their flying saucer, stationed outside town limits. Inside the craft, the space aliens explain that their mission was to seek out a representative of Earth and, they hope, the most intelligent. They chose Mr. Frisby because of the yarns they overheard, but when he explains that he is a country boy with a big mouth, the aliens are puzzled – the words "lies" and "exaggerations" are not in their vocabulary. Mr. Frisby is discontented when he learns what the space aliens want to do with him, but when he plays his harmonica, the aliens find themselves in pain – the instrument emits a death noise to the space visitors. In desperation for their lives, the aliens set Mr. Frisby free before they launch. When he returns to his general store, Frisby tells the story of his encounter, but the men laugh it off, assuming his story is another in the chapter of Frisby's tall tales.

"Mr. Somerset Frisby, who might have profited by reading an Aesop fable about a boy who cried wolf. Tonight's tall tale from the timberlands . . . of the Twilight Zone."

Trailer: *"As it happens to all men, a newcomer takes his first step into the Twilight Zone next week when Mr. Andy Devine joins us for a show called 'Hocus-Pocus and Frisby.' He plays the role of a storekeeper of the cracker barrel variety who stretches the truth like most people pull on taffy. This one is for laughs and for the congenital liars amongst you. Next week, Mr. Andy Devine, 'Hocus-Pocus and Frisby.'"*

Trivia, etc. As "Showdown with Rance McGrew" was getting ready for filming, Serling sent a complimentary shooting script to Frederic Louis Fox, in La Cañada, California, for his review. On October 15, Fox wrote to Serling. "Your satirical script is delightful! I loved reading it. Rance (short for Rancid, I assume) is a very badly spoiled boy. I might add, also, that his is a lot funnier than my guy. But I'm afraid you've posed a problem of ethics: You've taken whatever small seed I may have planted, nurtured it richly, in gestation, and brought forth a flowering peach. So how – in the name of integrity – can I dare to horn in on the fruit? As I recall, all I gave you was a quickie about a deceased hombre who, in righteous protest, crawled out of his pine box tract dwelling to destroy, with a gun, the comical image who portrayed him on the tubes. And as I remember it, he also punctured a few grey flannel balloons along the way."

On October 15, 1961, Fox was pleased with the Rance McGrew teleplay, based on his story idea. He returned the script to Serling, along with the following brief sketch, and asked if there was a possibility that he could also submit the 30-page script.

"MISTER TIBBS AND THE FLYING SAUCER"

Elderly Henry Tibbs is a latter-day Munchausen who runs a service station in a small town on Highway 66, and never has a chance to go anywhere, except in his fertile imagination. But, vicariously, Mister Tibbs is Walter Mitty, Frank Buck and Jules Verne. He regales his customers with fabulous tales of his experiences, and they, and Mister Tibbs, pretend to believe everything he tells them. Unbeknown to Mister Tibbs, his conversations are picked up by interplanetary radio, on Mars, and are sponsored there by Happy Joe, a dealer in used canal barges. Happy Joe sends a Martian emissary to visit Mister Tibbs, to take him to Mars to collect residuals on the radio broadcasts. But Tibbs settles instead for a trip around the world in a flying saucer. On his return, he is bursting to tell people about his fabulous, unfitness trip around the world. Then, to his dismay, he learns that his name is on the front page of the local newspaper that day. Over the years, Mister Tibbs has submitted material that has won him numerous honorable mentions – but today, of all days, he learns that he has finally won first prize in the Burlington Liars' Contest.

He has a small souvenir of his flying saucer trip, but he puts it in an attic trunk, closes the lid and locks it. With a wistful sigh, he says, "No one would have believed it."

The sketch was typed on a half-sheet of paper, and initialed at the bottom, F.L.F. Fox also suggested Ed Wynn to play the lead, but whether Serling attempted to meet the casting request remains unknown. (Wynn's health, by this time, was failing.) On October 18, Serling wrote back to Fox, telling him "'Mr. Tibbs' is a delight. If we go back into production for ten more films, I'll have one of our people contact your agent. Hang on and don't lose the faith."

Assigned a production number on January 30, 1962, Peter Brocco and Milton Selzer signed on to play the role of the two lead aliens before Andy Devine had inked his contract.. On February 12, 1962, Brocco and Selzer reported to the studio so William Tuttle and his crew could make molds of the actors' faces. Actor Larry Breitman underwent the same process on February 13. When Frisby punches one of the aliens, a mask containing the replica of one of the actors would be needed for the revealing of the alien's true form. The punching scene was done twice – one for each mask – Brocco and Selzer. The molds took 48 hours to create, and the time it took for the masks to be made from the molds took at least one week, which is most likely the reason the actors reported to the studio far in advance of filming.

On February 26, Andy Devine arrived for wardrobe fitting and to start rehearsals. On February 27, the actors playing the aliens were fitted for wardrobes. On the same day, a casting call asked for "four clean-cut" men to play aliens who stand in the background during Frisby's introduction inside the flying saucer. Bob O'Sullivan, Morris Drabin, Max Cutler, and Johnnie Albright were selected.

The "Hy-Test Rayton Gasoline" sign featured on the front of the pump at Frisby's general store was the same prop reused many times at M-G-M Studios. In the first season episode, "The Hitch-Hiker," Rayton Batteries were promoted on a sign at the gas station.

The cast must have gotten along very well – on the third and final day of filming, Devine, Selzer, Breitman and Brocco returned from lunch more than 15 minutes late. On March 8, 1962, retakes were filmed for added scenes involving Serling and the interior of the general store on Stage 20. The original opening narration Serling gave ran a few seconds too long and the film editors needed a shorter intro-duction. The former opener, which ended up on the cutting room floor:

"The reluctant gentleman with the sizeable mouth is Mr. Frisby. He has all the drive of a broken cam shaft and the aggressive vinegar of a corpse. As you've no doubt gathered, his big stock in trade is the tall tale; the outrageous falsehood; the bending of truth up to and beyond the breaking point. What he doesn't know is that the visitors out front are a very special breed, destined to change his life beyond anything even his fertile imagination could manufacture. The place is Pitchville Flats. The time is the present. But Mr. Frisby's on the first leg of a rather fanciful journey into the place we call . . . the Twilight Zone."

The barbershop is seen right by the general store, and one of the old men, a character named Mitchell played by Howard McNear, was not reprising his role of Floyd the barber on *The Andy Griffith Show* – regardless of what some trivia books state.

Once again, the flying saucer featured in this episode was the same from *Forbidden Planet* (1956) and a number of *Twilight Zone* episodes. The same clear globe in the center of the interior was also from the same motion picture and in the episode, "Third From the Sun."

Leonard Hoffman of *The Tucson Daily Citizen* reviewed this episode, commenting "this week's injection of whimsy makes for a mild diversion that doesn't measure up to the impact of straight shocker plots."

Production #4831 "THE TRADE-INS" (Initial telecast: April 20, 1962)
Copyright Registration: © Cayuga Productions, Inc., April 17, 1962, LP22267
Dates of Rehearsal: February 14 and 15, 1962
Dates of Filming: February 16, 19 and 20, 1962
Revised script #91 dated: January 22, 1962

Producer and Secretary: $1,625.00
Director: $1,250.00
Unit Manager and Secretary: $600.00
Agents Commission: $2,500.00
Below the line charges (M-G-M): $33,598.55
Total Production Costs: $52,877.70 *

Story and Secretary: $2,855.00
Cast: $7,682.50
Production Fee: $900.00
Legal and Accounting: $250.00
Below the line charges (other): $1,616.65

Cast: David Armstrong (the attendant); Terrence de Marney (gambler #1); Noah Keene (Mr. Vance); Theodore Marcuse (Mr. Farraday); Mary McMahon (receptionist); Alma Platt (Marie Holt); Joseph Schildkraut (John Holt); Edson Stroll (John Holt as a young man); and Billy Vincent (gambler #2).

Stock Music Cues: Etrange #3 (by Marius Constant, :09); Milieu #1 (by Constant, :16); Strange Return (by Jerry Goldsmith, :18); Dreams (by Wilfred Josephs, :24); Villers #1 (by Constant, :20); Villers #4 (by Constant, :01); Strange Return (by Goldsmith, :18); Perry Mason Background (by Fred Steiner, :04); Mist Lifts (by Goldsmith, :29); Sadness #3 – Sneak to Curtain (by Lucien Moraweck, :15); Piano Improvisation with Humming (CBS, :27); Improvised Humming (CBS, :12 and :09);

_____
* Total production costs and breakdown from production summary dated June 30, 1962.

Confession #2 (by Rene Garriguenc, :26); Memories (by Bernard Herrmann, :51); Grey Morning (by Goldsmith, :47); Religious Bridge – Walt Whitman (by Herrmann, :21); Strange Return (by Goldsmith, :32); Emotional #2 – Walt Whitman (by Herrmann, :42); Finale (by Herrmann, :13); Etrange #3 (by Constant, :08); and Milieu #2 (by Constant, :19).

Director of Photography: George T. Clemens, a.s.c.	Production Manager: Ralph W. Nelson
Art Directors: George W. Davis and Merrill Pye	Set Decorations: Keogh Gleason
Casting: Robert Walker	Assistant Director: E. Darrell Hallenbeck
Film Editor: Bill Mosher	Makeup: William Tuttle
Directed by Elliot Silverstein	Sound: Franklin Milton and Bill Edmondson
	Teleplay by Rod Serling

"Mr. and Mrs. John Holt – aging people who slowly, and with trembling fingers, turn the last pages of a book of life . . . and hope against logic and the preordained, that some magic printing press will add to this book another limited edition. But these two senior citizens happen to live in a time of the future where nothing is impossible – even the trading of old bodies for new. Mr. and Mrs. John Holt . . . in their twilight years . . . who are about to find . . . that there happens to be a zone with the same name."

Plot: In the far future, Mr. and Mrs. John Holt visit The New Life Corp., whose stock in trade is rebirth. The process is quick and painless. The customers are put to sleep, and will awake in a young body in the prime of health. After a tour through the facilities, they learn the price – $10,000 for the two of them. But they only have half the funds and wouldn't dream of

> **Production Schedule at M-G-M**
> Day 1 – Interior of General Store (Stage 20)
> Exterior of the General Store (Lot #3)
> Day 2 – Interior of General Store (Stage 20)
> Exterior of the Flying Saucer (Stage 24)
> Day 3 – Interior of the Flying Saucer (Stage 24)

making the change with just one of them – regardless of how much pain John is going through. In desperation to make the $10,000, John visits an illegal gambling establishment in an effort to double his money – at the risk of losing it all. Towards the end of the night, John has lost most of his money in a card game and when the men at the table learn of his motives, the card game turns in John's favor – an act of charity – giving the old man his $5,000 back. The next day, John is administered . . . the operation is a success. But seeing the hurt in his wife's eyes, John wants to return to his old body, pain or age be damned. He'll grow old with her as things were meant to be.

"From Kahlil Gibran's 'The Prophet': 'Love gives naught but itself and takes naught from itself. Love possesses not nor would it be possessed; for love is sufficient unto love.' Not a lesson . . . just a reminder from all the sentimentalists . . . in the Twilight Zone."

Trailer: *"We have a return visit next week from a most eminent performer, Joseph Schildkraut, and his vehicle is called 'The Trade-Ins.' It's the story of a future society in which new bodies may be traded for old. It's my own personal feeling that of all the various story areas we've tackled in the Twilight Zone, this has the most import* *and carries with it the most poignance. I hope you'll be able to be with us next week. Here in one cigarette a Chesterfield is all the flavor and taste of 21 of the world's finest tobaccos. Aged mild and then blended mild. The end result – tobacco too mild for a filter, pleasure too good to miss. Smoke for pleasure, smoke Chesterfield."*

Trivia, etc. The March 16, 1961 issue of *The Hollywood Reporter* announced that "Rod Serling is penning a 'Twilight Zone' to the measurements of Joseph Schildkraut and Ziva Rodann." The trade paper was a little late in reporting the news. By the time this script was assigned a production number (February 8, 1962) and scheduled for filming, Ziva Rodann was unavailable and Alma Platt had signed on for the role of Marie.

On February 15, a casting call for 20 boys, wearing their own swim trunks, ages 18 to 25, "good clean types with well proportioned muscular figures," reported to the studio. Five of the 20 were selected to play the male figures on display. Twenty women, wearing their own bathing suits, clean attractive types with well-proportioned figures, also reported to the studio and five were selected.

"To my way of thinking, there was a little bit of work on the script while we filmed," recalled Edson Stroll. "I know this might have been mentioned briefly, but to get the reaction on my face when I looked at Alma Platt, and realized she was hurting inside, the director wanted to shut off the sound in the studio and then shoot a gun in the background so my look of shock and surprise is real."

The entire episode was filmed on Stage 12, except for the third and last day with the gambling room on Stage 8. The scene where John Holt was on the verge of tears because of the pain he was suffering during the card game, was more than "acting." Schildkraut's wife, Marie McKay, died on Saturday, February 17. Rather than pre-empt the filming of the episode, he insisted on completing his scenes on February 19 and 20.

Serling's relationship with Schildkraut remained a healthy and happy one. In January of 1964, he donated $1,000 to Schildkraut as an investment in a stage production the actor was handling. Serling's faith in Schildkraut's talent was evidenced by his willingness to invest without even looking at a script.

The April 1962 issue of *Show* magazine reviewed, "Things, however, get out of joint until, with an osteopathic twist, Serling straightens them out."

Production #4830 "THE GIFT" (Initial telecast: April 27, 1962)
Copyright Registration: © Cayuga Productions, Inc., April 24, 1962, LP22268
Dates of Rehearsal: February 8 and 9, 1962
Dates of Filming: February 12, 13 and 14, 1962
Script #96 dated: February 7, 1962

Producer and Secretary: $1,625.00
Director: $1,370.00
Unit Manager and Secretary: $600.00
Agents Commission: $2,500.00
Below the line charges (M-G-M): $37,784.66
Total Production Costs: $58,436.62 *

Story and Secretary: $2,855.00
Cast: $8,185.53
Production Fee: $900.00
Legal and Accounting: $250.00
Below the line charges (other): $2,366.43

* Total production costs and breakdown from production summary dated June 30, 1962.

Cast: Henry Corden (Sanchez); Carmen Danton (woman #1); David Fresco (man #2); Geoffrey Horne (Williams); Lea Marmer (woman #2); Paul Mazurka (the police officer); Nico Minardos (the doctor); Cliff Osmond (Manuelo); Joe Perry (man #1); Vito Scotti (Rudolpho); Vladimir Sokoloff (the blind guitar player); and Edmund Vargas (Pedro).

Original Music Score Composed and Conducted by Laurindo Almeida (Score No. CPN6041): Etrange #3 (by Marius Constant, :09); Milieu #1 (by Constant, :16); The Ravens (1:01); Foot Prints (:30); This is Pedro (:16); Guitar Strums (1:09); The Stranger (:42); Blood and Wine (1:15); Look at Stars (:45); Judas (:13); Waiting for Gift (:18); For Good and All (1:00); The Search for Stranger (:34); Destroy the Gift (1:37); Etrange #3 (by Constant, :08); and Milieu #2 (by Constant, :18).

Director of Photography: George T. Clemens, a.s.c.	Production Manager: Ralph W. Nelson
Art Directors: George W. Davis and Merrill Pye	Set Decorations: Keogh Gleason
Casting: Robert Walker	Assistant Director: E. Darrell Hallenbeck
Sound: Franklin Milton and Bill Edmondson	Film Editor: Jason H. Bernie, a.c.e.
Teleplay by Rod Serling	Directed by Allen H. Miner

"The place is Mexico, just across the Texas border. A mountain village held back in time by its remoteness and suddenly intruded upon by the twentieth century. And this is Pedro – nine years old. A lonely, rootless little boy, who will soon make the acquaintance of a traveler from a distant place. We are at present forty miles from the Rio Grande. But any place – and all places, can be . . . the Twilight Zone."

Plot: Late one evening, south of the U.S.-Mexican border, a stranger visits the local bar and collapses from a gunshot wound. While the doctor heals the stranger in the back room, the town citizens listens to a story from the local sheriff regarding his efforts to wound someone or something that originated from the circular craft that supposedly crashed outside of town. Rumors spread through the streets that the stranger in the back room is a visitor from outer space. While many of the town citizens are either in fear of or angered by the visitor, a young boy named Pedro befriends the stranger with a welcome hand. Alone together, the visitor hands Pedro a gift and asks him to keep it a secret for the time being. The Army, meanwhile, arrives to take control of the situation. The spaceman attempts to flee, but is cornered and confronted in the alley. The gift Pedro brings to the people is burnt while gunfire erupts, killing the visitor. As the citizens prepare to return to their home, the doctor picks up the remains of the gift to discover it was a cure for cancer – the chemical compound burned away. They not only killed a man, but a dream as well.

"Madero, Mexico – the present. The subject – fear. The cure – a little more faith. An RX off a shelf . . . in the Twilight Zone."

Trailer: *"Next week on the Twilight Zone, we tell the story that we think might prove a rather haunting little item in the scheme of things. It tells of a small Mexican boy and a visitor from another planet, and it tells further what happens when this extra-terrestrial traveler is faced with some of the less-personable instincts of human beings – like fear, superstitions, and intolerance. Our story is called 'The Gift.'"*

Trivia, etc. The script for this episode was adapted from one of the unsold pilots, "I Shot An Arrow Into the Air," dated February 6, 1958, with revised pages dated February 18. The pilot script had been submitted to CBS weeks before. On January 27, 1958, CBS received the script for censorship purposes and made minimal changes – most notably, the deletion of words "damn," "helluva," "in God's name" and "hell." This was not uncommon with the network's request, and Serling had undergone this problem previously. "The big problem," Serling remarked for *TV Guide*, "is still censorship. In TV, anything controversial is any subject with two sides. I've found censorship always begins with the network. Then, it spreads to the advertising agency. Then the sponsor. Among them, when they get through, there isn't very much left. I've had script editors blue-pencil the word 'God' out of my scripts. There's no reason why profanity within reason should not be allowed on the networks after ten o'clock at night. What the hell – English, at least American, is like that."

The word "crazy" was deleted from one page, because it was a "trigger word" that the mental health people requested the network not use in that sense. Serling could certainly understand the network's concern with this request. Two days after the telecast of "The Time Element," Molly Mason, of Los Angeles, expressed her attitude toward Serling for his script, believing that the field of psychiatry was held up to ridicule. "I am very aware of the problems having to do with mental health in this country," Serling wrote back, "and I hope you believe me, Miss Mason, when I tell you that I would be the very last person to do anything to hinder the efforts of those working so terribly hard to help in this area."

For this episode of *The Twilight Zone*, Serling rewrote the hour-long teleplay in modified form, noting the concerns CBS had regarding the initial submission. Titled "The Guest," Serling's opening narrative in this draft said Pedro was 12-years-old and the setting was Madero, Mexico. When the episode was assigned a production number on January 30, 1962, it was retitled "The Visitor." On February 1, 1962, the title was changed again to "The Gift."

The entire primary filming of this episode was filmed on Stage 24 at M-G-M Studios. Rod Serling's on-screen appearance was filmed on Stage 20 with the hort standing in front of the exterior wall of the Mexican village. Additional scenes were later filmed for the exterior of the Mexican village on March 13, on Stage 18. Wild narrations of the crowd were recorded in Sync Room "B" on March 13, 1962, from 9 a.m. to 12:30 p.m.

Pedro recounts to the visitor the tale of Jesus Christ, who once came into the world to educate the meek. The bartender is referenced directly as "Judas," after the doctor learns that he surrendered information of the visitor's whereabouts to the authorities for payment in coins.

"I did some thirty movies over the years and a number of television and of all those, *The Twilight Zone* is the one I get more mail about," recalled Nico Minardos. "I'm getting fan mail from Switzerland, Ireland, Germany, as well as the United States. In those years we used to rehearse a couple days, and then film for three days. Rod wanted me to do the show and what I remember most was the excitement we all had of the show. We knew it was an allegory to Jesus Christ, which was the premise, and everyone was trying to remain calm for the crowd sequence."

In the mid-1960s, Serling wanted to make a theatrical motion picture titled *The Twilight Zone* and rewrote this story into a screenplay. The earliest news of the *Twilight Zone* movie was in an issue of *TV Guide*, which mentioned of the proposed feature film prematurely — given birth by an offhand remark Serling made at a luncheon. In a letter to Aldon Schwimmer of Ashley-Steiner, on August 26, 1964, Serling remarked, "I did this here movie treatment for the *Twilight Zone*, but I think it is bad. I know what

I want to write as a motion picture scenario, but when I do treatments of them, they never sound like I think the scripts will. I'm hanging on to it and not showing it to anyone." On a humorous note, Serling remarked that the script just needed a little sex added with a religious flavor, "and I got myself a movie."

Actor Vladimir Sokoloff, who plays the role of the blind guitar player, suffered a stroke the day after filming was completed for this episode and died. This episode of *The Twilight Zone* marked his final television appearance, having been seen on recently telecast episodes of *Thriller* and *The Dick Powell Show* weeks before.

Production #4834 "THE DUMMY" (Initial telecast: May 4, 1962)
Copyright Registration: © Cayuga Productions, Inc., May 1, 1962, LP22269
Date of Rehearsal: March 5, 1962
Dates of Filming: March 6, 7 and 8, 1962

Producer and Secretary: $1,625.00	Story and Secretary: $3,255.00
Director: $1,250.00	Cast: $6,853.76
Unit Manager and Secretary: $600.00	Production Fee: $900.00
Agents Commission: $2,500.00	Legal and Accounting: $250.00
Below the line charges (M-G-M): $33,498.60	Below the line charges (other): $1,626.62
Total Production Costs: $52,358.98 *	

Cast: Rudy Dolan (the emcee); Bethelynn Grey (a chorus girl); John Harmon (Georgie); Ralph Manza (the doorman); Bob McCord (man in audience); George Murdock (Willy, the ventriloquist); Cliff Robertson (Jerry Etherson); Frank Sutton (Frank Gaines, Jerry's agent); Sandra Warner (Noreen); and Edy Williams (a chorus girl).

Stock Music Cues: Etrange #3 (by Marius Constant, :09); Milieu #1 (by Constant, :16); Belfort #5 (by Constant, :22); Charleston Type (by George Clouston, 1:12); Try to Swing It (by Horst Jankowski, 2:00); Marne #1 (by Constant, :17); Belfort #7 (by Constant, :27); Bows (by Wilbur Hatch, :13); Soft Shoe (by Hatch, :21); I Only Have Eyes For You (by Harry Warren and Al Dubin, 1:12); "It" Girl (by Jeff Alexander, :25); F Story #3 (by Constant, :24); F Story #7 (by Constant, :59); F Story #3 (by Constant, :17); D Story #1 (by Constant, :43); Fight (aka I Am A Lawyer) (by Alex North, :28 and :59); F Story #3 (by Constant, :18); F Story #4 (by Constant, :13); F Story #7 (by Constant, :54); F Story #6 (by Constant, :16); Belfort #6 (by Constant, :15); Etrange #3 (by Constant, :08); and Milieu #2 (by Constant, :18).

Director of Photography: George T. Clemens, a.s.c.	Production Manager: Ralph W. Nelson
	Assistant Director: E. Darrell Hallenbeck
Art Directors: George W. Davis and Merrill Pye	Casting: Robert Walker
Set Decorations: Henry Grace and Keogh Gleason	Makeup: William Tuttle
	Film Editor: Jason H. Bernie, a.c.e.

---

* Total production costs and breakdown from production summary dated June 30, 1962.

Sound: Franklin Milton and Bill Edmondson   Directed by Abner Biberman
Teleplay by Rod Serling, based on an original story idea by Lee Polk.

"You're watching a ventriloquist named Jerry Etherson – a voice thrower par excellence. His alter ego, sitting atop his lap, is a brash stick of kindling with the sobriquet, 'Willy.' In a moment, Mr. Etherson and his knotty-pine partner will be booked in one of the out-of-the-way bistros – that small, dark, intimate place known as . . . the Twilight Zone."

Plot: The wooden half of a ventriloquist partnership longs to go solo and on occasion, breaks the routine on stage. Jerry has seen a psychiatrist, taken to the bottle, and pleaded for help from even his closest friends. Liquors and doctors cannot help because Willy really is a living and breathing force of nature. In an effort to dispose of his supposed hallucinations, Jerry replaces Willy with another wooden dummy. Late that evening, after the nightclub closes, Jerry feels like a new man because he's going to work with the new dummy on a permanent basis. As he walks alone through the dark alleys and streets of the city, he starts suffering from delusions of Willy's laughs. The voice gets so loud that Jerry races back to the nightclub and opening the trunk, smashes the doll into pieces – only to discover that he destroyed the wrong dummy. Willy is still intact. Getting down to business, Jerry is stuck with agreeing to a compromise. On a different nightclub stage a few evenings later, the ventriloquist act of Jerry and Willy entertain the audience with the same old jokes and routines – with Jerry and Willy having switched places.

"What's known in the parlance of the times as the old switcheroo. From boss to blockhead in a few uneasy lessons. And if you're given to nightclubbing on occasion, check this act. It's called 'Willy and Jerry' and they generally are booked into some of the clubs along the gray night way known . . . as the Twilight Zone."

Trailer: *"Next week on the Twilight Zone, a return visit from a illustrious young actor, Cliff Robertson. He stars in one of the strangest tales we've yet to throw at you. It's called "The Dummy," and it involves a ventriloquist and a piece of painted wood, a unique slab of carved pine who decides that lap-sitting is for the birds and who takes things into his own wooden hands. Now this one we recommend to the voice-throwers across the land. We hope we see you then. Chesterfield King? Extra length? Sure . . . and more. For only CK gives you the wonderful taste of 21 great tobaccos. Try a pack."*

Trivia, etc. Ever since the days of ventriloquism-gone-bad in motion pictures, a large number of people have attempted to do their own rendition of the killer dummy genre. Serling toyed around with the possibility of doing one for *The Twilight Zone*, but a number of fans submitted variations of the theme over the years and regrettably, without payment for their concept, was unable to utilize them. Since none of them truly impressed the playwright, it took a short story treatment submitted by *Zone* viewer Lee Polk to intrigue Serling's interest. Polk was an employee of WNDT, Channel 13, an affiliate of the Educational Broadcasting Corporation, in New York City. He submitted an idea involving a ventriloquist who suspects his wooden dummy is alive and suffers from the effects of the dummy improvising on stage. Serling was intrigued with the premise, and after making arrangements with Buck Houghton to secure the rights to the story, wrote a teleplay (script #97) giving Polk on-screen credit for his story. *

Serling's initial opening narration was longer than the finished footage seen in this episode:

"You're watching a ventriloquist named Jerry Etherson – a voice thrower par excellence. His alter ego,

sitting atop his lap, is a brash stick of kindling with the sobriquet, 'Willy.' In a moment, Mr. Etherson and his knotty-pine partner will come up with some gags not to be found in a script; some straight lines that are less a part of a nightclub then a nightmare, for Jerry Etherson and Willy are about to be booked in one of the out-of-the-way bistros – that small, dark, intimate place known as . . . the Twilight Zone."

The name "Willy" was lifted from previous radio scripts by Serling, who often reused names for fictional characters. On the February 17, 1951 radio broadcast of *Adventure Express*, broadcast over WLW in Cincinnati, Ohio, Serling's script featured a character named Willie (with a different spelling). In another radio script, "The Power of Abner Doubleday," rejected by the radio producer of *Dr. Christian*, the title character changed his name from Abner to Willie between script revisions.

Polk personally asked Serling to consider Wes Kenney, who produced and directed *Your First Impression* in Hollywood, the short-lived television program, and had directed many of Polk's scripts on the NBC Network, to helm this episode. By the time he placed his request, production had been completed.

Assigned a production number on February 12, 1962, the entire episode was filmed on Stage 19 at M-G-M, except for the exterior of the alley and the stage door on the second half of the third day, on Lot 1. During filming, George Murdock supplied the off-camera voice of Willy for Robertson to stay cued during filming. On March 9, from 1:00 to 3:00 p.m., Robertson recorded his own voice for Willy in Sync Room "B."

Laughter and chit-chat from the audience was recorded in the same Sync Room from 10:00 to 11:00 a.m. and 3:00 p.m. to 3:30 p.m. on March 29, 1962. There is a production sheet suggesting that canned laughter and audience was going to be used, but when this proved to "sound out of place with the film's atmosphere," it was decided to record original audience laughter.

"I watched my good friend Edgar Bergen perform with Charlie McCarthy and Mortimer Snerd, so I could reproduce the mannerisms of a ventriloquist," recalled Cliff Robertson. "I did my best, but the craft of ventriloquism was an art form you could not reproduce overnight. I don't think I did justice for puppeteers. But I did all the voices of the dummies."

"I did two of those *Twilight Zone* episodes," continued Robertson. "I had a reservation on an American Airlines or Pan-Am flight from New York to California for one of them. I believe it was 'The Dummy.' I was scheduled to arrive in Hollywood days before they really needed me. I rescheduled for a later flight and someone told me that I would get into trouble. But I just did not see any reason for flying in and waiting for my turn before the camera. I am glad now that I did it, because soon after that flight took off, the pilot had a heart attack and everyone perished. That episode of *The Twilight Zone* almost killed me."

On March 20, 1962, Jack Glass and his crew shot inserts of the dummy against the theater drape (and wall) beginning 10:00 a.m. (This same day, a half-hour earlier, they shot inserts of the school sign mounted on the brick wall from Stage 16 for "Changing of the Guard.")

Puppeteer Shari Lewis, then residing in New York City, had approached Rod Serling with the possibility of appearing in an episode of *The Twilight Zone*, after learning that he was planning to

---

* Apparently paperwork caused a brief bit of confusion regarding Lee Polk's name. While his name was Leon, which was how it was spelled initially on some paperwork, Polk explained to Serling that in both writing and directing at the television station where he worked, he was billed as "Lee Polk." Serling made sure the spelling was applied in accordance to Polk's request.

feature a ventriloquist in an upcoming episode. "I have racked my brain, files, and the public library for something close to you," Serling wrote to Lewis, "but with utter and dismaying candor, I must tell you you're a very special case and you require very special treatment. There is the feeling of pony-tailed moppet-ish that doesn't lend itself to the rather heavy melodrama that is part and parcel of my kit here.... Surely there must be something we can suddenly look at one another about and wax excited. The puppet thing we're doing isn't at all like you. It requires a toughness that is about as close to you as Lionel Barrymore playing Andy Hardy."

According to production sheets, the poster hanging outside the nightclub advertising the circus clown, The Great Pascal, was apparently an original, created specifically for this episode.

The May 1962 issue of *Show* featured a review of this episode. "The resemblance of this plot to an episode in an old and frequently rerun thriller *Dead of Night* (1945) is striking. A comparison, however, is not flattering to the newer version. Television writer Rod Serling has weakened

Jerry and Willy prepare for rehearsals.

his good moments with bad dialogue and given his plot one twist too many. That the man who wrote 'Patterns' and 'Requiem for a Heavyweight' should also turn out 'The Dummy' is perhaps partly explained by the fact that more than ninety scripts have now come off the *Twilight Zone* treadmill. Clearly, even a sturdy talent like Serling's can be worn to dullness by such a grueling grind."

On May 10, Lee Polk wrote to Serling, telling him "everyone I know who saw 'The Dummy' was properly chilled by the climax. Congratulations on a most effective program. I am appreciative of the opportunity of having been involved. The best news for we hard core fans is that you're staying on next season. You have all our many wishes for continued success. After all, to paraphrase W.C. Fields, a program that even makes room for an idea of mine can't be all bad."

On May 21, Serling replied to Polk, commenting that this episode got excellent reactions. "I hope you were not dismayed by its changing. This happens all the time and is hardly a reflection on the original writer's talent. It is just our attempt to more conveniently implement the shooting by inserting stuff and attitudes more conducive to a better shot show. Many thanks for your contribution and much good luck."

When this episode aired in syndication (and as late as certain PBS stations in the early half of the 1990s), Serling's teaser was cut short between his pitch for next week's episode and the Chesterfield King testimonial. However, the fade to black was not quick enough, making this the only episode of the series in syndication to catch him putting the cigarette into his mouth.

There is a two-page skit composed for this episode that was apparently never filmed. Whether it was written by Serling or Polk remains to be seen. There is no evidence of the authorship. A parody to the tune of "Don't Fence Me In," this skit was intended for the early stage performance with Jerry and Willy in this episode.

JERRY (singing)	*Oh, give me land, lots of land under starry skies above –*
WILLY	*This guy's a nut.*
JERRY (singing)	*Let me ride through the wide open country that I love –*
WILLY	*Go be my guest.*
(then, singing)	*Once he sat by himself in the evening breeze – took an axe then made me out of cotton wood trees. Now I'm bored to death just sitting on his knees –*
JERRY (singing)	*Don't fence me in.*
(then, continuing)	*Just turn me loose, let me straddle my old saddle underneath the western skies –*
WILLY (singing)	*I wish I could, but I'm wood –*
	This guy even rolls my eyes.
JERRY (singing)	*I wish to ride to the ridge where the West commences –*
WILLY (singing)	*And I'll stay East and maybe keep my senses –*
JERRY (singing)	*Can't look at hobbles and I can't stand fences –*
WILLY	*Trade in your lap.*
JERRY	*Don't fence me in.*
WILLY	*Which twin is the dummy?*
JERRY	*Don't fence me in.*
WILLY	*Is there a psychiatrist in the house?*
JERRY	*Don't fence me in.*

WILLY (singing, the triumphant ending) *Don't fence him in!*

Production #4813 "YOUNG MAN'S FANCY" (Initial telecast: May 11, 1962)

Copyright Registration: © Cayuga Productions, Inc., May 8, 1962, LP22956 (in notice: 1961)
Date of Rehearsal: May 31, 1961
Dates of Filming: June 1, 2 and 5, 1961
Script #69 dated: May 19, 1961, with revised pages dated May 26, 1961.

Producer and Secretary: $1,625.00	Story and Secretary: $2,755.00
Director: $1,354.12	Cast: $7,285.18
Unit Manager and Secretary: $600.00	Production Fee: $900.00
Agents Commission: $2,500.00	Legal and Accounting: $250.00
Below the line charges (M-G-M): $30,613.59	Below the line charges (other): $3,461.23
Total Production Costs: $51,344.12 *	

Cast: Helen Brown (Henrietta Walker); Ricky Kelman (Alex, 10 years old); Alex Nicol (Alex Walker); Wallace Rooney (Mr. Wilkinson); and Phyllis Thaxter (Virginia Laine-Walker).

Original Music Score Composed and Conducted by Nathan Scott (Score No. CPN6003): Etrange #3 (by Marius Constant, :09); Milieu #1 (by Constant, :16); Twenty-Five Years Ago (1:26); The Bride Enters (:27); The Old Clock (:34); The Stairs (:39); The Lady in Red (by Mort Dixon and Allie Wrudel, arr. by Nathan Scott, :05, :20 and 1:20); Crazy Clock (1:00); Clock-Watching (:12); Crazy Telephone (:59); Reaction, Part 1 (2:00); Reaction, Part 2 (1:51); Conclusion (:34); Etrange #3 (by Constant, :08); and Milieu #2 (by Constant, :18).

Director of Photography: George T. Clemens, a.s.c.	Production Manager: Ralph W. Nelson
Art Directors: George W. Davis and Phil Barber	Set Decorations: H. Web Arrowsmith
Casting: Stalmaster-Lister	Assistant Director: E. Darrell Hallenbeck
Film Editor: Jason H. Bernie, a.c.e.	Story Consultant: Richard McDonagh
Automobiles Supplied by the Ford Motor Company	Sound: Franklin Milton and Bill Edmondson
	Directed by John Brahm
	Teleplay by Richard Matheson

"You're looking at the house of the late Mrs. Henrietta Walker. This is Mrs. Walker herself, as she appeared twenty-five years ago. And this, except for isolated objects, is the living room of Mrs. Walker's house, as it appeared in that same year. The other rooms upstairs and down are much the same. The time, however, is not twenty-five years ago but now. The house of the late Mrs. Henrietta Walker is, you see, a house which belongs almost entirely to the past, a house which, like Mrs. Walker's clock here, has ceased to recognize the passage of time. Only one element is missing now . . . one remaining item in the estate of the late Mrs. Walker: her son, Alex, thirty-four years of age and up till twenty minutes ago, the so-called 'perennial bachelor.' With him is his bride, the former Miss Virginia Laine. They're returning from the city hall in order to get Mr. Walker's clothes packed, make final arrangements for the sale of the house, lock it up and depart on their honeymoon. Not a complicated set of tasks, it would appear, and yet the newlywed Mrs. Walker is about to discover that the old adage 'You can't go home again' has little meaning . . . in the Twilight Zone."

Plot: Virginia Laine waited 12 years to marry Alex Walker, a bachelor by habit and lifestyle who, until the age of 34, was unable to sever the apron strings bonded with his mother. One year after the old woman's death, the lovebirds are married, and Virginia longs to establish their own home – not the late mother's. Shortly before their departure for a honeymoon, Virginia discovers the house slowly transforming into what it once was. Realizing the dead woman is attempting to convince Alex to remain in the past, Virginia observes the radio turning on by itself, playing tunes from yesteryear. She ultimately meets the old woman face-to-face, promising her love for Alex is stronger, but the old woman explains that the transformation in the house is none of it is her doing – it is Alex who longs for the past. Before leaving the house, Virginia witnesses the transformation of her husband into a youth, who orders her to go away.

---

* Total production costs and breakdown from production summary dated February 28, 1962.

"Exit Miss Virginia Laine . . . formerly and most briefly . . . Mrs. Alex Walker. She has just given up a battle and in a strange way retreated. But this has been a retreat back to reality. Her opponent . . . Alex Walker, will now and forever hold a line that exists in the past. He has put a claim on a moment in time . . . and is not about to relinquish it. Such things do happen . . . in the Twilight Zone."

Trailer: *"Next week through the good offices of Mr. Richard Matheson, we tell you a story of a young man's fancy which is kind of a euphemistic description of a mortal combat between the living . . . and the dead; between the present and the past. Between Miss Phyllis Thaxter and Mr. Alex Nicol. The battleground is this old house and its front door will be open to you next week . . . on The Twilight Zone."*

Trivia, etc. Serling's closing narrative in the initial draft of Richard Matheson's script was not the same as recorded for this episode. Initially the lines read:

"The contest is ended now – a contest fought not only in space but in time. Mr. Alex Walker is gone, no longer in this house as it exists today. He has returned, in flesh, to that period of his life from which, emotionally, he had never really departed. Mrs. Henrietta Walker is also gone, back in the same era, having been forced to return there by a little boy whose will to remain forever a child is so powerful that time itself fell prey to it. As for the short-lived Mrs. Virginia Walker – now, once again, Miss Virginia Laine – she finds herself in an empty house, excluded and alone – the victim of a tragic warp in mind and time – as recorded in . . . The Twilight Zone."

Serling even rewrote the closing narration in which a revised page of the script describes "we hear Serling's voice over a long pan around the hall and other rooms, taking in all the old devices – telephone, radio, etc." This too was not recorded or used.

"Aftermath of a battle. A contest fought both in space and in time in which the victor and his mother have turned the present into the past. For further explanation of the phenomena check under B for Boy and M for Mother on file for your perusal . . . in the Twilight Zone."

The original title for this script was "The House," when submitted by Richard Matheson, first draft due contractually by April 28. It was assigned a production number on May 11, 1961.

The initial script called for the closing to be a bit different. After young Alex tells Virginia "Goodbye, lady," she catches her breath faintly as the door closes. Screaming his name, she lurches up the remaining steps and rushes toward Alex's room. Virginia flings open the door and freezes, gasping. Standing in the room as it looked in the 1930s, everything seen as through a shimmering haze, fading until there is only the 1961 room with no boy and no mother. Staring at the empty room with dazed, uncomprehending eyes, the camera tilts towards the heavens.

The title was changed to "Young Man's Fancy" officially on May 23, 1961, according to an M-G-M work order.

Alex's mention of Major Bowes and Fred Allen was an inside joke, referring to Charles Beaumont's former *Twilight Zone* opus, "Static," which featured sound clips from those two programs. The script also called for Alex to fondly recall his mother's favorite music was Eddie Duchin, and she used to be crazy about a record of his called "The Lady in Red." Matheson's instructions in the script states that if such a record did not exist, to substitute any Guy Lombardo recording from 1936 instead. "The Lady in Red" was available for use on the program and it is featured in the episode's soundtrack. The music was arranged by Nathan Scott specifically for this episode, with instructions on the score: "Eddie Duchin style."

While the music heard on the program was "The Lady in Red," the label on the record was "Lady Be Good," by George Gershwin. This may have been intentional – finding a record with a label for Eddie Duchin's "The Lady in

---

Production Schedule at M-G-M

Day 1 – Interior of Alex's and Mother's Bedroom (Stage 8)
Exterior of Walker House (Lot #2)
Interior of Living Room and Front Hall (Stage 16)

Day 2 – Interior of Walker's Living Room, Hall, Stairway, Dining Room and Kitchen (Stage 16)

Day 3 – Same as day 2

Red" might have been difficult to locate and secure for this episode, so the prop man probably chose "Lady Be Good" figuring the audience would have had a difficult time to read the label as it spun on the record player, and the title was close enough to pass without observation.

After reviewing the footage, it was decided by Buck Houghton to film insert shots with no people on the camera for the opening shot of the exterior of the house. This was filmed on Lot 2's Andy Hardy Street on the morning of June 15. On that same day, retakes were shot with Alex Nichol, Helen Brown, and a young boy named Richard Siebuhr, who was a member of the Screen Actors' Guild at the time. This was for a proposed revision of the closing scenes. Filmed on Stage 16 and directed by Richard L. Bare, the revised scenes were never used for the finished film. According to an interoffice memo dated June 21, while the revised scene met with Houghton's approval, the young boy playing the role of Alex as a small boy did not look like Ricky Kelman, whose picture was seen framed in previous scenes of the episode.

One of the paintings hanging on the wall, the bird and the eight-sided picture frame, is the same one hanging on the wall in "Living Doll."

Actor Ricky Kelman was spelled "Rickey" in the closing credits. While there is some question regarding the spelling of his first name because he was billed as "Rickey" in a number of other television guest spots, his name was "Ricky" on the opening title cards of *The Dennis O'Keefe Show*, in which he played series regular Randy Towne.

The May 1962 issue of *Show* magazine reviewed, "Mother was not one to change décor with the times, and every place Virginia looks there is a big, teary reminder of dear old Mater."

Richard Matheson commented later that he liked this episode very much except for the last few minutes. He felt the mother should have been more "scary-looking" since she was supposed to be a ghost.

Production #4826 "I SING THE BODY ELECTRIC" (Initial telecast: May 18, 1962)

Copyright Registration: © Cayuga Productions, Inc., May 15, 1962, LP22957 (in notice: 1961)
Date of Rehearsal: October 11, 1961
Dates of Filming: October 12, 13, 16 and 17, 1961

Producer and Secretary: $1,625.00
Director: $1,874.99
Unit Manager and Secretary: $600.00
Agents Commission: $2,500.00

Story and Secretary: $2,405.00
Cast: $8,664.67
Production Fee: $900.00
Legal and Accounting: $250.00

Below the line charges (M-G-M): $47,947.59   Below the line charges (other): $3,606.93
Total Production Costs: $70,374.18 *

Cast: Dave Armstrong (the truck driver); Susan Cane (Anne, age 19); Veronica Cartwright (Anne, age 11); Dana Dillaway (Karen, age 10); Charles Herbert (Tom, age 12); Josephine Hutchinson (the electric grandmother); Judee Morton (Karen, 18); Paul Nesbitt (Tom, age 20); Doris Packer (Nedra); Vaughn Taylor (the salesman); and David White (George Rogers).

Original Music Score Composed and Conducted by Nathan Van Cleave (Score No. CPN6044): Etrange #3 (by Marius Constant, :09); Milieu #1 (by Constant, :16); A Happy Home (:33); Something Old, Something New (1:34); We Should Investigate (:20); To the Factory (:39); Bits and Pieces (1:02); It's a Factory (1:04); Grandma (:57); The Kite (:49); Anne (:30); New Car (:15); Ann's the Problem (:59); Was It a VW? (:41); Back From the Dead (:44); The Passing Life (:32); But Who is to Say? (1:05); Etrange #3 (by Constant, :08); and Milieu #2 (by Constant, :18).

Director of Photography: George T. Clemens, a.s.c.
Art Directors: George W. Davis and Phil Barber
Set Decorations: Henry Grace and H. Web Arrowsmith
Sound: Franklin Milton and Bill Edmondson
Automobiles Supplied by the Ford Motor Company
Directed by James Sheldon and William Claxton

Production Manager: Ralph W. Nelson
Assistant Director: E. Darrell Hallenbeck
Casting: Stalmaster-Lister
Story Consultant: Richard McDonagh
Film Editor: Jason H. Bernie, a.c.e.
Teleplay by Ray Bradbury

"They make a fairly convincing pitch here. It doesn't seem possible though to find a woman who must be ten times better than mother in order to seem half as good . . . except, of course . . . in the Twilight Zone."

Plot: When a loving family loses their mother, the children find it difficult to cope with the loss. Because of his work schedule, the widowed father is unable to spend enough time with the children. The solution comes in the form of a robot in the shape of an elderly grandmother – courtesy of "I Sing the Body Electric" – a company specializing in replacing lost loved ones with surrogate robots. The children choose the hair color, the eyes, the ears and all the accessories, but Ann will not accept the grandmother as part of the family. Weeks and months pass and Ann claims the family is only playing "make believe" with a robot. Running into the street, Ann almost becomes a victim of an accident, but the quick-thinking grandmother pushes Ann out of the way. Ann watches as the robot rises to her feet, unharmed by the truck. When the grandmother promises never to leave her like her mother, Ann accepts the motherly figure. Many years later, as the children are now grown up and moving out, the grandmother says her goodbyes to the children she came to love, ready to move to a new family that could use her help.

"As of this moment, the wonderful electric grandmother moved into the lives of children and father. She became integral, important, she became of the essence. As of this moment, they would never see lightning,

---

* Total production costs and breakdown from production summary dated June 30, 1962.

never hear poetry read, never listen to foreign tongues, without thinking of her. Everything they would ever see, hear, taste, feel, would remind them of her. She was all life, and all life was wondrous, quick, electrical, like her. [pause for bridged scenes] *A fable? Most assuredly. But who's to say at some distant moment there might not be an assembly line producing a gentle product in the form of a grandmother whose stock in trade is love? Fable, sure . . . but who's to say?"*

Trailer: *"The name Ray Bradbury has become synonymous with a new horizon of American writing. Next week on the Twilight Zone, we present a typical Bradbury tale. It also has typical Bradbury ingredients, including a grand-mother built in a factory. Now if this doesn't intrigue you, then I'm simply not doing justice to a most intriguing tale. I hope you'll join us next week for 'I Sing the Body Electric.'"*

The Electric Grandmother
and her children.

Trivia, etc. The morning after this episode was telecast, television columnist Rick Du Brow, whose syndicated column appeared in such papers as the Traverse City, Michigan *Record-Eagle*, posted his review. "Last night's drama, about a firm which constructed a substitute grandmother to care for three young children and their widowed father, was written by top science fiction author Ray Bradbury. His contribution last night was, of course, minor, and was not especially outstanding. But it made the point that both he and *The Twilight Zone* have stressed in the past, directly or indirectly: The need to come to grips with the challenge, and to modify and humanize the super-machine age rather than fight it, so it can free us for more creative matters. And, above all, the need to keep on loving strongly, rather than becoming bland and impersonal like machines."

"I knew Rod Serling for many years before he started his series," recalled Ray Bradbury to author Matthew R. Bradley. "He came over to the house back in the late '50s, and he told me he was going to have his own TV series. I said, 'Well, if you're going to have a TV series, you'd better bone up on all the best fantasy writers.' So I gave him copies of books by Roald Dahl and John Collier, Richard Matheson, Charles Beaumont, and some of my own books, of course. I said, 'Read these and you'll know what the field of fantasy and science fiction is like, hunh?' So he read all these books, and he hired some of the writers, or if he didn't hire them he bought the story rights to some of the short stories, and started his series."

The September 14, 1959 issue of Syracuse, New York's *Post-Standard* reported that Ray Brad-bury had been one of three contributors for *The Twilight Zone* (along with Matheson and Beau-mont). Later that same month, columnist Charles Witbeck reported that "science fiction writers like Ray Bradbury will help Serling, and writers like Charles Beaumont and Louise Fletcher have already contributed." The announcement of Bradbury's involvement was accurate, but took three years and an exchange of negative opinions before this episode marked the science fiction legend's first (and only) contribution to the series.

Bradbury's association with Serling dated months before when, on March 15, 1959, he submitted a teleplay titled "I Sing the Body Electric," a story about young children living with their widowed father, in need of a grandmother who can be the ultimate substitute for their recently deceased kin, and the reaction the children take to the new member of the family. "Be brutal to me about it. I'm one of the few writers left in the world with a Rhino's skin," wrote Bradbury. "Call me at H-H-L, will you, when you've had a chance to digest this, and we'll set up a date for lunch."

On May 18, 1959, Serling returned the teleplay, with a heart-warming, and respectful rejection: "I'm returning 'I Sing the Body Electric,' which you'll very likely have use for yourself. I rather imagine that if you use it, you'll make me sorry as hell I didn't grab it while it was available."

Bradbury submitted other scripts, including "A Miracle of Rare Device," which was purchased with Cayuga funds, but never produced. According to a production report dated July 31, 1961, the story and secretary fee paid during that quarter (ending July 31) was $2,250 for the story. A progress report dated June 12, 1961 gave the same figures. Bradbury was contracted to submit a revised draft by May 8, 1961. "A Miracle of Rare Device" was assigned a production number, #4812, with Anton M. Leader directing. Filming dates scheduled were August 15, 16 and 17, with rehearsal dates August 11 and 14. The script never went to production.

The logistics of another Bradbury script, "Here There Be Tygers," could not be worked out, and the script was shelved.

Bradbury revised his 1959 draft of "I Sing the Body Electric," and resubmitted it again, but Serling in one letter to Buck Houghton, confessed that it needed more work and he had no heart to personally alter, revise or improve on "a master's privilege." When production for the third season of *The Twilight Zone* started, Serling began running out of ideas. He admitted this fact to newspaper columnists many times previous, so in desperation, he began pulling out old concepts and plot ideas and fleshing them into feasible scripts – including the revised script of Bradbury's. Production went into the script in October, but after viewing the rushes, both Houghton and Serling confessed that the film either needed to be refilmed or re-edited with additional footage.

"I'm not sure how this *Twilight Zone* will turn out," Bradbury commented for Hal Humphrey's syndicated television column in early May, a couple weeks before the episode aired. "It was shot six months ago. Then just recently it was necessary to reshoot some of it, and they called me only the day before to do the rewriting. I was exhausted from working on a new novel and told producer Buck Houghton he'd have to get somebody else to do it."

According to the same column, Bradbury refused to work regularly in television because of the medium's hurry-up pace. He preferred the magazine field, where his name pulled $3,000 per story and he could take his sweet time working each tale.

Earlier in the year, Bradbury wrote an original hour-long teleplay for *Alcoa Premiere*, titled "The Jail," which aired in February, dealing with a future society, Kafka-esque, where machines had taken over the decision-making for human beings, including administering justice in court. Though it was not publicly promoted, Alfred Hitchcock's Shamley Productions was responsible for the film, which served as a pilot for a proposed television series starring John Gavin. Viewers who saw the broadcast may recall a huge array of computers. "We borrowed them from the Burroughs people," Bradbury recalled. "I tried I.B.M., but they wouldn't cooperate because they felt it made the machine the 'heavy' of the piece."

Bradbury had contributed to a number of teleplays for other programs, including *Alfred Hitch-*

cock Presents, but praised Serling's attempts to bring good science fiction to the mainstream television audience. "Rod Serling, with the success of his *Twilight Zone*, did a great service for all of us in science fiction. Rod's an important TV name. He proved to the doubters that it could be done."

The production for this episode (script #88), however, suffered from a number of complications. Assigned a production number on October 2, 1961, director James Sheldon spent four days filming.

On November 30, 1961, the old lady's voice was recorded in Sync Room "B" from 10:00 to 10:30 a.m. The film was promptly edited and a rough draft was previewed for Serling and Houghton, who both admitted there were problems.

"This happened a number of times on *The Twilight Zone*," recalled Sheldon. "It was common for the rough cut to be viewed, and decisions made after. When they decided shots should be inserted or additional scenes needed to perk up the film, they would turn to whoever was directing an episode that day and ask them to film a number of inserts. They would ask the current director because oftentimes the initial director would have been off doing something else. Regarding the Bradbury story, it was not my choice. I complained about the script before we began shooting. I did not like what they gave me and there was little to work with. After they saw what we filmed, it was apparent they agreed with me and decided to re-shoot some of the scenes. But I was elsewhere doing some other project so they got someone else. Because of the Directors' Guild, they had to seek permission from me, and I gave it to them. That is why the two of us are credited for directing the episode."

> **Initial Production Schedule at M-G-M**
> Day 1 –   Interior of Living Room (Stage 10)
>   Exterior of Residential Street (Lot #2)
> Day 2 –   Exterior of Business Intersection and Exterior of Residential Street (Lot #2)
> Day 3 –   Interior of the Store (Stage 19)
> Day 4 –   Interior of Living Room and Dining Room (Stage 10)

Deciding that certain scenes needed to be re-shot, William Claxton was hired to direct the new segments on February 15, 16 and 19, 1962, filming numerous revised pages, dated February 12. According to a release schedule dated December 13, 1961, this episode was originally scheduled for broadcast on March 23, 1962. Going into an additional filming schedule, the broadcast date was pushed ahead.

The female arms in the store where the children selected the body parts for their electric grandmother, were not plastic. The following actresses stood behind the black wall and held their arms still for this episode: Shirley Swendsen, Randi Stevens, Kathy Petersen and Roberta Goodwins.

The sign on the side of the florist truck is "Ralph's Florist," a tip of the hat to Ralph W. Nelson.

Footage from both filming schedules was edited together, hence this episode credited two directors on the screen. Scenes from the first filming schedule originally had actress June Vincent as Aunt Nedra, but all of the footage featuring Vincent ended up on the cutting room floor.

The music heard in this episode is a completely different recording from what has been commercially released on LP and CD over the years. While they are mostly the same score, they are two different recordings. (The cue breakdown in this episode entry corresponds with the film seen today.) The alternate version includes an additional cue, titled "I Sing the Body Electric – Theme," which is not featured in the soundtrack of the film. This cue begins the "suite" on the commercially released recording, which lacks "A Happy Home." The two cues begin the same but end quite differently. The entire score was rerecorded because many of the cues are at different tempos than their counterparts, most likely due to having to reshoot several scenes which might have ended up at slightly different lengths than originally shot. Also of note: this is also the only *Twilight Zone* score recorded in stereo.

Production Schedule at M-G-M (Retakes)

Day 1 –   Interior of Living Room and Dining room, Interior of Hallway (sc. 4, 5, 33 and 65, Stage 22)

Day 2 –   Rod Serling's intro in Front of Wall of Living Room (Stage 12)

Day 3 –   Exterior of Florist Truck (Stage 12)

Days before the broadcast, the May 12, 1962 issue of *The Register and Post-Herald Weekender* put this episode among the seven "shows to watch" list for the upcoming television programs. "Writer Ray Bradbury has been the answer to a problem that's bugged all young married couples with children," the paper explained. "Need we add that Bradbury is a demon science fiction writer?"

Regardless of the improvements made to the telefilm, the finished script did not meet with Bradbury's approval. "Rod promised me that he would buy a couple of my scripts and that he wouldn't touch them," recalled Bradbury to author Mark Phillips. "'I Sing the Body Electric' turned out okay, but they took out the most important scene. In my script, the father asks the electric grandmother, 'Why are there electric grandmothers?' She gives him a moment of truth: she can do something no mother ever can. She can pay attention to all of the children equally. Only a machine could do that, and since the father may never find a new wife, somebody has to look after the children. The electric grandmother is the substitute for the mother that isn't there."

"When I saw that this scene was cut from the episode, I was furious!" continued Bradbury. "I called Rod the next day and said, 'For God's sake, why didn't you tell me?' He apologized and said that there hadn't been time to film it. I said, 'I had all of my friends come over to the house, and we sat down to watch the show, and the most important scene is gone! I don't want to work on your show anymore.' I told him that I couldn't trust him [as a producer]."

"Sometimes when I see one I think it is a little pretentious," recalled Serling about some of the lesser *Twilight Zone* efforts, for a reporter in *The Corpus Christi Caller-Times*. "That's a problem of making filmed shows. What one reads in the script is not always transferable."

This was not the first time one of Bradbury's stories was altered for television. He was once paid $10,000 for a script to be produced on the Shirley Temple television series. Apparently something in the script scared the producer. Later, Bradbury found out quite accidentally that another writer was paid an additional $7,000 to "doctor it up," and the reason it never aired was because of Bradbury's insistence that the story not air on the networks.

Most of Bradbury's stories, although perhaps "way out" in terms of setting, are designed to show man's foibles and how he might go about correcting them. "Since TV never has been famous for stimulating thought, it is natural that Ray's stuff causes mystification and suspicion by TV's brass," wrote Hal Humphrey in his May 5, 1962 column.

"A writer can get away with poorer quality on TV, but that very fact makes it impossible for him to grow, if he stays with TV," remarked Bradbury. "I don't think a writer should write for *Dr. Kildare* unless he has something in him that fits the series."

Bradbury had a number of short stories adapted for television films, and he also wrote teleplays for a number of programs, including *Steve Canyon, The Fireside Theater, Rendezvous* and *Alfred Hitchcock Presents*.

According to seminar notes by Jeanne Marshall (circa 1962-63), months after this episode was telecast, Serling told his students, "There are writers who write marvelous fiction, like Ray Bradbury, who cannot write drama (dialogue)."

The relationship between Bradbury and Serling went afoul after the telecast, with Bradbury having gone public about his disgust for the botched production. On September 13, 1962, Serling wrote to Bradbury, explaining that while they had straightened out their differences back in December of 1960, regarding Bradbury's accusations of Serling being a plagiarist, something new was thrown on the fire. On the afternoon of September 12, Serling was told by two people of a Los Angeles magazine that Bradbury had been in there, talked of Serling's deliberate theft of a story of his and the fact that Serling had been a constant defendant in a series of lawsuits regarding plagiarism. "I had thought that we had examined and re-examined most thoroughly the similarity of my pilot script to one of your published stories. Beyond the general concept of a man being alone in a town, nothing else in the story bore any resemblance to what you had done. The character, the direction, the flavor and the denouement of my script were totally unlike your story. As to the lawsuits which I'm 'constantly being badgered by,' there have been precisely three. They were directed, in order, at Charles Beaumont, Richard Matheson and George Clayton Johnson, and were specifically based on material written by these three. Nothing that I have written has been subject to any accusation of theft."

"Again I have to ask myself what motivates your behind-the-scenes back-biting. I have never once, in any conversation with anyone, had anything but praise for you as a man and as a talent," Serling continued. "It seems most odd, Ray, that you can produce this façade of friendship, break bread with Carol and me, phone on occasion, and then turn around to throw darts at me behind my back."

Weeks later, Bradbury attacked *The Twilight Zone* in a column personally written from his own typewriter, in place of a weekly syndicated column occupied by a vacationing Du Brow. "I wrote a *Twilight Zone* script about an electrical grandmother summoned in to raise a family after the mother dies. The point was my explanation of how a robot machine could be used to embody human and/or Christian principles, even as our heroes, servants, teachers embody them. This explanation was torn out of the script as being 'too slow,' thus ripping the heart out of the story and leaving everyone in the dark as to what it meant.

"Similarly, I was summoned to a series of meetings with various heads of a network earlier this year. I outlined a series of specials I wanted to do, which were received with great huzzahs, the throwing of confetti, dancing in the streets. I was told I was a grade-A genuine genius and sent happily home to await the signing of contracts. Silence followed. A week or so I began to realize there was no deal. Again they ran scared when confronted with something new. I never even received, in writing, a final rejection of my specials. I had to guess their verdict, when weeks had passed."

In the premiere issue of *Gamma* magazine (circa 1963), Serling added to the fire by commenting: "I know I've been knocked by some veteran science fiction writers who've spent the better part of their lives in this creative area – I've been called an opportunist who's taken this story form that these guys have sweated out for years and used my reasonably affluent name to just step all over them to get my show on the air. Well, I can say to these people this, I'm sorry they feel this way. *Zone* is an honest effort on my part. I tried not to step on any toes, but with a show such as this, you're almost bound to."

In the June 1963 issue of *Writer's Digest*, Serling was asked if he found the writers or if they found him. "Because *The Twilight Zone* has rather special requirements we have done far better using established science fiction writers. They know the story telling milieu and are also accomplished dramatists. At the moment they're supplying two-thirds of the story material for the show. Richard Matheson and Charles Beaumont are the best known. Earl Hamner, Jr. from Cincinnati has done some exceptionally good things for us. We were less fortunate with Ray Bradbury because, by and large, his material is harder to dramatize."

In May of 1969, Rod Serling looked back on this episode unpleasantly. "As to my attitude toward Bradbury's work, needless to say, I'm an admirer – a deep admirer," he confessed. "I have found, however, that he is much more effective on the page than he is on the proscenium. The lyrical quality of his work seems to lend itself to the printed page, rather than to spoken language. In the case of 'I Sing the Body Electric,' the words that seemed so beautiful in the story turned out archaic and wooden and somehow unbelievable when a person speaks them. But this, of course, is one man's opinion and it's hardly engraved on rock."

Production #4827 "CAVENDER IS COMING" (Initial telecast: May 25, 1962)

Copyright Registration: © Cayuga Productions, Inc., May 22, 1962, LP22958
Date of Rehearsal: January 22, 1962
Dates of Filming: January 23, 24, 25, 26 through 29, 1962
Script #90 dated: January 11, 1962

Producer and Secretary: $1,562.50
Director: $1,875.00
Unit Manager and Secretary: $600.00
Agents Commission: $2,500.00
Below the line charges (M-G-M): $70,652.52
Total Production Costs: $93,865.33 *

Story and Secretary: $2,855.00
Cast: $10,372.67
Production Fee: $900.00
Legal and Accounting: $250.00
Below the line charges (other): $2,297.64

Cast: Frank Behrens (Stout); Carol Burnett (Agnes Grep); Albert Carrier (the Frenchman); Maurice Dallimore (man #1); Diane Davis (the receptionist); Donna Douglas (woman #3); John Fiedler (field rep #3); Sandra Gould (woman #1); Pitt Herbert (field rep #2); G. Stanley Jones (field rep #4); Danny Kulick (the child); Marilyn Malloy (woman in automobile and double for Burnett); Adrienne Marden (woman #2); Bob McCord (man at party); Barbara Morrison (Matronly woman); Rory O'Brien (the little boy); William O'Connell (field rep #1); Norma Shattuck (the little girl); Roy Sickner (the bus driver); Howard Smith (Polk); Jesse White (Harmon Cavender); and Jack Younger (the truck driver).

Stock Music Cues: Etrange #3 (by Marius Constant, :09); Milieu #1 (by Constant, :16); Fight (by Bernard Green, :04); Whistle Gag (by Lyn Murray, :03); F Story #1 (by Constant, :12); For Me, Mink (by Lyn Murray :03); Big Check (by Fred Steiner, :16); For Me, Mink (by Murray, :03); F Story #1 (by Constant, :31 and :04); Travelling Lightly (by Bernard Green, :26); For Me, Mink (by Murray :03); Check #1 (by Steiner, :08); Nancy's Apartment (by Steiner, :09); Whistle Gag (by Murray, :06 and :08); Western Side Kick (by Green, :08); Opening of Story (by William Lava, :11);

---

* Total production costs and breakdown from production summary dated June 30, 1962.

Big Check (by Steiner, :15); A Story #1 (by Constant, :05); For Me, Mink (by Murray, :06 and :13); Whistle Gag (by Murray, :06); Black Forest Drive (by Horst Jankowski, :45); Montage (by Steiner, :11); Black Forest Drive (by Jankowski, :14); I Like My Wife Fat (by Jeff Alexander, :28); Whistle Gag (by Murray, :07); Serene Siren (by Green, :27); Sad But Funny (by Green, :08); Loving Wife (by Murray, :07); A Story #1 (by Constant, :05); Passing Days (by Steiner, :11); Big Check (by Steiner, :15); F Story #5 (by Constant, :31); Check #1 (by Steiner, :02); F Story #1 (by Constant, :18 and :04); Etrange #3 (by Constant, :08); and Milieu #2 (by Constant, :18). **

Director of Photography: George T.
    Clemens, a.s.c.
Art Directors: George W. Davis and Merrill Pye
Casting: Robert Walker
Sound: Franklin Milton and Bill Edmondson
Automobiles Supplied by Ford Motor Company

Production Manager: Ralph W. Nelson
Set Decorations: Keogh Gleason
Assistant Director: E. Darrell Hallenbeck
Film Editor: Bill Mosher
Directed by Chris Nyby
Teleplay by Rod Serling

"Small message of reassurance to that horizontal young lady: Don't despair, help is en route. It's coming in an odd form from a very distant place, but it's nonetheless coming . . . Submitted for your approval, the case of one Miss Agnes Grep, put on Earth with two left feet, an overabundance of thumbs and a propensity for falling down manholes. In a moment she will be up to her jaw in miracles wrought by apprentice angel Harmon Cavender, intent on winning his wings. And though it's a fact that both of them should have stood in bed – they will tempt all the fates by moving into the cold gray dawn . . . of the Twilight Zone."

Plot: An angel named Cavender is granted one final chance to earn his wings. His mission is to venture down to Earth and be the guardian angel for Agnes Grep, a woman best described as unstable and unresolved, and who cannot hold a job longer than a few hours. She is, however, well-loved by the tenants of the apartment house, a Thursday-night bowler, and always a few months behind in her rent. Offering aid and advice for a period for 24 hours, Cavender creates a number of miracles – independent wealth, a mansion, and making Agnes a prominent member of society. After tasting a bit of the high life, however, she longs for her friends, the junk-filled apartment she resided in, and the life she led before the divine intervention. Cavender is puzzled until Agnes begs for her life to be returned the way it was. She was happy before the miracles. Cavender consents and then returns to Heaven, where his superior explains that cash and contentment are not necessarily synonymous. Seeing how Agnes is happier than she was before, Cavender is assigned another lost soul.

"A word to the wise now to any and all who might suddenly feel the presence of a cigar-smoking helpmate who takes bankbooks out of thin air. If you're suddenly aware of any such celestial aids, it means that you're under the beneficent care of one Harmon Cavender, guardian angel. And this message from the Twilight Zone: lotsa luck!"

Trailer: *"Next week on the Twilight Zone, two incredibly talented people join forces to show us what happens when an accident-prone, discombooberated lady with six thumbs and two left feet meets a hapless*

** The music cue "Travelling Lightly" is supposed to be spelled that way, according to original music sheets.

guardian angel who knows more about martinis than miracles. Miss Carol Burnett and Mr. Jesse White. They're the choice ingredients to a very funny stew. Next week, 'Cavender Is Coming.'"

Trivia, etc. This episode was a rehash of "Mr. Bevis." In the first pilot, Mr. Bevis was the angel's permanent assignment. Though it didn't sell, Serling's intention was to keep the premise for this pilot, but focus the central character and title to the guardian angel, who each week would receive another assignment. Carol Burnett was billed as "special guest star" for this episode, but because the proposed series was designed as a starring vehicle for Jesse White, he received top billing. Serling did, however, write the script with Carol Burnett in mind and focused Cavender's first (and only) client on the comedic talents of Burnett.

John Fiedler recalled, inaccurately, to interviewer Tom Weaver, "It was a pilot for Carol Burnett. It was kind of like *Touched by an Angel*; she was gonna be a guardian angel and Jesse White and I would have been regulars. We would have been in Heaven, giving her assignments, and the idea that she'd go down and help somebody get out of a mess, sort of like that Michael Landon series. I don't know whether they decided not to do it or if that's when she got her own show."

On May 9, 1961, Serling appeared on *The Garry Moore Show*, telecast over CBS. He had wandered there on invitation just to watch them rehearse because they were doing a repeat of a take-off on *The Twilight Zone*. As Serling described to his former teacher, Helen Foley, in a letter dated June 9, 1961, "I guess they took one look at me and decided that I was kookie enough to play the role myself. Hence I got on. And once on, their smoke machine broke and I was practically asphyxiated. If you happen to have seen me, you can understand why I was a little tilt." It was on this program that Serling met Carol Burnett in person, and after a discussion, he agreed to write a script with a part specifically for her.

On October 16, George Spota of Martin Goodman Productions, Inc., a talent agency, wrote to Serling, thanking him and Houghton for extracting highlights of Jonathan Winters' talents during his appearance in "A Game of Pool." Spota also suggested that if they wanted Winters for an additional episode, an opening would be available in the spring. Spota also took advantage of the opportunity to discuss two other clients, Arlene Francis and Carol Burnett. Burnett had gone west with *The Garry Moore Show* during the month of March.

While the pilot was under consideration with the title "The Side of the Angels," a list of actors was drafted for consideration for the role of Cavender. Martin Balsam, Ronny Graham, Robert Q. Lewis, Arthur Malet, Alfred Ryder, Sam Wannamaker, Keenan Wynn and Tom Bosley were among the names, although Bosley was working in New York and that would have meant having him flown to the West Coast.

Other names considered; Brian Keith, Murray Hamilton, Tom Poston, Jack Carson, Larry Blyden, Orson Bean, Wally Cox, Bob Sweeney, Burgess Meredith, Art Carney, Buddy Ebsen, Buddy Hackett, Ray Walston, Jonathan Winters, William Bendix, Hans Conreid, Bert Lahr, Henry Morgan, Jack Klugman, Henry Jones, and Jesse White.

Paul Hartman was also under consideration for the male lead in *This Side of the Angels*, according to a letter dated December 15, 1961, from Wally Hiller to Buck Houghton.

Serling conceived of the script with Burnett in mind and then submitted a rough draft to George Spota of Martin Goodman Productions, Inc., asking for him to forward it to the comedian. On December 11, 1961, Spota congratulated Serling for "the fine story Carol Burnett tells me you

> **Production Schedule at M-G-M**
> Day 1 – Interior of the Westchester Home (Stage 27)
>   Interior of the Brownstone Apartment (Stage 20)
> Day 2 – Interior of the Brownstone Apartment Hall and Stairs (Stage 20)
> Day 3 – Exterior of the Theatre and New York Street (Lot #2)
>   Interior of the Bus and Exterior of the Brownstone Street (Lot #2)
> Day 4 – Interior of the Office Suite (Stage 10, same day Serling recorded)
> Day 5 – The Television Building and Interior of the Bus (Lot #1)
>   Interior of the Theater Lobby and Interior of Westchester Home
>   (added scenes, Stage 10)

have developed for her initial appearance on *The Twilight Zone*." Later that same month, Serling wrote to Spota, "I think the deal with Carol Burnett has been consummated and we're delighted beyond the telling. Thank you for your help in this."

On January 8, 1962, a production number was assigned to the film and dates of filming were scheduled for the month of February. With Carol Burnett signed for the pilot (and a commitment to appear on the series), it was brought to Serling and Houghton's attention that if the episode could be filmed in January, weeks earlier than intended, it would work with her schedule since the month of February might conflict with prior commitments. The dates were changed to January.

In early February 1962, Sam Kaplan received a letter from Seymour Peyser at United Artists relating to the use of the title, "The Side of the Angels," on the *Twilight Zone* spin-off. On the afternoon of February 8, 1962, Kaplan discussed the matter with Leo Lefcourt of CBS, and the men agreed that since United Artists already trademarked the title "The Side of the Angels," Rod Serling would have to come up with a new title.

While a final cut of the *Twilight Zone* presentation and title cards had not yet been completed, a separate sales presentation had been filmed using "The Side of the Angels" and could not be changed without abnormal costs, so the presentation was not altered.

By this time, a trailer for next week's episode had already been filmed, and Serling had announced on film that the show for next week would be "The Side of the Angels." As soon as Serling created the new title, "Cavender is Coming," the production crew took immediate steps to modify the trailer so that the new title replaced any references to United Artists' property.

The sales presentation, considered the unaired version of the pilot, titled "The Side of the Angels," contains a laugh track but the version that aired over the network, did not. Reruns, syndication prints and commercial releases, have not offered the unaired version. In 1960, CBS top brass admitted they did not like canned laughter (or technically augmented laughter) on their television programs. Some executives felt the illusion of a studio audience harmed the programs, but admitted it was necessary in some filmed shows because it improved the illusion of a comedian's television needs. The procedure of adding laughter to an episode meant someone spliced recorded laughter into the finished film. CBS usually had the option to refuse to air shows with canned laughter – it ensured this clause in its contracts – but in the contracts with Cayuga Productions there was no such stipulation.

The only involvement CBS had with the production was its request to include at least two Negro actors as pedestrians in the street, due to the rising complaints from African Americans regarding their lack of participation on television programs.

When Carol Burnett was 15 years old, her very first job was an usherette at a Warner Bros. theater in Hollywood. She recounted her experience to Serling, asking him to incorporate a scene in which she would play an usherette. "Mr. Batton was the manager's name," Burnett recalled. "Tall thin man, with a little bitty mustache . . . very Brooks brothers. I was paid 65-cents an hour and for that sum we worked like dogs. Mr. B was a nut on 'signals.' He never spoke, except to reprimand. He scared the hell out of everyone. When I started work there, I was as tall as I am now and had a loud voice . . . so I was made 'spot girl.' This is the girl who always stands in the middle of the lobby, framed in an amber spot, and bellows, 'Aisle two straight ahead, or the stairway to your right!' Mr. B never said, 'You will be the spot girl.' He simply put his right index finger on the palm of his left hand, made an about face, and exited the lobby cutting square corners all the way. I had to ask the head usher what that meant."

"I then proceeded to wear my vocal chords thin for three solid hours," she continued. "At the end of three hours, Mr. B marched up to me, slapped his wrist, and held up three fingers. This meant I was on a 30-minute break. I saluted, made an about face and cut square corners all the way to the john. This seemed to please him. Exactly 30 minutes later, a terrible buzzing sound rang through the ladies' room. The older and wiser usherettes said it was a Batton buzzing for us, so we marched upstairs, single file. Standing there, shoulder to shoulder, we could see Batton standing at attention clear across the lobby, beginning his signal routine. One girl got one finger, and she saluted and marched to aisle one; flashlight in hand. Another girl got two fingers, so she marched to aisle two, and so on. He made a 'C' with his fingers and the next girl took her position behind the candy stand. Then, of course, I received the finger on the palm bit, and returned to my battle position of 'The Spot.'"

"It went on like this for a couple of weeks," concluded Burnett. "We couldn't even ask if we could get a drink of water. Somehow, you would have to attract his attention, and then open your mouth and point frantically. He would either nod or shake his head. One day, after a break, I was waiting for the familiar spot signal, when he pulled a switch and gave that position to a new girl. I was terrified. What was he going to do with me? He then did a strange thing . . . there he was, at least 40 feet across the lobby, and he waved at me. I waved back. I thought he wanted to be friends. He waved again. I waved again. He ran toward me, eyes blazing with fury, grabbed hold of my maroon satin uniform top, and through clenched teeth said, 'That means box office, Stupid' . . . I was later fired because I wouldn't let some customers in on the last five minutes of *Strangers on a Train*."

On November 22, 1961, Serling completed the rough draft of the script and, for Burnett's benefit, incorporated her usherette experience in the opener of this *Twilight Zone* script. Serling also proposed Jonathan Winters as "Cavender" for this episode, but Winters proved unavailable at the time, so Jesse White was hired to play the role.

The original closer was considerably different from the one featured in the finished film:

"Chapter One in the saga of Harmon Cavender, the guardian angel. Proving, among other things, that happiness is relative; angels have their own problems and some people never had it so good. Tonight's excursion into the never-never land . . . of the Twilight Zone."

Carol Burnett was an avid television viewer of the *Dr. Kildare* program, and when she arrived on the M-G-M lot to film *The Twilight Zone*, she found that her favorite series was also filmed at the

Carol Burnett has man problems courtesy of Cavender.

same studio. "I bumped into him one day, accidentally, you understand. I almost attacked him," she recalled. Her strategy worked, which rewarded her with a luncheon invitation from Richard Chamberlain.

Apparently Chamberlain was not the only person she met at M-G-M that sparked a twinkle in her eye. She met up with *Father of the Bride* groom Burt Metcalfe, and the two split a steak in the studio commissary, both reminiscing back to 1955 when they were UCLA drama students and were lucky to split hotdogs.

Carol Burnett was flown to the West Coast for this production and stayed at the Beverly Hills Hotel. On January 22, she was picked up by station wagon and taken to the main wardrobe department at M-G-M. The pilot took five days to film – more than the usual amount for a *Twilight Zone* production, and the cost factor was much larger. Serling and Houghton decided that more care, time and expense should go into the film since it served as a pilot. Per contractual agreement, $20,000 of the total cost was not charged to Cayuga productions, but was borne by CBS as "new show development costs."

A $10,000 loan from the Cayuga general account was made to the production account in May of 1962 to cover production expenses for this episode. The overage in production had not yet been reimbursed by CBS in May, and the production account was short on funds. The loan was therefore made to the production account until that matter was settled and weeks later, CBS made good on its promise.

Production costs aside, the pilot was almost doomed, when, during the last week of May 1962, a man named Ray Williford at M-G-M claimed that in 1954, he developed a concept for a television series which he called "Guardian Angels, Inc.," which was in essence the basic format of this episode. Williford claimed that in 1957, during the production of *Saddle the Wind*, on which he worked and Serling scripted, he discussed this format with Serling on the set.

The purpose of Mr. Williford's claim was to try to work something out with Rod Serling and Cayuga since he felt that Serling "subconsciously" stole the idea. Sam Kaplan contacted Serling, who admitted he had no recollection of having had any discussions with Mr. Williford. Serling pointed out that he only appeared on the set for *Saddle the Wind* on two occasions during the entire course of production, and those were fairly brief.

Williford's basic idea for a "guardian angel" (even one who constantly goofs) had been used a number of times in features and was used in at least one television pilot previously, and such a premise crossed the desks at CBS a number of times. In a letter from Sam Kaplan wrote on June 4, 1962, he explained: "I laid into the fact that at this time, in Rod's opinion and in the opinion of the sales people in our organization, 'Cavender is Coming' will not sell as a series and that if there should be a surprise sale, it would be something short of a miracle."

On May 3, Serling wrote a letter to Carol Burnett, explaining the loss of his half-hour anthology, describing the experience, "I feel like Napoleon surveying the aftermath of Waterloo, except at least I get residuals – all he got was Elba. If this truly is the best of all possible worlds, I think I'll check with Greyhound to see if they have any trips to other galaxies."

Serling also added his valued opinion regarding the finished product, having recently previewed the final cut. "The show you did for us is not good and it's not bad – which makes it lousy. With a combination of talents like yours and Jesse's, it should have been walloping exceptional. That it isn't, points up to the fact that you were done wrong by all concerned. The script, I guess, is part of the trouble, but even more culpable is the direction. This was quite the most heavy-handed, ham fisted, squarest directing I've ever cried through. God knows when it's scheduled for – and I hope you'll be out on a ferry boat someplace and won't have to see it. I promise you that if given a second chance, ever, I'll make it up."

One of the usherettes in this episode is referred to by name, "Burnett," by Mr. Stout, in the lobby of the theater. This was, again, an inside joke referring to the guest star on stage.

All of the music scores by Lyn Murray and Fred Steiner in this episode were originally composed for *The Millionaire*, two episodes "Millionaire Tom Hampton" (initial telecast November 18, 1959) and "Millionaire Nancy Pearson" (December 15, 1959).

Television critic Leonard Hoffman of *The Tucson Daily Citizen* commented about this episode, "The humor comes off as a bit too mild as she portrays an optimistic girl who loses jobs as easily as she makes friends. Jesse White gets the most out of his role as an apprentice angel, who sees a chance to earn his wings by keeping her from being fired again. Fairly amusing, and delightfully so at the end."

Carol Burnett's association with *The Twilight Zone* did not end with the telecast of this episode. In early September 1962, Buck Houghton was working at Four Star Television for *The Richard Boone Show*. Staying in contact with Serling numerous times after their association with *The Twilight Zone* ended, he wrote to Serling, explaining that he and his wife, Wanda, went to Las Vegas for the first time to see Carol Burnett, then performing at the Sands. "It was well worth the trip," Houghton wrote. "She was her usual great."

Production #4835 "THE CHANGING OF THE GUARD"
(Initial telecast: June 1, 1962)
Copyright Registration: © Cayuga Productions, Inc., May 28, 1962, LP23014
Dates of Rehearsal: March 8 and 9, 1962
Dates of Filming: March 12, 13 and 14, 1962
Script #98 dated: February 26, 1962, with revised pages dated March 6, 8 and 9, 1962.
Shooting script dated: March 9, 1962

Producer and Secretary: $1,625.00	Story and Secretary: $2,855.00
Director: $1,250.00	Cast: $6,221.18
Unit Manager and Secretary: $540.00	Production Fee: $900.00
Agents Commission: $2,500.00	Legal and Accounting: $250.00
Below the line charges (M-G-M): $36,234.54	Below the line charges (other): $1,666.87
Total Production Costs: $54,042.59 *	

* Total production costs and breakdown from production summary dated June 30, 1962.

Cast: Jimmy Baird (boy #1); Philippa Bevans (Mrs. Landers); Bob Biheller (Graham); Bob Birchfield (student #1); Mike Brown (student #4); Tom Brown (student #3); James Browning (boy #8); Pat Close (boy #9); Buddy Hart (boy #6); John Hartsook (student #7); Rusty Havens (student #2); Russell Horton (boy #5); Kevin Jones (boy #2); Dennis Kerlee (boy #10); Tom Lowell (boy #4); Kevin O'Neal (Butler, aka Boy #3); Jim Pardue (student #5); Donald Pleasence (Professor Ellis Fowler); Robert Redd (student #6); Darryl Richard (boy #7); Liam Sullivan (the Headmaster); and Phil Susterick (student #8).

Stock Music Cues: Etrange #3 (by Marius Constant, :09); Milieu #1 (by Constant, :16); Gaudiamus Igitur (traditional, :16); Love Theme #4 (by Nathan Van Cleave, :34); Lost Love Part #3 (a.k.a. "Happy Return," by Lucien Moraweck, :27); Quiet Western Theme (by Van Cleave, :45); Lost Love Part #2 (by Moraweck, :37); Messiah (by George Frederic Handel, :39); Lost Love Part #2 (by Moraweck, :55); Lost Love Part #1 (by Moraweck, :35); Witness Chords #2 (by Moraweck, :06); Lost Love Part #1 (by Moraweck, :41); Reaction to Tag (by William Barnett, :15); F Story 6 (by Constant, :47); Romantic Melody #1 (by Fred Steiner, :47); F Story 6 (by Constant, :04); Romantic Melody #1 (by Steiner, :21); It Came Upon a Midnight Clear (traditional, :20); Romantic Melody #1 (by Steiner, :25); Etrange #3 (by Constant, :08); and Milieu #2 (by Constant, :18).

Director of Photography: George T. Clemens, a.s.c.
Art Directors: George W. Davis and Merrill Pye
Set Decorations: Henry Grace and Keogh Gleason
Sound: Franklin Milton and Bill Edmondson
Teleplay by Rod Serling

Production Manager: Ralph W. Nelson
Assistant Director: E. Darrell Hallenbeck
Casting: Robert Walker
Makeup: William Tuttle
Film Editor: Bill Mosher
Directed by Robert Ellis Miller

"Professor Ellis Fowler, a gentle, bookish guide to the young, who is about to discover that life still has certain surprises, and that the campus of the Rock Springs School for Boys lies on a direct path to another institution, commonly referred to as . . . the Twilight Zone."

Plot: On the final day of the first semester, just days before the Christmas holiday at the Rock Spring School for Boys, Professor Fowler is delivered a notice of termination. A member of the faculty for more than 50 years, the board considers him a teacher of incalculable value. As it must come to all men, youth must be served – a changing of the guard. Professor Fowler, however, feels he is an abject failure – an aging relic on deaf, young ears. He never accomplished anything with his poetry. In his final moments in the classroom alone, Professor Fowler contemplates suicide when he is visited by the specters of those who were once his students. After a brief discussion with the ghosts of his past, the professor learns that each of his students was a fine young man who left his mark on society. It was through his teaching that the boys learned about courage, loyalty, ethics and honesty. The professor hears their stories and realizes he was wrong when he stated that he moved nobody, motivated nobody and left no imprint. He was by their elbows from the moment they left his classroom. Content with this knowledge, Professor Fowler is grateful for the time he had to teach the youth, and now looks forward to a future of promising contentment.

"Professor Ellis Fowler – teacher. Who discovered, rather belatedly, something of his own value. A very small scholastic lesson . . . from the campus of . . . the Twilight Zone."

Trailer: *"Next week on the Twilight Zone, Mr. Donald Pleasence, visiting us from Broadway, brings his exceptional talents to a very special program. The story of an aging schoolmaster who finds some faith, some hope, and some mending glue for a few shattered dreams. But he finds it in that strange manner unique in the shadow regions of The Twilight Zone. Next week Donald Pleasence stars in 'The Changing of the Guard.'"*

Trivia, etc. The opening narration was much lengthier in an earlier draft of the script:

"What you've just seen is not just the end of a semester. It happens to be the end of an era. Professor Ellis Fowler, a teacher of literature, a gentle, bookish, guide to the young, is about to find a package under this Christmas tree . . . and not a pleasant one. He doesn't realize it yet, but after half a century of planting seeds of wisdom, and then watching the fruits of his harvest . . . he is to discover that he has come to the end of the field and is about to be discarded . . . and that the campus of the Rock Hill School for Boys lies on a direct path to another institution commonly referred to as . . . The Twilight Zone."

The ball got rolling for this episode when the script was assigned a production number on February 26. On March 7, a casting call for 32 boys (with the appearance of 15 to 17 years of age) gave Robert Walker, the casting director, his choice of eight boys to act as carolers, two for students in the hallway, and eight for classroom students. The call requested they be "good clean cut types." After the boys were selected for the roles, two were asked to remain as "alternatives on call" in case someone canceled or phoned in sick. Russell Hayes and Robert Mayon remained on call.

Three of the boys, Pat Close, Kevin O'Neal and Darryl Richard, were minors and therefore required a welfare worker on the set during the hours of filming.

The entire episode was filmed on Stage 16 at M-G-M except for Fowler's study and foyer, filmed on Stage 18 on the second day of filming. After principal production was completed, Jack Glass and his crew filmed insert shots of the school sign mounted on the brick wall from Stage 16 around 9:30 a.m. on March 20. (A half-hour later the same crew shot insert shots of the dummy against the wall in the alley). On April 10, a special effects man filmed the same school sign on the brick wall, this time with snow on the sign. It was the second insert shot that was used. On April 27, a group of kids was ushered into Sync Room "B" at M-G-M to sing the Christmas carol and provide the voices of juveniles in the hallway. This only took an hour to record, beginning at 9 a.m.

Clearance had to be made for the poems which were recited by Professor Fowler in this episode. Sam Kaplan of Ashley-Steiner, exchanged letters with Sol Rosenthal, an attorney, to secure a title report on the authors of the poems to ensure there would be no legal repercussion for the use of the poetry.

While the story took place in Rock Spring, Vermont, the quote Professor Fowler reads in this episode was "be ashamed to die until you have won some victory for humanity." Coined by Horace Mann, this was the motto of Serling's alma mater, Antioch College. Shortly after principal filming was completed for this episode, Serling accepted a teaching position at the college and moved to Ohio to try to teach aspiring writers quality in literature and screenplays. Shortly after completing his term, Serling told a reporter, "Recently I completed a term teaching playwriting classes at my alma mater, Antioch College. I wasn't a good teacher. I went back there to find out what was the truth, and I found out. The truth was at home and I should have stayed there."

"It's traditional, I know, for television editors to be inundated by euphemistic self-congratulatory notices of this show or that show, how it is essential that it must be watched, and how great it is," Serling wrote to a number of critics and editors of trade columns. "I hope you will forgive my succumbing to the ritual and at least accept my motives as honorable. On June 1st, *The Twilight Zone* will wind up its third season on the air with a production called, 'The Changing of the Guard.' It stars the fine British actor, Donald Pleasance, and is directed by Robert Ellis Miller. I think it is a poignant and moving story and is perhaps one of the best we've ever done on the show. I hope you have a chance to watch it."

Buck Houghton recalled how the casting director wanted Donald Pleasence for the role and arrangements were made to fly him from England for this episode – a choice Houghton later recalled was worth the expense. By the time the episode aired on CBS, Pleasence was receiving critical acclaim on Broadway for his performance in *The Caretaker*. He appeared on this episode under considerable makeup to give the appearance that he was old enough to justify retirement. This episode marked a satisfying conclusion to *Twilight Zone*'s third season, explaining that even in death, students can still educate their teachers.

SUMMER RERUNS

Unlike previous seasons, the opening title sequence was not re-edited to match the previous season. Therefore, all of the second season episodes that aired during the summer featured the sun setting sequence instead of the rotating satellite. For the telecast of June 15, the closing credits for "Eye of the Beholder" were re-edited to reflect a new title and avoid the potential lawsuit as described previously in the book. *The Twilight Zone* was not telecast on the evening of August 24, so that CBS could present "Money Talks," the final program in a short-run series on major economic issues in the country. Professor John R. Coleman of the Carnegie Institute of Technology was the host.

June 8, 1962	**Repeat** "The Odyssey of Flight 33"
June 15, 1962	**Repeat** "A Private World of Darkness"
June 22, 1962	**Repeat** "King Nine Will Not Return"
June 29, 1962	**Repeat** "The Trouble With Templeton"
July 6, 1962	**Repeat** "Dust"
July 13, 1962	**Repeat** "The Howling Man"
July 20, 1962	**Repeat** "A Most Unusual Camera"
July 27, 1962	**Repeat** "People Are Alike All Over"
August 3, 1962	**Repeat** "Nick of Time"
August 10, 1962	**Repeat** "The Silence"
August 17, 1962	**Repeat** "The Night of the Meek"
August 31, 1962	**Repeat** "A Hundred Yards Over the Rim"
September 7, 1962	**Repeat** "The Whole Truth"
September 14, 1962	**Repeat** "The Invaders"

Here is a list of the repeats telecast during the regular seasons, shown in between new productions.

June 24, 1960	**Repeat** "Mr. Denton on Doomsday"
December 30, 1960	**Repeat** "A Stop at Willoughby"
February 17, 1961	**Repeat** "A Passage for Trumpet"
March 17, 1961	**Repeat** "The After Hours"
April 14, 1961	**Repeat** "The Mighty Casey"
March 28, 1963	**Repeat** "The Thirty Fathom Grave"
April 25, 1963	**Repeat** "In His Image"

Music Trivia

Bernard Herrmann's arrangement of Marius Constant's opening and closing music cues that make up The Twilight Zone theme varied slightly from what was usually heard on most of the third season productions. An observant viewer with a keen ear may have picked up the two versions of the theme.

The following episodes feature Herrmann's arrangement for both the opening and closing music cues:

"Person or Persons Unknown"
"The Little People"
"Four O'Clock"
"Hocus-Pocus and Frisby"

The following episodes feature only Herrmann's arranged opening cues. The end credits are Constant's arrangement:

"The Trade-Ins"
"The Gift"
"The Dummy"
"Young Man's Fancy"
"I Sing the Body Electric"
"Cavender is Coming"
"The Changing of the Guard"

FOURTH SEASON PRODUCTION COSTS

Secretary's Salary: $1,260.00
Casting Director's Salary: $2,792.10
Office Supplies and Expense: $2,294.72
Payroll Taxes, etc.: $17,317.60

Unit Manager's Salary: $9,000.00
Guild Pension Plan: $15,593.47
Messenger Service: $863.85
Insurance: $6,399.50

Unassigned literary properties:
"The Happy Place" by Rod Serling, $6,000
"Trigger Man" by Harry Altshuler, $4,250.00, assigned production #4865

Adding the preproduction and unallocated costs, and the unassigned literary properties (totaling $10,250.00), and the costs of production for each episode, the total to produce the 18 episodes from the fourth season (including the $1,093.81 in expenses for the un-produced "The Next Impossible," previously assigned production #4863) totaled $2,005,025.12. All summary of production costs listed for fourth season episodes according to production files dated March 31, 1963.

Production #4851 "IN HIS IMAGE" (Initial telecast: January 3, 1963)
Copyright Registration: © Cayuga Productions, Inc., December 28, 1962, LP24877
Date of Rehearsal: July 30, 1962
Dates of Filming: July 31 and August 1, 2, 3, 6 and 7, 1962
Script #3 dated: July 9, 1962
Revised script dated: July 16 and 17, 1962
Shooting script dated: July 27, 1962

Producer and Secretary: $2,750.00
Director: $2,750.00
Unit Manager and Secretary: $700.00
Agents Commission: $6,000.00
Below the line charges (M-G-M): $72,644.12
Total Production Costs: $112,070.12

Story and Secretary: $4,300.00
Cast: $12,405.67
Production Fee: $4,000.00
Legal and Accounting: $250.00
Below the line charges (other): $6,270.33

Cast: Jamie Forster (the hotel clerk); Sherry Granato (the girl); George Grizzard (Alan Talbot / Walter Ryder, Jr.); Gail Kobe (Jessica Connelly); George Petrie (the driver); Wallace Rooney (the man); James Seay (the Sheriff); and Katherine Squire (the old woman).

Stock Music Cues: Etrange #3 (by Marius Constant, :09); Milieu #2 (by Constant, :21); Mother (by Jerry Goldsmith, :44); Alain #3 (by Constant, :20); Harp Chords (CBS, :01); The Cruel Past (by Goldsmith, :41); LD Story #2 (by Constant, :04); Autumn Love (by Goldsmith, :14 and :36); LD Story #2 (by Constant, :04 and :04); The Discussion (by Goldsmith, :11); Terror Struck (by Goldsmith, :39); Autumn Love (by Goldsmith, :14 and :41); LD Story #2 (by Constant, :04); Agony (by Rene Garriguenc, :05); Frigid Woman (by Goldsmith, :25); The Search #3 (by Lucien Moraweck, :16); LD Story #2 (by Constant, :04); Challenge (by Goldsmith, :16 and :11); The Discussion (by Goldsmith, :02); Secret Circle (by Goldsmith, :49); Moat Farm Murder (by Bernard Herrmann, :19); Hitch-Hiker (by Herrmann, :06); LD Story #2 (by Constant, :04); Menton 18 (by Constant, :21); Agony (by Garriguenc, :04); Shakedown (by Goldsmith, :19); Moat Farm Murder (by Herrmann, :07); Zephyr #1 (by Constant, :18); Agony (by Garriguenc, :06); Secret Circle (by Goldsmith, :54); Menton 18 (by Constant, :26); Alain #3 (by Constant, :25); Secret Circle (by Goldsmith, :42); Moat Farm Murder (by Herrmann, :18); Action Background (by Garriguenc, :02); Trial is On (by Leonard Rosenman, :06); Alain #3 (by Constant, :23); Kant #7 (by Constant, :25); The Telephone (by Herrmann, :07); Dirge (by Goldsmith, :16); Strange Return (by Goldsmith, :21); Etrange #3 (by Constant, :09); and Milieu #2 (by Constant, :31).

Director of Photography: George T. Clemens, a.s.c.
Art Direction: George W. Davis and Paul Groesse
Set Decoration: Henry Grace and Edward M. Parker
Directed by Perry Lafferty

Production Manager: Ralph W. Nelson
Film Editor: Edward Curtiss, a.c.e.
Assistant to Producer: John Conwell
Assistant Director: John Bloss
Produced by Herbert Hirschman
Sound: Franklin Milton and Joe Edmondson

Teleplay by Charles Beaumont, based on his short story, "The Man Who Made Himself," originally published in the February 1957 issue of *Imagination*.

"What you have just witnessed could be the end of a particularly terrifying nightmare. It isn't. It's the beginning. Although Alan Talbot doesn't know it, he's about to enter a strange, new world . . . too incredible to be real, too real to be a dream. It's called . . . the Twilight Zone."

Plot: Alan Talbot, tortured by the strange sounds in his head, murders a pestering old woman in the subway. Wanting to leave town with his romantic interest, Jessica, he decides to pay a visit to the aunt he hasn't seen in a while. Arriving in his hometown, Alan finds things are not exactly the same as they were when he left. Observing his impulse to murder, and his insistence that the town isn't the same, Jessica leaves him. Alan injures his wrist revealing fake skin and wires instead of blood vessels and veins. Following the clues, Alan looks up the residential addresses of Walter Ryder and pays him a visit. There, Alan is shocked to learn that he was born just eight days before. Walter explains that he fulfilled his childhood dream – to construct an artificial man. Escorting Alan to the "delivery room,"

Walter explains how he constructed Alan after years of research. He created the memories, including an aunt who never existed and hometown memories from 20 years previous. But something went wrong. A few days ago, Alan attacked Walter and ran off. Walter admits luck had a great deal to do with the making of Alan, but cannot explain the murderous impulses Alan continues to have. Maybe he made Alan a bit too human. Before Walter can dismantle Alan and discover what is causing the problem, Alan starts a brawl with Walter, smashing the lab to pieces. Back at Jessica's apartment, Walter visits her, apologizing for the nightmare the other day, and promises everything will be okay . . . while Alan lies partially dismantled on the floor back in the laboratory.

"In a way it can be said that Walter Ryder succeeded in his life's ambition. Even though the man he created was, after all, himself. There may be easier ways to self improvement, but sometimes it happens that the shortest distance between two points is a crooked line . . . through the Twilight Zone."

Trivia, etc. In October of 1958, before the first season of *The Twilight Zone* premiered, Serling had intentions of scripting an adaptation of Charles Beaumont's short story for use on the program. In a one-and-a-quarter-page plot synopsis titled "The Image," Serling changed the name of the protagonist to Jamison, who takes his girl to his hometown in Connecticut. There, every recollection that Jamison possessed appeared distorted and strangely different. Buildings he recalled are either not there or do not fit the description. His fear begins to assume serious proportions, scaring the girl, as he takes her back to New York. After burning himself, Jamison observes metallic objects sticking out of his thumb. Visiting a friend of his, Peters, Jamison discovers his friend is an exact duplicate. Only Jamison is made of plastic, wires and coils. He is electronically generated. Peters explains that as a shy man, he cannot get along with other people, so he tried to create something more perfect than himself. Jamison, running out of power, sits down and asks what he can do – describing the girl and the fact that they were going to be married. Peters does not say very much. The last scene, however, has Peters entertaining the girl at her apartment, and when he accidentally burns his thumb, flesh and blood are revealed.

For Serling to have written an adaptation (the plot synopsis was submitted to William Dozier, to give the CBS head an idea of the type of stories he wanted on *The Twilight Zone*), meant he approved of the Charles Beaumont story from the beginning, believing that it fit the thematic style of the program. Attempts to purchase the basic rights for adaptation failed, but with Beaumont himself jumping on board during the first season, Serling believed it was possible at some point in time for "The Man Who Made Himself" to be produced.

The opportunity knocked when Beaumont wrote this teleplay. Just like Serling's adaptation, Beaumont changed the names of the characters from his short story. Walter Cummings became Walter Ryder. Peter Nolan became Alan Talbot. Jessica Lang became Jessica Connelly.

Back in December of 1960, after viewing the episode, "The Lateness of the Hour," Beaumont was disturbed. "Immediately after 'The Lateness of the Hour,' I was deluged by friends and acquaintances who phoned to protest. They had all read my story in *In His Image* and many of them knew that I had submitted it to *Twilight Zone*. None of them said, 'That was something like your yarn' or 'I see Rod had the same idea,' but, instead: 'Where was your name?' and 'How come you changed the guy to a girl?' All took it absolutely for granted that the show was my story adaptation. All were shocked when I said that it wasn't my story, not really . . ."

Serling felt both stories were dissimilar beyond the central theme of the robot. In defense, Serling recalled another story in which Earthmen representing the world government apprehended a man getting off a spaceship who was also in the form of a human. They accused him of being a robot sent by an alien planet and possessing a hydrogen bomb within his innards that is set to blow up the Earth. The man protested his innocence and when faced with the further accusation that the 'man' whose image he has taken was killed in a space crash, he is shown photographs of the victim. The accused protests that the body lying in the wreckage in the photograph is actually the robot and that he himself is human. This he believes with all sincerity and the story ends with the readers discovering that the aliens have slipped into him certain memory tracks that make him believe that he is a man, when actually, he is a robot.

"I did two of those *Twilight Zone*s," recalled George Grizzard. "My part was much larger in the second, because it was the first hour-long production. Perry Lafferty was the director. You could tell he knew exactly what he was doing from day one. The scene where I fight my dual self was done through a process here they call 'split screen.' The camera was situated and bolted so it would stay in one place. Then they filmed me on one side of the screen, acting out the motions, as if I was talking to my other self. Then they filmed me on the other side, playing the other role. There was tape on the floor to mark the center of the screen. I would not cross the line. The fella who played my duplicate during the fight scenes [Joseph Sargent], read my lines off camera so the dialogue would be timed. When they put the film together, both halves were sliced to give the appearance that there really were two Georges on the screen."

The January 7, 1963 issue of *The Hollywood Reporter* reviewed this episode: "Debut of the new hour-long format for 'Twilight Zone' incorporated all the plusses – dramatic camera angles, mood lighting, hair-raising, anti-climaxes for suspense builds – that originally had made the half-hour version a prestige fantasy show from the start. Unfortunately, the second half didn't measure up to the suspense and excitement of the first half-hour, the explanation of the puzzle."

Variety commented: "The second half of the show, in which the solution was given, slipped into routine science fiction stuff. The man, played by George Grizzard, was passed off as an electronic creation of a scientific genius, also played by Grizzard. In short, another version of Frankenstein."

Production #4857 "THE THIRTY FATHOM GRAVE"
(Initial telecast: January 10, 1963)
Copyright Registration: © Cayuga Productions, Inc., January 7, 1963, LP24894 (in notice: 1962)
Date of Rehearsal: October 8, 1962
Dates of Filming: October 9, 10, 11, 12, 15 and 16, 1962
First draft dated: May 2, 1962 with revised pages dated June 13, 14, 15, and 22, 1962.
Second draft dated: June 22, 1962, with revised pages dated July 3, 1962.
Third draft dated: July 9, 1962 with revised pages dated September 14, 1962.
Revised excerpts dated: August 10, 15, 27, and September 14, 1962
Final revised draft dated: September 26, 1962 with revised pages dated August 1, 13, 15, 27, September 14 and 19, 1962.
Shooting script #1 dated: October 3, 1962 (with revised pages of the same date)

Producer and Secretary: $3,950.00   Story and Secretary: $10,201.05
Director: $3,618.30   Cast: $11,259.24

Unit Manager and Secretary: $700.00
Agents Commission: $6,000.00
Below the line charges (M-G-M): $72,204.65
Total Production Costs: $116,274.10

Production Fee: $4,000.00
Legal and Accounting: $250.00
Below the line charges (other): $4,090.86

Cast: Vince Bagetta (sailor #1); Bill Bixby (OOD); Tony Call (Lee Helmsman); Conlan Carter (Ensign Marmer); Forrest Compton (ASW Officer); John Considine (McClure); Louie Elias (sailor #2); Mike Kellin (Chief Bell); Charles Kuenstle (Sonar Operator); Derrik Lewis (Helmsman); Simon Oakland (Captain Beecham); Henry Scott (the Junior OOD); and David Sheiner (Doc Mathews).

Stock Music Cues: Etrange #3 (by Marius Constant, :09); Milieu #2 (by Constant, :21); Date and Place (by Fred Steiner, :22 and :15); Neuro (by Rene Garriguenc, :32); Date and Place (by Steiner, :24); Serling III (by Robert Drasnin, :20); Neuro (by Garriguenc, :17); Serling I (by Drasnin, :08); Date and Place (by Steiner, :04); Serling II (by Drasnin, :14); The Gadget (by Jerry Goldsmith, :15); Counterattack – Part 2 (by Goldsmith, :20); The Gadget (by Goldsmith, :58); Counterattack – Part 1 (by Goldsmith, :11); Neuro (by Garriguenc, :44); Counterattack – Part 2 (by Goldsmith, 1:27); Unison to SF Chords #3 (by Nathan Van Cleave, :10); The Hunter (by Goldsmith, :17); Neuro (by Garriguenc, :23); Jailbreak (by Goldsmith, 1:03); Unison to SF Chords #3 (by Van Cleave, :10); Serling III (by Drasnin, :11); Bits and Pieces (by Van Cleave, :20); The Factory (by Van Cleave, :10); Unison to SF Chords #3 (by Van Cleave, :10); Space Ship (by Goldsmith, :15); Unison to SF Chords #3 (by Van Cleave, :10); Serling III (by Drasnin, :05); Etrange #3 (by Constant, :09); and Milieu #2 (by Constant, :31).

Director of Photography: George T.
    Clemens, a.s.c.
Art Direction: George W. Davis and
    John J. Thompson
Set Decoration: Henry Grace and Don
    Greenwood, Jr.
Produced by Herbert Hirschman
Directed by Perry Lafferty

Production Manager: Ralph W. Nelson
Film Editor: Richard W. Farrell
Associate Producer: Murray Golden
Assistant to Producer: John Conwell
Assistant Director: John Bloss
Sound: Franklin Milton and Joe Edmondson
Teleplay by Rod Serling

"Incident one hundred miles off the coast of Guadalcanal. Time: the present. The United States naval destroyer on what has been a most uneventful cruise. In a moment, they're going to send a man down thirty fathoms to check on a noise maker. Someone or something tapping on metal. You may or may not read the results in a naval report, because Captain Beecham and his crew have just set a course that will lead this ship and everyone on it . . . into the Twilight Zone."

Plot: Somewhere in the South Pacific Ocean, the crew of a naval destroyer discovers what appears to be a sunken submarine, located about 30 fathoms below the surface. A strange sound originating from the sub is best described by the crew as "hammering." Determined to learn the identity of the sub and the origin of the sound, Captain Beecham sends a deep-sea diver named McClure down to investigate. McClure finds the sub partially buried about 15 feet in the sand, with significant shell

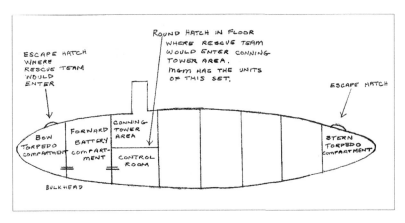

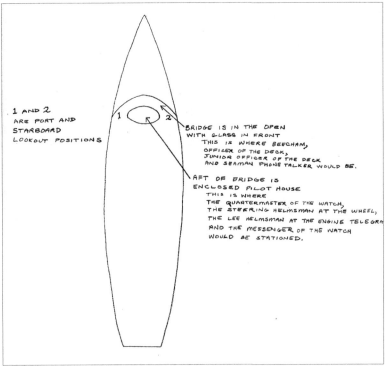

Ralph W. Nelson's sketches and layouts for the naval destroyer,
which he submitted to Rod Serling.

and machine gun damage. When McClure bangs on the sub, a reply bangs back. He returns empty handed, but lays odds there is someone alive inside. The identification number on the hull reveals the name of the sub, commissioned in 1941 and sunk in 1942 – only deepening the mystery. Chief Bell, in the meantime, takes ill with a strong impulse to keep moving, almost as if another force is guiding him. He starts having visions of ghosts beckoning him to join them – and the only evidence that his visions are not delusions is seaweed found on board. While the mission becomes salvage and rescue, McClure returns a third time to the sub and finds 20-year-old dog tags with Bell's name on them. Confronting Bell, the captain learns that he was the only survivor. The sub was sunk by enemy craft and Bell has spent the past 20 years blaming himself for the sinking. Screaming with delusions, Bell runs to the deck and dives overboard. After 10 hours, Beecham's crew is unable to find the body. When a rescue team from the Coast arrives to crack open the sub, they find the remains of eight men in the control room . . . one of them had a hammer in his hand.

"Small naval engagement. The month of April, 1963. Not to be found in any historical annals. Look for this one filed under 'H' for haunting . . . in the Twilight Zone."

Trailer: *"The ingredients, an American destroyer . . . the Pacific Ocean . . . and the ghostly sound of hammering from thirty fathoms below. They add up to a strange tale of the bizarre and nightmarish. Mike Kellin and Simon Oakland star in a very different kind of Twilight Zone which we call, 'The Thirty Fathom Grave.'"*

Trivia, etc. On March 15, 1960, J.B. Stewart, Commander, USN, Officer in Charge of the U.S. Navy Recruiting Aids Facility in Baltimore, Maryland, wrote to Rod Serling, offering him the opportunity to prepare a shooting script for a U.S. Navy recruiting film. Serling stated he would have accepted the job had his commitments at the time not been so demanding. Ironically, about two years later, Serling would begin scripting a telefilm using the U.S. Navy for his *Twilight Zone* series.

From March 28 to 30, 1962, Serling went to New York to meet with Ashley-Steiner, Hubbell Robinson and Robert Lewine at CBS to work out the preliminaries regarding the production of the hour-long series and how much of Serling's involvement would be required. (Serling also had a meeting in New York with Eagle Clothing regarding negotiations for the new season.)

By May of 1962, Serling had plot proposals for "The Bard" and "No Time Like the Past." He also submitted two hour-long scripts to Hubbell Robinson that same month, "The Happy Place" and "The Thirty Fathom Grave." "While I'll admit that a writer is perhaps the last in line to analytically and validly judge his work, I'm tremendously enthused by both efforts," Serling explained. "I ask only that you keep in mind that story material for *Twilight Zone* is very much 'camera' writing. That which may read as a slow and static movement, gains considerable momentum in its shooting." Robinson rejected "The Happy Place," but approved the other script for production.

Ralph W. Nelson got the ball rolling with production by making arrangements with the U.S. Navy to film on board a real naval destroyer. He paid a personal visit to the destroyer stationed in the harbor in mid-June 1962. After a couple of meetings with the local Navy public information office, Nelson relayed to Hirschman and Serling technical corrections that needed to be applied to the script. A frogman or scuba diver could not talk back and forth to the ship and the deepest they were allowed to go by Navy regulation was 135 feet, except in extreme emergency when they could drop to 190 feet for not more than five minutes. So the frogman or scuba diver from the initial script was substituted by a diver with a hard helmet and canvas suit, rather than the heavy typical leaded suits. This revision would grant the diver 30 fathoms and talk back and forth to the ship – but this would require an air hose for his supply of oxygen and air equipment on the deck. Serling made the necessary changes to the script to reflect this.

Serling was in Interlaken, New York, during this time, relaxing for the summer and preparing for his teaching job at Antioch. All communication with Ralph W. Nelson, the production manager, and Herbert Hirschman, the producer, was by phone and airmail letters.

On July 5, 1962, Nelson wrote several more notes to Serling, pointing out that "the fewer corrections Washington makes on the script, the faster we can get our requested cooperation. Washington will not okay a script except in final draft form." Nelson suggested they remove a speaking part where a steward says, "Coffee, Captain?" Nelson believed it was quite customary that any of the officers who would be in the wardroom could ask this question and get the coffee for the captain, so the steward would not be needed for the scene. Nelson gave Serling a couple of drawings of the destroyer bridge and pilot house to help envision the various scenes he had written. He also gave Serling a drawing of the submarine.

The closing in the initial draft set the time frame for July of 1962 (about the time Serling was completing the third draft). This would be later changed to April of 1963, working under the assumption that the episode would be telecast around that time. The initial draft also featured the wrecked conning tower area showing the skeletons of the deceased. Nelson told Serling that, "showing the skeletons is very distasteful and do not know what we could show because these skeletons would not be the clean bleached bones of a body in the desert and I'm sure we cannot portray clearly a mess of pulp." Serling revised a couple pages of the script to delete all references to the skeletons because of the Nelson's explanation about public reaction, and "especially because of the hundreds of bodies still entombed in the sunken *Arizona* in Pearl Harbor." Commander Coghlan of the local Navy office also expressed the same opinion and thought there would be trouble with Washington if the scene were left in the script. (CBS also sent a memo addressing the concern.)

Most of the scenes on the ship were shot on the destroyer, except for the captain's cabin and officers' wardroom and sick bay, which were built interiors at M-G-M. If the underwater scenes appeared to be from the same section of the sunken submarine, even after the sub supposedly shifted, the viewer is not mistaken. Because of the limitations of the underwater tank at Republic Studios, where the underwater scenes were shot, the submarine set for the diver could not be longer than 25 feet, limiting the amount of coverage the diver had to explore on the wreckage.

The Navy came up with a fictitious number for the submarine which was probably of the "S" class, which was a ship about 300 feet long and 25 feet amidships, rather than 16 feet amidships as indicated in the initial script. When it came to shooting exterior destroyer scenes, the movement on the water would have made the lights set aboard two or more barges constantly move; the technical problem was avoided by making all the night scenes become day scenes. "To fight the problem would have been with considerable expense and very likely the lack of cooperation from Washington and the destroyer Commander," Nelson explained.

The Navy was critical of Chief Bell screaming in one speech near the end of the episode. Serling defended the passage in a letter to Nelson on July 3, "What is the Navy's criticism of Bell talking about screaming, page 52, scene 147? It's a fairly important character point to dramatize cowardice. Do you think they'll let us retain it? I've left it in for the time being." By July 3, Serling revised a number of pages and told Nelson, "I've gone through this thing as best I could, making the changes that can be made at this long distance vantage point. There is some stuff with the diver down below that will have to be altered to correspond to the limitations that you've indicated."

Herbert Hirschman officially received Navy approval on the afternoon of September 19, 1962. The first draft of this script featured the ending as shown on film. When Serling composed a revised version, the ending was different – Bell disappeared into thin air, and the solution to the mystery revealed Bell as a ghost. After Hirschman read the script, he told Serling that the ending should revert to the original teleplay. "I believe making Bell a ghost throughout will mystify and confuse the audience," Hirschman explained. "I am certain that we would be best off to go back to a version of the Bell story as in the original script. That, somehow, in a scared funk he got out and away – perhaps leaving his buddies when he might have helped them. He should have died and the dead want him with them, and he joins them [at the bottom of the ocean]."

Production in early October went smoothly, with many of the scenes filmed on board the U.S.S. Edson (DD-946) while it was stationed at the docks in California. Bill Bixby could not remember his lines when speaking on the radio, because of the numbers and technicals he had to recite, so he read the words from a sheet of paper off camera.

According to a former draft, Serling's opening narration was varied from the final draft:

"Incident one hundred miles off the coast of Guadalcanal. A United States Naval destroyer on what has been a most uneventful cruise. In a moment, they're going to send a man down thirty fathoms to check on a noise-maker. Someone or something tapping on metal. You may or may not read the results in a Naval report because Captain Beecham and his crew have just set a course that will lead this ship and everyone on it . . . into the Twilight Zone."

When it was decided to feature clips of next week's episode, forcing Serling's teaser to be cut in length, the following proposed trailer was considered way too long and scrapped:

"The ingredients, an American destroyer . . . a Pacific Ocean . . . and the sound of hammering from thirty fathoms below. They add up to a strange and rather intriguing tale of the bizarre and the nightmarish. Mike Kellin and Simon Oakland star in a very different kind of Twilight Zone which we call 'The Thirty Fathom Grave.' This one is for sea-goers, navy buffs, and any and all who appreciate a few errant shivers during odd nocturnal moments. 'The Thirty Fathom Grave' . . . offered with the compliments of all the amateur funeral directors on . . . the Twilight Zone."

In late October of 1962, a beautiful inscribed silver service punch bowl was presented to the U.S.S. Edson, commemorating the small contribution made for this *Twilight Zone* episode. Commander M. J. Carpenter was instrumental in making the necessary arrangements for the film crew to board the Edson and film the scenes required. Commander Carpenter was also on the scene during filming and became acquainted with Perry Lafferty, John Bloss and Ralph W. Nelson very well during the preproduction. The silver service punch bowl remains with the ship to this day, supposedly displayed prominently and used at each ceremonial or festive shipboard function. "It was a major disappointment to me that my absence from the scene, while shooting on your ship, kept me from coming aboard and meeting you and your crew personally," Rod Serling wrote to Commander Carpenter on November 16, 1962. "I'm told, by my members and staff, that your treatment and cooperation was something special and unique. I wanted you to know how deeply grateful I was for this co-operation. Would you convey my thanks to the officers and crew of the U.S.S. Edson which must, of necessity, be one of the finest craft in the Navy. The caliber of its men certainly dictates this."

Variety reviewed: "The yarn was so thin that the hour had to be heavily padded with inconsequential naval routine. There was less progression to the drama than repetition of incidents until the climatic suggestion that the banging might not have been made by men more than 20 years dead. The nervous breakdown of the mate was the pretext for some hokey psychologizing that piled artificiality onto incredibility."

Production #4861 "VALLEY OF THE SHADOW" (Initial telecast: January 17, 1963)
© Cayuga Productions, Inc., January 12, 1963, LP24878 (in notice: 1962)
Dates of Rehearsal: October 30 and 31, 1962
Dates of Filming: November 1, 2, 5, 6, 7 and 8, 1962
Script dated: October 23, 1962
Shooting script dated: October 25, 1962

Producer and Secretary: $6,130.00
Director: $3,203.75
Unit Manager and Secretary: $920.00
Agents Commission: $6,000.00
Below the line charges (M-G-M): $57,860.73
Total Production Costs: $95,800.09

Story and Secretary: $4,321.05
Cast: $9,580.55
Production Fee: $4,000.00
Legal and Accounting: $250.00
Below the line charges (other): $3,534.01

Cast: Jacques Aubuchon (Connolly); Henry Beckman (townspeople #1); Bart Burns (townspeople #2); King Calder (townspeople #3); Suzanne Cupito (the girl); James Doohan (the father); Dabbs Greer (Evans); Sandy Kenyon (the gas station attendant); Bob McCord (man on porch); Ed Nelson (Philip Redfield); Pat O'Hara (townspeople #4); David Opatoshu (Dorn); and Natalie Trundy (Ellen Marshall).

Stock Music Cues: Etrange #3 (by Marius Constant, :09); Milieu #2 (by Constant, :21); New England Contry Scene (by Rene Garriguenc, 1:18); Over the Rim (by Fred Steiner, :08); Chris Walks (by Steiner, :37); Mrs. Joe (by Steiner, :24); Chris Walks (by Steiner, :08); Over the Rim (by Steiner, :05); Joe's Café (by Steiner, 1:24); Serling II (by Robert Drasnin, :30); Serling III (by Drasnin, :34); Shock Chords (by Lucien Moraweck, :06); Serling I (by Drasnin, :18); Serling II (by Drasnin, :53); Serling III (by Drasnin, :21); The Calendar (by Steiner, :20); Serling II (by Drasnin, :04); Over the Rim (by Steiner, :06); Serling II (by Drasnin, :23); Shadows – Western Suite (by Bernard Herrmann, 1:24); The Visit (by Jerry Goldsmith, :08); The Fight (by Goldsmith, :48); Joe's Café (by Steiner, :15); Curiosity (by Steiner, :12); Serling II (by Drasnin, :04); Over the Rim (by Steiner, :04); Chris Walks (by Steiner, :08); Serling I (by Drasnin, 1:19); Moat Farm Murder (by Herrmann, :10); The Road (by Steiner, :18); Serling I (by Drasnin, 1:02); The New Arrival (by Goldsmith, :08); Joe's Café (by Steiner, :55); Serling II (by Drasnin, :42); Over the Rim (by Steiner, :05); New Home (by Goldsmith, 1:03 and 1:38); Let Down (by Goldsmith, :21); Serling II (by Drasnin, :16); The Hallway (by Goldsmith, :11); Serling I (by Drasnin, :34); Joe's Café (by Steiner, :06); Chris Walks (by Steiner, :20); Chris Runs (by Steiner, :44); Joe's Café (by Steiner, :22); Over the Rim (by Steiner, :05); Shadows – Western Suite (by Herrmann, :39); Chris Walks (by Steiner, 1:21); New Home (by Goldsmith, :36); Etrange #3 (by Constant, :09); and Milieu #2 (by Constant, :31).

Director of Photography: Robert
    Pittack, a.s.c.
Art Direction: George W. Davis and
    John J. Thompson
Set Decoration: Henry Grace and Don
    Greenwood, Jr.

Production Manager: Ralph W. Nelson
Film Editor: Everett Dodd, a.c.e.
Associate Producer: Murray Golden
Assistant to Producer: John Conwell
Assistant Director: Ray De Camp
Sound: Franklin Milton and Joe Edmondson

Produced by Herbert Hirschman   Teleplay by Charles Beaumont
Directed by Perry Lafferty

> *"You've seen them. Little towns, tucked away far from the main roads. You've seen them, but have you thought about them? What do the people in these places do? Why do they stay? Philip Redfield never thought about them. If his dog hadn't gone after that cat, he would have driven through Peaceful Valley and put it out of his mind forever. But he can't do that now, because whether he knows it or not his friend's shortcut has led them right into the capital . . . of the Twilight Zone."*

Plot: Taking a back route to Albuquerque, Philip Redfield drives into Peaceful Valley (pop. 881), a small town not listed on any map or atlas. After witnessing a number of mysterious events that defy logic and wrecking his automobile when it hits an invisible wall, Redfield discovers he is trapped within city limits. The mayor of the town, seeing no other alternative, reveals to their guest the best kept secret in the world. A visitor from beyond paid the residents of Peaceful Valley a visit over a hundred years ago, offering the peace and harmony with the use of devices far more advanced than those of today. Since the world's history is paved in blood, this technology cannot be released to the outside world. Redfield, given the choice of death or assimilation, chooses to remain in the town as a citizen, to help retain the town's secret. As the days pass, he gets to know Ellen Marshal, one of the lovely citizens in town, who cries because with all the machines that provide her comfort, love cannot be manufactured. One afternoon, Ellen gives Redfield the opportunity to leave the town – with her by his side. Before leaving, Redfield uses the replicating machine to make a gun and the weapon to steal secret papers proving the town's existence. Driving outside of city limits in his newly-repaired car, he discovers it was all a test – the papers he stole are blank. Forced to return to Peaceful Valley, Redfield is tried and found guilty of his crime; he was made an example of what would happen if the advanced technology ever went public. Rather than execute Redfield, the mayor uses a device to wipe his memory clean and send him on his way out of town, without any knowledge of what has happened.

> *"You've seen them. Little towns, tucked away far from the main roads. You've seen them, but have you thought about them? Have you wondered what the people do in such places, why they stay? Philip Redfield thinks about them now and he wonders, but only very late at night, when he's between wakefulness and sleep . . . in the Twilight Zone."*

Trailer: *"Next on Twilight Zone a marvelously exciting excursion into a very strange place called Valley of the Shadow. It comes from the probing mind of Mr. Charles Beaumont and whether you are a science fiction buff, a fantasy lover, or just need fulfillness to escape, this one should fill most of your requirements."*

Trivia, etc. When it was decided to feature clips of next week's episode, forcing Serling's teaser to be cut in length, the following proposed trailer was considered way too long and scrapped:
> *"Next week on the Twilight Zone we dabble in physics, space, time and atoms, and we come up with an equation that could only come from the very probing mind of Mr. Charles Beaumont. I find it difficult to say very much about this show except to tell you that this one might very well stay with you for some time to come. It's a marvelously exciting excursion into a very strange place called 'Valley of the Shadow.' It stars Ed*

Nelson, Natalie Trundy and David Opatoshu. Whether you're a science fiction buff . . . a fantasy lover . . . or just needful of some escape . . . this one should fill most of your requirements. Next week on the Twilight Zone . . . 'Valley of the Shadow.' I hope you'll be able to join us for the trip."

The dirt road leading in and out of Peaceful Valley, with trees on both sides of the road, was the same featured in a number of episodes of *Combat!* and the classic teaser shot in *The Outer Limits* episode, "Children of Spider County," where the alien rescues the young man from the police. This same road is used again in the *Twilight Zone* episode, "Death Ship."

In the beginning of the episode, when the gas station attendant is filling Redfield's car with gasoline, a pair of cellar doors can be seen in the background. Though a lot of shrubbery was used to conceal the windows on the wall on both sides of the cellar doors, these are the same ones Buster Keaton used to enter the professor's laboratory in "Once Upon A Time." The blacksmith sign in this episode was also used in the previous episode, "Once Upon A Time." The corner of the building where Redfield parks in the beginning of the episode to fill up with gas might be recognizable to a few – it served as the front of Frisby's general store in the episode "Hocus-Pocus and Frisby."

The vehicle that is damaged by the invisible wall is a 1959 Chevrolet convertible. Beginning with production of the fourth season, Ford Motors was no longer supplying automobiles as "product placements." At least two Ford vehicles did grace the screen during this season – a 1957 Ford in "Printer's Devil" and a 1960 Ford in "In His Image."

Actress Suzanne Cupito is better known today as actress Morgan Brittany. "I loved doing *The Twilight Zone*," she recalled. "Because I was so young, I do not recall much of the production, but I must have left an impression because I was called in to do another episode and that one I remember very well. I receive fan letters from all over because I was on the show. I was treated like a queen at a recent *Twilight Zone* convention. If I had known then what I know today, I would have saved something worthwhile so my fans would know more about the series."

Production #4856 "HE'S ALIVE" (Initial telecast: January 24, 1963)

Copyright Registration: © Cayuga Productions, Inc., January 18, 1963, LP24895 (in notice: 1962)
Dates of Rehearsal: September 10, 11 and 12, 1962
Dates of Filming: September 13, 14, 17, 18, 19 and 20, 1962
First draft dated: August 20, 1959 with revised pages August 29 and September 11, 1962.
First revised script dated: August 31, 1962
Second revised script dated: September 11, 1962, with revised pages dated August 31, 1962.

Producer and Secretary: $3,350.00	Story and Secretary: $7,200.00
Director: $2,885.00	Cast: $11,164.79
Unit Manager and Secretary: $700.00	Production Fee: $4,000.00
Agents Commission: $6,000.00	Legal and Accounting: $250.00
Below the line charges (M-G-M): $66,663.39	Below the line charges (other): $3,102.38
Total Production Costs: $105,315.56	

Cast: Jay Adler (Gibbons); Wolfe Barzell (the proprietor); Howard Caine (Nick); Curt Conway (Adolph Hitler); Ludwig Donath (Ernst Ganz); Bernard Fein (the heckler); Barnaby Hale (Stanley); Dennis Hopper (Peter Vollmer); and Paul Mazursky (Frank).

Stock Music Cues: Etrange #3 (by Marius Constant, :09); Milieu #2 (by Constant, :21); Flashback (by Leonard Rosenman, :18); Jailbreak (by Goldsmith, :20); More Push-Push (by Nathan Scott, :30); The Telegram (by Rosenman, 1:02); Flashback (by Rosenman, :10); Celestial Call #3 (by Rosenman, 1:20); The Mob (by Nathan Van Cleave, :26); Reflection #3 (by Lucien Moraweck, :32); F Story #5 (by Constant, :30); How Heavy (by Van Cleave, :08); Iron Curtain (by Fred Steiner, :50); War Posters (by Van Cleave, :20); The Missing Colonel (by Rosenman, :13); The Enemy (by David Buttolph, :37); Heavy Curtains (by Bernard Herrmann, :03); The Producer (by Franz Waxman, :24); Onslaught (by Steiner, :37); House on K Street – Fade In (by Herrmann, :08); Snare Soli 8 (CBS, :08); Riot (by Van Cleave, :23); Desolation (by Van Cleave, :40); F Story #3 (by Constant, :47); House on K Street – Fade In (by Herrmann, :08); Snare Soli 8 (CBS, :08); Tough Guy (by Steiner, :21); House on K Street – Fade In (by Herrmann, :05); Reflections #3 (by Moraweck, 1:07); Desolation (by Van Cleave, 1:24); Riot (by Van Cleave, :15); Berlin Wall (by Van Cleave, 1:18); Etrange #3 (by Constant, :09); and Milieu #2 (by Constant, :31).

Dennis Hopper and Ludwig Dunath in "He's Alive."

Director of Photography: George T. Clemons., a.s.c.
Art Direction: George W. Davis and Edward Carfagno
Set Decoration: Henry Grace and Don Greenwood, Jr.
Produced by Herbert Hirschman
Directed by Stuart Rosenberg

Production Manager: Ralph W. Nelson
Film Editor: Richard W. Farrell
Associate Producer: Murray Golden
Assistant to Producer: John Conwell
Assistant Director: Ray De Camp
Sound: Franklin Milton and Joe Edmondson
Teleplay by Rod Serling

"Portrait of a bush league fuehrer named Peter Vollmer – a sparse little man who feeds off his self delusions and finds himself perpetually hungry for want of greatness in his diet. And like some goose-stepping predecessors, he searches for something to explain his hunger and to rationalize why a world passes him by without saluting. That something he looks for and finds is in a sewer. In his own twisted and distorted lexicon he calls it faith – strength – truth. But in just a moment Peter Vollmer will ply his trade on another kind of corner – a strange intersection in a shadow land called . . . the Twilight Zone."

Plot: Young Peter Vollmer peddles hate on street corners like popcorn – a philosophy reminiscent of the germs that built Dachau during the war. The only profit Vollmer gains from his racial bias against minorities are the cuts and bruises from citizens in the streets, not recognition and respect. Late one evening, a shadowy benefactor with a German accent introduces himself to Vollmer, offering advice that will make his ideals stronger in the community. Speak to them on their level and make their hate his hate, the mysterious man explains. If they are afraid, talk to them about their fears. If they are angry, give them objects for their anger. Only then will he make the mob an extension of himself. Vollmer follows the advice and as the weeks pass, citizens take notice. They begin to rally to his cause. When the benefactor reveals his true identity, that of Adolph Hitler, Vollmer continues to follow his advice, which leads to a series of cold-blooded murders. His desperation catches up to him when the police find enough evidence to convict Vollmer, but he attempts to flee. During the pursuit, the police are forced to shoot the young man. Lying in an alleyway bathed in his own blood, Vollmer discovers that he isn't made of steel – and the spirit of Hitler departs for another person to spread his message.

"Where will he go next? This phantom from another time. This resurrected ghost of a previous nightmare? Chicago. Los Angeles. Miami, Florida. Vincennes, Indiana. Syracuse, New York. Any place, every place . . . where there's hate. Where there's prejudice. Where there's bigotry. [a pause] *He's alive. He's alive so long as these evils exist. Remember that when he comes to your town. Remember it when you hear his voice speaking out through others. Remember it . . . when you hear a name called. A minority attacked. Any blind unreasoning assault on a people or any human being. He's alive . . . because through these things . . . we keep him alive."*

Trailer: *"We move next on Twilight Zone into a shadowy area that treads a very thin line between flesh and fantasy. You'll see a performance by Dennis Hopper that even from my rather very close-end perspective strikes me as an exceptional one. Our story is called 'He's Alive' and if this doesn't get you where you live, you'll find it close by in the suburbs."*

Trivia, etc. About the time this episode aired on network television, Rod Serling was asked in an interview for *Show Business Illustrated* what he wanted to do that he had not said on television. "I'd like to make comment on what I think is social evil. This is the function of the writer in a society," he replied. "I don't think you ever really could [on television]. I think you could do it in a kind of oblique way, but this is not to say that adult drama need always be a vehicle of social criticism. There should be a social platform for social comments, and what better one than a medium reaching so many people, which is so immediate and flexible?"

Serling began research for material related to the "He's Alive" (script #10) in late July. He contacted De Forest Research asking for information concerning the laws involved if an FBI agent warned a neo-Nazi, and whether the FBI, under the Presidential Directive of June 26, 1939, and/or on instructions from the Attorney General, can investigate an organization involved with white supremacy. On August 3, Kellam De Forest mailed to Serling material related to the various federal laws regarding sedition and registration.

"'He's Alive' is going extremely well," Hirschman reported to Serling on September 19, 1962. "The dailies have been excellent. The performances and Stu Rosenberg's work are both very exciting. The way it now looks, this should be one of our very good shows."

Months before this episode went before the cameras, the California State Commission for Human Rights was picketed by actors who accused it of having failed to investigate the portrayal of Negroes on television programs. The broadcasting networks were also under fire. About the time this episode went into production, a committee of the New York Society for Ethical Culture charged the broadcasting companies for not keeping abreast of the American scene where Negroes were concerned. "Children are exposed to a lily-white screen and women's serials have less than token depiction of the Negro," a report by the society's committee on integration said.

In a letter dated June 22, 1962, Serling informed Herbert Hirschman that "in line with the networks most exemplary policy on portraying Negroes legitimately, Ralph Nelson tells me there could be a Negro on the bridge – either as an Ensign or Lieutenant J.G. This is not indicated in the script but I wish you'd make a note about it for casting." Apparently the request was not fulfilled in "The Thirty Fathom Grave" (the script Serling was discussing in his letter), but a police officer in this episode (with no speaking lines), was portrayed by an African American. Dr. Lawrence Plotkin, assistant professor of psychology at City College in New York, was quick to point out after the broadcast that the network's attempt to incorporate Negroes in roles was done without thought – citing "He's Alive" as an example, though pointing out that in the real world, Negro police officers were paired together and were rarely paired with a white officer.

In early October, a couple weeks after filming was completed, Hirschman and Serling discussed over the phone the length of the episode – too much footage had been filmed. Serling spent a good bit of early October with a persistent idea that this could possibly be released as a theatrical entry. Serling questioned whether it would be against CBS policy to have two separate cuts of this film, each with a separate score and dubbing. "I have no idea of CBS's policy on this," Serling wrote to Hirschman on October 15, "nor am I very sure in my own mind as to just how appropriate this film would be for theatre release. I do think, however, that if the rest of the footage is on a par with the opening sequences that I saw, I'd hate to see valuable footage cut away and made irreplaceable." He requested Hirschman to figure out how much extra cost would be involved in the double cutting and double scoring, but since the CBS contract would not have granted him the opportunity without further expense to the network, the option was promptly dropped. This might also explain why this is the only episode of the series in which Serling never uses the words "The Twilight Zone" during the closing scenes.

The previous opening narration reveals Peter Vollmer's last name as Collier in an earlier draft. The name change went into effect with the revision of September 11, 1962. The unused narration is reprinted:

"Portrait of a bush league fuehrer named Peter Collier – a sparse little man who feeds off his self delusions and finds himself perpetually hungry for want of greatness in his diet. And like some goose-stepping predecessors, he looks for something to explain his hunger and to rationalize why a world passes him by without saluting. He finds it in a sewer. He refers to it as faith, strength, truth – when it is nothing but garbage. The garbage of bigotry, prejudice, hate. (a pause) But in just a moment, Peter Collier will ply his trade on another kind of corner. A strange intersection in a shadow land called . . . the Twilight Zone."

When it was decided to feature clips of next week's episode, forcing Serling's teaser to be cut in length, the following proposed trailer was considered way too long and scrapped:

"Next week on the Twilight Zone we move into another shadowy area that trods a very thin line between flesh and fantasy. It's the story of a nickel-and-dime Fuehrer whose business is hate and prejudice . . . and whose clientele, unfortunately, is any man or woman willing to close a mind and open an ear to the kind of street corner poison all too readily available any time at any place. You'll see a performance by Dennis Hopper, in this particular program, that – even from my rather close in perspective – strikes me as an exceptional one. Our

story is called 'He's Alive,' and if this one doesn't get you where you live . . . you'll find it close by in the suburbs. Next week on the Twilight Zone, Dennis Hopper, Ludwig Donath and Kurt Conway in . . . 'He's Alive.'"

A number of concerns at CBS was addressed in the form of a list of suggested revisions for censorship, and the production crew was instructed not to feature any Nazi swastikas on the program. The symbol was replaced with a hand holding a torch (much like a symbol for the Olympics) and a lightning bolt behind the torch.

In the August 1986 issue of *The Twilight Zone Magazine*, Hal Erickson wrote an article titled "All the Little Hitlers" and reported that within a week after the telecast, Serling and his staff received 4,000 angry letters classified as "hate mail." After sifting through two separate collections containing an estimated total of 1,800 fan letters spanning the years of 1959 to 1964, only 12 specifically mentioned this episode. Erickson's article never cited the source for his statistic. Whether this was a fact or an assumption remains unknown. One thing is for certain. Had this episode received more "hate mail" than the rest of the hour-long productions, it is likely that "He's Alive" would never have been rerun by the network.

On January 27, Mr. and Mrs. Clifford Cole of Orange, California, wrote to Serling, commenting: "both of us felt that it was among the best television shows we had ever seen. I am an ordained minister of the Christian Church (Disciples of Christ) and feel that some of the sentences in the show could bear repeating." On January 29, Clive Hoffman, director of communication at The National Conference of Christians and Jews in Los Angeles, wrote to Serling with compliments. "We are most gratified by your excellent presentation on the *Twilight Zone* last week. It was a most informative and penetrating study of bigotry in its most fanatical form. Its impact must have been felt by all who watched and I am sure that the good done was immeasurable."

Production #4858 "MUTE" (Initial telecast: January 31, 1963)

© Cayuga Productions, Inc., January 25, 1963, LP24896 (in notice: 1962)
Dates of Rehearsal: September 27 and 28, 1962
Dates of Filming: October 1, 2, 3, 4, 5 and 8, 1962
Script #11 dated: September 7, 1962
Revised excerpts dated: September 18 and 26, 1962
Shooting script dated: October 1, 1962 with cut and paste revisions.

Producer and Secretary: $3,350.00
Director: $2,885.00
Unit Manager and Secretary: $700.00
Agents Commission: $6,000.00
Below the line charges (M-G-M): $63,118.11
Total Production Costs: $103,494.43

Story and Secretary: $4,300.00
Cast: $10,112.50
Production Fee: $4,000.00
Legal and Accounting: $250.00
Below the line charges (other): $8,778.82

Cast: Barbara Baxley (Cora Wheeler); Oscar Beregi (Professor Karl Werner); Robert Boon (Holger Nielsen); Claudia Bryar (Frau Nielsen); William Challee (man at the bus stop); Irene Dailey (Miss Frank); Percy Helton (Tom Poulter); Ann Jillian (Ilse Nielsen); Frank Overton (Sheriff Harry Wheeler); and Eva Soreny (Frau Werner).

Original Music Composed and Conducted by Fred Steiner (Score No. CPN6070): Etrange #3 (by Marius Constant, :09); Milieu #2 (by Constant, :21); Peasant Waltz (traditional, :35); The Mute (:57); German Corners (:21); Emergency (:13); Meet Ilsa (2:10); Ilsa's Parents (:47); Ilsa's Vision (:26); Ilsa Weeps (:17); Ilsa's Thought (:10); Strange Girl (:29); Distorted Voices (:40); Cora's Plea (1:55); Ilsa's Vision #2 (:20); Cora's Burden (:26); The Letters (:26); Cora Troubled (1:02); Purloined Letter (:48); Ilsa's Vision #3 (:17); Ilsa's Flight (1:14); Ilsa's Room (:38); Thought Voice (:11); Meet Miss Frank (:42); School Music (:44); Schoolmates (1:30; Ilsa Remembers (:58); Ilsa's Lesson (:34); Teacher Goofs (:35); Day's End (:11); German Corners #2 (:27); Cora Troubled #2 (:48); The Werners (1:08); Lesson #2 (:19); No Message (1:10); Ilsa Speaks (1:13); Farewell to Ilsa (:50); Etrange #3 (by Constant, :09); and Milieu #2 (by Constant, :31).

Director of Photography: Robert Pittack, a.s.c.	Production Manager: Ralph W. Nelson
Art Direction: George W. Davis and Edward Carfagno	Film Editor: Eda Warren, a.c.e.
Set Decoration: Henry Grace and Don Greenwood, Jr.	Associate Producer: Murray Golden
Produced by Herbert Hirschman	Assistant to Producer: John Conwell
	Assistant Director: Ray De Camp
	Sound: Franklin Milton and Joe Edmondson
	Directed by Stuart Rosenberg

Teleplay by Richard Matheson, based on his short story of the same name, which was originally published in *The Fiend in You* (edited by Charles Beaumont, Ballantine, 1962).

"What you're witnessing is the curtain-raiser to a most extraordinary play; to wit, the signing of a pact, the commencement of a project. The play itself will be performed almost entirely offstage. The final scenes are to be enacted a decade hence and with a different cast. The main character of these final scenes is Ilse, the daughter of Professor and Mrs. Nielsen, age two. At the moment she lies sleeping in her crib, unaware of the singular drama in which she is to be involved. Ten years from this moment, Ilse Nielsen is to know the desolating terror of living simultaneously in the world . . . and in the Twilight Zone."

Plot: When a house outside of a small Pennsylvania town burns to the ground, Sheriff Harry Wheeler and his wife Cora adopt the sole survivor – a 12-year-old girl named Ilse Nielsen. The Wheelers are unaware that Ilse was part of an experiment that began 10 years before in Dusseldorf, Germany, where prominent scientists were to train their offspring to communicate telepathically. Having lost a daughter of her own by accident years previous, Cora begins to develop an attachment to the girl. Harry, however, insists the Ilse needs to go to school in the meantime, believing that she might learn to talk if she grows up with people other than her parents, who apparently deprived her of an education. While the schoolteacher slowly gets Ilse speaking normally, the Werners arrive from Germany to take custody of the child. Ilse, however, cries out her name in front of the Werners, revealing the change in behavior. The couple agrees to return to Germany, leaving Ilse with the Wheelers, believing that love is more important than telepathic abilities – and certainly stronger.

"It has been noted in a book of proven wisdom that perfect love casteth out fear. While it's unlikely that this observation was meant to include that specific fear which follows the loss of extrasensory perception, the principle remains, as always, beautifully intact. Case in point, that of Ilse Nielsen, former resident . . . of the Twilight Zone."

Trailer: *"The talented author Richard Matheson pays a return visit to Twilight Zone with a story called 'Mute.' It provides an exceptional challenge to the acting talents of Barbara Baxley, Frank Overton, and an unusual twelve-year-old named Ann Jillian."*

Trivia, etc. When it was decided to feature clips of next week's episode, forcing Serling's teaser to be cut in length, the following proposed trailer was considered way too long and scrapped:

"Next week Richard Matheson pays a return visit to the Twilight Zone, and the extremely talented author provides us with an exceptional vehicle for the talents of Frank Overton and Barbara Baxley in a story called 'Mute.' It probes into the recesses of a child's mind and reveals a pattern of strangeness and tension characteristic of the Twilight Zone . . . and also very characteristic of the mind of one Richard Matheson who has provided us on a number of occasions with some of our more intriguing entries. Next week, then, an exercise in five-dimensional logic in the best of the science fiction tradition. 'Mute'. . . on the Twilight Zone."

One of the bird portraits hanging on the wall in the Wheeler dining room is the same hanging on the wall in "Living Doll."

The Wheeler house was located on Lot 2 at M-G-M, also known as the Philadelphia Story House, which was the same used for the 1940 motion picture, *The Philadelphia Story.* The front doorway is the same where Cary Grant pushes Katharine Hepburn to the ground. The same house was also used for "The Parallel," with only a few changes made, including the house number. This is the same house Bob Frazier walks up to and knocks on the door in "Stopover in a Quiet Town."

In the original short story, the telepathic child was a small boy, not a small girl. When Matheson was asked to write the script, he was asked to change the sex.

The town center where Ilse runs away and gathers a crowd is also located on Lot 2 at M-G-M, the same public park that can be seen in "Walking Distance," "A Stop at Willoughby," "No Time Like the Past" and "I Sing the Body Electric."

Actress Ann Jillian's name was spelled "Ann Jilliann" in the closing credits, which happened in a number of her early television programs.

Production #4850 "DEATH SHIP" (Initial telecast: February 7, 1963)

Copyright Registration: © Cayuga Productions, Inc., February 1, 1963, LP24897 (in notice: 1962)
Dates of Rehearsal: August 23, 1962
Dates of Filming: August 24, 27, 28, 29, 30 and 31, 1962
Script #4 dated: July 10, 1962

Producer and Secretary: $2,750.00	Story and Secretary: $4,300.00
Director: $2,750.00	Cast: $10,009.00
Unit Manager and Secretary: $700.00	Production Fee: $4,000.00
Agents Commission: $6,000.00	Legal and Accounting: $250.00
Below the line charges (M-G-M): $91,172.58	Below the line charges (other): $3,544.86
Total Production Costs: $125,476.44	

Cast: Fredrick Beir (Lieutenant Michael Carter); Ross Elliott (Kramer); Jack Klugman (Captain Paul Ross); Tammy Marihugh (Jeannie Mason); Ross Martin (Lieutenant Theodore Mason); Sara Taft (Mrs. Nolan); and Mary Webster (Ruth Mason).

Stock Music Cues: Etrange #3 (by Marius Constant, :09); Milieu #2 (by Constant, :21); Tales of the Universe (by David Raksin, :39); Fantasies (by Wilfred Josephs, :36); Loire #2 (by Constant, :08); Menton 4 (by Constant, :10); Hope – Walt Whitman Suite (by Bernard Herrmann, :16); Deserted Mansion (by Lucien Moraweck, :29); Shock Chord (by Moraweck, :12); Villers #4 (by Constant, :21); The Jungle (by Nathan Van Cleave, :22); Fantasies (by Josephs, :41); Back to the Scene of the Crime (by Leonard Rosenman, :56); Waiting for a Phone Call (by Rosenman, :14); Pasacaglia King (by Fred Steiner, :21); Captain Embry (by Steiner, :42); Second Vision (by Steiner, :18); The Prediction (by Jerry Goldsmith, 1:21); Return to the Past (by Goldsmith, 1:27); Wild Knife Chord (by Bernard Herrmann, :10); The Assassination (by Goldsmith, :55); The Prediction (by Goldsmith, 1:04); Prayer (by Steiner, :12); Grandma (by Van Cleave, :41); New Car (by Van Cleave, :10); D Story #2 (by Constant, :21); The Jungle (by Van Cleave, :31); Dead Phones (by Steiner, :09); Confusion (by Rosenman, :05); Jets (by Steiner, :27); Confusion (by Rosenman, :10); Hammer Blows of Fate (by Rene Garriguenc, :20); Memories (by Herrmann, :43); Heartbreak (by Goldsmith, :38); Frigid Woman (by Goldsmith, :23); Strange Rider (by Steiner, :25); Struggle (by Steiner, :35); First Vision (by Steiner, :27); Dolly Finds Him (by Nathan Scott, :10); Action Background (by Rene Garriguenc, :03); Ford's Theater (by Goldsmith, :43); Struggle (by Steiner, 1:03); Deserted Mansion (by Moraweck, :26); Cerebellum II (by Jeff Alexander, :40); Captain Embry A (by Steiner, :37); Tales of the Universe (by David Raskin, :59); Etrange #3 (by Constant, :09); and Milieu #2 (by Constant, :31).

Director of Photography: Robert
  Pittack, a.s.c.
Art Direction: George W. Davis and
  Edward Carfagno
Set Decoration: Henry Grace and
  Edward M. Parker
Directed by Don Medford

Production Manager: Ralph W. Nelson
Film Editor: Richard W. Farrell, a.c.e.
Assistant to Producer: John Conwell
Assistant Director: Ray De Camp
Sound: Franklin Milton and Joe Edmondson
Produced by Herbert Hirschman

Teleplay by Richard Matheson, based on his short story of the same name, originally published in the March 1953 issue of *Fantastic Story Magazine*.

"Picture of the spaceship E-89. Cruising above the thirteenth planet of star system fifty-one. The year 1997. In a little while, supposedly, the ship will be landed and specimens taken: vegetable, mineral and, if any, animal. These will be brought back to overpopulated Earth, where technicians will evaluate them and, if everything is satisfactory, stamp their findings with the word 'inhabitable' and open up yet another planet for colonization. These are the things that are supposed to happen. [scene between narration] *Picture of the crew of the spaceship E-89: Captain Ross, Lieutenant Mason, Lieutenant Carter. Three men who have just reached a place which is as far from home as they will ever be. Three men who in a matter of minutes will be plunged into the darkest nightmare reaches . . . of the Twilight Zone."*

Plot: While exploring the surface of another planet, Lieutenant Mason observes a blip on the radar screen, and Captain Ross authorizes an investigation. Upon landing, they discover the wreckage of a spacecraft much like their own and the bodies of three crewmembers – exact duplicates of their own. Unable to conceive of a rational explanation, each has a theory. Captain Ross suspects they went through a time warp and are witnessing a probable future. Staying on the planet will ensure their safety. Lieutenant Carter experiences a hallucination of returning home, finding a funeral veil on his wife's bed and a telegram reporting his death. Mason, too, experiences a hallucination of his own – meeting with his wife and daughter, knowing full well that they have been dead for some time. Unable to make radio contact with Earth Station 1217, Captain Ross believes in Mason's theory that man isn't the only form of life in the universe. Aliens on this planet want to create hallucinations to prevent the spacemen from reporting back to Earth about the planet's existence. Diluted fear is the only thing keeping them from taking off. Realizing they have no alternative, the men start the engines. Back in space, Captain Ross, assured that hallucinations were all they encountered, insists on returning to the planet to pick up specimens. Returning to the planet, they find the wreckage still there. Lieutenant Mason finally figures the solution – they already crashed. They are restless ghosts who will not rest until all three of them admit this fact. Captain Ross, stubborn, insists they will continue trying to find an explanation.

"Picture of a man who will not see anything he does not choose to see – including his own death. A man of such indomitable will that even the two men beneath his command are not allowed to see the truth; which truth is, that they are no longer among the living. That the movements they make and the words they speak have all been made and spoken countless times before – and will be made and spoken countless times again . . . perhaps even unto eternity. Picture of a latter-day Flying Dutchman sailing . . . into the Twilight Zone.

Trailer: *"Mr. Richard Matheson lets his typewriter pay us a return visit next time out on Twilight Zone with a story called 'Death Ship.' Now this one is for science fiction aficionados, ghost story buffs and any and all who file away clues with an eye toward out-guessing the writer. Next on Twilight Zone Misters Jack Klugman, Ross Martin and Fred Beir, take an extended trip through space in a death ship."*

Trivia, etc. Rehearsals were only for the first day, August 23, consisting of the three leads. The rehearsals were only conducted for the scenes inside the spaceship cabin, since most of the story took place in the cabin. On the evening of the fifth day, August 30, the exterior of the Carter Home was shot on Lot 3 with just actor Fredrick Beir.

At the bottom of the telegram, the words "J. Bloss – Space Exploration" is printed. This was a tip of the hat to John Bloss, who served as the assistant director for a number of hour-long episodes.

This episode also makes use of a number of props left over from the 1956 motion picture, *Forbidden Planet*. The spaceship E-89 is the same as the United Planets Cruiser C-57D from the movie. The space uniforms in this production are the same worn by the crewmembers of the United Planets Cruiser.

On February 8, the day after this episode aired over the network, Richard Matheson wrote a brief note expressing his joy at seeing the final production come to form.

Dear Rod,
A note to let you know that old malcontent Matheson is, at long last, content indeed. 'Death Ship' was, as you would say, a corker. I was almost dazed by the extreme quality of it in every single department – marvelously perceptive directing, three superb pieces of acting (not to mention the flawless contributions of the actors in the lesser roles), great photography and special effects, even a perfect score (which, because I saw no credit, I assume was canned). All in all, a

highly satisfying and, to me, very close to a haunting experience. Extremely satisfying to me. Such a production really gives one hope.
Best,
Dick

Matheson's opening statement in his letter was in reference to his complaint during the third season regarding productions that he felt could have been better. His dissatisfaction was curbed by this hour-long production. On February 12, Rod Serling wrote back his reply, sharing Matheson's excitement with "Death Ship." Serling admitted the film was intriguing and beautifully directed. "I had one carping criticism of the performances during the teaser. I thought they were too high, too emotional and too unrestrained," he explained. "But this was covered for by a corker of a first act and all the ensuing stuff that followed. I really thought it a beautiful job of writing and a marvelous job of production. The garland goes out to Old Man Matheson for doing it again! And speaking of doing it again – it appears we might go back to a half-hour form. Can we count on you?"

A number of science fiction fans would notice the similarity between this story and Bradbury's short story "Mars is Heaven," which Matheson himself would later adapt in the filmed miniseries, *The Martian Chronicles* (1980). When asked about this, Matheson told author Matthew R. Bradley, "Everyone did a story about Martians being defenseless and using mental means to get their invaders put away at that time, but there were no aliens in 'Death Ship.' It was just the will power of the captain. I didn't think it was ambiguous at all. In the last commentary, [Serling] said, 'a man who is so powerful and convinced that he just refused to let reality impinge on him,' and then they started it all over again. . . . I kind of like ['Death Ship'], actually, because it had such a good cast and it had a lot of honest emotion in it, so it wasn't bad at all."

Production #4855 "JESS-BELLE" (Initial telecast: February 14, 1963)
Copyright Registration: © Cayuga Productions, Inc., February 8, 1963, LP24898 (in notice: 1962)
Dates of Filming: September 18, 19, 20, 21, 24, 25, 26, 27 and 28, 1962
Script #5 dated: August 24, September 5 and 12, 1962

Producer and Secretary: $3,350.00
Director: $2,750.00
Unit Manager and Secretary: $700.00
Agents Commission: $6,000.00
Below the line charges (M-G-M): $78,534.70
Total Production Costs: $120,100.64

Story and Secretary: $4,200.00
Cast: $12,540.38
Production Fee: $4,000.00
Legal and Accounting: $250.00
Below the line charges (other): $7,775.56

Cast: James Best (Billy-Ben Turner); Jim Boles (Obed Miller); Laura Devon (Ellwyn Glover); Anne Francis (Jess-Belle); Virginia Gregg (Ossie Stone); Helen Kleeb (Mattie Glover); Jon Lormer (the minister); George Mitchell (Luther Glover); and Jeanette Nolan (Granny Hart).

Original Music Composed and Conducted by Nathan Van Cleave (Score No. CPN6077):
Etrange #3 (by Marius Constant, :09); Milieu #2 (by Constant, :21); Leather Breeches (traditional, arr. by Bobby Bruce, :11); Country Dance Waltz (by Bobby Bruce, 2:29); Tell Your Love (:47); Tell

Your Love (by Van Cleave and Earl Hamner, :17); Happy Woman (:14); No Title (CBS, :24); The Potion (2:21); Country Dance Waltz (by Bruce, :25); The Witching Moon (1:29); Two in Torment (1:05); Two in Torment (by Van Cleave and Earl Hamner, :15); Panther's Claw (:14); Hi Billie (:25); Midnight (1:04); Forever A Witch (1:14); Forever A Witch (by Van Cleave and Earl Hamner, :18); Watch it Billie (:45); There Goen Hunten (:40); How Did You Pay, Jess? (:46); The Panther Hunt (1:18); The Ring (1:29); Well Miss Ossie (:07); Well Miss Ossie (by Van Cleave and Earl Hamner, :18); The Wedding (:56); Spooks Afoot (1:46); Drat That Mouse (:20); The Witch is Dead (1:56); A Falling Star (:18); A Falling Star (by Van Cleave and Earl Hamner, :18); Etrange #3 (by Constant, :09); and Milieu #2 (by Constant, :31). *

Director of Photography: Robert Pittack, a.s.c.	Production Manager: Ralph W. Nelson
Art Direction: George W. Davis and Edward Carfagno	Film Editor: Edward Curtiss, a.c.e.
Set Decoration: Henry Grace and Don Greenwood, Jr.	Associate Producer: Murray Golden
Produced by Herbert Hirschman	Assistant to Producer: John Conwell
Directed by Buzz Kulik	Assistant Director: John Bloss
	Sound: Franklin Milton and Joe Edmondson
	Teleplay by Earl Hamner, Jr.

"The Twilight Zone has existed in many lands, in many times. It has its roots in history, in something that happened long, long ago and got told about and handed down from one generation of folk to the other. In the telling the story gets added to and embroidered on, so that what might have happened in the time of the Druids is told as if it took place yesterday in the Blue Ridge Mountains. Such stories are best told by an elderly grandfather on a cold winter's night by the fireside . . . in the southern hills . . . of the Twilight Zone."

Plot: When Billy-Ben Turner and Ellwyn Glover announce their engagement, Jess-Belle turns to Granny Hart, who, according to backwoods folk, practices witchcraft. Jess-Belle promises anything in order to have Billy-Ben fall in love with her. Granny Hart gives Jess-Belle a potion that bewitches him, causing a break up of the engagement. Every midnight to sunrise, in payment for the potion, Jess-Belle turns into a mountain lion. When Jess-Belle returns to Granny Hart, she discovers her soul was also part of the bargain, and there can be no turning back. Jess-Belle's mother, upon learning the price her daughter paid, locks her up in a room one night in order to keep the hunting party from finding the cat – but she fails. The cat escapes from the back window and the hunting party shoots the animal, which fades away into a cloud of smoke. One year later, with the Jess-Belle dead and the spell broken, the love between Billy-Ben and Ellwyn Glover is mended. Jess-Belle's mother, however, pays Billy-Ben a visit to inform him that her daughter isn't dead – witches just change into another form. On their wedding night, the lovebirds discover this fact, so Billy-Ben pays Granny Hart in cash to learn just how to kill a witch. Using the clothes of Jess-Belle, Billy-Ben makes a life-size figure and then it in the heart with silver. Jess-Belle reappears in the clothes and disappears, leaving Billy-Ben and Ellwyn alone together.

---

* The proper spelling of the music cue "There Goen Hunten" remains in question. While it fits with the country slang featured in this film, the spelling may be "There Goes Hutten" or "There Goen Hutten."

Trailer: *"Next week we'll delve into the realm of American folklore and through the offices of a fine writer named Earl Hamner, Jr., we peruse a little witchcraft to bring you a story called 'Jess-Belle.' This exercise in terror and talisman stars Anne Francis and James Best."*

Trivia, etc. When it was decided to feature clips of next week's episode, forcing Serling's teaser to be cut in length, the following proposed trailer was considered way too long and scrapped:

"Next week on the Twilight Zone we move into the strange realm of American folklore. And through the offices of a fine writer named Earl Hamner, Jr., we peruse a little witchcraft and bring you a story called 'Jess-Belle.' This is an exercise in terror and talisman . . . The kind of story you might expect to hear from some aged grandfather – presented to you, perhaps, a little tongue-in-cheek . . . perhaps with a gentle, wafting smile – as one might tell a ghost story to a child. But this particular ghost story leaves its humor in the foothills and we move on and up from there to a tale of rather stunning effect. Anne Francis and James Best head a fine cast in next week's presentation of 'Jess-Belle.'"

"Herb Hirschman took over Buck's job on *The Twilight Zone* and Herb phoned me one day and asked if I had any script lying around somewhere," recalled Earl Hamner, Jr. "I said 'No, but I can write you one if you need it.' Herb didn't think I could write one that fast but I did. I wrote the first act in one day and then took it to Herb." By July 12, Hamner had submitted the outline for "Jess-Belle" and was awaiting a decision. It was approved days after, and by August 1, Hamner had been commissioned to write the script. He also wrote the lyrics to which Nathan Van Cleave composed an accompanying score.

This was the only episode of the series not to feature Serling's closing narration. There had been a number of teleplays written for *The Twilight Zone* to overlook any form of narration, because the authors knew Serling himself would write one himself. Instead of a closing narration because the authors knew Serling himself would write one.

"I did three of those *Twilight Zones*," recalled James Best. "My favorite was probably the Jeff Myrtlebank episode, but I liked the one I did with Anne Francis. We kissed a lot for the one scene, but that was acting of course. Most of the episode, as I recall, was filmed at the studio. I recall teaching one of the actresses, maybe it was Laura Devon, how to speak a southern drawl so she would blend in with the country folk."

Production #4862 "MINIATURE" (Initial telecast: February 21, 1963)

© Cayuga Productions, Inc., February 15, 1963, LP24899 (in notice: 1962)
Date of Rehearsal: October 16, 1962
Dates of Filming: October 17, 18, 19, 22, 23 and 24, 1962
Script #9 dated: August 27, 1962, with revised pages dated October 4 and 16, 1962.

Producer and Secretary: $3,380.00
Director: $2,750.00
Unit Manager and Secretary: $720.00
Agents Commission: $6,000.00
Below the line charges (M-G-M): $84,991.37
Total Production Costs: $122,522.18

Story and Secretary: $4,323.12
Cast: $11,997.31
Production Fee: $4,000.00
Legal and Accounting: $250.00
Below the line charges (other): $4,110.38

Cast: Richard Angarola (the suitor); Barbara Barrie (Myra); Joan Chambers (Harriet); Robert Duvall (Charley Parkes); Claire Griswold (the doll); Pert Kelton (Mrs. Parkes); John McLiam (the guard); Barney Phillips (Diemel); Nina Roman (the maid); Chet Stratton (the guide); Lennie Weinrib (Buddy); and William Windom (Dr. Wallman).

Original Music Composed and Conducted by Fred Steiner (Score No. CPN6080): Etrange #3 (by Marius Constant, :09); Milieu #2 (by Constant, :21); Charlie's Tune (1:12); Charlie's Tune #2 (by Steiner, :58); Piano Sonata in "A" Major (by A. Mozart, :47); Doll House (:24); Piano Sonata in "A" Major (by Mozart, 1:01 and :07); Charlie's Tune #3 (1:02); Piano Sonata in "A" Major (by Mozart, :15); Ready Charlie (:07); Piano Sonata in "A" Major (by Mozart, :12); Spring Song (by Felix Mendelssohn, arr. by Steiner, :34); Piano Conata in "A" Major (by Mozart, :18); Flower Song (by Gustav Lange, arr. by Steiner, :34); Charlie's Nose (:07); Melody in F (by Anton Rubinstein, arr. by Steiner, 1:05); Charlie Chases (:26); Charlie's Sister, Interloping "Spring Song" (by Mendelsohn, arr. by Steiner, :35); La Donna E Mobile-Rigoletto (by Giuseppe Verdi, 1:00); Santa Lucia (traditional, 2:05);Charlie Vacation (:41); Pique Dame Overture (by Franz Von Suppe, arr. by Steiner, :23); Martha Overture Excerpt (by Von Flotow, arr. by Steiner, 1:10); Charlie Flips (:19); Charlie's Doll (:19); Doll's House #2 (:19); Charlie Alone (:13); Charlie's Gone, Part 1 (:11); Charlie's Gone, Part 2 (:39); Piano Sonata in "A" Major (by Mozart, :29); Flower Song (by Gustav Lange, arr. by Steiner, :21 and :48); Charlie's House, based on Piano Sonata in "A" Major (by Mozart, arr. by Steiner, :38); Etrange #3 (by Constant, :09); and Milieu #2 (by Constant, :31).

Director of Photography: Robert Pittack, a.s.c.	Production Manager: Ralph W. Nelson
	Film Editor: Edward Curtiss, a.c.e.
Art Direction: George W. Davis and Edward Carfagno	Associate Producer: Murray Golden
	Assistant to Producer: John Conwell
Set Decoration: Henry Grace and Don Greenwood, Jr.	Assistant Director: Ray De Camp
	Sound: Franklin Milton and Joe Edmondson
Produced by Herbert Hirschman	Teleplay by Charles Beaumont
Directed by Walter E. Grauman	

"To the average person, a museum is a place of knowledge, a place of beauty and truth and wonder. Some people come to study, others to contemplate, others to look for the sheer joy of looking. Charley Parkes has his own reasons. He comes to the museum to get away from the world. It isn't really the sixty-cent cafeteria meal that has drawn him here every day . . . it's the fact that here in these strange, cool halls he can be alone for a little while . . . really and truly alone. Anyway, that's how it was before he got lost and wandered into the Twilight Zone."

Plot: While visiting the Burton County Museum one afternoon, Charley Parkes observes a young female doll in the model of a 19th century town house, playing the piano. While no one else observes the phenomenon, Charley won't dismiss the music. After losing his job, Charley chooses to spend his mornings and afternoons at the museum display, instead of seeking employment. Concerned, his family seeks help by arranging for him to meet a woman his age and make arrangements for him to start a new job. All of this fails and Charley's hallucinations grow out of proportion when he smashes the glass on the display in an effort to reach out to the female doll. His family arranges for a visit to a psychiatrist where the good doctor explains to them how Charley had too much pressure to cope with and fashioned a make-believe world of his own. Weeks later, Charley is released from the sanitarium. Making a desperate attempt to see the doll, he flees back to the Museum to revisit the doll house and confess his love for the female piano player. After contacting the psychiatrist and the police, Charley's family arrives at the museum, but discover he is nowhere to be seen ... while the security guard observes a doll that looks like Charley, smiling, sitting in the miniature house next to the female figure.

Robert Duvall bestows a kiss
on his imaginary friend.

"They never found Charley Parkes, because the guard didn't tell them what he saw in the glass case. He knew what they'd say, and he knew they'd be right, too, because seeing is not always believing . . . especially if what you see happens to be an odd corner . . . of the Twilight Zone."

Trailer: *"Next on Twilight Zone, a most unusual program called 'Miniature.' The very eminent Charles Beaumont takes us into a brand new realm of science fiction and fantasy that is the same time intriguing and strangely believable."*

Trivia, etc. When it was decided to feature clips of next week's episode, forcing Serling's teaser to be cut in length, the following proposed trailer was considered way too long and scrapped:

"Next week on the Twilight Zone, a return visit from the very eminent Charles Beaumont. His typewriter provides a most intriguing program which is called 'Miniature.' This one we find ourselves hard-pressed to describe without telegraphing to you what are the rather unusual set of circumstances that you'll find yourself watching. Let's just say, by way of a rather selectively controlled introduction, that 'Miniature' takes us into a brand new realm of science fiction and fantasy that is at the same time intriguing and strangely believable. I hope you'll be able to join us next week when the Twilight Zone presents Robert Du Val and Pert Kelton in a production of Charles Beaumont's 'Miniature.'"

A production note included with the script, "The miniature house should be arranged so that the three rooms – parlor, bedroom, living room – may be fully depicted, while all other rooms are either eliminated or barely indicated. When we are dealing with scenes within the house, the feeling should be that of a model magnified. The action within the house must be highly stylized at all times, danced or pantomimed rather than acted. The point is to provide a sharp contrast with the real world, with which the protagonist cannot cope. Therefore, the more stylized the house itself, the better. If a staircase to a cut-away bedroom could be arranged, it would be ideal."

In mid-July 1962, Charles Beaumont submitted the script to Herbert Hirschman, who then sent the script to Serling during the last few days of July. "I would be interested in getting your reaction," Hirschman commented. "Charlie impressed upon me that this is not necessarily the accurate framework of the script but just a reassurance that there is enough material for an hour. Considering my regard for his writing ability, I would be inclined to agree. I would like your reaction to the story, however."

On August 2, Serling replied his liking of the Beaumont story. "I hope you put Charles to work immediately. I have a couple of concerns that are minor, but knowing his talent – I think these will be ironed out in the script."

By mid-November, the rough cut was seven to eight hundred feet over length and Serling had to choose the scenes that needed to be edited to fit the television schedule.

Leonard Weinrib, billed as "Lennie Weinrib" in the closing credits, who played the role of Buddy in this episode, was a professional voice actor who played roles on radio dramas throughout the 1950s, and cartoon characters in the years following the initial telecast of this *Twilight Zone*. Weinrib leads a cult following for playing the title role in *H.R. Pufnstuf*.

On March 25, 1963, David Leanse of the law offices of Leanse & Janger in Los Angeles, California, submitted a letter addressed to Sam Kaplan of Ashley-Steiner, asserting a claim of plagiarism and wrongful appropriation against Cayuga Productions. Mr. Leanse made the claim on behalf of his client, Clyde Ware, whose two-act script titled "The Thirteenth Mannequin," originally written for a half-hour format, had been submitted to Cayuga Productions in the Spring of 1961.

The script was submitted to Cayuga Productions by an authorized and recognized literary agent named Ben Conway for a proposed segment on *The Twilight Zone*. Correspondence was exchanged between Conway and Buck Houghton, who was then the producer for the television series, and Richard McDonagh, who was then the story editor, regarding the submission of the property. Leanse signed a release form on April 19, 1961, so the teleplay could be reviewed, but after Houghton and McDonagh reviewed the script, "The Thirteenth Mannequin" was rejected.

Ware's story was about a character called "the old man," who lived with his daughter, Louise, and son-in-law, Bill Dickson, and worked as a night watchman in a department store which had a display of 12 mannequins, grouped and costumed as members of a community. The old man spent his working hours talking to the plastic figures, as if they were "friends" of equal stature. As the night watchman, he was granted the privacy no other employee of the department store had during the overnight hours. Louise and Bill were kind to the old man, but questioning his mental health, made arrangements for him to be committed. Late one evening, after leaving for work, the old man discovers that Bill has phoned for the family doctor, to ensure the commitment papers are in line. The old man is fully aware of their intentions. He proceeds to consult with his "friends," the mannequins. By morning, the old man has strained his heart to the breaking point and collapses. His body is found on the floor. Bill and the doctor examine the old man, shaking their heads. A few minutes later, they are shocked to see workmen delivering a thirteenth mannequin, a grandfather figure reminiscent of the old man, set to join the ranks of his "friends."

The *Twilight Zone* episode titled "Miniature" utilized an original story and teleplay written by Charles Beaumont, pursuant to an employment agreement between Cayuga Productions and Beaumont dated July 27, 1962. Beaumont brought in the story idea in the summer of 1962 and discussed the plot with Herbert Hirschman, then producing the show. On the basis of the oral presentation, Cayuga purchased the story and assigned him the screenplay.

After the official notice of the infringement claim was served, on March 27, Robert Myers of the Firemans Fund Insurance Company was notified by Gerald Saltsman of Ashley-Steiner. Rod Serling was unaware of the claim until he received a duplicate copy of the letter mailed to Sam Kaplan, and on April 9, when Saltsman forwarded Serling the necessary paperwork related to the suit.

On April 10, Serling drafted the following reply to David Leanse, ensuring him that he never read "The Thirteenth Mannequin," and possessed no knowledge as to who at Cayuga did read it. Serling assured Leanse that for the most part, material submitted to him was sent back unread since most of the writing was done on an assignment basis. It was rare that Cayuga utilized the submissions of either agents or the writers themselves. "Knowing Mr. Beaumont's personal integrity, not to mention his own professional status, it is my educated guess that what has occurred is the very commonplace occurrence of a coincidental similarity of approach to an oft used theme," Serling assured him. "I'm rather certain that if the two scripts are analyzed concurrently this coincidence will present itself and Mr. Ware will note a gratuitous similarity – not an overt act of literary piracy. Had anyone in my organization been positively disposed toward "The Thirteenth Mannequin," it would have been purchased at the time of its submission." Serling pointed out that it would have been unrealistic and impractical to have spirited the script away in a drawer and then paid another writer to appropriate it two years later.

While many suits of infringement were attempted because of the various stories presented on *The Twilight Zone*, the dollar amount asked for in damages was usually minor, and the insurance companies weighed the difference between fighting the case or settling out of court – whichever proved to be more economical. Settling out of court was not necessarily an admission of guilt. Each suit was analyzed, and a decision was made by the insurance company and its respective clients. Regarding this particular instance, however, the dollar amount was too much for the insurance company to settle out of court, so the matter was brought to trial.

Inasmuch as Clyde Ware's work had never been published and had not been copyrighted under the federal act, it was still protected from infringement under the state law. Neither state law nor the federal statute prohibited anyone from borrowing another's theme or ideas, as such. Copyright protection extended only to the representation or expression of those ideas.

The case went before the arbitrator on July 20. In early August, the case went to court. On August 16, 1963, Gerald Saltsman wrote to William Froug, then producer of the final season of *Twilight Zone*. "In view of the Superior Court's ruling this week in the 'Miniature' suit holding invalid Cayuga's release agreement, I would suggest that Cayuga not accept the submission of any unsolicited materials nor read any such materials until we can get a reading from the attorneys as to the ramifications of the court's decision and have an opportunity to revise the release agreement."

Charles Beaumont was summoned to appear in court to help defend the allegation. On September 10, Beaumont received from Robert Gordon, the attorney representing Cayuga Productions, a copy of "The Thirteenth Mannequin," which the writer was able to see with his own eyes for the first time. Though Gordon felt the lawsuit had very little merit, Beaumont took the time to read Ware's script and gave Gordon his thoughts with respect to similarities and dissimilarities between the two, from the point of view both in general storyline and literary structure. The only similarity between the two works was the theme or idea of a man who found happiness with an inanimate figure, whom he treated as a real person. (This theme is at least as old as Ovid's myth of *Pygmalion* and *Galatea*.)

After reviewing the facts, Judge Carlos M. Teran of the Superior Court of Los Angeles County, ruled that the defendants did not use Ware's property to compose "Miniature," and thus, under the terms of the contract (sign of release) as pleaded, the defendants were not obligated to pay damages.

Years later, on August 11, 1967, the issue regarding "Miniature" and "The Thirteenth Manne-quin" returned to the court room. David Leanse and Irwin O. Spiegel of Simon & Leanse, represented Clyde Ware again, who now requested an appeal from the former judgment by Teran. The Court of Appeals of California, Second Appellate District, reviewed the former ruling, but again, after examination of the unsold script and the television film, the judgment was affirmed, and the Columbia Broadcasting System, Inc. (now owner of *The Twilight Zone*) remained defiant. Even with the lawsuit dismissed and affirmed, the whole affair was a bit of an annoyance to CBS, who decided to withhold the episode from syndication and reruns. It wasn't until 1984 that the episode would be telecast since its initial 1963 airing, as part of a television special. The 1984 airing gave fans of *The Twilight Zone* cause to celebrate: all of the sequences in the doll house that were animated through the eyes of Charley were colorized – a fad many film studios assumed would catch on, and give a younger audience a willing exposure to view films they disregarded in black and white form.

Production #4864 "PRINTER'S DEVIL" (Initial telecast: February 28, 1963)

© Cayuga Productions, Inc., February 22, 1963, LP24900 (in notice: 1962)
Date of Rehearsal: November 12, 1962
Dates of Filming: November 13, 14, 15, 16, 19 and 20, 1962
Script dated: November 8 and 9, 1962

Shooting script dated: November 13, 1962
Story and Secretary: $4,301.50
Cast: $15,517.43
Production Fee: $4,000.00
Legal and Accounting: $250.00
Below the line charges (other): $3,285.52

Producer and Secretary: $3,380.00
Director: $2,500.00
Unit Manager and Secretary: $720.00
Agents Commission: $6,000.00
Below the line charges (M-G-M): $68,910.13
Total Production Costs: $108,864.58

Cast: Patricia Crowley (Jackie Benson); Camille Franklin (Molly); Doris Kemper (the landlady); Burgess Meredith (Mr. Smith); Robert Sterling (Douglas Winter); Ray Teal (Mr. Franklin); and Charles Thompson (Andy Praskins).

Stock Music Cues: Etrange #3 (by Marius Constant, :09); Milieu #2 (by Constant, :21); Bolie Jackson (by Jerry Goldsmith, 1:13); The Cruel Past (by Goldsmith, 1:26); Broken Fist (by Goldsmith, :11); Concrete World (by Goldsmith, :15); Broken Fist (by Goldsmith, :34); Letter to Home (by Fred Steiner, 1:22); CBS Electronic Seal (by Riedel, :05); Nostalgia (by James Moody and Tommy Reilly (:30); Harp Chords (CBS, :02); Tension (by Tommy Morgan, :44); Big Dipper (by Bruce Campbell, :52); Lonely Lady (by Campbell, 2:01); Bits and Pieces (by Nathan Van Cleave, :13, :11 and :38); Trial is On (by Leonard Rosenman, :07); Suspicion (by Rosenman, :15); Bits and Pieces (by Van Cleave, :13); The Magic (by Goldsmith, :04); Perry Mason Montage (by William A. Barnett, :50); Blue Danube Waltz (by Johann Strauss Jr, :13); Bits and Pieces (by Van Cleave, :10); The Magic (by Goldsmith, :06); Shadows (by Goldsmith, :08); Blue Danube Waltz (by Strauss Jr, :09); Convening Jury (by Rosenman, :15); Drovers (by Leith Stevens, :08); Nostalgia (by Moody and Reilly, :29); Bits and Pieces (by Van Cleave, :14); Nostalgia (by Moody and Reilly, :22); CBS Electronic Seal (by Riedel, :05); Showdown (by Tommy Morgan, 1:42); Loy Wanders (by Steiner, :08); Suspense (by Morgan, :38); Blue Danube Waltz (by Strauss Jr, :06); Wild Knife Chord (by Bernard Herrmann, :05); The Squaw (by Steiner, :35); Loy Wanders (by Steiner, :08); Stalking (by Morgan, :10); Hardy Agrees (by Steiner,

:26); Stalking (by Morgan, :10); Blue Danube Waltz (by Strauss Jr, :14); Shadows (by Goldsmith, :25); Tension (by Morgan, :35); CBS Electronic Seal (by Riedel, :04); Stalking (by Morgan, :41); CBS Electronic Seal (by Riedel, :05); Danger (by Morgan, :31); Nostalgia (by Moody and Reilly, :27); Trial is On (by Rosenman, :07); Suspense (by Morgan, :29); Loy Wanders (by Steiner, :08); Suspense (by Morgan, :36); Passage of Time #6 (by Rene Garriguenc, :04); Dead Phone Nervous (by Goldsmith, :40); The Appointment (by Goldsmith, :21); Jackie's Escape (by Goldsmith, :43); The Gun Nervous (by Goldsmith, :50); Shadow "A" (by Goldsmith, :15); Shadows (by Goldsmith, :15); Jackie's Escape (by Goldsmith, :16); Dolly Finds Him (by Nathan Scott, :11); The Plot (by Goldsmith, :02); Deep Thoughts (by Goldsmith, :05); Passage of Time #16 (by Garriguenc, :05); Suspicion (by Rosenman, :12); Bull's Lesson (by Steiner, :18); Etrange #3 (by Constant, :09); and Milieu #2 (by Constant, :31).

Publicity photo with Meredith, Sterling and Crowley.

Director of Photography: George T. Clemens, a.s.c.
Film Editor: Richard W. Farrell
Art Direction: George W. Davis and John J. Thompson
Set Decoration: Henry Grace and Don Greenwood, Jr.
Produced by Herbert Hirschman

Production Manager: Ralph W. Nelson
Associate Producer: Murray Golden
Assistant to Producer: John Conwell
Assistant Director: John Bloss
Sound: Franklin Milton and Joe Edmondson
Directed by Ralph Senensky

Teleplay by Charles Beaumont, based on his short story "The Devil, You Say?," originally published in the January 1951 issue of *Amazing Stories*.

"Take away a man's dream, fill him with whiskey and despair, send him to a lonely bridge, let him stand there all by himself looking down at the black water, and try to imagine the thoughts that are in his mind. You can't, I can't. But there's someone who can – and that someone is seated next to Douglas Winter right now. The car is headed back toward town, but its real destination . . . is the Twilight Zone"

Plot: Douglas Winter, editor of the Dansburg Courier, finds himself at the bottom of the barrel. Circulation is down, creditors are calling on him, and his staff is walking out on him – ever since The Gazette, a rival newspaper, came into town with its modern equipment and staff of a dozen reporters. Moments after Doug considers suicide as a means of escape, he meets an eccentric old man named Mr. Smith, who can operate a Linotype as if the machine was a part of his anatomy. To ensure his position, Smith even pays off the Courier's debts. Weeks later, the Courier has tripled circulation, beat the rival newspaper to every sensational scoop and made good with future creditors. Alone in the office one evening, Smith and Doug exchange words and the old man reveals his true identity – he is the Devil. Smith offers to continue his services, making Doug the most powerful newspaper editor in the country, if he signs his soul over to him. Doug does so and soon regrets his decision when he discovers that predictions on the linotype come true before they happen. After Jacqueline Benson, Doug's fiancée, leaves him, the Devil attempts to finalize the arrangement by forcing Doug to commit suicide – an agreement to save Jacqueline's life from a future auto accident. While Miss Benson rides to her doom, Doug chooses another option, typing a story on the modified Linotype, rendering the arrangement between him and Mr. Smith null and void.

"*Exit the infernal machine . . . and with it his satanic majesty, Lucifer, Prince of Darkness, otherwise known as Mr. Smith. He's gone, but not for good . . . that wouldn't be like him. He's gone for bad. And he might be back, with another ticket . . . to the Twilight Zone.*"

Trailer: "*Some rather special ingredients to a bizarre brew served up next on the Twilight Zone. An oddball printing press, an editor with a stringer from the lower regions, are just a few as we bring you Robert Sterling, Patricia Crowley and special guest star Burgess Meredith, in Charles Beaumont's 'Printer's Devil.'*"

Trivia, etc. Director Ralph Senensky was new to *The Twilight Zone* with this episode and considered working with Meredith a pleasure. "I was very proud of the way it turned out," he said. "Burgess Meredith told me that director John Huston called him the day after the episode aired, commending him on the show."

Much of the stock music was originally composed for episodes of *Have Gun-Will Travel* and *Gunsmoke*.

The Devil's comment that "You're not the first editor I've helped," is a joke referring to the legendary William Randolph Hearst.

Production #4853 "NO TIME LIKE THE PAST" (Initial telecast: March 7, 1963)

© Cayuga Productions, Inc., March 1, 1963, LP24901 (in notice: 1962)
Date of Rehearsal: August 7, 1962
Dates of Filming: August 8, 9, 10, 13, 14 and 15, 1962
Script #6 dated: July 20, 1962
Revised draft dated: July 24, 1962 with revised pages dated July 23, August 2, 6 and 8, 1962.
Revised excerpts dated: January 7, 8, 10 and 11, 1963

Producer and Secretary: $2,750.00	Story and Secretary: $7,320.00
Director: $4,940.63	Cast: $17,765.50
Unit Manager and Secretary: $1,200.00	Production Fee: $4,000.00
Agents Commission: $6,000.00	Legal and Accounting: $250.00
Below the line charges (M-G-M): $107,740.70	Below the line charges (other): $3,506.74
Total Production Costs: $155,473.57	

Cast: Dana Andrews (Paul Driscoll); Malcolm Atterbury (Professor Eliot); Marjorie Bennett (Mrs. Chamberlain); Patricia Breslin (Abigail Sloan); Robert Cornthwaite (Hanford); Bob McCord (town citizen in street); Tudor Owen (Captain of the Lusitania); Robert F. Simon (Harvey); Lindsay Workman (the bartender); James Yagi (the Japanese Police Captain); and John Zaremba (the horn player).

Stock Music Cues: Etrange #3 (by Marius Constant, :09); Milieu #2 (by Constant, :21); House on K Street – Fade In (by Bernard Herrmann, :07); Vibrating Rubber Band (CBS, :03); Electronic Effects (CBS, :25 and :16); Villers #5 (by Constant, :21); Electronic Effects (CBS, :22); Tratonium #38 (by George Haentschel, :15); Two Mandarin Gongs (CBS, :05); In a Japanese Temple (by Tak Shinto, :22); Wild Knife Chord (by Herrmann, :08); Electronic Effects (CBS, :10); Espace Sidereal (by Pierre Henry, :09); House on K Street – Fade In (by Herrmann, :09); Military Drums (CBS, :22); Jungle (by Nathan Van Cleave, :22); Menace Ahead #1 (by Lucien Moraweck, :09); Electronic Effects (CBS, :10); Espace Sidereal (by Pierre Henry, :09); American Scene (by Fred Steiner, :12); The Fire (by Jerry Goldsmith, :20); Action Background (by Rene Garriguenc, :04); Second Vision (by Steiner, :21); House on K Street – Fade In (by Herrmann, :06); Electronic Effects (CBS, :09); Espace Sidereal (by Pierre Henry, :08); Vibrating Rubber Band (CBS, :03); Electronic Effects (CBS, :13 and :13); Tratonium #38 (by Haentschel, :12); Remember (by Goldsmith, 1:08); Good Morning (by Goldsmith, :21); More Push-Push (by Nathan Scott, :34); Alone in 1888 (by Scott, :12); More Push-Push (by Scott, :26); Alone in 1888 (by Scott, :12); Old William (by Goldsmith, :10 and :30); Passage of Time #3 (by Garriguenc, :08); Action Background (by Garriguenc, :05); The Fight (by Goldsmith, :15); Autumn Love (by Goldsmith, :21 and :58); Curtain (by Herrmann, :10); Morning (by Steiner, :26); More Push-Push (by Scott, :03); Friendly Talk (by Goldsmith, :48); Morning (by Steiner, :25); Sweet Genevieve (by Henry Tucker and George Cooper, :31); Columbia, the Gem of the Ocean (by Thomas A. Becket, :59); Board Meeting (by Scott , :39); Columbia, the Gem of the Ocean (by Becket, 1:38); Fed Up (by Scott, :10); Shut Your Mouth! (by Scott, :07); Morning (by Goldsmith, :13); Contemplation (by Goldsmith, :33); Columbia, the Gem of the Ocean (by Becket, 1:28); Counter Attack (by Goldsmith, :07); Ford's Theater "A" (by Goldsmith, :22); The Victor (by Goldsmith, :15); Lonely Moment (by Goldsmith, 1:29); Morning (by Steiner, :26); Electronic Effects (CBS, :13); Espace Sidereal (by Pierre Henry, :09); Autumn Love (by Goldsmith, :37); Harp Chords (CBS, :02); Etrange #3 (by Constant, :09); and Milieu #2 (by Constant, :31).

Director of Photography: Robert Pittack, a.s.c.
Art Direction: George W. Davis and William Ferrari
Set Decoration: Henry Grace and Edward M. Parker
Teleplay by Rod Serling

Production Manager: Ralph W. Nelson
Film Editor: Eda Warren, a.c.e.
Associate Producer: Murray Golden
Assistant to Producer: John Conwell
Assistant Director: Ray De Camp
Sound: Franklin Milton and Joe Edmondson
Directed by Justus Addiss

"Exit one Paul Driscoll, a creature of the 20th century. He puts to a test a complicated theorem of space-time continuum . . . but he goes a step further, or tries to. Shortly, he will seek out three moments of the past in a desperate attempt to alter the present. One of the odd and fanciful functions in a shadow land known as . . . the Twilight Zone."

Plot: Paul Driscoll classifies the late 20th century as a cesspool of prejudice and violence and applies his scientific mind to construct a time machine, giving him the opportunity to change horrific disasters of the past. He intends to change the present day so the world will be a better place to live. He fails in his attempts to warn the inhabitants of Hiroshima in August 1945 the crew of the Lusitania in 1915, and he tries to assassinate Adolph Hitler in 1939. Realizing that he cannot change any of the events of the past, he decides to "retire" in a world without fear. He travels to Homeville, Indiana, July 1881, as a resident, to enjoy a life of peace and quiet. There, he meets Miss Abigail, the local schoolteacher, and the two fall in love. His attempt to escape from a world of germ warfare and nuclear fallout is substituted by men pioneering westward, cutting down trees and Indians as fast as they can. The country grows strong by filling its graveyards, and Driscoll realizes the world is "viral as the Devil because mankind likes to spill blood." Aware of the town's history, Driscoll soon discovers that a kerosene lantern thrown from a runaway wagon will set fire to the schoolhouse. Driscoll is forced to refrain from interfering with the natural course of time – even if it means the serious injury of 12 schoolchildren and the risk of the loss of his new love. Deciding to take time in his own hands, Driscoll attempts to prevent the "accident," only to become the cause of the damage. Realizing he cannot change what is already history, Driscoll understands that the past is not for interlopers or passersby wishing to become a part of it. Driscoll leaves Abigail, explaining that he has overstayed his welcome and returns to the nightmarish future, accepting that he cannot change the past . . . but perhaps he can put the same effort into changing the future and making it a better world.

"*Incident on a July afternoon, 1881. A man named Driscoll, who came and went and, in the process learned a simple lesson. Perhaps best said by a poet named Lathbury, who wrote: 'Children of yesterday, heirs of tomorrow. What are you weaving? Labor and sorrow? Look to your looms again, faster and faster – fly the great shuttles prepared by the master. Life's in the loom, room for it, room.' Tonight's tale of clocks and calendars . . . in the Twilight Zone.*"

Trailer: "*For our next show, Mr. Dana Andrews makes his first visit to the Twilight Zone in a show called 'No Time Like the Past.' You'll see him as a discontented inhabitant of the 20th century, who goes back in time, back to what we assume to be the inviolate past and violates it. A walloping performance, a strange and oddball theme, and an ending most unexpected in the tradition of . . . the Twilight Zone.*"

Trivia, etc. Rod Serling wrote a one-page plot synopsis dated October 1958 titled "You Must Go Home Again." In this plot proposal, the time is a distant future which sees Earth wrecked by war, turmoil and misery. A decorated military solider of his time, recovering from wounds suffered in battle, is called in by his superior officer and told that he has been given a month to relax and recuperate. He may spend that month any way he so desires. Since there has been talk of experimenting in time travel, he asks that he be permitted to visit to a distant age. The higher ranking officer concurs and suggests time periods which would prove interesting. Perhaps watch the Pharaoh build the pyramids or see Helen of Troy. The young officer shakes his head. He would prefer to visit the North American continent in the late 19th century. A small country town in Illinois just before the turn of the century.

There, he enjoys the quiet, the sedateness and the gentle living of that time. The long summer evenings with the band concerts in the park, the cotton candy and the lemonade. The laughing, gentle residents welcome him in his guise as a "stranger from another state." As days go by he discovers he is useful to the community because he can cure chicken pox and fix lights and offer wonderful new inventions. Toward the end of his fourth week, another stranger greets him in his room and tells him that it's time to go back. The soldier thinks up several excuses to himself because he cannot admit, not even to himself, that the thought of leaving is adamant and concerned. The soldier hears out the plea from the visitor. Think of his family and his loved ones. Think of his country. Think of the Army that he's served, that he owes an allegiance to. The soldier agrees but at the very last instant he changes his mind. When we see him last, he's walking down the main street on his way to a Fourth of July picnic. Reality to him has been the nightmare, only his dream had been real, and this is what he chooses to live.

While the synopsis never became an actual episode of *The Twilight Zone*, elements from the tale were incorporated in "Walking Distance," "A Stop at Willoughby" and of course, "No Time Like the Past."

Serling composed the initial draft before the new opening titles were designed for the fourth season. The script opens with a description of the satellite top disappearing in the distance.

The production of this episode suffered from a number of rewrites and poor production. The 1881 sequences pretty much remained the same, but the rest of the episode, Driscoll's purpose for going back in time and the method by which he traveled, varied from one revision to another. Many of the revisions were made at the insistence of Herbert Hirschman. In the initial draft, set in a near future, Driscoll, in his early 40s, has invented a time machine and succeeds in sending a chair back to the week of October 8, 1871, the day of the Great Chicago Fire. Having taught under Professor Weiner at college, Driscoll reveals to his friend how he sent a number of items into the past; a paperweight to November 1918, a book to Munich in 1923, and a pen to Geneva, Switzerland, 1920, when the League of Nations began. All of these items returned with little or no damage. He sent an ashtray to Hiroshima, Japan, in August of 1945. The ashtray never came back.

Having succeeded in sending material objects into the past, Driscoll has decided to send himself back to Homeville, Indiana, July, 1881. His reason – he does not like the surroundings, the background, and the threat of extinction from nuclear war, as revealed in the evening news broadcast on television. The human race is suffering from the effects of nuclear fallout, and humans cope by taking tranquillizers three times a day – a race of pack rats climbing all over one another for a dubious place in the sun.

The initial draft had Paul Driscoll travel through time via use of an energy belt, which Driscoll wore around his waist. Because of the complications resulting in production (mostly by Hirschman's insistence that the script was unacceptable), Serling rewrote a number of pages, calling for picking up scenes 41 through 45, dissolving out on Weiner and dissolving to a shot of Homeville, Indiana, as Driscoll begins to materialize. This idea was scrapped and the footage of Driscoll appearing in Indiana ultimately ended up on the cutting room floor. In the finished film, partially as a result of the numerous revisions and filming additional footage, no scene with Driscoll physically materializing or dematerializing while traveling through time is shown. Ultimately, the belt idea was scrapped, replaced with a standard time-machine.

The initial script also called for the school building to be burned to the ground, but Hirschman wrote to Serling on August 1, explaining the need to change part of the script. "The description of the school building fire won't coincide with the set that we are forced to use, namely a brick building, and hence I would change 'until it burned down' to 'and gutted by fire.'"

On July 27, 1962, Herbert Hirschman wrote to Serling in Interlaken, New York, to make a few suggestions for the script that he had written, dated July 20. "I think there is one aspect of the story which you agreed might be helped that you might think about, and forward to me, and that is the reference somewhere in dialogue to the effect that although problems and tragedies of 1881 don't begin to compare in magnitude to those of the present (namely, the strong possibility of the total destruction of the world) we might mention that each age has its own problems. Even in remote and quiet communities, problems and tragedies arise which to the people concerned are of tremendous magnitude, and that you can't run away from problems which have to be faced no matter where you go, either geographically or in time."

"I forgot one other point that needs covering in 'No Time Like The Past,'" he concluded. "This is the matter of Driscoll's clothes. I would suggest something like this: Scene 27, Professor Weiner's speech, 'Money, the books you'll want, some clothes more fitting to the era than those you are wearing.' And in scene 31, some comment that under his trench coat Driscoll is wearing clothes of the 1880s, and a remark perhaps that he got them from a theatrical costumer." These changes Hirschman suggested were implemented in revised pages of the script.

On July 24, Serling revised the opening scenes of the script. Driscoll locates and visits Professor Weiner, who was the subject of an article in the recent alumni magazine. Driscoll recalls how the professor, dying from an incurable disease, was once working on a time machine years previous and now asks the favor of being a human guinea pig. The professor confesses that he had sent small items into the past and brought them back, but he had not experimented yet with a human being. Driscoll explains that he is disenchanted with the twentieth century. He found a book in the library, a study of nineteenth century Midwest America. It talks of a certain place called Homeville, Indiana, 1881.

Professor Weiner reveals to Driscoll the items he sent into the past (the same items described in the previous draft), explaining to his guest that a human being can also become damaged from the experience. Driscoll is willing to take the risk, and the professor agrees to give his ex-student a ticket to the past.

On August 6, Serling revised the opening a third time. This version is closer to the second, but with Hirschman's suggestions to have Professor Weiner order Driscoll to dress in clothing that fits the century, money and books. Driscoll leaves to gather the items he requires. He returns the next day with a bag carrying $1000 in gold pieces, each dated prior to 1875. He also included medicine, a few books, and a change of clothes, in keeping with the times.

The name of the character was previously Dr. Jacoby in other scripts, but changed to Dr. Malone as of a memo dated August 2. The name was changed to Professor Eliot on August 6, and later changed to Professor Weiner.

Serling composed a fourth alternate opener on November 16, 1962. In this revision, Driscoll leaves instructions for his secretary via a Dictaphone, to donate his funds to various charities across the city. Then Driscoll goes to the Professor and requests he be sent back in time.

After viewing the rough cut of the finished product, it was decided that most of the scenes would need to be refilmed. The 1881 scenes in Indiana pretty much remained intact while the rest of the scenes were replaced with Driscoll's failed attempts to warn victims of oncoming disasters and his scenes with Harvey, the lab assistant who transports Driscoll to the past.

On December 4, 1962, Serling wrote to Ralph W. Nelson, "The last word I got from CBS as to re-shooting on 'No Time Like the Past,' was that they definitely expect re-shooting to take place but have not yet come up with a new concept. They're working on it and said they'd send me something."

On December 5, Robert F. Lewine of CBS informed Serling that "It would be dishonest of me not to report to you that I have been disappointed in some of the episodes that I've seen in rough cut. I think that errors were made either in direction or in story continuity and in some instances just plain, old-fashioned judgment. We find it necessary to do some substantial revising of 'No Time Like the Past'."

By early November, Serling had already recorded the narration, which would later be revised and edited into the final product:

Mr. Paul Driscoll . . . a creature of the present . . . who hungers to put in a claim to the past. In a moment we'll take a journey with Mr. Driscoll when he takes the pace and poison of the twentieth century and tries to exchange it for a moment already passed. One of the bizarre transactions that can be found taking place in an odd marketplace known as . . . The Twilight Zone.

Retakes were filmed on February 1 and 4, 1963. These included scenes of Driscoll and his assistant Harvey in the lab, Driscoll's attempt to warn the authorities of Hiroshima, the crew of the Lusitania and an assassination attempt on Adolph Hitler.

A number of music cues for this episode was taken from *House on K Street*, an original music score by Bernard Herrmann. *House on K Street* was an unsold pilot scripted by Lawrence Menkin and produced by Sam Gallu for CBS-TV. When the network purchased the pilot, they also purchased all rights to the music score and catalogued it as part of the CBS stock music library.

"Columbia, the Gem of the Ocean" and "Sweet Genevieve" were musical pieces selected solely because they were in the public domain. "Columbia, the Gem of the Ocean" was the unofficial national anthem for the United States until "The Star-Spangled Banner" became the national anthem officially in 1931, so the song fit historically with the time period.

The Thompson Brothers Restaurant was named after the art director, John J. Thompson. Because so much of the episode was refilmed after Hirschman's departure, and Bert Granet had taken over the reins, it was decided not to credit any producer on-screen for this production.

The horse-drawn carriage that was featured in this episode (which Driscoll tries to alter to prevent the fire from starting) is the same carriage featured in the 1967 movie, *The Fastest Guitar Alive*, repainted to avoid similarities.

One scene in this episode caused a concern with the Metropolitan Dairy Institute. Paul asked Harvey in the opening scenes if he checked his milk in the morning and whether there was any Strontium 90 within the contents. This prompted a letter on March 8, 1963, from Barnett Bildersee of the Bildersee Public Relations in New York:

My Dear Mr. Serling:
My telephone has been ringing today with calls from distressed members of the Metropolitan Dairy Institute which is the public information arm of the milk industry in the New York area. What disturbed them was the dialogue in last night's *Twilight Zone* presentation referring to Strontium 90 in milk. The industry has no thought of censorship. All it asks is a sense of responsibility.

The levels of Strontium 90 in milk are low, far within every accepted level of safety. No one – not even a fictional physicist – could drink milk with dangerous quantities of Strontium 90 because it never would be offered for consumption. In effect, and no doubt unwittingly, the reference constituted a "libel of product." The atmosphere we breathe, the water we drink and foods generally contain Strontium 90 in varying degrees, just as milk does, according to the amount of fallout. Yet milk – one of the most important elements of the national diet and one considered indispensable for the proper nutrition of our youth was the only product singled out for mention by name.

This letter is written only to prevent a repetition of such an unfortunate reference and I hope I may have your assurances to that end.
Sincerely yours,
Barnett Bildersee

On April 10, Rod Serling drafted a reply, reassuring her that it was not his intention to cast any doubts on the health-giving properties of milk or to suggest that there was anything suspect in its drinking. He assured Bildersee that he was a "dedicated dairy user" and an almost "compulsive milk drinker." He also explained that the mention of Strontium 90 in milk on the program was a passing side remark commentative on what might be the future dangers in a society in which there has resulted an atmospheric danger because of constant nuclear testing. "I wish you would inform the Metropolitan Diary Institute that this very negative labeling of a product was a most inadvertent one and never meant to plant even a remote seed of doubt and certainly not to libel a product. If a personal letter to this effect is required, I should be most happy to comply. You must tell them that the choice of 'milk' as a dramatic point is gratuitous and certainly not overt." The matter was promptly dropped after receipt of Serling's letter.

Production #4859 "THE PARALLEL" (Initial telecast: March 14, 1963)

© Cayuga Productions, Inc., March 9, 1963, LP24903
Dates of Rehearsal: January 28 and 29, 1963
Dates of Filming: January 30 and February 1, 4, 5 and 6, 1963
Script dated: October 2, 1962, with revised pages dated January 8 and 9, 1963.
Revised excerpts dated: January 23 and 29, 1963

Producer and Secretary: $600.00	Story and Secretary: $345.15
Director: $2,750.00	Cast: $10,847.92
Unit Manager and Secretary: $1,000.00	Production Fee: $4,000.00
Agents Commission: $6,000.00	Legal and Accounting: $100.00
Below the line charges (M-G-M): $61,665.02	Below the line charges (other): $1,316.23
Total Production Costs: $88,624.32	

Cast: Philip Abbott (General Eaton); Frank Aletter (Colonel William Connacher); Paul Comi (the psychiatrist); Steve Forrest (Robert Gaines); Morgan Jones (the Captain); Shari Lee Bernath (Maggie Gaines); William Sargent (the project manager); and Jacqueline Scott (Helen Gaines).

Stock Music Cues: Etrange #3 (by Marius Constant, :09); Milieu #2 (by Constant, :21); Solemn

Finish (by Goldsmith, :21); Ran Afoul (by Goldsmith, :15); Nocturnal Interlude (by Goldsmith, :16); The Picture (by Nathan Van Cleave, :40); Fantasies Part 1 (by Wilfred Josephs, :26); Harp Glissando On C (CBS, :02); Light Rain (by Constant, :42); Brouillard (by Constant, :13); Kant #1 (by Constant, :08); Wild Knife Chord (by Bernard Herrmann, :07); Neuro (by Garriguenc, :35); The Picture (by Van Cleave, 1:13); Light Dramatic #1 (by Garriguenc, :17); Two Unison Horns on C (CBS, :04); Jud's Song (by Steiner, :28); Belfort #8 (by Constant, :16); Moat Farm Murder (by Herrmann, :22 and :24); Unison to SF Chord #1 (by Van Cleave, :20); Menton 18 (by Constant, :23); The Prediction (by Goldsmith, 1:25); Missing Colonel (by Leonard Rosenman, :43); The Old Woman (by Goldsmith, 1:41); The Prediction (by Goldsmith, :10); Third Act Opening (by Van Cleave, :26); Figures in the Fog (by Goldsmith, :15); Sneak and Punctuation #3 (by Rene Garriguenc, :14); The Discussion (by Goldsmith, :27); Zephyr #1 (by Constant, :20); Foggy Hill (by Moraweck, :12); Passage of Time #16 (by Garriguenc, :06); Eerie Dream (by Moraweck, :29); Mausoleum Part 3 (by Wilfred Josephs, :59); The Fight (by Goldsmith, :05); Belfort #6 (by Constant, :04); Kant #1 (by Constant, :08); Wild Knife Chord (by Herrmann, :09); Neuro (by Garriguenc, :35); A Story #1 (by Constant, :04); Fantasies Part 1 (by Josephs, :44); Western Pastoral Sneak #1 (by Garriguenc, :16); Quiet Western Scene (by Van Cleave, :53); Etrange #3 (by Constant, :09); and Milieu #2 (by Constant, :31).

Director of Photography: Robert Pittack, a.s.c.	Production Manager: Ralph W. Nelson
Art Direction: George W. Davis and Paul Groesse	Film Editor: Al Clark, a.c.e.
	Assistant to Producer: John Conwell
Set Decoration: Henry Grace and Frank R. McKelvy	Assistant Director: Ray De Camp
	Sound: Franklin Milton and Joe Edmondson
Teleplay by Rod Serling	Produced by Bert Granet
	Directed by Alan Crosland, Jr.

"In the vernacular of space . . . this is T-minus one hour. Sixty minutes before a human being named Major Robert Gaines is lifted off from the Mother Earth and rocketed into the sky . . . farther and longer than any man ahead of him. Call this one, one of the first faltering steps of man to sever the umbilical cord of gravity and stretch out a fingertip toward an unknown. Shortly we'll join this astronaut named Gaines and embark on an adventure. Because the environs overhead . . . the stars . . . the sky – the infinite space . . . are all part of a vast question mark known as . . . the Twilight Zone."

Plot: Major Robert Gaines returns to Earth after being the first man to spend one week orbiting the planet – and having lost communication on radar and radio for a total of six hours. The U.S. Air Force is mystified because the spacecraft was found 40-plus miles away from where he blasted off, without a scratch or dent to the craft. Gaines does not recall how he gained re-entry because he passed out after the 15th orbit. While the Air Force investigates, Gaines finds things are not what they used to be at home: a fence in the front yard that wasn't there before; his rank isn't major, but colonel; even his wife suspects something out of place when she kisses him. The brass at the air base start to suspect the same theory as Gaines – that somehow he fell into a parallel world not too different from our own – but with slight differences. Examining the spacecraft, Gaines finds himself back inside, making his descent to the Earth he left almost two weeks previous. In the hospital, he discovers that he was out of communication for only six hours – but he couldn't have spent a full week on another world. In the hallway, Colonel Connacher learns that they just received a brief minute-and-a-half communication from someone identifying himself as Colonel Robert Gaines.

"Major Robert Gaines . . . a latter-day voyageur just returned from an adventure. Submitted to you without any recommendations as to belief or disbelief. You can accept or reject; you pays your money and you takes your choice. But credulous or incredulous, don't bother to ask anyone for proof that it could happen. The obligation is a reverse challenge. (a pause). Prove that it couldn't. This happens to be . . . the Twilight Zone."

Trailer: *"Next on Twilight Zone we take a page out of a book on the space age, and we project as to a couple of degrees as to what conceivably might happen to an astronaut if suddenly and inexplicably, in the middle of an orbit, he disappears. Our story tells you how, why and where. It stars Steve Forrest. It's called 'The Parallel.'"*

Trivia, etc. Months before the first draft of this script was written, John Glenn became the first American to orbit the Earth. Science fiction had become science fact. He had piloted the first American manned orbital mission aboard the Friendship 7, lasting four hours, 55 minutes and 23 seconds.

Inspired by the recent news item that man was finally reaching out past the Earth's atmosphere, Serling wrote the first draft of "The Parallel," which concerned an American astronaut who made a daring orbital flight around the Earth. The first draft was completed in early-to-mid 1962, and the script was then submitted to the De Forest Research Group, which explained three points of interest, all suggestions of changes so the drama would be more down-to-Earth.

1. Loss of Radio – When radio communication is broken between capsule and ground, the procedure is as follows: The priority network at Cape Canaveral attempts to make contact by calling, "Cape Com calling ___(name of capsule)___. This is done every minute until contact is made."
2. Loss of Radar – It is improbable that all ground stations would lose radar and the ionization factor has also been eliminated, insofar as loss of radar is concerned. A "science fiction" reason could be, "Due to the sun spot activity the electromagnetic disturbances on Earth could become so severe that it would cancel out a target on a radar scope."
3. Procedure In Case of Loss of Radio Communication – The astronaut is instructed to proceed with his flight unless otherwise instructed. With loss of radio he would be unable to receive instructions so he would continue on his orbital path.

Serling's initial opening narration was different from what we hear today:
In the vernacular of space . . . This is T-minus 4 hours – 240 minutes before a human being named Major Robert Gaines is lifted off from the Mother Earth and rocketed into the sky . . .
On November 8, 1962, Serling informed Ralph W. Nelson that Herbert Hirschman "had no interest in this script – disliked it, didn't understand it, and didn't want to do it. He told me that this was pretty much your feeling as well. I was somewhat shattered by this since I loved the idea and thought we could do a good job on it."

On December 5, 1962, Robert F. Lewine of CBS told Serling in the form of a letter that "Boris confirms the fact that 'Parallel' was rejected and that it would require a very substantial rewrite before it can be used."

On December 13, Boris Kaplan admitted that while he and Hirschman had reservations about this script, Bert Granet, who became the new producer, "read the script and liked it unequivocally. "Bob Lewine also read it and his opinion was equally strong. With some rewriting, the script might just become more effective."

In early January of 1963, Serling revised a number of script pages and the film was scheduled for production. It was at the suggestion of Alan Crosland, who had just recently filmed an episode of *The Virginian*, that Steve Forrest play the lead. Crosland had just worked with Forrest on the television series.

"I was thrilled to be doing the show because it was one of the most popular shows on the air at the time – and rightfully so, with its wonderful scripts," recalled Jacqueline Scott. "This was a particularly special episode since, as you know, Rod Serling wrote it. I was happy to be working again with Steve Forest since we had done the pilot of the *Wide Country* together. An added bonus to the whole experience was that Rod Serling called me afterwards and said that he had never written a script for a woman but was going to write one for me. It never materialized but the idea of it was a lovely compliment."

Promotion went beyond the stars for this episode. The March 4, 1963 issue of *The Hollywood Reporter* reported that the Air Force recruiting office tapped Steve Forrest to narrate a 10-minute film, utilizing clips from this episode of *The Twilight Zone*. Forrest was the younger brother of actor Dana Andrews, who appeared in the episode that aired the week before, "No Time Like the Past."

On July 11, 1963, Ralph W. Nelson wrote to Rod Serling: "A couple of days ago Jerry Saltsman called me regarding a possible plagiarism claim on 'The Parallel,' and today Jerry sent me a copy of the letter from a certain Steven Masino's attorney. . . . Upon the advice of Jerry Saltsman, with 'The Parallel' rerun going on the air next Thursday, July 12, I contacted CBS and this rerun is being canceled for the time being, due to the possibility of punitive damages. 'In His Image' will be rerun in its place on July 18, and 'Printer's Devil' will have its second rerun on September 12. As you know, 'The Thirty Fathom Grave' will have its second rerun on September 19, and this is the show in which we need the one-minute trailer telling of the new season of half-hour shows starting on Friday, September 27."

On the same day, CBS and Cayuga Productions received a letter drafted from the law offices of Irwin O. Spiegel in Beverly Hills. Stephen Masino, author of an unpublished story titled "The Carbon Copy," was asserting a claim of appropriation and wrongful use against Cayuga Productions. Masino claimed that his literary property was submitted to Cayuga Productions on three separate occasions during the year of 1961, for the sole purpose of selling the story for an episode on *Twilight Zone*. Having viewed the episode titled "The Parallel," Masino claimed that the broadcast used substantial parts and portions of "The Carbon Copy."

On the morning of July 11, Gerald Saltsman, associate resident counsel of Ashley-Steiner, phoned Robert Gordon, the attorney representing the firm, to inform him of the notice received from the law office of Irwin O. Spiegel. "Our client, Cayuga Productions, Inc. will, of course, look to Firemans Fund Insurance Company to indemnify and defend in accordance with the Producer's Liability Insurance Policy with Cayuga Productions, Inc. carries," Saltsman wrote.

After digging into his files, Serling found a copy of an undated release signed by Masino. The release accompanied a synopsis of the story, "The Carbon Copy." Copies of all correspondence between employees of Cayuga Productions and Stephen Masino and his agent regarding the submission of the story were also taken out of the files and given to Gerald Saltsman for consulting.

In September of 1963, Masino's claim against Cayuga Productions, Inc. involving "The Parallel" episode had been settled out of court for $6,500. The insurance company's attorney made sure that as part of the agreement Cayuga could now utilize "The Parallel" episode free from any further claims by Masino. The network restriction on reruns was lifted.

Though the first draft of the script was already written in October of 1962, on January 22, 1963, Hugh Hefner, editor-publisher of *Playboy* magazine, wrote to Serling, suggesting a plot idea for *Twilight Zone*. The premise was not too different from this episode. "One can imagine a situation in which a guy returns home from an extended space trip in which he has aged no more than a couple of years, and returning to his house he is disturbed to the extent to which familiar things now seem unfamiliar to him," Hefner proposed. "But perhaps he has been injured slightly in his return from the trip, and blames the strangeness on a head injury that causes lapses of memory, or perhaps the implications in a crash-landing return to Earth suggest that whatever is wrong may actually be wrong with him – that doctors have worked some remarkable plastic surgery to piece him back together from a crash without telling him."

"These thoughts might crowd in upon his conscious when he first returns home," Hefner continued. "For his wife is there, but she doesn't recognize him. This might prompt the self-doubt and a staring at his face in a nearby mirror. His wife appears very much as he remembers her from before the trip, and yet there's a difference somehow – a difference that he can't put his finger on. But worst of all, she doesn't recognize him, doesn't know him, states flatly, in fact, that's he has never been married. And then he discovers, to his horror, that her name is not even the right one – which convinces him that he must really be off his nut, or dead, or something.

"At which point, of course, his actual wife comes in – a very old and senile woman – and the woman in her middle thirties to whom he has been talking is, of course, his own daughter, the unborn child that his wife was carrying when he first left Earth – 35 years ago by Earth time, but only two or three, as it passed ever so much more slowly in his speeding rocket."

Production #4860 "I DREAM OF GENIE" (Initial telecast: March 21, 1963)

Copyright Registration: © Cayuga Productions, Inc., March 15, 1963, LP24902 (in notice: 1962)
Dates of Rehearsal: October 23 and 24, 1962
Dates of Filming: October 25, 26, 29, 30, 31 and November 1, 1962
Retakes: February 5, 1963
First draft: undated
Second draft titled "Do Unto Others" dated: October 16, 1962
Revised draft dated: October 19, 1962, with revised pages dated October 25, 29 and 30, 1962.

Producer and Secretary: $3,380.00
Director: $5,080.00
Unit Manager and Secretary: $720.00
Story and Secretary: $4,321.05
Cast: $13,152.18
Production Fee: $4,000.00

Agents Commission: $6,000.00

Below the line charges (M-G-M): $61,784.15

Total Production Costs: $101,608.10

Legal and Accounting: $250.00

Below the line charges (other): $2,920.72

Cast: Jack Albertson (the genie); Robert Ball (the clerk); Patricia Barry (Ann); Bob Hastings (Sam); Joyce Jameson (the Starlet); Mark Miller (Roger); James Millhollin (Masters, the salesman); Howard Morris (George P. Hanley); Milton Parsons (the scientist); and Loring Smith (Mr. Eli T. Watson).

Original Music Score Composed and Conducted by Fred Steiner (Score No. CPN6085A): Etrange #3 (by Marius Constant, :09); Milieu #2 (by Constant, :21); Bottles (:14); Meet George Hanley (:51); George's Desk (:40); Meet Ann (:42); Ann Flirts (:39); George's Tune (:55); Magic Box (:44); Attila Barks (1:07); Genie Enters (:28); Genie Exits (:09); Which One? (:11); George Muses (1:04); Ann's Tune (:38); Ann's Tune #2 (:20); Try to Swing It (by Horst Jankowski, 1:24); Poor George (:18); Bad Girl (:20); What Now (:08); Mad George (:18); Tycoon (:42); Glad Tycoon (:27); Bad Tycoon (:23); Mad Tycoon (:28); George Spins (:12); George Walks (:24); Another Dream (:14); George's March (:16); George Panics (:24); George Decides (:57); Tramp and Lamp (:21); New Genie (:26); Etrange #3 (by Constant, :09); and Milieu #2 (by Constant, :31).

Director of Photography: George T. Clemens, a.s.c.

Art Direction: George W. Davis and John J. Thompson

Set Decoration: Henry Grace and Don Greenwood, Jr.

Produced by Herbert Hirschman

Directed by Robert Gist

Production Manager: Ralph W. Nelson

Film Editor: Eda Warren, a.c.e.

Associate Producer: Murray Golden

Assistant to Producer: John Conwell

Assistant Director: John Bloss

Sound: Franklin Milton and Joe Edmondson

Teleplay by John Furia, Jr.

"Meet Mr. George P. Hanley, a man life treats without deference, honor or success. Waiters serve his soup cold. Elevator operators close doors in his face. Mothers never bother to wait up for the daughters he dates. George is a creature of humble habits and tame dreams. He's an ordinary man, Mr. Hanley, but at this moment the accidental possessor of a very special gift – the kind of gift that measures men against their dreams. The kind of gift most of us might ask for first and possibly regret to the last ... if we, like Mr. George P. Hanley ... were about to plunge head-first and unaware into our own personal Twilight Zone."

Plot: As the proud possessor of a magic lamp with a genie in it, George Hanley discovers that he will be granted one – and only one – wish. Because George observed a fellow employee win the heart of the beautiful secretary, receive a promotion and a raise all on the same day, he wonders if he really wants true happiness. Before giving George the opportunity to make his wish, the genie offers a suggestion: think on it and sleep on it. George does so, contemplating his three options: love, wealth or power. Through a series of dreams, George visits a brief glimpse of a life of wealth and finds that money won't buy happiness. He dreams of being married to the secretary-turned-movie star, but the she thinks more of herself than of her husband. He dreams of being president of the United States, but the decisions he is forced to make remind George that power isn't everything. Deciding that neither love, wealth or power is worth the effort, George wishes for something original . . . he takes the place of the genie in the lamp.

"Mr. George P. Hanley. Former vocation: jerk. Present vocation: genie. George P. Hanley, a most ordinary man whom life treated without deference, honor or success . . . but a man wise enough to decide on a most extraordinary wish that makes him the contented, permanent master of his own altruistic Twilight Zone."

Trailer: *"A new author joins the ranks of the Twilight Zone crew, when John Furia Jr. gives us several stunningly new twists to a classic character in 'I Dream of Genie.' Join Howard Morris, Patricia Barry and Loring Smith as they take their trip into the Twilight Zone."*

Trivia, etc. When it was decided to feature clips of next week's episode, forcing Serling's teaser to be cut in length, the following proposed trailer was considered way too long and scrapped:

"A new author joins the ranks of the Twilight Zone crew next week when John Furia Jr. gives us several stunningly new twists to the idea of that classic character who makes his appearance once or twice during an eon and calls himself a genie. This one is for the wishful thinkers amongst you who do a bit of daydreaming on occasion when visiting an old curio shop and while gazing, perhaps hopefully, at an old jug, let your imaginations run to the extent that . . . well . . . what if after a rub or two . . . a little smoke might appear . . . and then you're in business . . . or in trouble. In Mr. Furia's story . . . trouble is of the essence. This one is of the essence. This one is a walloping good story with a very, very exceptionally odd twist. Howard Morris and Patricia Barry take their trips into the Twilight Zone in next week's production of 'I Dream of Genie.'"

M-G-M prop numbers show the helmet and uniform George wears in one of his visions is the same worn by Steve Forrest in "The Parallel."

To publicize this episode, *TV Guide* featured a three-page article with actress Patricia Barry and the colorful characters she played on various television programs. In *Thriller*, she had portrayed an aging movie love-goddess who finds that when beauty passes, she has nothing left to sustain her; an engaging femme fatale hot-footing it after Fred MacMurray; and an apprehensive woman expecting her first child on *Dr. Kildare*. She liked her parts "slightly larger than life," she explained. The same issue of *TV Guide* featured a news brief adjoining the article, reporting that Patricia Barry would play four roles in the upcoming "I Dream of Genie" episode of the *Twilight Zone*.

A letter to Rod Serling from Ralph W. Nelson dated November 29, 1962, verified that there were intentions to reshoot the genie appearance and disappearance sequence in this episode, "because of the faggot-like performance of the actor who played Genie." This was not a simple proposal. It meant digging out the same wardrobe, reproducing the set, and getting the necessary actors together on the same day. This was an expensive procedure, and ultimately the scenes were never reshot. According to an interoffice memo, it was suggested that had CBS decided to start broadcasting the hour-long shows in late January instead of early January, there would have been enough time for the production crew to possibly reshoot the scenes.

By December 12, Boris and Herb looked over the film (twice) and admitted that unless there was more time to re-edit the episode (which there was not), it hardly seemed worth reshooting.

"Herbert Hirschman, who was the producer of *Twilight Zone*, asked me to contribute a script," recalled John Furia. "We had worked together before, but I hesitated. I was not comfortable about approaching the idea in the science fiction format the *Twilight Zone* had established. I played with the idea of a man who imagines the possibilities – and the consequences – before choosing his one wish. Hirschman liked my proposal so I wrote the teleplay. What pleased me most was not seeing how the film turned out when it was telecast, but [that] Serling quoted the introduction I wrote, almost verbatim."

While some of the *Twilight Zone* staff disregarded the finished product, some viewers found the production entertaining. The day after this episode was initially telecast, Naomi Kellison, director of the Program Bureau at Roosevelt University in Chicago, wrote to Serling, "To say congratulations and thank you for the excellent show on *Twilight Zone* last night. 'I Dream of Genie' was so delightful and well-done it deserves many awards."

Production #4866 "THE NEW EXHIBIT" (Initial telecast: April 4, 1963)
© Cayuga Productions, Inc., April 1, 1963, LP25538
Date of Rehearsal: February 7, 1963
Dates of Filming: February 8, 11, 12, 13, 14 and 15, 1963
Script dated: January 14, 1963

Story and Secretary: $4,301.44
Cast: $14,804.88
Production Fee: $4,000.00
Legal and Accounting: $250.00
Below the line charges (other): $643.61

Director: $50.00
Unit Manager and Secretary: $720.00
Agents Commission: $6,000.00
Below the line charges (M-G-M): $60,746.61
Total Production Costs: $91,516.54

Cast: Martin Balsam (Martin Lombard Senescu); Ed Barth (sailor #1); Billy Beck (Hare); David Bond (Jack the Ripper); Lennie Bremen (the van man); Phil Chambers (the gas man); Craig Curtis (sailor #2); Marcel Hillarie (the guide at Marchand's): Will Kuluva (Mr. Ferguson); Maggie Mahoney (Emma Senescu); Bob McCord (Burke); William Mims (Dave, Martin's brother); Bob Mitchell (Albert W. Hicks); and Milton Parsons (Henri Desire Landru).

Stock Music Cues: Etrange #3 (by Marius Constant, :09); Milieu #2 (by Constant, :21); Neutral #3 (:14); Ich Rut' Zu Dir (by Johann Sebastian Bach, 4:38); Moat Farm Murder (by Bernard Herrmann, :09); Menton 18 (by Constant, :27); Harp Chords (CBS, :02); Strange Return (by Goldsmith, :28); Blood Fever #1 (by Lyn Murray, :41); The Meeting (by Goldsmith, :04); Brothers Lime #3 (by Murray, :23); Blood Fever #1 (by Murray, :23); Dramatic Tension Tag – Elegy (by Nathan Van Cleave, :21); Meditation (by Goldsmith, :47); Howe's Place (by Steiner, :09); Moat Farm Murder (by Herrmann, :08); I'm Alone (by Steiner, 1:01); Unloaded Gun (by Murray, :10); Puzzles (by Steiner, :50); Sand (by Steiner, :25); Blood Fever #1 (by Murray, :11); Brothers Lime #3 (by Murray, :41); Moat Farm Murder (by Herrmann, :09); The Station (by Herrmann, :16); Unloaded Gun (by Murray, :09); Light Dramatic #8 (by Rene Garriguenc, :42); Blood Fever #1 (by Murray, :22); Brothers Lime #4 (by Murray, :18); Brothers Lime #5 (by Murray, :32); Brothers Lime #3 (by Murray, :08); Moat Farm Murder (by Herrmann, :08); The Station (by Herrmann, :16); Eerie #6 (Tension) (by Moraweck, :30); Moat Farm Murder (by Herrmann, :10 and :32); Strange Return (by Goldsmith, :22); Low Bass Notes (CBS, :02); Etrange #3 (by Constant, :09); and Milieu #2 (by Constant, :31).

Director of Photography: George T.
  Clemens, a.s.c.

Art Direction: George W. Davis and
  Paul Groesse

Set Decoration: Henry Grace and
  Frank R. McKelvy

Production Manager: Ralph W. Nelson

Film Editor: Everett Dodd, a.c.e.

Assistant to Producer: John Conwell

Assistant Director: John Bloss

Sound: Franklin Milton and Joe Edmondson

Produced by Bert Granet

Teleplay by Jerry Sohl, based on an original story idea by Charles Beaumont.
Directed by John Brahm

"Martin Lombard Senescu. A gentle man. The dedicated curator of 'Murderer's Row' in Ferguson's Wax Museum. He ponders the reasons why ordinary men are driven to commit mass murder. What Mr. Senescu does not know is that the ground work has already been laid for his own special kind of madness and torment . . . found only in the Twilight Zone."

Plot: Mr. Ferguson of the Ferguson Wax Museum has sold the building to a developer to make way for a supermarket. Martin Senescu, the caretaker of the wax figures, treasures the works of art, offering to store them in his climate-controlled basement until a solution can be found and the figures can be put back on display. Martin's wife, Emma, takes a dislike to the unwelcome visitors when the electric bills start to grow as a result of the air conditioning required to keep the figures in excellent condition. Late one night, in an attempt to dispose of the figures, she visits the basement to shut down the air conditioning. The knife of Jack-the-Ripper cuts her short of accomplishing her mission. When Martin discovers what has happened, he buries her body in the basement. When Martin's brother, Dave, suspects something out of the ordinary, he breaks into the basement to find the wax figures – and receives a hatchet to the head, courtesy of Albert Hicks. After disposing of the second body, Martin receives a visit from Mr. Ferguson, who gives Martin great news. Another museum is interested in buying the figures. When Martin goes upstairs to make some tea, Mr. Ferguson begins taking measurements – and is strangled by Henri Desire Landru. Martin returns to find the dead body and, forced to cover a third crime, threatens the wax figures. The dummies come to life in the form of Martin's hallucinations explaining the solution to the crimes: it was he who committed the murderous acts. Months later, the new exhibit at Marchand's includes Jack-the-Ripper, Henri Desire Landru and Martin Lombard Senescu . . . a featured attraction of murderer's row at the wax museum.

"The New Exhibit became very popular at Marchand's. But of all the figures, none was ever regarded with more dread than that of Martin Lombard Senescu. 'It was something about the eyes' people said. It's the look that one often gets after taking a quick walk . . . through the Twilight Zone."

Trivia, etc. On September 14, 1962, Joe Castor of Castor and Associates, Los Angeles, wrote to Rod Serling:

Thanks, Rod, for your kind letter.
I write you now to determine the possibility of a basis of mutuality between your *Twilight Zone* and the Movieland Wax Museum.

In this museum are fifty wax figures of famous movie personalities, i.e., Valentino, Monroe, Lollobrigida, Laurel and Hardy, Ward Bond, etc. All figures are in settings (see enclosures) from one of their most famous roles. As you would say about Kuppenheimer "Class shows." The Museum epitomizes class – as an example to establish the Sunset Blvd. scene appropriately the creator bought a Rolls as part of the permanent set to show Eric Von Stroheim holding open the door for Gloria Swanson while Holden awaits her. The place is housed in a beautiful building – one of the most extravagant in southern California.

It is my ambition that to satisfy your creative ability and my financial aggrandizement (grin) your typewriter and the Museum might get together on some truly quid pro quo basis.

What do you think . . .

Best personal regards,

Respectfully,

Joe Castor

On September 27, Serling drafted a reply clarifying Castor's proposal of a *Twilight Zone* episode in which a Wax Museum could be used as the background. Serling assured him that this might be a possibility when and if they continued shooting beyond the contracted thirteen hour-long episodes. "There is also the constant risk of whether or not a proper story line can be developed so that you get valid drama without the obvious inclusion of a specific place that for the sake of its inclusion," he explained. After additional episodes were contracted, Serling approached Charles Beaumont with the idea and with the assistance of Jerry Sohl, a script was typed out.

Initial plans for this episode were to have people standing still or keeping the screen moving like Douglas Heyes accomplished in "Elegy," but Serling confessed that having wax figures adds to the illusion. Charles Beaumont was paid $4,100 for this script, under Serling's exclusive creative control, with the stipulation that should it not work out, Beaumont would be obligated to write another script at no additional cost. "Aside from the financial agreement by Cayuga Productions in connection with this deal, I must say that it would be most unorthodox for Charlie Beaumont to report to you directly with his material and bypass or ignore Bert Granet who has been contracted by CBS to produce the final block of five shows," wrote Boris Kaplan. "In my opinion, this is an untenable and unprofessional position in which to place a producer, and must perforce weaken his effectiveness as far as the show is concerned. Because of the obvious problems posed by this situation, we defer advising Bert of your desired script procedure until you get here so that you can be a part of the notification of him of the role you will expect him to play."

The reason for Serling's decision was because of the extraneous script conference Beaumont had to ordeal just days before. Serling believed Beaumont was extremely capable of writing two scripts, one of them being the wax museum story, in proper time, or share the assignment with Richard Matheson. But Beaumont's condition was getting worse. Beaumont was suffering from what some would later refer to as Alzheimer's, and the disease was gradually robbing him of his memory and coordination. Jerry Sohl was brought in to assist Beaumont, and while Beaumont received credit on screen, Sohl wrote every word of the 60-page script.

"He was able to come up with an idea and sell it," recalled Jerry Sohl for interviewer Steve Boisson. "But beyond the fact that these museum people were murderers, he had no story. And instead of plotting out the story, we really just chewed the fat. He seemed to waiver and talk about other things than the story. It was rather unsettling for me. He said, 'It's up to you how you do this.' So I did it. And it didn't take very long."

All of the Lyn Murray music cues were originally composed for the *Gunsmoke* episode, "Unloaded Gun," initially telecast on January 14, 1961.

The stairway in the opening shot of this episode, in which Mr. Ferguson is giving the tour of the museum, is the same used in the opening shots of "The Masks."

Production #4867 "OF LATE I THINK OF CLIFFORDVILLE" (Initial telecast: April 11, 1963)

© Cayuga Productions, Inc., April 5, 1963, LP25024
Date of Rehearsal: February 14, 1963
Dates of Filming: February 15, 18, 19, 20, 21 and 22, 1963
Script dated January 28, 1963 with revised pages dated February 5, 6 and 11, 1963

Story and Secretary: $700.00
Cast: $10,897.04
Production Fee: $4,000.00
Legal and Accounting: $250.00
Below the line charges (other): $154.97

Director: $2,817.50
Unit Manager and Secretary: $720.00
Agents Commission: $6,000.00
Below the line charges (M-G-M): $68,82.49
Total Production Costs: $94,362.00

Cast: John Anderson (Mr. Sebastian Deidrich); Christine Burke (Joanna Gibbons); John Harmon (Clark); Wright King (Hecate, the custodian); Julie Newmar (Miss Devlin); Guy Raymond (Mr. Gibbons); Albert Salmi (William Feathersmith); and Hugh Sanders (Mr. Cronk).

Stock Music Cues: Etrange #3 (by Marius Constant, :09); Milieu #2 (by Constant, :21); Solemn Finish (by Jerry Goldsmith, :21); Mist Lifts (by Goldsmith, :29); Now We Move (by Nathan Van Cleave, :22); Warming Up (by Fred Steiner, :04); Rosie's Man (by Steiner, :17); Mist Lifts (by Goldsmith, :29); The Old Woman (by Goldsmith, 1:44); Attempted Murder (by Lucien Moraweck, :24); Horn Stings on G (CBS, :04); A Story #1 (by Constant, :04); Tramontane #1 (by Constant, :12); A Story #1 (by Constant, :06); Mendel Shaves (by Steiner, :06); Now We Move (by Van Cleave, :22); The Road (by Steiner, :11); Fantasies (by Wilfred Josephs, :38); The Road (by Steiner, :11); Broken Dream (by Steiner, :12); Dapper Emile (by Goldsmith, :22); The Wedding (by Goldsmith, :13); Mendel Shaves (by Steiner, :08); Every Little Movement (by Otto Harbach and Karl Hoschna, 1:08); The Old Woman (by Goldsmith, :22); Rosie's Man (by Steiner, :23); Warming Up (by Steiner, :04); The Wedding (by Goldsmith, :11); Bushwhack (by Steiner, :17); F Story #8 (by Constant, 1:13); Rosie's Man (by Steiner, :08); A Story #1 (by Constant, :01); Now We Move (by Van Cleave, :22); Loy's Arrest (by Steiner, :17); Ashland Scene (by Steiner, :31); Rosie's Man (by Steiner, :17); The Old Woman (by Goldsmith, 1:10); Summer Sadness (by Goldsmith, :22); Low Bass Note on E (CBS, :02); Etrange #3 (by Constant, :09); and Milieu #2 (by Constant, :31).

Director of Photography: Robert
    Pittack, a.s.c.
Art Direction: George W. Davis and

Production Manager: Ralph W. Nelson
Film Editor: Richard W. Farrell
Assistant to Producer: John Conwell

Paul Groesse

Set Decoration: Henry Grace and
Frank R. McKelvy

Directed by David Lowell Rich.

Assistant Director: Ray De Camp

Sound: Franklin Milton and Joe Edmondson

Produced by Bert Granet

Teleplay by Rod Serling, based on the short story "Blind Alley" by Malcolm Jameson, originally published in the June 1943 issue of *Unknown Worlds*.

"Witness . . . a murder. The killer is Mr. William Feathersmith, a robber baron whose body composition is made up of a refrigeration plant covered by thick skin. In a moment, Mr. Feathersmith will proceed in his daily course of conquest and calumny with yet another business dealing. But this one will be one of those bizarre transactions that take place in an odd marketplace known as . . . the Twilight Zone."

Plot: Business tycoon William Feathersmith is a predatory animal who has become synonymous with Genghis Khan when it comes to conquering other companies for his empire. Without a heart of compassion, he applies a form of cruelty in the way he does his business, driving people to poverty and hopelessness. Having just secured the last available company, he discovers that the fun was accumulating his wealth, not having it. He's bored now – no purpose, no drive – it was the desperate struggle to possess, not the possession itself. Recalling his old hometown, Cliffordville, Indiana, Feathersmith longs for the days of the past. Through a business transaction with Miss Devlin, he travels back to 1910, looking much younger, and retaining the memories and knowledge of the past 40 years. He would have sold his soul for the chance, but they already have that, so he liquidates most of his fortune for the opportunity. As he strikes a number of business transactions, in an effort to start his new company, he discovers that his habit of gloating comes back with a taste of irony. He tells people about radios, television, storage batteries, plastics and other features without which he cannot function or operate as a success. Possibilities of investments fail to get the attention of anyone, except for a laugh. Miss Devlin eventually makes an appearance – giving him a taste of his own medicine, gloating over his loss and her gain. He pleads to return to 1963, and Miss Devlin, out of sympathy, allows him to return, provided the changes he made go into effect. Back in 1963, Feathersmith now finds himself as the janitor of the Hecate Company and the man who was once the janitor when Feathersmith had control, is the new president of the same empire . . . gloating over the failures of others, including the janitor.

Julie Newmar and Albert Salmi agree to a business proposition.

"Mr. William J. Feathersmith, tycoon, who tried the track one more time and found it muddier than he remembered . . . proving with at least a degree of conclusiveness that nice guys don't always finish last, and some people should quit when they're ahead. Tonight's tale of iron men and irony, delivered f.o.b. . . . from the Twilight Zone."

Trailer: *Next on Twilight Zone, a trip back into time with Albert Salmi, John Anderson and guest star Julie Newmar. But this trip is an off-beat, very adventuresome and totally unexpected itinerary. It's called, "Of Late I Think of Cliffordville."*

Trivia, etc. In the earliest draft of the script, Serling's opening narration was originally longer:

"Witness . . . a murder. A willful, predatory case of homicide. The victim is a Mr. Sebastian Dietrich – age seventy-seven. The killer is Mr. William Feathersmith. A robber baron whose body composition is made up of a refrigeration plant covered by thick skin. In a moment, Mr. Feathersmith will proceed in his daily course of conquest and calumny with yet another business dealing. But this one will be one of those bizarre transactions that take place in an odd marketplace known as . . . The Twilight Zone."

The line Feathersmith remarks on the train, shortly after going back into time, "the Devil you say?" was an in-joke Serling placed in the script. "The Devil, You Say?" was Charles Beaumont's first short story, published in the January 1951 issue of *Amazing Stories*. The same short story was adapted into an hour-long teleplay, "Printer's Devil."

The doors to Feathersmith's office are the same from the episode, "Mr. Bevis." The doors had, since then, been painted darker in color and the center door knobs were replaced with new ones.

In an interview with Mark Phillips, John Anderson recalled, "All I remember was that Albert Salmi, who played this devilish character, had to laugh maniacally whenever he pulled a devious deed. However, Al couldn't laugh on cue. All David Rich, the director, could get out of him was a very heavy, totally unconvincing, 'HA! HA! HA!' David, a wonderful man, came up to me and said, 'John, what am I going to do with Al? I can't use that laugh.' I said, 'Jesus, David, I don't know, but it sure ain't working, is it?' I suggested that they lay down a sound track of somebody else's laughter. That's what they must have done, because they sure as hell couldn't use what ol' Al was giving 'em!"

"There was lots of schmaltz with that episode," recalled Wright King. "I enjoyed the switch, of course, and doing both the young and aged Hecate character. Frank Tuttle, famed M-G-M makeup man, did the aging bald head on me, covered by the black Homberg hat in that final scene. I kept it intact to surprise my wife at home. Al Salmi was larger than life and I assumed his laugh was too. Regarding David Rich, our director on this one, I go back a long way with David to live television days on several *Big Town* shows. He's the brother of John Rich, the director of *Gunsmoke*."

Serling was teaching at the college during the time this episode was produced. One month before this episode went to film, Serling had one of his students read the story for him, while he composed the adaptation.

This episode was based on the short story, "Blind Alley," by Malcolm Jameson. While it was later anthologized in *Rod Serling's Triple W*, the original tale was devoted to the primitive ways of the past, and Feathersmith's inability to adjust to the absence of modern conveniences, which he took for granted before he struck his deal. He dies an old man, having never requested to regain his youth. For the *Twilight Zone* version, Feathersmith does negotiate in the bargain to retain his youth.

The original story also dealt with a male Satan, not a female. Feathersmith asked about his soul being thrown into the purchase price, but Satan explains that there was no need for that.

"Dear me, no," responded Satan cheerily, with a friendly pat on the knee. "We've owned that outright for many, many years. Money's all we need. You see, if anything happened to you as you are, the government would get about three quarters of it and the lawyers the rest. We hate to see that three quarters squandered in subversive work – such as improved housing and all that rot."

The January 28, 1963 script described a sign reading "Sam Demon – Wishes, Prognostications – Time Travel" on the glass door and the devilish character is referenced in the script as Samuel Demon. While the Devil was a male in the initial script, the sex was changed to a woman beginning with the February 6, 1963 revision, and the name of the company was revised to "Devlin's Travel Service."

Saturday Night Live featured a skit once that involved the switching of a C.E.O. and a janitor who worked for him, courtesy of supernatural events, in a spoof of this *Twilight Zone* episode. The switching of the roles happens multiple times in the sketch.

Production #4854 "THE INCREDIBLE WORLD OF HORACE FORD" (Initial telecast: April 18, 1963)

Copyright Registration: © Cayuga Productions, Inc., April 18, 1963, LP25536 (in notice: 1962)
Dates of Rehearsal: September 3 and 4, 1962
Dates of Filming: September 5, 6, 7, 10, 11 and 12, 1962
Script #8 dated: August 14, 1962
Revised script dated: August 30, 1962

Producer and Secretary: $3,350.00
Director: $2,750.00
Unit Manager and Secretary: $700.00
Legal and Accounting: $150.00
Below the line charges (other): $3,392.31

Story and Secretary: $5,300.00
Cast: $12,657.94
Production Fee: $4,000.00
Below the line charges (M-G-M): $67,910.09
Total Production Costs: $100,210.34

Cast: Mary Carver (Betty O'Brien); Jerry Davis (Henry "Hermie" Brandt); Pat Hingle (Horace Maxwell Ford); Nan Martin (Laura Ford); Phillip Pine (Leonard O'Brien); Vaughn Taylor (Mr. Judson); Jim E. Titus (Horace Ford, age 10); and Ruth White (Mrs. Ford).

Stock Music Cues: Etrange #3 (by Marius Constant, :09); Milieu #2 (by Constant, :21); The Park (by Bernard Herrmann, :16); Menton 18 (by Constant, :28); The Faro Game (by Herrmann, :22); No Joking (by Steiner, :15); The Park (by Herrmann, :25 and 1:15); Second Act Opening (by Nathan Van Cleave, :16); The Park (by Herrmann, 1:21); Beer Barrel Polka (by Lew Brown, W.A. Timm, and Jaromir Vejvoda:43); Maya (by Van Cleave, :09); Poor Cale (by Steiner, :17); The Road (by Steiner, :11); Letter to Home (by Steiner, :35); Isham Goes (by Steiner, :18); Poor Cale (by Steiner, :17); Unloaded Gun (by Lyn Murray, :10); Brothers Lime #3 (by Murray, :29); Brothers Lime (by Murray, :31); The Park (by Herrmann, :35); A Mercy Bullet (by Rene Garriguenc, :43); Beer Barrel Polka (by Brown, Timm and Velvoda, :39); Blinded Eyes (by Steiner, 2:11); Terror Struck (by Goldsmith, :13); Blood Fever #1 (by Murray, :22); Poor Cale (by Steiner, :17); Unloaded Gun (by Murray, :15); Passage of Time #3 (by Rene Garriguenc, :08); A Mercy Bullet (by Garriguenc, :32); Letter to Home (by Steiner,

1:02); Unloaded Gun (by Murray, :06); Blood Fever #1 (by Murray, 1:19); Beer Barrel Polka (by Brown, Timm and Vejvoda, :39); Knockout (by Goldsmith, :12); Poor Cale (by Steiner, :28); Terror Struck (by Goldsmith, :56); String Effects (CBS, :06); Italian Folk Song (traditional, 1:17); Cale Conks Out (by Steiner, :07); Knockout (by Goldsmith, :16); Blinded Eyes (by Steiner, :14); Heartbreak (by Goldsmith, :39); Tycho – Outer Space Suite (by Herrmann, :05); Martin's Summer (by Herrmann, :29); Coney Island (by Van Cleave, :16); Etrange #3 (by Constant, :09); and Milieu #2 (by Constant, :31).

Director of Photography: George T.
    Clemens, a.s.c.
Assistant to Producer: John Conwell
Art Direction: George W. Davis and
    Edward Carfagno
Set Decoration: Henry Grace and
    Edward M. Parker
Directed by Abner Biberman

Production Manager: Ralph W. Nelson
Associate Producer: Murray Golden
Film Editor: Eda Warren, a.c.e.
Assistant Director: John Bloss
Sound: Franklin Milton and Joe Edmondson
Produced by Herbert Hirschman
Teleplay by Reginald Rose

"Mr. Horace Ford . . . who has a preoccupation with another time. A time of childhood . . . a time of growing up . . . a time of street games, stickball and hide-and-go-seek. He has a reluctance to go check out a mirror and see the nature of his image . . . proof positive that the time he dwells in . . . has already passed him by. But in a moment or two, he'll discover that mechanical toys and memories and daydreaming and wishful thinking and all manner of odd and special events, can lead one into a special province, uncharted and unmapped. A country of both shadow and substance known as . . . the Twilight Zone."

Plot: A toy designer of 15 years named Horace Ford longs for the days when he was 10-years-old and the fond times on Randolph Street. Under constant pressure from his employer, Horace attempts to escape to memory lane when he takes a walk down Randolph Street. Oddly, he finds the street is not as is it today, but as it once was, complete with the same friends he spent his childhood with. Returning to the real world, he tells his wife, who shares the same opinion of his boss, and is concerned over his well-being. She pleads for him to see a doctor. On the evening of his 38th birthday, Horace is fired for being inadequate in his work performance, and instead of making an appearance at his surprise birthday party, he ventures back to Randolph Street to revisit his youth. In a confrontation with the small boys, he discovers that he has been gone too long and he is no longer wanted. Horace is forced to admit that every memory he had from his childhood was lie. His stories and memories of the past were nothing but a favored unbearable nightmare that he kept locked up, disguised as the days he longed to have. After the boys knock this into his consciousness, Horace is rescued by his wife, who realizes that his longing for the past was a calling. Arm in arm, they return home . . . with Horace content to live in the present.

"Exit Mr. and Mrs. Horace Ford . . . who have lived through a bizarre moment not to be calibrated on normal clocks or watches. Time has passed, to be sure . . . but it's the special time in the special place known as . . . the Twilight Zone."

Trailer: *"On our next excursion into The Twilight Zone, we borrow an imposing array of talent and call on the services of a distinguished author named Reginald Rose. And some exceptionally fine acting talent in the* *persons of Mr. Pat Hingle, Miss Nan Martin and Miss Ruth White. The apprehensible story is called 'The Incredible World of Horace Ford' and it's an incredible world indeed."*

Trivia, etc. In August of 1959, a little less than two months before the premiere of *The Twilight Zone*, Russell Stoneham of CBS Television forwarded to Rod Serling a kinescope of the *Studio One* broadcast of the same name, written by Reginald Rose. In late August or early September, Serling reviewed the production and though he admitted the story would fit the mold of *The Twilight Zone*, the episode "Walking Distance" was already filmed and in the can. He did not want two films of the same plot appearing on the series, so he returned the kinescope to CBS, with a promise to explore the prospect of using the teleplay at a future date.

A few years later, Edith Efron wrote an editorial titled "Can a TV Writer Keep His Integrity?" The article was a backhand slap at Rod Serling, who had made numerous comments in the public eye about quality television. Serling promptly wrote a reply to the editorial. In the May 12, 1962 issue of *TV Guide*, he remarked: "Should *TV Guide* have any further interest in me, I would count it a personal favor if they'd refrain from sending Miss Edith Efron with her lace-handled hatchet to do the job." Reginald Rose, meanwhile, praised Efron for her candor. "I've just seen the *TV Guide* piece and I'm writing to thank you for all the effort you put into making it an interesting and excellent article. I only wish it could have been longer . . ."

In the same month, Rose wrote to Serling personally to convey his appreciation and friendship, citing the only reason for the letter to *TV Guide* was to encourage Serling to venture away from science fiction and return to his dramatic roots from the *Playhouse 90* and *Studio One* years. While Rose did not share the same passion for the field of fantasy, he did acknowledge Serling's success and wished him all the best. "If you promise not to be sore about the *TV Guide* article, I'll tell you a funny story," Rose wrote. "My rotten kid, age ten, had a birthday party last week, and what do you think my rotten kid demanded as entertainment? 'Dear old dad,' said he, 'I want you to show to my chums and me three *Twilight Zones*.' So I did . . . The dirty rotten kid."

Serling had deep respect for Reginald Rose, praising the playwright for his many achievements, and decided to get even with Rose (humorously), by starting a series of gears in motion that would bring Rose's former *Studio One* teleplay, "The Incredible World of Horace Ford," to *Twilight Zone*.

Director Abner Biberman, who previously directed "The Dummy," received this script on the recommendation of Ralph W. Nelson of CBS. Nelson contacted John B. Bennett of The Jaffe Agency, Inc. in Hollywood, and through Nelson's insistence, Bennett contracted Herbert Hirschman on July 3, 1962, explaining to Hirschman that Biberman would be available after August 20 or 21st, after he finished commitments for *Empire* and *Adam Fable*. With Biberman's two Emmy nominations, Hirschman agreed to assign a *Twilight Zone* episode to the director.

After reading the script, however, Hirschman informed Serling of his opinion. "It is a strange play. One level it is a classic description of schizophrenia, but this is disturbed by the concrete evidence of fantasy when the little boy brings back the Mickey Mouse watch. Unquestionably this brief element of fantasy into what is otherwise an absorbing psychological study is what disturbed many of the viewers seven years ago, and frankly it disturbs me to some small degree. Also, I have a feeling that the script, aside from this strange element, is a little thin and incomplete in that it is a straight line of a man's retreating into a dream world. The other problem present is that it's about a quarter of the way through the play before we enter any area that could be considered *Twilight Zone*."

Hirschman phoned Reginald Rose to make the necessary arrangements to purchase the rights, and assess Rose's reaction to his concerns. The rights were secured and the director and the script fell into place.

In late December 1962, after a rough cut was made, the original ending was not favored by the network, especially Robert Lewine. The end of the story stops when Hermy returns the Mickey Mouse watch one final time, suggesting Horace had traveled back in time to his childhood for good. This was also how the original *Studio One* production ended. Lewine remarked in a stern letter that "the meaning of the play is not clear."

On January 2, 1963, Hirschman wrote a reply to Lewine, suggesting the alternative of re-shooting the last few scenes. "Start with the 1934 street with the people in wardrobe of the period, old cars, etc. Shooting down on the street sign, we see Hermy running through the crowd. A few beats behind him comes Laura (Horace's wife). She has obviously lost sight of Hermy. As she makes her way down the busy street she comes to the alley, looks in and sees Horace the boy lying on the ground. She goes over to him, recognizes him as her husband, is horrified, and frantically tugging and yanking at him, and perhaps in dialogue also, trying to call him back. She shakes him vigorously and the boy transforms into Horace Ford the man. A scene is then played in the alley which could contain all the thoughts and dialogue which are present in the version already shot. At the end of the scene, Horace and Laura walk out into the street on their way home, only now the street is 1963, people in present day clothes, set dressing and cars accordingly up to the moment. As they walk down the street and past the sign, we could still bring in Hermy Brandt looking after them. Very close to the same effect could be obtained somewhat more simply by using what has already been shot up to the time that Laura finds Horace the boy in the alley and re-shooting from there to the end."

This alternative ending Hirschman suggested was, more or less, what was filmed and edited into the final cut, which appears on the finished episode today.

The network's concern for a story that did not conclude on a rational level was founded. When the original *Studio One* presentation earned the network a large number of letters (over 1,000 in the first three days following the telecast) asking for a clarification regarding the ending, Reginald Rose himself was forced to defend his play, reasoning that the viewers probably did not understand that the story dealt in fantasy, and perhaps was unable to distinguish whose fantasy it was. This serves as an excellent example of why the CBS Television Network, in 1958, was cautious about "The Time Element" and *The Twilight Zone* in general.

"Pat and I have been great friends. We did stage work together," recalled Nan Martin. "They flew me in from New York to do 'Horace Ford.' I was flown in for a lot of television. We were known as the Jeanette MacDonald and Nelson Eddy of the stage and screen because we worked together so often. I met Rod when he came on the set. He was a very nice man. Kind of shy. But here I am, an actress, and I was in awe for Rod Serling! [pause] We were doing the street scene where Pat relives his childhood with the street kids. I was off camera with everyone else and he played the part so well that I had chills on my back. I told someone next to me how I felt and they agreed with me."

To help establish the time period of 1934, a movie poster of the M-G-M classic *O'Shaughnessy's Boy* was pasted on the wall. The movie, starring Ben Hendricks and Jackie Cooper, was released from the same studio where *The Twilight Zone* was produced.

Production #4868 "ON THURSDAY WE LEAVE FOR HOME"
(Initial telecast: May 2, 1963)
© Cayuga Productions, Inc., April 26, 1963, LP25083
Date of Rehearsal: February 25, 1963
Dates of Filming: February 26, 27, 28 and March 1, 4 and 5, 1963
First draft dated: February 11, 1963 with revised pages on February 18, 1963.
Second draft dated: February 20, 1963 with revised pages February 23 and 25, 1963.

Story and Secretary: $200.00
Cast: $15,683.09
Production Fee: $4,000.00
Legal and Accounting: $250.00
Total Production Costs: $115,656.54

Director: $2,817.50
Unit Manager and Secretary: $720.00
Agents Commission: $6,000.00
Below the line charges (M-G-M): $85,985.95

Cast: Russ Bender (Hank); Anthony Benson (colonist #4); James Broderick (Al); Lew Gallo (Lt. Engle); Jo Helton (Julie); Paul Langton (George); Madge Kennedy (colonist #1); Daniel Kulick (Jo-Jo); Tim O'Connor (Colonel Sloane); Shirley O'Hara (colonist #3); Mercedes Shirley (Joan); John Ward (colonist #2); and James Whitmore (Captain William Benteen).

Stock Music Cues: Etrange #3 (by Marius Constant, :09); Milieu #2 (by Constant, :21); Electronic Effects (CBS, :22); The Hospital (by Bernard Herrmann, :50); The Doctor (by Herrmann, :23); The Unknown (by Fred Steiner, :36); The Hospital (by Herrmann, :41); Harp Chords (CBS, :01); The Station (by Herrmann, :21); The Door (by Herrmann, :07); Bergson #1 (by Constant, :20); Squaw Man (by Steiner, :21); Goodbye Keith (by William Lava, :06); Charlie Passes (by Steiner, :56); Quiet Western Scene (by Nathan Van Cleave, 2:55); Hope – Walt Whitman Suite (by Herrmann, :05); Warming Up (by Steiner, :03); Pantomime Chords (by Leonard Rosenman, :36); The Cruel Past (by Goldsmith, :52); Transition #4 (by William Barnett, :07); The Sun (by Herrmann, :26); The Telephone (by Herrmann, :43); The Bookrack (by Herrmann, :10); The Sun (by Herrmann, :38); The Bookrack (by Herrmann, :15); The Station (by Herrmann, :29); Culley Works (by Steiner, :42); The Man (by Herrmann, :35); The Door (by Herrmann, :08); The Sun (by Herrmann, :45); Strange Rider (by Steiner, 1:01); The Door (by Herrmann, :09); Charlie Passes (by Steiner, :29); The Sun (by Herrmann, :10); Charlie Passes (by Steiner, :15); Lavinia (by Steiner, :11); Perry Mason Background (by Steiner, :02); Squaw Man (by Steiner, :22); Reckoning Star Chords (by Goldsmith, :02); Jud's Song (by Steiner, :23); The Bookrack (by Herrmann, :06); The Breakdown (by Herrmann, :39); The Phone Booth (by Herrmann, :15); The Station (by Herrmann, :25); Rosie's Farm (by Steiner, :13); The Phone Booth (by Herrmann, :40); The Victor (by Goldsmith, :21); Etrange #3 (by Constant, :09); and Milieu #2 (by Constant, :31).

Director of Photography: George T. Clemens, a.s.c.
Art Direction: George W. Davis and Paul Groesse
Set Decoration: Henry Grace and

Production Manager: Ralph W. Nelson
Film Editor: Al Clark, a.c.e.
Assistant to Producer: John Conwell
Assistant Director: John Bloss
Sound: Franklin Milton and Joe Edmondson

Frank R. McKelvy   Produced by Bert Granet
Teleplay by Rod Serling   Directed by Buzz Kulik

"This is William Benteen – who officiates on a disintegrating outpost in space. The people are a remnant society who left the Earth looking for a millennium – a place without war, without jeopardy, without fear. And what they found was a lonely, barren place whose only industry was survival. And this is what they have done for three decades – survive. Until the memory of the Earth they came from has become an indistinct and shadowed recollection of another time and another place. One month ago, a signal from Earth announced that a ship would be coming to pick them up and take them home. In just a moment, we'll hear more of that ship . . . more of that home . . . and what it takes out of mind and body to reach it. This is the Twilight Zone."

Plot: In August of 1991, the Pilgrim I, the first spaceship sent up to colonize the outer regions, carrying a crew of 113 people, crash-landed on a barren planet in the hopes of colonizing a new home. Discovering too late that they cannot plant new roots there, they look to the guidance of Captain Benteen, who comforted them, guided them and kept them alive. After 30 years of survival, a spaceship from Earth arrives to transport the survivors, now a population of 187. Amongst the cheers, Captain Benteen longs to continue as their guide and consultant when they return home – against the wishes of the survivors who intend to meet and settle with their relatives. When the captain of the rescue ship insists that the survivors should live free to do what they want and go where they want, as God meant for them, he finds himself against Benteen, who prefers to remain with his "children" as their leader. Benteen starts to preach to the survivors with a religious fervor that the Earth is not a Garden of Eden. His cries are accepted by the majority as delusions, and the survivors board the ship. Benteen, realizing the situation, causes his own damnation when, moments after the ship takes off, he discovers he's preaching to a crowd of one – himself – and his pleas become cries for help.

> **Blooper!** Shortly after the initial commercial break, in the cave, during a discussion between Benteen and George, the microphone can be seen on the bottom corner of the screen. Obviously, this blooper should not have made it to the final cut, but apparently no one during production caught this error.

"William Benteen, who had prerogatives; he could lead, he could direct, dictate, judge, legislate. It became a habit, then a pattern, and finally a necessity. William Benteen; once a God, now a population of one."

Trailer: *"On Twilight Zone next week, a most unusual and provocative story in which we call upon the talents of James Whitmore as a mayor of a town – a little mild on the face of it except when we supply the following addenda: This town is on an asteroid ten billion miles from Earth. Our story is called 'On Thursday We Leave for Home.'"*

Trivia, etc. "It's my real conviction that this is an above-average item with consistently fine performances in which Mr. Whitmore is unique. I think it is probably one of the best *Twilight Zones* that we've ever done," explained Serling to a number of newspaper columnists, hoping television reviewers would tune in for what was perhaps one of the best episodes of the fourth season.

The opening narration in the first draft (dated February 11, 1963) was lengthier than the final draft:

"This is a village without a name. On a planet that needs no name. Fifty years earlier, at the end of the Twentieth Century, a space ship called the 'Pioneer I' landed a hundred people on its barren, lonely landscape. They had only one mission – that was to survive. And this they did – they and their children, and then their children's children, until the memory of the Earth they came from became an indistinct and shadowed memory of another place and another time. They built their homes, made their food, married, delivered their children, and survived. And Earth, racked with wars and with the normal Earthly preoccupations of the killing off of one another – began to forget them . . . lose contact with them . . . and finally to abandon them. One month ago, a signal from Earth announced that a ship would be coming to pick them up and take them home. (a pause) *In just a moment we'll hear more of that ship . . . more of that home . . . and what it takes out of mind and body to reach it. This is the Twilight Zone."*

"They constructed the entire set for that episode," recalled Tim O'Connor for *Starlog Magazine.* "There was no possible way the camera could have moved without picking up the landscape they designed. The set was enormous! M-G-M studios was like a production factory back then. They saved every costume, every prop and the mountain set they built stood there for years so it could be reused. Some executive must have choked when they saw the budget. I am not surprised they didn't tear the set down after we finished that episode."

The character of Lt. Engle, played by actor Lew Gallo, was a nod to Fred Engel of Ashley-Steiner. The crew of the spaceship (yes, the same flying saucer from *Forbidden Planet*) are wearing the same uniforms (with the same insignias) worn by the cast of "Death Ship" and *Forbidden Planet.*

On May 6, 1963, Mel Bloom (of the Kumin-Olenick Agency) wrote a brief note to Rod Serling: "Last Thursday night's *Twilight Zone* was one of the most wonderful experiences I have ever received from television. May I offer you my congratulations on what was to me TV's most glorious moment."

Production #4869 "PASSAGE ON THE LADY ANNE" (Initial telecast: May 9, 1963)
© Cayuga Productions, Inc., May 3, 1963, LP25539
Dates of Rehearsal: March 4 and 5, 1963
Dates of Filming: March 6, 7, 8, 11, 12 and 13, 1963
Script dated: February 19, 1963
Revised script dated: March 1, 1963

Story and Secretary: $4,320.00
Cast: $13,803.08
Production Fee: $4,000.00
Legal and Accounting: $250.00
Below the line charges (other): $75.43

Director: $2,750.00
Unit Manager and Secretary: $720.00
Agents Commission: $6,000.00
Below the line charges (M-G-M): $66,501.37
Total Production Costs: $88,169.88

Cast: Colin Campbell (Addicott); Gladys Cooper (Mrs. McKenzie); Cyril Delevanti (officer #1); Wilfrid Hyde-White (Mr. McKenzie); Don Keefer (Mr. Spierto); Cecil Kellaway (Burgess); Alan Napier (Captain Protheroe); Lee Philips (Alan Ransome); Jack Raine (officer #2); and Joyce Van Patten (Eileen Ransome).

An hour-long episode of *The Twilight Zone* was not telecast on the evening of May 16. Instead, a half-hour episode from the third season titled "Still Valley" was presented. The remaining half hour, (9:30 – 10 p.m.) was devoted to a TV special titled "Faith 7."

Original Music Composed by Rene Garriguenc and Conducted by Lud Gluskin (Score No. CPN6091): Etrange #3 (by Marius Constant, :09); Milieu #2 (by Constant, :21); Light Metropolitan (:51); Two Tickets (:54); On the Dock (:34); The Ramsoms Go Aboard (1:35); Leave the Ship (:41); First Day Aboard (1:45); Old Passengers (:37); I'm Leaving You (:44); I Dreamt I Dwelt in Marble Halls (by Michael William Balfe, arr. by Lucien Moraweck, 1:49); You Won't Have to Die (:12); Drovers (by Leith Stevens, :04); Darling Nellie Grey (by S.R. Hanby, arr. by Lucien Moraweck, 3:23); Last Rose of Summer (traditional, arr. by Lucien Moraweck, 4:22); Believe Me, If All Those Endearing Young Charms (traditional, arr. by Lucien Moraweck, :50); Eileen Disappears (1:39); Alan Runs (:34); Alan Searches (2:25); Alan Despairs (:30); Alan Finds Eileen (1:18); Roses from the South (by Johann Strauss, arr. By Rene Garriguenc, :37); Every Little Movement (by Otto Harbach and Karl Hoschna, :13); Off the Ship (4:22); Etrange #3 (by Constant, :09); and Milieu #2 (by Constant, :31).

Director of Photography: Robert Pittack, a.s.c.
Art Direction: George W. Davis and Paul Groesse
Set Decoration: Henry Grace and Frank R. McKelvy
Directed by Lamont Johnson

Production Manager: Ralph W. Nelson
Film Editor: Everett Dodd, a.c.e.
Assistant to Producer: John Conwell
Assistant Director: Ray De Camp
Sound: Franklin Milton and Joe Edmondson
Produced by Bert Granet

Teleplay by Charles Beaumont, based on his short story "Song for a Lady," originally published in *Night Ride and Other Journeys* (Bantam, 1960).

"Portrait of a honeymoon couple getting ready for a journey – with a difference. These newlyweds have been married for six years, and they're not taking this honeymoon to start their life, but rather to save it, or so Eileen Ransome thinks. She doesn't know why she insisted on a ship for this voyage, except that it would give them some time and she'd never been on one before – certainly never one like the 'Lady Anne.' The tickets read 'New York to Southampton' but this old liner is going somewhere else. Its destination . . . the Twilight Zone."

Plot: In a desperate attempt to save their marriage, Eileen and Alan Ransome book passage on "The Lady Anne," a decades-old luxury liner from the past en route to London. Against the wishes of the passengers, Eileen and Alan — the only young couple aboard — remain on the ship, intent on enjoying and making the most of their vacation. As the marriage finally meets a rocky conclusion, they agree that divorce is imminent. Making the best of the trip, Alan soon realizes what it was that sparked the relationship in the first place and attempts to make up for his error. Reconciling their petty differences, the married couple begin acting like honeymooners and confess their appreciation to the elderly passengers, and the ship itself, for saving their marriage. The good news, however, comes with a price. "The Lady Anne" is retiring after this final voyage, so the passengers agree in unison to jettison the young couple. Placed in a lifeboat, Eileen and Alan are given a fond bon voyage as "The Lady Anne" and its elderly passengers depart into the fog never to be seen again.

"The Lady Anne never reached port. After they were picked up by a cutter a few hours later, as Captain Protheroe had promised, the Ransomes searched the newspapers for news – but there wasn't any news. The Lady Anne with all her crew and all her passengers vanished . . . without a trace. But the Ransomes knew what had happened, they knew that the ship had sailed off to a better port . . . a place called . . . the Twilight Zone."

Trailer: *"Next on Twilight Zone, an exercise from the typewriter of Charles Beaumont. A sea voyage into the darker regions of the zone. Our stars in alphabetical order: Gladys Cooper, Wilfred Hyde-White, Cecil Kellaway, Lee Phillips and Joyce Van Patton."*

Trivia, etc. The original trailer was intended to read:

On Twilight Zone next week, an exercise from the typewriter of Charles Beaumont. A sea voyage into the darker regions of the zone. Our cast: Gladys Cooper, Wilfred Hyde-White, Cecil Kellaway, Lee Phillips and Joyce Van Patton . . . in the story, 'Song for a Lady.'

The February 19 draft of the script was titled "Song for a Lady," the same name as the short story it was based on. Beginning with the March 1 revision, the script was now titled "Passage on the Lady Anne."

According to an issue of *The Hollywood Reporter*, Oscar-nominee Ed Begley was going to fly to the West Coast from New York to play the role of Burgess for this *Twilight Zone* episode, then return to the East Coast for an episode of the *U.S. Steel Hour*. For reasons unknown, Begley never arrived in California, and Cecil Kellaway signed on for the role.

According to another issue of *The Hollywood Reporter*, James Coburn was asked to play the role of Alan Ransome. Coburn was also asked to play a role in an episode of *Dr. Kildare*. A scheduling conflict occurred and he was never able to commit to either of the two, leaving the part of Alan open for Lee Philips.

Rather than have the closing credits flip from page to page on the screen, this is the only episode to feature the credits scrolling from bottom to top. The error was a result of a newly-hired hand under the supervision of Everett Dodd, who was unaware of the format for *Twilight Zone*.

The Leith Stevens music cue, "Drovers," was originally composed for an episode of *Rawhide* titled "Incident of the Dancing Death," initially telecast on April 4, 1960.

Many of the sets featured in this episode (on board the boat) were seen previously on *Marie Antoinette* (1938), the film starring Norma Shearer. Costumes worn in this episode were borrowed from the costume department, and Joyce Van Patten recalled wearing a costume that still had actress Eleanor Parker's name inside from a previous M-G-M motion picture.

"Lamont Johnson, the director, had been an actor before changing professions. I have always thought that working with a director/actor was very helpful. A sort of short-hand exists and for me, a relaxation," recalled Joyce Van Patten. "Lee Philips was a good friend of mine, and his wife was one of my dearest friends. Monty was a real gentleman. However, the greatest gift was that amazing group of great character actors they had put together. Gladys Cooper was so real and funny and she and Wilfred Hyde-White were full of fun and tons of gossip. I could not wait to get to work and see those dynamos, the energy, the wit. It was amazing! They had it in for Cecil Kellaway and talked behind his back giggling like school kids."

Production #4852 "THE BARD" (Initial telecast: May 23, 1963)
Copyright Registration: © Cayuga Productions, Inc., May 17, 1963, LP25537 (in notice: 1962)
Dates of Filming: August 16, 17, 20, 21, 22 and 23, 1962
Script #100 dated: June 13, 1962 with revised pages dated June 15 and 28, August 1 and 10, 1962

Producer and Secretary: $2,750.00
Director: $2,750.00
Unit Manager and Secretary: $700.00
Legal and Accounting: $250.00
Below the line charges (other): $4,493.31

Story and Secretary: $7,205.95
Cast: $13,504.71
Production Fee: $4,000.00
Below the line charges (M-G-M): $50,700.48
Total Production Costs: $86,354.45

Cast: Clegg Hoyt (the bus driver); William Lanteau (Dolan); Henry Lascoe (Mr. Gerald Hugo); John McGiver (Mr. Shannon); Howard McNear (Mr. Bramhoff); Doro Merande (Sadie Polodney); Marge Redmond (the secretary); Burt Reynolds (Rocky Rhodes); Judy Strangis (Cora); Jack Weston (Julius Moomer); and John Williams (William Shakespeare).

Original Music Score Composed and Conducted by Fred Steiner (Score No. CPN6083): Etrange #3 (by Marius Constant, :09); Milieu #2 (by Constant, :21); Meet Julius (:14); Julius' Ideas (:57); Julius' Talent (:20); Black Magic (:44); Julius' Tune (:32); Julius Walks (:24); Magic Book (1:01); Magic on a Bus (:44); Eject Julius (:39); Rotten Kid (:35); More Magic (:20); Meet Will (:08); His Humor (by G. Farnaby, 1:00); Julius Faints (:11); Will Appears (:09); Walshingham (by John Bull, :20); Will's Fanfare (:05); Will's Fanfare – A (:03); Will's Fanfare – B (:05); Will's Fanfare – C (:05); Will's Fanfare – D (:07); Big Shot (:12); Julius Knocks (:09); Julius Reads (:28); Julius' Fanfare (:02); Julius' Fanfare – A (:02); Julius' Fanfare – B (:03); Julius' Fanfare – C (:18); Julius' Dance (:17); Wills' Fanfare (:05); Julius Pleads (:18); Will's Fanfare – A (:05); Truncated Fanfare (:03); Julius Runs (:25); Pavana (by John Bull, :20); Will's Fanfare – A (:10); Will's Punch (:01); Fanfare – C (:02); Fanfare – D (:02); Will Goeth (:10); Poor Julius (:48); Ghost Writers (:42); Tell Tale (:15); Etrange #3 (by Constant, :09); and Milieu #2 (by Constant, :31).

Director of Photography: George T.
    Clemens, a.s.c.
Art Direction: George W. Davis and
    Edward Carfagno
Set Decoration: Henry Grace and
    Edward M. Parker
Teleplay by Rod Serling

Production Manager: Ralph W. Nelson
Film Editor: Edward Curtiss, a.c.e.
Assistant to Producer: John Conwell
Assistant Director: John Bloss
Sound: Franklin Milton and Joe Edmondson
Produced by Herbert Hirschman
Directed by David Butler

"You've just witnessed opportunity . . . if not knocking, at least scratching plaintively on a closed door. Mr. Julius Moomer . . . a would-be writer who, if talent came twenty-five cents a pound, would be worth less than

carfare. But in a moment, Mr. Moomer – through the offices of some black magic – is about to embark on a brand-new career. And although he may never get a writing credit on the Twilight Zone, he's to become an integral character in it."

Plot: Thanks to a book on black magic, Julius Moomer, a wanna-be television playwright, finds himself in the presence of William Shakespeare. Suspecting there is a benefit to employing black magic, Moomer asks Shakespeare to write a script for a television pilot Moomer was commissioned to do. A comedy of errors takes shape when the sponsor, their advertising agency, a producer and the network purchase the script, believing Moomer is the author. Shakespeare, however, takes it personally when Moomer steals the credit, instead of sharing it. After seeing the rehearsal and the changes made to his teleplay because of sponsor interference, Shakespeare is furious and returns from whence he came. Moomer, upset because his chances of becoming a successful playwright are thwarted, returns to his apartment with a bright idea and conjures up a number of figures in American history for a two-and-a-half hour television spectacular.

Rocky Rhodes (Burt Reynolds) tries to explain to William Shakespeare (John Williams) how a real drama should be acted out.

"Mr. Julius Moomer, a streetcar conductor with delusions of authorship. And if the tale, just told, seems a little tall . . . remember a thing called poetic license . . . and another thing called . . . the Twilight Zone."

Trivia, etc. "As a rule, TV can't do comedy well," Serling told reporter J.P. Shanley in 1956. "It's one thing to take a comedian with built-in humor. People are waiting to laugh at him. It's another matter to take a one-hour comedy script, particularly broad comedy. There's a total lack of spontaneity on the part of the audience. Comedy is something you've got to share with people."

This was not Serling's first attempt to bring comedy to *The Twilight Zone.* More satire on the state of affairs regarding television production, and a sponsor's lack of concern for quality for the sake of product placement, Serling drafted his proposal in the form of a 54-page plot synopsis to Herbert Hirschman. What hurt the episode most were the numerous script revisions and production issues that went along with the film, as Serling kept revising page after page in an effort to convince Hirschman to approve the script.

After reviewing the rough draft, Sam Kaplan wrote to Serling on June 25, 1962. Kaplan felt a few areas should be re-examined. "We have so much going for us in 'The Bard' that it is possible the sponsor and agency stereotypes in our script vitiate the humor of the basic situation," he wrote. "I think if they were played straighter and more realistically, Moomer's and Shakespeare's dilemma would be that much more intriguing, and equally comedic."

"The only other point I would like to make is that the female character in the bookshop seems to be a mirror-image of Moomer from the way she talks to the way she acts," Kaplan concluded. "I understand your desire to portray her as a 'character,' and a wild one at that. But since she sounds so much like Moomer, I wonder if you wouldn't have more fun with an individual who was still 'way out,' but possibly a bird-like creature who is the complete antithesis of Moomer. I am sure there are other possibilities which your fertile brain can uncover far better than I can – granted you agree that a counterpoint to Moomer would be more effective than the prototype we have now."

By the first of August, Hirschman insisted on drastic changes, claiming it was too comical and whimsical for the *Twilight Zone*. In late July, he sent Serling a list of 16 concerns, most of which he felt were a primary reason for discarding the script altogether. The quiz show joke Moomer suggests early in the episode, about the embalmer, was "too far out." Hirschman felt the joke about the onion soup bit was "a bit heavy handed." Hirschman disliked Moomer's comments to the little girl, referring to her as a "dirty kid" and suggesting she take a "flying jump." Hirschman also requested Serling change the scene with the sponsor, Shannon, by eliminating his cigar because *Twilight Zone* might be sponsored by a cigarette sponsor. Obviously, Hirschman's attempt to revise the script to satisfy both the network and the sponsors was exactly what Serling was trying to spoof. (The name of the advertising executive, Mr. Shannon, was originally Mr. Blumberg in the earlier draft.)

On August 2, Serling wrote to Hirschman, "By the time you will have read what I've done on 'The Bard' and I'm reasonably certain that you are, as yet, dissatisfied with it. Let me put it this way, Herb: It's a wild story. The dialogue is wild. The humor is farfetched. The comedy is broad stroked. I frankly wouldn't have it any other way. When we first launched this thing together, I told you that I would certainly not want you in the capacity of a rubber stamp to support my opinions constantly. You're too fine a talent and too sensitive a man to have latched onto that kind of a position which would be untenable to you. But I also said that there would be moments when I would have to get up on my hind legs and say, 'no more' – and I'm afraid this is the situation with 'The Bard.' This is one I'm afraid I must ask you to swallow wholesale and then spit it out – but swallow it, you guys must! Please forgive my perfunctory hard-nosedness about this one – but I can't rewrite it anymore. Not a scene, not a line."

Hirschman, however, requested more rewrites. Serling revised pages for the script four separate times, each addressing concerns Hirschman continued to outline in writing. Some of the changes included eliminating the speaking line for the policeman. "It's a hundred bucks well saved and I don't think it's necessary," Hirschman explained. (Actors who spoke lines were paid more than actors who stood in the background.) Other changes Hirschman requested were ignored by Serling, such as giving Moomer a "better magic incantation, more real."

On August 20, halfway through filming, Hirschman commented favorably to Serling: "'The Bard' seems to be going very well, and certainly the people on the stage as well as those who have seen the dailies find it amusing." Serling's attempt to poke jabs at television sponsors and their advertising agencies, went over well with the network executives. In this episode, the fictional sponsor deleted the suicide in Shakespeare's script, because of censorship issues, unaware that the drama was scripted by the Bard himself. The line delivered suggesting a change in a fictional character's occupation be a medical doctor because "doctor stories are very big this season," went over very well with Boris Kaplan, who complimented Serling in his letter briefing him on the production.

In mid-December 1962, the rough cut of this film was previewed. The network was dissatisfied. Hirschman, by this time, was out of the picture except for his contractual obligation to finish production on the films he started. The film was edited again, and Boris Kaplan personally sat in with the cutter to make certain changes and eliminations to curb the broadness in direction and acting on the part of Moomer, the woman in the book shop, the agency men, and the character of the sponsor. The finished film was originally scheduled for telecast on May 16, 1963, but was pushed ahead a week because of the early uncertainty about completing the final cut in time.

According to an interoffice memo dated July 27, 1962, Hirschman and the casting director attempted to get Cyril Ritchard to do William Shakespeare. Ritchard was unavailable, so John Williams was hired for the role. The character of Gerald Hugo may have been named after the Hugo Awards, which Serling had received by the time he composed this teleplay.

Jack Weston had already signed for the lead by late July for the second of his two appearances on the *Twilight Zone*. To learn his trade, Weston dropped out of high school after his father was killed and went to work as an usher at Loew's Park. At the same time, he played stock roles at the Cleveland Playhouse. He later enrolled at the American Theater Wing in New York, where he worked with Rod Steiger, Lee Marvin and other students at the Wing. Pursuing TV production to Hollywood in 1957, Weston and his wife, Marge, headed west in a Volkswagen. Near Grand Junction, Iowa, the car hit a soft shoulder and turned over twice. Marge got a slight cut as her only injury, but Weston, fretting over the sale of the car for junk, decided it was an omen. "We flipped a quarter to decide whether to go on, or back to New York," he recalled. It came up heads, and a month later he was at work for an episode of *Gunsmoke*. Had the quarter come up tails, someone else would have played the role of Julius Moomer.

During the opening scene in which Moomer is talking to the secretary, Hugo learns from a client by phone that they want something with black magic. Though the dialogue is barely audible, Serling's script reveals what Hugo spoke: "Hello, Sid. Well you never know. Comme ci comme ca. Oh, really? Yeah, I know. I heard some talk of it a few days ago. Yeah, it sounded like a very good idea. Well, I just got a rough idea of the format, that's all. Well, let me hear it. Maybe I can come up with somebody. Black what? Black magic? Well, it's different – I'll give it that. I see. I see."

Though there is no paperwork to verify the assumption, it has been suggested the character of Julius Moomer was named after Julius Golden of Atlantic/Bernstein Associates, the advertising agency representing Eagle Clothing, who supplied many of the suits Serling wore on-screen. Serling was in contact a number of times with Julius Golden, whenever exchanges between Eagle and Serling were required.

The ridiculous story proposals Moomer pitches to his Gerald Agent are the same Art Carney pitched to his agent in "The Velvet Alley," a teleplay scripted by Rod Serling and telecast on *Playhouse 90* on January 22, 1959. Among the program proposals was a guardian angel series much like "Mr. Bevis" and "Cavender is Coming."

In the final episode of *The Sopranos*, titled "Made in America," initially telecast June 10, 2007, a scene from this episode can be glimpsed on the television screen in the Soprano living room.

SUMMER RERUNS

May 30, 1963	**Repeat** "Jess-Belle"
June 6, 1963	**Repeat** "The Mute"
June 13, 1963	**Repeat** "Valley of the Shadow"
June 27, 1963	**Repeat** "Printer's Devil"
July 4, 1963	**Repeat** "The Incredible World of Horace Ford"
July 11, 1963	**Repeat** "The New Exhibit"
July 18, 1963	**Repeat** "In His Image"
July 25, 1963	**Repeat** "I Dream of Genie"
August 1, 1963	**Repeat** "He's Alive"
August 8, 1963	**Repeat** "Passage on the Lady Anne"
August 15, 1963	**Repeat** "Death Ship"
August 22, 1963	**Repeat** "The Bard"
August 29, 1963	**Repeat** "Of Late I Think of Cliffordville"
September 5, 1963	**Repeat** "On Thursday We Leave for Home"
September 12, 1963	**Repeat** "Printer's Devil"
September 19, 1963	**Repeat** "The Thirty Fathom Grave" *

The Twilight Zone was not telecast on the evening of June 20, 1963. Instead, CBS offered "Shakespeare in the Park: Antony and Cleopatra." This special two-and-a-half hour broadcast of a New York Shakespeare production starred Colleen Dewhurst, Michael Higgins and Ramon Bieri. Performed at Central Park's Delacorte Theatre, it was presented by the WCBS-TV Public Affairs Department, in cooperation with the New York Shakespeare Festival and the City of New York. According to seven rerun schedules dated from March 26 to July 15, 1963, "No Time Like the Past" was originally slated for telecast on this date.

---

* This particular telecast varied from the other hour-long summer reruns. Instead of a preview for next week's presentation, it now featured a one-minute trailer previewing the new season of half-hour shows which began Friday, September 27.

FIFTH SEASON PRODUCTION COSTS

Secretary's Salary: $835.00
Guild Pension Plan: $17,049.72
Messenger Service: $320.35
Other Taxes – Unsecured Property: $14,789.60
Total of all Abandoned Literary Properties: $12,290.00 (all according to May 31, 1964 report)

Unit Manager's Salary: $6,465.00
Office Supplies and Expense: $3,134.75
Payroll Taxes, etc.: $20,841.63

According to the October 31, 1963 production files, the total preproduction and unallocated costs were $50,955.36. Adding these costs and the unassigned literary properties (totaling $3,625.00), the costs of production for each episode, the total cost to produce the first 25 episodes from the fifth and final season (including the $278.20 for the un-produced "What the Devil?" and $326.55 for the un-produced "The Doll") totaled $1,353,757.20.

According to the May 31, 1964 production files, the total preproduction and unallocated costs was $77,672.64. Adding the preproduction and unallocated costs, and the costs of production for each episode, the total cost to produce the 36 episodes from the fifth and final season (including the $420.47 for the un-produced "The Doll," $85.33 for "Many, Many Monkeys" and the $343.30 for "What the Devil?") totaled $2,109,974.71.

Unless noted otherwise, all summary of production costs listed for fifth season episodes are according to production files dated May 31, 1964.

Production #2607 "IN PRAISE OF PIP" (Initial telecast: September 27, 1963)
Copyright Registration: © Cayuga Productions, Inc., September 19, 1963, LP27129
Date of Rehearsal: June 18, 1963
Dates of Filming: June 19, 20, 21 and 24, 1963
Script dated: May 6, 1963 with revised pages dated May 10, 12, 16, 17 and 20, 1963.
Revised script dated: June 17, 1963

Producer and Secretary: $1,626.02
Director: $1,750.00

Story and Secretary: $3,310.00
Cast: $8,504.99

Unit Manager and Secretary: $726.01
Agents Commission: $2,500.00
Below the line charges (M-G-M): $45,517.43
Total Production Costs: $71,354.72

Production Fee: $1,800.00
Legal and Accounting: $250.00
Below the line charges (other): $5,370.27

Cast: Bobby Diamond (Pip, Army Private); Ross Elliott (the doctor); Connie Gilchrist (Mrs. Feeny); Gerald Gordon (the lieutenant); Russell Horton (George Reynold); Jack Klugman (Max Phillips); S. John Launer (Moran); Kreg Martin (the gunman, a.k.a. the torpedo); Bob McCord (shooting gallery operator); Billy Mumy (young Pip); and Stuart Nisbet (the surgeon).

Original Music Score Composed by Rene Garriguenc and Conducted by Lud Gluskin (Score No. CPN6099): Etrange #3 (by Marius Constant, :09); Milieu #2 (by Constant, :21); Viet Nam (:51); Good Intentions (1:04); The Mirror (:22); Transition – Pip (:19); Franz Schubert Medley (by Franz Schubert, 1:10); The Fight – Pip (:26); The Gate Opens (:31); Pip (:45); Montage – Pip (2:34); House of Mirrors (:26); Pip Leaves (1:03); Max Dies (:35); Die Fledermaus (by Johann Strauss (:45); Pip Remembers (:40); and Milieu #2 (by Constant, arr. by Herrmann, :21).

Director of Photography: George T.
    Clemens, a.s.c.
Art Directors: George W. Davis and
    Walter Holscher
Set Decorations: Henry Grace and
    Robert R. Benton
Sound: Franklin Milton and Philip N. Mitchell

Production Manager: Ralph W. Nelson
Film Editor: Thomas W. Scott
Casting: Patricia Rose
Assistant Director: Charles Bonniwell, Jr.
Produced by Bert Granet
Directed by Joseph M. Newman
Teleplay by Rod Serling

"Submitted for your approval, one Max Phillips – a slightly-the-worst-for-wear maker of book . . . whose life has been as drab and undistinguished as a bundle of dirty clothes. And though it's very late in his day – he has an errant wish that the rest of his life might be sent out to a laundry to come back shiny and clean; this to be a gift of love to a son named Pip. Mr. Max Phillips, homo-sapien, who is soon to discover that man is not as wise as he thinks – said lesson to be learned in . . . the Twilight Zone."

Production Schedule at M-G-M and on Location
Day 1 –   Interior of Max's Bedroom (Stage 19)
           Exterior of Pacific Ocean Park (on location)
Day 2 –   Interior of Hospital and Operating Room (Stage 7)
           Interior of Max's Bedroom (Stage 19)
           Exterior of Pacific Ocean Park (on location)
Day 3 –   Exterior of the Midway and the House of Mirrors (Stage 19)
           Black Velvet Shots and Interior of Max's Bedroom (Stage 19)
Day 4 –   Interior of Moran Hotel Room (Stage 19)

Plot: Max Phillips, a small-time bookie, receives a telegram from the Army reporting the critical wounding of his son, Pip, presently serving overseas. Remorseful for the way he raised his son in a bad environment, defies his boss in an attempt to save the life of a young man about to enter the same profession. Wounded from a bullet in the chest, Max wanders into a midway where he fondly spent time with his son and envisions an hour with his son Pip – now 10 years old – riding the merry-go-round, eating cotton candy, and playing cat and mouse in the hall of mirrors. When the hour expires, young Pip explains he's dying and needs to go back – having granted Max the opportunity to revisit the past. In desperation, Max pleads with God to take his life in place of his son and then collapses. Days later, Pip, who has recovered, visits the midway recalling the fondness he had for his father.

"Very little comment here, save for this small aside. That the ties of flesh are deep and strong; that the capacity to love is a vital, rich, and all-consuming function of the human animal. (a pause) *And that you can find nobility and sacrifice and love wherever you may seek it out. Down the block . . . in the heart . . . or . . . in the Twilight Zone."*

Trivia, etc. This was not Rod Serling's first exploration into a war drama that offered hope for a wounded soldier. On December 24, 1950, Serling's radio script, "Choose One Gift," was broadcast over radio station WLW in Ohio. The holiday story concerned a soldier named Rierden, who suffered life-threatening wounds while stationed overseas during the Korean War. The doctors and nurses do not have much hope for the soldier, but their primary concern is the number of wounded that continues to grow every day. Their emotions are stretched to the breaking point, and they pray to God for relief. Towards the end of the drama, it appears a little Divine intervention prevails as the wounded soldier recovers and brings them a most welcome gift for Christmas – the gift of hope.

On May 8, 1963, Patricia Rose, casting director for *Twilight Zone*, submitted this script to William McCaffrey, an agent representing Art Carney, proposing he play the role of "Max Phillips." The top salary on *Twilight Zone* by this time was $3,500 for an actor or actress playing the lead, and it was offered to Carney with the usual Favorite Nations Clause and sole star billing, including residuals for reruns. "'In Praise of Pip' is a favorite script of Rod Serling," Rose wrote in her letter, "who would love to have Mr. Carney play the role." Carney was unable to commit, so the role was offered to Jack Klugman.

An actor named Paul Geary was interviewed for the role of George in this episode. He did not get the part (Russell Horton did), but Geary was so intrigued by the script that he asked for permission to use it in the Richard Boone Workshop. The private workshop was for actors wanting to experiment with "method acting" and other forms of acting, and was not available for public or commercial viewing. Permission was granted.

All of the exterior scenes of the park were filmed on location at Pacific Ocean Park in Santa Monica, California. To film on location cost Cayuga $1,500, plus permit fees. All of the scenes that take place at the midway, including the interior of the House of Mirrors, were filmed on Stage 19 at M-G-M. The cost to recreate the House of Mirrors was $850. (The most expensive set was Moran's hotel room, $954.) *

---

* Pacific Ocean Park was the same place George Clayton Johnson and Charles Beaumont would visit repeatedly to ride the bumper cars and slam hell out of each other.

Jack Klugman in between takes
for "In Praise of Pip."

Serling originally intended to use one the following two trailers. Unsure at the time of composition if this was going to be the opening presentation of the season or not, it was decided that one of them had to be recorded anyway, for the sake of reruns.

"Next week on the Twilight Zone a very special outing with an actor of consummate skill named Jack Klugman. It's a change of pace. A change of scene. And it's a story with a somewhat haunting quality. On the Twilight Zone next week . . . 'In Praise of Pip.'"

"Next on the Twilight Zone, a rather special excursion into an area full of cotton candy, roller coasters, and that brief and incredible moment known as growing up. It stars one of the most versatile and skilled actors on the American scene – Mr. Jack Klugman – and it is perhaps one of the most moving episodes to come down that shadowy pike where we generally do our walking. Submitted for your approval next time – 'In Praise of Pip' on . . . the Twilight Zone."

On Tuesday, May 28, 1963, Serling reported to Stage 21 at M-G-M Studios around 8 a.m. for filming of the teasers, trailers and promos for some of the fifth-season episodes that were already in the can, including "Steel," "The Last Night of a Jockey," and "In Praise of Pip." As Serling was undecided which of the last two would be the season opener, of two separate one-minute promos were filmed:

Promo #1 *"Next week, Twilight Zone begins its fifth season on the air, continuing an itinerary of imaginative story-telling. We'll investigate all the nooks and all the crannies of man's imagination. So, if you're a science fiction buff or simply someone who likes to pack up reality and shove it under a bed on occasion – I think we're for you. For our first show we enlist the aid of a fine performer named Jack Klugman and a charming little guy named Billy Mumy, and bring you a story that is perhaps one of the most intriguing and one of the gentlest we've ever done in the Twilight Zone. It's called 'In Praise of Pip.' From all of us on Twilight Zone to all of you – we're delighted to be back. We hope to please, to entertain, to intrigue. We'll probably leave as many questions as we leave answers – but this is the nature of the Twilight Zone and the things it talks about. First stop on that strange itinerary – 'In Praise of Pip'."*

Promo #2 *"Next week, Twilight Zone begins its fifth season on the air, continuing an itinerary of imaginative story-telling. We'll investigate all the nooks and all the crannies of man's imagination. So, if you're a science fiction buff or simply someone who likes to pack up reality and shove it under a bed on occasion – I think we're for you. For our first show we enlist the aid of the most versatile and certainly one of the most talented ever to trod a board or fill up a camera lens. A little giant named . . . Mickey Rooney. He appears in one of the most intriguing tales we've ever told on the Twilight Zone. It's called 'The Last Night of a Jockey.' From all of us on Twilight Zone to all of you – we're delighted to be back. We hope to please, to entertain, to intrigue. We'll probably leave as many questions as we leave answers – but this is the nature of the Twilight Zone and the things it talks about. First stop on that strange itinerary – 'The Last Night of a Jockey.'"*

In early July 1963, Serling was leaning toward featuring "In Praise of Pip" as the first episode of the season.

Serling was on the set during the second and fourth days of filming, so his onscreen introduction was filmed on Stage 7 on the second day, and additional scenes on Stage 19 on the final day. These scenes, however, were never used. He visited the West Coast on the first full week of September to oversee the production of other half-hour episodes, conduct meetings with staff, and be filmed for the teasers, trailers and narration for "The Last Night of Jockey" and "Living Doll." Since it was decided in mid-August that "In Praise of Pip" was going to be the season opener, the one-minute trailer for the opening of the season did not have to be re-shot. Serling's promos were necessary by no later than September 5 or September 6 so the films could be cut in, dubbed and shipped to meet the Canadian station air dates which preceded the U.S. network airings. Bill Froug rewrote the teaser material for the "Living Doll" so that the film would fit the required length.

A press release sent out to periodicals responsible for television listings, described the episode as: "There's enough action, a good visual bit in a fun house with mirrors, and Jack Klugman's performance as a bookie (he really looks like one), to please *Twilight Zone* fans." When this episode was rerun on July 3, 1964, the television critic for *The New York Oneonta Star*, commented in his column that this was "worth a second look."

The opening scene featured a schoolhouse that has been converted into a hospital for wounded patients brought in for treatment. The set decoration costs for the "converted schoolhouse" was $325, though it isn't established in the scene that the hospital was a converted schoolhouse.

While the doctor comments that "Pip" was an odd name, Serling once again borrowed the name from a Charles Dickens novel. Serling's original script had Pip serving in Laos. The network corrected him, noting that there were no American soldiers stationed in Laos and suggesting Vietnam as an alternative. (There is a more explicit reference to Vietnam in "I Am the Night – Color Me Black.") The opening images of the Green Beret captain and the wounded son are probably the first fictional depiction of the United States Army Special Forces in popular culture. The script called for the legend "Vietnam – The Present" shot over the opening scene, but "Vietnam" was all that appears on the screen.

This *Twilight Zone* presentation contains what is probably the first reference to a Vietnam War casualty on an American dramatic program. *Variety* was quick to comment, "Penned by Rod Serling, it was slick without too much depth, sentimental without true emotion ringing out, violent, as a peg rather than a necessary element ..."

"The performers were excellent," *Variety* continued. "Jack Klugman, as the focal point, the smalltime bookie who makes a fantasy pact with God, carried more conviction to the role than called for in the script. Connie Gilchrist, in a bit part, was moving as the landlady with the heart of gold. Billy Mumy as young Pip had the quality to make the viewer choke up, as he plays with his father Klugman, one of whom is about to die. For all that, when the half-hour was ended, the viewer felt he was fed a pat tale, an affliction which bothers the short stories of O. Henry today despite their style and sentiment."

Production #2602 "STEEL" (Initial telecast: October 4, 1963)

© Cayuga Productions, Inc., September 26, 1963, LP27860
Dates of Rehearsals: May 23 and 24, 1963
Dates of Filming: May 27, 28 and 29, 1963
Script dated: April 16, 1963, with revised pages dated May 3, 1963.
Revised script dated: May 20, 1963

Producer and Secretary: $1,626.02
Director: $1,500.00
Unit Manager and Secretary: $726.01
Agents Commission: $2,500.00
Below the line charges (M-G-M): $31,157.06
Total Production Costs: $54,702.87

Story and Secretary: $2,410.00
Cast: $7,307.34
Production Fee: $1,800.00
Legal and Accounting: $250.00
Below the line charges (other): $5,426.44

Cast: Jimmy Ames (the announcer); Larry Barton (voice in the crowd); Slim Bergman (man in crowd); Merritt Bohn (Nolan, the local promoter); Lou Cavalier (man in crowd); Chuck Hicks (Maynard Flash); Frank London (Maxwell); Joe Mantell (Pole); Lee Marvin (Steel Kelly); Tipp McClure (Battling Maxo); Bob McCord (Maynard Flash's handler); Bob Peterson (voice in the crowd); and Edwin Rochelle (voice in the crowd).

Original Music Score Composed and Conducted by Nathan Van Cleave (Score No. CPN6095): Etrange #3 (by Marius Constant, :09); Milieu #2 (by Constant, :21); The Arrival (1:23); Sports Item (1:03); Silent Arena (:44); Yes-Sir, Sir (:28); Test Run (1:07); Go for Broke (1:39); The Resolve (:12); To the Test (:42); Meet the B7 (:39); Now the Bread (1:40); Resurgent Spirit (1:15); and Milieu #2 (by Constant, arr. by Herrmann, :21).

Director of Photography: George T.
    Clemens, a.s.c.
Art Directors: George W. Davis and
    Walter Holscher
Set Decorations: Henry Grace and
    Robert R. Benton
Sound: Franklin Milton and Philip N. Mitchell

Production Manager: Ralph W. Nelson
Film Editor: Thomas W. Scott
Casting: Patricia Rose
Makeup: William Tuttle
Assistant Director: Charles Bonniwell, Jr.
Produced by Bert Granet
Directed by Don Weis

Teleplay by Richard Matheson, based on his short story of the same name, originally published in the May 1956 issue of *The Magazine of Fantasy and Science Fiction.*

"Sports item, circa 1974: Battling Maxo, B2, heavyweight, accompanied by his manager and handler, arrives in Maynard, Kansas, for a scheduled six-round bout. Battling Maxo is a robot, or to be exact, an android. Definition: 'an automaton resembling a human being.' Only these automatons have been permitted in the ring since prizefighting was legally abolished in 1968. This is the story of that scheduled six-round bout, more specifically the story of two men shortly to face that remorseless truth: that no law can be passed which will abolish cruelty or desperate need – nor, for that matter, blind animal courage. Location for the facing of said truth a small, smoke-filled arena just this side . . . of the Twilight Zone."

Set Decoration Production Costs
Interior of the Café $686
Interior Corridor of the Arena $1,693
Interior of the Ring and the Arena
    (including 5 neon signs) $625
Total $3,004

Plot: In the near future, robots have replaced human beings in the professional prizefight ring. Steel Kelly and Pole, owners and managers of the Battling Maxo, an outdated model, have arranged for a fight against one of the newer models. Intending to pay for updated parts and repairs if they can pull through the next fight, they attempt to force their machine against a superior one. When the model breaks down due to a technical glitch, Kelly and Pole find themselves in a tough position. Their solution? Steel Kelly takes the place of the robot, hoping no one will catch on to the ruse. In an effort to prove his superiority to a machine that once replaced him in the ring, Steel takes the beatings and the audience cries for blood. Before the first round is over, Steel lies helpless on the ground and the winner is proclaimed. While Pole takes Steel back to the locker room, the audience shouts names at the "robot," unaware that the weak structure has more animal courage than they think. Pole fetches the money – half of it for a one-rounder – and Steel, picking up from where they left off, starts to figure out what repairs can be made to the robot.

"Portrait of a losing side. Proof positive that you can't out-punch machinery. Proof, also, of something else. That no matter what the future brings, man's capacity to rise to the occasion will remain unaltered; his potential for tenacity and optimism continues, as always, to out-fight, out-point and out-live any and all changes made by his society. For which three cheers and a unanimous decision – rendered from the Twilight Zone."

Trailer: *"Next on Twilight Zone we dabble into the manly arts with a show called 'Steel' written especially for us by Richard Matheson. This one isn't just for prize fighting buffs – because the story is above and beyond anything remotely involving the Marquis of Queensbury. Rather, it's a tender, touching, and tough analysis of some very bizarre people. Lee Marvin and Joe Mantell take a walk in the Twilight Zone next in 'Steel.'"*

Trivia, etc. The September 13, 1963 issue of *The Stroudsburg Daily Record* reported *"Twilight Zone,* returning to its original half-hour format, opens its fifth season with Lee Marvin starring in 'Steel,' story of a manager of a prizefighting robot that breaks down just before an important bout." If this information is correct (and would have originated from a press release issued from the CBS Television Network), this episode was at one time intended to be the season opener, instead of "In Praise of Pip." How the newspaper made the error remains unknown, but either the newspaper made a mistake, or it never received the official notice from the CBS Press Department.

In an early draft of the script, Matheson dated the episode a century earlier in Serling's opening narration, which was lengthier than what was used for the episode:

"Battling Maxo is a robot – or to be exact, an android. Definition: An automation resembling a human being. Only these automatons have been permitted in the ring since prize fighting was legally abolished in 1968. This is the story of that scheduled ten-round bout. More specifically, the story of two men shortly to face the remorseless truth that no law can be passed which will abolish cruelty or desperate need – nor, for that matter, blind, animal courage. Location for the facing of said truth: a small, smoke-filled arena just this side of the Twilight Zone."

Pre-production began on May 21, when Tipp McClure reported to the makeup and costume department for fittings and mask molds so he could be transformed into the Battling Maxo. He also visited the prop shop for measurements and fittings.

The entire episode was filmed on Stage 21 at M-G-M, except for the exterior of Maynard Street, the scene involving the removal of the robot fighter from the bus, which was on Lot 2. Serling's trailer was shot on the second day as he visited the set to check out how production was coming along.

A professional welterweight boxer named Johnny Indrisano was hired to rehearse with the actors and instruct players how to fight – or at the very least, give the appearance of a fight. Indrisano held the claim to fame of defeating champions Lou Brouillard and Jackie Fields in the ring, but never received a title shot. He retired with a record of 37 wins (with only two KOs), and nine defeats. After his retirement, Indrisano had a successful career as a referee, stunt man and bit-part actor in numerous motion pictures, including *Some Like It Hot* (1959) and *Guys and Dolls* (1955).

A former bodyguard for Mae West, Indrisano later turned his Hollywood career to a boxing coach for movie actors and advisor on films featuring boxing scenes. Among the stars he trained were Mickey Rooney, Cary Grant, Spencer Tracy, John Garfield, Robert Ryan, Robert Taylor, Ricardo Montalban, William Lundigan and Jimmy Durante. In 1953, he appeared on the television series *You Asked For It*, where he portrayed champion boxer John L. Sullivan for a recreation of the Sullivan/La Savant fight in Paris. Indrisano appeared as a referee on two television broadcasts: in the episode "The Champ," on *The Rebel*, and in the episode "The Last Round" on *One Step Beyond*.

"I knew Lee Marvin for a long time and he was a real man and a great guy," recalled Chuck Hicks. "During the fight scenes while filming, we were both fighting the plastic that covered our faces. The eyes were getting fogged up and it was hard to see. I ended up hitting Lee a couple of times, but the tough Marine that he was never complained. He always would say, 'Don't worry about it Chuck, I know your problem.' Yeah, he was a drinker, but a real great man underneath that plastic and skin."

In the September 1981 issue of *The Twilight Zone Magazine*, Richard Matheson recounted how he attended the script reading and afterwards as the cast gathered for rehearsals, he watched Lee Marvin attempt to get emotionally into the story by reproducing crowd noises and traffic sounds on the newly constructed set.

On June 5, 1963, insert shots were filmed of the electronic box that would be attached to the back of the mechanical boxer. A still shot of the tool case and boxing gloves for the closing titles was also filmed on the same day. The music scores were dubbed on July 24, finishing the majority of the production.

The television critic for *The Tucson Daily Citizen* reviewed this episode as a "provocatively novel plot that counters unbelievability with a sensible alternative to bloodshed." *The Lima News* called this "a farfetched script, which would get a poor review from any sports writer worth his salt."

Production #2605 "NIGHTMARE AT 20,000 FEET"
(Initial telecast: October 11, 1963)
© Cayuga Productions, Inc., October 4, 1963, LP27130
Dates of Filming: July 12 through 16, 1963
Script dated: April 25, 1963

Producer and Secretary: $1,626.02	Story and Secretary: $2,660.00
Director: $1,375.00	Cast: $9,770.08
Unit Manager and Secretary: $726.01	Production Fee: $1,800.00
Agents Commission: $2,500.00	Legal and Accounting: $250.00
Below the line charges (M-G-M): $55,813.23	Below the line charges (other): $3,374.82
Total Production Costs: $79,895.16	

Cast: Dave Armstrong (police officer); Slim Bergman (a passenger); Nick Cravat (the gremlin); Extelle Ettere (a passenger); Madeline Finochio (a passenger); Ed Haskett (a passenger); Hath Howard (a passenger); Edward Kemmer (the copilot); Asa Maynor (the stewardess); Bob McCord (a passenger); Beryl McCutcheon (a passenger); Jean Olson (a passenger); William Shatner (Bob Wilson); and Christine White (Ruth Wilson).

Stock Music Cues: Etrange #3 (by Marius Constant, :09); Milieu #2 (by Constant, :21); Onslaught (by Fred Steiner, :35); The Station (by Bernard Herrmann, :07 and :07); Struggle (by Steiner, :36); Moat Farm Murder (by Herrmann, :31); Goodbye Keith (by William Lava, :06); Moat Farm Murder (by Herrmann, :04); Second Vision (by Steiner, :21); Puzzles (by Steiner, :46); Forboding Preamble (by Lyn Murray, :11); Moat Farm Murder (by Herrmann, :16); Struggle (by Steiner, :36); Goodbye Keith (by Lava, :06); The Sun (by Herrmann, 1:04); Moat Farm Murder (by Herrmann, :21 and :32); The Station (by Herrmann, :47); Dead Phones (by Steiner, :18); Moat Farm Murder (by Herrmann, :29 and :19); Ford's Theater (by Jerry Goldsmith, :17); Moat Farm Murder (by Herrmann, :16); Goodbye Keith (by Lava, :06); Dirge (by Goldsmith, :14); Now We Move (by Nathan Van Cleave, :17); A Story #1 (by Constant, :03); Magdalena Curtain (by Murray, :05); and Milieu #2 (by Constant, arr. by Herrmann, :21).

William Shatner in "Nightmare at 20,000 Feet"

Director of Photography: Robert W.
   Pittack, a.s.c.
Art Directors: George W. Davis and
   Walter Holscher
Set Decorations: Henry Grace and
   Robert R. Benton
Sound: Franklin Milton and Philip N. Mitchell

Production Manager: Ralph W. Nelson
Film Editor: Thomas W. Scott
Casting: Patricia Rose
Makeup: William Tuttle
Assistant Director: Charles Bonniwell, Jr.
Produced by Bert Granet
Directed by Richard Donner

Teleplay by Richard Matheson, based on his short story of the same name, originally published in *Alone at Night* (Ballantine Books, 1962, edited by M. and D. Congdon).

"Portrait of a frightened man: Mr. Robert Wilson, thirty-seven, husband, father, and salesman on sick leave. Mr. Wilson has just been discharged from a sanitarium where he spent the last six months recovering from a nervous breakdown, the onset of which took place on an evening not dissimilar to this one ... on an airliner very much like the one in which Mr. Wilson is about to be flown home ... the difference being that, on that evening half a year ago, Mr. Wilson's flight was terminated by the onslaught of his mental breakdown. Tonight, he's traveling all the way to his appointed destination – which, contrary to Mr. Wilson's plan – happens to be in the darkest corner ... of the Twilight Zone."

Plot: Robert Wilson, accompanied by his wife, Ruth, is flying back home one evening, having been released from a sanitarium for a severe case of nerves. Flying through a storm, Robert suddenly notices what appears to be a man on the wing of the aircraft. Regardless of the warnings, neither his wife, the steward-ess or the copilot believe him. Robert's problem grows when he realizes that it wasn't a man outside – but a gremlin – and witnesses the creature tampering with one of the plane's engines. Robert insists he is not having another nervous breakdown, but his wife gives him a pill to ease his nerves, hoping he will sleep peacefully until the plane lands safely. Minutes later, after his wife and everyone else on board falls asleep, he spits out the pill and sneaks down the aisle to secure a gun from an armed officer. Tightening his seat belt, he opens the emergency glass and amongst the chaos and screams of the passengers, Robert man-ages to shoot the gremlin off the wing. Back on the ground, Robert is taken away in a straitjacket . . . but content with the knowledge that he will soon be released when the inspectors find evidence that proves the engine plate was tampered with.

"The flight of Mr. Wilson has ended now. A flight not only from point A to point B, but also from the fear of recurring mental breakdown. Mr. Wilson has that fear no longer, though, for the moment, he is, as he said, alone in this assurance. Happily, his conviction will not remain isolated too much longer . . . for happily, tangible manifestation is very often left as evidence of trespass, even from so intangible a quarter . . . as the Twilight Zone."

Trivia, etc. The wing section was secured by M-G-M from a plane that was being taken out of ser-vice. The transport of the plane wing from Douglas Aircraft in Santa Monica to M-G-M Studios was $435. The exterior airline set cost $1,650, while full-size effects set construction cost $1,441. An eight-blade Ritter wind machine, the same kind used for the *Twilight Zone* episode "The 7th is Made Up of Phantoms," cost Cayuga $180 in rental fees. Three extra special effects men were required to operate the machine and the gremlin's wires, costing a total of $716 in employment costs. With ad-ditional costs involved, the exterior of the airliner cost a total of $4,800.

On July 8, 1963, Nick Cravat visited the Cayuga office to discuss the role he would play in this epi-sode. After a full understanding of what he would be subjected to, high winds, water splashing on him, makeup on the face, and so on, he then went to wardrobe for a fitting and then to the makeup department so a preliminary mask could be made for the facial features. Before the day was over, Cravat visited Ralph Swartz regarding fittings for the wires, which would be used to keep him suspended on the plane wing.

Nick Cravat was hired for the role of the gremlin because of his past expertise as an acrobatic circus performer (who once partnered with actor Burt Lancaster, performing as "Lang and Cravat"). His athletic prowess helped meet the physical demands of the role.

Actress Christine White, who had appeared in "The Prime Mover," also played the role of Abi-gail Adams in *Ichabod and Me*, a short-run television comedy for which Serling had written a script. He and White remained friends for a number of years, and it was through their friendship that he arranged for her casting in this episode.

Matheson had wished that William Shatner and Pat Breslin, the same couple from "Nick of Time," would play the leads, as he envisioned the two when he wrote the script. On July 11, Wil-liam Shatner went to wardrobe before joining Christine White for a script reading. On the evening of that same day, Ralph W. Nelson wrote to Rod Serling, explaining that this episode "is rehearsing today and testing all of the effects in the airplane set. This set certainly looks like it will work out very, very well. Dick Donner is directing it."

"I got the job directing 'Nightmare' because I was doing a lot of television shows for M-G-M at that time," recalled Richard Donner in a phone interview. "I remember the initial sit-down with the producer and we discussed how this was going to be put together. We had rain hitting the actor in the gremlin suit, wind, and lightning. That was one of those moments I realized I had something material to make out of a simple television script. I recall we ran behind by the evening of the last day, so we kept filming all through the night. Someone needed to use the set the next day so we could not have possibly returned to finish the job the next day."

The entire episode was filmed on Stage 14 at M-G-M Studios. "Someone must have complained about the long hours," Donner continued, "because I almost lot my job there. After they viewed the rough cut, Bill Froug, I think he was responsible for making the studio heads change their minds, but Bill let me keep my job and assigned me a few more [episodes]."

All of the extras in this episode, the passengers on board the plane, were hired for scale – and informed in advance to bring topcoats and hats. "All should be smartly dressed for traveling aboard a modern airliner," they were instructed. According to CBS policy, one Negro was hired to play the role of a sailor on board the plane.

"[William Shatner] was a great nut. We were always putting each other on and having the time of our lives," Donner revealed in an interview with Robert Martin for the July 1981 issue of *The Twilight Zone Magazine*. "On that last night of shooting, he was visited on the set by Edd Byrnes, 'Kookie' from *77 Sunset Strip*. We were all exhausted – it was quite late – and when my back was turned, Shatner and Byrnes decided to stage a fight. I happened to look up at the wing of the airplane and saw this fight going on. I started running over, of course, and just when I got there I saw Byrnes hit Shatner, who went over the wing of the airplane, down forty feet to the [water] tank below! What I didn't know was that they had dressed a dummy in Shatner's clothes. All I could think at the time was, screw Shatner, now I have to re-shoot this whole thing! But Shatner is a wonderful guy. I enjoyed working with him tremendously."

After filming was completed, the wing section was stored by M-G-M, according to an interoffice memo: "as per Maj. Alberts of Air Force, Hollywood Office."

Much of the music for this episode was lifted from Bernard Herrmann's music score from the premiere episode, "Where is Everybody?" while some small segments were lifted from Fred Steiner's music score for "King Nine Will Not Return," another episode involving an airplane.

The Tucson Daily Citizen reviewed this episode as "the only redeeming quality of this farfetched half-hour is the acting of William Shatner, as the only passenger in a plane who can see an inhuman creature tampering with the engine."

This was one of three episodes to be remade for *Twilight Zone – The Movie* (1983). Richard Matheson recalled to interviewer Tom Weaver: "In my story, and in the original *Twilight Zone* episode, the guy had had a mental breakdown, but George Miller thought to make it just a guy who was afraid of flying. I can't say that I liked the characterization, but I must admit that John Lithgow was marvelous – I mean, to start out at 99 percent of hysteria and build from that is a little difficult, but he somehow managed to do it! Visually that episode was marvelous, although a lot of it I didn't care for. And I thought the monster in the movie was much better than in the television show." *

For the movie version, Gregory Peck was originally slated for the role of the nervous passenger,

---

* In the June 1984 issue of *The Twilight Zone Magazine*, Matheson was quoted as saying "I thought the monster on the wing was somewhat ludicrous. It looked rather like a surly teddy bear."

so Matheson wrote the script for the movie in which Peck was like the character he played in *Twelve O'Clock High* (1949), having already been familiar with gremlins. Suddenly, without advance notice, Peck was unavailable and director George Miller decided to go with John Lithgow.

This episode influenced a number of salutes and spoofs including an episode of *The Simpsons* in which Bart witnesses a gremlin outside his bus window. The bus driver, of course, did not see the gremlin every time he humored the young lad's screams. On *The Bernie Mac Show*, Bernie eats a slice of undercooked turkey and suffers his own "nightmare" when he dreams Vanessa is a gremlin on the wing of an airplane. In the motion picture, *Ace Ventura: When Nature Calls* (1995), actor Jim Carrey looks out the window of an airplane and imitating William Shatner, claims he sees something on the wing. Shatner himself made an appearance on *The Muppet Show* when Miss Piggy sees a gremlin on the wing – and Shatner informs her that it's no use – he's been trying to tell people for years. On the television sitcom *3rd Rock from the Sun*, William Shatner makes a guest appearance, arriving at an airport, making reference to having seen something on the wing of the airplane.

The 1979 album, *Extensions*, performed by The Manhattan Transfer, featured two tracks, back to back, titled "Twilight Zone," which reached No. 12 on the Billboard's Disco Chart. That musical number also made reference to this episode and "The Obsolete Man," "The Last Flight" and "Will the Real Martian Please Stand Up?" The 1990 album *Cure for Sanity*, performed by the pop rock group Pop Will Eat Itself, features a song titled "Nightmare at 20,000 Feet."

There are a number of other spoofs and salutes (some of the 1983 motion picture, not the television episode), and there will no doubt be a number of others in the coming years, suggesting this episode remains one that will continue to leave a lasting impression on viewers.

Production #2609 "A KIND OF A STOPWATCH"
(Initial telecast: October 18, 1963)
Copyright Registration: © Cayuga Productions, Inc., October 11, 1963, LP27555
Date of Rehearsal: July 17, 1963
Dates of Filming: July 18, 19 and 22, 1963
First script dated: June 10, 1963, with revised pages dated June 14, 1963.
Second script dated: June 14, 1963 with revised pages dated July 8, 1963.
Third script dated: July 9, 1963
Shooting script dated: July 15, 1963 with revised pages dated July 16, 1963.

Producer and Secretary: $1,626.02
Director: $1,500.00
Unit Manager and Secretary: $726.01
Agents Commission: $2,500.00
Below the line charges (M-G-M): $39,980.22
Total Production Costs: $62,790.10

Story and Secretary: $3,810.00
Cast: $4,917.18
Production Fee: $1,800.00
Legal and Accounting: $250.00
Below the line charges (other): $5,680.67

Cast: Sam Balter (the TV announcer); Leon Belasco (Potts); Ken Drake (a barroom customer); Richard Erdman (Patrick McNulty); Herbie Faye (Joe, the bartender); Ray Kellogg (the attendant); Bob McCord (one of the frozen figures); Roy Roberts (Mr. Cooper); Doris Singleton (the secretary); and Richard Wessel (Charlie, the barroom customer).

Original Music Score Composed and Conducted by Nathan Van Cleave (Score No. CPN6103): Etrange #3 (by Marius Constant, :09); Milieu #2 (by Constant, :21); Biggest Bore on Earth (:38); Heh-Heh-Heh! (:18); You're Fired (:04); The First Time (:29); The First Test (:16); And So To Bed (:30); First Goldfish Event (:05); And So To Rise (:38); Second Goldfish Event (:10); Real Life Montage (:05); Stopwatch Montage (:41); I'll Just Show Him (1:12); Mr. Cooper (:06); I Can Stop Anything (:28); Double Take (:03); Now to Work (:20); Disaster (:59); Tutti Fine (:14); Etrange #3 (by Constant, :09); and Milieu #1 (by Constant, :22).

Director of Photography: Robert
   Pittack, a.s.c.
Art Directors: George W. Davis and
   Walter Holscher
Set Decorations: Henry Grace and
   Robert R. Benton
Sound: Franklin Milton and Philip N. Mitchell

Production Manager: Ralph W. Nelson
Film Editor: Richard Heermance, a.c.e.
Casting: Patricia Rose
Assistant Director: Charles Bonniwell, Jr.
Produced by Bert Granet
Directed by John Rich

Teleplay by Rod Serling, based on an original unpublished short story by Michael D. Rosenthal.

"Submitted for your approval, or at least your analysis – one Patrick Thomas McNulty who at age forty-one is the biggest bore on Earth. He holds a ten-year record for the most meaningless words spewed out during a coffee break. And it's very likely that, as of this moment, he would have gone through life in precisely this manner – a dull, argumentative bigmouth who sets back the art of conversation a thousand years. I say he very likely would have except for something that will soon happen to him. Something that will considerably alter his existence . . . and ours. Now you think about that now . . . because this is – the Twilight Zone."

Plot: Mr. McNulty is the perfect conversation piece . . . unto himself. A constant bore, McNulty's sole purpose in life is to make suggestions for ways to improve the way society lives, but the only success he manages to accomplish is to clear out the patrons from a local bar who tire of his constant chattering. After a year of suggestions, McNulty fails to impress his boss, who promptly fires him for lack of contribution to the company. Late that evening, while McNulty drinks in celebration of his dismissal, he is given an old family heirloom from a drunk – a stopwatch. Playing with the gadget, McNulty soon discovers that the ticker, when pressed, stops time in its tracks. When McNulty fails to get his job back, offering the watch to his boss as an incentive, the former employee uses the gadget for practical jokes. When he tires of the petty exhibition, he gets what is probably the first practical idea in his life – he can use the stopwatch to become wealthy. Drunk with power, McNulty visits a local bank and freezes time to begin robbing the vault with a load of cash. As he attempts to exit the bank, he accidentally drops the stopwatch – which cracks upon impact. Attempting to make amends by clicking the button, the stopwatch fails to work. Fearing that he might lose the one gift that might have given him recognition, McNulty runs through the streets of town, the office of his former employer and the local bar, finding himself trapped in a world frozen in time. A world that fails to notice (or care) about the presence of McNulty and will probably be better off without him.

"Mr. Patrick Thomas McNulty . . . who had a gift of time. He used it . . . and he misused it . . . and now he's just been handed the bill. Tonight's tale of motion . . . and McNulty . . . in the Twilight Zone."

Trailer: *"Next time on the Twilight Zone, we probe into the element of time and present a very oddball opus entitled 'A Kind of a Stopwatch.' We tell the story of a man, a stopwatch, and an incredible deviation from the norm . . . said norm being the usual twenty-four hour day . . . said deviation involving what happens when a stopwatch is pushed, and everything stops, not just time. To titillate and intrigue, 'A Kind of a Stopwatch,' next, on Twilight Zone."*

Trivia, etc. The script for this episode was adapted from an unpublished short story by Jerry McNeely, which in turn was based on an idea by Michael D. Rosenthal. His one-page plot synopsis was proposed to Cayuga Productions through an agency, Bick and Siegel Associates in Beverly Hills. On January 16, 1963, Jerome Siegel sent the five-paragraph plot summary along with the following letter:

Dear Rod,
The one page idea which you see attached is such an arresting one that I am sending it to you directly. It, in its turn, was sent to me by Jerry McNeely, who writes a good many of the *Kildare* shows and whose work on *Studio One* I believe you know. Please let me know what you think.
    And best wishes to you in the coming year.
Sincerely,
Jerome S. Siegel

THE STOP-WATCH
Story idea by Jerry McNeeley, based on an idea by Michael D. Rosenthal.

An ineffectual man purchases a second-hand chronometer because he is always arriving late for work. One of the devices on the chronometer is a stop-watch, the mechanism for which is apparently broken. Accidentally, the man discovers how to make the stop-watch work – and when he punches the button, not only does the hand stop, but time as well. Everything in the world is suspended in frozen animation, except the man himself and objects he touches. When he punches the button again, time resumes.

Frightened at first, gradually he gains confidence in using the device, playing harmless pranks on people who have been unkind to him in the past. For example, he stops time while his boss is in an important conference, goes in and removes his boss' shirt, then starts time again.

He becomes bolder, more self-assertive and, eventually, greedy. He conceives a plan to become wealthy by committing the perfect crime. He will stop time in New York, drive across the country, helping himself to gasoline and food on the way, rob several large California banks, return to New York and start time again. The effect, so far as the California bank is concerned, will be that the money simply vanished before everyone's eyes. And he can never be implicated because he can prove he was in New York all the time.

The plan comes off without a hitch but, during the trip, he becomes terribly upset at the loneliness of being the only moving thing in the world of statues. It preys on his mind, and several times he almost starts his watch just to be able to talk with someone. Therefore he is tremendously relieved to see moving people again when it is over. Soon, however, he is making bigger plans – to take over the world itself. And he sets methodically to the task.

But on the verge of success, he drops his watch and the springs go whanging off in every direction. He looks around, horrified: he is condemned to live permanently in solitude among statues – there is no way he can start time again.

This episode was assigned a production number on June 3, 1963, under the title "The Stop Watch." The title was revised to "A Kind of a Stop Watch" seven days later, according to an M-G-M work order dated June 10, 1963. Weeks before this episode was even assigned a production number, on May 20, 1963, Bert Granet, Ralph W. Nelson and Rod Serling considered a number of filmed stock footages that could be used for this episode. It was suggested that the action be day shots and not evening shots, for clarity purposes. Among the suggestions:

1. Boat shooting rapids	22. Kids jumping rope
2. Oil well gusher	23. Ballet dancer
3. An avalanche	24. Automobile race
4. A ski tow	25. Record in a jukebox
5. Ski jumper after take-off	26. Storm at sea
6. Diver leaving high platform	27. Line of dancing girls
7. Rush hour in the subway	28. Cattle stampede
8. Train around a curve	29. Falling tree – "timber"
9. A golfer swinging	30. Beer drinker
10. Elevator indicator	31. Roller coaster
11. A football game	32. Fire hose splashing
12. A building on fire	33. Twist contest
13. Atom bomb explosion	34. Seaplane landing
14. Freeway traffic	35. Boxing knockout
15. Cavalry charge	36. Circus aerialist
16. Trampoline jumpers	37. Volcano erupting
17. Ferris wheel	38. Seaplane landing
18. Salmon jumping	39. Newspapers printing off the press
19. Square dancing	40. Monkey jumping from tree to tree
20. A large stamp press	41. Movie on TV screen with fast action
21. Building being wrecked	42. Tornado spout traveling across the country

Serling completed the first draft of the script on June 10, 1963. Four days later, he revised it and sent the revision to the usual – sponsor, advertising agency, producer, and of course, Bert Granet, who, on June 25, 1963, wrote Serling regarding a few essential problems he found in the script. "There is a little bit of disappointment around about Stopwatch. I think this primarily stems from the fact that McNulty's characterization, being an absolute bore, gets off to a bad start and an unpleasant teaser." Serling was about to leave for a four-week vacation, so his attempt to complete a number of scripts before the end of the month was hampered by having to revise a number of pages on the spot.

In the earliest draft, Potts (the little man with the stop-watch), hands McNulty the device, but Granet suggested that Potts appear to be a bit of a lush, "and maybe because of McNulty's generosity in buying him a drink, he gives him the watch." The change was made in later drafts of the

Production Schedule at M-G-M

Day 1 –   Interior and Exterior of the Bar (Stage 19)
Day 2 –   Interior and Exterior of Bar and Interior of
                  McNulty's Apartment (Stage 19)
                  Interior and Exterior of Bank (Stage 9)
Day 3 –   Interior Outer Office and Interior of
                  Cooper's Office (Stage 9)

script. One suggestion, however, was not seen eye-to-eye with Serling, "I personally would stress recognition," explained Granet. "I do not think for a moment McNulty would ever part with his stopwatch nor permit it to be mass-manufactured. When they ignore him, naturally he puts the stopwatch to work."

An early draft of this script reveals a different closing narration by Rod Serling:

"Mr. Patrick Thomas McNulty ... who had a gift of time. He used it ... and he misused it ... and now he's just been handed the bill. Mr. Thomas McNulty who now controls the Earth and everything on it. He will eat well ... live well ... and have everything at his beck and call. But the thing he wanted most ... the thing that gave him the most acute hunger ... his desperate need for a sympathetic ear – this he will never have again. Tonight's tale of motion ... and McNulty ... in the Twilight Zone."

On July 12, Ralph W. Nelson had a meeting with John Rich, the director, to verify how various scenes in the script were going to be filmed beginning the week after. The cast was selected that same week and Richard Erdman was hired to play the lead. Erdman was among the cast of the Serling-scripted *Saddle the Wind*. "I never met Rod Serling on the set of *Saddle the Wind* (1958) at M-G-M but we both lived in Pacific Palisades and attended a number of charities," recalled Erdman. "It was a fun script and a frantic shoot. I worked with John Rich many times previous, and he was a last-minute placement – under the condition that I star in the lead because, well, we worked well together. It was so frantic and I had so many lines to remember that I recall we would shoot a scene, we would refer to the script and shoot a few more lines, and then go back to the script again."

A casting call for extras to play the role of bank customers required the actors to arrive at the studio in dress as if they were visiting their own bank. Per CBS policy, one Negro woman bank teller was required at the United Fidelity Bank.

The wild narration of the baseball announcer for the television in the bar scene was recorded separately on August 5. Sam Balter supplied the voice. All of the close-up scenes with McNulty's hand clicking the stopwatch were not part of the principal filming. Two weeks after shooting completed, a stopwatch was rented and Bob McCord, a stand-in for the majority of the *Twilight Zone* episodes, offered a hand (no pun intended) to click the stopwatch a number of times for close-up inserts. The inserts were filmed in August, and the rented stopwatch was returned to its owner late that afternoon, who also rented out the railing and floor used for the bank scenes used during the initial filming.

Some of the photos hanging on the wall in the bar are the same featured in the bar scenes in "What You Need."

On October 29, days after the initial telecast, Roger L. Vernon of Evanston, Illinois, wrote to Serling, (in care of Bantam Books in New York). "The *Twilight Zone* story 'A Kind of Stopwatch' is fantastically like a story in this book of mine. My story is called simply: 'The Stopwatch.' I know that you did not write the story in question for television, a fact that makes me personally happy since I have long admired you and your work. I know of you as a man with a wide reputation for fairness. After consulting with my publishers, they suggest that infringement actions are difficult unless there is a slavish imitation of the total expression." *

On December 30, Rod Serling replied to Roger Vernon, explaining that the list of similarities were not at all unusual considering the very nature of the story. Serling pointed out that if a person was in the process of overtly copying someone else's story, they would not use a similar title but rather go far afield. As to the idea of time stopping, Serling pointed out that he received no less than 20 stories with this as a central theme. "The one I chose and then adapted seemed to be the freshest and cleverest in its approach," he explained.

> **Set Decoration Production Costs**
> Interior of Cooper's Office $1,108
> Interior of McNulty's Apartment $380
> Interior of Joe's Bar $1,215
> Interior of the Bank $515
> Total $3,218

Coincidentally, on January 15, just months before this episode went to film, John Guedel (of John Guedel Productions in Los Angeles) wrote to Serling with two story ideas for the *Twilight Zone* series. His second was similar in notion. "I have a most remarkable wristwatch," Guedel wrote in his letter. "When I set it three hours ahead, I move time three hours ahead. When I set it back, I move time back. There have been a lot of stories about moving time around, but with the ability to continually change it back and forth a few hours one way or the other – it would really upset society. I'm particularly intrigued as to how it would be handled by the greedy (a killing in the stock market), or by the good (Don't drive the car along the road tonight)."

Another letter writer submitted a similar idea in February of 1960, suggesting a modern electronic clock, that records the time, day and year. When he rewound the clock 30 or 40 years, the owner traveled with the clock to that time period. When he moved the day, time and year ahead, he forward in time. When he plugs the clock back into the wall, he returns to his own time. One evening after an argument with his wife, he slams into his room and dials the clock with a vengeance to pre-Tom Edison days, such as possibly the Civil War, and only then discovers that there are no sockets to plug it into – and he is stuck in the past for good.

When this episode was rebroadcast in June of 1964, *The Lima News* commented, "it's well worth watching again just to catch its sardonic ending."

On the episode "Death Becomes Him," on the television sitcom *Wings*, initially telecast October 10, 1995, the character of Brian comes up with a solution to their problem by suggesting they stop time – and comments how he saw it work on *The Twilight Zone*. On another television comedy, *The Simpsons*, the broadcast of November 2, 2003, featured the annual "Treehouse of Horror" presentation, offering a spoof of this *Twilight Zone* episode, titled "Stop the World, I Want to Goof Off." Bart and Milhouse find themselves in possession of a stopwatch with the same non-scientific property. After using the stopwatch to pull a number of practical jokes, they break the watch and find themselves in a world frozen in time. The kids spend the next fifteen years trying to repair the watch, until they finally succeed.

---

* The short story titled "The Stop Watch" in question was one of nine short stories that appeared in Roger Lee Vernon's book, *The Space Frontiers*, published by New American Library in 1955.

Production #2616 "THE LAST NIGHT OF A JOCKEY"
(Initial telecast: October 25, 1963)
© Cayuga Productions, Inc., October 21, 1963, LP27556
Date of rehearsal: August 12, 1963
Dates of Filming: August 13, 14 and 15, 1963
Script dated: June 21, 1963
Second script dated: August 7, 1963 with revised pages August 14, 1963.

Producer and Secretary: $2,126.02	Story and Secretary: $3,310.00
Director: $1,500.00	Cast: $5,975.00
Unit Manager and Secretary: $726.01	Production Fee: $1,800.00
Agents Commission: $2,500.00	Legal and Accounting: $250.00
Below the line charges (M-G-M): $36,396.35	Below the line charges (other): $2,743.83
Total Production Costs: $2,743.83	

Cast: Mickey Rooney (Michael Grady)

Stock Music Cues: Etrange #3 (by Marius Constant, :09); Milieu #2 (by Constant, :21); Missing Pills (by Jerry Goldsmith, :21); Perry Mason Background (by Fred Steiner, :04); Bolie Jackson (by Goldsmith, 1:03); Low Bas Notes (CBS, :02); Missing Pills (by Goldsmith, :21); The Waiting (by Bernard Herrmann, 1:01); Missing Pills (by Goldsmith, :36); Finale "O" (by Constant, :25); The Waiting (by Herrmann, :08 and :13); Finale (by Constant, :11); Trial is On (by Leonard Rosenman, :07); Safecracker (by Wilfred Josephs, :51); The Waiting (by Herrmann, :41 and :54); Aftermath (by D.B. Ray, :47); Finale (by Constant, :26); Low Bass Notes (CBS, :01); and Milieu #2 (by Constant, arr. by Herrmann, :21).

Director of Photography: George T. Clemens, a.s.c.	Production Manager: Ralph W. Nelson
	Film Editor: Thomas W. Scott
Art Directors: George W. Davis and Malcolm Brown	Casting: Patricia Rose
	Assistant Director: Charles Bonniwell, Jr.
Set Decorations: Henry Grace and Robert R. Benton	Sound: Franklin Milton and Joe Edmondson
	Produced by William Froug
Directed by Joseph M. Newman	Teleplay by Rod Serling

"*The name is Grady. Five feet short in stockings and boots; a slightly distorted offshoot of a good breed of humans who race horses. He happens to be one of the rotten apples – bruised and yellowed by dealing in dirt; a short man with a short memory who's forgotten that he's worked for the sport of kings –and helped turn it into a cesspool – used and misused by the two-legged animals who've hung around sporting events since the days of the Coliseum. So this is Grady on his last night as a jockey. Behind him are Hialeah, Hollywood Park and Saratoga. Rounding the far turn and coming up fast on the rail . . . is the Twilight Zone.*"

Plot: Having been suspended for 60 days for rigging a horse race, Grady, a jockey, drinks himself into a stupor in his apartment. He soon finds himself talking to his "alter ego," arguing whether or not his large aspirations were worth the expense. Always wanting to be a big shot, his dream has been to be big – not the half-pint that receives his due when he is on a horse. Having suffered the lowest form of defeat, Grady is granted his wish – he wakes to find himself a foot or two taller. His heart's desire for stature and size fits Grady's approval. Shortly after, he receives a phone call from a lawyer of the racing commission and learns that his suspension has been lifted. But having accepted the new size, he is now too tall to race another horse and finds himself the victim of his own success in another attempt to cheat the system. Out of anger, Grady tears the room apart, begging to be small again – unaware that when he was small, he was great. It was when, as a little man, he won an honest race that he was a giant.

"The name is Grady. Ten feet tall. A slightly distorted offshoot of a good breed of humans who race horses. Unfortunately, for Mr. Grady, he learned too late that you don't measure size with a ruler; you don't figure height with a yardstick; and you never judge a man by how tall he looks in a mirror. The giant is as he does. You can make a pari-mutuel bet on this – win, place or show . . . in or out . . . of the Twilight Zone."

Trailer: *"Next on Twilight Zone, a gentleman of merited talents in a story written especially for him. Mr. Mickey Rooney appears in 'The Last Night of a Jockey.' He plays the role of a diminutive little man screaming for help from the bottom of a barrel. And out of it what he receives is unexpected and quite incredible. On the Twilight Zone, a cast of one – Mr. Mickey Rooney. I hope you'll be able to be with us."*

Trivia, etc. This was not the first time Mickey Rooney carried a one-man performance throughout an entire television drama. An earlier one-man performance by Rooney in "Eddie," an episode of the *Alcoa-Goodyear Theater*, earned him an Emmy nomination in 1958. Rooney had portrayed a bookie desperately trying to raise money to pay off debts so he would not be killed. William Froug, who received a Screen Producers' Guild award for producing "Eddie," was also the producer of this teleplay – a reunion for both men.

Rod Serling was a good and personal friend of Mickey Rooney, and the two knew each other when Rooney played the role of Sammy Hogart in the Serling-scripted, "The Comedian," dramatized on *Playhouse 90*. Months before this episode was filmed, in March of 1963, Serling was instrumental in arranging for Rooney to perform an act on stage at a dinner honoring Steve Allen, sponsored by the American Civil Liberties Union. Serling approached Jim Pollack, who produced the affair, to get in touch with Mickey Rooney for the gala. It was because of his friendship with Rooney and his awareness of the *Alcoa-Goodyear Theater* production that Serling had Rooney in mind when he created this teleplay.

In the earliest draft, the main character was named Brady – not Grady. The name changed with the revision of August 7. Serling often reused the names of fictional characters, and borrowed this name from a radio script he wrote in 1950 for *Stars Over Hollywood*, titled "Grady Everett for the People." The story concerned a politician named Grady Everett, running for office and willing to do anything to accomplish the votes of the populace wanting to see an honest man as governor.

The shooting script for this *Twilight Zone* featured a scene that ended up on the cutting room floor. The voice of a landlord, from behind the door, asks Grady for the rent money that was due, and the ex-jockey promises to make good on his debt by morning. The voice of his "alter ego," overhearing the conversation, then teases Grady about the six-dollar rent, reminding him that was what he used to make in tips. The voice from behind the door was actor Vic Perrin, playing the role of the landlord. Perrin remained on the set for the entire three-day shoot, supplying the off-camera voice of Grady's conscience during both rehearsal and filming. When the finished film was edited for a final cut, Perrin's lines were replaced with Rooney's voice. Sig Frohlich was on hand as a stand-in (a photo double) for Rooney. Rooney and director, Joseph M. Newman, decided to slip an inside-joke in this episode when Grady refers to the man on the phone as "Mr. Newman," instead of the name in the original script, which was Hannicheck.

Filmed entirely on Stage 19 at M-G-M, three separate sets were created to help establish the illusion that Grady had grown in size. Each set contained the interior of Grady's bedroom, each of a different size, with rented furniture for each set, all scaled down to size. The first bedroom cost a total of $300 in the rental of furniture and props. The second bedroom cost $1,000, since much of the furniture had to be custom-built. The third and final bedroom cost $600. To help create the illusion of nighttime, rather than dim down the lights, a dark lining was rented for $240 and draped overhead.

The CBS Program Practices Department in Hollywood received the first draft of the script on June 25, 1963. Thomas W. Downer of the department read the script and on July 3, submitted a two-page request for a number of changes, and detailed the reasons. The first was the opener in which Grady called himself a "dwarf" in the mirror. "Dwarf is an accepted medical term describing a condition that must be harshly cruel to some persons so afflicted," the report explained. "To use it in this sense implies an opprobrium that need not (as your story points out) shadow the life of a person of small stature. Slang words such as half-pint, shrimp, and the like, lacking medical authority, would seem to convey the desired meaning without the offense." Serling made the appropriate changes, so in the finished film, Grady refers to himself as a "runt" and a "shrimp" when looking at himself in the mirror.

When Grady talks to the female over the phone, he refers to her as a "no good alley cat." Originally the words "cheap little alley cat" were in the script, but Serling changed it at Downer's suggestion because the phrase "implies a sexual promiscuity we would prefer go unnoticed." Other suggestions by Downer were to change Grady's reference to God, replacing it with the word "crud" in the middle of one speech; delete the word "pigs" because it was "offensive"; and that the voice not refer to Grady's "gut," suggesting to replace the term with "knot up your insides."

Considered by many fans as a remake of the previous *Twilight Zone* opus, "Nervous Man in a Four Dollar Room," this episode was an excellent example of what Serling meant when he told a reporter a year previous for *The Fresno Bee* that, "Sometimes I think we have tried everything, and there is the danger now that I will be imitative of myself." Even though critics argued that Serling's production line had "consistently remained high and imaginative," he found himself tiring from the chores demanded of him. "Before the show I would tackle writing jobs in a leisurely way. Now if I spend more than five days working out a *Twilight* show, it goes out the window."

Production #2620 "GENTLEMEN, BE SEATED"

In early March of 1963, Charles Beaumont approached Serling with the idea of adapting his short story, *Gentlemen, Be Seated*, originally published in a 1960 issue of *Rogue* magazine. The story takes place in a possible futuristic world where the powers-that-be found a solution to prejudice, war and poverty. Human emotion has been suppressed through scientific means, and police patrol the streets seeking out those who fight against the policy, believing that the suppression of emotion – especially laughter – is a God-given right. An employee named James Kinkaid has a private meeting in the office of his boss, William Biddle, and is shocked to learn that his employer is a member of the secret Society for the Preservation of Laughter (S.P.O.L.). The society members enjoy the comforts of laughing at jokes and slapstick, and as a gesture of good will, Biddle takes Kinkaid to the next meeting at a "laugh-easy" (somewhat akin to a Prohibition-era speakeasy, only where illegal yuks are served, not banned booze).

At the meeting, Kinkaid is subjected to one-liners, jokes, limericks and slapstick, but as much as he tries, laughter does not come easy. Kinkaid suspected the meeting was a test to check his vulnerability and returns home, realizing it was not a test and that he disappointed his boss, who confided in him with a treasonable secret. Returning to work the next day, Kinkaid is determined to laugh for his boss, only causing his termination at the office for displaying public smiles. Kinkaid spends his remaining evenings seeking out the society and fails, suffering a personal damnation having felt the pleasures of laughter in a laughless society.

The plot idea was approved by Rod Serling and Bert Granet, and Beaumont was commissioned to write a script for *The Twilight Zone*. Beaumont quickly did so, and on April 10, 1963, having consulted Granet, addressed a few issues regarding the script. The first was a slow opening that did not emphasize the sobriety of that particular society until much later in the script. "My guess here is that if we were to establish through colloquy between Kinkaid and Biddle that this particular society was a drab, colorless, neutral kind of place and that Kinkaid had a glimmer of a sense of humor and the capacity to enjoy, might be desperately sought after objectives an audience would feel much more toward the ensuing tests that Kinkaid has to undergo," Serling explained.

Serling also suggested the laugh-easy where the slapstick occurs be revised. "I feel, as does Bert, that there should be a step-by-step process of unexpected slapstick accidents not tossed at Kinkaid, but at others. His inability to laugh at a pie in his own face is hardly unique." Serling also suggested the elimination of the Keystone Cops figures that performed at the laugh-easy, explaining how difficult it would be to do on camera, and just leave the slapstick to the members of the club. It was also suggested to let the story take place in a bar, because of the numerous opportunities to generate the slapstick – first with the bar stool crumbling, then seltzer water in the face, perhaps a dribble glass, and a pie coming out of nowhere. Serling, looking to save money and time, knew full well that reproducing a bar was far less expensive than an original laugh-easy, especially since "A Kind of a Stop Watch" was getting ready to go into production and props could be reused.

It is through Kinkaid's inability to laugh at genuine humor that both he and the audience realize that he's a lost soul and a part of a present-day society that has altered him beyond repair. Serling felt the changes would emphasize this dramatic point and add to the poignancy oof the ending – Kincaid going back to the dark street to seek out laughter.

Beaumont made the changes as Serling suggested and submitted a revised script. On July 16, 1963, the episode was assigned a production number (#2620). Because William Froug replaced Bert Granet, the Beaumont script was reviewed, and Froug shelved the script and canceled all plans for production.

Production #2621 "LIVING DOLL" (Initial telecast: November 1, 1963)
© Cayuga Productions, Inc., October 26, 1963, LP27131
Date of Rehearsal: August 16, 1963
Dates of Filming: August 19, 20 and 21, 1963
Script dated: August 14, 1963, with revised pages dated August 15, 1963.

Producer and Secretary: $2,126.02   Story and Secretary: $2,660.00
Director: $1,500.00   Cast: $6,512.50

Telly Savalas takes a break
between filming scenes.

Unit Manager and Secretary: $726.01
Production Fee: $1,800.00
Agents Commission: $2,500.00
Legal and Accounting: $250.00
Below the line charges (M-G-M): $31,002.24
Below the line charges (other): $4,442.48
Total Production Costs: $53,519.25

Cast: June Foray (voice of Talky Tina); Mary LaRoche (Annabelle); Telly Savalas (Erich Streator); and Tracy Stratford (Christie).

Original Music Composed and Conducted by Bernard Herrmann (Score No. CPN6104): Etrange #3 (by Marius Constant, :09); Milieu #2 (by Constant, :21); Tina Arrives (:34); Tina Talks (:29); Eric Throws the Doll (:42); Supper (:14); Tina Talks Again (:43); Tina Threatens (:23); In the Cellar (:58); I'm Going to Kill You (:07); Talking Doll (:12); Tina Disappears (:24); Eric Finds Tina (:43); Destroy Tina (1:31); Indestructible Tina (1:07); Finale (:55); Etrange #3 (by Constant, :09); and Milieu #1 (by Constant, :22).

Director of Photography: Robert
 Pittack, a.s.c.
Art Directors: George W. Davis and
 Malcolm Brown
Set Decorations: Henry Grace and
 Robert R. Benton
Directed by Richard C. Sarafian

Production Manager: Ralph W. Nelson
Film Editor: Richard Heermance, a.c.e.
Casting: Patricia Rose
Assistant Director: Charles Bonniwell, Jr.
Sound: Franklin Milton and Joe Edmondson
Produced by William Froug

Teleplay by Jerry Sohl, based on an original story idea by Charles Beaumont.

"Talky Tina, a doll that does everything, a lifelike creation of plastic and springs and painted smile. To Erich Streator, she is a most unwelcome addition to his household, but without her he'd never enter . . . the Twilight Zone."

Plot: Annabelle buys her daughter, Christie, a department store doll named Talky Tina, much to the disappointment of Christie's stepfather, Erich. Annabelle is unable to bear children with Erich, so he vents blind hatred for his stepdaughter. Confronted with the doll in private, Erich discovers the wind-up toy has a vocabulary all of its own – expressing her dislike for the stepfather. Erich suspects his wife and stepdaughter are playing an elaborate practical joke on him, but soon rules this out when he rationalizes the situation. In a number of attempts to destroy the doll, he discovers his efforts are hopeless, forcing him to dispose of Talky Tina in the garage trash can. When Annabelle starts packing to leave, he finds the only solution to his domestic issues is to return the doll to Christie. Late that evening, after everyone is sound asleep, he wakes to the sound of a windup toy roaming the hallway. Setting out to investigate, he trips over the doll and falls down a flight of stairs. Annabelle cries out to the dead body of Erich and finds the doll lying next to his body. Talky Tina warns Annabelle to be nice to her.

Set Decoration Production Costs
Interior of Garage $500
Interior of Lower Floor $900
Interior of Girl's Bed Room $100
Interior of Annabelle's Bedroom $100
Total $1,600

"Of course we all know dolls can't really talk, and they certainly can't commit murder. But to a child caught in the middle of turmoil and conflict, a doll can become many things: friend, defender, guardian. Especially a doll like Talky Tina who did talk and did commit murder, in the misty region of . . . the Twilight Zone."

Trailer: *"Next on Twilight Zone, a show that might very aptly be called 'the living end,' and with comparable aptness is called 'Living Doll.' It's written by colleague and cohort Charles Beaumont, and stars Telly Savalas and co-stars Mary Lou Roche. Mr. Beaumont supplies us with a little world involving a man and a doll. It comes well recommended. Next time out, 'Living Doll.'"*

Trivia, etc. While Charles Beaumont received on-screen credit for this episode, Jerry Sohl was responsible for writing the teleplay. "I think Chuck Beaumont and I were walking along and saying, 'Suppose we had a doll that talked, and could answer our questions and reprimand us. Just think of all the things that doll could do,' recalled Sohl to interviewer Matthew R. Bradley. "Not anything animal or carnival, but in speaking. So, we got on that track. It was no problem at all, once we had worked out the idea. A couple of months passed, and I said, 'Gee, it's about time that I did 'Living Doll,' because Beaumont was in no condition to do it. I usually wrote most of Beaumont's stuff, at that stage of the game."

The doll was not custom-made for this episode. Talky Tina was actually Brikette, a doll manufactured by the Vogue Doll Company and introduced to the market in 1959. Standing 22 inches tall, with a twist-and-turn waist, freckles, green eyes and orange hair, Brikette was discontinued in 1961. After contacting the manufacturing company, Cayuga Productions secured permission, proposing that the doll be altered with a different dress and equipped to talk when wound up. Naturally, the voice of the doll was looped in after production, so the gimmicked doll on the show contained a fake wind-up key on the back.

The voice of the doll was supplied by June Foray, character voice actor best-remembered as the voice of Rocky, the Flying Squirrel on *The Rocky and Bullwinkle Show*. "I was the voice for a line of dolls called Chatty Cathy and I think they hired me to do the voice of Talky Tina because they wanted the same kind of voice," recalled Foray. "Talky Tina was evil and she would say 'My name is Talky Tina, and I am going to kill you.' I thought it was creepy how they wanted me to play this nice voice throughout and threaten Telly Savalas with killing him . . . the same way Tina would say how much she loved him."

"I started out on radio first, which led to a job with Walt Disney, then Warner Bros. and Chuck Jones," continued Foray. "I was doing voices for so many cartoons by the time they wanted me to be Talky Tina that it was just another job. Now I get calls and letters from fans all the time about Talky Tina."

Felix Silla, best known for playing the role of Cousin Itt on *The Addams Family* and Twiki the robot on *Buck Rogers*, was a stand-in for Tracy Stratford. A stuntman doubled for Telly Savalas during the climax when Erich tumbles down the stairs.

This script was assigned a production number on July 15, 1963. The garage scenes were filmed on Stage 4, and all exterior scenes were shot on Lot 2 at M-G-M Studios. If the interior of the Streator home (the living room) seems familiar, it should. The living room set was filmed on Stage 16 and, before being taken down, was reused (replacing the furniture, props, paintings, etc.) for the living room scenes in "Ring-A-Ding Girl," "Ninety Years Without Slumbering" and "Black Leather Jackets."

On the October 29, 1992 telecast of *The Simpsons*, the Halloween episode featured a spoof of "Living Doll" substituting Talky Tina with a Krusty the Klown doll, that comes to life and literally attempts to kill Homer.

In the 2004 motion picture, *The Terminal*, the character of Mulroy tells Viktor Navorski, played by Tom Hanks, about *The Twilight Zone*, making references to this episode and "Nightmare at 20,000 Feet."

Production #2603 "THE OLD MAN IN THE CAVE"
(Initial telecast: November 8, 1963)
© Cayuga Productions, Inc., November 1, 1963, LP27132
Date of Rehearsal: May 31, 1963
Dates of Filming: June 3, 4 and 5, 1963
Script undated with revised pages dated April 16, 17, 18 and May 7, 1963.

Producer and Secretary: $1,626.02
Director: $1,375.00
Unit Manager and Secretary: $726.01
Agents Commission: $2,500.00
Below the line charges (M-G-M): $39,204.39
Total Production Costs: $63,179.38

Story and Secretary: $4,560.00
Cast: $7,387.40
Production Fee: $1,800.00
Legal and Accounting: $250.00
Below the line charges (other): $3,750.56

Cast: John Anderson (Goldsmith); Ann Cameron (weary survivor); Violet Cane (weary survivor); Brandon Carrol (man #2); James Coburn (Major French); John Craven (man #1); Morris Drabin (weary survivor); Lennie Geer (Douglas); Sid Goldie (weary survivor); Betty Graeff (weary survivor); Sandee Hobin (weary survivor); Josie Lloyd (Evelyn); Sandra Lynne (weary survivor); John Marley (Jason); Mary Lee Martin (weary survivor); Natalie Masters (woman #1); Sol Murgie (weary survivor); Eva Pearson (weary survivor); Warren Powers (weary survivor); Irene Sale (weary survivor); Wade Shannon (weary survivor); Barbara Walker (weary survivor); Frank Watkins (Harber); and Don Wilbanks (Furman).

Stock Music Cues: Etrange #3 (by Marius Constant, :09); Milieu #2 (by Constant, :21); To the Rescue (by Bernard Herrmann, :24); Moat Farm Murder (by Herrmann, :42); Walt Whitman (by Herrmann, 31); Rain Clouds – Western Suite (by Herrmann, :35); Harp Chords (CBS, :02); To the Rescue (by Hermann, :24); Horn Stings on C Sharp (CBS, :05); Bridge and Neutral Suspicion (by

Rene Garriguenc, :30); The Search #3 (by Lucien Moraweck, :15); Third Act Opening (by Nathan Van Cleave, :23); Moat Farm Murder (by Herrmann, :24); Walt Whitman (by Herrmann, :49); Passage of Time #16 (by Garriguenc, :05); To the Rescue (by Herrmann, :26); Night Suspense (by Herrmann, :27); Second Narration (by Leonard Rosenman, :12); First Hospital Scene (by Rosenman, :13); Bridge and Neutral Suspense (by Garriguenc, :36); To the Rescue (by Herrmann, :25); Second Narration (by Rosenman, :09); First Hospital Scene (by Rosenman, :15); Moat Farm Murder (by Herrmann, :22); Second Vision (by Fred Steiner, :14); Walt Whitman (by Herrmann, :12); Moat Farm Murder (by Herrmann, :26); Celestial #4 (by Rosenman, :19); Moat Farm Murder (by Herrmann, :11); Sand (by Steiner, :10); Walt Whitman (by Herrmann, :29); Los Bass Notes (CBS, :02); and Milieu #2 (by Constant, arr. by Herrmann, :21).

Director of Photography: Robert Pittack, a.s.c.

Art Directors: George W. Davis and Walter Holscher

Set Decorations: Henry Grace and Robert R. Benton

Sound: Franklin Milton and Philip N. Mitchell

Production Manager: Ralph W. Nelson

Film Editor: Richard Heermance, a.c.e.

Casting: Patricia Rose

Assistant Director: Charles Bonniwell, Jr.

Produced by Bert Granet

Directed by Alan Crosland, Jr.

Teleplay by Rod Serling, based on the short story "The Old Man" by Henry Slesar, originally published in the 1962 issue of *The Diner's Club Magazine.*

"What you're looking at is a legacy that man left to himself. A decade previous he pushed his buttons and a nightmarish moment later woke up to find that he had set the clock back a thousand years. His engines, his medicines, his science were buried in a mass tomb . . . covered over by the biggest gravedigger of them all – a bomb. And this is the Earth ten years later. A fragment of what was once a whole; a remnant of what was once a race. The year is 1974, and this is . . . the Twilight Zone."

Plot: In the 10th illustrious year after the bomb, radioactivity and plague have killed off most of mankind, but a group of survivors in a ghost town has managed to survive following the advice from an old man in a cave. Peace and harmony are disturbed one afternoon by the arrival of a group of ex-soldiers who claim to be members of the Central States Committee, sent to organize what is left of humanity. But Goldsmith, the representative of the survivors, doesn't acknowledge any authority because in the past, a similar constabulary never had a headquarters. Major French insists on meeting the old man personally, in an effort to exercise authority and discipline and to prove to the band of survivors that no such deity could be responsible for their survival. After convincing the people to enjoy the food that the old man claimed was contaminated, he urges them to visit the cave and like an angry mob, they enter to find no old man – just a large computer. First throwing stones, they begin smashing the sensors and tearing out the wires until the machine no longer operates. The next morning, Goldsmith wanders the streets paved with dead men and women and ponders whether this is the destiny of mankind.

"Mr. Goldsmith . . . Survivor. An eyewitness to man's imperfection. An observer of the very human trait of greed and a chronicler of the last chapter – the one reading 'suicide.' Not a prediction of what is to be . . . just a projection of what could be. This has been . . . the Twilight Zone."

Trailer: *"Next on Twilight Zone, a journey into a future moment. A nightmarish, frightening moment in time when man sits in his own rubble and surveys the legacy he's left to himself. James Coburn and John Anderson star in 'The Old Man in the Cave.' Recommended viewing for the more imaginative amongst you . . . on the Twilight Zone."*

Trivia, etc. Based on the short story "The Old Man" by Henry Slesar, the short story was called to Rod Serling's attention by Sybil S. Gurner of Los Angeles. She also brought to Serling's attention a whimsically macabre story by Peter S. Beagle, titled "Come, Lady Death," originally appearing in the September 1963 issue of *Atlantic Monthly*.

According to a release schedule dated September 25, 1963, this episode was slated for telecast on December 6, 1963. Earliest drafts indicated Serling wanted the story to take place in 1973, but the year was changed to 1974 by the time the final revised pages were composed.

Production began on the morning of May 14, 1963, at 9 a.m., at the Cayuga Productions office. The meeting consisted of Bert Granet, producer; Ralph W. Nelson, production manager; Charles Bonniwell, assistant director; Mildred Zaske, producer's secretary; Walter Holscher, art director; Robert Benton, set decorator; Kitty Majer (also Kitty Mager and Kitty Major), women's wardrobe; Norman Burza, men's wardrobe; Harry Edwards, prop master; Don Trew, trans.; Patricia Rose, casting; and Ralph Schwartz, special effects. The meeting lasted three hours, with directors Alan Crosland, Jr., Ida Lupino and Don Siegel. All of the technicals for "The Old Man in the Cave," "The Masks" and "Uncle Simon" were worked out, so when the day came to start rehearsals and filming, sets would be standing, costumes would be chosen, and the cast would have been selected for the major roles.

Set Decoration Production Costs	
Exterior of the Village Street	$980
Exterior of the Cave	$1,285
Interior of the Cave	$260
Store Front	$135
Total	$2,660

The first nine episodes to be scored during the fifth season featured a different rendition of the closing theme. This was lifted from Bernard Herrmann's version which he recorded specifically for "Little Girl Lost." Those episodes include "Uncle Simon," "The 7th is Made Up of Phantoms," "The Masks," "Steel," "Nightmare at 20,000 Feet," "The Last Night of a Jockey," "In Praise of Pip," "The Old Man in the Cave" and "Night Call."

The night scenes were shot on June 4, shortly after sunset, on the exterior of the Village Street on Lot 3 at M-G-M. Part of the cast and crew stayed on the set until dark, and Cayuga paid for a total of 70 hot dinners at an expense of $165.00 to be served at 6 p.m. Tables and chairs were set up for the cast and crew.

All of the extras featured in this episode were hired stand-ins, who visited the Cayuga office at M-G-M on Wednesday, May 28 for interviews. It was explained they needed to represent a group who had been living in a contaminated area due to atomic fallout, hollow-eyed, frail and on the verge of starvation. One heavyset woman was considered overweight and was sent back home. The rest of the stand-ins were instructed to report to Lot 3 on June 3 under the following conditions: not to wear any makeup or nail polish, keep unkept hair free of any preparation and appear in stingy and worn clothing.

Vehicles required for this episode included a Jaguar Sedan, a sports car, a pickup truck, Plymouth convertible, and a jeep, for a total rental fee of $110. Drivers to handle the vehicles cost $51. Alterations made to the cars to give the appearance of suffering the effects of a nuclear holocaust cost Cayuga $100. According to studio paperwork, the same jeep made an appearance in two separate episodes of *Combat!*

Production #2604
"UNCLE SIMON"
(Initial telecast:
November 15, 1963)

© Cayuga Productions, Inc., November 7, 1963, LP27749
Date of Rehearsal: June 6, 1963
Dates of Filming: June 7, 10 and 11, 1963
Script dated: April 19, 1963, with revised pages dated April 22, May 16 and 31, 1963.

Production Schedule at M-G-M

Day 1 –   Exterior of the Village Street (Lot #3)
Day 2 –   Exterior of the Village Street (Lot #3, day and night shots)
Day 3 –   Limbo Set (Stage 27 for Serling)
             Interior of the Cave (Stage 27)
             Exterior of the Cave (Stage 26)

Producer and Secretary: $1,626.02
Director: $1,625.00
Unit Manager and Secretary: $726.01
Agents Commission: $2,500.00
Below the line charges (M-G-M): $34,511.10
Total Production Costs: $55,286.74

Story and Secretary: $3,310.00
Cast: $5,901.89
Production Fee: $1,800.00
Legal and Accounting: $250.00
Below the line charges (other): $3,036.72

Cast: Constance Ford (Barbara Polk); Sir Cedric Hardwicke (Uncle Simon); and Ian Wolfe (Schwimmer).

Stock Music Cues: Etrange #3 (by Marius Constant, :09); Milieu #2 (by Constant, :21); Allison's Confession (by Fred Steiner, :38); Moment of Grief #3 (by D.B. Ray, :10 and :20); Harp Chords (CBS, :02); Alain #3 (by Constant, :19); The Discussion (by Goldsmith, :16); Into Darkness (by Lucien Moraweck, :13, :06 and :42); Shock Chords (by Moraweck, :06); Moment of Grief #1 (by D.B. Ray, :58); Trial is On (by Rosenman, :04); Hitch-Hiker (by Herrmann, :08); Concrete World (by Goldsmith, :44); The Plot (by Goldsmith, :37); Menace Ahead #1 (by Moraweck, :08); Meeting on the Roof (by Goldsmith, :24); Alain #3 (by Constant, :24); Into Darkness (by Moraweck, :15, :07 and :29); Moat Farm Murder (by Herrmann, :190; Broken Fist (by Goldsmith, :32); and Milieu #2 (by Constant, arr. by Herrmann, :21).

Director of Photography: Robert
    Pittack, a.s.c.
Art Directors: George W. Davis and
    Walter Holscher
Set Decorations: Henry Grace and
    Robert R. Benton
Sound: Franklin Milton and Philip N. Mitchell

Production Manager: Ralph W. Nelson
Film Editor: Thomas W. Scott
Casting: Patricia Rose
Assistant Director: Charles Bonniwell, Jr.
Produced by Bert Granet
Directed by Don Siegel
Teleplay by Rod Serling

"Dramatis personae – Mr. Simon Polk, a gentleman who has lived out his life in a gleeful rage. And the young lady who has just beat the hasty retreat is Mr. Polk's niece, Barbara. She has lived her life as if during each ensuing hour she had a dentist's appointment. There is yet a third member of the company soon to be seen. He now resides in the laboratory and he is the kind of character to be found only in . . . the Twilight Zone."

Plot: Barbara has spent the past 25 years faithfully serving her Uncle Simon, an old man who spends much of his time tinkering with a project in the laboratory, which he keeps locked at all times. He verbally abuses his niece because he has not an ounce of love in his heart. In an exchange of opinions, Barbara confesses that her only reason for staying is for the day when Uncle Simon dies -- to return from the funeral and celebrate with a bottle of wine. Uncle Simon believes she stays for the hope of a future financial convenience – and he isn't far from the truth. One afternoon, when he raises his cane toward Barbara, Uncle Simon loses his balance and falls down a flight of stairs, breaking his back. Instead of phoning for help, Barbara stands above the ancient albatross and before he passes on, gleefully cheers for the death of her verbal abuser. Weeks later, Uncle Simon's will is read. Everything is hers – the money and the house – under the condition that she remains, removes nothing and tends to the care of his latest experiment. A member of a law firm will visit the house weekly to ensure that this provision has been kept, else all of Uncle Simon's belongings will be donated to the local university. Uncle Simon's experiment turns out to be a mechanical man – a robot – that eventually develops the attributes programmed, gradually maturing to possess human characteristics. Before long, Barbara realizes that she cannot push this metal man around. Not only does he possess the same personality as her late uncle, but the same voice as well . . .

"Dramatis personae. A metal man who will go by the name of 'Simon' whose life, as well as his body, has been stamped out for him. And the woman who tends to him . . . the lady Barbara who has discovered belatedly, that all bad things don't come to an end, and that once a bed is made – it's quite necessary that you sleep in it. Tonight's uncomfortable little exercise in avarice and automatons . . . from the Twilight Zone."

Trailer: *"Next on the Twilight Zone, the distinguished Sir Cedric Hardwicke lends us his considerable talent along with the very accomplished Miss Constance Ford. They appear in what can most aptly be described as one of the shockers on our schedule. The play is called 'Uncle Simon.' – and this, we submit, is a relative you've never met before. It's a story with a final curtain I doubt anyone can predict. Next on Twilight Zone, 'Uncle Simon.'"*

Trivia, etc. When this episode was filmed, there was an additional scene that took place immediately after Uncle Simon's death at the bottom of the stairs. Barbara watches him die and lifts her head to laugh. The scene then abruptly cuts to the study where Barbara, with a tear-stained face, cries into a handkerchief. A plainclothes police officer is asking her questions so he can complete his report. Barbara tells the officer that she heard a crash, went to open the basement door and found the body of her Uncle at the bottom of the stairs. She tells the officer that Uncle Simon was already dead when she found him. The officer offers his condolences and comments, "I can imagine how close you two were." She looks up as if searching for another meaning, then seeing the sympathetic face, remarks, "You have no idea, Lieutenant." Before the officer leaves, he comments how the deceased was a brilliant old man, recalling how his father was a student at the university where Uncle Simon

A History of Robby the Robot

Robby the Robot was the most expensive prop created for the 1956 movie, *Forbidden Planet*, at an estimated cost of $125,000. M-G-M, like any major movie studio, did not waste props and costumes – especially at such a great cost. Producers for various television programs were optioned to rent the costume and the equipment that operated the costume's features. The design of Robby was created by art directors Arthur Lonergan and A. Arnold Gillespie, modeled after producer Nicholas Nayfack's ideas. Production illustrator Mentor Huebner refined the look of Robby from Gillespie's sketches. In late December of 1954, Bob Kinoshita, head draftsman of the art department produced the working blueprints. The costume was designed so the man inside could see out of the voice box below the glass head. (If you look carefully, Dion Hansen can be seen inside the voice box in this episode.)

After technicals were completed on the blueprints, the drawings were turned over to Jack Gaylord, head of M-G-M's prop shop, who was responsible for supervising the molding and assembly of Robby's plastic parts. (Metal would have been too heavy for a man to walk in and was not as flexible as plastic.) Glen Robinson, a mechanical effects expert, worked with Gaylord in engineering the electrical system that operated the complex tools on the side of Robby's head and the chest panel. Wires, motors, a glass blower and other electrical gimmicks were attached to the costume. All of the electrical apparatus were powered from a cable that could be plugged into either heel of the robot's costume. (If you pay close attention to the episode, you'll see this cable has been cleverly concealed.)

once taught. After the officer leaves, Barbara rushes into the room to smash the ash trays and pipes across the room, and runs up the stairs to proclaim her freedom. This scene involving the police officer never made the final cut. Actor John McLiam played the role.

Serling originally concluded his trailer with "It's a story in the best of O. Henry traditions with a final curtain I doubt anyone can predict." Shortly after composing the trailer, Serling finished the script for "The Long Morrow" and realizing that episode fit the O. Henry description, revised the ending of the trailer for this episode to prevent repetition.

According to a release schedule dated September 25, 1963, this episode was slated for initial telecast on December 13, 1963.

"It's increasingly difficult, if you've got a name, to find character parts that are sufficiently important," remarked Sir Cedric Hardwicke. "The older dramatists wrote plays that made demands on actors. Today, they don't. The idiots who write today would be very happy to do without actors. I have trouble finding plays that are even readable, let alone actable." To underscore his enthusiasm for the part of Uncle Simon and his further disdain for an apparent majority of screenwriters, he said, "I think more playwrights have been saved by inarticulate actors than you can imagine. In the movies, you hear everything they say."

Constance Ford, who had played a major role in the "Joey Menotti" production on *Kraft Television Theater*, also scripted by Serling, makes her first and only visit in this *Twilight Zone* episode. She had attempted to get a role on the program many times previous, apparently keeping in touch with Serling. On September 27, 1960, she sent a telegram to Serling asking him to watch *Thriller* that evening. She admitted the script was not as good as the "Joey Menotti" script, "but it's the most fun I've had with a part since then," she remarked.

Don Siegel's first directorial job for television was a medical drama, *The Doctor*. Of

Set Decoration Production Costs
Interior of Simon Polk's House $465
Interior of the Cellar and Stairs including the Lab $1,822
Interior of Uncle Simon's Bedroom $558
Total $2,845

the three episodes he directed, two of them were scripted by Rod Serling: "No Gods to Serve" (October 5, 1952) and "Those Who Wait" (October 19, 1952). While Siegel since directed other television programs, such as *The Lineup*, *Frontier* and *Bus Stop*, and the 1956 motion picture, *Invasion of the Body Snatchers*, this marked the return collaboration of Serling and Siegel.

The entire episode was filmed on Stage 18. The stairway leading down to the cellar (where Uncle Simon takes his death fall) was specially constructed for this episode. Amongst the superb acting of Constance Ford and Sir Cedric Hardwicke, the robot took center stage and proved to be the most expensive and time-consuming effect for the entire production. Not only was the robot instructed to carry on a personality that plagues Barbara, but it had to be convincing enough to make the viewers believe that he could reside in the house as a resident and not as a stack of moving metal.

The voice of Robby did not originate from the costume. Actor Vic Perrin's voice was recorded in a sound studio at M-G-M and is the voice you hear except for the very end, when Sir Cedric Hardwicke's voice comes through the soundtrack. Scott Hale was hired as the dialogue director for this episode to ensure that the voice of the robot came through clearly on the recording. (It remains a puzzle as to why Vic Perrin, a professional actor for thousands of radio broadcasts and who could have handled the task on a professional level, was in need of a dialogue director.) The robot was not required for the scenes filmed on the first day, but three special effects men were required for the second and third day of filming, to help operate the robot, at a cost of $304. This included powering the electricity for the lights and moving gadgets on the costume.

For this *Twilight Zone* episode, the chest box was replaced with a different one from what appeared in *Forbidden Planet* (1956). The steel bucket head inside the glass dome on top of Robby's head was a temporary one – the original components were replaced after filming was completed. A battery pack was required for certain scenes, which only lasted a few brief minutes for the film, requiring certain scenes to be completed without multiple takes.

Because of the cost factor in designing and constructing Robby, for more than three decades he made appearances in numerous motion pictures and television programs. Besides the motion picture, *The Invisible Boy* (1957), he made appearances on *The Perry Como Show* (circa 1960s), *The Gale Storm Show* (December 13, 1958), as Lurch's replacement in *The Addams Family* (March 18, 1966) and a dream sequence in *Hazel* (September 27, 1962). Robby made an appearance in two television episodes of *Lost in Space*, "War of the Robots" (May 9, 1966) and "Condemned of Space" (September 6, 1967). On television's *The Thin Man*, Robby appeared in the episode "Robot Gent" initially telecast on November 15, 1957, also filmed at M-G-M.

On June 18, additional insert shots were filmed of the robot in the closet and at the bottom of the stairs. On the same day, the camera crew filmed a still shot of the robot for the closing title credits and a still shot of a canteen, map and note for production #2606.

The grandfather clock in this episode is the same that is prominently featured in the hallway of the episode, "Young Man's Fancy."

As with all of the previous episodes of the *Twilight Zone* series, the sponsor was granted time to look over all the scripts before filming commenced. This was a contractual obligation, so the sponsor could approve or object to any questionable material that could jeopardize the company's image or legal status. While the American Tobacco Company (the present sponsor) approved such scripts as "The Masks," "Steel" and "The Old Man in the Cave" without a question, one scene in this episode raised a concern.

In a letter addressed to Bert Granet, dated May 9, 1963, Larry Algeo of Batten, Barton, Durstine & Osborn, Inc., the advertising agency representing American Tobacco, wrote that this episode "has several references and scenes which make tobacco and pipe smoking appear most unsavory." The letter cited such examples as the line delivered by Barbara, " . . . get rid of your ugly smelling pipe ashes . . ." Other objectionable scenes included Barbara backhanding the pipes off the desk, stamping on them and breaking them into pieces, flinging the ashtray against the wall, and the robot's knocking used tobacco on the floor.

"We hope you will make every effort to alter these so that American Tobacco will have no objection," the letter requested. Algeo offered a number of substitutes, "Perhaps open books, scientific papers, and manuscripts strewn around could be substituted. Or various bits of wire, tubes and electronic gear. Even smelly, dirty, open and spilled chemical bottles and jars. Or if you want something more personal, how about apple cores, banana peels and grape stems? Even old clothing thrown around might help."

On May 10, Bert Granet composed the following reply: "Dramatically speaking, it seems to me that there is a misinterpretation of the meaning of the pipe and tobacco in the story. First, I would like to point out that the prototypes of the character are many nuclear physicists and scientists who are preoccupied pipe smokers, i.e. Einstein, Oppenheimer, Steinmetz. What untidiness accrued in their nature was, and is, a preoccupation with the more important things in their lives."

"It is Barbara, his niece, a partial psychotic, who objects to his smoking, which is obviously a joy to him, since there are so many pipes present," Granet continued. "Barbara, then, of course is adverse to a symbol that gives him constant happiness. None of your suggestions to replace the pipe has its personal nature. It would be distasteful to me for someone to be munching and strewing fruit through a show. Now would these fruit peels have a reason to be about when the robot supplants Uncle Simon, whereas the pipes serve as a positive reminder of what he loved and she hated."

A columnist for *The San Francisco Daily Review* regarded this episode as "another cutie from the pen of the creator-host of the series, Rod Serling." *The Tucson Daily Citizen* reviewed this episode as "a novel thriller with a surprise macabre finish."

Production #2622 "PROBE 7, OVER AND OUT"
(Initial telecast: November 29, 1963)
© Cayuga Productions, Inc., November 25, 1963, LP27133
(Copyrighted under the title "Probe Seven, Over and Out")
Date of Rehearsal: August 22, 1963
Dates of Filming: August 23, 26 and 27, 1963
Script dated: August 1, 1963, with revised pages dated August 3 and 5, 1963.

First revised script dated: August 7, 1963
Second revised script dated: August 21, 1963

Producer and Secretary: $2,126.02
Director: $1,500.00
Unit Manager and Secretary: $726.01
Agents Commission: $2,500.00
Below the line charges (M-G-M): $39,595.98
Total Production Costs: $61,355.50

Story and Secretary: $3,310.00
Cast: $6,594.65
Production Fee: $1,800.00
Legal and Accounting: $250.00
Below the line charges (other): $2,952.84

Cast: Richard Basehart (Colonel Adam Cook); Antoinette Bower (Eve Norda); Harold Gould (General Larrabee); and Barton Heyman (Lieutenant Blane).

Stock Music Cues: Etrange #3 (by Marius Constant, :09); Milieu #2 (by Constant, :21); First Narration (by Leonard Rosenman, :22); Confusion (by Rosenman, :47); No Trace (by Rosenman, :01); Mr. Wellington (by Goldsmith, :28); Return to the Past (by Goldsmith, :15); The Assassination (by Goldsmith, 16); The Wound (by Goldsmith, :13); Mr. Wellington (by Goldsmith, :22); The Prediction (by Goldsmith, :11); Knock Out (by Goldsmith, :15); The Victor (by Goldsmith, :43); Return to the Past (by Goldsmith, :47); Second Vision (by Steiner, :21); Counterattack – Part 1 (by Goldsmith, :43); F Story #1 (by Constant, :04); The Assassination (by Goldsmith, :04 and 1:12); The Prediction (by Goldsmith, :11); The Assassination (by Goldsmith, :16); Cerebrum #2 (by Jeff Alexander, :54); Old William (by Goldsmith, :23); Etrange #3 (by Constant, :09); and Milieu #2 (by Constant, :21).

Director of Photography: Robert
    Pittack, a.s.c.
Art Directors: George W. Davis and
    Malcolm Brown
Set Decorations: Henry Grace and
    Robert R. Benton
Sound: Franklin Milton and Joe Edmondson

Production Manager: Ralph W. Nelson
Film Editor: Thomas W. Scott
Casting: Patricia Rose
Assistant Director: Charles Bonniwell, Jr.
Produced by William Froug
Directed by Ted Post
Teleplay by Rod Serling

"One Colonel Cook – a traveler in space. He's landed on a remote planet several million miles from his point of departure. He can make an inventory of his plight by just one 360-degree movement of head and eyes. Colonel Cook has been set adrift in an ocean of space in a metal lifeboat that has been scorched and destroyed and will never fly again. He survived the crash but his ordeal is yet to begin. Now he must give battle to loneliness. Now Colonel Cook must meet the unknown. It's a small planet set deep in space, but for Colonel Cook . . . it's the Twilight Zone."

Plot: Colonel Adam Cook crash-lands his spacecraft, Probe 7, on a remote planet. His ship will never fly again. While the planet features plant life and an atmosphere similar to home, there is an intelligent being moving about in the bushes. Through the limited means of power, he manages to communicate with his superiors. His commanding officer explains that war back home is imminent, and more than likely, within the next 24 hours, there will be no survivors – the planet will be suffering a little "wholesale dying." It's only a question now of how long before all of humanity is extinct. Colonel Cook meets up with the stranger outside, and discovers she is a woman of the same breed.

Set Decoration Production Costs
Exterior of the Spaceship $700
Interior of the Spaceship $2,000
Interior of the General's Office for TV Insert $100
Total $2,800

While she does not speak his language, she is the sole survivor of a planet that left its orbit and faced Armageddon. After a brief confrontation with Eve Norda, he realizes that survival means moving to a different part of the planet where vegetation is more abundant. Before leaving, however, he attempts to communicate so she will join him in his trek. She refers to the dirt as "earth" and she hands him a freshly picked apple off a tree . . . a gift from Eve to Adam.

"Do you know these people? Names familiar, are they? They lived a long time ago. Perhaps they're part fable. Perhaps they're part fantasy. And perhaps the place they're walking to now is not really called Eden. We offer it only as a presumption, This has been the Twilight Zone."

Trailer: *"Next on Twilight Zone, an eminent performer of stage and screen Mr. Richard Basehart, in an oddball excursion we call 'Probe 7, Over and Out.' On occasion we'll come up with a wild and wooly adenoma, but this particular opus has an unpredictable ending that we doubt even the most seasoned Tee Vee fans would be able to pick up, before it happens on your screen. Next on Twilight Zone, 'Probe 7, Over and Out.'"*

Trivia, etc. Days before this episode went into production, on August 5, 1963, Rod Serling wrote to William Froug, telling him, "I am simply delighted that you're aboard. I think this could be the beginning of some very good times." Serling also enclosed the slightly revised version of "Probe 7" with an explanation: "I did not putz around with any of the lines that are so definitely 'Earth-like', but I did add a beat in act two to give it a little more bulk and movement. If you'll drop me a note giving me your ideas on line changes, or if you'd like to do those line changes yourself – it would be just fine."

"Richard Basehart and Antoinette Bower were professional actors who worked together. Of all the episodes I filmed . . . that was a breeze," recalled director Ted Post. "I recall the script was nothing out of the ordinary. Rod told me that he felt it could have been better. He granted me an exclusive to do what I could to improve the scenes. With actors like Richard and Antoinette, that was never a problem."

In what became the first episode assigned to production (August 6, 1963) when Froug replaced Bert Granet, who was originally a temporary replacement for Hirschman, the entire episode was filmed on Lot 3 and Lot 14 at M-G-M Studios.

"In a rare spirit of cooperation" commented Bob Stahl in an issue of *TV Guide*, "CBS's *Twilight Zone* has purchased a spaceship mock-up created originally for ABC's *The Outer Limits*." The set described in the magazine was the downed spacecraft Adam Cook took shelter in. Daystar Productions, which produced *The Outer Limits*, went to a bit of expense to construct the spaceship, which was used for the episode "Specimen: Unknown," originally telecast on February 24, 1964. Daystar and Cayuga arranged for the purchase of the fake wreckage for use on this episode.

In the early draft of this script, Serling's opening narration was longer:

"One Colonel Cook – a traveler in space. He's landed on a remote planet several million miles from his point of departure. He can make an inventory of his plight by just one 360-degree movement of head and eyes. Colonel Cook has been set adrift in an ocean of space in a metal lifeboat that has been scorched and destroyed and will never fly again. He has survived the crash. He has lived through the impact of flaming metal smashing against the atmosphere and what was beyond. But his ordeal is yet to begin. Now he must give battle to loneliness. Now he must stand up and face what awaits him on the other side of the bulkhead. Now Colonel Cook must meet the unknown. (a pause) *It's a small planet set deep in space – but for Colonel Cook it's . . . the Twilight Zone"*

Basehart and Bower reported for makeup and wardrobe fittings on the morning of August 22. Filming only took three days, but on September 6, Serling and Froug viewed the rough cut, and because the film was considerably over length, they chose which scenes needed to be removed.

Harold Gould recorded his voice in Sync Room "B" on October 8, which was used for the last transmission that is heard coming from the ship at the end of act one, and Bower's lines were re-recorded because the microphone was unable to pick up her voice clearly on film. Richard Basehart reported to the same studio on October 9 for looping of his voice. Antoinette Bower's voice was recorded in October, having returned to the West Coast after hurrying away after the initial production.

"This is not what I call a behind-the-scenes story, but for myself, I always think that anyone in this profession would subscribe to 'what happens on the set stays on the set.' It is a fact that we have selective memories – and heaven knows what happens to memories from well over four-and-a-half decades ago," recalled Antoinette Bower. "I'm not much of a nostalgia fan and I just wouldn't want to think about it. Except that in the case of 'Probe 7, Over and Out' – beyond the pleasure of working with Richard Basehart and director Ted Post's not entirely tongue-in-cheek instructions to run around the back lot for real breathlessness . . . there is something I will never forget. I worried through the entire show about being able to make a charter flight to Washington for the August 28 march. It looked at one point as if we might run over schedule: on the other hand, I was desperate to get to the march. In the end, we wrapped in time but in my anxious mind, it was too tight. The flight left that evening (August 27), later than expected because we waited for Harry Belafonte to finish his show at the Greek Theater. I made it in time. No need to say the event was unforgettable. It was extraordinary. It was one of the times one truly felt fond of the human race."

According to a release schedule dated September 25, 1963, this episode was slated for initial telecast on November 15, 1963.

A column in *The Daily Review Sunday Previewer* ruined the ending for television viewers when, on the morning of the telecast, the paper described the plot as "something of a futuristic version of the story of Adam and Eve."

Production #2606 "THE 7ᵀᴴ IS MADE UP OF PHANTOMS"
(Initial telecast: December 6, 1963)

© Cayuga Productions, Inc., December 2, 1963, LP27134
Date of Rehearsal: June 12, 1963
Dates of Filming: June 13, 14 and 17, 1963
Script dated: April 30, 1963, with revised pages dated May 16, 1963.

Producer and Secretary: $1,626.02
Director: $1,375.00
Unit Manager and Secretary: $726.01
Agents Commission: $2,500.00
Below the line charges (M-G-M): $38,055.33
Total Production Costs: $56,979.67

Story and Secretary: $3,313.52
Cast: $4,484.39
Production Fee: $1,800.00
Legal and Accounting: $250.00
Below the line charges (other): $2,849.40

Cast: Randy Boone (Pvt. McCluskey); Robert Bray (Captain Dennet); Lew Brown (the sergeant); Ron Foster (Sgt. Connors); Wayne Mallory (the scout); Greg Morris (Lieutenant Woodward); Jeffrey Morris (the radio operator); Warren Oates (Cpl. Langsford); and Jacque Shelton (the Corporal).

Stock Music Cues: Etrange #3 (by Marius Constant, :09); Milieu #2 (by Constant, :21); Village Death (by Jerry Goldsmith, :21); Dramatic (by Dimitri Tiomkin, arr. by Hill Bowen); Punctuation (by Lucien Moraweck, :05); Village Death (by Goldsmith, :14); Albany – Ethan Allen Suite (by Bernard Herrmann, :30); The Meeting – Ethan Allen Suite (by Herrmann, :32); The Robbery (by Goldsmith, :04); Village Death (by Goldmith, :16); The Meeting (by Goldsmith, :14); Village Death (by Goldsmith, :24); The Meeting Hair (by Goldsmith, :21); Guilty Party (by Goldsmith, :22); Camp Before Battle (by Leonard Rosenthal, :15 and :36); East Horizon (by Herrmann, :21); The Watchers (by Goldsmith, :40); Passage of Time #6 (by Garriguenc, :05); Goodbye Keith (by William Lava, :06); Sand Storm (by Herrmann, :24 and :21); Open Spaces (by Herrmann, :37 and :18); Knock Out (by Goldsmith, :08); Angie's Farewell (by Goldsmith, :04); Peg's Sorrow (by Goldsmith, :37); and Milieu #2 (by Constant, arr. by Herrmann, :21).

Director of Photography: George T.
   Clemens, a.s.c.
Art Directors: George W. Davis and
   Walter Holscher
Set Decorations: Henry Grace and
   Robert R. Benton
Sound: Franklin Milton and Philip N. Mitchell

Production Manager: Ralph W. Nelson
Film Editor: Richard Heermance, a.c.e.
Casting: Patricia Rose
Assistant Director: Charles Bonniwell, Jr.
Produced by Bert Granet
Directed by Alan Crosland, Jr.
Teleplay by Rod Serling

"June 25th, 1964 or – if you prefer, June 25th, 1876. The cast of characters in order of their appearance. A patrol of General Custer's Cavalry and a patrol of National Guardsmen on a maneuver. Past and present are about to collide head on . . . as they are wont to do in a very special bivouac area known as . . . the Twilight Zone."

Plot: Three National Guard soldiers on patrol on the grounds of Little Big Horn overhear rifle fire and investigate. After finding a Sioux teepee and a water canteen belonging to the 7th Cavalry, the men soon discover their regiment is making the same maneuvers as Marcus Reno's scouts made back in 1876. McCluskey fires into a dust cloud where the sounds of an attack by the Sioux originates, and an Indian's horse without a rider appears out of nowhere. Believing that time stands still on hallowed ground, the three-man squad traces the historical route, and Corporal Langsford finds six deserted

Indian teepees. McCluskey gets shot in the back with an arrow, so the men set out to find the 7th Cavalry and run smack into the middle of the battle at Little Bighorn. Drawing their guns, the men race down the hill to help assist General Custer and his men. Hours later, the National Guard arrives on the battleground to find an empty tank and the battlefield monument at the West Point Cemetery with the names of Conners, McCluskey and Langsford on the decades-old monument.

"Sergeant William Conners, Trooper Michael McCluskey and Trooper Richard Langsford —who, on a hot afternoon in June, made a charge over a hill and never returned. Look for this one under 'P' for Phantom, in a historical ledger located in a reading room known as . . . the Twilight Zone."

Trailer: *"Next on Twilight Zone: Three National Guardsmen on a maneuver traveling across the same ground formerly occupied by General Custer, in an outfit called the 7th Cavalry. Time in its infinite complexity, meshes – and what evolves is a stunningly different story about soldiers and Indians suspended in limbo, between then and now. On Twilight Zone next, 'The 7th is Made Up of Phantoms.'"*

Trivia, etc. Thirteen years before this telecast, Rod Serling wrote a series of scripts for a radio program titled *Our America* (exact dates remain unknown, but earliest and latest dates are September and October 1951). The program featured historic dramas of notable American historical figures such as Jefferson Davis and Lewis and Clark. One of the episodes dramatized a recreation of General Custer and his encounter with the Sioux at Little Bighorn and this episode offered Serling a chance to revisit the same historical events that he wrote for radio years before.

The entire episode was filmed at Albertson's Ranch, located outside Hollywood. Albertson Ranch was purchased by Fred Albertson from William Randolph Hearst in 1943, and shortly after, the Albertson Company used the vast acreage as a movie ranch. *Bonanza* and *Gunsmoke* were among the many television series that frequented the grounds. Albertson's Ranch was in a very dangerous fire area due to a drought, so the cast and crew were ordered to obey all smoking regulations during their tenure on the ranch. Cans for cigarette butts were furnished. Trucks and other equipment were checked regularly to be sure no gas spillage occurred. If the water wagon left the set for refilling, the cast and crew were instructed: "there would be no smoking by any personnel until the truck arrives."

Numerous vehicles and equipment had to be rented for this episode. A wind machine cost $30 and a man specially trained to operate it cost $117. One jeep cost $45, one jeep trailer cost $25, an M-3 tank cost $750, and the commander's car cost $180. Two-way radios had to be purchased for the show (not rented) at a cost of $50. A night watchman was hired to guard the props and equipment at the ranch at a cost of $175. The fee to film on Albertson Ranch was $450, and the contract with the owner included an additional fee of $100 to cover the cost of mowing the grass. According to studio paperwork, the same jeep and M-3 tank had made appearances in episodes of *Combat!*

Honoring CBS' policy to employ Negro actors in roles whenever possible, two black lieutenants were hired to play a lieutenant and a radio operator – one was Greg Morris, who would later become a regular on the television series *Mission: Impossible*. The original draft of this script stated the story took place on June 24, not June 25.

The television critic for *The Wisconsin State Journal* described this episode as "a western ghost story with an odd but believable script by Rod Serling, which youngsters should really enjoy."

On January 8, 1963, Captain James L. O'Neill wrote a letter addressed to Serling (in care of CBS). "The *Twilight Zone* has scored another first in the field of entertainment," O'Neill wrote. "Both the Division Commander, Maj. Gen. Charles Billingslea, and Lt. Col. James Keown, present 7th U.S. Cavalry Commander here at Fort Benning, Georgia, have talked quite a bit about the above referenced show since its showing in the area. I am certain that you are aware of the great tradition attached to the U.S. Cavalry and especially to the colorful Garry Owen unit." Rod Serling appreciated the letter, since Fort Benning held fond and nostalgic memories for him. In early 1943, Serling was at the same Parachute School.

The battlefield monument and West Point Cemetery was reconstructed on the Albertson Ranch, consulting photos of the real monument located in Big Horn County, Montana. The original marble obelisk was constructed in 1881, and the production crew was able to reproduce the monument flawlessly. The cost to reproduce the grave markers, the fence and the monument was $1,600. The names of the fictional characters that supposedly died at the scene of the Custer Battlefield were superimposed on the original monument, so as the camera zooms in on the list, some of the actual names of the 261 men of the 7th Cavalry are seen.

Originally Serling intended to use the following for the trailer, but it was considered too lengthy, and needed to be trimmed:

"The ingredients for our next Twilight Zone is as follows: Three National Guardsmen on a maneuver traveling across the same ground formerly occupied by General Custer and the outfit named the 7th Cavalry. Time, in its infinite complexity, meshes – and what evolves is a stunningly different story with soldiers and Indians suspended in limbo between then and the now. On the Twilight Zone next time – 'The 7th is Made Up of Phantoms.' I hope you can make it."

Production #2614 "A SHORT DRINK FROM A CERTAIN FOUNTAIN"
(Initial telecast: December 13, 1963)
Copyright Registration: © Cayuga Productions, Inc., December 9, 1963, LP27861
Date of Rehearsal: July 23, 1963
Dates of Filming: July 24, 25 and 26, 1963
Script dated: June 14, 1963

Producer and Secretary: $1,626.02
Director: $1,500.00
Unit Manager and Secretary: $726.01
Agents Commission: $2,500.00
Below the line charges (M-G-M): $32,086.73
Total Production Costs: $53,231.66

Story and Secretary: $3,710.00
Cast: $6,455.61
Production Fee: $1,800.00
Legal and Accounting: $250.00
Below the line charges (other): $2,577.29

Cast: Walter Brooke (Dr. Raymond Gordon); Ruta Lee (Flora Gordon); Tim Matheson (Harmon as a teenager); and Patrick O'Neal (Harmon Gordon).

Stock Music Cues: Etrange #3 (by Marius Constant, :09); Milieu #2 (by Constant, :21); Natural Rock (by Bruce Campbell, 1:17); The Old Woman (by Goldsmith, :46); Harp Chords (CBS, :01); Tarn #1 (by Constant, :22); Heartbreak (by Goldsmith, :39); Mother (by Goldsmith, 1:03); Bergson

#1 (by Constant, :21); The Arrest (by Goldsmith, :18); Meeting on the Roof (by Goldsmith, :33); Bergson #1 (by Constant, :21); F Story #1 (by Constant, :44); F Story #3 (by Constant, :45); F Story #1 (by Constant, :05); Concrete World (by Goldsmith, :11); Terror Struck (by Goldsmith, :14); Mother (by Goldsmith, :58); New Hope (by Goldsmith, :26); Low Bass Notes (CBS, :02); Etrange #3 (by Constant, :09); and Milieu #2 (by Constant, :21).

Director of Photography: George T. Clemens, a.s.c.	Production Manager: Ralph W. Nelson
Art Directors: George W. Davis and Walter Holscher	Film Editor: Thomas W. Scott
Set Decorations: Henry Grace and Robert R. Benton	Casting: Patricia Rose
	Assistant Director: Charles Bonniwell, Jr.
	Producer: Bert Granet
	Directed by Bernard Girard

Sound: Franklin Milton and Philip N. Mitchell
Teleplay by Rod Serling, based on an unpublished short story titled "Ah, Youth!" by Lou Holz.

"Picture of an aging man who leads his life, as Thoreau said – in quiet desperation – because Harmon Gordon is enslaved by a love affair with a wife forty years his junior. Because of this, he runs when he should walk; he surrenders when simple pride dictates a stand; he pines away for the lost morning of his life – when he should be enjoying the evening. In short, Mr. Harmon Gordon seeks a fountain of youth, and who's to say he won't find it? This happens to be . . .the Twilight Zone."

Plot: Harmon Gordon is a walking mausoleum who cannot keep up with the pace of his younger wife, Flora. She wants to be married to a younger man, but won't leave Harmon because of his money. Desperate, Harmon calls on his brother, Raymond, a scientist who has made an incredible breakthrough with a cellular serum that rejuvenates the youth and health of animals. He's willing to be a human guinea pig for Flora's sake. After a discussion about ethics and age, Raymond agrees and returns to the penthouse with the experimental serum. Raymond confesses his opinion of Flora, a conniving, covetous broad, made of asbestos with no heart, and promises that if Harmon dies as a result of the injection, he'll take out his anger against the predatory alley cat. Harmon accepts his brother's opinion and the injection. In the morning, Harmon wakes to find the serum taking effect. He is now 30 years younger. Flora likes the change at first, preparing to make plans for their evenings out, but Harmon's condition continues and the ground rules change. He soon becomes a teenager, and Flora pleads to know what is happening. Raymond informs her that as bizarre as the situation is, she is to stay and take care of her husband – regardless of his age. If she leaves, she loses everything. Flora agrees to the terms and begins making preparations on how she will spend her remaining years with Harmon, now two years old.

"It happens to be a fact: as one gets older, one does get wiser. If you don't believe it – ask Flora. Ask her any day of the ensuing weeks of her life – as she takes notes during the coming years. And realizes that the worm has turned. Youth has taken over. It's simply the way the calendar crumbles . . . in the Twilight Zone."

Trailer: *"No one likes to age, but it's a natural process like death and taxes and the weather, but next time on Twilight Zone, we tell the story about what happens when a certain man doesn't age. As a matter of fact,* *he grows younger. Patrick O'Neal stars in 'A Short Drink From a Certain Fountain' and if this one doesn't pull you up by the shoulders, I don't think anything will. I hope we see you next time."*

Trivia, etc. A bit of mystery surrounds this episode. The October 1985 issue of *The Twilight Zone Magazine* featured an article about censorship titled "Censorship: Another Dimension Behind the Twilight Zone," by Hal Erickson. In his article, he stated, "When Flora told a doctor to 'blow it out your black bag,' CBS blew the whistle." Having reviewed over 150 censorship reports and letters from a representative of CBS, there has been no paper stating the network ever blew the whistle on material in any *Twilight Zone* script. Regarding this particular episode, the network had no major issues regarding the content that couldn't be addressed in the form of a polite suggestion or request. Teleplays broadcast over any network – documentaries, dramas, comedies – were always subject to review by the censorship department for two reasons. One, to protect the network legally from material that might prove damaging on moral, political or religious

Patrick O'Neal and Ruta Lee
pose for the photographer.

grounds. Two, content that might be taken out of context would be asked for clarification or a suggestion for a substitute. The network preferred to avoid any issues that might give a viewer cause to file a suit for damages or bring a flood of complaints.

The suggestions in the report were merely that – suggestions. Whether the writers or producers made the changes was entirely their decision. The network could hold the production company liable for damages if the concerns were not addressed. While some suggestions may have appeared on the front as ridiculous, the network had its reasons and in many cases, the producers and writers discovered something about illicit broadcast content they normally would have learned the hard way. It was in the interest of both parties to review first drafts and then make revisions for a second draft. The network never blew any whistles about the content on *The Twilight Zone*. There was never any tension between the producers and network. It was a standard business practice that, to this day, is still justified on legal grounds.

The Program Policies Department of CBS received the first draft of the script on June 19, 1963, and after their review, submitted a list of revisions dated July 3. Among the requests was removing the word "damned" from Raymond's speech early in the script, along with a number of references to "God" be removed. Flora's graphic comment of "blow it out your black bag" was deemed "unacceptable" by CBS, so Serling shortened the line to just "blow it." Regarding the discussion of ethics between Harmon and Raymond, and of Raymond's willingness to experiment on a fellow human, the network asked that they identify Raymond as a scientist or a medical researcher rather than a physician. The concern over this discussion was explained by CBS as trying to "avoid a debate with the American Medical Association."

In an early draft of this script, the closing narration was a bit different, and lengthier:

"S-s-s-s-h. Harmon Gordon is sleeping. He's taking a little nap. He'll wake up soon and impatiently demand a lollipop or a stuffed toy or some attention. Youth is like that. It demands. If you don't believe it – ask Flora. Ask her any day of the ensuing weeks of her life – as she takes notes during the coming years. And realizes that the worm has turned. The oppressed has become the persecutor. Youth has taken over. It's simply the way the calendar crumbles . . . in the Twilight Zone."

The entire episode was filmed on Stage 3, for a total cost of $1,491 for set decoration for the apartment and bedroom scenes. A casting call netted a small, but brief role for a baby boy, 2-years of age with dark colored hair.

Tim Matheson, who played the role of Harmon as a teenager, recalled how he and other minors were hired to play roles on television. "As a minor I was limited to the hours I could be on the set. Labor laws enforced that. How it worked was the child and their parents or legal guardians would visit the Board of Education, and apply for a permit. After which the parents or legal guardians, and someone chosen from a list of teachers, would be on the set the entire time. We would be limited to four hours of work per day, one hour of lunch and three hours of school. They were strict with that. For this episode, filmed in the summer, there was no need for school so I could be used a total of seven hours with a one hour lunch break. I couldn't be used past 6 p.m. without approval, so there were certain hours I could not work without exception."

"What I recall most were the grand days of M-G-M Studios when it was magnificent," Matheson continued. "Walking through the commissary was the best because I could catch glimpses of movie stars relaxing on break. Usually they were in the studios, so passing them in the street or outside the studios was rare . . . but the commissary was fun."

Back in May of 1960, Blanche Gaines forwarded to Rod Serling an original story outline by Jerome Ross titled "A Drink of Water." The story was about a man who discovers that he could prolong life indefinitely through the use of treated water, and while reliving a moment of his youth, discovers the negative qualities of being young and realizes too late that he made a mistake. Serling wrote to Ross on May 12, rejecting the idea for two reasons. One, the story did not fit the mold of *The Twilight Zone*, because, as Serling explained, he felt the story was too realistic and did not contain a hint of fantasy or at least the suggestion of fantasy or the unreal. Two, there were so many elements in the story he explained, "I'm afraid one will get in the way of the other instead of presenting a clear-cut, down-the-line plot development."

Buck Houghton looked over the story, and both men reevaluated the plot, suggesting Ross rewrite the outline. On May 20, 1960, Ross, who resided in New York City, wrote to Serling. "On learning of your definite interest, I've reworked it, boiled it down, so that it can easily be told in half an hour, with the emphasis on only two main characters, an elderly couple. As reworked it becomes a quite simple, clear-cut development."

Serling wrote back on May 24, explaining that while Houghton remained fascinated by the idea, he could not see how it can be dramatized in a 24-minute frame. On May 23, Serling elaborated with Blanche Gaines, "I showed it to both our producer and our new editor Del Reisman, neither of whom felt that the thing could be compressed to any realistic degree for our shooting purposes."

On speculation, so the script would retain the chief element of the story, without veering too far from the original plot, Ross wrote a teleplay based on the synopsis and resubmitted his proposal. Serling submitted it to Del Reisman, the editor and associate producer, who, in June 1960, made the final decision – he shelved it.

Ross had also submitted another plot synopsis in the spring of 1960, "The Man Who Likes Children." Serling felt it "was a honey." But the story got killed by a sponsor quirk. "General Foods who occupy one half of the show, take a dim view of anything that suggests horror and obviously the masks in the piece which are so integral to it would hardly pass muster with these food people."

In a letter dated August 20, 1962, Hirschman reminded Serling that the rights to the Jerome Ross story that had been temporarily shelved could be purchased and adapted into an hour-long teleplay. Serling again felt the story was acceptable, especially for an hour-long teleplay, but for reasons unknown, the story remained shelved. When arrangements were finalized to guarantee *The Twilight Zone* would revert to the half-hour format, Serling optioned to script an episode about the fountain of youth premise. Jerome Ross' story, however, was not adapted into a script. Instead, a submission by Louis Holz was accepted, met with Serling's approval, and a teleplay was drafted in the spring and summer of 1963.

In Serling's early draft of the script, the character of Raymond was originally Robert. The names Harmon and Flora, of course, were names Serling used repeatedly in other teleplays on the series. The title of this episode, during production and on the scripts was "A Drink From a Certain Fountain."

On January 3, 1964, Saul Cohen, Esq., of the law offices of Selvin, Cohen and Rosen, submitted a letter addressed to CBS Television asserting a possible claim of appropriation and wrongful use against Cayuga Productions with respect to this episode. Saul Cohen's claim was in question so Gerald H. Saltsman, associate resident counsel for Ashley-Steiner, forwarded the claim to A. Victor Sinclair of Rathbone, King and Seeley regarding Cayuga's insurance policy (policy/certificate No. L-71738). For the final season of the series, Cayuga was insured by Lloyd's. Standard policy whenever any such claim came to their attention was that reruns for episodes alleged as infringements were withheld until the matter was cleared.

Serling never stole anyone's idea for this episode, which was based on an unpublished story idea titled, "Ah, Youth!" by Louis Holz. Holz was a chief of security review at the Air Research & Development Command in Los Angeles. He had submitted a few stories to Cayuga in October of 1960, and after a brief discussion regarding "The Odyssey of Flight 33," (see that episode entry for more details), Serling purchased "Ah, Youth!" in good faith and in the hopes that one day he might be able to compose a teleplay adapted from the unpublished story. The suit was a temporary nuisance, causing this episode to be withdrawn from reruns and syndication until 1984, when CBS included this film as part of a two-hour holiday special.

Production #2615 "NINETY YEARS WITHOUT SLUMBERING"
(Initial telecast: December 20, 1963)
© Cayuga Productions, Inc., December 16, 1963, LP27862
Date of Rehearsal: September 9, 1963
Dates of Filming: September 10, 11 and 12, 1963

Carolyn Kearney and Ed Wynn share a family bond in between takes of "Ninety Years Without Slumbering."

Script dated: June 24, 1963 under the title of "The Grandfather Clock"
Revised excerpt dated: July 9, 1963
Revised script dated: August 23, 1963 under the title of "Tick of Time"

Producer and Secretary: $2,126.02
Story and Secretary: $3,910.00
Director: $1,500.00
Cast: $7,362.50
Unit Manager and Secretary: $726.01
Production Fee: $1,800.00
Agents Commission: $2,500.00
Legal and Accounting: $250.00
Below the line charges (M-G-M): $27,885.92
Below the line charges (other): $5,298.59
Total Production Costs: $53,359.04

Cast: Carol Byron (Carol Chase); James Callahan (Doug Kirk); Chuck Hicks (mover #2); Carolyn Kearney (Marnie Kirk); John Pickard (the policeman); William Sargent (Dr. Mel Avery); Dick Wilson (mover #1); and Ed Wynn (Sam Forstmann).

Original Music Score Composed and Conducted by Bernard Herrmann (Score No. CPN6113): Etrange #3 (by Marius Constant, :09); Milieu #2 (by Constant, :21); Grandfather's Clock (traditional, 1:05); Ninety Years #1 (1:06); Ninety Years #2 (:32); Ninety Years #3 (:28); Ninety Years #4 (1:08); Ninety Years #5 (:10); Ninety Years #6 (:54); Ninety Years #7 (:15); Ninety Years #8 (:25); Ninety Years #9 (1:56); Ninety Years #10 (:18); Ninety Years #11 (3:30); Ninety Years #12 (:35); Ninety Years Finale (:14); Etrange #3 (by Constant, :09); and Milieu #1 (by Constant, :22).

Director of Photography: Robert
    Pittack, a.s.c.
Art Directors: George W. Davis and
    Malcolm Brown
Set Decorations: Henry Grace and
    Robert R. Benton
Sound: Franklin Milton and Joe Edmondson

Production Manager: Ralph W. Nelson
Film Editor: Richard Heermance, a.c.e.
Casting: Patricia Rose
Assistant Director: Charles Bonniwell, Jr.
Produced by William Froug
Directed by Roger Kay

Teleplay by Richard De Roy, based on an original story by Johnson Smith (a pseudonym for George Clayton Johnson).

"Each man measures his time. Some with hope, some with joy, some with fear. But Sam Forstmann measures his allotted time by a grandfather's clock, a unique mechanism whose pendulum swings between

life and death, a very special clock that keeps a special kind of time . . . in the Twilight Zone."

Plot: Sam Forstmann, age 76, a clockmaker by trade, spends his retirement tending to a grandfather clock that was presented to his father on the day of his birth. The old man's preoccupation with the clock concerns his relatives, who believe his tinkering with the timepiece has become an obsession. Sam claims that when the clock stops

ticking, so will his heart. At the insistence of his in-laws, he agrees to pass on the clock to a new owner – the next-door neighbors. But when the neighbors leave for a week-long trip and fail to tell the old man, he attempts to break in the house to wind it up. The police arrive and escort him home, where Sam finally accepts the fact that he is soon going to die. Late that evening, Sam admits to himself that he has a grandchild coming soon, and perhaps what he really needs is a new preoccupation. He confesses to his daughter that when the clock stopped this evening, he was born again – and looks forward to a bright, new future.

"Clocks are made by men. God creates time. No man can prolong his allotted hours – he can only live them to the fullest, in this world or . . . in the Twilight Zone."

Trailer: *"Next time a new author joins the ranks of the elves and gremlins who supply the imaginative material on the Twilight Zone. His name is Richard De Roy and his story is in the best tradition of the program. It stars one of the gentlest and certainly the most able of America's actors. A beloved little fixture on the American scene named Ed Wynn. Next time out on the Twilight Zone, Ed Wynn stars in 'Ninety Years Without Slumbering.'"*

Trivia, etc. The script for this episode was assigned a production number on June 19, 1963, titled "The Grandfather Clock." When the script was revised under a new title, "Tick of Time," it was dated August 23, but an M-G-M work order officially changed the name of the production to "Tick of Time" on August 26. On September 5, an M-G-M work order referred to this episode as "Ninety Years Without Slumbering." Oddly enough, a press release issued by CBS dated October 6, announced Ed Wynn's appearance on *Twilight Zone* in the episode "Tick of Time."

"I was at dinner with Bert Granet and Rod and they were discussing how to do a few hour-long episodes," recalled George Clayton Johnson. "I met with Bert Granet one morning with some people where he told me that the show was going to make a return to a half hour. By then I had submitted the script to the show and Bill Froug had replaced Bert Granet. Bill had purchased the story and he hired a writer of his, Richard DeRoy, to write the script. It broke my heart that Bill wouldn't let me write the script. As an exercise, it was disappointing. The story line was in many ways . . . well, I felt I would have found a more clever way to do that. The actors were perfect. I was tempted to have my name removed from the credits, but I never did. I was tempted for them to use a pseudonym I used instead, but then I thought, 'Oh, what the hell' and let it go up there." The pseudonym Johnson used was Johnson Smith, a pen name he used a number of times.

Set Decoration Production Costs
Interior of the Kirk Home $800
Interior of Sam's Bedroom $200
Interior of the Doctor's Office $100
Exterior of the Homes and Streets $100
Interior of Chase Home $300
Total $1,500

Except for the nighttime scene outside the Chase home, which was filmed on Lot 2 at M-G-M, the entire episode was filmed on Stage 16.

"Ed Wynn being up in years at the time, when he had to go up and down the stairs [on the set], I had to help him," recalled actress Carolyn Kearney to author and interviewer Tom Weaver. "He would lean on me, and then he would say, 'Oh, but you're pregnant! Don't want to hurt you.' I said, 'But Mr. Wynn, I'm really not pregnant, I'm playing pregnant. You can lean on me any time you want to!' 'Oh, that's right, that's right!' – he laughed, he liked that. I just had a big ol' pad in my tummy, to make me look pregnant. I had actually just had a baby, so I knew how it felt! So I do remember he had a hard time going up and down the stairs. The director had him do it quite often, and we were getting very winded, and I said, 'Well, let's take a little time out and take a breath,' and so we did. I remember that he was very eager – he had to be pushing 80, but he was eager and he was interested. I think that's what kept him going, his eagerness and his interest."

"Rod Serling was on the set, because he was also the producer," continued Kearney. "He was there and he was very protective of Ed Wynn. He wanted to make sure that Ed Wynn had his chair and he wanted to make sure that Ed Wynn was well taken care of and that they didn't work him too hard. Roger Kay didn't do any of that, but Rod Serling was very instrumental in making sure that he was well taken care of. Roger Kay was a little frenetic, and not taking the time that Robert Florey and some of the other directors did. Roger Kay was sort of 'rushed' and you can't do anything good if you rush. Keenan Wynn, Ed Wynn's son, was also there to support his dad. I think he was worried about his father, because his father was in ill health, and Keenan Wynn was like, 'Now, Dad, I'm gonna be right here . . .'"

"Ed Wynn was more charming off camera than on," recalled James Callahan. "I was not an enthusiast for his movies. I couldn't even recall the names of any films except that TV thing he did called 'Requiem for a Heavyweight,' but I had respect for him as an actor. The first impression I got from him was an old man, crying for retirement, being forced to do that program. Seemed like he wanted to do it. Maybe to amuse himself. But when the director called action, he was a professional and I was taken back at how he transformed himself from an old man to an actor playing an old man. You had to be there to understand."

"Everyone was a joy to work with. No complications whatsoever," Callahan continued. "Ed was in poor health. You could see it. Everyone knew it. Remember that scene where you see a close-up of Ed's face through the clock as he's cleaning the gears? They had to get him a chair to sit on while they filmed that scene so he wouldn't stand up. He couldn't stand very long. In between takes he was always sitting."

Bob McCord, a stand-in and background extra for more episodes of *The Twilight Zone* than anyone else, substituted for Ed Wynn in a couple shots. The scene in which Ed Wynn's spirit rises up and speaks to his other self – on the set, Keenan Wynn was actually the person that Ed Wynn was speaking to in the scenes where [in the finished episode] Ed Wynn was talking to himself.

Months after filming was completed, Ed Wynn sent Serling a personal note thanking him for the opportunity to appear in another *Twilight Zone* and the gracious assistance given to him on the set while his health was in decline. Serling wrote a reply on December 26: "The Wynn legacy to Serling has been an incredible talent of longevity and a dignity and grace that are in most short supply these days."

On January 12, 1964, Walter Kempler, M.D., psychiatrist and director of The Kempler Institute in Los Angeles, whose motto was "Psychotherapy within the family, education and research," wrote to Serling, expressing his distaste for this particular episode of the *Twilight Zone*. "My objections are not serious and I submit them in the hope that psychiatrists could be consulted in such programs to present a better image of the psychiatrist and at the same time avoid mis-leading the population about psychological phenomena. First of all, as a psychiatrist, I would have guessed the patient's obsessional fantasy almost from the outset. Then I would never have recommended to his family that he take the 'iron cure' and treat his harmless obsession by urging him to give up the clock. I might have told him it was a crazy notion but that he could have it if he wished and would have then urged the family to temper their judgment of this life-long obsession."

"Adaptation in the aged is a most dangerous thing," he continued. "To remove a life-long obsession from a person of this age is impossible. It seems to me that for the sake of drama it is not necessary to distort psychological mechanisms too greatly. Many people who view this program may be led to attempt similar maneuvers with elderly people and the results could be disastrous. These people can be thrown into extremely severe depressive episodes and premature psychological, if not physical death."

Serling's reply was, in short, a defense and temporary solution. "I was not the author of this script, so this will be a kind of middle-man defense – if, indeed, it is a defense at all. In a half-hour program we very often have to take exceptional liberties in the treatment of peripheral characters. On certain occasions damage is unfortunately done to particular professional images simply by being forced to short shrift the characterizations. I've taken the liberty of sending your letter to the author of the script in the hope that he'll give you a personal response and, I'm rather sure, an apology."

Production #2623 "RING-A-DING GIRL" (Initial telecast: December 27, 1963)
Copyright Registration: © Cayuga Productions, Inc., December 22, 1963, LP29473
Dates of Filming: August 28, 29 and 30, 1963
First script dated: August 19, 1963
Revised script dated: August 23, 1963 with revised pages dated August 27, 1963.

Producer and Secretary: $2,126.02
Director: $1,750.00
Unit Manager and Secretary: $726.01
Agents Commission: $2,500.00
Below the line charges (M-G-M): $28,990.52
Total Production Costs: $49,218.98

Story and Secretary: $2,660.00
Cast: $4,655.20
Production Fee: $1,800.00
Legal and Accounting: $250.00
Below the line charges (other): $3,761.23

Cast: Bill Hickman (the pilot); Betty Lou Gerson (Cici); David Macklin (Bud Powell); Maggie McNamara (Bunny Blake); George Mitchell (Dr. Floyd); Mary Munday (Hildy Powell); Hank Patterson (Mr. Gentry); Vic Perrin (Jimmy, the State Trooper); and Bing Russell (Ben Braden).

Stock Music Cues: Etrange #3 (by Marius Constant, :09); Milieu #2 (by Constant, :21); Party Preparations (by Nathan Scott, :21); Allison's Confession (by Fred Steiner, :14); Martenot #2 (CBS, :24); Eerie Background (by Moraweck, :24, :23 and :24); Low Bass Note (CBS, :01); Easy Moment (by Jerry Goldsmith, :29); Allison's Confession (by Steiner, :15); Martenot #2 (CBS, :23); Eerie Background (by Moraweck, :23 and :22); Challenge (by Goldsmith, :15); Martenot #2 (CBS, :19);

Eerie Background (by Moraweck, :20 and :20); Terror Struck (by Goldsmith, :14); Rural Bounce (by Goldsmith, :23); Easy Moment (by Goldsmith, :32); Allison's Confession (by Steiner, :05); Martenot #2 (CBS, :22); Eerie Background (by Moraweck, :20 and :20); Lonely Moment (by Goldsmith, :22); Martenot #2 (CBS, :20); Eerie Background (by Moraweck, :20 and :20); Morning (by Steiner, :20); Heartbreak (by Goldsmith, :43); Jud's Song (by Steiner, :29); Harp Chords (CBS, :02); Etrange #3 (by Constant, :09); and Milieu #2 (by Constant, :21).

Director of Photography: George T. Clemens, a.s.c.	Production Manager: Ralph W. Nelson
Art Directors: George W. Davis and Walter Holscher	Film Editor: Richard Heermance, a.c.e.
Set Decorations: Henry Grace and Robert R. Benton	Casting: Patricia Rose
Sound: Franklin Milton and Joe Edmondson	Assistant Director: Charles Bonniwell, Jr.
	Produced by William Froug
	Directed by Alan Crosland, Jr.
	Teleplay by Earl Hamner, Jr.

"Introduction to Bunny Blake. Occupation: film actress. Residence: Hollywood, California, or anywhere in the world that cameras happen to be grinding. Bunny Blake is a public figure; what she wears, eats, thinks, says is news. But underneath the glamour, the makeup, the publicity, the build-up, the costuming ... is a flesh-and-blood person, a beautiful girl about to take a long and bizarre journey ... into the Twilight Zone."

Plot: Movie actress Barbara "Bunny" Blake, nicknamed the "Ring-A-Ding Girl," returns to her hometown of Howardville for a 24-hour vacation. The town is having the annual Founder's Day picnic this afternoon and her sister invites Bunny to the event. Bunny, however, wants the picnic to be postponed for a later date, so she can visit friends in their homes without the inconvenience of crowds and autograph seekers. Bunny seeks out her old friends, school superintendents and Ben Brady of the local television station, making arrangements to perform a one-woman show at the high school, causing most of the citizens to choose between the picnic and the performance. Later that afternoon, a transcontinental passenger plane crashes into the park where the picnic was originally planned. It turns out that a greater disaster was averted since most of the town's citizens had chosen to see Bunny Blake on stage, instead of being

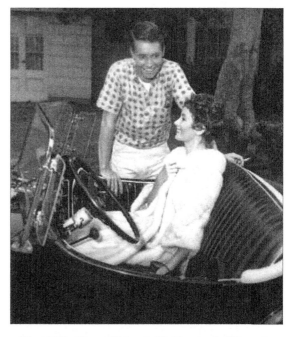

David Macklin and Maggie McNamara in "Ring-A-Ding Girl." Photo courtesy of David Macklin.

in the park. But Bunny Blake vanishes after the plane crash – and her body is recovered from the wreckage, having been a passenger on board the plane the entire time.

"We are all travelers. The trip starts in a place called birth . . . and ends in that lonely town called death. And that's the end of the journey, unless you happen to exist for a few hours, like Bunny Blake, in the misty regions . . . of the Twilight Zone."

Trailer: *"Next time we enlist the aid of a very talented scribe, Earl Hamner, Jr. He's written a story called 'Ring-A-Ding Girl' and in the milieu of fantasy this one is strictly a blue-ribbon entry. It stars Maggie McNamara and it involves a movie actress, a publicity tour, a strange flight, an airplane, and some occult occurrences designed to send shivers through you like a fast subway train. Next time out on the Twilight Zone, 'Ring-A-Ding Girl.'"*

Trivia, etc. The first draft of the script was titled "There Goes Bunny Blake," based on a story treatment titled "The Return of Hildy Blake." On August 20, the script was assigned a production number and the title then changed to "The Return of Bunny Blake." The episode title was not changed to "Ring-A-Ding Girl" until after production was completed. "The Return of Bunny Blake" was the working title during the entire production. The reason for the title change remains unknown, but it may have had something to do with the similarity of an Evelyn Piper novel titled *Bunny Lake is Missing.* Ironically, *Zone* staffer Charles Beaumont was given the writing assignment for Otto Preminger's motion picture in 1959, but it was shelved and never used; years later someone else wrote a screenplay based on the novel.

Almost every scene in the entire episode was filmed on Stage 16, using the same living room set featured in "Black Leather Jackets," "Living Doll" and "Ninety Years Without Slumbering" (with different furniture and props). The only exception is the park scene with actor Vic Perrin in the phone booth. That outside scene was filmed on Lot 2 at M-G-M. Production sheets stated the scenes filmed on Lot 2 could be filmed regardless of rain or shine.

"I am afraid most of my comments on working in that episode are a bit negative," recalled David Macklin. "First of all I didn't care for the script or my character. I was getting much bigger parts. But it was slow and I went for the money. My first experience was make-up where some old hack gave me the worst make-up I have ever experienced. It seemed he didn't think I was important enough to give the kind of make-up he did on Maggie and Mary. Maybe he didn't have time after doing them and thought he would catch up on the kid. Anyway, he simply smeared pancake all over my face including my mouth, eyelashes and brows. I had the sense to remove the make-up from those areas but I still looked lousy. It was that show that taught me to bring my own make-up to the set."

"Then I went to wardrobe and they dressed me in the worst shirt ever seen on television," Macklin continued. "That show also taught me to be more discriminating about wardrobe. Mr. Gossland was rather aloof and gave no help or encouragement. In fact I think his coverage of the final scene stinks. I didn't get a reaction shot and should have. On the positive side, Maggie and Mary were a delight to work with and I loved that car. Poor Maggie, she had to wear that one dress through the whole show and they never cleaned it. It was getting a little ripe near the end. I had no idea, at the time that I was working on a classic TV show [and] that a lot of people would like the segment. I certainly had no idea it would be rerun so much. I wouldn't be surprised if it were the most run TV show ever . . . and I receive no residuals, bah! Ironically, I didn't know at the time that I would get more mail for this program than any other."

The August 29, 1963, of *The Hollywood Reporter* was late in reporting Mary Munday had signed for a co-starring role in "There Goes Bunny Blake."

This was one of three episodes that were copyrighted from Canada, and registered as "Twilight Zone" and not "The Twilight Zone."

Production #2625 "YOU DRIVE" (Initial telecast: January 3, 1964)

Copyright Registration: © Cayuga Productions, Inc., December 28, 1963, LP28070
Date of Rehearsal: September 12, 1963
Dates of Filming: September 13, 16 and 17, 1963
First script dated: September 6, 1963
Shooting script dated: September 10, 1963

Producer and Secretary: $2,126.02	Story and Secretary: $2,660.00
Director: $1,685.00	Cast: $6,025.53
Unit Manager and Secretary: $726.01	Production Fee: $1,800.00
Agents Commission: $2,500.00	Legal and Accounting: $250.00
Below the line charges (M-G-M): $33,733.23	Below the line charges (other): $3,883.52
Total Production Costs: $55,389.31	

Cast: Totty Ames (Muriel Hastings, woman observer); Edward Andrews (Oliver Pope); Mike Gorfain (the newsboy); Kevin Hagen (Pete Ratcliffe); John Hanek (the policeman); and Hellena Westcott (Lillian Pope).

Stock Music Cues: Etrange #3 (by Marius Constant, :09); Milieu #2 (by Constant, :21); Ostinato Suspense Motion (by Constant, :22); String Flareouts (CBS, :04); Night Vigil (by Lucien Moraweck, :10); The Discovery (by Bernard Herrmann, :06); The Gun Nervous (by Goldsmith, :16); Dead Phone Nervous (by Goldsmith, :10); The Image (by Goldsmith, :08); Jackie's Escape (by Goldsmith, :08); New Man (by Goldsmith, :04); The Appointment (by Goldsmith, :17); Shadows (by Herrmann, :09); Old William (by Goldsmith, :53); The Discovery (by Herrmann, :06); The Fire (by Goldsmith, :32); The Discovery (by Hermann, :06); Old William (by Goldsmith, 1:00); The Fire (by Goldsmith, :22); The Discovery (by Herrmann, :06); The Wine (by Goldsmith, :07 and :07); Old William (by Goldsmith, :07); Return to the Past (by Goldsmith, :20); The Fire (by Goldsmith, :24); The Homecoming (by Goldsmith, :06 and :25); Jackie's Escape (by Goldsmith, :23); The Image (by Goldsmith, :23); The Discovery (by Herrmann, :06); The Meeting (by Goldsmith, :04); Jackie's Escape (by Goldsmith, :16); The Appointment (by Goldsmith, :04); Old William (by Goldsmith, :59); Police

Blooper! When Oliver and his wife consult the newspaper, the accident supposedly occurred at 3rd and Park. This fact was mentioned twice on the program. When Oliver faced the car in the garage and the radio turned on by itself, the news report on the radio mentioned the accident taking place at 3rd and Elm.

Station (by Goldsmith, :06); Algebra Rock (by Wilbur Hatch, 1:18); Old William (by Goldsmith, :34 and :14); The Image (by Goldsmith, :04); Police Station (by Goldsmith, :23); The Image (by Goldsmith, :10); The Knock (by Goldsmith, :11); Shadows (by Goldsmith, :31); Jackie's Escape (by Goldsmith, :28); Counterattack – Part 2 (by Goldsmith, :40); 26 Stings or Accents (by Garriguenc, :04); The Gun Nervous (by Goldsmith, :42); Etrange #3 (by Constant, :09); and Milieu #1 (by Constant, :22).

Director of Photography: George T. Clemens, a.s.c.
Art Directors: George W. Davis and Malcolm Brown
Set Decorations: Henry Grace and Robert R. Benton
Sound: Franklin Milton and Joe Edmondson

Production Manager: Ralph W. Nelson
Film Editor: Thomas W. Scott
Casting: Patricia Rose
Assistant Director: Charles Bonniwell, Jr.
Produced by William Froug
Directed by John Brahm
Teleplay by Earl Hamner, Jr.

"Portrait of a nervous man: Oliver Pope by name, office manager by profession. A man beset by life's problems: his job, his salary, the competition to get ahead. Obviously, Mr. Pope's mind is not on his driving . . . Oliver Pope, businessman–turned–killer on a rain–soaked street in the early evening of just another day during just another drive home from the office. The victim, a kid on a bicycle, lying injured, near death. But Mr. Pope hasn't time for the victim, his only concern is for himself. Oliver Pope, hit-and-run driver, just arrived at a crossroad in his life, and he's chosen the wrong turn. The hit occurred in the world he knows, but the run will lead him straight into . . . the Twilight Zone."

Plot: Driving home from work one evening, Oliver Pope accidentally hits a delivery boy and flees the scene of the crime. He reads in the paper the next morning that the child is under intensive care and later dies of his injuries. As the hours pass, Oliver's conscience gets a nudge in the form of his automobile, which begins taking on a life of its own. Flashing the lights and honking the horn, the auto attempts to drive Oliver into a confession. When his wife takes the car to a mechanic, the

Filmed on Location
Residence at 4183 Keystone Ave, Culver City
Residence at 4169 Motor Ave. Culver City
Residence at 4160 Motor Ave. Culver City
Residence at 4220 Motor Ave. Culver City
Vinton Street, Motor Avenue, Braddock Street and two other miscellaneous streets

car stalls at the same intersection of the hit-and-run. Late one evening, the car starts blaring the radio, and Oliver responds by smashing the electronics. When the lights start flashing, he smashes the bulbs. When the horn begins to sound, he rips out the wires. The next morning, Oliver decides to walk to work – and the automobile starts a campaign of psychological warfare by following him, giving chase through the streets. Almost running him over, Oliver finally relents and agrees to ride in the car, which drives him to the local police station. Out of options, Oliver enters the station to make a confession.

"All persons attempting to conceal criminal acts involving their cars are hereby warned: check first to see

that underneath that chrome there does not lie a conscience, especially if you're driving along a rain-soaked highway . . . . in the Twilight Zone."

Trailer: *"On Twilight Zone next time, again the services of Earl Hamner, Jr. in a strange story, a strange conclusion and a very unusual brand of justice, dramatizing a show called 'You Drive.' It's the story of a hit-and-run driver and a very special kind of an automobile. The consummately fine actor named Edward Andrews lives out a nightmare partly of his own making. On Twilight Zone, 'You Drive.' I hope you're going to watch it with us."*

Trivia, etc. While the car appeared normal enough on the exterior, the interior was something else. The 1956 Ford was found by M-G-M Studios transportation men in a used car lot. When purchased, it had a spruced-up engine and two bullet holes in a side panel. The studio invested $1,000 in special engineering so the car could drive itself, or at least give that impression for the cameras.

While some scenes featured Andrews in the driver's seat, when the car moved on its own, the real driver was Hal Grist, who handled the controls from a prone position. To rig the automobile for the role, the partition between the trunk and rear seat was removed and a mattress was installed so the driver could lie down to handle the controls. A rudder bar was attached to the steering assembly and a special mirror arrangement was installed, permitting the driver to see ahead. While the cast was rehearsing on September 12 in the studio, the technical crew test drove the specially rigged automobile in the evening on a deserted lot to ensure there would be no problems during filming.

The first day of filming was on Stage 28 at M-G-M Studios. Most of the second and third day were devoted to filming on location in Culver City. (For the complicated and risky scenes, Bill Clark doubled for Andrews in the vehicle.) To film on location, Cayuga had to purchase Culver City Business Permits at a total of $40 ($20 per day of filming). Police officers were provided to maintain local traffic, provided courtesy of arrangements made through Captain Lugo of the local police department. Lugo also granted permission to film outside the police station, though some studio paperwork claims the exterior of the police station was located at rival television network NBC. Filming at another studio seems unlikely, and the notation is possibly a clerical error.

Mr. Kronenthal granted permission for Cayuga to film at the corner of Victory Park, in Culver City, where the hit-and-run scene was filmed. A number of street residences were caught on camera, so Cayuga paid the residents of those houses a fee for permission. The fee varied from residence to residence. Helen Freeman was paid $25 while Ruth Jacobson was paid $50. (It's possible if a resident was married, two signatures were required for permission, thus $50 instead of $25.)

Production #2624 "THE LONG MORROW" (Initial telecast: January 10, 1964)

Copyright Registration: © Cayuga Productions, Inc., January 3, 1964, LP28071 (in notice: 1963)
Date of Rehearsal: September 18, 1963
Dates of Filming: September 19, 20 and 23, 1963
Script dated: August 27, 1963, with revised pages dated September 5, 1963.
Revised shooting draft dated: September 17, 1963

Producer and Secretary: $2,126.02   Story and Secretary: $3,310.00
Director: $1,500.00   Cast: $4,800.00

Unit Manager and Secretary: $726.01
Agents Commission: $2,500.00
Below the line charges (M-G-M): $29,213.79
Total Production Costs: $49,776.09

Production Fee: $1,800.00
Legal and Accounting: $250.00
Below the line charges (other): $3,550.27

Cast: Edward Binns (General Walters); Mariette Hartley (Sandra Horn); Robert Lansing (Commander Douglas Stansfield); George Macready (Dr. Bixler); Donald Spruance (man #1); and William Swan (the technician).

Stock Music Cues: Etrange #3 (by Marius Constant, :09); Milieu #2 (by Constant, :21); Strange Return (by Jerry Goldsmith, :40); Light Rain (by Constant, :07); Silent Flight (by Goldsmith, :43); Ambush (by Fred Steiner, :09); The Unknown (by Steiner, :36 and :10); Strange Return (by Goldsmith, :40); Autumn Love (by Goldsmith, 1:14, :37 and :30); Silent Flight (by Goldsmith, :55); Now We Move (by Nathan Van Cleave, :23); The Unknown (by Steiner, :11); Autumn Love (by Goldsmith, :15 and :17); Morning (by Steiner, :20); Light Rain (by Constant, :08); Strange Return (by Goldsmith, :26); Morning (by Steiner, :26); Now We Move (by Steiner, :39); Harp Effects (CBS, :36); Autumn Love (by Goldsmith, :17); Morning (by Steiner, :20); Strange Return (by Goldsmith, :31); Etrange #3 (by Constant, :09); and Milieu #1 (by Constant, :22).

Director of Photography: George T.
    Clemens, a.s.c.
Art Directors: George W. Davis and
    Malcolm Brown
Set Decorations: Henry Grace and
    Robert R. Benton
Directed by Robert Florey

Production Manager: Ralph W. Nelson
Film Editor: Richard Heermance, a.c.e.
Casting: Patricia Rose
Assistant Director: Charles Bonniwell, Jr.
Sound: Franklin Milton and Joe Edmondson
Produced by William Froug
Teleplay by Rod Serling

"It may be said with a degree of assurance that not everything that meets the eye is as it appears. Case in point – the scene you're watching. This is not a hospital . . . not a morgue . . . not a mausoleum . . . not an undertaker's parlor of the future. What it is, is the belly of a spaceship. It is en route to another planetary system . . . an incredible distance from the Earth. This is the crux of our story – a flight into space. It is also the story of the things that might happen to human beings who take a step beyond, unable to anticipate everything that might await them out there . . . [bridge between scenes] . . . Commander Douglas Stansfield, astronaut, a man about to embark on one of history's longest journeys: forty years out into endless space and hopefully back again. This is the beginning, the first step toward man's longest leap into the unknown. Science has solved the mechanical details, and now it's up to one human being to breathe life into blueprints and computers . . . to prove once and for all that man can live half a lifetime in the total void of outer space, forty years alone in the unknown. This is Earth. Ahead lies a planetary system. The vast region in between is . . . the Twilight Zone."

Plot: Set in the near future, an astronaut named Douglas Stansfield is assigned to an experimental interplanetary space flight to an unexplored solar system with a planet that "may" support other life. His destination is 141 light years (a rough estimate) round trip, which will take about 40 years. The custom-built craft is designed with an interstellar drive. As the sole occupant, a special glass case will be designed to put Stansfield into hibernation – so he will age no more than a few weeks during his entire trip. Stansfield's career choice is set back by a romantic fling with Sandra Horn, a young employee of the Space Agency. Very much apart from protocol, they know their relationship is only temporary, yet Stansfield still sets out on his trip, bidding his love a fond farewell. Almost 40 years later, Stansfield's ship is making a return and makes contact with the new commander in charge of the Space Agency. The arrival is greeted with a shocking surprise. Knowing her life would be dull and meaningless without him, Sandra had made arrangements to be put into a similar hibernation chamber days after Stansfield's takeoff. Today, she is still in her early 30s, but Stansfield, however, has a surprise for Sandra. Six months into the flight, he woke from the hibernation chamber and spent the past 40 years dreaming of his young love, knowing they would be the same age when he arrived home. Though she insisted that their love will continue to grow, Stansfield has 40 years of wisdom to his name, and tells her to leave – he no longer places a premium on love.

"Commander Douglas Stansfield. One of the forgotten pioneers of the space age. He's been pushed aside by the flow of progress and the passage of years . . . and the ferocious travesty of fate. Tonight's tale of the ionosphere and irony . . . delivered from . . . the Twilight Zone."

Trailer: *"Next on the Twilight Zone, a rather probing study in ice, irony, and the ionosphere. A show titled, 'The Long Morrow.' It stars Robert Lansing and Mariette Hartley and it tells the story of an incredible trip into space with the sole occupant of the craft living in suspended animation. This one is for space addicts and the romantically inclined. On the Twilight Zone – 'The Long Morrow.'"*

Trivia, etc. One scene in the first draft of the script was eliminated for the second draft. A low bell rings constantly and the door to the glass case opened automatically. Color returned to Stansfield's face and the temperature gauge rose slowly. A small speaker near the receptacle featured a voice, recorded, coming through clearly. "This is a prerecorded time check and periodic duty reminder. Repeat. This is a prerecorded time check and duty recorder. You have been in space for exactly one month, 11 days, 13 hours, 22 minutes. This is one of 131 interval moments when course, speed, temperature, must all be manually checked." Stansfield walks over to the bank of equipment, swinging his arms back and forth restoring circulation. He checks several readings, checks a radar screen, looks over grid-lines and pushes another button.

The voice then reminds Stansfield that if he returns to the receptacle, the closing of the lid will automatically put him back in suspension. He walks over to the receptacle, puts his hand on the side as if to go back in, stares at it, turns, and moves back across the room to an instrument panel. He pushes several buttons and then pulls down a microphone. "This is Solar-2 Probe calling Earth . . . calling Earth." A light flashes and a distant static voice can be heard – totally indistinguishable. Stansfield speaks into the microphone again. "You're obviously hearing me but I'm too far away to receive you. I'll make an assumption I'm coming through clearly enough to be understood. The following information should be relayed to my Base and to Dr. Bixler in charge of our project. I'm . . I'm not going back into the receptacle. I'm going to . . . I'm going to try to stay alive and awake." Standfield explains that the food stores, placed in the ship to cover an emergency breakdown of the freezing equipment, are ample to carry him through. He will try to make periodic checks until he reaches his destination . . . and the same during his return trip.

He pushes another button and moves the microphone away. Walking over to the receptacle, he removes a metal object from the wall, like a crowbar, and smashes it down on the glass receptacle, breaking it. "I'll sleep eight hours at a time, thank you. Eight hours at a time. And if I age, I age. And if I starve, I starve. And if I die of loneliness . . . so be it. So be it. Sandy, my dear . . . you're the old woman in the lace shawl. I'll be the old man in the worn space suit. God willing . . . I'll be the old man."

A series of facial shots helps span the passing years. While this scene was removed for the second draft of the script, it does explain the details involving Stansfield's efforts to remain out of the chamber during his space flight. During the actual film, there is no reference to Stansfield periodically monitoring the controls, checking the gauges and returning to the chamber, leaving the audience with the question of how he could have possibly woke out of the chamber on route to his destination. There is no reference to him being woken from suspended animation except for when he reached his destination, and his arrival back on Earth.

Playing the role of the doctor was George Macready, who usually played the role of heavies, but nonetheless called himself a "character man." In this *Twilight Zone* episode, he played the role of a doctor working on the good side. "I like heavies, though," he told a reporter for *TV Guide*. "It's enjoyable to have the upper hand – for a while. I try to achieve a different approach to each character. Then, too, I think there's a bit of evil in all of us."

Macready was a newspaperman in New York, studied drama on the side and began banging on casting directors' doors. In 1928 he picked up a small part in *Macbeth*. He acted with Katherine Cornell (in *Romeo and Juliet* and *The Barretts of Wimpole Street*) and with Helen Hayes (in *Victoria Regina*). Entering the movies in 1942, he became the embodiment of the sinister aristocrat with the scar on his cheek, playing the role with variations in numerous pictures. He was also one of the first movie actors to try television. In 1948 he did his first live show for *Kraft Theater* in New York and stuck with television. In May of 1960, he played the role of Captain Richter in Serling's "In the Presence of Mine Enemies," the final telecast of the *Playhouse 90* series.

A production number was assigned on August 27, 1963, and the entire episode was filmed on Stage 29. The premise of a man in suspended animation in a glass case to escape the passing years was applied in previously in "The Rip Van Winkle Caper." Serling would reuse the same concept, this time involving four astronauts instead of one, traveling through space, in *Planet of the Apes* (1968).

This episode of *Twilight Zone* was loosely adapted from O. Henry's "The Gift of the Magi." It was not the first time Serling was involved in an adaptation. Sometime circa 1948, he played the role of Jim Young, in a radio adaptation (which he also scripted) dramatized locally from WMRN in Marion, Ohio. This was the same radio station for which Serling wrote a number of 15-minute radio scripts titled *The Sutton and Lightner Personal Album*, which was sponsored by Sutton & Lightner, located at 131 South Prospect Street. It told the tale of a young couple, in a poor economic condition, who wish to purchase something special for each other for the holiday. She sells her long hair to afford the money to buy him a chain for his prized watch. He sells his prized watch to buy a set of combs for her hair.

In November of 1960, Serling was approached by the Board of National Measures of the United Presbyterian Church of the U.S.A., located in New York City, to possibly adapt a teleplay from the O. Henry short story. After much correspondence, negotiations and rights clarifications, Serling did so, submitting the script on March 8, 1961.

Television critics across the country were quick to pick up on the variation-on-a-theme, inspired by "The Gift of the Magi." The television critic for *The Lima News* remarked, "The twist here is decidedly O. Henry." The same review also described the plot as "a moving love story which has some pungent comments on the speed of progress in space exploration."

"I was head of the drama club at Staples High School in Westport, Connecticut," recalled Mariette Hartley. "It seemed everyone at the school saw 'Requiem for a Heavyweight' so I decided to write to him and see if he would be interested in coming to our club and talk about television drama. And he did! He came to the school and boy was I the shining star for that week, I'll tell you!"

"Oh yes, years later I was acting professionally and made the move to Hollywood. I was probably one of the last people to be signed to a studio contract at M-G-M. Of course, I had spent time waiting to be told what my next picture was. There was an afternoon I was on the back lot. I cannot recall if Rod Serling was riding in a limousine or in a golf cart between sound stages, but I waved and caught his attention. I got him to stop for a moment and introduced myself, and he remembered me. I was bold enough to ask him for a part in a *Twilight Zone* and he said there might be an opening and get back to me. A few friends were with me at the time and I remember them laughing at me for the stunt I pulled, but I showed them, didn't I?"

Production #2612 "THE SELF-IMPROVEMENT OF SALVADORE ROSS" (Initial telecast: January 17, 1964)

Copyright Registration: © Cayuga Productions, Inc., January 13, 1964, LP28072
Date of Rehearsal: July 26, 1963
Dates of Filming: July 30 and 31, and August 1, 1963
Script dated: June 7, 1963 with revised pages dated July 23 and 25, 1963.

Producer and Secretary: $1,626.02
Director: $1,625.00
Unit Manager and Secretary: $726.01
Agents Commission: $2,500.00
Below the line charges (M-G-M): $31,934.49
Total Production Costs: $52,098.24

Story and Secretary: $3,410.00
Cast: $5,331.25
Production Fee: $1,800.00
Legal and Accounting: $250.00
Below the line charges (other): $2,895.47

Cast: Seymour Cassel (Jerry); Douglass Dumbrille (Mr. Halpert); Don Gordon (Salvadore Ross); Colin Kenny (the derelict); Gail Kobe (Leah Maitland); Doug Lambert (Mr. Albert); J. Pat O'Malley (the hospital patient); Kathleen O'Malley (the nurse); and Vaughn Taylor (Mr. Maitland).

Stock Music Cues: Etrange #3 (by Marius Constant, :09); Milieu #2 (by Constant, :21); Loneliness (by D.B. Ray, :11 and :11); Home (by Jerry Goldsmith, :03 and :16); Peg's Sorrow (by Goldsmith, :18); Low Bass Notes (CBS, :01); Solemn Finish (by Goldsmith, :21); A Story #1 (by Constant, :03); Unison Horn Note on C (CBS, :04); Aftermath (by D.B. Ray, :40); Bathroom (by Franz Waxman, :23); A Story #1 (by Constant, :04); Bergson #1 (by Constant, :22 and :22); Bathroom (by Franz Waxman, :12); Belfort #3 (by Constant, :27); Bergson #5 (by Constant, :14); Bathroom (by Waxman, :12); Sand (by Fred Steiner, :24); Morning (by Steiner, :22); Challenge (by Goldsmith, :18); Summer Love (by Goldsmith, :56 and :13); Perry Mason Background (by Steiner, :03); Sand (by Steiner, :16);

Dirge (by Goldsmith, :25); Low Bass Notes (CBS, :02); Etrange #3 (by Constant, :09); and Milieu #2 (by Constant, :21).

Director of Photography: George T. Clemens, a.s.c.
Art Directors: George W. Davis and Walter Holscher
Set Decorations: Henry Grace and Robert R. Benton
Sound: Franklin Milton and Philip N. Mitchell

Production Manager: Ralph W. Nelson
Film Editor: Richard Heermance, a.c.e.
Casting: Patricia Rose
Assistant Director: Charles Bonniwell, Jr.
Produced by Bert Granet
Directed by Don Siegel

Teleplay by Jerry McNeely, based on the short story of the same name by Henry Slesar, originally published in the May 1961 issue of *The Magazine of Fantasy and Science Fiction*.

"Confidential personnel file on Salvadore Ross. Personality: a volatile mixture of fury and frustration. Distinguishing physical characteristic: a badly-broken hand which will require emergency treatment at the nearest hospital. Ambition: shows great determination toward self-improvement. Estimate of potential success: a sure bet for a listing in Who's Who . . . in the Twilight Zone."

Plot: Admitted to a hospital for a broken hand, Salvadore Ross discovers that he possesses a weird bargaining power that grants him the opportunity to exchange medical symptoms. Having lived in the slums of the city where a man has to bargain, trade, steal and borrow to make a living, he puts his gift to good use by offering a millionaire the opportunity to purchase a number of years. Salvadore gains 40 plus years to his age, the aged millionaire becomes young again, and Salvadore profits with a million dollars and a luxury penthouse. Selling a year or two among various juveniles, he gains back his youth and still makes a profit. Visiting the apartment of an ex-girlfriend named Leah, Salvadore attempts to win her hand through her father, thanks to a few "self-improvements." Salvadore has no compassion and Leah tries to explain that compassion is not something he can buy. Unable to comprehend, he offers her father $100,000 for his compassion – in hopes of winning her heart . . . and in doing so, performs the same switch. Finally gaining Leah's respect, and her love, he asks her father for forgiveness and compassion – the latter of which her father no longer possesses – and pulls out a gun and shoots Salvadore Ross.

Set Decoration Production Costs
Exterior of the City Street $410
Interior of the Hospital Ward $265
Interior of the Bar $25
Interior of the Rooming House and Hall $230
Exterior of the Alley $50
Interior of the Apartment, Garage and Elevator $340
Interior of the Halpert Apartment $687
Interior of the Maitland Apartment $140
Total $2,147

"The Salvadore Ross program for self-improvement. The all-in-one, sure-fire success course that lets you lick the bully, learn the language, dance the tango and anything else you want to do . . . or think you want to do. Money-back guarantee. Offer limited to . . . the Twilight Zone."

Trailer: *"Next time out on the Twilight Zone, an unusual little item from the pen of Jerry McNeely, based on a story by Henry Slesar, and called intriguingly enough, 'The Self-Improvement of Salvadore Ross.' This one poses the question, if you don't like what you are, how do you go about changing? Don Gordon portrays a man who really goes to the root when it comes to some basic changing, and the results are most unexpected."*

Trivia, etc. Jerry McNeely was a professor of the University of Wisconsin speech department, whose credits included writing original scripts for *Hall of Fame*, *Studio One*, *Climax!*, and at least four scripts for *Dr. Kildare*. He submitted a short story that was purchased and adapted for "A Kind of a Stopwatch," and having got his foot in the door, so to speak, he managed to secure the task of adapting Henry Slesar's short story for this *Twilight Zone* production, his first and only teleplay for the series.

The street scenes were shot on Lot 2 at M-G-M, while the rest of the episode was filmed on Stage 19. Serling's narration and trailer were filmed on Lot 2 on the second day of filming.

Gail Kobe tore her pantyhose on the set, so a new pair had to be purchased for her (a cost of $3.00 against Cayuga funds). The ones torn were her own, so the production company allowed her to take the new pair home with her. According to a recent CBS policy, a Negro was hired to play a pedestrian and be able to drive an automobile if called on.

Actor Ted Jacques was hired to play the role of a bartender named Stan for scene 17, which ended up on the cutting room floor. In the scene, the interior of a bar, Salvadore is suffering from a cough and asks the bartender how much money he has in the till. Stan says "no touches today" (referring to money). Sal looks at Stan's bald head and asks how much it would be worth to have a full set of hair. Stan agrees to the trade, but asks when the switcheroo would occur and Salvadore says he doesn't know exactly. Of course, the bartender will be pleased by morning, but the television audience never gets to see the bar scene, or the results of the exchange.

In the spring of 1974, Henry Slesar wrote a script for an episode of the radio program, *The CBS Radio Mystery Theater*, titled "A Bargain in Blood." The hour-long radio drama was an adaptation of Slesar's story "The Self-Improvement of Salvadore Ross." Ken Roberts played the lead, Evelyn Juster played Ruth Maitland, and Mandel Kramer played her father, Mr. Maitland.

Production #2613 "WHAT THE DEVIL?"
Television script by Arch Oboler, dated June 11, 1963.

"Traffic incident on an Arizona highway. Menacing ingredients as they stand . . . An impatient man in a hot sports car with an urging lady at his elbow. But to compound the menace . . . The following geographical item. The road's in Arizona and it runs west to California. But it's also one of the main thoroughfares that runs in and out . . . of the Twilight Zone!"

Plot: Millie and Frank, driving a Jaguar across the desert, witness a hellish hit-and-run that kills the driver of one of the vehicles. In shock, the two start to suspect the fleeing driver may have seen them and now set his sights on the witnesses. Their suspicions are confirmed when, further down the road, the huge truck takes chase. The words "Danger, High Explosives" are on the side of the vehicle, but the driver misses his mark and the couple manages to get away. Frank tells Millie he caught a glimpse of the driver, and she laughs when he tells her it was the Devil. In a game of cat and mouse, they manage to switch vehicles, hoping the driver is looking for the Jaguar and not a station wagon. Millie, meanwhile, discovers that Frank committed a brutal act before leaving on the trip, and the driver may be a form of conscience. Ultimately, the truck catches up and once again, gives chase, hits-and-runs, this time taking the lives of Millie and Frank, the police arrive on the scene to find the car flattened. One of the officers is puzzled when he points out to his partner the hoof prints burned in the pavement, "like something walked around watching them burn!"

"A wisp of smoke on a lonely Arizona road. They say the Gods grind small. But sometimes, they say, the Gods stay their hands and permit the Evil One to finish the grinding . . . in the Twilight Zone."

Trivia, etc. Rod Serling respected the craft of radio writing and admired such legends as Norman Corwin and Arch Oboler. So it is no surprise that when Oboler approached Serling with an idea for *The Twilight Zone*, the playwright was all ears. From 1942 to 1943, Oboler scripted a total of 52 episodes for a horror program titled *Lights Out!*, sponsored by Ironized Yeast and broadcast over the CBS. The premiere episode, aired on October 6, 1942, was a radio play titled "What the Devil?" and this *Twilight Zone* teleplay was a faithful adaptation of the radio version. Gloria Blondell and Wally Maher played the leads for the radio version.

Serling insisted the script be purchased from Oboler, and Bert Granet went along with Serling's decision. (A letter dated October 2, 1963, from Granet to Serling, suggests that this arrangement was a fiasco, and Granet disliked the idea from the start, keeping silent to please Serling for a decision that ultimately never went before the cameras.)

Assigned a production number on June 11, 1963, the television script was clearly intended to be filmed for the fifth season of *The Twilight Zone*. The attempt was short-lived. An M-G-M work order dated August 13, 1963 announced the cancellation of this production, and most of the copies of the scripts were returned to Oboler. Serling retained at least two copies for his records, and donated one to UCLA. According to tax paperwork and financial records, secretarial and other expenses cost Cayuga Productions a total of $420.47. No paperwork has been found to verify how much Arch Oboler was paid (if he was paid at all) for his teleplay, which would have been an additional expense to Cayuga.

Shortly after the telecast of the 1971 made-for-TV movie *Duel*, directed by Steven Spielberg, Arch Oboler threatened to sue the director, claiming plagiarism. Oboler felt that the story and script for the movie mirrored too close to his radio and television script, and wanted to sue for infringement. The case was ultimately dropped, but Oboler felt scorned for many years, crying victim on radio interviews during the late 1970s and early 1980s.

The script for the movie was adapted by Richard Matheson from his own short story, originally published in *Playboy*. The idea came to Matheson from a real-life experience, in which Matheson was tailgated by a trucker on his way home from a golfing match with writer friend Jerry Sohl, on the same day as the Kennedy assassination.

Production #2617 "THE DOLL"
Television script by Richard Matheson, dated June 27, 1963.

"An exchange of smiles in a little side-street doll shop; one, the smile of a nameless female doll, the other, that of Mr. John Walters, forty-two, unmarried – and a very lonely man. Shortly, Mr. Walters is to purchase said doll and take it from the shop; this much, he already knows. What he doesn't know is that, having left the shop, his path will be directed on a straight line – right across the border of the Twilight Zone."

Plot: A bachelor named John Walters purchases a doll for his 12-year-old niece and discovers by accident that she has outgrown the fascination for toy dolls. Believing the face on the doll is too beautiful a craftsmanship to return, John takes it home with him. As the weeks pass, John strikes up a friendship with the non-responsive doll, assigning the female figure the name of Mary and carries on a one-sided conversation. One afternoon, returning to Liebemacher's shop where he purchased the doll, John discovers that there was a model of inspiration – and her name is Mary Dickinson, a school teacher. John learns where she lives, but hesitates paying her a visit for fear that she might think of him as a stalker or a psycho. Ultimately, he builds up the courage to call on her, and Mary welcomes him in. As they introduce themselves, John discovers that she, too, lives by herself – and also is lonely. She has a doll on her mantle she named John. After noticing her doll strikes a similarity to his facial features, he realizes that Liebemacher, in German, means "maker of love."

"Sir Edwin Arnold said it: 'Somewhere there waited in this world of ours / For one lone soul, another lonely soul – Each chasing each through all the weary hours – and meeting strangely at one sudden goal.' To which it might be added: Especially when assisted by one Mr. Liebemacher and the more accommodating influences – of the Twilight Zone."

Trivia, etc. This script was assigned a production number on June 28, 1963. Revised pages of the script are dated July 10. Filming dates were slated for sometime during the last week of August running into the first week of September. For reasons unknown, production never went before the cameras. On September 20, 1963, Ralph W. Nelson officially reported that the production had been canceled.

William Froug took over the producing after Bert Granet, and it was Froug's decision not to do this script. As Richard Matheson remarked years later, Froug "didn't like my writing." According to production files dated May 31, 1964, Cayuga invested a total of $420.47 in assorted expenses for this production.

Ironically, Matheson's teleplay was filmed for an episode of television's *Amazing Stories* two decades later, initially telecast on May 4, 1986. On September 21, 1986, this episode helped secure three Emmy Awards. John Lithgow won an Emmy for "Outstanding Guest Performer in a Drama Series" for his performance as John Walters, John McPherson won an Emmy for "Outstanding Cinematography for a Series," and Bernadette (Bunny) Parker won an Emmy for "Outstanding Hairstyling for a Series."

Production #2618 "NUMBER 12 LOOKS JUST LIKE YOU"
(Initial telecast: January 24, 1964)

Copyright Registration: © Cayuga Productions, Inc., January 20, 1964, LP28073
Date of Rehearsal: September 24, 1963
Dates of Filming: September 25, 26 and 27, 1963
Script dated: July 8, 1963, "The Beautiful People"
Script dated: September 4, 1963
Revised script dated: September 23 and 24, 1963

Producer and Secretary: $2,126.02
Director: $1,500.00
Unit Manager and Secretary: $726.01
Agents Commission: $2,500.00
Below the line charges (M-G-M): $32,127.42
Total Production Costs: $54,404.33

Story and Secretary: $2,660.00
Cast: $7,312.51
Production Fee: $1,800.00
Legal and Accounting: $250.00
Below the line charges (other): $3,402.37

Cast: Pam Austin (Valerie / Number 8 / Marilyn after the transformation); Richard Long (Uncle Rock / Jack / Doctor Rex / Professor Sig / Dr. Tom / Number 17); Suzy Parker (Lana Cuberle / Grace, the maid / Eva Simmons / Jane / Number 12 / Nurse Doe / patient on stretcher); and Collin Wilcox (Marilyn Cuberle).

Stock Music Cues: Etrange #3 (by Marius Constant, :09); Milieu #2 (by Constant, :21); Brave New World (by Bernard Herrmann, :16, :17, :49, :16 and :16); The Knife Invaders (by Jerry Goldsmith, :11); Brave New World (by Herrmann, :06, :16 and :20); Curiosity (by Fred Steiner, :08 and :26); Brave New World (by Herrmann, :07); Chris Walks (by Steiner, :32 and :31); The Knife Invaders (by Goldsmith, :23); Chris Jr. (by Steiner, :42); The Road (by Steiner, :10); Curiosity (by Steiner, :07); Brave New World (by Herrmann, :15); Loire #2 (by Constant, :08); Brave New World (by Herrmann, :48); Low Bass Notes (CBS, :02); Etrange #3 (by Constant, :09); and Milieu #1 (by Constant, :22).

Director of Photography: Charles
    Wheeler, a.s.c.
Art Directors: George W. Davis and
    Malcolm Brown
Set Decorations: Henry Grace and
    Robert R. Benton
Directed by Abner Biberman

Production Manager: Ralph W. Nelson
Film Editor: Thomas W. Scott
Casting: Patricia Rose
Assistant Director: Charles Bonniwell, Jr.
Sound: Franklin Milton and Edmondson
Produced by William Froug

Teleplay by John Tomerlin, based on the short story "The Beautiful People" by Charles Beaumont, originally published in the September 1952 issue of *If*.

"Given the chance, what young girl wouldn't happily exchange a plain face for a lovely one? What girl could refuse the opportunity to be beautiful? For want of a better estimate, let's call it the year 2000. At any rate, imagine a time in the future when science has developed a means of giving everyone the face and body he dreams of. It may not happen tomorrow, but it happens now . . . in the Twilight Zone."

Richard Long adores Pam Austin
(or is she Number 8?)

Plot: In a future society where cosmetics and plastic surgery have replaced braces and contact lenses, young children at the age of 19 are required to go through a "transformation," granting them the opportunity to be surgically altered to resemble one of a limited number of fashion models. Marilyn, at the age of 18, chooses not to look like everyone else. In a society without ugliness, there can be no beauty, she debates. Isn't being the same as everybody, the same as being nobody? Her actions puzzle her mother and the doctor, who send Marilyn to a psychiatrist for evaluation. Marilyn's insistence is misinterpreted as teenage rebellion, brought on by a loving father who taught her that conforming in a society can lead to malcontent. Marilyn's ideas, however, are thrown out the back door when she finds herself transformed into Model No. 8 and she now admires and accepts her new-found beauty.

"Portrait of a young lady in love . . . with herself. Improbable? Perhaps. But in an age of plastic surgery, body building and an infinity of cosmetics, let us hesitate to say impossible. These and other strange blessings may be waiting in the future, which after all . . . is the Twilight Zone."

Trailer: *"On our next outing Charles Beaumont comes through with another delightful flight of futuristic fantasy, about a society of another time in which you literally can't tell the players without a score card. They all appear in identical mold. The column will cause Richard Long and special guest star Suzy Parker to appear in a program called 'Number 12 Looks Just Like You.' I hope you're around to catch the similarity."*

Trivia, etc. On July 8, 1963, the script titled "The Beautiful People" was assigned a production number. On September 5, the title was officially changed to "Number 12 Looks Just Like You." This entire episode was filmed on Stage 29 at M-G-M. If the hospital corridors of this episode appear to be the same hallways in "The Long Morrow," they should. Principal filming was completed on "The Long Morrow" on September 23, and the cast and crew for this production began rehearsals on the same stage on September 24. Costs to design the interior of the Cuberle home was $1,000 and costs to design the hospital rooms and the corridor was $1,100.

"Chuck [Beaumont] and I first met when he was beginning," explained John Tomerlin to interviewer Steve Boisson. "About two years later he got going so fast that he would accept more assignments than he could do. He was very prolific and he was always saying yes because he'd spent a long time, as most beginning writers do, having people say no. When he got overburdened he'd usually ask Bill Nolan or me to do stuff for him, usually articles for magazines."

Charles Beaumont was suffering from the effects of what would later be suspected as Pick's or Alzheimer's disease, so the writer phoned John Tomerlin to help him adapt the short story. As with "The New Exhibit," Beaumont received on-screen credit, and Tomerlin remained uncredited. "I actually did that script in two days. I never made an effort to see the show because I'd heard they kind of screwed it up. But it was a great story and it made a very good script."

TV Guide featured a two-page spread of Suzy Parker modeling in seven different costumes, representing the different characters she would play on the upcoming episode. "I am enchanted," Parker told a rep at *TV Guide*, speaking of the chance to play characters ranging from maid to matron. "When I played in a *Burke's Law*, I didn't get to see many of my costars. Here I see them all." Suzy Parker was once referred to as "the first supermodel." She is billed as "special guest star" for this episode. The split screen process was used for this episode, as well as stand-ins for scenes in which the backs of duplicate models were featured on the same screen.

This episode was originally intended for broadcast on January 10, but got pushed ahead a couple weeks. The caption accompanying the two-page spread in *TV Guide* erroneously announced a January 10 airdate before it received notice of the change.

Producer William Froug originally offered the male lead to actor Lloyd Bochner, who had already been a *Twilight Zone* veteran as Mr. Chambers in "To Serve Man." A script was mailed to Bochner, but for reasons that remain unknown, he was unable to commit, so the role was offered to Richard Long.

The Tucson Daily Citizen reviewed this episode: "This one will chill you up to the surprise finish." A reviewer for *The San Antonio Express* did not think so favorably, remarking that this show "is great fun until a let-down at the end."

Serling had originally composed a different trailer for this episode:

"On our next outing Charles Beaumont comes through with another delightful flight and futuristic fantasy, about a society of another time in which you literally can't tell the players without a score card. They all appear in identical mold. Collin Wilcox, Richard Long, and special guest star Suzy Parker appear in a program called 'Number 12 Looks Just Like You.' I hope you're around to catch the similarity."

A six-piece band from Bergen County, New Jersey, named their band after this episode of *The Twilight Zone*. The music group *The Number Twelve Looks Like You* has released a number of hit singles and albums since 2003.

Production #2628 "BLACK LEATHER JACKETS"
(Initial telecast: January 31, 1964)
Copyright Registration: © Cayuga Productions, Inc., January 27, 1964, LP28074 (in notice: 1963)
Date of Rehearsal: October 4, 1963
Dates of Filming: October 7, 8, 9 and 11, 1963
Script dated: October 2, 1963

Producer and Secretary: $1,626.01	Story and Secretary: $2,500.00
Director: $1,500.00	Cast: $6,581.56
Unit Manager and Secretary: $726.01	Production Fee: $1,800.00
Agents Commission: $2,500.00	Legal and Accounting: $250.00

Below the line charges (M-G-M): $35,479.33   Below the line charges (other): $5,973.00
Total Production Costs: $58,935.91

Cast: Michael Conrad (Sheriff Harper); Shelly Fabares (Ellen Tillman); Michael Forest (Steve); Tom Gilleran (Fred); Irene Harvey (Martha Tillman); Wayne Hefley (mover #1); Lee Kinsolving (Scott); Denver Pyle (Stu Tillman); and Jerry Schumacher (mover #2).

Original Music Score Composed and Conducted by Nathan Van Cleave (Score No. 6125): Etrange #3 (by Marius Constant, :09); Milieu #2 (by Constant, :21); Three There Are (1:33); The Eyes Have It (:43); Start the Story (:19) Anybody Home (:47); Wait a Minute (1:03); The Watch (:08); Be At Ease (:59); Proceed (:27); It's My Fault (1:13); Treason (:22); Who Are You? (:36); The Insignia (:56); Don't Fight Them Son (:32); Etrange #3 (by Constant, :09); and Milieu #1 (by Constant, :22).

Director of Photography: George T. Clemens, a.s.c.
Art Directors: George W. Davis and Malcolm Brown
Set Decorations: Henry Grace and Robert R. Benton
Directed by Joseph W. Newman

Production Manager: Ralph W. Nelson
Film Editor: Thomas W. Scott
Casting: Patricia Rose
Produced by William Froug
Assistant Director: Charles Bonniwell, Jr.
Sound: Franklin Milton and Joe Edmondson
Teleplay by Earl Hamner, Jr.

"Three strangers arrive in a small town. Three men in black leather jackets in an empty rented house. We'll call them Steve and Scott and Fred, but their names are not important; their mission is . . . as three men on motorcycles lead us into . . . the Twilight Zone."

Plot: Mr. and Mrs. Tillman, and teenage daughter Ellen, observe three young men moving into the vacant house across the street. The young men ride motorcycles and wear black leather jackets, suggesting trouble for the neighborhood. When radio and television reception is interfered with, Mr. Tillman suspects foul play and blames the new neighbors. Ellen takes a liking to one of the boys, Scott, who gives her a ride to the library when she misses the bus. Scott soon realizes that the planet has more to offer than unreasonable hate and racism. In desperation, Scott takes her into his confidence – explaining that he is a member of an advanced race from outer space, who have been taking key positions for colonization. Within the next 24 hours, the water reservoir will be contaminated with a bacteria that will cause fatalities across the land. Ellen races back home in disbelief and tells her father, who phones the police. Scott, in the meantime, attempts to convince Central Command that this planet offers more love than hate, but his efforts are thwarted when the authorities arrive to take him away – the authorities have been taken over by the alien race.

"Portrait of an American family on the eve of invasion from outer space. Of course, we know it's merely fiction and yet, think twice when you drink your next glass of water. Find out if it's from your local reservoir, or possibly it came direct to you . . . from the Twilight Zone."

Trailer: *"Earl Hamner, Jr. brings his typewriter and his fertile mind back into the Twilight Zone next time with* *a program about . . . visitors. On the surface they're beatniks, a few raunchy-looking characters on motorcycles roar into town one day. But once you meet them you won't forget them. They're quite different from what they appear. On the Twilight Zone, Lee Kinsolving, Shelly Fabares and Michael Forest star in 'Black Leather Jackets.'"*

Trivia, etc. When this episode was assigned a production number on October 4, 1963, the name on the script and the production was "Love Story." All of the exterior shots were filmed on Lot 2 at M-G-M, while the interior scenes were filmed on Stage 16. The street corner where the motorcyclists park in the opening scene is the same sidewalk featured in the premiere episode of *The Outer Limits* (the shoe store in this *Twilight Zone* episode was known as "Babcock's" in *The Outer Limits*).

The redecorated living room was the same featured in other fifth season episodes such as "Ninety Years Without Slumbering" and "Ring-A-Ding Girl." This might explain why the costs for set decoration are a bit odd. The cost to decorate and furnish the living room was $650, but the cost involved for the vacant home was $800. The cost for the exterior of the main street was $850 and the interior of the sheriff's office was $75!

A production number was assigned to this script on October 4, 1963. Motorcycles were rented for the four-day shoot. The cost was $25 for the first day, $50 for the second day, and $75 for the last two days – a total of $225 in rental fees. Someone was hired for "technical motorcycle supervision" at $25 per day. Actor Michael Forest recalled working on the set for this episode, to interviewer Tom Weaver, "We played aliens on motorcycles in that, and I used to ride motorcycles. They gave me a bike that had a regular foot clutch, which was the old-fashioned kind that I was used to riding. So they gave me this 1939 Harley frame with a brand-new engine and a foot clutch – they call it a 'suicide clutch.' The other bikes had the hand clutch, which of course all bikes have now. It was fun because they were *very* hot bikes, and we did 'wheelies' a couple of times, which we weren't supposed to do. But we got fooling around, and it was a fun episode to do."

Raymond Hampton drove the bus seen in the background of the opening scene, on Lot 2 at M-G-M on October 7. Ray Pourchot was the photo double for a few scenes. Bob McCord was the man who supplied his eyeball for the alien leader known as "The Mask," and his inserts were filmed on October 10. Actress Barbara Walker provided the hand insert on the same day for the shot of the wristwatch. Extras for the street scenes included a Negro man and a Negro woman, as requested by the casting director, but their appearances are either too far in the background to be noticed or ended up on the cutting room floor during editing. The grandfather clock in the living room is the same Hazel Court has in her living room in "The Fear."

Many fans of the *Twilight Zone* series have commented that the giant eyeball on the screen was ineffective for shock appeal. The original script described the character as "The Mask," and referenced as: "Over the heads of the three men we see the screen where a Being of some kind is visible. It is a head, a metallic mask with slits for eyes, a nose and lips."

Bloopers! Before Rod Serling appears on the screen, a close-up shot of the doorknob turning by itself is seen. This insert shot features a reflection of a stage light, even though the scene called for darkness, because the space visitors also closed the window blinds. Towards the end of the episode, when Ellen turns to enter her house, leaving Scott in the front yard, the shadow of a boom mike on the white post can be seen moving out of camera range.

The image being disrupted on the television set is *To Tell the Truth*, a quiz program that was also carried by CBS at the time. One of the sponsors for the series, Jif peanut butter, is also featured on the disrupted television screen.

Serling originally composed a different trailer for this episode:

"*The exceptionally fine writer, Earl Hamner, Jr. brings his typewriter and his fertile mind back into the Twilight Zone next time with a program about . . . visitors. On the surface they're beatniks, a few raunchy-looking characters on motorcycles roar into town one night. But once you meet them you won't forget them. They're quite different from what they appear. On the Twilight Zone, Lee Kinsolving, Shelly Fabares and Michael Forest star in 'Black Leather Jackets.'*"

After viewing this episode, Edwin Matesky, a television columnist, was prompted to write a review about the science fiction stories presented on the program during the past few weeks, including "Probe 7, Over and Out," "Number 12 Looks Just Like You" and "The Long Morrow," concluding they were "underdone, sometimes mediocre, type of science fiction. From the level of great science fiction, à la Ray Bradbury or Isaac Asimov or hour-long Serling, *Twilight Zone* has tumbled for the most part into the bleak, pedestrian world of pulp science fiction."

The Abilene Reporter-News remarked this episode was "more *Outer Limits* than anything else."

Production #2610 "NIGHT CALL" (Initial telecast: February 7, 1964)

© Cayuga Productions, Inc., February 3, 1964, LP28075 (in notice: 1963)
Date of Rehearsal: July 5, 1963
Dates of Filming: July 8, 9 and 10, 1963
Script dated: June 5, 1963

Producer and Secretary: $1,626.02	Story and Secretary: $2,660.00
Director: $1,250.00	Cast: $4,400.00
Unit Manager and Secretary: $726.01	Production Fee: $1,800.00
Agents Commission: $2,500.00	Legal and Accounting: $250.00
Below the line charges (M-G-M): $27,717.68	Below the line charges (other): $3,175.01
Total Production Costs: $46,104.72	

Cast: Martine Bartlett (Miss Finch); Gladys Cooper (Miss Elva Keene); Ken Drake (voice of Brian Douglas); and Nora Marlowe (Marge Phillips).

Stock Music Cues: Etrange #3 (by Marius Constant, :09); Milieu #2 (by Constant, :21); Secret Circle (by Jerry Goldsmith, :43); The Robbery (by Goldsmith, :05); Rosie's Farm (by Fred Steiner, :48); Solemn Finish (by Goldsmith, :24); Neutral (by Rene Garriguenc, :12); Religious Bridge – Walt Whitman (by Bernard Herrmann, :17); Now We Move (by Nathan Van Cleave, :22); Neutral #3 (by Garriguenc, :12); F Story #7 (by Constant, :43); Loire #2 (by Constant, :14); Jud's Song (by Steiner, :30); Dirge (by Goldsmith, :08); Summer Sadness (by Goldsmith, :24); Harp Strings (CBS, :02); and Milieu #2 (by Constant, arr. by Herrmann, :21).

Director of Photography: Robert Pittack, a.s.c.	Production Manager: Ralph W. Nelson Film Editor: Richard Heermance, a.c.e.

Art Directors: George W. Davis and
    Walter Holscher
Set Decorations: Henry Grace and
    Robert R. Benton
Sound: Franklin Milton and Philip N. Mitchell

Casting: Patricia Rose
Assistant Director: Charles Bonniwell, Jr.
Produced by Bert Granet
Directed by Jacques Tourneur

Teleplay by Richard Matheson, based on his short story "Sorry, Right Number," originally published in the November 1953 issue of *Beyond Fantasy Fiction*.

"Miss Elva Keene lives alone on the outskirts of London Flats – a tiny rural community in Maine. Up until now, the pattern of Miss Keene's existence has been that of lying in her bed or sitting in her wheelchair reading books, listening to a radio, eating, napping, taking medication and waiting for something different to happen. Miss Keene doesn't know it yet, but her period of waiting has just ended, for something different is about to happen to her, and has in fact already begun to happen, via two most unaccountable telephone calls in the middle of a stormy night. Telephone calls routed directly through . . . the Twilight Zone."

Plot: Miss Keene, an old woman living just outside town, finds herself plagued by a number of mysterious phone calls that may or may not be a crude practical joke. A bitter and demanding person, she orders the operator in town to put a trace on the calls, but is dissatisfied with the answer she receives. On the evening of the third night, Miss Keene, still a victim of the moans and groans coming from the receiver, orders the voice to leave her alone. In the morning, a telephone repairman comes out to inspect the line and reveals that the line has been down for days as a result of the recent thunderstorm. The difficulty originates from a fallen wire at the local cemetery. Ordering her housekeeper to drive her, Miss Keene finds the wire hanging over the grave of her late fiancé. Back at home, she picks up the phone and attempts to talk to her loved one . . . but discovers that he is doing what he was told, as he always did when she bossed him about. Miss Keene, a victim of her own damnation, cries in desperation.

"According to the Bible, God created the heavens and the Earth. It is man's prerogative – and woman's – to create their own particular and private hell. Case in point, Miss Elva Keene, who in every sense has made her own bed and now must lie in it . . . sadder but wiser, by dint of a rather painful lesson in responsibility. Transmitted from . . . the Twilight Zone."

Trailer: *"Next time out on the Twilight Zone, Richard Matheson provides us with a tour-de-force in suspense and the unexpected with a show called 'Night Call.' It stars one of the most eminent actresses of our time, Miss Gladys Cooper . . . and it poses the kind of question that arises when a telephone keeps ringing and you realize that the caller has not been on Earth for a number of years. I hope this intrigues because I think the show will. Next time out, 'Night Call.'"*

Trivia, etc. Richard Matheson recalled to interviewer Tom Weaver his fascination for director Jacques Tourneur. "I was a fan of his from way back – I wrote letters to Val Lewton when I was 17, about *Cat People*. I'd always been a tremendous fan of Tourneur's; as a matter of fact, even before *Comedy of Terrors* (1963), I had talked with Bert Granet about hiring him to do one of my *Twilight Zones*. They said the one reason they didn't want him was because he was a movie director, and it would take him too long. Well, they hired him anyway, and Tourneur was so organized that he shot the shortest *Twilight Zone* shooting schedule ever – I think he had done it in like 28 hours. The man was a master, and he had great taste, too."

Matheson's preferred title for the story on which the episode was based is "Long Distance Call," but it was first published as "Sorry, Right Number" (the editors often gave his stories titles he didn't like); the title was presumably changed to "Night Call" since there was already a *Twilight Zone* episode of that name. Matheson's script was titled "Long Distance Call" when assigned the production number on June 5, 1963. Five days later, an M-G-M work order dated June 10 officially changed the name of the production to "Night Call."

"The idea just occurred to me that some disabled old lady was getting phone calls from a dead man," Richard Matheson recalled. "I ended the story on a very dark note, where he says, 'I'll be right over.' Which leaves the reader with the feeling of just what is coming over to her house? But it's a flat ending. I thought the new ending I put on it for *The Twilight Zone* was a lot better. I thought it made much more sense, because her personality was so abrasive that, for it to turn out that she had caused this man to die in the first place, and now she wanted him more than ever. And he just said, 'You told me not to come over. I always do what you say.' I thought that was much stronger; it made much more of a character study."

Except for the exterior of the Keene house and the cemetery, which was filmed on Lot 3, all of the scenes (including the telephone office) for this episode were shot on Stage 19 at M-G-M.

Production costs for the special effects (rain, wind and lightning) cost a total of $250. On July 16, days after principal filming was completed, Ken Drake reported to Stage 14 to supply the voice of Brian. The recording session lasted 45 minutes beginning 12:30 p.m.

This episode was originally scheduled to air on the evening of November 22, 1963. Regularly scheduled programming for all networks was canceled that evening for news coverage of President Kennedy's assassination. (Regularly scheduled programming did not return until Monday.) This episode was rescheduled for the month of February.

Lyrics of the song "Killers," performed by the rock group, "Iron Maiden," referenced this particular episode of the *Twilight Zone*.

Production #2629 "FROM AGNES – WITH LOVE"
(Initial telecast: February 14, 1964)
Copyright Registration: © Cayuga Productions, Inc., February 10, 1964, LP28076 (in notice: 1963)
Copyrighted under the title: "From Agnes, With Love"
Date of Rehearsal: October 10, 1963
Dates of Filming: October 11, 14 and 15, 1963
Script dated: October 4, 1963, with revised pages dated October 10 and 11, 1963.

Producer and Secretary: $1,626.02
Director: $1,500.00
Unit Manager and Secretary: $726.01
Agents Commission: $2,500.00
Below the line charges (M-G-M): $33,991.45
Total Production Costs: $57,952.14

Story and Secretary: $2,540.00
Cast: $6,175.00
Production Fee: $1,800.00
Legal and Accounting: $250.00
Below the line charges (other): $6,843.66

Cast: Raymond Bailey (the supervisor); Wally Cox (James Elwood); Byron Kane (the assistant);

Don Keefer (Fred Danziger); Nan Peterson (the secretary); Sue Randall (Millie); and Ralph Taeger (Walter Holmes).

Original Music Score Composed and Conducted by Nathan Van Cleave: Etrange #3 (by Marius Constant, :09); Milieu #2 (by Constant, :21); Down the Hall (:13); Femme Fatale (:10); To Work (:10); She Called Me Jim (:23); Hello Mr. Elwood (:21); Lonely Lady (by Bruce Campbell, 1:01); Mother (:13); The Roses (:13); Me (:25); Project Venus (:06); To Work (:05); Lonely Lady (by Campbell, 2:41); Natural Rock (by Campbell, :38); Door Slam (:17); Kiss Off (:36); Etrange #3 (by Constant, :09); and Milieu #1 (by Constant, :22).

Director of Photography: George T. Clemens, a.s.c.	Production Manager: Ralph W. Nelson
Art Directors: George W. Davis and Malcolm Brown	Film Editor: Richard Heermance, a.c.e.
	Casting: Patricia Rose
Set Decorations: Henry Grace and Robert R. Benton	Assistant Director: Charles Bonniwell, Jr.
	Sound: Franklin Milton and Joe Edmondson
Directed by Richard Donner	Produced by William Froug
	Teleplay by Bernard C. Schoenfeld

"James Elwood: master programmer, in charge of Mark 502-741, commonly known as 'Agnes,' the world's most advanced electronic computer. Machines are made by men for man's benefit and progress, but when man ceases to control the products of his ingenuity and imagination, he not only risks losing the benefit but he takes a long and unpredictable step into . . . the Twilight Zone."

Plot: Computer expert James Elwood thinks of nothing but electrodes, computations and Millie – a young secretary who works at the same government office where Elwood is employed. Having just been promoted to operational supervisor for a mechanical oracle of wisdom known as "Agnes," he strikes a friendship with the computer. It becomes apparent that Agnes can compute rocket to air science ratios, space velocity and complicated equations – including love. Working on the advice from the electronic brain, the lovelorn scientist attempts to woo Millie, but strikes out with every opportunity. After introducing Millie to a senior programmer named Walter, Elwood discovers his chances with the secretary are out the door. The computer's advice was correct, but not in Elwood's favor . . . because the computer was jealous. Agnes wants Elwood all to herself because she is in love with the supervisor. Before the evening is through, Elwood cracks under the strain like the programmer before him.

"Advice to all future male scientists: be sure you understand the opposite sex, especially if you intend being a computer expert. Otherwise, you may find yourself, like poor Elwood, defeated by a jealous machine, a most dangerous sort of female, whose victims are forever banished . . . to the Twilight Zone."

Trailer: *"Bernard C. Schoenfeld pays us his first visit on the Twilight Zone next time with his script entitled, 'From Agnes – With Love.' Delightful and diminutive Wally Cox lends his sizable talent to a charming science fiction comedy called, 'From Agnes – With Love.' You've heard about thinking machines. On our program next time, you'll see a machine that does considerably more than just think. Wally Cox stars in 'From Agnes – With Love' on the Twilight Zone."*

Set Decoration Production Costs
Interior of the Supervisor's Office $635
Interior of the Corridor $25
Interior of Agnes' Suite $890
Interior of Millie's Office $445
Interior of Elwood's Apartment $75
Total $2,070

Trivia, etc. A brief in the December 7, 1963 issue of *TV Guide* reported that Serling, among his other projects, "also hopes to make a series out of a coming *Twilight Zone* about Wally Cox and a computer." This Valentine offering served as a pilot, helping Serling meet a contractual obligation with CBS to provide a number of pilots every year, exclusively for CBS-TV. Since no potential sponsors expressed an interest beyond the initial telecast, a regular series never came to be.

The Tucson Daily Citizen reviewed this episode as "a humorous approach to the weird possibilities of automation."

When Walter is first introduced to Millie, the music coming over the radio fits the scene, titled "Lonely Lady." In the scene where Elwood returns to Walter's apartment, the music which Millie is dancing to is Bruce Campbell's "Natural Rock" – the same music heard over the jukebox in the drug store scene in "Walking Distance."

The entire episode was filmed on Stage 3 at M-G-M. Assigned a production number on October 4, 1963, Richard Donner quickly made arrangements with the technical staff to design a computer that not only fit the description of the script, but would also serve as a perfect companion for Wally Cox. Scene six in the script describes the computer: "Elwood hangs up his jacket, crosses to Agnes, starts getting the huge computer ready for the day's work. He pushes buttons, turns dials, checks tape, etc. – the Emperor of his domain . . . Elwood sits down at the control desk, pushes the clear-all-registers button. We hear Agnes' obedient humming, as Elwood picks up the microphone. The typewriter taps as he speaks."

Agnes was not made pre-existing props at the studio. According to three separate invoices dated October 4, 8 and 10, 1963, from Maxwell Smith at 1741 Berkeley Street, in Santa Monica, the following parts (totaling a little more than $600) were ordered to construct the computer:

4 large computer indicator cabinets
1 computer control console
1 Creed computer typewriter and
    punched tape unit
1 Dumont 392A Oscilloscope #1x32
1 Electromec Oscilloscope
1 Transmitter Control #4042
1 GCA Quad Radar Indicator
2 Computer Test Sets
1 Neutron Monitor
3 rack panel cases
1 Large aluminum case
1 Box Machine Screws and Cup Washers
1 Radar Transmitter Indicator with Hood
1 box push button switches

1 TV monitor screen
3 rolls of paper tape
1 roll of typewriter paper
2 additional TV monitors
1 Dumont 392S Oscilloscope #2x49
1 Norelco Electronic Counter
1 Computer Unit
1 RM Oscilloscope
1 Test Fire Set (3 section case)
1 Monitor with 2 ports
4 stainless steel Herm Sld. Cases
1 Communications Rack Cabinet
1 Rack Cab. For Mounting Panels (40")
11 Light Assemblies
1 triple panel cabinet

6 10" x 12" control panels

10 19" control panels

1 large indicator meter

2 SAC control panels

Production #2608 "SPUR OF THE MOMENT" (Initial telecast: February 21, 1964)

© Cayuga Productions, Inc., February 17, 1964, LP28077 (in notice: 1963)

Date of Rehearsal: June 24, 1963

Dates of Filming: June 25, 26, 27 and 28, 1963

Script dated: May 20, 1963, formerly titled "Pale Rider"

Script dated: June 14, 1963, with revised pages dated May 27 and June 26, 1963.

June 14 draft now dated "Spur of the Moment"

Producer and Secretary: $1,626.02

Story and Secretary: $2,660.00

Director: $1,750.00

Cast: $8,119.59

Unit Manager and Secretary: $726.01

Production Fee: $1,800.00

Agents Commission: $2,500.00

Legal and Accounting: $250.00

Below the line charges (M-G-M): $36,860.06

Below the line charges (other): $5,161.09

Total Production Costs: $61,452.77

Cast: Roger Davis (David Mitchell); Robert Hogan (Robert Blake); Marsha Hunt (Mrs. Henderson); Diana Hyland (Anne Henderson); Philip Ober (Mr. Henderson); and Jack Raine (Reynolds, the butler).

Original Music Composed by Rene Garriguenc and Conducted by Lud Gluskin (Score No. CPN6120): Etrange #3 (by Marius Constant, :09); Milieu #2 (by Constant, :21); Spur Cue #1 (:25); Spur Cue #1A (:45); Spur Cue #2 (1:16); Spur Cue #3 (:41); Spur Cue #4 (:29); Spur Cue #4A (1:04); Spur Cue #5 (:35); Spur Cue #6 (1:56); Mitzi (by Rene Garriguenc, 2:11); Spur Cue #6A (:43); Spur Cue #7 (:09); Spur Cue #8 (:35); Spur Cue #9 (:59); Etrange #3 (by Constant, :09); and Milieu #1 (by Constant, :22).

Director of Photography: Robert
    Pittack, a.s.c.

Production Manager: Ralph W. Nelson

Film Editor: Richard Heermance, a.c.e.

Art Directors: George W. Davis and
    Walter Holscher

Casting: Patricia Rose

Assistant Director: Charles Bonniwell, Jr.

Set Decorations: Henry Grace and
    Robert R. Benton

Produced by Bert Granet

Directed by Elliot Silverstein

Sound: Franklin Milton and Philip N. Mitchell

Teleplay by Richard Matheson

"This is the face of terror: Anne Marie Henderson, eighteen years of age, her young existence suddenly marred by a savage and wholly unanticipated pursuit by a strange, nightmarish figure of a woman in black, who has appeared as if from nowhere and now at driving gallop chases the terrified girl across the countryside . . . as if she means to ride her down and kill her – and then suddenly and inexplicably stops, to watch in malignant silence as her prey takes flight. Miss Henderson has no idea whatever as to the motive for this pursuit; worse, not the vaguest notion regarding the identity of her pursuer. Soon enough, she will be given the solution

to this twofold mystery, but in a manner far beyond her present capacity to understand. A manner enigmatically bizarre in terms of time and space . . . which is to say, an answer from . . . the Twilight Zone."

Plot: Anne Henderson, a young woman of prominent breeding and wealth, is riding through the countryside one afternoon until she sees a mad woman dressed in black, shouting her name. Out of fright, she races back home. After searching the grounds of the estate, no one is able to find the mysterious figure, who apparently vanished like the wind. Back home, Anne finds her life in turmoil when she is forced to choose either the wealthy and ambitious Robert Blake with a promising future or a young man named David, of whom her parents disapprove. David has no promising future or prominent social status, but she chooses love over family's wishes. Almost 25 years later, residing in the same mansion, Anne regrets the choices she made and the consequences of her decisions. David has caused her family fortune to go bankrupt and her parents fear the worst. Pondering whether her life might have been better had she chosen to marry the boy her parents preferred, she sets out every day riding the horse, dressed in black, attempting to deliver a haunted warning she hopes her younger self would one day heed.

"This is the face of terror: Anne Marie Mitchell, forty-three years of age, her desolate existence once more afflicted by the hope of altering her past mistake . . . a hope which is, unfortunately, doomed to disappointment. For warnings from the future to the past must be taken in the past; today may change tomorrow, but once today is gone tomorrow can only look back in sorrow that the warning was ignored. Said warning as of now stamped 'not accepted' and stored away in the dead file in the recording office . . . of the Twilight Zone."

Trailer: *"Next on the Twilight Zone, the stalwart typewriter of Richard Matheson brings us a most intriguing tale of riders, pale horses, and peeks into the future. It stars Diana Hyland and it concerns itself with some very unlooked for and some unpredicted events. It's called 'Spur of the Moment' and it's recommended for those of you who'd like to take a look at the next page of the calendar before it's time. On Twilight Zone next, 'Spur of the Moment.'"*

Trivia: For the initial telecast, the closing theme music did not end when the on-screen credits concluded. The music was heard over a photographic Red Cross appeal. For reruns, the music was rerecorded (or speeded up) to ensure it ended when the closing credits concluded.

While many public service announcements appeared on screen after the closing credits, the initial telecast marked the only time the closing theme was heard over a public service announcement. This was a favor for Harold E. Abramson, Hollywood representative of the American National Red Cross, who asked Serling to find some way to work some mention of Red Cross services into the television series. Since it was the practice and policy of CBS to handle all spots and announcements to appear over credit rolls or as adjuncts to given television programs, and because Serling found it difficult to incorporate a Red Cross worker into a script, he contacted someone at the network, urging them to make the arrangements. [*]

The first draft of this script was titled "Pale Rider" when assigned a production number on May 20. On an M-G-M work order dated June 3, the title was officially changed to "Spur of the Moment."

---

[*] A poster promoting the Red Cross was displayed on the wall in the subway in the episode "In His Image."

The horse riding scenes consisted of two women doubling for actress Hyland. Donna Hall was the riding double for the scenes requiring a 43-year-old Anne Henderson, and Patty Elder was the riding double for the scenes requiring an 18-year-old Anne.

The interior of the mansion was filmed on Stage 25. Scenes shot outside of the Henderson mansion were filmed on Lot 2 at M-G-M. (This was the same mansion Agent Luis D. Spain worked as a chauffer in the episode, "The Invisibles," on *The Outer Limits*.) The exterior of Gazebo Hill and Gazebo Road were filmed on Lot 3. All of the horse riding scenes on the countryside were conducted on the second day of filming, shot on location on Beanfield granted by the Anne V. Crawford Estate, with the courtesy of Mrs. Florence Thompson. To shoot on the property, permission was granted by agreement through the Standard Oil Company through Mr. Lynn Price and Mr. Dave Anderson. Cost for permission was $35 per day for two days, though all of the horse riding scenes were completed on the afternoon of June 26. (Cayuga paid for two days in advance, just in case the weather was not cooperative for the first day.) A 600-amp gas generator was needed to power the equipment for outdoor filming, a total of $41 rental, not counting the cost of gas. The fourth and last day of filming was devoted to filming scenes of the exterior of the mansion on Lot 2. The cost of set decoration for the living room of the Henderson Mansion was $430. The Rolls Royce was a rental of $50 for the day. An extra makeup artist was required for filming at an additional cost of $156 to Cayuga.

The music in this episode by Rene Garriguenc was composed on December 12, 1963. Inspired by western adventure pictures, the riding scenes featured an adrenaline-paced score during the horse-riding sequences.

"Michael Parks was going to be on that show, and I took his place," recalled Roger Davis. "I remember I was doing two shows back-to-back so having returned from one show, I showed up on the set and didn't know my lines. I walked over to a man who looked okay in my book, and asked him if he could do me a favor and feed me my lines and cue me when I needed to, and he said 'no problem.' Turned out he was the producer working for Serling at the time! The makeup was time-consuming, and as a young man it wasn't easy to make me look much older."

"I liked that story," recalled Richard Matheson in an interview with Matthew R. Bradley. "The only thing I didn't like was that, I thought, in the beginning they gave it away. You should not have seen her face when she was chasing the young girl. It should have been just a scary figure in black, in the background."

The Tucson Daily Citizen complimented: "Diana Hyland is quite good as the self-centered girl . . . An obvious plot that makes a solid point." *The Valley Independent* reviewed: "This one combines elements of Margaret Mitchell and Tennessee Williams, with the *Twilight Zone*."

Production #2638 "AN OCCURRENCE AT OWL CREEK BRIDGE"
(Initial telecast: February 28, 1964)

Producer and Secretary: $300.00	Story and Secretary: $800.00
Director: $1,250.00	Cast: $125.00
License: $20,000.00	Below the line charges (M-G-M): $281.17
Below the line charges (other): $5,856.14	Total Production Costs: $28,612.31

Cast: Louis Adelin (a Union soldier); Anne Cornaly (Mrs. Farquhar, the wife); Pierre Danny (a Union soldier); Stephanie Fey (a Union soldier); Roger Jacquet (Peyton Farquhar); Anker Larsen (a Union soldier); and Jean-François Zeller (a Union soldier).

Stock Music Cues (and original score): Etrange #3 (by Marius Constant, :09); Milieu #2 (by Constant, :21); original music score from the original film short is included (see trivia); Etrange #3 (by Constant, :09); and Milieu #1 (by Constant, :22).

Director of Photography: Jean Boffety
Art Direction: Denise de Casablanca and
    Robert Enrico
Film Editors: Denise de Casablanca and
    Robert Enrico
Production Managers: Pierre Lobreau and
    Gerard Berger

Music by Henri Lanoë.
Camera Operator: Christian Guillouet
Assistant Director: Nat Lilenstein
Sound: Jean Neny
Directed by Robert Enrico
Produced by Marcel Ichac
    and Paul de Roubaix

Screenplay by Robert Enrico, based on the short story of the same name by Ambrose Bierce, originally published in the July 13, 1890 issue of *The San Francisco Examiner*, later reprinted in *Tales of Soldiers and Civilians* (1891).

"Tonight a presentation so special and unique that for the first time in the five years we've been presenting The Twilight Zone, we're offering a film shot in France by others. Winner of the Cannes Film Festival of 1962, as well as other international awards, here is a haunting study of the incredible, from the past master of the incredible, Ambrose Bierce. Here is the French production of 'An Occurrence At Owl Creek Bridge.'"

Plot: The American Civil War. Peyton Farquhar stands upon a railroad bridge in northern Alabama, looking down into the swift water 20 feet below. The man's hands are behind his back, the wrists bound with a cord. Captured by the Union Army, he has been found guilty of treason and will face a swift hanging. Farquhar had been tricked by a Federal scout, disguised as a Confederate soldier, into attempting the sabotage of Owl Creek Bridge. During the hanging, however, the rope breaks and Farquhar plunges into the water. Free from his bonds, he dodges bullets and travels through an uninhabited and seemingly unending forest, attempting to reach his home located miles away. Urged on by the thought of his wife and children, he safely makes it back home. Reaching for his wife, he suddenly feels a searing pain in his neck, and everything goes black. His escape was merely a dream, envisioned between the time the plank beneath his feet fell away and the noose broke his neck.

"'An Occurrence At Owl Creek Bridge,' in two forms – as it was dreamed and as it was lived . . . and died. This is the stuff of fantasy, the thread of imagination, the ingredients . . . of The Twilight Zone."

Trailer: *"Next time on the Twilight Zone, a departure from the norm. A program shot in its entirety in France. A film so special and so unique, that for the first time in the five years we've been presenting the Twilight Zone, we're offering a film shot by others. Adapted and directed by Robert Enrico, winner of the Cannes Film Festival, 1962, as well as other major international awards. Ambrose Bierce's 'An Occurrence at Owl Creek Bridge.'"*

Trivia, etc. In what the September 23, 1962 issue of *The London Observer* regarded as "stunning" and "a hallucinatory film," this French short produced by Marcel Ichal and Paul de Robaix won first prize for short subjects at the Cannes Film Festival in 1962. Director Jean Bofferty consulted Matthew Brady's Civil War pictures to construct a surreal world of dreamscapes and unusual photography.

Perhaps no other film short presented at the Cannes Film Festival that decade made a larger impression than *La Rivière du Hibou* (English Translation: "Incident at Owl Creek"), adapted from an Ambrose Bierce story titled "An Occurrence at Owl Creek Bridge."

The September 1962 issue of *Films and Filming* reviewed: "This is another fragment of time out of war, and it is not simply its time (under the half-hour) or its war (American, Civil) that call to mind the Sanders' rightly honored episode of truce. It has something of the same innocence, too. In the grey light before sunrise, in a woody Alabama gorge, they are hanging a man. We watch him escape and run for home and wife. There is little dialogue and no character-drawing to divert us from the action which, gripping the imagination throughout, is told principally by camera and soundtrack . . . The ritual sounds of death – the fixing of the rope, the tying of restless arms and feet, the giving and receiving of grey orders – are blown up, brutally resonant in the morning stillness, and set in counterpoint to the ritual sounds of life awakening in the surrounding woods."

"Robert Enrico and his cameraman achieve a natural polyphony of light and sound – sunlight and the incessant chatter of living things – through which the condemned man races, a primitive again," concluded the same review. "He rolls and laughs deliriously on the shingle; he marvels anew at the miracle of his own hand, at an open flower, at a centipede even. The photography is breathtaking, conveying marvelously the right sense of things seen for the very first time. The climax is short, sharp and a bit flash, strictly irrelevant to the coolly observed poetics of the rest, and the film neither seeks nor achieves any real humanity; but within its imposed limits it is a complete success."

This film won an Academy Award in 1963 for the category of Best Live Action Short Film. One month later, the April 1963 issue of *Show* reviewed the film, commenting: "The photography caresses the trees and water with lovely effect; the sound track heightens the innocent cries of the birds and chirps of the cricket; while the camera calmly focuses on the man standing on the bridge with the noose around his neck, waiting to be hanged."

It was in the same month of April that Windsor Lewis of Cappagariff Productions in New York wrote to Rod Serling inviting him to come attend a private screening of the French film. Serling wrote back, explaining that he would be in New York on Wednesday, May 8, and staying at the Waldorf. "Please phone me there so we can make a date to look at the film. I'm looking forward to it," replied Serling. During Serling's stay in the Big Apple that week, Serling's enthusiasm grew after watching the film, he gave Lewis the phone number and address to Ted Ashley of Ashley-Steiner. He informed Lewis that the legal and business arrangements regarding a deal to have the film used as a possible segment for *Twilight Zone* would have to be secured through Ashley.

Throughout the month of June, Windsor Lewis attempted to contact Ted Ashley, even making arrangements for the rep to come attend a private screening himself, but as Lewis explained, "it never worked out." Serling's enthusiasm waned a bit, until July 18, when Lewis wrote a follow-up letter to Serling, explaining the situation.

On July 25, Serling offered his apologies. He was unable to interest the network in any cash outlay for the film unless the price would be below production costs. In Serling's opinion, the figure they proposed was really insufficient to broach to Lewis as a legitimate deal. "So I've given up on the whole affair, but with real regret," Serling remarked. "The film was unquestionably one of the finest produced and directed items I've seen in a good, long time. I'm truly sorry we can't consummate an agreement."

On August 2, Serling wrote to Joseph Weill, explaining, "I obviously read Windsor Lewis' dialogue incorrectly. I felt that the sense of our meeting indicated that the price tag for *An Occurrence at*

Owl Creek Bridge to be far too high for a legitimate offering by the Network. Your letter makes me think that perhaps an arrangement could be worked out. I immediately contacted Robert Lewine at CBS-Television here in Hollywood. He has authorized me to make the following offer: $20,000 for one presentation of the film in the continental United States, said airing to be scheduled within the next ten months. Future reruns would, of course, have to be re-negotiated ... I would be delighted if you would transmit this offer to Windsor Lewis and let me know of his reaction."

Lewis agreed with the price tag. A 35mm print was mailed to William Froug at Metro-Goldwyn-Mayer Studios, by air mail special delivery, on August 27, 1963. Upon arrival, the French picture was screened by Froug, Boris Kaplan and an executive at CBS on August 29. By this time, Serling was in full support for the film and insisted that they themselves could not match the quality of the French short, especially at the price being offered. Ralph W. Nelson had reservations about the photography and made arrangements with the CBS engineers to run it on a closed circuit to make sure that the dark and impressionistic scenes would be suitable for American televising. The film passed the test.

Throughout the month of September 1963, Gerald Saltsman of Ashley-Steiner, acting as an agent for Cayuga, conducted negotiations with Joseph Weill of Cappa Gariff, Inc., owners of the 29-minute film. Windsor Lewis' position with the film was completed – leaving the legalities in the capable hands of Joseph Weill. After a number of discussions, an agreement was reached between both parties, under the following terms and conditions:

1. Gariff licensed to Cayuga the film for one network broadcast plus the right to re-peat once on the network. Cayuga had the right to broadcast the film in the United States, its possessions and territories, and Bermuda.
2. Gariff not only supplied a fine-grain print of the 29-minute film short, printed and developed pursuant to the exact specifications which Cayuga required, but also supplied the following items:
    (a) separate dialogue track
    (b) music and sound effect tracks
    (c) a separate unit of background pictures behind the titles, such as the back ground before titles were super-imposed.
    (d) all negatives in Gariff's possession, from which still photographs could be printed
    (e) music cue sheets (there was only one)
3. The work print supplied to Cayuga would be non-returnable.
4. The shipping of the negative and duty thereon would be at Gariff's expense. The expense to make a copy of the negatives for CBS, so Gariff could retain the origi-nals, would be at Gariff's expense.
5. Cayuga had the right to delete, re-edit, reform and arrange the continuity as it saw fit. This also included the right to delete or alter the whatever credits or title it so desired.

On September 9 and 10, two M-G-M work orders assigned a production number to "Incident at Owl Creek." The cost of the film was a total sum of $20,000. The estimated cost for re-cutting the French film for use as a *Twilight Zone* episode was $5,925, according to an interoffice memo from Ralph W. Nelson, dated September 11, 1963. The estimate was based on the costs and labor involved to edit the film, using separate sound tracks of narration, sound effects and music. The estimated cost did not include CBS's 2 percent cost control, duty and shipping charges, Ashley-Steiner's fee, Cayuga's fee, George Amy's fee, Ralph W. Nelson and his secretary fees, and any fee for Rod Serling for photography of a contemplated opening with Serling breaking the fourth wall, as he had for previous episodes. Financial paperwork from two separate sources verify the $20,000 figure.

Editing began in late September 1963. George Amy, the film program coordinator, determined what footage would be used for the end credits, which ran a total of 20 feet of film. Paperwork sent to George Amy specifically stated that on card #11 in the closing credits, there was to be no Westrex bug or copyright identification. The end credits were decided and finalized on November 25, 1963, suggesting the finished film was completed by early December.

The arrangement for presenting the film on *The Twilight Zone* did not include complete owner-ship. Cayuga purchased the negatives to edit as deemed necessary for the format of the television series and permission for two broadcasts. Reruns beyond the two would require a new or amended contract or a new agreement with a fee due to the distributors and owners of the French film. Not wanting to waste the opportunity to broadcast the film a second time, this episode was rerun on September 11, 1964. After CBS purchased the rights to *The Twilight Zone* in early 1965, it was made quite clear that CBS would not own the right to include this episode in syndication packages because the network was obligated to honor the contract Cayuga Productions made in September of 1963.

Serling's initial introduction was a bit different from what we see today:

"Tonight on the Twilight Zone, a special event. A program made outside of the United States that seems to us to be so different, so effective, and so meaningful that we offer it to you now. A haunting study of the incredible from the past master of the incredible – Ambrose Bierce. What you will now see is the French production of . . . 'An Occurrence at Owl Creek Bridge.'"

The arrangement between Joseph Weill and Cayuga Productions was apparently favorable enough to give Serling the option to purchase additional foreign films. On February 6, Weill wrote to Serling, explaining, "We have available two others of the same quality, dramatic intensity and in-terest as Owl Creek. They were made by the same director with as much integrity as he infused into Owl Creek. They are available immediately for this year, or could be made available for next season's programming. If you have any interest in seeing them with a view of making a similar deal, we would be happy to forward prints to California."

On February 27, the day before this episode was telecast, Serling replied favorably. He confessed that at the moment, the prospects for the *Twilight Zone* continuing a sixth season appeared to be dim. "On the off chance that something happens to save us at the last moment, I would very much appreci-ate looking at the two films that you make mention of. Could you mail them directly to William Froug, Cayuga Productions, M-G-M Studios, Culver City, California?" On March 9, *The Mocking Bird* (1962) and *Chickamauga* (1962), two shorts made by Robert Enrico, were shipped to the West Coast for re-view. Because CBS would not renew the series for an additional season, the shorts were never used. *

When the film was edited to fit the time space allotted for *Twilight Zone*, a seven-page script was drawn up, citing which scenes would be included in the final cut, and which scenes would not. The sound effects, dialogue (French accent with the English language) and music were edited together

_____

* All three shorts were adaptations of Ambrose Bierce stories. In 1963, they were edited into a feature-length motion picture, *Au coeur de la vie*, which won Enrico a "Best Director" award at the San Sebastián International Film Festival in 1963.

from the duplicate tracks. Henri Lanoë, who wrote the guitar ballad, "Live Livin' Man," would later become a celebrated film editor. Lanoë recalled to the author by letter how he came about composing the song for the film short. "When I was young, I studied music. With my background, I myself composed the music you hear in the short film. *La Riviere Du Hibou* was directed by Robert Enrico, which took the Palme d'Or at Cannes here in France. My music was, in part, the success of the film. Looking back at that and other films I have been a part of, I can say that my background in music has helped me a lot, because as an editor, the relationship between musician, director and editor must blend." (Original letter was in French. It was translated by a friend of the author.)

The music was on a separate track and edited into the shorter version. This included "Live Livin' Man," three guitar music cues and three drums. The music cues were named as follows: Drums (1:02); Guitars (:48); Battente 1 (:53); Battente 2 (:35); Battente 3 (:41); Battente 4 (:05); Guitars (:16) and Guitars Finis (:05). Keeping the music in track with the newly-edited film was important, so the director's original vision could remain. The sounds of gunshots were deliberately altered to sound like cannonballs. The slow vocals for the escape scene was retained. The music score should not be confused with "An Occurrence At Owl Creek Bridge," credited to David M. Gordon, Ruth Layne Gordon, Melvin L. Gordon and Dave Kahn, which was composed specially for the film version presented on the television series, *Alfred Hitchcock Presents*.

Ironically, Paul F. Schedler, a lawyer in Spokane, Washington, wrote to Serling in March of 1961, proposing Ambrose Bierce's short story, which "might make a suitable vehicle for your fascinating program." Schedler even cited *The Collected Writings of Ambrose Bierce*, published by Citadel Press, New York, 1946; page 9. *Alfred Hitchcock Presents* had already filmed their own version of the Bierce story back in 1959, and this was probably the reason why Serling never chose to adapt it for *The Twilight Zone* previous to the 1964 presentation.

On February 1, 1964, CBS sent out a press release to newspapers announcing that *Twilight Zone* would be presenting the French film as part of the series' lineup on February 28. "The small amount of dialogue in the film would be in English," the network explained. Serling said that he chose the film as an episode in the series "for its classic expression of the unknown world of the imagination."

The March 24, 1964 issue of *New York World-Telegram and Sun* reviewed the telecast, "The effects are startling, always moving, because we see, feel and hear as the nameless man does. There are the ever present bird-songs during the pantomime of preparation for the hanging . . . With an economy and skill in camera work, the film describes and suggests the multifarious and the marvelous in all life."

The Tucson Daily Citizen told its readers "this is highly recommended." One television critic, having viewed this telecast, commented "it has an unusual camera technique that makes you feel this was filmed a hundred years ago."

Production #2626 "QUEEN OF THE NILE" (Initial telecast: March 6, 1964)
© Cayuga Productions, Inc., February 29, 1964, LP28078 (in notice: 1963)
Date of Rehearsal: September 30, 1963
Dates of Filming: October 1, 2 and 3, 1963
Script dated: September 12, 1963

Producer and Secretary: $2,016.02	Story and Secretary: $2,540.00
Director: $1,750.00	Cast: $7,016.20

Unit Manager and Secretary: $616.01
Agents Commission: $2,500.00
Below the line charges (M-G-M): $31,993.12
Total Production Costs: $56,849.64

Production Fee: $1,800.00
Legal and Accounting: $250.00
Below the line charges (other): $6,368.29

Cast: Ann Blyth (Pamela Morris); Frank Ferguson (Krueger); Celia Lovsky (Viola Draper); Lee Philips (Jordan Herrick); Ruth Phillips (Charlotte, the maid); and James Tyler (Mr. Jackson).

Original Music Score Composed by Lucien Moraweck and Conducted by Lud Gluskin (Score No. CPN6124): Etrange #3 (by Marius Constant, :09); Milieu #2 (by Constant, :21); The Egyptian Statue (1:14); Dead Man (by Jerry Goldsmith, :34); D Story #4 (by Constant, :30); The Mother (:36); Dead Man (by Goldsmith, :25); Mother's Loyalty (:45 and :43); Pamela's Entrance (:20); Disintegration (:50); Dead Man (by Goldsmith, :25); The Terrace (:06); Mother's Revelation #1 (:10); Mother's Revelation #2 (:04); Egyptian Scarab (:03); Dead Man (by Goldsmith, :44); Pamela's Estate (:10); Egyptian Scarab (1:18); The Terrace (:06); Egyptian Statues (:04); Egyptian Scarab (:31); The Death Pill (:24); Moat Farm Murder (by Herrmann, :31, :16, :24, :26, :10 and :40); Disintegration (:26); Dead Man (:20); Private Eye (:09); Etrange #3 (by Constant, :09); and Milieu #1 (by Constant, :22).

Director of Photography: Charles Wheeler
Art Directors: George W. Davis and
    Malcolm Brown
Set Decorations: Henry Grace and
    Robert R. Benton
Sound: Franklin Milton and Joe Edmondson

Production Manager: Ralph W. Nelson
Film Editor: Richard Heermance, a.c.e.
Casting: Patricia Rose
Assistant Director: Charles Bonniwell, Jr.
Produced by William Froug
Directed by John Brahm

Teleplay by Jerry Sohl, based on an original story by Charles Beaumont.

"Jordan Herrick, syndicated columnist whose work appears in more than a hundred newspapers. By nature a cynic, a disbeliever, caught for the moment by a lovely vision. He knows the vision he's seen is no dream; she is Pamela Morris, renowned movie star, whose name is a household word and whose face is known to millions. What Mr. Herrick does not know is that he has also just looked into the face . . . of the Twilight Zone."

Plot: Movie actress Pamela Morris, with a passion for Egyptian artifacts, makes a few advances on an inquisitive magazine writer named Jordan Herrick. He seeks information about the starlet in the hopes of writing a biography for his column. Herrick falls under her spell, and as he begins to investigate Pamela's past, he is shocked to learn that the old woman Pamela claims is her mother is really her daughter. Pamela's first film wasn't in 1940 – her first dates as early as 1920. After privately confronting her with these puzzling facts, he listens to her confession. Pamela possesses the secret of eternal youth; a rare Egyptian scarab whose power was known only by the pharaohs. After drugging Herrick to unconsciousness, Pamela uses the scarab to suck the life out of him; his body at first ages into a skeleton, and then withers away to dust. Placing the scarab on her chest, she absorbs the youth and replaces the bug where it cannot be found, just in time for the next young man to pay a visit to her estate.

"Everybody knows Pamela Morris, the beautiful and eternally young movie star. Or does she have another name, even more famous . . . an Egyptian name from centuries past? It's best not to be too curious, lest you wind up like Jordan Herrick, a pile of dust and old clothing, discarded in the endless eternity . . . of the Twilight Zone."

Trailer: *"Twilight Zone regular Charles Beaumont brings us our next offering, a tale of age and youth and a beautiful woman. Our star is Ann Blyth. Our story – 'Queen of the Nile.' They say that beauty is only skin deep and when a surface is scratched, what you might conceivably find underneath is something quite apart from beauty. This is the rather intriguing basis of our next presentation. On the Twilight Zone – Miss Ann Blyth in 'Queen of the Nile.' "*

Trivia, etc. While Charles Beaumont is credited on the screen for writing the teleplay, every word of the script was composed by Jerry Sohl. Beaumont was very ill by this time and Sohl insisted on leaving his name off the script so Beaumont (and later his widow) would receive the residuals. It is apparent that the plot idea originated with Sohl. Someone had found a scarab ring and given it to him, pointing out how scary the bug looked. As Sohl thought about it, the ring proved to be the inspiration for "Queen of the Nile."

This episode was assigned a production number on September 13, 1963. All of the scenes filmed outside the mansion and around the swimming pool were shot on Lot 2, and the interior of Pamela Morris' mansion was filmed on Stage 18 at M-G-M. Hand inserts were filmed on October 2 – supplied by Bob McCord. On October 15, additional insert shots were filmed with McCord and Barbara Walker.

All of the Egyptian-styled statues and props were borrowed from a warehouse at M-G-M for a rental fee and were returned after primary filming was completed. Receipts and paperwork suggest that Cayuga never paid for the use of the statues and props. A clerical error may have been made and the studio may not have caught the mistake. To date, no paperwork has been found to verify payment for the use of the props.

Music cues titled "Dead Man" and "Private Eye" by Jerry Goldsmith were originally composed and conducted for an episode of *Perry Mason* titled "The Case of the Blushing Pearls," initially telecast on October 24, 1959.

The March 1964 issue of *Show* reviewed this episode, commenting: "Serling's forte is the tale with a twist, and his talent, the ability to get the very best writers on the air. 'The Queen of the Nile' illustrates both precepts nicely. It is written by Charles Beaumont, who is very big with the science fiction and horror fiction crowd, and stars Ann Blyth as an apparently ageless movie star, noted for her eternal beauty. In typical *Sunset Boulevard* fashion, the vamp lures a young writer into her lair. The lair, in this case, is furnished by early Cleopatra, and the reason for the décor is the heart of the script. Miss Blyth, it seems, has been around long enough to know a Cleopatra period piece from a movie prop, and the ensuing developments, if not horrendous, are twisty indeed."

The swimming pool was located at Cohn Park on Lot 2 at M-G-M. This was the same swimming pool featured in "The Bewitchin' Pool," "A Thing About Machines" and "The Trouble With Templeton." The outside of the mansion where Jordan drives up to is the same where Bartlett Finchley resides in "A Thing About Machines."

On October 25, 1963, plans were prepared by Ralph W. Nelson and William Froug regarding the last of Serling's photography for the remainder of the fifth season episodes. Having viewed the films, Froug suggested to Serling that he view "You Drive," "The Bewitchin' Pool" and the final cut on "An Occurrence at Owl Creek Bridge" before Serling locked himself down to composing the narrations. On Monday, November 11, 1963, Serling reported to the studios to film the following list, under the direction of Robert Florey:

(1)   A retake teaser for "You Drive" and opening narration for the same episode.
(2)   Narration for "The Bewitchin' Pool" which Froug felt was needed over the body of the show.
(3)   Trailer for "Ring-A-Ding-Girl" as this was not previously shot because the title "There Goes Bunny Blake" had not been cleared.
(4)   Teaser, trailer and end narration for "The Long Morrow."
(5)   Teaser, trailer and end narration for "Queen of the Nile."
(6)   Teaser, trailer and end narration for "Black Leather Jackets."
(7)   Teaser, trailer and end narration for "From Agnes, With Love."
(8)   Teaser, trailer and end narration for "Number 12 Looks Just Like You."
(9)   Twenty second opening for "An Occurrence at Owl Creek Bridge," trailer and end narration.
(10) BBC programs #3 through #7, 5 openings, bridges and closings.

This was a common practice for many of the third and fifth season episodes. Since Serling could not be on the set for each episode as they were being produced, many of his on-screen narrations were done in batches, with the camera panning to a stop as he delivered his lines. In the editing room, the film editor would put the two films together, giving a seamless appearance that the camera simply spun around to the other end of the room where Serling supposedly had been standing during the entire scene. (One mistake occurs in "Stopover in a Quiet Town" when a bit of the backstage lights are captured on film and carelessly overlooked just a fraction of a second before Serling appears on camera.)

Production #2627 "WHO AM I?"
Television script by Jerry Sohl.

"Witness one Glenn Holbrook, a man long accustomed to his own face, now understandably confused by what he sees in the mirror. Who is this stranger who stares back at him? Mr. Holbrook will never know, for a basic rule of cause and effect has been suddenly changed; it changed the moment he entered . . . The Twilight Zone."

Plot: Glenn Holbrook wakes one morning to discover that his face is not the same. While his wife, his boss and the employees all say Glenn looks no different than the day before, he knows something is very wrong. He never had the scar on his cheek, the brown eyes, and other distinguishing features. After failing to spend the entire day trying to convince everyone that the face he wears belongs to someone else, he visits a psychiatrist who tries to reason with him. Glenn ultimately retires to bed, content on the fact that regardless of what caused the phenomena, he will have to live with this new face for the rest of his life. When he wakes the next morning, he discovers to his horror that his face has changed again . . . and like the day before, his wife claims there is nothing wrong.

Trivia, etc. When Charles Beaumont began exhibiting symptoms of memory loss and slurred speech, his colleagues initially assumed it was due to his heavy drinking. As the months passed, Beaumont's symptoms grew and it became increasingly clear that something was very wrong. With deep respect for Beaumont, Rod Serling insisted that any stories conceived by the writer receive proper screen credit – and against the rules of the Writers' Guild, agreed to allow luminaries John Tomerlin, Ocee Ritch and Jerry Sohl to write the teleplays. Beaumont often assigned the tasks, but Serling was obviously involved according to a number of letters exchanged between the two, spanning 1962 through 1964. Even with his condition worse than the year before, Beaumont would still pitch a storyline to *Twilight Zone* producers, who would then commission him to create a feasible script.

For "Who Am I?" Beaumont was paid $2,500 for the story treatment and teleplay. After meeting up secretly with Jerry Sohl, Beaumont worked out the plot details and Sohl did the rest. Assigned a production number on September 30, 1963, the entire production was officially closed 24 hours later, according to an M-G-M work order dated October 1. The script, which contains no closing narration for Rod Serling, was never filmed. *

Production #2635 "WHAT'S IN THE BOX" (Initial telecast: March 13, 1964)
Copyright Registration: © Cayuga Productions, Inc., March 9, 1964, LP28079
Date of Rehearsal: January 31, 1964
Dates of Filming: February 3, 4 and 5, 1964
Script dated: January 21, 1964
Revised script dated: January 29, 1964, with revised pages dated January 31, 1964.

Producer and Secretary: $1,610.00
Director: $1,375.00
Unit Manager and Secretary: $710.00
Agents Commission: $2,500.00
Below the line charges (M-G-M): $30,888.90
Total Production Costs: $3,312.71

Story and Secretary: $2,688.14
Cast: $7,026.25
Production Fee: $1,800.00
Legal and Accounting: $250.00
Below the line charges (other): $3,312.71

Cast: Douglas Bank (the prosecutor); Joan Blondell (Phyllis Britt); Ted Christy (the Panther Man); William Demarest (Joe Britt); Sandra Gould (the woman); Sterling Holloway (the TV repairman); Herbert Lytton (Dr. Saltman); Tony Miller (the announcer); Ron Stokes (the car salesman); John L. Sullivan (the Russian Duke); and Howard Wright (the judge).

Stock Music Cues: Etrange #3 (by Marius Constant, :09); Milieu #2 (by Constant, :21); The Giant Killer (by Jerry Goldsmith, :16); The Gun (by Goldsmith, :26); The Caper (by Goldsmith, :20); Horn String on G (CBS, :04); The Gun (by Goldsmith, :22); Mistral (by Constant, :52); Trouble Ahead Tag (by Gold-

---

* Jerry Sohl also wrote a teleplay titled "Pattern for Doomsday" for the *Twilight Zone*. The tale told of Jody Hallum, a gambler, who makes a desperate attempt to survive, when he is given the news that a huge rock in space is hurtling toward Earth. Adapted from a brief story synopsis written by Beaumont, this author found no production material verifying the teleplay was ever purchased by Cayuga or assigned a production number. More than likely there was a verbal agreement to accept the teleplay based on the synopsis. It is doubtful that Sohl would have spent hours typing a teleplay on a whim, and since it was clearly written for *Twilight Zone*, the script is considered an unproduced feature.

smith, :17); The Gun (by Goldsmith, :16); The Caper (by Goldsmith, :11); The Image (by Goldsmith, :29); Mistral (by Constant, :52); The Caper (by Goldsmith, :08); The Giant Killer (by Goldsmith, :19); Low Bass Note (CBS, :02); Etrange #3 (by Constant, :09); and Milieu #1 (by Constant, :22).

Director of Photography: George T. Clemens, a.s.c.
Art Directors: George W. Davis and Eddie Imazu
Set Decorations: Henry Grace and Frank R. McKelvy
Directed by Richard L. Bare

Production Manager: Ralph W. Nelson
Film Editor: Richard W. Farrell
Casting: Larry Stewart
Assistant Director: Marty Moss
Sound: Franklin Milton and Joe Edmondson
Produced by William Froug
Teleplay by Martin M. Goldsmith

"Portrait of a TV fan. Name: Joe Britt. Occupation: cab driver. Tonight, Mr. Britt is going to watch a really big show. Something special for the cabbie who has seen everything. Joe Britt doesn't know it, but his flag is down and his meter's running – and he's in high gear on his way . . . to the Twilight Zone."

Plot: After several years of marriage, Joe Britt and his wife Phyllis have made it an evening ritual to get into a fight. Late one afternoon, after a long day of driving the cab, Britt discovers the repairman has fixed his television set and added a few modifications. Every time he turns the set on, Joe witnesses his life dramatized on the screen, including the petty cause of their domestic squabbles. Whenever he calls on his wife to look at the screen, she sees only static. Joe eventually sees a flash-forward, in which he and Phyllis get into another fight that ends with Joe pushing her out the window to her death. The family doctor thinks Joe is suffering from stress. Phyllis, however, has had enough and begins to pack her bags. Heated words are exchanged, resulting in a fight that mirrors the scene depicted on the television screen. Phyllis is pushed out the window, and the police arrive to arrest Joe for murder.

"The next time your TV set is on the blink, when you're in the need of a first-rate repairman, may we suggest our own specialist? Factory-trained, prompt, honest, twenty-four-hour service. You won't find him in the phone book, but his office is conveniently located . . . in the Twilight Zone."

Trailer: *"Next time out we do a little biting of the hand that feeds, and we tell you a delightful yarn that has to do with television. Not normal television, mind you, but a wacky tale about a TV set that predicts the future. It's written by Martin Goldsmith and stars three eminently talented people who make their first visit to the Zone: Joan Blondell, William Demarest, and Sterling Holloway. On the Twilight Zone next time, 'What's in the Box.'"*

Trivia, etc. *The Tucson Daily Citizen* reviewed this episode, "Bill Demarest is very good as a harassed man, bedeviled by a nagging wife. Good in a bit as a weird television repairman is Sterling Holloway."

In Serling's first draft, the name of the protagonist was Joe Brice. As of the January 29, 1964 draft, the name was changed officially to Joe Britt. In the original draft, the closing narration was different from what Serling later revised for the finished film:

"Joe Brice, cabdriver, two-bit Romeo, and star of Channel Ten, made his debut in October. But his final show was during the week of June third – live, from the prison at Ossining, and also, incidentally, from the Twilight Zone.

Next to Bob McCord, Beryl McCutcheon was probably featured in more *Twilight Zone* episodes than anyone else. Under contract to M-G-M Studios, she appeared in bit parts as a showgirl, a secretary, a bridesmaid, a college co-ed, and a female pedestrian. As a stunt double for female parts on *The Twilight Zone*, she also made numerous appearances as a pedestrian in the background scenes, a passenger on an airliner, and other assorted non-speaking roles that awarded her the position of being the female actress to appear in more *Twilight Zone* episodes than any other woman. She makes an appearance in this episode as Phyllis for the stunt involving the death scene out the window.

Production #2601 "THE MASKS" (Initial telecast: March 20, 1964)
© Cayuga Productions, Inc., March 16, 1964, LP29196 (in notice: 1963)
Date of Rehearsal: May 20, 1963
Dates of Filming: May 21, 22 and 23, 1963
Script dated: March 22, 1963, with revised pages dated April 10, 15, and May 3, 15 and 20, 1963.

Producer and Secretary: $1,626.02
Director: $1,375.00
Unit Manager and Secretary: $726.01
Agents Commission: $2,500.00
Below the line charges (M-G-M): $33,657.99
Total Production Costs: $55,157.52

Story and Secretary: $3,310.00
Cast: $7,843.84
Production Fee: $1,800.00
Legal and Accounting: $250.00
Below the line charges (other): $2,068.66

Cast: Willis Bouchey (Dr. Samuel Thorne); Virginia Gregg (Emily Harper); Brooke Hayward (Paula Harper); Robert Keith (Jason Foster); Maide Norman (the maid); Milton Selzer (Wilfred Harper); Alan Sues (Wilfred Harper Jr.); and Bill Walker (Jeffrey, the servant).

Stock Music Cues: Etrange #3 (by Marius Constant, :09); Milieu #2 (by Constant, :21); Menton 18 (by Constant, :26); Harp Glissandi (CBS, :02); Dreams (by Wilfred Josephs, :22); Sad Departure (by Goldsmith, :18); Dreams (by Josephs, :32); Belfort #5 (by Constant, :16); Fight for the Old Elm Grove (by Lyn Murray, :21); The Discussion (by Goldsmith, :12); Dreams (by Josephs, :32); Maya (by Nathan Van Cleave, :22); The Picture (by Van Cleave, :14); Magdalena #1 (by Lyn Murray, :08); The Funhouse (by Van Cleave, :49); Loire (by Constant, :07); Return to Desolation (by Murray, :46); Now We Move (by Van Cleave, :22); Harp Chord (CBS, :02); and Milieu #2 (by Constant, arr. by Herrmann, :21).

Director of Photography: George T.
    Clemens, a.s.c.
Art Directors: George W. Davis and
    Walter Holscher
Set Decorations: Henry Grace and
    Robert R. Benton
Sound: Franklin Milton and Philip N. Mitchell

Production Manager: Ralph W. Nelson
Film Editor: Richard Heermance, a.c.e.
Casting: Patricia Rose
Assistant Director: Charles Bonniwell, Jr.
Produced by Bert Granet
Directed by Ida Lupino
Teleplay by Rod Serling

"Mr. Jason Foster – a tired ancient who on this particular Mardi Gras evening will leave the Earth. But before departing he has some things to do – some services to perform, some debts to pay, and some justice

to mete out. This is New Orleans – Mardi Gras time . . . It is also . . . the Twilight Zone."

Plot: Old man Foster is dying from the hardening of the arteries and a sick heart, which comes from age and greedy relatives. His only reason for living is the inner strength brought on by cross-brained orneriness and a drive to entertain his rich, greedy relatives, who have recently paid him a personal visit on Mardi Gras, solely waiting for him to kick off so they can inherit. After a good meal, they all retire to the lounge where Foster introduces them to a set of masks created by an old Cajun. Besides the artistic virtue, the masks have special properties, he explains, and forces each of them to wear the masks that reflect the cruelty they display. He guarantees delivery of his entire estate on condition that they wear the masks until midnight. If they remove the masks, they lose any chance of inheritance. For hours the family pleads against the old man's wishes, but at midnight the old man dies and the masks are removed. The family is shocked when they discover that the masks branded them with the image of the caricatures they portrayed – while the old man dies a comfortable death, content knowing he achieved his vengeance.

"Mardi Gras incident. The dramatis personae being four people who came to celebrate. And in a sense let themselves go. This they did with a vengeance. They now wear the faces of all that was inside them, and they'll wear them for the rest of their lives. Said lives now to be spent in shadow. Tonight's tale of men, the macabre and masks . . . on the Twilight Zone."

Trailer: *"Next on Twilight Zone we move into New Orleans for the Mardi Gras, and we do it with a vengeance. Robert Keith and Milton Selzer appear in a bizarre story of men, masquerades and masks. This is a small shocker to wind up a week – and if it doesn't send you to a psychiatrist, it'll send you, at least, to a mirror. On Twilight Zone next . . . 'The Masks.'"*

Trivia, etc. In the earlier drafts from March and April, the ending to the script was slightly different. After the family removes their masks to reveal the side-effects, the audience gets an abrupt cut to the front entrance hall, where the butler stands transfixed, listening to the screams from behind closed doors. He very slowly closes his eyes, lowers his head and makes a silent prayer. The grandfather clock strikes two and the butler enters the study, followed by a gnarled little old man. "Mr. Foster told me that I should pick up the masks any time after midnight," he explains. He picks up the masks that have been strewn across the room. After getting the fourth one he turns towards Foster, looks at him briefly, points to him, and looks toward the butler questionably.

"Mr. Foster is dead," the butler explains. "He died at midnight. He left word that I was to let you in . . . you were to take the masks back with you." The old man walks over to Foster, gently moving the dead man's head back and removes the death mask. Underneath is a face in repose and peace. "This is the mask of death. The true one. The endless sleep of peace." The butler and the old man make for the door while the camera pans to the top of the stairs where the four people are huddled together, and Serling's closing narration concludes the episode. (In another draft similar to the above, the old man picks up the masks and then points to Foster, who is already unmasked and dead. The butler comments that Foster already removed his mask. The old man smiled slightly, "Mais non. He did not. He merely exchanged.")

The entire episode was filmed on Stage 27 at M-G-M. In a cost-saving effort, two of the walls featured in this episode were moved to Stage 18 for use in the episode "Uncle Simon." The cost of set design and construction for John's bedroom was $1,107. The interior of the New Orleans mansion was $706. The stairs in the lobby of the New Orleans mansion were also reused for a scene in "Uncle Simon." An insert shot of the grandfather clock against backing was filmed on the morning of June 5, 1963.

Despite the history of stage activity, including her appearance in "The Sixteen Millimeter Shrine," Ida Lupino took to the director's chair for this episode – marking the only episode of the series to be directed by a woman. She fell into directing in 1949, when she and Collier Young (her husband at the time) were producing their first picture together, *Not Wanted*. The director became ill on the first day of shooting and Lupino, who had had a hand in drafting the script, was rushed into the breach.

"Directing is much easier than acting," she explained. "The actor deals in false emotions, produced on cue. The director has his problems, but they are all normal. He doesn't have to smile into a camera while suffering through an early morning grouch."

"She is a trouper," recalled fellow television director Roy Kellino. "She will stand all day on a recently broken ankle because she knows that if the picture goes into another day of shooting, it will cost more money. I admire Miss Lupino tremendously." Producer Bert Granet admired her too, for the same reasons. The largest concern a producer had was keeping the production – and the budget – on schedule.

Assigned a production number on March 21, 1963, this episode required the use of masks and pre-styled makeup. On May 8, 1963, all five principal players were brought in for makeup tests. Molds were made of the actors' faces to create the masks and prosthetics that would later be created for the production. The reason for the makeup tests two weeks before filming was the time involved to create the masks and ensure their completion before production began.

"They had to do a life mask with the cast in advance," recalled Brooke Hayward. "After we were done filming, Ida Lupino told us we could keep the masks, because they would not be needed. I used to have my mask for many years but I don't recall what happened to it since. Rod Serling was on the set much of the time. He was involved with a lot of what was filmed on stage. He was terrific, a really nice man."

Filming of this episode was almost shot in the order the scenes appeared in the finished film. The first day consisted of all the scenes in Foster's bedroom and the interior of the corridor. The second day consisted of filming the interior of the New Orleans mansion entry hall and the interior of the study. On the morning of the third day, all of the actors had to report to the studio early, wearing the prosthetics and makeup, so the concluding scenes of this episode – the revealing of the damage done by the masks – could be shot. The application and removal of the makeup was time-consuming, so leaving the most complex scenes for the final day ensured a swift production.

Bill Walker, who played Jeffrey, the Negro servant, and Maide Norman, the maid, went for wardrobe fitting on the afternoon of the first day of filming, since their scenes were limited to the second and third day.

This episode was originally slated for initial telecast on March 13, 1964, but pushed ahead when the tentative release schedule was revised to make room for "An Occurrence at Owl Creek Bridge."

Canned music scores were dubbed on July 24, closing production and awaiting Serling's approval. Critics loved the episode. *The Tucson Daily Citizen* alerted their readers that this episode was worth watching, noting it contained "a rather terrifying climax that's worth waiting for." Lupino's creative direction stands out – one scene in particular has the servant holding living flowers and the edit fades to the next scene where the doctor is taking Jason Foster's pulse.

Production #2630 "I AM THE NIGHT – COLOR ME BLACK"
(Initial telecast: March 27, 1964)

Copyright Registration: © Cayuga Productions, Inc., March 23, 1964, LP29221
Date of Rehearsal: January 31, 1964
Dates of Filming: February 3, 4 and 5, 1964
First script dated: December 18, 1963
Revised script dated: January 23, 1964, with revised pages February 5 and 6, 1964.

Producer and Secretary: $1,610.00
Director: $1,500.00
Unit Manager and Secretary: $710.00
Agents Commission: $2,500.00
Below the line charges (M-G-M): $31,201.67
Total Production Costs: $55,017.00

Story and Secretary: $6,460.00
Cast: $5,578.11
Production Fee: $1,800.00
Legal and Accounting: $250.00
Below the line charges (other): $3,407.22

Cast: Douglas Bank (man #1); Terry Becker (Jagger); Michael Constantine (Sheriff Charlie Koch); Ivan Dixon (Reverend Anderson); Paul Fix (Colbey); Elizabeth Harrower (the woman); George Lindsey (Deputy Pierce); Bob McCord (town citizen at lynching); Eve McVeagh (Ella Koch); and Ward Wood (man #2).

Stock Music Cues: Etrange #3 (by Marius Constant, :09); Milieu #2 (by Constant, :21); The Cellar – Collector's Item (by Bernard Herrmann, :52); The Hitch-Hiker (by Herrmann, 1:02); The Station (by Herrmann, :18); The Door (by Herrmann, :10); The Sun (by Herrmann, :14); Now We Move (by Nathan Van Cleave, :32 and :17); The Station (by Herrmann, :17); The Sun (by Herrmann, :14 and :44); The Phone (by Herrmann, :34); Unison Horn Notes (CBS, :06); Now We Move (by Van Cleave, :34); Etrange #3 (by Constant, :09); and Milieu #1 (by Constant, :22).

Director of Photography: George T.
    Clemens, a.s.c.
Art Directors: George W. Davis and
    Eddie Imazu
Set Decorations: Henry Grace and
    Frank R. McKelvy
Sound: Franklin Milton and Joe Edmondson

Production Manager: Ralph W. Nelson
Film Editor: Richard Heermance, a.c.e.
Casting: Larry Stewart
Assistant Director: Marty Moss
Produced by William Froug
Directed by Abner Biberman
Teleplay by Rod Serling

"Sheriff Charlie Koch, on the morning of an execution. As a matter of fact, it's 7:30 in the morning. Logic and natural laws dictate that at this hour there should be daylight. It is a simple rule of physical science that the sun should rise at a certain moment and supersede the darkness. But at this given moment Sheriff Charlie Koch, a deputy named Pierce, a condemned man named Jagger, and a small, inconsequential village will shortly find out that there are causes and effects that have no precedent. Such is usually the case . . . in the Twilight Zone."

Plot: On the morning of a public execution, sunlight fails to shine upon a small southern town. Scientists cannot figure out why the town has been thrown into darkness, when sunlight beats down on the surrounding areas. The city editor suspects the hanging is unjustified and wonders if the execution has something to do with the darkness. The sheriff's deputy perjured himself on the stand, the editor suspects. The sheriff, wanting to be reelected, allowed the trial to go on without justification. Since the victim was well-loved by the townfolk for his efforts in front-yard cross burning, Jagger, the condemned man, was found guilty of first-degree murder. At the time of the execution, citizens gather to watch the hanging, shouting for blood as Jagger walks the steps leading up to the gallows. The minister, who wants to do what's right, leans with the majority in an effort to keep from being run out of town, and the hanging goes on as scheduled. Turning to the crowd, Reverend Anderson explains to the crowd that the blackness is all the hate. Meanwhile, the radio news reports the darkness is spreading – in South Vietnam, over the Berlin wall, and anywhere the hatred is too strong to be contained.

"A sickness known as hate; not a virus, not a microbe, not a germ, but a sickness nonetheless; highly contagious, deadly in its effects. Don't look for it in the Twilight Zone. Look for it in a mirror. Look for it before the light goes out altogether."

Trailer: *"Next time out on the Twilight Zone, we do a probe in depth into a current cancer known as hatred. And we tell you the story of a little mid-western village which wakes up on a violent morning to discover that there is no morning. No light, no sun. Only a frightening and pervading darkness. It stars Michael Constantine and Paul Fix. And it's called 'I Am the Night – Color Me Black.'"*

Trivia, etc. On the evening of May 25, 1956, Serling's teleplay titled "Noon on Doomsday" was dramatized on *The U.S. Steel Hour*, which began in his mind as a dramatization of the 1955 Emmett Till kidnapping-murder case in Mississippi, and ended up (with poor critical reception) as a demonstration of narrow-mindedness in a small town. "Our problem is the ritual one of covering up our tracks," recalled Serling. "You state something without anyone realizing what it is you're stating. I take the blame for that one. It had a lot of phony writing in it – calling a spade a heart."

While advertisers and networks imposed taboos, Serling had discovered that censorship problems with his scripts could be mellowed with the right approach. "By and large I think the trend is to considerably more freedom in treatment and themes," commented Serling in an interview with columnist Dave Jampel. "I think the public has indicated that it doesn't associate controversy with a product. It doesn't associate a theme with a box top. You compromise as best you know how. You try to make the social-point you want to make within the allowable frame of reference. If you want to tell a story of racial prejudice, for example, you don't set it in Birmingham, but in an unidentifiable place. You tell it somewhat obliquely, but nonetheless make the point you want to make. It wears a different costume and a different make, but the act is the same. There is a traditional trick covering what we've been doing for years on *The Twilight Zone*, we tell it completely in parable. If we do a story about the psychology of mob violence, we tell it as a science fiction story, but the psychology remains the same."

A welter of publicity came about from *The U.S. Steel Hour* presentation, many generated by the White Citizens Councils. Up until this time, Serling's teleplays were considered "non-controversial." This play helped establish him with a record for touching on subjects the networks were afraid to dramatize for fear of public backlash. With this *Twilight Zone*, Serling attempted to revisit the past with a script not too dissimilar from "Noon on Doomsday." Adding an element of fantasy (the mysterious darkness), the Programming Practices Department of CBS did not have any complaints regarding the lynching – only suggesting deleting or replacing minor phrases and words that could be misinterpreted as slang, to avoid complaints from viewers.

The entire episode was filmed in a studio, including the scenes at the public execution. Terry Becker recalled having the flu during filming and was in very bad shape. Rather than call in sick, he made it to the studio and did the best he could. George Lindsey recalled how the crew was blowing earth around on the set, to give the illusion that the episode was taking place outside and not in. When the actors were not on camera, they had to wear nose-mouth filters.

The voice heard over the radio was actor Larry Thor, who signed with CBS as an announcer in 1948. Speaking only Icelandic until the age of seven, the Canadian-born voice actor was the announcer for numerous radio and television series such as *Suspense* and *Crime Classics*. Thor is probably best remembered for his role as plainclothes detective Danny Clover on radio's *Broadway Is My Beat*.

When a student at Bingham Central High School in Utah wrote to Serling in March of 1958, asking for biographical information for her research paper concerning his rise to fame, he sent her a polite letter giving a very brief biography about his career and personal life. Among his comments were, "My pet peeves are phony commercials on television, the late Senator McCarthy and the Ku Klux Klan."

"The idea may send some fans away but stick with it, the drama is worth it," the television critic for *The San Antonio Light* remarked. Producer William Froug wrote a teleplay for *Twilight Zone*, dated a few days after Serling's script, with a similar premise, titled "Many, Many Monkeys." (See Production #2634.) Both scripts were similar in nature, and after discussion between both parties, it was decided that only one would be produced, and Froug's script was shelved.

Production #2634 "MANY, MANY MONKEYS"
Script written by William Froug, dated January 20, 1964.

"A city hospital. A night like any other night. But inside these sterile walls, down these shadowed corridors, an unexpected visitor walks ... A stranger bearing unwelcome tidings ... Someone never seen before, by this hospital or any other. The stranger's name? Unknown. A disease so new the textbooks haven't recorded it. This, then is the first case history ... Documented from the medical files of ... The Twilight Zone."

Plot: Jean Reed pays a visit to a New York hospital in hopes that a team of surgeons can explain the cause of her recent blindness. After taking off the sunglasses, the surgeons and nurses are shocked to see that her face has grown a thin layer of skin over each of the eye sockets. While Jean waits in a hospital room, one of the nurses, Claire, takes pity on the patient and offers a hand of friendship. When Dr. Edward Peterson arrives, he is shocked to learn that Jean's illness is spreading – two nurses, an intern and an orderly are blindly rushing toward the admitting area. They too have a thin layer of skin covering their eyes. Dr. Mark Friedman arrives to consult with Peterson about this sudden epidemic, suggesting nuclear fallout from a bomb may be the cause. The radio and television news reports an estimated 500 cases have broken out in the city. Reports from London are no different. Meanwhile, back in the hospital room, Claire comforts Jean, telling her that the situation reminds her of a poem, "See no evil, speak no evil, hear no evil." The blind reminds her of monkeys. "We've shut our eyes, our ears, even our brains to our own hate. Something bigger than a bomb has finally made us see ourselves for what we really are ... and that flash of insight has blinded us all." A phone call at the hospital reveals that Jean's husband is also blind, and Jean has deserted him in a time of need. If Claire's theory is correct, then Jean brought on her own blindness. Current news on the radio verifies there was no bomb or fallout. In fact, there is hope – in London a permanent cure is nothing more than skillful surgery. However, the surgeon in the New York hospital, realizing that Nurse Claire's theory is the correct diagnosis, chooses not to cure Jean. He advises the patient to go home and make amends with her husband – it is a cure that no operation could provide.

Trivia, etc. The original script did not feature any closing narration, suggesting that Froug was going to leave the closing comments to Serling. Dated a few days after "I Am the Night – Color Me Black," the script mirrored a similar concept, people being thrown into darkness because of the hatred that can no longer be bottled inside. It was decided that only one would be produced, according to production notes by William Froug. This script was put aside so Serling's would be produced. When *The Twilight Zone* was revived in the 1980s, this script was filmed and later publicized as "an unproduced telefeature" and "lost episode" of *The Twilight Zone*. At least one source erroneously remarked that CBS bought the script and, finding the subject matter disturbing, would not allow it to be produced. But, in fact, the script was never submitted to the network for review.

Production #2631 "SOUNDS AND SILENCES" (Initial telecast: April 3, 1964)

© Cayuga Productions, Inc., March 27, 1964, LP29222
Date of Rehearsal: February 12, 1964
Dates of Filming: February 13, 14 and 17, 1964
Script dated: November 19, 1963
Revised draft dated: December 18, 1963

Producer and Secretary: $1,610.00
Director: $1,500.00
Unit Manager and Secretary: $710.00
Agents Commission: $2,500.00
Below the line charges (M-G-M): $32,689.56
Total Production Costs: $52,774.87

Story and Secretary: $3,310.00
Cast: $4,700.00
Production Fee: $1,800.00
Legal and Accounting: $250.00
Below the line charges (other): $3,705.31

Cast: Renee Aubrey (the secretary); William Benedict (Conklin); Francis De Sales (the doctor); Michael Fox (the psychiatrist); John McGiver (Roswell G. Flemington); and Penny Singleton (Mrs. Flemington).

Stock Music Cues: Etrange #3 (by Marius Constant, :09); Milieu #2 (by Constant, :21); Anchors Aweigh (by George D. Lottman, Charles A. Zimmerman and Alfred H. Miles, :54); Sailor's Hornpipe (traditional, arr. by Lyn Murray, :22); Hornpipe Suite (traditional, arr. by Lucien Moraweck, :11); Unison Horns on C (CBS, :04); Sailor's Hornpipe (traditional, arr. by Lyn Murray, :13); Etrange #3 (by Constant, :09); and Milieu #1 (by Constant, :22).

Director of Photography: George T.
    Clemens, a.s.c.
Art Directors: George W. Davis and

Production Manager: Ralph W. Nelson
Film Editor: Richard W. Farrell
Casting: Larry Stewart

Eddie Imazu
Set Decorations: Henry Grace and
    Frank R. McKelvy
Sound: Franklin Milton and Joe Edmondson

Assistant Director: Marty Moss
Produced by William Froug
Directed by Richard Donner
Teleplay by Rod Serling

"This is Roswell G. Flemington. Two hundred and twenty pounds of gristle, lung tissue and sound decibels. He is, as you have perceived, a noisy man. One of a breed who substitutes volume for substance; sound for significance; and shouting to cover up the readily apparent phenomenon that he is nothing more than an overweight and aging perennial Sea Scout whose noise-making is in inverse ratio to his competence and to his character. But soon our would-be admiral of the fleet will embark on another voyage. This one is an uncharted and twisting stream that heads for a distant port called . . . the Twilight Zone."

Plot: Roswell Flemington, owner of a model ship company and ex-naval officer from the war, spends his hours playing recordings of battleships so loud that objects rock back and forth. His idiosyncrasy of listening to loud sounds is now an obsession, and he runs his household and office like a battleship. After his wife of 20 years finally leaves him, Roswell starts suffering from an acute strain of nerves, in which even the most minor of sounds roars like thunder. A doctor checks out his ears, but finds nothing wrong. A psychiatrist explains to Roswell that it's all just a figment of his imagination. When Roswell believes his problem is mind over matter, he finds himself cured . . . until he shuts out all the sounds from his head. What he hears now is total silence – and begins smashing bookshelves and bottles throughout his room, hoping to hear something even if it is the sound of his own voice.

"When last heard from, Mr. Roswell G. Flemington was in a sanitarium pleading with the medical staff to make some noise. They, of course, believe the case to be a rather tragic aberration – a man's mind becoming unhinged. And for this they'll give him pills, therapy and rest. Little do they realize that all Mr. Flemington is suffering from is a case of poetic justice. Tonight's tale of sounds and silences . . . from the Twilight Zone."

Trailer: *"Next time out we bring you a few decibels of sound in a bizarre opus of a man who breaks ear drums for a living. We welcome to the program two fine talents. Mr. John McGiver and Miss Penny Singleton, who will prove the following point: namely that too much of a good thing can have nightmarish results, and that all things are not necessarily as they meet the eye or the ear. On the Twilight Zone next, 'Sounds and Silences.'"*

Trivia, etc. Many years previous, when Serling proposed the radio series *It Happens to You*, he wrote a script titled "The Gallant Breed of Men." The story told of Captain Peter Bruce, an ex-captain in the merchant marine who, guided by his conscience, makes a choice that most men would not make in order to save another man. His flamboyant personality was loud and boisterous. For this *Twilight Zone* episode, he made Roswell Flemington an ex-naval officer, a walking loudspeaker, but without a conscience. *

"John McGiver, a very funny man, makes *The Twilight Zone* worth your time," a television critic for *The Appleton Post-Crescent* wrote. "There are no great messages in Rod Serling's script, but it is an amusing look at a man who runs both home and office as a taut ship." *The Mansfield News Journal* remarked: "Character actor John McGiver gives the story a special flavor playing the obnoxious fel-

---

* In the proposed script, "The Gallant Breed of Men," the name of the ex-captain's wife was Nan.

low. McGiver doesn't miss a beat." (In Serling's original draft of the script, he labeled Roswell as 217 pounds "of gristle, lung tissue and sound," not 220.)

When Serling defended his reputation as an author of original teleplays, and not a plagiarist as he was accused of a number of times, he wrote to one doubter, "I can tell you quite unequivocally, that I have never – in the course of some seventeen years of writing – ever – repeat, ever – deliberately, knowingly or overtly taken another man's work and substituted it as my own. In all areas of science fiction – and this is my experience after five years on the air – it is rare that we do a show in which at least ten people do not accost us, waving material of their own, and accuse us of plagiarism, conscious or otherwise. There is no question but that when you deal in this kind of storytelling, you automatically handle certain ideas in precisely the same manner that other science fictionaires do. It's unhappy and unfortunate but I think it's to be quite expected."

Shortly after viewing this episode, one viewer who submitted a script of the same name to Cayuga Productions about a man who heard sounds in a deafening roar and then tortured with complete silence, contacted an attorney, Irwin O. Spiegel, Esq. On April 22, 1964, Spiegel sent a letter addressed to Serling and CBS threatening a suit for plagiarism. After a few weeks of exchanges between attorneys representing both parties, an out-of-court settlement was made for a total of $3,500.

Production #2636 "CAESAR AND ME" (Initial telecast: April 10, 1964)
Copyright Registration: © Cayuga Productions, Inc., April 6, 1964, LP29223
Date of Rehearsal: February 18, 1964
Dates of Filming: February 19, 20 and 21, 1964
Script dated: January 23, 1964
Revised draft dated: January 28, 1964
Shooting script dated: February 14, 1964, with revised pages dated February 18, 1964.

Producer and Secretary: $1,610.00	Story and Secretary: $1,545.00
Director: $1,500.00	Cast: $6,145.00
Unit Manager and Secretary: $710.00	Production Fee: $1,800.00
Agents Commission: $2,500.00	Legal and Accounting: $250.00
Below the line charges (M-G-M): $34,291.47	Below the line charges (other): $5,113.32
Total Production Costs: $55,464.79	

Cast: Jackie Cooper (Jonathan West); Susanne Cupito (Susan); Don Gazzaniga (the detective); Ken Konopka (Mr. Miller); Sidney Marion (the night watchman); Bob McCord (man in theater); Stafford Repp (the pawnbroker); Sarah Selby (Mrs. Cudahy); and Olan Soulé (the employment agent).

Original Music Score Composed and Conducted by Richard Shores: Etrange #3 (by Marius Constant, :09); Milieu #2 (by Constant, :21); Down and Out (:18); No Claim (:26); Caesar Talks (:05); Marking Time (:27); Episode (:17); Hey Pal (:03); Episode A (:17); Maybe (:03); Audition (:11); Living Doll (:10); No Job (:12); Now What (1:01); The Robbery (1:04); What A Way (1:07); Susan and Caesar (:17); I Dare You (:16); Easy Street (:45); Once More (1:31); Night Watchman (:30); Very Big in Dublin (:39); Caught (:40); We're A Team (1:46); Etrange #3 (by Constant, :09); and Milieu #1 (by Constant, :22).

Director of Photography: George T.
 Clemens, a.s.c.
Art Directors: George W. Davis and
 Eddie Imazu
Set Decorations: Henry Grace and
 Frank R. McKelvy
Directed by Robert Butler

Production Manager: Ralph W. Nelson
Film Editor: Richard Heermance, a.c.e.
Casting: Larry Stewart
Assistant Director: Marty Moss
Sound: Franklin Milton and Joe Edmondson
Produced by William Froug
Teleplay by Adele T. Strassfield

"Jonathan West, ventriloquist, a master of voice manipulation. A man late of Ireland, with a talent for putting words into other people's mouths. In this case the other person is a dummy, aptly named Caesar – a small splinter with large ideas, a wooden tyrant with a mind and voice of his own, who is about to talk Jonathan West into the Twilight Zone."

Plot: A ventriloquist named Jonathan West, a recent arrival from Ireland, has been unable to get a job and is behind in his rent. Caesar, the wooden half of the partnership, walks and talks by himself and convinces Jonathan that the only way he'll make any money is to steal it. At first, Jonathan insists on earning money the honest way – but no one wants to hire him. Desperate to make good on his bills, Jonathan goes along with Caesar and breaks into a delicatessen. Susan, the landlady's niece, suspects the dummy is alive, and makes a few attempts to prove her theory. The next evening, Caesar convinces Jonathan to break into the nightclub after hours and steal the money from the safe. Susan, learning about the robbery in the newspapers, places an anonymous phone call to the police. Jonathan receives a visit from a pair of detectives. After the arrest, Susan meets with the dummy privately and the two discuss plans to run off to New York with the stolen loot – but something needs to be done about her aunt first.

"Little girl and a wooden doll . . . a lethal dummy in the shape of a man. But everybody knows dummies can't talk – unless, of course, they learn their vocabulary in the Twilight Zone."

Trailer: *"Next time on the Twilight Zone, we move into a very dark corner of the odd and the unpredictable with a story called 'Caesar and Me.' It's written by Adele T. Strassfield and it stars one of the most talented young men on the acting scene today, Jackie Cooper. Here's one that may stay with you after the lights are out. It's a story of a ventriloquist and his dummy, and this one is designed for the cold chills and the hot fevers."*

Trivia, etc. This marked the only *Twilight Zone* episode to be scripted by a woman. Adele Strassfield was the assistant and secretary of producer William Froug. In

Jackie Cooper exchanges opinions with
Caesar, his better half.

an interview with columnist Fred H. Russell for *The Bridgeport Post*, Strassfield wasn't aware of being a "first" for the series and did not try to account for her feat in breaking into a previously all-male world.

"I just had an idea about a ventriloquist who is controlled by his own dummy and becomes the victim of a dreadful little girl. I told Mr. Froug about it, and he said to go ahead with the script," she recalled. William Froug, naturally, helped work on the teleplay which went under the name of "Caesar's Husband" for the first draft.

Jackie Cooper thought it would be interesting to play the character as a naïve Irishman, and as director Robert Butler recalled, "He was very effective. We had him on a dolly so that when we filmed him from the hip up, we could make the dummy pace back and forth across the room, weaving his spell over Jackie."

Young Morgan Brittany, billed as Suzanne Cupito in this episode, recalled how her hair was cut short for the role. "I had long hair for a long time, but someone, maybe it was the director, I still don't know to this day, wanted my hair short to match a style that was popular with other little girls," recalled Brittany. "I guess they wanted me to play the role of a tomboy or a spoiled brat, so I had to look the part."

The décor and walls featured in the theater where Jonathan tries out his routine with potential employers is the same featured in previous *Twilight Zone* episodes, "The Mirror" and "A Piano in the House."

The Wisconsin State Journal labeled this episode as "a little horror tale, suited to its 26-minute span."

Production #2639 "THE JEOPARDY ROOM" (Initial telecast: April 17, 1964)

Copyright Registration: © Cayuga Productions, Inc., April 13, 1964, LP29224
Date of Rehearsal: February 24, 1964
Dates of Filming: February 25, 26 and 27, 1964
Script dated: February 14, 1964, with revised pages dated February 20, 1964.

Producer and Secretary: $1,610.00
Director: $1,500.00
Unit Manager and Secretary: $710.00
Agents Commission: $2,500.00
Below the line charges (M-G-M): $28,537.70
Total Production Costs: $48,241.37

Story and Secretary: $3,310.00
Cast: $4,770.00
Production Fee: $1,800.00
Legal and Accounting: $250.00
Below the line charges (other): $3,253.67

Cast: Robert Kelljan (Boris); Martin Landau (Major Ivan Kuchenko); and John Van Dreelen (Commissar Vassiloff).

Stock Music Cues: Etrange #3 (by Marius Constant, :09); Milieu #2 (by Constant, :21); Puzzles (by Fred Steiner, :07); The Last Killing (by Jerry Goldsmith, :53); The Killing (by Goldsmith, :09); Puzzles (by Steiner, :07); Guilty Party (by Goldsmith, :33); The Fire (by Goldsmith, :24); Unison Horns of F Sharp (CBS, :06); The Last Killing (by Goldsmith, :53); The Killing (by Goldsmith, :06); Into Darkness (by Lucien Moraweck, :47); The Robbery (by Goldsmith, :05); The Last Killing (by Goldsmith, :40); The Killing (by Goldsmith, :09); Silent Flight (by Goldsmith, 1:08 and 1:08); Neutral

Suspense (by Goldsmith, :29); String Effects (CBS, :07); The Last Killing (by Goldsmith, :32); Sick Boy (by Goldsmith, :15); Gun Fight (by Goldsmith, :23); Gunfighters (by Goldsmith, :04); Puzzles (by Steiner, :07); Religious Professional #1 (by Rene Garriguenc, :35); Rosie's Man (by Steiner, :12); Sand (by Steiner, :04); Etrange #3 (by Constant, :09); and Milieu #1 (by Constant, :22).

Director of Photography: George T. Clemens, a.s.c.
Art Directors: George W. Davis and Eddie Imazu
Set Decorations: Henry Grace and Frank R. McKelvy
Directed by Richard Donner

Production Manager: Ralph W. Nelson
Film Editor: Richard W. Farrell
Casting: Larry Stewart
Assistant Director: Marty Moss
Sound: Franklin Milton and Joe Edmondson
Produced by William Froug
Teleplay by Rod Serling

"The cast of characters: a cat and a mouse. This is the latter, the intended victim who may or may not know that he is to die, be it by butchery or bullet. His name is Major Ivan Kuchenko. He has, if events go according to certain plans, perhaps three or four more hours of living. But an ignorance shared by both himself and his executioner is of the fact that both of them have taken a first step . . . into the Twilight Zone."

Plot: Major Kuchenko, a former political prisoner who recently escaped from a 12-year sentence, arrives in a neutral country in hopes of being rescued. Since he has information that would prove an embarrassment to a foreign country, the Commissar, an imaginative executioner, watches his intended victim with intense scrutiny. To simply shoot Kuchenko would be an injustice; he prefers to kill his victim with some finesse and subtlety. To suffer a bad death is the work of a butcher; to suffer a good death is the work of an artist. Kuchenko wakes to find a recording in his room that says a booby trap has been planted in the room. If he finds it and cuts the wires before it goes off, he can go free. If he tries to make an escape, or put the lights out, he will be shot by a sniper. For three hours Kuchenko searches for the small explosive, but fails. Ten minutes before the detonation, in desperation, Kuchenko makes a run for the door and with luck, dodges the bullets. Back in the room, the Commissar, disappointed, picks up all evidence of his deed, only to find himself the victim of his own device.

"Major Ivan Kuchenko, on his way west, on his way to freedom. A freedom bought and paid for by a most stunning ingenuity. And exit one Commissar Vassiloff, who forgot that there are two sides to an argument . . . and two parties on the line. This has been . . . the Twilight Zone."

Trailer: *"Next time out, you'll share a study in depth of human terror with Martin Landau and John Van Dreelen. You'll stay in a hotel room of a European city which has been booby-trapped with a plastic bomb. You'll walk around this room with violent death resting on your shoulder. It could be anywhere . . . a picture, a chair, a faucet, or simply the carpet you're walking on. Next time out on the Twilight Zone, 'The Jeopardy Room.'"*

Trivia, etc. This story dates back to July 10, 1961, when Rod Serling drafted an incomplete script titled "Method of Execution," for possible use on *The Twilight Zone.* The story tells of two men, Commissar Kirsch and "a big, sheep-like man" named Bulgov, who plot to kill a Czech democrat who has recently gained power and influence over the people. Kirsch is the mastermind, while Bulgov is an expert in explosives, who, guided by his partner-in-crime, plants a number of small explosives about the room. Their intention is to assassinate their victim with flair. As Kirsch explains, "Killing a human being is an art in itself. It would be relatively simple to jump into an arena with a Tommy gun. The beauty of the kill lies in the way the matador sights with his weapon and then drives it home between the eyes. Of course . . . a Tommy gun would render the bull just as dead. But there lies the distinction between butchery and art." After planting a number of bombs throughout the room (window shades, rocking chair, coat hanger, etc.), they exit, leaving their victim to suffer a gruesome demise – or so they think. It is here that the script ends, without an entrance by the intended victim. The title originates from a comment spoken by the assassin, "A bizarre and novel method of execution."

In early 1964, Serling dusted off his partial script and completed a new revision, starting from the beginning, eliminating the concept of multiple detonation devices down to one – the telephone. *The Lima News* was quick to point out that while this episode was "a horrifying and suspended half-hour. There are no weird excursions into unreality here." While this was not the first episode to dismiss an element of fantasy, it was the last.

"I met Rod again on the set of 'The Jeopardy Room' and I could tell he was different from the western episode I did before," recalled Martin Landau. "He looked tired, felt tired and I think he was tired of fighting the networks and sponsors just to keep the show going. I could see it in his face, but it wasn't until years later that I learned how hard he fought them . . . The filming was no different than most of the television shows I did. We had a day to rehearse, which was not common with other shows, but the role was larger than the Denton episode. I was glad – and I still am – to have been a part of it."

Most of the music cues written by Jerry Goldsmith originated from his original composition for "Love Thy Neighbor," an episode of *Gunsmoke* initially telecast on January 28, 1961.

Production #2611 "STOPOVER IN A QUIET TOWN"
(Initial telecast: April 24, 1964)
© Cayuga Productions, Inc., April 20, 1964, LP29197 (in notice: 1963)
Date of Rehearsal: June 28, 1963
Dates of Filming: July 1, 2 and 3, 1963
Script dated: June 11, 1963

Producer and Secretary: $1,626.02	Story and Secretary: $2,660.00
Director: $1,250.00	Cast: $6,023.47
Unit Manager and Secretary: $726.01	Production Fee: $1,800.00
Agents Commission: $2,500.00	Legal and Accounting: $250.00
Below the line charges (M-G-M): $35,659.80	Below the line charges (other): $3,027.60
Total Production Costs: $55,522.90	

Cast: Denise Lynn (the little girl); Nancy Malone (Millie Frazier); Barry Nelson (Bob Frazier); and Karen Norris (the mother).

Stock Music Cues: Etrange #3 (by Marius Constant, :09); Milieu #2 (by Constant, :21); The Club (by Jerry Goldsmith, :40); Suspicion (by Leonard Rosenman, :40); Space Ship (by Goldsmith, :21); Knife (by Goldsmith, :05 and :05); The Gadgets (by Goldsmith, :59); The Knife (by Goldsmith, :30); Counterattack – Part 1 (by Goldsmith, :10); Magdalena Curtain #3 (by Lyn Murray, :05); The Magic (by Goldsmith, :15); The Gadget (by Goldsmith, :28); The Club (by Goldsmith, :10 and :14); Mr. Wellington (by Goldsmith, :22); The Homecoming (by Goldsmith, :34); The Victor (by Goldsmith, :14); Counterattack – Part 2 (by Goldsmith, :18); Police Station (by Goldsmith, :15); The Knife (by Goldsmith, :06); Villers #5 (by Constant, :17); Space Ship (by Goldsmith, :20); The Club (by Goldsmith, :45); The Mound (by Goldsmith, :10); Counterattack – Part 2 (by Goldsmith, :45); Unison Horns of D Sharp (CBS, :07); Counterattack – Part 2 (by Goldsmith, :24 and :08); Goodbye Keith (by William Lava, :07); Concrete World (by Goldsmith, :20); Counterattack – Part 2 (by Goldsmith, :21); Comedy Tag #4 (by Guy Luypaertz, :05); Etrange #3 (by Constant, :09); and Milieu #2 (by Constant, :21).

Director of Photography: Robert
  Pittack, a.s.c.
Art Directors: George W. Davis and
  Walter Holscher
Set Decorations: Henry Grace and
  Robert R. Benton
Sound: Franklin Milton and
  Philip N. Mitchell

Production Manager: Ralph W. Nelson
Film Editor: Thomas W. Scott
Casting: Patricia Rose
Assistant Director: Charles Bonniwell, Jr.
Produced by Bert Granet
Directed by Ron Winston
Teleplay by Earl Hamner, Jr.

"Bob and Millie Frazier, average young New Yorkers who attended a party in the country last night and on the way home . . . took a detour. Most of us on waking in the morning know exactly where we are; the rooster or the alarm clock brings us out of sleep into the familiar sights, sounds, aromas of home and the comfort of a routine day ahead. Not so with our young friends. This will be a day like none they've ever spent . . . and they'll spend it . . . in the Twilight Zone."

Plot: Bob and Millie Frazier wake to find themselves in a house belonging to someone else, in a neighborhood far away from their New York apartment. Their surroundings, however, are something of a mystery: food in the fridge is fake, as are the telephone and drawers in the house. Outside, Bob and Millie wander the streets of Centerville to discover that the animals and trees are fake. Cars have no engines. Their attempt to ride out of town by train brings them right back to where they started. All the time the Fraziers are trying to unravel the mystery of their surroundings, they hear a little girl giggle . . . but a child they cannot find. In desperation, the Fraziers decide to walk out of town . . . only to discover the solution: they are the new pets of a giant girl, whose father brought them all the way from Earth. They were placed in a miniature replica of an Earth town, and Bob and Millie will now have to deal with their new surroundings – that is, until the girl returns to play with them after she finishes her dinner.

"The moral of what you've just seen is clear. If you drink, don't drive. And if your wife has had a couple, she shouldn't drive either. You might both just wake up with a whale of a headache in a deserted village . . . in the Twilight Zone."

Trailer: *"Next time out on the Twilight Zone, we enlist the talented typewriter of Earl Hamner, Jr. . . . and present a stunningly conceived show called 'Stopover in a Quiet Town.' It will star Barry Nelson and Nancy Malone and it will provide the kind of shock ending that punches the emotional eye with unexpected force. Next time, 'Stopover in a Quiet Town.'"*

Trivia, etc. The original title of this production was "Strangers in Town." The title did not become "Stopover in a Quiet Town" officially until an M-G-M work order dated July 24, 1963, revealed the new title and asked everyone involved with production to make the proper changes.

Nancy Malone was paid $1,500 for her role as Millie Frazier. She also received round-trip transportation from New York to Los Angeles. She received star billing in second position on a separate card. Malone agreed to do the role and signed the necessary documents upon her arrival in California. All the paperwork related to her employment was dated June 28, the same morning rehearsals were conducted. "I loved doing the show," recalled Nancy Malone. "Rod Serling was on the set and he wanted to make sure Barry Nelson and I were comfortable. He told me he was working on a stage production of 'Requiem for a Heavyweight' for Broadway. I took advantage of the opportunity and told him I wanted to do something with him, and he remembered our meeting and my request, because I got a large role for the stage production."

Barry Nelson was paid $3,500 for his role of Bob Frazier. He received first star billing on a separate card. Nelson took up residence in both New York and Bel Air, California, and since he was already on the West Coast, there was no need to pay for any airfare. Nelson signed for the role on June 20.

"It was a very quick shoot," recalled Nelson. "In fact, most of television was very quick. You had to. You try to put on thirty something episodes a year. I did a lot of television. I was a contract player at M-G-M for a while. We filmed on the M-G-M backlot which I knew almost as well as the neighborhood I grew up in. They did not have to do much to prepare since the script called for everything to be fake. The trees, the phone and the fake food. I remember they drove the car on the lot and having read the script, the part where it said I was to open the front hood and discover there was no engine underneath, I had to ask the director what I was supposed to do. He told me, 'Don't worry about that. Just pretend you are trying to start the car and it won't turn.' I said, 'Yes, but the engine is still there.' He told me they were going to capture [a view of] the missing engine later and have it inserted into the film. Well . . . I felt about two feet tall after he explained it to me."

"I get asked all the time about that episode," remarked Earl Hamner Jr. "People ask me where the idea came for that episode. And I am ashamed to say that I can never give a definite answer. I was writing scripts for the program, and I guess I created it quickly and it sold and today fans keep reminding me about that one."

The Tuscon Daily Citizen remarked this episode contained, "eerie suspense, the kind that implies violence never seen." *The Lima News* remarked this episode, "will raise the eyebrows and blood pressure of its fans who delight in science fiction or have experienced a hangover."

The opening scenes (interior of the house) were filmed on Stage 20. A blooper appears before Serling makes his screen appearance – a moving shadow can be seen quite clearly on the refrigerator. The passenger coach was filmed on Stage 12. The exterior scenes (street, front lawn, the church, waiting platform, etc.) were filmed on Lot 2 of M-G-M. The bulletin on the church reveals "Rev. Kosh Gleason," a tip of the hat to Keogh Gleason, who was the set designer. The special effect for the climax involving the child's hand was done with a blue screen, at an estimated cost of $60 for the effect, filmed on the afternoon of July 3.

This episode was originally slated for telecast on February 28, 1964 (according to a release schedule dated January 8, 1964). It was pushed ahead a few weeks to make room for "An Occurrence at Owl Creek Bridge" for that date.

"Stopover in a Quiet Town" was referenced in the song "The Twilight Zone," featured in the 1976 album titled *2112* ("Twenty-One Twelve"), performed by the Canadian progressive rock group band, Rush. The single was written by Geddy Lee, Alex Lifeson and Neil Peart.

Production #2640 "THE ENCOUNTER" (Initial telecast: May 1, 1964)
Copyright Registration: © Cayuga Productions, Inc., April 27, 1964, LP29198
Dates of Filming: March 2, 3 and 4, 1964
Script dated: February 24, 1964, with revised pages dated February 27, 1964.

Story and Secretary: $2,660.00
Cast: $4,334.38
Production Fee: $1,800.00
Legal and Accounting: $250.00
Below the line charges (other): $2,615.26

Director: $1,500.00
Unit Manager and Secretary: $600.00
Agents Commission: $2,500.00
Below the line charges (M-G-M): $26,317.94
Total Production Costs: $42,577.58

Cast: Neville Brand (Fenton) and George Takei (Arthur "Taro" Takamuri).

Stock Music Cues: Etrange #3 (by Marius Constant, :09); Milieu #2 (by Constant, :21); Algebra Rock (by Bruce Campbell, 2:58); In a Japanese Temple (by Tak Shindo, :41); The Robbery (by Jerry Goldsmith, :05); In a Japanese Temple (by Shindo, :24 and :24); Struggle (by Fred Steiner, :42); Second Vision (by Steiner, :21); Moat Farm Murder (by Bernard Herrmann, :11); In a Japanese Temple (by Shindo, :41); The Robbery (by Goldsmith, : 05); Moat Farm Murder (by Herrmann, :21); Mist Lifts (by Goldsmith, :30); Puzzles (by Steiner, :54); Struggle (by Steiner, :42); Second Vision (by Steiner, :21); Climactic Close (by Herrmann, :21); Howe's Place (by Steiner, :07); Broken Fist (by Goldsmith, :23); In a Japanese Temple (by Shindo, :17); Summer Sadness (by Goldsmith, :21); Rosie's Man (by Steiner, :12); Etrange #3 (by Constant, :09); and Milieu #1 (by Constant, :22).

Director of Photography: George T. Clemens, a.s.c.
Art Directors: George W. Davis and Eddie Imazu
Set Decorations: Henry Grace and Frank R. McKelvy
Directed by Robert Butler

Production Manager: Ralph W. Nelson
Film Editor: Richard Heermance, a.c.e.
Casting: Larry Stewart
Assistant Director: Marty Moss
Sound: Franklin Milton and Joe Edmondson
Produced by William Froug
Teleplay by Martin M. Goldsmith

"Two men alone in an attic: a young Japanese-American and a seasoned veteran of yesterday's war. It's twenty-odd years since Pearl Harbor, but two ancient opponents are moving into position for a battle in an attic crammed with skeletons – souvenirs, mementos, old uniforms and rusted medals – ghosts from the dim reaches of the past that will lead us . . . into the Twilight Zone."

Plot: One hot summer day, Arthur Takamuri, a Japanese-American, is hired by Mr. Fenton, a war veteran, to help clean out the dusty attic. Fenton finds a genuine Samurai sword and confesses that he picked it up as a souvenir from the war and tried his best to get rid of it over the years. Words engraved on the sword state the original owner will be avenged. Fenton starts to recollect the violent days of the war, and Arthur suddenly is trying to defend himself with the sword. Before either of them get seriously wounded, the men figure the beer and the heat must be getting to their heads. Arthur tries to excuse himself, but the door is apparently jammed shut – even Fenton cannot open it. Arthur, forced to spend some time in the attic, suffers flashbacks of his youth when his father was responsible for signaling the planes that bombed Pearl Harbor. After revealing their differences, they come to realize their situation . . . the final page of the war has yet to turn. Drunk and angry, Fenton coaxes the young boy into stabbing him with the sword so he can stop living the pathetic life he leads today. A struggle causes Fenton to get stabbed by the sword. Arthur, pulling the blade out of the dead body, jumps out the window, shouting "banzai" . . . as the door to the attic slowly opens.

"Two men in an attic, locked in mortal embrace. Their common bond and their common enemy: guilt. A disease all too prevalent among men, both in and out . . . of the Twilight Zone."

Trivia, etc. "Some people thought that it was racist," recalled director Robert Butler to author Mark Phillips. "The American-vs.-the Japanese theme could have been too volatile. It wasn't your typical TV." The plot concerned a beer-drinking Marine, who took one drink too many and voiced his opinion for a war that burned an ever-lasting mark. A Japanese gardener was hired to help clean out the attic, and took one of the Marine's comments to heart, resulting in a confrontation that ultimately killed the men. "It's a very harsh show," Butler remarked. "I'm sure it was considered too hot to handle. It's raw conflict, and it gave both the actors and myself a terrific opportunity. We didn't have to spend time on any production linguistics. We spent time on developing the theme, the characters and the drama. For me, it conveyed a tragic circumstance. How unfortunate that these two people should meet in peace-time and rekindle that same volatility. Each of the individuals is a fine person, but the fates have thrown them together. Physically, it was a small show – two individuals in a small attic – but it was also huge because it dealt with the nature of fateful, inevitable conflict. These men had been stained by history, and they were unable to be harmonious with each other. That was the tragedy."

"That episode is unique because it has never been rerun on television because of the controversy," recalled George Takei. "In it, I played a young Japanese-American gardener who confronts a war veteran, and we ultimately kill each other. Civil Liberties took offense to my comments on the show about my Japanese-American father, guiding the Japanese bombers into Pearl Harbor. History buffs and Civil Liberties raised enough complaints and that is why the episode has never been shown on television since. . . . I got the role because my agent at the time, who was handling me, got me any role that called for a Japanese or Japanese-American. I did a *Perry Mason* and a *Playhouse 90* before the *Twilight Zone*. I met Rod Serling on the set when I was there, and Neville Brand who I admired from his *Playhouse 90* days. It was an honor to work with Neville and meet Rod . . . and I am still proud of having been on the *Twilight Zone*. People still ask me today about it."

Robert Butler was the assistant director for the *Playhouse 90* episode, "Made in Japan," in which Takei played an important role. According to Takei, Butler was the man responsible for casting the Japanese-American gardener. Butler recalled a behind-the-scenes misunderstanding during filming.

"There was either something in the script or the character – I don't recall which – that I felt needed some clarity. I talked to producer William Froug about it. He got very impatient with my position, and we argued about it. He was left feeling that I simply didn't like the show, period. I simply wanted to be clear on a story point, but I remember being misunderstood. In any case, the episode turned out to be a terrific little piece."

Neville Brand was originally slated for the first season episode, "Execution," but came down with the flu on the first morning of filming. His role was replaced by Albert Salmi. Illness or not, Brand was one of many actors requested by the viewers. On September 19, 1961, Mrs. Virginia Decker wrote to Serling. "Would like to see Ken Tobey and Neville Brand; especially Neville Brand. He is one of the most talented actors in Hollywood, but so little is seen of him. If the casting is out of your hands, please mention my suggestions to the 'powers that be.' Maybe I'll be lucky enough to see Neville Brand on *The Twilight Zone.*" With this episode, her wish was granted.

In his attitude towards heavies, Neville Brand insisted "the roles I've played are not strictly heavies. That's because I really have to like the guy and believe in him before I can play him. There's no secret to this business. You just make your guy come out a human being. Even Al Capone had his charms."

This episode of *Twilight Zone* marked Brand's only contribution – and it mirrored his own WWII experience on celluloid. "I picked up an emotional stutter when I served in the war," he recalled. "I was fighting in Dieppe and Omaha Beach. When I got out of service, a friend suggested I get into acting at the American Theater Wing in New York, partly as an attempt to remedy my problem. It worked and here I am playing roles on camera. I admit that most of the characters I played are disagreeable, but that is as far as I will go. I could never play Mussolini or Hitler or heavies in that sense, because I don't see any humanity in them."

The original opening narration was different from what Serling would later compose and recite:

"Portrait of a young Japanese-American and an aging Marine. It's twenty-odd years since Pearl Harbor, but two ancient opponents are moving into position for a battle in an attic crammed with skeletons – souvenirs, mementos, old uniforms and rusted medals – ghosts from the dim reaches of the Twilight Zone."

Regardless of the controversy, this episode was never rerun and never offered as part of any syndication package. Until the 1980s, when Columbia House began offering *The Twilight Zone* on VHS videos, this film was rarely available for viewing. It is available today on commercial home video and DVD packages.

Production #2637 "MR. GARRITY AND THE GRAVES"
(Initial telecast: May 8, 1964)
Copyright Registration: © Cayuga Productions, Inc., May 4, 1964, LP29199

Story and Secretary: $3,510.00
Cast: $8,060.96
Production Fee: $1,800.00
Legal and Accounting: $250.00
Below the line charges (other): $2,556.42

Director: $1,500.00
Unit Manager and Secretary: $600.00
Agents Commission: $2,500.00
Below the line charges (M-G-M): $35,952.59
Total Production Costs: $56,729.97

Cast: Stanley Adams (Jensen); Edgar Dearing (Lightning Peterson); John Dehner (Jared Garrity); Percy Helton (Lapham); Norman Leavitt (Sheriff Gilchrist); Bob McCord (town citizen); John

Mitchum (Ace); Kate Muztagh (Zelda Gooberman); J. Pat O'Malley (Gooberman); and Patrick O'Moore (the man).

Original Music Score Composed and Played by Tommy Morgan (Score No. CPN6144): Etrange #3 (by Marius Constant, :09); Milieu #2 (by Constant, :21); Enter Garrity (:39); Hello Garrity (:47); What's His Name (:22); Garrity (:21); Garrity Wails (:16); Happiness is Comin' (:07); Waiting for Garrity (:51); Jensen's First Up (:28); Garrity Wails (:13); Garrity Wails Again (:16); Good Job Garrity (:45); Rod Agrees (:18); Etrange #3 (by Constant, :09); and Milieu #1 (by Constant, :22).

Director of Photography: George T. Clemens, a.s.c.
Art Directors: George W. Davis and Eddie Imazu
Set Decorations: Henry Grace and Frank R. McKelvy
Directed by Ted Post

Production Manager: Ralph W. Nelson
Film Editor: Richard Heermance, a.c.e.
Casting: Larry Stewart
Assistant Director: Marty Moss
Sound: Franklin Milton and Joe Edmondson
Produced by William Froug

Teleplay by Rod Serling, based on a magazine article titled "Alta – Boomtown to Boomtown," by Mike Korologos.

"Introducing Mr. Jared Garrity, a gentleman of commerce, who in the latter half of the nineteenth century plied his trade in the wild and wooly hinterlands of the American West. And Mr. Garrity, if one can believe him, is a resurrector of the dead . . . which, on the face of it, certainly sounds like the bull is off the nickel. But to the scoffers amongst you, and you ladies and gentlemen from Missouri, don't laugh this one off entirely – at least until you've seen a sample of Mr. Garrity's wares, and an example of his services. The place is Happiness, Arizona, the time about 1890. And you an I have just entered a saloon where the bar whiskey is brewed, bottled and delivered . . . from the Twilight Zone."

Plot: The wild, wild west of 1890. Up until 10 months ago, Happiness, Arizona, was a town scarred from more than 100 deaths as a result of unfair gunplay and needless killings — 128 people were shot to death (and one who died of natural causes), but thanks to an elected sheriff and a newly-built jail house and gallows, the town took to law and order like decent God-fearing men take to the Bible. Enter stage left Mr. Garrity, a man who makes his trade by supplying a rare service – he resurrects the dead. The town citizens scoff at the notion, until they witness an example of Mr. Garrity's abilities on a dog that got killed under a wagon train in the streets. As a service to the reformed town citizens, Mr. Garrity announces that he will resurrect all 128 recently deceased from boot hill shortly before midnight. Late that evening, one-by-one, the town citizens start to plead with Mr. Garrity to keep their loved ones six feet under. Time has changed and so have people's lives. Mr. Garrity charges for undoing his services and after reaping the rewards, heads for the nearest road out of town. Thanks to a dog that plays dead and a partner who can play the part of a resurrected loved one, Garrity and company makes haste for the next town gullible enough to fall for the scheme. As the wagon rides past the cemetery, the recently departed push aside the earth and make for town.

"Exit Mr. Garrity, a would-be charlatan, a make-believe con man and a sad mis-judger of his own

talents. Respectfully submitted from an empty cemetery on a dark hillside that is one of the slopes leading to . . . the Twilight Zone."

Trailer: *"Next time out we move into the area of graveyards and the dear departed and we tell you a story about a most distinctive type of fellow, who happily enough has an equally distinctive profession . . . he raises the dead. On the Twilight Zone next time, John Dehner, Stanley Adams and J. Pat O'Malley lend selective talents to a little item called 'Mr. Garrity and the Graves.'"*

Trivia, etc. "I was the first Paladin for *Have Gun – Will Travel*," Dehner recalled. "That was the radio version. I probably did more radio westerns than television. Warner Bros. hired me to play in *The Roaring 20s* and from then on television was a second income. I loved the radio . . . but television offered more money and my close friends, with whom I worked on radio, were making the switch. That *Twilight Zone* I did where I played the con man and supposedly brought the dead to life was on a quick shooting schedule. We also shot scenes by the graveyard at night. One of the cameramen was using a generator to power the lights and he was having trouble keeping the generator running. [laughs] We did a shot by a wagon that was perfect and right before the director called for a cut, the lights went out."

Larry Stewart, the casting director for the final season, recalled how brilliant Serling was when it came to composing the first draft of his scripts: "He'd come in at 9 a.m. and say, 'On my way over here, I was thinking, what would happen if everybody suddenly walked out of Boot Hill in an Old Western town?' He'd go in his office, close the door and by noon, he had completed a teleplay. We usually shot his first draft. I had never seen anybody write that fast."

A magazine article by Mike Korologos, titled "Alta – Boomtown to Boomtown," caught the attention of Rod Serling, who read with fascination how the city of Alta, Utah, was slowly becoming one of America's premiere ski resorts. There was one section of the article that fascinated him. About a hundred years previous, Alta boasted a number of silver mines, breweries and saloons, attracting a sizeable number of brutal gunslingers, brassy dance hall queens, crooked gamblers and fervid miners. A stranger wandered into town one afternoon, having learned that over 100 people had been killed in Alta's saloons alone, while untold numbers of others had been killed in the streets, shootouts and mining accidents. The stranger proposed an unholy proposition. He claimed he had the power to resurrect the dead, and intended to bring back to life all the loved ones who had been too soon committed to the hereafter. The man, who claimed to posses Christ-like powers, was really a con artist.

"Like so many triumphs, my involvement with the show came in a very round-about way: As a hungry-for-by-lines sports writer for *The Salt Lake Tribune* in 1963, I wrote a story about Alta, Utah, the famous ski area near Salt Lake City," recalled Mike Korologos. "It told of 'a mysterious stranger' who came to town (in its silver-mining hey-days of the 1870s when it had 26 saloons, five breweries and averaged a murder a night) and offered to raise the dead at the base of Rustler Mountain. At first, the townsfolk were delighted with the idea but later decided a general resurrection would be followed by a number of inconveniences: widows and widowers who had remarried feared the return of the dead might disturb the domestic arrangements. And those who had inherited property (silver-rich mines) soon recognized the dead have no business out of the cemetery. The stranger kept insisting; the locals kept resisting. Eventually, the townsfolk took up a collection of $2,500 and presented it to the stranger hoping he would leave town. He did. I found the story of the Alta stranger in an old tour guide, titled *American Guide Series, 1941*. Anyway, the Alta Ski Area's newsletter, *The Alta Powder News*, reprinted the story sometime that ski season. I'm told that Rod Serling was a guest at one of the Alta lodges and read my piece in the newsletter. Soon thereafter I received an offer from the show's producer to sell the story."

On January 20, 1964, Gerald Saltsman of Ashley-Steiner wrote to Mike Korologos, care of *The Salt Lake Tribune*. "An excerpt from this story was called to our attention as a possible basis for the *Twilight Zone* 30-minute program which appears on CBS every Friday night. We would be interested in purchasing all rights in this story, which would be adapted into teleplay form by Mr. Rod Serling. If you are, and can so warrant, the complete owner of the story, we will pay you the sum of $150.00 for all rights thereto."

On January 22, Mike Korologos wrote back, expressing interest, but the price had to be $500. He also phoned Saltsman to inquire whether or not he would receive appropriate screen credit on the television program, and Saltsman agreed, adding "we will make every effort to let you know when the program will be shown." On January 27, Saltsman mailed to Korologos an original and six copies of the contract between Cayuga Productions and Korologos. The check for $500 was mailed on February 4, and Saltsman contacted Bill Froug about Korologos' request to submit other story ideas, none of which never reached the submission stage since the series was not renewed shortly after production for this episode was completed.

"I offered a story about the so-called 'man in the yellow slicker,'" recalled Korologos. "He was a ghostly figure often 'seen' in fleeting appearances by miners in the silver mines of Park City, Utah. A yellow slicker is the rain coat underground miners wore to deflect the waters dripping on them. Nothing ever came of that offer."

"To a starving sports writer making about $90 a week, I was in awe," Korologos continued. "The program that aired with my credit line pertained to a mining town in the desert of Arizona, not the mountains of Utah. In addition, the 'stranger' in the film had a trained dog that he used. At a certain command, the dog would roll over and play dead; then the stranger would do his service and the dog would rise up and appear to be resurrected. We had a black-white TV and the entire family gathered to watch the program. It seemed my name passed along the small TV screen so quickly when the credits rolled that we hardly had time to relish the excitement. We didn't have a video recorder and were saddened that we couldn't play it again and again. But that isn't the end of the story: Some 20 years later, I am visited by one Thurl Bailey, then a star for the Utah Jazz basketball team of the NBA. I was impressed to get a visit from such a luminary – why he wanted to meet with me, I had no idea. Turns out, Thurl is a *Twilight Zone* fanatic and, I was told, had a copy of every one of the shows. In reviewing a videotape of the show that listed my credit, a mutual friend was startled to see my name roll by while watching the program with Bailey. She let out a yelp, 'I know him!' Bailey was esthetic as he wanted to meet someone who had written a *Twilight Zone* episode. Our mutual friend told him how to contact me. We had a long chat about the show, etc. During our visit, I mentioned how disappointed I was in not ever having a copy of the show and he offered to give me one, copied from his vast collection. I am forever thankful to him for that kind gesture."

The original title of this script (first draft) was "Mr. Graniety and the Graves," but was later changed by the second draft. When this episode was copyrighted, it was registered under the title of "Garrity and the Graves," sans "Mr." *The Bridgeport Post* reviewed this episode as "a tough show to do and it comes off quite nicely."

Production #2632 "THE BRAIN CENTER AT WHIPPLE'S"
(Initial telecast: May 15, 1964)

Copyright Registration: © Cayuga Productions, Inc., May 11, 1964, LP29200
Date of Rehearsal: March 5, 1964
Dates of Filming: March 6, 9 and 10, 1964
Script dated: January 6, 1964
Revised script dated: February 24, 1964

Producer and Secretary: $1,610.00
Director: $1,500.00
Unit Manager and Secretary: $600.00
Agents Commission: $2,500.00
Below the line charges (M-G-M): $33,491.74
Total Production Costs: $49,304.20

Story and Secretary: $3,310.00
Cast: $3,825.00
Production Fee: $1,800.00
Legal and Accounting: $250.00
Below the line charges (other): $2,917.46

Cast: Burt Conroy (the watchman); Jack Crowder (the technician); Richard Deacon (Wallace V. Whipple); Ted de Corsia (Mr. Dickerson); Dion Hansen (the robot); Shawn Michaels (the bartender); and Paul Newlan (Hanley).

Stock Music Cues: Etrange #3 (by Marius Constant, :09); Milieu #2 (by Constant, :21); Short Fanfare (by Rene Challan, :04); The World Today – Newsreel March (by Willis Schaeffer, 1:59); F Story #8 (by Constant, :44); Edna's Theme (by Fred Steiner, :05); F Story #8 (by Constant, :20); A Story #1 (by Constant, :04); F Story #8 (:57); A Story #1 (by Constant, :05); F Story #8 (by Constant, :13); A Story #1 (by Constant, :05); D Story #1 (by Constant, :27); F Story #8 (by Constant, :27); A Story #1 (by Constant, :05); F Story #8 (by Constant, :05); A Story #1 (by Constant, :04 and :07); D Story #1 (by Constant, :18); F Story #8 (by Constant, :18); Etrange #3 (by Constant, :09); and Milieu #1 (by Constant, :22).

Director of Photography: George T.
    Clemens, a.s.c.
Art Directors: George W. Davis and
    Eddie Imazu
Set Decorations: Henry Grace and
    Frank R. McKelvy
Directed by Richard Donner

Production Manager: Ralph W. Nelson
Film Editor: Richard W. Farrell
Casting: Larry Stewart
Assistant Director: Marty Moss
Sound: Franklin Milton and Joe Edmondson
Produced by William Froug
Teleplay by Rod Serling

"These are the players, with or without a scorecard: in one corner, a machine; in the other, one Wallace V. Whipple, man. And the game? It happens to be the historical battle between flesh and steel, between the brain of man and the product of man's brain. We don't make book on this one, and predict no winner, but we can tell you that for this particular contest there is standing room only . . . in the Twilight Zone."

Plot: The W.V. Whipple Manufacturing Corporation employs 283,000 people. Making room for progress, Mr. Whipple purchases and installs the X109-B14 modified transistor machine, which eliminates 61,000 jobs and $4 million in expenditures. Mr. Whipple insists that in order to beat his competition, he will now operate the plant by replacing his faithful staff, factory-by-factory, with similar automated "brain" machines. Walter Hanley, the plant manager, regrets the wholesale firing, explaining to Whipple that replacing human pride for the sake of efficiency isn't worth the increased profits. Men have to eat and work. As the months pass, more automated machines replace human jobs and the parking lots grow empty. Hanley, forced to do all the firing, turns in his resignation when he discovers that he, too, is being replaced. Months later, Whipple himself faces karma when his penchant for automation leads to his own dismissal, and the board of directors finds the perfect substitute – a robot with no heart.

"There are many bromides applicable here – too much of a good thing, tiger by the tail, as you sow so shall ye reap. The point is that too often man becomes clever instead of becoming wise, he becomes inventive but not thoughtful – and sometimes, as in the case of Mr. Whipple, he can create himself right out of existence. Tonight's tale of oddness and obsolescence . . . from the Twilight Zone."

Trailer: *"The subject next time is automation. Our area of concern – the replacement of men by machines. It happens to be not only a current industrial phenomena, but potentially a sizable can of peas that once opened . . . carries with it some very special story material. On the Twilight Zone next time we open that can of peas, and present a battle between the men and the machines. Richard Deacon and Paul Newlan star in 'The Brain Center at Whipple's.'"*

Trivia, etc. The fear of machines replacing human beings has been a constant query over the past few decades. One of these earliest efforts in television history was on the evening of October 26, 1960. A machine-written Western play-let, in which a sheriff and a bandit have a gun duel, was televised by CBS. The machine, an electronic computer called TX-O, was developed by the Massachusetts Institute of Technology. The two-minute playlet was presented on *Tomorrow*, a science series, with a one-hour program called "The Thinking Machine." David Wayne, the actor, was seen visiting M.I.T. and talking to scientists about machines that seem capable of reasoning. After Wayne watched the TX-O type out an "original" western, the script, which was without dialogue, was performed by two actors.

The idea of asking M.I.T. for a machine-written script originated with Thomas H. Wolf, executive producer for *Tomorrow*. TX-O was provided with a dramatic situation in which a robber with newly stolen money enters a hideout shack and is overtaken there by the sheriff. The machine, which was "told" that objects in the shack included money, a table, a glass and a bottle of whiskey, then typed out the chain of action and arrived at its denouement. Critics did not find much flaw in the program itself, but were left asking for more details about the computer – not the means by which it "could" replace people in the script writing department.

Thankfully, Rod Serling was still writing scripts for television without the fear of machines taking his place, so in early 1964, he completed the first draft, titled "Automation." The title would later be revised to "The Brain Center at Whipple's" with the February 24 draft.

"I have the uneasy feeling that people think of me as the world's worst sourpuss," commented Richard Deacon, a regular on *The Dick Van Dyke Show*, who made his non-comic starring debut in this episode. The two had attended the same high school together in Binghamton, New York. "After seeing all he had me do in this show," Deacon commented, "I wondered what I'd done to Rod in school to deserve it. If I didn't wear glasses and have 40 years of unpaved road on my head, I probably wouldn't be working at all." With critics of automation worried about people going out of style, Deacon remarked that for this episode, "there is more truth than fiction in the show."

"As soon as someone comes into my [fictional] office, I start talking," Deacon continued. "It was a real chore for me – I even hired a dialogue coach to help." In the CBS press release, Deacon was asked whether he preferred dramatic or comedy roles; he declined to take sides. "I just like to work," he said.

"Robby had been in the M-G-M lot," recalled Donner in the July 1981 issue of *The Twilight Zone Magazine*. "We redressed him a little, painted him differently, and put another light on top of his head. He was in fairly good condition; in those days studios had great pride in their prop and wardrobe departments, so when you went to get something, there was no problem."

In most areas of the state of Oregon, this episode of *Twilight Zone* was broadcast at 7:30, before any of the usual prime-time programs, because the regular time slot was occupied by a special telecast of the Oregon Primary. With the state laws permitting vote-counting during the day for release at 8 p.m, poll-closing time, both CBS and NBC offered special early coverage direct from Portland, with programs shuffling time slots for Pacific Coast viewers to see the latest returns live.

By request of network policy, Cayuga hired a Negro for the role of one of the technicians in this episode.

The Valley Independent remarked that this was "better than most that come off the *Twilight* assembly line."

On May 20, 1964, Patrick E. Gorman, international secretary-treasurer of the Amalgamated Meat Cutters and Butcher Workmen of North America (located in Illinois) wrote the following letter to Serling:

Dear Mr. Serling,
Without doubt, the *Twilight Zone* episode I witnessed at Louisville this past Friday was the strongest drama of this particular type that has ever been produced. It dealt with automation, and while I do not recall the title, it was something like 'Nerve Center at Whittaker,' or something to that effect.

There will be something like 2,500 delegates attending the Convention of our International Union at the Diplomat Hotel in Hollywood, Florida, beginning on Monday, July 13th. The hit of the Convention would be if we could secure the film to show it to the delegates in the assembled meeting.

Whatever cost would be involved, our International Union would be agreeable to pay same. I believe that this one episode of the *Twilight Zone* will be remembered for a long time by everyone who viewed it. Will you kindly let me hear from you?

With all good wishes, I remain,
Sincerely Yours,
Patrick E. Gorman

On June 17, Rod Serling wrote a reply to Mr. Gorman, thanking him for the letter, and suggested he write to John Reynolds, Vice President of CBS Television – Television City – Hollywood, California, and mention their exchange of correspondence. "I'm sure that he'll see to it that you receive a copy of the film. If you run into any kind of trouble or delay, please contact me."

On June 23, Patrick Gorman sent a Western Union telegram to John Reynolds, with the same request. On June 30, Rod Serling wrote a letter to John Reynolds, commenting that he no doubt received a wire from the Butcher's Union requesting the loan-out of the *Twilight Zone* episode. "Since I rather assured the gentleman that a copy of the film could be made available to him, I'm hopeful that you'll be able to handle this. Public relations, I always say, John – public relations!"

On July 1, 1964, Sam Kaplan of Ashley-Steiner in Los Angeles, drafted a letter to Serling, as to a resolution of the request.

Dear Rod,

I received a phone call from CBS yesterday during which Frank Rohner explained that CBS had received a request from the Meat-Cutters Union to make available to them a *Twilight Zone* episode for exhibition at their convention, or something of that sort. CBS understands that the approach had originally been made to you and that your response was to the effect that you had no objection but that the matter had to be handled through CBS.

Apparently the episode requested deals with automation and consequential technological unemployment. In CBS' opinion, it would be better not to make the film available since the wisdom of feeding this kind of material to a union is subject to serious question particularly since network [program sponsors] are manufacturers.

CBS indicated that they would send a general reply to the Meat-Cutters Union to the effects that they were unable to clear the film due to union involvements, contractual commitments, etc. I took the liberty of telling them that you would take no objection to this response and, indeed, feel that it would be in your interests to avoid becoming enmeshed in any kind of union campaign against technological unemployment.

My best to Carolyn and the kids, and I must admit, as I peer at Claire over a pile of papers, that I envy you in your retreat.

Sincerely,

Sam Kaplan

In March of 1974, Rod Serling was in Houston, in association with Mutual Broadcasting System, during the National Association of Broadcasters Convention. He was promoting his new radio program, *Zero Hour*, which he was heavily involved with. He addressed Mutual's annual national convention at the Rice Hotel on March 17. Robert R. Rees sat down with Serling for a brief interview and when asked what he thought about the Stanley Kubrick film, *2001 – A Space Odyssey*, Serling commented, "It was a nice production, but it was too long. I particularly liked the idea of giving the computer a brain. Reasoning for computers is not too far away. Here they gave it logic and it developed its own." Apparently Serling's reason for automation was still founded 10 years after this *Twilight Zone* was initially telecast.

In 2002, Ipecac Recordings released an album performed by the heavy metal rock group, "The Melvins," titled *Hostile Ambient Takeover*. The sixth track on the album featured a song titled "The Brain Center at Whipples," named after this particular episode.

Production #2641 "COME WANDER WITH ME" (Initial telecast: May 22, 1964)
Copyright Registration: © Cayuga Productions, Inc., May 18, 1964, LP29201
Date of Rehearsal: March 16, 1964
Dates of Filming: March 17, 18 and 19, 1964
Script dated: March 9, 1964

Story and Secretary: $2,500.00

Cast: $3,812.50

Production Fee: $1,800.00

Legal and Accounting: $250.00

Below the line charges (other): $4,462.11

Director: $1,500.00

Unit Manager and Secretary: $600.00

Agents Commission: $2,500.00

Below the line charges (M-G-M): $40,853.41

Total Production Costs: $58,278.02

Cast: Bonnie Beecher (Mary Rachel); John Bolt (Billy Rayford); Gary Crosby (Floyd Burney); and Hank Patterson (the old man).

Original Music Score Composed and Conducted by Jeff Alexander: Etrange #3 (by Marius Constant, :09); Milieu #2 (by Constant, :21); Duet (1:27); Dirty Old Man (:08); Come Wander With Me (by Jeff Alexander and Tony Wilson, 1:03); Come Wander With Me Opening (:41); Come Wander With Me (by Alexander and Wilson, :42); Come Wander Sweetener #1 (:29); Guitar #1 (:03); Guitar #2 (:04); Guitar #3 (:23); Guitar #4 (:05); Guitar #5 (:03); Come Wander With Me (by Alexander and Wilson, 1:01); Guitar #6 (:40); Come Wander With Me Woods Version (by Alexander and Wilson, :31); Come Wander With Me Leadin (by Alexander and Wilson, :53); Come Wander With The Rayfords (by Alexander and Wilson, :31); Come Wander With Me Prophesy (by Alexander and Wilson, :33); Come Wander Chase #1 (:16); Come Wander With Me (by Alexander and Wilson, :36); Chase #2 (:48); Guitar #7 (:05); Melody (by W.A. Mozart, :57); La Traviata (by G. Verdi, :52); Artist's Life (by Johann Strauss, :47); There's a Tavern in the Town (by William H. Hill, :42); Improvisation #8 (by William Borda Gomez, :37); Two Voice Invention (by Rene Garriguenc, :32); In the Sweet Bye and Bye (traditional, :27); Blue Danube (by Johann Strauss Jr., :22); Come Wander With Me Closing (:19); Etrange #3 (by Constant, :09); and Milieu #1 (by Constant, :22).

Director of Photography: Fred Mandl, a.s.c.

Art Directors: George W. Davis and Eddie Imazu

Set Decorations: Henry Grace and
    Jerry Wunderlich

Sound: Franklin Milton and Joe Edmondson

Directed by Richard Donner

Production Manager: Ralph W. Nelson

Film Editor: Richard W. Farrell

Casting: Larry Stewart

Assistant Director: Marty Moss

Produced by William Froug

Teleplay by Anthony Wilson

"Mr. Floyd Burney, a gentleman songster in search of song, is about to answer the age-old question of whether a man can be in two places at the same time. As far as his folk song is concerned, we can assure Mr. Burney he'll find everything he's looking for, although the lyrics may not be all to his liking. But that's sometimes the case – when the words and music are recorded . . . in the Twilight Zone."

Plot: Floyd Burney, a.k.a. "The Rock-A-Billy Kid," is a boorish rock n' roll singer in search of authentic folk music in a remote area of a thick forest. Though he is ignorant of the warnings of others, he meets young Mary Rachel, a country girl who sings "Come Wander With Me" – a song she describes as sacred. The song belongs to someone else and cannot be bought with a price tag. Promising her a future with riches and love, Floyd makes her record the lyrics on a tape, It doesn't take long for him to discover that the song is about him. She tries to explain that the events leading to his death, including the murder of her admirer, Billy Rayford, and an old man, were revealed in the lyrics. His attempt to steal Mary Rachel's song is the motive of the deaths. The song belongs to both of them and no matter what they do, he'll continue to die the same tragic fate repeatedly – so long as his death is told in song and verse.

"In retrospect, it may be said of Mr. Floyd Burney that he achieved that final dream of the performer: eternal top-name billing – not on the fleeting billboards of the entertainment world, but forever recorded among the folk songs . . . of the Twilight Zone."

Trailer: *"On the Twilight Zone's next trip, we move into the area of authentic folk singing . . . but this is folk singing like you've probably never heard before. The words and the music in this item are haunting indeed, and this one provides one of the more odd excursions into the places of shadow. Gary Crosby and Bonnie Beecher star in a most unusual tale by Anthony Wilson. It's called 'Come Wander With Me.'"*

Trivia, etc. "When we filmed that particular episode, I had just seen *Sunday in Seville*, and I insisted that the entire thing have that misty, backwoods look," recalled director Richard Donner in the July 1981 issue of *The Twilight Zone Magazine*. "We had so much smoke in the back lot that the fire department came out; and then the production department got mad at us because we'd lose shots when the wind would come up. Gary Crosby's agent sent him in to us at a time when we were considering someone totally different. He had practically memorized the script before he came into my office. He did a reading for me that was so brilliant that I immediately said, 'that's it – Gary Crosby.' He is a very flexible, very good actor."

The grave marker with Burney's name was one of the many grave markers used in "Mr. Garrity and the Graves." Burney's name was put on the back of the marker, while the front side (not depicted on camera) featured the markings from the previous production.

The bridge which Floyd Burney drives on in the opening scene is the same featured in *The Outer Limits* episode, "The Children of Spider County." The bridge on the other program was not partially destroyed like it is depicted here in this *Twilight Zone* episode. Both programs were filmed at M-G-M so it was common for different production companies to film on the same lots. Another connection between this episode and *The Outer Limits*: M-G-M prop numbers show that some of the guitars hanging in the pawnshop in the episode "Controlled Experiment" were the same hanging in the wooden shack in this episode.

The Post-Standard in Syracuse, New York, commented this episode was "a pretty fair vehicle for young Gary Crosby." When interviewed by Joseph Finnigan of the *Tele-Views* in early May 1964, Crosby remarked that this episode gave him the opportunity to "do a little bit of acting instead of saying lines and running for my life." Crosby previously played little roles on other television series, usually of the sugar-and-spice variety, parts that called for singing and dancing with music in the background.

"They were the old three guys and three girls bit," he explained. "Mostly the fellows were in uniform."

Crosby played a bellhop on Bill Dana's comedy program, but this episode gave him the opportunity to expand his horizons as an actor. The eldest of Bing Crosby's sons, Gary, like most of the stars who appeared on *Twilight Zone*, never saw the final cut before it went to air. "I'm waiting to see it," he explained to a reporter days before the broadcast. "I'll either have pride in myself or run and hide out. I'm praying. But I think it came off pretty good."

The song "Come Wander With Me," was composed by Jeff Alexander (score) and Anthony Wilson (lyrics). Bonnie Beecher sung the song for the soundtrack, which was incorporated into the story. Beecher made her acting debut with this episode, leading to her appearance on other programs such as *The Invaders*, *Gunsmoke*, *Burke's Law* and *The Fugitive*.

According to William Froug, Liza Minnelli was the first choice to play the role of Mary Rachel, but no paperwork has been found to substantiate this statement. Froug consented to a number of interviews over the years, but his recollections regarding *Twilight Zone* were –repeatedly – not always accurate.

The song "Come Wander With Me" has been featured in the soundtrack of the 2003 motion picture, *The Brown Bunny*, directed by Vincent Gallo. The song was also used as background accompaniment for a television commercial in 2006 for a Dutch insurance company, RVS.

Production #2633 "THE FEAR" (Initial telecast: May 29, 1964)
Copyright Registration: © Cayuga Productions, Inc., May 25, 1964, LP29225
Date of Rehearsal: March 20, 1964
Dates of Filming: March 20, 23, 24 and 25, 1964
Script dated: January 15, 1964

Story and Secretary: $155.01
Cast: $3,545.31
Production Fee: $1,800.00
Legal and Accounting: $250.00
Below the line charges (other): $2,662.55

Director: $1,750.00
Unit Manager and Secretary: $600.00
Agents Commission: $2,500.00
Below the line charges (M-G-M): $52,273.76
Total Production Costs: $63,036.63

Cast: Hazel Court (Charlotte Scott) and Peter Mark Richman (Trooper Robert Franklin).

Stock Music Cues: Etrange #3 (by Marius Constant, :09); Milieu #2 (by Constant, :21); Curiosity (by Fred Steiner, :37); The Road (by Steiner, :08); Maya (by Nathan Van Cleave, :30); Chris Walks (by Steiner, :37); Curiosity (by Steiner, :10 and 1:47); Maya (by Van Cleave, :30); Loire #2 (by Constant, :10); Chris Walks (by Steiner, :10); Curiosity (by Steiner, 1:47); Chris Runs (by Steiner, :17); Maya (by Van Cleave, :30); Loire #2 (by Constant, :10); Mrs. Joe (by Steiner, :23); Chris Runs (by Steiner, :58); Chris Runs (by Steiner, :18); Struggle (by Steiner, :07); The Fun House (by Van Cleave, 1:22); Chris Jr. (by Steiner, :19); The Calendar (by Steiner, :20); The Road (by Steiner, :28); Etrange #3 (by Constant, :09); and Milieu #1 (by Constant, :22).

Director of Photography: Fred Mandl, a.s.c.
Art Directors: George W. Davis and Eddie Imazu
Set Decorations: Henry Grace and

Production Manager: Ralph W. Nelson
Film Editor: Richard Heermance, a.c.e.
Casting: Larry Stewart

Jerry Wunderlich

Sound: Franklin Milton and Joe Edmondson

Directed by Ted Post

Assistant Director: Marty Moss

Produced by William Froug

Teleplay by Rod Serling

"The major ingredient of any recipe for fear is the unknown. And here are two characters about to partake of the meal. Miss Charlotte Scott, a fashion editor, and Mr. Robert Franklin, a state trooper. And the third member of the party: the unknown, that has just landed a few hundred yards away. This person or thing is soon to be met. This is a mountain cabin, but it is also a clearing in the shadows known as . . . the Twilight Zone."

Plot: Charlotte Scott, a fashion editor from New York, has retired to a mountain cabin for a little relaxation after suffering a nervous breakdown back home. When Charlotte swore she saw bright lights in the sky, Trooper Rob Franklin makes a late-night house call and witnesses the same phenomena. Ruling out all possible explanations, Franklin searches the woods and discovers tree limbs knocked down. Something gigantic in size brushes past the house. Large fingerprints are found on the side of his patrol car. Frightened, they contemplate their options, and he agrees to stay the evening to ensure her protection. In the morning, they find a huge footprint on the grounds, and panicking, Miss Scott attempts to flee, stumbling right in front of a one-eyed space alien standing 500 feet high. Rather than run, Franklin shoots the creature, only to discover the hoax was a huge air-filled balloon. Puzzled, they find a small spacecraft containing two small aliens, who attempted to scare the human race with an elaborate ruse. Having failed in their mission, the aliens take off in fear of their lives.

"Fear of course, is extremely relative. It depends on who can look down and who must look up. It depends on other vagaries like the time, the mood, the darkness. But it's been said before, with great validity, that the worst thing there is to fear is fear itself. Tonight's tale of terror and tiny people . . . on the Twilight Zone."

Trailer: *"We go wild next time with some science fiction ingredients that should do a sizable job of shocking. Miss Hazel Court and Mr. Mark Richman lend talents to a piece called 'The Fear.' If you ever wondered what nature of beast might come out of the sky in an inter-planetary invasion, watch the Twilight Zone next time. You'll get your answer in the most visual terms."*

Trivia, etc. Back on July 8, 1959, months before the premiere of *The Twilight Zone*, Rod Serling wrote to his brother Bob, giving him a brief update of life in Hollywood. Among his comments was a note regarding his meeting with director Don Taylor, and his wife, Hazel Court. Court left an impression with Serling, so her casting for this episode may have been influenced by Serling himself.

The first draft of this script was titled "The Fear Itself." The title was abbreviated soon after. Serling's original narration in the earliest draft was longer:

"The major ingredient of any recipe for fear is the unknown. And here are two characters about to partake of the meal. Miss Charlotte Scott, a fashion editor recovering from a nervous breakdown . . and Mr. Robert Franklin, a state trooper – a gentleman of only average imagination who up to now has dealt only in unimaginative realities. And the third member of the party the unknown, that has just landed a few hundred yards away. This person . . . or thing . . . is soon to be met. This is a mountain cabin near

Lake Arrowhead, California, but it is also a clearing in the shadows known as . . . the Twilight Zone."

"I do not recall much about the filming of that episode. It only lasted a couple days and that was 40 or so years ago," commented Peter Mark Richman. "I remember being instructed to shoot in the air at a giant that wasn't there. To pretend a giant space being is looking down on you was not a challenge. I just looked up and reacted naturally. I don't think I've ever heard a bad word about Rod Serling. Hazel Court and I became good friends and we stayed in touch a number of times after *The Twilight Zone*. I did a lot of television but that was one I enjoyed very much."

"'The Fear' was one of the many times I have worked with Ted Post, the director," continued Richman. "We did *Combat!*, a television movie called *Yuma* and I hired Ted to direct a feature I wrote, produced and starred in: *4 Faces*, as yet unreleased – although it has been in many film festivals and was nominated for a Prism Award. Ted is one of the top pros in this business who has done more film than there are Carter's Liver Pills. In fact, I just went to his 90th birthday. I could not speak enough praise for him . . . That was a classic Serling script and is always shown when they have a festival of Rod Serling, who was a dear man. 'The Fear' was shot on the back lot of M-G-M Studios where I did my first series starring as Nick Cain in *Cain's Hundred*. The studio was bustling then with major TV activity. It was a great time and afforded actors the opportunity to play varying roles."

The (Plymouth) police car in this episode is the same featured in "I Am the Night – Color Me Black." *The Bridgeport Post* remarked this episode would give the audience "some puzzling, uneasy moments."

Production #2619 "THE BEWITCHIN' POOL" (Initial telecast: June 19, 1964)

Copyright Registration: © Cayuga Productions, Inc., June 15, 1964, LP29220 (in notice: 1963)
Date of Rehearsal: September 3, 1963
Dates of Filming: September 4, 5, 6 and 9, 1963
Script dated: July 9, 1963
Revised script dated: August 19, 1963

Producer and Secretary: $2,126.02
Director: $1,500.00
Unit Manager and Secretary: $726.01
Agents Commission: $2,500.00
Below the line charges (M-G-M): $44,692.09
Total Production Costs: $66,415.32

Story and Secretary: $2,660.00
Cast: $6,780.48
Production Fee: $1,800.00
Legal and Accounting: $250.00
Below the line charges (other): $3,380.73

Cast: Tod Andrews (Gil Sherwood); Mary Badham (Sport Sherwood); Harold Gould (the radio announcer); Dee Hartford (Gloria Sherwood); Kim Hector (Whitt); Georgia Simmons (Aunt T); and Tim Stafford (Jeb Sherwood).

Stock Music Cues: Etrange #3 (by Marius Constant, :09); Milieu #2 (by Constant, :21); Walt Whitman Suite (by Bernard Herrman, :32); Eerie Nightmare (by Lucien Moraweck, :09); The Fight (by Jerry Goldsmith, :27); Terror-Struck (by Goldsmith, :33); Harp Glissando (CBS, :03); Autumn Mist (by Goldsmith, :42); Eerie Nightmare (by Moraweck, :20); Saturday Night (by Goldsmith, :32 and :32); Nice Old Man (by Nathan Van Cleave, :09); Drunk at Six (by Goldsmith, :21); Nice Old Man (by Van

The Twilight Zone was not telecast on the evening of June 5, 1964. Instead, another episode of the ongoing series, *CBS Reports*, was presented during this time slot. This 90-minute special titled "D-Day Plus 20 Years: Eisenhower Returns to Normandy" commemorated the anniversary of the historic events of that day. The special was designed to recapture the sights, sounds and emotions of the greatest military invasion in history through the eyes and words of the man who shouldered the full responsibility for its outcome – the former Supreme Commander of the Allied Expeditionary Force, Gen. Dwight D. Eisenhower.

On the evening of June 12, 1964, a repeat of "Steel" was telecast.

Cleave, :06); Laramie Hoedown (by Goldsmith, :10); Drunk at Six (by Goldsmith, :21); Bridge Fantasy (by Dino Marinuzzi, :02); The Factory (by Van Cleave, :09); Bits and Pieces (by Van Cleave, :06); Walt Whitman Suite (by Herrmann, :08); Saturday Night (by Goldsmith, :32); Good Morning (by Goldsmith, :06); Rural Bounce (by Goldsmith, :41); A Clever Trick (by Goldsmith, :29); Mohawk Story Portage (by Lyn Murray, :13); Drunk at Six (by Goldsmith, :21); Nocturnal Interlude (by Goldsmith, :14); Drunk at Six (by Goldsmith, :21); Bridge Fantasy (by Gino Marinuzzi, :01); Walt Whitman Suite (by Herrmann, :08); Drunk at Six (by Goldsmith, :21); Walt Whitman Suite (by Herrmann, :47); Eerie Nightmare (by Moraweck, :09); The Fight (by Goldsmith, :43); Walt Whitman Suite (by Herrmann, :27); Saturday Night (by Goldsmith, :35); Hop and a Skip (by Goldsmith, :02); Etrange #3 (by Constant, :09); and Milieu #1 (by Constant, :22).

Director of Photography: George T. Clemens, a.s.c.
Art Directors: George W. Davis and Malcolm Brown
Set Decorations: Henry Grace and Robert R. Benton
Directed by Joseph M. Newman

Production Manager: Ralph W. Nelson
Film Editor: Thomas W. Scott
Casting: Patricia Rose
Assistant Director: Charles Bonniwell, Jr.
Sound: Franklin Milton and Joe Edmondson
Produced by William Froug
Teleplay by Earl Hamner, Jr

"A swimming pool not unlike any other pool. A structure built of tile and cement and money. A backyard toy for the affluent, wet entertainment for the well-to-do. But to Jeb and Sport Sherwood, this pool holds mysteries not dreamed of by the building contractor – not guaranteed in any sales brochure. For this pool has a secret exit that leads to a never neverland, a place designed for junior citizens who need a long voyage away from reality, into the bottomless regions . . . of the Twilight Zone."

Plot: Diving deep into the swimming pool, two young children, Sport and Jeb, surface to find themselves in another world where children can escape from uncaring parents. In this world, witches and kind grannies reside – and chocolate cake is served for breakfast. After spending time with Aunt T and other children, Sport and Jeb learn that some children have come to stay – and after time, they no longer hear the call of their parents. Here they stay in perfect harmony. Sport and Jeb return through the swimming pool, unable to explain how they were able to travel to another world. A few days later, the parents inform the children that there will be a divorce – and have to choose with whom they will live. Unable to cope with the situation, Sport and Jeb dive into the swimming pool and return to the other world. Content with their new surroundings, the call and cry of their parents fade in the distance as they continue to eat chocolate cake with Aunt T and the other children.

"Introduction to a perfect setting. Colonial mansion, spacious grounds, heated swimming pool. All the luxuries money can buy. Introduction to two children, brother and sister. Names: Jeb and Sport. Healthy, happy, normal youngsters. Introduction to a mother: Gloria Sherwood by name, glamorous by nature. Introduction to a father: Gil Sherwood, handsome, prosperous, the picture of success. The man who has achieved every man's ambition: beautiful children, beautiful home, beautiful wife. Idyllic? Obviously. But don't look too carefully. Don't peek behind the facade. The idol might have feet of clay."

"A brief epilogue for concerned parents. Of course, there isn't any such place as the gingerbread house of Aunt T, and we grownups know there's no door at the bottom of a swimming pool that leads to a secret place. But who can say how real the fantasy world of lonely children can become? For Jeb and Sport Sherwood, the need for love turned fantasy into reality. They found a secret place . . . in the Twilight Zone."

Trivia, etc. "I hope to this day that my script was not the cause for the show's demise," joked Earl Hamner, Jr. "I was in a mood swing one morning after learning that the divorce rate had gone up, and more importantly, the children that were affected. I wanted to write a commentary about this so I came up with 'The Bewitchin' Pool.'"

The original title of this script was "The Marvelous Pool." Assigned a production number on July 10, 1963, a director sufficient enough to handle the production was not yet found by the end of July, so the production was canceled. According to a late July interoffice memo, this episode was going to be filmed in four days, two days in early August and two days in mid-August. As Froug explained in a letter to Serling: "We are still figuring to have the hiatus starting August 2 and will start shooting again on August 15 with Earl Hamner's 'The Marvelous Pool.' Because there are children who work in practically every scene, this one I'm going to schedule as a four-day show with short shooting hours, which means that it would cost very little more than the average three-day show with over-time shooting."

Complications prevented the production from going before the cameras, and on August 19, an M-G-M work order reported the script: "Will Not Be Produced." On August 19, the script was revised to adhere to a lower budgetary figure for production costs and on August 20, the title was changed officially to "The Bewitchin' Pool." Joseph M. Newman was assigned to direct, but on August 31, a studio memo incorrectly reported this production as canceled. On September 1, another memo was issued to correct the mistake, reporting "canceled in error." An interoffice memo dated August 29, 1963, stated that "The Bewitchin' Pool" would start shooting next Tuesday.

The scene at the swimming pool is the same pool at Cohn Park on the M-G-M lot, part of Lot 2 at the studio. This was the same swimming pool featured in "Queen of the Nile" and "The Trouble With Templeton."

Stand-ins included Frank Delfino for Tim Stafford, Myra Jones for Dee Hartford, Bob McCord for Tod Andrews, and Laurel Clanton was the stand-in for Mary Badham's swimming and diving scenes. A casting call for young children required one Oriental boy and one Oriental girl, one Mexican boy and one Mexican girl, and one Negro boy and one Negro girl.

After reviewing the daily rushes, William Froug expressed a concern over the soundtrack in

Set Decoration Production Costs
Exterior of the Mansion and Pool $100
Exterior of the Swimming Hole and Farm House $200
Interior of the Farm House $400
Total $700

the developed film. Noises in the background were picked up on the mike, and Mary Badham's voice stood out above all the other actors. On September 10 and September 11, Mary Badham reported to Sync Room "B" at M-G-M to rerecord her dialogue so it could be dubbed onto the finished film. Her voice, once again, stood out and a decision to hire June Foray. Foray reported to the studio November 12 to dub Badham's voice. (Foray supplied the voice for Badham in the "real world" scenes and not the Aunt T scenes.) On December 30, Kim Hector reported to Sync Room "B" and Tim Herton reported to Sync Room "A." Loops and wild narrations with Tod Anderson were recorded on the morning of December 31, in Sync Room "B."

After viewing the rough cut, William Froug asked Howard Adamson, who was responsible for drawing up a release schedule, to remove this episode from the March 20, 1964 intended airdate and reschedule to June, making this the final original episode to be telecast over CBS.

The television critic for the Connecticut *Bridgeport Post* commented this story was "a difficult one to put over on TV, with moments of more than routine interest."

The Twilight Zone was not telecast on the evening of August 28, 1964. A curtain raiser for the World Golf Championship coverage titled "It's a Big World" was broadcast, with Cary Middlecoff and Pat Harrington, Jr.

"The Jeopardy Room" was originally scheduled for broadcast on the evening of September 18. Though a number of published reference guides cite this as being the final episode of *The Twilight Zone* during the summer reruns, that information is inaccurate. A political broadcast, sponsored by Citizens for Barry Goldwater, was broadcast that evening.

Willis James of Newark, Ohio, after tuning in to CBS that same evening, wrote a letter to the editor of his local newspaper asking how many people turned in Friday night expecting to see *Twilight Zone*, which was listed, and were surprised to see something different. "The question is, rather, how many people watched it without even knowing the difference," James wrote. "For indeed, what better place could they schedule the Republican candidate? The entire business is almost like one of those way-out Rod Serling science fiction dramas. You know, about a weirdo who doesn't know what century he is living in, who inhabits a misty dream world where everything is simple and uncomplicated, where all frustrations are satisfied, where the most difficult problems are solved by a push of the button, where we are always good and they are always bad, where black is black and white is white, and nothing in between."

AN EXTENDED SUMMER OF *THE TWILIGHT ZONE*

On March 26, 1965, *The New York Herald Tribune* mentioned, "CBS will revive the hour-long version of Rod Serling's *Twilight Zone* as a summer rerun feature Sunday nights beginning May 16. The dramas will replace *For the People*, the latest CBS attempt to woo viewers away from NBC's *Bonanza*. *Twilight Zone* will run until September, when CBS plans – unless there is a change of mind – to pit *Perry Mason* against *Bonanza*." Telecast on Sunday evenings from 9 to 10 p.m., the following is a list of those summer reruns, marking the final episodes broadcast on the network before going into syndication. *Twilight Zone* was not telecast on the evening of June 20, so that "The Hollow Crown," a documentary about the English monarchy as depicted in world literature, would be presented.

May 16, 1965	**Repeat** "On Thursday We Leave for Home"
May 23, 1965	**Repeat** "No Time Like the Past"
May 30, 1965	**Repeat** "The New Exhibit"
June 6, 1965	**Repeat** "Jess-Belle"
June 13, 1965	**Repeat** "In His Image"
June 27, 1965	**Repeat** "The Bard"
July 4, 1965	**Repeat** "Of Late I Think of Cliffordville"
July 11, 1965	**Repeat** "Printer's Devil"
July 18, 1965	**Repeat** "I Dream of Genie"
July 25, 1965	**Repeat** "The Incredible World of Horace Ford"
August 1, 1965	**Repeat** "Mute"
August 8, 1965	**Repeat** "He's Alive"
August 15, 1965	**Repeat** "Valley of the Shadow"
August 22, 1965	**Repeat** "Passage on the Lady Anne"
August 29, 1965	**Repeat** "The Thirty Fathom Grave"
September 5, 1965	**Repeat** "Death Ship"

SUMMER RERUNS

June 26, 1964	**Repeat** "A Kind of a Stopwatch"
July 3, 1964	**Repeat** "In Praise of Pip"
July 10, 1964	**Repeat** "Uncle Simon"
July 17, 1964	**Repeat** "Nightmare at 20,000 Feet"
July 24, 1964	**Repeat** "Probe 7 – Over and Out"
July 31, 1964	**Repeat** "The 7th is Made Up on Phantoms"
August 7, 1964	**Repeat** "The Long Morrow"
August 14, 1964	**Repeat** "You Drive"
August 21, 1964	**Repeat** "The Fear"
September 4, 1964	**Repeat** "Number 12 Looks Just Like You"
September 11, 1964	**Repeat** "An Occurrence at Owl Creek Bridge"

APPENDIX A: PRODUCTION CREDITS

PRODUCTION CREW, FIRST SEASON (as of June 30, 1959)

Art Director: Bill Ferrari
Assistant Bookkeeper: Hene Bercovich
Assistant Cameraman: Paul Uhl
Assistant Cutter: Marshall Borden and Pierre Jalbert
Assistant to Mr. Kaplan: Gerald Saltsman
Best Boy: Si Reuben
Bookkeeper: Gretchen Fremdling
Boom Man: Mike Clark
CBS Business Affairs: Jack Foreman and Leo Lefcourt
CBS Production Manager: Dewey Starkey
Camera Operator: Jack Swain
Casting Director: Mildred Gusse
Cayuga Productions, Inc.: Ashley-Steiner: Sam Kaplan
Cayuga Suprv. Film Editor: Joseph Gluck
Chief Accountant: Bill Freedman
Executive Producer for CBS: William Self
Executive Producer for Cayuga: Rod Serling
Film Editor: Bill Mosher
Film Program Co-ordinator: George Amy
First Assistant Director: Edward Denault
First Cameraman: George Clemens
Gaffer: Paul Keller
Hair Dresser: Eve Kreyer
Key Grip: Richard Hagar

Makeup Man: Bob Keats
M-G-M Camera: Ray Johnson
M-G-M Production: Arvid Griffen and Al Alt
M-G-M Transportation: Jack Allison
Mixer: Jean Valentine
Producer: Buck Houghton
Property Master: Jack Pollyea
Publicity: Ernest Sloman
Recorder: Don Raubiere
Script Supervisor: Betty Andrews
Second Assistant Director: Kurt Neumann
Second Grip: Ford Clark
Second Prop Man: Robert Schultz
Secretary to Mr. Self: Mary Jane Maney
Secretary: Lillian Gallo and Betty Rosher
Set Decorator: Rudy Butler
Story Editor: Del Reisman
Supervising Music Editor: Eugene Feldman
Supervising Negative Cutter: Lamar Weisner
Supervising Sound Effects Editor: Gene Eliot
Unit Production Manager: Ralph W. Nelson
Wardrobe Lady: Ann Helfgott
Wardrobe Man: Beau Vanden Ecker

PRODUCTION CREW, THIRD SEASON (as of May 12, 1961)

Art Director: Phil Barber and Merrill Pye
Assistant Cameraman: Joe Raue
Assistant to Mr. Bernie: Howard Apfel

Assistant to Mr. Kaplan: Gerald Saltsman
Assistant to Mr. Mosher: Walter Mulconery
Best Boy: Jack Stein
Bookkeeper: Hene Bercovich
Boom Man: Mel Rennings
CBS Business Affairs: Leo Lefcourt, Robert
    Norvet and Harold Hourihan
CBS Press Relations: Dick Isreal
CBS Production Manager: Sid Van Keuren
Cable Man: Steve Shearer and Charles
    Regan
Camera Operator: Charles Wheeler and
    Jimmy King
Casting Director: James Lister
Cayuga Productions, Inc.: Ashley-Steiner:
    Sam Kaplan
Cayuga Supervising Film Editor: Jason H.
    Bernie, a.c.e.
Chief Accountant: Bill Freedman
Executive Producer for Cayuga: Rod Serling
Film Editor: Bill Mosher
Film Program Co-ordinator: George Amy
First Assistant Director: E. Darrell
    Hallenbeck
First Cameraman: George Clemens
Gaffer: Cam Rogers
Hair Dresser: Billie Southern
Insurance: Lynn Welvart, Ebenstein & Co.
Key Grip: Richard Hagar
Makeup Man: Bob Keats
McCann-Erickson Agency: Ted Robertson
    and Joe Santley
M-G-M Camera: Ray Johnson
M-G-M Location: Dutch Horton and
    Bernice Burrows
M-G-M Production: Arvid Griffen, Bob
    Foss and Mike Glick
M-G-M Transportation: Jack Allison
M-G-M Wardrobe: Kitty Mager
Producer: Buck Houghton
Property Master: Bob Henderson and Dick
    Neblett
Recorder: Howard Voss

Rod Serling's Secretary: Patricia Temple
Script Supervisor: Betty Crosby
Second Assistant Director: Bill Finnegan
Second Grip: Albert Robison
Second Prop Man: Jerry Graham and Harry
    Edwards
Secretary: Virginia Gregory and Marsha
    Fullmer
Set Decorator: H. Web Arrowsmith and
    Keogh Gleason
Sound Mixer: Bill Edmondson
Special Effects: Virgil Beck
Story Editor: Richard McDonagh
Supervising Music Editor: Scott Perry, Jr.
Supervising Sound Effects Editor: John
    Mills
Unit Production Manager: Ralph W. Nelson
Wardrobe Lady: Marie Rose
Wardrobe Man: Beau Vanden Ecker and
    Grady Hunt

PRODUCTION CREW, FIFTH SEASON (as of August 1, 1963)

Art Director: Malcolm Brown
Assistant Cameraman: Joe Raue and Bunny
    Levitt
Assistant Film Editors: Alex Beaton and
    Dale Varnum
Assistant to Mr. Kaplan: Gerald Saltsman
Best Boy: Jack Stein
Bookkeeper: Hene Bercovich
Boom Man: Mel Rennings (also listed
    onscreen as Malcolm Rennings)
CBS Business Affairs: Leo Lefcourt and
    Harold Hourihan
CBS Press Relations: Dick Isreal
CBS Production Manager: Sid Van Keuren
Cable Man: Charles Regan
Camera Operator: Jimmy King
Cameraman: Robert W. Pittack
Casting Director: Patricia Rose
Cayuga Productions, Inc.: Ashley-Steiner:
    Sam Kaplan

Cayuga Suprv. Film Editor: Tommy Scott
Chief Accountant: Bill Freedman
Craft Service Man (Special Effects): Elmo Evans
Executive Producer for Cayuga: Rod Serling
Film Editor: Richard Heermance
Film Program Co-ordinator: George Amy
First Assistant Director: Charles Bonniwell, Jr.
First Cameraman: George Clemens
Gaffer: Cam Rogers
Hair Dresser: Billie Southern
Insurance: Lynn Welvart, Ebenstein & Co.
Key Grip: Richard Hagar
Makeup Man: Bob Keats
McCann-Erickson Agency: Ted Robertson and Joe Santley
M-G-M Camera: Ray Johnson
M-G-M Location: Dutch Horton and Bernice Burrows
M-G-M Production: Arvid Griffen, Bob Foss and Mike Glick

M-G-M Transportation: Jack Allison
Producers: William Froug
Property Master: Harry Edwards
Recorder: Ted Mann
Rod Serling's Secretary: Marjorie Langsford
Script Supervisor: Betty Crosby
Second Assistant Director: Major Roup
Second Grip: Al Hunter
Second Prop Man: John Ricardo
Secretary: Shirley Pullan and Dawn Forrester
Set Decorator: Robert Benton
Sound Mixer: Philip Mitchell
Special Effects: Ralph Swartz
Standby Driver: Don Trew
Story Editor: Richard McDonagh
Supervising Music Editor: Gene Feldman
Supervising Sound Effects Editor: Gene Eliot
Unit Production Manager: Ralph W. Nelson
Wardrobe Lady: (various)
Wardrobe Man: Norman Burza

APPENDIX B: *THE TWILIGHT ZONE* BOOKS

The contract with Bantam Books featured a provision prohibiting Rod Serling from exploiting any other publication rights for a period of three years from the date of initial publication. However, he reserved the right to publish summaries or digests of the stories for the purpose of exploiting the television series, motion picture and legitimate stage rights. He was granted an advance against royalties of $4,000 for the task of adapting his scripts into short story form. Serling took on the task, admitting in a letter that such a book would enhance the popularity of the television series. The copyrights remained with Serling, not the publisher, but Bantam Books was responsible for undertaking the obligation to secure copyright registration. (All copyright notifications inside each book clearly stated the copyright was registered under the name of Cayuga Productions.)

The origin of these books began when Sam Kaplan of Ashley-Steiner was approached by Merle Goldberg, a representative from Bantam Books, in late May and early June of 1959. In late June, Kaplan discussed the contract with Serling over the phone and then negotiated the terms of the contract to Goldberg so the deal could be finalized. The books were issued in paperback form, with hardcover format initially not considered.

Dick Roberts of Bantam Books, Inc. was the editor who oversaw book production and reviewed each of Serling's stories, tweaking a few words here and there to ensure the quality of the books contents. Tim Horan, the promotion director, reviewed each of the three books and consulted with Serling personally to arrange publicity.

A total of three books were contracted, one due for each year of the contract. All of the stories were adaptations of Serling-scripted teleplays that had previously aired over the CBS-TV. The first of the three was *Stories from the Twilight Zone*, first printing April 1960. The stories included "The Mighty Casey," "Escape Clause," "Walking Distance," "The Fever," "Where is Everybody?" and "The Monsters are Due on Maple Street." There were 151 pages and it cost 35 cents. The cover of the book featured a photo of Rod Serling, sitting behind his typewriter, with a cigarette in hand. (Could this have been an endorsement for Oasis cigarettes?)

According to a royalty report dated March 31, 1963, for sales up to December 31, 1962, *Stories from The Twilight Zone* sold a total of 432,000 copies. Serling's royalties were 1.4 cents for the first 150,000 copies sold in both foreign and U.S. sales, 2.1 cents for each book sold over the 150,000 (which totaled 213,100), and 1.4 cents for all sales in Canada (13,200), Foreign (11,700) and to the Teen Age Book Club (44,000). Total gross royalties for Serling by December 31, 1962, were $7,539.70.

Oscar Dystel, managing editor of Bantam Books, Inc., confessed to Serling in a letter dated September 20, 1960, that "this title caught all of us unawares. We had no idea it would take off as fast as it did and we promise you that we'll do better with the next edition." Serling expressed a concern when, having read a number of fan letters, and personally browsed book shops, he discovered that it was not being sold at Newark, Idlewild, Chicago, Columbus and Los Angeles airports. Dystel explained, "I was completely mystified and upset by your report . . . I'm passing this little tidbit on to our sales manager. I'm really astonished."

The second was *More Stories from The Twilight Zone*, first printing April 1961. Serling was contracted to deliver all the stories to the publisher by November 1, 1960. The stories included "The Lonely," "Mr. Dingle, The Strong," "A Thing About Machines," "The Big, Tall Wish," "A Stop at Willoughby," "The Odyssey of Flight 33" and "Dust." Running a total of 149 pages, the paperback sold for 35 cents cover price.

According to a royalty report dated March 31, 1963, for sales up to December 31, 1962, *More Stories from The Twilight Zone* sold 367,100 copies. His royalties were 1.4 cents for the first 150,000 copies sold in both foreign and U.S. sales, 2.1 cents for each book sold over the 150,000 (which totaled 139,500), and 1.4 cents for all sales in Canada (15,700), Foreign (12,500) and to the Teen Age Book Club (49,400). Total gross royalties for Serling by December 31, 1962 were $6,115.90. *

The third book, *New Stories from The Twilight Zone*, went into the first printing in May of 1962. The stories included adaptations of "The Whole Truth," "The Shelter," "Showdown with Rance McGrew," "The Night of the Meek," "The Midnight Sun" and "The Rip Van Winkle Caper," making a total of 122 pages.

During the second half of 1962, shortly after the third paperback was released to bookshelves, all of the stories from the three publications were reprinted together for a green hardcover book from Nelson Doubleday, Inc., in Garden City, New York. Totaling 314 pages, the reprint — titled *From the Twilight Zone* — offered fans another chance to read the story adaptations. In April of 1966, Serling received a check for $288.23 representing his share of proceeds from the hardcover book still being published by Doubleday & Co., as part of the Book Club Division.

All of the above were also reprinted in October of 1986 by Bantam, with an introduction by T.E.D. Klein. This reprint was 418 pages, and retailed for $9.95.

In September of 1962, a representative of Grosset & Dunlap contacted Murray Benson, director of licensing at CBS Films, Inc., expressing an interest in a hardcover book based on *The Twilight Zone*. Since Serling had been working with a paperback publisher, this option was considered. "It would be our thought to take eight or ten of your scripts, not previously published, and turn them over to a top flight writer who would adapt them into short story form," wrote Benson to Serling

---

* The following are the release months and years for each printing of the second paperback. By December 31, 1962, the book had recently gone into its eighth printing. First printing was April 1961; second printing, May 1961; third printing, June 1961; fourth printing, July 1961; fifth printing, October 1961; sixth printing, January 1962; seventh printing, April 1962; eighth printing, December 1962; ninth printing, July 1964; tenth printing, September 1964; eleventh printing, September 1965; and twelfth printing, September 1966. Inside the front cover of the September 1966 edition, Bantam printed the unaccredited praise, "Rod Serling can take his place with Ray Bradbury as tops in the field."

on September 12. "The financial arrangements would, of course, be subject to your approval and we could work on the same basis in terms of payment as in the comic book income."

On September 26, Serling, then residing in Yellow Springs, Ohio, informed Benson that he had already been in correspondence with Robert Bernstein at Random House, the same man responsible for sending Serling a couple of Hitchcock anthologies. "They were tremendously well done things and if we're to go into some kind of hardcover, I wish you'd check it out with Random House first," Serling explained.

The deal with Random House fell through, and Serling agreed to the terms of Grosset & Dunlap. This fourth book gave Serling more freedom than the previous three paperbacks. Handing over a number of television scripts to Murray Benson, Serling did not have to adapt any of his stories. That job was handed to Walter B. Gibson, creator and author of *The Shadow* pulp magazines. This 207 page hardcover book, titled *The Twilight Zone* (also listed in reference guides as *Rod Serling's The Twilight Zone*), featured mostly ghost stories. "Back There" and "Judgment Night" were the only adaptations of Serling's teleplays. The remaining eleven stories were originals by Gibson. The illustrations were by Earl E. Mayan, who featured a photo image of Gibson on the inside of the front cover.

On October 29, 1963, Murray Benson forwarded to Gerald Saltsman of Ashley-Steiner-Famous Artists, Inc. a check for $2,500. This was Cayuga's 50 percent share of the advance received from Grosset & Dunlap in connection with the hardcover book. This was a standard practice with networks and television production companies – since Cayuga controlled 50 percent interest in the series, 50 percent of the profits were handed over to Cayuga for any approved products bearing the name *Twilight Zone*.

"You will be pleased to know the book is doing extremely well with every indication that at least 50,000 copies will be sold this year," Benson told Saltsman. "Incidentally, we are definitely proceeding with the Literary Guild of America for a hardcover book club reprinting of the first three paperbacks published by Bantam Books. The retail price will definitely be above the $1.75 category, probably $1.98." This same hardcover would be reprinted in 1965 by Tempo in New York, retitled *Chilling Stories from Rod Serling's The Twilight Zone* and featuring only 10 of the 13 short stories. The two adaptations from Serling's teleplays were included.

The year after, 1964, a sequel was written titled *Twilight Zone Revisited*, a 208-page hardcover containing 13 new stories, again written by Walter B. Gibson. "Beyond the Rim" was an adaptation of "A Hundred Yards Over the Rim" and "Mirror Image," "The Purple Testament" and "The Man in the Bottle" were also adapted into short stories. The remaining nine were originals by Gibson. Earl E. Mayan again illustrated.

Years later, a paperback book titled *Rod Serling's Twilight Zone: Stories from the Supernatural, Selected Stories*, was published. Running 159 pages, the book again credited Gibson and Mayan for their efforts and reprinted ten of the short stories, only featuring one adaptation from Serling's teleplays, "Back There."

APPENDIX C: *THE TWILIGHT ZONE* COMIC BOOKS

In early 1961, Western Publishing made arrangements with the CBS Marketing Department to produce a series of comic books, using *The Twilight Zone* name. Under its Dell Comics imprint, Western succeeded in releasing four issues from late 1961 through early 1962, retailing for 15 cents. The first two were published as part of the long-running *Four Color* anthology series.

In late 1962, Western struck a second agreement with CBS and began issuing another series of comic books, restarting the numbering system with #1, under the Gold Key imprint. This second series of issues ran until 1982. The first issue of the second series was released in November of 1962, and sold for a retail price of 12 cents. The retail price rose to 15 cents beginning with issue #26, released July 1968; 20 cents beginning with issue 50, released July 1973; and 25 cents beginning with issue 57, released July 1974. By the time the final issue (#92) was released May of 1982, the retail price was 60 cents. There was a publishing hiatus between issue 91 (June 1979) and 92 (May 1982).

A circulation statement from spring of 1972 stated *The Twilight Zone* comic books averaged a circulation of 199,000. Issues 84 and 85 historically marks the first two comic books to ever feature the work of Frank Miller.

None of the plots were adapted from the television scripts. The stories were all original. In issue 8, one story concerned a scientist, driven by a strange compulsion to seek an incredible creature in the forbidding mountains of Tibet. In issue 6, a downed bomber crew trekked across the trackless desert, following a magic amulet to treachery in a strange oasis. Issues 1 through 8 have a pin-up back cover, with the same painting as the front without copy and logo.

The Twilight Zone comics were still going strong two years after the television series concluded, as evidenced by a royalty statement totaling $517.69 payable to Rod Serling, dated October 19, 1966.

In 1974, Western Publishing offered "Dan Curtis Giveaways #3: The Twilight Zone." This 24-page comic was a free giveaway, part of a set of nine 6-by-3-inch mini comic books, intended for use as premiums for bubble gum. For this particular issue, the story was titled "Long Laugh the King" and featured the character of Mirtho the Magnificent.

On a side note, Marvel Comics made an intentional attempt to grab some of the *Twilight Zone* audience by introducing a series of comic books titled, *Amazing Adult Fantasy*, which was billed on the front cover as "The Comic Magazine That Respects Your Intelligence." Originally the comic was *Amazing Adventures*, but beginning with issue 7, released December 1961, the title was changed and the "intelligence" billing was added to the front cover. After eight issues, concluding with issue 14, released July 1962, the comic book changed format again and was called simply *Amazing Fantasy* beginning with issue 15.

Issue #1 © CBS, Ent. Reprinted with permission.

Dell Four Color, Issue #1173 (March – May 1961, 36 pages)
"The Specter of Youth" 10 pages, Reed Crandall (Pencils) and Ben Oda (Letters).
   Reprinted: Twilight Zone #21
"The Phantom Lighthouse" 12 pages, Reed Crandall (Pencils and Inks) and Ben Oda (Letters).
   Reprinted: Twilight Zone #21
"Doom by Prediction" 10 pages, Reed Crandall (Pencils and Inks) and Ben Oda (Letters).
   Reprinted: Twilight Zone #25 and Mystery Digest #18
"Journeys in the Twilight Zone" 1 page, George Evans (Pencils and Inks) and Ben Oda (Letters).
   Reprinted: Twilight Zone #29 and Mystery Digest #18
"Travelers in Twilight Zone" 1 page, George Evans (Pencils and Inks) and Ben Oda (Letters).
   Reprinted: Twilight Zone #26 and Mystery Digest #21

Dell Four Color, Issue #1288 (February – April 1962, 36 pages)
"The Bridegroom" 10 pages, George Evans (Pencils and Inks) and Ben Oda (Letters).
   Reprinted: Twilight Zone #26 and Mystery Digest #3, 18 and 24
"The Secret Weapon" 10 pages, George Evans (Pencils and Inks) and Ben Oda (Letters).
"Voices From the Twilight Zone" 2 pages, George Evans (Pencils and Inks) and Ben Oda (Letters).
   Reprinted: Twilight Zone #25 and Mystery Digest #3 and 18
"The Joiner" 10 pages, George Evans (Pencils), Reed Crandall (Inks) and Ben Oda (Letters).
   Reprinted: Twilight Zone #26
"Voyage Into the Twilight Zone" 1 page, George Evans (Pencils and Inks) and Ben Oda (Letters).
   Reprinted: Mystery Digest #6
"Calling the Twilight Zone" 1 page, George Evans (Pencils and Inks) and Ben Oda (Letters).
   Reprinted: Twilight Zone #33 and Mystery Digest #3

Notes: Regarding issue #1288, the last story was replaced by advertisements in some copies of that comic. The cover art was reprinted for Twilight Zone #26.

Dell, Issue #01-860-207 (May – July 1962, 36 pages)
Credits: Mike Sekowsky (Pencils), Frank Giacoia (Inks) and Ben Oda (Letters).
"The Man From Nowhere" 11 pages
"Beyond the Window" 11 pages
"Hard-Luck Harvey" 10 pages

"Luck in the Twilight Zone" 1 page
>   **Reprinted:** Mystery Digest #6

"Lost in the Twilight Zone" 1 page
>   **Reprinted:** Twilight Zone #33 and Mystery Digest #3 and 24

Dell, Issue #12-860-210 (August – October 1962, 36 pages)

Credits: George Evans (Pencils), George Evans and Frank Giacoia (Inks) and Ben Oda (Letters).

"The Ring" 11 pages
>   **Reprinted:** Twilight Zone #27 and Mystery Digest #3 and 24

"The Collector" 10 pages
>   **Reprinted:** Twilight Zone #27 and Mystery Digest #3

"The Time Machine" 11 pages
>   **Reprinted:** Twilight Zone #32 and Mystery Digest #9 and 24

"Creatures From the Twilight Zone" 1 page
>   **Reprinted:** Mystery Digest #9

"Time Travel into The Twilight Zone" 1 page
>   **Reprinted:** Twilight Zone #32 and Mystery Digest #3

The Twilight Zone, Issue #1 (November 1962, 36 pages)

"Frozen Worlds of Space" 1 page, Joe Certa (Pencils) and Joe Certa (Inks).

"Perilous Journey" 10 pages, Reed Crandall (Pencils), Reed Crandall (Inks) and Ben Oda (Letters).
>   **Reprinted:** Twilight Zone #92 and Mystery Digest #3

"Do Not Touch Exhibit" 10 pages, Reed Crandall (Pencils), George Evans and Reed Crandall (Inks) and Ben Oda (Letters).
>   **Reprinted:** Twilight Zone #92 and Mystery Digest #6

"Wings of Death" 1 page text story, Joe Certa (Pencils and Inks).
>   **Reprinted:** Twilight Zone #92 and Mystery Digest #6

"Voyage to Nowhere" 11 pages, Reed Crandall (Pencils) and Ben Oda (Letters).
>   **Reprinted:** Twilight Zone #92 and Mystery Digest #3

"Custer's Last Stand" 1 page text story, Tom Gill (Pencils and Inks).

The Twilight Zone, Issue #2 (February 1963, 36 pages)

"The Sea #8: Island Life" 1 page text

"The Lost Colonie" 9 pages, Alberto Giolitti (Pencils and Inks) and Ben Oda (Letters).
>   **Reprinted:** Twilight Zone #28 and Mystery Digest #12

"The Living Fossil" 1 page text story, Mel Crawford (Pencils and Inks) and Ben Oda (Letters).
>   **Reprinted:** Twilight Zone #28

"Journey Into Jeopardy" 10 pages, Alberto Giolitti (Pencils and Inks) and Ben Oda (Letters).
>   **Reprinted:** Mystery Digest #6

"The Ray Phobos" 11 pages, Alberto Giolitti (Pencils and Inks) and Ben Oda (Letters).
>   **Reprinted:** Mystery Digest #6

"The Sea #10: Coral Reef Fish" 1 page text

Notes: Regarding Issue #2, each of the one-page text stories were part of an ongoing series subtitled "Keys of Knowledge," hoping to educate the youth who read the comic books. Many of the one-page text stories in future issues were also part of that series.

The Twilight Zone, Issue #3 (May 1963, 36 pages)

"Roads and Vehicles #3: Primitive Transportation" 1 page, Joe Certa (Pencils and Inks).

"The Last Battle" 11 pages, Mike Sekowsky (Pencils), Mike Peppe (Inks) and Ben Oda (Letters).
>   **Reprinted:** Mystery Digest #3

"The Ghost in the Drifting Tomb" 1 page text story, Joe Certa (Pencils and Inks).
>   **Reprinted:** Mystery Digest #12

"Birds of a Feather" 9 pages, Mike Sekowsky (Pencils), Mike Peppe (Inks) and Ben Oda (Letters).
>   **Reprinted:** Mystery Digest #6

"The Queen is Dead – Long Live the Queen" 11 pages, Alex Toth (Pencils and Inks) and Ben Oda (Letters).
>   **Reprinted:** Mystery Digest #3

"Roads and Vehicles #6: The Roman Road" 1 page, Jack Sparling (Pencils and Inks).

The Twilight Zone, Issue #4 (August 1963, 36 pages)

"Electricity #1: The Ancients and the Early Experiments" 1 page, Tom Gill (Pencils and Inks).

"The Secret of the Key" 10 pages, Alex Toth (Pencils and Inks) and Ben Oda (Letters).
>   **Reprinted:** Mystery Digest #3

"Experiment in Purple" 8 pages, Mike Sekowsky (Pencils), Mike Peppe (Inks) and Ben Oda (Letters).
>   **Reprinted:** Mystery Digest #3

"The Captive" 4 pages, Alex Toth (Pencils and Inks) and Ben Oda (Letters).
>   **Reprinted:** Twilight Zone #25, Mystery Digest #12, #21

"Ordeal of Bluebird 3" 9 pages, Mike Sekowsky (Pencils), Mike Peppe (Inks) and Ben Oda (Letters).
>   **Reprinted:** Mystery Digest #3

"Trail of Tears" 1 page text story

"Electricity #2: Lightning Conductors" 1 page, Tom Gill (Pencils and Inks).

The Twilight Zone, Issue #5 (November 1963, 36 pages)

"Archeology #11: Cuneiform Writing" 1 page text story

"The Legacy of Hans Burkel" 10 pages, Mike Sekowsky (Pencils), Mike Peppe (Inks) and Ben Oda (Letters).
>   **Reprinted:** Mystery Digest #6

"Poor Little Sylvester" 8 pages, Tom Gill (Pencils and Inks) and Ben Oda (Letters).
>   **Reprinted:** Mystery Digest #9

"The Shadow of Fate" 4 pages, Mike Sekowsky (Pencils), Mike Peppe (Inks) and Ben Oda (Letters).
>   **Reprinted:** Mystery Digest #6

"Journey to the Frozen Past" 1 page text story, Mel Crawford (Pencils and Inks).
>   **Reprinted:** Mystery Digest #6

"The Fortune Hunters" 9 pages, Frank Thorne (Pencils and Inks) and Ben Oda (Letters).

"Astronomy #6: Sunspots" 1 page text

The Twilight Zone, Issue #6 (February 1964, 36 pages)

"Seagoing Vessels #20: The Whaling Bark" 1 page, Jack Sparling (Pencils and Inks)

"Captives of the Mirage" 17 pages, Tuska and Heck (Pencils) and Ben Oda (Letters).

> **Reprinted:** Mystery Digest #9

"The Strange Sleep" 1 page text, Mel Crawford (Pencils and Inks).

> **Reprinted:** Mystery Digest #3

"Night People of London" 4 pages, Mike Sekowsky (Pencils), Mike Peppe (Inks) and Ben Oda (Letters).

> **Reprinted:** Mystery Digest #9

"The Last Sixty Seconds" 10 pages, Mike Sekowsky (Pencils), Mike Peppe (Inks) and Ben Oda (Letters).

> **Reprinted:** Mystery Digest #3

"Roads and Vehicles #41: Pioneer Motorists" 1 page text, Jack Sparling (Pencils and Inks).

The Twilight Zone, Issue #7 (May 1964, 36 pages)

"Roads and Vehicles #25: Classic Roman Vehicles" 1 page, Jack Sparling (Pencils and Inks).

"Shield of Medusa" 15 pages, Frank Thorne (Pencils and Inks) and Ben Oda (Letters).

> **Reprinted:** Mystery Digest #6

"Human Radio Receivers" 1 page

> **Reprinted:** Mystery Digest #12

"Menace From Out There" 4 pages, Fred Fredericks (Pencils, Inks and Letters).

> **Reprinted:** Mystery Digest #18

"The Man Who Haunted Himself" 12 pages

> **Reprinted:** Mystery Digest #12

"Seagoing Vessels #13: The Frigate" 1 page, Jerry Robinson (Pencils and Inks).

The Twilight Zone, Issue #8 (August 1964, 36 pages)

"Astronomy #9: Earth's Neighbors" 1 page

"Hamilton's Creature" 14 pages, Fred Fredericks (Pencils, Inks and Letters).

"Raptures" 1 page text story

"The Night Stalker of Paris" 4 pages, Mel Crawford (Pencils and Inks) and Ben Oda (Letters).

> **Reprinted:** Mystery Digest #12

"Iron Man #1" 13 pages, Mike Peppe (Inks) and Ben Oda (Letters).

> **Reprinted:** In Mystery Digest #12

"Domestic Animals #13: The Bulldog" 1 page, Ray Bailey (Pencils and Inks).

The Twilight Zone, Issue #9 (November 1964, 36 pages)

"Our Changing Weather #4: Winds" 1 page, Joe Certa (Pencils) and Joe Certa (Inks).

"The Street Where Evil Dwelt" 12 pages, Fred Fredericks (Pencils, Inks and Letters).

> **Reprinted:** Mystery Digest #6

"The Pharaoh's Curse" 1 page, Joe Certa (Pencils and Inks).

Reprinted: Mystery Digest #12

"The Doom Days" 4 pages, Fred Fredericks (Pencils, Inks and Letters).

    Reprinted: Mystery Digest #6

"Creatures on Canvas" 15 pages. Fred Fredericks (Pencils, Inks and Letters).

    Reprinted: Mystery Digest #9

"Trees #15: Southern White Oaks" 1 page, Jack Sparling (Pencils and Inks).

The Twilight Zone, Issue #10 (February 1965, 36 pages)

"Architecture #2: Ancient Monuments" 1 page

"The Bewitching Window" 8 pages, Frank Thorne (Pencils and Inks) and Ben Oda (Letters).

    Reprinted: Mystery Digest #15

"Lost Acre" 7 pages, Frank Thorne (Pencils and Inks) and Ben Oda (Letters).

    Reprinted: Mystery Digest #6

"The Men on the Moon" 1 page, Fred Fredericks (Pencils and Inks).

"The Patient Workers" 1 page, Frank Thorne (Pencils and Inks) and Ben Oda (Letters).

"The Demon Light" 10 pages, Frank Thorne (Pencils and Inks) and Ben Oda (Letters).

    Reprinted: Mystery Digest #9

"The Mystic Book" 4 pages, Frank Thorne (Pencils and Inks) and Ben Oda (Letters).

"The Midas Wheel" 1 page, Frank Thorne (Pencils and Inks) and Ben Oda (Letters).

    Reprinted: Mystery Digest #18

"The People of Asia #1: The Laotians" 1 page, Joe Certa (Pencils and Inks).

The Twilight Zone, Issue #11 (May 1965, 36 pages)

"Bridges and Man #4: Roman Bridges and Builders" 1 page, Joe Certa (Pencils and Inks).

"The Gremlins" 9 page, Hy Eisman (Pencils and Inks) and Ben Oda (Letters).

"The Island Vision" 6 pages, Frank Bolle (Pencils and Inks) and Ben Oda (Letters).

    Reprinted: Mystery Digest #9

"The Wanted One" 1 page, Joe Certa (Pencils and Inks) and Ben Oda (Letters).

    Reprinted: Mystery Digest #18

"The Jinx Breakers" 1 page, Fred Fredericks (Pencils and Inks).

    Reprinted: Mystery Digest #9

"(Wanted . . . Alive!) Doomsday in Dusterville" 9 pages, Joe Certa (Pencils and Inks) and Ben Oda (Letters).

    Reprinted: Mystery Digest #12

"Ghost Ship of the Skies" 7 pages, Frank Bolle (Pencils and Inks) and Ben Oda (Letters).

"The Vision" 1 page, Joe Certa (Pencils and Inks) and Ben Oda (Letters).

"The Magic Makers" 1 page text story

    Reprinted: Mystery Digest #9

The Twilight Zone, Issue #12 (August 1965, 36 pages)

"Architecture #6: The Assyrians" 1 page, Joe Certa (Pencils and Inks).

"The Shadow with Claws" 15 pages, Angelo Torres (Pencils and Inks) and Ben Oda (Letters).

    Reprinted: Mystery Digest #12

"The Haunted Sentry Box" 1 page
> **Reprinted:** Mystery Digest #9

"The Revolt of the Machines" 4 pages, Al Williamson (Pencils and Inks) and Ben Oda (Letters).
> **Reprinted:** Mystery Digest #9

"The Voice in the Mist" 1 page, Joe Certa (Pencils and Inks) and Ben Oda (Letters).
> **Reprinted:** Mystery Digest #12

"They Dwell Among Us" 11 pages, Don Heck (Pencils) and Ben Oda (Letters).
> **Reprinted:** Mystery Digest #18

"People of Asia #3: The Iranians" 1 page text story, Joe Certa (Pencils and Inks).

The Twilight Zone, Issue #13 (November 1965, 36 pages)

"The Man Who Could Read the Future" 15 pages, Frank Bolle (Pencils and Inks) and Ben Oda (Letters).
> **Reprinted:** Mystery Digest #15

"The Spectral Lights" 1 page text story, Joe Certa (Pencils and Inks).

"The Man With My Face" 4 pages, Al McWilliams (Pencils and Inks) and Ben Oda (Letters).
> **Reprinted:** Mystery Digest #9

"Way Out West – On Mars!" 9 pages, Reed Crandall (Pencils) and Ben Oda (Letters).
> **Reprinted:** Mystery Digest #9

The Twilight Zone, Issue #14 (February 1966, 36 pages)

"The Ship That Vanished" 1 page, Joe Certa (Pencils and Inks).

"The Day That Vanished" 11 pages, Reed Crandall (Pencils and Inks) and Ben Oda (Letters).
> **Reprinted:** Mystery Digest #12

"The Death Car" 4 pages, Alberto Giolitti (Pencils and Inks) and Ben Oda (Letters).
> **Reprinted:** Mystery Digest #12

"The Amazing Mr. Home" 1 page text story
> **Reprinted:** Mystery Digest #12

"The Lost Genius" 5 pages, Joe Orlando (Pencils and Inks) and Ben Oda (Letters).
> **Reprinted:** Mystery Digest #12

"The Lost Oasis" 9 pages, Angelo Torres (Pencils and Inks) and Ben Oda (Letters).
> **Reprinted:** Mystery Digest #9

"A Nightmare Tale" 1 page, Joe Certa (Pencils and Inks) and Ben Oda (Letters).
> **Reprinted:** Mystery Digest #9

"The Thing From the Sky" 1 page, Joe Certa (Pencils and Inks) and Ben Oda (Letters).

The Twilight Zone, Issue #15 (May 1966, 36 pages)

"The Flaming Ship" 1 page, Joe Certa (Pencils and Inks).

"Moment of Decision" 9 pages, Joe Orlando (Pencils and Inks) and Ben Oda (Letters).
> **Reprinted:** Mystery Digest #15

"Wipe Out the Future" 6 pages, Andre LeBlanc (Pencils and Inks) and Ben Oda (Letters).
> **Reprinted:** Mystery Digest #15

"Wheel of Light" 1 page, Mike Roy (Pencils), Mike Peppe (Inks) and Ben Oda (Letters).
"The Cipher Manuscript" 1 page text story
"Perfect Preservation" 4 pages, Mike Roy (Pencils), Mike Peppe (Inks) and Ben Oda (Letters).
"The Vision of Mystir" 9 pages, Reed Crandall (Pencils and Inks) and Ben Oda (Letters).
"The Prophet" 1 page, Ben Oda (Letters).

The Twilight Zone, Issue #16 (July 1966, 36 pages)
"Prophecy of Doom" 1 page, Joe Certa (Pencils and Inks).
"Nightmare for an Astronaut" 11 pages, Joe Orlando (Pencils and Inks) and Ben Oda (Letters).
   Reprinted: Mystery Digest #15
"The Ghost Gunner" 4 pages, Angelo Torres (Pencils and Inks) and Ben Oda (Letters).
"The Wisdom of the Beast" 1 page, Joe Certa (Pencils and Inks) and Ben Oda (Letters).
"Footprints in the Night" 1 page text story, Joe Certa (Pencils and Inks).
"The Perfect Criminal" 5 pages, Jose Delbo (Pencils and Inks) and Ben Oda (Letters).
   Reprinted: Mystery Digest #12
"When the Ball is Over" 8 pages, Frank Bolle (Pencils and Inks).
   Reprinted: Mystery Digest #18
"The Warning" 1 page, Joe Certa (Pencils and Inks).

The Twilight Zone, Issue #17 (September 1966, 36 pages)
"The Masquerader" 11 pages, Joe Orlando (Pencils) and Ben Oda (Letters).
   Reprinted: Mystery Digest #15
"Once Upon a Dream" 4 pages, Tom Gill (Pencils and Inks) and Ben Oda (Letters).
   Reprinted: Mystery Digest #15
"He Walked on Water" 1 page, Joe Certa (Pencils and Inks) and Ben Oda (Letters).
"The Ship That Knew" 1 page, Joe Certa (Pencils and Inks) and Ben Oda (Letters).
   Reprinted: Mystery Digest #15
"The Sleeping Doctor" 1 page text story, Joe Certa (Pencils and Inks).
"Crystal Clear" 4 pages, Win Mortimer (Pencils and Inks) and Ben Oda (Letters).
"Mars, Dead or Alive" 9 pages, Nevio Zaccara (Pencils and Inks).
   Reprinted: Mystery Digest #18

The Twilight Zone, Issue #18 (October 1966, 36 pages)
"The Mysterious Gambler" 1 page text story, Joe Certa (Pencils and Inks).
"Second Hand Clothes" 11 pages, Ben Oda (Letters).
"When the Lights Go Out" 4 pages, Joe Certa (Pencils and Inks) and Ben Oda (Letters).
"Dead Man's Train" 1 page, Joe Certa (Pencils and Inks) and Ben Oda (Letters).
"Man in the Green Coat" 1 page, Joe Certa (Pencils and Inks) and Ben Oda (Letters).
"The Green Children" 1 page text story, Joe Certa (Pencils and Inks).
"Programmed Vacation" 6 pages, Joe Certa (Pencils and Inks) and Ben Oda (Letters).
   Reprinted: Mystery Digest #15
"The Impressionist" 7 pages, Alberto Giolitti (Pencils and Inks) and Ben Oda (Letters).
   Reprinted: Mystery Digest #15

"Strange Reunion" 1 page, Joe Certa (Pencils and Inks) and Ben Oda (Letters).

The Twilight Zone, Issue #19 (January 1967, 36 pages)
"Crime-A-Day Town" 11 pages, Mike Roy (Pencils and Inks) and Ben Oda (Letters).
"Into World's Beyond" 4 pages, Andre LeBlanc (Pencils and Inks) and Ben Oda (Letters).
"Big Foot" 1 page, Joe Certa (Pencils and Inks) and Ben Oda (Letters).
"Visitors From Elsewhere" 1 page text story, Joe Certa (Pencils and Inks).
"The Man Who Mastered Yoga" 6 pages, Joe Orlando (Pencils) and Ben Oda (Letters).
    Reprinted: Mystery Digest #15
"Our Man on Planet Ergo" 7 pages, Joe Certa (Pencils and Inks) and Ben Oda (Letters).

The Twilight Zone, Issue #20 (March 1967, 36 pages)
"The Phantom Bullets" 1 page, Joe Certa (Pencils and Inks).
"The Plague" 9 pages, Joe Orlando (Pencils and Inks) and Ben Oda (Letters).
"The Wonderful Lulu Hearst" 1 page text story
"The Prodigy" 4 pages, Andre LeBlanc (Pencils and Inks) and Ben Oda (Letters).
"The Day That Couldn't Get Lost" 5 pages, Sal Trapani (Pencils and Inks) and Ben Oda (Letters).
"The Portal" 5 pages, Russ Jones (Pencils and Inks) and Ben Oda (Letters).

The Twilight Zone, Issue #21 (May 1967, 36 pages)
"Specter of Youth" 10 pages, Reed Crandall (Pencils).
    Reprinted: Twilight Zone #1173
"Mystifying Disappearances" 4 pages, Andre LeBlanc (Pencils and Inks).
"Vanishing Island" 1 page text story, Joe Certa (Pencils and Inks).
"The Phantom Lighthouse" 11 pages, Reed Crandall (Pencils and Inks).
    Reprinted: Twilight Zone #1173

The Twilight Zone, Issue #22 (July 1967, 36 pages)
"The Cat Was Black" 1 page, Joe Certa (Pencils and Inks).
"The Death Mask" 9 pages, Al McWilliams (Pencils and Inks).
"The Phantoms from the Past" 4 pages, Andre LeBlanc (Pencils and Inks).
    Reprinted: Mystery Digest #15
"Survival" 5 pages, Nevio Zaccara (Pencils and Inks) and Ben Oda (Letters).
"The Curse of James Henry" 7 pages, Joe Orlando (Pencils and Inks) and Ben Oda (Letters).
    Reprinted: Mystery Digest #15
"The Echoes" 1 page, Joe Certa (Pencils and Inks).

The Twilight Zone, Issue #23 (October 1967, 36 pages)
"The Human Pet" 9 pages, Joe Orlando (Pencils and Inks).
"The Incredible Illusion" 1 page text story
"Terror From the Sky" 4 pages, Andre LeBlanc (Pencils and Inks) and Ben Oda (Letters).
    Reprinted: Mystery Digest #15
"The Visitor" 6 pages, Luis Dominguez (Pencils and Inks).

"The Method Marshall" 6 pages, Tom Gill (Pencils and Inks).

The Twilight Zone, Issue #24 (January 1968, 36 pages)

"The Shield of Evil" 14 pages, Sam Citron (Pencils and Inks).

"The Invisible Ones" 5 pages, Andre LeBlanc (Pencils and Inks).

"The Nightmare" 1 page text story, Joe Certa (Pencils and Inks).

"Mind Over Matter" 6 pages

"The Faces" 1 page text story, Joe Certa (Pencils and Inks).

The Twilight Zone, Issue #25 (April 1968, 36 pages)

"Tombstone Valley" 9 pages, Luis Dominguez (Pencils and Inks) and Ben Oda (Letters).
    Reprinted: Mystery Digest #21

"The Ghost in the Drifting Tomb" 1 page text story, Joe Certa (Pencils and Inks).

"The Captive" 4 pages, Alex Toth (Pencils and Inks) and Ben Oda (Letters).
    Reprinted: Twilight Zone #4

"Voices From the Twilight Zone" 2 pages, George Evans (Pencils and Inks) and Ben Oda (Letters).
    Reprinted: Twilight Zone #1288

"Doom by Prediction" 10 pages, Reed Crandall (Pencils) and Ben Oda (Letters).
    Reprinted: Twilight Zone #1173

The Twilight Zone, Issue #26 (July 1968, 36 pages)

"The Bridegroom" 10 pages, George Evans (Pencils and Inks) and Ben Oda (Letters).
    Reprinted: Twilight Zone #1288

"Journeys Into Oblivion" 4 pages, Andre LeBlanc (Pencils and Inks).
    Reprinted: Mystery Digest #18 and #24

"Travelers in the Twilight Zone" 1 page, George Evans (Pencils and Inks) and Jon D'Agostino (Letters).
    Reprinted: Twilight Zone #1173

"The Visions" 1 page text story, Joe Certa (Pencils and Inks).

"The Joiner" 10 pages, Reed Crandall (Pencils), George Evans (Inks) and Ben Oda (Letters).
    Reprinted: Twilight Zone #1288

"Dinosauria: Iguanadon" 1 page, Jack Sparling (Pencils and Inks).

The Twilight Zone, Issue #27 (December 1968, 36 pages)

"The Ring" 11 pages, George Evans (Pencils and Inks) and Ben Oda (Letters).
    Reprinted: Dell Twilight Zone #12-860-210

"The House of Evil" 1 page text story, Joe Certa (Pencils and Inks).

"Unidentified Aircraft" 2 pages, Art Saaf (Pencils and Inks).
    Reprinted: Mystery Digest #18

"The Scrapfaggot Witch" 2 pages, Art Saaf (Pencils and Inks) and Jon D'Agostino (Letters).
    Reprinted: Mystery Digest #18

"The Collector" 10 pages, George Evans (Pencils), Frank Frazetta (Inks) and Ben Oda (Letters).
    Reprinted: Dell Twilight Zone #12-860-210

"Pteranodon" 1 page, Jack Sparling (Pencils and Inks).

Reprinted: Donald Duck (1962 series) #122 (November 1968)

The Twilight Zone, Issue #28 (March 1969, 36 pages)

"The Lost Colonie" 9 pages, Alberto Giolitti (Pencils and Inks) and Ben Oda (Letters).
>   **Reprinted:** Twilight Zone #2

"The Living Fossil" 1 page text story, Mel Crawford (Pencils and Inks).
>   **Reprinted:** Twilight Zone #2

"Strange Visit at Sea" 4 pages, Sal Trapani (Pencils and Inks).
>   **Reprinted:** Mystery Digest #24

"The Captive Town" 12 pages, Luis Dominguez (Pencils and Inks) and Ben Oda (Letters).

The Twilight Zone, Issue #29 (June 1969, 36 pages)

"Captain Clegg's Treasure" 9 pages, Ben Oda (Letters).
>   **Reprinted:** Mystery Digest #24

"The Curse of Anne Machen" 1 page text story

"Past, Present . . . Eternity" 4 pages, Joe Certa (Pencils and Inks) and Ben Oda (Letters).
>   **Reprinted:** Mystery Digest #18

"Trapped Between Lives" 11 pages, Art Saaf (Pencils) and Ben Oda (Letters).
>   **Reprinted:** Mystery Digest #21

"Journeys Into the Twilight Zone" 1 page, George Evans (Pencils and Inks) and Ben Oda (Letters).
>   **Reprinted:** Dell Twilight Zone #1173.

The Twilight Zone, Issue #30 (September 1969, 36 pages)

"Tall Timber" 9 pages, Joe Certa (Pencils and Inks) and Ben Oda (Letters).

"The Vanishing Hero" 1 page text story, Joe Certa (Pencils and Inks).

"In the Cards" 4 pages, Bob Jenney (Pencils and Inks) and Ben Oda (Letters).
>   **Reprinted:** Mystery Digest #24

"Made in Hong Kong" 6 pages, Sal Trapani (Inks) and Ben Oda (Letters).
>   **Reprinted:** Mystery Digest #21

"The Phantom Balloon" 6 pages, Win Mortimer (Pencils and Inks) and Ben Oda (Letters).
>   **Reprinted:** Mystery Digest #24

The Twilight Zone, Issue #31 (December 1969, 36 pages)

"The Voices" 9 pages, Jose Delbo (Pencils and Inks) and Ben Oda (Letters).

"The Inner Warning" 1 page text story, Joe Certa (Pencils and Inks).

"A Different Point of View" 4 pages, Ben Oda (Letters).
>   **Reprinted:** Mystery Digest #21

"The Most Menacing Man Alive" 12 pages, Frank Bolle (Pencils and Inks) and Jon D'Agostino (Letters).
>   **Reprinted:** Mystery Digest #18 and #24

The Twilight Zone, Issue #32 (March 1970, 36 pages)

"Voice in the Wind" 9 pages, Ed Robbins (Pencils and Inks).
"Secret of the Death-Ship" 1 page text story, Joe Certa (Pencils and Inks).
"A Spell in the Night" 4 pages, Joe Certa (Pencils and Inks) and Jon D'Agostino (Letters).
  Reprinted: Mystery Digest #18 and #24
"The Time Machine" 11 pages, George Evans (Pencils and Inks) and Ben Oda (Letters).
  Reprinted: Dell Twilight Zone #12-860-210
"Time Travel into the Twilight Zone" 1 page, George Evans (Pencils and Inks) and Ben Oda (Letters).
  Reprinted: Dell Twilight Zone #12-860-210

The Twilight Zone, Issue #33 (June 1970, 36 pages)
"The Bounty Hunters" 9 pages, Sal Trapani (Inks).
"Calling the Twilight Zone" 1 page, George Evans (Pencils and Inks) and Ben Oda (Letters).
  Reprinted: Dell Twilight Zone #1288
"The Bookworm" 4 pages, Joe Certa (Pencils and Inks).
  Reprinted: Mystery Digest #21
"Lost in the Twilight Zone" 1 page, Mike Sekowsky (Pencils), Frank Giacoia (Inks) and Ben Oda (Letters).
  Reprinted: Twilight Zone #01-860-207
"The Killer Doll" 1 page text story, Joe Certa (Pencils and Inks).
"Manolete's Last Fight" 10 pages, Ed Robbins (Pencils and Inks).
  Reprinted: Mystery Digest #24

The Twilight Zone, Issue #34 (September 1970, 36 pages)
"Beware the Kewpie Doll" 9 pages, John Celardo (Pencils and Inks).
  Reprinted: Mystery Digest #18
"Dream of Gold" 1 page text story, Joe Certa (Pencils and Inks).
  Reprinted: Mystery Digest #24
"Mirage" 4 pages, Oscar Novelle (Pencils and Inks).
"The Unseen Thing" 12 pages, Alberto Giolitti (Pencils and Inks) and Ben Oda (Letters).
  Reprinted: Mystery Digest #21
"Your Future: As a Cosmetologist / As an Air Traffic Controller" 1 page text story, Dan Spiegle (Pencils and Inks).

The Twilight Zone, Issue #35 (December 1970, 36 pages)
"The Singing Sword" 9 pages, Alberto Giolitti (Pencils and Inks) and Ben Oda (Letters).
  Reprinted: Mystery Digest #24
"Death Drinks a Toast" 1 page text story, Joe Certa (Pencils and Inks).
"A Thing About Cats" 4 pages, Jack Sparling (Pencils and Inks).
  Reprinted: Mystery Digest #21
"To the Death" 6 pages, Ed Robbins (Pencils and Inks) and Ben Oda (Letters).
"The Shivering Stars" 6 pages, Alberto Giolitti (Pencils and Inks) and Ben Oda (Letters).
  Reprinted: Mystery Digest #21
"Your Future: As an Oceanographer / As an Interior Designer and Decorator" 1 page text story, Dan

Spiegle (Pencils and Inks).

The Twilight Zone, Issue #36 (March 1971, 36 pages)
"All's Quiet on the Eastern Front" 9 pages, John Celardo (Pencils and Inks).
    Reprinted: Mystery Digest #21
"The Man With the ESP Eyes" 1 page text story, John Celardo (Pencils and Inks).
    Reprinted: Mystery Digest #21
"For Love of Money" 4 pages, Jack Sparling (Pencils and Inks).
    Reprinted: Mystery Digest #21
"Cemetery Scene" 6 pages, Ed Robbins (Pencils and Inks).
"Fortune and Men's Eyes" 6 pages, Frank Bolle (Pencils, Inks and Letters).
    Reprinted: Mystery Digest #21

The Twilight Zone, Issue #37 (May 1971, 36 pages)
"The Man Beast of Paris" 8 pages, Paul S. Newman (Script) and Luis Dominguez (Pencils and Inks).
    Reprinted: Mystery Digest #24
"Enigma in the Sky" 1 page text story, Paul S. Newman (Script) and Joe Certa (Pencils and Inks).
"The Tall Corn" 4 pages, Len Wein (Script) and Jack Sparling (Pencils and Inks).
"The Threshold" 6 pages, Len Wein (Script) and Luis Dominguez (Pencils and Inks).
"The Fall Guy" 6 pages, Len Wein (Script) and John Celardo (Pencils and Inks).

The Twilight Zone, Issue #38 (July 1971, 36 pages)
"A Date With Death" 8 pages, Luis Dominguez (Pencils and Inks).
"Return from the Grave" 1 page text story, Joe Certa (Pencils and Inks).
"The Cat With the Evil Eye" 4 pages, Win Mortimer (Pencils and Inks).
"Buried Alive" 6 pages, Frank Bolle (Pencils and Inks).
"The General's Statue" 6 pages, Joe Certa (Pencils and Inks).

The Twilight Zone, Issue #39 (September 1971, 36 pages)
"The Youngest Witch" 8 pages, John Celardo (Pencils and Inks).
"Plane of Death" 1 page text story, Joe Certa (Pencils and Inks).
"Wedding March" 4 pages, Oscar Novelle (Pencils and Inks).
"Fool's Gold" 6 pages, Alan Weiss (Pencils and Inks).
"Escape Artist" 6 pages, Jack Sparling (Pencils and Inks).

Note: All of the stories in issue #39 were later reprinted for issue #79.

The Twilight Zone, Issue #40 (November 1971, 36 pages)
"A Charmed Life" 8 pages, Jack Sparling (Pencils and Inks).
"Door to Oblivion" 1 page text story
"Premonition" 4 pages, Oscar Novelle (Pencils and Inks).
"The Missing Link" 6 pages, Joe Certa (Pencils and Inks) and Ben Oda (Letters).
"The Last Voyage" 6 pages, Len Wein (Script) and Luis Dominguez (Pencils and Inks).

Note: All of the stories in issue #40 were later reprinted for issue #73.

The Twilight Zone, Issue #41 (January 1972, 36 pages)
"Guilt Has a Thousand Eyes" 6 pages, Dan Spiegle (Pencils and Inks) and Bill Spicer (Letters).
"Harbinger of Death" 1 page text story
"A Matter of Time" 6 pages, Len Wein (Script) and Jack Sparling (Pencils and Inks).
"The Chimpanzee" 1 page, Frank Bolle (Pencils and Inks).
"The Magic Herb" 4 pages, Win Mortimer (Pencils and Inks).
"Long Laugh the King" 8 pages, John Celardo (Pencils and Inks).

The Twilight Zone, Issue #42 (March 1972, 36 pages)
"The Haunted Taxi" 8 pages, Luis Dominguez (Pencils and Inks).
"Torture Revisited" 1 page text story, Joe Certa (Pencils and Inks).
"The Possible Dream" 4 pages, Jack Sparling (Pencils and Inks).
"At the End of His Rope" 6 pages, Mike Vosburg (Pencils and Inks).
"The Day of the Palio" 6 pages, Cambiotti (Pencils and Inks) and Ben Oda (Letters).

The Twilight Zone, Issue #43 (May 1972, 36 pages)
"The Man Who Kidnapped Death" 8 pages, John Celardo (Pencils and Inks).
"Three Tombstones" 1 page text story, Joe Certa (Pencils and Inks).
"This is Your – Pizzazz – Captain Speaking" 4 pages, Tom Gill (Pencils and Inks).
"Ten Seconds to Live" 6 pages, Jack Sparling (Pencils and Inks).
"The Face of Justice" 6 pages

The Twilight Zone, Issue #44 (July 1972, 36 pages)
"The Camera Doesn't Lie" 8 pages
"The Mysterious Grass" 1 page text story, Joe Certa (Pencils and Inks).
"The Call" 4 pages, Oscar Novelle (Pencils and Inks).
"The Swampscott Explosion" 6 pages, John Celardo (Pencils, Inks and Letters).
"The Science Teacher" 6 pages, Luis Dominguez (Pencils and Inks).

The Twilight Zone, Issue #45 (September 1972, 36 pages)
"A Call for Mr. Travers" 8 pages, Luis Dominguez (Pencils and Inks).
"What's In a Name?" 1 page text story, Joe Certa (Pencils and Inks).
"The Experiment" 4 pages, Jack Sparling (Pencils and Inks).
"The Curse of Deal Bay" 6 pages, Adolpho Buylla (Pencils and Inks).
"Art for Art's Sake" 6 pages, John Celardo (Pencils and Inks).

Note: All of the stories in issue #45 were later reprinted for issue #71.

The Twilight Zone, Issue #46 (November 1972, 36 pages)
"Dream of the Devil" 8 pages, Luis Dominguez (Pencils and Inks).
"The Severed Head" 1 page text story, Joe Certa (Pencils and Inks).

"Passage of the Doomed" 4 pages, Joe Certa (Pencils and Inks).

"Scene of the Crime" 6 pages, Win Mortimer (Pencils and Inks) and Ben Oda (Letters).

"The Great Sale" 6 pages, Wayne Howard (Pencils) and Sal Trapani (Inks).

The Twilight Zone, Issue #47 (January 1973, 36 pages)

"And Where It Stops, Nobody Knows" 9 pages, Rich Buckler (Pencils) and Sal Trapani (Inks).

"Golden Dreams" 1 page text story, Joe Certa (Pencils and Inks).

"The Man Who Hated Mankind" 4 pages, Jack Sparling (Pencils and Inks).

"Something New in Town" 6 pages, Jack Sparling (Pencils and Inks).

"The Space Prize" 6 pages, John Celardo (Pencils and Inks).

The Twilight Zone, Issue #48 (March 1973, 36 pages)

"Nightmare in Miniature" 8 pages, Luis Dominguez (Pencils and Inks).

"Fiery Death" 1 page text story, Joe Certa (Pencils and Inks).

"The Numbers Game" 4 pages, Luis Dominguez (Pencils and Inks).

"The Killer Light" 7 pages, Joe Certa (Pencils and Inks) and Gaspar Saladino (Letters).

"Perfect Partners" 6 pages, Stanley Pitt (Pencils) and Reginald Pitt (Inks).

Note: All of the stories in issue #48 were later reprinted for issue #86.

The Twilight Zone, Issue #49 (May 1973, 36 pages)

"Color Him Dead" 8 pages, Adolpho Buylla (Pencils and Inks).

"Oh, You Beautiful Doll" 1 page text story, Joe Certa (Pencils and Inks).

"The Man on the 13th Floor" 4 pages, Frank Bolle (Pencils, Inks and Letters).

"The Supreme Penalty" 6 pages, Oscar Novelle (Pencils and Inks).

"Proceed at Your Own Risk" 6 pages, Mike Sekowsky (Pencils).

The Twilight Zone, Issue #50 (July 1973, 36 pages)

"Water, Water Everywhere" 8 pages, Adolpho Buylla (Pencils and Inks).

"3 Dreams of Death" 1 page text story, Joe Certa (Pencils and Inks).

"Nature's Way" 4 pages, Walter Simonson (Pencils and Inks).

    Reprinted: Twilight Zone #83

"Join the Club" 6 pages, Luis Dominguez (Pencils and Inks).

    Reprinted: Twilight Zone #83

"The Vampire of East 29th Street" 6 pages, Frank Bolle (Pencils, Inks and Letters).

    Reprinted: Twilight Zone #83

The Twilight Zone, Issue #51 (August 1973, 36 pages)

"The Yesterday Window" 8 pages, Frank Bolle (Pencils, Inks and Letters).

"The Torment of Esther Cox" 1 page text story, Joe Certa (Pencils and Inks).

"The Manuscript" 4 pages, Oscar Novelle (Pencils and Inks).

"Time Is On His Hands" 6 pages, Jack Sparling (Pencils and Inks) and Gaspar Saladino (Letters).

"Telephone From the Tomb" 6 pages, Al Williamson (Pencils and Inks).

The Twilight Zone, Issue #52 (September 1973, 36 pages)
"Dream of Death" 8 pages, Jose Delbo (Pencils and Inks).
"Grandma is Missing" 1 page, Joe Certa (Pencils and Inks).
"Night Owl" 4 pages, Jack Sparling (Pencils and Inks).
"Don't Call Me" 6 pages, Frank Bolle (Pencils and Inks).
"Seeing Eye Man" 6 pages, John Celardo (Pencils and Inks).

The Twilight Zone, Issue #53 (November 1973, 36 pages)
"The Expert" 8 pages, Adolpho Buylla (Pencils and Inks).
"Who's Afraid of the Ju-Ju Man?" 5 pages, Luis Dominguez (Pencils and Inks).
"The Isle of the Dead" 6 pages
"Those Good Ol' Days" 6 pages, Jack Abel (Pencils and Inks) and Ben Oda (Letters).

The Twilight Zone, Issue #54 (January 1974, 36 pages)
"Why So Pale, Henry Lad?" 8 pages, John Celardo (Pencils and Inks).
"Ultra-Crepi-Clarian" 1 page text story, Joe Certa (Pencils and Inks).
"The Prisoner" 4 pages, Walter Simonson (Pencils and Inks) and Gaspar Saladino (Letters).
"Caldwell's Last Stand" 6 pages, Luis Dominguez (Pencils and Inks).
"The Copy Machine" 6 pages, John Warner (Script) and Jack Sparling (Pencils and Inks).

The Twilight Zone, Issue #55 (March 1974, 36 pages)
"Now You See It" 8 pages, John Celardo (Pencils and Inks).
"Forget Me Not" 5 pages, Jack Abel (Pencils and Inks).
"Musk's Daughter" 6 pages, Walt Simonson (Pencils and Inks).
"Clothes Make the Woman" 6 pages, Frank Bolle (Pencils and Inks).

The Twilight Zone, Issue #56 (May 1974, 36 pages)
"The Vandals" 8 pages, Adolpho Buylla (Pencils and Inks).
"The Sorcerer's Apprentice" 4 pages, John Celardo (Pencils and Inks).
"A Taste pf Immortality" 6 pages, Luis Dominguez (Pencils and Inks).
"The Night of the Ravens" 7 pages, Adolpho Buylla (Pencils and Inks).

The Twilight Zone, Issue #57 (July 1974, 36 pages)
"What Do You Want to Come Back As?" 8 pages, Frank Bolle (Pencils and Inks).
"The Three Wishes?" 6 pages
"The Spell of the Hat" 4 pages, Oscar Novelle (Pencils and Inks).
"The Haunted Church" 1 page text story
"The Medallion" 6 pages, George Roussos (Pencils and Inks).

The Twilight Zone, Issue #58 (August 1974, 36 pages)
"A Rage to Dance" 7 pages, Amador Garcia (Pencils and Inks).

"Nothing Sacred" 6 pages, Jose Delbo (Pencils and Inks).
"Portrait of an Artist" 6 pages, Luis Dominguez (Pencils and Inks).
"The Cartoonist" 6 pages, Frank Bolle (Pencils and Inks).

The Twilight Zone, Issue #59 (September 1974, 36 pages)
"The Plague" 8 pages, John Warner (Script) and Frank Bolle (Pencils and Inks).
"The Stand-In" 5 pages, Freff (Script) and Adolpho Buylla (Pencils).
"Shock Treatment" 6 pages, Arnold Drake (Script) and Jose Delbo (Pencils).
"The Golden Glove" 6 pages, John Warner (Script) and Jack Sparling (Pencils).

The Twilight Zone, Issue #60 (November 1974, 36 pages)
"Stay Tuned" 6 pages, Ricardo Villamonte (Pencils and Inks).
"The Race" 5 pages, Jack Sparling (Pencils and Inks).
"A Dream of Conquest" 6 pages, Adolpho Buylla (Pencils and Inks).
"Please Wait for the Death Tone" 8 pages, Jack Sparling (Pencils and Inks).

The Twilight Zone, Issue #61 (January 1975, 36 pages)
"Coming Attractions" 8 pages, Jose Delbo (Pencils and Inks).
"School Spirits" 5 pages, Win Mortimer (Pencils and Inks).
"The Candidate" 5 pages, Jack Sparling (Pencils and Inks).
"The Last Starship" 7 pages, Jose Delbo (Pencils and Inks).

The Twilight Zone, Issue #62 (March 1975, 36 pages)
"An Expensive Date" 7 pages, Adolpho Buylla (Pencils and Inks).
"The Bounty Hunter" 6 pages, Ricardo Villamonte (Pencils and Inks).
"The Howling Dog" 6 pages, Jack Sparling (Pencils and Inks).
"Planet Death" 6 pages, Esphidy Menhalim (Letters).

The Twilight Zone, Issue #63 (May 1975, 36 pages)
"No Perfect Crime" 8 pages, Frank Bolle (Pencils and Inks).
"In Their Own Time" 4 pages, Jack Sparling (Pencils and Inks).
"Going Up?" 6 pages, Jose Delbo (Pencils and Inks).
"Last Request" 7 pages, Adolpho Buylla (Pencils and Inks).

The Twilight Zone, Issue #64 (July 1975, 36 pages)
"The Weather Picture" 7 pages, Jack Sparling (Pencils and Inks).
"An Object of Fear" 6 pages, Jack Sparling (Pencils and Inks).
"The Graffiti Wants You" 5 pages, Esphidy Menhalim (Letters).
"Raise the Dead" 7 pages, Ricardo Villamonte (Pencils and Inks).

The Twilight Zone, Issue #65 (August 1975, 36 pages)
"The Unseen" 7 pages, Jose Luis Garcia-Lopez (Pencils and Inks).
"Over My Dead Body" 6 pages, Fred Carrillo (Pencils and Inks) and Esphidy Menhalim (Letters).

"The Silver Ghost" 6 pages, Alex Nino (Pencils and Inks) and Esphidy Menhalim (Letters).
"Big Foot" 5 pages, Jose Delbo (Pencils and Inks).
"The Unmoveable Coffin" 1 page, Joe Certa (Pencils and Inks).

The Twilight Zone, Issue #66 (September 1975, 36 pages)

"Photographic Memory" 8 pages, Frank Bolle (Pencils and Inks).
"Perchance to Dream" 6 pages, Freff (Script) and Jose Delbo (Pencils and Inks).
"The Inheritors" 6 pages, Amador Garcia (Pencils and Inks).
"Thar's Gold in Them Thar Hills" 6 pages, Ricardo Villamonte (Pencils and Inks).

The Twilight Zone, Issue #67 (November 1975, 36 pages)

"Unburied Alive" 8 pages, Jose Luis Garcia-Lopez (Pencils and Inks).
"No Witness to Death" 4 pages, Joe Certa (Pencils and Inks).
"The Challenger" 6 pages, Freff (Script) and Ricardo Villamonte (Pencils and Inks).
"Somewhere Far From Trouble" 6 pages, Frank Cirocco (Pencils, Inks and Letters).

The Twilight Zone, Issue #68 (January 1976, 36 pages)

"The Second Will" 6 pages
"A Lease on Death" 3 pages, Frank Bolle (Pencils and Inks).
"The Wide Open Spaces" 7 pages, Jack Sparling (Pencils and Inks).
"Discovery" 7 pages

The Twilight Zone, Issue #69 (March 1976, 36 pages)

"The Numbers Game" 10 pages, Jack Sparling (Pencils and Inks).
"A Trip to Limbo" 7 pages, Amador Garcia (Pencils and Inks).
"The Man Who Didn't Exist" 6 pages, Frank Bolle (Pencils and Inks).

The Twilight Zone, Issue #70 (May 1976, 36 pages)

"The Tyranny of Time" 8 pages, Jose Luis Garcia-Lopez (Pencils and Inks).
"Agatha's Baby" 5 pages, Frank Bolle (Pencils and Inks).
"Plain Jane" 6 pages, Amador Garcia (Pencils and Inks).
"Frost: Bite" 4 pages

The Twilight Zone, Issue #71 (July 1976, 36 pages)

"A Call for Mr. Travers" 8 pages, Luis Dominguez (Pencils and Inks).
"What's In A Name?" 1 page text story, Joe Certa (Pencils and Inks).
"The Experiment" 4 pages, Jack Sparling (Pencils and Inks).
"The Curse of Seal Bay" 6 pages, Adolpho Buylla (Pencils and Inks).
"Art for Art's Sake" 6 pages, John Celardo (Pencils and Inks).

Note: The contents of issue #71 is a reprint of issue #45.

The Twilight Zone, Issue #72 (August 1976, 36 pages)

"Cave of the Time-Mists" 8 pages, Bill Ziegler (Pencils and Inks) and Bill Spicer (Letters).
"Your Daily Horror-Scope" 8 pages, Jack Sparling (Pencils and Inks).
"Sorry, the President Cannot See You Today" 7 pages, Jack Sparling (Pencils and Inks).

The Twilight Zone, Issue #73 (September 1976, 36 pages)
"A Charmed Life" 8 pages, Jack Sparling (Pencils and Inks)
"Door to Oblivion" 1 page text story
"Premonition" 4 pages, Oscar Novelle (Pencils and Inks).
"The Missing Link" 6 pages, Joe Certa (Pencils and Inks) and Ben Oda (Letters).
 "The Last Voyage" 6 pages, Luis Dominguez (Pencils and Inks).

Note: The contents of issue #73 is a reprint of issue #40.

The Twilight Zone, Issue #74 (November 1976, 36 pages)
"Game of Doom" 7 pages, Frank Bolle (Pencils and Inks).
"The Sorcerer's Ring" 8 pages, Bill Ziegler (Pencils and Inks) and Bill Spicer (Letters).
"The Mummy's Mirror" 8 pages, Bill Ziegler (Pencils and Inks) and Bill Spicer (Letters).

The Twilight Zone, Issue #75 (January 1977, 36 pages)
"The Return of Wulfstein" 10 pages, Bill Ziegler (Pencils and Inks) and Bill Spicer (Letters).
"Each Autumn I Die" 6 pages, Frank Bolle (Pencils and Inks).
"The Fish" 6 pages, Frank Bolle (Pencils and Inks).
"Modern Day Rainmaker: Fact or Fiction" 1 pages, Carlos Garzon (Pencils and Inks) and Ben Oda
(Letters).

The Twilight Zone, Issue #76 (March 1977, 36 pages)
"Ride the High Country" 3 pages, Bob McLeod (Pencils and Inks).
"The Gift" 5 pages, Jose Delbo (Pencils and Inks).
"Poster Man" 4 pages, Joe Certa (Pencils and Inks).
"The Game Show" 8 pages, Jack Sparling (Pencils and Inks).
"Return of the Dream" 3 pages

The Twilight Zone, Issue #77 (May 1977, 36 pages)
"Honeymoon on Elk Mountain" 8 pages, Bob McLeod (Pencils).
"Mirror Image" 6 pages, Frank Bolle (Pencils and Inks).
"Death Plot" 6 pages, Frank Bolle (Pencils and Inks).
"The Visit" 3 pages, Joe Certa (Pencils and Inks).

The Twilight Zone, Issue #78 (July 1977, 36 pages)
"The Missing Mirage" 8 pages, Frank Bolle (Pencils and Inks).
"The Shakespeare Factor" 10 pages, Al McWilliams (Pencils, Inks and Letters).
"Too Many Murderers" 5 pages, Jack Sparling (Pencils and Inks).

The Twilight Zone, Issue #79 (August 1977, 36 pages)
"The Youngest Witch" 8 pages, John Celardo (Pencils and Inks).
"Plane of Death" 1 page text story, Joe Certa (Pencils and Inks).
"Wedding March" 4 pages, Oscar Novelle (Pencils and Inks).
"Fool's Gold" 6 pages, Alan Weiss (Pencils and Inks).
"Escape Artist" 6 pages, Jack Sparling (Pencils and Inks).

Note: The contents of issue #79 is a reprint of issue #39, including the cover art.

The Twilight Zone, Issue #80 (September 1977, 36 pages)
"Poacher's Dream" 7 pages, Al McWilliams (Pencils, Inks and Letters).
"Beware of the Deep Blue Sea" 8 pages, Juan Ortiz (Pencils and Inks).
"Instant Replay" 8 pages, Frank Bolle (Pencils and Inks).

The Twilight Zone, Issue #81 (November 1977, 36 pages)
"No Joking Matter" 10 pages, Luis Dominguez (Pencils and Inks).
"The Little Rich Man" 8 pages, Dan Spiegle (Pencils and Inks) and Bill Spicer (Letters).
"Heart of Stone" 5 pages, Juan Ortiz (Pencils and Inks).

The Twilight Zone, Issue #82 (January 1978, 36 pages)
"Every Dog Has His Day" 6 pages, Jack Sparling (Pencils and Inks).
"The Fate Changer" 6 pages, Al McWilliams (Pencils and Inks) and Al McWilliams (Letters).
"The Fast Ball" 7 pages, Jose Delbo (Pencils and Inks).
"Back Where You Came From" 4 pages, Juan Ortiz (Pencils and Inks).

The Twilight Zone, Issue #83 (April 1978, 52 pages)
"Two Faces of Evil" 7 pages, Jack Sparling (Pencils and Inks).
"The Last Voyage of the Dolphin" 3 pages, Juan Ortiz (Pencils and Inks).
"The Wooden Witness" 7 pages, John Celardo (Pencils and Inks).
"Hide and Seek" 6 pages, Frank Bolle (Pencils and Inks).
"Nature's Way" 4 pages, Walter Simonson (Pencils and Inks).
    Reprinted: Twilight Zone #50
"Join the Club" 6 pages, Luis Dominguez (Pencils and Inks).
    Reprinted: Twilight Zone #50
"The Vampire of East 29th Street" 6 pages, Frank Bolle (Pencils, Inks and Letters).
    Reprinted: Twilight Zone #50

The Twilight Zone, Issue #84 (June 1978, 52 pages)
"Raptures of the Deep" 6 pages, Adolpho Buylla (Pencils and Inks).
"Mike Royal Feast" 3 pages
"Nightowl" 4 pages, Jack Sparling (Pencils and Inks).
    Reprinted: Twilight Zone #52

"Don't Call Me" 6 pages, Frank Bolle (Pencils and Inks).
    Reprinted: Twilight Zone #52
"I Did It!" 6 pages, Al McWilliams (Pencils and Inks).
"The Seeing-Eye Man" 6 pages, John Celardo (Pencils and Inks).
    Reprinted: Twilight Zone #52
"Makeover" 8 pages, Frank Bolle (Pencils and Inks).

The Twilight Zone, Issue #85 (July 1978, 36 pages)
"Soundproof Room" 8 pages, Frank Bolle (Pencils and Inks).
"Endless Cloud" 5 pages, Frank Miller (Pencils and Inks).
"An Actor's Life For Me" 5 pages, Frank Bolle (Pencils and Inks).
"The Bad Joke" 5 pages, Bob Jenney (Pencils and Inks).

The Twilight Zone, Issue #86 (August 1978, 36 pages)
"Nightmare in Miniature" 8 pages, Luis Dominguez (Pencils and Inks).
"Fiery Death" 1 page text story, Joe Certa (Pencils and Inks).
"The Numbers Game" 4 pages, Luis Dominguez (Pencils and Inks).
"The Killer Light" 7 pages, Joe Certa (Pencils and Inks) and Gaspar Saladino (Letters).
"Perfect Partners" 6 pages, Stanley Pitt (Pencils) and Reginald Pitt (Inks).

Note: All of the content in issue #86 were reprinted from issue #48.

The Twilight Zone, Issue #87 (October 1978, 36 pages)
"Headed for Catastrophe" 8 pages, Mel Crawford (Pencils and Inks).
"Nostalgia Trip" 7 pages, Frank Bolle (Pencils and Inks).
"Cover Artist" 7 pages, Jack Sparling (Pencils and Inks).

The Twilight Zone, Issue #88 (December 1978, 36 pages)
"The Meek Shall Inherit" 10 pages, Frank Bolle (Pencils and Inks).
"Farewell Performance" 8 pages, Mike Roy (Pencils and Inks).
"Super Star" 2 pages, Sal Trapani (Pencils and Inks).

The Twilight Zone, Issue #89 (February 1979, 36 pages)
"Star Pupil" 4 pages, Jack Sparling (Pencils and Inks).
"The Prettiest Child" 6 pages, Mike Roy (Pencils and Inks).
"Overly Charming" 7 pages, Jack Sparling (Pencils and Inks).
"The Hangman's Noose" 5 pages, Jack Sparling (Pencils and Inks).

The Twilight Zone, Issue #90 (April 1979, 36 pages)
"Horror Movie" 6 pages, Frank Bolle (Pencils and Inks).

"Falcon's Curse" 6 pages
"A Loss of Face" 5 pages, Win Mortimer (Pencils and Inks).
"Bradley Manor"

The Twilight Zone, Issue #91 (June 1979, 36 pages)
"Soldier of Death" 6 pages, Mike Roy (Pencils and Inks).
"Design for Treachery" 6 pages, Win Mortimer (Pencils and Inks).
"Good Samaritan" 8 pages, Jack Sparling (Pencils and Inks).
"Look Alike" 6 pages, Jack Sparling (Pencils and Inks).

The Twilight Zone, Issue #92 (May 1982, 36 pages)
"Perilous Journey" 10 pages, Reed Crandall (Pencils and Inks) and Ben Oda (Letters).
"Do Not Touch Exhibit" 10 pages, George Evans (Pencils and Inks) and Ben Oda (Letters).
"Wings of Death" 1 page text story, Joe Certa (Pencils and Inks).
"Voyage to Nowhere" 11 pages, Reed Crandall (Pencils) and Ben Oda (Letters).

Note: All of the content in issue #92 were reprinted from issue #1.

APPENDIX D: LIST OF STATIONS CARRYING
THE TWILIGHT ZONE: THE FIRST SEASON

Live Stations

Albany, N.Y.	WTEN-TV	Lansing, Mich.	WJIM-TV
Indianapolis, Ind.	WISH-TV	Cadillac, Mich.	WWTV
Albuquerque, N.M.	KGGM-TV	Las Vegas, Nev.	KLAS-TV
Jackson, Miss.	WJTV-TV	Cape Girardeau, Mo.	KFVS-TV
Amarillo, Texas	KFDA-TV	Lewiston, Idaho	KLEW-TV
Jacksonville, Fla.	WJXT-TV	Carthage-	
Atlanta, Ga.	WAGA-TV	Watertown, N.Y.	WCNY-TV
Jefferson City, Mo.	KRCG-TV	Lincoln, Nebr.	KOLN-TV
Augusta, Ga.	WRDW-TV	Lexington, Kentucky	WKYT-TV
Johnson City, Tenn.	WJHL-TV	Cedar Rapids, Iowa	WMT-TV
Bakersfield, Cal.	KBAK-TV	Little Rock, Ark.	KTHV-TV
Joplin, Mo.	KODE-TV	Champaign, Ill.	WCIA-TV
Baltimore, M.D.	WMAR-TV	Los Angeles, Cal.	KNXT-TV
Kalamazoo, Mich.	WKZO-TV	Charleston, S.C.	WCSC-TV
Bangor, M.E.	WABI-TV	Louisville, Kentucky	WHAS-TV
Kansas City, Mo.	KCMO-TV	Charleston –	
Binghamton, N.Y.	WNBF-TV	Huntington, W.Va.	WHTN-TV
Kearney, Nebr.	KHOL-TV	Macon, Ga.	WMAZ-TV
Birmingham, Ala.	WBRC-TV	Madison, Wisc.	WISC-TV
Klamath Falls, Ore.	KOTI-TV	Charlotte, N.C.	WBTV
Bismark, N.D.	KBMB-TV	Marquette, Mich.	WDMJ-TV
Knoxville, Tenn.	WBIR-TV	Chattanooga, Tenn.	WDEF-TV
Boise, Idaho	KBOI-TV	Mason City, Iowa	KGLO-TV
La Crosse, Wisc.	WKBT-TV	Chicago, Ill.	WBBM-TV
Boston, Mass.	WNAC-TV	Medford, Ore.	KBES-TV
Lafayette, La.	KLFY-TV	Cincinnati, Ohio	WKRC-TV
Buffalo, N.Y.	WBEN-TV	Memphis, Tenn.	WREC-TV

Cleveland, Ohio	WJW-TV	Richmond, Va.	WRVA-TV
Miami, Florida	WTVJ-TV	Harlingen, Tex.	KGBT-TV
Columbia, S.C.	WNOK-TV	Roanoke, Va.	WDBJ-TV
Missoula, Mont.	KMSO-TV	Harrisburg, Pa.	WHP-TV
Columbus, Ga.	WRBL-TV	Rochester, N.Y.	WVET-TV
Mobile, Ala.	WKRG-TV	Hartford, Conn.	WTIC-TV
Columbus, Miss.	WCBI-TV	Rock Island, Ill.	WHBF-TV
New Orleans, La.	WWL-TV	Hayes City, Nebr.	KHPL-TV
Columbus, Ohio	WBNS-TV	Sacramento, Cal.	KBET-TV
New York, N.Y.	WCBS-TV	Salt Lake City, Utah	KSL-TV
Corpus Christi, Tex.	KZTV-TV	Holyoke – Springfield,	
Norfolk, Va.	WTAR-TV	Mass.	WHYN-TV
Dallas, Texas	KRLD-TV	Salisbury, Md.	WBOC-TV
Oak Hill, W. Va.	WOAY-TV	Hutchinson –	
Dayton, Ohio	WHIO-TV	Wichita, Kan.	KTVH-TV
Oklahoma City, Okla.	KWTV-TV	Saginaw, Mich.	WKNX-TV
Denver, Colo.	KLZ-TV	San Antonio, Tex.	KENS-TV
Omaha, Nebr.	WOW-TV	San Diego, Cal.	KFMB-TV
Des Moines, Iowa	KRNT-TV	Tampa, Fla.	WTVT-TV
Orlando, Fla.	WDBO-TV	San Francisco, Cal.	KPIX-TV
Detroit, Mich.	WJBK-TV	Savannah, Ga.	WTOC-TV
Pasco, Wash.	KEPR-TV	Shreveport, La.	KSLA-TV
Ephrata, Wash.	KBAS-TV	Scranton, Pa.	WDAU-TV
Peoria, Ill.	WMBD-TV	Sioux City, Iowa	KVTV-TV
Erie, Pa.	WSEE-TV	South Bend, Ind.	WSBT-TV
Philadelphia, Pa.	WCAU-TV	Spartanburg, W. Va.	WSPA-TV
Eureka, Cal.	KIEM-TV	Spokane, Wash.	KXLY-TV
Phoenix, Ariz.	KOOL-TV	St. Joseph, Mo.	KFEQ-TV
Evansville, Ind.	WEHT-TV	St. Louis, Mo.	KMOX-TV
Pittsburgh, Pa.	KDKA-TV	Syracuse, N.Y.	WHEN-TV
Fresno, Cal.	KFRE-TV	Toledo, Ohio	WTOL-TV
Portland, Me.	WGAN-TV	Tucson, Ariz.	KOLD-TV
Ft. Meyers, Fla.	WINK-TV	Tulsa, Okla.	KOTV-TV
Portland, Ore.	KOIN-TV	Valley City, N.D.	KXJB-TV
Ft. Wayne, Ind.	WANE-TV	Washington, D.C.	WTOP-TV
Providence, R.I.	WPRO-TV	Yakima, Wash.	KIMA-TV
Galveston –		Youngstown, Ohio	WKBN-TV
Houston, Tex.	KGUL-TV	Texarkana, Tex.	KCMC-TV
Quincy, Ill.	KHQA-TV	Terre-Haute, Ind.	WTHI-TV
Green Bay, Wisc.	WBAY-TV	Thomasville, Ga. –	
Raleigh – Durham, N.C.	WTVD-TV	Tallahassee, Fla.	WCTV
Greensboro, N.C.	WFMY-TV		

Delayed Stations

		(Local Time)	(Delayed)
Altoona, Pa.	WFBG-TV	8:30 p.m., Fri.	0 day
Baton Rouge, La.	WAFB-TV	10:05 p.m., Mon.	10 days
Beaumont, Tex.	KFDA-TV	10:30 p.m., Fri.	7 days
Big Spring, Tex.	KEDY-TV	10:30 p.m., Thurs.	6 days
Billings, Mont.	KOOK-TV	11:00 p.m., Tues.	4 days
Bryan, Tex.	KBTX-TV	10:40 p.m., Fri.	7 days
Carlsbad, N.M.	KAVE-TV	8:30 p.m., Sat.	15 days
Cheyenne, Wyo.	KFBC-TV	10:15 pm., Tues.	11 days
Chico, Cal.	KHSL-TV	11:00 p.m., Fri.	0 day
Clarksburg, W. Va.	WBOY-TV	10:00 p.m., Sat.	8 days
Clovis, N.M.	KICA-TV	8:00 p.m., Thurs.	6 days
Colorado Springs, Colo.	KKTV	9:00 p.m., Sat.	8 days
Dickinson, N.D.	KDIX	10:00 p.m., Sun.	16 days
Dothan, Ala.	WTVY	9:00 p.m., Fri.	21 days
Duluth, Minn.	KDAL-TV	10:30 p.m., Sat.	1 day
El Paso, Tex.	KROD-TV	10:00 p.m., Tues.	11 days
Great Falls, Mont.	KFBB-TV	11:00 p.m., Tues.	11 days
Greenville, N.C.	WNCT	10:00 p.m., Wed.	5 days
Hay Springs, Nebr.	KDUH-TV	10:30 p.m., Fri.	0 day
Idaho Falls, Idaho	KID-TV	11:00 p.m., Tues.	4 days
Lubbock, Tex.	KDUB-TV	10:30 p.m., Thurs.	6 days
Meridian, Miss.	WTOK-TV	8:00 p.m., Fri.	28 days
Midland-Odessa, Tex.	KOSA-TV	10:30 p.m., Mon.	3 days
Milwaukee, Wisc.	WITI-TV	10:00 p.m., Sun.	2 days
Minneapolis, Minn.	WCCO	9:00 p.m., Fri.	0 days
Minot, N.D.	KEMC	10:30 p.m., Sun.	9 days
Montgomery, Ala.	WCOV-TV	9:30 p.m., Wed.	12 days
Nashville, Tenn.	WLAC-TV	10:15 p.m., Sun.	2 days
Parkesburg, W. Va.	WTAP-TV	10:30 p.m., Thurs.	13 days
Rapid City, S.D.	KOTA-TV	10:30 p.m., Fri.	0 day
Roswell, N.M.	KSWS-TV	10:00 p.m., Wed.	12 days
San Angelo, Cal.	KCTV	9:30 p.m., Fri.	0 day
Scottsbluff, Nebr.	KSTF-TV	10:15 p.m., Tues.	11 days
Seattle-Tacoma, Wash.	KIRO	10:30 p.m., Tues.	4 days
Springfield, Mo.	KTTS-TV	10:00 p.m., Wed.	12 days
Steubenville, Ohio	WSTV-TV	8:00 p.m., Wed.	5 days
Sweetwater-Abilene, Tex.	KPAR-TV	9:00 p.m., Fri.	7 days
Topeka, Kans.	WIBW-TV	9:30 p.m., Wed.	5 days
Waco, Tex.	KWTX-TV	10:40 p.m., Fri.	7 days
Wichita Falls, Tex.	KSYD-TV	10:30 p.m., Thurs.	6 days

All of the above was for the network show of December 11, 1959.

For the network show of March 4, 1960, the same list above was in effect, with the additional delayed stations:

Billings, Mont.	KOOK-TV	11:00 p.m., Tues.	4 days
Butte, Mont.	KXLF-TV	11:00 p.m., Tues.	4 days
Missoula, Mont.	KMSO-TV	10:00 p.m., Thurs.	19 days

SELECTED BIBLIOGRAPHY

Resources

The CBS Inc. Television and Film Music Collection consists of music manuscripts, logs, books, printed music, sound recordings and business papers relating to documentaries, feature films, miniseries, television programs and made-for-television movies. The productions fall under the CBS Television Network, CBS Entertainment Division, CBS Productions Network, and, in a few cases, earlier manifestations of these divisions. Included in the collection are materials by composers such as Jeff Alexander, Bill Conti, Jerry Goldsmith, Bernard Herrmann, Henry Mancini, Lyn Murray, Alex North, Fred Steiner, Dimitri Tiomkin, Franz Waxman and John Williams. Productions represented include TV series such as *Gilligan's Island*, *Gunsmoke*, *Have Gun-Will Travel*, *Perry Mason*, *Rawhide*, and *The Twilight Zone*. The music cues featured in this book came from this source, and then polished with the help of Paul Giammarco, Carson Cohen, Phil Sternenberg and Matt Vandermast.

The production costs originate from a complete set of books in my personal collection, issued monthly from June 30, 1958 to May 31, 1964, from the office of Freedman & Freedman of Beverly Hills, California. William Freedman was Serling's personal business manager and accountant, who worked closely with Serling and the producers for Cayuga Productions to ensure accurate records were kept. The production costs for many episodes varied month by month due to the cost of film duplication, negatives, retakes and other factors. Few pages were missing, but the inevitable gaps still remain. The author makes no claim that the figures are final. He merely cites the source for the information.

The opening and closing narrations were taken direct from the actual films. Spelling of words (including slang) was verified from the scripts and various papers composed separately from the scripts. Punctuation may vary from one episode to another – the scripts were also consulted. To the best of the author's ability, the narratives are as complete and accurate according to these sources.

Casting call sheets reveal the actors and actresses who appeared before the camera. The proper spelling of many actors varied from one television production to another. In some cases, actors are listed in reference guides under assumed names. The casting call sheets occasionally listed the actor twice under two different spellings. (Bill or William? McCoog or MacCoog?) Attempts have been made to verify the accurate spelling, keeping in mind that regardless of the source, some actors went by two different names so what appears to be a misspelling may not necessarily be.

The proper spelling of fictional characters was verified by the scripts in the author's personal collection, and by scripts housed in the homes of private collectors for secondary verification. Finals shooting drafts were consulted, since names of characters often changed between drafts. Whenever a script was unavailable, a relative of the scriptwriter was consulted to ensure the proper spelling.

Periodicals

Numerous periodicals are cited as source material throughout the book. Reprinted below are periodicals that were consulted for reference, but not cited within the pages, and were recommended by my good friend Matthew R. Bradley.

* *American Cinematographer* (June 1988), "'Walking Distance' From *The Twilight Zone*"
* *Filmfax* #42 (Dec. 1993/Jan. 1994), "And in the Beginning Was the Word . . . : An Interview with Screenwriter Richard Matheson"
* *Filmfax* #48 (Jan./Feb. 1995; discusses Nolan's unproduced *Twilight Zone* script), "Nolan's Run: The Screenwriting Career of Logan's Papa" (Interview)
* *Filmfax* #75-76 (Oct. 1999/Jan. 2000), "Enter *The Twilight Zone* with Richard Matheson" (Interview)
* *Filmfax* #75-76 (Oct. 1999/Jan. 2000), "Richard Matheson's *The Twilight Zone* Scripts" (Review)
* *Filmfax* #75-76 (Oct. 1999/Jan. 2000), "Sohl Man: An Interview with Jerry Sohl"
* *Filmfax* #75-76 (Oct. 1999/Jan. 2000), #77 (Feb./Mar. 2000), and #78 (April/May 2000), "The Third Gremlin: An Interview with George Clayton Johnson"
* *Filmfax* #78 (April/May 2000), "Altair Ego: An Out-of-This-World Interview with Anne Francis"
* *Filmfax* #101 (Jan./Mar. 2004), "Filet of Sohl: The Classic Scripts and Stories of Jerry Sohl" (Review)
* *New York Review of Science Fiction, The* #160 (December 2001)
* *Outré* Vol. 1 #3 (Summer 1995), "Rod Serling: A Portrait in Twilight" (by William F. Nolan)
* *Outré* Vol. 1 #4 (Fall 1995), "The Illustrative Man: An Interview with SF Legend Ray Bradbury"
* *Outré* Vol. 1 #5 (Winter 1996), "Richard Matheson, Profile in Friendship: The Incredible Thinking Man"
* *Twilight Zone Magazine, The* (a total 58 issues were consulted, dated 1981 to 1989)

Books

After observing a few errors in books concerning *The Twilight Zone*, and finding the same errors recurring in later publications, the author decided not to consult any previously published books on the subject. Rather, the author relied on information provided only through archival material, correspondence, interoffice memos, telegrams, tax forms, corporation paperwork, and other first-generation sources he considered reliable. Many of these items were purchased by the author on eBay. Other materials are preserved in the hands of private collectors, who allowed the author access to their private archives. Some previously published books have been mentioned within these pages and were done so solely for the purpose of correcting the errors that continue to be reprinted. Books that were consulted and used as reference for this publication include:

* Billips, Connie and Arthur Pierce. *Lux Presents Hollywood: A Show-by-Show History of the Lux Radio Theatre and the Lux Video Theatre, 1934-1957.* Jefferson, North Carolina, McFarland & Company, Inc., 1995.

* Conklin, Groff. *The Classic Book of Science Fiction.* New York: Bonanza Books, 1982.

* Cox, Jim. *Radio Speakers: Narrators, News Junkies, Sports Jockeys, Tattletales, Tipsters, Toastmasters and Coffee Klatch Couples . . .* Jefferson, North Carolina, McFarland & Company, Inc., 2007.

* Dunning, John. *On the Air: The Encyclopedia of Old-Time Radio.* New York: Oxford University Press, 1998.

* Grams Jr., Martin. *Alfred Hitchcock Presents Companion, The.* Churchville, Maryland: OTR Publishing, 2002.

*Grams Jr., Martin. *Radio Drama: American Programs, 1932-1962.* Jefferson, North Carolina, McFarland & Company, Inc., 2000.

* Matheson, Richard. *Shock III.* New York: Dell, 1966.

* Matheson, Richard. *The Shores of Space.* New York: Bantam Books, 1957.

* O'Neil, Thomas. *The Emmys: Star Wars, Showdowns, and the Supreme Test of TV's Best.* New York: Penguin Books, 1992.

* Pohl, Frederik. *Star of Stars.* New York: Ballantine Books, 1960.

* Weaver, Tom. *Eye on Science Fiction.* Jefferson, North Carolina, McFarland & Company, Inc., 2003.

Interviews

The author conducted a large number of interviews with the cast and crew over a 10-year period. These were accomplished in person at celebrity conventions across the country and recorded to ensure the actors were quoted precisely. Other interviews were conducted through personal visits to their homes, exchanges by e-mail, postal mail, and phone calls. To reprint all of the interviews in their complete form would have taken an entire book by itself, perhaps two volumes. The author chose to reprint only selected passages from those interviews – brief quotes that would help give the reader further insight into the subject at hand, without reprinting quotations that might otherwise be repetitive. It is the author's intention that one day, all of the interviews may be collected into a single volume or donated to a website dedicated to *The Twilight Zone*, for appreciative fans to enjoy.

TITLE INDEX

INDEX

Bender, Russ 231, 493, 593
Bendix, William 33, 532
Benedek, Lazlo 53
Benedict, William 690
Bennett, Constance 57
Bennett, John B. 591
Bennett, Marjorie 285, 480, 570
Bennington Evening Banner, The (newspaper) 290
Benny, Jack 129, 130, 137
Benson, Anthony 593
Benson, Murray 150, 157, 424, 723, 724
Benson, Shelby 251
Benton, Gene 488
Benton, Robert R. 604, 608, 611, 615, 620, 624, 627-
    629, 634, 637, 640, 644, 648, 651, 653, 657, 661,
    664, 667, 669, 671, 679, 684, 697, 714, 721
Bercovich, Hene 101, 719, 720
Beregi, Oscar 392, 443, 556
Berg, Gertrude 58
Bergen, Edgar 518
Berger, Gerard 674
Bergman, Slim 608, 610
Berman, Bayard F. 25
Berman, Shelley 294, 401, 404
Bernard, Barry 205
Bernard, Joseph 421
Bernarth, Shari Lee 576
Bernie Mac Show, The (television program) 614
Bernie, Jason H. 392, 399, 402, 411, 419, 421, 428, 438,
    446, 453, 456, 463, 465, 471, 488, 491, 493, 496,
    503, 506, 514, 516, 521, 524, 720
Bernstein, Leonard 124
Bernstein, Robert 506, 724
Bernstein, Ted 137
Best Science Fiction (magazine) 41
Best, Edna 58
Best, James 434, 436, 437, 485-487, 561, 563
Bester, Alfred 105
Better Publications (magazine publisher) 43
Betty Hutton Show, The (television program) 64
Bevans, Clem 508
Bevans, Phillipa 537
Beverly Hills Federal Savings & Loan Association 100
Bewitched (television program) 367
Beyond Fantasy Fiction (magazine) 667
Biberman, Abner 517, 590, 591, 661, 687
Bierce, Ambrose 211, 674, 675
Bieri, Ramon 602
Big Town (television program) 588
Biheller, Bob 537
Bikel, Theodore 505, 507
Bildersee, Barnett 575, 576
Billingslea, Maj. Gen. Charles 639
Billy Rose's Playbill Theater 286
Binghamton Press, The (newspaper) 94

Binns, Edward 226, 653
Birch, John 412, 413
Birchfield, Bob 537
Birds of Prey (television program) 157
Bishop, Joey 404, 504
Bixby, Bill 545, 549
Bixby, Jerome 438, 441
Black Saddle (television program) 478
Black, Karen 362
Blackmer, Sidney 426
Blake, Bob 57
Blake, J.W. 291, 292
Blake, Larry 343
Blanchard, Mari 57
Blasetti, Alessandro 40
Blassingame, Lurton 46
Bliss, Lela 196
Bloch, Robert 81
Blondell, Gloria 659
Blondell, Joan 682
Bloom, Mel 595
Bloss, John 542, 545, 549, 560, 562, 569, 581, 584, 590,
    593, 598
Blue Book (magazine) 250
Blue Cross Animal Hospital 102
Bluebook Magazine 39, 74
Blumgarten, James 347
Blyden, Larry 278, 279, 477, 532
Blyth, Ann 679, 680
Bob Hope Show, The (television program) 141
Bobbins, Stephen 352
Bouchey, Willis 684
Bochner, Lloyd 488, 491, 492, 663
Boffety, Jean 674
Bohn, Merritt 168, 608
Boisson, Steve 383, 585, 662
Boles, Jim 418
Bolle, Frank 730-732, 735, 737-745
Bolt, John 709
Bonanza (television program) 638, 716
Bond, David 583
Bond, Nelson 6, 74
Boniga, Jack 477
Bonigul, Jack 251, 418
Bonniwell Jr., Charles 604, 608, 611, 615, 620, 624, 627-
    629, 634, 637, 640, 644, 648, 651, 653, 657, 661,
    664, 667, 669, 671, 679, 684, 697, 714, 721
Boon, Robert 443, 556
Boone, Pat 119
Boone, Randy 637
Boone, Richard 605
Booth, Billy 282
Booth, Deena Lynn 190
Booth, Nesdon 188, 190, 191, 382
Booth, Nesdon Faye 190

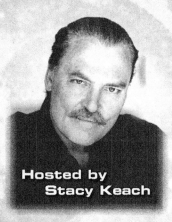

ABOUT THE AUTHOR

Dubbed as the "young Isaac Asimov" by Ivan Shreve of Thrilling Days of Yesteryear, Martin Grams Jr. authored or co-authored over a dozen books about radio and television. He wrote a number of magazine articles for *Filmfax, Scarlet Street, the Old-Time Radio Digest* and SPERDVAC's *Radiogram*. He contributed chapters, essays, short stories and appendices for various books including Ken Mogg's *The Alfred Hitchcock Story* (1999), Bear Manor Media's *It's That Time Again* (all three volumes, 2002 - 2005), Midnight Marquee's *Vincent Price* (1998), Arthur Anderson's *Let's Pretend* (2004), and Ben Ohmart's Alan Freed biography (2009).

Martin is the recipient of the 1999 Ray Stanich Award, the 2005 Parley E. Baer Award and the 2005 Stone/Waterman Award. His name appears in the acknowledgments of over 100 books about radio and television. Author/historian Jack French dedicated his 2004 book, Private Eyelashes, to Martin among a list of other historians and researchers. A consultant for two publishing companies, he has plans to continue writing books for a number of years. Since 2006, he has been the Events Coordinator for the Mid-Atlantic Nostalgia Convention held annually every September in Maryland. He presently lives in Delta, Pennsylvania, with his wife and three cats.

Also By Martin Grams Jr.
The History of the Cavalcade of America (1999, Morris Publishing)
The CBS Radio Mystery Theater: An Episode Guide and Handbook (1999, McFarland Publishing)
The Have Gun - Will Travel Companion (2000, OTR Publishing, LLC)
The Alfred Hitchcock Presents Companion (2001, OTR Publishing, LLC)
The Sound of Detection: Ellery Queen's Adventures in Radio (2002, OTR Publishing, LLC)
Inner Sanctum Mysteries: Behind the Creaking Door (2002, OTR Publishing, LLC)
The I Love A Mystery Companion (2003, OTR Publishing, LLC)
Information Please (2003, Bear Manor Media)
Gang Busters: The Crime Fighters of American Broadcasting (2004, OTR Publishing, LLC)
The Railroad Hour (2006, Bear Manor Media)
The Radio Adventures of Sam Spade (2007, OTR Publishing, LLC)
I Led Three Lives: The True Story of Herbert A. Philbrick's Television Program (2007, Bear Manor Media)
Car 54, Where Are You? (2009, Bear Manor Media)

Printed in Great Britain
by Amazon

47640988R00454